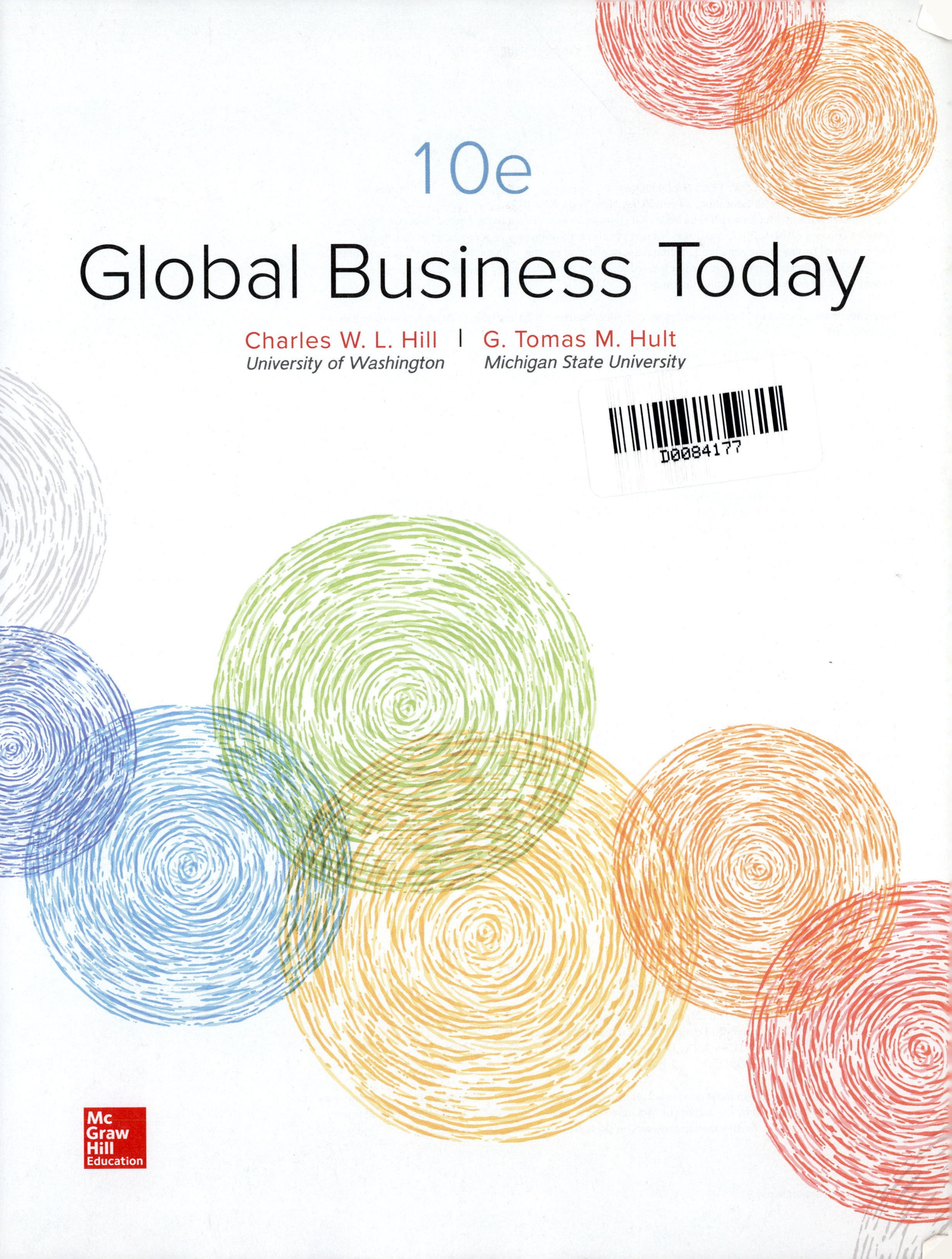

10e

Global Business Today

Charles W. L. Hill | G. Tomas M. Hult
University of Washington   Michigan State University

Mc Graw Hill Education

GLOBAL BUSINESS TODAY, TENTH EDITION
Published by McGraw-Hill Education, 2 Penn Plaza, New York, NY 10121.

This book is printed on acid-free paper.

1 2 3 4 5 6 7 8 9 LMN 21 20 19 18 17

ISBN 978-1-259-68669-6
MHID 1-259-68669-8

Chief Product Officer, SVP Products & Markets: *G. Scott Virkler*
Vice President, General Manager, Products & Markets: *Michael Ryan*
Vice President, Content Design & Delivery: *Betsy Whalen*
Managing Director: *Susan Gouijnstook*
Director: *Michael Ablassmeir*
Executive Brand Manager: *Anke Weekes*
Director, Product Development: *Meghan Campbell*
Lead Product Developer: *Kelly Delso*
Product Developer: *Gabriela G. Velasco*
Freelance Product Developer: *Tracey Douglas*
Director of Digital Content: *Kristy DeKat*
Senior Digital Product Analyst: *Kerry Shanahan*
Senior Marketing Manager: *Michael Gedatus*
Director, Content Design & Delivery: *Terri Schiesl*
Program Manager: *Mary Conzachi*
Content Project Managers: *Mary E. Powers* (Core), *Keri Johnson* (Assessment)
Buyer: *Laura M. Fuller*
Design: *Matt Diamond*
Content Licensing Specialists: *Lori Hancock* (Image), *Shannon Manderscheid* (Text)
Cover Image: *aleksandarvelasevic/Getty Images*
Compositor: *Aptara, Inc.*
Printer: *LSC Communications*

Library of Congress Cataloging-in-Publication Data

Names: Hill, Charles W. L., author. | Hult, G. Tomas M., author.
Title: Global business today / Charles W.L. Hill, University of Washington, G. Tomas M. Hult, Michigan State University.
Description: Tenth edition. | New York, NY : McGraw-Hill Education, [2018]
Identifiers: LCCN 2016040841| ISBN 9781259686696 (alk. paper) | ISBN 1259686698 (alk. paper)
Subjects: LCSH: International business enterprises—Management. | International trade. | Investments, Foreign. | Capital market.
Classification: LCC HD62.4 .H548 2018 | DDC 658/.049—dc23 LC record available at https://lccn.loc.gov/2016040841

mheducation.com/highered

For my mother June Hill, and the memory of my father, Mike Hill
—Charles W. L. Hill
For Gert & Margareta Hult, my parents
—G. Tomas M. Hult

about the authors

Charles W. L. Hill

University of Washington

Charles W. L. Hill is the Hughes M. and Katherine Blake Professor of Strategy and International Business at the Foster School of Business, University of Washington. The Foster School has a Center for International Business Education and Research (CIBER), one of only 17 funded by the U.S. Department of Education.

Professor Hill received his PhD from the University of Manchester in the United Kingdom. In addition to the University of Washington, he has served on the faculties of the University of Manchester, Texas A&M University, and Michigan State University.

Professor Hill has published over 50 articles in peer-reviewed academic journals including the *Academy of Management Journal, Academy of Management Review, Strategic Management Journal,* and *Organization Science*. He has also published several textbooks including *International Business* (McGraw-Hill) and *Global Business Today* (McGraw-Hill). His work is among the most widely cited in international business and strategic management.

Professor Hill has taught in the MBA, Executive MBA, Technology Management MBA, Management, and PhD programs at the University of Washington. During his time at the University of Washington, he has received over 25 awards for teaching excellence, including multiple Charles E. Summer Outstanding Teaching Awards, most recently in 2016.

Professor Hill works on a private basis with a number of organizations. His clients have included Microsoft, where he has been teaching in-house executive education courses for two decades. He has also consulted for a variety of other large companies (e.g., AT&T Wireless, Boeing, BF Goodrich, Group Health, Hexcel, Microsoft, Philips Healthcare, Philips Medical Systems, Seattle City Light, Swedish Health Services, Tacoma City Light, Thompson Financial Services, WRQ, and Wizards of the Coast).

Professor Hill has served on the advisory board of several start-up companies. For recreation, Professor Hill enjoys mountaineering, rock climbing, skiing, and competitive sailing.

G. Tomas M. Hult

Michigan State University

G. Tomas M. Hult is the John W. Byington Endowed Chair, Professor of Marketing and International Business, and Director of the International Business Center in the Eli Broad College of Business at Michigan State University. The Eli Broad College of Business has a Center for International Business Education and Research (CIBER), one of only 17 funded by the U.S. Department of Education. Professor Hult serves as the CIBER Director, and he is also currently President of the 17-university CIBER coalition.

Professor Hult is an elected Fellow of the Academy of International Business (AIB), one of only about 80 scholars worldwide receiving this honor. He also serves as the Executive Director and Foundation President of AIB. Professor Hult serves on the U.S. District Export Council and holds board member positions of the International Trade Center of Mid-Michigan, Global Business Club of Mid-Michigan, and the Sheth Foundation.

Several studies have ranked Professor Hult as one of the most cited scholars in the world in business and management. He has served as editor of *Journal of the Academy of Marketing Science* and has published more than 60 articles in premier business journals, including *Journal of International Business Studies, Academy of Management Journal, Strategic Management Journal, Journal of Management, Journal of Marketing, Journal of the Academy of Marketing Science, Journal of Retailing, Journal of Operations Management, Decision Sciences,* and *IEEE.*

Professor Hult has also published several books: *International Business* (2017), *Second Shift* (2017), *Global Business Today* (2016), *Global Supply Chain Management* (2014), *Total Global Strategy* (2012), and *Extending the Supply Chain* (2005). He is a regular contributor of articles in the popular press (e.g., *Time, Fortune, World Economic Forum, The Conversation*).

Professor Hult is a well-known keynote speaker on international business, international marketing, global supply chain management, global strategy, and marketing strategy. He teaches in doctoral, master's, and undergraduate programs at Michigan State University, and he is a visiting professor at Leeds University (United Kingdom) and Uppsala University (Sweden).

He also teaches frequently in executive development programs and has developed a large clientele of the world's top multinational corporations (e.g., ABB, Albertsons, Avon, BG, Bechtel, Bosch, BP, Defense Logistics Agency, Domino's, FedEx, Ford, FreshDirect, General Motors, Grocery-Gateway, HSBC, IBM, Michigan Economic Development Corporation, Masco, NASA, Raytheon, Shell, Siemens, State Farm, Steelcase, Tech Data, and Xerox).

Tomas Hult is a dual citizen of the United States and Sweden, and lives in Okemos, Michigan, with his wife, Laurie, and their children, Daniel and Isabelle. Tennis, golf, and traveling are his favorite recreational activities.

brief contents

the proven choice for international business

Current. Application Rich, Relevant. Accessible and Student Focused.

Global Business Today (GBT), the worldwide market leader among international business products, has set a new standard for international business teaching. We have focused on creating resources that:

- Are comprehensive, state of the art, and timely.
- Are theoretically sound and practically relevant.
- Focus on applications of international business concepts.
- Tightly integrate the chapter topics throughout.
- Are fully integrated with results-driven technology.
- Take full and integrative advantage of globalEDGE.msu.edu—the Google-ranked #1 web resource for "international business resources."

International Business (now in its 11th edition, 2017), also co-authored by Charles W.L. Hill and G. Tomas M. Hult, is a more comprehensive and case-oriented version that lends itself to the core course in international business for those courses that want a deeper focus on the global monetary system, structure of international business, international accounting, and international finance.

GBT has always endeavored to be current, relevant, application rich, and accessible and student focused. Our goal has always been to cover macro and micro issues equally and in a relevant, practical, accessible, and student focused approach. We believe that anything short of such a breadth and depth of coverage is a serious deficiency. Many of the students in these international business courses will soon be working in global businesses, and they will be expected to understand the implications of international business for their organization's strategy, structure, and functions in the context of the global marketplace. We are proud and delighted to have put together this international business learning experience for the leaders of tomorrow.

Over the years, and through now 10 editions, Dr. Charles Hill has worked hard to adhere to these goals. Since the ninth edition, Charles' coauthor, Dr. Tomas Hult, follows the same approach. In deciding what changes to make, we have been guided not only by our own reading, teaching, and research but also by the invaluable feedback we received from professors and students around the world, from reviewers, and from the editorial staff at McGraw-Hill Education. Our thanks go out to all of them.

Comprehensive and Up-to-Date

To be relevant and comprehensive, an international business package must

- Explain how and why the world's cultures, countries, and regions differ.
- Cover economics and politics of international trade and investment.
- Tackle international issues related to ethics, corporate social responsibility, and sustainability.
- Explain the functions and form of the global monetary system.
- Examine the strategies and structures of international businesses.
- Assess the special roles of the various functions of an international business.

Comprehensiveness and up-to-date also require coverage of the major theories. It has always been a goal to incorporate the insights gleaned from recent academic scholarship into the book. Consistent with this goal, insights from the following research, as a sample of theoretical streams used in the book, have been incorporated:

- New trade theory and strategic trade policy.
- The work of Nobel Prize–winning economist Amartya Sen on economic development.
- Samuel Huntington's influential thesis on the "clash of civilizations."
- Growth theory of economic development championed by Paul Romer and Gene Grossman.
- Empirical work by Jeffrey Sachs and others on the relationship between international trade and economic growth.
- Michael Porter's theory of the competitive advantage of nations.
- Robert Reich's work on national competitive advantage.
- The work of Nobel Prize–winner Douglass North and others on national institutional structures and the protection of property rights.
- The market imperfections approach to foreign direct investment that has grown out of Ronald Coase and Oliver Williamson's work on transaction cost economics.
- Bartlett and Ghoshal's research on the transnational corporation.
- The writings of C. K. Prahalad and Gary Hamel on core competencies, global competition, and global strategic alliances.
- Insights for international business strategy that can be derived from the resource-based view of the firm and complementary theories.
- Paul Samuelson's critique of free trade theory.
- Conceptual and empirical work on global supply chain management—logistics, purchasing (sourcing), operations, and marketing channels.

In addition to including leading-edge theory, in light of the fast-changing nature of the international business environment we have made every effort to ensure that this product is as up-to-date as possible. A significant amount has happened in the world since we began revisions of this book. By 2016, almost $4 trillion per day were flowing across national borders. The size of such flows fueled concern about the ability of short-term speculative shifts in global capital markets to destabilize the world economy.

The world continued to become more global. Several Asian economies, most notably China and India, continued to grow their economies at a rapid rate. New multinationals continued to emerge from developing nations in addition to the world's established industrial powers. Increasingly, the globalization of the world economy affected a wide range of firms of all sizes, from the very large to the very small. And unfortunately, global terrorism and the attendant geopolitical risks keep emerging in various places globally, many new and inconceivable just a decade ago. These represent a threat to global economic integration and activity.

WHAT'S NEW IN THE 10TH EDITION The success of the first nine editions of *Global Business Today* was based in part on the incorporation of leading-edge research into the text, the use of the up-to-date examples and statistics to illustrate global trends and enterprise strategy, and the discussion of current events within the context of the appropriate theory. Building on these strengths, our goals for the 10th edition have focused on the following:

1. Incorporate new insights from scholarly research.
2. Make sure the content covers all appropriate issues.
3. Make sure the text is up-to-date with current events, statistics, and examples.
4. Add new and insightful opening and closing cases in most chapters.
5. Incorporate value-added globalEDGE™ features in every chapter.
6. Connect every chapter to a focus on managerial implications.
7. Incorporate a new *Did You Know?* feature in every chapter that links to mini-video cases.

As part of the overall revision process, changes have been made to every chapter in the book. All statistics have been updated to incorporate the most recently available data, which typically refer to 2014 and 2015. For example, new examples, cases, and boxes have been added and older examples updated to reflect new developments.

Importantly, every chapter of the 10th edition of *Global Business Today* has again incorporated value-added globalEDGE™ features in every chapter. The Google number-one-ranked globaledge.msu.edu site (for "international business resources") is used in each chapter to add value to the chapter material and provide up-to-date data and information. This feature was added for the ninth edition, and the marketplace (e.g., professors, instructors, and students) really liked the practical and up-to-date materials covered via globalEDGE™ and the integration into *Global Business Today*. This GBT-*globalEDGE™* integration keeps chapter material constantly and dynamically updated for teachers who want to infuse globalEDGE™ material into the chapter topics, and it keeps students abreast of current developments in international business.

In addition to updating all descriptive statistics, figures, and maps to incorporate most recently published data, a chapter-by-chapter selection of changes for the 10th edition include the following:

CHAPTER 1: GLOBALIZATION

- New Opening Case: Uber, Going Global from Day One
- New Management Focus: Boeing's Global Production System
- New Management Focus: The Dalian Wanda Group
- New Closing Case: Medical Tourism and the Globalization of Health Care

CHAPTER 2: NATIONAL DIFFERENCES IN POLITICAL, ECONOMIC, AND LEGAL SYSTEMS

- New Opening Case: Economic Transformation in Vietnam
- New Country Focus: Putin's Russia
- New Country Focus: Corruption in Brazil
- New Closing Case: Venezuela under Hugo Chavez and Beyond

CHAPTER 3: NATIONAL DIFFERENCES IN ECONOMIC DEVELOPMENT

- New Opening Case: The Political and Economic Evolution of Indonesia
- New Closing Case: Political and Economic Reform in Myanmar

CHAPTER 4: DIFFERENCES IN CULTURE

- New Opening Case: World Expo 2020 in Dubai, UAE
- Revised focus on business and culture
- New Closing Case: Best Buy and eBay in China

CHAPTER 5: ETHICS, CORPORATE SOCIAL RESPONSIBILITY, AND SUSTAINABILITY

- New Opening Case: UNCTAD Sustainable Development Goals
- Revised focus on corporate social responsibility and sustainability
- New Management Focus: Apple's Manufacturing—Always Ethical?
- Revised Closing Case: Making Toys Globally

CHAPTER 6: INTERNATIONAL TRADE THEORY

- New Opening Case: The Trans Pacific Partnership
- New Closing Case: Creating the World's Biggest Free Trade Zone
- The appendix, International Trade and the Balance of Payments, has been updated to include the most recently available balance-of-payments data

CHAPTER 7: GOVERNMENT POLICY AND INTERNATIONAL TRADE

- New Opening Case: Is China Dumping Its Excess Steel Production?
- New section: Multilateral and Bilateral Trade Agreements
- New Closing Case: Sugar Subsidies Drive Candy Makers Abroad

CHAPTER 8: FOREIGN DIRECT INVESTMENT

- New Opening Case: Burberry Shifts Its Strategy in Japan
- New Closing Case: Volkswagen in Russia

CHAPTER 9: REGIONAL ECONOMIC INTEGRATION

- New Opening Case: The Push Toward Free Trade in Africa
- New section: Regional Trade Blocs in Africa
- New Closing Case: Regional Trade Deals and the Mexican Auto Industry

CHAPTER 10: THE FOREIGN EXCHANGE MARKET

- New Opening Case: Apple's Earnings Hit by the Strong Dollar
- New Management Focus: Embraer and the Gyrations of the Brazilian Real
- New Closing Case: Subaru's Sales Boom Thanks to Weaker Yen

CHAPTER 11: THE INTERNATIONAL MONETARY SYSTEM

- New Opening Case: China's Exchange Rate Regime
- New Country Focus: The IMF and Iceland's Economic Recovery
- New Closing Case: The IMF and Ukraine's Economic Crisis

CHAPTER 12: THE STRATEGY OF INTERNATIONAL BUSINESS

- New Opening Case: AB InBev and Beer Globally
- New Management Focus: Ford Creating Value
- Revision of Management Focus boxes
- New Closing Case: IKEA and Its Strategy of International Business

CHAPTER 13: ENTERING FOREIGN MARKETS

- New Opening Case: Cutco Corporation—Sharpening Your Market Entry
- Revision to Entry Modes section
- Revision of Management Focus boxes
- New Closing Case: Starbucks' Foreign Entry Strategy

CHAPTER 14: EXPORTING, IMPORTING, AND COUNTERTRADE

- New Opening Case: Two Men and a Truck
- Added readiness to export and import material
- New Management Focus: Ambient Technologies and the Panama Canal
- Revision of Management Focus boxes
- Added material on globalEDGE™ Diagnostic Tools
- New Closing Case: Exporting Desserts

CHAPTER 15: GLOBAL PRODUCTION AND SUPPLY CHAIN MANAGEMENT

- New Opening Case: Amazon—A Leader in Global Supply Chain Management
- Revised integration of the supply chain (logistics, purchasing, production, and operations)
- Revised section on Global Supply Chain Functions
- New Management Focus: H&M and Their Order Timing
- Revision of Management Focus boxes
- Revised Closing Case: Apple: The Best Supply Chains in the World?

CHAPTER 16: GLOBAL MARKETING AND R&D

- New Opening Case: Domino's Global Marketing
- Revised section Configuring the Marketing Mix
- New Management Focus: Global Branding of Marvel's Movies
- Revision of Management Focus boxes
- New Closing Case: Burberry's Reinventing Its Global Marketing

CHAPTER 17: GLOBAL HUMAN RESOURCE MANAGEMENT

- Revised Opening Case: A Global Team at Mary Kay Inc.
- Revision of Management Focus boxes
- New Closing Case: Siemens and Global Competitiveness

Beyond Uncritical Presentation and Shallow Explanation

Many issues in international business are complex and thus necessitate considerations of pros and cons. To demonstrate this to students, we have adopted a critical approach that presents the arguments for and against economic theories, government policies, business strategies, organizational structures, and so on.

Related to this, we have attempted to explain the complexities of the many theories and phenomena unique to international business so the student might fully comprehend the statements of a theory or the reasons a phenomenon is the way it is. We believe that these theories and phenomena are explained in more depth in this work than they are in the competition, which seem to use the rationale that a shallow explanation is little better than no explanation. In international business, a little knowledge is indeed a dangerous thing.

Practical and Rich Applications

We have always believed that it is important to show students how the material covered in the text is relevant to the actual practice of international business. This is explicit in the later chapters of the book, which focus on the practice of international business, but it is not always obvious in the first half of the book, which considers macro topics. Accordingly, at the end of each chapter in Parts Two, Three, and Four—where the focus is on the environment of international business, as opposed to particular firms—there is a section titled **Focus on Managerial Implications**. In this section, the managerial implications of the material discussed in the chapter are clearly explained. Additionally, most chapters have at least one **Management Focus** box. The purpose of these boxes is to illustrate the relevance of chapter material for the practice of international business.

A new **Did You Know?** feature in each chapter challenges students to view the world around them through the lens of international business (e.g., Did you know that sugar prices in the United States are much higher than sugar prices in the rest of the world?). The authors recorded short videos explaining the phenomenon.

In addition, each chapter begins with an **opening case** that sets the stage for the chapter and ends with a **closing case** that illustrates the relevance of chapter material for the practice of international business.

To help students go a step further in expanding their application-level understanding of international business, each chapter incorporates two **globalEDGE research tasks** designed and written by Tomas Hult. The exercises dovetail with the content just covered.

Integrated Progression of Topics

A weakness of many texts is that they lack a tight, integrated flow of topics from chapter to chapter. This book explains to students in Chapter 1 how the book's topics are related to each other. Integration has been achieved by organizing the material so that each chapter builds on the material of the previous ones in a logical fashion.

PART ONE Chapter 1 provides an overview of the key issues to be addressed and explains the plan of the book. Globalization of markets and globalization of production is the core focus.

PART TWO Chapters 2 through 4 focus on country differences in political economy and culture, and Chapter 5 on ethics, corporate social responsibility, and sustainability issues in international business. Most international business textbooks place this material at a later point, but we believe it is vital to discuss national differences first. After all, many of the central issues in international trade and investment, the global monetary system, international business strategy and structure, and international business functions arise out of national differences in political economy and culture.

PART THREE Chapters 6 through 9 investigate the political economy of global trade and investment. The purpose of this part is to describe and explain the trade and investment environment in which international business occurs.

PART FOUR Chapters 10 and 11 describe and explain the global monetary system, laying out in detail the monetary framework in which international business transactions are conducted.

PART FIVE In Chapters 12 and 13, attention shifts from the environment to the firm. In other words, we move from a macro focus to a micro focus at this stage of the book. We examine strategies that firms adopt to compete effectively in the international business environment.

PART SIX In Chapters 14 through 17, the focus narrows further to investigate business functions and related operations. These chapters explain how firms can perform their key functions —exporting, importing, and countertrade; global production; global supply chain management; global marketing; global research and development (R&D); human resource management—to compete and succeed in the international business environment.

Throughout the book, the relationship of new material to topics discussed in earlier chapters is pointed out to the students to reinforce their understanding of how the material comprises an integrated whole. We deliberately bring a management focus to the macro chapters (Chapters 1 through 11). We also integrate macro themes in covering the micro chapters (Chapters 12 through 17).

Acknowledgments

Numerous people deserve to be thanked for their assistance in preparing this book. First, thank you to all the people at McGraw-Hill Education who have worked with us on this project:

Anke Braun Weekes, Executive Brand Manager
Gabriela G. Velasco, Product Developer
Michael Gedatus, Senior Marketing Manager
Brittany Bernholdt, Marketing Coordinator
Mary Powers, Content Project Manager (Core)
Evan Roberts, Content Project Manager (Assessment)
Jennifer Pickel, Senior Buyer
Srdjan Savanovic, Designer
Lori Hancock, Content Licensing Specialist (Image)
DeAnna Dausener, Content Licensing Specialist (Text)

Second, our thanks go to the reviewers who provided good feedback that helped shape this book:

Yeqing Bao, *University of Alabama, Huntsville*
Jacobus F. Boers, *Georgia State University*
Peter Buckley, *Leeds University*
Ken Chinen, *California State University, Sacramento*
Macgorine A. Cassell, *Fairmont State University*
David Closs, *Michigan State University*
Ping Deng, *Maryville University of St. Louis*
Betty J. Diener, *Barry University*
Abiola O. Fanimokun, *Pennsylvania State University, Fayette*
John Finley, *Columbus State University*
Pat Fox, *Marion Technical College*

David Frayer, *Michigan State University*
Michael Harris, *East Carolina University*
Jan Johanson, *Uppsala University*
Tunga Kiyak, *Michigan State University*
Anthony C. Koh, *University of Toledo*
Steve Lawton, *Oregon State University*
Ruby Lee, *Florida State University*
Joseph W. Leonard, *Miami University*
David N. McArthur, *Utah Valley University*
Sunder Narayanan, *New York University*
Eydis Olsen, *Drexel University*
Daria Panina, *Texas A&M University*
Hoon Park, *University of Central Florida*
Dr. Mahesh Raisinghani, *Texas Women's University*
Brian Satterlee, *EdD, DBA, Liberty University*
Michael Volpe, *University of Maryland*
Macgorine A. Cassell, *Fairmont State University*
Ping Deng, *Maryville University of St. Louis*
Betty J. Diener, *Barry University*
Pat Fox, *Marion Technical College*
Connie Golden, *Lakeland Community College*
Laura Kozloski Hart, *Barry University*
Chip Izard, *Richland College*
Vishakha Maskey, *West Liberty University*
Shelly McCallum, *Saint Mary's University of Minnesota*
Emily A. Morad, *Reading Area Community College*
Tim Muth, *Florida Institute of Technology*
Dwight Shook, *Catawba Valley Community College*
James Whelan, *Manhattan College*
Man Zhang, *Bowling Green State University*
Martin Grossman, *Bridgewater State University*
Sara B. Kimmel, *Mississippi College*
Candida Johnson, *Holyoke Community College*
Kathy Hastings, *Greenville Technical College*
Brenda Sternqvist, *Michigan State University*
Katarina Lagerstrom, *Uppsala University*
William Hernández Requejo, *University of California, Irvine*
Manveer Mann, *Montclair State University*
Debra Vaughn, *Athens State University*
Dan Himelstein, *University of California, Berkeley*
Gerald Groshek, *University of Redlands*
Manuel G. Serapio, *University of Colorado, Denver*
Eren Ozgen, *Troy University*
Edmund Bednarz, *American International College*
John T. Finley, *Columbus State University*
Diane Griffin, *Forsyth Technical Community College*
Keith Kelley, *University of Michigan, Flint*
Athanasios Mihalakas, *SUNY, Brockport*
Miguel Angel Zúñiga, *Morgan State University*
Marvin Kirby Roberts III, *University of Texas, Austin*
Yeqing Bao, *University of Alabama, Huntsville*
Gary L. Lefort, *American International College*

A special thanks to David Closs, and David Frayer for allowing us to borrow elements of the sections on Strategic Roles for Production Facilities; Make-or-Buy Decisions; Global Supply Chain Functions; Coordination in Global Supply Chains; and Interorganizational Relationships for chapter 17 of this text from Tomas Hult, David Closs, and David Frayer (2014), Global Supply Chain Management, New York: McGraw-Hill.

Required=Results

©Getty Images/iStockphoto

McGraw-Hill Connect® Learn Without Limits

Connect is a teaching and learning platform that is proven to deliver better results for students and instructors.

Connect empowers students by continually adapting to deliver precisely what they need, when they need it, and how they need it, so your class time is more engaging and effective.

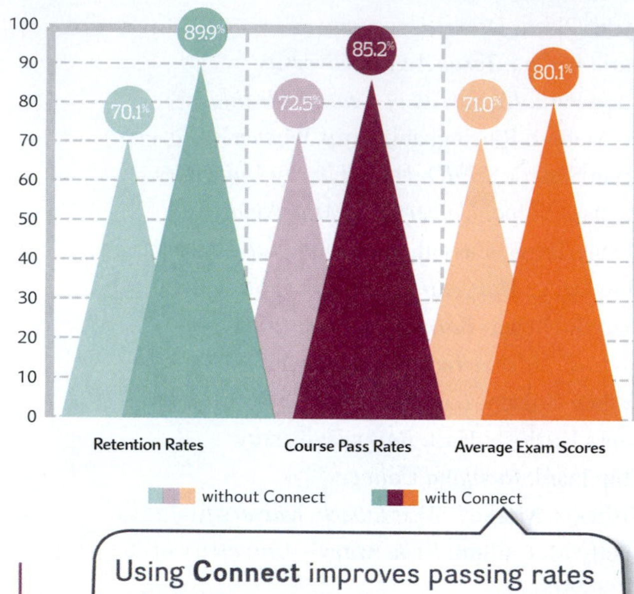

Using **Connect** improves passing rates by **12.7%**, and retention by **19.8%**.

73% of instructors who use **Connect** require it; instructor satisfaction **increases** by 28% when **Connect** is required.

Analytics

Connect Insight®

Connect Insight is Connect's new one-of-a-kind visual analytics dashboard that provides at-a-glance information regarding student performance, which is immediately actionable. By presenting assignment, assessment, and topical performance results together with a time metric that is easily visible for aggregate or individual results, Connect Insight gives the user the ability to take a just-in-time approach to teaching and learning, which was never before available. Connect Insight presents data that helps instructors improve class performance in a way that is efficient and effective.

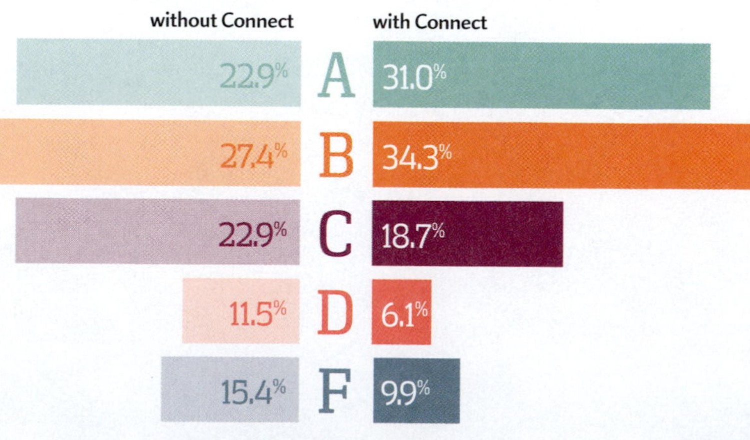

Adaptive

THE ADAPTIVE READING EXPERIENCE DESIGNED TO TRANSFORM THE WAY STUDENTS READ

More students earn **A's** and **B's** when they use McGraw-Hill Education **Adaptive** products.

SmartBook®

Proven to help students improve grades and study more efficiently, SmartBook contains the same content as the print book, but actively tailors that content to the needs of the individual. SmartBook's adaptive technology provides precise, personalized instruction on what the student should do next, guiding the student to master and remember key concepts, targeting gaps in knowledge and offering customized feedback, and driving the student toward comprehension and retention of the subject matter. Available on smartphones and tablets, SmartBook puts learning at the student's fingertips—anywhere, anytime.

Applied

A variety of application exercises within Connect require students to apply what they have learned in a real-world scenario. These online exercises help students assess their understanding of the concepts at a higher level. Exercises include video cases, decision making scenarios/ cases from real-world companies, case analysis exercises, business models, processes, and problem solving cases.

Over **5.7 billion questions** have been answered, making McGraw-Hill Education products more intelligent, reliable, and precise.

www.mheducation.com

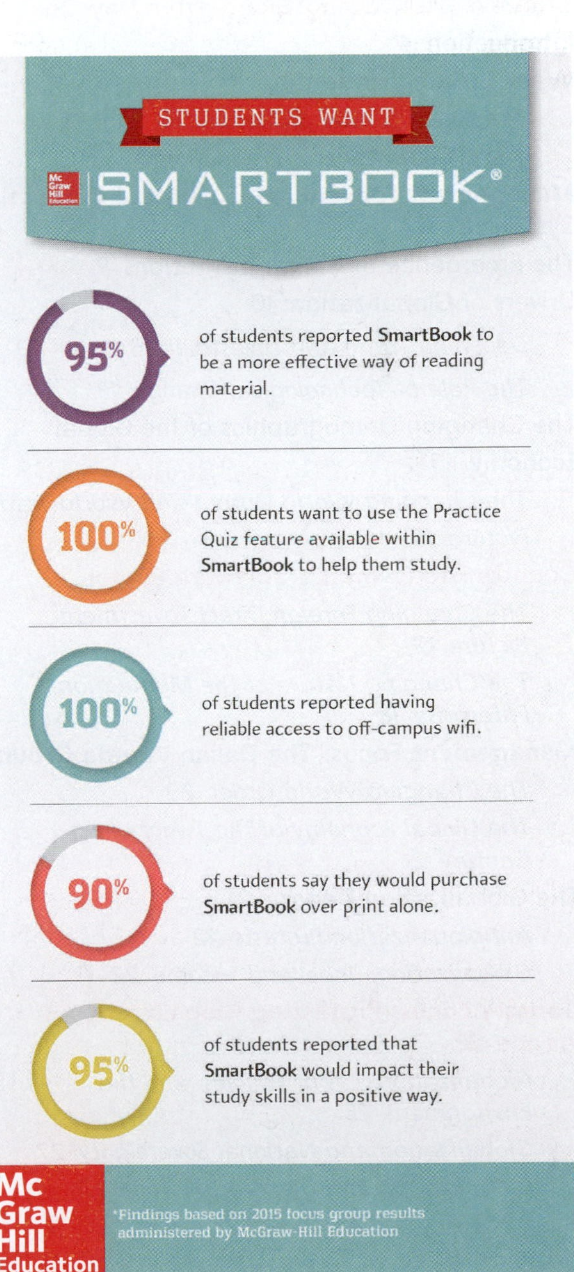

contents

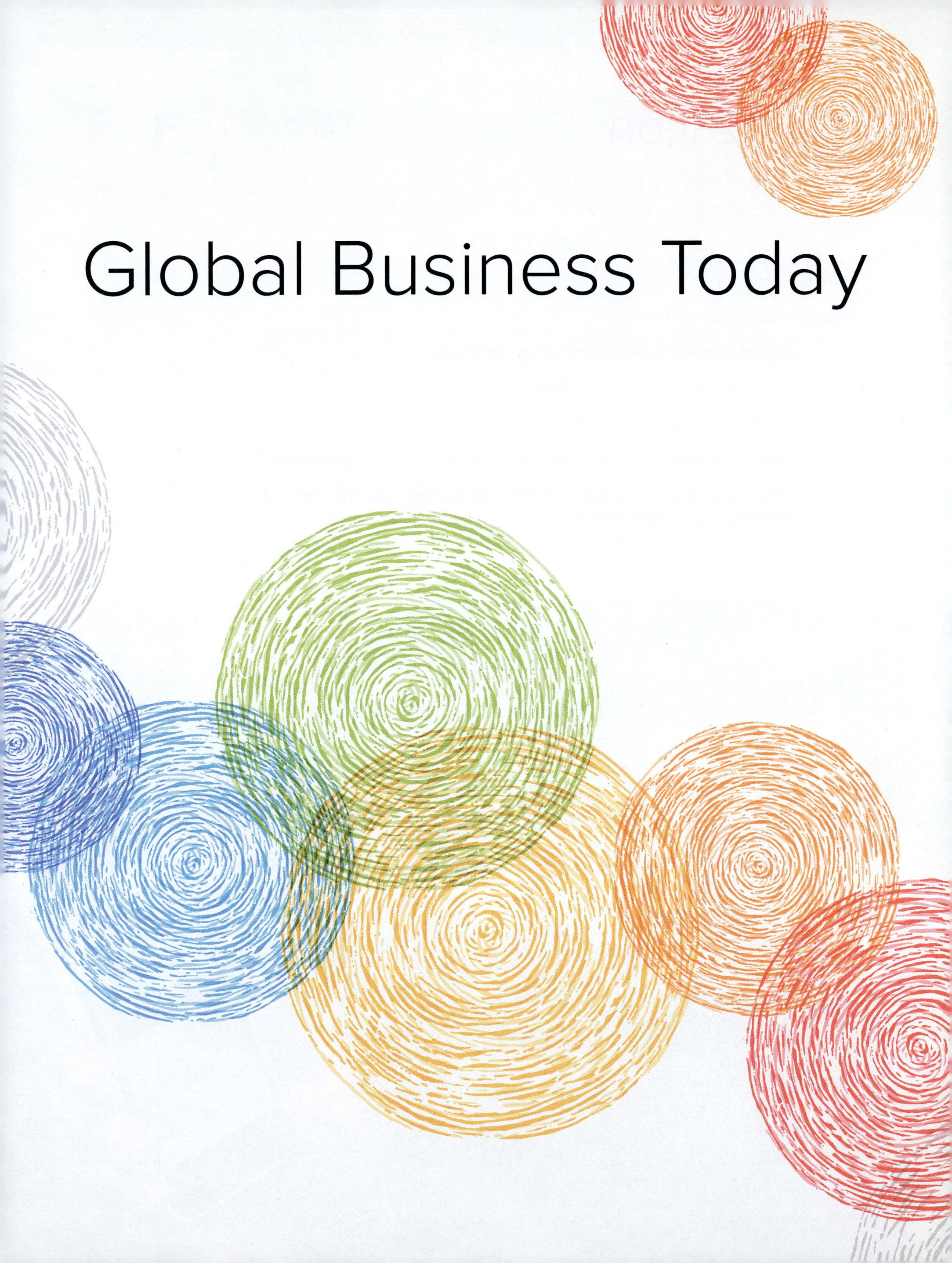

Global Business Today

Globalization

learning objectives

After reading this chapter, you will be able to:

- **LO1-1** Understand what is meant by the term *globalization*.
- **LO1-2** Recognize the main drivers of globalization.
- **LO1-3** Describe the changing nature of the global economy.
- **LO1-4** Explain the main arguments in the debate over the impact of globalization.
- **LO1-5** Understand how the process of globalization is creating opportunities and challenges for management practice.

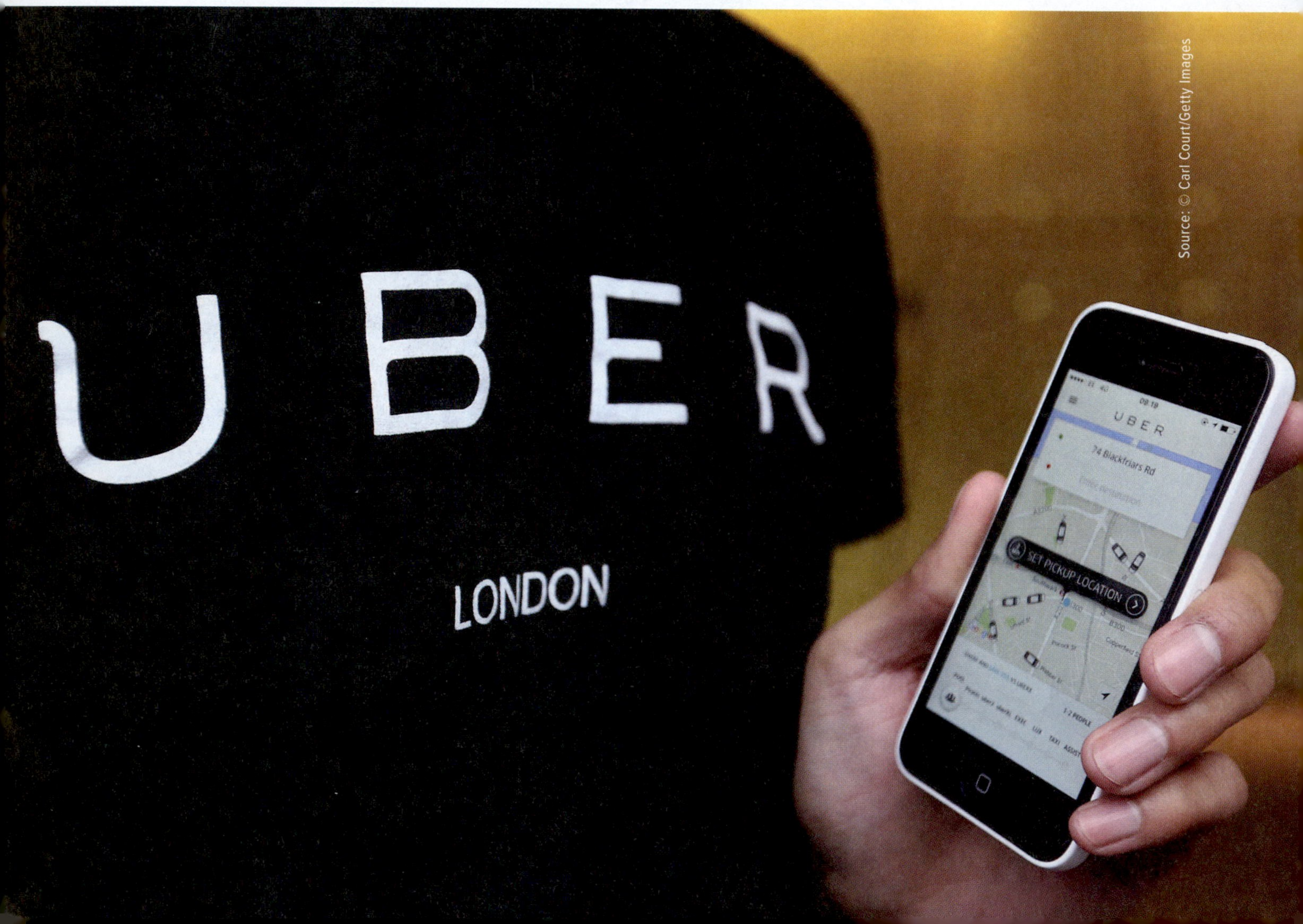

Source: © Carl Court/Getty Images

Uber: Going Global from Day One

opening case

Uber, the controversial San Francisco–based ride for hire service, has made a virtue out of disrupting the established taxi business. From a standing start in 2009, the company has spread across the globe like wildfire. Uber's strategy has been to focus on major metropolitan areas around the world. By early 2016, this strategy had taken Uber into 375 cities in 68 countries. The privately held company is rumored to be generating annual revenues of around $10 billion.

At the core of Uber's business is a smartphone app that allows customers to hail a ride from the comfort of their own home, a restaurant, or a bar stool. The app shows cars in the area, notifies the rider when a car is on the way, and tracks the progress of the car on screen using GPS mapping technology. The rider pays via the app using a credit card, so no cash changes hands. The driver takes 80 percent of the fee and Uber 20 percent. The price for the ride is determined by Uber using an algorithm that sets prices in order to match the demand for rides with the supply of cars on the road. Thus if demand exceeds supply, the price for a ride will rise, inducing drivers to get on the road. Uber does not own any cars. Its drivers are independent contractors with their own vehicles. The company is in effect a twenty-first century version of an old-style radio taxi dispatch company. Interestingly, Uber's founders got their idea for the app-based service one snowy night in Paris when they were unable to find a taxi.

Historically, taxi markets around the globe have been tightly regulated by metropolitan authorities. The stated purpose of these regulations has often included (1) limiting the supply of taxis in order to boost demand for other forms of public transportation, (2) limiting the supply of taxis in order to reduce traffic congestion, (3) ensuring the safety of riders by only allowing licensed taxis to offer rides, (4) ensuring that the prices charged are "fair," and (5) guaranteeing a reasonable rate of return to the owners of taxi licenses.

In practice, widespread restrictions on the supply of taxi licenses have created shortages in many cities, making it difficult to find a taxis, particularly at busy periods. In New York, the number of licenses barely increased from 11,787 in 1945 to 13,437 in 2014, even though the population expanded significantly. In Paris, the number of licenses was 14,000 in 1937, and had only increased to 15,900 by 2014, even though both the population and the number of visitors to the city had surged. The number of taxis in Milan was frozen between 1974 and 2014, despite Milan having a ratios of taxis to inhabitants that was one of the lowest for any major city. Whenever metropolitan authorities have tried to increase the number of taxis in a city, they have often been meet by strong resistance from established taxi companies. When the French

–continued

tried to increase the number of taxis in Paris in 2007, a strike among transportation workers shut down the city and forced the government to back off.

Uber's strategy has been to break these regulations, establishing its service first, and then fighting attempts by regulators to shut the service down. In pursuing this strategy, Uber has often used social networks to enlisted the support of its riders, getting them to pressure local governments to change their regulations and allow Uber to continue offering its service. In many cities, the strategy has worked, even in the face of protests from established taxi companies and their drivers. In London, for example, when taxi drivers went on strike to pressure the government to restrict Uber, Uber reported a surge in downloads for its app and thousands of new riders.

However, this confrontational strategy has not always worked well. The government of Vancouver, Canada, reacted to the unauthorized entry of Uber by banning it outright. So did the local authorities in Brussels in Belgium, Delhi in India, and a host of other cities around the globe. In Paris, the government has tried to limit Uber by imposing several restrictions that make it harder for Uber to do business there. To complicate matters, Uber drivers in Paris have unionized—something that they cannot do in the United States due to their status as independent contractors. They went on strike when Uber tried to lower fares. Similar protests by Uber drivers have occurred in other cities. Overall, there is a sense that Uber's abrasive strategy has not always worked well, particularly outside of the United States where locals see Uber as a brash American startup that pays scant attention to local laws, customs, and culture.

Uber is also witnessing the emergence of local rivals in some countries, such as India and China, where startups using a smartphone app and a business model similar to Uber are gaining traction. In China, local rival Didi Kuaidi has raised $4 billion in venture capital and claims that by mid-2016, it will be operating in over 400 cities in China. Didi already has a 90 percent market share in Beijing, where the company fields over 1 million daily ride requests. ●

Sources: Alyson Shontel, "Uber Is Generating a Staggering Amount of Revenue," *Business Insider*, November 15, 2014. Carmel DeAmicic, "Leaked Doc: Uber Nears $2 Billion in Revenue," Recode, August 21, 2015. Kara Swisher, "Uber and Uber Man," *Vanity Fair*, December 2014. Nitish Kulkarni, "Uber Hits Roadblock in India After Being Denied Permission to Operate in Delhi," Tech Crunch, September 16, 2015. Brian Solomon, "Uber Seems to Be Getting Its Butt Kicked in China," *Forbes*, December 1, 2015.

Introduction

Over the past five decades, a fundamental shift has been occurring in the world economy. We have been moving away from a world in which national economies were relatively self-contained entities, isolated from each other by barriers to cross-border trade and investment; by distance, time zones, and language; and by national differences in government regulation, culture, and business systems. We are moving toward a world in which barriers to cross-border trade and investment are declining; perceived distance is shrinking due to advances in transportation and telecommunications technology; material culture is starting to look similar the world over; and national economies are merging into an interdependent, integrated global economic system. The process by which this transformation is occurring is commonly referred to as *globalization*.

The rise of Uber discussed in the opening case is one illustration of the trend toward globalization. From a standing start in 2009, Uber has built a global ride for hire taxi service that by early 2016 could be found in over 357 cities in 68 countries. Uber customers visiting London, New York, Athens, Paris, or Hong Kong can now quickly find rides by using the Uber app on their smartphone. Uber has rapidly built a global brand. Its strategy was to go global from day one. In doing so, it is similar to many other modern technology business such as Facebook, Google, and Amazon that have also rapidly built a global presence. At the same time, it has not always been smooth sailing for Uber. Local authorities have banned or placed tight restrictions on Uber's service in many cities around the world. Uber's brash American ways have not always endeared themselves to local regulators, drivers, and customers. It is perhaps true, as critics have noted, that Uber might have done even better internationally if it had adapted its entry strategy to take local differences in regulations, culture, and political realities into account. This matters not only because it may have slowed down Uber's growth rate but also because it has opened the doors to foreign rivals who have used similar technology to Uber but seem more adept at working with local regulators and drivers.

More generally, globalization now has an impact on almost everything we do. The average American, for example, might drive to work in a car that was designed in Germany and assembled in Mexico by Ford from components made in the United States and Japan, which were fabricated from Korean steel and Malaysian rubber. He may have filled the car with gasoline at a Shell service station owned by a British-Dutch multinational company. The gasoline could have been made from oil pumped out of a well off the coast of Africa by a French oil company that transported it to the United States in a ship owned by a Greek shipping line. While driving to work, the American might talk to his stockbroker (using a hands-free, in-car speaker) on an Apple iPhone that was designed in California and assembled in China using chip sets produced in Japan and Europe, glass made by Corning in Kentucky, and memory chips from South Korea. He could tell the stockbroker to purchase shares in Lenovo, a multinational Chinese PC manufacturer whose operational headquarters is in North Carolina and whose shares are listed on the New York Stock Exchange.

This is the world in which we live. It is a world where the volume of goods, services, and investments crossing national borders has expanded faster than world output for more than half a century. It is a world where more than $5 trillion in foreign exchange transactions are made every day, where $19 trillion of goods and $5 trillion of services are sold across national borders every year.[1] It is a world in which international institutions such as the World Trade Organization and gatherings of leaders from the world's most powerful economies continue to work for even lower barriers to cross-border trade and investment. It is a world where the symbols of material and popular culture are increasingly global: from Coca-Cola and Starbucks to Sony PlayStations, Facebook, Netflix video streaming service, IKEA stores, and Apple iPads and iPhones. It is also a world in which vigorous and vocal groups protest against globalization, which they blame for a list of ills from unemployment in developed nations to environmental degradation and the Westernization or Americanization of local culture.

For businesses, this globalization process has produced many opportunities. Firms can expand their revenues by selling around the world and/or reduce their costs by producing in nations where key inputs, including labor, are cheap. The global expansion of enterprises has been facilitated by generally favorable political and economic trends. Since the collapse of communism over a quarter of a century ago, the pendulum of public policy in many nations has swung toward the free market end of the economic spectrum. Regulatory and administrative barriers to doing business in foreign nations have been reduced, while those nations have often transformed their economies, privatizing state-owned enterprises, deregulating markets, increasing competition, and welcoming investment by foreign businesses. This has allowed businesses both large and small, from both advanced nations and developing nations, to expand internationally.

As globalization unfolds, it is transforming industries and creating anxiety among those who believed their jobs were protected from foreign competition. Historically, while many workers in manufacturing industries worried about the impact foreign competition might have on their jobs, workers in service industries felt more secure. Now, this too is changing. Advances in technology, lower transportation costs, and the rise of skilled workers in developing countries imply that many services no longer need to be performed where they are delivered. Today, many individual U.S. tax returns are compiled in India. Indian accountants, trained in U.S. tax rules, perform work for U.S. accounting firms.[2] They access individual tax returns stored on computers in the United States, perform routine calculations, and save their work so that it can be inspected by a U.S. accountant,

What Will Happen to the United States?

The United States has the largest and most technologically powerful economy in the world, with a per capita GDP (gross domestic product) of $49,100. The 2013 GDP was valued at $16.72 trillion. Most of the labor force (79.4 percent) is employed in the services sector, with 19.5 percent employed in manufacturing industries, and only 1.1 percent in the agricultural area. China, India, and the European Union have labor forces larger than that of the United States, which ranks fourth in the world. Data show that the United States has become much more of a service economy over the years. Will the United States continue to increase its service sector at the cost of manufacturing and agriculture?

Source: U.S. Central Intelligence Agency, *World Factbook*, March 3, 2014. www.cia.gov.

who then bills clients. As the best-selling author Thomas Friedman has argued, the world is becoming flat.[3] People living in developed nations no longer have the playing field tilted in their favor. Increasingly, enterprising individuals based in India, China, or Brazil have the same opportunities to better themselves as those living in western Europe, the United States, or Canada.

In this text, we will take a close look at the issues introduced here and many more. We will explore how changes in regulations governing international trade and investment, when coupled with changes in political systems and technology, have dramatically altered the competitive playing field confronting many businesses. We will discuss the resulting opportunities and threats and review the strategies that managers can pursue to exploit the opportunities and counter the threats. We will consider whether globalization benefits or harms national economies. We will look at what economic theory has to say about the outsourcing of manufacturing and service jobs to places such as India and China and look at the benefits and costs of outsourcing, not just to business firms and their employees but also to entire economies. First, though, we need to get a better overview of the nature and process of globalization, and that is the function of this first chapter.

LO 1-1
Understand what is meant by the term *globalization*.

What Is Globalization?

As used in this text, **globalization** refers to the shift toward a more integrated and interdependent world economy. Globalization has several facets, including the globalization of markets and the globalization of production.

globalization
Trend away from distinct national economic units and toward one huge global market.

globalization of markets
Moving away from an economic system in which national markets are distinct entities, isolated by trade barriers and barriers of distance, time, and culture, and toward a system in which national markets are merging into one global market.

THE GLOBALIZATION OF MARKETS

The **globalization of markets** refers to the merging of historically distinct and separate national markets into one huge global marketplace. Falling barriers to cross-border trade and investment have made it easier to sell internationally. It has been argued for some time that the tastes and preferences of consumers in different nations are beginning to converge on some global norm, thereby helping create a global market.[4] Consumer products such as Citigroup credit cards, Coca-Cola soft drinks, video games, McDonald's hamburgers, Starbucks coffee, IKEA furniture, and Apple iPhones are frequently held up as prototypical examples of this trend. The firms that produce these products are more than just benefactors of this trend; they are also facilitators of it. By offering the same basic product worldwide, they help create a global market.

A company does not have to be the size of these multinational giants to facilitate, and benefit from, the globalization of markets. In the United States, for example, according to the International Trade Administration, more than 295,000 small and medium-size firms with fewer than 500 employees exported in 2013, accounting for 98 percent of the companies that exported that year. More generally, exports from small and medium-sized companies accounted for 33 percent of the value of U.S. exports of manufactured goods in 2013.[5] Typical of these is B&S Aircraft Alloys, a New York company whose exports account for 40 percent of its $8 million annual revenues.[6] The situation is similar in several other nations. For example, in Germany, the world's largest exporter, a staggering 98 percent of small and midsize companies have exposure to international markets, via either exports or international production.[7]

International Business Resources

globalEDGE™ offers the latest and most comprehensive international business and trade content for a wide range of topics. Whether conducting extensive market research, looking to improve your international knowledge, or simply browsing, you're sure to find what you need to sharpen your competitive edge in today's rapidly changing global marketplace. The easy, convenient, and free globalEDGE™ website's tagline is "Your Source for Global Business Knowledge." It was developed and is maintained by a 30-member team in the International Business Center at Michigan State University under the supervision of Tomas Hult, Tunga Kiyak, and Sarah Singer. For example, related to this chapter on globalization, take a look at the always up-to-date "Globalization" resources on the site at globaledge.msu.edu/global-resources/globalization. There is even a quick guide to the world history of globalization to browse!

Despite the global prevalence of Citigroup credit cards, McDonald's hamburgers, Starbucks coffee, and IKEA stores, it is important not to push too far the view that national markets are giving way to the global market. As we shall see in later chapters, significant differences still exist among national markets along many relevant dimensions, including consumer tastes and preferences, distribution channels, culturally embedded value systems, business systems, and legal regulations. Uber, for example, the fast-growing ride for hire service, is finding that it needs to refine its entry strategy in many foreign cities in order to take differences in the regulatory regime into account (see the Opening Case). These differences frequently require companies to customize marketing strategies, product features, and operating practices to best match conditions in a particular country.

The most global of markets are not typically markets for consumer products—where national differences in tastes and preferences can still be important enough to act as a brake on globalization—but markets for industrial goods and materials that serve universal needs the world over. These include the markets for commodities such as aluminum, oil, and wheat; for industrial products such as microprocessors, DRAMs (computer memory chips), and commercial jet aircraft; for computer software; and for financial assets from U.S. Treasury bills to Eurobonds and futures on the Nikkei index or the euro. That being said, it is increasingly evident that many newer high-technology consumer products, such as Apple's iPhone, are being successfully sold the same way the world over.

In many global markets, the same firms frequently confront each other as competitors in nation after nation. Coca-Cola's rivalry with PepsiCo is a global one, as are the rivalries between Ford and Toyota; Boeing and Airbus; Caterpillar and Komatsu in earthmoving equipment; General Electric and Rolls-Royce in aero engines; Sony, Nintendo, and Microsoft in video-game consoles; and Samsung and Apple in smartphones. If a firm moves into a nation not currently served by its rivals, many of those rivals are sure to follow to prevent their competitor from gaining an advantage.[8] As firms follow each other around the world, they bring with them many of the assets that served them well in other national markets—their products, operating strategies, marketing strategies, and brand names—creating some homogeneity across markets. Thus, greater uniformity replaces diversity. In an increasing number of industries, it is no longer meaningful to talk about "the German market," "the American market," "the Brazilian market," or "the Japanese market"; for many firms, there is only the global market.

THE GLOBALIZATION OF PRODUCTION

The **globalization of production** refers to the sourcing of goods and services from locations around the globe to take advantage of national differences in the cost and quality of **factors of production** (such as labor, energy, land, and capital). By doing this, companies hope to lower their overall cost structure or improve the quality or functionality of their product offering, thereby allowing them to compete more effectively. For example, Boeing has made extensive use of outsourcing to foreign suppliers. Consider Boeing's 777: eight Japanese suppliers make parts for the fuselage, doors, and wings; a supplier in Singapore makes the doors for the nose landing gear; three suppliers in Italy manufacture wing flaps; and so on.[9] In total, some 30 percent of the 777, by value, is built by foreign companies. And, for its most recent jet airliner, the 787, Boeing has pushed this trend even further; some 65 percent of the total value of the aircraft is outsourced to foreign companies, 35 percent of which goes to three major Japanese companies.

globalization of production

Trend by individual firms to disperse parts of their productive processes to different locations around the globe to take advantage of differences in cost and quality of factors of production.

factors of production

Inputs into the productive process of a firm, including labor, management, land, capital, and technological know-how.

Part of Boeing's rationale for outsourcing so much production to foreign suppliers is that these suppliers are the best in the world at their particular activity. A global web of suppliers yields a better final product, which enhances the chances of Boeing winning a greater share of total orders for aircraft than its global rival, Airbus. Boeing also outsources some production to foreign countries to increase the chance that it will win significant orders from airlines based in that country. For a more detailed look at the globalization of production at Boeing, see the accompanying Management Focus.

Did You Know?

Did you know that your iPhone was assembled in China? It's not what you might think.

Visit your instructor's Connect® course and click on SmartBook® or visit www. learnsmartadvantage .com to view a short video explanation from the authors.

Early outsourcing efforts were primarily confined to manufacturing activities, such as those undertaken by Boeing and Apple. Increasingly, however, companies are taking advantage of modern communications technology, particularly the Internet, to outsource service activities to low-cost producers in other nations. The Internet has allowed hospitals to outsource some radiology work to India, where images from MRI scans and the like are read at night while U.S. physicians

management FOCUS

Boeing's Global Production System

Executives at the Boeing Corporation, America's largest exporter, say that building a large commercial jet aircraft like the 747 or 787 involves bringing together more than a million parts in flying formation. Forty-five years ago, when the early models of Boeing's venerable 737 and 747 jets were rolling off the company's Seattle-area production lines, foreign suppliers accounted for only 5 percent of those parts on average. Boeing was vertically integrated and manufactured many of the major components that went into the planes. The largest parts produced by outside suppliers were the jet engines, where two of the three suppliers were American companies. The lone foreign engine manufacturer was the British company Rolls-Royce.

Fast-forward to the modern era, and things look very different. In the case of its latest aircraft, the super-efficient 787 Dreamliner, 50 outside suppliers spread around the world account for 65 percent of the value of the aircraft. Italian firm Alenia Aeronautica makes the center fuselage and horizontal stabilizer. Kawasaki of Japan makes part of the forward fuselage and the fixed trailing edge of the wing. French firm Messier-Dowty makes the aircraft's landing gear. German firm Diehl Luftahrt Elektronik supplies the main cabin lighting. Sweden's Saab Aerostructures makes the access doors. Japanese company Jamco makes parts for the lavatories, flight deck interiors, and galleys. Mitsubishi Heavy Industries of Japan makes the wings. KAA of Korea makes the wing tips. And so on.

Why the change? One reason is that 80 percent of Boeing's customers are foreign airlines, and to sell into those nations, it often helps to be giving business to those nations. The trend started in 1974 when Mitsubishi of Japan was given contracts to produce inboard wing flaps for the 747. The Japanese reciprocated by placing big orders for Boeing jets. A second rationale was to disperse component part production to those suppliers who are the best in the world at their particular activity. Over the years, for example, Mitsubishi has acquired considerable expertise in the manufacture of wings, so it was logical for Boeing to use Mitsubishi to make the wings for the 787. Similarly, the 787 is the first commercial jet aircraft to be made almost entirely out of carbon fiber, so Boeing tapped Japan's Toray Industries, a world-class expert in sturdy but light carbon-fiber composites, to supply materials for the fuselage. A third reason for the extensive outsourcing on the 787 was that Boeing wanted to unburden itself of some of the risks and costs associated with developing production facilities for the 787. By outsourcing, it pushed some of those risks and costs onto suppliers, who had to undertake major investments in capacity to ramp up to produce for the 787.

So what did Boeing retain for itself? Engineering design, marketing and sales, and final assembly are done at its Everett plant north of Seattle, all activities where Boeing maintains it is the best in the world. Of major component parts, Boeing made only the tail fin and wing to body fairing (which attaches the wings to the fuselage of the plane). Everything else was outsourced.

As the 787 moved through development in the 2000s, however, it became clear that Boeing had pushed the outsourcing paradigm too far. Coordinating a globally dispersed production system this extensive turned out to be very challenging. Parts turned up late, some parts didn't "snap together" the way Boeing had envisioned, and several suppliers ran into engineering problems that slowed down the entire production process. As a consequence, the date for delivery of the first jet was pushed back more than four years, and Boeing had to take millions of dollars in penalties for late deliveries. The problems at one supplier, Vought Aircraft in North Carolina, were so severe that Boeing ultimately agreed to acquire the company and bring its production in-house. Vought was co-owned by Alenia of Italy and made parts of the main fuselage.

There are now signs that Boeing is rethinking some of its global outsourcing policy. For its next jet, a new version of its popular wide-bodied 777 jet, the 777X, which will use the same carbon-fiber technology as the 787, Boeing will bring wing production back in-house. Mitsubishi and Kawasaki of Japan produce much of the wing structure for the 787 and for the original version of the 777. However, recently Japan's airlines have been placing large orders with Airbus, breaking with their traditional allegiance to Boeing. This seems to have given Boeing an opening to bring wing production back in-house. Boeing executives also note that Boeing has lost much of its expertise in wing production over the last 20 years due to outsourcing, and bringing it back in-house for new carbon-fiber wings might enable Boeing to regain these important core skills and strengthen the company's competitive position.

Sources: K. Epstein and J. Crown, "Globalization Bites Boeing," *Bloomberg Businessweek*, March 12, 2008; H. Mallick, "Out of Control Outsourcing Ruined Boeing's Beautiful Dreamliner," *The Star*, February 25, 2013; P. Kavilanz, "Dreamliner: Where in the World Its Parts Come From," *CNN Money*, January 18, 2013; S. Dubois, "Boeing's Dreamliner Mess: Simply Inevitable?," *CNN Money*, January 22, 2013; A. Scott and T. Kelly, "Boeing's Loss of a $9.5 Billion Deal Could Bring Jobs Back to the U.S.," *Business Insider*, October 14, 2013.

sleep; the results are ready for them in the morning. Many software companies, including Microsoft, now use Indian engineers to perform test functions on software designed in the United States. The time difference allows Indian engineers to run debugging tests on software written in the United States when U.S. engineers sleep, transmitting the corrected code back to the United States over secure Internet connections so it is ready for U.S. engineers to work on the following day. Dispersing value-creation activities in this way can compress the time and lower the costs required to develop new software programs. Other companies, from computer makers to banks, are outsourcing customer service functions, such as customer call centers, to developing nations where labor is cheaper. In another example from health care, workers in the Philippines transcribe American medical files (such as audio files from doctors seeking approval from insurance companies for performing a procedure). Some estimates suggest the outsourcing of many administrative procedures in health care, such as customer service and claims processing, could reduce health care costs in America by as much as $70 billion.[10]

The economist Robert Reich has argued that as a consequence of the trend exemplified by companies such as Boeing, Apple, and Microsoft, in many cases it is becoming irrelevant to talk about American products, Japanese products, German products, or Korean products. Increasingly, according to Reich, the outsourcing of productive activities to different suppliers results in the creation of products that are global in nature, that is, "global products."[11] But as with the globalization of markets, companies must be careful not to push the globalization of production too far. As we will see in later chapters, substantial impediments still make it difficult for firms to achieve the optimal dispersion of their productive activities to locations around the globe. These impediments include formal and informal barriers to trade between countries, barriers to foreign direct investment, transportation costs, issues associated with economic and political risk, and the sheer managerial challenge of coordinating a globally dispersed supply chain (an issue for Boeing with the 787, as discussed in the Management Focus). For example, government regulations ultimately limit the ability of hospitals to outsource the process of interpreting MRI scans to developing nations where radiologists are cheaper.

test PREP

Use SmartBook to help retain what you have learned. Access your Instructor's Connect course to check out SmartBook or go to learnsmartadvantage.com for help.

Nevertheless, the globalization of markets and production will probably continue. Modern firms are important actors in this trend, their very actions fostering increased globalization. These firms, however, are merely responding in an efficient manner to changing conditions in their operating environment—as well they should.

General Agreement on Tariffs and Trade (GATT)
International treaty that committed signatories to lowering barriers to the free flow of goods across national borders and led to the WTO.

World Trade Organization (WTO)
The organization that succeeded the General Agreement on Tariffs and Trade (GATT) as a result of the successful completion of the Uruguay Round of GATT negotiations.

International Monetary Fund (IMF)
International institution set up to maintain order in the international monetary system.

World Bank
International institution set up to promote general economic development in the world's poorer nations.

The Emergence of Global Institutions

As markets globalize and an increasing proportion of business activity transcends national borders, institutions are needed to help manage, regulate, and police the global marketplace and to promote the establishment of multinational treaties to govern the global business system. Over the past half century, a number of important global institutions have been created to help perform these functions, including the **General Agreement on Tariffs and Trade (GATT)** and its successor, the World Trade Organization; the International Monetary Fund and its sister institution, the World Bank; and the United Nations. All these institutions were created by voluntary agreement between individual nation-states, and their functions are enshrined in international treaties.

The **World Trade Organization (WTO)** (like the GATT before it) is primarily responsible for policing the world trading system and making sure nation-states adhere to the rules laid down in trade treaties signed by WTO member states. As of 2016, 162 nations that collectively accounted for 98 percent of world trade were WTO members, thereby giving the organization enormous scope and influence. The WTO is also responsible for facilitating the establishment of additional multinational agreements among WTO member states. Over its entire history, and that of the GATT before it, the WTO has promoted the lowering of barriers to cross-border trade and investment. In doing so, the WTO has been the instrument of its member states, which have sought to create a more open global business system unencumbered by barriers to trade and investment between countries. Without an institution such as the WTO, the globalization of markets and production is unlikely to have proceeded as far as it has. However, as we shall see in this chapter and in Chapter 7 when we look closely at the WTO, critics charge that the organization is usurping the national sovereignty of individual nation-states.

The **International Monetary Fund (IMF)** and the **World Bank** were both created in 1944 by 44 nations that met at Bretton Woods, New Hampshire. The IMF was established to maintain order in the international monetary system; the World Bank was set up to promote economic development. In the more than six decades since their creation, both institutions have emerged as significant players in the global economy. The World Bank is the

Can the International Court of Justice Be Effective?

The International Court of Justice (www.icj-cij.org) is the principal judicial organ of the United Nations (UN). Of the six principal organs of the UN, it is the only one not located in New York (United States); instead, the seat of the Court is at the Peace Palace in The Hague (Netherlands). The court's role is to settle, in accordance with international law, legal disputes submitted to it by countries and to give advisory opinions on legal questions referred to it by authorized United Nations organs and specialized agencies. But, how effective can the UN International Court of Justice really be in the global marketplace with its many legal systems?

Source: www.icj-cij.org/court.

How Important is the EU Among the Group of Twenty (G20)?

There have been nine G20 Leaders' Summits since they started in 2008. The Group of Twenty includes 19 prominent countries and the European Union. At the "Leaders' Level," following leadership by the United States, United Kingdom, Canada, South Korea, and France from 2008 to 2011, the more recent leadership has included three emerging markets (Mexico in 2012; Russia in 2013; Turkey in 2015) in a four-year span (with Australia the leader in 2014). G20 members represent about 85 percent of global GDP, 80 percent of global trade, and about two-thirds of the world's population. Now, is it really right for the G20 to include 19 countries and all of the EU countries, or should the EU countries be selected individually?

Source: www.g20.org/index.php/en/numeralia.

less controversial of the two sister institutions. It has focused on making low-interest loans to cash-strapped governments in poor nations that wish to undertake significant infrastructure investments (such as building dams or roads).

The IMF is often seen as the lender of last resort to nation-states whose economies are in turmoil and whose currencies are losing value against those of other nations. During the past two decades, for example, the IMF has lent money to the governments of troubled states, including Argentina, Indonesia, Mexico, Russia, South Korea, Thailand, and Turkey. More recently, the IMF took a proactive role in helping countries cope with some of the effects of the 2008–2009 global financial crisis. IMF loans come with strings attached, however; in return for loans, the IMF requires nation-states to adopt specific economic policies aimed at returning their troubled economies to stability and growth. These requirements have sparked controversy. Some critics charge that the IMF's policy recommendations are often inappropriate; others maintain that by telling national governments what economic policies they must adopt, the IMF, like the WTO, is usurping the sovereignty of nation-states. We will look at the debate over the role of the IMF in Chapter 11.

United Nations (UN)

An international organization made up of 193 countries headquartered in New York City, formed in 1945 to promote peace, security, and cooperation.

The **United Nations (UN)** was established October 24, 1945, by 51 countries committed to preserving peace through international cooperation and collective security. Today, nearly every nation in the world belongs to the United Nations; membership now totals 193 countries. When states become members of the United Nations, they agree to accept the obligations of the UN Charter, an international treaty that establishes basic principles of international relations. According to the charter, the UN has four purposes: to maintain international peace and security, to develop friendly relations among nations, to cooperate in solving international problems and in promoting respect for human rights, and to be a center for harmonizing the actions of nations. Although the UN is perhaps best known for its peacekeeping role, one of the organization's central mandates is the promotion of higher standards of living, full employment, and conditions of economic and social progress and development—all issues that are central to the creation of a vibrant global economy. As much as 70 percent of the work of the UN system is devoted to accomplishing this mandate. To do so, the UN works closely with other international institutions such as the World Bank. Guiding the work is the belief that eradicating poverty and improving the well-being of people everywhere are necessary steps in creating conditions for lasting world peace.[12]

Group of Twenty (G20)

Established in 1999, the G20 comprises the finance ministers and central bank governors of the 19 largest economies in the world, plus representatives from the European Union and the European Central Bank.

Another institution in the news is the **Group of Twenty (G20)**. Established in 1999, the G20 comprises the finance ministers and central bank governors of the 19 largest economies in the world, plus representatives from the European Union and the European Central Bank. Collectively, the G20 represents 90 percent of global GDP and 80 percent of international global trade. Originally established to formulate a coordinated policy response to financial crises in developing nations, in 2008 and 2009 it became the forum through which major nations attempted to launch a coordinated policy response to the global financial crisis that started in America and then rapidly spread around the world, ushering in the first serious global economic recession since 1981.

LO 1-2

Recognize the main drivers of globalization.

Drivers of Globalization

Two macro factors underlie the trend toward greater globalization.[13] The first is the decline in barriers to the free flow of goods, services, and capital that has occurred since the end of World War II. The second factor is technological change, particularly the dramatic developments in recent decades in communication, information processing, and transportation technologies.

international trade

Occurs when a firm exports goods or services to consumers in another country.

DECLINING TRADE AND INVESTMENT BARRIERS

During the 1920s and 1930s, many of the world's nation-states erected formidable barriers to international trade and foreign direct investment. **International trade** occurs when a firm exports goods or services

	1913	1950	1990	2014
France	21%	18%	5.9%	1.5%
Germany	20	26	5.9	1.5
Italy	18	25	5.9	1.5
Japan	30	—	5.3	1.3
Holland	5	11	5.9	1.5
Sweden	20	9	4.4	1.5
United Kingdom	—	23	5.9	1.5
United States	44	14	4.8	1.5

TABLE

Average Tariff Rates on Manufactured Products as Percentage of Value

Sources: The 1913–1990 data are from "Who Wants to Be a Giant?," *The Economist: A Survey of the Multinationals*, June 24, 1995, pp. 3–4. The 2014 data are from World Development Indicators 2015, World Bank.

to consumers in another country. **Foreign direct investment (FDI)** occurs when a firm invests resources in business activities outside its home country. Many of the barriers to international trade took the form of high tariffs on imports of manufactured goods. The typical aim of such tariffs was to protect domestic industries from foreign competition. One consequence, however, was "beggar thy neighbor" retaliatory trade policies, with countries progressively raising trade barriers against each other. Ultimately, this depressed world demand and contributed to the Great Depression of the 1930s.

foreign direct investment (FDI)
Direct investment in business operations in a foreign country.

Having learned from this experience, the advanced industrial nations of the West committed themselves after World War II to progressively reducing barriers to the free flow of goods, services, and capital among nations.[14] This goal was enshrined in the General Agreement on Tariffs and Trade. Under the umbrella of GATT, eight rounds of negotiations among member states worked to lower barriers to the free flow of goods and services. The first round of negotiations went into effect in 1948. The most recent negotiations to be completed, known as the Uruguay Round, were finalized in December 1993. The Uruguay Round further reduced trade barriers; extended GATT to cover services as well as manufactured goods; provided enhanced protection for patents, trademarks, and copyrights; and established the World Trade Organization to police the international trading system.[15] Table 1.1 summarizes the impact of GATT agreements on average tariff rates for *manufactured* goods. As can be seen, average tariff rates have fallen significantly since 1950 and now stand at about 1.5 percent. Comparable tariff rates in 2014 for China and India were 4.8 and 7.1 percent, respectively.

In addition to the GATT and WTO, there have been a large number of regional trade agreements between two or more countries that have been implemented in recent decades. These included the North American Free Trade Agreement (NAFTA) and the European Union (EU), as well as numerous bilateral agreements, such as a 2012 free trade agreement between the United States and South Korea. In 1960, there were only two such regional agreements in the world. As of early 2016, there were 267 in force.

In addition to reducing trade barriers, many countries have also been progressively removing restrictions to foreign direct investment. According to the United Nations, some 80 percent of the 1,440 changes made worldwide between 2000 and 2013 in the laws governing foreign direct investment created a more favorable environment for FDI.[17]

Such trends have been driving both the globalization of markets and the globalization of production. The lowering of barriers to international trade enables firms to view the world, rather than a single country, as their market. The lowering of trade and investment barriers also allows firms to base production at the optimal location for that activity. Thus, a firm might design a product in one country, produce component parts in two other countries, assemble the product in yet another country, and then export the finished product around the world.

According to WTO, the value of world trade in merchandised goods has grown consistently faster than the growth rate in the world economy since since 1950 (see Figure 1.1). As a consequence, by 2014 the value of world trade was 180 times larger than in 1950, whereas the world economy was 9.3 times larger. This trend has continued into the modern era. Between

1.1 FIGURE

Value of World Trade and World Production, 1950–2014 (Index 2005 = 100).

Source: World Trade Organization, 2016.

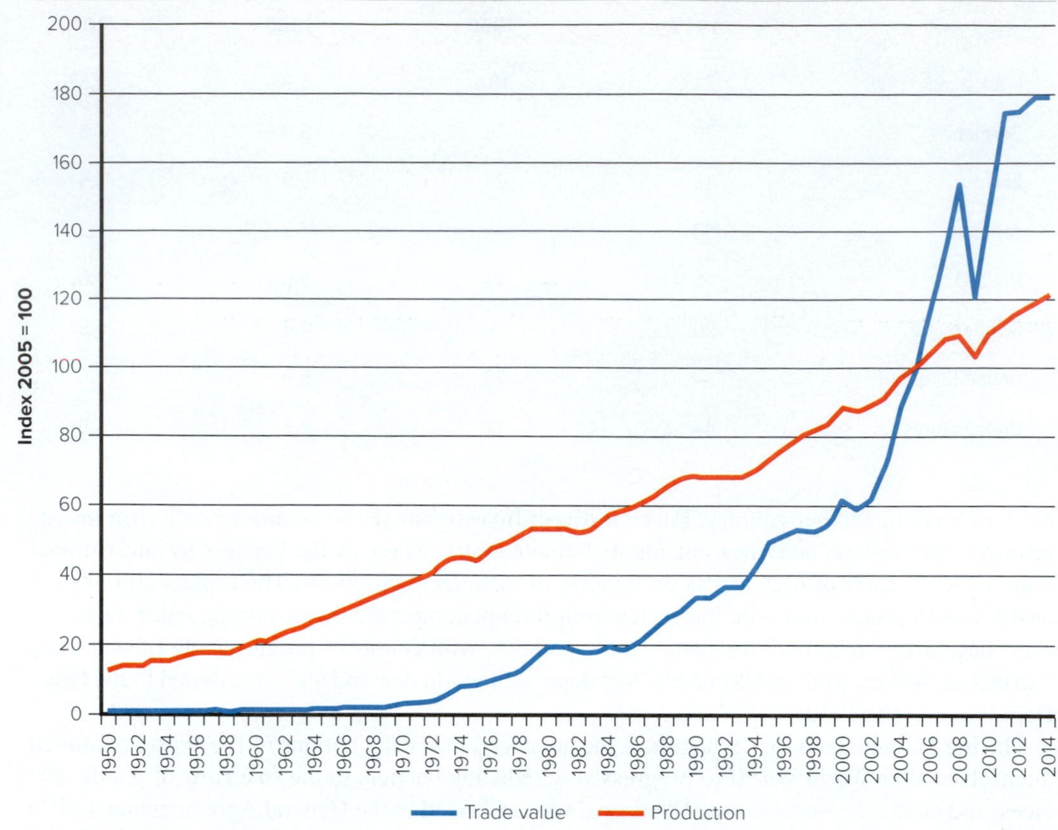

1990 and 2014, the value of world trade has increased 5.3 times whereas the world economy has increased 1.75 times after adjusting for inflation.[18] Since the mid-1980s, the value of international trade in services has also grown robustly and now accounts for about 20 percent of the value of all international trade. Increasingly, international trade in services has been driven by advances in communications, which allow corporations to outsource service activities to different locations around the globe. For example, many corporations in the developed world outsource customer service functions, from software testing to customer call centers, to developing nations where labor costs are lower.

The difference in the growth rates of world production and world trade is why studying international business is so important. While we produce more goods and services today compared with before, a far greater proportion of that production is being traded across national borders than at any time in modern history. Moreover, the knowledge society that we live in has resulted in consumers knowing more than ever before about goods and services being produced worldwide. This is driving demand for internationally traded goods. Thus the larger the difference between the growth rates of world trade and world production, the greater the extent of globalization and the more important it becomes to understand international business.

The fact that the volume of world trade has been growing faster than world GDP implies several things. First, more firms are doing what Boeing does with the 777 and 787: dispersing parts of their production process to different locations around the globe to drive down production costs and increase product quality. Second, the economies of the world's nation-states are becoming ever more intertwined. As trade expands, nations are becoming increasingly dependent on each other for important goods and services. Third, the world has become significantly wealthier since 1990. The implication is that rising trade is the engine that has helped pull the global economy along.

Evidence also suggests that foreign direct investment is playing an increasing role in the global economy as firms increase their cross-border investments. The average yearly outflow of FDI increased from $14 billion in 1970 to $1.35 trillion in 2014.[19] Even though the 2014 figure was below the peak of $1.9 billion in foreign direct investment recorded in 2007, the long-term trends remain positive. As a result of the strong FDI flow, by 2014 the global stock of FDI was about $26 trillion. More than 80,000 parent companies had more than 800,000 affiliates in foreign markets that collectively employed more than 75 million people abroad and generated value accounting for about 11 percent of global GDP. The foreign affiliates of multinationals had $36 trillion in global sales, higher than the value of global exports of goods and services, which stood at close to $23.4 trillion.[20]

Commercial jet travel has reduced the time needed to get from one location to another, effectively shrinking the globe.

Source: © Glow Images RF

The globalization of markets and production and the resulting growth of world trade, foreign direct investment, and imports all imply that firms are finding their home markets under attack from foreign competitors. This is true in China, where U.S. companies such as Apple, General Motors, and Starbucks are expanding their presence. It is true in the United States, where Japanese automobile firms have taken market share away from General Motors and Ford over the past three decades, and it is true in Europe, where the once-dominant Dutch company Philips has seen its market share in the consumer electronics industry taken by Japan's Panasonic and Sony and Korea's Samsung and LG. The growing integration of the world economy into a single, huge marketplace is increasing the intensity of competition in a range of manufacturing and service industries.

However, declining barriers to cross-border trade and investment cannot be taken for granted. As we shall see in subsequent chapters, demands for "protection" from foreign competitors are still often heard in countries around the world, including the United States. Although a return to the restrictive trade policies of the 1920s and 1930s is unlikely, it is not clear whether the political majority in the industrialized world favors further reductions in trade barriers. Indeed, the global financial crisis of 2008–2009 and the associated drop in global output that occurred led to more calls for trade barriers to protect jobs at home. If trade barriers decline no further, this may slow the rate of globalization of both markets and production.

THE ROLE OF TECHNOLOGICAL CHANGE

The lowering of trade barriers made globalization of markets and production a theoretical possibility. Technological change has made it a tangible reality. Since the end of World War II, the world has seen major advances in communication, information processing, and transportation technology, including the explosive emergence of the Internet.

Microprocessors and Telecommunications

Perhaps the single most important innovation has been development of the microprocessor, which enabled the explosive growth of high-power, low-cost computing, vastly increasing the amount of information that can be processed by individuals and firms. The microprocessor also underlies many recent advances in telecommunications technology. Over the past 30 years, global communications have been revolutionized by developments in satellite, optical fiber, wireless technologies, and the Internet. These technologies rely on the microprocessor to encode, transmit, and decode the vast amount of information that flows along these electronic highways. The cost of microprocessors continues to fall, while their power increases (a phenomenon known as **Moore's law**, which predicts that the power of microprocessor technology doubles and its cost of production falls in half every 18 months).[21]

Moore's law
The power of microprocessor technology doubles and its costs of production fall in half every 18 months.

The Internet

The explosive growth of the Internet since 1994 when the first web browser was introduced is the latest expression of this development. In 1990, fewer than 1 million users were connected to the Internet. By 1995, the figure had risen to 50 million. By 2015, the Internet had 3.3 billion users, or 46% of the global population.[22] The Internet has developed into the information backbone of the global economy. In North America alone, e-commerce retail sales surpassed $340 billion in 2015 (up from almost nothing in 1998), while global e-commerce sales surpassed $1 trillion for the first time in 2012.[23] Viewed globally, the Internet has emerged as an equalizer. It rolls back some of the constraints of location, scale, and time zones.[24] The Internet makes it much easier for buyers and sellers to find each other, wherever they may be located and whatever their size. It allows businesses, both small and large, to expand their global presence at a lower cost than ever before. Just as important, it enables enterprises to coordinate and control a globally dispersed production system in a way that was not possible 25 years ago.

Transportation Technology

In addition to developments in communications technology, several major innovations in transportation technology have occurred since the 1950s. In economic terms, the most important are probably the development of commercial jet aircraft and superfreighters and the introduction of *containerization*, which simplifies transshipment from one mode of transport to another. The advent of commercial jet travel, by reducing the time needed to get from one location to another, has effectively shrunk the globe. In terms of travel time, New York is now "closer" to Tokyo than it was to Philadelphia in the colonial days.

Containerization has revolutionized the transportation business, significantly lowering the costs of shipping goods over long distances. Because the international shipping industry is responsible for carrying about 90 percent of the *volume* of world trade in goods, this has been an extremely important development.[25] Before the advent of containerization, moving goods from one mode of transport to another was very labor intensive, lengthy, and costly. It could take days and several hundred longshore workers to unload a ship and reload goods onto trucks and trains. With the advent of widespread containerization in the 1970s and 1980s, the whole process can now be executed by a handful of longshore workers in a couple of days. As a result of the efficiency gains associated with containerization, transportation costs have plummeted, making it much more economical to ship goods around the globe, thereby helping drive the globalization of markets and production. Between 1920 and 1990, the average ocean freight and port charges per ton of U.S. export and import cargo fell from $95 to $29 (in 1990 dollars).[26] Today, the typical cost of transporting a 20-foot container from Asia to Europe carrying more than 20 tons of cargo is about the same as the economy airfare for a single passenger on the same journey. As a result, in 2012 the shipping cost of a $700 TV set was just $10 and that of a $150 vacuum cleaner just $1.[27] The cost of shipping freight per ton-mile on railroads in the United States also fell from 3.04 cents in 1985 to 2.3 cents in 2000, largely as a result of efficiency gains from the widespread use of containers.[28] An increased share of cargo now goes by air. Between 1955 and 1999, average air transportation revenue per ton-kilometer fell by more than 80 percent.[29] Reflecting the falling cost of airfreight, by the early 2000s air shipments accounted for 28 percent of the value of U.S. trade, up from 7 percent in 1965.[30]

Implications for the Globalization of Production

As transportation costs associated with the globalization of production have declined, dispersal of production to geographically separate locations has become more economical. As a result of the technological innovations discussed earlier, the real costs of information processing and communication have fallen dramatically in the past two decades. These developments make it possible for a firm to create and then manage a globally dispersed production system, further facilitating the globalization of production. A worldwide communications network has become essential for many international businesses. For example, Dell uses the Internet to coordinate and control a globally dispersed production system to such an extent that it holds only three days' worth of inventory at its assembly locations. Dell's Internet-based system records orders for computer equipment as they are submitted by customers via the company's website and then immediately transmits the resulting orders for components to various suppliers around the world, which have a real-time look at Dell's order flow and can adjust their production schedules accordingly. Given the low cost of airfreight, Dell can use air transportation to speed up the delivery of critical components to meet unanticipated demand shifts without delaying the shipment of final product to consumers. Dell has also used modern communications technology to outsource its customer service operations to India. When U.S. customers call Dell with a service inquiry, they are routed to Bangalore in India, where English-speaking service personnel handle the call.

Implications for the Globalization of Markets

In addition to the globalization of production, technological innovations have facilitated the globalization of markets. Low-cost global communications networks, including those built on top of the Internet, are helping create electronic global marketplaces. As noted earlier, low-cost transportation has made it more economical to ship products around the world, thereby helping create global markets. In addition, low-cost jet travel has resulted in the mass movement of people between countries. This has reduced the cultural distance between countries and is bringing about some convergence of consumer tastes and preferences. At the same time, global communications networks and global media are creating a worldwide culture. U.S. television networks such as CNN and HBO are now received in many countries, Hollywood films are shown the world over, while non-U.S. news networks such as the BBC and Al Jazeera also have a global footprint. In any society, the media are primary conveyors of culture; as global media develop, we must expect the evolution of something akin to a global culture. A logical result of this evolution is the emergence of global markets for consumer products. Clear signs of this are apparent. It is now as easy to find a McDonald's restaurant in Tokyo as it is in New York, to buy an iPad in Rio as it is in Berlin, and to buy Gap jeans in Paris as it is in San Francisco.

Despite these trends, we must be careful not to overemphasize their importance. While modern communications and transportation technologies are ushering in the "global village," significant national differences remain in culture, consumer preferences, and business practices. A firm that ignores differences among countries does so at its peril. We shall stress this point repeatedly throughout this text and elaborate on it in later chapters.

Use SmartBook to help retain what you have learned. Access your Instructor's Connect course to check out SmartBook or go to learnsmartadvantage.com for help.

The Changing Demographics of the Global Economy

Describe the changing nature of the global economy.

Hand in hand with the trend toward globalization has been a fairly dramatic change in the demographics of the global economy over the past 30 years. As late as the 1960s, four stylized facts described the demographics of the global economy. The first was U.S. dominance in the world economy and world trade picture. The second was U.S. dominance in world foreign direct investment. Related to this, the third fact was the dominance of large, multinational U.S. firms on the international business scene. The fourth was that roughly half the globe—the centrally planned economies of the communist world—was off-limits to Western international businesses. As will be explained here, all four of these qualities either have changed or are now changing rapidly.

THE CHANGING WORLD OUTPUT AND WORLD TRADE PICTURE In the early 1960s, the United States was still by far the world's dominant industrial power. In 1960, the United States accounted for 38.3 percent of world output, measured by gross domestic product (GDP). By 2014, the United States accounted for 22.4 percent of world output, still the world's largest industrial and commercial power but down significantly in relative size (see Table 1.2). Nor was the United States the only developed nation to see its relative standing slip. The same occurred to Germany, France, and the United Kingdom—all nations that were among the first to industrialize. This change in the U.S. position was not an absolute decline because the U.S. economy grew significantly between 1960 and 2014 (the economies of Germany, France, and the United Kingdom also grew during this time). Rather, it was a relative decline, reflecting the faster economic growth of several other economies, particularly in Asia. For example, as can be seen from Table 1.2, from 1960 to 2014, China's share of world output increased from a trivial amount to 13.3 percent, making it the world's

The Changing Demographics of World Output and Trade

Sources: Output data from World Bank database, 2016. Trade data from WTO Statistical Database, 2015.

Country	Share of World Output, 1960 (%)	Share of World Output, 2014 (%)	Share of World Exports, 2014 (%)
United States	38.3%	22.4%	9.2%
Germany	8.7	5.0	8.4
France	4.6	3.6	3.1
Italy	3.0	2.8	2.9
United Kingdom	5.3	3.0	2.7
Canada	3.0	2.3	2.7
Japan	3.3	5.9	3.9
China	NA	13.3	13.2

second-largest economy. Other countries that markedly increased their share of world output included Japan, Thailand, Malaysia, Taiwan, Brazil, and South Korea.

By the end of the 1980s, the U.S. position as the world's leading trading nation was being challenged. Over the past 30 years, U.S. dominance in export markets has waned as Japan, Germany, and a number of newly industrialized countries such as South Korea and China have taken a larger share of world exports. During the 1960s, the United States routinely accounted for 20 percent of world exports of manufactured goods. But as Table 1.2 shows, the U.S. share of world exports of goods and services had slipped to 9.2 percent by 2014, behind that of China.

As emerging economies such as China, India, Russia, and Brazil continue to grow, a further relative decline in the share of world output and world exports accounted for by the United States and other long-established developed nations seems likely. By itself, this is not bad. The relative decline of the United States reflects the growing economic development and industrialization of the world economy, as opposed to any absolute decline in the health of the U.S. economy.

Most forecasts now predict a continued rise in the share of world output accounted for by developing nations such as China, India, Russia, Indonesia, Thailand, South Korea, Mexico, and Brazil, and a commensurate decline in the share enjoyed by rich industrialized countries such as Great Britain, Germany, Japan, and the United States. If current trends continue, the Chinese economy could ultimately be larger than that of the United States on a purchasing power parity basis, while the economy of India will approach that of Germany. The World Bank has estimated that today's developing nations may account for more than 60 percent of world economic activity by 2025, while today's rich nations, which currently account for more than 55 percent of world economic activity, may account for only about 38 percent. Forecasts are not always correct, but these suggest that a shift in the economic geography of the world is now under way, although the magnitude of that shift is not totally evident. For international businesses, the implications of this changing economic geography are clear: Many of tomorrow's economic opportunities may be found in the developing nations of the world, and many of tomorrow's most capable competitors will probably also emerge from these regions. A case in point has been the dramatic expansion of India's software sector, which is profiled in the accompanying Country Focus.

country FOCUS

India's Software Sector

Some 25 years ago, a number of small software enterprises were established in Bangalore, India. Typical of these enterprises was Infosys Technologies, which was started by seven Indian entrepreneurs with about $1,000 among them. Infosys now has annual revenues of $8.25 billion and some 170,000 employees, but it is just one of more than 100 software companies clustered around Bangalore, which has become the epicenter of India's fast-growing information technology sector. From a standing start in the mid-1980s, by 2014–2015 this sector was generating export sales of almost $100 billion.

The growth of the Indian software sector has been based on four factors. First, the country has an abundant supply of engineering talent. Every year, Indian universities graduate some 400,000 engineers. Second, labor costs in the Indian software sector have historically been low. As recently as 2008, the cost to hire an Indian graduate was roughly 12 percent of the cost of hiring an American graduate (however, this gap is narrowing fast with pay in the sector now only 30–40 percent less than in the United States). Third, many Indians are fluent in English, which makes coordination between Western firms and India easier. Fourth, due to time differences, Indians can work while Americans sleep.

Initially, Indian software enterprises focused on the low end of the software industry, supplying basic software development and testing services to Western firms. But as the industry has grown in size and sophistication, Indian firms have moved up the market. Today, the leading Indian companies compete directly with the likes of IBM and EDS for large software development projects, business process outsourcing contracts, and information technology consulting services. Over the past 15 years, these markets have boomed, with Indian enterprises capturing a large slice of the pie. One response of Western firms to this emerging competitive threat has been to invest in India to garner the same kind of economic advantages that Indian firms enjoy. IBM, for example, has invested $2 billion in its Indian operations and now has 150,000 employees located there, more than in any other country. Microsoft, too, has made major investments in India, including a research and development (R&D) center in Hyderabad that employs 4,000 people and was located there specifically to tap into talented Indian engineers who did not want to move to the United States.

Sources: "America's Pain, India's Gain: Outsourcing," *The Economist*, January 11, 2003, p. 59; "The World Is Our Oyster," *The Economist*, October 7, 2006, pp. 9–10; "IBM and Globalization: Hungry Tiger, Dancing Elephant," *The Economist*, April 7, 2007, pp. 67–69; P. Mishra, "New Billing Model May Hit India's Software Exports," *Live Mint*, February 14, 2013; "India's Outsourcing Business: On the Turn," *The Economist*, January 19, 2013.

THE CHANGING FOREIGN DIRECT INVESTMENT PICTURE

Reflecting the dominance of the United States in the global economy, U.S. firms accounted for 66.3 percent of worldwide foreign direct investment flows in the 1960s. British firms were second, accounting for 10.5 percent, while Japanese firms were a distant eighth, with only 2 percent. The dominance of U.S. firms was so great that books were written about the economic threat posed to Europe by U.S. corporations.[31] Several European governments, most notably France, talked of limiting inward investment by U.S. firms.

However, as the barriers to the free flow of goods, services, and capital fell, and as other countries increased their shares of world output, non-U.S. firms increasingly began to invest across national borders. The motivation for much of this foreign direct investment by non-U.S. firms was the desire to disperse production activities to optimal locations and to build a direct presence in major foreign markets. Thus, beginning in the 1970s, European and Japanese firms began to shift labor-intensive manufacturing operations from their home markets to developing nations where labor costs were lower. In addition, many Japanese firms invested in North America and Europe—often as a hedge against unfavorable currency movements and the possible imposition of trade barriers. For example, Toyota, the Japanese automobile company, rapidly increased its investment in automobile production facilities in the United States and Europe during the late 1980s and 1990s. Toyota executives believed that an increasingly strong Japanese yen would price Japanese automobile exports out of foreign markets; therefore, production in the most important foreign markets, as opposed to exports from Japan, made sense. Toyota also undertook these investments to head off growing political pressures in the United States and Europe to restrict Japanese automobile exports into those markets.

One consequence of these developments is illustrated in Figure 1.2, which shows how the stock of foreign direct investment by the world's six most important national sources—the United States, the United Kingdom, Germany, the Netherlands, France, and Japan—changed between 1980 and 2013. (The **stock of foreign direct investment (FDI)** refers to the total cumulative value of foreign investments.) Figure 1.2 also shows the stock accounted for by firms from developing economies. The share of the total stock accounted for by U.S. firms declined from about 38 percent in 1980 to 24.4 percent in 2014. Meanwhile, the shares accounted for by the world's developing nations increased markedly. The rise in the share of FDI stock accounted for by developing nations reflects a growing trend for firms from these countries to invest outside their borders. In 2014, firms based in developing nations accounted for 18.7 percent of the stock of foreign direct investment, up from around 1 percent in 1980. Firms based in Hong Kong, South Korea, Singapore, Taiwan, India, Brazil, and mainland China accounted for much of this investment.

stock of FDI
The total accumulated value of foreign-owned assets at a given time.

Figure 1.3 illustrates two other important trends—the sustained growth in cross-border flows of foreign direct investment that occurred during the 1990s and the increasing importance of developing nations as the destination of foreign direct investment. Throughout the 1990s, the amount of investment directed at both developed and developing nations increased dramatically,

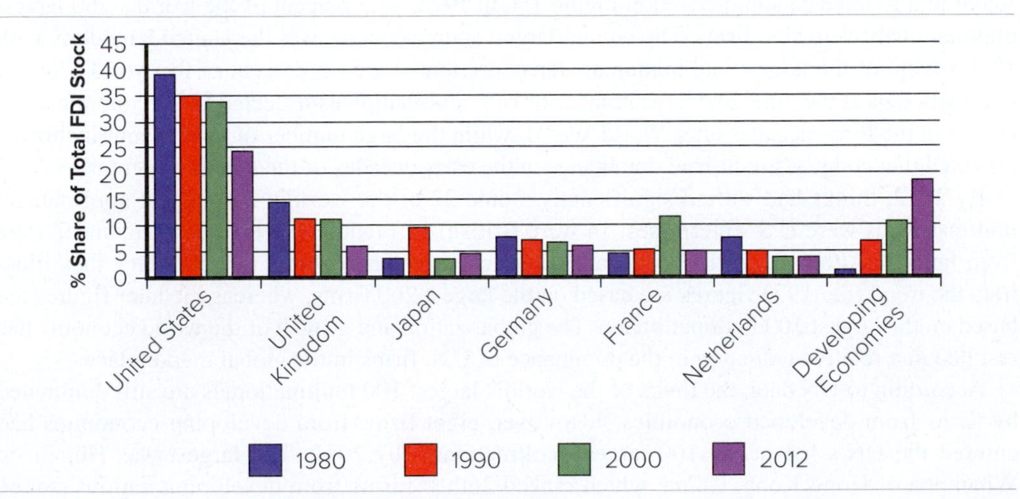

FIGURE

Percentage Share of Total FDI Stock, 1980–2014.

Source: C. W. L. Hill and G. T. M. Hult, *International Business: Competing in the Global Marketplace*. (New York, NY: McGraw-Hill Education, 2017).

FIGURE

FDI Inflows, 1980–2014.

Source: C. W. L. Hill and G. T. M. Hult, *International Business: Competing in the Global Marketplace.* (New York, NY: McGraw-Hill Education, 2017).

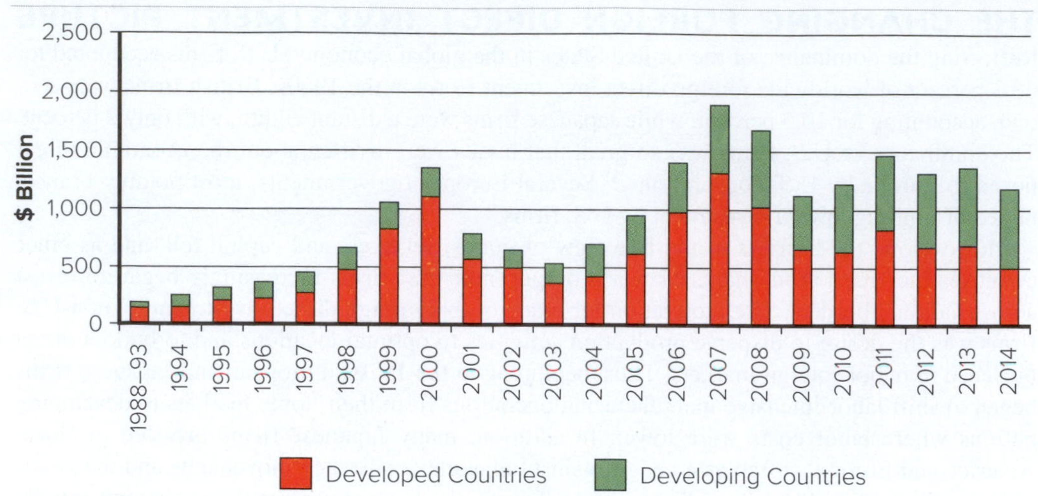

a trend that reflects the increasing internationalization of business corporations. A surge in foreign direct investment from 1998 to 2000 was followed by a slump from 2001 to 2003, associated with a slowdown in global economic activity after the collapse of the financial bubble of the late 1990s and 2000. The growth of foreign direct investment resumed in 2004 and continued through 2007, when it hit record levels, only to slow again in 2008 and 2009 as the global financial crisis took hold. However, throughout this time period, the growth of foreign direct investment into developing nations remained robust. Among developing nations, the largest recipient has been China, which in 2014 received a record $129 billion in inflows, followed by the likes of Brazil, Mexico, and India. As we shall see later in this text, the sustained flow of foreign investment into developing nations is an important stimulus for economic growth in those countries, which bodes well for the future of countries such as China, Mexico, and Brazil—all leading beneficiaries of this trend.

THE CHANGING NATURE OF THE MULTINATIONAL ENTERPRISE

multinational enterprise (MNE)

A firm that owns business operations in more than one country.

A **multinational enterprise (MNE)** is any business that has productive activities in two or more countries. Since the 1960s, two notable trends in the demographics of the multinational enterprise have been (1) the rise of non-U.S. multinationals and (2) the growth of mini-multinationals.

Non-U.S. Multinationals

In the 1960s, global business activity was dominated by large U.S. multinational corporations. With U.S. firms accounting for about two-thirds of foreign direct investment during the 1960s, one would expect most multinationals to be U.S. enterprises. According to the data summarized in Figure 1.4, in 1973, 48.5 percent of the world's 260 largest multinationals were U.S. firms. The second-largest source country was the United Kingdom, with 18.8 percent of the largest multinationals. Japan accounted for 3.5 percent of the world's largest multinationals at the time. The large number of U.S. multinationals reflected U.S. economic dominance in the three decades after World War II, while the large number of British multinationals reflected that country's industrial dominance in the early decades of the twentieth century.

By 2012, things had shifted significantly. Some 22 of the world's 100 largest nonfinancial multinationals were U.S. enterprises; 14 were British, 14 French, 10 were German, and 7 were from Japan.[32] Although the 1973 data are not strictly comparable with the later data, they illustrate the trend (the 1973 figures are based on the largest 260 firms, whereas the later figures are based on the largest 100 multinationals). The globalization and growth of the world economy has resulted in a relative reduction in the dominance of U.S. firms in the global marketplace.

According to UN data, the ranks of the world's largest 100 multinationals are still dominated by firms from developed economies.[33] However, eight firms from developing economies had entered the UN's list of the 100 largest multinationals by 2012. The largest was Hutchison Whampoa of Hong Kong, China, which ranked 26th.[34] Firms from developing nations can be

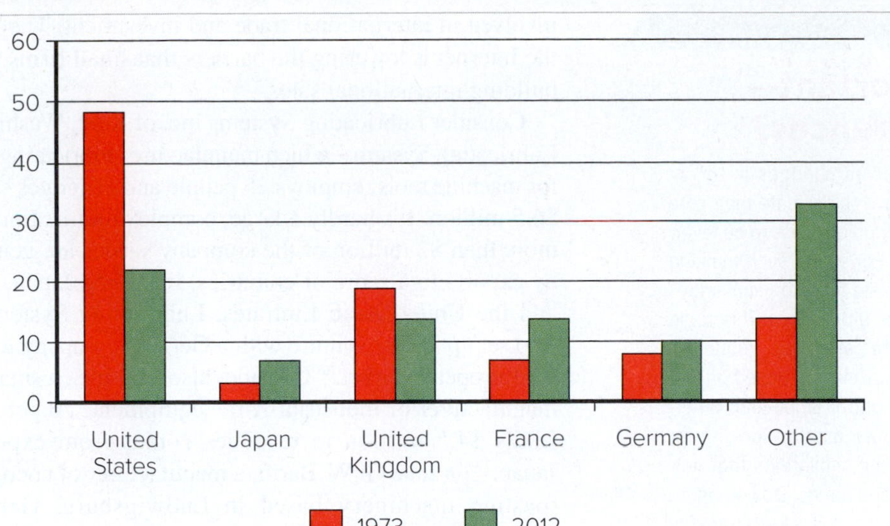

FIGURE

National Share of Largest Multinationals, 1973 and 2012.

Source: C. W. L. Hill and G. T. M. Hult, *International Business: Competing in the Global Marketplace.* (New York, NY: McGraw-Hill Education, 2017).

expected to emerge as important competitors in global markets, further shifting the axis of the world economy away from North America and western Europe and challenging the long dominance of Western companies. One such rising competitor, Dalian Wanda Group, is profiled in the accompanying Management Focus.

The Rise of Mini-Multinationals Another trend in international business has been the growth of medium-size and small multinationals (mini-multinationals).[35] When people think of international businesses, they tend to think of firms such as ExxonMobil, General Motors, Ford, Panasonic, Procter & Gamble, Sony, and Unilever—large, complex multinational corporations with operations that span the globe. Although most international trade and investment are still conducted by large firms, many medium-size and small businesses are becoming increasingly

The Dalian Wanda Group

The Dalian Wanda Group is perhaps the world's largest real estate company, although as yet it is little known outside of China. Established in 1988, Dalian Wanda Group is the largest owner of five-star hotels in the world. The company's real estate portfolio includes 133 Wanda shopping malls and 84 hotels. It also has extensive activities in the film business, sports holdings, tourism, and children's entertainment. The stated ambition of Dalian Wanda is to become a world-class multinational by 2020 with assets of $200 billion, revenue of $100 billion, and net profits of $10 billion.

In 2012, Dalian Wanda made a significant step in this direction when it acquired the U.S. cinema chain AMC Entertainment Holdings for $2.6 billion. At the time, the acquisition was the largest ever of a U.S. company by a Chinese enterprise, surpassing the $1.8 billion takeover of IBM's PC business by Lenovo in 2005. AMC is the second-largest cinema operator in North America, where movie goers spend more than $10 billion a year on tickets. After the acquisition was completed, the headquarters of AMC remained in Kansas City. Dalian, however, indicated that it would inject capital into AMC to upgrade is theaters to show more IMAX and 3D movies.

In 2015, Wanda followed its AMC acquisition with the purchase of Hoyts Group, an Australian cinema operator with over 150 cinemas. By combining AMC's movie theaters with Hoyts and its already extensive movie properties in China, Dalian Wanda has become the largest cinema operator in the world with over 500 cinemas. This puts Wanda in a strong position when negotiating distribution terms with movie studios.

Wanda is also expanding its international real estate operations. In 2014, it announced that it won a bid for a prime plot of land in Beverly Hills, Los Angeles. Wanda plans to invest $1.2 billion to construct a mixed-use development. The company also has a sizable project in Chicago, where it is investing $900 million to build the third-tallest building in the city. In addition, Wanda has has real estate projects in Spain, Australia, and London.

Sources: Keith Weir, "China's Dalian Wanda to Acquire Australia's Hoyts for $365.7 Million", *Reuters,* June 24, 2015; Zachary Mider, "China's Wanda to Buy AMC Cinema Chain for $2.6 Billion," *Bloomberg Business,* May 21, 2012; Wanda Group Corporate, http://www.wanda-group.com/.

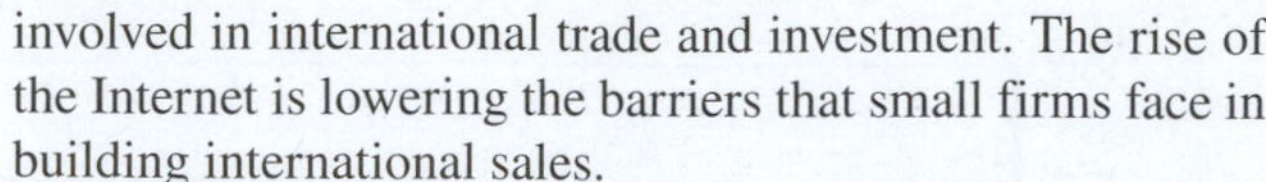

Which Is More Important—Similarities or Differences?

International strategy has seen significant changes in recent years. Multinational enterprises now have to evaluate their core uniqueness and how they can drive their uniqueness to be leveraged in the global marketplace better. For some, such thinking may represent a major shift in thinking—to focus on similarities across nations and customers instead of differences. This could be an important shift because companies and their people are trained to look for differences and form strategies based on satisfying the needs of customers with slight or significant differences across the globe. In the future, we may be looking for similarities first and then focusing on the similarities that outweigh the differences in tastes, wants, and needs. Do you agree that focusing on similarities across countries is a better way to developing strategy than focusing on differences?

Source: globalEDGE.msu.edu/content/gbr/gbr7-2.pdf.

involved in international trade and investment. The rise of the Internet is lowering the barriers that small firms face in building international sales.

Consider Lubricating Systems Inc. of Kent, Washington. Lubricating Systems, which manufactures lubricating fluids for machine tools, employs 25 people and generates sales of $6.5 million. It's hardly a large, complex multinational, yet more than $2 million of the company's sales are generated by exports to a score of countries, including Japan, Israel, and the United Arab Emirates. Lubricating Systems has also set up a joint venture with a German company to serve the European market.[36] Consider also Lixi Inc., a small U.S. manufacturer of industrial X-ray equipment; 70 percent of Lixi's $4.5 million in revenues comes from exports to Japan.[37] Or take G. W. Barth, a manufacturer of cocoa-bean roasting machinery based in Ludwigsburg, Germany. Employing just 65 people, this small company has captured 70 percent of the global market for cocoa-bean roasting machines.[38] International business is conducted not just by large firms but also by medium-size and small enterprises.

THE CHANGING WORLD ORDER

Between 1989 and 1991, a series of democratic revolutions swept the communist world. For reasons that are explored in more detail in Chapter 3, in country after country throughout eastern Europe and eventually in the Soviet Union itself, Communist Party governments collapsed. The Soviet Union receded into history, having been replaced by 15 independent republics. Czechoslovakia divided itself into two states, while Yugoslavia dissolved into a bloody civil war, now thankfully over, among its five successor states.

Many of the former communist nations of Europe and Asia seem to share a commitment to democratic politics and free market economics. For half a century, these countries were essentially closed to Western international businesses. Now, they present a host of export and investment opportunities. Two decades later, the economies of many of the former communist states are still relatively undeveloped, and their continued commitment to democracy and market-based economic systems cannot be taken for granted. Disturbing signs of growing unrest and totalitarian tendencies continue to be seen in several eastern European and central Asian states, including Russia, which has shown signs of shifting back toward greater state involvement in economic activity and authoritarian government.[39] Thus, the risks involved in doing business in such countries are high, but so may be the returns.

In addition to these changes, quieter revolutions have been occurring in China, other states in Southeast Asia, and Latin America. Their implications for international businesses may be just as profound as the collapse of communism in eastern Europe. China suppressed its pro-democracy movement in the bloody Tiananmen Square massacre of 1989. Despite this, China continues to move progressively toward greater free market reforms. If what is occurring in China continues for two more decades, China may move from third world to industrial superpower status even more rapidly than Japan did. If China's GDP per capita grows by an average of 6 to 7 percent, which is slower than the 8 to 10 percent growth rate achieved during the past decade, then by 2030 this nation of 1.3 billion people could boast an average GDP per capita of about $23,000, roughly the same as that of Chile or Poland today.

The potential consequences for international business are enormous. On the one hand, China represents a huge and largely untapped market. Reflecting this, between 1983 and 2015, annual foreign direct investment in China increased from less than $2 billion to $129 billion annually. On the other hand, China's new firms are proving to be very capable competitors, and they could take global market share away from Western and Japanese enterprises (e.g., see the Management Focus on the Wanda Group). Thus, the changes in China are creating both opportunities and threats for established international businesses.

As for Latin America, both democracy and free market reforms have been evident there too. For decades, most Latin American countries were ruled by dictators, many of whom seemed to view Western international businesses as instruments of imperialist domination. Accordingly, they restricted direct investment by foreign firms. In addition, the poorly managed economies of Latin America were characterized by low growth, high debt, and hyperinflation—all of which discouraged investment by international businesses. In the past two decades, much of this has changed. Throughout most of Latin America, debt and inflation are down, governments have sold state-owned enterprises to private investors, foreign investment is welcomed, and the region's economies have expanded. Brazil, Mexico, and Chile have led the way. These changes have increased the attractiveness of Latin America, both as a market for exports and as a site for foreign direct investment. At the same time, given the long history of economic mismanagement in Latin America, there is no guarantee that these favorable trends will continue. Indeed, Bolivia, Ecuador, and most notably Venezuela have seen shifts back toward greater state involvement in industry in the past few years, and foreign investment is now less welcome than it was during the 1990s. In these nations, the government has seized control of oil and gas fields from foreign investors and has limited the rights of foreign energy companies to extract oil and gas from their nations. Thus, as in the case of eastern Europe, substantial opportunities are accompanied by substantial risks.

THE GLOBAL ECONOMY OF THE TWENTY-FIRST CENTURY

As discussed, the past quarter century has seen rapid changes in the global economy. Barriers to the free flow of goods, services, and capital have been coming down. As their economies advance, more nations are joining the ranks of the developed world. A generation ago, South Korea and Taiwan were viewed as second-tier developing nations. Now they boast large economies, and firms based there are major players in many global industries, from shipbuilding and steel to electronics and chemicals. The move toward a global economy has been further strengthened by the widespread adoption of liberal economic policies by countries that had firmly opposed them for two generations or more. In short, current trends indicate the world is moving toward an economic system that is more favorable for international business.

But it is always hazardous to use established trends to predict the future. The world may be moving toward a more global economic system, but globalization is not inevitable. Countries may pull back from the recent commitment to liberal economic ideology if their experiences do not match their expectations. There are clear signs, for example, of a retreat from liberal economic ideology in Russia. If Russia's hesitation were to become more permanent and widespread, the liberal vision of a more prosperous global economy based on free market principles might not occur as quickly as many hope. Clearly, this would be a tougher world for international businesses.

Also, greater globalization brings with it risks of its own. This was starkly demonstrated in 1997 and 1998, when a financial crisis in Thailand spread first to other East Asian nations and then to Russia and Brazil. Ultimately, the crisis threatened to plunge the economies of the developed world, including the United States, into a recession. We explore the causes and consequences of this and other similar global financial crises in Chapter 11. Even from a purely economic perspective, globalization is not all good. The opportunities for doing business in a global economy may be significantly enhanced, but as we saw in 1997–1998, the risks associated with global financial contagion are also greater. Indeed, during 2008–2009, a crisis that started in the financial sector of America, where banks had been too liberal in their lending policies to homeowners, swept around the world and plunged the global economy into its deepest recession since the early 1980s, illustrating once more that in an interconnected world a severe crisis in one region can affect the entire globe. Still, as explained later in this text, firms can exploit the opportunities associated with globalization while reducing the risks through appropriate hedging strategies.

Use SmartBook to help retain what you have learned. Access your Instructor's Connect course to check out SmartBook or go to learnsmartadvantage.com for help.

The Globalization Debate

Explain the main arguments in the debate over the impact of globalization.

Is the shift toward a more integrated and interdependent global economy a good thing? Many influential economists, politicians, and business leaders seem to think so.[40] They argue that falling barriers to international trade and investment are the twin engines driving the global economy toward greater prosperity. They say increased international trade and cross-border investment will result in lower prices for goods and services. They believe that globalization stimulates economic growth, raises the incomes of consumers, and helps create jobs in all countries that participate in the global trading system. The arguments of those who support globalization are covered in detail in Chapters 6, 7, and 8. As we shall see, there are good theoretical reasons for believing that declining barriers to international trade and investment do stimulate economic growth, create jobs, and raise income levels. Moreover, as described in Chapters 6, 7, and 8, empirical evidence lends support to the predictions of this theory. However, despite the existence of a compelling body of theory and evidence, globalization has its critics.[41] Some of these critics are vocal and active, taking to the streets to demonstrate their opposition to globalization. Here, we look at the nature of protests against globalization and briefly review the main themes of the debate concerning the merits of globalization. In later chapters, we elaborate on many of these points.

ANTIGLOBALIZATION PROTESTS Popular demonstrations against globalization date to December 1999, when more than 40,000 protesters blocked the streets of Seattle in an attempt to shut down a World Trade Organization meeting being held in the city. The demonstrators were protesting against a wide range of issues, including job losses in industries under attack from foreign competitors, downward pressure on the wage rates of unskilled workers, environmental degradation, and the cultural imperialism of global media and multinational enterprises, which was seen as being dominated by what some protesters called the "culturally impoverished" interests and values of the United States. All of these ills, the demonstrators claimed, could be laid at the feet of globalization. The World Trade Organization was meeting to try to launch a new round of talks to cut barriers to cross-border trade and investment. As such, it was seen as a promoter of globalization and a target for the protesters. The protests turned violent, transforming the normally placid streets of Seattle into a running battle between "anarchists" and Seattle's bemused and poorly prepared police department. Pictures of brick-throwing protesters and armored police wielding their batons were duly recorded by the global media, which then circulated the images around the world. Meanwhile, the WTO meeting failed to reach agreement, and although the protests outside the meeting halls had little to do with that failure, the impression took hold that the demonstrators had succeeded in derailing the meetings.

Emboldened by the experience in Seattle, antiglobalization protesters have made a habit of turning up at major meetings of global institutions. Smaller-scale protests have periodically occurred in several countries, such as France, where antiglobalization activists destroyed a McDonald's restaurant in 1999 to protest the impoverishment of French culture by American imperialism (see the accompanying Country Focus for details). While violent protests may give the antiglobalization effort a bad name, it is clear from the scale of the demonstrations that support for the cause goes beyond a core of anarchists. Large segments of the population in many countries believe that globalization has detrimental effects on living standards, wage rates, and the environment. Indeed, the strong support for Donald Trump in the 2016 U.S. presidential primary season was primarily based on his repeated assertions that trade deals had exported U.S. job overseas and created unemployment and low wages in America.

Both theory and evidence suggest that many of these fears are exaggerated; both politicians and businesspeople need to do more to counter these fears. Many protests against globalization are tapping into a general sense of loss at the passing of a world in which barriers of time and distance, and significant differences in economic institutions, political institutions, and the level of development of different nations produced a world rich in the diversity of human cultures. However, while the rich citizens of the developed world may have the luxury of mourning the fact that they can now see McDonald's restaurants and Starbucks coffeehouses on their vacations to exotic locations such as Thailand, fewer complaints are heard from the citizens of those countries, who welcome the higher living standards that progress brings.

GLOBALIZATION, JOBS, AND INCOME One concern frequently voiced by globalization opponents is that falling barriers to international trade destroy manufacturing jobs in wealthy advanced economies such as the United States and western Europe. Critics argue that falling trade barriers allow firms to move manufacturing activities to countries where wage rates are much lower.[42] Indeed, due to the entry of China, India, and states from eastern Europe into the global trading system, along with global population growth, estimates suggest

country FOCUS

Protesting Globalization in France

One night in August 1999, 10 men under the leadership of local sheep farmer and rural activist José Bové crept into the town of Millau in central France and vandalized a McDonald's restaurant under construction, causing an estimated $150,000 in damage. These were no ordinary vandals, however, at least according to their supporters, for the "symbolic dismantling" of the McDonald's outlet had noble aims, or so it was claimed. The attack was initially presented as a protest against unfair American trade policies. The European Union (EU) had banned imports of hormone-treated beef from the United States, primarily because of fears that it might lead to health problems (although EU scientists had concluded there was no evidence of this). After a careful review, the World Trade Organization stated the EU ban was not allowed under trading rules that the EU and United States were party to and that the EU would have to lift it or face retaliation. The EU refused to comply, so the U.S. government imposed a 100 percent tariff on imports of certain EU products, including French staples such as foie gras, mustard, and Roquefort cheese. On farms near Millau, Bové and others raised sheep whose milk was used to make Roquefort. They felt incensed by the American tariff and decided to vent their frustrations on McDonald's.

Bové and his compatriots were arrested and charged. About the same time in the Languedoc region of France, California winemaker Robert Mondavi had reached agreement with the mayor and council of the village of Aniane and regional authorities to turn 125 acres of wooded hillside belonging to the village into a vineyard. Mondavi planned to invest $7 million in the project and hoped to produce top-quality wine that would sell in Europe and the United States for $60 a bottle. However, local environmentalists objected to the plan, which they claimed would destroy the area's unique ecological heritage. José Bové, basking in sudden fame, offered his support to the opponents, and the protests started. In May 2001, the socialist mayor who had approved the project was defeated in local elections in which the Mondavi project had become the major issue. He was replaced by a communist, Manuel Diaz, who denounced the project as a capitalist plot designed to enrich wealthy U.S. shareholders at the cost of his villagers and the environment. Following Diaz's victory, Mondavi announced he would pull out of the project. A spokesperson noted, "It's a huge waste, but there are clearly personal and political interests at play here that go way beyond us."

So, are the French opposed to foreign investment? The experience of McDonald's and Mondavi seems to suggest so, as does the associated news coverage, but look closer and a different reality seems to emerge. Today McDonald's has more than 1,200 restaurants in France. McDonald's employs 69,000 workers in the country. France is the most profitable market for McDonald's after the United States. In short, 15 years after the protests, France is a major success story for McDonald's. Moreover, France has long been one of the most favored locations for inward foreign direct investment, receiving more than $660 billion of foreign investment between 2000 and 2013, which makes it one of the top destinations for foreign investment in Europe. American companies have always accounted for a significant percentage of this investment. French enterprises have also been significant foreign investors; some 1,100 French multinationals have about $1.1 trillion of assets in other nations. For all of the populist opposition to globalization, French corporations and consumers appear to be embracing it.

Sources: "Behind the Bluster," *The Economist,* May 26, 2001; "The French Farmers' Anti-Global Hero," *The Economist,* July 8, 2000; C. Trueheart, "France's Golden Arch Enemy?" *Toronto Star,* July 1, 2000; J. Henley, "Grapes of Wrath Scare Off U.S. Firm," *The Economist,* May 18, 2001, p. 11; United Nations, *World Investment Report,* 2014. New York & Geneva: United Nations, 2011; Rob Wile, "The True Story of How McDonald's Conquered France," *Business Insider,* August 22, 2014.

that the pool of global labor may have quadrupled between 1985 and 2005, with most of the increase occurring after 1990.[43] Other things being equal, we might conclude that this enormous expansion in the global labor force, when coupled with expanding international trade, would have depressed wages in developed nations.

This fear is often supported by anecdotes. For example, D. L. Bartlett and J. B. Steele, two journalists for the *Philadelphia Inquirer* who gained notoriety for their attacks on free trade, cite the case of Harwood Industries, a U.S. clothing manufacturer that closed its U.S. operations, where it paid workers $9 per hour, and shifted manufacturing to Honduras, where textile workers received 48 cents per hour.[44] Because of moves such as this, argue Bartlett and Steele, the wage rates of poorer Americans have fallen significantly over the past quarter of a century.

In the past few years, the same fears have been applied to services, which have increasingly been outsourced to nations with lower labor costs. The popular feeling is that when corporations such as Dell, IBM, or Citigroup outsource service activities to lower-cost foreign suppliers—as all three have done—they are "exporting jobs" to low-wage nations and contributing to higher unemployment and lower living standards in their home nations (in this case, the United States). Some U.S. lawmakers have responded by calling for legal barriers to job outsourcing.

Supporters of globalization reply that critics of these trends miss the essential point about free trade agreements—the benefits outweigh the costs.[45] They argue that free trade will result in countries specializing in the production of those goods and services that they can produce most efficiently, while importing goods and services that they cannot produce as efficiently. When a country embraces free trade, there is always some dislocation—lost textile jobs at Harwood

Industries or lost call-center jobs at Dell—but the whole economy is better off as a result. According to this view, it makes little sense for the United States to produce textiles at home when they can be produced at a lower cost in Honduras or China. Importing textiles from China leads to lower prices for clothes in the United States, which enables consumers to spend more of their money on other items. At the same time, the increased income generated in China from textile exports increases income levels in that country, which helps the Chinese purchase more products produced in the United States, such as pharmaceuticals from Amgen, Boeing jets, microprocessors made by Intel, Microsoft software, and Cisco routers.

The same argument can be made to support the outsourcing of services to low-wage countries. By outsourcing its customer service call centers to India, Dell can reduce its cost structure and thereby its prices for PCs. U.S. consumers benefit from this development. As prices for PCs fall, Americans can spend more of their money on other goods and services. Moreover, the increase in income levels in India allows Indians to purchase more U.S. goods and services, which helps create jobs in the United States. In this manner, supporters of globalization argue that free trade benefits *all* countries that adhere to a free trade regime.

If the critics of globalization are correct, three things must be shown. First, the share of national income received by labor, as opposed to the share received by the owners of capital (e.g., stockholders and bondholders), should have declined in advanced nations as a result of downward pressure on wage rates. Second, even though labor's share of the economic pie may have declined, this does not mean lower living standards if the size of the total pie has increased sufficiently to offset the decline in labor's share—in other words, if economic growth and rising living standards in advanced economies have offset declines in labor's share (this is the position argued by supporters of globalization). Third, the decline in labor's share of national income must be due to moving production to low-wage countries, as opposed to improvement in production technology and productivity.

Several studies shed light on these issues.[46] First, the data suggest that over the past two decades, the share of labor in national income has declined. However, detailed analysis suggests the share of national income enjoyed by *skilled labor* has actually *increased,* suggesting that the fall in labor's share has been due to a fall in the share taken by *unskilled labor*. A study by the IMF suggested the earnings gap between workers in skilled and unskilled sectors has widened by 25 percent over the past two decades.[47] Another study that focused on U.S. data found that exposure to competition from imports led to a decline in real wages for workers who performed *unskilled* tasks, while having no discernible impact on wages in skilled occupations. The same study found that skilled and unskilled workers in sectors where exports grew saw an increase in their real wages.[48] These figures suggest that *unskilled labor* in sectors that have been exposed to more efficient foreign competition probably has seen its share of national income decline over the past three decades.

However, this does not mean that the *living standards* of unskilled workers in developed nations have declined. It is possible that economic growth in developed nations has offset the fall in the share of national income enjoyed by unskilled workers, raising their living standards. Evidence suggests that real labor compensation has expanded in most developed nations since the 1980s, including the United States. Several studies by the Organisation for Economic Co-operation and Development (OECD), whose members include the 34 richest economies in the world, conclude that while the gap between the poorest and richest segments of society in OECD countries has widened, in *most* countries real income levels have increased for all, including the poorest segment. In one study, the OECD found that between 1985 and 2008, real household income (adjusted for inflation) increased by 1.7 percent annually among its member states. The real income level of the poorest 10 percent of the population increased at 1.4 percent on average, while that of the richest 10 percent increased by 2 percent annually (i.e., while everyone got richer, the gap between the most affluent and the poorest sectors of society widened). The differential in growth rates was more extreme in the United States than most other countries. The study found that the real income of the poorest 10 percent of the population grew by just 0.5 percent a year in the United States between 1985 and 2008, while that of the richest 10 percent grew by 1.9 percent annually.[49]

As noted earlier, globalization critics argue that the decline in unskilled wage rates is due to the migration of low-wage manufacturing jobs offshore and a corresponding reduction in demand for unskilled workers. However, supporters of globalization see a more complex picture. They maintain that the weak growth rate in real wage rates for unskilled workers owes far more to a technology-induced shift within advanced economies away from jobs where the only qualification was a willingness to turn up for work every day and toward jobs that require significant education and skills. They point out that many advanced economies report a shortage of highly skilled workers and an excess supply of unskilled workers. Thus, growing income inequality is a result of the wages for skilled workers being bid up by the labor market and the wages for unskilled workers being discounted. In fact, evidence suggests that technological change has had a bigger impact than globalization on the declining share of national income enjoyed by labor.[50] This suggests that a solution to the problem of slow real income growth among the unskilled is to be found not in limiting free trade and globalization but in increasing society's investment in education to reduce the supply of unskilled workers.[51]

Finally, it is worth noting that the wage gap between developing and developed nations is closing as developing nations experience rapid economic growth. For example, one estimate suggests that wages in China will approach Western levels in two decades.[52] To the extent that this is the case, any migration of unskilled jobs to low-wage countries is a temporary phenomenon representing a structural adjustment on the way to a more tightly integrated global economy.

GLOBALIZATION, LABOR POLICIES, AND THE ENVIRONMENT

A second source of concern is that free trade encourages firms from advanced nations to move manufacturing facilities to less developed countries that lack adequate regulations to protect labor and the environment from abuse by the unscrupulous.[53] Globalization critics often argue that adhering to labor and environmental regulations significantly increases the costs of manufacturing enterprises and puts them at a competitive disadvantage in the global marketplace vis-à-vis firms based in developing nations that do not have to comply with such regulations. Firms deal with this cost disadvantage, the theory goes, by moving their production facilities to nations that do not have such burdensome regulations or that fail to enforce the regulations they have.

If this were the case, we might expect free trade to lead to an increase in pollution and result in firms from advanced nations exploiting the labor of less developed nations.[54] This argument was used repeatedly by those who opposed the 1994 formation of the North American Free Trade Agreement (NAFTA) among Canada, Mexico, and the United States. They painted a picture of U.S. manufacturing firms moving to Mexico in droves so that they would be free to pollute the environment, employ child labor, and ignore workplace safety and health issues, all in the name of higher profits.[55]

Supporters of free trade and greater globalization express doubts about this scenario. They argue that tougher environmental regulations and stricter labor standards go hand in hand with economic progress.[56] In general, as countries get richer, they enact tougher environmental and labor regulations.[57] Because free trade enables developing countries to increase their economic growth rates and become richer, this should lead to tougher environmental and labor laws. In this view, the critics of free trade have got it backward: free trade does not lead to more pollution and labor exploitation; it leads to less. By creating wealth and incentives for enterprises to produce technological innovations, the free market system and free trade could make it easier for the world to cope with pollution and population growth. Indeed, while pollution levels are rising in the world's poorer countries, they have been falling in developed nations. In the United States, for example, the concentration of carbon monoxide and sulfur dioxide pollutants in the atmosphere decreased by 60 percent between 1978 and 1997, while lead concentrations decreased by 98 percent—and these reductions have occurred against a background of sustained economic expansion.[58]

A number of econometric studies have found consistent evidence of a hump-shaped relationship between income levels and pollution levels (see Figure 1.5.).[59] As an economy grows and income levels rise, initially pollution levels also rise. However, past some point, rising income levels lead to demands for greater environmental protection, and pollution levels then fall. A seminal study by Grossman and Krueger found that the turning point generally occurred before per capita income levels reached $8,000.[60]

FIGURE 1.5

Income Levels and Environmental Pollution.

Source: Hill, C. W. L.; Hult, G. T. M., *International Business: Competing in the Global Marketplace*. New York, NY: McGraw-Hill Education, 2017.

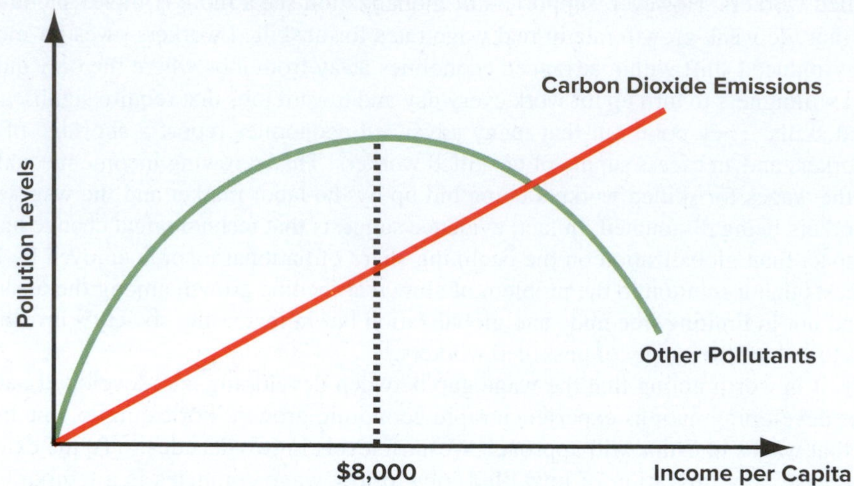

While the hump-shaped relationship depicted in Figure 1.5 seems to hold across a wide range of pollutants—from sulfur dioxide to lead concentrations and water quality—carbon dioxide emissions are an important exception, rising steadily with higher-income levels. Given that carbon dioxide is a heat-trapping gas and given that there is good evidence that increased atmospheric carbon dioxide concentrations are a cause of global warming, this should be of serious concern. The solution to the problem, however, is probably not to roll back the trade liberalization efforts that have fostered economic growth and globalization but to get the nations of the world to agree to policies designed to limit carbon emissions. In the view of most economists, the most effect way to do this would be to put a price on carbon intensive energy generation through a carbon tax. To ensure that this tax does not harm economic growth, economists argue that it should be revenue neutral, with increases in carbon taxes offset by reductions in income or consumption taxes.[61]

Although UN-sponsored talks have had reduction in carbon dioxide emissions as a central aim since the 1992 Earth Summit in Rio de Janeiro, until recently there has been little success in moving toward the ambitious goals for reducing carbon emissions laid down in the Earth Summit and subsequent talks in Kyoto, Japan, in 1997 and in Copenhagen in 2009. In part, this is because the largest emitters of carbon dioxide, the United States and China, failed to reach agreements about how to proceed. China, a country whose carbon emissions are increasing at a rapid rate, has until recently shown little appetite for tighter pollution controls. As for the United States, political divisions in Congress and a culture of denial have made it difficult for the country to even acknowledge, never mind move forward with, legislation designed to tackle climate change. However, in late 2014 America and China struck a historic deal under which both countries agreed to potentially significant reductions in carbon emissions. This was followed by a broadly based multilateral agreement reached in Paris in 2015 that has committed the nations of the world to carbon reduction targets. If these agreements hold, progress may be made on this important issue.

Notwithstanding this, supporters of free trade point out that it is possible to tie free trade agreements to the implementation of tougher environmental and labor laws in less developed countries. NAFTA, for example, was passed only after side agreements had been negotiated that committed Mexico to tougher enforcement of environmental protection regulations. Thus, supporters of free trade argue that factories based in Mexico are now cleaner than they would have been without the passage of NAFTA.[62]

They also argue that business firms are not the amoral organizations that critics suggest. While there may be some rotten apples, most business enterprises are staffed by managers who are committed to behave in an ethical manner and would be unlikely to move production offshore just so they could pump more pollution into the atmosphere or exploit labor. Furthermore, the relationship between pollution, labor exploitation, and production costs may not be that suggested by critics. In general, a well-treated labor force is productive, and it is productivity rather than base wage rates that often has the greatest influence on costs. The vision of greedy managers who shift production to low-wage countries to exploit their labor force may be misplaced.

GLOBALIZATION AND NATIONAL SOVEREIGNTY Another concern voiced by critics of globalization is that today's increasingly interdependent global economy shifts economic power away from national governments and toward supranational organizations such as the World Trade Organization, the European Union, and the United Nations. As perceived by critics, unelected bureaucrats now impose policies on the democratically elected governments of nation-states, thereby undermining the sovereignty of those states and limiting the nation's ability to control its own destiny.[63]

The World Trade Organization is a favorite target of those who attack the headlong rush toward a global economy. As noted earlier, the WTO was founded in 1995 to police the world trading system established by the General Agreement on Tariffs and Trade. The WTO arbitrates trade disputes between its 162 member states. The arbitration panel can issue a ruling instructing a member state to change trade policies that violate GATT regulations. If the violator refuses to comply with the ruling, the WTO allows other states to impose appropriate trade sanctions on the transgressor. As a result, according to one prominent critic, U.S. environmentalist, consumer rights advocate, and sometime presidential candidate Ralph Nader:

> Under the new system, many decisions that affect billions of people are no longer made by local or national governments but instead, if challenged by any WTO member nation, would be deferred to a group of unelected bureaucrats sitting behind closed doors in Geneva (which is where the headquarters of the WTO are located). The bureaucrats can decide whether or not people in California can prevent the destruction of the last virgin forests or determine if carcinogenic pesticides can be banned from their foods; or whether European countries have the right to ban dangerous biotech hormones in meat.... At risk is the very basis of democracy and accountable decision making.[64]

In contrast to Nader, many economists and politicians maintain that the power of supranational organizations such as the WTO is limited to what nation-states collectively agree to grant. They argue that bodies such as the United Nations and the WTO exist to serve the collective interests of member states, not to subvert those interests. Supporters of supranational organizations point out that the power of these bodies rests largely on their ability to persuade member states to follow a certain action. If these bodies fail to serve the collective interests of member states, those states will withdraw their support and the supranational organization will quickly collapse. In this view, real power still resides with individual nation-states, not supranational organizations.

GLOBALIZATION AND THE WORLD'S POOR Critics of globalization argue that despite the supposed benefits associated with free trade and investment, over the past 100 years or so the gap between the rich and poor nations of the world has gotten wider. In 1870, the average income per capita in the world's 17 richest nations was 2.4 times that of all other countries. In 1990, the same group was 4.5 times as rich as the rest. In 2013, the 34 member states of the Organisation for Economic Co-operation and Development (OECD), which includes most of the world's rich economies, had an average gross national income (GNI) per person of $38,896, whereas the world's 40 least developed countries had a GNI of just $888 per capital—implying that income per capita in the world's 34 richest nations was 45 times that in the world's 40 poorest.[65]

While recent history has shown that some of the world's poorer nations are capable of rapid periods of economic growth—witness the transformation that has occurred in some Southeast Asian nations such as South Korea, Thailand, and Malaysia—there appear to be strong forces for stagnation among the world's poorest nations. A quarter of the countries with a GDP per capita of less than $1,000 in 1960 had growth rates of less than zero from 1960 to 1995, and a third had growth rates of less than 0.05 percent.[66] Critics argue that if globalization is such a positive development, this divergence between the rich and poor should not have occurred.

Although the reasons for economic stagnation vary, several factors stand out, none of which has anything to do with free trade or globalization.[67] Many of the world's poorest countries have suffered from totalitarian governments, economic policies that destroyed wealth rather than facilitated its creation, endemic corruption, scant protection for property rights, and prolonged civil war. A combination of such factors helps explain why countries such as Afghanistan, Cuba, Haiti, Iraq, Libya, Nigeria, Sudan, Syria, North Korea, and Zimbabwe have failed to improve the economic lot of their citizens during recent decades. A complicating factor is the rapidly expanding populations in many of these countries. Without a major change in government, population growth may exacerbate their problems. Promoters of free trade argue that the best way for these countries to improve their lot is to lower their barriers to free trade and investment and to implement economic policies based on free market economics.[68]

Many of the world's poorer nations are being held back by large debt burdens. Of particular concern are the 40 or so "highly indebted poorer countries" (HIPCs), which are home to some 700 million people. Among these countries, the average government debt burden has been as high as 85 percent of the value of the economy, as measured by gross domestic product, and the annual costs of serving government debt consumed 15 percent of the country's export earnings.[69] Servicing such a heavy debt load leaves the governments of these countries with little left to invest in important public infrastructure projects, such as education, health care, roads, and power. The result is the HIPCs are trapped in a cycle of poverty and debt that inhibits economic development. Free trade alone, some argue, is a necessary but not sufficient prerequisite to help these countries bootstrap themselves out of poverty. Instead, large-scale debt relief is needed for the world's poorest nations to give them the opportunity to restructure their economies and start the long climb toward prosperity. Supporters of debt relief also argue that new democratic governments in poor nations should not be forced to honor debts that were incurred and mismanaged long ago by their corrupt and dictatorial predecessors.

In the late 1990s, a debt relief movement began to gain ground among the political establishment in the world's richer nations.[70] Fueled by high-profile endorsements from Irish rock star Bono (who has been a tireless and increasingly effective advocate for debt relief), the Dalai Lama, and influential Harvard economist Jeffrey Sachs, the debt relief movement was instrumental in persuading the United States to enact legislation in 2000 that provided $435 million in debt relief for HIPCs. More important perhaps, the United States also backed an IMF plan to sell some of its gold reserves and use the proceeds to help with debt relief. The IMF and World Bank have now picked up the banner and have embarked on a systematic debt relief program.

For such a program to have a lasting effect, however, debt relief must be matched by wise investment in public projects that boost economic growth (such as education) and by the adoption of economic policies that facilitate investment and trade. Consistent with this, in June 2005, the finance ministers from several of the world's richest economies (including the United States) agreed to provide enough funds to the World Bank and IMF to allow them to cancel a further $55 billion in debt owed by the HIPCs. The goal was to enable the HIPCs to redirect resources from debt payments to health and education programs, and for alleviating poverty.

The richest nations of the world also can help by reducing barriers to the importation of products from the world's poorest nations, particularly tariffs on imports of agricultural products and textiles. High-tariff barriers and other impediments to trade make it difficult for poor countries to export more of their agricultural production. The World Trade Organization has estimated that if the developed nations of the world eradicated subsidies to their agricultural producers and removed tariff barriers to trade in agriculture, this would raise global economic welfare by $128 billion, with $30 billion of that going to poor nations, many of which are highly indebted. The faster growth associated with expanded trade in agriculture could significantly reduce the number of people living in poverty according to the WTO.[71]

Despite the large gap between the rich and poor nations, there is some evidence that progress is being made. In 2000, the United Nations adopted what were known as the *Millennium Goals*. These were eight economic and human development goals for the world. One of these goals was to cut in half the number of people living in extreme poverty, defined as less than $1.25 a day, between 1995 and 2015. This goal was actually achieved in 2010, five years ahead of schedule.

Some 1.2 billion people were pulled out of poverty, the majority in China and India, two countries that have been rapidly integrated into the global economy. This represents the greatest reduction in extreme poverty in human history. It's hard to escape the conclusion that globalization and lower barriers to cross-border trade and investment were major factors behind this remarkable achievement.

test PREP

Use SmartBook to help retain what you have learned. Access your Instructor's Connect course to check out SmartBook or go to learnsmartadvantage.com for help.

Managing in the Global Marketplace

LO 1-5

Understand how the process of globalization is creating opportunities and challenges for business managers.

international business

Any firm that engages in international trade or investment.

Much of this text is concerned with the challenges of managing in an international business. An **international business** is any firm that engages in international trade or investment. A firm does not have to become a multinational enterprise, investing directly in operations in other countries, to engage in international business, although multinational enterprises are international businesses. All a firm has to do is export or import products from other countries. As the world shifts toward a truly integrated global economy, more firms—both large and small—are becoming international businesses. What does this shift toward a global economy mean for managers within an international business?

As their organizations increasingly engage in cross-border trade and investment, managers need to recognize that the task of managing an international business differs from that of managing a purely domestic business in many ways. At the most fundamental level, the differences arise from the simple fact that countries are different. Countries differ in their cultures, political systems, economic systems, legal systems, and levels of economic development. Despite all the talk about the emerging global village and despite the trend toward globalization of markets and production, as we shall see in this text, many of these differences are very profound and enduring.

Differences among countries require that an international business vary its practices country by country. Marketing a product in Brazil may require a different approach from marketing the product in Germany; managing U.S. workers might require different skills from managing Japanese workers; maintaining close relations with a particular level of government may be very important in Mexico and irrelevant in Great Britain; the business strategy pursued in Canada might not work in South Korea; and so on. Managers in an international business must not only be sensitive to these differences but also adopt the appropriate policies and strategies for coping with them. Much of this text is devoted to explaining the sources of these differences and the methods for successfully coping with them.

A further way in which international business differs from domestic business is the greater complexity of managing an international business. In addition to the problems that arise from the differences between countries, a manager in an international business is confronted with a range of other issues that the manager in a domestic business never confronts. The managers of an international business must decide where in the world to site production activities to minimize costs and maximize value added. They must decide whether it is ethical to adhere to the lower labor and environmental standards found in many less developed nations. Then they must decide how best to coordinate and control globally dispersed production activities (which, as we shall see later in the text, is not a trivial problem). The managers in an international business also must decide which foreign markets to enter and which to avoid. They must choose the appropriate mode for entering a particular foreign country. Is it best to export its product to the foreign country? Should the firm allow a local company to produce its product under license in that country? Should the firm enter into a joint venture with a local firm to produce its product in that country? Or should the firm set up a wholly owned subsidiary to serve the market in that country? As we shall see, the choice of entry mode is critical because it has major implications for the long-term health of the firm.

Conducting business transactions across national borders requires understanding the rules governing the international trading and investment system. Managers in an international business must also deal with government restrictions on international trade and investment. They must find ways to work within the limits imposed by specific governmental interventions. As this text explains, even though many governments are nominally committed to free trade, they often intervene to regulate cross-border trade and investment. Managers within international businesses must develop strategies and policies for dealing with such interventions.

Cross-border transactions also require that money be converted from the firm's home currency into a foreign currency and vice versa. Because currency exchange rates vary in response to changing economic conditions, managers in an international business must develop policies for dealing with exchange rate movements. A firm that adopts the wrong policy can lose large amounts of money, whereas one that adopts the right policy can increase the profitability of its international transactions.

In sum, managing an international business is different from managing a purely domestic business for at least four reasons: (1) countries are different, (2) the range of problems confronted by a manager in an international business is wider and the problems themselves more complex than those confronted by a manager in a domestic business, (3) an international business must find ways to work within the limits imposed by government intervention in the international trade and investment system, and (4) international transactions involve converting money into different currencies.

In this text, we examine all these issues in depth, paying close attention to the different strategies and policies that managers pursue to deal with the various challenges created when a firm becomes an international business. Chapters 2, 3, and 4 explore how countries differ from each other with regard to their political, economic, legal, and cultural institutions. Chapter 5 takes a detailed look at the ethical issues, corporate social responsibility, and sustainability issues that arise in international business. Chapters 6 through 9 look at the global trade and investment environment within which international businesses must operate. Chapters 10 and 11 review the global monetary system. These chapters focus on the nature of the foreign exchange market and the emerging global monetary system. Chapters 12 and 13 explore the strategy, organization, and market entry choices of an international business. Chapters 14 through 17 look at the management of various functional operations within an international business, including exporting, importing, countertrade, production, supply chain management, marketing, R&D, and human resources. By the time you complete this text, you should have a good grasp of the issues that managers working in international business have to grapple with on a daily basis, and you should be familiar with the range of strategies and operating policies available to compete more effectively in today's rapidly emerging global economy.

test PREP

Use SmartBook to help retain what you have learned. Access your Instructor's Connect course to check out SmartBook or go to learnsmartadvantage.com for help.

Key Terms

globalization, p. 6
globalization of markets, p. 6
globalization of production, p. 7
factors of production, p. 7
General Agreement on Tariffs and Trade (GATT), p. 9
World Trade Organization (WTO), p. 9
International Monetary Fund (IMF), p. 9
World Bank, p. 9
United Nations (UN), p. 10
Group of Twenty (G20), p. 10
international trade, p. 10
foreign direct investment (FDI), p. 11
Moore's law, p. 13
stock of foreign direct investment (FDI), p. 17
multinational enterprise (MNE), p. 18
international business, p. 29

Summary

This chapter has shown how the world economy is becoming more global and reviewed the main drivers of globalization, arguing that they seem to be thrusting nation-states toward a more tightly integrated global economy. It looked at how the nature of international business is changing in response to the changing global economy, discussed concerns raised by rapid globalization, and reviewed implications of rapid globalization for individual managers. The chapter made the following points:

1. Over the past three decades, we have witnessed the globalization of markets and production.
2. The globalization of markets implies that national markets are merging into one huge marketplace. However, it is important not to push this view too far.

3. The globalization of production implies that firms are basing individual productive activities at the optimal world locations for the particular activities. As a consequence, it is increasingly irrelevant to talk about American products, Japanese products, or German products because these are being replaced by "global" products.
4. Two factors seem to underlie the trend toward globalization: declining trade barriers and changes in communication, information, and transportation technologies.
5. Since the end of World War II, barriers to the free flow of goods, services, and capital have been lowered significantly. More than anything else, this has facilitated the trend toward the globalization of production and has enabled firms to view the world as a single market.
6. As a consequence of the globalization of production and markets, in the last decade, world trade has grown faster than world output, foreign direct investment has surged, imports have penetrated more deeply into the world's industrial nations, and competitive pressures have increased in industry after industry.
7. The development of the microprocessor and related developments in communication and information processing technology have helped firms link their worldwide operations into sophisticated information networks. Jet air travel, by shrinking travel time, has also helped link the worldwide operations of international businesses. These changes have enabled firms to achieve tight coordination of their worldwide operations and to view the world as a single market.
8. In the 1960s, the U.S. economy was dominant in the world, U.S. firms accounted for most of the foreign direct investment in the world economy, U.S. firms dominated the list of large multinationals, and roughly half the world—the centrally planned economies of the communist world—was closed to Western businesses.
9. By the 2000s, the U.S. share of world output had been cut in half, with major shares now being accounted for by western European and Southeast Asian economies. The U.S. share of worldwide foreign direct investment had also fallen by about two-thirds. U.S. multinationals were now facing competition from a large number of Japanese and European multinationals. In addition, the emergence of mini-multinationals was noted.
10. One of the most dramatic developments of the past 30 years has been the collapse of communism in eastern Europe, which has created enormous opportunities for international businesses. In addition, the move toward free market economies in China and Latin America is creating opportunities (and threats) for Western international businesses.
11. The benefits and costs of the emerging global economy are being hotly debated among businesspeople, economists, and politicians. The debate focuses on the impact of globalization on jobs, wages, the environment, working conditions, national sovereignty, and extreme poverty in the world's poorest nations.
12. Managing an international business is different from managing a domestic business for at least four reasons: (*a*) countries are different, (*b*) the range of problems confronted by a manager in an international business is wider and the problems themselves more complex than those confronted by a manager in a domestic business, (*c*) managers in an international business must find ways to work within the limits imposed by governments' intervention in the international trade and investment system, and (*d*) international transactions involve converting money into different currencies.

Critical Thinking and Discussion Questions

1. Describe the shifts in the world economy over the past 30 years. What are the implications of these shifts for international businesses based in Great Britain? North America? Hong Kong?
2. "The study of international business is fine if you are going to work in a large multinational enterprise, but it has no relevance for individuals who are going to work in small firms." Evaluate this statement.
3. How have changes in technology contributed to the globalization of markets and production? Would the globalization of production and markets have been possible without these technological changes?
4. "Ultimately, the study of international business is no different from the study of domestic business. Thus, there is no point in having a separate course on international business." Evaluate this statement.
5. How does the Internet affect international business activity and the globalization of the world economy?
6. If current trends continue, China may be the world's largest economy by 2030. Discuss the possible implications of such a development for (*a*) the world trading system, (*b*) the world monetary system, (*c*) the business strategy of today's European and U.S.-based global corporations, and (*d*) global commodity prices.

7. Reread the Management Focus on Boeing and answer the following questions:
   a. What are the benefits to Boeing of outsourcing manufacturing of components of the Boeing 787 to firms based in other countries?
   b. What are the potential costs and risks to Boeing of outsourcing?
   c. In addition to foreign subcontractors and Boeing, who else benefits from Boeing's decision to outsource component part manufacturing assembly to other nations? Who are the potential losers?
   d. If Boeing's management decided to keep all production in America, what do you think the effect would be on the company, its employees, and the communities that depend on it?
   e. On balance, do you think that the kind of outsourcing undertaken by Boeing is a good thing or a bad thing for the American economy? Explain your reasoning.

globalEDGE Research Task

globalEDGE.msu.edu

Use the globalEDGE™ website (globaledge.msu.edu) to complete the following exercises:

1. As the drivers of globalization continue to pressure both the globalization of markets and the globalization of production, we continue to see the impact of greater globalization on worldwide trade patterns. HSBC, a large global bank, analyzes these pressures and trends to identify opportunities across markets and sectors through its *trade forecasts.* Visit the HSBC Global Connections site and use the trade forecast tool to identify which export routes are forecasted to see the greatest growth over the next 15 to 20 years. What patterns do you see? What types of countries dominate these routes?
2. You are working for a company that is considering investing in a foreign country. Investing in countries with different traditions is an important element of your company's long-term strategic goals. As such, management has requested a report regarding the attractiveness of alternative countries based on the potential return of FDI. Accordingly, the ranking of the top 25 countries in terms of FDI attractiveness is a crucial ingredient for your report. A colleague mentioned a potentially useful tool called the Foreign Direct Investment (FDI) Confidence Index. The FDI Confidence Index is a regular survey of global executives conducted by A.T. Kearney. Find this index and provide additional information regarding how the index is constructed.

Medical Tourism and the Globalization of Health Care — Closing case

You might think that health care is one of the industries least vulnerable to dislocation from globalization. Like many service businesses, surely health care is delivered where it is purchased? If an American goes to a hospital for an MRI scan, won't a local radiologist read that scan? If the MRI scan shows that surgery is required, surely the surgery will be done at a local hospital in the United States? Until recently, this was true, but we are now witnessing globalization in this traditionally most local of industries.

Consider the MRI scan: The United States has a shortage of radiologists, the doctors who specialize in reading and interpreting diagnostic medical images, including X-rays, CT scans, MRI scans, and ultrasounds. Demand for radiologists is reportedly growing twice as fast as the rate at which medical schools are graduating radiologists with the skills and qualifications required to read medical images. This imbalance between supply and demand means that radiologists are expensive; an American radiologist can earn as much as $400,000 a year. Back in the early 2000s, an Indian radiologist working at the prestigious Massachusetts General Hospital, Dr. Sanjay Saini, thought he had found a clever way to deal with the shortage and expense—send images over the Internet to India where they could be interpreted by radiologists. This would reduce the workload on America's radiologists and cut costs. A radiologist in India might earn one-tenth what his or her U.S. counterpart earns. Plus, because India is on the opposite side of the globe, the images could be interpreted while it was nighttime in the United States and be ready for the attending physician when he or she arrived for work the following morning.

As for the surgery, here too we are witnessing an outsourcing trend. Consider Howard Staab, a 53-year-old uninsured self-employed carpenter from North Carolina. Mr. Staab had surgery to repair a leaking heart valve—in India. Mr. Staab flew to New Delhi, had the operation, and afterward toured the Taj Mahal, the price of which was bundled with that of the surgery. The cost, including airfare, totaled $10,000. If Mr. Staab's surgery had been performed in the United States, the cost would have been $60,000 and there would have been no visit to the Taj Mahal.

Howard Staab is not alone. Driven by a desire to access low-cost health care, some 150,000 Westerners visit India every year for medical treatments. In general, medical procedures in India cost about 10–20 percent less than in the United States. The Indian industry generates $2 billion in revenues every year from foreign patients. In another example, after years of living in pain, Robert Beeney, a 64-year-old from San Francisco, was advised to get his hip joint replaced. After doing some research, Mr. Beeney elected instead for joint resurfacing, which was not covered by his insurance. Instead of going to a nearby hospital, he flew to Hyderabad in southern India and had the surgery done for $6,600, a fraction of the $25,000 the procedure would have cost in the United States.

Mr. Beeney had his surgery performed at a branch of the Apollo hospital chain. Apollo, which was founded by Dr. Prathap C. Reddy, a surgeon trained at Massachusetts General Hospital, runs a chain of 50 state-of-the-art hospitals throughout Asia. Eight of Apollo's hospitals have the highest level of international accreditation. Apollo's main hospitals in India are estimated to treat some 50,000 international patients from 55 countries every year, mainly from nations in Southeast Asia and the Persian Gulf, although a growing number are from western Europe and North America.

Will demand for American health services soon collapse as work moves offshore to places like India? That seems unlikely. Regulations, personal preferences, and practical considerations mean that the majority of health services will always be performed in the country where the patient resides. For example, the U.S. government–sponsored medical insurance program, Medicare, will not pay for services done outside the country.

Moreover, in an interesting countertrend, U.S. medical providers also seem to be benefiting from medical tourism, particularly from China, where health care services are poor and lag far behind U.S. levels. Over the past decade, middle-class Chinese have flocked to South Korea for plastic surgery and to the United States, Singapore, and India for treatment of life-threatening conditions. When Lin Tao was diagnosed with a lethal spinal tumor in 2012, rather than risk treatment in his native Hangzhou, China, he flew to San Francisco and paid $70,000 for treatment at University of California, San Francisco Medical Center. UCSF Medical Center says that its Chinese population has grown by more than 25 percent in each of the past few years. Similarly, Massachusetts General Hospital is expecting its Chinese patients to more than double in 2015 over 2014. As China gets wealthier, ever more Chinese are apparently willing to spend more to get better treatment overseas, and America's world-class hospitals are benefiting from this trend.

Sources: G. Colvin, "Think Your Job Can't Be Sent to India?," *Fortune,* December 13, 2004, p. 80; A. Pollack, "Who's Reading Your X-Ray," *The New York Times,* November 16, 2003, pp. 1, 9; S. Rai, "Low Costs Lure Foreigners to India for Medical Care," *The New York Times,* April 7, 2005, p. C6; J. Solomon, "Traveling Cure: India's New Coup in Outsourcing," *The Wall Street Journal,* April 26, 2004, p. A1; J. Slater, "Increasing Doses in India," *Far Eastern Economic Review,* February 19, 2004, pp. 32–35; U. Kher, "Outsourcing Your Heart," *Time,* May 29, 2006, pp. 44–47; Anuradha Raghunathan, "The Reddy Sisters Have India's Apollo Hospitals Covered in Four Ways," *Forbes Asia,* January 8, 2014; Fanfan Wang, "Desperate Chinese Seek Medical Care Abroad," *The Wall Street Journal,* September 6, 2014; Apollo Hospital Group, Patients Beyond Borders, April 2015. www.patientsbeyondborders.com.

CASE DISCUSSION QUESTIONS

1. What are the benefits to American medical providers of outsourcing certain well-defined tasks such as an interpreting an MRI scan to foreign providers based in countries such as India? What are the costs?
2. Who are the primary beneficiaries of the growth of medical tourism? Who might lose from this trend?
3. What are the practical limits to outsourcing health care provision to other countries?
4. On balance, do you think that the kind of outsourcing undertaken by American health care providers is a good thing or a bad thing for the American economy? Explain your reasoning.

Endnotes

1. Figures from World Trade Organization, Statistics Database, 2013.
2. Thomas L. Friedman, *The World Is Flat* (New York: Farrar, Straus and Giroux, 2005).
3. Ibid.
4. T. Levitt, "The Globalization of Markets," *Harvard Business Review,* May–June 1983, pp. 92–102.
5. U.S. Department of Commerce, Internal Trade Administration, "Profile of U.S. Exporting and Importing Companies, 2012–2013," April 2015.
6. C. M. Draffen, "Going Global: Export Market Proves Profitable for Region's Small Businesses," *Newsday,* March 19, 2001, p. C18.
7. B. Benoit and R. Milne, "Germany's Best Kept Secret: How Its Exporters Are Betting the World," *Financial Times,* May 19, 2006, p. 11.
8. See F. T. Knickerbocker, *Oligopolistic Reaction and Multinational Enterprise* (Boston: Harvard Business School Press, 1973); R. E. Caves, "Japanese Investment in the U.S.: Lessons for the Economic Analysis of Foreign Investment," *The World Economy* 16 (1993), pp. 279–300.
9. I. Metthee, "Playing a Large Part," *Seattle Post-Intelligencer,* April 9, 1994, p. 13.
10. "Operating Profit," *The Economist,* August 16, 2008, pp. 74–76.
11. R. B. Reich, *The Work of Nations* (New York: Knopf, 1991).
12. United Nations, "The UN in Brief," www.un.org/Overview/brief.html.
13. J. A. Frankel, "Globalization of the Economy," National Bureau of Economic Research, working paper no. 7858, 2000.
14. J. Bhagwati, *Protectionism* (Cambridge, MA: MIT Press, 1989).
15. F. Williams, "Trade Round Like This May Never Be Seen Again," *Financial Times,* April 15, 1994, p. 8.
16. W. Vieth, "Major Concessions Lead to Success for WTO Talks," *Los Angeles Times,* November 14, 2001, p. A1; "Seeds Sown for Future Growth," *The Economist,* November 17, 2001, pp. 65–66.
17. United Nations, *World Investment Report, 2014* (New York and Geneva: United Nations, 2014).
18. World Trade Organization, *International Trade Statistics 2014* (Geneva: WTO, 2014).

19. United Nations Conference on Trade and Investment, "Global FDI Flows Declined in 2014," *Global Investment Trends Monitor,* January 29, 2015.
20. United Nations, *World Investment Report, 2014.*
21. Moore's law is named after Intel founder Gordon Moore.
22. Data compiled from various sources and listed at www.internetworldstats.com/stats.htm.
23. From www.census.gov/mrts/www/ecomm.html. See also S. Fiegerman, "Ecommerce Is Now a Trillion Dollar Industry," *Mashable Business*, February 5, 2013.
24. For a counterpoint, see "Geography and the Net: Putting It in Its Place," *The Economist,* August 11, 2001, pp. 18–20.
25. International Chamber of Shipping, Key Facts, www.ics-shipping.org/shipping-facts/key-facts.
26. Frankel, "Globalization of the Economy."
27. R. Wile, "Here's What It Costs to Ship 7 Everyday Goods across the Ocean," *Business Insider,* September 19, 2012.
28. Data from Bureau of Transportation Statistics, 2001.
29. John G. Fernald and Victoria Greenfield, "The Fall and Rise of the Global Economy," *Chicago Fed Letter*, April 2001, Number 164.
30. Data located at www.bts.gov/publications/us_international_trade_and_freight_transportation_trends/2003/index.html.
31. N. Hood and J. Young, *The Economics of the Multinational Enterprise* (New York: Longman, 1973).
32. United Nations, *World Investment Report, 2014.*
33. Ibid.
34. Ibid.
35. S. Chetty, "Explosive International Growth and Problems of Success Among Small and Medium Sized Firms," *International Small Business Journal,* February 2003, pp. 5–28.
36. R. A. Mosbacher, "Opening Up Export Doors for Smaller Firms," *Seattle Times,* July 24, 1991, p. A7.
37. "Small Companies Learn How to Sell to the Japanese," *Seattle Times,* March 19, 1992.
38. W. J. Holstein, "Why Johann Can Export, but Johnny Can't," *BusinessWeek,* November 3, 1991. Archived at www.businessweek.com/stories/1991-11-03/why-johann-can-export-but-johnny-cant.
39. N. Buckley and A. Ostrovsky, "Back to Business—How Putin's Allies Are Turning Russia into a Corporate State," *Financial Times,* June 19, 2006, p. 11.
40. J. E. Stiglitz, *Globalization and Its Discontents* (New York: W. W. Norton, 2003); J. Bhagwati, *In Defense of Globalization* (New York: Oxford University Press, 2004); Friedman, *The World Is Flat.*
41. See, for example, Ravi Batra, *The Myth of Free Trade* (New York: Touchstone Books, 1993); William Greider, *One World, Ready or Not: The Manic Logic of Global Capitalism* (New York: Simon & Schuster, 1997); D. Radrik, *Has Globalization Gone Too Far?* (Washington, DC: Institution for International Economics, 1997).
42. E. Goldsmith, "The Winners and the Losers," in *The Case Against the Global Economy,* ed. J. Mander and E. Goldsmith (San Francisco: Sierra Club, 1996); Lou Dobbs, *Exporting America* (New York: Time Warner Books, 2004).
43. For an excellent summary, see "The Globalization of Labor," Chapter 5, in *IMF, World Economic Outlook 2007* (Washington, DC: IMF, April 2007). Also see R. Freeman, "Labor Market Imbalances," Harvard University working paper, www.bos.frb.org/economic/conf/conf51/conf51d.pdf.
44. D. L. Bartlett and J. B. Steele, "America: Who Stole the Dream," *Philadelphia Inquirer,* September 9, 1996.
45. For example, see Paul Krugman, *Pop Internationalism* (Cambridge, MA: MIT Press, 1996).
46. For example, see B. Milanovic and L. Squire, "Does Tariff Liberalization Increase Wage Inequality?," National Bureau of Economic Research, working paper no. 11046, January 2005; B. Milanovic, "Can We Discern the Effect of Globalization on Income Distribution?," *World Bank Economic Review* 19 (2005), pp. 21–44. Also see the summary in Thomas Piketty, "The Globalization of Labor," in *Capital in the Twenty First Century* (Cambridge, MA: Harvard University Press, 2014).
47. See Piketty, "The Globalization of Labor."
48. A. Ebenstein, A. Harrison, M. McMillam, and S. Phillips, "Estimating the Impact of Trade and Offshoring on American Workers Using the Current Population Survey," *Review of Economics and Statistics* 67 (October 2014), pp. 581–95.
49. M. Forster and M. Pearson, "Income Distribution and Poverty in the OECD Area," *OECD Economic Studies* 34 (2002); Moffett, "Income Inequality Increases"; OECD, "Growing Income Inequality in OECD Countries," *OECD Forum,* May 2, 2011.
50. See Piketty, "The Globalization of Labor."
51. See Krugman, *Pop Internationalism;* and D. Belman and T. M. Lee, "International Trade and the Performance of U.S. Labor Markets," in *U.S. Trade Policy and Global Growth,* ed. R. A. Blecker (New York: Economic Policy Institute, 1996).
52. Freeman, "Labor Market Imbalances."
53. E. Goldsmith, "Global Trade and the Environment," in *The Case Against the Global Economy,* eds. J. Mander and E. Goldsmith (San Francisco: Sierra Club, 1996).
54. P. Choate, *Jobs at Risk: Vulnerable U.S. Industries and Jobs Under NAFTA* (Washington, DC: Manufacturing Policy Project, 1993).
55. Ibid.
56. B. Lomborg, *The Skeptical Environmentalist* (Cambridge, UK: Cambridge University Press, 2001).
57. H. Nordstrom and S. Vaughan, *Trade and the Environment, World Trade Organization Special Studies No. 4* (Geneva: WTO, 1999).
58. Figures are from "Freedom's Journey: A Survey of the 20th Century. Our Durable Planet," *The Economist,* September 11, 1999, p. 30.
59. For an exhaustive review of the empirical literature, see B. R. Copeland and M. Scott Taylor, "Trade, Growth and the Environment," *Journal of Economic Literature,* March 2004, pp. 7–77.
60. G. M. Grossman and A. B. Krueger, "Economic Growth and the Environment," *Quarterly Journal of Economics* 110 (1995), pp. 353–78.
61. For an economic perspective on climate change, see William Nordhouse, *The Climate Casino* (Princeton, NJ: Yale University Press, 2013).
62. Krugman, *Pop Internationalism.*

63. R. Kuttner, "Managed Trade and Economic Sovereignty," in *U.S. Trade Policy and Global Growth,* ed. R. A. Blecker (New York: Economic Policy Institute, 1996).

64. Nader, Ralph; Wallach, Lori, "GATT, NAFTA, and the Subversion of the Democratic Process," *U.S. Trade Policy and Global Growth*, R. A. Blecker, ed. New York: Economic Policy Institute, 1996, pp. 93–94

65. Lant Pritchett, "Divergence, Big Time," *Journal of Economic Perspectives* 11, no. 3 (Summer 1997), pp. 3–18. The data are from the World Bank's *World Development Indicators,* 2015.

66. Ibid.

67. W. Easterly, "How Did Heavily Indebted Poor Countries Become Heavily Indebted?" *World Development,* October 2002, pp. 1677–96; and J. Sachs, *The End of Poverty* (New York: Penguin Books, 2006).

68. See D. Ben-David, H. Nordstrom, and L. A. Winters, *Trade, Income Disparity and Poverty: World Trade Organization Special Studies No. 5* (Geneva: WTO, 1999).

69. William Easterly, "Debt Relief," *Foreign Policy,* November–December 2001, pp. 20–26.

70. Jeffrey Sachs, "Sachs on Development: Helping the World's Poorest," *The Economist,* August 14, 1999, pp. 17–20.

71. World Trade Organization, *Annual Report 2003* (Geneva: WTO, 2004).

Part 2 National Differences

National Differences in Political, Economic, and Legal Systems

learning objectives

After reading this chapter, you will be able to:

- **LO2-1** Understand how the political systems of countries differ.
- **LO2-2** Understand how the economic systems of countries differ.
- **LO2-3** Understand how the legal systems of countries differ.
- **LO2-4** Explain the implications for management practice of national differences in political economy.

Source: © Hoang Dinh Nam/Getty Images

Economic Transformation in Vietnam

opening case

Vietnam is a country undergoing transformation from a centrally planned socialist economy to a system that is more market orientated. The transformation dates back to 1986, a decade after the end of the Vietnam War that reunited the north and south of the country under Communist rule. At that time, Vietnam was one of the poorest countries in the world. Per capita income stood at just $100 per person, poverty was endemic, price inflation exceeded 700 percent, and the Communist Party exercised tight control over most forms of economic and political life. To compound matters, Vietnam struggled under a trade embargo imposed by the United States after the end of the Vietnam War.

Recognizing that central planning and government ownership of the means of production were not raising the living standards of the population, in 1986 the Communist Party embarked upon the first of a series of reforms that over the next two decades were to transform much of the economy. Agricultural land was privatized and state farm collectives were dismantled. As a result, farm productivity surged. Following this, rules restricting the establishment of private enterprises were relaxed. Many price controls were removed. State-owned enterprises were privatized. Barriers to foreign direct investment were lowered, and Vietnam entered into trade agreements with its neighbors and its old enemy the United States, culminating in the country joining the World Trade Organization in 2007. Today Vietnam is one of the signatories of the Trans Pacific Partnership, a trade agreement that, if ratified, could further liberalize its economy.

The impact of these reforms has been dramatic. Vietnam achieved annual economic growth rates of around 7 percent for the first 20 years of its reform program. Although growth rates fell to 5 percent in the aftermath of the 2008–09 global financial crisis, by 2015 Vietnam was once again achieving growth rates of around 7 percent. Living standards have surged, with GDP per capita on a purchasing parity basis reaching $5,700 in 2014. The country is now a major exporter of textiles and agricultural products, with an expanding electronics sector. State-owned enterprises now only account for 40 percent of total output, down from a near monopoly in 1985. Moreover, with a population approaching a 100 million and an average age of just 30, Vietnam is emerging as a potentially significant market for consumer goods.

For all of this progress, significant problems still remain. The country is too dependent upon exports of commodities, the prices of which can be very volatile. Vietnam's remaining state-owned enterprises are inefficient and burdened with high levels of debt. Rather than let prices be set by market forces, the government has recently reintroduced some price controls. On the political front, the Communist Party has maintained a tight grip on power, even as the economy has transitioned to a market-based system. Vietnam bans all independent political parties, labor unions, and human rights organizations. Government

–continued

critics are routinely harassed and can be arrest and detained for long periods without trial. The courts lack independence and are used as a political tool by the Communist Party to punish critics. There is no freedom of assembly or freedom of the press.

To compound matters, corruption is rampant in Vietnam. Transparency International, a nongovernmental organization that evaluates countries based on perceptions of how corrupt they are, ranks Vietnam 112 out of the 167 countries it ranks. Corruption is not a new problem in Vietnam. There is a well-established tradition of public officials selling their influence and favoring their families. However, critics say that the problem was exacerbated by privatization processes that provided opportunities for government officials to appoint themselves and family members as executives of formerly state-owned companies. Although the ruling Communist Party has launched anticorruption initiatives, these seem to be largely symbolic efforts. Many observers believe that widespread corruption has a negative impact on new business formation and is hamstringing economic growth. ●

Sources: "Crying over Cheap Milk," "*The Economist*, November 21, 2015. "Gold Stars," *The Economist*, January 23, 2016; Nick Davis, "Vietnam 40 Years on," *The Guardian*, April 22, 2015; Vietnam, *CIA Fact Book*, 2016; Human Rights Watch, "Vietnam," *World Report* 2015.

Introduction

International business is much more complicated than domestic business because countries differ in many ways. Countries have different political, economic, and legal systems. They vary significantly in their level of economic development and future economic growth trajectory. Cultural practices can vary dramatically, as can the education and skill levels of the population. All these differences can and do have major implications for the practice of international business. They have a profound impact on the benefits, costs, and risks associated with doing business in different countries; the way in which operations in different countries should be managed; and the strategy international firms should pursue in different countries. The main function of this chapter and the next two is to develop an awareness of and appreciation for the significance of country differences in political systems, economic systems, legal systems, economic development, and societal culture. Another function of the three chapters is to describe how the political, economic, legal, and cultural systems of many of the world's nation-states are evolving and to draw out the implications of these changes for the practice of international business.

This chapter focuses on how the political, economic, and legal systems of countries differ. Collectively, we refer to these systems as constituting the political economy of a country. We use the term **political economy** to stress that the political, economic, and legal systems of a country are interdependent; they interact with and influence each other, and in doing so, they affect the level of economic well-being. In Chapter 3, we build on the concepts discussed here to explore in detail how differences in political, economic, and legal systems influence the economic development of a nation-state and its likely future growth trajectory. In Chapter 4, we look at differences in societal culture and at how these differences influence the practice of international business. Moreover, as we will see in Chapter 4, societal culture has an influence on the political, economic, and legal systems in a nation and thus its level of economic well-being. We also discuss how the converse may occur: how political, economic, and legal systems may also shape societal culture.

Political Economy

The political, economic, and legal systems of a country.

The opening case illustrates some of the issues discussed in this chapter. Vietnam emerged from the Vietnam War as a communist nation in which a totalitarian government exercised tight control over most aspects of political and economic life. The government favored a command economy in which resources were allocated by central planning. Most enterprises were owned by the government. Independent entrepreneurial activity was severely limited. This form of political and economic system did not serve Vietnam well. The economy stagnated and living standards remained very low. In response, the government shifted away from a command economy and toward a market-based system. This transformation, which is ongoing, delivered almost three decades of robust economic growth. At the same time, Vietnam is still ruled by the Communist

Get Insights by Country

The "Get Insights by Country" section of globalEDGE™ (globaledge.msu.edu/global-insights/by/country) is your source for information and statistical data for nearly every country around the world (more than 200 countries). As related to Chapter 2 of the text, globalEDGE™ has a wealth of information and data on national differences in political economy. These differences are available across a dozen menu categories in the country sections (e.g., economy, history, government, culture, risk). The "Executive Memos" on each country page are also great for abbreviated fingertip access to current information. At a minimum, we suggest that you take a look at the country pages of the United Kingdom and Sweden because the authors of this text are from those countries—have you figured out who is from the UK and who is from Sweden yet?

Party, which has a monopoly on power. Political opposition is suppressed and corruption is rampant. This arguably limits the ability of the country to reach its full economic potential and makes doing business in Vietnam more challenging and less attractive than might otherwise be the case.

Political Systems

LO 2-1
Understand how the political systems of countries differ.

The political system of a country shapes its economic and legal systems.[1] As such, we need to understand the nature of different political systems before discussing economic and legal systems. By **political system**, we mean the system of government in a nation. Political systems can be assessed according to two dimensions. The first is the degree to which they emphasize collectivism as opposed to individualism. The second is the degree to which they are democratic or totalitarian. These dimensions are interrelated; systems that emphasize collectivism tend to lean toward totalitarianism, whereas those that place a high value on individualism tend to be democratic. However, a large gray area exists in the middle. It is possible to have democratic societies that emphasize a mix of collectivism and individualism. Similarly, it is possible to have totalitarian societies that are not collectivist.

Political System
System of government in a nation.

COLLECTIVISM AND INDIVIDUALISM

Collectivism refers to a political system that stresses the primacy of collective goals over individual goals.[2] When collectivism is emphasized, the needs of society as a whole are generally viewed as being more important than individual freedoms. In such circumstances, an individual's right to do something may be restricted on the grounds that it runs counter to "the good of society" or to "the common good." Advocacy of collectivism can be traced to the ancient Greek philosopher Plato (427–347 B.C.), who, in *The Republic,* argued that individual rights should be sacrificed for the good of the majority and that property should be owned in common. Plato did not equate collectivism with equality; he believed that society should be stratified into classes, with those best suited to rule (which for Plato, naturally, were philosophers and soldiers) administering society for the benefit of all. In modern times, the collectivist mantle has been picked up by socialists.

Collectivism
A political system that emphasizes collective goals as opposed to individual goals.

Socialism

Modern **socialists** trace their intellectual roots to Karl Marx (1818–1883), although socialist thought clearly predates Marx (elements of it can be traced to Plato). Marx argued that the few benefit at the expense of the many in a capitalist society where individual freedoms are not restricted. While successful capitalists accumulate considerable wealth, Marx postulated that the wages earned by the majority of workers in a capitalist society would be forced down to subsistence levels. He argued that capitalists expropriate for their own use the value created by workers, while paying workers only subsistence wages in return. According to Marx, the pay of workers does not reflect the full value of their labor. To correct this perceived wrong, Marx advocated state ownership of the basic means of production, distribution, and exchange (i.e., businesses). His logic was that if the state owned the means of production, the state could ensure that workers were fully compensated for their labor. Thus, the idea is to manage state-owned enterprise to benefit society as a whole, rather than individual capitalists.[3]

Socialists
Those who believe in public ownership of the means of production for the common good of society.

Communists
Those who believe socialism can be achieved only through revolution and totalitarian dictatorship.

Social Democrats
Those committed to achieving socialism by democratic means.

In the early twentieth century, the socialist ideology split into two broad camps. The **communists** believed that socialism could be achieved only through violent revolution and totalitarian dictatorship, whereas the **social democrats** committed themselves to achieving socialism by democratic means, turning their backs on violent revolution and dictatorship. Both versions of socialism waxed and waned during the twentieth century. The communist version of socialism reached its high point in the late 1970s, when the majority of the world's population lived in communist states. The countries under Communist Party rule at that time included the former Soviet Union; its eastern European client nations (e.g., Poland, Czechoslovakia, Hungary); China; the Southeast Asian nations of Cambodia, Laos, and Vietnam; various African nations (e.g., Angola and Mozambique); and the Latin American nations of Cuba and Nicaragua. By the mid-1990s, however, communism was in retreat worldwide. The Soviet Union had collapsed and had been replaced by a collection of 15 republics, many of which were at least nominally structured as democracies. Communism was swept out of eastern Europe by the largely bloodless revolutions of 1989. Although China is still nominally a communist state with substantial limits to individual political freedom, in the economic sphere, the country has moved sharply away from strict adherence to communist ideology. The same is true in Vietnam, where the communist government has overseen a shift away from state control of economic activity and toward a market-based economic system (see the opening case). Old-style communism, with state control over all economic activity, hangs on in only a handful of small fringe states, most notably North Korea.

Social democracy also seems to have passed a high-water mark, although the ideology may prove to be more enduring than communism. Social democracy has had perhaps its greatest influence in a number of democratic Western nations, including Australia, France, Germany, Great Britain, Norway, Spain, and Sweden, where social democratic parties have often held political power. Other countries where social democracy has had an important influence include India and Brazil. Consistent with their Marxist roots, many social democratic governments after World War II nationalized private companies in certain industries, transforming them into state-owned enterprises to be run for the "public good rather than private profit." In Great Britain by the end of the 1970s, for example, state-owned companies had a monopoly in the telecommunications, electricity, gas, coal, railway, and shipbuilding industries, as well as substantial interests in the oil, airline, auto, and steel industries.

Privatization
The sale of state-owned enterprises to private investors.

However, experience demonstrated that state ownership of the means of production ran counter to the public interest. In many countries, state-owned companies performed poorly. Protected from competition by their monopoly position and guaranteed government financial support, many became increasingly inefficient. Individuals paid for the luxury of state ownership through higher prices and higher taxes. As a consequence, a number of Western democracies voted many social democratic parties out of office in the late 1970s and early 1980s. They were succeeded by political parties, such as Britain's Conservative Party and Germany's Christian Democratic Party, that were more committed to free market economics. These parties sold state-owned enterprises to private investors (a process referred to as **privatization**). Even where social democratic parties regained the levers of power, as in Great Britain in 1997 when the left-leaning Labor Party won control of the government, they too now seem committed to continued private ownership.

Individualism
An emphasis on the importance of guaranteeing individual freedom and self-expression.

Individualism

The opposite of collectivism, **individualism** refers to a philosophy that an individual should have freedom in his or her economic and political pursuits. In contrast to collectivism, individualism stresses that the interests of the individual should take precedence over the interests of the state. Like collectivism, individualism can be traced to an ancient Greek philosopher, in this case Plato's disciple Aristotle (384–322 B.C.). In contrast to Plato, Aristotle argued that individual diversity and private ownership are desirable. In a passage that might have been taken from a speech by contemporary politicians who adhere to a free market ideology, he argued that private property is more highly productive than communal property and will thus stimulate progress. According to Aristotle, communal property receives little care, whereas property that is owned by an individual will receive the greatest care and therefore be most productive.

Individualism was reborn as an influential political philosophy in the Protestant trading nations of England and the Netherlands during the sixteenth century. The philosophy was refined in the work of a number of British philosophers, including David Hume (1711–1776), Adam Smith (1723–1790), and John Stuart Mill (1806–1873). Individualism exercised a profound influence on those in the American colonies that sought independence from Great Britain. Indeed, the concept underlies the ideas expressed in the Declaration of Independence. In the twentieth century, several Nobel Prize–winning economists—including Milton Friedman, Friedrich von Hayek, and James Buchanan—championed the philosophy.

Individualism is built on two central tenets. The first is an emphasis on the importance of guaranteeing individual freedom and self-expression. The second tenet of individualism is that the welfare of society is best served by letting people pursue their own economic self-interest, as opposed to some collective body (such as government) dictating what is in society's best interest. Or, as Adam Smith put it in a famous passage from *The Wealth of Nations,* "an individual who intends his own gain is led by an invisible hand to promote an end that was no part of his intention. Nor is it always worse for the society that it was no part of it. By pursuing his own interest, he frequently promotes that of the society more effectually than when he really intends to promote it. This author has never known much good done by those who effect to trade for the public good."[4]

What About People's Future Rights?

Individualism versus collectivism is a century-old debate topic and an inherently interesting issue. For example, does an individual's life belong to him or her or to the community, society, or country in which he or she resides? Most people have a direct and immediate answer, but there is no consensus on which answer depending on which country you reside in or which personal "compass" you subscribe to. Everyone has tendencies toward being both individualistic and collectivistic but prefers one way more than the other. So, which of these ideas—individualism or collectivism—do you think is correct, and which cultural belief do you prefer and why?

Source: Objective Standard, March 3, 2014. www.theobjectivestandard.com.

The central message of individualism, therefore, is that individual economic and political freedoms are the ground rules on which a society should be based. This puts individualism in conflict with collectivism. Collectivism asserts the primacy of the collective over the individual; individualism asserts the opposite. This underlying ideological conflict shaped much of the recent history of the world. The Cold War, for example, was in many respects a war between collectivism, championed by the former Soviet Union, and individualism, championed by the United States. From the late 1980s until about 2005, the waning of collectivism was matched by the ascendancy of individualism. Democratic ideals and market economics replaced socialism and communism in many states. Since 2005, there have been some signs of a small swing back toward left-leaning socialist ideas in several countries, including several Latin America nations such as Venezuela, Bolivia, and Paraguay, along with Russia (see the Country Focus for details). Also, the global financial crisis of 2008–2009 caused some reevaluation of the trends towards individualism, and it remains possible that the pendulum might tilt back the other way.

DEMOCRACY AND TOTALITARIANISM

Democracy and totalitarianism are at different ends of a political dimension. **Democracy** refers to a political system in which government is by the people, exercised either directly or through elected representatives. **Totalitarianism** is a form of government in which one person or political party exercises absolute control over all spheres of human life and prohibits opposing political parties. The democratic–totalitarian dimension is not independent of the individualism–collectivism dimension. Democracy and individualism go hand in hand, as do the communist version of collectivism and totalitarianism. However, gray areas exist; it is possible to have a democratic state in which collective values predominate, and it is possible to have a totalitarian state that is hostile to collectivism and in which some degree of individualism—particularly in the economic sphere—is encouraged. For example, China and Vietnam have seen a move toward greater individual freedom in the economic sphere, but those countries are stilled ruled by parties that have a monopoly on political power and constrain political freedom.

Democracy
Political system in which government is by the people, exercised either directly or through elected representatives.

Totalitarianism
Form of government in which one person or political party exercises absolute control over all spheres of human life and opposing political parties are prohibited.

Democracy

The pure form of democracy, as originally practiced by several city-states in ancient Greece, is based on a belief that citizens should be directly involved in decision making. In complex, advanced societies with populations in the tens or hundreds of millions, this is impractical. Most modern democratic states practice **representative democracy**. In a representative democracy, citizens periodically elect individuals to represent them. These elected representatives then form a government whose function is to make decisions on behalf of the electorate. In a representative democracy, elected representatives who fail to perform this job adequately will be voted out of office at the next election.

Representative Democracy
A political system in which citizens periodically elect individuals to represent them in government.

country FOCUS

Putin's Russia

The modern Russian state was born in 1991 after the dramatic collapse of the Soviet Union. Early in the post-Soviet era, Russia embraced ambitious policies designed to transform a communist dictatorship with a centrally planned economy into a democratic state with a market-based economic system. The policies, however, were imperfectly implemented. Political reform left Russia with a strong presidency that—in hindsight—had the ability to subvert the democratic process. On the economic front, the privatization of many state-owned enterprises was done in such a way as to leave large shareholdings in the hands of the politically connected, many of whom were party officials and factory managers under the old Soviet system. Corruption was also endemic, and organized crime was able to seize control of some newly privatized enterprises. In 1998, the poorly managed Russian economy went through a financial crisis that nearly bought the country to its knees.

Fast-forward to 2016, and Russia still has a long way to go before it resembles a modern democracy with a functioning free market–based economic system. On the positive side, the economy grew at a healthy clip during most of the 2000s, helped in large part by high prices for oil and gas, Russia's largest exports (in 2013 oil and gas accounted for 75 percent of all Russian exports). Between 2000 and 2013, Russia's gross domestic product (GDP) per capita more than doubled when measured by purchasing power parity. The country now boasts the world's ninth-largest economy. Thanks to government oil revenues, public debt is also low by international standards—at just 9.2 percent of GDP (in the United States, by comparison, public debt amounts to 70 percent of GDP). Indeed, Russia has run a healthy trade surplus on the back of strong oil and gas exports for the last decade.

On the other hand, the economy is overly dependent on commodities, particularly oil and gas. This was exposed in mid-2014 when the price of oil started to tumble as a result of rapidly increasing supply from the United States. Between mid-2014 and early 2016, the price of oil fell from $110 a barrel to around $27. This drove a freight train through Russia's public finances. Much of Russia's oil and gas production remains in the hands of enterprises in which the state still has a significant ownership stake. The government has a controlling ownership position in Gazprom and Rosneft, two of the country's largest oil and gas companies. The government used the rise in oil and gas revenues between 2004 and 2014 to increase public spending through state-led investment projects and increases in wages and pensions for government workers. While this boosted private consumption, there has been a dearth of private investment, and productivity growth remains low. This is particularly true among many state-owned enterprises that collectively still account for about half of the Russian economy. Now with oil prices tumbling, Russia is having to issue ever more debt to finance public spending.

Russian private enterprises are also hamstrung by bureaucratic red tape and endemic corruption. The World Bank ranks Russia 92nd in the world in terms of the ease of doing business and 88th when it comes to starting a business (for comparison, the United States is ranked 4th and 20th, respectively). Transparency International, which ranks countries by the extent of corruption, ranked Russia 119 out of 167 nations in 2015. The state and state-owned enterprises are famous for pushing work to private enterprises that are owned by political allies, which further subverts market-based processes.

On the political front, Russia is becoming less democratic with every passing year. Since 1999, Vladimir Putin has exerted increasingly tight control over Russian politics, either as president or as prime minister. Under Putin, potential opponents have been sidelined, civil liberties have been progressively reduced, and the freedom of the press has been diminished. For example, in response to opposition protests in 2011 and 2012, the Russian government passed laws increasing its control over the Internet, dramatically raising fines for participating in "unsanctioned" street protests, and expanded the definition of treason to further limit opposition activities. Vocal opponents of the régime—from business executives who do not tow the state line to protest groups such as the punk rock protest band Pussy Riot—have found themselves jailed on dubious charges. To make matters worse, Putin has recently been tightening his grip on the legal system. In late 2013, Russia's parliament, which is dominated by Putin supporters, gave the president more power to appoint and fire prosecutors, thereby diminishing the independence of the legal system.

Freedom House, which produces an annual ranking tracking freedom in the world, classifies Russia as "not free" and gives it low scores for political and civil liberties. Freedom House notes that in the March 2012 presidential elections, Putin benefited from preferential treatment by state-owned media, numerous abuses of incumbency, and procedural "irregularities" during the vote count. Putin won 63.6 percent of the vote against a field of weak, hand-chosen opponents, led by Communist Party leader Gennadiy Zyuganove, with 17.2 percent of the vote. Under a Putin-inspired 2008 constitutional amendment, the term of the presidency was expanded from four years to six. Putin will be eligible for another six-year term in 2018.

In 2014, Putin burnished his growing reputation for authoritarianism when he took advantage of unrest in the neighboring country of Ukraine to annex the Crimea region and to support armed revolt by Russian-speaking separatists in eastern Ukraine. Western powers responded to this aggression by imposing economic sanctions on Russia. Taken together with the rapid fall in oil prices, this pushed the once-booming Russian economy into a recession. In 2014, the economy grew by just 0.6 percent, while the Russian ruble tumbled, losing half of its value against other major currencies. Despite economic weaknesses, however, there is no sign that Putin's hold on power has been diminished; in fact, quite the opposite seems to have occurred.

Sources: "Putin's Russia: Sochi or Bust," *The Economist*, February 1, 2014; "Russia's Economy: The S Word," *The Economist*, November 9, 2013; Freedom House, Freedom in the World 2015: Russia, www.freedomhouse.org; K. Hille, "Putin Tightens Grip on Legal System," *Financial Times*, November 27, 2013.

To guarantee that elected representatives can be held accountable for their actions by the electorate, an ideal representative democracy has a number of safeguards that are typically enshrined in constitutional law. These include (1) an individual's right to freedom of expression, opinion, and organization; (2) a free media; (3) regular elections in which all eligible citizens are allowed to vote; (4) universal adult suffrage; (5) limited terms for elected representatives; (6) a fair court system that is independent from the political system; (7) a nonpolitical state bureaucracy; (8) a nonpolitical police force and armed service; and (9) relatively free access to state information.[5]

Totalitarianism

In a totalitarian country, all the constitutional guarantees on which representative democracies are built—an individual's right to freedom of expression and organization, a free media, and regular elections—are denied to the citizens. In most totalitarian states, political repression is widespread, free and fair elections are lacking, media are heavily censored, basic civil liberties are denied, and those who question the right of the rulers to rule find themselves imprisoned or worse.

Four major forms of totalitarianism exist in the world today. Until recently, the most widespread was **communist totalitarianism**. Communism, however, is in decline worldwide, and most of the Communist Party dictatorships have collapsed since 1989. Exceptions to this trend (so far) are China, Vietnam, Laos, North Korea, and Cuba, although most of these states exhibit clear signs that the Communist Party's monopoly on political power is eroding. In many respects, the governments of China, Vietnam, and Laos are communist in name only because those nations have adopted wide-ranging, market-based economic reforms. They remain, however, totalitarian states that deny many basic civil liberties to their populations. On the other hand, there are signs of a swing back toward communist totalitarian ideas in some states, such as Venezuela, where the government of the late Hugo Chávez displayed totalitarian tendencies. The same is true in Russia, where the government of Vladimir Putin has become increasingly totalitarian over time (see the Country Focus).

A second form of totalitarianism might be labeled **theocratic totalitarianism**. Theocratic totalitarianism is found in states where political power is monopolized by a party, group, or individual that governs according to religious principles. The most common form of theocratic totalitarianism is based on Islam and is exemplified by states such as Iran and Saudi Arabia. These states limit freedom of political and religious expression with laws based on Islamic principles.

A third form of totalitarianism might be referred to as **tribal totalitarianism**. Tribal totalitarianism has arisen from time to time in African countries such as Zimbabwe, Tanzania, Uganda, and Kenya. The borders of most African states reflect the administrative boundaries drawn by the old European colonial powers rather than tribal realities. Consequently, the typical African country contains a number of tribes (e.g., in Kenya there are more than 40 tribes). Tribal totalitarianism occurs when a political party that represents the interests of a particular tribe (and not always the majority tribe) monopolizes power. In Kenya, for example, politicians from the Kikuyu tribe long dominated the political system.

A fourth major form of totalitarianism might be described as **right-wing totalitarianism**. Right-wing totalitarianism generally permits some individual economic freedom but restricts individual political freedom, frequently on the grounds that it would lead to the rise of communism. A common feature of many right-wing dictatorships is an overt hostility to socialist or communist ideas. Many right-wing totalitarian governments are backed by the military, and in some cases, the government may be made up of military officers. The fascist regimes that ruled Germany and Italy in the 1930s and 1940s were right-wing totalitarian states. Until the early 1980s, right-wing dictatorships, many of which were military dictatorships, were common throughout Latin America (e.g., Brazil was ruled by a military dictatorship between 1964 and 1985). They were also found

Communist Totalitarianism
A version of collectivism advocating that socialism can be achieved only through a totalitarian dictatorship.

Theocratic Totalitarianism
A political system in which political power is monopolized by a party, group, or individual that governs according to religious principles.

Tribal Totalitarianism
A political system in which a party, group, or individual that represents the interests of a particular tribe (ethnic group) monopolizes political power.

Right-Wing Totalitarianism
A political system in which political power is monopolized by a party, group, or individual that generally permits individual economic freedom but restricts individual political freedom, including free speech, often on the grounds that it would lead to the rise of communism.

Is Representative Democracy the Best Way?

Chile is a country in South America that borders the South Pacific Sea. Neighboring countries include Argentina, Bolivia, and Peru—also representative democracies. Chile has a strategic location relative to sealanes between the Atlantic and Pacific Oceans, including the Strait of Magellan, the Beagle Channel, and the Drake Passage. Chile has a market-oriented economy in which the prices of goods and services are determined in a free price system. The government system is a republic (and it returned to a democracy in 1990). The chief of state and head of government is the president. Presidential and congressional elections are held periodically, with each election since the post-Pinochet era (which ended in 1988) being viewed as free and fair. How often do you believe elections should be held for the head of state?

Source: http://globalEDGE.msu.edu/countries/chile/government.

in several Asian countries, particularly South Korea, Taiwan, Singapore, Indonesia, and the Philippines. Since the early 1980s, however, this form of government has been in retreat. Most Latin American countries are now genuine multiparty democracies. Similarly, South Korea, Taiwan, and the Philippines have all become functioning democracies, as has Indonesia.

Pseudo-Democracies Many of the world's nations are neither pure democracies nor iron-clad totalitarian states. Rather they lie between pure democracies and complete totalitarian systems of government. They might be described as imperfect or pseudo-democracies, where authoritarian elements have captured some or much of the machinery of state and use this in an attempt to deny basic political and civil liberties. In the Russia of Vladimir Putin, for example, elections are still held, people compete through the ballot box for political office, and the independent press does not always tow the official line. However, Putin has used his position to systematically limit the political and civil liberties of opposition groups. His control is not yet perfect, though. Voices opposing Putin are still heard in Russia, and in theory, elections are still contested. But in practice, it is becoming increasingly difficult to challenge a man and régime that has systematically extended its political, legal, and economic power over the past 15 years (see the Country Focus).

Use SmartBook to help retain what you have learned. Access your Instructor's Connect course to check out SmartBook or go to learnsmartadvantage.com for help.

Economic Systems

Understand how the economic systems of countries differ.

It should be clear from the previous section that political ideology and economic systems are connected. In countries where individual goals are given primacy over collective goals, we are more likely to find market-based economic systems. In contrast, in countries where collective goals are given preeminence, the state may have taken control over many enterprises; markets in such countries are likely to be restricted rather than free. We can identify three broad types of economic systems: a market economy, a command economy, and a mixed economy.

Market Economy

An economic system in which the interaction of supply and demand determines the quantity in which goods and services are produced.

MARKET ECONOMY

In the archetypal pure **market economy,** all productive activities are privately owned, as opposed to being owned by the state. The goods and services that a country produces are not planned by anyone. Production is determined by the interaction of supply and demand and signaled to producers through the price system. If demand for a product exceeds supply, prices will rise, signaling producers to produce more. If supply exceeds demand, prices will fall, signaling producers to produce less. In this system, consumers are sovereign. The purchasing patterns of consumers, as signaled to producers through the mechanism of the price system, determine what is produced and in what quantity.

For a market to work in this manner, supply must not be restricted. A supply restriction occurs when a single firm monopolizes a market. In such circumstances, rather than increase output in response to increased demand, a monopolist might restrict output and let prices rise. This allows the monopolist to take a greater profit margin on each unit it sells. Although this is good for the monopolist, it is bad for the consumer, who has to pay higher prices. It also is probably bad for the welfare of society. Because a monopolist has no competitors, it has no incentive to search for ways to lower production costs. Rather, it can simply pass on cost increases to consumers in the form of higher prices. The net result is that the monopolist is likely to become increasingly inefficient, producing high-priced, low-quality goods, and society suffers as a consequence.

Given the dangers inherent in monopoly, one role of government in a market economy is to encourage vigorous free and fair competition between private producers. Governments do this by banning restrictive business practices designed to monopolize a market (antitrust laws serve this function in the United States and European Union). Private ownership also encourages vigorous competition and economic efficiency. Private ownership ensures that entrepreneurs have a right to the profits generated by their own efforts. This gives entrepreneurs an incentive to search for better ways of serving consumer needs. That may be through introducing new products, by developing more efficient production processes, by pursuing better marketing and after-sale service, or simply through managing their businesses more efficiently than their competitors. In turn, the constant improvement in product and process that results from such an incentive has been argued to have a major positive impact on economic growth and development.[6]

Kim Jong-un, the leader of the Democratic People's Republic of Korea, inspecting a factory. North Korea functions as a centralized, single party, and tightly controlled dictatorial command economy. Source: © AFP/Getty Images

COMMAND ECONOMY In a pure **command economy**, the government plans the goods and services that a country produces, the quantity in which they are produced, and the prices at which they are sold. Consistent with the collectivist ideology, the objective of a command economy is for government to allocate resources for "the good of society." In addition, in a pure command economy, all businesses are state owned, the rationale being that the government can then direct them to make investments that are in the best interests of the nation as a whole rather than in the interests of private individuals. Historically, command economies were found in communist countries where collectivist goals were given priority over individual goals. Since the demise of communism in the late 1980s, the number of command economies has fallen dramatically. Some elements of a command economy were also evident in a number of democratic nations led by socialist-inclined governments. France and India both experimented with extensive government planning and state ownership, although government planning has fallen into disfavor in both countries.

Command Economy
An economic system where the allocation of resources, including determination of what goods and services should be produced, and in what quantity, is planned by the government.

While the objective of a command economy is to mobilize economic resources for the public good, the opposite often seems to have occurred. In a command economy, state-owned enterprises have little incentive to control costs and be efficient because they cannot go out of business. Also, the abolition of private ownership means there is no incentive for individuals to look for better ways to serve consumer needs; hence, dynamism and innovation are absent from command economies. Instead of growing and becoming more prosperous, such economies tend to stagnate.

MIXED ECONOMY Mixed economies can be found between market and command economies. In a mixed economy, certain sectors of the economy are left to private ownership and free market mechanisms, while other sectors have significant state ownership and government planning. Mixed economies were once common throughout much of the developed world, although they are becoming much less so. Until the 1980s, Great Britain, France, and Sweden were mixed economies, but extensive privatization has reduced state ownership of businesses in all three nations. A similar trend occurred in many other countries where there was once a large state-owned sector, such as Brazil, Italy, and India (although there are still state-owned enterprises in all of these nations). As a counterpoint, the involvement of the state in economic activity has been on the rise again in countries such as Russia and Venezuela, where authoritarian regimes have seized control of the political structure, typically by first winning power through democratic means and then subverting those same structures to maintain their grip on power.

In mixed economies, governments also tend to take into state ownership troubled firms whose continued operation is thought to be vital to national interests. For example, in 2008 the U.S. government took an 80 percent stake in AIG to stop that financial institution from collapsing, the theory being that if AIG did collapse, it would have very serious consequences for the entire financial system. The U.S. government usually prefers market-oriented solutions to economic problems, and in the AIG case, the intention was to sell the institution back to private investors as soon as possible. The United States also took similar action with respect to a number of other troubled private enterprises, including Citigroup and General Motors. In all these cases, the government stake was seen as nothing more than a short-term action designed to stave off economic collapse by injecting capital into troubled enterprises in highly unusually circumstances. As soon as it was able to, the government sold these stakes. In early 2010, for example, the U.S. government sold its stake in Citigroup. The government stake in AIG was sold off in 2012, and by 2014, it had also disposed of its stake in GM.

test PREP

Use SmartBook to help retain what you have learned. Access your Instructor's Connect course to check out SmartBook or go to learnsmartadvantage.com for help.

LO 2-3

Understand how the legal systems of countries differ.

Legal Systems

Legal System

System of rules that regulate behavior and the processes by which the laws of a country are enforced and through which redress of grievances is obtained.

The **legal system** of a country refers to the rules, or laws, that regulate behavior along with the processes by which the laws are enforced and through which redress for grievances is obtained. The legal system of a country is of immense importance to international business. A country's laws regulate business practice, define the manner in which business transactions are to be executed, and set down the rights and obligations of those involved in business transactions. The legal environments of countries differ in significant ways. As we shall see, differences in legal systems can affect the attractiveness of a country as an investment site or market.

Like the economic system of a country, the legal system is influenced by the prevailing political system (although it is also strongly influenced by historical tradition). The government of a country defines the legal framework within which firms do business, and often the laws that regulate business reflect the rulers' dominant political ideology. For example, collectivist-inclined totalitarian states tend to enact laws that severely restrict private enterprise, whereas the laws enacted by governments in democratic states where individualism is the dominant political philosophy tend to be pro-private enterprise and pro-consumer.

Here, we focus on several issues that illustrate how legal systems can vary—and how such variations can affect international business. First, we look at some basic differences in legal systems. Next we look at contract law. Third, we look at the laws governing property rights with particular reference to patents, copyrights, and trademarks. Then we discuss protection of intellectual property. Finally, we look at laws covering product safety and product liability.

DIFFERENT LEGAL SYSTEMS

There are three main types of legal systems—or legal traditions—in use around the world: common law, civil law, and theocratic law.

Common Law

Common Law

A system of law based on tradition, precedent, and custom; when law courts interpret common law, they do so with regard to these characteristics.

The common law system evolved in England over hundreds of years. It is now found in most of Great Britain's former colonies, including the United States. **Common law** is based on tradition, precedent, and custom. *Tradition* refers to a country's legal history, *precedent* to cases that have come before the courts in the past, and *custom* to the ways in which laws are applied in specific situations. When law courts interpret common law, they do so with regard to these characteristics. This gives a common law system a degree of flexibility that other systems lack. Judges in a common law system have the power to interpret the law so that it applies to the unique circumstances of an individual case. In turn, each new interpretation sets a precedent that may be followed in future cases. As new precedents arise, laws may be altered, clarified, or amended to deal with new situations.

Civil Law

A **civil law system** is based on a detailed set of laws organized into codes. When law courts interpret civil law, they do so with regard to these codes. More than 80 countries—including Germany, France, Japan, and Russia—operate with a civil law system. A civil law system tends to be less adversarial than a common law system because the judges rely on detailed legal codes rather than interpreting tradition, precedent, and custom. Judges under a civil law system have less flexibility than those under a common law system. Judges in a common law system have the power to interpret the law, whereas judges in a civil law system have the power only to apply the law.

Theocratic Law

A **theocratic law system** is one in which the law is based on religious teachings. Islamic law is the most widely practiced theocratic legal system in the modern world, although usage of both Hindu and Jewish law persisted into the twentieth century. Islamic law is primarily a moral rather than a commercial law and is intended to govern all aspects of life.[7] The foundation for Islamic law is the holy book of Islam, the Koran, along with the Sunnah, or decisions and sayings of the Prophet Muhammad, and the writings of Islamic scholars who have derived rules by analogy from the principles established in the Koran and the Sunnah. Because the Koran and Sunnah are holy documents, the basic foundations of Islamic law cannot be changed. However, in practice, Islamic jurists and scholars are constantly debating the application of Islamic law to the modern world. In reality, many Muslim countries have legal systems that are a blend of Islamic law and a common or civil law system.

Although Islamic law is primarily concerned with moral behavior, it has been extended to cover certain commercial activities. An example is the payment or receipt of interest, which is considered usury and outlawed by the Koran. To the devout Muslim, acceptance of interest payments is seen as a grave sin; the giver and the taker are equally damned. This is not just a matter of theology; in several Islamic states, it has also become a matter of law. In the 1990s, for example, Pakistan's Federal Shariat Court, the highest Islamic lawmaking body in the country, pronounced interest to be un-Islamic and therefore illegal and demanded that the government amend all financial laws accordingly. In 1999, Pakistan's Supreme Court ruled that Islamic banking methods should be used in the country after July 1, 2001.[8] By the late 2000s, there were some 500 Islamic financial institutions in the world, and as of 2014 they collectively managed more than $1 trillion in assets. In addition to Pakistan, Islamic financial institutions are found in many of the Gulf states, Egypt, Malaysia, and Iran.[9]

Do You Agree with the Unique System of Islamic Banking?

How can a banking system operate without interest (*riba* in Arabic)? The basic economic idea is that commercial risk should be shared. In the Western approach, interest guarantees the banker a return, so on a collateralized loan, the banker avoids much of the commercial risk that's inherent in business. No matter what happens to the business, the banker gets a return. In contrast, Islam requires that the banker share this commercial risk. If the business venture is successful, the banker shares the profit. If the venture doesn't do well, neither does the banker. The value of community in Islam is stronger than the value of individual profit. As a result, Islamic Banking was born in the mid-1970s and has grown ever since, now to the point of having millions of clients, a resilient code of ethics, and engagement from many conventional banks around the world. What do you think? Should the banker be paid regardless of entrepreneurial success, or is the Islamic Banking system a better way to share commercial risk?

Source: www.dib.ae/islamic-banking.

Civil Law System
A system of law based on a very detailed set of written laws and codes.

Theocratic Law System
A system of law based on religious teachings.

DIFFERENCES IN CONTRACT LAW

The difference between common law and civil law systems can be illustrated by the approach of each to contract law (remember, most theocratic legal systems also have elements of common or civil law). A **contract** is a document that specifies the conditions under which an exchange is to occur and details the rights and obligations of the parties involved. Some form of contract regulates many business transactions. **Contract law** is the body of law that governs contract enforcement. The parties to an agreement normally resort to contract law when one party feels the other has violated either the letter or the spirit of an agreement.

Contract
A document that specifies the conditions under which an exchange is to occur and details the rights and obligations of the parties involved.

Contract Law
The body of law that governs contract enforcement.

Because common law tends to be relatively ill specified, contracts drafted under a common law framework tend to be very detailed with all contingencies spelled out. In civil law systems, however, contracts tend to be much shorter and less specific because many of the issues are already covered in a civil code. Thus, it is more expensive to draw up contracts in a common law jurisdiction, and resolving contract disputes can be very adversarial in common law systems. But common law systems have the advantage of greater flexibility and allow judges to interpret a contract dispute in light of the prevailing situation. International businesses need to be sensitive to these differences; approaching a contract dispute in a state with a civil law system as if it had a common law system may backfire, and vice versa.

When contract disputes arise in international trade, there is always the question of which country's laws to apply. To resolve this issue, a number of countries, including the United States, have ratified the **United Nations Convention on Contracts for the International Sale of Goods (CISG)**. The CISG establishes a uniform set of rules governing certain aspects of the making and performance of everyday commercial contracts between sellers and buyers who have their places of business in different nations. By adopting the CISG, a nation signals to other adopters that it will treat the convention's rules as part of its law. The CISG applies automatically to all contracts for the sale of goods between different firms based in countries that have ratified the convention, unless the parties to the contract explicitly opt out. One problem with the CISG, however, is that as of 2015, only 83 nations have ratified the convention (the CISG went into effect in 1988).[10] Some of the world's important trading nations, including India and the United Kingdom, have not ratified the CISG.

United Nations Convention on Contracts for the International Sale of Goods (CISG)
A set of rules governing certain aspects of the making and performance of commercial contracts between sellers and buyers who have their places of businesses in different nations.

When firms do not wish to accept the CISG, they often opt for arbitration by a recognized arbitration court to settle contract disputes. The most well known of these courts is the International Court of Arbitration of the International Chamber of Commerce in Paris, which handles more than 500 requests per year from more than 100 countries.[11]

PROPERTY RIGHTS AND CORRUPTION

In a legal sense, the term *property* refers to a resource over which an individual or business holds a legal title, that is, a resource that it owns. Resources include land, buildings, equipment, capital, mineral rights, businesses, and intellectual property (ideas, which are protected by patents, copyrights, and trademarks). **Property rights** refer to the legal rights over the use to which a resource is put and over the use made of any income that may be derived from that resource.[12] Countries differ in the extent to which their legal systems define and protect property rights. Almost all countries now have laws on their books that protect property rights. Even China, still nominally a communist state despite its booming market economy, finally enacted a law to protect the rights of private property holders in 2007 (the law gives individuals the same legal protection for their property as the state has).[13] However, in many countries these laws are not enforced by the authorities, and property rights are violated. Property rights can be violated in two ways: through private action and through public action.

Property Rights
Bundle of legal rights over the use to which a resource is put and over the use made of any income that may be derived from that resource.

Private Action

In terms of violating property rights, **private action** refers to theft, piracy, blackmail, and the like by private individuals or groups. Although theft occurs in all countries, a weak legal system allows a much higher level of criminal action. For example, in the chaotic period following the collapse of communism in Russia, an outdated legal system, coupled with a weak police force and judicial system, offered both domestic and foreign businesses scant protection from blackmail by the "Russian Mafia." Successful business owners in Russia often had to pay "protection money" to the Mafia or face violent retribution, including bombings and assassinations (about 500 contract killings of businessmen occurred per year in the 1990s).[14]

Private Action
Violation of property rights through theft, piracy, blackmail, and the like by private individuals or groups.

Russia is not alone in having organized crime problems (and the situation in Russia has improved since the 1990s). The Mafia has a long history in the United States (Chicago in the 1930s was similar to Moscow in the 1990s). In Japan, the local version of the Mafia, known as the *yakuza,* runs protection rackets, particularly in the food and entertainment industries.[15] However, there was a big difference between the magnitude of such activity in Russia in the 1990s and its limited impact in Japan and the United States. The difference arose because the legal enforcement apparatus, such as the police and court system, was weak in Russia following the collapse of communism. Many other countries from time to time have had problems similar to or even greater than those experienced by Russia.

Public Action and Corruption

Public action to violate property rights occurs when public officials, such as politicians and government bureaucrats, extort income, resources, or the property itself from property holders. This can be done through legal mechanisms such as levying excessive taxation, requiring expensive licenses or permits from property holders, taking assets

Public Action
The extortion of income or resources of property holders by public officials, such as politicians and government bureaucrats.

into state ownership without compensating the owners, or redistributing assets without compensating the prior owners. It can also be done through illegal means, or corruption, by demanding bribes from businesses in return for the rights to operate in a country, industry, or location.[16]

Corruption has been well documented in every society, from the banks of the Congo River to the palace of the Dutch royal family, from Japanese politicians to Brazilian bankers, and from Indonesian government officials to the New York City Police Department. The government of the late Ferdinand Marcos in the Philippines was famous for demanding bribes from foreign businesses wishing to set up operations in that country. The same was true of government officials in Indonesia under the rule of former President Suharto. No society is immune to corruption. However, there are systematic differences in the extent of corruption. In some countries, the rule of law minimizes corruption. Corruption is seen and treated as illegal, and when discovered, violators are punished by the full force of the law. In other countries, the rule of law is weak and corruption by bureaucrats and politicians is rife. Corruption is so endemic in some countries that politicians and bureaucrats regard it as a perk of office and openly flout laws against corruption. This seems to have been the case in Brazil until recently; the situation there may be evolving in a more positive direction.

According to Transparency International, an independent nonprofit organization dedicated to exposing and fighting corruption, businesses and individuals spend some $400 billion a year worldwide on bribes related to government procurement contracts alone.[17] Transparency International has also measured the level of corruption among public officials in different countries.[18] As can be seen in Figure 2.1, the organization rated countries such as Denmark and Sweden as clean; it rated others, such as Russia, India, and Venezuela, as corrupt. Somalia ranked last out of all 167 countries in the survey (the country is often described as a "failed state").

Economic evidence suggests that high levels of corruption significantly reduce the foreign direct investment, level of international trade, and economic growth rate in a country.[19] By

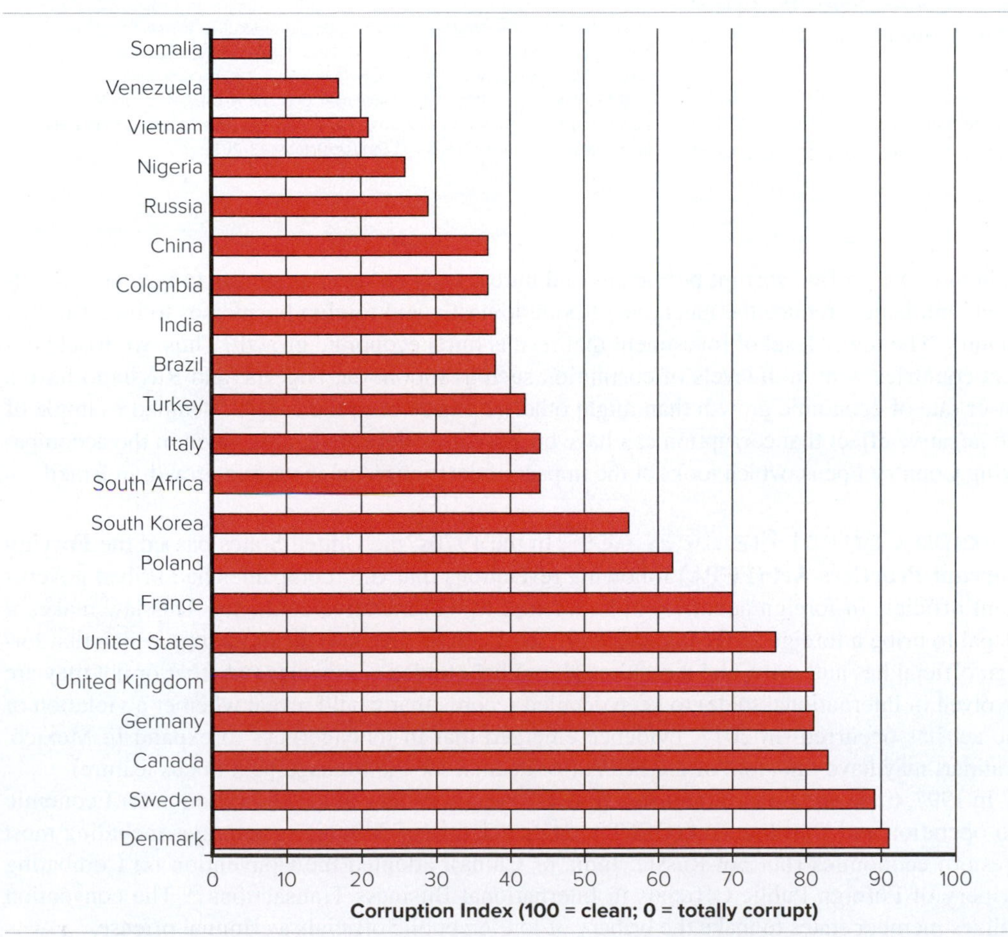

FIGURE

Rankings of corruption by country, 2015.

Source: Constructed by the author from raw data from Transparency International, Corruption Perceptions Index 2015.

management FOCUS

Did Walmart Violate the Foreign Corrupt Practices Act?

In the early 2000s, Walmart wanted to build a new store in San Juan Teotihuacan, Mexico, barely a mile from ancient pyramids that drew tourists from around the world. The owner of the land was happy to sell to Walmart, but one thing stood in the way of a deal: the city's new zoning laws. These prohibited commercial development in the historic area. Not to be denied, executives at the headquarters of Walmart de Mexico found a way around the problem: They paid a $52,000 bribe to a local official to redraw the zoning area so that the property Walmart wanted to purchase was placed *outside* the commercial-free zone. Walmart then went ahead and built the store, despite vigorous local opposition, opening it in late 2004.

A former lawyer for Walmart de Mexico subsequently contacted Walmart executives at the company's corporate headquarters in Bentonville, Arkansas. He told them that Walmart de Mexico routinely resorted to bribery, citing the altered zoning map as just one example. Alarmed, executives at Walmart started their own investigation. Faced with growing evidence of corruption in Mexico, top Walmart executives decided to engage in damage control, rather than coming clean. Walmart's top lawyer shipped the case files back to Mexico and handed over responsibility for the investigation to the general council of Walmart de Mexico. This was an interesting choice as the very same general council was alleged to have authorized bribes. The general council quickly exonerated fellow Mexican executives, and the internal investigation was closed in 2006.

For several years nothing more happened; then, in April 2012, the *New York Times* published an article detailing bribery by Walmart. The *Times* cited the changed zoning map and several other examples of bribery by Walmart: for example, eight bribes totaling $341,000 enabled Walmart to build a Sam's Club in one of Mexico City's most densely populated neighborhoods without a construction license, an environmental permit, an urban impact assessment, or even a traffic permit. Similarly, thanks to nine bribe payments totaling $765,000, Walmart built a vast refrigerated distribution center in an environmentally fragile flood basin north of Mexico City, in an area where electricity was so scarce that many smaller developers were turned away.

Walmart responded to the *New York Times* article by ramping up a second internal investigation into bribery that it had initiated in 2011. By mid-2015, there were reportedly more than 300 outside lawyers working on the investigation, and it had cost more than $612 million in fees. In addition, the U.S. Department of Justice and the Securities and Exchange Commission both announced that they had started investigations into Walmart's practices. In November 2012, Walmart reported that its own investigation into violations had extended beyond Mexico to include China and India. Among other things, it was looking into the allegations by the *Times* that top executives at Walmart, including former CEO Lee Scott Jr., had deliberately squashed earlier investigations. While the investigations are still ongoing, in late 2015, people familiar with the matter stated that the federal investigation had not uncovered evidence of widespread bribery and that the investigation would probably result in a smaller case than initially thought.

Sources: David Barstow, "Vast Mexican Bribery Case Hushed Up by Wal-Mart after Top Level Struggle," *The New York Times*, April 21, 2012; Stephanie Clifford and David Barstow, "Wal-Mart Inquiry Reflects Alarm on Corruption," *The New York Times*, November 15, 2012; Nathan Vardi, "Why Justice Department Could Hit Wal-Mart Hard over Mexican Bribery Allegations," *Forbes*, April 22, 2012; Phil Wahba, "Walmart Bribery Probe by Feds Finds No Major Misconduct in Mexico," *Fortune*, October 18, 2015.

siphoning off profits, corrupt politicians and bureaucrats reduce the returns to business investment and, hence, reduce the incentive of both domestic and foreign businesses to invest in that country. The lower level of investment that results hurts economic growth. Thus, we would expect countries with high levels of corruption such as Indonesia, Nigeria, and Russia to have a lower rate of economic growth than might otherwise have been the case. A detailed example of the negative effect that corruption can have on economic development is given in the accompanying Country Focus, which looks at the impact of corruption on economic growth in Brazil.

Foreign Corrupt Practices Act (FCPA)
U.S. law regulating behavior regarding the conduct of international business in the taking of bribes and other unethical actions.

Foreign Corrupt Practices Act

In the 1970s, the United States passed the **Foreign Corrupt Practices Act (FCPA)** following revelations that U.S. companies had bribed government officials in foreign countries in an attempt to win lucrative contracts. This law makes it illegal to bribe a foreign government official to obtain or maintain business over which that foreign official has authority, and it requires all publicly traded companies (whether or not they are involved in international trade) to keep detailed records that would reveal whether a violation of the act has occurred. In 2012, evidence emerged that in its eagerness to expand in Mexico, Walmart may have run afoul of the FCPA (for details, see the Management Focus feature).

Did You Know?
Did you know that it's illegal for Americans to bribe public officials to gain business in a foreign country, even if bribery is commonplace in that nation?

Visit your instructor's Connect® course and click on SmartBook® or visit www. learnsmartadvantage .com to view a short video explanation from the authors.

In 1997, trade and finance ministers from the member states of the Organisation for Economic Co-operation and Development (OECD), an association of 34 major economies including most Western economies (but not Russia, India or China), adopted the Convention on Combating Bribery of Foreign Public Officials in International Business Transactions.[20] The convention obliges member states to make the bribery of foreign public officials a criminal offense.

country FOCUS

Corruption in Brazil

Brazil is the seventh-largest economy in the world with a gross domestic product of $2.25 trillion. The country has a democratic government and an economy characterized by moderately free markets, although the country's largest oil producer (Petrobras) and one of its top banks (Banco do Brazil) are both state owned. Many economists, however, have long felt that the country has never quite lived up to its considerable economic potential. A major reason for this has been an endemically high level of corruption that favors those with political connections and discourages investment by more ethical businesses.

Transparency International, a nongovernmental organization that evaluates countries based on perceptions of how corrupt they are, ranked Brazil 76 out of the 169 countries it looked at in its 2015 report. The problems it identifies in Brazil include public officials who demand bribes in return for awarding government contracts and "influence peddling," in which elected officials use their position in government to obtain favors or preferential treatment. Consistent with this, according to a study by the World Economic Forum, Brazil ranks 135th out of 144 countries in the proper use of public funds.

Over the last decade, several corruption scandals have come to light that serve to emphasize Brazil's corruption problem. In 2005, a scandal known as the *mensalao* (the monthly payoff scandal) broke. The scandal started when a midlevel postal official was caught on film pocketing a modest bribe in exchange for promises to favor certain businesses in landing government contracts. Further investigation uncovered a web of influence peddling in which fat monthly payments were given to lawmakers willing to back government initiatives in National Congress. After a lengthy investigation, in late 2012 some 25 politicians and business executives were found guilty of crimes that included bribery, money laundering, and corruption.

The public uproar surrounding the *mensalao* scandal was just starting to die down when in March 2014 another corruption scandal captured the attention of Brazilians. This time it involved the state-owned oil company, Petrobras. Under a scheme that seems to have been operating since 1997, construction firms wanting to do business with Petrobras agreed to pay bribes to the company's executives. Many of these executives were themselves political appointees. The executives would inflate the value of contracts they awarded, adding a 3 percent "fee," which was effectively a kickback. The 3 percent fee was shared among Petrobras executives, construction industry executives, and politicians. The construction companies established shell companies to make payments and launder the money. According to prosecutors investigating the case, the total value of bribes may have exceeded $3.7 billion.

Four former Petrobras officials and at least 23 construction company executives have been charged with crimes that include corruption and money laundering. In addition, Brazil's Supreme Court has given prosecutors the go-ahead to investigate 48 current or former members of Congress, including the former Brazilian President Fernando Collor de Mello. The Brazilian president, Dilma Rousseff, was also tainted by the scandal. In June 2016 she was suspended from the Presidency pending an impeachment trial . She was chair of Petrobras during the time this was occurring. She is also a member of the governing Workers' Party, several members of which seem to have been among the major beneficiaries of the kickback scandal. Although there is no evidence that Rousseff knew of the bribes or profited from them, her ability to govern effectively has been severely damaged by association. The scandal has so rocked Brazil that it has pushed the country close to a recession.

If there is a bright spot in all of this, it is that the scandals are coming to light. Backed by Supreme Court rulings and public outrage, corrupted politicians, government officials, and business executives are being prosecuted. In the past, that was far less likely to occur.

Sources: Will Conners and Luciana Magalhaes, "Brazil Cracks Open Vast Bribery Scandal," *The Wall Street Journal,* April 7, 2015; Marc Margolis, "In Brazil's Trial of the Century, Lula's Reputation Is at Stake," *Newsweek,* July 27, 2012; "The Big Oily," *The Economist,* January 3, 2015; Donna Bowater, "Brazil's Continuing Corruption Problem", *BBC News,* September 18, 2015.

Both the U.S. law and OECD convention include language that allows exceptions known as facilitating or expediting payments (also called *grease payments* or *speed money*), the purpose of which is to expedite or to secure the performance of a routine governmental action.[21] For example, they allow small payments made to speed up the issuance of permits or licenses, process paperwork, or just get vegetables off the dock and on their way to market. The explanation for this exception to general antibribery provisions is that while grease payments are, technically, bribes, they are distinguishable from (and, apparently, less offensive than) bribes used to obtain or maintain business because they merely facilitate performance of duties that the recipients are already obligated to perform.

Intellectual Property
Products of the mind, ideas (e.g., books, music, computer software, designs, technological know-how); intellectual property can be protected by patents, copyrights, and trademarks.

Patent
Grants the inventor of a new product or process exclusive rights to the manufacture, use, or sale of that invention.

Copyrights
The exclusive legal rights of authors, composers, playwrights, artists, and publishers to publish and disperse their work as they see fit.

Trademarks
The designs and names, often officially registered, by which merchants or manufacturers designate and differentiate their products.

THE PROTECTION OF INTELLECTUAL PROPERTY **Intellectual property** refers to property that is the product of intellectual activity, such as computer software, a screenplay, a music score, or the chemical formula for a new drug. Patents, copyrights, and trademarks establish ownership rights over intellectual property. A **patent** grants the inventor of a new product or process exclusive rights for a defined period to the manufacture, use, or sale of that invention. **Copyrights** are the exclusive legal rights of authors, composers, playwrights, artists, and publishers to publish and disperse their work as they see fit. **Trademarks** are designs and names, officially registered, by which merchants or manufacturers designate and differentiate their products (e.g., Christian Dior clothes). In the high-technology "knowledge" economy of the twenty-first century, intellectual property has become an increasingly important source of economic value for businesses. Protecting intellectual property has also become increasingly problematic, particularly if it can be rendered in a digital form and then copied and distributed at very low cost via pirated DVDs or over the Internet (e.g., computer software, music, and video recordings).[22]

The philosophy behind intellectual property laws is to reward the originator of a new invention, book, musical record, clothes design, restaurant chain, and the like for his or her idea and effort. Such laws stimulate innovation and creative work. They provide an incentive for people to search for novel ways of doing things, and they reward creativity. For example, consider innovation in the pharmaceutical industry. A patent will grant the inventor of a new drug a 20-year monopoly in production of that drug. This gives pharmaceutical firms an incentive to undertake the expensive, difficult, and time-consuming basic research required to generate new drugs (it can cost $1 billion in R&D and take 12 years to get a new drug on the market). Without the guarantees provided by patents, companies would be unlikely to commit themselves to extensive basic research.[23]

World Intellectual Property Organization

An international organization whose members sign treaties to agree to protect intellectual property.

Paris Convention for the Protection of Industrial Property

International agreement to protect intellectual property.

The protection of intellectual property rights differs greatly from country to country. Although many countries have stringent intellectual property regulations on their books, the enforcement of these regulations has often been lax. This has been the case even among many of the 185 countries that are now members of the **World Intellectual Property Organization**, all of which have signed international treaties designed to protect intellectual property, including the oldest such treaty, the **Paris Convention for the Protection of Industrial Property**, which dates to 1883 and has been signed by more than 170 nations. Weak enforcement encourages the piracy (theft) of intellectual property. China and Thailand have often been among the worst offenders in Asia. Pirated computer software is widely available in China. Similarly, the streets of Bangkok, Thailand's capital, are lined with stands selling pirated copies of Rolex watches, Levi's jeans, DVDs, and computer software.

The computer software industry is an example of an industry that suffers from lax enforcement of intellectual property rights. Estimates suggest that violations of intellectual property rights cost personal computer software firms revenues equal to $63 billion in 2011.[24] According to the Business Software Alliance, a software industry association, in 2011 some 42 percent of all software applications used in the world were pirated. One of the worst large countries was China, where the piracy rate in 2011 ran at 77 percent and cost the industry more than $9.8 billion in lost sales, up from $444 million in 1995. The piracy rate in the United States was much lower at 19 percent; however, the value of sales lost was significant because of the size of the U.S. market, reaching an estimated $9.8 billion in 2011.[25]

How Important Are Intellectual Property Rights?

Burundi is a landlocked country in the Great Lake region of Eastern Africa. Neighboring countries include Rwanda, Tanzania, and the Democratic Republic of the Congo. Burundi is hilly and mountainous, with access to Lake Tanganyika. The government system is a republic, with the chief of state and head of government being the president. Burundi has a traditional economic system in which the allocation of available resources is made on the basis of primitive methods, and many citizens engage in subsistence agriculture. At the same time, Burundi was last of the 131 countries ranked in the 2013 International Property Rights Index (IPRI). The IPRI is conducted by a partnership of 74 international organizations. The IPRI takes into account legal and political environment, physical property rights, and intellectual property rights. How much should companies focus on intellectual property rights in deciding where to (1) produce their products and (2) sell their products? Does it differ if you produce or sell in the country?

Source: www.internationalpropertyrightsindex.org.

International businesses have a number of possible responses to violations of their intellectual property. They can lobby their respective governments to push for international agreements to ensure that intellectual property rights are protected and that the law is enforced. Partly as a result of such actions, international laws are being strengthened. As we shall see in Chapter 7, the most recent world trade agreement, signed in 1994, for the first time extends the scope of the General Agreement on Tariffs and Trade to cover intellectual property. Under the new agreement, known as the Trade-Related Aspects of Intellectual Property Rights (TRIPS), as of 1995 a council of the World Trade Organization is overseeing enforcement of much stricter intellectual property regulations. These regulations oblige WTO members to grant and enforce patents lasting at least 20 years and copyrights lasting 50 years after the death of the author. Rich countries had to comply with the

management FOCUS

Starbucks Wins Key Trademark Case in China

Starbucks has big plans for China. It believes the fast-growing nation will become the company's second-largest market after the United States. Starbucks entered the country in 1999, and by the end of 2012, it had opened more than 400 stores. But in China, copycats of well-established Western brands are common. Starbucks faced competition from a look-alike, Shanghai Xing Ba Ke Coffee Shop, whose stores closely matched the Starbucks format, right down to a green-and-white Xing Ba Ke circular logo that mimics Starbucks' ubiquitous logo. The name also mimics the standard Chinese translation for Starbucks. *Xing* means "star," and *Ba Ke* sounds like "bucks."

In 2003, Starbucks decided to sue Xing Ba Ke in Chinese court for trademark violations. Xing Ba Ke's general manager responded by claiming it was just an accident that the logo and name were so similar to that of Starbucks. He claimed the right to use the logo and name because Xing Ba Ke had registered as a company in Shanghai in 1999, before Starbucks entered the city. "I hadn't heard of Starbucks at the time," claimed the manager, "so how could I imitate its brand and logo?"

However, in January 2006, a Shanghai court ruled that Starbucks had precedence, in part because it had registered its Chinese name in 1998. The court stated that Xing Ba Ke's use of the name and similar logo was "clearly malicious" and constituted improper competition. The court ordered Xing Ba Ke to stop using the name and to pay Starbucks $62,000 in compensation. While the money involved here may be small, the precedent is not. In a country where violation of trademarks has been common, the courts seem to be signaling a shift toward greater protection of intellectual property rights. This is perhaps not surprising because foreign governments and the World Trade Organization have been pushing China hard recently to start respecting intellectual property rights.

Sources: M. Dickie, "Starbucks Wins Case against Chinese Copycat," *Financial Times*, January 3, 2006, p. 1; "Starbucks: Chinese Court Backs Company over Trademark Infringement," *The Wall Street Journal*, January 2, 2006, p. A11; "Starbucks Calls China Its Top Growth Focus," *The Wall Street Journal*, February 14, 2006, p. 1.

rules within a year. Poor countries, in which such protection generally was much weaker, had five years of grace, and the very poorest have 10 years.[26] (For further details of the TRIPS agreement, see Chapter 7.)

In addition to lobbying governments, firms can file lawsuits on their own behalf. For example, Starbucks won a landmark trademark copyright case in China against a copycat that signaled a change in the approach in China (see the accompanying Management Focus for details). Firms may also choose to stay out of countries where intellectual property laws are lax, rather than risk having their ideas stolen by local entrepreneurs. Firms also need to be on the alert to ensure that pirated copies of their products produced in countries with weak intellectual property laws don't turn up in their home market or in third countries. U.S. computer software giant Microsoft, for example, discovered that pirated Microsoft software, produced illegally in Thailand, was being sold worldwide as the real thing.

PRODUCT SAFETY AND PRODUCT LIABILITY

Product safety laws set certain safety standards to which a product must adhere. **Product liability** involves holding a firm and its officers responsible when a product causes injury, death, or damage. Product liability can be much greater if a product does not conform to required safety standards. Both civil and criminal product liability laws exist. Civil laws call for payment and monetary damages. Criminal liability laws result in fines or imprisonment. Both civil and criminal liability laws are probably more extensive in the United States than in any other country, although many other Western nations also have comprehensive liability laws. Liability laws are typically the least extensive in less developed nations. A boom in product liability suits and awards in the United States resulted in a dramatic increase in the cost of liability insurance. Many business executives argue that the high costs of liability insurance make American businesses less competitive in the global marketplace.

Product Safety Laws
Set certain safety standards to which a product must adhere.

Product Liability
Involves holding a firm and its officers responsible when a product causes injury, death, or damage.

In addition to the competitiveness issue, country differences in product safety and liability laws raise an important ethical issue for firms doing business abroad. When product safety laws are tougher in a firm's home country than in a foreign country or when liability laws are more lax, should a firm doing business in that foreign country follow the more relaxed local standards or should it adhere to the standards of its home country? While the ethical thing to do is undoubtedly to adhere to home-country standards, firms have been known to take advantage of lax safety and liability laws to do business in a manner that would not be allowed at home.

Use SmartBook to help retain what you have learned. Access your Instructor's Connect course to check out SmartBook or go to learnsmartadvantage.com for help.

FOCUS ON MANAGERIAL IMPLICATIONS

THE MACRO ENVIRONMENT INFLUENCES MARKET ATTRACTIVENESS

LO 2-4
Explain the implications for management practice of national differences in political economy.

The material discussed in this chapter has two broad implications for international business. First, the political, economic, and legal systems of a country raise important ethical issues that have implications for the practice of international business. For example, what ethical implications are associated with doing business in totalitarian countries where citizens are denied basic human rights, corruption is rampant, and bribes are necessary to gain permission to do business? Is it right to operate in such a setting? A full discussion of the ethical implications of country differences in political economy is reserved for Chapter 5, where we explore ethics in international business in much greater depth.

Second, the political, economic, and legal environments of a country clearly influence the attractiveness of that country as a market or investment site. The benefits, costs, and risks associated with doing business in a country are a function of that country's political, economic, and legal systems. The overall attractiveness of a country as a market or investment site depends on balancing the likely long-term benefits of doing business in that country against the likely costs and risks. Because this chapter is the first of two dealing with issues of political economy, we will delay a detailed discussion of how political economy impacts the benefits, costs, and risks of doing business in different nation-states until the end of the next chapter, when we have a full grasp of all the relevant variables that are important for assessing benefits, costs, and risks.

For now, other things being equal, a nation with democratic political institutions, a market-based economic system, and strong legal system that protects property rights and limits corruption is clearly more attractive as a place in which to do business than a nation that lacks democratic institutions, where economic activity is heavily regulated by the state, and where corruption is rampant and the rule of law is not respected. On this basis, for example, a country like Canada is a better place in which to do business than the Russia of Vladimir Putin (see the Country Focus on Putin's Russia). That being said, the reality is often more nuanced and complex. For example, China lacks democratic institutions, corruption is widespread, property rights are not always respected, and even though the country has embraced many market-based economic reforms, there are still large numbers of state-owned enterprises, yet many Western businesses feel that they must invest in China. They do so despite the risks because the market is large, the nation is moving toward a market-based system, economic growth has been strong (although it faltered in 2015–2016), legal protection of property rights has been improving, and China is already the second largest economy in the world and could ultimately replace the United States as the world's largest. Thus, China is becoming increasingly attractive as a place in which to do business, and given the future growth trajectory, significant opportunities may be lost by not investing in the country. We will explore how changes in political economy impact the attractiveness of a nation as a place in which to do business in the next chapter.

Key Terms

political economy, p. 38
political system, p. 39
collectivism, p. 39
socialists, p. 39
communists, p. 40
social democrats, p. 40
privatization, p. 40
individualism, p. 40
democracy, p. 41
totalitarianism, p. 41
representative democracy, p. 41
communist totalitarianism, p. 43
theocratic totalitarianism, p. 43
tribal totalitarianism, p. 43
right-wing totalitarianism, p. 43
market economy, p. 44
command economy, p. 45
legal system, p. 46
common law, p. 46
civil law system, p. 47
theocratic law system, p. 47
contract, p. 47
contract law, p. 47
United Nations Convention on Contracts for the International Sale of Goods (CISG), p. 48
property rights, p. 48
private action, p. 48
public action, p. 48
Foreign Corrupt Practices Act (FCPA), p. 50
intellectual property, p. 51

patent, p. 51
copyrights, p. 51
trademarks, p. 51
World Intellectual Property Organization, p. 52
Paris Convention for the Protection of Industrial Property, p. 52
product safety laws, p. 53
product liability, p. 53

Summary

This chapter has reviewed how the political, economic, and legal systems of countries vary. The potential benefits, costs, and risks of doing business in a country are a function of its political, economic, and legal systems. The chapter made the following points:

1. Political systems can be assessed according to two dimensions: the degree to which they emphasize collectivism as opposed to individualism and the degree to which they are democratic or totalitarian.
2. Collectivism is an ideology that views the needs of society as being more important than the needs of the individual. Collectivism translates into an advocacy for state intervention in economic activity and, in the case of communism, a totalitarian dictatorship.
3. Individualism is an ideology that is built on an emphasis of the primacy of the individual's freedoms in the political, economic, and cultural realms. Individualism translates into an advocacy for democratic ideals and free market economics.
4. Democracy and totalitarianism are at different ends of the political spectrum. In a representative democracy, citizens periodically elect individuals to represent them, and political freedoms are guaranteed by a constitution. In a totalitarian state, political power is monopolized by a party, group, or individual, and basic political freedoms are denied to citizens of the state.
5. There are three broad types of economic systems: a market economy, a command economy, and a mixed economy. In a market economy, prices are free of controls, and private ownership is predominant. In a command economy, prices are set by central planners, productive assets are owned by the state, and private ownership is forbidden. A mixed economy has elements of both a market economy and a command economy.
6. Differences in the structure of law between countries can have important implications for the practice of international business. The degree to which property rights are protected can vary dramatically from country to country, as can product safety and product liability legislation and the nature of contract law.

Critical Thinking and Discussion Questions

1. Free market economies stimulate greater economic growth, whereas state-directed economies stifle growth. Discuss.
2. A democratic political system is an essential condition for sustained economic progress. Discuss.
3. What is the relationship between corruption in a country (i.e., government officials taking bribes) and economic growth? Is corruption always bad?
4. You are the CEO of a company that has to choose between making a $100 million investment in Russia or Poland. Both investments promise the same long-run return, so your choice is driven by risk considerations. Assess the various risks of doing business in each of these nations. Which investment would you favor and why?
5. Read the Management Focus feature titled Did Walmart Violate the Foreign Corrupt Practices Act? What is your opinion? If you think it did, what do you think the consequences will be for Walmart?

globalEDGE Research Task

globalEDGE.msu.edu

Use the globalEDGE™ website (globaledge.msu.edu) to complete the following exercises:

1. The definition of words and political ideas can have different meanings in different contexts worldwide. In fact, the *Freedom in the World* survey published by Freedom House evaluates the state of political rights and civil liberties around the world. Provide a description of this survey and a ranking (in terms of "freedom") of the world's country leaders and laggards. What factors are taken into consideration in this survey?
2. As the chapter discusses, differences in political, economic, and legal systems have considerable impact on the benefits, costs, and risks of doing business in various countries. The World Bank's "Doing Business Indicators" measure the extent of business regulations in countries around the world. Compare Brazil, Ghana, India, New Zealand, the United States, Sweden, and Turkey in terms of how easily contracts are enforced, how property can be registered, and how investors can be protected. Identify in which area you see the greatest variation from one country to the next.

Venezuela Under Hugo Chávez and Beyond — closing case

On March 5, 2013, Hugo Chávez, the president of Venezuela, died after losing a battle against cancer. Chávez had been president of Venezuela since 1999. A former military officer who was once jailed for engineering a failed coup attempt, Chávez was a self-styled democratic socialist who won the presidential election by campaigning against corruption, economic mismanagement, and the "harsh realities" of global capitalism. When he took office in February 1999, Chávez claimed he had inherited the worst economic situation in the country's recent history. He wasn't far off the mark. A collapse in the price of oil, which accounted for 70 percent of the country's exports, left Venezuela with a large budget deficit and forced the economy into a deep recession.

Soon after taking office, Chávez worked to consolidate his hold over the apparatus of government. By 2012, Freedom House, which annually assesses political and civil liberties worldwide, concluded Venezuela was only "partly free" and that freedoms were being progressively curtailed. In 2006, for example, Parliament, which was dominated by his supporters, gave him the power to legislate by decree for 18 months. In late 2010, Chávez yet again persuaded the National Assembly to grant him the power to rule by decree for another 18 months.

On the economic front, the economy shrank in the early 2000s, while unemployment remained persistently high (at 15 to 17 percent) and the poverty rate rose to more than 50 percent of the population. A 2003 study by the World Bank concluded Venezuela was one of the most regulated economies in the world and that state controls over business activities gave public officials ample opportunities to enrich themselves by demanding bribes in return for permission to expand operations or enter new lines of business. Despite Chávez's anticorruption rhetoric, Transparency International, which ranks the world's nations according to the extent of public corruption, noted that corruption increased under Chávez. In 2012, Transparency International ranked Venezuela 165th out of 174 nations in terms of level of corruption.

Consistent with his socialist rhetoric, Chávez progressively took various enterprises into state ownership and required that other enterprises be restructured as "workers' cooperatives" in return for government loans. In addition, the government took over large rural farms and ranches that Chávez claimed were not sufficiently productive and turned them into state-owned cooperatives.

In mid-2000, the world oil market bailed Chávez out of mounting economic difficulties. Oil prices started to surge from the low $20s in 2003, reaching $150 a barrel by mid-2008. Venezuela, the world's fifth-largest producer, reaped a bonanza. On the back of surging oil exports, the economy grew at a robust rate. Chávez used the oil revenues to boost government spending on social programs, many of them modeled after programs in Cuba. These included ultra-cheap gasoline and free housing for the poor.

In 2006, he announced plans to reduce the stakes held by foreign companies in oil projects in the Orinoco regions, to increase the royalties they had to pay to the Venezuelan government, and to give the state-run oil company a majority position. Simultaneously, he replaced professional managers at the state-owned oil company with his supporters, many of whom knew little about the oil business. They extracted profits to support Chávez's social programs but at the cost of low investments in the oil company, and over time its output started to fall.

Notwithstanding his ability to consolidate political power, on the economic front, Venezuela's performance under Chávez was mixed. His main achievements were to reduce poverty, which fell from 50 percent to 28 percent by 2012, and to bring down unemployment from 14.5 percent at the start of his rule to 7.6 percent in February 2013. Profits from oil helped Chávez achieve both these goals. However, despite strong global demand and massive reserves, oil production in Venezuela fell by a third between 2000 and 2012 as foreign oil companies exited the country and the state-run oil company failed to make up the difference. Inflation surged and was running at around 28 percent per annum between 2008 and 2012, one of the highest rates in the world. To compound matters, the budget deficit expanded to 17 percent of GDP in 2012 as the government spent heavily to support its social programs and various subsidies.

Following Chávez's death, his handpicked successor, Nicolas Maduro, took over the presidency. Maduro continued the policies introduced by Chávez. Things did not go well. By 2014, the country was in a recession. The economy contracted by 4 percent, while inflation surged to around 65 percent. The situation continued to deteriorate in 2015. Exacerbated by a sharp fall in oil prices and hence government revenues, the economy shrunk by 10 percent, the worst decline in the world. By 2015, widespread shortages of basic goods had emerged. Unemployment was rising. Inflation increased to 275 percent (the highest in the world). The poverty rate was back up over 30 percent. To cap this litany of disaster, the value of the Venezuelan currency, the bolivar, fell from 64 per U.S. dollar in 2014 to 960 per dollar by early 2016. The economy looked to be on the brink of total collapse.

Parliamentary elections held in December 2015 resulted in large losses for the ruling United Socialist Party. For the first time since 1999, the opposition gained a majority of seats in Parliament, although Maduro still holds the presidency. As yet, he shows no sign of changing course.

Sources: D. Luhnow and P. Millard, "Chávez Plans to Take More Control of Oil away from Foreign Firms," *The Wall Street Journal,* April 24, 2006, p. A1; R. Gallego, "Chávez's Agenda Takes Shape," *The Wall Street Journal,* December 27, 2005, p. A12; "The Sickly Stench of Corruption: Venezuela," *The Economist,* April 1, 2006, p. 50; "Chávez Squeezes the Oil Firms," *The Economist,* November 12, 2005, p. 61; "Glimpsing the Bottom of the Barrel: Venezuela," *The Economist,* February 3, 2007, p. 51; "The Wind Goes Out of the Revolution—Defeat for Hugo Chávez," *The Economist,* December 8, 2007, pp. 30–32; "Oil Leak," *The Economist,* February 26, 2011, p. 43; "Medieval Policies," *The Economist,* August 8, 2011, p. 38; "Now for the Reckoning," *The Economist,* May 5, 2013. "Heading For a Crash," *The Economist,* January 23, 2016; Matt O'Brian, "Venezuela Is on the Brink of Complete Economic Collapse," *The Washington Post,* January 29, 2016.

CASE DISCUSSION QUESTIONS

1. Under Chávez's leadership, what kind of economic system was put in place in Venezuela? How would you characterize the political system?
2. How do you think that Chávez's unilateral changes to contracts with foreign oil companies will affect future investment by foreigners in Venezuela?

3. How will the high level of public corruption in Venezuela affect future growth rates?
4. During the latter part of Chávez's rule, Venezuela benefited from high oil prices. Since 2014, however, oil prices have fallen substantially. What has the affect of this has been on government finances and the Venezuelan economy?
5. During the Chávez years, many foreign multinationals exited Venezuela or reduced their exposure there. What do you think the impact of this has been on Venezuela? What needs to be done to reverse the trend?
6. By early 2016, Venezuela's economy appeared to be on the brink of total collapse. What do you think needs to be done to reverse this?

Endnotes

1. As we shall see, there is not a strict one-to-one correspondence between political systems and economic systems. A. O. Hirschman, "The On-and-Off Again Connection between Political and Economic Progress," *American Economic Review* 84, no. 2 (1994), pp. 343–48.
2. For a discussion of the roots of collectivism and individualism, see H. W. Spiegel, *The Growth of Economic Thought* (Durham, NC: Duke University Press, 1991). A discussion of collectivism and individualism can be found in M. Friedman and R. Friedman, *Free to Choose* (London: Penguin Books, 1980).
3. For a classic summary of the tenets of Marxism, see A. Giddens, *Capitalism and Modern Social Theory* (Cambridge, UK: Cambridge University Press, 1971).
4. Smith, Adam, *The Wealth of Nations, Vol. 1*. London: Penguin Books, p. 325.
5. R. Wesson, *Modern Government—Democracy and Authoritarianism,* 2nd ed. (Englewood Cliffs, NJ: Prentice Hall, 1990).
6. For a detailed but accessible elaboration of this argument, see Friedman and Friedman, *Free to Choose.* Also see P. M. Romer, "The Origins of Endogenous Growth," *Journal of Economic Perspectives* 8, no. 1 (1994), pp. 2–32.
7. T. W. Lippman, *Understanding Islam* (New York: Meridian Books, 1995).
8. "Islam's Interest," *The Economist,* January 18, 1992, pp. 33–34.
9. M. El Qorchi, "Islamic Finance Gears Up," *Finance and Development,* December 2005, pp. 46–50; S. Timewell, "Islamic Finance—Virtual Concept to Critical Mass," *The Banker,* March 1, 2008, pp. 10–16; Lydia Yueh, "Islamic Finance Growing Fast, But Can It Be More Than a Niche Market?", *BBC News,* April 14, 2014.
10. This information can be found on the UN's treaty website at www.uncitral.org/uncitral/en/uncitral_texts/sale_goods/1980CISG.html.
11. International Court of Arbitration, www.iccwbo.org/index_court.asp.
12. D. North, *Institutions, Institutional Change, and Economic Performance* (Cambridge, UK: Cambridge University Press, 1991).
13. "China's Next Revolution," *The Economist,* March 10, 2007, p. 9.
14. P. Klebnikov, "Russia's Robber Barons," *Forbes,* November 21, 1994, pp. 74–84; C. Mellow, "Russia: Making Cash from Chaos," *Fortune,* April 17, 1995, pp. 145–51; "Mr. Tatum Checks Out," *The Economist,* November 9, 1996, p. 78.
15. K. van Wolferen, *The Enigma of Japanese Power* (New York: Vintage Books, 1990), pp. 100–105.
16. P. Bardhan, "Corruption and Development: A Review of the Issues," *Journal of Economic Literature,* September 1997, pp. 1320–46.
17. Transparency International, "Global Corruption Report, 2014," www.transparency.org, 2014.
18. Ibid.
19. J. Coolidge and S. Rose Ackerman, "High Level Rent Seeking and Corruption in African Regimes," World Bank policy research working paper no. 1780, June 1997; K. Murphy, A. Shleifer, and R. Vishny, "Why Is Rent-Seeking So Costly to Growth?," *AEA Papers and Proceedings*, May 1993, pp. 409–14; M. Habib and L. Zurawicki, "Corruption and Foreign Direct Investment," *Journal of International Business Studies* 33 (2002), pp. 291–307; J. E. Anderson and D. Marcouiller, "Insecurity and the Pattern of International Trade," *Review of Economics and Statistics* 84 (2002), pp. 342–52; T. S. Aidt, "Economic Analysis of Corruption: A Survey," *The Economic Journal* 113 (November 2003), pp. 632–53; D. A. Houston, "Can Corruption Ever Improve an Economy?," *Cato Institute* 27 (2007), pp. 325–43.
20. Details can be found at www.oecd.org/corruption/oecdantibriberyconvention.htm.
21. D. Stackhouse and K. Ungar, "The Foreign Corrupt Practices Act: Bribery, Corruption, Record Keeping and More," *Indiana Lawyer,* April 21, 1993.
22. For an interesting discussion of strategies for dealing with the low cost of copying and distributing digital information, see the chapter on rights management in C. Shapiro and H. R. Varian, *Information Rules* (Boston: Harvard Business School Press, 1999). Also see C. W. L. Hill, "Digital Piracy," *Asian Pacific Journal of Management,* 2007, pp. 9–25.
23. Douglass North has argued that the correct specification of intellectual property rights is one factor that lowers the cost of doing business and, thereby, stimulates economic growth and development. See North, *Institutions, Institutional Change, and Economic Performance.*
24. Business Software Alliance, "Ninth Annual BSA Global Software Piracy Study," May 2012, www.bsa.org.
25. Ibid.
26. "Trade Tripwires," *The Economist,* August 27, 1994, p. 61.

Part 2 National Differences

National Differences in Economic Development

learning objectives

After reading this chapter, you will be able to:

LO3-1 Explain what determines the level of economic development of a nation.

LO3-2 Identify the macropolitical and macroeconomic changes occurring worldwide.

LO3-3 Describe how transition economies are moving toward market-based systems.

LO3-4 Explain the implications for management practice of national difference in political economy.

Source: © Toonman/Shutterstock.com

The Political and Economic Evolution of Indonesia

opening case

Indonesia is a vast country. Its 260 million people are spread out over some 17,000 islands that span an arc 3,200 miles long from Sumatra in the west to Irian Jaya in the east. It is the most populous Muslim nation—some 86 percent of the population count themselves as Muslims—but also one of the most ethnically diverse. More than 500 languages are spoken in the country, and separatists are active in a number of provinces.

For 30 years, the strong arm of President Suharto held this sprawling nation together. Suharto was a virtual dictator who was backed by the military establishment. Under his rule, the Indonesian economy grew steadily, but there was a cost. Suharto brutally repressed internal dissent. He was also famous for "crony capitalism," using his command of the political system to favor the business enterprises of his supporters and family. In the end, Suharto was overtaken by massive debts that Indonesia had accumulated during the 1990s. In 1997, the Indonesian economy went into a tailspin. The International Monetary Fund stepped in with a $43 billion rescue package. When it was revealed that much of this money found its way into the personal coffers of Suharto and his cronies, people took to the streets in protest, and he was forced to resign.

After Suharto, Indonesia moved rapidly toward a vigorous democracy. In 2004, the country's first directly elected president, Susilo Bambang Yudhoyono, took power. Yudhoyono was elected to a second term in 2009. In 2014, he was succeeded by the current president, Joko Widodo. Freedom House, which tracks the state of political freedom around the world, notes that Indonesia has "free and fair elections," although they criticize the country for restrictions on civil liberties, freedom of movement, and freedom of the press. Freedom House also notes that Indonesia has high levels of public corruption. Transparency International, which ranks countries according to their level of corruption, has given Indonesia a poor score. It ranked Indonesia 88 out of the 168 nations in 2015 with a score of just 36 out of a possible 100.

On the economic front, progress has been somewhat halting. Although Indonesia has consistently grown its economy, growth has been at a lower rate than in other large developing nations such as India and China. Economic liberalism has never really taken hold in Indonesia. Many industries are sheltered from foreign competition by protectionist policies. These policies have their roots in the widespread belief that foreigners have long plundered Indonesia's resources while leaving the country impoverished. In 2014, the list of industries protected from foreign competition was expanded to include onshore oil extraction and e-commerce. To compound matters, the government has frequently imposed price controls and heavily subsidized certain goods, most notably gasoline, all of which distorts the market mechanism.

Moreover, several sectors are still dominated by inefficient state-run enterprises. There are over 140 state-run enterprises in Indonesia accounting for about 20 percent of the county's gross domestic product.

–continued

State-owned enterprises are widespread in energy, power production, transportation, aviation, agriculture, banking, and telecommunications. The country also suffers from chronically poor infrastructure, much of which is managed by state-owned enterprises. There are simply not enough power stations, roads, ports, etc. Indonesia has five times the population of the United Kingdom but only half the power generating capacity. Due to poor transportation infrastructure, logistics costs in Indonesia are 50 percent more than in Thailand and twice as much as in Malaysia.

In 2014, Indonesia's new president, Joko Widodo, pledged to liberalize the economy and improve infrastructure. In early 2015, Widodo abolished the state subsidy on gasoline, allowing the market to set prices. The subsidy was costing the government almost $20 billion a year, or 15 percent of total government outlays. Widodo also announced plans to boost public infrastructure, investing in 5 deep-sea and 24 feeder ports, 10 airports, 25 hydroelectric dams, 2,000 kilometers of roads, and 10 industrial parks. These acts were followed by a number of measures designed to deregulate the economy. Import restrictions on some goods were removed, the time required to process investment permits was reduced substantially, and some onerous business regulations were abolished. Widodo has also repeatedly signaled that Indonesia will be more welcoming to foreign investment than hitherto.

Despite these measures, Indonesia still faces significant economic headwinds. One major problem: the economy is overly dependent upon commodities, the prices of which have fallen sharply in the wake of economic slowdown in China. Then there is the persistently high level of corruption, which continues to burden and distort business activity in the country. There is also no move to reduce the number of state-owned enterprises. Many critics feel that for Indonesia to unleash its full potential, it must do more to reduce corruption, privatize inefficient state-owned companies, further deregulate its economy, continue to improve its infrastructure, and do more to attract long-term foreign investors. •

Sources: Freedom House, "Freedom in the World 2015"; "A Survey of Indonesia: Time to Deliver," *The Economist*, December 11, 2004; "Spicing up Growth," *The Economist*, May 9, 2015; "The Unstimulating Stimulus," *The Economist*, October 17, 2015; CIA World Factbook, 2015; Mukul Raheja, "The Dire Need for Reform of Indonesian SOEs," *Jakarta Post*, February 26, 2014.

Introduction

In Chapter 2, we described how countries differ with regard to their political systems, economic systems, and legal systems. In this chapter, we build on this material to explain how these differences influence the level of economic development of a nation and, thus, how attractive it is as a place for doing business. We also look at how economic, political, and legal systems are changing around the world and what the implications of this are for the future rate of economic development of nations and regions. The past three decades have seen a general move toward more democratic forms of government, market-based economic reforms, and adoption of legal systems that better enforce property rights. Taken together, these trends have helped foster greater economic development around the world and have created a more favorable environment for international business. In the final section of this chapter, we pull all this material together to explore how differences in political, economic, and legal institutions affect the benefits, costs, and risks of doing business in different nations.

The opening case, which looks at changes in the political and economic structure of Indonesia over the last 20 years, highlights many of the issues that we discuss here. For decades, Indonesia was a dictatorship run by former President Suharto with the backing of the military. Since the early 2000s, it has become a democratic state, although one where civil liberties are still somewhat limited. While this has helped the country to improve its economy, Indonesia continues to underperform other large developing nations such as China and India. The reasons include a failure to embrace market-orientated policies, persistently high levels of corruption, poor infrastructure, and a high number of inefficient state-owned enterprises. Most observers believe that for Indonesia to reach its full potential, it must enact more economic reforms, deregulate markets, improve its infrastructure, privatize state-owned enterprises, and reduce corruption. The current government is starting to do some of these things, although there is a long way to go.

Differences in Economic Development

LO 3-1

Explain what determines the level of economic development of a nation.

Different countries have dramatically different levels of economic development. One common measure of economic development is a country's **gross national income (GNI)** per head of population. GNI is regarded as a yardstick for the economic activity of a country; it measures the total annual income received by residents of a nation. Map 3.1 summarizes the GNI per capita of the world's nations in 2014. As can be seen, countries such as Japan, Sweden, Switzerland, the United States, and Australia are among the richest on this measure, whereas the large developing countries of China and India are significantly poorer. Japan, for example, had a 2014 GNI per capita of $42,000, but China achieved only $7,400 and India just $1,570.[1]

Gross National Income (GNI)
Measures the total annual income received by residents of a nation.

GNI per person figures can be misleading because they don't consider differences in the cost of living. For example, although the 2014 GNI per capita of Switzerland at $90,680 exceeded that of the United States by a wide margin ($55,200), the higher cost of living in Switzerland meant that U.S. citizens could actually afford almost as many goods and services as the average Swiss citizen. To account for differences in the cost of living, one can adjust GNI per capita by purchasing power. Referred to as a **purchasing power parity (PPP)** adjustment, it allows a more direct comparison of living standards in different countries. The base for the adjustment is the cost of living in the United States. The PPP for different countries is then adjusted (up or down) depending on whether the cost of living is lower or higher than in the United States. For example, in 2014 the GNI per capita for China was $7,400, but the PPP per capita was $13,170, suggesting that the cost of living was lower in China and that $7,400 in China would buy as much as $13,170 in the

Purchasing Power Parity (PPP)
An adjustment in gross domestic product per capita to reflect differences in the cost of living.

ARCTIC OCEAN

ATLANTIC OCEAN

PACIFIC OCEAN

PACIFIC OCEAN

INDIAN OCEAN

GNI per Capita in U.S. Dollars

- Low Income: $765 or less
- Lower Middle Income: $765–$3,035
- Upper Middle Income: $3,035–$9,385
- Lower High Income: $9,385–$20,000
- Upper High Income: $20,001 or more
- No data

The values for the class intervals above are taken from the World Bank's cutoff figures for high-income, upper-middle-income, lower-middle-income, and low-income economies.

Scale: 1 to 174,385,000

0 1000 2000 Miles

0 1000 2000 3000 Kilometers

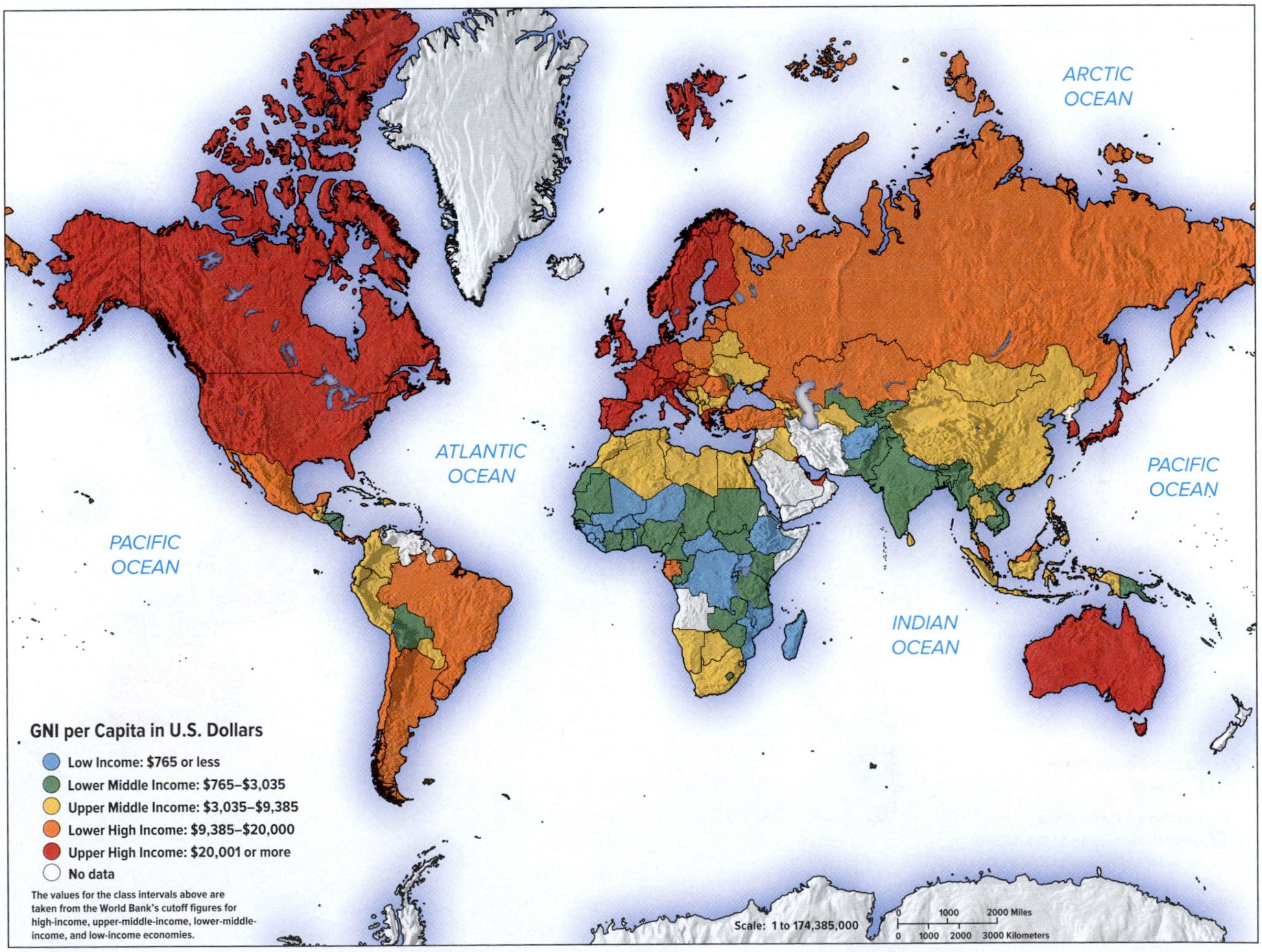

3.1 MAP

GNI per Capita, 2014.

3.1 TABLE

Economic Data for Select Countries

Source: World Development Indicators Online, 2016.

Country	GNI per Capita, 2014 ($)	GNI PPP per Capita, 2014 ($)	Annual Average GDP Growth Rate, 2005–2014 (%)	Size of Economy GDP, 2014 ($ billions)
Brazil	$11,530	$15,590	3.41%	$2,346
China	7,400	13,170	9.99	10,355
Germany	47,640	46,480	1.32	3,868
India	1,570	5,630	7.69	2,049
Japan	42,000	37,920	0.61	4,601
Nigeria	2,970	5,710	6.04	569
Poland	13,690	23,930	3.84	545
Russia	13,220	24,710	3.46	1,861
Switzerland	90,680	59,610	2.09	701
United Kingdom	43.430	39,040	1.34	2,989
United States	55,200	55,860	1.58	17,419

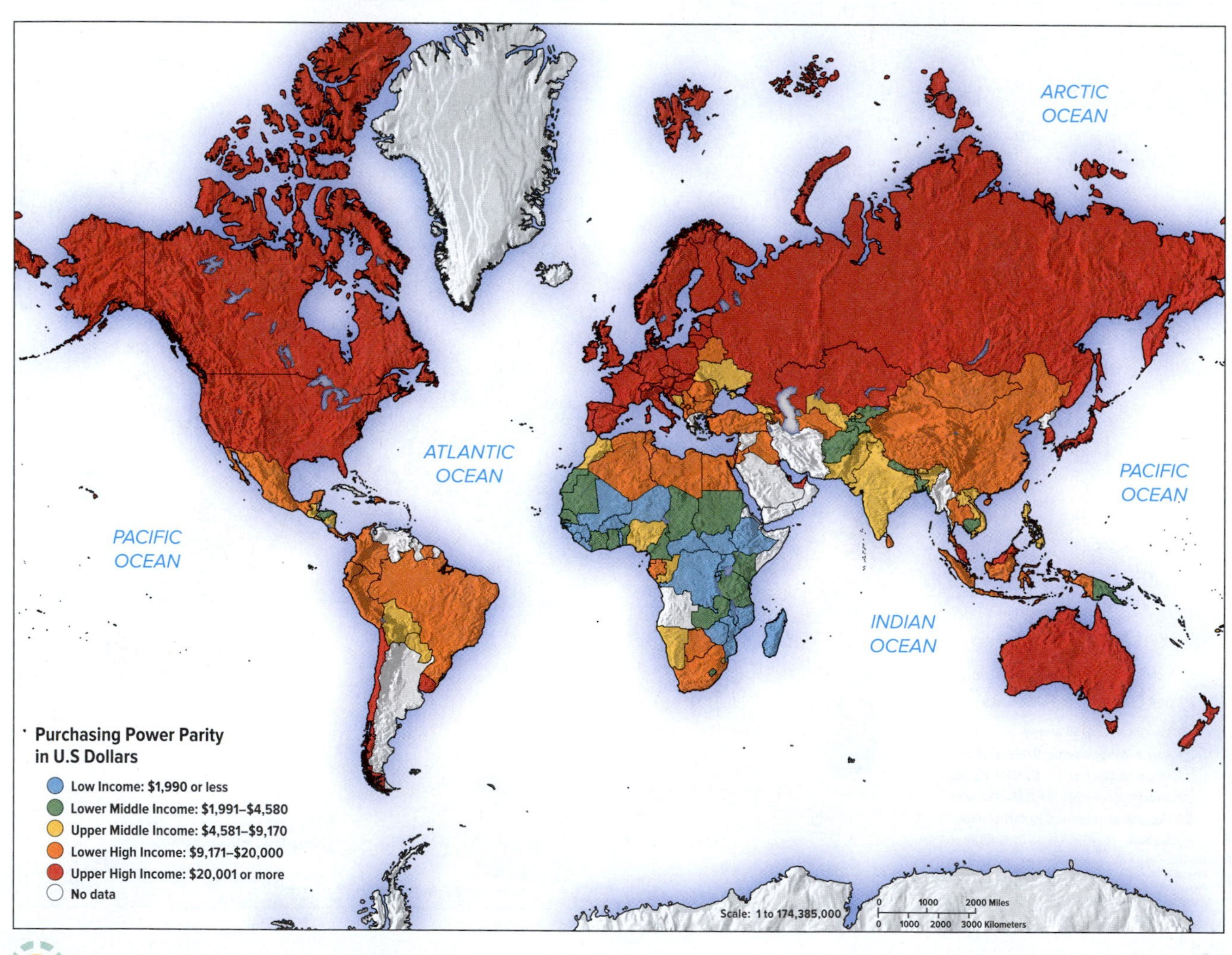

3.2 MAP

GNI PPP per Capita, 2014.

United States. Table 3.1 gives the GNI per capita measured at PPP in 2014 for a selection of countries, along with their GNI per capita and their growth rate in gross domestic product (GDP) from 2004 to 2014. Map 3.2 summarizes the GNI PPP per capita in 2014 for the nations of the world.

As can be seen, there are striking differences in the standards of living among countries. Table 3.1 suggests the average Indian citizen can afford to consume only about 10 percent of the goods and services consumed by the average U.S. citizen on a PPP basis. Given this, we might conclude that despite having a population of 1.2 billion, India is unlikely to be a very lucrative market for the consumer products produced by many Western international businesses. However, this would be incorrect because India has a fairly wealthy middle class of close to 250 million people, despite its large number of poor citizens. In absolute terms, the Indian economy now rivals that of Russia.

Did You Know?

Did you know that the United States has an economy that is 70 percent larger than that of China and has four times the standard of living?

Visit your instructor's Connect® course and click on SmartBook® or visit www. learnsmartadvantage .com to view a short video explanation from the authors.

To complicate matters, in many countries the "official" figures do not tell the entire story. Large amounts of economic activity may be in the form of unrecorded cash transactions or barter agreements. People engage in such transactions to avoid paying taxes, and although the share of total economic activity accounted for by such transactions may be small in developed economies such as the United States, in some countries (India being an example), they are reportedly very significant. Known as the *black economy or shadow economy,* estimates suggest that in India it may be around 50 percent of GDP, which implies that the Indian economy is half as big again as the figures reported in Table 3.1. Estimates produced by the European Union suggest that in 2012 the shadow economy accounted for around 10 percent of GDP in the United Kingdom and France, but 24 percent in Greece and as much as 32 percent in Bulgaria.[2]

The GNI and PPP data give a static picture of development. They tell us, for example, that China is much poorer than the United States, but they do not tell us if China is closing the gap. To assess this, we have to look at the economic growth rates achieved by countries. Table 3.1 gives the rate of growth in gross domestic product (GDP) per capita achieved by a number of countries between 2005 and 2014. Map 3.3 summarizes the annual average percentage growth rate in GDP from 2005 to 2014. Although countries such as China and India are currently relatively poor, their economies are already large in absolute terms and growing far more rapidly than those of many advanced nations. They are already huge markets for the products of international businesses. In 2010, China overtook Japan to become the second-largest economy in the world after the United States. Indeed, if both China and the United States maintain their current economic growth rates, China will become the world's largest economy sometime during the next decade. On current trends, India too will be among the largest economies in the world. Given that potential, many international businesses are trying to establish a strong presence in these markets.

What If We Were a Community of 100 People?

The "Miniature Earth" project was developed by Allysson Luca in 2001 as a way to better illustrate and create understanding of differences in the world. He thought that reducing the world's population to a community of only 100 people would be a useful and easy-to-understand illustration of various dynamics in the global marketplace. And this Miniature Earth captures a variety of issues related to the political economy and economic development that are discussed in Chapter 3. At the basic level, if the earth were a community of 100 people, 61 people would be Asian, 13 African, 12 European, 8 North American, 5 South American, and 1 would be from Oceania. Twenty people would own 75 percent of the financial wealth. If you could decide, how would you redistribute wealth among the 100 people? Make some richer, make the wealth among people more even, or let market forces distribute wealth as we have it now?

Source: www.miniature-earth.com.

Country Comparator

The "Country Comparator" tool on globalEDGE™ (globaledge.msu.edu/comparator) includes data from as early as 1960 to the most recent year. Using this tool, it is easy to compare countries across a variety of macro variables to better understand the economic changes occurring in countries. As related to Chapter 3, the globalEDGE™ Country Comparator tool is an effective way to statistically get an overview of the political economy and economic development by country worldwide. Comparisons of up to 20 countries at a time can be made in table format. Sometimes we talk about the BRIC countries when referring to Brazil, Russia, India, and China—in essence, we broadly classify them as "superstar" emerging markets, but are they really that similar? Using the Country Comparator tool on globalEDGE™, we find that the GDP adjusted for purchasing power parity is by far the greatest in Russia. Where do you think Brazil, India, and China fall on the GDP PPP scale?

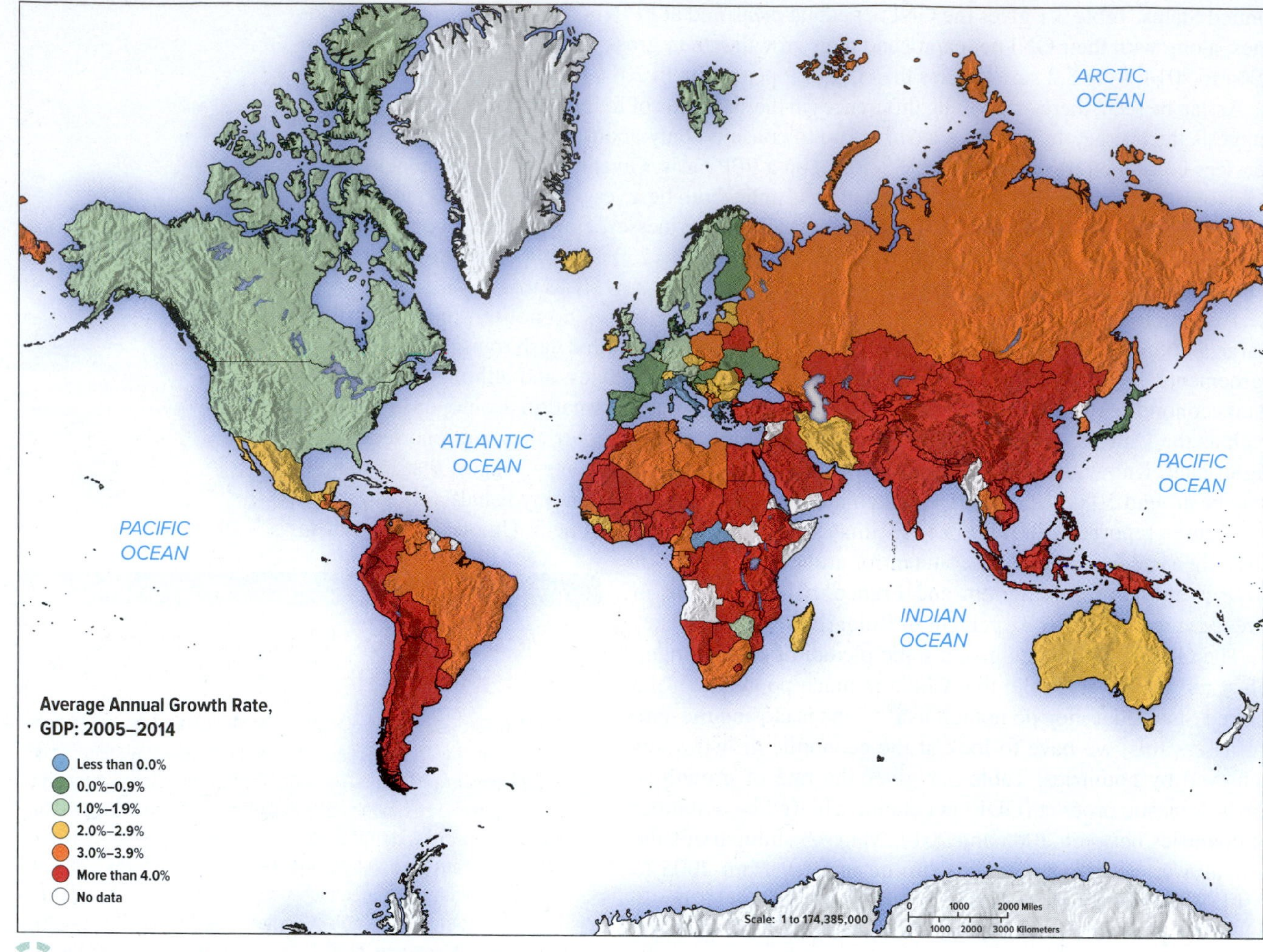

3.3 MAP

Average Annual Growth Rate in GDP (%) 2005–2014.

BROADER CONCEPTIONS OF DEVELOPMENT: AMARTYA SEN

The Nobel Prize–winning economist Amartya Sen has argued that development should be assessed less by material output measures such as GNI per capita and more by the capabilities and opportunities that people enjoy.[3] According to Sen, development should be seen as a process of expanding the real freedoms that people experience. Hence, development requires the removal of major impediments to freedom: poverty as well as tyranny, poor economic opportunities as well as systematic social deprivation, and neglect of public facilities as well as the intolerance of repressive states. In Sen's view, development is not just an economic process but a political one too, and to succeed requires the "democratization" of political communities to give citizens a voice in the important decisions made for the community. This perspective leads Sen to emphasize basic health care, especially for children, and basic education, especially for women. Not only are these factors desirable for their instrumental value in helping achieve higher income levels, but they are also beneficial in their own right. People cannot develop their capabilities if they are chronically ill or woefully ignorant.

Human Development Index (HDI)
An attempt by the United Nations to assess the impact of a number of factors on the quality of human life in a country.

Sen's influential thesis has been picked up by the United Nations, which has developed the **Human Development Index (HDI)** to measure the quality of human life in different nations. The HDI is based on three measures: life expectancy at birth (a function of health care); educational attainment (measured by a combination of the adult literacy rate and enrollment in primary, secondary, and tertiary education); and whether average incomes, based on PPP estimates, are sufficient to meet the basic needs of life in a country (adequate food, shelter, and health care).

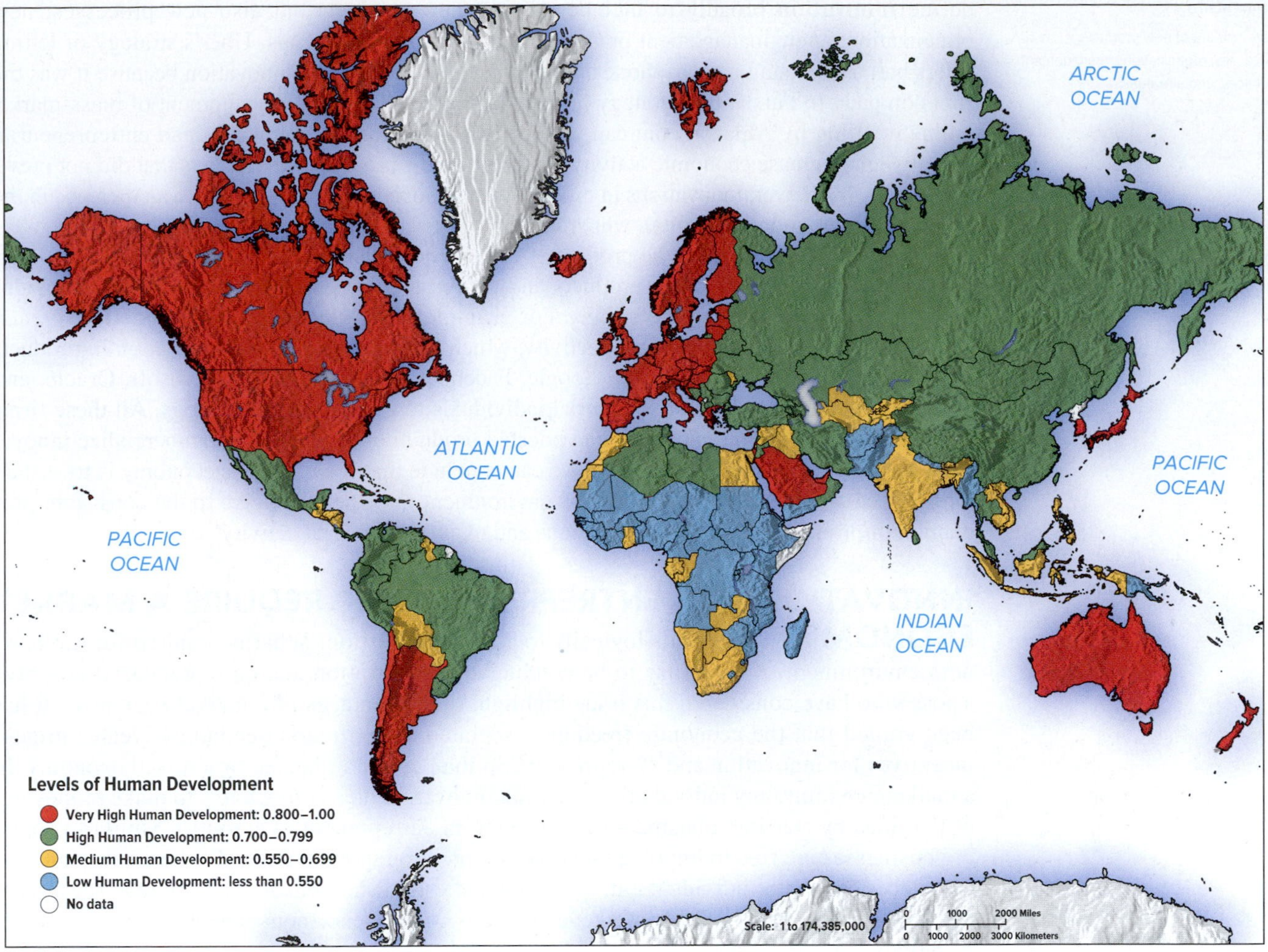

3.4 MAP

Human Development Index, 2014.

As such, the HDI comes much closer to Sen's conception of how development should be measured than narrow economic measures such as GNI per capita—although Sen's thesis suggests that political freedoms should also be included in the index, and they are not. The HDI is scaled from 0 to 1. Countries scoring less than 0.5 are classified as having low human development (the quality of life is poor); those scoring from 0.5 to 0.8 are classified as having medium human development; and those that score above 0.8 are classified as having high human development. Map 3.4 summarizes the HDI scores for 2014.

test PREP

Use SmartBook to help retain what you have learned. Access your Instructor's Connect course to check out SmartBook or go to learnsmartadvantage.com for help.

Political Economy and Economic Progress

It is often argued that a country's economic development is a function of its economic and political systems. What then is the nature of the relationship between political economy and economic progress? Despite the long debate over this question among academics and policymakers, it is not possible to give an unambiguous answer. However, it is possible to untangle the main threads of the arguments and make a few generalizations as to the nature of the relationship between political economy and economic progress.

INNOVATION AND ENTREPRENEURSHIP ARE THE ENGINES OF GROWTH There is substantial agreement among economists that innovation and entrepreneurial activity are the engines of long-run economic growth.[4] Those who make this argument

Innovation

Development of new products, processes, organizations, management practices, and strategies.

define **innovation** broadly to include not just new products but also new processes, new organizations, new management practices, and new strategies. Thus, Uber's strategy of letting riders hail a cab using a smartphone application can be seen as an innovation because it was the first company to pursue this strategy in its industry. Similarly, the development of mass-market online retailing by Amazon.com can be seen as an innovation. Innovation and entrepreneurial activity help increase economic activity by creating new products and markets that did not previously exist. Moreover, innovations in production and business processes lead to an increase in the productivity of labor and capital, which further boosts economic growth rates.[5]

Entrepreneurs

Those who first commercialize innovations.

Innovation is also seen as the product of entrepreneurial activity. Often, **entrepreneurs** first commercialize innovative new products and processes, and entrepreneurial activity provides much of the dynamism in an economy. For example, the U.S. economy has benefited greatly from a high level of entrepreneurial activity, which has resulted in rapid innovation in products and process. Firms such as Apple, Google, Facebook, Amazon, Dell, Microsoft, Oracle, and Uber were all founded by entrepreneurial individuals to exploit new technology. All these firms created significant economic value and boosted productivity by helping commercialize innovations in products and processes. Thus, we can conclude that if a country's economy is to sustain long-run economic growth, the business environment must be conducive to the consistent production of product and process innovations and to entrepreneurial activity.

INNOVATION AND ENTREPRENEURSHIP REQUIRE A MARKET ECONOMY This leads logically to a further question: What is required for the business environment of a country to be conducive to innovation and entrepreneurial activity? Those who have considered this issue highlight the advantages of a market economy.[6] It has been argued that the economic freedom associated with a market economy creates greater incentives for innovation and entrepreneurship than either a planned or a mixed economy. In a market economy, any individual who has an innovative idea is free to try to make money out of that idea by starting a business (by engaging in entrepreneurial activity). Similarly, existing businesses are free to improve their operations through innovation. To the extent that they are successful, both individual entrepreneurs and established businesses can reap rewards in the form of high profits. Thus, market economies contain enormous incentives to develop innovations.

In a planned economy, the state owns all means of production. Consequently, entrepreneurial individuals have few economic incentives to develop valuable new innovations because it is the state, rather than the individual, that captures most of the gains. The lack of economic freedom and incentives for innovation was probably a main factor in the economic stagnation of many former communist states and led ultimately to their collapse at the end of the 1980s. Similar stagnation occurred in many mixed economies in those sectors where the state had a monopoly (such as coal mining and telecommunications in Great Britain). This stagnation provided the impetus for the widespread privatization of state-owned enterprises that we witnessed in many mixed economies during the mid-1980s and that is still going on today (*privatization* refers to the process of selling state-owned enterprises to private investors; see Chapter 2 for details).

A study of 102 countries over a 20-year period provided evidence of a strong relationship between economic freedom (as provided by a market economy) and economic growth.[7] The study found that the more economic freedom a country had between 1975 and 1995, the more economic growth it achieved and the richer its citizens became. The six countries that had persistently high ratings of economic freedom from 1975 to 1995 (Hong Kong, Switzerland, Singapore, the United States, Canada, and Germany) were also all in the top 10 in terms of economic growth rates. In contrast, no country with persistently low economic freedom achieved a respectable growth rate. In the 16 countries for which the index of economic freedom declined the most during 1975 to 1995, gross domestic product fell at an annual rate of 0.6 percent.

INNOVATION AND ENTREPRENEURSHIP REQUIRE STRONG PROPERTY RIGHTS Strong legal protection of property rights is another requirement for a business environment to be conducive to innovation, entrepreneurial activity, and hence economic growth.[8] Both individuals and businesses must be given the opportunity to profit from innovative ideas. Without strong property rights protection, businesses and individuals run the risk that the profits from their innovative efforts will be expropriated, either by criminal elements or by the state. The state can expropriate the profits from innovation through legal means, such as excessive taxation, or through illegal means, such as demands from state bureaucrats for kickbacks in return for granting an individual or firm a license to do business in a certain area (i.e., corruption). According to the Nobel Prize–winning economist Douglass North, throughout history many governments have displayed a tendency to engage in such behavior.[9] Inadequately enforced property rights reduce the incentives for innovation and entrepreneurial activity—because the profits from such activity are "stolen"—and hence reduce the rate of economic growth.

The influential Peruvian development economist Hernando de Soto has argued that much of the developing world will fail to reap the benefits of capitalism until property rights are better defined and protected.[10] De Soto's arguments are interesting because he says the key problem is not the risk of expropriation but the chronic inability of property owners to establish legal title to the property they own. As an example of the scale of the problem, he cites the situation in Haiti, where individuals must take 176 steps over 19 years to own land legally. Because most property in poor countries is informally "owned," the absence of legal proof of ownership means that property holders cannot convert their assets into capital, which could then be used to finance business ventures. Banks will not lend money to the poor to start businesses because the poor possess no proof that they own property, such as farmland, that can be used as collateral for a loan. By de Soto's calculations, the total value of real estate held by the poor in third world and former communist states amounted to more than $9.3 trillion in 2000. If those assets could be converted into capital, the result could be an economic revolution that would allow the poor to bootstrap their way out of poverty. Interestingly enough, the Chinese seem to have taken de Soto's arguments to heart. Despite still being nominally a communist country, in October 2007 the government passed a law that gave private property owners the same rights as the state, which significantly improved the rights of urban and rural landowners to the land that they use (see the accompanying Country Focus).

country FOCUS

Emerging Property Rights in China

On October 1, 2007, a new property law took effect in China, granting rural and urban landholders far more secure property rights. The law was a much-needed response to how China's economy has changed over the past 30 years as it transitions from a centrally planned system to a more dynamic market-based economy where two-thirds of economic activity is in the hands of private enterprises.

Although all land in China still technically belongs to the state—an ideological necessity in a country where the government still claims to be guided by Marxism—urban landholders had been granted 40- to 70-year leases to use the land, while rural farmers had 30-year leases. However, the lack of legal title meant that landholders were at the whim of the state. Large-scale appropriation of rural land for housing and factory construction had rendered millions of farmers landless. Many were given little or no compensation, and they drifted to the cities where they added to a growing underclass. In both urban and rural areas, property and land disputes had become a leading cause of social unrest. According to government sources, in 2006 there were about 23,000 "mass incidents" of social unrest in China, many related to disputes over property rights.

The 2007 law, which was 14 years in gestation due to a rearguard action fought by left-wing Communist Party activists who objected to it on ideological grounds, gives urban and rural land users the right to automatic renewal of their leases after the expiration of the 30- to 70-year terms. In addition, the law requires that land users be fairly compensated if the land is required for other purposes, and it gives individuals the same legal protection for their property as the state. Taken together with a 2004 change in China's constitution, which stated that private property "was not to be encroached upon," the new law significantly strengthens property rights in China.

Nevertheless, the law has its limitations; most notably, it still falls short of giving peasants marketable ownership rights to the land they farm. If they could sell their land, tens of millions of underemployed farmers might find more productive work elsewhere. Those who stayed could acquire bigger landholdings that could be used more efficiently. Also, farmers might be able to use their landholdings as security against which they could borrow funds for investments to boost productivity.

Sources: "China's Next Revolution—Property Rights in China," *The Economist*, March 10, 2007, p. 11; "Caught between the Right and Left," *The Economist*, March 10, 2007, pp. 25–27; Z. Keliang, Z and L. Ping, "Rural Land Rights under the PRC Property Law," *China Law and Practice*, November 2007, pp. 10–15.

THE REQUIRED POLITICAL SYSTEM Much debate surrounds which kind of political system best achieves a functioning market economy with strong protection for property rights.[11] People in the West tend to associate a representative democracy with a market economic system, strong property rights protection, and economic progress. Building on this, we tend to argue that democracy is good for growth. However, some totalitarian regimes have fostered a market economy and strong property rights protection and have experienced rapid economic growth. Five of the fastest-growing economies of the past 30 years—China, South Korea, Taiwan, Singapore, and Hong Kong—had one thing in common at the start of their economic growth: undemocratic governments. At the same time, countries with stable democratic governments, such as India, experienced sluggish economic growth for long periods. In 1992, Lee Kuan Yew, Singapore's leader for many years, told an audience, "I do not believe that democracy necessarily leads to development. I believe that a country needs to develop discipline more than democracy. The exuberance of democracy leads to undisciplined and disorderly conduct which is inimical to development."[12]

However, those who argue for the value of a totalitarian regime miss an important point: If dictators made countries rich, then much of Africa, Asia, and Latin America should have been growing rapidly during 1960 to 1990, and this was not the case. Only a totalitarian regime that is committed to a market system and strong protection of property rights is capable of promoting economic growth. Also, there is no guarantee that a dictatorship will continue to pursue such progressive policies. Dictators are rarely benevolent. Many are tempted to use the apparatus of the state to further their own private ends, violating property rights and stalling economic growth. Given this, it seems likely that democratic regimes are far more conducive to long-term economic growth than are dictatorships, even benevolent ones. Only in a well-functioning, mature democracy are property rights truly secure.[13] Nor should we forget Amartya Sen's arguments reviewed earlier. Totalitarian states, by limiting human freedom, also suppress human development and therefore are detrimental to progress.

ECONOMIC PROGRESS BEGETS DEMOCRACY While it is possible to argue that democracy is not a necessary precondition for a free market economy in which property rights are protected, subsequent economic growth often leads to establishment of a democratic regime. Several of the fastest-growing Asian economies adopted more democratic governments during the past three decades, including South Korea and Taiwan. Thus, although democracy may not always be the cause of initial economic progress, it seems to be one consequence of that progress.

A strong belief that economic progress leads to adoption of a democratic regime underlies the fairly permissive attitude that many Western governments have adopted toward human rights violations in China. Although China has a totalitarian government in which human rights are violated, many Western countries have been hesitant to criticize the country too much for fear that this might hamper the country's march toward a free market system. The belief is that once China has a free market system, greater individual freedoms and democracy will follow. Whether this optimistic vision comes to pass remains to be seen.

Democracy in the Arab World: New Realities in an Ancient Land?

Democracy is finally making an appearance in the ancient lands of the Middle East, as witnessed by the recent uprisings known as the "The Arab Spring." Wissam Yafi, an expert in technology and international development, believes geo-economic, geosocial, technological, and geo-political forces will lead to inevitable changes in the Arab world. Economic forces will make these governments cut many of the social services offered, putting people out of work, which will lead toward democratic alternatives. Technology is another major binding force connecting populations across the Middle East, which will mean less censorship—something that has been widespread in many parts of the Arab world. People will continue to challenge the status quo as rapid urbanization, population growth, and movements toward self-determination grow. Wissam Yafi has a lot of guesses on what will happen. Do you agree with his forecasts?

Source: carnegieendowment.org.

GEOGRAPHY, EDUCATION, AND ECONOMIC DEVELOPMENT While a country's political and economic systems are probably the big engine driving its rate of economic development, other factors are also important. One that has received attention is geography.[14] But the belief that geography can influence economic policy, and hence economic growth rates, goes back to Adam Smith. The influential economist Jeffrey Sachs argues that

> throughout history, coastal states, with their long engagements in international trade, have been more supportive of market institutions than landlocked states, which have tended to organize themselves as hierarchical (and often militarised) societies. Mountainous states, as a result of physical isolation, have often neglected market-based trade. Temperate climes have generally supported higher densities of population and thus a more extensive division of labour than tropical regions.[15]

Sachs's point is that by virtue of favorable geography, certain societies are more likely to engage in trade than others and are thus more likely to be open to and develop market-based economic systems, which in turn promotes faster economic growth. He also argues that, irrespective of the economic and political institutions a country adopts, adverse geographic conditions—such as the high rate of disease, poor soils, and hostile climate that afflict many tropical countries—can have a negative impact on development. Together with colleagues at Harvard's Institute for International Development, Sachs tested for the impact of geography on a country's economic growth rate between 1965 and 1990. He found that landlocked countries grew more slowly than coastal economies and that being entirely landlocked reduced a country's growth rate by roughly 0.7 percent per year. He also found that tropical countries grew 1.3 percent more slowly each year than countries in the temperate zone.

Education emerges as another important determinant of economic development (a point that Amartya Sen emphasizes). The general assertion is that nations that invest more in education will have higher growth rates because an educated population is a more productive population. Anecdotal comparisons suggest this is true. In 1960, Pakistanis and South Koreans were on equal footing economically. However, just 30 percent of Pakistani children were enrolled in primary schools, while 94 percent of South Koreans were. By the mid-1980s, South Korea's GNP per person was three times that of Pakistan.[16] A survey of 14 statistical studies that looked at the relationship between a country's investment in education and its subsequent growth rates concluded investment in education did have a positive and statistically significant impact on a country's rate of economic growth.[17] Similarly, the work by Sachs discussed earlier suggests that investments in education help explain why some countries in Southeast Asia, such as Indonesia, Malaysia, and Singapore, have been able to overcome the disadvantages associated with their tropical geography and grow far more rapidly than tropical nations in Africa and Latin America.

 **test PREP**

Use SmartBook to help retain what you have learned. Access your Instructor's Connect course to check out SmartBook or go to learnsmartadvantage.com for help.

States in Transition

 **LO 3-2**

Identify the macropolitical and macroeconomic changes occurring worldwide.

The political economy of many of the world's nation-states has changed radically since the late 1980s. Two trends have been evident. First, during the late 1980s and early 1990s, a wave of democratic revolutions swept the world. Totalitarian governments fell and were replaced by democratically elected governments that were typically more committed to free market capitalism than their predecessors had been. Second, there has been a move away from centrally planned and mixed economies and toward a more free market economic model.

Image of Nigeria, where a peaceful transfer of power occurred after elections in March 2015. Muhammadu Buhari is the new president of Nigeria, taking office on May 29, 2015.

Source: © Anadolu Agency/Getty Images

THE SPREAD OF DEMOCRACY One notable development of the past 30 years has been the spread of democracy (and, by extension, the decline of totalitarianism). Map 3.5 reports on the extent of totalitarianism in the world as determined by Freedom House.[18] This map charts political freedom in 2016, grouping countries into three broad groupings: free, partly free, and not free. In "free" countries, citizens enjoy a high degree of political and civil freedoms. "Partly free" countries are characterized by some restrictions on political rights and civil liberties, often in the context of corruption, weak rule of law, ethnic

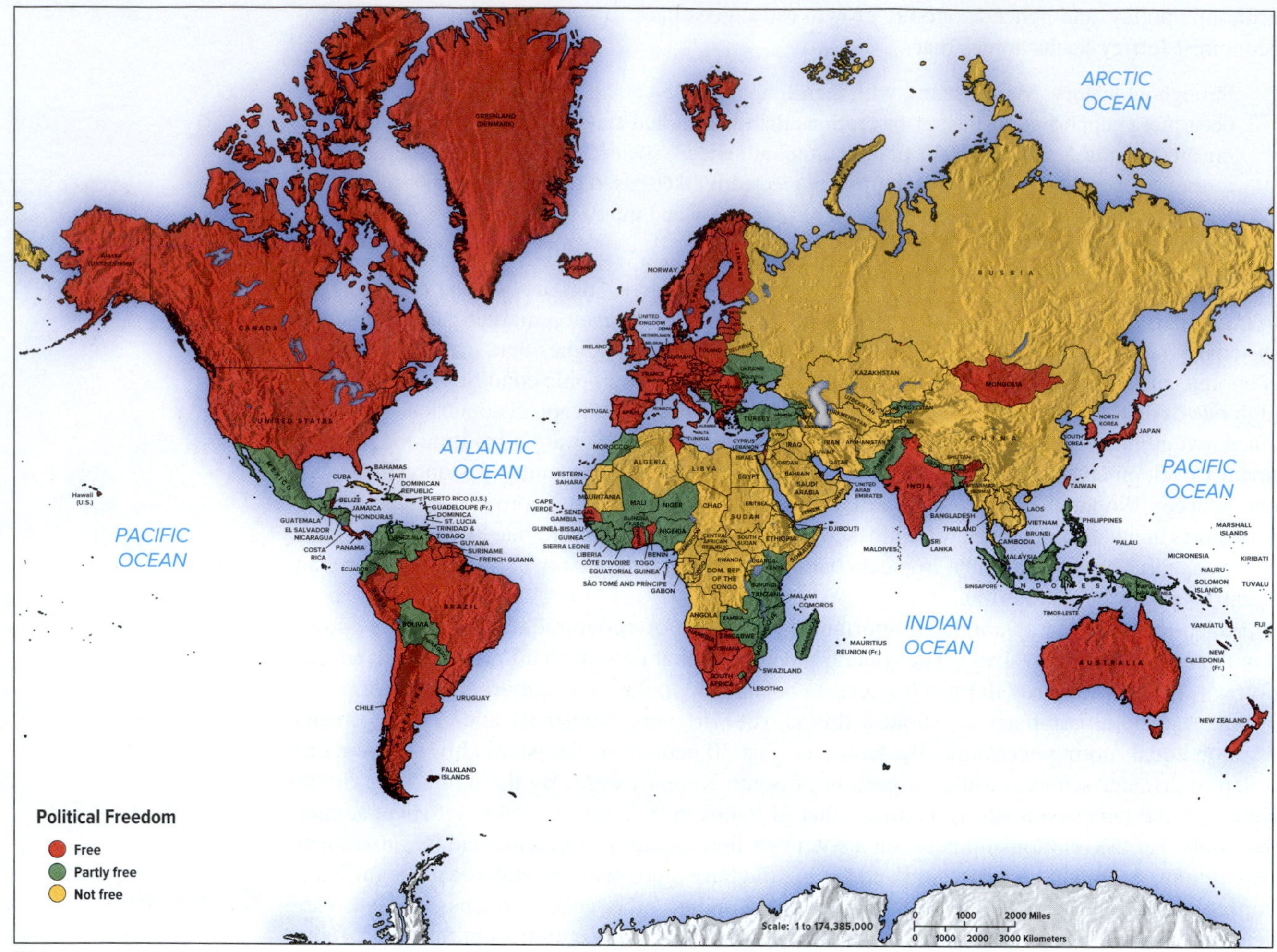

3.5 MAP

Freedom in the World in 2016.

The Freedom House Survey Team, "Freedom in the World 2016," www.freedomhouse.org.

strife, or civil war. In "not free" countries, the political process is tightly controlled and basic freedoms are denied.

Freedom House classified some 86 countries as free in 2016, accounting for about 40 percent of the world's nations. These countries respect a broad range of political rights. Another 59 countries accounting for 24 percent of the world's nations were classified as partly free, while 50 countries representing approximately 36 percent of the world's nations were classified as not free. The number of democracies in the world has increased from 69 nations in 1987 to 125 in 2015. But not all democracies are free, according to Freedom House, because some democracies still restrict certain political and civil liberties. For example, although Russia is nominally a democracy, it has consistently been rated "not free" since the early 2000s. According to Freedom House,

> Russia's step backwards into the Not Free category is the culmination of a growing trend . . . to concentrate political authority, harass and intimidate the media, and politicize the country's law-enforcement system.[19]

Similarly, Freedom House argues that democracy was restricted in Venezuela under the leadership of the late Hugo Chávez, a trend that continued under his successor.

Many of the newer democracies are to be found in eastern Europe and Latin America, although there also have been notable gains in Africa during this time, including South Africa and

Nigeria. Entrants into the ranks of the world's democracies during the last 25 years include Mexico, which held its first fully free and fair presidential election in 2000 after free and fair parliamentary and state elections in 1997 and 1998; Senegal, where free and fair presidential elections led to a peaceful transfer of power; Myanmar, where in 2015, after decades of rule by a military dictatorship, the opposition party won a landslide victory in elections that were mostly free and fair; and Nigeria, where in 2015 for the first time the opposition won an election and there was a peaceful transfer of power.

Three main reasons account for the spread of democracy.[20] First, many totalitarian regimes failed to deliver economic progress to the vast bulk of their populations. The collapse of communism in eastern Europe, for example, was precipitated by the growing gulf between the vibrant and wealthy economies of the West and the stagnant economies of the communist East. In looking for alternatives to the socialist model, the populations of these countries could not have failed to notice that most of the world's strongest economies were governed by representative democracies. Today, the economic success of many of the newer democracies—such as Poland and the Czech Republic in the former communist bloc, the Philippines and Taiwan in Asia, and Chile in Latin America—has strengthened the case for democracy as a key component of successful economic advancement.

Second, new information and communication technologies—including satellite television, desktop publishing, and, most important, the Internet and associated social media—have reduced a state's ability to control access to uncensored information. These technologies have created new conduits for the spread of democratic ideals and information from free societies. Today, the Internet is allowing democratic ideals to penetrate closed societies as never before.[21] Young people who utilized Facebook and Twitter to reach large numbers of people very quickly and coordinate their actions organized the demonstrations in 2011 that led to the overthrow of the Egyptian government.

Third, in many countries, economic advances have led to the emergence of increasingly prosperous middle and working classes that have pushed for democratic reforms. This was certainly a factor in the democratic transformation of South Korea. Entrepreneurs and other business leaders, eager to protect their property rights and ensure the dispassionate enforcement of contracts, are another force pressing for more accountable and open government.

Despite this, it would be naive to conclude that the global spread of democracy will continue unchallenged. Democracy is still rare in large parts of the world. In sub-Saharan Africa in 2015, only 9 countries were considered free, 20 were partly free, and 20 were not free. Among the post-communist countries in eastern and central Europe and the former Soviet Union, only 13 are classified as free (primarily in eastern Europe). And there are only 2 free state among the 18 nations of the Middle East and North Africa. Although the wave of unrest that spread across the Middle East during 2011–2013 created hope for change, with the exception of Tunisia, this as not been realized.

Moreover, there are disturbing signs that authoritarianism is gaining ground in several countries where political and civil liberties have been progressively limited in recent years, including Russia, Ukraine, Indonesia, and Venezuela. An increasingly autocratic Russia annexed the Crimea region from the Ukraine in 2014 and has actively supported pro-Russian rebels in eastern Ukraine. Libya, where there was hope that a democracy might be established, appears to have slipped into anarchy. In Egypt, after a brief flirtation with democracy, the military stepped in, removing the government of Mohamed Morsi, after Morsi and his political movement, the Muslim Brotherhood, had exhibited its own authoritarian tendencies. The military-backed government, however, has also acted in an authoritarian manner, effectively reversing much of the progress that had occurred after the revolution of 2011.

Is World Peace Through Commerce Possible?

Interested in world peace? Business students worldwide can participate in Peace Through Commerce's "Matrix of Peace," an integrated program that shows how business schools can promote peace. The program is sponsored by the Association to Advance Collegiate Schools of Business (AACSB International), the global accrediting organization of business schools. Peace Through Commerce is built on the premise that peace is achieved and maintained by an interdependent system of commerce, consciousness, and laws and structure. As the AACSB puts it: "If we educate students that it is their responsibility to advance society, over a generation we may be able to have more impact than governments have had." What do you think? Can business people advance global societies more than governments if educated according to the framework of the "Matrix of Peace"?

Source: www.peacethroughcommerce.com.

THE NEW WORLD ORDER AND GLOBAL TERRORISM The end of the Cold War and the "new world order" that followed the collapse of communism in eastern Europe and the former Soviet Union, taken together with the demise of many authoritarian regimes in Latin America, gave rise to intense speculation about the future shape of global geopolitics. Two decades ago, author Francis Fukuyama argued, "We may be witnessing . . . the end of history as such: that is, the end point of mankind's ideological evolution and the universalization of Western liberal democracy as the final form of human government."[22] Fukuyama goes on to say that the war of ideas may be at an end and that liberal democracy has triumphed.

Others questioned Fukuyama's vision of a more harmonious world dominated by a universal civilization characterized by democratic regimes and free market capitalism. In a controversial book, the late influential political scientist Samuel Huntington argued there is no "universal" civilization based on widespread acceptance of Western liberal democratic ideals.[23] Huntington maintained that while many societies may be modernizing—they are adopting the material paraphernalia of the modern world, from automobiles and Facebook to Coca-Cola and smartphones—they are not becoming more Western. On the contrary, Huntington theorized that modernization in non-Western societies can result in a retreat toward the traditional, such as the resurgence of Islam in many traditionally Muslim societies. He wrote,

> The Islamic resurgence is both a product of and an effort to come to grips with modernization. Its underlying causes are those generally responsible for indigenization trends in non-Western societies: urbanization, social mobilization, higher levels of literacy and education, intensified communication and media consumption, and expanded interaction with Western and other cultures. These developments undermine traditional village and clan ties and create alienation and an identity crisis. Islamist symbols, commitments, and beliefs meet these psychological needs, and Islamist welfare organizations, the social, cultural, and economic needs of Muslims caught in the process of modernization. Muslims feel a need to return to Islamic ideas, practices, and institutions to provide the compass and the motor of modernization.[24]

Thus, the rise of Islamic fundamentalism is portrayed as a response to the alienation produced by modernization.

In contrast to Fukuyama, Huntington envisioned a world split into different civilizations, each of which has its own value systems and ideology. Huntington predicted conflict between the West and Islam and between the West and China. While some commentators originally dismissed Huntington's thesis, in the aftermath of the terrorist attacks on the United States on September 11, 2001, Huntington's views received new attention. The dramatic rise of the Islamic State (ISIS) in war-torn Syria and neighboring Iraq during 2014–2015 has drawn further attention to Huntington's thesis, as has the growing penchant for ISIS to engage is terrorist acts outside of the Middle east, most notably in Paris in 2015.

If Huntington's views are even partly correct, they have important implications for international business. They suggest many countries may be difficult places in which to do business, either because they are shot through with violent conflicts or because they are part of a civilization that is in conflict with an enterprise's home country. Huntington's views are speculative and controversial. More likely than his predictions coming to pass is the evolution of a global political system that is positioned somewhere between Fukuyama's universal global civilization based on liberal democratic ideals and Huntington's vision of a fractured world. That would still be a world, however, in which geopolitical forces limit the ability of business enterprises to operate in certain foreign countries.

As for terrorism, in Huntington's thesis, global terrorism is a product of the tension between civilizations and the clash of value systems and ideology. The terror attacks undertaken by al-Qaeda and ISIS are consistent with this view. Others point to terrorism's roots in long-standing conflicts that seem to defy political resolution—the Palestinian, Kashmir, and Northern Ireland conflicts being obvious examples. It is also true that much of the terrorism perpetrated by al-Qaeda affiliates in Iraq during the 2000s and more recently by ISIS in Iraq and Syria can be understood in part as a struggle between radicalized Sunni and Shia factions within Islam. Moreover, substantial amount of terrorist activity in some parts of the world, such as Colombia, has been interwoven with the illegal drug trade. As former U.S. Secretary of State Colin Powell has maintained, terrorism represents one of the major threats to world peace and economic progress in the twenty-first century.[25]

THE SPREAD OF MARKET-BASED SYSTEMS

Paralleling the spread of democracy since the 1980s has been the transformation from centrally planned command economies to market-based economies. More than 30 countries that were in the former Soviet Union or the eastern European communist bloc have changed their economic systems. A complete list of countries where change is now occurring also would include Asian states such as China and Vietnam, as well as African countries such as Angola, Ethiopia, and Mozambique.[26] There has been a similar shift away from a mixed economy. Many states in Asia, Latin America, and western Europe have sold state-owned businesses to private investors (privatization) and deregulated their economies to promote greater competition.

The rationale for economic transformation has been the same the world over. In general, command and mixed economies failed to deliver the kind of sustained economic performance that was achieved by countries adopting market-based systems, such as the United States, Switzerland, Hong Kong, and Taiwan. As a consequence, even more states have gravitated toward the market-based model.

Map 3.6, based on data from the Heritage Foundation, a politically conservative U.S. research foundation, gives some idea of the degree to which the world has shifted toward market-based economic systems (given that the Heritage Foundation has an overt political agenda and generally supports the "Tea Party" wing of the Republican Party, its work should be viewed with caution). The Heritage Foundation's index of economic freedom is based on 10 indicators, including the extent to which the government intervenes in the economy, trade policy, the degree to which property rights are protected, foreign investment regulations, taxation rules, freedom from corruption, and labor freedom. A country can score between 100 (freest) and 0 (least free) on each of these indicators. The higher a country's average score across all 10 indicators, the more closely its economy represents the pure market model. According to the 2016 index, which is summarized in Map 3.6, the world's freest economies are (in rank order) Hong Kong, Singapore, New Zealand, Switzerland, Australia, Canada, Chile, Ireland, Estonia, the United Kingdom and the

Rapid economic development has taken place in China and Vietnam since the shift toward a more market-based system.
Source: © Per-Anders Pettersson/Terra/Corbis

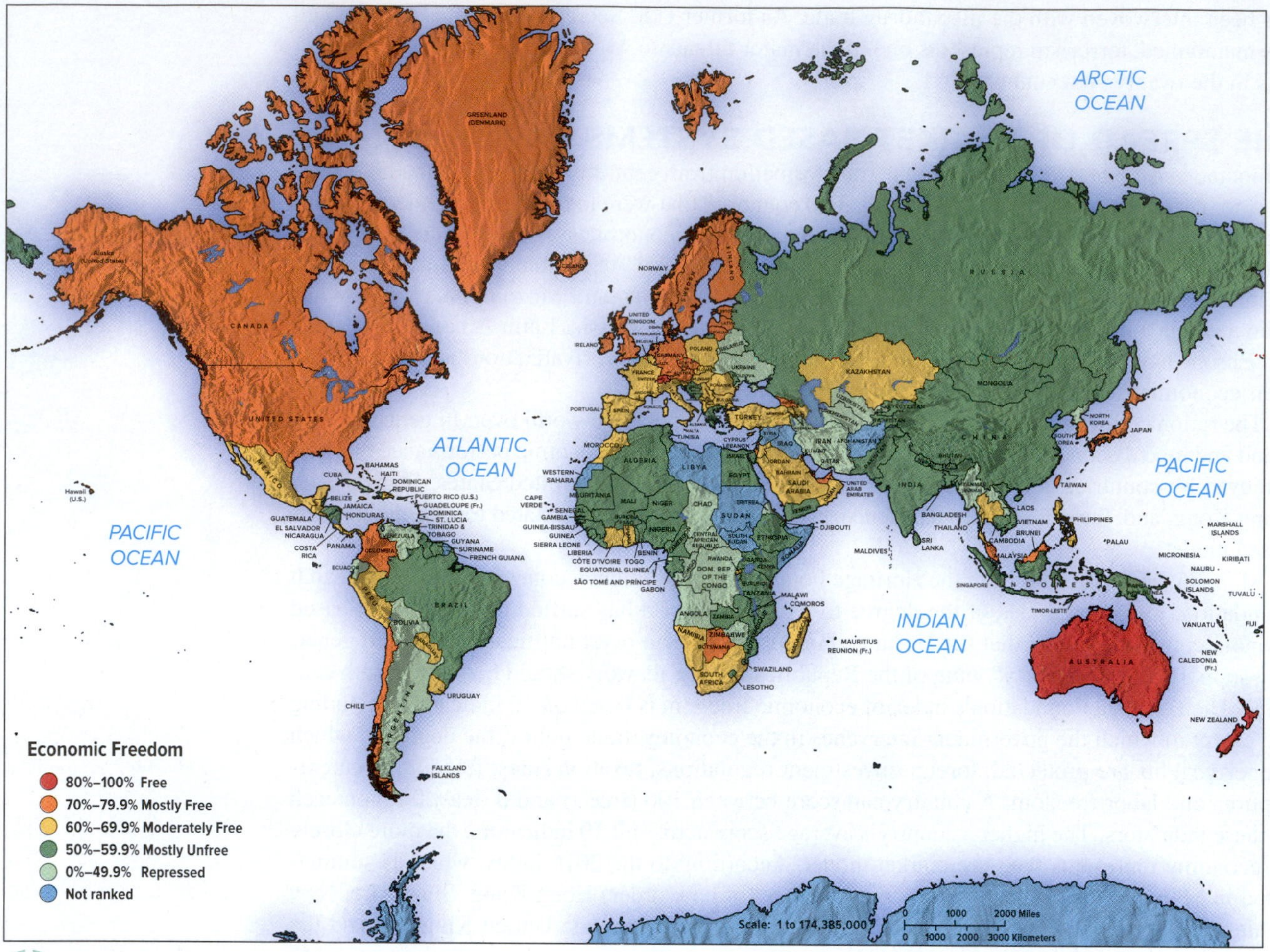

Economic Freedom
- 80%–100% Free
- 70%–79.9% Mostly Free
- 60%–69.9% Moderately Free
- 50%–59.9% Mostly Unfree
- 0%–49.9% Repressed
- Not ranked

Scale: 1 to 174,385,000

3.6 MAP

Distribution of Economic Freedom, 2016.

Source: The Freedom House Survey Team, "Freedom in the World 2016." www.freedomhouse.org.

United States. Germany came in at 17, Japan at 22, Mexico at 62, France at 75, Brazil at 122, India at 123, China at 144, and Russia at 153. The economies of Zimbabwe, Venezuela, Cuba, and North Korea are to be found at the bottom of the rankings.[27]

test PREP

Use SmartBook to help retain what you have learned. Access your Instructor's Connect course to check out SmartBook or go to learnsmartadvantage.com for help.

Economic freedom does not necessarily equate with political freedom, as detailed in Map 3.6. For example, the two top states in the Heritage Foundation index, Hong Kong and Singapore, cannot be classified as politically free. Hong Kong was reabsorbed into communist China in 1997, and the first thing Beijing did was shut down Hong Kong's freely elected legislature. Singapore is ranked as only partly free on Freedom House's index of political freedom due to practices such as widespread press censorship.

LO 3-3

Describe how transition economies are moving toward market-based systems.

The Nature of Economic Transformation

The shift toward a market-based economic system often entails a number of steps: deregulation, privatization, and creation of a legal system to safeguard property rights.[28]

Deregulation

Removal of government restrictions concerning the conduct of a business.

DEREGULATION

Deregulation involves removing legal restrictions to the free play of markets, the establishment of private enterprises, and the manner in which private enterprises operate. Before the collapse of communism, the governments in most command economies exercised tight control over prices and output, setting both through detailed state planning. They also prohibited private enterprises from operating in most sectors of the economy, severely restricted direct investment by foreign enterprises, and limited international trade. Deregulation in these cases involved removing price controls, thereby allowing prices to be set by the interplay between demand and supply; abolishing laws regulating the establishment and operation of private enterprises; and relaxing or removing restrictions on direct investment by foreign enterprises and international trade.

In mixed economies, the role of the state was more limited; but here, too, in certain sectors the state set prices, owned businesses, limited private enterprise, restricted investment by foreigners, and restricted international trade. For these countries, deregulation has involved the same kind of initiatives that we have seen in former command economies, although the transformation has been easier because these countries often had a vibrant private sector. India is an example of a country that has substantially deregulated its economy over the past two decades (see the Country Focus on India).

country FOCUS

India's Economic Transformation

After gaining independence from Britain in 1947, India adopted a democratic system of government. The economic system that developed in India after 1947 was a mixed economy characterized by a large number of state-owned enterprises, centralized planning, and subsidies. This system constrained the growth of the private sector. Private companies could expand only with government permission. It could take years to get permission to diversify into a new product. Much of heavy industry, such as auto, chemical, and steel production, was reserved for state-owned enterprises. Production quotas and high tariffs on imports also stunted the development of a healthy private sector, as did labor laws that made it difficult to fire employees.

By the early 1990s, it was clear this system was incapable of delivering the kind of economic progress that many Southeast Asian nations had started to enjoy. In 1994, India's economy was still smaller than Belgium's, despite having a population of 950 million. Its GDP per capita was a paltry $310, less than half the population could read, only 6 million had access to telephones, and only 14 percent had access to clean sanitation; the World Bank estimated that some 40 percent of the world's desperately poor lived in India, and only 2.3 percent of the population had an annual household income in excess of $2,484.

The lack of progress led the government to embark on an ambitious economic reform program. Starting in 1991, much of the industrial licensing system was dismantled, and several areas once closed to the private sector were opened, including electricity generation, parts of the oil industry, steelmaking, air transport, and some areas of the telecommunications industry. Investment by foreign enterprises, formerly allowed only grudgingly and subject to arbitrary ceilings, was suddenly welcomed. Approval was made automatic for foreign equity stakes of up to 51 percent in an Indian enterprise, and 100 percent foreign ownership was allowed under certain circumstances. Raw materials and many industrial goods could be freely imported, and the maximum tariff that could be levied on imports was reduced from 400 percent to 65 percent. The top income tax rate was also reduced, and corporate tax fell from 57.5 percent to 46 percent in 1994, and then to 35 percent in 1997. The government also announced plans to start privatizing India's state-owned businesses, some 40 percent of which were losing money in the early 1990s.

Judged by some measures, the response to these economic reforms has been impressive. The Indian economy expanded at an annual rate of about 6.3 percent from 1994 to 2004 and then accelerated to 7 to 8 percent annually during 2005–2014. Foreign investment, a key indicator of how attractive foreign companies thought the Indian economy was, jumped from $150 million in 1991 to a record $34.4 billion in 2014. In the first half of 2015, India overtook both China and the United States to become the top destination for foreign investment, with $31 billion invested in just six months. In the information technology sector, India has emerged as a vibrant global center for software development with sales of $147 billion and exports of $99 billion in 2015, up from sales of just $150 million in 1990. In pharmaceuticals, too, Indian companies are emerging as credible players in the global marketplace, primarily by selling low-cost, generic versions of drugs that have come off patent in the developed world.

However, the country still has a long way to go. Attempts to further reduce import tariffs have been stalled by political opposition from employers, employees, and politicians who fear that if barriers come down, a flood of inexpensive Chinese products will enter India. The privatization program continues to hit speed bumps—the latest in September 2003 when the Indian Supreme Court ruled that the government could not privatize two state-owned oil companies without explicit approval from the parliament. State-owned firms still account for 38 percent of national output in the non-farm sector, yet India's private firms are 30 to 40 percent more productive than state-owned enterprises. There has also been strong resistance to reforming many of India's laws that make it difficult for private business to operate efficiently. For example, labor laws make it almost impossible for firms with more than 100 employees to fire workers, creating a disincentive for entrepreneurs to increase their enterprises beyond 100 employees. Other laws mandate that certain products can be manufactured only by small companies, effectively making it impossible for companies in these industries to attain the scale required to compete internationally.

Sources: "India's Breakthrough Budget?," *The Economist*, March 3, 2001; "America's Pain, India's Gain," *The Economist*, January 11, 2003, p. 57; Joanna Slater, "In Once Socialist India, Privatizations Are Becoming More Like Routine Matters," *The Wall Street Journal*, July 5, 2002, p. A8; "India's Economy: Ready to Roll Again?," *The Economist*, September 20, 2003, pp. 39–40; Joanna Slater, "Indian Pirates Turned Partners," *The Wall Street Journal*, November 13, 2003, p. A14; "The Next Wave: India," *The Economist*, December 17, 2005, p. 67; M. Dell, "The Digital Sector Can Make Poor Nations Prosper," *Financial Times*, May 4, 2006, p. 17; "What's Holding India Back," *The Economist*, March 8, 2008, p. 11; "Battling the Babu Raj," *The Economist*, March 8, 2008, pp. 29–31. Lyengar, Rishi, "India Tops Foreign Investment Rankings Ahead of U.S. and China," *Time*, October 11, 2015.

PRIVATIZATION Hand in hand with deregulation has come a sharp increase in privatization. Privatization, as we discussed in Chapter 2, transfers the ownership of state property into the hands of private individuals, frequently by the sale of state assets through an auction.[29] Privatization is seen as a way to stimulate gains in economic efficiency by giving new private owners a powerful incentive—the reward of greater profits—to search for increases in productivity, to enter new markets, and to exit losing ones.[30]

The privatization movement started in Great Britain in the early 1980s when then–Prime Minister Margaret Thatcher started to sell state-owned assets such as the British telephone company, British Telecom (BT). In a pattern that has been repeated around the world, this sale was linked with the deregulation of the British telecommunications industry. By allowing other firms to compete head to head with BT, deregulation ensured that privatization did not simply replace a state-owned monopoly with a private monopoly. Since the 1980s, privatization has become a worldwide phenomenon. More than 8,000 acts of privatization were completed around the world between 1995 and 1999.[31] Some of the most dramatic privatization programs occurred in the economies of the former Soviet Union and its eastern European satellite states. In the Czech Republic, for example, three-quarters of all state-owned enterprises were privatized between 1989 and 1996, helping push the share of gross domestic product accounted for by the private sector up from 11 percent in 1989 to 60 percent in 1995.[32]

Despite this three-decade trend, large amounts of economic activity are still in the hands of state-owned enterprises in many nations. In China, for example, state-owned companies still dominate the banking, energy, telecommunications, health care, and technology sectors. Overall, they account for about 40 percent of the country's GDP. In a report released in early 2012, the World Bank cautioned China that unless it reformed these sectors—liberalizing them and privatizing many state-owned enterprises—the country runs the risk of experiencing a serious economic crisis.[33]

As privatization has proceeded, it has become clear that simply selling state-owned assets to private investors is not enough to guarantee economic growth. Studies of privatization in central Europe have shown that the process often fails to deliver predicted benefits if the newly privatized firms continue to receive subsidies from the state and if they are protected from foreign competition by barriers to international trade and foreign direct investment.[34] In such cases, the newly privatized firms are sheltered from competition and continue acting like state monopolies. When these circumstances prevail, the newly privatized entities often have little incentive to restructure their operations to become more efficient. For privatization to work, it must also be accompanied by a more general deregulation and opening of the economy. Thus, when Brazil decided to privatize the state-owned telephone monopoly, Telebrás Brazil, the government also split the company into four independent units that were to compete with each other and removed barriers to foreign direct investment in telecommunications services. This action ensured that the newly privatized entities would face significant competition and thus would have to improve their operating efficiency to survive.

Is Selling in China a Good Strategy?

If China and the United States continue to grow like they did in recent years, some estimates indicate that China will be the world's largest economy by 2030. Let's assume this is true. Then China is clearly a country to take a closer look at—not just to outsource from (i.e., build factories in the country, produce products, and then sell those products to other parts of the world), but also to sell into to target their increasing customer base with purchasing power. Between 2000 and 2011, for example, the U.S. increased exports to China by 542 percent, roughly three times that of the increase to Brazil (which was ranked second in increase during the same time period). Also, by 2020 China is expected to have some 190 million customers in the middle- and upper-income categories, making this the largest population segment of any country's middle-/upper-income citizens. If you were a global manager for a company, would you concentrate on selling your products in China without having a production facility in the country?

Source: solutions.mckinsey.com/insightschina.

LEGAL SYSTEMS As noted in Chapter 2, a well-functioning market economy requires laws protecting private property rights and providing mechanisms for contract enforcement. Without a legal system that protects property rights and without the machinery to enforce that system, the incentive to engage in economic activity can be reduced substantially by private and public entities, including organized crime, that expropriate the profits generated by the efforts of private-sector entrepreneurs. For example, when communism collapsed in eastern Europe, many countries lacked the legal structure required to protect property rights, all property having been held by the state. Although many nations have made big strides toward instituting the required system, it may be years before the legal system is functioning as smoothly as it does in the West. For example, in most eastern European nations, the title to urban and agricultural property is often uncertain because of incomplete and inaccurate records, multiple pledges on the same property, and unsettled claims resulting from demands for restitution from owners in the pre-communist era. Also, although most countries have improved their commercial codes, institutional weaknesses still undermine contract enforcement. Court capacity is often inadequate, and procedures for resolving contract disputes out of court are often lacking or poorly developed.[35] Nevertheless, progress is being made. In 2004, for example, China amended its constitution to state that "private property was not to be encroached upon," and in 2007 it enacted a new law on property rights that gave property holders many of the same protections as those enjoyed by the state (see the Country Focus on China's emerging property rights).[36]

 **test PREP**

Use SmartBook to help retain what you have learned. Access your Instructor's Connect course to check out SmartBook or go to learnsmartadvantage.com for help.

Implications of Changing Political Economy

The global changes in political and economic systems discussed earlier have several implications for international business. The long-standing ideological conflict between collectivism and individualism that defined the twentieth century is less in evidence today. The West won the Cold War, and Western ideology is now widespread. Although command economies remain and totalitarian dictatorships can still be found around the world, the tide has been running in favor of free markets and greater democracy for 30 years. It remains to be seen, however, whether the global financial crisis of 2008–2009 and the recession that followed will lead to a retrenchment. Certainly many commentators have blamed the problems that led to this crisis on a lack of regulation, and some reassessment of Western political ideology seems likely.

Notwithstanding the crisis of 2008–2009, the trends of the past 30 years have enormous implications for business. For nearly 50 years, half of the world was off-limits to Western businesses. Now much of that has changed. Many of the national markets of eastern Europe, Latin America, Africa, and Asia may still be underdeveloped, but they are potentially enormous. With a population of more than 1.3 billion, the Chinese market alone is potentially bigger than that of the United States, the European Union, and Japan combined. Similarly, India, with about 1.2 billion people, is a potentially huge market. Latin America has another 600 million potential consumers. It is unlikely that China, Russia, Vietnam, or any of the other states now moving toward a market system will attain the living standards of the West soon. Nevertheless, the upside potential is so large that companies need to consider making inroads now. For example, if China and the United States continue to grow at the rates they did during 1996–2015, China will surpass the United States to become the world's largest national economy within the next two decades.

Just as the potential gains are large, so are the risks. There is no guarantee that democracy will thrive in many of the world's newer democratic states, particularly if these states have to grapple with severe economic setbacks. Totalitarian dictatorships could return, although they are unlikely to be of the communist variety. Although the bipolar world of the Cold War era has vanished, it may be replaced by a multipolar world dominated by a number of civilizations. In such a world, much of the economic promise inherent in the global shift toward market-based economic systems may stall in the face of conflicts between civilizations. While the long-term potential for economic gain from investment in the world's new market economies is large, the risks associated with any such investment are also substantial. It would be foolish to ignore these. The financial system in China, for example, is not transparent, and many suspect that Chinese banks hold a high proportion of nonperforming loans on their books. If true, these bad debts could trigger a significant financial crisis during the next decade in China, which would dramatically lower growth rates.

 **test PREP**

Use SmartBook to help retain what you have learned. Access your Instructor's Connect course to check out SmartBook or go to learnsmartadvantage.com for help.

BENEFITS, COSTS, RISKS, AND OVERALL ATTRACTIVENESS OF DOING BUSINESS INTERNATIONALLY

LO 3-4
Explain the implications for management practice of national difference in political economy.

As noted in Chapter 2, the political, economic, and legal environments of a country clearly influence the attractiveness of that country as a market or investment site. In this chapter, we argued that countries with democratic regimes, market-based economic policies, and strong protection of property rights are more likely to attain high and sustained economic growth rates and are thus a more attractive location for international business. It follows that the benefits, costs, and risks associated with doing business in a country are a function of that country's political, economic, and legal systems. The overall attractiveness of a country as a market or investment site depends on balancing the likely long-term benefits of doing business in that country against the likely costs and risks. Here, we consider the determinants of benefits, costs, and risks.

Benefits

In the most general sense, the long-run monetary benefits of doing business in a country are a function of the size of the market, the present wealth (purchasing power) of consumers in that market, and the likely future wealth of consumers. While some markets are very large when measured by number of consumers (e.g., China and India), low living standards may imply limited purchasing power and therefore a relatively small market when measured in economic terms. International businesses need to be aware of this distinction, but they also need to keep in mind the likely future prospects of a country. In 1960, South Korea was viewed as just another impoverished third world nation. By 2014, it had the world's 13th-largest economy. International firms that recognized South Korea's potential in 1960 and began to do business in that country may have reaped greater benefits than those that wrote off South Korea.

Coca-Cola has ramped up spending on marketing and advertising in emerging markets such as China.
Source: © Keith Bedford/Bloomberg/Getty Images

By identifying and investing early in a potential future economic star, international firms may build brand loyalty and gain experience in that country's business practices. These will pay back substantial dividends if that country achieves sustained high economic growth rates. In contrast, late entrants may find that they lack the brand loyalty and experience necessary to achieve a significant presence in the market. In the language of business strategy, early entrants into potential future economic stars may be able to reap substantial first-mover advantages, while late entrants may fall victim to late-mover disadvantages.[37] (**First-mover advantages** are the advantages that accrue to early entrants into a market. **Late-mover disadvantages** are the handicaps that late entrants might suffer.) This kind of reasoning has been driving significant inward investment into China, which may become the world's largest economy by 2030 if it continues growing at current rates (China is already the world's second-largest national economy). For more than two decades, China has been the largest recipient of foreign direct investment in the developing world as international businesses—including General Motors, Volkswagen, Coca-Cola, and Unilever—try to establish a sustainable advantage in this nation.

First-Mover Advantages
Advantages accruing to the first to enter a market.

Late-Mover Disadvantages
Handicaps experienced by being a late entrant in a market.

A country's economic system and property rights regime are reasonably good predictors of economic prospects. Countries with free market economies in which property rights are protected tend to achieve greater economic growth rates than command economies or economies where property rights are poorly protected. It follows that a country's economic system, property rights regime, and market size (in terms of population) probably constitute reasonably good indicators of the potential long-run benefits of doing business in a country. In contrast, countries where property rights are not well respected and where corruption is rampant tend to have lower levels of economic growth. We must be careful about generalizing too much from this, however, because both China and India have achieved high growth rates despite relatively weak property rights regimes and high levels of corruption. In both countries, the shift toward a market-based economic system has produced large gains despite weak property rights and endemic corruption.

Costs

A number of political, economic, and legal factors determine the costs of doing business in a country. With regard to political factors, a company may pushed to pay off politically powerful entities in a country before the government allows it to do business there. The need to pay what are essentially bribes is greater in closed totalitarian states than in open democratic societies where politicians are held accountable by the electorate (although this is not a hard-and-fast distinction). Whether a company should actually pay bribes in return for market access should be determined on the basis of the legal and ethical implications of such action. We discuss this consideration in Chapter 5, when we look closely at the issue of business ethics.

With regard to economic factors, one of the most important variables is the sophistication of a country's economy. It may be more costly to do business in relatively primitive or undeveloped economies because of the lack of infrastructure and supporting businesses. At the extreme, an international firm may have to provide its own infrastructure and supporting business, which obviously raises costs. When McDonald's decided to open its first restaurant in Moscow, it found that to serve food and drink indistinguishable from that served in McDonald's restaurants elsewhere, it had to vertically integrate backward to supply its own needs. The quality of Russian-grown potatoes and meat was too poor. Thus, to protect the quality of its product, McDonald's set up its own dairy farms, cattle ranches, vegetable plots, and food-processing plants within Russia. This raised the cost of doing business in Russia, relative to the cost in more sophisticated economies where high-quality inputs could be purchased on the open market.

As for legal factors, it can be more costly to do business in a country where local laws and regulations set strict standards with regard to product safety, safety in the workplace, environmental pollution, and the like (because adhering to such regulations is costly). It can also be more costly to do business in a country like the United States, where the absence of a cap on damage awards has meant spiraling liability insurance rates. It can be more costly to do business in a country that lacks well-established laws for regulating business practice (as is the case in many of the former communist nations). In the absence of a well-developed body of business contract law, international firms may find no satisfactory way to resolve contract disputes and, consequently, routinely face large losses from contract violations. Similarly, local laws that fail to adequately protect intellectual property can lead to the theft of an international business's intellectual property and lost income.

Risks

Political Risk
The likelihood that political forces will cause drastic changes in a country's business environment that will adversely affect the profit and other goals of a particular business enterprise.

As with costs, the risks of doing business in a country are determined by a number of political, economic, and legal factors. **Political risk** has been defined as the likelihood that political forces will cause drastic changes in a country's business environment that adversely affect the profit and other goals of a business enterprise.[38] So defined, political risk tends to be greater in countries experiencing social unrest and disorder or in countries where the underlying nature of a society increases the likelihood of social unrest. Social unrest typically finds expression in strikes, demonstrations, terrorism, and violent conflict. Such unrest is more likely to be found in countries that contain more than one ethnic nationality, in countries where competing ideologies are battling for political control, in countries where economic mismanagement has created high inflation and falling living standards, or in countries that straddle the "fault lines" between civilizations.

Social unrest can result in abrupt changes in government and government policy or, in some cases, in protracted civil strife. Such strife tends to have negative economic implications for the profit goals of business enterprises. For example, in the aftermath of the 1979 Islamic revolution in Iran, the Iranian assets of numerous U.S. companies were seized by the new Iranian government without compensation. Similarly, the violent disintegration of the Yugoslavian federation into warring states, including Bosnia, Croatia, and Serbia, precipitated a collapse in the local economies and in the profitability of investments in those countries.

More generally, a change in political regime can result in the enactment of laws that are less favorable to international business. In Venezuela, for example, the populist socialist politician Hugo Chávez held power from 1998 until his death in 2013. Chávez declared himself to be a "Fidelista," a follower of Cuba's Fidel Castro. He pledged to improve the lot of the poor in Venezuela through government intervention in private business and frequently railed against American imperialism, all of which is of concern to Western enterprises doing business in the country. Among other actions, he increased the royalties that foreign oil companies operating in Venezuela had to pay the government from 1 to 30 percent of sales.

Economic Risk
The likelihood that events, including economic mismanagement, will cause drastic changes in a country's business environment that adversely affect the profit and other goals of a particular business enterprise.

Other risks may arise from a country's mismanagement of its economy. An **economic risk** can be defined as the likelihood that economic mismanagement will cause drastic changes in a country's business environment that hurt the profit and other goals of a particular business enterprise. Economic risks are not independent of political risk. Economic mismanagement may give rise to significant social unrest and, hence, political risk. Nevertheless, economic risks are worth emphasizing as a separate category because there is not always a one-to-one relationship between economic mismanagement and social unrest. One visible indicator of economic mismanagement tends to be a country's inflation rate. Another is the level of business and government debt in the country.

The collapse in oil prices that occurred in 2014–2015 exposed economic mismanagement and increased economic risk in a number countries that had been overly dependent upon oil revenues to finance profligate government spending. In countries such as Russia, Saudi Arabia, and Venezuela, high oil prices had enabled national governments to spend lavishly on social programs and public sector infrastructure. As oil prices collapsed, these countries saw government revenues tumble. Budget deficits began to climb sharply, their currencies fell on foreign exchange markets, price inflation began to accelerate as the price of imports rose, and their economies started to contract, increasing unemployment and creating the potential for social disruption. None of this was good for those countries, and nor did it benefit foreign business that had invested in those economies.

On the legal front, risks arise when a country's legal system fails to provide adequate safeguards in the case of contract violations or to protect property rights. When legal safeguards are weak, firms are more likely to break contracts or steal intellectual property if they perceive it as being in their interests to do so. Thus, a **legal risk** can be defined as the likelihood that a trading partner will opportunistically break a contract or expropriate property rights. When legal risks in a country are high, an international business might hesitate entering into a long-term contract or joint-venture agreement with a firm in that country. For example, in the 1970s when the Indian government passed a law requiring all foreign investors to enter into joint ventures with Indian companies, U.S. companies such as IBM and Coca-Cola closed their investments in India. They believed that the Indian legal system did not provide adequate protection of intellectual property rights, creating the very real danger that their Indian partners might expropriate the intellectual property of the American companies—which for IBM and Coca-Cola amounted to the core of their competitive advantage.

Legal Risk
The likelihood that a trading partner will opportunistically break a contract or expropriate intellectual property rights.

Overall Attractiveness

The overall attractiveness of a country as a potential market or investment site for an international business depends on balancing the benefits, costs, and risks associated with doing business in that country (see Figure 3.1). Generally, the costs and risks associated with doing business in a foreign country are typically lower in economically advanced and politically stable democratic nations and greater in less developed and politically unstable nations. The calculus is complicated, however, because the potential long-run benefits are dependent not only on a nation's current stage of economic development or political stability but also on likely future economic growth rates. Economic growth appears to be a function of a free market system and a country's capacity for growth (which may be greater in less developed nations). This leads us to conclude that, other things being equal, the benefit–cost–risk trade-off is likely to be most favorable in politically stable developed and developing nations that have free market systems and no dramatic upsurge in either inflation rates or private-sector debt. It is likely to be least favorable in politically unstable developing nations that operate with a mixed or command economy or in developing nations where speculative financial bubbles have led to excess borrowing.

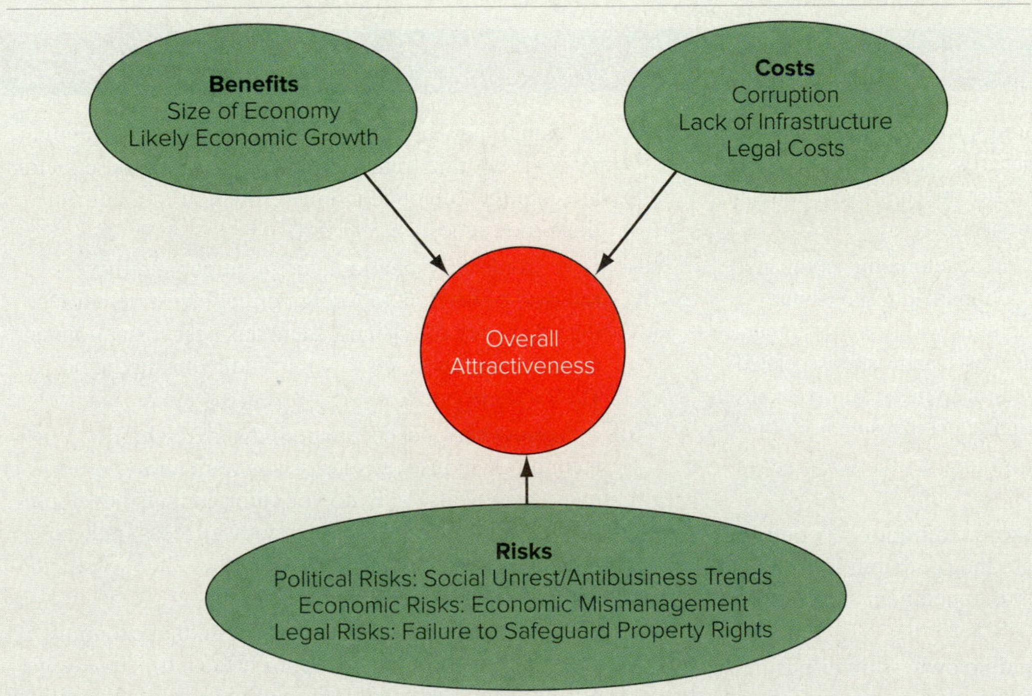

3.1 FIGURE
Country Attractiveness.

Key Terms

gross national income (GNI), p. 61
purchasing power parity (PPP), p. 61
Human Development Index (HDI), p. 64
innovation, p. 66
entrepreneurs, p. 66
deregulation, p. 74
first-mover advantages, p. 79
late-mover disadvantages, p. 79
political risk, p. 80
economic risk, p. 80
legal risk, p. 81

Summary

This chapter reviewed how the political, economic, and legal systems of countries vary. The potential benefits, costs, and risks of doing business in a country are a function of its political, economic, and legal systems. The chapter made the following points:

1. The rate of economic progress in a country seems to depend on the extent to which that country has a well-functioning market economy in which property rights are protected.
2. Many countries are now in a state of transition. There is a marked shift away from totalitarian governments and command or mixed economic systems and toward democratic political institutions and free market economic systems.
3. The attractiveness of a country as a market and/or investment site depends on balancing the likely long-run benefits of doing business in that country against the likely costs and risks.
4. The benefits of doing business in a country are a function of the size of the market (population), its present wealth (purchasing power), and its future growth prospects. By investing early in countries that are currently poor but are nevertheless growing rapidly, firms can gain first-mover advantages that will pay back substantial dividends in the future.
5. The costs of doing business in a country tend to be greater where political payoffs are required to gain market access, where supporting infrastructure is lacking or underdeveloped, and where adhering to local laws and regulations is costly.
6. The risks of doing business in a country tend to be greater in countries that are politically unstable, subject to economic mismanagement, and lacking a legal system to provide adequate safeguards in the case of contract or property rights violations.

Critical Thinking and Discussion Questions

1. What is the relationship among property rights, corruption, and economic progress? How important are anticorruption efforts in the effort to improve a country's level of economic development?
2. You are a senior manager in a U.S. automobile company considering investing in production facilities in China, Russia, or Germany. These facilities will serve local market demand. Evaluate the benefits, costs, and risks associated with doing business in each nation. Which country seems the most attractive target for foreign direct investment? Why?
3. Reread the Country Focus on India, and answer the following questions:
    a. What kind of economic system did India operate under during 1947–1990? What kind of system is it moving toward today? What are the impediments to completing this transformation?
    b. How might widespread public ownership of businesses and extensive government regulations have affected (*i*) the efficiency of state and private businesses and (*ii*) the rate of new business formation in India during the 1947–1990 time frame? How do you think these factors affected the rate of economic growth in India during this time frame?
    c. How would privatization, deregulation, and the removal of barriers to foreign direct investment affect the efficiency of business, new business formation, and the rate of economic growth in India during the post-1990 time period?
    d. India now has pockets of strengths in key high-technology industries such as software and pharmaceuticals. Why do you think India is developing strength in these areas? How might success in these industries help generate growth in the other sectors of the Indian economy?
    e. Given what is now occurring in the Indian economy, do you think the country represents an attractive target for inward investment by foreign multinationals selling consumer products? Why?

globalEDGE Research Task

globalEDGE.msu.edu

Use the globalEDGE™ website (globaledge.msu.edu) to complete the following exercises:

1. Increased instability in the global marketplace can introduce unanticipated risks in a company's daily transactions. As such, your company must evaluate these *commercial transaction* risks for its foreign operations in Argentina, China, Egypt, Poland, and South Africa. A risk analyst at your firm said that you could evaluate both the political and commercial risk of these countries simultaneously. Provide a commercial transaction risk overview of all five countries for top management. In your evaluation, indicate possible corrective measures in the countries with considerably high political and/or commercial risk.
2. Managers at your firm are very concerned about the influence of terrorism on its long-term strategy. To counter this issue, the CEO has indicated you must identify the countries where *terrorism threat* and political risk are minimal. This will provide the basis for the development of future company facilities, which need to be built in all major continents in the world. Include recommendations on which countries in each continent would serve as a good candidate for your company to further analyze.

Political and Economic Reform in Myanmar

closing case

For decades, the Southeast Asian nation of Myanmar (formerly known as Burma) was an international pariah. Ruled by a brutal military dictatorship since the 1960s, political dissent was not tolerated, the press was tightly controlled, and opposition parties were shut down. Much economic activity was placed in the hands of the state—which effectively meant the hands of the military elite, who siphoned off economic profits for their own benefit. Corruption was rampant. In the 1990s, America and the European Union imposed sweeping economic sanctions on the country to punish the military junta for stealing elections and jailing opponents. The de facto leader of the country's democratic opposition movement, Nobel Peace Prize–winner Aung San Suu Kyi, was repeatedly placed under house arrest from 1989 through 2010.

None of this was good for the country's economy. Despite having a wealth of natural resources, including timber, minerals, oil, and gas, the economy stagnated while its Southeast Asian neighbors flourished. By 2012, Myanmar's GDP per capita was $1,400. In neighboring Thailand, it was $10,000 per capita. The economy was still largely rural, with 70 percent of the country's nearly 60 million people involved in agriculture. This compares with 8.6 percent in Thailand. Few people own cars or cell phones, and there are no major road or rail links between Myanmar and its neighbors—China, India, and Thailand.

In 2010, the military again won elections that were clearly rigged. Almost no one expected any changes, but the new president, Thein Sein, was to defy expectations. The government released hundreds of political prisoners, removed restrictions on the press, freed Aung San Suu Kyi, and allowed opposition parties to contest seats in a series of by-elections. When Aung San Suu Kyi won a by-election, thrashing her military-backed opponent, they let her take the seat, raising hopes that Myanmar was at last joining the modern world. In response, both America and the European Union began to lift their sanctions.

Thein Sein also started to initiate much-needed economic reforms. Even before the 2010 elections, the military had begun to quietly privatize state-owned enterprises, although many were placed in the hands of cronies of the regime. In 2012, Thein Sein stated that the government would continue to reduce its role in a wide range of sectors, including energy, forestry, health care, finance, and telecommunications. Land reforms are also under way. The government also abandoned the official fixed exchange rate for the Myanmar currency, the kyat, replacing it with a managed float. From 2001 to 2012, the official exchange rate for the kyat varied between 5.75 and 6.70 per U.S. dollar, while the black-market rate was between 750 and 1,335 per U.S. dollar. The official fixed exchange rate had effectively priced Myanmar's exports out of the world market, although it did benefit the military elite who were able to exchange their worthless kyat for valuable U.S. dollars on very favorable terms. Implemented in April 2012, the managed float valued the kyat at 818 per U.S. dollar. The dramatic fall in the value of the kyat is expected to stimulate demand for exports from Myanmar and help the economy grow.

To further encourage economic growth, the government signaled that it would welcome foreign direct investment and encouraged foreign enterprises to enter into partnerships with domestic enterprises in its underdeveloped telecommunications sector. General Electric and IBM are among the companies stating that they may invest in the country. Between 2010 and 2014, Myanmar recorded the largest increase in inward FDI of any country in Southeast Asia apart from the Philippines, although admittedly from a low base.

In November 2015, general elections were held in Myanmar. These were the first free and fair elections in 25 years. The results were stunning. The opposition party, the National League for Democracy, led by Anug San Suu Kyi, won 81 percent of the seats in parliament, sweeping the military-backed government out of office. It now seems likely that Myanmar will finally emerge from its isolation.

Sources: Lex Rieffel, "Myanmar's Economy Confronts Tough Policy Challenges," *East Asian Forum,* July 31, 2012; "Opening Soon: Myanmar Gets Ready for Business," *The Economist,* March 3, 2012; "Myanmar on the Move," *The Economist,* November 21, 2012; CIA World Factbook, 2015, www.cia.gov/library/publications; "An Unfinished Peace," *The Economist,* March 11, 2015; "A New Era," *The Economist,* November 14, 2015.

CASE DISCUSSION QUESTIONS

1. What explains the economic stagnation of Myanmar until very recently?
2. What do you think motivated the government of Myanmar to start undertaking political and economic reforms from 2010 onward?
3. How would you characterize the nature of the economic reforms now being implemented in Myanmar? What is the government trying to do here? What do you think the results will be?
4. What potential impediments do you think might stand in the way of further improvements in Myanmar?
6. In November 2015, the democratic opposition won a landslide victory in a general election. How do you think this will impact upon Myanmar's economic growth trajectory going forward? What are the risks here?

Endnotes

1. World Bank, *World Development Indicators Online*, 2016.
2. P. Sinha and N. Singh, "The Economy's Black Hole," *The Times of India*, March 22, 2010. EU estimates for 2012 can be found at http://ec.europa.eu/europe2020/pdf/themes/07_shadow_economy.pdf.
3. A. Sen, *Development as Freedom* (New York: Knopf, 1999).
4. G. M. Grossman and E. Helpman, "Endogenous Innovation in the Theory of Growth," *Journal of Economic Perspectives* 8, no. 1 (1994), pp. 23–44; P. M. Romer, "The Origins of Endogenous Growth," *Journal of Economic Perspectives* 8, no. 1 (1994), pp. 2–22.
5. W. W. Lewis, *The Power of Productivity* (Chicago: University of Chicago Press, 2004).
6. F. A. Hayek, *The Fatal Conceit: Errors of Socialism* (Chicago: University of Chicago Press, 1989).
7. J. Gwartney, R. Lawson, and W. Block, *Economic Freedom of the World: 1975–1995* (London: Institute of Economic Affairs, 1996).
8. D. North, *Institutions, Institutional Change, and Economic Performance* (Cambridge, UK: Cambridge University Press, 1991). See also K. M. Murphy, A. Shleifer, and R. Vishney, "Why Is Rent Seeking So Costly to Growth?," *American Economic Review* 83, no. 2 (1993), pp. 409–14; K. E. Maskus, "Intellectual Property Rights in the Global Economy," Institute for International Economics, 2000.
9. North, *Institutions, Institutional Change and Economic Performance*.
10. H. de Soto, *The Mystery of Capital: Why Capitalism Triumphs in the West and Fails Everywhere Else* (New York: Basic Books, 2000).
11. A. O. Hirschman, "The On-and-Off Again Connection between Political and Economic Progress," *American Economic Review* 84, no. 2 (1994), pp. 343–48; A. Przeworski and F. Limongi, "Political Regimes and Economic Growth," *Journal of Economic Perspectives* 7, no. 3 (1993), pp. 51–59.
12. Hirschman, A.O., "The On-and-Off Again Connection between Political and Economic Progress," *American Economic Review*, vol. 84, no. 2, 1994, p. 343–48.
13. For details of this argument, see M. Olson, "Dictatorship, Democracy, and Development," *American Political Science Review*, September 1993.
14. For example, see Jared Diamond's Pulitzer Prize–winning book, *Guns, Germs, and Steel* (New York: Norton, 1997). Also see J. Sachs, "Nature, Nurture and Growth," *The Economist*, June 14, 1997, pp. 19–22; J. Sachs, *The End of Poverty* (New York: Penguin Books, 2005).
15. Sachs, J., "Nature, Nurture and Growth," *The Economist*, June 14, 1997, p. 19–22.
16. "What Can the Rest of the World Learn from the Classrooms of Asia?," *The Economist*, September 21, 1996, p. 24.
17. J. Fagerberg, "Technology and International Differences in Growth Rates," *Journal of Economic Literature* 32 (September 1994), pp. 1147–75.
18. See The Freedom House Survey Team, "Freedom in the World 2015" and associated materials, www.freedomhouse.org.
19. "Russia Downgraded to Not Free," *Freedom House* (Press Release), December 20, 2004, www.freedomhouse.org.
20. Freedom House, "Democracies Century: A Survey of Political Change in the Twentieth Century, 1999," www.freedomhouse.org.
21. L. Conners, "Freedom to Connect," *Wired*, August 1997, pp. 105–6.
22. Fukuyama, F., "The End of History," *The National Interest*, vol. 16, Summer 1989, p. 18.
23. S. P. Huntington, *The Clash of Civilizations and the Remaking of World Order* (New York: Simon & Schuster, 1996).
24. Ibid., p. 116.
25. U.S. National Counterterrorism Center, *Reports on Incidents of Terrorism, 2005*, April 11, 2006.
26. S. Fisher, R. Sahay, and C. A. Vegh, "Stabilization and the Growth in Transition Economies: The Early Experience," *Journal of Economic Perspectives* 10 (Spring 1996), pp. 45–66.
27. M. Miles et al., *2016 Index of Economic Freedom* (Washington, DC: Heritage Foundation, 2016).
28. International Monetary Fund, *World Economic Outlook: Focus on Transition Economies* (Geneva: IMF, October 2000).
29. J. C. Brada, "Privatization Is Transition—Is It?," *Journal of Economic Perspectives*, Spring 1996, pp. 67–86.
30. See S. Zahra et al., "Privatization and Entrepreneurial Transformation," *Academy of Management Review* 3, no. 25 (2000), pp. 509–24.

31. N. Brune, G. Garrett, and B. Kogut, "The International Monetary Fund and the Global Spread of Privatization," *IMF Staff Papers* 51, no. 2 (2003), pp. 195–219.

32. Fischer et al., "Stabilization and Growth in Transition Economies."

33. "China 2030," World Bank, 2012.

34. J. Sachs, C. Zinnes, and Y. Eilat, "The Gains from Privatization in Transition Economies: Is Change of Ownership Enough?," CAER discussion paper no. 63 (Cambridge, MA: Harvard Institute for International Development, 2000).

35. M. S. Borish and M. Noel, "Private Sector Development in the Visegrad Countries," World Bank, March 1997.

36. "Caught between Right and Left," *The Economist*, March 8, 2007.

37. For a discussion of first-mover advantages, see M. Liberman and D. Montgomery, "First-Mover Advantages," *Strategic Management Journal* 9 (Summer Special Issue, 1988), pp. 41–58.

38. S. H. Robock, "Political Risk: Identification and Assessment," *Columbia Journal of World Business*, July–August 1971, pp. 6–20.

Differences in Culture

learning objectives

After reading this chapter, you will be able to:

- LO4-1 Explain what is meant by the culture of a society.
- LO4-2 Identify the forces that lead to differences in social culture.
- LO4-3 Identify the business and economic implications of differences in culture.
- LO4-4 Recognize how differences in social culture influence values in business.
- LO4-5 Demonstrate an appreciation for the economic and business implications of cultural change.

Source: © Ashok Saxena/Alamy Stock Photo

World Expo 2020 in Dubai, UAE

opening case

The United Arab Emirates (UAE) was established in 1971 and is a country located in the Middle East. The country is often called "the Emirates" or simply "UAE." UAE borders the Gulf of Oman and the Persian Gulf. Neighboring countries include Oman and Saudi Arabia, and UAE shares sea borders with Quatar, Iran, and Pakistan. Strategically, UAE is in an important location along the southern approaches to the Strait of Hormuz, a transit point for the world's crude oil. UAE is also in the top 10 countries for the largest oil reserves in the world.

The geography of UAE includes lots of rolling sand dunes of desert and also mountains in the eastern part of the country. The government consists of a federation with specified powers delegated to the UAE federal government and other powers reserved to the member emirates (equivalent to principalities). The chief of state is the president and the head of government is the prime minister. UAE has an open-market economy in which the prices of products and services are set using a free price system.

The foundation for this market economy lies in the collaboration between the seven emirates that are part of the UAE. They include the emirates of Abu Dhabi, Ajman, Dubai, Fujairah, Ras al-Khaimah, Sharjah, and Umm al-Quwain. Each emirate is governed by a hereditary emir, a system similar to succession planning in countries with royalty (king or queen) as the head of state. These emirs jointly make up the Federal Supreme Council, which serves as the highest legislative and executive body in the UAE. One of the seven emirs is selected as the president of the United Arab Emirates. The capital of the country is Abu Dhabi, Islam is the official religion, and Arabic is the official language. Most people have heard of Abu Dhabi and Dubai because they are the country's centers of commercial and cultural activities. Dubai is UAE's most populous city, with more than 2 million people, and it has emerged as a true global city with an eclectic cultural makeup. It also has a strategic location as a business gateway for the Middle East and Africa for multinational enterprises from all of the world's continents.

Dubai has frequently been rated as one of the best places to live in the Middle East (although it is also one of the most expensive). The emirate of Dubai has been ruled by the Al Maktoum family since 1833; the emirate is considered a constitutional monarchy. In 2013, the Norway-based Global Network for Rights and Development ranked UAE as the 14th country in its annual International Human Rights Indicator report. This was a first among Arab countries, with the next Arab country on the list, Tunisia, at a distant 72nd place. Only about 10 percent of the population in Dubai are Arabs, with the remaining 90 percent being expatriates. Most of the expatriates are from Asia, with India (50 percent) and Pakistan (16 percent) prominently featured. The largest group of Westerners is from the United Kingdom.

–continued

With this eclectic cultural background, Dubai's bid to host the World Expo 2020 with a theme of "connecting minds, creating the future" makes sense both logically and strategically. The theme resonates well with issues related to culture. In essence, the theme illustrates and acknowledges differences in culture (as does this chapter), and the theme supports the notion that we strive to emphasize similarities across the globe. Today, multinational enterprises have to evaluate their core uniqueness and how they can leverage this strategic uniqueness in the global marketplace. The leveraging of the uniqueness typically requires a focus on similarities across cultures instead of differences. Connecting minds is a great way to illustrate how people, companies, and countries can stress the importance of looking for similarities first and then focus on the similarities that outweigh the differences in creating strategic options.

As with any World Expo, the expectation is that the world will be treated to an important event in the year 2020 in Dubai. The Expo on "connecting minds, creating the future" will span six months, following the World Expo 2017 in Astana, Kazakhstan. The expectation is also that countries will showcase who they are and what they can do in the spirit of today's era of "nation branding." Tracing history, the best-known first World Expo was held in the Crystal Palace in Hyde Park, London (United Kingdom), in 1851 under the title "Great Exhibition of the Works of Industry of All Nations." Since 1928, the Bureau International des Expositions (International Exhibitions Bureau) has served as an international sanctioning body for the World Expo. These Expo showcases have generally gone through three eras: the era of industrialization (1851–1938), the era of cultural exchange (1939–1987), and the era of nation branding (1988–present).

The theme for Dubai's World Expo 2020 is a direct connection to its cultural values and beliefs in facilitating connections and pioneering new ideas. The organizers expect 70 percent of the 25 million visitors to originate outside UAE, making it the most globally oriented World Expo in the event's long history. The idea is that the global community will come together and explore creative and pioneering solutions to three key drivers of global development: sustainability, mobility, and opportunity. As viewed by the World Expo 2020 organizing team, sustainability centers on lasting sources of energy and water. Mobility focuses on smart systems of logistics and transportation. And opportunity refers to new paths to economic development. •

Sources: Expo 2020, http://expo2020dubai.ae/en; globalEDGE™—United Arab Emirates. globaledge.msu.edu/countries/united-arab-emirates; A. Ahmed, "After Winning Expo, Emirate Fumes at Allies It Says Didn't Back It," *The New York Times*, January 6, 2014; S. Potter, "Expo 2020 Win to Boost Dubai Sukuk on Spending: Islamic Finance," *Bloomberg Businessweek*, November 27, 2013; "Dubai—It's Bouncing Back," *The Economist*, November 23, 2013.

Introduction

Cross-Cultural Literacy
Understanding how the culture of a country affects the way business is practiced.

In Chapters 2 and 3, we saw how national differences in political, economic, and legal systems influence the benefits, costs, and risks associated with doing business in different countries. In this chapter, we explore how differences in culture across and within countries can affect international business strategies and operations of small, medium, and large companies. Several themes run through this chapter. The first is that business success in a variety of countries requires cross-cultural literacy. By **cross-cultural literacy**, we mean an understanding of how cultural differences across and within nations can affect the way business is practiced. Global communications, global brands, fast cycle times, worldwide markets, technology, and global supply chains characterize today's world. This is an era in which the global village seems to be just around the corner. At the same time, it is sometimes easy to forget how different various cultures really are, even today.[1] Underneath the veneer of modernism and globalization, deep cultural differences often remain.[2]

The opening case deals with precisely this point. While the UAE is a well-known "headquarters" in the Middle East for business, the country is a clash of cultures between the many foreign workers and their lifestyles and the natives and their stricter beliefs regarding religion, social issues, and society. For example, the culture in Dubai (and all of the United Arab Emirates) is predominantly Islamic. The Islamic religion touches all aspects of everyday life in the UAE. These include day-to-day activities, festivals, cuisine, dresses, weddings, and other customs. This ultimately becomes a cultural clash between the very westernized and modernized shores of

Dubai, for example, and the emirate remaining close to its cultural heritage. In this chapter, we argue that it is important for foreign businesses to gain an understanding of the culture that prevails in those countries where they do business and that success requires a foreign enterprise to adapt to the culture of its host country.[3]

Another theme developed in this chapter is that a relationship may exist between culture and the cost of doing business in a country or region. Different cultures are more or less supportive of the capitalist mode of production and may increase or lower the costs of doing business. For example, some observers have argued that cultural factors lowered the costs of doing business in Japan and helped explain Japan's rapid economic ascent during the 1960s to 1980s.[4] Similarly, cultural factors can sometimes raise the costs of doing business. Historically, class divisions were an important aspect of British culture, and for a long time, firms operating in Great Britain found it difficult to achieve cooperation between management and labor. Class divisions led to a high level of industrial disputes in that country during the 1960s and 1970s and raised the costs of doing business relative to the costs in countries such as Germany, Japan, Norway, Sweden, and Switzerland, where class conflict was historically less prevalent.

The British example, however, brings us to another theme we explore in this chapter. Culture is not static. It can and does evolve, although the rate at which culture can change is the subject of some dispute. Generally, culture evolves as behaviors of people become ingrained in their values and norms. This means that after some time, when a person has behaved a certain way for a while, that person (and perhaps those around the person) adopts a cultural value mindset consistent with the type of behavior illustrated by the person's actions. Interestingly, this also involves how people view time.

Culture in society evolves when large population segments in a country or region adopt cultural values based on common ways of behaving. This cultural evolution is the reason important aspects of British culture have changed significantly over the past 30 years, and the changes have been reflected in weaker class distinctions and a lower level of industrial disputes.[5] Finally, it is important to note that multinational enterprises can themselves be engines of cultural change. In India, for example, McDonald's and other Western fast-food companies facilitated change in the dining culture of that nation, drawing them away from traditional restaurants and toward fast-food outlets.

Did You Know?
Did you know arriving late is expected in some cultures?

Visit your Connect SmartBook® to view a short video explanation from the authors.

What Is Culture?

LO 4-1
Explain what is meant by the culture of a society.

Scholars have never been able to agree on a simple definition of *culture*. In the 1870s, anthropologist Edward Tylor defined culture as "that complex whole which includes knowledge, belief, art, morals, law, custom, and other capabilities acquired by man as a member of society."[6] Since then hundreds of other definitions have been offered. At the basic level, Florence Kluckhohn and Fred Strodtbeck's values orientation theory illustrates that all culture definitions must answer a limited number of universal problems, that the value-based solutions are limited in number and universally known, and that different cultures have different preferences among them.[7] Following their work, other prominent culture specialists have supported the idea of a universal set of human values serving as the basis for culture, such as Milton Rokeach with his work on "the nature of human values" and Shalom Schwartz with his work on the "theory of basic human values."[8] Also supportive of this finite set of human values, Geert Hofstede, an expert on cross-cultural differences and management, defined culture as "the collective programming of the mind which distinguishes the members of one human group from another. Culture, in this sense, includes systems of values; and values are among the building blocks of culture."[9] Another complementary definition of culture comes from sociologists Zvi Namenwirth and Robert Weber, who see culture as a system of ideas and argue that these ideas constitute a design for living.[10]

Geert Hofstede, often viewed as the foremost expert on cross-cultural differences in international business, presents his work in Istanbul, Turkey, at the Academy of International Business conference in 2013.

Source: © Academy of international business (AIB)

Culture
A system of values and norms that are shared among a group of people and that when taken together constitute a design for living.

In our view, we subscribe to the definitions of both Hofstede and Namenwirth and Weber by viewing **culture** as a system of values and norms that are shared among a group of people and

Values

Abstract ideas about what a society believes to be good, right, and desirable.

Norms

Social rules and guidelines that prescribe appropriate behavior in particular situations.

Society

Group of people who share a common set of values and norms.

that when taken together constitute a design for living. By **values**, we mean abstract ideas about what a group believes to be good, right, and desirable. Put differently, values are shared assumptions about how things ought to be.[11] By **norms**, we mean the social rules and guidelines that prescribe appropriate behavior in particular situations. We shall use the term **society** to refer to a group of people sharing a common set of values and norms. While a society may be equivalent to a country, some countries harbor several societies or subcultures (i.e., they support multiple cultures), and some societies embrace more than one country (e.g., the Scandinavian countries of Denmark, Norway, and Sweden are often viewed as culturally being a part of one society in terms of the business marketplace).

VALUES AND NORMS

Values form the bedrock of a culture. They provide the context within which a society's norms are established and justified. They may include a society's attitudes toward such concepts as individual freedom, democracy, truth, justice, honesty, loyalty, social obligations, collective responsibility, the role of women, love, sex, marriage, and so on. Values are not just abstract concepts; they are invested with considerable emotional significance. People argue, fight, and even die over values such as freedom. Values are also often reflected in the political and economic systems of a society. As we saw in Chapter 2, democratic free market capitalism is a reflection of a philosophical value system that emphasizes individual freedom.[12]

Folkways

Routine conventions of everyday life.

Norms are the social rules that govern people's actions toward one another. Norms can be subdivided further into two major categories: folkways and mores. Both of these terms were coined by William Graham Sumner, an early American sociologist, in 1906. **Folkways** are the routine conventions of everyday life. Generally, folkways are actions of little moral significance. Rather, they are social conventions concerning things such as the appropriate dress code in a particular situation, good social manners, eating with the correct utensils, neighborly behavior, and the like. Although folkways define the way people are expected to behave, violation of them is not normally a serious matter. People who violate folkways may be thought of as eccentric or ill-mannered, but they are not usually considered to be evil or bad. In many countries, foreigners may initially be excused for violating folkways. However, with the increasing availability of information on folkways for the various countries in the world, businesspeople are increasingly expected to know about dress code in a particular situation, good social and professional manners, eating with the correct utensils, and general business etiquette. The evolution of norms now demand in many cases that business partners at least try to behave according to the folkways norms in the country in which they are doing business.

Planning on Doing Business Internationally?

If a company is planning to start exporting a product, there are two basic questions that need to be asked. Is the product ready to be exported? And, is the company ready to export the product? Culturally, the product is either ready for a global market or not (and, if not, the company can modify it if the market is important enough). Company readiness is much more culturally sensitive. Having the appropriate cultural knowledge and skills are important. If you have the basic information about a company, you can use globalEDGE™'s diagnostic tool called CORE (Company Readiness to Export) to assess both product and company readiness to be exported. Try it out; how much better do you think Microsoft, which is everywhere in the world, will score compared with Questcor Pharmaceuticals (questcor.com), which was ranked number one on *Forbes*' list of "America's Best Small Companies" in 2013?

Sources: globalEDGE's CORE diagnostic tool, http://globalEDGE.msu.edu; Badenhausen, K., "America's Best Small Companies," *Forbes*, October 9, 2013.

A good example of folkways concerns attitudes toward time in different countries. People are keenly aware of the passage of time in the United States and northern European cultures such as Germany, Netherlands, and the Scandinavian countries. Businesspeople are very conscious about scheduling their time and are quickly irritated when their time is wasted because a business associate is late for a meeting or if they are kept waiting. They talk about time as though it were money, as something that can be spent, saved, wasted, and lost.[13] Alternatively, in many Arabic, Latin, and African cultures, time has a more elastic character. Keeping to a schedule is viewed as less important than finishing an interaction with people. For example, an American businessperson might feel slighted if he or she is kept waiting for 30 minutes outside the office of a Latin American executive before a meeting. However, the Latin American person may simply be completing an interaction with an associate and view the information gathered from this as more important than sticking to a rigid schedule. The Latin American executive intends no disrespect, but due to a mutual misunderstanding about the importance of time, the American may see things differently. Similarly, Saudi Arabian attitudes toward time have been shaped by their nomadic Bedouin heritage, in which precise time played no real role and arriving somewhere "tomorrow" might mean next week. Like Latin Americans, many Saudis are unlikely to understand Westerners' obsession with precise time and schedules. Both Saudis and Westerners' need to adjust their expectations accordingly.

Folkways also include rituals and symbolic behavior. Rituals and symbols are the most visible manifestations of a culture and constitute the outward expression of deeper values. For example, upon meeting a foreign business executive, a Japanese executive will hold his business card in both hands and bow while presenting the card to the foreigner.[14] This ritual behavior is loaded with deep cultural symbolism. The card specifies the rank of the Japanese executive, which is a very important piece of information in a hierarchical society such as Japan. The bow is a sign of respect, and the deeper the angle of the bow, the greater the reverence one person shows for the other. The person receiving the card is expected to examine it carefully (Japanese often have business cards with Japanese printed on one side and English printed on the other), which is a way of returning respect and acknowledging the card giver's position in the hierarchy. The foreigner is also expected to bow when taking the card and to return the greeting by presenting the Japanese executive with his or her own card, similarly bowing in the process. To not do so and to fail to read the card that he or she has been given, instead casually placing it in a jacket, pocket, or purse, violates this important folkway and is considered rude.

Mores is a term that refers to norms that are more widely observed, have greater moral significance than other norms, and are central to the functioning of a society and to its social life. This means that mores have a much greater significance than folkways. Accordingly, violating mores can bring serious retribution, ill will, and collapse of any business deal in the making. Mores include such factors as indictments against theft, adultery, incest, and cannibalism. In many societies, certain mores have been enacted into law. Specifically, all advanced societies have laws against theft, incest, and cannibalism. However, there are also many differences among cultures. In the United States, for example, drinking alcohol is widely accepted, whereas in Saudi Arabia the consumption of alcohol is viewed as violating important social mores and is punishable by imprisonment (as some Western citizens working in Saudi Arabia have discovered). In some way, mores are being implemented differently depending on where you are and who you are. For example, like Saudi Arabia, the United Arab Emirates have laws against drinking alcohol in public places, but alcohol is often present and a part of business relationships involving Westerners in Dubai and elsewhere in the country (especially in the bars of luxury hotels).

Mores

Norms seen as central to the functioning of a society and to its social life.

CULTURE, SOCIETY, AND THE NATION-STATE We have defined a society as a group of people who share a common set of values and norms; that is, people who are bound together by a common culture. There is not a strict one-to-one correspondence between a society and a nation-state. Nation-states are political creations. While these nation-states are often studied for their "national identity," "national character," and even "competitive advantage of nations," in reality they may contain a single culture or several cultures.[15] Representative of a single culture setting, the French nation can be thought of as the political embodiment of French culture. However, the nation of Canada has at least three cultures—an Anglo culture, a French-speaking "Quebecois" culture, and a Native American culture. Similarly, many of the 55 African nations have important cultural differences among tribal groups, as exhibited in the early 1990s when Rwanda dissolved into a bloody civil war between two tribes, the Tutsis and Hutus. Africa is not alone in this regard. India, for example, is composed of many distinct cultural groups with their own rich history and traditions (e.g., Andhras, Gonds, Gujaratis, Marathas, Oriya, Rajputs, and Tamils).

At the other end of the scale are cultures that embrace several nations. Several scholars argue that we can speak of an Islamic society or culture that is shared by the citizens of many different nations in the Middle East, Asia, and Africa. As you will recall from Chapter 3, this view of expansive cultures that embrace several nations underpins Samuel Huntington's view of a world that is fragmented into different civilizations, including Western, Islamic, and Sinic (Chinese).[16]

To complicate things further, it is also possible to talk about culture at different levels. It is reasonable to talk about "American society" and "American culture," but there are several

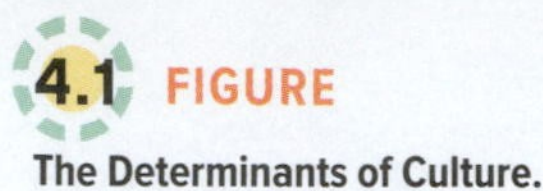

The Determinants of Culture.

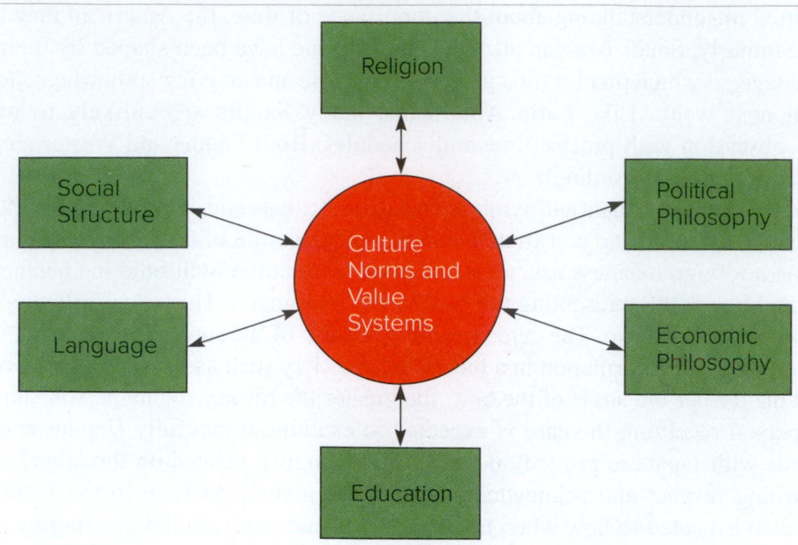

societies within America, each with its own culture. For example, in the United States of America, which is one country, one can talk about African American culture, Cajun culture, Chinese American culture, Hispanic culture, Indian culture, Irish American culture, and Southern culture. The relationship between culture and country is often ambiguous. Even if a country can be characterized as having a single homogeneous culture, often that national culture is a mosaic of subcultures. To abide by these cultural nuances, businesspeople should be aware of the delicate issues pertaining to folkways, as appropriate, and not violate mores in the country in which they intend to do business. Increased globalization has meant an increased number of business relationships across countries and cultures but not necessarily an increased culturally homogeneity in all parts of the world. Culture is still a complex phenomenon with multiple dimensions and multiple levels.[17]

Identify the forces that lead to differences in social culture.

THE DETERMINANTS OF CULTURE

The values and norms of a culture do not emerge fully formed. They evolve over time in response to a number of factors, including prevailing political and economic philosophies, the social structure of a society, and the dominant religion, language, and education (see Figure 4.1). We discussed political and economic philosophies in Chapter 2. Such philosophies clearly influence the value systems of a society. For example, the values found in communist North Korea toward freedom, justice, and individual achievement are clearly different from the values found in the United States, precisely because each society operates according to different political and economic philosophies. In the next sections of this chapter, we discuss the influence of social structure, religion, language, and education. The chain of causation runs both ways. While factors such as social structure and religion clearly influence the values and norms of a society, the values and norms of a society can influence social structure and religion.

test PREP

Use SmartBook to help retain what you have learned. Access your Instructor's Connect course to check out SmartBook or go to learnsmartadvantage.com for help.

Social Structure

Social Structure

The basic social organization of a society.

A society's **social structure** refers to its basic social organization, and this social organization is both emergent from and determinant of the behaviors of individuals. Although social structure consists of many different aspects, two dimensions are particularly important when explaining differences among cultures. The first is the degree to which the basic unit of a social organization is the individual, as opposed to the group. In general, Western societies tend to emphasize the importance of the individual, whereas groups tend to figure much larger in many other societies. The second dimension is the degree to which a society is stratified into classes or castes. Some societies are characterized by a relatively high degree of social stratification and relatively low mobility between strata (e.g., Indian); other societies are characterized by a low degree of social stratification and high mobility between strata (e.g., American).

INDIVIDUALS AND GROUPS

A **group** is an association of two or more individuals who have a shared sense of identity and who interact with each other in structured ways on the basis of a common set of expectations about each other's behavior.[18] Human social life is group life. Individuals are involved in families, work groups, social groups, recreational groups, and so on. In a way, social media have expanded the boundaries and what is included in group life and placed an added emphasis on what we can call the extended social groups. When research on social structure was developed, social media clearly did not enter into the equation of what was possible in terms of group life. This new form of social media group life has unique possibilities that affect both individuals within a social group and the group itself. For example, consumers are significantly more likely to buy from the brands they follow on Twitter and Facebook due to group influences. However, while groups are found in all societies, some societies differ according to the degree to which the group is viewed as the primary means of social organization.[19] In some societies, individual attributes and achievements are viewed as being more important than group membership; in others, the reverse is true.

Group

An association of two or more individuals who have a shared sense of identity and who interact with each other in structured ways on the basis of a common set of expectations about each other's behavior.

The Individual

In Chapter 2, we discussed individualism as a political philosophy. However, individualism is more than just an abstract political philosophy. In many Western societies, the individual is the basic building block of social organization. This is reflected not just in the political and economic organization of society but also in the way people perceive themselves and relate to each other in social and business settings. The value systems of many Western societies, for example, emphasize individual achievement. The social standing of individuals is not so much a function of whom they work for as of their individual performance in whatever work setting they choose. More and more, individuals are regarded as "independent contractors" even though they belong to and work for a company. These individuals, in essence, build their personal brands by the knowledge, skills, and experience that they have; which often translates to increased salaries and promotions at the current company or another company that believes that it can benefit from that person's capabilities. In science, the label "star scientist" has become synonymous with these individualistic high-producers of innovative products based on their knowledge, skills, and experience.[20]

LO 4-3

Identify the business and economic implications of differences in culture.

The emphasis on individual performance in many Western societies has both beneficial and harmful aspects. In the United States, the emphasis on individual performance finds expression in an admiration of rugged individualism, entrepreneurship, and innovation. One benefit of this is the high level of entrepreneurial activity in the United States and other Western societies. Entrepreneurial individuals in the United States have created many new products and new ways of doing business (e.g., personal computers, photocopiers, computer software, biotechnology, supermarkets, and discount retail stores). One can argue that the dynamism of the U.S. economy owes much to the philosophy of individualism. Highly individualistic societies are often synonymous with people who are capable and have the capacity to constantly innovate by their creative ideas for products and services.

Individualism also finds expression in a high degree of managerial mobility between companies, as our "personal brand" example illustrated earlier, and this is not always a good thing. Although moving from company to company may be good for individual managers who are trying to build impressive résumés, it is not necessarily a good thing for companies. The lack of loyalty and commitment to an individual company and the tendency to move on for a better offer can result in managers who have good general skills but lack the knowledge, experience, and network of interpersonal contacts that come from years of working within the same company. An effective manager draws on company-specific experience, knowledge, and a network of contacts to find solutions to current problems, and companies may suffer if their managers lack these attributes. One positive aspect of high managerial mobility is that executives are exposed to different ways of doing business. The ability to compare business practices helps executives identify how good practices and techniques developed in one firm might be profitably applied to other firms.

Is Social Class Determined by Income?

In the text, we said that a class system is a less rigid form of social stratification in which social mobility is possible. It is a form of open stratification in which the position a person has by birth can be changed through his or her own achievements or luck. Social class can broadly be divided into three levels, including upper (or rich), middle, and lower (or poor). These levels appear to be tied to income, but does a high income automatically bring power and prestige? Is it the income that should determine social class, or is it the social class that will determine the income? Or, is income just a small portion of social class status?

Source: D. Francis, "Where Do You Fall in the American Economic Class System?" *US News and World Report*, September 13, 2012.

The Group In contrast to the Western emphasis on the individual, the group is the primary unit of social organization in many other societies. For example, in Japan, the social status of an individual has traditionally been determined as much by the standing of the group to which he or she belongs as by his or her individual performance.[21] In traditional Japanese society, the group was the family or village to which an individual belonged. Today, the group has frequently come to be associated with the work team or business organization to which an individual belongs. In a now-classic study of Japanese society, Nakane noted how this expresses itself in everyday life:

> When a Japanese faces the outside (confronts another person) and affixes some position to himself socially he is inclined to give precedence to institution over kind of occupation. Rather than saying, "I am a typesetter" or "I am a filing clerk," he is likely to say, "I am from B Publishing Group" or "I belong to S company."[22]

Nakane goes on to observe that the primacy of the group to which an individual belongs often evolves into a deeply emotional attachment in which identification with the group becomes all-important in one's life. One central value of Japanese culture is the importance attached to group membership. This may have beneficial implications for business firms. Strong identification with the group is argued to create pressures for mutual self-help and collective action. If the worth of an individual is closely linked to the achievements of the group (e.g., firm), as Nakane maintains is the case in Japan, this creates a strong incentive for individual members of the group to work together for the common good. Some argue that the success of some Japanese enterprises in the global economy has been based partly on their ability to achieve close cooperation between individuals within a company and between companies. This has found expression in the widespread diffusion of self-managing work teams within Japanese organizations; the close cooperation among different functions within Japanese companies (e.g., among manufacturing, marketing, and R&D); and the cooperation between a company and its suppliers on issues such as design, quality control, and inventory reduction.[23] In all these cases, cooperation is driven by the need to improve the performance of the group (i.e., the business firm).

The primacy of the value of group identification also discourages managers and workers from moving from company to company. Lifetime employment in a particular company was long the norm in certain sectors of the Japanese economy (estimates suggest that between 20 and 40 percent of all Japanese employees have formal or informal lifetime employment guarantees). Over the years, managers and workers build up knowledge, experience, and a network of interpersonal business contacts. All these things can help managers perform their jobs more effectively and achieve cooperation with others.

However, the primacy of the group is not always beneficial. Just as U.S. society is characterized by a great deal of dynamism and entrepreneurship, reflecting the primacy of values associated with individualism, some argue that Japanese society is characterized by a corresponding lack of dynamism and entrepreneurship. Although the long-run consequences are unclear, one implication is that the United States could continue to create more new industries than Japan and continue to be more successful at pioneering radically new products and new ways of doing business. By most estimates, the United States has led the world in innovation for some time, especially radically new products and services, and the country's individualism is a strong contributor to this innovative mindset. At the same time, some group-oriented countries such as Japan also do well in innovation, especially nonradical "normal" innovations, according to the GE Global Innovation Barometer.[24] This is an indication that multiple paths to being innovative exists in both individualistic and group-oriented cultures, drawing from the uniqueness of the particular culture and what core competencies are reflected in the culture.[25]

Identify the forces that lead to differences in social culture.

Social Strata
Hierarchical social categories often based on family background, occupation, and income.

SOCIAL STRATIFICATION

All societies are stratified on a hierarchical basis into social categories—that is, into **social strata**. These strata are typically defined on the basis of socioeconomic characteristics such as family background, occupation, and income. Individuals are born into a particular stratum. They become a member of the social category to which their parents belong. Individuals born into a stratum toward the top of the social hierarchy tend to have better life chances than those born into a stratum toward the bottom of the hierarchy. They are likely to have better education, health, standard of living, and work opportunities. Although all societies are stratified to some degree, they differ in two related ways. First, they differ from each other with regard to the degree of mobility between social strata. Second, they differ with regard to the significance attached to social strata in business contexts. Overall, social stratification is based on four basic principles:[26]

1. Social stratification is a trait of society, not a reflection of individual differences.
2. Social stratification carries over a generation to the next generation.
3. Social stratification is generally universal but variable.
4. Social stratification involves not just inequality but also beliefs.

Social Mobility The term **social mobility** refers to the extent to which individuals can move out of the strata into which they are born. Social mobility varies significantly from society to society. The most rigid system of stratification is a caste system. A **caste system** is a closed system of stratification in which social position is determined by the family into which a person is born, and change in that position is usually not possible during an individual's lifetime. Often, a caste position carries with it a specific occupation. Members of one caste might be shoemakers, members of another might be butchers, and so on. These occupations are embedded in the caste and passed down through the family to succeeding generations. Although the number of societies with caste systems diminished rapidly during the twentieth century, one partial example still remains. India has four main castes and several thousand subcastes. Even though the caste system was officially abolished in 1949, two years after India became independent, it is still a force in rural Indian society where occupation and marital opportunities are still partly related to caste (for more details, see the accompanying Country Focus on the caste system in India today).[27]

Social Mobility
The extent to which individuals can move out of the social strata into which they are born.

Caste System
A system of social stratification in which social position is determined by the family into which a person is born, and change in that position is usually not possible during an individual's lifetime.

country FOCUS

India Still Has a Caste System

Modern India is a country of dramatic contrasts. Its information technology (IT) sector is among the most vibrant in the world with companies such as Tata Consultancy Services, Cognizant Technology Solutions, Infosys, and Wipro emerging as powerful global players. Cognizant is an interesting company in that it was founded as a technology arm of Dun & Bradstreet (USA) in 1994 but is typically considered an Indian IT company because a majority of its employees are based in India. In fact, many IT companies locate or operate in India because of its strong IT knowledge, human capital, and culture.

Traditionally, India has had one of the strongest caste systems in the world. Somewhat sadly, this caste system still exists today, and many Indians actually prefer it this way! At the core, the caste system has no legality in India, and discrimination against lower castes is illegal. India has also enacted numerous new laws and social initiatives to protect and improve living conditions of lower castes in the country. Historically, however, India's caste system was an impediment to social mobility. But the stranglehold on people's socioeconomic conditions is steadily becoming a fading memory among the educated, urban middle-class Indians who make up the majority of employees in the high-tech economy. Unfortunately, the same is not true in rural India, where some 70 percent of the nation's population still resides. There caste remains a pervasive influence.

For example, a young female engineer at Infosys who grew up in a small rural village and is a *dalit* (sometimes called a "scheduled caste") recounts how she never entered the house of a *Brahmin,* India's elite priestly caste, even though half of her village were *Brahmins*. When a *dalit* was hired to cook at the school in her native village, *Brahmins* withdrew their children from the school. The engineer herself is the beneficiary of a charitable training scheme that Infosys launched in 2006. Her caste, making up about 16 percent of the country (or around 165 million people), is among the poorest in India, with some 91 percent making less than $100 a month, compared to 65 percent of *Brahmins*.

To try to correct this historic inequality, politicians have talked for years about extending the employment quota system to private enterprises. The government has told private companies to hire more *dalits* and members of tribal communities and warned that "strong measures" will be taken if companies do not comply. Private employers are resisting attempts to impose quotas, arguing with some justification that people who are guaranteed a job by a quota system are unlikely to work very hard.

At the same time, progressive employers realize they need to do something to correct the inequalities, and unless India taps into the lower castes, it may not be able to find the employees required to staff rapidly growing high-technology enterprises. Thus, the Confederation of Indian Industry recently introduced a package of *dalit*-friendly measures, including scholarships for bright lower-caste children. Building on this, Infosys is leading the way among high-tech enterprises. The company provides special training to low-caste engineering graduates who have failed to get a job in industry after graduation. While the training does not promise employment, so far almost all graduates who completed the seven-month training program have been hired by Infosys and other enterprises. Infosys programs are privatized version of the education offered in India to try to break down India's caste system.

Sources: B. Hardzinski; S. Grillot; and M.Addison, "Breaking Down India's Caste System through Education," *KGOU,* November 29, 2013, http://kgou.org; "With Reservations: Business and Caste in India," *The Economist,* October 6, 2007, pp. 81–83; Eric Bellman, "Reversal of Fortune Isolates India's Brahmins," *The Wall Street Journal,* December 24, 2007, p. 4.

Class System

A system of social stratification in which social status is determined by the family into which a person is born and by subsequent socioeconomic achievements; mobility between classes is possible.

A **class system** is a less rigid form of social stratification in which social mobility is possible. It is a form of open stratification in which the position a person has by birth can be changed through his or her own achievements or luck. Individuals born into a class at the bottom of the hierarchy can work their way up; conversely, individuals born into a class at the top of the hierarchy can slip down.

While many societies have class systems, social mobility within a class system varies from society to society. For example, some sociologists have argued that Britain has a more rigid class structure than certain other Western societies, such as the United States.[28] Historically, British society was divided into three main classes: the upper class, which was made up of individuals whose families for generations had wealth, prestige, and occasionally power; the middle class, whose members were involved in professional, managerial, and clerical occupations; and the working class, whose members earned their living from manual occupations. The middle class was further subdivided into the upper-middle class, whose members were involved in important managerial occupations and the prestigious professions (e.g., lawyers, accountants, doctors), and the lower-middle class, whose members were involved in clerical work (e.g., bank tellers) and the less prestigious professions (e.g., schoolteachers).

The British class system exhibited significant divergence between the life chances of members of different classes. The upper and upper-middle classes typically sent their children to a select group of private schools, where they wouldn't mix with lower-class children and where they picked up many of the speech accents and social norms that marked them as being from the higher strata of society. These same private schools also had close ties with the most prestigious universities, such as Oxford and Cambridge. Until fairly recently, Oxford and Cambridge guaranteed a certain number of places for the graduates of these private schools. Having been to a prestigious university, the offspring of the upper and upper-middle classes then had an excellent chance of being offered a prestigious job in companies, banks, brokerage firms, and law firms run by members of the upper and upper-middle classes.

In contrast, the members of the British working and lower-middle classes typically went to state schools. The majority left at age 16, and those who went on to higher education found it more difficult to get accepted at the best universities. When they did, they found that their lower-class accent and lack of social skills marked them as being from a lower social stratum, which made it more difficult for them to get access to the most prestigious jobs.

Because of this, the class system in Britain perpetuated itself from generation to generation, and mobility was limited. Although upward mobility was possible, it could not normally be achieved in one generation. While an individual from a working-class background may have established an income level that was consistent with membership in the upper-middle class, he or she may not have been accepted as such by others of that class due to accent and background. However, by sending his or her offspring to the "right kind of school," the individual could ensure that his or her children were accepted.

According to some commentators, modern British society is now rapidly leaving behind this class structure and moving toward a classless society. However, sociologists continue to dispute this finding and present evidence that this is not the case. For example, one study reported that state schools in the London Borough (suburb) of Islington, which now has a population of 215,000, had only 79 candidates for university, while one prestigious private school alone, Eton, sent more than that number to Oxford and Cambridge.[29] This, according to the study's authors, implies that "money still begets money." They argue that a good school means a good university, a good university means a good job, and merit has only a limited chance of elbowing its way into this tight little circle. In another recent survey of the empirical literature, a sociologist noted that class differentials in educational achievement have changed surprisingly little over the last few decades in many societies, despite assumptions to the contrary.[30]

The class system in the United States is less pronounced than in Britain and mobility is greater. Like Britain, the United States has its own upper, middle, and working classes. However, class membership is determined to a much greater degree by individual economic achievements, as opposed to background and schooling. Thus, an individual can, by his or her own economic achievement, move smoothly from the working class to the upper class in a lifetime. Successful individuals from humble origins are highly respected in American society.

Another society for which class divisions have historically been of some importance has been China, where there has been a long-standing difference between the life chances of the rural peasantry and urban dwellers. Ironically, this historic division was strengthened during the high point of communist rule because of a rigid system of household registration that restricted most Chinese to the place of their birth for their lifetime. Bound to collective farming, peasants were cut off from many urban privileges—compulsory education, quality schools, health care, public housing, varieties of foodstuffs, to name only a few—and they largely lived in poverty. Social mobility was thus very limited. This system crumbled following reforms of the a few decades ago, and as a consequence, migrant peasant laborers have flooded into China's cities looking for work. Sociologists now hypothesize that a new class system is emerging in China based less on the rural-urban divide and more on urban occupation.[31]

LO 4-3
Identify the business and economic implications of differences in culture.

Significance From a business perspective, the stratification of a society is significant if it affects the operation of business organizations. In American society, the high degree of social mobility and the extreme emphasis on individualism limit the impact of class background on business operations. The same is true in Japan, where most of the population perceives itself to be middle class. In a country such as Great Britain, however, the relative lack of class mobility and the differences between classes have resulted in the emergence of class consciousness. **Class consciousness** refers to a condition by which people tend to perceive themselves in terms of their class background, and this shapes their relationships with members of other classes.

Class Consciousness
A tendency for individuals to perceive themselves in terms of their class background.

This has been played out in British society in the traditional hostility between upper-middle-class managers and their working-class employees. Mutual antagonism and lack of respect historically made it difficult to achieve cooperation between management and labor in many British companies and resulted in a relatively high level of industrial disputes. However, the past two decades have seen a dramatic reduction in industrial disputes, which bolsters the arguments of those who claim that the country is moving toward a classless society. Alternatively, as noted earlier, class consciousness may be reemerging in urban China, and it may ultimately prove to be significant there.

test PREP
Use SmartBook to help retain what you have learned. Access your Instructor's Connect course to check out SmartBook or go to learnsmartadvantage.com for help.

An antagonistic relationship between management and labor classes, and the resulting lack of cooperation and high level of industrial disruption, tends to raise the costs of production in countries characterized by significant class divisions. In turn, this can make it more difficult for companies based in such countries to establish a competitive advantage in the global economy.

Religious and Ethical Systems

LO 4-2
Identify the forces that lead to differences in social culture.

Religion may be defined as a system of shared beliefs and rituals that are concerned with the realm of the sacred.[32] An **ethical system** refers to a set of moral principles, or values, that are used to guide and shape behavior.[33] Most of the world's ethical systems are the product of religions. Thus, we can talk about Christian ethics and Islamic ethics. However, there is a major exception to the principle that ethical systems are grounded in religion. Confucianism and Confucian ethics influence behavior and shape culture in parts of Asia, yet it is incorrect to characterize Confucianism as a religion.

Religion
A system of shared beliefs and rituals concerned with the realm of the sacred.

Ethical System
A set of moral principles, or values, that is used to guide and shape behavior.

The relationship among religion, ethics, and society is subtle and complex. Among the thousands of religions in the world today, four dominate in terms of numbers of adherents: Christianity with roughly 2.20 billion adherents, Islam with around 1.60 billion adherents, Hinduism with 1.10 billion adherents (primarily in India), and Buddhism with about 535 million adherents (see Map 4.1). Although many other religions have an important influence in certain parts of the modern world (e.g., Shintoism in Japan, with roughly 40 million followers, and Judaism, which has 18 million adherents and accounts for 75 percent of the population of Israel), their numbers pale in comparison with these dominant religions (although as the precursor of both Christianity and Islam, Judaism has an indirect influence that goes beyond its numbers). We review these four religions, along with Confucianism, focusing on their potential economic and business implications.

Some scholars have theorized that the most important business implications of religion center on the extent to which different religions shape attitudes toward work and entrepreneurship and the degree to which the religious ethics affects the costs of doing business in a country. However, it is hazardous to make sweeping generalizations about the nature of the relationship between religion and ethical systems and business practice. While some professionals argue that there is a

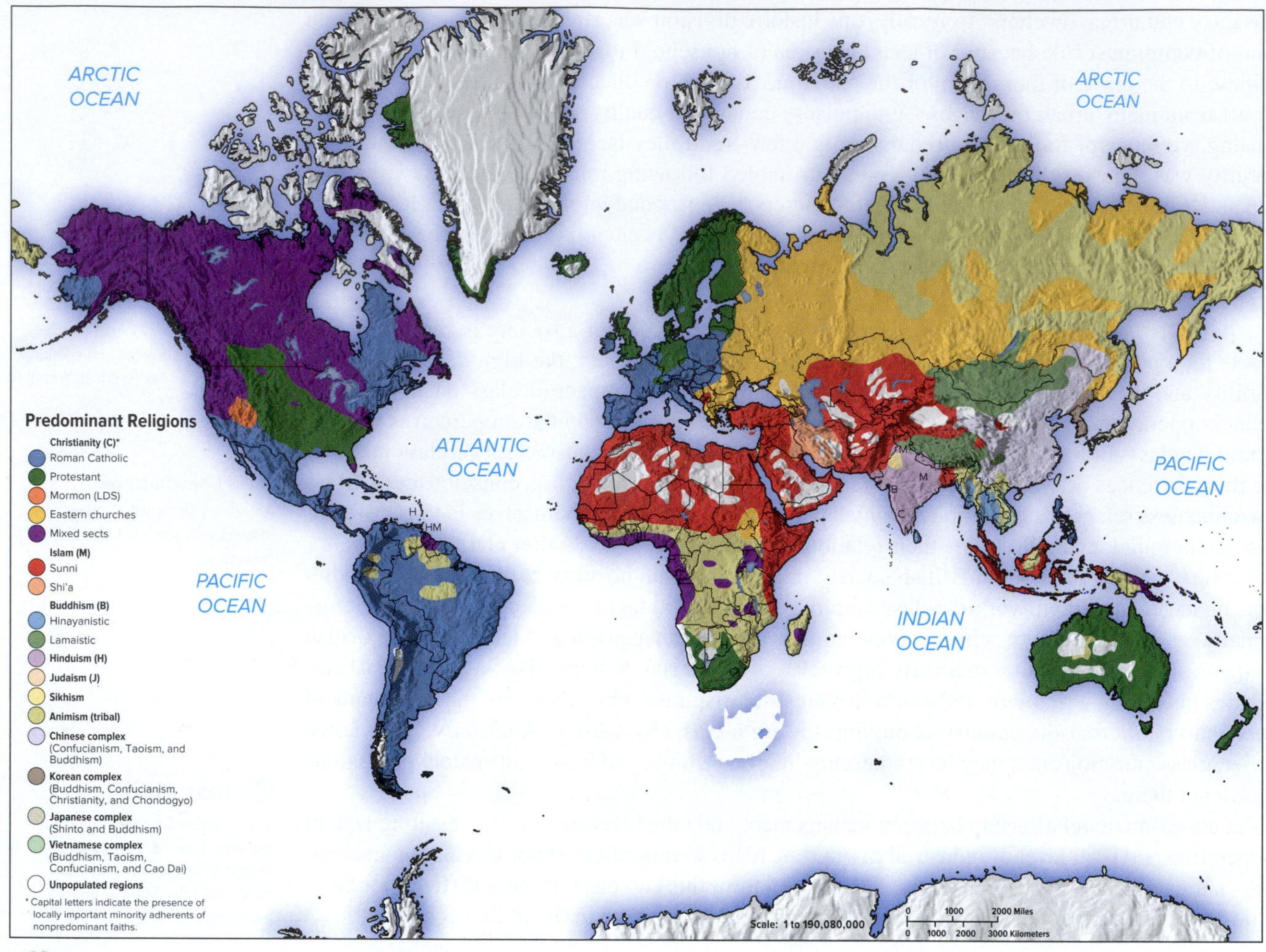

4.1 MAP

World Religions.

Source: "Map 14," Allen, John L., *Student Atlas of World Politics*, 10th ed. McGraw-Hill Education.

relationship between religious and ethical systems and business practice in a society, in a world where nations with Catholic, Protestant, Muslim, Hindu, and Buddhist majorities all show evidence of entrepreneurial activity and sustainable economic growth, it is important to view such proposed relationships with a degree of skepticism. The proposed relationships may exist, but their impact may be small compared with the impact of economic policy. On the other hand, research by economists Robert Barro and Rachel McCleary does suggest that strong religious beliefs, particularly beliefs in heaven, hell, and an afterlife, have a positive impact on economic growth rates, irrespective of the particular religion in question.[34] Barro and McCleary looked at religious beliefs and economic growth rates in 59 countries. Their conjecture was that higher religious beliefs stimulate economic growth because they help sustain aspects of individual behavior that lead to higher productivity.

CHRISTIANITY Christianity is the most widely practiced religion in the world with some 2.20 billion followers. The vast majority of Christians live in Europe and the Americas, although their numbers are growing rapidly in Africa. Christianity grew out of Judaism. Like Judaism, it is a monotheistic religion (monotheism is the belief in one God). A religious division in the eleventh century led to the establishment of two major Christian organizations—the Roman Catholic Church and the Orthodox Church. Today, the Roman Catholic Church accounts for more than half of all Christians, most of whom are found in southern Europe and Latin America. The Orthodox Church, while less influential, is still of major importance in several countries (e.g., Greece and Russia). In the sixteenth century, the Reformation led to a further split with Rome; the result was Protestantism. The nonconformist nature of Protestantism has facilitated the emergence of numerous denominations under the Protestant umbrella (e.g., Baptist, Methodist, Calvinist).

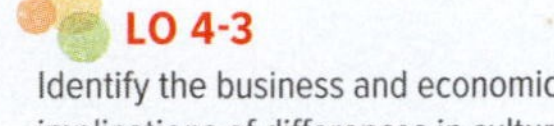

Identify the business and economic implications of differences in culture.

Economic Implications of Christianity

Several sociologists have argued that of the main branches of Christianity—Catholic, Orthodox, and Protestant—the latter has the most important economic implications. In 1904, prominent German sociologist Max Weber made a connection between Protestant ethics and "the spirit of capitalism" that has since become famous.[35] Weber noted that capitalism emerged in western Europe, where

> business leaders and owners of capital, as well as the higher grades of skilled labor, and even more the higher technically and commercially trained personnel of modern enterprises, are overwhelmingly Protestant.[36]

Weber theorized that there was a relationship between Protestantism and the emergence of modern capitalism. He argued that Protestant ethics emphasizes the importance of hard work and wealth creation (for the glory of God) and frugality (abstinence from worldly pleasures). According to Weber, this kind of value system was needed to facilitate the development of capitalism. Protestants worked hard and systematically to accumulate wealth. However, their ascetic beliefs suggested that rather than consuming this wealth by indulging in worldly pleasures, they should invest it in the expansion of capitalist enterprises. Thus, the combination of hard work and the accumulation of capital, which could be used to finance investment and expansion, paved the way for the development of capitalism in western Europe and subsequently in the United States. In contrast, Weber argued that the Catholic promise of salvation in the next world, rather than this world, did not foster the same kind of work ethic.

Protestantism also may have encouraged capitalism's development in another way. By breaking away from the hierarchical domination of religious and social life that characterized the Catholic Church for much of its history, Protestantism gave individuals significantly more freedom to develop their own relationship with God. The right to freedom of form of worship was central to the nonconformist nature of early Protestantism. This emphasis on individual religious freedom may have paved the way for the subsequent emphasis on individual economic and political freedoms and the development of individualism as an economic and political philosophy. As we saw in Chapter 2, such a philosophy forms the bedrock on which entrepreneurial free market capitalism is based. Building on this, some scholars claim there is a connection between individualism, as inspired by Protestantism, and the extent of entrepreneurial activity in a nation.[37] Again, we must be careful not to generalize too much from this historical sociological view. While nations with a strong Protestant tradition such as Britain, Germany, and the United States were early leaders in the Industrial Revolution, nations with Catholic or Orthodox majorities show significant and sustained entrepreneurial activity and economic growth in the modern world.

Identify the forces that lead to differences in social culture.

ISLAM

With about 1.60 billion adherents, Islam is the second largest of the world's major religions. Islam dates to A.D. 610 when the Prophet Muhammad began spreading the word, although the Muslim calendar begins in A.D. 622 when, to escape growing opposition, Muhammad left Mecca for the oasis settlement of Yathrib, later known as Medina. Adherents of Islam are referred to as Muslims. Muslims constitute a majority in more than 40 countries and inhabit a nearly contiguous stretch of land from the northwest coast of Africa, through the Middle East, to China and Malaysia in the Far East.

Islam has roots in both Judaism and Christianity (Islam views Jesus Christ as one of God's prophets). Like Christianity and Judaism, Islam is a monotheistic religion. The central principle of Islam is that there is but the one true omnipotent God (Allah). Islam requires unconditional acceptance of the uniqueness, power, and authority of God and the understanding that the objective of life is to fulfill the dictates of His will in the hope of admission to paradise. According to Islam, worldly gain and temporal power are an illusion. Those who pursue riches on earth may gain them, but those who forgo worldly ambitions to seek the favor of Allah may gain the greater treasure: entry into paradise. Other major principles of Islam include (1) honoring and respecting parents, (2) respecting the rights of others, (3) being generous but not a squanderer, (4) avoiding killing except for justifiable causes, (5) not committing adultery, (6) dealing justly and equitably with others, (7) being of pure heart and mind, (8) safeguarding the possessions of orphans, and

(9) being humble and unpretentious.[38] Obvious parallels exist with many of the central principles of both Judaism and Christianity.

Islam is an all-embracing way of life governing the totality of a Muslim's being.[39] As God's surrogate in this world, a Muslim is not a totally free agent but is circumscribed by religious principles—by a code of conduct for interpersonal relations—in social and economic activities. Religion is paramount in all areas of life. The Muslim lives in a social structure that is shaped by Islamic values and norms of moral conduct. The ritual nature of everyday life in a Muslim country is striking to a Western visitor. Among other things, orthodox Muslim ritual requires prayer five times a day (business meetings may be put on hold while the Muslim participants engage in their daily prayer ritual), demands that women should be dressed in a certain manner, and forbids the consumption of pork and alcohol.

Islamic Fundamentalism

The past three decades have witnessed the growth of a social movement often referred to as Islamic fundamentalism.[40] In the West, Islamic fundamentalism is associated in the media with militants, terrorists, and violent upheavals, such as the bloody conflict occurring in Algeria, the killing of foreign tourists in Egypt, and the September 11, 2001, attacks on the World Trade Center and Pentagon in the United States. This characterization is misleading. Just as Christian fundamentalists are motivated by sincere and deeply held religious values firmly rooted in their faith, so are Islamic fundamentalists. A small minority of radical "fundamentalists" who have hijacked the religion to further their own political and violent ends perpetrates the violence that the Western media associates with Islamic fundamentalism. (Some Christian "fundamentalists" have done exactly the same, including Jim Jones and David Koresh.) The vast majority of Muslims point out that Islam teaches peace, justice, and tolerance, not violence and intolerance, and that Islam explicitly repudiates the violence that a radical minority practices.

The rise of Islamic fundamentalism has no one cause. In part, it is a response to the social pressures created in traditional Islamic societies by the move toward modernization and by the influence of Western ideas, such as liberal democracy, materialism, equal rights for women, and attitudes toward sex, marriage, and alcohol. In many Muslim countries, modernization has been accompanied by a growing gap between a rich urban minority and an impoverished urban and rural majority. For the impoverished majority, modernization has offered little in the way of tangible economic progress, while threatening the traditional value system. Thus, for a Muslim who cherishes his or her traditions and feels that his or her identity is jeopardized by the encroachment of alien Western values, Islamic fundamentalism has become a cultural anchor.

Fundamentalists demand commitment to traditional religious beliefs and rituals. The result has been a marked increase in the use of symbolic gestures that confirm Islamic values. In areas where fundamentalism is strong, women have resumed wearing floor-length, long-sleeved dresses and covering their hair; religious studies have increased in universities; the publication of religious tracts has increased; and public religious orations have risen.[41] Also, the sentiments of some fundamentalist groups are often anti-Western. Rightly or wrongly, Western influence is blamed for a range of social ills, and many fundamentalists' actions are directed against Western governments, cultural symbols, businesses, and even individuals.

In several Muslim countries, fundamentalists have gained political power and have used this to try to make Islamic law (as set down in the Koran, the bible of Islam) the law of the land. There are grounds for this in Islam doctrine. Islam makes no distinction between church and state. It is not just a religion; Islam is also the source of law, a guide to statecraft, and an arbiter of social behavior. Muslims believe that every human endeavor is within the purview of the faith—and this includes political activity—because the only purpose of any activity is to do God's will.[42] (Some Christian fundamentalists also share this view.) Muslim fundamentalists have been most successful in Iran, where a fundamentalist party has held power since 1979, but they also have had an influence in many other countries, such as Afghanistan (where the Taliban established an extreme fundamentalist state until removed by the U.S.-led coalition in 2002), Algeria, Egypt, Pakistan, Saudi Arabia, and the Sudan.

LO 4-3
Identify the business and economic implications of differences in culture.

Economic Implications of Islam

The Koran establishes some explicit economic principles, many of which are pro–free enterprise.[43] The Koran speaks approvingly of free enterprise and of earning legitimate profit through trade and commerce (the Prophet Muhammad himself was once a trader). The protection of the right to private property is also embedded within Islam, although Islam asserts that all property is a favor from Allah (God), who created and so owns everything. Those who hold property are regarded as trustees rather than owners in the Western sense of the word. As trustees, they are entitled to receive profits from the property but are admonished to use it in a righteous, socially beneficial, and prudent manner. This reflects Islam's concern with social justice. Islam is critical of those who earn profit through the exploitation of others. In the Islamic view of the world, humans are part of a collective in which the wealthy and successful have obligations to help the disadvantaged. Put simply, in Muslim countries, it is fine to earn a profit, so long as that profit is justly earned and not based on the exploitation of others for one's own advantage. It also helps if those making profits undertake charitable acts to help the poor. Furthermore, Islam stresses the importance of living up to contractual obligations, keeping one's word, and abstaining from deception. For a closer look at how Islam, capitalism, and globalization can coexist, see the accompanying Country Focus about the region around Kayseri in central Turkey.

Given the Islamic proclivity to favor market-based systems, Muslim countries are likely to be receptive to international businesses as long as those businesses behave in a manner that is consistent with Islamic ethics, customs, and business practices. Businesses that are perceived as making an unjust profit through the exploitation of others, by deception, or by breaking contractual obligations are unlikely to be welcomed in an Islamic country. In addition, in Islamic countries where fundamentalism is on the rise, hostility toward Western-owned businesses is likely to increase.

One economic principle of Islam prohibits the payment or receipt of interest, which is considered usury. This is not just a matter of theology; in several Islamic states, it is also a matter of law. The Koran clearly condemns interest, which is called *riba* in Arabic, as exploitative and unjust. For many years, banks operating in Islamic countries conveniently ignored this condemnation, but starting in the 1970s with the establishment of an Islamic bank in Egypt, Islamic banks opened in

country FOCUS

Turkey and Islam

For years now, Turkey has been lobbying the European Union to allow it to join the free trade bloc as a member state. If the EU says yes, it will be the first Muslim state in the union. But this is unlikely to happen any time soon; after all, it has been half a century in the making!

Many critics in the EU worry that Islam and Western-style capitalism do not mix well and that, as a consequence, allowing Turkey into the EU would be a mistake. However, a close look at what is going on in Turkey suggests this view may be misplaced. Consider the area around the city of Kayseri in central Turkey. Many dismiss this poor, largely agricultural region of Turkey as a non-European backwater, far removed from the secular bustle of Istanbul. It is a region where traditional Islamic values hold sway. And yet it is a region that has produced so many thriving Muslim enterprises that it is sometimes called the "Anatolian Tiger." Businesses based here include large food manufacturers, textile companies, furniture manufacturers, and engineering enterprises, many of which export a substantial percentage of their production.

Local business leaders attribute the success of companies in the region to an entrepreneurial spirit that they say is part of Islam. They point out that the Prophet Muhammad, who was himself a trader, preached merchant honor and commanded that 90 percent of a Muslim's life be devoted to work in order to put food on the table. Outside observers have gone further, arguing that what is occurring around Kayseri is an example of Islamic Calvinism, a fusion of traditional Islamic values and the work ethic often associated with Protestantism in general and Calvinism in particular.

However, not everyone agrees that Islam is the driving force behind the region's success. Saffet Arslan, the managing director of Ipek, the largest furniture producer in the region (which exports to more than 30 countries), says another force is at work: globalization! According to Arslan, over the past three decades, local Muslims who once eschewed making money in favor of focusing on religion are now making business a priority. They see the Western world, and Western capitalism, as a model, not Islam, and because of globalization and the opportunities associated with it, they want to become successful.

If there is a weakness in the Islamic model of business that is emerging in places such as Kayseri, some say it can be found in traditional attitudes toward the role of women in the workplace and the low level of female employment in the region. According to a report by the European Stability Initiative, the same group that holds up the Kayseri region as an example of Islamic Calvinism, the low participation of women in the local workforce is the Achilles' heel of the economy and may stymie the attempts of the region to catch up with the countries of the European Union.

Sources: "Turkey's Future Forward to the Past: Can Turkey's Past Glories Be Revived by Its Grandiose Islamist President?," *The Economist*, January 3, 2015. www.economist.com; Bilefsky, D., "Turks Knock on Europe's Door with Evidence That Islam and Capitalism Can Coexist," *The New York Times*, August 27, 2006, p. 4; European Stability Initiative, *Islamic Calvinists*, September 19, 2005, archived at www.esiweb.org.

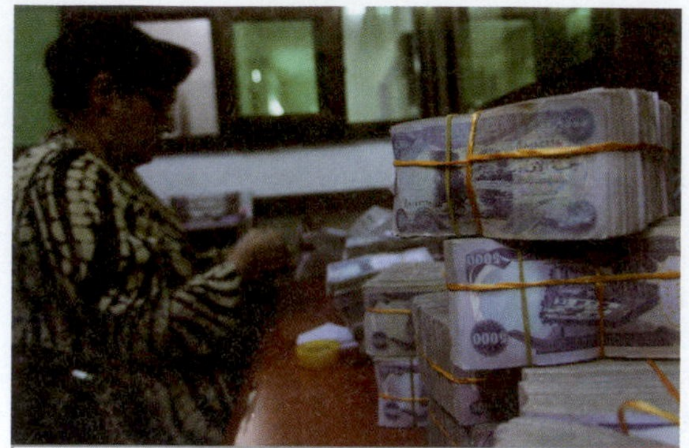

Islamic banks function differently than conventional banks in the world, as the Islamic banks cannot pay or charge interest.

Source: © Ali Al Saadi/AFP/Getty Images

predominantly Muslim countries. Now there are hundreds of Islamic banks in more than 50 countries with assets of around $1.6 trillion; plus more than $1 trillion is managed by mutual funds that adhere to Islamic principles.[44] Even conventional banks are entering the market: both Citigroup and HSBC, two of the world's largest financial institutions, now offer Islamic financial services. While only Iran and the Sudan enforce Islamic banking conventions, in an increasing number of countries, customers can choose between conventional banks and Islamic banks.

Conventional banks make a profit on the spread between the interest rate they have to pay to depositors and the higher interest rate they charge borrowers. Because Islamic banks cannot pay or charge interest, they must find a different way of making money. Islamic banks have experimented with two different banking methods—the *mudarabah* and the *murabaha.*[45]

A *mudarabah* contract is similar to a profit-sharing scheme. Under *mudarabah,* when an Islamic bank lends money to a business, rather than charging that business interest on the loan, it takes a share in the profits that are derived from the investment. Similarly, when a business (or individual) deposits money at an Islamic bank in a savings account, the deposit is treated as an equity investment in whatever activity the bank uses the capital for. Thus, the depositor receives a share in the profit from the bank's investment (as opposed to interest payments) according to an agreed-upon ratio. Some Muslims claim this is a more efficient system than the Western banking system because it encourages both long-term savings and long-term investment. However, there is no hard evidence of this, and many believe that a *mudarabah* system is less efficient than a conventional Western banking system.

The second Islamic banking method, the *murabaha* contract, is the most widely used among the world's Islamic banks, primarily because it is the easiest to implement. In a *murabaha* contract, when a firm wishes to purchase something using a loan—let's say a piece of equipment that costs $1,000—the firm tells the bank after having negotiated the price with the equipment manufacturer. The bank then buys the equipment for $1,000, and the borrower buys it back from the bank at some later date for, say, $1,100, a price that includes a $100 markup for the bank. A cynic might point out that such a markup is functionally equivalent to an interest payment, and it is the similarity between this method and conventional banking that makes it so much easier to adopt.

LO 4-2
Identify the forces that lead to differences in social culture.

HINDUISM Hinduism has approximately 1.10 billion adherents, most of them on the Indian subcontinent. Hinduism began in the Indus Valley in India more than 4,000 years ago, making it the world's oldest major religion. Unlike Christianity and Islam, its founding is not linked to a particular person. Nor does it have an officially sanctioned sacred book such as the Bible or the Koran. Hindus believe that a moral force in society requires the acceptance of certain responsibilities, called *dharma*. Hindus believe in reincarnation, or rebirth into a different body, after death. Hindus also believe in *karma,* the spiritual progression of each person's soul. A person's karma is affected by the

globalEDGE | **Culture on globalEDGE**

The "Culture" section of globalEDGE™ (globaledge.msu.edu/global-resources/culture) offers a variety of sources, information, and data on culture and international business. In addition, the "Insights by Country" section (globaledge.msu.edu/global-insights/by/country), with coverage of more than 200 countries, has country-specific culture issues (e.g., what to do and not to do when visiting a country). These globalEDGE™ culture resources are nice complements to the material in Chapter 4. In this chapter, we cover a lot of material on culture, and Geert Hofstede's research has been the most influential on culture and business. globalEDGE™ has "The Hofstede Centre" as one of its cultural reference sources. This reference focuses on Hofstede's research on cultural dimensions, including scores on countries, regions, charts, and graphs. Are you interested in the scores for a country we do not illustrate in Table 4.1? If so, check out "The Hofstede Centre" and its "Culture Compass," and see what the scores are for your favored country.

way he or she lives. The moral state of an individual's karma determines the challenges he or she will face in the next life. By perfecting the soul in each new life, Hindus believe that an individual can eventually achieve *nirvana,* a state of complete spiritual perfection that renders reincarnation no longer necessary. Many Hindus believe that the way to achieve nirvana is to lead a severe ascetic lifestyle of material and physical self-denial, devoting life to a spiritual rather than material quest.

LO 4-3
Identify the business and economic implications of differences in culture.

Economic Implications of Hinduism

Max Weber, famous for expounding on the Protestant work ethic, also argued that the ascetic principles embedded in Hinduism do not encourage the kind of entrepreneurial activity in pursuit of wealth creation that we find in Protestantism.[46] According to Weber, traditional Hindu values emphasize that individuals should be judged not by their material achievements but by their spiritual achievements. Hindus perceive the pursuit of material well-being as making the attainment of nirvana more difficult. Given the emphasis on an ascetic lifestyle, Weber thought that devout Hindus would be less likely to engage in entrepreneurial activity than devout Protestants.

Mahatma Gandhi, the famous Indian nationalist and spiritual leader, was certainly the embodiment of Hindu asceticism. It has been argued that the values of Hindu asceticism and self-reliance that Gandhi advocated had a negative impact on the economic development of postindependence India.[47] But we must be careful not to read too much into Weber's rather old arguments. Modern India is a very dynamic entrepreneurial society, and millions of hardworking entrepreneurs form the economic backbone of the country's rapidly growing economy, especially in the information technology sector.[48]

Historically, Hinduism also supported India's caste system. The concept of mobility between castes within an individual's lifetime makes no sense to traditional Hindus. Hindus see mobility between castes as something that is achieved through spiritual progression and reincarnation. An individual can be reborn into a higher caste in his or her next life if he or she achieves spiritual development in this life. Although the caste system has been abolished in India, as discussed earlier in the chapter, it still casts a long shadow over Indian life.

LO 4-2
Identify the forces that lead to differences in social culture.

BUDDHISM

Buddhism, with some 535 million adherents, was founded in the sixth century B.C. by Siddhartha Gautama in what is now Nepal. Siddhartha renounced his wealth to pursue an ascetic lifestyle and spiritual perfection. His adherents claimed he achieved nirvana but decided to remain on earth to teach his followers how they, too, could achieve this state of spiritual enlightenment. Siddhartha became known as the Buddha (which means "the awakened one"). Today, most Buddhists are found in Central and Southeast Asia, China, Korea, and Japan. According to Buddhism, suffering originates in people's desires for pleasure. Cessation of suffering can be achieved by following a path for transformation. Siddhartha offered the Noble Eightfold Path as a route for transformation. This emphasizes right seeing, thinking, speech, action, living, effort, mindfulness, and meditation. Unlike Hinduism, Buddhism does not support the caste system. Nor does Buddhism advocate the kind of extreme ascetic behavior that is encouraged by Hinduism. Nevertheless, like Hindus, Buddhists stress the afterlife and spiritual achievement rather than involvement in this world.

LO 4-3
Identify the business and economic implications of differences in culture.

Economic Implications of Buddhism

The emphasis on wealth creation that is embedded in Protestantism is historically not found in Buddhism. Thus, in Buddhist societies, we do not see the same kind of cultural stress on entrepreneurial behavior that Weber claimed could be found in the Protestant West. But unlike Hinduism, the lack of support for the caste system and extreme ascetic behavior suggests that a Buddhist society may represent a more fertile ground for entrepreneurial activity than a Hindu culture. In effect, innovative ideas and entrepreneurial activities may take hold throughout society independent of which caste a person may belong to, but again, each culture is uniquely oriented toward its own types of entrepreneurial behavior.

In Buddhism, societies were historically more deeply rooted to their local place in the natural world.[49] This means that economies were more localized, with relations between people and also between culture and nature being relatively unmediated. In the modern economy, complex technologies and large-scale social institutions have led to a separation between people and also between people and the natural world. Plus, as the economy grows, it is difficult to understand and appreciate the potential effects people have on the natural world. Both of these separations are the antithetical to the Buddha's teachings.

Interestingly, recent trends actually bring in the "Zen" orientation from Buddhism into business in the Western world.[50] By 2013, there were 657 live trademarks containing the word *Zen* in them in the United States alone, according to the U.S. Patent and Trademark Office. "In business, 'Zen' is often a synonym for ordinary nothingness," blogged Nancy Friedman, a corporate copywriter who consults with businesses on naming and branding. She said that "*Zen* can be combined with *mail* to describe 'an incoming e-mail message with no message or attachments.' *Zen spin* is a verb meaning 'to tell a story without saying anything at all.' And *to zen* a computing problem means to figure it out in an intuitive flash—perhaps while you're plugged into the earphones of your ZEN MP3 player, now available from Creative with a 16Gb capacity."[51]

LO 4-2
Identify the forces that lead to differences in social culture.

CONFUSIANISM

Confucianism was founded in the fifth century B.C. by K'ung-Fu-tzu, more generally known as Confucius. For more than 2,000 years until the 1949 communist revolution, Confucianism was the official ethical system of China. While observance of Confucian ethics has been weakened in China since 1949, many people still follow the teachings of Confucius, principally in China, Korea, and Japan. Confucianism teaches the importance of attaining personal salvation through right action. Although not a religion, Confucian ideology has become deeply embedded in the culture of these countries over the centuries and, through that, has an impact on the lives of many millions more.[52] Confucianism is built around a comprehensive ethical code that sets down guidelines for relationships with others. High moral and ethical conduct and loyalty to others are central to Confucianism. Unlike religions, Confucianism is not concerned with the supernatural and has little to say about the concept of a supreme being or an afterlife.

LO 4-3
Identify the business and economic implications of differences in culture.

Economic Implications of Confucianism

Some scholars maintain that Confucianism may have economic implications as profound as those Weber argued were to be found in Protestantism, although they are of a different nature.[53] Their basic thesis is that the influence of Confucian ethics on the culture of China, Japan, South Korea, and Taiwan, by lowering the costs of doing business in those countries, may help explain their economic success. In this regard, three values central to the Confucian system of ethics are of particular interest: loyalty, reciprocal obligations, and honesty in dealings with others.

In Confucian thought, loyalty to one's superiors is regarded as a sacred duty—an absolute obligation. In modern organizations based in Confucian cultures, the loyalty that binds employees to the heads of their organization can reduce the conflict between management and labor that we find in more class-conscious societies. Cooperation between management and labor can be achieved at a lower cost in a culture where the virtue of loyalty is emphasized in the value systems.

However, in a Confucian culture, loyalty to one's superiors, such as a worker's loyalty to management, is not blind loyalty. The concept of reciprocal obligations is important. Confucian ethics stresses that superiors are obliged to reward the loyalty of their subordinates by bestowing blessings on them. If these "blessings" are not forthcoming, then neither will be the loyalty. This Confucian ethic is central to the Chinese concept of *guanxi,* which refers to relationship networks supported by reciprocal obligations.[54] *Guanxi* means relationships, although in business settings it can be better understood as connections. Today, Chinese will often cultivate a *guanxiwang,* or "relationship network," for help. Reciprocal obligations are the glue that holds such networks together. If those obligations are not met—if favors done are not paid back or reciprocated—the reputation of the transgressor is tarnished, and the person will be less able to draw on his or her *guanxiwang* for help in the future. Thus, the implicit threat of social sanctions is often sufficient to ensure that favors are repaid, obligations are met, and relationships are honored. In a society that lacks a rule-based legal tradition, and thus legal ways of redressing wrongs such as violations of business agreements, *guanxi* is an important mechanism for building long-term business relationships and getting business done in China. For an example of the importance of *guanxi,* read the Management Focus on advertising in China.

A third concept found in Confucian ethics is the importance attached to honesty. Confucian thinkers emphasize that although dishonest behavior may yield short-term benefits for the transgressor, dishonesty does not pay in the long run. The importance attached to honesty has major economic implications. When companies can trust each other not to break contractual obligations, the costs of doing business are lowered. Expensive lawyers are not needed to resolve

management FOCUS

Advertising in China

In 1993, New Yorker Dan Mintz moved to China as a freelance film director with no contacts, no advertising experience, and no Mandarin skills. By 2009, the company he subsequently founded in China, DMG, had emerged as one of China's fastest-growing advertising agencies with a client list that includes Budweiser, Unilever, Sony, Nabisco, Audi, Volkswagen, China Mobile, and dozens of other Chinese brands. Mintz attributes his success in part to what the Chinese call *guanxi*.

Guanxi literally means relationships, although in business settings it can be better understood as connections. *Guanxi* has its roots in the Confucian philosophy of valuing social hierarchy and reciprocal obligations. Confucian ideology has a 2,000-year-old history in China. Confucianism stresses the importance of relationships, both within the family and between master and servant. Confucian ideology teaches that people are not created equal. In Confucian thought, loyalty and obligations to one's superiors (or to family) are regarded as a sacred duty, but at the same time, this loyalty has its price. Social superiors are obligated to reward the loyalty of their social inferiors by bestowing "blessings" upon them; thus, the obligations are reciprocal. Chinese will often cultivate a *guanxiwang,* or "relationship network," for help. There is a tacit acknowledgment that if you have the right *guanxi,* legal rules can be broken, or at least bent.

Mintz, who is now fluent in Mandarin, cultivated his *guanxiwang* by going into business with two young Chinese who had connections, Bing Wu and Peter Xiao. Wu, who works on the production side of the business, was a former national gymnastics champion, which translates into prestige and access to business and government officials. Xiao comes from a military family with major political connections. Together, these three have been able to open doors that long-established Western advertising agencies could not. They have done it in large part by leveraging the contacts of Wu and Xiao and by backing up their connections with what the Chinese call *Shi li,* the ability to do good work.

A case in point was DMG's campaign for Volkswagen, which helped the German company become ubiquitous in China. The ads used traditional Chinese characters, which had been banned by Chairman Mao during the cultural revolution in favor of simplified versions. To get permission to use the characters in film and print ads—a first in modern China—the trio had to draw on high-level government contacts in Beijing. They won over officials by arguing that the old characters should be thought of not as "characters" but as art. Later, they shot TV spots for the ad on Shanghai's famous Bund, a congested boulevard that runs along the waterfront of the old city. Drawing again on government contacts, they were able to shut down the Bund to make the shoot. Steven Spielberg had been able to close down only a portion of the street when he filmed *Empire of the Sun* there in 1986. DMG has also filmed inside Beijing's Forbidden City, even though it is against the law to do so. Using his contacts, Mintz persuaded the government to lift the law for 24 hours. As Mintz has noted, "We don't stop when we come across regulations. There are restrictions everywhere you go. You have to know how get around them and get things done."*

Today, DMG Entertainment is a Chinese-based production and distribution company. While it began as an advertising agency in 1993, the company started distributing non-Chinese movies in the Chinese market in the late 2000s (e.g., *Iron Man 3,* the sixth-highest-grossing film of all time in China) as well as producing Chinese films, the first being *Founding of a Republic* in 2009. This is a movie that marked the 60th anniversary of the People's Republic of China. In these new activities, DMG is also enjoying *guanxi* in the country. *Variety* reported that DMG benefited from "strong connections" with Chinese government officials and the state-run China Film Group Corporation.

*M. Graser, "Featured Player," *Variety,* October 18, 2004, p. 6.

Sources: A. Busch, "China's DMG and Valiant Entertainment Partner to Expand Superhero Universe," *Deadline Hollywood,* March 12, 2015; J. Bryan, "The Mintz Dynasty," *Fast Company,* April 2006, pp. 56–62; M. Graser, "Featured Player," *Variety,* October 18, 2004, p. 6.; C. Coonan, "DMG's Dan Mintz: Hollywood's Man in China," *Variety,* June 5, 2013.

contract disputes. In a Confucian society, people may be less hesitant to commit substantial resources to cooperative ventures than in a society where honesty is less pervasive. When companies adhere to Confucian ethics, they can trust each other not to violate the terms of cooperative agreements. Thus, the costs of achieving cooperation between companies may be lower in societies such as Japan relative to societies where trust is less pervasive.

For example, it has been argued that the close ties between the automobile companies and their component parts suppliers in Japan are facilitated by a combination of trust and reciprocal obligations. These close ties allow the auto companies and their suppliers to work together on a range of issues, including inventory reduction, quality control, and design. The competitive advantage of Japanese auto companies such as Toyota may in part be explained by such factors.[55] Similarly, the combination of trust and reciprocal obligations is central to the workings and persistence of *guanxi* networks in China.

test PREP

Use SmartBook to help retain what you have learned. Access your Instructor's Connect course to check out SmartBook or go to learnsmartadvantage.com for help.

Language

One obvious way in which many countries differ is language. By language, we mean both the spoken and the unspoken means of communication. Language is one of the defining characteristics of a culture. Oftentimes, learning a language also entails learning a culture and vice versa. Some would even argue that a person cannot get entrenched in a culture without knowing its dominant language.

Can You Speak the Most Important Languages?

Mastering your own native language is critically important to doing business in your own home country. Mastering the language of a foreign country (or subcultures) with which you want to do business is also an added value in any cross-cultural relationship. English leads the way in terms of business languages, but which languages are important after English? Spanish? No, not necessarily. The three languages that are important for business after English are Mandarin Chinese, French, and Arabic. Spanish is fifth, so it is clearly important, but not as useful as English, Mandarin, French, and Arabic because of the number of people who speak these languages. Do you agree with the rank order of these languages? Why or why not? Did you know that you can now learn a new language online? Check out the Language Resources on globalEDGE™ (globalEDGE.msu.edu/global-resources/ language-resources), and learn a new language (including Mandarin, French, Arabic, and Spanish).

Source: S. Kim, "Top 3 Useful Foreign Languages for Business Excludes Spanish," *ABC News*, September 1, 2011. http://abcnews.go.com/blogs.

SPOKEN LANGUAGE Language does far more than just enable people to communicate with each other. The nature of a language also structures the way we perceive the world. The language of a society can direct the attention of its members to certain features of the world rather than others. The classic illustration of this phenomenon is that whereas the English language has but one word for snow, the language of the Inuit (Eskimos) lacks a general term for it. Instead, because distinguishing different forms of snow is so important in the lives of the Inuit, they have 24 words that describe different types of snow (e.g., powder snow, falling snow, wet snow, drifting snow).[56]

Because language shapes the way people perceive the world, it also helps define culture. Countries with more than one language often have more than one culture. Canada has an English-speaking culture and a French-speaking culture. Tensions between the two can run quite high, with a substantial proportion of the French-speaking minority demanding independence from a Canada "dominated by English speakers." The same phenomenon can be observed in many other countries. Belgium is divided into Flemish and French speakers, and tensions between the two groups exist; in Spain, a Basque-speaking minority with its own distinctive culture has been agitating for independence from the Spanish-speaking majority for decades; on the Mediterranean island of Cyprus, the culturally diverse Greek- and Turkish-speaking populations of the island continuously engage in some level of conflict. Based on the open conflict the countries had in the 1970s, the island is now partitioned into two parts. While it does not necessarily follow that language differences create differences in culture and, therefore, separatist pressures (e.g., witness the harmony in Switzerland, where four languages are spoken), there certainly seems to be a tendency in this direction.[57]

Mandarin (Chinese) is the mother tongue of the largest number of people, followed by English and Hindi, which is spoken in India. However, the most widely spoken language in the world is English, followed by French, Spanish, and Mandarin (i.e., many people speak English as a second language). And, English is increasingly becoming the language of international business. When Japanese and German businesspeople get together to do business, it is almost certain that they will communicate in English. However, although English is widely used, learning the local language yields considerable advantages. Most people prefer to converse in their own language, and being able to speak the local language can build rapport and goodwill, which may be very important for a business deal. International businesses that do not understand the local language can make major blunders through improper translation.

For example, the Sunbeam Corporation used the English words for its "Mist-Stick" mist-producing hair-curling iron when it entered the German market, only to discover after an expensive advertising campaign that *mist* means excrement in German. General Motors was troubled by the lack of enthusiasm among Puerto Rican dealers for its new Chevrolet Nova. When literally translated into Spanish, *nova* means star. However, when spoken it sounds like "no va," which in Spanish means "it doesn't go." General Motors changed the name of the car to Caribe.[58] Ford made a similar and somewhat embarrassing mistake in Brazil. The Ford Pinto may well have been a good car, but the Brazilians wanted no part of a car called "pinto," which is slang for tiny male genitals in Brazil. Even the world's largest furniture manufacturer, IKEA from Sweden, ran into branding issues when it named a plant pot "Jättebra" (which means great or superbly good in Swedish). Unfortunately, *Jättebra* resembles the Thai slang word for sex! As one final example, and there are numerous, of companies using product names, advertising slogans, and branding campaigns that translate poorly, Pepsi's slogan "come alive with the Pepsi Generation" did not quite work in China. People in China took it literally to mean "bring your ancestors back from the grave."

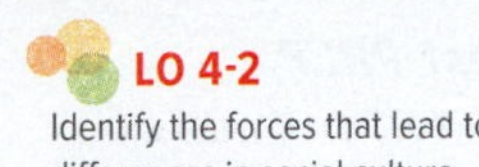

LO 4-2

Identify the forces that lead to differences in social culture.

UNSPOKEN LANGUAGE Unspoken language refers to nonverbal communication. We all communicate with each other by a host of nonverbal cues. The raising of eyebrows, for example, is a sign of recognition in most cultures, while a smile is a sign of joy. Many nonverbal cues, however, are culturally bound. A failure to understand the nonverbal cues of another culture can lead to a communication failure. For example, making a circle with the thumb and the forefinger is a friendly gesture in the United States, but it is a vulgar sexual invitation in Greece and Turkey. Similarly, while most Americans and Europeans use the thumbs-up gesture to indicate that "it's all right," in Greece the gesture is obscene.

Another aspect of nonverbal communication is personal space, which is the comfortable amount of distance between you and someone you are talking with. In the United States, the customary distance apart adopted by parties in a business discussion is five to eight feet. In Latin America, it is three to five feet. Consequently, many North Americans unconsciously feel that Latin Americans are invading their personal space and can be seen backing away from them during a conversation. Indeed, the American may feel that the Latin is being aggressive and pushy. In turn, the Latin American may interpret such backing away as aloofness. The result can be a regrettable lack of rapport between two businesspeople from different cultures.

test PREP

Use SmartBook to help retain what you have learned. Access your Instructor's Connect course to check out SmartBook or go to learnsmartadvantage.com for help.

Education

LO 4-2

Identify the forces that lead to differences in social culture.

Formal education plays a key role in a society. Formal education is the medium through which individuals learn many of the language, conceptual, and technical skills that are indispensable in a modern society. Formal education also supplements the family's role in socializing the young into the values and norms of a society. Values and norms are taught both directly and indirectly. Schools generally teach basic facts about the social and political nature of a society. They also focus on the fundamental obligations of citizenship. Cultural norms are also taught indirectly at school. Respect for others, obedience to authority, honesty, neatness, being on time, and so on, are all part of the "hidden curriculum" of schools. The use of a grading system also teaches children the value of personal achievement and competition.[59]

From an international business perspective, one important aspect of education is its role as a determinant of national competitive advantage.[60] The availability of a pool of skilled and knowledgeable workers is a major determinant of the likely economic success of a country. In analyzing the competitive success of Japan since 1945, for example, Michael Porter notes that after the war, Japan had almost nothing except for a pool of skilled and educated human resources:

> With a long tradition of respect for education that borders on reverence, Japan possessed a large pool of literate, educated, and increasingly skilled human resources. . . . Japan has benefited from a large pool of trained engineers. Japanese universities graduate many more engineers per capita than in the United States. . . . A first-rate primary and secondary education system in Japan operates based on high standards and emphasizes math and science. Primary and secondary education is highly competitive. . . . Japanese education provides most students all over Japan with a sound education for later education and training. A Japanese high school graduate knows as much about math as most American college graduates.[61]

Porter's point is that Japan's excellent education system is an important factor explaining the country's postwar economic success. Not only is a good education system a determinant of national competitive advantage, but it is also an important factor guiding the location choices of international businesses. The recent trend to outsource information technology jobs to India, for example, is partly due to the presence of significant numbers of trained engineers in India, which in turn is a result of the Indian education system. By the same token, it would make little sense to base production facilities that require highly skilled labor in a country where the education system was so poor that a skilled labor pool was not available, no matter how attractive the country might seem on other dimensions. It might make sense to base production operations that require only unskilled labor in such a country.

The general education level of a country is also a good index of the kind of products that might sell in a country and of the type of promotional material that should be used. As a direct

test PREP

Use SmartBook to help retain what you have learned. Access your Instructor's Connect course to check out SmartBook or go to learnsmartadvantage.com for help.

LO 4-4

Recognize how differences in social culture influence values in business.

Power Distance

Theory of how a society deals with the fact that people are unequal in physical and intellectual capabilities. High power distance cultures are found in countries that let inequalities grow over time into inequalities of power and wealth; low power distance cultures are found in societies that try to play down such inequalities as much as possible.

Individualism Versus Collectivism

Theory focusing on the relationship between the individual and his or her fellows; in individualistic societies, the ties between individuals are loose and individual achievement is highly valued; in societies where collectivism is emphasized, ties between individuals are tight, people are born into collectives, such as extended families, and everyone is supposed to look after the interests of his or her collective.

Uncertainty Avoidance

Extent to which cultures socialize members to accept ambiguous situations and to tolerate uncertainty.

Masculinity Versus Femininity

Theory of the relationship between gender and work roles. In masculine cultures, sex roles are sharply differentiated and traditional "masculine values" such as achievement and the effective exercise of power determine cultural ideals; in feminine cultures, sex roles are less sharply distinguished, and little differentiation is made between men and women in the same job.

Long-Term Versus Short-Term Orientation

The theory of the extent to which a culture programs its citizens to accept delayed gratification of their material, social, and emotional needs. It captures attitudes toward time, persistence, ordering by status, protection of face, respect for tradition, and reciprocation of gifts and favors.

example, a country where more than 70 percent of the population is illiterate is unlikely to be a good market for popular books. But perhaps more importantly, promotional material containing written descriptions of mass-marketed products is unlikely to have an effect in a country where almost three-quarters of the population cannot read. It is far better to use pictorial promotions in such circumstances.

Culture and Business

Of considerable importance for an international business with operations in different countries is how a society's culture affects the values found in the workplace. Management process and practices may need to vary according to culturally determined work-related values. For example, if the cultures of Brazil and Great Britain or the United States and Sweden result in different work-related values, an international business with operations in both countries should vary its management process and practices to account for these differences.

The most famous study of how culture relates to values in the workplace was undertaken by Geert Hofstede.[62] As part of his job as a psychologist working for IBM, Hofstede collected data on employee attitudes and values for more than 116,000 individuals; respondents were matched on occupation, age, and gender. These data later on enabled him to compare dimensions of culture across 50 countries. Hofstede initially isolated four dimensions that he claimed summarized different cultures[63]—power distance, uncertainty avoidance, individualism versus collectivism, and masculinity versus femininity—and then, later on, he added a fifth dimension inspired by Confucianism that he called long-term versus short-term orientation.[64]

The fifth dimension was added as a function of the data obtained via the Chinese Value Survey (CVS), an instrument developed by Michael Harris Bond based on discussions with Hofstede in relation to a joint article they wrote.[65] Bond used input from "Eastern minds," as Hofstede called it, to develop CVS. (Bond references Chinese scholars as helping him create the values that exemplify this new long-term versus short-term orientation.) In his original research, Bond called this new dimension "Confucian work dynamism," but Hofstede said that in practical terms, the dimension refers to a long-term versus short-term orientation.

Hofstede's **power distance** dimension focused on how a society deals with the fact that people are unequal in physical and intellectual capabilities. According to Hofstede, high power distance cultures were found in countries that let inequalities grow over time into inequalities of power and wealth. Low power distance cultures were found in societies that tried to play down such inequalities as much as possible.

The **individualism versus collectivism** dimension focused on the relationship between the individual and his or her fellows. In individualistic societies, the ties between individuals were loose, and individual achievement and freedom were highly valued. In societies where collectivism was emphasized, the ties between individuals were tight. In such societies, people were born into collectives, such as extended families, and everyone was supposed to look after the interest of his or her collective.

Hofstede's **uncertainty avoidance** dimension measured the extent to which different cultures socialized their members into accepting ambiguous situations and tolerating uncertainty. Members of high uncertainty avoidance cultures placed a premium on job security, career patterns, retirement benefits, and so on. They also had a strong need for rules and regulations; the manager was expected to issue clear instructions, and subordinates' initiatives were tightly controlled. Lower uncertainty avoidance cultures were characterized by a greater readiness to take risks and less emotional resistance to change.

Hofstede's **masculinity versus femininity** dimension looked at the relationship between gender and work roles. In masculine cultures, sex roles were sharply differentiated, and traditional "masculine values," such as achievement and the effective exercise of power, determined cultural ideals. In feminine cultures, sex roles were less sharply distinguished, and little differentiation was made between men and women in the same job.

The **long-term versus short-term orientation** dimension refers to the extent to which a culture programs its citizens to accept delayed gratification of their material, social, and emotional needs. It captures attitudes toward time, persistence, ordering by status, protection of face, respect for tradition, and reciprocation of gifts and favors. The label refers to these "values" being derived from Confucian teachings.

Hofstede created an index score for each of these five dimensions that ranged from 0 to 100 and scored high for high individualism, high power distance, high uncertainty avoidance, high masculinity, and high for long-term orientation.[66] He averaged the score for all employees from a given country.

Interestingly, there is movement to add a sixth dimension to Hofstede's work. Geert Hofstede, working with Michael Minkov's analysis of the World Values Survey, added a promising new dimension called indulgence versus restraint (IND) in 2010.[67] On January 17, 2011, Hofstede delivered a webinar for SIETAR Europe called "New Software of the Mind" to introduce the third edition of *Cultures and Organizations*, in which the research results of Minkov were included to support this sixth dimension. In addition, in a keynote delivered at the annual meeting of the Academy of International Business (http://aib.msu.edu) in Istanbul, Turkey, on July 6, 2013, Hofstede again presented results and theoretical rationale to support the *indulgence versus restraint dimension. Indulgence* refers to a society that allows relatively free gratification of basic and natural human drives related to enjoying life and having fun. *Restraint* refers to a society that suppresses gratification of needs and regulates it by means of strict social norms.

Table 4.1 summarizes data for 15 selected countries for the five established dimensions of individualism versus collectivism, power distance, uncertainty avoidance, masculinity versus femininity, and long-term versus short-term orientation (the Hofstede data were collected for 50 countries and the Bond data were collected for 23 countries; since those two researchers' data collection, numerous other researchers have also added to the country samples). Western nations such as the United States, Canada, and Great Britain score high on the individualism scale and low on the power distance scale. At the other extreme are a group of Latin American and Asian countries that emphasize collectivism over individualism and score high on the power distance scale. Table 4.1 also reveals that Japan's culture has strong uncertainty avoidance and high masculinity. This characterization fits the standard stereotype of Japan as a country that is male dominant and where uncertainty avoidance exhibits itself in the institution of lifetime

Work-Related Values for 15 Selected Countries

Hofstede, Geert, "The Cultural Relativity of Organizational Practices and Theories," *Journal of International Business Studies*, vol. 14, Fall 1983, p. 75–89.

	Power Distance	Uncertainty Avoidance	Individualism	Masculinity	Long-Term Orientation
Australia	36	51	90	61	31
Brazil	69	76	38	49	65
Canada	39	48	80	52	23
Germany (F.R.)	35	65	67	66	31
Great Britain	35	35	89	66	25
India	77	40	48	56	61
Japan	54	92	46	95	80
Netherlands	38	53	80	14	44
New Zealand	22	49	79	58	30
Pakistan	55	70	14	50	00
Philippines	94	44	32	64	19
Singapore	74	8	20	48	48
Sweden	31	29	71	5	33
Thailand	64	64	20	34	56
United States	40	46	91	62	29

employment. Sweden and Denmark stand out as countries that have both low uncertainty avoidance and low masculinity (high emphasis on "feminine" values).

Hofstede's results are interesting for what they tell us in a very general way about differences between cultures. Many of Hofstede's findings are consistent with standard stereotypes about cultural differences. For example, many people believe Americans are more individualistic and egalitarian than the Japanese (they have a lower power distance), who in turn are more individualistic and egalitarian than Mexicans. Similarly, many might agree that Latin countries place a higher emphasis on masculine value—they are machismo cultures—than the Nordic countries of Denmark and Sweden.

As might be expected, East Asian countries such as Japan and Thailand scored high on long-term orientation, while nations such as the United States and Canada scored low. Hofstede and his associates went on to argue that their evidence suggested that nations with higher economic growth rates scored high on long-term orientation and low on individualism—the implication being Confucianism is good for growth. However, subsequent studies have shown that this finding does not hold up under more sophisticated statistical analysis.[68] Since the economy has come back from the downturn in 2008, countries with high individualism and short-term orientation such as the United States have attained high growth rates, while some Confucian cultures such as Japan have had stagnant economic growth.

However, we should be careful about reading too much into Hofstede's research. It has been criticized on a number of points.[69] First, Hofstede assumes there is a one-to-one correspondence between culture and the nation-state, but as we discussed earlier, many countries have more than one culture. Hofstede's results do not capture this distinction. Second, the research may have been culturally bound. The research team was composed of Europeans and Americans. The questions they asked of IBM employees—and their analysis of the answers—may have been shaped by their own cultural biases and concerns. So it is not surprising that Hofstede's results confirm Western stereotypes because it was Westerners who undertook the research. The later addition of the long-term versus short-term dimension illustrates this point.

Third, Hofstede's informants worked not only within a single industry, the computer industry, but also within one company, IBM. At the time, IBM was renowned for its own strong corporate culture and employee selection procedures, making it possible that the employees' values were different in important respects from the values of the cultures from which those employees came. Also, certain social classes (such as unskilled manual workers) were excluded from Hofstede's sample. A final caution is that Hofstede's work is now beginning to look dated. Cultures do not stand still; they evolve, albeit slowly. What was a reasonable characterization in the late 1960s and early 1970s may not be so today.

Still, just as it should not be accepted without question, Hofstede's work should not be dismissed either. As such, it represents a starting point for managers trying to figure out how cultures differ and what that might mean for management practices. Also, several other scholars have found strong evidence that differences in culture affect values and practices in the workplace, and Hofstede's basic results have been replicated using more diverse samples of individuals in different settings.[70] Nevertheless, managers should use the results with caution. One reason for caution is the plethora of new cultural values surveys and data points that are starting to become important additions to Hofstede's work. However, in many cases, they build on or are related to

How Strong Is Your National Identity?

As we have found out in this chapter, a lot of measures exist to assess cultural values and norms. Self-assessment is one of the best ways to better know yourself, and we encourage you to take a rigorous cultural personality test such as what Hofstede has developed. But let's have some easy fun! How strong is your personal national identity? On a scale from 1 to 7, with 1 being "strongly disagree" and 7 being "strongly agree" (and with scores of 2, 3, 4, 5, and 6 being in between those two extremes), rate yourself on these four questions:

1. My country has a strong historical heritage (national heritage).
2. People from my country are proud of their nationality (cultural homogeneity).
3. A true native of my country would never reject their religious beliefs (belief system).
4. It is always best to purchase products made from my home country (consumer ethnocentrism).

If you scored above 23 in total for the four questions, you have a strong "national identity"; if you scored below 9, you have a weak "national identity." Most people fall in between these two extremes.

Sources: B. Keillor and T. Hult, "A Five-Country Study of National Identity: Implications for International Marketing Research and Practice," *International Marketing Review,* 1999, p. 65–82; B. Keillor, T. Hult, R. Erffmeyer, and E. Babakus, "NATID: The Development and Application of a National Identity Measure for Use in International Marketing," *Journal of International Marketing,* vol. 4, 1996.

Hofstede's tone-setting work. Two additional cultural values frameworks that have been examined and have been related to work-related and/or business-related issues are the Global Leadership and Organizational Behavior Effectiveness instrument and the World Values Survey.

The *Global Leadership and Organizational Behavior Effectiveness (GLOBE)* instrument is designed to address the notion that a leader's effectiveness is contextual.[71] It is embedded in the societal and organizational norms, values, and beliefs of the people being led. The initial GLOBE findings from 62 societies involving 17,300 middle managers from 951 organizations build on findings by Hofstede and other culture researchers. The GLOBE research established nine cultural dimensions: power distance, uncertainty avoidance, humane orientation, institutional collectivism, in-group collectivism, assertiveness, gender egalitarianism, future orientation, and performance orientation.

The *World Values Survey (WVS)* is a research project spanning more than 100 countries that explores people's values and norms, how they change over time, and what impact they have in society and business.[72] The WVS includes dimensions for support for democracy; tolerance of foreigners and ethnic minorities; support for gender equality; the role of religion and changing levels of religiosity; the impact of globalization; attitudes toward the environment, work, family, politics, national identity, culture, diversity, and insecurity; and subjective well-being.

Despite Hofstede's work along with findings from GLOBE, WVS, and others, culture is just one of many factors that might influence the economic success of a nation. While culture's importance should not be ignored, neither should it be overstated. The Hofstede framework is the most significant and studied framework of culture as it relates to work values and business that we have ever seen. But some of the newer culture frameworks (e.g., GLOBE, WVS) are also becoming popular in the literature, and they have potential to complement and perhaps even supplant Hofstede's work with additional validation and connection to work-related values, business, and marketplace issues. At the same time, the factors discussed in Chapters 2 and 3—economic, political, and legal systems—are probably more important than culture in explaining differential economic growth rates over time.

test PREP

Use SmartBook to help retain what you have learned. Access your Instructor's Connect course to check out SmartBook or go to learnsmartadvantage.com for help.

Cultural Change

LO 4-5

Demonstrate an appreciation for the economic and business implications of cultural change.

An important point we want to make in this chapter on culture is that culture is not a constant; it evolves over time.[73] Changes in value systems can be slow and painful for a society. In the 1960s, for example, American values toward the role of women, love, sex, and marriage underwent significant changes. Much of the social turmoil of that time reflected these changes. Change, however, does occur and can often be quite profound. At the beginning of the 1960s, the idea that women might hold senior management positions in major corporations was not widely accepted. Many scoffed at the idea. Today, of course, it is a reality, and most people in the United States could not fathom it any other way.

For example, in 2012 Virginia ("Ginny") Rometty became the CEO of IBM; and Mary Teresa Barra became the CEO of General Motors in 2014. Barra, as but one of many examples (in 2015, 23 of the CEO positions at S&P 500 companies were held by women), was named to the *Time 100,* and *Forbes* named her one of the World's 100 Most Powerful Women. No one in the mainstream of American society now questions the development or the capability of women in the business world. American culture has changed (although it is still more difficult for women to gain senior management positions than men).

Mary T. Barra became the chief executive officer (CEO) of General Motors (GM) on January 15, 2014. She is the first CEO of a major global automaker. Source: © Bill Pugliano/Getty Images

For another illustration of cultural change, consider Japan. Some academics argue that a major cultural shift has been occurring in Japan, with a move toward greater individualism.[74] The model Japanese office worker, or "salaryman," is characterized as being loyal to his boss and the organization to the point of giving up evenings, weekends, and vacations to serve the organization, which is the collective the employee is a member of. However, a new generation of office workers may not fit this model. An individual from the new generation is likely to be more direct than the traditional Japanese. He acts more like a Westerner, a *gaijin.* He does not live for the company and will move on if he gets the offer of a better job. He is not keen on overtime, especially if he has a date. He has his own plans for his free time, and they may not include drinking or playing golf with the boss.[75]

Several studies have suggested that economic advancement and globalization may be important factors in societal change.[76] There is evidence that economic progress is accompanied by a shift in values away from collectivism and toward individualism.[77] Thus, as Japan has become richer, the cultural emphasis on collectivism has declined and greater individualism is being witnessed. One reason for this shift may be that richer societies exhibit less need for social and material support structures built on collectives, whether the collective is the extended family or the paternalistic company. People are better able to take care of their own needs. As a result, the importance attached to collectivism declines, while greater economic freedoms lead to an increase in opportunities for expressing individualism.

The culture of societies may also change as they become richer because economic progress affects a number of other factors, which in turn influence culture. For example, increased urbanization and improvements in the quality and availability of education are both a function of economic progress, and both can lead to declining emphasis on the traditional values associated with poor rural societies. The World Values Survey, which we mentioned earlier, has documented how values change. The study linked these changes in values to changes in a country's level of economic development.[78] According to this research, as countries get richer, a shift occurs away from "traditional values" linked to religion, family, and country, and toward "secular rational" values. Traditionalists say religion is important in their lives. They have a strong sense of national pride; they also think that children should be taught to obey and that the first duty of a child is to make his or her parents proud. They say abortion, euthanasia, divorce, and suicide are never justified. At the other end of this spectrum are secular rational values.

Another category in the World Values Survey is quality of life attributes. At one end of this spectrum are "survival values," the values people hold when the struggle for survival is of paramount importance. These values tend to stress that economic and physical security are more important than self-expression. People who cannot take food or safety for granted tend to be xenophobic, are wary of political activity, have authoritarian tendencies, and believe that men make better political leaders than women. "Self-expression" or "well-being" values stress the importance of diversity, belonging, and participation in political processes.

As countries get richer, there seems to be a shift from "traditional" to "secular rational" values, and from "survival values" to "well-being" values. The shift, however, takes time, primarily because individuals are socialized into a set of values when they are young and find it difficult to change as they grow older. Substantial changes in values are linked to generations, with younger people typically being in the vanguard of a significant change in values.

With regard to globalization, some have argued that advances in transportation and communication technologies; the dramatic increase in trade that we have witnessed since World War II; and the rise of global corporations such as Hitachi, Disney, Microsoft, IBM, Google, and Levi Strauss (whose products and operations can be found around the globe) are helping create conditions for the merging or convergence of cultures.[79] With McDonald's hamburgers in China, The Gap in India, iPods in South Africa, and MTV everywhere helping foster a ubiquitous youth culture and with countries around the world climbing the ladder of economic progress, some argue that the conditions for less cultural variation have been created. There may be, in other words, a slow but steady convergence occurring across different cultures toward some universally accepted values and norms: This is known as the *convergence* hypothesis.[80]

Having said this, we must not ignore important countertrends, such as the shift toward Islamic fundamentalism in several countries; the continual separatist movement in Quebec, Canada; or ethnic strains and separatist movements in Russia. Such countertrends in many ways are a reaction to the pressures for cultural convergence. In an increasingly modern and materialistic world, some societies are trying to reemphasize their cultural roots and uniqueness. Cultural change is not unidirectional, with national cultures converging toward some homogeneous global entity. It is also important to note that while some elements of culture change quite rapidly—particularly the use of material symbols—other elements change slowly if at all. Thus, just because people the world over wear jeans, eat at McDonald's, use smartphones, watch their national version of *American Idol*, and drive Ford cars to work, we should not assume that they have also adopted American (or Western) values—for often they have not.[81] To illustrate, consider that many Westerners eat Chinese food, watch Chinese martial arts movies, and take classes in kung fu, but their values are still those of Westerners. Thus, a distinction needs to be made between the visible material aspects of culture and the deep structure, particularly core social values and norms. The deep structure changes only slowly, and differences here are often far more persistent than we might suppose.

Use SmartBook to help retain what you have learned. Access your Instructor's Connect course to check out SmartBook or go to learnsmartadvantage.com for help.

FOCUS ON MANAGERIAL IMPLICATIONS

CROSS-CULTURAL LITERACY AND COMPETITIVE ADVANTAGE

International business is different from national business because countries and societies are different. In this chapter, we have seen just how different societies can be. Societies differ because their cultures vary. Their cultures vary because of profound differences in social structure, religion, language, education, economic philosophy, and political philosophy. Three important implications for international business flow from these differences. The first is the need to develop cross-cultural literacy. There is a need not only to appreciate that cultural differences exist but also to appreciate what such differences mean for international business. A second implication centers on the connection between culture and national competitive advantage. A third implication looks at the connection between culture and ethics in decision making. In this section, we explore the first two of these issues in depth. The connection between culture and ethics is explored in Chapter 5.

Cross-Cultural Literacy

One of the biggest dangers confronting a company that goes abroad for the first time is the danger of being ill-informed. International businesses that are ill-informed about the practices of another culture are likely to fail. Doing business in different cultures requires adaptation to conform to the value systems and norms of that culture. Adaptation can embrace all aspects of an international firm's operations in a foreign country. The way in which deals are negotiated, the appropriate incentive pay systems for salespeople, the structure of the organization, the name of a product, the tenor of relations between management and labor, the manner in which the product is promoted, and so on are all sensitive to cultural differences. What works in one culture might not work in another (see the closing case on Best Buy and eBay in China, for example).

To combat the danger of being ill-informed, international businesses should consider employing local citizens to help them do business in a particular culture. They must also ensure that home-country executives are cosmopolitan enough to understand how differences in culture affect the practice of business. Transferring executives overseas at regular intervals to expose them to different cultures will help build a cadre of cosmopolitan executives. An international business must also be constantly on guard against the dangers of *ethnocentric behavior.* **Ethnocentrism** is a belief in the superiority of one's own ethnic group or culture. Hand in hand with ethnocentrism goes a disregard or contempt for the culture of other countries. Unfortunately, ethnocentrism is all too prevalent; many Americans are guilty of it, as are many French people, Japanese people, British people, and so on. Ugly as it is, ethnocentrism is a fact of life, one that international businesses must be on guard against.

Ethnocentrism
Behavior that is based on the belief in the superiority of one's own ethnic group or culture; often shows disregard or contempt for the culture of other countries.

Simple examples illustrate how important cross-cultural literacy can be. Anthropologist Edward T. Hall has described how Americans, who tend to be informal in nature, react strongly to being corrected or reprimanded in public.[82] This can cause problems in Germany, where a cultural tendency toward correcting strangers can shock and offend most Americans. For their part, Germans can be a bit taken aback by the tendency of Americans to call people by their first name. This is uncomfortable enough among executives of the same rank, but it can be seen as insulting when a young and junior American executive addresses an older and more senior German manager by his or her first name without having been invited to do so. Hall concludes it can take a long time to get on a first-name basis with a German; if you rush the process, you will be perceived as overfriendly and rude—and that may not be good for business.

Hall also notes that cultural differences in attitude to time can cause myriad problems. He notes that in the United States, giving a person a deadline is a way of increasing the urgency or relative importance of a task. However, in the Middle East, giving a deadline can have exactly the opposite effect. The American who insists an Arab business associate make his mind up in a hurry is likely to be perceived as overly demanding and exerting undue pressure. The result may be exactly the opposite of what the American intended, with the Arab going slow as a reaction to the American's arrogance and rudeness. For his part, the American may believe that an Arab associate is being rude if he shows up late to a meeting because he met a friend in the street and stopped to talk. The American, of course, is very concerned about time and scheduling. But for the Arab, who lives in a society where social networks are a major source of information and maintaining relationships is important, finishing the discussion with a friend is more important than adhering to a strict schedule. Indeed, the Arab may be puzzled as to why the American attaches so much importance to time and schedule.

Culture and Competitive Advantage

One theme that surfaces in this chapter is the relationship between culture and national competitive advantage.[83] Put simply, the value systems and norms of a country influence the costs of doing business in that country. The costs of doing business in a country influence the ability of firms to establish a competitive advantage in the global marketplace. We have seen how attitudes toward cooperation between management and labor, toward work, and toward the payment of interest are influenced by social structure and religion. It can be argued that the class-based conflict between workers and management in class-conscious societies, when it leads to industrial disruption, raises the costs of doing business in that society. Similarly, we have seen how some sociologists have argued that the ascetic "other-worldly" ethics of Hinduism may not be as supportive of capitalism as the ethics embedded in Protestantism and Confucianism. Also, Islamic laws banning interest payments may raise the costs of doing business by constraining a country's banking system.

Japan presents an interesting case study of how culture can influence competitive advantage. Some scholars have argued that the culture of modern Japan lowers the costs of doing business relative to the costs in most Western nations. Japan's emphasis on group affiliation, loyalty, reciprocal obligations, honesty, and education all boost the competitiveness of Japanese companies. The emphasis on group affiliation and loyalty encourages individuals to identify strongly with the companies in which they work. This tends to foster an ethic of hard work and cooperation between management and labor "for the good of the company." Similarly, reciprocal obligations and honesty help foster an atmosphere of trust between companies and their suppliers. This encourages them to enter into long-term relationships with each other to work on inventory reduction, quality control, and design—all of which have been shown to improve an organization's competitiveness. This level of cooperation has often been lacking in the West, where the relationship between a company and its suppliers tends to be a short-term one structured around competitive bidding rather than one based on long-term mutual commitments. In addition, the availability of a pool of highly skilled labor, particularly engineers, has helped Japanese enterprises develop cost-reducing process innovations that have boosted their productivity.[84] Thus, cultural factors may help explain the success enjoyed by many Japanese businesses in the global marketplace. Most notably, it has been argued that the rise of Japan as an economic power during the second half of the twentieth century may be in part attributed to the economic consequences of its culture.[85]

It also has been argued that the Japanese culture is less supportive of entrepreneurial activity than, say, American society. In many ways, entrepreneurial activity is a product of an individualistic mindset, not a classic characteristic of the Japanese. This may explain why American enterprises, rather than Japanese corporations, dominate industries where entrepreneurship and innovation are highly valued, such as computer software and biotechnology. Of course, obvious and significant exceptions to this generalization exist. Masayoshi Son recognized the potential of software far faster than any of Japan's corporate giants; set up his company, Softbank, in 1981; and over the past 30 years has built it into Japan's top software distributor. Similarly, dynamic entrepreneurial individuals established major Japanese companies such as Sony and Matsushita. But these examples may be the exceptions that prove the rule, for as yet there has been no surge in entrepreneurial high-technology enterprises in Japan equivalent to what has occurred in the United States.

For international business, the connection between culture and competitive advantage is important for two reasons. First, the connection suggests which countries are likely to produce the most viable competitors. For example, we might argue that U.S. enterprises are likely to see continued growth in aggressive, cost-efficient competitors from those Pacific Rim nations where a combination of free market economics, Confucian ideology, group-oriented social structures, and advanced education systems can all be found (e.g., South Korea, Taiwan, Japan, and, increasingly, China).

Second, the connection between culture and competitive advantage has important implications for the choice of countries in which to locate production facilities and do business. Consider a hypothetical case when a company has to choose between two countries, A and B, for locating a production facility. Both countries are characterized by low labor costs and good access to world markets. Both countries are of roughly the same size (in terms of population), and both are at a similar stage of economic development. In country A, the education system is undeveloped, the society is characterized by a marked stratification between the upper and lower classes, and there are six major linguistic groups. In country B, the education system is well developed, social stratification is lacking, group identification is valued by the culture, and there is only one linguistic group. Which country makes the best investment site?

Country B probably does. In country A, conflict between management and labor, and between different language groups, can be expected to lead to social and industrial disruption, thereby raising the costs of doing business.[86] The lack of a good education system also can be expected to work against the attainment of business goals.

The same kind of comparison could be made for an international business trying to decide where to push its products, country A or B. Again, country B would be the logical choice because cultural factors suggest that in the long run, country B is the nation most likely to achieve the greatest level of economic growth.

But as important as culture is to people, companies, and society, it is probably less important than economic, political, and legal systems in explaining differential economic growth between nations. Cultural differences are significant, but we should not overemphasize their importance in the economic sphere. For example, earlier we noted that Max Weber argued that the ascetic principles embedded in Hinduism do not encourage entrepreneurial activity. While this is an interesting academic thesis, recent years have seen an increase in entrepreneurial activity in India, particularly in the information technology sector, where India is rapidly becoming an important global player. The ascetic principles of Hinduism and caste-based social stratification have apparently not held back entrepreneurial activity in this sector.

Key Terms

cross-cultural literacy, p. 88
culture, p. 89
values, p. 90
norms, p. 90
society, p. 90
folkways, p. 90
mores, p. 91
social structure, p. 92
group, p. 93
social strata, p. 94
social mobility, p. 95
caste system, p. 95
class system, p. 96
class consciousness, p. 97
religion, p. 97
ethical system, p. 97
power distance, p. 108
individualism versus collectivism, p. 108
uncertainty avoidance, p. 108
masculinity versus femininity, p. 108
long-term versus short-term orientation, p. 108
ethnocentrism, p. 113

Summary

This chapter looked at the nature of social culture and studied some implications for business practice. The chapter made the following points:

1. Culture is a complex whole that includes knowledge, beliefs, art, morals, law, customs, and other capabilities acquired by people as members of society.
2. Values and norms are the central components of a culture. Values are abstract ideals about what a society believes to be good, right, and desirable. Norms are social rules and guidelines that prescribe appropriate behavior in particular situations.

3. Values and norms are influenced by political and economic philosophy, social structure, religion, language, and education.
4. The social structure of a society refers to its basic social organization. Two main dimensions along which social structures differ are the individual–group dimension and the stratification dimension.
5. In some societies, the individual is the basic building block of social organization. These societies emphasize individual achievements above all else. In other societies, the group is the basic building block of social organization. These societies emphasize group membership and group achievements above all else.
6. All societies are stratified into different classes. Class-conscious societies are characterized by low social mobility and a high degree of stratification. Less class-conscious societies are characterized by high social mobility and a low degree of stratification.
7. Religion may be defined as a system of shared beliefs and rituals that is concerned with the realm of the sacred. Ethical systems refer to a set of moral principles, or values, that are used to guide and shape behavior. The world's major religions are Christianity, Islam, Hinduism, and Buddhism. Although not a religion, Confucianism has an impact on behavior that is as profound as that of many religions. The value systems of different religious and ethical systems have different implications for business practice.
8. Language is one defining characteristic of a culture. It has both spoken and unspoken dimensions. In countries with more than one spoken language, we tend to find more than one culture.
9. Formal education is the medium through which individuals learn skills and are socialized into the values and norms of a society. Education plays an important role in the determination of national competitive advantage.
10. Geert Hofstede studied how culture relates to values in the workplace. He isolated five dimensions that he claimed summarized different cultures: power distance, uncertainty avoidance, individualism versus collectivism, masculinity versus femininity, and long-term versus short-term orientation.
11. Culture is not a constant; it evolves. Economic progress and globalization seem to be two important engines of cultural change.
12. One danger confronting a company that goes abroad for the first time is being ill-informed. To develop cross-cultural literacy, international businesses need to employ host-country nationals, build a cadre of cosmopolitan executives, and guard against the dangers of ethnocentric behavior.
13. The value systems and norms of a country can affect the costs of doing business in that country.

Critical Thinking and Discussion Questions

1. Outline why the culture of a country might influence the costs of doing business in that country. Illustrate your answer with examples.
2. Do you think that business practices in an Islamic country are likely to differ from business practices in a Christian country? If so, how?
3. What are the implications for international business of differences in the dominant religion or ethical system of a country?
4. Choose two countries that appear to be culturally diverse. Compare the cultures of those countries, and then indicate how cultural differences influence (*a*) the costs of doing business in each country, (*b*) the likely future economic development of that country, and (*c*) business practices.
5. Reread the Country Focus about Islamic capitalism in Turkey. Then answer the following questions:
   a. Can you see anything in the values and norms of Islam that is hostile to business?
   b. What does the experience of the region around Kayseri teach about the relationship between Islam and business?
   c. What are the implications of Islamic values toward business for the participation of a country such as Turkey in the global economy or becoming a member of the European Union?
6. Reread the Management Focus on advertising in China and answer the follow questions:
   a. Why do you think it is so important to cultivate *guanxi* and *guanxiwang* in China?
   b. What does the experience of DMG tells us about the way things work in China? What would likely happen to a business that obeyed all the rules and regulations, rather than trying to find a way around them as Dan Mintz apparently does?
   c. What ethical issues might arise when drawing on *guanxiwang* to get things done in China? What does this suggest about the limits of using *guanxiwang* for a Western business committed to high ethical standards?

globalEDGE Research Task

globalEDGE.msu.edu

Use the globalEDGE™ website (globaledge.msu.edu) to complete the following exercises:

1. You are preparing for a business trip to Chile, where you will need to interact extensively with local professionals. Therefore, you would like to collect information regarding local culture and business practices prior to your departure. A colleague from Latin America recommends you visit the Centre for Intercultural Learning and read through the country insights provided for Chile. Prepare a short description of the most striking cultural characteristics that may affect business interactions in this country.
2. Typically, cultural factors drive the differences in business etiquette encountered during international business travel. In fact, Middle Eastern cultures exhibit significant differences in business etiquette when compared to Western cultures. Prior to leaving for your first business trip to the region, a colleague informed you that a guide named ***Business Etiquette around the World*** may help you. Using this guide, identify five tips regarding business etiquette in the Middle Eastern country of your choice.

Best Buy and eBay in China

closing case

The People's Republic of China opened up to foreign direct investments (FDI) in the late 1970s. Since that time, numerous companies have tried to establish operations and sell their products to customers in China. Many more companies will try in the years to come: China is expected to have some 190 million people in the middle- and upper-income categories by 2020. This is an increase from only about 17 million people in these income brackets as recently as in 2010. China's purchasing power for virtually all products and services has strong potential, and foreign companies will seek these market opportunities. What have we learned culturally that can help companies establish themselves in China's marketplace?

Some background on China can serve as a starting point for better understanding the culture in China and what some well-known companies such as Best Buy and eBay have done to target the Chinese marketplace. The motivation for many foreign companies to enter China—beyond those that have been there for a few decades for reasons of low-cost production—was the triple growth of the Chinese economy that was seen from 2000 to 2010.

With this growth, China overtook Japan to become the second-largest economy in the world behind only the United States, and its large population makes for an enormous target market. Investment from foreign companies was the largest driver of China's growth in this period. However, many companies also increased their exports to China. The United States, for example, saw its companies increase exports to China by 542 percent from 2000 to 2011 (from about $16.2 billion to $103.9 billion), while total exports to the rest of the world by U.S. companies increased by only 80 percent in the same time period.

Interestingly, while foreign investments grew, domestic consumption as a share of the Chinese economy declined from 46 percent to 33 percent in the same time period. This consumption decline—coupled with slower growth globally and, ultimately, the worldwide economic downturn that started in 2008—raised questions about China's momentum. Right now, around 85 percent of mainstream Chinese consumers are living in the top 100 wealthiest cities. By the year 2020, these advanced and developing cities will have relatively few customers who are lower than the middle- and upper-income brackets by Chinese standards. The expectation is that these consumers will be able to afford a range of products and services, such as flat-screen televisions and overseas travel, making the Chinese customer much more of a target for a wide variety of consumption. This begs the question, can the unprecedented Chinese growth really continue, and would it come from increased consumption?

The resounding answer is yes, according to research conducted by McKinsey & Company. McKinsey found that barring another major economic shock similar to what we saw in 2008, China's gross domestic product (GDP) will continue to grow, albeit not at the historic levels seen between 2000 and 2010, when it grew about 10.4 percent annually. The growth from 2010 to 2020 is expected to be about 7.9 percent per year, which is still far above the expected growth for the United States (2.8 percent annually), Japan (1.2 percent annually), and Germany (1.7 percent annually)—the three countries among the top four worldwide economies along with China. And the key is that consumption will now be the driving force behind the growth instead of foreign investment. The consumption forecast opens up opportunities for foreign companies to engage with Chinese consumers who are expected to have more purchasing power and discretionary spending.

But culturally translating market success from one country or even a large number of countries to the Chinese marketplace is not necessarily as straightforward as it may seem. Often, a combination of naiveté, arrogance, and cultural misunderstanding have led many well-known companies to fail in China. Lack of an understanding of issues such as local demands, buying habits, consumption values, and Chinese customers' personal beliefs led to struggles for companies that had been very successful elsewhere in the world. Let's take a brief look at Best Buy and eBay as two examples.

Best Buy, the mega-store mainly focused on consumer electronics, was founded in 1966 as an audio specialty store. Best Buy entered China in 2006 by acquiring a majority interest in China's fourth-largest appliance retailer, Jiangsu Five Star Appliance, for $180 million. But culture shock hit Best Buy, best described by Shaun Rein, the founder of China Market Research Group. He pointed to a few reasons for this culture shock and lack of success. First, the Chinese will not pay for Best Buy's overly expensive products unless they are a brand like Apple. Second, there is too much piracy in the Chinese market, and this reduces demand for electronics products at competitive market prices. Third, like many Europeans, the Chinese do not want to shop at huge mega-stores. So, these three seemingly easy-to-understand cultural issues created difficulties for Best Buy. Solving these issues, Best Buy believed that it would have to develop and implement a different business model for the Chinese market than it has used, for example, in the United States. Now, how far should a company go outside its normal business model to adhere to cultural values and beliefs of a new market? Strategically moving forward, Best Buy opted to close all of its Best Buy–branded stores in China and focus on its wholly owned local Jiangsu Five Star chain of stores. But will this new strategic business model be successful with the new makeup of customers in China expected by 2020?

eBay, the popular e-business site focused on consumer-to-consumer purchases, was founded in 1995. The company was one of the true success stories that lived through the dot-com bubble in the 1990s. It is now a multibillion-dollar business with operations in more than 30 countries. But China's unique culture created problems for eBay in that market. Contrary to the widespread cultural issues that faced Best Buy, one company in particular (TaoBao) and one feature more specifically (built-in instant messaging) shaped a lot of the problems that eBay ran into in China. Some 200 million shoppers are using TaoBao to buy products, and the company accounts for almost 80 percent of online transaction value in China. TaoBao is owned by the powerful Alibaba Group.

Uniquely, TaoBao's built-in instant messaging system has been cited as a main reason for its edge over eBay in China. Basically, customers wanted to be able to identify a seller's online status and communicate with them directly and easily—a function not seamlessly incorporated into eBay's China system. Clearly, built-in instant text messaging is a solvable obstacle in doing business in China. It sounds easy now when we know about it but may not always be the case when we take into account all the little things that are important in a market. How can a foreign company entering China ensure that it tackles the most important "little" things that end up being huge barriers to success as we approach the year 2020, when China is expected to have significantly increased purchasing power among its middle class?

Sources: B. Carlson, "Why Big American Businesses Fail in China," *GlobalPost,* September 22, 2013; Y. Atsmon, M Magni, L. Li, W. Liao, "Meet the 2020 Chinese Consumer," *McKinsey Consumer*; Shopper Insights, March 2012; "Exports to China by State 2000–2011," *The US-China Business Council,* 2012; A. Groth, "Best Buy's Overseas Strategy Is Failing in Europe and China," *Business Insider,* November 4, 2011.

CASE DISCUSSION QUESTIONS

1. Will China maintain its strong economic growth in the years to come? Some suggest it will until 2050. What do you think?
2. If China will go from 17 million to 190 million middle-income people by the year 2020, would the scenario presented Best Buy in 2006 not be applicable anymore? That is, the culture shock in 2006 was that the Chinese would not pay for Best Buy's overly expensive products unless they are a brand like Apple. Would newly rich Chinese customer engage in this purchasing by 2020?
3. With Alibaba's ownership of the very popular TaoBao online shopping system (similar to eBay and Amazon) and its spread across the world, will a Western-based online shopping culture ultimately infiltrate China?

Endnotes

1. D. Barry, *Exporters! The Wit and Wisdom of Small Businesspeople Who Sell Globally* (Washington, DC: International Trade Administration, U.S. Department of Commerce, 2013); T. Hult, D. Ketchen, D. Griffith, C. Finnegan, T. Padron-Gonzalez, F. Harmancioglu, Y. Huang, M. Talay, and S. Cavusgil, "Data Equivalence in Cross-Cultural International Business Research: Assessment and Guidelines," *Journal of International Business Studies*, 2008, pp. 1027–44; S. Ronen and O. Shenkar, "Mapping World Cultures: Cluster Formation, Sources, and Implications," *Journal of International Business Studies*, 2013, pp. 867–97.
2. This is a point made effectively by K. Leung, R. S. Bhagat, N. R. Buchan, M. Erez, and C. B. Gibson, "Culture and International Business: Recent Advances and Their Implications for Future Research," *Journal of International Business Studies,* 2005, pp. 357–78. Several research articles and books also support the notion that significant cultural differences still exist in the world; for example, T. Hult, D. Closs, and D. Frayer, *Global Supply Chain Management: Leveraging Processes, Measurements, and Tools for Strategic Corporate Advantage* (New York: McGraw-Hill, 2014).
3. M. Y. Brannen, "When Micky Loses Face: Recontextualization, Semantic Fit, and the Semiotics of Foreignness," *Academy of Management Review,* 2004, pp. 593–616.
4. See R. Dore, *Taking Japan Seriously* (Stanford, CA: Stanford University Press, 1987).
5. Data come from J. Monger, "International Comparison of Labor Disputes in 2004," *Labor Market Trends,* April 2006, pp. 117–28.
6. E. B. Tylor, *Primitive Culture* (London: Murray, 1871).
7. F. Kluckhohn and F. Strodtbeck, *Variations in Value Orientations* (Evanston, IL: Row, Peterson, 1961); C. Kluckhohn, "Values and Value Orientations in the Theory of Action," in T. Parsons and E. A. Shils (Eds.), *Toward a General Theory of Action* (Cambridge, MA: Harvard University Press, 1951).
8. M. Rokeach, *The Nature of Human Values* (New York: Free Press, 1973); S. Schwartz, "Universals in the Content and

Structure of Values: Theory and Empirical Tests in 20 Countries," in M. Zanna (Ed.), *Advances in Experimental Social Psychology*, vol. 25 (New York: Academic Press, 1992), pp. 1–65.

9. G. Hofstede, *Culture's Consequences: International Differences in Work-Related Values* (Beverly Hills, CA: Sage, 1984), p. 21.
10. J. Z. Namenwirth and R. B. Weber, *Dynamics of Culture* (Boston: Allen & Unwin, 1987), p. 8.
11. R. Mead, *International Management: Cross-Cultural Dimensions* (Oxford: Blackwell Business, 1994), p. 7.
12. G. Hofstede, *Culture's Consequences: Comparing Values, Beliefs, Behaviors, Institutions and Organizations Across Nations* (Thousand Oaks, CA: Sage, 2001).
13. E. T. Hall and M. R. Hall, *Understanding Cultural Differences* (Yarmouth, ME: Intercultural Press, 1990).
14. E. T. Hall and M. R. Hall, *Hidden Differences: Doing Business with the Japanese* (New York: Doubleday, 1987).
15. B. Keillor and T. Hult, "A Five-Country Study of National Identity: Implications for International Marketing Research and Practice," *International Marketing Review*, 1999, pp. 65–82; T. Clark, "International Marketing and National Character: A Review and Proposal for an Integrative Theory," *Journal of Marketing*, 1990, pp. 66–79; M. E. Porter, *The Competitive Advantage of Nations* (New York: Free Press, 1990).
16. S. P. Huntington, *The Clash of Civilizations* (New York: Simon & Schuster, 1996).
17. F. Vijver, D. Hemert, and Y. Poortinga, *Multilevel Analysis of Individuals and Cultures* (New York: Taylor & Francis, 2010).
18. M. Thompson, R. Ellis, and A. Wildavsky, *Cultural Theory* (Boulder, CO: Westview Press, 1990).
19. M. Douglas, *In the Active Voice* (London: Routledge, 1982), pp. 183–254.
20. L. Zucker and M. Darby, "Star-Scientist Linkages to Firms in APEC and European Countries: Indicators of Regional Institutional Differences Affecting Competitive Advantage," *International Journal of Biotechnology*, 1999, pp. 119–31.
21. C. Nakane, *Japanese Society* (Berkeley: University of California Press, 1970).
22. Ibid.
23. For details, see M. Aoki, *Information, Incentives, and Bargaining in the Japanese Economy* (Cambridge, UK: Cambridge University Press, 1988); and M. L. Dertouzos, R. K. Lester, and R. M. Solow, *Made in America* (Cambridge, MA: MIT Press, 1989).
24. Global Innovation Barometer 2013 is a product by Ideas Lab and supported by General Electric (GE). The GE Global Innovation Barometer explores how business leaders around the world view innovation and how those perceptions are influencing business strategies in an increasingly complex and globalized environment. It is the largest global survey of business executives dedicated to innovation. GE expanded the global study in 2013, surveying more than 3,000 executives in 25 countries www.ideaslaboratory.com/projects/innovation-barometer-2013/.
25. P. Skarynski and R. Gibson, *Innovation to the Core: A Blueprint for Transforming the Way Your Company Innovates* (Boston, MA: Harvard Business School Press, 2008); L. Edvinsson and M. Malone, *Intellectual Capital: Realizing Your Company's True Value by Finding Its Hidden Brainpower* (New York: Harper Collins, 1997); T. Davenport and L. Prusak, *Working Knowledge: How Organizations Manage What They Know* (Boston, MA: Harvard Business School Press, 1998).
26. G. Macionis and L. John, *Sociology* (Toronto, Ontario: Pearson Canada, Inc., 2010), pp. 224–25.
27. E. Luce, *The Strange Rise of Modern India* (Boston: Little, Brown, 2006); D. Pick and K. Dayaram, "Modernity and Tradition in the Global Era: The Re-invention of Caste in India," *International Journal of Sociology and Social Policy,* 2006, pp. 284–301.
28. For an excellent historical treatment of the evolution of the English class system, see E. P. Thompson, *The Making of the English Working Class* (London: Vintage Books, 1966). See also R. Miliband, *The State in Capitalist Society* (New York: Basic Books, 1969), especially Chapter 2. For more recent studies of class in British societies, see Stephen Brook, *Class: Knowing Your Place in Modern Britain* (London: Victor Gollancz, 1997); A. Adonis and S. Pollard, *A Class Act: The Myth of Britain's Classless Society* (London: Hamish Hamilton, 1997); J. Gerteis and M. Savage, "The Salience of Class in Britain and America: A Comparative Analysis," *British Journal of Sociology,* June 1998.
29. Adonis and Pollard, *A Class Act.*
30. J. H. Goldthorpe, "Class Analysis and the Reorientation of Class Theory: The Case of Persisting Differentials in Education Attainment," *British Journal of Sociology,* 2010, pp. 311–35.
31. Y. Bian, "Chinese Social Stratification and Social Mobility," *Annual Review of Sociology* 28 (2002), pp. 91–117.
32. N. Goodman, *An Introduction to Sociology* (New York: HarperCollins, 1991).
33. O. C. Ferrell, J. Fraedrich, and L. Ferrell, *Business Ethics: Ethical Decision Making and Cases* (Mason, OH: Cengage Learning, 2012).
34. R. J. Barro and R. McCleary, "Religion and Economic Growth across Countries," *American Sociological Review,* October 2003, pp. 760–82; R. McCleary and R. J. Barro, "Religion and Economy," *Journal of Economic Perspectives,* Spring 2006, pp. 49–72.
35. M. Weber, *The Protestant Ethic and the Spirit of Capitalism* (New York: Scribner's, 1958, original 1904–1905). For an excellent review of Weber's work, see A. Giddens, *Capitalism and Modern Social Theory* (Cambridge, UK: Cambridge University Press, 1971).
36. M. Weber, *The Protestant Ethic and the Spirit of Capitalism,* p. 35.
37. A. S. Thomas and S. L. Mueller, "The Case for Comparative Entrepreneurship," *Journal of International Business Studies* 31, no. 2 (2000), pp. 287–302; S. A. Shane, "Why Do Some Societies Invent More than Others?," *Journal of Business Venturing* 7 (1992), pp. 29–46.
38. See S. M. Abbasi, K. W. Hollman, and J. H. Murrey, "Islamic Economics: Foundations and Practices," *International Journal of Social Economics* 16, no. 5 (1990), pp. 5–17; R. H. Dekmejian, *Islam in Revolution: Fundamentalism in the Arab World* (Syracuse, NY: Syracuse University Press, 1995).
39. T. W. Lippman, *Understanding Islam* (New York: Meridian Books, 1995).
40. Dekmejian, *Islam in Revolution.*

41. M. K. Nydell, *Understanding Arabs* (Yarmouth, ME: Intercultural Press, 1987).
42. Lippman, *Understanding Islam.*
43. The material in this section is based largely on Abbasi et al., "Islamic Economics."
44. "Sharia Calling," *The Economist*, November 12, 2010; N. Popper, "Islamic Banks, Stuffed with Cash, Explore Partnerships in West," *The New York Times*, December 26, 2013.
45. "Forced Devotion," *The Economist,* February 17, 2001, pp. 76–77.
46. For details of Weber's work and views, see Giddens, *Capitalism and Modern Social Theory.*
47. See, for example, the views expressed in "A Survey of India: The Tiger Steps Out," *The Economist,* January 21, 1995.
48. "High-Tech Entrepreneurs Flock to India," *PBS News Hour*, February 9, 2014, www.pbs.org/newshour/bb/high-tech-entrepreneurs-flock-india, accessed March 7, 2014.
49. H. Norberg-Hodge, "Buddhism in the Global Economy," International Society for Ecology and Culture, www.localfutures.org/publications/online-articles/buddhism-in-the-global-economy, accessed March 7, 2014.
50. P. Clark, "Zen and the Art of Startup Naming," *Bloomberg Businessweek*, August 30, 2013, www.businessweek.com/articles/2013-08-30/zen-and-the-art-of-startup-naming, accessed March 7, 2014.
51. Ibid.
52. Hofstede, *Culture's Consequences.*
53. See Dore, *Taking Japan Seriously*; C. W. L. Hill, "Transaction Cost Economizing as a Source of Comparative Advantage: The Case of Japan," *Organization Science* 6 (1995).
54. C. C. Chen, Y. R. Chen, and K. Xin, "Guanxi Practices and Trust in Management," *Organization Science* 15, no. 2 (March–April 2004), pp. 200–10.
55. See Aoki, *Information, Incentives, and Bargaining*; J. P. Womack, D. T. Jones, and D. Roos, *The Machine That Changed the World* (New York: Rawson Associates, 1990).
56. This hypothesis dates back to two anthropologists, Edward Sapir and Benjamin Lee Whorf. See E. Sapir, "The Status of Linguistics as a Science," *Language* 5 (1929), pp. 207–14; B. L. Whorf, *Language, Thought, and Reality* (Cambridge, MA: MIT Press, 1956).
57. The tendency has been documented empirically. See A. Annett, "Social Fractionalization, Political Instability, and the Size of Government," *IMF Staff Papers* 48 (2001), pp. 561–92.
58. D. A. Ricks, *Big Business Blunders: Mistakes in Multinational Marketing* (Homewood, IL: Dow Jones–Irwin, 1983).
59. Goodman, *An Introduction to Sociology.*
60. Porter, *The Competitive Advantage of Nations.*
61. Ibid., pp. 395–97.
62. G. Hofstede, "The Cultural Relativity of Organizational Practices and Theories," *Journal of International Business Studies,* Fall 1983, pp. 75–89; G. Hofstede, *Cultures and Organizations: Software of the Mind* (New York: McGraw-Hill USA, 1997); Hofstede, *Culture's Consequences.*
63. Hofstede, "The Cultural Relativity of Organizational Practices and Theories"; Hofstede, *Cultures and Organizations.*
64. Hofstede, *Culture's Consequences.*
65. G. Hofstede and M. Bond, "Hofstede's Culture Dimensions: An Independent Validation Using Rokeach's Value Survey," *Journal of Cross-Cultural Psychology,* 15 (December 1984), pp. 417–33.
66. The factor scores for the long-term versus short-term orientation, using Bond's survey, were brought into a 0–100 range by a linear transformation (LTO = 50 × F + 50, in which F is the factor score). However, the data for China came in after Hofstede and Bond had standardized the scale, and they put China outside the range at LTO = 118 (which indicates a very strong long-term orientation).
67. G. Hofstede, G. J. Hofstede, and M. Minkov, *Cultures and Organizations: Software of the Mind*, 3d ed. (New York: McGraw-Hill, 2010).
68. R. S. Yeh and J. J. Lawrence, "Individualism and Confucian Dynamism," *Journal of International Business Studies* 26, no. 3 (1995), pp. 655–66.
69. For a more detailed critique, see Mead, *International Management,* pp. 73–75.
70. For example, see W. J. Bigoness and G. L. Blakely, "A Cross-National Study of Managerial Values," *Journal of International Business Studies,* December 1996, p. 739; D. H. Ralston, D. H. Holt, R. H. Terpstra, and Y. Kai-Cheng, "The Impact of National Culture and Economic Ideology on Managerial Work Values," *Journal of International Business Studies* 28, no. 1 (1997), pp. 177–208; P. B. Smith, M. F. Peterson, and Z. Ming Wang, "The Manager as a Mediator of Alternative Meanings," *Journal of International Business Studies* 27, no. 1 (1996), pp. 115–37; L. Tang and P. E. Koves, "A Framework to Update Hofstede's Cultural Value Indices," *Journal of International Business Studies* 39 (2008), pp. 1045–63.
71. R. House, P. Hanges, M. Javidan, P. Dorfman, and V. Gupta, *Culture, Leadership, and Organizations: The GLOBE Study of 62 Societies* (Thousand Oaks, CA: Sage, 2004); J. Chhokar, F. Brodbeck, and R. House, *Culture and Leadership across the World: The GLOBE Book of In-Depth Studies of 25 Societies* (New York: Routledge, 2012).
72. R. Inglehart, *Modernization and Postmodernization: Cultural, Economic, and Political Change in 43 Societies* (Princeton, NJ: Princeton University Press, 1997). Information and data on the World Values Survey can be found at www.worldvaluessurvey.org.
73. For evidence of this, see R. Inglehart, "Globalization and Postmodern Values," *The Washington Quarterly,* Winter 2000, pp. 215–28.
74. Mead, *International Management,* chap. 17.
75. "Free, Young, and Japanese," *The Economist,* December 21, 1991.
76. Namenwirth and Weber, *Dynamics of Culture;* Inglehart, "Globalization and Postmodern Values."
77. G. Hofstede, "National Cultures in Four Dimensions," *International Studies of Management and Organization* 13, no. 1 (1983), pp. 46–74; Tang and Koves, "A Framework to Update Hofstede's Cultural Value Indices."
78. See Inglehart, "Globalization and Postmodern Values." For updates, go to http://wvs.isr.umich.edu/index.html.

79. Hofstede, "National Cultures in Four Dimensions."
80. D. A. Ralston, D. H. Holt, R. H. Terpstra, and Y. Kai-Chung, "The Impact of National Culture and Economic Ideology on Managerial Work Values," *Journal of International Business Studies,* 2007, pp. 1–19.
81. See Leung et al., "Culture and International Business."
82. Hall and Hall, *Understanding Cultural Differences.*
83. Porter, *The Competitive Advantage of Nations.*
84. See Aoki, *Information, Incentives, and Bargaining;* Dertouzos et al., *Made in America;* Porter, *The Competitive Advantage of Nations,* pp. 395–97.
85. See Dore, *Taking Japan Seriously;* Hill, "Transaction Cost Economizing as a Source of Comparative Advantage."
86. For empirical work supporting such a view, see Annett, "Social Fractionalization, Political Instability, and the Size of Government."

Ethics, Corporate Social Responsibility, and Sustainability

learning objectives

After reading this chapter, you will be able to:

- **LO5-1** Understand the ethical issues faced by international businesses.
- **LO5-2** Recognize an ethical dilemma.
- **LO5-3** Identify the causes of unethical behavior by managers.
- **LO5-4** Describe the different philosophical approaches to ethics.
- **LO5-5** Explain how managers can incorporate ethical considerations into their decision making.

Source: © Ozdel/Anadolu Agency/Getty Images

UNCTAD Sustainable Development Goals

opening case

The United Nations Conference on Trade and Development (UNCTAD) was established in 1964 to promote development-friendly integration of countries into the world economy. UNCTAD has progressively evolved into an authoritative, knowledge-based institution working on helping to shape policy debates and thinking on development. A core of this focus is on ensuring that countries' domestic policies and international actions are mutually supportive in bringing about sustainable development.

On September 15, 2015, a large number of countries worldwide adopted the "2030 Agenda for Sustainable Development" and its 17 "Sustainable Development Goals" (SDGs) to end poverty, protect the planet, and ensure prosperity for all. Each goal has a set of specific targets to be achieved in the 15 years that follow. Importantly, the idea is that for the 17 goals to be achieved in this time frame, everyone needs to participate and do their part, including governments, the private sector of businesses, civil society, and all people.

The 17 SDGs include: (1) no poverty, (2) zero hunger, (3) good health and well-being, (4) quality education, (5) gender equality, (6) clean water and sanitation, (7) affordable and clean energy, (8) decent work and economic growth, (9) industry, innovation and infrastructure, (10) reduced inequalities, (11) sustainable cities and communities, (12) responsible consumption and production, (13) climate action, (14) life below water, (15) life on land, (16) peace, justice and strong institutions, and (17) partnerships for the goals.

These SDGs are described in detail by UNCTAD in various forms, such as at http://www.un.org/sustainabledevelopment. However, a brief overview of some of the current status of certain SDGs can serve nicely as a precursor to what has to be done to achieve each SDG by 2030. For example, with respect to SGD 1, while extreme poverty rates have been reduced by more than half in the last 25 years, more than 800 million people still live in extreme poverty. And, for SDG 2, globally one in every nine people, also some 800 million people, are undernourished. Quality education (SDG 4)—a driver of global competitiveness—is a major goal; currently, there are 103 million youth worldwide who lack basic literacy skills.

These three Sustainable Development Goals that were highlighted in the previous paragraph illustrate the task at hand for the world and its countries to end poverty, protect the planet, and ensure prosperity for all. Plus, SGD 17 makes it very clear that revitalizing global partnerships are critical for sustainable development to reach the aspirations that have been set forth in the UNCTAD "2030 Agenda for Sustainable Development." These partnerships should include governments, the private business sector, and civil society. UNCTAD has said that these inclusive partnerships also have to build on principles and values, a shared vision, and shared goals that place people and the planet at the center. •

Sources: United Nations, "Sustainable Development Goals—17 Goals to Transform Our World," www.un.org; James Zhan, "Investing in Sustainable Development Goals," *CFI.co*, October 9, 2014. cfi.co/finance.

Introduction

The opening case describes the 17 Sustainable Development Goals (SDGs) that were adopted in the "2030 Agenda for Sustainable Development" by the United Nations Conference on Trade and Development (UNCTAD) and its 193 member countries. The general idea is that the 17 SDGs represent an unprecedented opportunity for the world to bring together its countries, companies, and societies—from bottom-of-the-pyramid countries to the richest nations—in an effort to improve the lives of everyone everywhere. The SDGs place greater demands on the scientific community than did the eight UNCTAD Millennium Development Goals (MDGs), which they replaced in 2015.[1]

As noted in the opening case, the 17 Sustainable Development Goals cover a broad spectrum of issues focused on ending poverty, protecting the planet, and ensuring prosperity for all. There is clear evidence that some companies and countries are less oriented than others toward sustainable development in their manufacturing, sharing of resources, and investment in people. In many cases, the 17 Sustainable Development Goals become a voluntary standard and not a regulation that can be enforced worldwide, certainly not at the company and private enterprise levels.

For example, we know that some toy manufacturers have been violating safety regulations for almost 30 years and many will continue to do so in the future; time will tell, assuming we can track the ingredients in the materials being used to make toys. But what we do know is that about a third of the toys that are exported out of China currently are tainted with heavy metals above the norm. Unfortunately, it is not illegal to use lead, for example, in plastics at this time; it is an ethical issue and perhaps also a sustainability issue—and usually a voluntary one—that some companies tackle and others choose to side-step, given the large size of market opportunities in the toy industry. A basic question then is: Can it be considered unethical to manufacture toys that include heavy metals that are bad for children to ingest and come in contact with when using the toys in their proper way? What about corporate social responsibility among a country's companies or the companies' sustainable business practices?

Ethics, corporate social responsibility, and sustainability are intertwined issues facing countries, companies, and societies. These "social" issues arise frequently in international business, often because business practices and regulations differ from nation to nation. With regard to lead pollution, for example, what is allowed in Mexico is outlawed in the United States. Ultimately, differences can create dilemmas for businesses. Understanding the nature of these dilemmas and deciding the course of action to pursue when confronted with them is a central theme in this chapter.

The core starting point for the chapter is ethics. Ethics serves as the foundation for what people do or do not and ultimately what companies engage in globally. As such, companies' involvement in corporate social responsibility practices and sustainability initiatives can be traced to the ethical foundation of its employees and other stakeholders, such as customers, shareholders, suppliers, regulators, and communities.[2]

Module on International Ethics

globalEDGE™ has a series of interactive educational modules for businesspeople, policy officials, and students. These modules focus on issues pertinent to international business and include a case study or anecdotes, a glossary of terms, quiz questions, and a list of references, when applicable. The combination of our textbook on international business and the free globalEDGE™ online course modules serves as an excellent resource to prepare for NASBITE's Certified Global Business Professional Credential (the CGBP includes a testing focus on management, marketing, supply chain management, and finance). Achieving the industry-leading CGBP credential ensures that employees are able to practice global business at the professional level required in today's competitive environment. As related to this chapter, check out globalEDGE™'s online module on international ethics at globaledge.msu.edu/reference-desk/online-course-modules. View the questions in the module as a quick test on your understanding of the main issues in international ethics and your readiness to achieve the CGBP credential.

The term *ethics* refers to accepted principles of right or wrong that govern the conduct of a person, the members of a profession, or the actions of an organization. **Business ethics** are the accepted principles of right or wrong governing the conduct of businesspeople, and an **ethical strategy** is a strategy, or course of action, that does not violate these accepted principles. This chapter looks at how ethical issues should be incorporated into decision making in an international business. The chapter also reviews the reasons for poor ethical decision making and discusses different philosophical approaches to business ethics. Then, using the ethical decision-making process as platform, we include a series of illustrations via Management Focus boxes throughout the chapter, including issues related to Apple, Unocal, Daimler, Stora Enso, and Umicore. The chapter closes by reviewing the different processes that managers can adopt to make sure that ethical considerations are incorporated into decision making in international business and how these decisions filter into corporate social responsibility and sustainability efforts.

Business Ethics
The accepted principles of right or wrong governing the conduct of businesspeople.

Ethical Strategy
A course of action that does not violate a company's business ethics.

Ethics and International Business

LO 5-1
Understand the ethical issues faced by international businesses.

Many of the ethical issues in international business are rooted in the fact that political systems, law, economic development, and culture vary significantly from nation to nation. What is considered normal practice in one nation may be considered unethical in another. Because they work for an institution that transcends national borders and cultures, managers in a multinational firm need to be particularly sensitive to these differences. In the international business setting, the most common ethical issues involve employment practices, human rights, environmental regulations, corruption, and the moral obligation of multinational corporations.

EMPLOYMENT PRACTICES

When work conditions in a host nation are clearly inferior to those in a multinational's home nation, which standards should be applied? Those of the home nation, those of the host nation, or something in between? While few would suggest that pay and work conditions should be the same across nations, how much divergence is acceptable? For example, while 12-hour workdays, extremely low pay, and a failure to protect workers against toxic chemicals may be common in some less developed nations, does this mean that it is okay for a multinational to tolerate such working conditions in its subsidiaries there or to condone it by using local subcontractors?

Some time ago, Nike found itself in the center of a storm of protests when news reports revealed that working conditions at many of its subcontractors were very poor. Typical of the allegations were those detailed in a *48 Hours* program. The report painted a picture of young women who worked with toxic materials six days a week in poor conditions for only 20 cents an hour at a Vietnamese subcontractor. The report also stated that a living wage in Vietnam was at least $3 a day, an income that could not be achieved at the subcontractor without working substantial overtime. Nike and its subcontractors were not breaking any laws, but this report and others like it raised questions about the ethics of using sweatshop labor to make what were essentially fashion accessories. It may have been legal, but was it ethical to use subcontractors who, by developed-nation standards, clearly exploited their workforce? Nike's critics thought not, and the company found itself the focus of a wave of demonstrations and consumer boycotts. These exposés surrounding Nike's use of subcontractors forced the company to reexamine its policies. Realizing that even though it was breaking no law, its subcontracting policies were perceived as unethical, Nike's management established a code of conduct for Nike subcontractors and instituted annual monitoring by independent auditors of all subcontractors.[3]

As the Nike case demonstrates, a strong argument can be made that it is not okay for a multinational firm to tolerate poor working conditions in its foreign operations or those of subcontractors. However, this still leaves unanswered the question of which standards should be applied. We shall return to and consider this issue in more detail later in the chapter. For now, note that establishing minimal acceptable standards that safeguard the basic rights and dignity of employees, auditing foreign subsidiaries and subcontractors on a regular basis to make sure those standards are met, and taking corrective action if they are not up to standards are a good way to guard against ethical abuses. For another example of problems with working practices among suppliers, read the accompanying Management Focus, which looks at working conditions related to Apple and its manufacturing.

management FOCUS

Apple's Manufacturing—Always Ethical?

In mid-2006, news reports surfaced suggesting there were systematic labor abuses at a factory in China that makes the iPhone and iPod for Apple, Inc. According to the reports, workers at Hongfujin Precision Industry were paid as little as $50 a month to work 15-hour shifts making Apple products. There were also reports of forced overtime and poor living conditions for the workers, many of them young women who had migrated from the countryside to work at the plant and lived in company-owned dormitories.

The 2006 articles were the work of two Chinese journalists, Wang You and Weng Bao, employed by *China Business News,* a state-run newspaper. The target of the reports, Hongfujin Precision Industry, was reportedly China's largest export manufacturer with overseas sales totaling $14.5 billion. Hongfujin is owned by Foxconn, a large Taiwanese conglomerate whose customers (in addition to Apple) include Intel, Dell, and Sony Corporation. The Hongfujin factory is a small city in its own right, with clinics, recreational facilities, buses, and 13 restaurants that serve the 200,000 employees.

Upon hearing the news, Apple management responded quickly, pledging to audit the operations to make sure Hongfujin was complying with Apple's code on labor standards for subcontractors. Managers at Hongfujin took a somewhat different tack; they filed a defamation suit against the two journalists, suing them for $3.8 million in a local court, which promptly froze the journalists' personal assets pending a trial. Clearly, the management of Hongfujin was trying to send a message to the journalist community: criticism would be costly. The suit sent a chill through the Chinese journalist community because Chinese courts have shown a tendency to favor powerful, locally based companies in legal proceedings.

Within six weeks, Apple had completed its audit. The company's report suggested that although workers had not been forced to work overtime and were earning at least the local minimum wage, many had worked more than the 60 hours a week allowed for by Apple and their housing was substandard. Under pressure from Apple, management at Hongfujin agreed to bring practices in line with Apple's code, committing to building new housing for employees and limiting work to 60 hours a week.

However, Hongfujin did not immediately withdraw the defamation suit. In an unusually bold move in a country where censorship is still common, *China Business News* gave its unconditional backing to Wang and Weng. The Shanghai-based news organization issued a statement arguing that what the two journalists did "was not a violation of any rules, laws, or journalistic ethics." The Paris-based Reporters Without Borders also took up the case of Wang and Weng, writing a letter to Apple's then-CEO, the late Steve Jobs, stating, "We believe that all Wang and Weng did was to report the facts and we condemn Foxconn's reaction. We therefore ask you to intercede on behalf of these two journalists so that their assets are unfrozen and the lawsuit is dropped."

Once again, Apple moved quickly, pressuring Foxconn behind the scenes to drop the suit. Foxconn agreed to do so and issued a "face-saving" statement saying the two sides had agreed to end the dispute after apologizing to each other "for the disturbances brought to both of them by the lawsuit." The experience shed a harsh light on labor conditions in China. At the same time, the response of the Chinese media, and *China Business News* in particular, point toward the emergence of some journalistic freedoms in a nation that has historically seen news organizations as a mouthpiece for the state.

More recent news may indicate new ethical concerns at Apple's production facilities in China. In a 2014 story by BBC News, Apple was again at the center of issues related to workers' hours, ID cards, housing arrangements, work meetings, and juvenile workers at its Pegatron facilities on the outskirts of Shanghai. Apple disagreed strongly with the portrayal of the Pegatron factory's working conditions and stated in the BBC News article that "We are aware of no other company doing as much as Apple to ensure fair and safe working conditions."*

*R. Bilton, "Apple Failing to Protect Chinese Factory Workers," *BBC News,* December 18, 2014.

Sources: R. Bilton, "Apple Failing to Protect Chinese Factory Workers," *BBC News,* December 18, 2014; E. Kurtenbach, "The Foreign Factory Factor," *Seattle Times,* August 31, 2006, pp. C1, C3; E. Kurtenbach, "Apple Says It's Trying to Resolve Dispute over Labor Conditions at Chinese iPod Factory," *Associated Press Financial Wire,* August 30, 2006; "Chinese iPod Supplier Pulls Suit," *Associated Press Financial Wire,* September 3, 2006.

HUMAN RIGHTS Questions of human rights can arise in international business. Basic human rights still are not respected in a large number of nations. Rights taken for granted in developed nations, such as freedom of association, freedom of speech, freedom of assembly, freedom of movement, freedom from political repression, and so on, are by no means universally accepted (see Chapter 2 for details). One of the most obvious historic examples was South Africa during the days of white rule and apartheid, which did not end until 1994. This may seem like a long time ago, but the effects of the old system—despite it ending in 1994—still linger to this day.

The apartheid system denied basic political rights to the majority nonwhite population of South Africa, mandated segregation between whites and nonwhites, reserved certain occupations exclusively for whites, and prohibited blacks from being placed in positions where they would manage whites. Despite the odious nature of this system, businesses from developed nations operated in South Africa. In the decade prior to apartheid's abolishment, however, many questioned the ethics of doing so. They argued that inward investment by foreign multinationals, by boosting the South African economy, supported the repressive apartheid regime.

Several businesses started to change their policies in the 1990s and 2000s,[4] and gearing up for the 2020s and beyond when the assumption is that most business would follow the idea of, for example, the United Nation's Sustainable Development Goals which were established in September 2015. In doing so, more and more companies are now competing on being ethical as a core philosophy promoted to customers. General Motors, which had significant activities in South Africa, was at the forefront of this trend. GM adopted what came to be called the *Sullivan principles,* named after Leon Sullivan, an African American Baptist minister and a member of GM's board of directors. Sullivan argued that it was ethically justified for GM to operate in South Africa so long as two conditions were fulfilled. First, the company should not obey the apartheid laws in its own South African operations (a form of passive resistance). Second, the company should do everything within its power to promote the abolition of apartheid laws. Sullivan's principles were widely adopted by US firms operating in South Africa. Their violation of the apartheid laws was ignored by the South African government, which clearly did not want to antagonize important foreign investors.

After 10 years, Leon Sullivan concluded that simply following the principles was not sufficient to break down the apartheid regime and that any American company, even those adhering to his principles, could not ethically justify their continued presence in South Africa. Over the next few years, numerous companies divested their South African operations, including Exxon, General Motors, IBM, and Xerox. At the same time, many state pension funds signaled they would no longer hold stock in companies that did business in South Africa, which helped persuade several companies to divest their South African operations. These divestments, coupled with the imposition of economic sanctions from the United States and other governments, contributed to the abandonment of white minority rule and apartheid in South Africa and the introduction of democratic elections in 1994. Thus, adopting an ethical stance was argued to have helped improve human rights in South Africa.[5]

Although change has come in South Africa, many repressive regimes still exist in the world. Is it ethical for multinationals to do business in them? It is often argued that inward investment by a multinational can be a force for economic, political, and social progress that ultimately improves the rights of people in repressive regimes. This position was first discussed in Chapter 2, when we noted that economic progress in a nation could create pressure for democratization. In general, this belief suggests it is ethical for a multinational to do business in nations that lack the democratic structures and human rights records of developed nations. Investment in China, for example, is frequently justified on the grounds that although China's human rights record is often questioned by human rights groups and although the country is not a democracy, continuing inward investment will help boost economic growth and raise living standards. These developments will ultimately create pressures from the Chinese people for more participatory government, political pluralism, and freedom of expression and speech.

There is a limit to this argument. As in the case of South Africa, some regimes are so repressive that investment cannot be justified on ethical grounds. Another example would be Myanmar (formerly known as Burma). Ruled by a military dictatorship for more than 45 years, Myanmar has one of the worst human rights records in the world. Beginning in the mid-1990s, many companies exited Myanmar, judging the human rights violations to be so extreme that doing business there cannot be justified on ethical grounds. (In contrast, the accompanying Management Focus looks at the controversy surrounding one company, Unocal, which chose to stay in Myanmar.) However, a cynic might note that Myanmar has a small economy and that divestment carries no great economic penalty for firms, unlike, for example, divestment from China. Interestingly, after decades of pressure from the international community, in 2012 the military government of Myanmar finally acquiesced and allowed limited democratic elections to be held.

ENVIRONMENTAL POLLUTION Ethical issues arise when environmental regulations in host nations are inferior to those in the home nation. Many developed nations have substantial regulations governing the emission of pollutants, the dumping of toxic chemicals, the use of toxic materials in the workplace, and so on. Those regulations are often lacking in developing nations, and, according to critics, the result can be higher levels of pollution from the operations of multinationals than would be allowed at home.

Should a multinational feel free to pollute in a developing nation? To do so hardly seems ethical. Is there a danger that amoral management might move production to a developing nation precisely because costly pollution controls are not required and the company is, therefore, free to despoil the

management FOCUS

Unocal and Total Collaboration

A couple of decades ago, Unocal, an oil and gas enterprise based in California, took a 29 percent stake in a partnership with the French oil company Total and state-owned companies from both Myanmar and Thailand to build a gas pipeline from Myanmar to Thailand. At the time, the $1 billion project was expected to bring Myanmar about $200 million in annual export earnings, a quarter of the country's total. The gas used domestically would increase Myanmar's generating capacity by 30 percent. This investment was made when a number of other American companies were exiting Myanmar. Myanmar's government, a military dictatorship, had a reputation for brutally suppressing internal dissent. Citing the political climate, the apparel companies Levi Strauss and Eddie Bauer had both withdrawn from the country. However, as far as Unocal's management was concerned, the giant infrastructure project would generate healthy returns for the company and, by boosting economic growth, a better life for Myanmar's now 53 million people. Moreover, while Levi Strauss and Eddie Bauer could easily shift production of clothes to another low-cost location, Unocal argued it had to go where the oil and gas were located.

However, Unocal's investment quickly became highly controversial. Under the terms of the contract, the government of Myanmar was contractually obliged to clear a corridor for the pipeline through Myanmar's tropical forests and to protect the pipeline from attacks by the government's enemies. According to human rights groups, the Myanmar army forcibly moved villages and ordered hundreds of local peasants to work on the pipeline in conditions that were no better than slave labor. Those who refused suffered retaliation. News reports cited the case of one woman who was thrown into a fire, along with her baby, after her husband tried to escape from troops forcing him to work on the project. The baby died and she suffered burns. Other villagers reported being beaten, tortured, raped, and otherwise mistreated when the alleged slave labor conditions were occurring.

Human rights activists brought a lawsuit against Unocal in the United States on behalf of 15 Myanmar villagers who had fled to refugee camps in Thailand. The suit claimed that Unocal was aware of what was going on, even if it did not participate or condone it, and that awareness was enough to make Unocal in part responsible for the alleged crimes. The presiding judge dismissed the case, arguing that Unocal could not be held liable for the actions of a foreign government against its own people—although the judge did note that Unocal was indeed aware of what was going on in Myanmar. The plaintiffs appealed, and the case wound up at a superior court. Ultimately, the case was settled out of court for an undisclosed amount. Unocal itself was acquired by Chevron in 2005.

Sources: Jim Carlton, "Unocal Trial for Slave Labor Claims Is Set to Start Today," *The Wall Street Journal,* December 9, 2003, p. A19; Seth Stern, "Big Business Targeted for Rights Abuse," *Christian Science Monitor,* September 4, 2003, p. 2; "Trouble in the Pipeline," *The Economist,* January 18, 1997, p. 39; Evelyn Iritani, "Feeling the Heat: Unocal Defends Myanmar Gas Pipeline Deal," *Los Angeles Times,* February 20, 1995, p. D1; "Unocal Settles Myanmar Human Rights Cases," *Business and Environment,* February 16, 2005, pp. 14–16.

Early-morning smog hangs over office towers in Shanghai, China. Companies are faced with ethical decisions in moving to host nations where environmental regulations are less stringent.

Source: © Atiger/Shutterstock.com

environment and perhaps endanger local people in its quest to lower production costs and gain a competitive advantage? What is the right and moral thing to do in such circumstances: pollute to gain an economic advantage, or make sure that foreign subsidiaries adhere to common standards regarding pollution controls?

These questions take on added importance because some parts of the environment are a public good that no one owns but anyone can despoil. No one owns the atmosphere or the oceans, but polluting both, no matter where the pollution originates, harms all.[6] The atmosphere and oceans can be viewed as a global commons from which everyone benefits but for which no one is specifically responsible. In such cases, a phenomenon known as the *tragedy of the commons* becomes applicable. The tragedy of the commons occurs when a resource held in common by all but owned by no one is overused by individuals, resulting in its degradation. The phenomenon was first named by Garrett Hardin when describing a particular problem in sixteenth-century England. Large open areas, called commons, were free for all to use as pasture. The poor put out livestock on these commons and supplemented their meager incomes. It was advantageous for each to put out more and more livestock, but the social consequence was far more livestock than the commons could handle. The result was overgrazing, degradation of the commons, and the loss of this much-needed supplement.[7]

Should the United States Have Jurisdiction over Foreign Firms?

The Foreign Corrupt Practices Act (FCPA) is not just imposed on U.S. companies with operations globally. It also has jurisdiction over foreigners operating in the country. Settling a FCPA investigation, Siemens—Europe's largest engineering company and the largest electronics company in the world—was fined $800 million by the U.S. Department of Justice and the U.S. Securities and Exchange Commission. Together with various penalties imposed in Germany, Siemens' home country, the penalties total $1.6 billion. The settlement involved at least 4,200 allegedly corrupt payments totaling some $1.4 billion over six years to foreign officials in numerous countries. Meetings, negotiations, and bank account transfers were taking place in the United States between Siemens and officials from other countries. Is it appropriate that the U.S. government can use the FCPA to investigate and fine foreign companies doing business in other countries?

Sources: U.S. Department of Justice, www.justice.gov; "Siemens: A Giant Awakens," *The Economist*, September 10, 2010; J. Ewing, "Siemens Settlement: Relief, But Is It Over?" *BusinessWeek*, December 15, 2008.

Corporations can contribute to the *global tragedy of the commons* by moving production to locations where they are free to pump pollutants into the atmosphere or dump them in oceans or rivers, thereby harming these valuable global commons. While such action may be legal, is it ethical? Again, such actions seem to violate basic societal notions of ethics and corporate social responsibility. This issue is taking on greater importance as concerns about human-induced global warming move to center stage. Most climate scientists argue that human industrial and commercial activity is increasing the amount of carbon dioxide in the atmosphere; carbon dioxide is a greenhouse gas, which reflects heat back to the earth's surface, warming the globe; and as a result, the average temperature of the earth is increasing. The accumulated scientific evidence from numerous databases supports this argument.[8] Consequently, societies around the world are starting to restrict the amount of carbon dioxide that can be emitted into the atmosphere as a by-product of industrial and commercial activity. However, regulations differ from nation to nation. Given this, is it ethical for a company to try to escape tight emission limits by moving production to a country with lax regulations, given that doing so will contribute to global warming? Again, many would argue that doing so violates basic ethical principles.

CORRUPTION As noted in Chapter 2, corruption has been a problem in almost every society in history, and it continues to be one today.[9] There always have been and always will be corrupt government officials. International businesses can and have gained economic advantages by making payments to those officials. A historical and classic example concerns a well-publicized incident in the 1970s. Carl Kotchian, the president of Lockheed, made a $12.6 million payment to Japanese agents and government officials to secure a large order for Lockheed's TriStar jet from Nippon Air. When the payments were discovered, U.S. officials charged Lockheed with falsification of its records and tax violations. Although such payments were supposed to be an accepted business practice in Japan (they might be viewed as an exceptionally lavish form of gift-giving), the revelations created a scandal there too. The government ministers in question were criminally charged, one committed suicide, the government fell in disgrace, and the Japanese people were outraged. Apparently, such a payment was not an accepted way of doing business in Japan! The payment was nothing more than a bribe, paid to corrupt officials, to secure a large order that might otherwise have gone to another manufacturer, such as Boeing. Kotchian clearly engaged in unethical behavior—and to argue that the payment was an "acceptable form of doing business in Japan" was self-serving and incorrect.

management FOCUS

Daimler, Chrysler, and Bribes

In 1998, Daimler, one of the world's largest manufacturers of automobiles, purchased the Chrysler Corporation for what was a reported $38 billion. Soon afterward, a former Chrysler auditor identified suspicious payments being made by subsidiaries. For example, in 2002 Daimler's Chinese subsidiary paid $25,000 to a Texas company listed at a residential apartment complex in Houston. The auditor suspected that such payments were bribes and reported the issue to the U.S. Securities and Exchange Commission (SEC), which then teamed up with the U.S. Department of Justice (DOJ) and began an investigation.

The investigation took eight years. During that time, investigators uncovered a pattern of corruption so widespread that an SEC official described it as "standard operating practice at Daimler." In the case of the $25,000 payment, the Texas company was a shell organization established to launder the money, and the payment was to be passed on to the wife of a Chinese government official who was involved in contract negotiations for about $1.3 million in commercial vehicles. In another case, bribes were given to secure the sale of passenger and commercial vehicles to government entities in Russia. Daimler overcharged for the cars on invoices and passed the overpayments to bank accounts in Latvia controlled by the Russian officials responsible for the purchase decision. In certain cases, Daimler made bribes from "cash desks," allowing employees to take out large amounts of currency to make payments to foreign officials.

In total, the investigation uncovered hundreds of such payments in at least 22 countries that were linked to the sale of vehicles valued at $1.9 billion. The SEC stated, "The bribery was so pervasive in Daimler's decentralized corporate structure that it extended outside of the sales organization to internal audit, legal, and finance departments. These departments should have caught and stopped the illegal sales practices, but instead they permitted or were directly involved in the company's bribery practices."

Threatened with court proceedings in the United States, in 2010 Daimler entered into a consent decree with the SEC under which it agreed to pay $185 million in criminal and civil fines. While subsidiaries of Daimler in Germany and Russia pleaded guilty to corruption charges, the corporate parent and the Chinese subsidiary will avoid indictment so long as they live up to an agreement to halt such practices.

Some 10 years after Daimler bought Chrysler (some say it was a merger of equals) and became a target of the SEC because of a Chrysler employee's whistle-blower actions, Daimler sold off Chrysler in 2007 to Cerberus Capital Management for $6 billion, and the name was changed to simply "Daimler AG." Since Chrysler's bankruptcy filing in the United States in 2009, the company has been controlled as a unit by Italian automaker Fiat. Chrysler Automobiles, with main offices in Auburn Hills, Michigan, has shown strong improvements in sales and profits in recent years.

Sources: M. Wayland, "Fiat Chrysler-UAW Profit Sharing Increases to $2750," *Detroit News*, February 3, 2015; A. R. Sorkin, "Daimler to Pay $185 Million to Settle Corruption Charges," *The New York Times*, March 24, 2010; "Corruption: Daimler Settles with DOJ; SEC Wades in: Germany Next," *Chiefofficers.net*, March 25, 2010.

Foreign Corrupt Practices Act (FCPA)
U.S. law regulating behavior regarding the conduct of international business in the taking of bribes and other unethical actions.

The Lockheed case was the impetus for the 1977 passage of the **Foreign Corrupt Practices Act (FCPA)** in the United States, discussed in Chapter 2. The act outlawed the paying of bribes to foreign government officials to gain business. Some U.S. businesses immediately objected that the act would put U.S. firms at a competitive disadvantage (there is no evidence that has occurred).[10] The act was subsequently amended to allow for "facilitating payments." Sometimes known as *speed money* or *grease payments*, facilitating payments are *not* payments to secure contracts that would not otherwise be secured, nor are they payments to obtain exclusive preferential treatment. Rather they are payments to ensure receiving the standard treatment that a business ought to receive from a foreign government but might not due to the obstruction of a foreign official. The accompanying Management Focus looks at what happened when the German company Daimler ran afoul of the FCPA.

Convention on Combating Bribery of Foreign Public Officials in International Business Transactions
An OECD convention that establishes legally binding standards to criminalize bribery of foreign public officials in international business transactions and provides for a host of related measures that make this effective.

In 1997, the trade and finance ministers from the member states of the Organisation for Economic Co-operation and Development (OECD) followed the U.S. lead and adopted the **Convention on Combating Bribery of Foreign Public Officials in International Business Transactions**.[11] The convention, which went into force in 1999, obliges member states and other signatories to make the bribery of foreign public officials a criminal offense. The convention excludes facilitating payments made to expedite routine government action from the convention.

While facilitating payments, or *speed money*, are excluded from both the Foreign Corrupt Practices Act and the OECD convention on bribery, the ethical implications of making such payments are unclear. From a pragmatic standpoint, giving bribes, although a little evil, might be the price that must be paid to do a greater good (assuming the investment creates jobs where none existed and assuming the practice is not illegal). Several economists advocate this reasoning, suggesting that in the context of pervasive and cumbersome regulations in developing countries, corruption may improve efficiency and help growth! These economists theorize that in a country where preexisting political structures distort or limit the workings of the market mechanism, corruption in the form of black-marketeering, smuggling, and side payments to government bureaucrats to "speed up" approval for business investments may enhance welfare.[12] Arguments such as this persuaded the U.S. Congress to exempt facilitating payments from the FCPA.

In contrast, other economists have argued that corruption reduces the returns on business investment and leads to low economic growth.[13] In a country where corruption is common, unproductive bureaucrats who demand side payments for granting the enterprise permission to operate may siphon off the profits from a business activity. This reduces businesses' incentive to invest and may retard a country's economic growth rate. One study of the connection between corruption and economic growth in 70 countries found that corruption had a significant negative impact on a country's growth rate.[14] Another study found that firms that paid more in bribes are likely to spend more, not less, management time with bureaucrats negotiating regulations and that this tended to raise the costs of the firm.[15]

Given the debate and the complexity of this issue, we again might conclude that generalization is difficult and the demand for speed money creates a genuine ethical dilemma. Yes, corruption is bad, and yes, it may harm a country's economic development, but yes, there are also cases where side payments to government officials can remove the bureaucratic barriers to investments that create jobs. However, this pragmatic stance ignores the fact that corruption tends to corrupt both the bribe giver and the bribe taker. Corruption feeds on itself, and once an individual starts down the road of corruption, pulling back may be difficult, if not impossible. This argument strengthens the ethical case for never engaging in corruption, no matter how compelling the benefits might seem.

Many multinationals have accepted this argument. The large oil multinational BP, for example, has a zero-tolerance approach toward facilitating payments. Other corporations have a more nuanced approach. For example, Dow Corning used to formally state a few years ago in its Code of Conduct that "in countries where local business practice dictates such [facilitating] payments and there is no alternative, facilitating payments are to be for the minimum amount necessary and must be accurately documented and recorded."[16] This statement recognized that business practices and customs differ from country to country. At the same time, Dow Corning allowed for facilitating payments when "there is no alternative," although they were also stated to be strongly discouraged. More recently, the latest version of Dow Corning's Code of Conduct has removed the section on "international business guidelines" altogether, so our assumption has to be that the company is taking a stronger zero-tolerance approach at this time.

Dow Corning may have simply realized that the nuances between a bribe and a facilitating payment are very unclear in interpretation. Many U.S. companies have sustained FCPA violations due to facilitating payments that were made but did not fall within the general rules allowing such payments. For example, in 2008 the global freight forwarder Con-way paid a $300,000 penalty for making hundreds of what could be considered small payments to various customs officials in the Philippines. In total, Con-way distributed some $244,000 to these officials who were induced to violate customs regulations, settle disputes, and not enforce fines for administrative violations.[17]

Use SmartBook to help retain what you have learned. Access your Instructor's Connect course to check out SmartBook or go to learnsmartadvantage.com for help.

Ethical Dilemmas

Recognize an ethical dilemma.

The ethical obligations of a multinational corporation toward employment conditions, human rights, corruption, and environmental pollution are not always clear-cut. However, what is becoming clear-cut is the businesses are feeling more and more of the marketplace pressures from customers and other stakeholders to be transparent in their ethical decision making and operations. At the same time, there are no universal worldwide agreement about what constitutes accepted ethical principles. From an international business perspective, some argue that what is ethical depends on one's cultural perspective.[18] In the United States, it is considered acceptable to execute murderers, but in many cultures, this is not acceptable—execution is viewed as an affront to human dignity, and the death penalty is outlawed. Many Americans find this attitude very strange, but, for example, many Europeans find the American approach barbaric. For a more business-oriented example, consider the practice of "gift-giving" between the parties to a business negotiation. While this is considered right and proper behavior in many Asian cultures, some Westerners view the practice as a form of bribery, and, therefore unethical, particularly if the gifts are substantial.

Child labor is still common in many poor nations.

Source: © Ata Mohammad Adnan/Moment/Getty Images

Managers often confront very real ethical dilemmas where the appropriate course of action is not clear. For example, imagine that a visiting American executive finds that a foreign subsidiary in a poor nation has hired a 12-year-old girl to work on a factory floor. Appalled to find that the subsidiary is using child labor in direct violation of the company's own ethical code, the American instructs the local manager to replace the child with an adult. The local manager dutifully complies. The girl, an orphan, who is the only breadwinner for herself and her six-year-old brother, is unable to find another job, so in desperation she turns to prostitution. Two years later, she dies of AIDS.

Had the visiting American understood the gravity of the girl's situation, would he still have requested her replacement? Perhaps not! Would it have been better, therefore, to stick with the status quo and allow the girl to continue working? Probably not, because that would have violated the reasonable prohibition against child labor found in the company's own ethical code. What then would have been the right thing to do? What was the obligation of the executive given this ethical dilemma?

Ethical Dilemma
A situation in which there is no ethically acceptable solution.

There are no easy answers to these questions. That is the nature of **ethical dilemmas**—situations in which none of the available alternatives seems ethically acceptable.[19] In this case, employing child labor was not acceptable, but given that she was employed, neither was denying the child her only source of income. What this American executive needs, what all managers need, is a moral compass, or perhaps an ethical algorithm, to guide them through such an ethical dilemma to find an acceptable solution. Later, we will outline what such a moral compass, or ethical algorithm, might look like. For now, it is enough to note that ethical dilemmas exist because many real-world decisions are complex, difficult to frame, and involve first-, second-, and third-order consequences that are hard to quantify. Doing the right thing, or even knowing what the right thing might be, is often far from easy.[20]

test PREP

Use SmartBook to help retain what you have learned. Access your Instructor's Connect course to check out SmartBook or go to learnsmartadvantage.com for help.

LO 5-3
Identify the causes of unethical behavior by managers.

The Roots of Unethical Behavior

Examples are plentiful of managers behaving in a manner that might be judged unethical in an international business setting. Why do managers behave in an unethical manner? There is no simple answer to this question because the causes are complex, but some generalizations can be made and these issues are rooted in six determinants of ethical behavior: personal ethics, decision-making processes, organizational culture, unrealistic performance goals, leadership, and societal culture (see Figure 5.1).[21]

5.1 FIGURE
Determinants of Ethical Behavior.

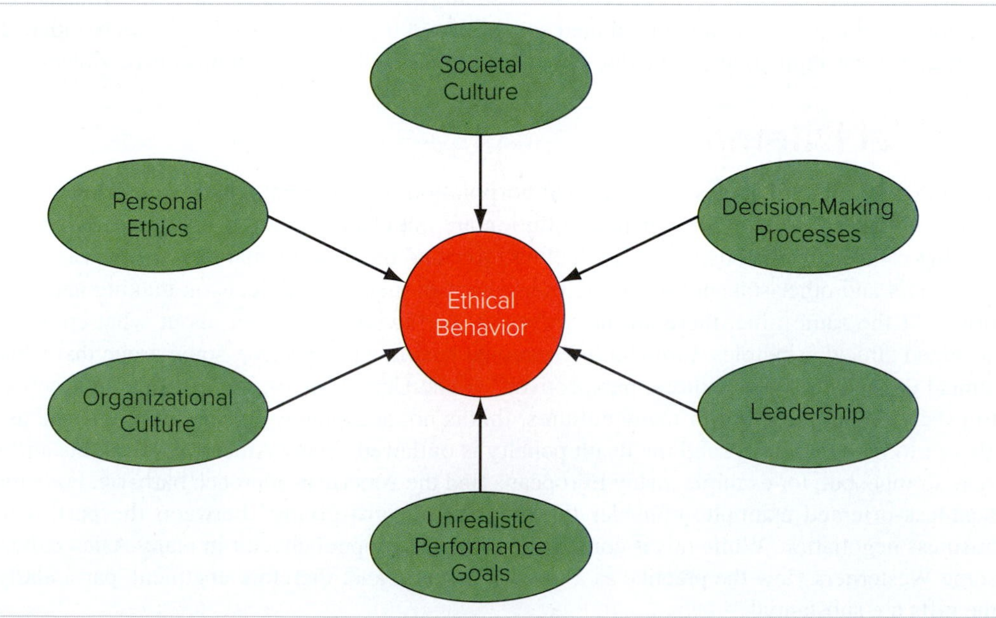

PERSONAL ETHICS Societal business ethics are not divorced from *personal ethics,* which are the generally accepted principles of right and wrong governing the conduct of individuals. As individuals, we are typically taught that it is wrong to lie and cheat—it is unethical—and that it is right to behave with integrity and honor and to stand up for what we believe to be right and true. This is generally true across societies. The personal ethical code that guides our behavior comes from a number of sources, including our parents, our schools, our religion, and the media. Our personal ethical code exerts a profound influence on the way we behave as businesspeople. An individual with a strong sense of personal ethics is less likely to behave in an unethical manner in a business setting. It follows that the first step to establishing a strong sense of business ethics is for a society to emphasize strong personal ethics.

Home-country managers working abroad in multinational firms (expatriate managers) may experience more than the usual degree of pressure to violate their personal ethics. They are away from their ordinary social context and supporting culture, and they are psychologically and geographically distant from the parent company. They may be based in a culture that does not place the same value on ethical norms important in the manager's home country, and they may be surrounded by local employees who have less rigorous ethical standards. The parent company may pressure expatriate managers to meet unrealistic goals that can only be fulfilled by cutting corners or acting unethically. For example, to meet centrally mandated performance goals, expatriate managers might give bribes to win contracts or might implement working conditions and environmental controls that are below minimal acceptable standards. Local managers might encourage the expatriate to adopt such behavior. Due to its geographic distance, the parent company may be unable to see how expatriate managers are meeting goals or may choose not to see how they are doing so, allowing such behavior to flourish and persist.

DECISION-MAKING PROCESSES Several studies of unethical behavior in a business setting have concluded that businesspeople sometimes do not realize they are behaving unethically, primarily because they simply fail to ask, "Is this decision or action ethical?"[22] Instead, they apply a straightforward business calculus to what they perceive to be a business decision, forgetting that the decision may also have an important ethical dimension. The fault lies in processes that do not incorporate ethical considerations into business decision making. This may have been the case at Nike when managers originally made subcontracting decisions. Those decisions were probably made based on good economic logic. Subcontractors were probably chosen based on business variables such as cost, delivery, and product quality, but the key managers simply failed to ask, "How does this subcontractor treat its workforce?" If they thought about the question at all, they probably reasoned that it was the subcontractor's concern, not theirs.

To improve ethical decision making in a multinational firm, the best starting point is to better understand how individuals make decisions that can be considered ethical or unethical in an organizational environment.[23] Two assumptions must be taken into account. First, too often it is assumed that individuals in the workplace make ethical decisions in the same way as they would if they were home. Second, too often it is assumed that people from different cultures make ethical decisions following a similar process (see Chapter 4 for more on cultural differences). Both of these assumptions are problematic. First, within an organization, there are very few individuals who have the freedom (e.g., power) to decide ethical issues independent of pressures that may exist in an organizational setting (e.g., should we make a facilitating payment or resort to bribery?). Second, while the process for making an ethical decision may largely be the same in many countries, the relative emphasis on certain issues are unlikely to be the same. Some cultures may stress organizational factors (e.g., Japan), while others stress individual personal factors (e.g., the United States), yet some may base it purely on opportunity (e.g., Myanmar) and others base it on the importance to their superiors, for example (e.g., India).

ORGANIZATIONAL CULTURE The culture in some businesses does not encourage people to think through the ethical consequences of business decisions. This brings us to the third cause of unethical behavior in businesses: an organizational culture that deemphasizes business ethics, reducing all decisions to the purely economic. The term **organizational culture** refers to the values and norms that are shared among employees of an organization. You will

Organizational Culture
The values and norms shared among an organization's employees.

recall from Chapter 4 that *values* are abstract ideas about what a group believes to be good, right, and desirable, while *norms* are the social rules and guidelines that prescribe appropriate behavior in particular situations. Just as societies have cultures, so do business organizations. Together, values and norms shape the culture of a business organization, and that culture has an important influence on the ethics of business decision making.

The Management Focus on corruption at Daimler and Chrysler, for example, strongly suggests that paying bribes to secure business contracts was long viewed as an acceptable way of doing business within that company. It was, in the words of an investigator, "standard business practice" that permeated much of the organization, including departments such as auditing and finance that were supposed to detect and halt such behavior. It can be argued that such a widespread practice could have persisted only if the values and norms of the organization implicitly approved of paying bribes to secure business.

UNREALISTIC PERFORMANCE GOALS A fourth cause of unethical behavior has already been hinted at: pressure from the parent company to meet unrealistic performance goals that can be attained only by cutting corners or acting in an unethical manner. In the Daimler case, for example, bribery may have been viewed as a way to hit challenging performance goals. The combination of an organizational culture that legitimizes unethical behavior, or at least turns a blind eye to such behavior, and unrealistic performance goals may be particularly toxic. In such circumstances, there is a greater than average probability that managers will violate their own personal ethics and engage in unethical behavior. Conversely, an organization culture can do just the opposite and reinforce the need for ethical behavior. At Hewlett-Packard, for example, Bill Hewlett and David Packard, the company's founders, propagated a set of values known as The HP Way. These values, which shape the way business is conducted both within and by the corporation, have an important ethical component. Among other things, they stress the need for confidence in and respect for people, open communication, and concern for the individual employee.

LEADERSHIP The Hewlett-Packard example suggests a fifth root cause of unethical behavior: leadership. Leaders help establish the culture of an organization, and they set the example, rules, and guidelines that others follow as well as the structure and processes for operating both strategically and in daily operations. Employees often operate and work within a defined structure with a mindset very much similar to the overall culture of the organization that employs them.

Additionally, employees in a business often take their cue from business leaders, and if those leaders do not behave in an ethical manner, the employees might not either. It is not just what leaders say that matters but what they do or do not do. What message, then, did the leaders at Daimler send about corrupt practices? Presumably, they did very little to discourage them and may have encouraged such behavior.

SOCIETAL CULTURE Societal culture may well have an impact on the propensity of people and organizations to behave in an unethical manner. One study of 2,700 firms in 24 countries found that there were significant differences among the ethical policies of firms headquartered in different countries.[24] Using Hofstede's dimensions of social culture (see Chapter 4), the study found that enterprises headquartered in cultures where individualism and uncertainty avoidance are strong were more likely to emphasize the importance of behaving ethically than firms headquartered in cultures where masculinity and power distance are important cultural attributes. Such analysis suggests that enterprises headquartered in a country such as Russia, which scores high on masculinity and power distance measures, and where corruption is endemic, are more likely to engage in unethical behavior than enterprises headquartered in Scandinavia.

Use SmartBook to help retain what you have learned. Access your Instructor's Connect course to check out SmartBook or go to learnsmartadvantage.com for help.

Describe the different philosophical approaches to ethics.

Philosophical Approaches to Ethics

In this section, we look at several different philosophical approaches to business ethics in the global marketplace. Basically, all individuals adopt a process for making ethical (or unethical) decisions. This process is based on their personal philosophical approach to ethics—that is, the underlying moral fabric of the individual.

We begin with what can best be described as straw men, which either deny the value of business ethics or apply the concept in a very unsatisfactory way. Having discussed and, we hope you agree, dismissed the straw men, we move on to consider approaches that are favored by most moral philosophers and form the basis for current models of ethical behavior in international businesses.

STRAW MEN

Straw men approaches to business ethics are raised by business ethics scholars primarily to demonstrate that they offer inappropriate guidelines for ethical decision making in a multinational enterprise. Four such approaches to business ethics are commonly discussed in the literature. These approaches can be characterized as the Friedman doctrine, cultural relativism, the righteous moralist, and the naive immoralist. All these approaches have some inherent value, but all are unsatisfactory in important ways. Nevertheless, sometimes companies adopt these approaches.

The Friedman Doctrine

The Nobel Prize–winning economist Milton Friedman wrote an article in the *New York Times* in 1970 that has since become a classic straw man example that business ethics scholars outline only to then tear down.[25] Friedman's basic position is that "the social responsibility of business is to increase profits," so long as the company stays within the rules of law. He explicitly rejects the idea that businesses should undertake social expenditures beyond those mandated by the law and required for the efficient running of a business. For example, his arguments suggest that improving working conditions beyond the level required by the law *and* necessary to maximize employee productivity will reduce profits and are therefore not appropriate. His belief is that a firm should maximize its profits because that is the way to maximize the returns that accrue to the owners of the firm, its shareholders. If the shareholders then wish to use the proceeds to make social investments, that is their right, according to Friedman, but managers of the firm should not make that decision for them.

"When in Rome, Behave Like a Swede," Really?

You would think that as one of the authors of this book is from Sweden, it seemed convenient to revise the ancient proverb "when in Rome, do as the Romans" to "when in Rome, behave like a Swede." But instead this slightly reworded saying was coined in an article in *The Economist*. As just one example, IKEA, the Swedish furniture giant, as mentioned in the article, has gone to great lengths to fight corruption worldwide. In that spirit, the argument is for the case that doing the right thing is smart business. But we all know—even the Swedish author of this book (!)—that the global marketplace can be a jungle: It's eat or be eaten. Now if we go back to the ancient proverb, the meaning of it basically suggests that we should behave as those around us and conform to the culture in the foreign society in which we are doing business. So, what is your preference: Do you prefer "when in Rome, do as the Romans" or "when in Rome, behave like a Swede"?

Sources: "The Corruption Eruption," *The Economist*, April 29, 2010; Ethical Business Ethics, May 6, 2010. http://ethicalbusinessethics.blogspot.com.

Although Friedman is talking about social responsibility and "ethical custom," rather than business ethics per se, many business ethics scholars equate social responsibility with ethical behavior and thus believe Friedman is also arguing against business ethics. However, the assumption that Friedman is arguing against ethics is not quite true, for Friedman does argue that there is only one social responsibility of business: to increase the profitability of the enterprise so long as it stays within the law, which is taken to mean that it engages in open and free competition without deception or fraud.[26]

> There is one and only one social responsibility of business—to use its resources and engage in activities designed to increase its profits so long as it stays within the rules of the game, which is to say that it engages in open and free competition without deception or fraud.[27]

In other words, Friedman argues that businesses should behave in a socially responsible manner, according to ethical custom and without deception and fraud.

Critics charge that Friedman's arguments break down under examination. This is particularly true in international business, where the "rules of the game" are not well established and

Are Human Rights a Moral Compass?

The Universal Declaration of Human Rights (UDHR) was adopted by the United Nations General Assembly on December 10, 1948, in Paris, France. The Preamble of UDHR starts by stating that "Whereas recognition of the inherent dignity and of the equal and inalienable rights of all members of the human family is the foundation of freedom, justice and peace in the world . . . ." The day on which UDHR was adopted, December 10, is known as "International Human Rights Day," and this day is also the one on which the Nobel Peace Prize is awarded annually. One human right that we discuss in the text is the right to free speech; by the same token, we have an obligation to respect free speech. But are there issues, situations, or reasons where free speech should not be granted?

Sources: "The Universal Declaration of Human Rights," United Nations, www.un.org/en/documents/udhr; the official site of the Nobel Prize, www.nobelprize.org.

differ from country to county. Consider again the case of sweatshop labor. Child labor may not be against the law in a developing nation, and maximizing productivity may not require that a multinational firm stop using child labor in that country, but it is still immoral to use child labor because the practice conflicts with widely held views about what is the right and proper thing to do. Similarly, there may be no rules against pollution in a less developed nation and spending money on pollution control may reduce the profit rate of the firm, but generalized notions of morality would hold that it is still unethical to dump toxic pollutants into rivers or foul the air with gas releases. In addition to the local consequences of such pollution, which may have serious health effects for the surrounding population, there is also a global consequence as pollutants degrade those two global commons so important to us all: the atmosphere and the oceans.

Cultural Relativism

The belief that ethics are culturally determined and that firms should adopt the ethics of the cultures in which they operate.

Cultural Relativism Another straw man often raised by business ethics scholars is **cultural relativism**, which is the belief that ethics are nothing more than the reflection of a culture—all ethics are culturally determined—and that accordingly, a firm should adopt the ethics of the culture in which it is operating.[28] This approach is often summarized by the maxim *when in Rome, do as the Romans.* As with Friedman's approach, cultural relativism does not stand up to a closer look. At its extreme, cultural relativism suggests that if a culture supports slavery, it is okay to use slave labor in a country. Clearly, it is not! Cultural relativism implicitly rejects the idea that universal notions of morality transcend different cultures, but, as we argue later in the chapter, some universal notions of morality are found across cultures.

While dismissing cultural relativism in its most sweeping form, some ethicists argue there is residual value in this approach.[29] We agree. As we noted in Chapter 3, societal values and norms do vary from culture to culture, and customs do differ, so it might follow that certain business practices are ethical in one country but not another. Indeed, the facilitating payments allowed in the Foreign Corrupt Practices Act can be seen as an acknowledgment that in some countries, the payment of speed money to government officials is necessary to get business done, and, if not ethically desirable, it is at least ethically acceptable.

Righteous Moralist

One who claims that a multinational's home-country standards of ethics are the appropriate ones for companies to follow in foreign countries.

The Righteous Moralist A **righteous moralist** claims that a multinational's home-country standards of ethics are the appropriate ones for companies to follow in foreign countries. This approach is typically associated with managers from developed nations. While this seems reasonable at first blush, the approach can create problems. Consider the following example: An American bank manager was sent to Italy and was appalled to learn that the local branch's accounting department recommended grossly underreporting the bank's profits for income tax purposes.[30] The manager insisted that the bank report its earnings accurately, American style. When he was called by the Italian tax department to the firm's tax hearing, he was told the firm owed three times as much tax as it had paid, reflecting the department's standard assumption that each firm underreports its earnings by two-thirds. Despite his protests, the new assessment stood. In this case, the righteous moralist has run into a problem caused by the prevailing cultural norms in the country where he was doing business. How should he respond? The righteous moralist would argue for maintaining the position, while a more pragmatic view might be that in this case, the right thing to do is to follow the prevailing cultural norms because there is a big penalty for not doing so.

The main criticism of the righteous moralist approach is that its proponents go too far. While there are some universal moral principles that should not be violated, it does not always follow that the appropriate thing to do is adopt home-country standards. For example, U.S. laws set down strict guidelines with regard to minimum wage and working conditions. Does this mean it is ethical to apply the same guidelines in a foreign country, paying people the same as they are paid in the United States, providing the same benefits and working conditions? Probably not, because doing so might nullify the reason for investing in that country and therefore deny locals the benefits of inward investment by the multinational. Clearly, a more nuanced approach is needed.

Naive Immoralist

One who asserts that if a manager of a multinational sees that firms from other nations are not following ethical norms in a host nation, that manager should not either.

The Naive Immoralist A **naive immoralist** asserts that if a manager of a multinational sees that firms from other nations are not following ethical norms in a host nation, that manager should not either. The classic example to illustrate the approach is known as the drug lord problem. In one variant of this problem, an American manager in Colombia routinely pays off the local drug lord to guarantee that her plant will not be bombed and that none of her employees will be kidnapped. The manager argues that such payments are ethically defensible because everyone is doing it.

The objection is twofold. First, to say that an action is ethically justified if everyone is doing it is not sufficient. If firms in a country routinely employ 12-year-olds and make them work 10-hour days, is it therefore ethically defensible to do the same? Obviously not, and the company does have a clear choice. It does not have to abide by local practices, and it can decide not to invest in a country where the practices are particularly odious. Second, the multinational must recognize that it does have the ability to change the prevailing practice in a country. It can use its power for a positive moral purpose. This is what BP is doing by adopting a zero-tolerance policy with regard to facilitating payments. BP is stating that the prevailing practice of making facilitating payments is ethically wrong, and it is incumbent upon the company to use its power to try to change the standard. While some might argue that such an approach smells of moral imperialism and a lack of cultural sensitivity, if it is consistent with widely accepted moral standards in the global community, it may be ethically justified.

UTILITARIAN AND KANTIAN ETHICS

In contrast to the straw men just discussed, most moral philosophers see value in utilitarian and Kantian approaches to business ethics. These approaches were developed in the eighteenth and nineteenth centuries, and although they have been largely superseded by more modern approaches, they form part of the tradition on which newer approaches have been constructed.

The utilitarian approach to business ethics dates to philosophers such as David Hume (1711–1776), Jeremy Bentham (1748–1832), and John Stuart Mill (1806–1873). **Utilitarian approaches to ethics** hold that the moral worth of actions or practices is determined by their consequences.[31] An action is judged desirable if it leads to the best possible balance of good consequences over bad consequences. Utilitarianism is committed to the maximization of good and the minimization of harm. Utilitarianism recognizes that actions have multiple consequences, some of which are good in a social sense and some of which are harmful. As a philosophy for business ethics, it focuses attention on the need to weigh carefully all the social benefits and costs of a business action and to pursue only those actions where the benefits outweigh the costs. The best decisions, from a utilitarian perspective, are those that produce the greatest good for the greatest number of people.

Utilitarian Approaches to Ethics

These hold that the moral worth of actions or practices is determined by their consequences.

Many businesses have adopted specific tools such as cost–benefit analysis and risk assessment that are firmly rooted in a utilitarian philosophy. Managers often weigh the benefits and costs of an action before deciding whether to pursue it. An oil company considering drilling in the Alaskan wildlife preserve must weigh the economic benefits of increased oil production and the creation of jobs against the costs of environmental degradation in a fragile ecosystem. An agricultural biotechnology company such as Monsanto must decide whether the benefits of genetically modified crops that produce natural pesticides outweigh the risks. The benefits include increased crop yields and reduced need for chemical fertilizers. The risks include the possibility that Monsanto's insect-resistant crops might make matters worse over time if insects evolve a resistance to the natural pesticides engineered into Monsanto's plants, rendering the plants vulnerable to a new generation of superbugs.

The utilitarian philosophy does have some serious drawbacks as an approach to business ethics. One problem is measuring the benefits, costs, and risks of a course of action. In the case of an oil company considering drilling in Alaska, how does one measure the potential harm done to the region's ecosystem? The second problem with utilitarianism is that the philosophy omits the consideration of justice. The action that produces the greatest good for the greatest number of people may result in the unjustified treatment of a minority. Such action cannot be ethical, precisely because it is unjust. For example, suppose that in the interests of keeping down health insurance costs, the government decides to screen people for the HIV virus and deny insurance coverage to those who are HIV positive. By reducing health costs, such action might produce significant benefits for a large number of people, but the action is unjust because it discriminates unfairly against a minority.

Kantian ethics is based on the philosophy of Immanuel Kant (1724–1804). **Kantian ethics** holds that people should be treated as ends and never purely as *means* to the ends of others. People are not instruments, like a machine. People have dignity and need to be respected

Kantian Ethics

The belief that people should be treated as ends and never as means to the ends of others.

as such. Employing people in sweatshops, making them work long hours for low pay in poor working conditions, is a violation of ethics, according to Kantian philosophy, because it treats people as mere cogs in a machine and not as conscious moral beings that have dignity. Although contemporary moral philosophers tend to view Kant's ethical philosophy as incomplete—for example, his system has no place for moral emotions or sentiments such as sympathy or caring—the notion that people should be respected and treated with dignity resonates in the modern world.

Rights Theories

Twentieth-century theories that recognize that human beings have fundamental rights and privileges that transcend national boundaries and cultures.

RIGHTS THEORIES Developed in the twentieth century, **rights theories** recognize that human beings have fundamental rights and privileges that transcend national boundaries and cultures. Rights establish a minimum level of morally acceptable behavior. One well-known definition of a fundamental right construes it as something that takes precedence over or "trumps" a collective good. Thus, we might say that the right to free speech is a fundamental right that takes precedence over all but the most compelling collective goals and overrides, for example, the interest of the state in civil harmony or moral consensus.[32] Moral theorists argue that fundamental human rights form the basis for the *moral compass* that managers should navigate by when making decisions that have an ethical component. More precisely, they should not pursue actions that violate these rights.

Universal Declaration of Human Rights

A United Nations document that lays down the basic principles of human rights that should be adhered to.

The notion that there are fundamental rights that transcend national borders and cultures was the underlying motivation for the United Nations **Universal Declaration of Human Rights**, adopted in 1948, which has been ratified by almost every country on the planet and lays down basic principles that should always be adhered to irrespective of the culture in which one is doing business.[33] Echoing Kantian ethics, Article 1 of this declaration states:

> All human beings are born free and equal in dignity and rights. They are endowed with reason and conscience and should act towards one another in a spirit of brotherhood.

Article 23 of this declaration, which relates directly to employment, states:

1. Everyone has the right to work, to free choice of employment, to just and favorable conditions of work, and to protection against unemployment.
2. Everyone, without any discrimination, has the right to equal pay for equal work.
3. Everyone who works has the right to just and favorable remuneration ensuring for himself and his family an existence worthy of human dignity, and supplemented, if necessary, by other means of social protection.
4. Everyone has the right to form and to join trade unions for the protection of his interests.

Clearly, the rights to "just and favorable conditions of work," "equal pay for equal work," and remuneration that ensures an "existence worthy of human dignity" embodied in Article 23 imply that it is unethical to employ child labor in sweatshop settings and pay less than subsistence wages, even if that happens to be common practice in some countries. These are fundamental human rights that transcend national borders.

It is important to note that along with *rights* come *obligations.* Because we have the right to free speech, we are also obligated to make sure that we respect the free speech of others. The notion that people have obligations is stated in Article 29 of the Universal Declaration of Human Rights:

1. Everyone has duties to the community in which alone the free and full development of his personality is possible.

Within the framework of a theory of rights, certain people or institutions are obligated to provide benefits or services that secure the rights of others. Such obligations also fall on more than one class of moral agent (a *moral agent* is any person or institution that is capable of moral action such as a government or corporation).

For example, to escape the high costs of toxic waste disposal in the West, in the late 1980s several firms shipped their waste in bulk to African nations, where it was disposed of at a much lower cost. In 1987, five European ships unloaded toxic waste containing dangerous poisons in Nigeria. Workers wearing sandals and shorts unloaded the barrels for $2.50 a day and placed them in a dirt lot in a residential area. They were not told about the contents of the barrels.[34] Who bears the obligation for protecting the rights of workers and residents to safety in a case like this? According to rights theorists, the obligation rests not on the shoulders of one moral agent but on the shoulders of all moral agents whose actions might harm or contribute to the harm of the workers and residents. Thus, it was the obligation not just of the Nigerian government but also of the multinational firms that shipped the toxic waste to make sure it did no harm to residents and workers. In this case, both the government and the multinationals apparently failed to recognize their basic obligation to protect the fundamental human rights of others.

JUSTICE THEORIES Justice theories focus on the attainment of a just distribution of economic goods and services. A **just distribution** is one that is considered fair and equitable. There is no one theory of justice, and several theories of justice conflict with each other in important ways.[35] Here, we focus on one particular theory of justice that is both very influential and has important ethical implications. The theory is attributed to philosopher John Rawls.[36] Rawls argues that all economic goods and services should be distributed equally except when an unequal distribution would work to everyone's advantage.

Just Distribution
A distribution of goods and services that is considered fair and equitable.

According to Rawls, valid principles of justice are those with which all persons would agree if they could freely and impartially consider the situation. Impartiality is guaranteed by a conceptual device that Rawls calls the *veil of ignorance.* Under the veil of ignorance, everyone is imagined to be ignorant of all of his or her particular characteristics, for example, race, sex, intelligence, nationality, family background, and special talents. Rawls then asks what system people would design under a veil of ignorance. Under these conditions, people would unanimously agree on two fundamental principles of justice.

The first principle is that each person be permitted the maximum amount of basic liberty compatible with a similar liberty for others. Rawls takes these to be political liberty (e.g., the right to vote), freedom of speech and assembly, liberty of conscience and freedom of thought, the freedom and right to hold personal property, and freedom from arbitrary arrest and seizure.

The second principle is that once equal basic liberty is ensured, inequality in basic social goods—such as income and wealth distribution, and opportunities—is to be allowed *only* if such inequalities benefit everyone. Rawls accepts that inequalities can be just if the system that produces inequalities is to the advantage of everyone. More precisely, he formulates what he calls the *difference principle,* which is that inequalities are justified if they benefit the position of the least-advantaged person. So, for example, wide variations in income and wealth can be considered just if the market-based system that produces this unequal distribution also benefits the least-advantaged members of society. One can argue that a well-regulated, market-based economy and free trade, by promoting economic growth, benefit the least-advantaged members of society. In principle at least, the inequalities inherent in such systems are therefore just (in other words, the rising tide of wealth created by a market-based economy and free trade lifts all boats, even those of the most disadvantaged).

In the context of international business ethics, Rawls's theory creates an interesting perspective. Managers could ask themselves whether the policies they adopt in foreign operations would be considered just under Rawls's veil of ignorance. Is it just, for example, to pay foreign workers less than workers in the firm's home country? Rawls's theory would suggest it is, so long as the inequality benefits the least-advantaged members of the global society (which is what economic theory suggests). Alternatively, it is difficult to imagine that managers operating under a veil of ignorance would design a system where foreign employees were paid subsistence wages to work long hours in sweatshop conditions and where they were exposed to toxic materials. Such working conditions are clearly unjust in Rawls's framework, and therefore, it is unethical to adopt them. Similarly, operating under a veil of ignorance, most people would probably design a system that imparts some protection from environmental degradation to important global commons, such as the oceans, atmosphere, and tropical rain forests. To the extent that this is the case, it follows that it is unjust, and by extension unethical, for companies to pursue actions that contribute toward extensive degradation of these commons. Thus, Rawls's veil of ignorance is a conceptual tool that contributes to the moral compass that managers can use to help them navigate through difficult ethical dilemmas.

test PREP

Use SmartBook to help retain what you have learned. Access your Instructor's Connect course to check out SmartBook or go to learnsmartadvantage.com for help.

FOCUS ON MANAGERIAL IMPLICATIONS

MAKING ETHICAL DECISIONS INTERNATIONALLY

LO 5-5

Explain how managers can incorporate ethical considerations into their decision making.

What, then, is the best way for managers in a multinational firm to make sure that ethical considerations figure into international business decisions?

How do managers decide on an ethical course of action when confronted with decisions pertaining to working conditions, human rights, corruption, and environmental pollution? From an ethical perspective, how do managers determine the moral obligations that flow from the power of a multinational? In many cases, there are no easy answers to these questions: many of the most vexing ethical problems arise because there are very real dilemmas inherent in them and no obvious correct action. Nevertheless, managers can and should do many things to make sure that basic ethical principles are adhered to and that ethical issues are routinely inserted into international business decisions.

Here, we focus on seven actions that an international business and its managers can take to make sure ethical issues are considered in business decisions: (1) favor hiring and promoting people with a well-grounded sense of personal ethics; (2) build an organizational culture and exemplify leadership behaviors that place a high value on ethical behavior; (3) put decision-making processes in place that require people to consider the ethical dimension of business decisions; (4) institute ethical officers in the organization; (5) develop moral courage; (6) make corporate social responsibility a cornerstone of enterprise policy; and (7) pursue strategies that are sustainable.

Hiring and Promotion

It seems obvious that businesses should strive to hire people who have a strong sense of personal ethics and would not engage in unethical or illegal behavior. Similarly, you would expect a business to not promote people, and perhaps to fire people, whose behavior does not match generally accepted ethical standards. However, actually doing so is very difficult. How do you know that someone has a poor sense of personal ethics? In our society, we have an incentive to hide a lack of personal ethics from public view. Once people realize that you are unethical, they will no longer trust you.

Is there anything that businesses can do to make sure they do not hire people who subsequently turn out to have poor personal ethics, particularly given that people have an incentive to hide this from public view (indeed, the unethical person may lie about his or her nature)? Businesses can give potential employees psychological tests to try to discern their ethical predispositions, and they can check with prior employees regarding someone's reputation (e.g., by asking for letters of reference and talking to people who have worked with the prospective employee). The latter is common and does influence the hiring process. Promoting people who have displayed poor ethics should not occur in a company where the organizational culture values the need for ethical behavior and where leaders act accordingly.

Not only should businesses strive to identify and hire people with a strong sense of personal ethics, but it also is in the interests of prospective employees to find out as much as they can about the ethical climate in an organization. Who wants to work at a multinational such as Enron, which ultimately entered bankruptcy because unethical executives had established risky partnerships that were hidden from public view and that existed in part to enrich those same executives?

Organizational Culture and Leadership

Code of Ethics

A business's formal statement of ethical priorities.

To foster ethical behavior, businesses need to build an organizational culture that values ethical behavior. Three things are particularly important in building an organizational culture that emphasizes ethical behavior. First, the businesses must explicitly articulate values that emphasize ethical behavior. Many companies now do this by drafting a **code of ethics**, which is a formal statement of the ethical priorities a business adheres to. Often, the code of ethics draws heavily on documents such as the UN Universal Declaration of Human Rights, which itself is grounded in Kantian and rights-based theories of moral philosophy. Others have incorporated ethical statements into documents that articulate the values or mission of the business. For example, the food and consumer products multinational Unilever has a code of ethics that includes the following points:[37]

> **Employees:** Unilever is committed to diversity in a working environment where there is mutual trust and respect and where everyone feels responsible for the performance and reputation of our company. We will recruit, employ, and promote employees on the sole basis of the qualifications and abilities needed for the work to be performed. We are committed to safe and healthy working conditions for all employees. We will not use any form of forced, compulsory, or child labor. We are committed to working with employees to develop and enhance each individual's skills and capabilities. We respect the dignity of the individual and the right of employees to freedom of association. We will maintain good communications with employees through company-based information and consultation procedures.
>
> **Business Integrity:** Unilever does not give or receive, whether directly or indirectly, bribes or other improper advantages for business or financial gain. No employee may offer, give, or receive any gift or payment which is, or may be construed as being, a bribe. Any demand for, or offer of, a bribe must be rejected immediately and reported to management. Unilever accounting records and supporting documents must accurately describe and reflect the nature of the underlying transactions. No undisclosed or unrecorded account, fund, or asset will be established or maintained.

It is clear from these principles that, among other things, Unilever will not tolerate substandard working conditions, use child labor, or give bribes under any circumstances. Note also the reference to respecting the dignity of employees, a statement that is grounded in Kantian ethics. Unilever's principles send a very clear message about appropriate ethics to managers and employees.

Having articulated values in a code of ethics or some other document, leaders in the business must give life and meaning to those words by repeatedly emphasizing their importance *and then acting on them.* This means using every relevant opportunity to stress the importance of business ethics and making sure that key business decisions not only make good economic sense but also are ethical. Many companies have gone a step further by hiring independent auditors to make sure they are behaving in a manner consistent with their ethical codes. Nike, for example, has hired independent auditors to make sure that subcontractors used by the company are living up to Nike's code of conduct.

Finally, building an organizational culture that places a high value on ethical behavior requires incentive and reward systems, including promotions that reward people who engage in ethical behavior and sanction those who do not. At General Electric, for example, the former CEO Jack Welch has described how he reviewed the performance of managers, dividing them into several different groups. These included overperformers who displayed the right values and were singled out for advancement and bonuses and overperformers who displayed the wrong values and were let go. Welch was not willing to tolerate leaders within the company who did not act in accordance with the central values of the company, even if they were in all other respects skilled managers.[38]

Decision-Making Processes

In addition to establishing the right kind of ethical culture in an organization, businesspeople must be able to think through the ethical implications of decisions in a systematic way. To do this, they need a moral compass, and both rights theories and Rawls's theory of justice help provide such a compass. Beyond these theories, some experts on ethics have proposed a straightforward practical guide—or ethical algorithm—to determine whether a decision is ethical.[39] According to these experts, a decision is acceptable on ethical grounds if a businessperson can answer yes to each of these questions:

- Does my decision fall within the accepted values or standards that typically apply in the organizational environment (as articulated in a code of ethics or some other corporate statement)?
- Am I willing to see the decision communicated to all stakeholders affected by it—for example, by having it reported in newspapers, on television, or via social media?

- Would the people with whom I have a significant personal relationship, such as family members, friends, or even managers in other businesses, approve of the decision?

Stakeholders

The individuals or groups that have an interest, stake, or claim in the actions and overall performance of a company.

Internal Stakeholders

People who work for or own the business such as employees, directors, and stockholders.

External Stakeholders

Individuals or groups that have some claim on a firm such as customers, suppliers, and unions.

Others have recommended a five-step process to think through ethical problems (this is another example of an ethical algorithm).[40] In step 1, businesspeople should identify which stakeholders a decision would affect and in what ways. A firm's **stakeholders** are individuals or groups that have an interest, claim, or stake in the company, in what it does, and in how well it performs.[41] They can be divided into internal stakeholders and external stakeholders. **Internal stakeholders** are individuals or groups who work for or own the business. They include primary stakeholders such as employees, the board of directors, and shareholders. **External stakeholders** are all the other individuals and groups that have some direct or indirect claim on the firm. Typically, this group comprises primary stakeholders such as customers, suppliers, governments, and local communities as well as secondary stakeholders such as special-interest groups, competitors, trade associations, mass media, and social media.[42]

All stakeholders are in an exchange relationship with the company.[43] Each stakeholder group supplies the organization with important resources (or contributions), and in exchange each expects its interests to be satisfied (by inducements).[44] For example, employees provide labor, skills, knowledge, and time and in exchange expect commensurate income, job satisfaction, job security, and good working conditions. Customers provide a company with its revenues and in exchange want quality products that represent value for money. Communities provide businesses with local infrastructure and in exchange want businesses that are responsible citizens and seek some assurance that the quality of life will be improved as a result of the business firm's existence.

Stakeholder analysis involves a certain amount of what has been called *moral imagination*.[45] This means standing in the shoes of a stakeholder and asking how a proposed decision might impact that stakeholder. For example, when considering outsourcing to subcontractors, managers might need to ask themselves how it might feel to be working under substandard health conditions for long hours.

Step 2 involves judging the ethics of the proposed strategic decision, given the information gained in step 1. Managers need to determine whether a proposed decision would violate the *fundamental rights* of any stakeholders. For example, we might argue that the right to information about health risks in the workplace is a fundamental entitlement of employees. Similarly, the right to know about potentially dangerous features of a product is a fundamental entitlement of customers (something tobacco companies violated when they did not reveal to their customers what they knew about the health risks of smoking). Managers might also want to ask themselves whether they would allow the proposed strategic decision if they were designing a system under Rawls's veil of ignorance. For example, if the issue under consideration was whether to outsource work to a subcontractor with low pay and poor working conditions, managers might want to ask themselves whether they would allow such action if they were considering it under a veil of ignorance, where they themselves might ultimately be the ones to work for the subcontractor.

The judgment at this stage should be guided by various moral principles that should not be violated. The principles might be those articulated in a corporate code of ethics or other company documents. In addition, certain moral principles that we have adopted as members of society—for instance, the prohibition on stealing—should not be violated. The judgment at this stage will also be guided by the decision rule that is chosen to assess the proposed strategic decision. Although maximizing long-run profitability is the decision rule that most businesses stress, it should be applied subject to the constraint that no moral principles are violated—that the business behaves in an ethical manner.

Step 3 requires managers to establish moral intent. This means the business must resolve to place moral concerns ahead of other concerns in cases where either the fundamental rights of stakeholders or key moral principles have been violated. At this stage, input from top management might be particularly valuable. Without the proactive encouragement of top managers, middle-level managers might tend to place the narrow economic interests of the company before the interests of stakeholders. They might do so in the (usually erroneous) belief that top managers favor such an approach.

Step 4 requires the company to engage in ethical behavior. Step 5 requires the business to audit its decisions, reviewing them to make sure they were consistent with ethical principles, such as those stated in the company's code of ethics. This final step is critical and often overlooked. Without auditing past decisions, businesspeople may not know if their decision process is working and if changes should be made to ensure greater compliance with a code of ethics.

Ethics Officers

To make sure that a business behaves in an ethical manner, firms now must have oversight by a high-ranking person or people known to respect legal and ethical standards. These individuals—often referred to as ethics officers—are responsible for managing their organizations ethics and legal compliance programs. They are typically responsible for (1) assessing the needs and risks that an ethics program must address; (2) developing and distributing a code of ethics; (3) conducting training programs for employees; (4) establishing and maintaining a confidential service to address employees' questions about issues that may be ethical or unethical; (5) making sure that the organization is in compliance with government laws and regulations; (6) monitoring and auditing ethical conduct; (7) taking action, as appropriate, on possible violations; and (8) reviewing and updating the code of ethics periodically.[46] Because of these broad topics covered by the ethics officer, in many businesses ethics officers act as an internal ombudsperson with responsibility for handling confidential inquiries from employees, investigating complaints from employees or others, reporting findings, and making recommendations for change.

For example, United Technologies, a multinational aerospace company with worldwide revenues of more than $30 billion, has had a formal code of ethics since 1990.[47] United Technologies has some 450 business practices officers (the company's name for ethics officers). They are responsible for making sure the code is followed. United Technologies also established an ombudsperson program in 1986 that lets employees inquire anonymously about ethics issues. The program has received some 60,000 inquiries since 1986, and more than 10,000 cases have been handled by an ombudsperson.

Moral Courage

It is important to recognize that employees in an international business may need significant *moral courage*. Moral courage enables managers to walk away from a decision that is profitable but unethical. Moral courage gives an employee the strength to say no to a superior who instructs her to pursue actions that are unethical. Moral courage gives employees the integrity to go public to the media and blow the whistle on persistent unethical behavior in a company. Moral courage does not come easily; there are well-known cases where individuals have lost their jobs because they blew the whistle on corporate behaviors they thought unethical, telling the media about what was occurring.[48]

However, companies can strengthen the moral courage of employees by committing themselves to not retaliate against employees who exercise moral courage, say no to superiors, or otherwise complain about unethical actions. For example, consider the following excerpt from Unilever's "Our Principles":

> Any breaches of the Code must be reported in accordance with the procedures specified by the Chief Legal Officer. The Board of Unilever will not criticize management for any loss of business resulting from adherence to these principles and other mandatory policies and instructions. The Board of Unilever expects employees to bring to their attention, or to that of senior management, any breach or suspected breach of these principles. Provision has been made for employees to be able to report in confidence and no employee will suffer as a consequence of doing so.[49]

This statement gives permission to employees to exercise moral courage. Companies can also set up ethics hotlines, which allow employees to anonymously register a complaint with a corporate ethics officer.

Corporate Social Responsibility

Multinational corporations have power that comes from their control over resources and their ability to move production from country to country. Although that power is constrained not only by laws and regulations but also by the discipline of the market and the competitive process, it is substantial. Some moral philosophers argue that with power comes the social responsibility for multinationals to give something back to the societies that enable them to prosper and grow.

Did You Know?

Did you know corporate social responsibility is not as new as it seems?

Visit your Connect SmartBook® to view a short video explanation from the authors.

Corporate Social Responsibility (CSR)
Refers to the idea that businesspeople should consider the social consequences of economic actions when making business decisions and that there should be a presumption in favor of decisions that have both good economic and social consequences.

Sustainable Strategies
Strategies that not only help the multinational firm make good profits but that do so without harming the environment, while simultaneously ensuring that the corporation acts in a socially responsible manner with regard to its multiple stakeholders.

The concept of **corporate social responsibility (CSR)** refers to the idea that businesspeople should consider the social consequences of economic actions when making business decisions and that there should be a presumption in favor of decisions that have both good economic and social consequences.[50] In its purest form, corporate social responsibility can be supported for its own sake simply because it is the right way for a business to behave. Advocates of this approach argue that businesses, particularly large successful businesses, need to recognize their *noblesse oblige* and give something back to the societies that have made their success possible. *Noblesse oblige* is a French term that refers to honorable and benevolent behavior considered the responsibility of people of high (noble) birth. In a business setting, it is taken to mean benevolent behavior that is the responsibility of *successful* enterprises. This has long been recognized by many businesspeople, resulting in a substantial and venerable history of corporate giving to society, with businesses making social investments designed to enhance the welfare of the communities in which they operate.

Power itself is morally neutral; how power is used is what matters. It can be used in a positive way to increase social welfare, which is ethical, or it can be used in a manner that is ethically and morally suspect. Managers at some multinationals have acknowledged a moral obligation to use their power to enhance social welfare in the communities where they do business. BP, one of the world's largest oil companies, has made it part of the company policy to undertake "social investments" in the countries where it does business.[51] In Algeria, BP has been investing in a major project to develop gas fields near the desert town of Salah. When the company noticed the lack of clean water in Salah, it built two desalination plants to provide drinking water for the local community and distributed containers to residents so they could take water from the plants to their homes. There was no economic reason for BP to make this social investment, but the company believes it is morally obligated to use its power in constructive ways. The action, while a small thing for BP, is a very important thing for the local community. For another example of corporate social responsibility in practice, see the Management Focus feature on the Finnish company Stora Enso.

Is Sustainability Bad for Profits?

Most customers prefer that the companies they buy products and services from engage in business-focused sustainability practices. Eighty-three percent of the respondents in the Public Opinion Survey on Sustainability said that they think companies should try to accomplish their performance goals while also trying to improve society and the environment. At the same time, multinational firms are overwhelmed about the varied stakeholder needs they face. And, the Global Reporting Initiative, with its some 80 equally important sustainability indicators, is not giving companies a clear set of sustainability proprieties. Meanwhile, sustainability executives in companies have not exactly been elevated to the importance levels of other top managers. If you had to pay more for a product, like gasoline for your automobile, how much more would you be willing to pay to buy from a highly rated sustainability-oriented company —5 percent, 10 percent, 25 percent, 40 percent?

Sources: Epstein-Reeves, J., "The Pain of Sustainability," *Forbes*, January 18, 2012; "Consumers Expect Action from Companies on Sustainability," *Second Annual Public Opinion Survey on Sustainability*, http://dowelldogood.net; *Global Reporting Initiative*.www.globalreporting.org.

Sustainability

As managers in international businesses strive to translate ideas about corporate social responsibility into strategic actions, many are gravitating toward strategies that are viewed as *sustainable*. By **sustainable strategies,** we refer to strategies that not only help the multinational firm make good profits, but that also do so without harming the environment while simultaneously ensuring that the corporation acts in a socially responsible manner with regard to its stakeholders.[52] The core idea of *sustainability* is that the organization—through its actions—does not exert a negative impact on the ability of future generations to meet their own economic needs and that its actions impart long-run economic *and* social benefits on stakeholders.[53]

A company pursuing a sustainable strategy would not adopt business practices that deplete the environment for short-term economic gain because doing so would impose a cost on future generations. In other words, international businesses that pursue sustainable strategies try to ensure that they do not precipitate or participate in a situation that results in a tragedy of the commons Thus, for example, a company pursuing a sustainable strategy would try to reduce its carbon footprint (CO_2 emissions) so that it does not contribute to global warming.

Nor would a company pursuing a sustainable strategy adopt policies that negatively affect the well-being of key

management FOCUS

Corporate Social Responsibility at Stora Enso

Stora Enso is a Finnish pulp and paper manufacturer that was formed by the merger of Swedish mining and forestry products company Stora and Finnish forestry products company Enso-Gutzeit Oy in 1998. The company is headquartered in Helsinki, the capital of Finland, and it has approximately 29,000 employees. In 2000, the company bought Consolidated Papers in North America. Stora Enso also expanded into South America, Asia, and Russia. By 2005, Stora Enso had become the world's largest pulp and paper manufacturer as measured by production capacity. However, the North American operations were sold in 2007 to NewPage Corporation.

Stora Enso has a long-standing tradition of corporate social responsibility on a global scale. As part of the company's section "Global Responsibility in Stora Enso," the company states that "for Stora Enso, Global Responsibility means realizing concrete actions that will help us fulfil [*sic*] our Purpose, which is to do good for the people and the planet." Stora Enso continues to state:

> Our purpose "do good for the people and the planet" is the ultimate reason why we run our business. It is the overriding rule that guides us in all that we do: producing and selling our renewable products, buying trees from a local forest-owner in Finland, selling electricity generated at Stora Enso Skoghall Mill, or managing our logistics on a global scale.*

Interestingly, Stora Enso also asserts that it realizes that this statement is rather bold and perhaps not even fully believable. But the company suggests that it makes the company accountable for its actions; that is, setting its purpose boldly in writing. At the same time, Stora Enso positions the company as though it has always been attending to the "socially responsible" needs of doing good for the people and the planet. It illustrates this by maintaining that it has created and enhanced communities around its mills, developed innovative systems to reduce the use of scarce resources, and maintained good relationships with key stakeholders such as forest owners, their own employees, governments, and local communities near its mills.

Tracing to its past and reflecting on its future, Stora Enso has adopted three lead areas for its global responsibility strategy: people and ethics, forests and land use, and environment and efficiency. For people and ethics, the company focuses on conducting business in a socially responsible manner throughout its global value chain. For forests and land use, it focuses on an innovative and responsible approach on forestry and land use to make it a preferred partner and a good local community citizen. For the environment and efficiency, the focus is on resource-efficient operations that help the company achieve superior environmental performance related to its products.

While a number of companies have corporate social responsibility statements incorporated as part of their websites, annual reports, and talking points, Stora Enso also presents clear targets and performance goals that are assessed by established metrics. Its overall operations are guided by corporate-level targets for environmental and social performance, aptly named Stora Enso's Global Responsibility Key Performance Indicators (KPIs). Targets are publicly listed in a document titled "Targets and Performance" and include two to five basic categories of measures for each of the three lead areas. For people and ethics, the dimensions cover health and safety, human rights, ethics and compliance, sustainable leadership, and responsible sourcing. For forests and land use, the dimensions cover efficiency of land use and sustainable forestry. For environment and efficiency, the dimensions cover climate and energy, material efficiency, and process water discharges. The "Targets and Performance" document also lists performance in the prior year, targets in the current year, and strategic objectives related to each dimension.

*J. Smith, "The World's Most Sustainable Companies," *Forbes*, January 24, 2014.

Sources: "Global Responsibility in Stora Enso," *www.storaenso.com;* K. Vita, "Stora Enso Falls as UBS Plays Down Merger Talk: Helsinki Mover," *Bloomberg Businessweek*, September 30, 2013; M. Huuhtanen, "Paper Maker Stora Enso Selling North American Mills," *USA Today*, September 21, 2007.

stakeholders such as employees and suppliers because managers would recognize that in the long run, this would harm the company. The company that pays its employees so little that it forces them into poverty, for example, may find it hard to recruit employees in the future and may have to deal with high employee turnover, which imposes its own costs on an enterprise. Similarly, a company that drives down the prices it pays to its suppliers so far that the suppliers cannot make enough money to invest in upgrading their operations may find that in the long run, its business suffers poor-quality inputs and a lack of innovation among its supplier base.

Stora Enso, profiled in the Management Focus, is in essence pursuing sustainable strategies because, through its actions, it is trying to make sure that forest resources are well managed and available for future generations and that the communities with which it interacts benefit from its presence and will, therefore, support the company going forward. For another example, consider Starbucks. Starbucks has a goal of ensuring that 100 percent of its coffee is ethically sourced. By this, it means that the farmers who grow the coffee beans it purchases use sustainable farming methods that do not harm the environment and that they treat their employees well and pay them fairly. Starbucks agronomists work directly with farmers in places such as Costa Rica and Rwanda to make sure that they use environmentally responsible farming methods. The company also provides loans to farmers to help them upgrade their production methods. As a result of these policies, by 2012 some 93 percent of Starbucks coffee beans were ethically sourced.

Sustainability at Umicore

In introducing Umicore as the most sustainable multinational firm in the world for 2013 on its Global 100 Index, Doug Morrow, vice president of research at Corporate Knights, a Toronto-based media company, said that sustainability is "recognizing that a corporation's long-term interests are intellectually and financially consistent with resource efficiency, proactive health and safety practices, and responsible leadership." "Sustainability is when what is good for a company is also good for the planet, and vice-versa,"* added the editor in chief of Corporate Knights, Toby Heaps.

Umicore NV, formerly Union Minière until 2001, is a multinational materials technology company headquartered in Brussels, Belgium. The company was founded in 1989 as a merger of four companies in the mining and smelting industries. Subsequent to the merger, Umicore reshaped itself to focus on technology-related businesses such as refining and recycling of precious metals along with the manufacturing of specialized products from precious metals. As a solid and respected company, Umicore has been included as a component of Belgium's benchmark BEL20 index since its inception in 1991 (BEL20 is the benchmark stock market index of Euronext Brussels, the Brussels Stock Exchange).

Umicore's core business areas or divisions are Catalysis, Energy Materials, Performance Materials, and Recycling. Catalysis is involved with abatement of global automotive emissions and production of compounds for use in chemicals, life science, and pharmaceutical industries. The materials produced by Energy Materials can be found in a number of applications used in the production and storage of clean energy. Performance Materials applies its technology and know-how to the unique properties of precious and other metals (to achieve safer products). Recycling treats complex waste streams containing precious and other nonferrous metals.

Across these four business areas, Umicore clearly defines its sustainability objectives and goals, which address market orientation, multiple stakeholders, and corporate social responsibility. The company's financial objective is to achieve double-digit revenue growth, with the goal of generating an average return on capital employed of more than 15 percent annually. Such a goal is market oriented with a clear, bottom-line financial expectation for performance. For corporate social responsibility, the focus is on two issues. Environmentally, Umicore focuses on reducing its carbon footprint by 20 percent, reducing the impact of metal emissions on water and air by 20 percent, and investing in tools to better understand and measure life cycles of its products. Socially, Umicore focuses on achieving zero lost-time accidents, reducing body concentrations of metals to which employees have exposure, and individual employee development. Umicore also takes a strong stand in its stakeholder management, stating that all of its sites are expected to identify key stakeholders and engage with the local community.

*J. Smith, "The World's Most Sustainable Companies," Forbes, January 24, 2014.

Sources: J. Smith, "The World's Most Sustainable Companies," *Forbes*, January 23, 2014; Umicore's Sustainability, www.umicore.com; J. Martens, "Umicore Gains after Maintaining Profit Forecast: Brussels Mover," *Bloomberg Businessweek*, July 30, 2013.

An important aspect of the sustainable strategies pursued by both Stora Enso and Starbucks is that they have helped both companies gain a competitive advantage and, therefore, make more money for their shareholders. In the case of Starbucks, its ethical sourcing policies send a powerful signal to its customers about the kind of company Starbucks wants to be. This resonates well with the company's customer base and strengthens the Starbucks brand, resulting in more store traffic and higher sales and profits. So even though it may cost Starbucks some money up front to shift to an ethical sourcing policy, the benefits in terms of a more powerful brand outweigh the costs. For another example of a multinational that is pursuing a sustainable strategy, see the Management Focus feature about sustainability at Umicore, a Belgian company.

The basic point here is that well-crafted sustainable strategies can be good for all primary stakeholders, such as shareholders, the environment, suppliers, local communities, employees, and customers. Business need not be a zero-sum game, where increasing the returns to one stakeholder group (e.g., shareholders) requires the imposition of costs on other stakeholder groups (e.g., the environment, suppliers, employees).

As the examples we have given illustrate, it is possible to pursue sustainable strategies that result in a positive-sum game where all stakeholders benefit. To be sure, pursuing such strategies may impose some short-term costs on the multinational as it increases investments in better environmental practices, better employee working conditions, and safer products, and as it requires suppliers to adopt similar policies. In the long run, however, there is good evidence that all stakeholders can benefit from such an approach and, indeed, that such an approach may help the company compete more effectively in the global marketplace. Good ethical practices are good for business!

Key Terms

business ethics, p. 125
ethical strategy, p. 125
Foreign Corrupt Practices Act (FCPA), p. 130
Convention on Combating Bribery of Foreign Public Officials in International Business Transactions, p. 130
ethical dilemma, p. 132
organizational culture, p. 133
cultural relativism, p. 136
righteous moralist, p. 136
naive immoralist, p. 136
utilitarian approach to ethics, p. 137
Kantian ethics, p. 137
rights theories, p. 138
Universal Declaration of Human Rights, p. 138
just distribution, p. 139
code of ethics, p. 140
stakeholders, p. 142
internal stakeholders, p. 142
external stakeholders, p. 142
corporate social responsibility (CSR), p. 144
sustainable strategies, p. 144

Summary

This chapter discussed the source and nature of ethical issues in international businesses, the different philosophical approaches to business ethics, and the steps managers can take to ensure that ethical issues are respected in international business decisions. The chapter made the following points:

1. The term *ethics* refers to accepted principles of right or wrong that govern the conduct of a person, the members of a profession, or the actions of an organization. Business ethics are the accepted principles of right or wrong governing the conduct of businesspeople, and an ethical strategy is one that does not violate these accepted principles.
2. Ethical issues and dilemmas in international business are rooted in the variations among political systems, law, economic development, and culture from nation to nation.
3. The most common ethical issues in international business involve employment practices, human rights, environmental regulations, corruption, and social responsibility of multinational corporations.
4. Ethical dilemmas are situations in which none of the available alternatives seems ethically acceptable.
5. Unethical behavior is rooted in poor personal ethics, societal culture, the psychological and geographic distances of a foreign subsidiary from the home office, a failure to incorporate ethical issues into strategic and operational decision making, a dysfunctional culture, and failure of leaders to act in an ethical manner.
6. Moral philosophers contend that approaches to business ethics such as the Friedman doctrine, cultural relativism, the righteous moralist, and the naive immoralist are unsatisfactory in important ways.
7. The Friedman doctrine states that the only social responsibility of business is to increase profits, as long as the company stays within the rules of law. Cultural relativism contends that one should adopt the ethics of the culture in which one is doing business. The righteous moralist monolithically applies home-country ethics to a foreign situation, while the naive immoralist believes that if a manager of a multinational sees that firms from other nations are not following ethical norms in a host nation, that manager should not either.
8. Utilitarian approaches to ethics hold that the moral worth of actions or practices is determined by their consequences, and the best decisions are those that produce the greatest good for the greatest number of people.
9. Kantian ethics state that people should be treated as ends and never purely as *means* to the ends of others. People are not instruments, like a machine. People have dignity and need to be respected as such.
10. Rights theories recognize that human beings have fundamental rights and privileges that transcend national boundaries and cultures. These rights establish a minimum level of morally acceptable behavior.
11. The concept of justice developed by John Rawls suggests that a decision is just and ethical if people would allow it when designing a social system under a veil of ignorance.
12. To make sure that ethical issues are considered in international business decisions, managers should (*a*) favor hiring and promoting people with a well-grounded sense of personal ethics; (*b*) build an organizational culture and exemplify leadership behaviors that place a high value on ethical behavior; (*c*) put decision-making processes in place that require people to consider the ethical dimension of business decisions; (*d*) establish ethics officers in the organization with responsibility for ethical decision making; (*e*) be morally courageous and encourage others to do the same; (*f*) make corporate social

responsibility a cornerstone of enterprise policy; and (g) pursue strategies that are sustainable.

13. Multinational corporations that are practicing business-focused sustainability integrate a focus on market orientation, addressing the needs of multiple stakeholders, and adhering to corporate social responsibility principles.

Critical Thinking and Discussion Questions

1. A visiting American executive finds that a foreign subsidiary in a less developed country has hired a 12-year-old girl to work on a factory floor, in violation of the company's prohibition on child labor. He tells the local manager to replace the child and tell her to go back to school. The local manager tells the American executive that the child is an orphan with no other means of support, and she will probably become a street child if she is denied work. What should the American executive do?
2. Drawing on John Rawls's concept of the veil of ignorance, develop an ethical code that will (*a*) guide the decisions of a large oil multinational toward environmental protection and (*b*) influence the policies of a clothing company in their potential decision of outsourcing its manufacturing operations.
3. Under what conditions is it ethically defensible to outsource production to the developing world where labor costs are lower when such actions also involve laying off long-term employees in the firm's home country?
4. Do you think facilitating payments (*speed payments*) should be ethical?
5. A manager from a developing country is overseeing a multinational's operations in a country where drug trafficking and lawlessness are rife. One day, a representative of a local "big man" approaches the manager and asks for a "donation" to help the big man provide housing for the poor. The representative tells the manager that in return for the donation, the big man will make sure that the manager has a productive stay in his country. No threats are made, but the manager is well aware that the big man heads a criminal organization that is engaged in drug trafficking. He also knows that the big man does indeed help the poor in the rundown neighborhood of the city where he was born. What should the manager do?
6. Milton Friedman stated in his famous article in the *New York Times* in 1970 that "the social responsibility of business is to increase profits."* Do you agree? If not, do you prefer that multinational corporations adopt a focus on corporate social responsibility or sustainability practices?
7. Reread the Management Focus on Unocal, and answer the following questions:
   a. Was it ethical for Unocal to enter into a partnership with a brutal military dictatorship for financial gain?
   b. What actions could Unocal have taken, short of not investing at all, to safeguard the human rights of people affected by the gas pipeline project?

*M. Friedman, "The Social Responsibility of Business Is to Increase Profits," *The New York Times Magazine*, September 13, 1970.

globalEDGE Research Task

globalEDGE.msu.edu

Use the globalEDGE™ website (**globaledge.msu.edu**) to complete the following exercises:

1. Promoting respect for universal human rights is a central dimension of many countries' foreign policy. As history has shown, human rights abuses are an important concern worldwide. Some countries are more ready to work with other governments and civil society organizations to prevent abuses of power. Begun in 1977, the annual *Country Reports on Human Rights Practices* are designed to assess the state of democracy and human rights around the world, call attention to violations, and—where needed—prompt needed changes in U.S. policies toward particular countries. Find the latest annual *Country Reports on Human Right Practices* for the BRIC countries (Brazil, China, India, and Russia), and create a table to compare the findings under the "Worker Rights" sections. What commonalities do you see? What differences are there?
2. The use of bribery in the business setting is an important ethical dilemma many companies face both domestically and abroad. The Bribe Payers Index is a study published every three years to assess the likelihood of firms from 28 leading economies to win business overseas by offering bribes. It also ranks industry sectors based on the prevalence of bribery. Compare the five industries thought to have the largest problems with bribery with those five that have the least problems. What patterns do you see? What factors make some industries more conducive to bribery than others?

Making Toys Globally

closing case

Toys for children are made in numerous countries and then exported to buyers throughout the world. In some countries, such as the United States, certain protection exists to make sure that toys are safe for children. The U.S. Consumer Product Safety Commission (CPSC) regularly issues recalls of toys that have the potential to expose children to danger such as lead or other heavy metals. For example, lead may be found in the paint used on toys and in the plastic used to make the toys. If ingested (e.g., children chewing on toys), lead is poisonous and can damage the nervous system and cause brain disorders. Lead is also a neurotoxin that can accumulate in both soft tissue and bones in the body.

For these reasons, lead was banned in house paint, on toys marketed to children, and in dishes or cookware in the United States in 1978. In addition, in an agreement between China's General Administration of Quality Supervision, Inspection and Quarantine (AQSIQ) and CPSC, the Chinese agreed to take immediate action in 2007 to eliminate the use of lead paint on Chinese manufactured toys that are exported to the United States. With China's prominence as a toy manufacturing country, this agreement was a step toward making safe products for children.

Still, lead continues to be a hazard in a quarter of all U.S. homes with children under age six. In fact, a wide range of toys and children's products, including many market-leading and reputable brands, often contain either lead or other heavy metals (e.g., arsenic, cadmium, mercury, antimony, or chromium). Estimates exist that suggest that one-third of Chinese toys contain heavy metals. This is a major problem given that China manufactures 80 percent of the toys sold in the United States. Researchers from Greenpeace and IPEN conducted a study by buying 500 toys and children's products in five Chinese cities. They tested the products with handheld X-ray scanners and found that 163 of the toys were tainted with heavy metals above the norm (32.6 percent). "These contaminated toys not only poison children when chewed or touched, but can enter the body through the air they breathe," said Ada Kong Cheuk-san at Greenpeace.

While lead in the paint on toys has not been eliminated, the focus on cleaning up lead in the paint has been given front-page coverage ever since the agreement to eliminate it in 2007. It is certainly not gone, but at least more and more people are paying attention. Several organizations—both governmental and private—are examining lead-based paint in toys on a continual basis. For example, the *New York Times* and *Consumer Reports* recently found that dangerous products for children are still widely available. The Ecology Center has created a website called HealthyStuff.org that contains a database of toys and other products that have been tested for dangerous chemicals.

While lead in paint seems to be in focus, the use of lead in plastics has not been banned! Lead is used to soften the plastic and make it more flexible to allow it to go back to its original shape after children play with the toys. Plus, lead may also be used in plastic toys to stabilize molecules from heat. Unfortunately, when the plastic is exposed to sunlight, air, and detergents, for example, the chemical bond between the lead and plastics breaks down and forms dust that can enter the human body. Another unfortunate part about lead is that it is invisible to the naked eye and has no detectable smell. This means that children may be exposed to lead from toys (and other consumer products) through normal playing activity (e.g., hand-to-mouth activity). As everyone with children knows, children often put toys, fingers, and other objects in their mouth, exposing themselves to lead paint or dust.

Children are also more vulnerable to lead than adults; there is no safe level of lead for children. The worldwide toy industry has published a voluntary standard of 90 parts per million for lead in toys, which, of course, is greater than a ban on lead in paint used for toys and in the materials used to make the toys (such as plastics). But since 2007, the world has at least seen stricter standards—either voluntary or regulated standards—that make it safer for children to play with newly purchased toys. The CPSC in the United States, the European Union, and China's AQSIQ are actively monitoring and seemingly enforcing stricter standards. But, according to Scott Wolfson of the CPSC, many toy manufacturers have been violating safety regulations for almost 30 years. So, are toys safer now than they were before 2007, and are they really safe to play with throughout the world? What do we do with the old toys?

Sources: M. Moore, "One Third of Chinese Toys Contain Heavy Metals," *The Telegraph*, December 8, 2011; P. Kavilanz, "China to Eliminate Lead Paint in Toy Exports," *CNN Money*, September 11, 2007; U.S. Centers for Disease Control and Prevention. www.cdc.gov; "U.S. Prosecutes Importers of Toys Containing Lead, Phthalates," *AmeriScan*, February 26, 2014.

CASE DISCUSSION QUESTIONS

1. How realistic do you think it is to create a world standard for toys with respect to their safety and use by children?
2. Should we ban products from a country that does not follow standards similar to what the U.S. Consumer Product Safety Commission suggests for the United States? Is the CPSC overprotective? Should each country have its own guidelines? Why or why not?
3. If there are health risks associated with lead poisoning, what about related areas such as lead in drinking water (e.g., the issue that came to the forefront in the 2016 U.S. presidential campaign regarding water supply in Flint, Michigan)?
4. Is lead in toys a financial, or cost, issue? Why have we not seen the toy industry monitor and do something about the lead problem, even though we have known about it for more than 30 years?

Endnotes

1. Y. Lu, N. Nakicenovic, M. Visbeck, and A-S. Stevance, "Policy: Five Priorities for the UN Sustainable Development Goals," *Nature*, April 20, 2015. "Sustainable Development Goals," accessed March 14, 2016, http://www.un.org/sustainabledevelopment/
2. T. Hult, "Market-Focused Sustainability: Market Orientation Plus!," *Journal of the Academy of Marketing Science* 39, pp. 1–6, 2011; T. Hult, J. Mena, O. C. Ferrell, and L. Ferrell, "Stakeholder Marketing: A Definition and Conceptual Framework," *AMS Review* 1 (2011), pp. 44–65.
3. S. Greenhouse, "Nike Shoe Plant in Vietnam Is Called Unsafe for Workers," *The New York Times,* November 8, 1997; V. Dobnik, "Chinese Workers Abused Making Nikes, Reeboks," *Seattle Times,* September 21, 1997, p. A4.
4. R. K. Massie, *Loosing the Bonds: The United States and South Africa in the Apartheid Years* (New York: Doubleday, 1997).
5. Not everyone agrees that the divestment trend had much influence on the South African economy. For a counterview, see S. H. Teoh, I. Welch, and C. P. Wazzan, "The Effect of Socially Activist Investing on the Financial Markets: Evidence from South Africa," *The Journal of Business* 72, no. 1 (January 1999), pp. 35–60.
6. Peter Singer, *One World: The Ethics of Globalization* (New Haven, CT: Yale University Press, 2002).
7. Garrett Hardin, "The Tragedy of the Commons," *Science* 162, no. 1 (1968), pp. 243–48.
8. For a summary of the evidence, see S. Solomon, D. Qin, M. Manning, Z. Chen, M. Marquis, K. B. Averyt, M. Tignor, and H. L. Miller, eds., *Contribution of Working Group I to the Fourth Assessment Report of the Intergovernmental Panel on Climate Change* (Cambridge, UK: Cambridge University Press, 2007).
9. J. Everett, D. Neu, and A. S. Rahaman, "The Global Fight against Corruption," *Journal of Business Ethics* 65 (2006), pp. 1–18.
10. R. T. De George, *Competing with Integrity in International Business* (Oxford, UK: Oxford University Press, 1993).
11. Details can be found at www.oecd.org/corruption/oecdantibriberyconvention.
12. B. Pranab, "Corruption and Development," *Journal of Economic Literature* 36 (September 1997), pp. 1320–46.
13. A. Shleifer and R. W. Vishny, "Corruption," *Quarterly Journal of Economics,* no. 108 (1993), pp. 599–617; and I. Ehrlich and F. Lui, "Bureaucratic Corruption and Endogenous Economic Growth," *Journal of Political Economy* 107 (December 1999), pp. 270–92.
14. P. Mauro, "Corruption and Growth," *Quarterly Journal of Economics,* no. 110 (1995), pp. 681–712.
15. D. Kaufman and S. J. Wei, "Does Grease Money Speed up the Wheels of Commerce?," World Bank policy research working paper, January 11, 2000.
16. http://ethics.iit.edu.
17. B. Vitou, R. Kovalevsky, and T. Fox, "Time to Call a Spade a Spade: Facilitation Payments and Why Neither Bans nor Exemption Work," http://thebriberyact.com/2011/02/03/time-to-call-a-spade-a-spade-facilitation-payments-why-neither-bans-nor-exemptions-work, accessed March 8, 2014.
18. This is known as the "when in Rome perspective." T. Donaldson, "Values in Tension: Ethics Away from Home," *Harvard Business Review,* September–October 1996.
19. De George, *Competing with Integrity in International Business.*
20. For a discussion of the ethics of using child labor, see J. Isern, "Bittersweet Chocolate: The Legacy of Child Labor in Cocoa Production in Cote d'Ivoire," *Journal of Applied Management and Entrepreneurship* 11 (2006), pp. 115–32.
21. S. W. Gellerman, "Why Good Managers Make Bad Ethical Choices," in *Ethics in Practice: Managing the Moral Corporation,* ed. K. R. Andrews (Cambridge, MA: Harvard Business School Press, 1989).
22. D. Messick and M. H. Bazerman, "Ethical Leadership and the Psychology of Decision Making," *Sloan Management Review* 37 (Winter 1996), pp. 9–20.
23. O. C. Ferrell, J. Fraedrich, and L. Ferrell, *Business Ethics*, 9th ed. (Mason, OH: Cengage, 2013).
24. B. Scholtens and L. Dam, "Cultural Values and International Differences in Business Ethics," *Journal of Business Ethics,* 2007.
25. M. Friedman, "The Social Responsibility of Business Is to Increase Profits," *The New York Times Magazine,* September 13, 1970. Reprinted in T. L. Beauchamp and N. E. Bowie, *Ethical Theory and Business,* 7th ed. (Englewood Cliffs, NJ: Prentice Hall, 2001).
26. Friedman, M., "The Social Responsibility of Business Is to Increase Profits," *The New York Times Magazine*, September 13, 1970.
27. Friedman, M., "The Social Responsibility of Business Is to Increase Profits," *The New York Times Magazine,* September 13, 1970.
28. For example, see Donaldson, "Values in Tension: Ethics Away from Home." See also N. Bowie, "Relativism and the Moral Obligations of Multinational Corporations," in T. L. Beauchamp and N. E. Bowie, *Ethical Theory and Business,* 7th ed. (Englewood Cliffs, NJ: Prentice Hall, 2001).
29. For example, see De George, *Competing with Integrity in International Business.*
30. This example is often repeated in the literature on international business ethics. It was first outlined by A. Kelly in "Case Study—Italian Style Mores," in T. Donaldson and P. Werhane, *Ethical Issues in Business* (Englewood Cliffs, NJ: Prentice Hall, 1979).
31. See Beauchamp and Bowie, *Ethical Theory and Business.*
32. T. Donaldson, *The Ethics of International Business* (Oxford: Oxford University Press, 1989).
33. Found at www.un.org/Overview/rights.html.
34. Donaldson, *The Ethics of International Business.*
35. See Chapter 10 in Beauchamp and Bowie, *Ethical Theory and Business.*
36. J. Rawls, *A Theory of Justice,* rev. ed. (Cambridge, MA: Belknap Press, 1999).
37. www.unilever.com.
38. J. Bower and J. Dial, "Jack Welch: General Electrics Revolutionary," Harvard Business School Case 9-394-065, April 1994.

39. For example, see R. E. Freeman and D. Gilbert, *Corporate Strategy and the Search for Ethics* (Englewood Cliffs, NJ: Prentice Hall, 1988); T. Jones, "Ethical Decision Making by Individuals in Organizations," *Academy of Management Review* 16 (1991), pp. 366–95; J. R. Rest, *Moral Development: Advances in Research and Theory* (New York: Praeger, 1986).
40. Freeman and Gilbert, *Corporate Strategy and the Search for Ethics;* Jones, "Ethical Decision Making by Individuals in Organizations"; Rest, *Moral Development.*
41. See E. Freeman, *Strategic Management: A Stakeholder Approach* (Boston: Pitman Press, 1984); C. W. L. Hill and T. M. Jones, "Stakeholder-Agency Theory," *Journal of Management Studies* 29 (1992), pp. 131–54; J. G. March and H. A. Simon, *Organizations* (New York: Wiley, 1958).
42. Hult et al., "Stakeholder Marketing."
43. Hult, "Market-Focused Sustainability: Market Orientation Plus!"; Hult et al., "Stakeholder Marketing."
44. Hill and Jones, "Stakeholder-Agency Theory"; March and Simon, *Organizations.*
45. De George, *Competing with Integrity in International Business.*
46. Ferrell et al., *Business Ethics.*
47. The code can be accessed at United Technologies website, www.utc.com/profile/ethics/index.htm.
48. C. Grant, "Whistle Blowers: Saints of Secular Culture," *Journal of Business Ethics,* September 2002, pp. 391–400.
49. "Our Principles," Unilever, www.unilever.com.
50. S. A. Waddock and S. B. Graves, "The Corporate Social Performance–Financial Performance Link," *Strategic Management Journal* 8 (1997), pp. 303–19; I. Maignan, O. C. Ferrell, and T. Hult, "Corporate Citizenship: Cultural Antecedents and Business Benefits," *Journal of the Academy of Marketing Science* 27 (1999), pp. 455–69.
51. Details can be found at BP's website, www.bp.com.
52. Hult, "Market-Focused Sustainability: Market Orientation Plus!"
53. M. Clarkson, "A Stakeholder Framework for Analyzing and Evaluating Corporate Social Performance," *Academy of Management Review* 20 (1995), pp. 92–117; R. Freeman, *Strategic Management: A Stakeholder Approach* (Marshfield: Pitman, 1984); T. Hult, J. Mena, O. Ferrell, and L. Ferrell, "Stakeholder Marketing: A Definition and Conceptual Framework," *AMS Review* 1 (2011), pp. 44–65.

International Trade Theory

learning objectives

After reading this chapter, you will be able to:

- **LO6-1** Understand why nations trade with each other.
- **LO6-2** Summarize the different theories explaining trade flows between nations.
- **LO6-3** Recognize why many economists believe that unrestricted free trade between nations will raise the economic welfare of countries that participate in a free trade system.
- **LO6-4** Explain the arguments of those who maintain that government can play a proactive role in promoting national competitive advantage in certain industries.
- **LO6-5** Understand the important implications that international trade theory holds for management practice.

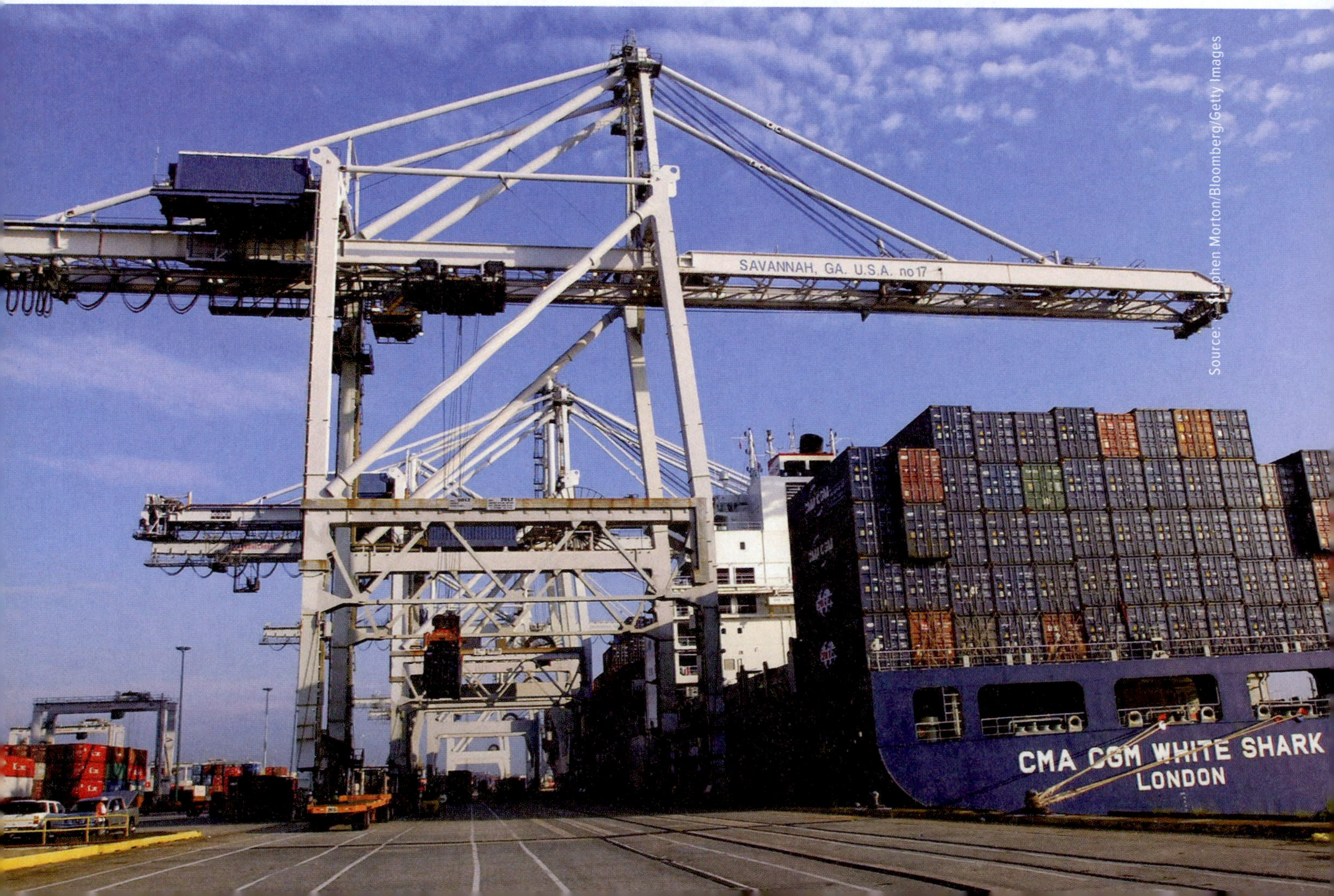

Source: Stephen Morton/Bloomberg/Getty Images

The Trans Pacific Partnership

opening case

On February 4, 2016, ministers from 12 governments signed off on the Trans Pacific Partnership (TPP), a free trade deal between 12 countries including the United States, Japan, Australia, South Korea, Chile, Canada, Mexico, and Vietnam. China was not part of the deal. Together these countries account for 36 percent of the world's GDP and 26 percent of world trade. In the United States, critics of the deal were quick to register their opposition. Donald Trump, a contender for the Republican presidential nomination, said that the "TPP is a terrible deal." Bernie Sanders, one of the leading Democratic contenders, called it "disastrous" and "a victory for Wall Street and other big corporations," Many other politicians, wary of the fact that 2016 was a general election year in the United States, were also quick to criticize the deal. On the other hand, the administration of Barack Obama heralded the TPP as a historic deal of major importance. Editorials in influential publications such as *The Wall Street Journal* and *The Economist* urged the U.S. Congress to ratify the deal.

So what does the deal try to do? The TPP will eliminate or reduce about 18,000 tariffs, taxes, and non-tariff barriers such as quotas on trade between the 12 member countries. By expanding market access and lowering prices for consumers, economists claim that the deal will boost economic growth rates among TPP countries and add about $285 billion to global GDP by 2025. Since the United States already has very low tariff barriers, most of the tariff reductions will occur in other countries.

U.S. agriculture looks to be a big beneficiary. The TPP would eliminate import tariffs as high as 40 percent on U.S. poultry products and fruit, and 35 percent on soybeans, all products where the United States has a comparative advantage in production. Cargill, Inc., a giant U.S. grain exporter and meat producer, urged lawmakers to support the pact. A number of large efficient U.S. manufacturers also came out in support of the deal, which eliminates import tariffs as high as 59 percent on U.S. machinery exports to TPP countries. Boeing, the country's largest exporter, said that the deal would help it compete overseas, where it gets 70 percent of its revenue. Several technology companies including Intel voiced support for the deal, pointing out that it would eliminate import taxes as high as 35 percent on the sale of information and communication technology to some other TPP countries.

On the other hand, some U.S. companies urged Congress to vote against the deal. Ford opposed the deal because it would phase out a 2.5 percent tariff on imports of Japanese cars into the United States and a 25 percent tariff on imports of light trucks—even though under the agreement, those tariffs would be phased down over 30 years. Labor unions were quick to oppose the deal, arguing that it would result in further losses of U.S. manufacturing jobs and lead to lower wages. The tobacco company Philip Morris

–continued

opposed the deal because it would *prevent* tobacco companies from suing foreign governments over anti-smoking measures that restrict tobacco companies from using their logos and brands to market tobacco products. Several big drug companies also opposed the deal because it only protected new biotechnology products from generic competition for five years, rather than the 12 years they had before.

Data supporting these various claims and counterclaims was offered by a number of independent studies, including those from the World Bank, the Institute of International Economics (IIE), and Tuft's University. Both the World Bank and the IIE concluded that by creating more overseas demand for American goods and services, by 2030 the TPP would raise U.S. wages slightly above what they would have been without the deal. The IIE study estimated that the TPP would increase annual U.S. exports by $357 billion, or 9 percent, by 2030. The IIE study also calculated that overall, there would be no job losses in the United States. Although some sectors would see job losses, the IIE suggested that these would be offset by job gains elsewhere. The study from Tufts University was the most pessimistic, estimating that the deal would result in the loss of 450,000 jobs in the United States over 10 years. To put this in context, between 2010 and 2015, the U.S. economy created 13 million new jobs, so the worst-case estimate of losses amounted to no more than two months of job growth during the 2010–2015 period. ●

Sources: Caitlin McGee, "Controversial TPP Pact Signed amid New Zealand Protests," *Aljazeera*, February 4, 2016; Catherine Ho, "Fact Checking the Campaigns for and against the TPP Trade Deal," *Washington Post*, February 11, 2016; Tripp Mickle and Theo Francis, "Trade Pact Sealed," *The Wall Street Journal*, October 6, 2015; Peter Petri and Michael Plummer, "The Economic Effects of the Trans Pacific Partnership: New Estimates," *Peterson Institute for International Economics*, working paper 16-2, January 1, 2016.

Introduction

The Trans Pacific Partnership (TPP) between 12 countries that was profiled in the opening case of this chapter is an attempt to unlock the gains that many economists believe flow from free trade across international borders. Economists have long argued that free trade stimulates economic growth and raises living standards across the board. As the opening case illustrates, the economic arguments concerning the benefits of free trade in goods and services are not abstract academic ones. International trade theories have shaped the economic policy of many nations for the past 60 years. They have been the driver behind the formation of the World Trade Organization and regional trade blocs such as the European Union and the North American Free Trade Agreement. They underlie the current push to ratify the TPP, as well as ongoing negotiations between the United States and the European Union to establish a trans-Atlantic free trade area. It is important to understand, therefore, what these theories are and why they have been so successful at shaping the economic policy of so many nations and the environment in which international businesses compete. As the opening case clearly demonstrates, managers have a stake in the outcome of trade deals.

This chapter has two goals that go to the heart of the debate over the benefits—and the costs—of free trade. The first is to review a number of theories that explain why it is beneficial for a country to engage in international trade. The second goal is to explain the pattern of international trade that we observe in the world economy. With regard to the pattern of trade, we will be primarily concerned with explaining the pattern of exports and imports of goods and services between countries. The pattern of foreign direct investment between countries is discussed in Chapter 8.

An Overview of Trade Theory

We open this chapter with a discussion of mercantilism. Propagated in the sixteenth and seventeenth centuries, mercantilism advocated that countries should simultaneously encourage exports and discourage imports. Although mercantilism is an old and largely discredited doctrine, its echoes remain in modern political debate and in the trade policies of many countries. Next, we will look at Adam Smith's theory of absolute advantage. Proposed in 1776, Smith's theory was the first to explain why unrestricted free trade is beneficial to a country. **Free trade** refers to a situation in which a government does not attempt to influence through quotas or duties what its citizens can buy from another country or what they can produce and sell to another country. Smith argued that the invisible hand of the market mechanism, rather than government policy, should determine what a country imports and what it exports. His arguments imply that such a laissez-faire stance toward trade was in the best interests of a country. Building on Smith's work are two additional theories that we review. One is the theory of comparative advantage, advanced by the nineteenth-century English economist David Ricardo. This theory is the intellectual basis of the modern argument for unrestricted free trade. In the twentieth century, Ricardo's work was refined by two Swedish economists, Eli Heckscher and Bertil Ohlin, whose theory is known as the Heckscher-Ohlin theory.

Free Trade
The absence of barriers to the free flow of goods and services between countries.

THE BENEFITS OF TRADE

LO 6-1
Understand why nations trade with each other.

The great strength of the theories of Smith, Ricardo, and Heckscher-Ohlin is that they identify with precision the specific benefits of international trade. Common sense suggests that some international trade is beneficial. For example, nobody would suggest that Iceland should grow its own oranges. Iceland can benefit from trade by exchanging some of the products that it can produce at a low cost (fish) for some products that it cannot produce at all (oranges). Thus, by engaging in international trade, Icelanders are able to add oranges to their diet of fish.

The theories of Smith, Ricardo, and Heckscher-Ohlin go beyond this commonsense notion, however, to show why it is beneficial for a country to engage in international trade *even for products it is able to produce for itself.* This is a difficult concept for people to grasp. For example, many people in the United States believe that American consumers should buy products made in the United States by American companies whenever possible to help save American jobs from foreign competition. The same kind of nationalistic sentiments can be observed in many other countries.

However, the theories of Smith, Ricardo, and Heckscher-Ohlin tell us that a country's economy may gain if its citizens buy certain products from other nations that could be produced at home. The gains arise because international trade allows a country to *specialize* in the manufacture and export of products that can be produced most efficiently in that country, while importing products that can be produced more efficiently in other countries. Thus, it may make sense for the United States to specialize in the production and export of commercial jet aircraft, because the efficient production of commercial jet aircraft requires resources that are abundant in the United States, such as a highly skilled labor force and cutting-edge technological know-how. On the other hand, it may make sense for the United States to import textiles from Bangladesh because the efficient production of textiles requires a relatively cheap labor force—and cheap labor is not abundant in the United States.

Of course, this economic argument is often difficult for segments of a country's population to accept. With their future threatened by imports, U.S. textile companies and their employees have tried hard to persuade the government to limit the importation of textiles by demanding quotas and tariffs. Although such import controls may benefit particular groups, such as textile businesses and their employees, the theories of Smith, Ricardo, and Heckscher-Ohlin suggest that the economy as a whole is hurt by such action. One of the key insights of international trade theory is that limits on imports are often in the interests of domestic producers but not domestic consumers.

Did You Know?
Did you know that sugar prices in the United States are much higher than sugar prices in the rest of the world?

Visit your Connect SmartBook® to view a short video explanation from the authors.

THE PATTERN OF INTERNATIONAL TRADE

The theories of Smith, Ricardo, and Heckscher-Ohlin help explain the pattern of international trade that we observe in the world economy. Some aspects of the pattern are easy to understand. Climate and natural resource endowments explain why Ghana exports cocoa, Brazil exports coffee, Saudi Arabia exports oil, and China exports crawfish. However, much of the observed pattern of international trade is more difficult to explain. For example, why does Japan export automobiles, consumer electronics, and machine tools? Why does Switzerland export chemicals, pharmaceuticals, watches, and jewelry? Why does Bangladesh export garments? David Ricardo's theory of comparative advantage offers an explanation in terms of international differences in labor productivity. The more sophisticated Heckscher-Ohlin theory emphasizes the interplay between the proportions in which the factors of production (such as land, labor, and capital) are available in different countries and

globalEDGE — Trade Tutorials

In this chapter, we discuss benefits and costs associated with free trade, discuss the benefits of international trade, and explain the pattern of international trade in today's world economy. The general idea is that international trade theories explain why it can be beneficial for a country to engage in trade across country borders, even though countries are at different stages of development, have different product needs, and produce different types of products. International trade theory assumes that countries—through their governments, laws, and regulations—engage in more or less trade across borders. In reality, the vast majority of trade happens across borders by companies from different countries. As related to this chapter, check out globalEDGE™'s "trade tutorials" section where lots of information, data, and tools are compiled related to trading internationally (globaledge.msu.edu/global-resources/trade-tutorials). The potpourri of trade resources includes export tutorials, online course modules, a glossary, a free trade agreement tariff tool, and much more. The glossary includes lots of terms related to trade. For example, "trade surplus" is defined as a situation in which a country's exports exceeds its imports (i.e., it represents a net inflow of domestic currency from foreign markets). The opposite is called trade deficit and is considered a net outflow, but how is it really defined? The globalEDGE™ glossary can help.

the proportions in which they are needed for producing particular goods. This explanation rests on the assumption that countries have varying endowments of the various factors of production. Tests of this theory, however, suggest that it is a less powerful explanation of real-world trade patterns than once thought.

One early response to the failure of the Heckscher-Ohlin theory to explain the observed pattern of international trade was the product life-cycle theory. Proposed by Raymond Vernon, this theory suggests that early in their life cycle, most new products are produced in and exported from the country in which they were developed. As a new product becomes widely accepted internationally, however, production starts in other countries. As a result, the theory suggests, the product may ultimately be exported back to the country of its original innovation.

New Trade Theory

The observed pattern of trade in the world economy may be due in part to the ability of firms in a given market to capture first-mover advantages.

In a similar vein, during the 1980s, economists such as Paul Krugman developed what has come to be known as the new trade theory. **New trade theory** (for which Krugman won the Nobel Prize in economics in 2008) stresses that in some cases, countries specialize in the production and export of particular products not because of underlying differences in factor endowments but because in certain industries the world market can support only a limited number of firms. (This is argued to be the case for the commercial aircraft industry.) In such industries, firms that enter the market first are able to build a competitive advantage that is subsequently difficult to challenge. Thus, the observed pattern of trade between nations may be due in part to the ability of firms within a given nation to capture first-mover advantages. The United States is a major exporter of commercial jet aircraft because American firms such as Boeing were first movers in the world market. Boeing built a competitive advantage that has subsequently been difficult for firms from countries with equally favorable factor endowments to challenge (although Europe's Airbus has succeeded in doing that). In a work related to the new trade theory, Michael Porter developed a theory referred to as the theory of national competitive advantage. This attempts to explain why particular nations achieve international success in particular industries. In addition to factor endowments, Porter points out the importance of country factors such as domestic demand and domestic rivalry in explaining a nation's dominance in the production and export of particular products.

Switzerland has long had a national competitive advantage in the manufacture of watches.

Source: © Imaginechina/Corbis Wire/Corbis

TRADE THEORY AND GOVERNMENT POLICY

Although all these theories agree that international trade is beneficial to a country, they lack agreement in their recommendations for government policy. Mercantilism makes a crude case for government involvement in promoting exports and limiting imports. The theories of Smith, Ricardo, and Heckscher-Ohlin form part of the case for unrestricted free trade. The argument for unrestricted free trade is that both import controls and export incentives (such as subsidies) are self-defeating and result in wasted resources. Both the new trade theory and Porter's theory of national competitive advantage can be interpreted as justifying some limited government intervention to support the development of certain export-oriented industries. We discuss the pros and cons of this argument, known as strategic trade policy, as well as the pros and cons of the argument for unrestricted free trade, in Chapter 7.

Use SmartBook to help retain what you have learned. Access your Instructor's Connect course to check out SmartBook or go to learnsmartadvantage.com for help.

Mercantilism

Summarize the different theories explaining trade flows between nations.

The first theory of international trade, mercantilism, emerged in England in the mid-sixteenth century. The principle assertion of mercantilism was that gold and silver were the mainstays of national wealth and essential to vigorous commerce. At that time, gold and silver were the currency of trade between countries; a country could earn gold and silver by exporting goods. Conversely, importing goods from other countries would result in an outflow of gold and silver to those countries. The main tenet of **mercantilism** was that it was in a country's best interests to maintain a trade surplus, to export more than it imported. By doing so, a country would accumulate gold and silver and, consequently, increase its national wealth, prestige, and power. As the English mercantilist writer Thomas Mun put it in 1630:

Mercantilism

An economic philosophy advocating that countries should simultaneously encourage exports and discourage imports.

> The ordinary means therefore to increase our wealth and treasure is by foreign trade, wherein we must ever observe this rule: to sell more to strangers yearly than we consume of theirs in value.[1]

Consistent with this belief, the mercantilist doctrine advocated government intervention to achieve a surplus in the balance of trade. The mercantilists saw no virtue in a large volume of trade. Rather, they recommended policies to maximize exports and minimize imports. To achieve this, imports were limited by tariffs and quotas, while exports were subsidized.

The classical economist David Hume pointed out an inherent inconsistency in the mercantilist doctrine in 1752. According to Hume, if England had a balance-of-trade surplus with France (it exported more than it imported), the resulting inflow of gold and silver would swell the domestic money supply and generate inflation in England. In France, however, the outflow of gold and silver would have the opposite effect. France's money supply would contract, and its prices would fall. This change in relative prices between France and England would encourage the French to buy fewer English goods (because they were becoming more expensive) and the English to buy more French goods (because they were becoming cheaper). The result would be a deterioration in the English balance of trade and an improvement in France's trade balance, until the English surplus was eliminated. Hence, according to Hume, in the long run no country could sustain a surplus on the balance of trade and so accumulate gold and silver as the mercantilists had envisaged.

The flaw with mercantilism was that it viewed trade as a zero-sum game. (A **zero-sum game** is one in which a gain by one country results in a loss by another.) It was left to Adam Smith and David Ricardo to show the shortsightedness of this approach and to demonstrate that trade is a positive-sum game, or a situation in which all countries can benefit. Unfortunately, the mercantilist doctrine is by no means dead. Neo-mercantilists equate political power with economic power and economic power with a balance-of-trade surplus. Critics argue that many nations have adopted a neo-mercantilist strategy that is designed to simultaneously boost exports and limit imports.[2] For example, critics charge that China long pursued a neo-mercantilist policy, deliberately keeping its currency value low against the U.S. dollar in order to sell more goods to the United States and other developed nations, and thus amass a trade surplus and foreign exchange reserves (see the accompanying Country Focus).

Zero-Sum Game

A situation in which an economic gain by one country results in an economic loss by another.

Use SmartBook to help retain what you have learned. Access your Instructor's Connect course to check out SmartBook or go to learnsmartadvantage.com for help.

Absolute Advantage

Summarize the different theories explaining trade flows between nations.

In his 1776 landmark book *The Wealth of Nations,* Adam Smith attacked the mercantilist assumption that trade is a zero-sum game. Smith argued that countries differ in their ability to produce goods efficiently. In his time, the English, by virtue of their superior manufacturing processes, were the world's most efficient textile manufacturers. Due to the combination of

country FOCUS

Is China a Neo-mercantilist Nation?

China's rapid rise in economic power (it is now the world's second-largest economy) has been built on export-led growth. The country takes raw material imports and, using relatively cheap labor, converts them to products that it sells to developed nations. For years, the country's exports have been growing faster than its imports. This has lead some critics to claim that China is pursuing a neo-mercantilist policy, trying to amass record trade surpluses and foreign currency that will give it economic power over developed nations. By the end of 2014, its foreign exchange reserves exceeded $3.8 trillion, some 60 percent of which were held in U.S.-denominated assets such as U.S. treasury bills. Observers worry that if China ever decides to sell its holdings of U.S. currency, this could depress the value of the dollar against other currencies and increase the price of imports into America.

Throughout most of the last three decades, China's exports grew faster than its imports, leading some to argue that China has been limiting imports by pursuing an import substitution policy, encouraging domestic investment in the production of products such as steel, aluminum, and paper, that it had historically imported from other nations. The trade deficit with America has been a particular cause for concern. In 2015, this reached a record $366 billion. At the same time, China long resisted attempts to let its currency float freely against the U.S. dollar. Many claim that China's currency has been too cheap and that this keeps the prices of China's goods artificially low, which fuels the country's exports.

So, is China a neo-mercantilist nation that is deliberately discouraging imports and encouraging exports to increase its trade surplus and accumulate foreign exchange reserves, which might give it economic power? The facts of the matter are less clear than the rhetoric. China started to allow the value of the *yuan* (China's currency) to appreciate against the dollar in July 2005, albeit at a slow pace. In July 2005, one U.S. dollar purchased 8.11 yuan. By March 2015, one U.S. dollar purchased 6.57 yuan.

Moreover, in 2015 and early 2016, the rate of growth in China started to slow significantly. China's stock market fell sharply, and capital started to leave the country, with investors selling yuan and buying U.S. dollars. To stop the yuan from declining in value against the U.S. dollar, China was spending about $100 million of its foreign exchange reserves every month to buy yuan on the open market. Far from allowing its currency to decline against the U.S. dollar, thereby giving a boost to its exports, China was now trying to support its value, an action that is perhaps inconsistent with the charges that the country is pursuing a neo-mercantilist policy.

Sources: A. Browne, "China's Wild Swings Can Roil the Global Economy," *The Wall Street Journal,* October 24, 2005, p. A2; S. H. Hanke, "Stop the Mercantilists," *Forbes,* June 20, 2005, p. 164; G. Dyer and A. Balls, "Dollar Threat as China Signals Shift," *Financial Times,* January 6, 2006, p. 1; W. Chong, "China's Trade Surplus to U.S. to Narrow," *China Daily,* December 7, 2009; A. Wang and K. Yao, "China's Trade Surplus Dips, Taking Heat off Yuan," *Reuters,* January 9, 2011; Aaron Back, "China's Trade Surplus Shrank in '11,'" *The Wall Street Journal,* January 11, 2012; Richard Silk, "China's Foreign Exchange Reserves Jump Again," *The Wall Street Journal,* October 15, 2013; Terence Jeffrey, "US Merchandise Trade Deficit with China Hit Record in 2015", cnsnews.com, February 9, 2016.

favorable climate, good soils, and accumulated expertise, the French had the world's most efficient wine industry. The English had an *absolute advantage* in the production of textiles, while the French had an *absolute advantage* in the production of wine. Thus, a country has an **absolute advantage** in the production of a product when it is more efficient than any other country at producing it.

Absolute Advantage

A country has an absolute advantage in the production of a product when it is more efficient than any other country at producing it.

According to Smith, countries should specialize in the production of goods for which they have an absolute advantage and then trade these goods for those produced by other countries. In Smith's time, this suggested the English should specialize in the production of textiles, while the French should specialize in the production of wine. England could get all the wine it needed by selling its textiles to France and buying wine in exchange. Similarly, France could get all the textiles it needed by selling wine to England and buying textiles in exchange. Smith's basic argument, therefore, is that a country should never produce goods at home that it can buy at a lower cost from other countries. Smith demonstrates that by specializing in the production of goods in which each has an absolute advantage, both countries benefit by engaging in trade.

Consider the effects of trade between two countries, Ghana and South Korea. The production of any good (output) requires resources (inputs) such as land, labor, and capital. Assume that Ghana and South Korea both have the same amount of resources and that these resources can be used to produce either rice or cocoa. Assume further that 200 units of resources are available in each country. Imagine that in Ghana it takes 10 resources to produce 1 ton of cocoa and 20 resources to produce 1 ton of rice. Thus, Ghana could produce 20 tons of cocoa and no rice, 10 tons of rice and no cocoa, or some combination of rice and cocoa between these two extremes. The different combinations that Ghana could produce are represented by the line GG′ in Figure 6.1. This is referred to as Ghana's *production possibility frontier (PPF)*. Similarly, imagine that in South Korea it takes 40 resources to produce 1 ton of cocoa and 10 resources to

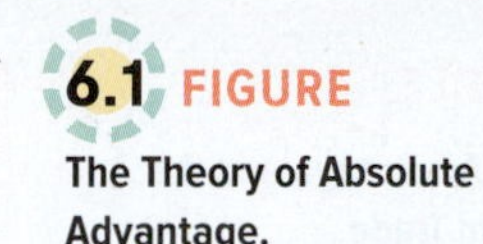

FIGURE

The Theory of Absolute Advantage.

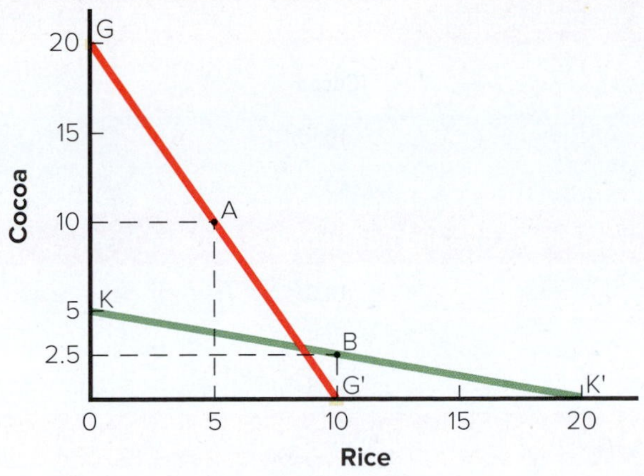

produce 1 ton of rice. Thus, South Korea could produce 5 tons of cocoa and no rice, 20 tons of rice and no cocoa, or some combination between these two extremes. The different combinations available to South Korea are represented by the line KK′ in Figure 6.1, which is South Korea's PPF. Clearly, Ghana has an absolute advantage in the production of cocoa. (More resources are needed to produce a ton of cocoa in South Korea than in Ghana.) By the same token, South Korea has an absolute advantage in the production of rice.

Now consider a situation in which neither country trades with any other. Each country devotes half its resources to the production of rice and half to the production of cocoa. Each country must also consume what it produces. Ghana would be able to produce 10 tons of cocoa and 5 tons of rice (point A in Figure 6.1), while South Korea would be able to produce 10 tons of rice and 2.5 tons of cocoa (point B in Figure 6.1). Without trade, the combined production of both countries would be 12.5 tons of cocoa (10 tons in Ghana plus 2.5 tons in South Korea) and 15 tons of rice (5 tons in Ghana and 10 tons in South Korea). If each country were to specialize in producing the good for which it had an absolute advantage and then trade with the other for the good it lacks, Ghana could produce 20 tons of cocoa, and South Korea could produce 20 tons of rice. Thus, by specializing, the production of both goods could be increased. Production of cocoa would increase from 12.5 tons to 20 tons, while production of rice would increase from 15 tons to 20 tons. The increase in production that would result from specialization is therefore 7.5 tons of cocoa and 5 tons of rice. Table 6.1 summarizes these figures.

By engaging in trade and swapping 1 ton of cocoa for 1 ton of rice, producers in both countries could consume more of both cocoa and rice. Imagine that Ghana and South Korea swap cocoa and rice on a one-to-one basis; that is, the price of 1 ton of cocoa is equal to the price of 1 ton of rice. If Ghana decided to export 6 tons of cocoa to South Korea and import 6 tons of rice in return, its final consumption after trade would be 14 tons of cocoa and 6 tons of rice. This is 4 tons more cocoa than it could have consumed before specialization and trade and 1 ton more rice. Similarly, South Korea's final consumption after trade would be 6 tons of cocoa and 14 tons of rice. This is 3.5 tons more cocoa than it could have consumed before specialization and trade and 4 tons more rice. Thus, as a result of specialization and trade, output of both cocoa and rice would be increased, and consumers in both nations would be able to consume more. Thus, we can see that trade is a positive-sum game; it produces net gains for all involved.

Which Products Should Always Be Produced at Home?

One of the key insights of international trade theory is that limits on imports are often in the interests of domestic producers but not domestic consumers. This is especially true if Adam Smith's theory of absolute advantage is in play, where one country is better at producing a product than another country. The reason is that consumers typically want the best products they can get for the amount of money they are willing to pay. But what about the comparative advantage theory that was originally conceptualized by David Ricardo and then refined by Eli Heckscher and Bertil Ohlin? Comparative advantage theory argues that a country should consider not producing products that it can actually produce reasonably well if the country can produce something else even more efficiently. In reality, not a single country has stopped all production of products they produce less efficiently than some other country. The reason is that countries always engage in a strategic balancing act! They prefer to be as efficient as possible (engage in international trade when advantageous) while also being as self-sufficient as possible (produce inside their country). So, what types of products should always be produced in the home country and which products should always be considered for importing if other countries can produce them more efficiently?

6.1 TABLE

Absolute Advantage and the Gains from Trade

	Cocoa	Rice
Resources Required to Produce 1 Ton of Cocoa and Rice		
Ghana	10	20
South Korea	40	10
Production and Consumption Without Trade		
Ghana	10.0	5.0
South Korea	2.5	10.0
Total production	12.5	15.0
Production with Specialization		
Ghana	20.0	0.0
South Korea	0.0	20.0
Total production	20.0	20.0
Consumption after Ghana Trades 6 Tons of Cocoa for 6 Tons of South Korean Rice		
Ghana	14.0	6.0
South Korea	6.0	14.0
Increase in Consumption as a Result of Specialization and Trade		
Ghana	4.0	1.0
South Korea	3.5	4.0

LO 6-2
Summarize the different theories explaining trade flows between nations.

Comparative Advantage

David Ricardo took Adam Smith's theory one step further by exploring what might happen when one country has an absolute advantage in the production of all goods.[3] Smith's theory of absolute advantage suggests that such a country might derive no benefits from international trade. In his 1817 book *Principles of Political Economy,* Ricardo showed that this was not the case. According to Ricardo's theory of comparative advantage, it makes sense for a country to specialize in the production of those goods that it produces most efficiently and to buy the goods that it produces less efficiently from other countries, even if this means buying goods from other countries that it could produce more efficiently itself.[4] While this may seem counterintuitive, the logic can be explained with a simple example.

Assume that Ghana is more efficient in the production of both cocoa and rice; that is, Ghana has an absolute advantage in the production of both products. In Ghana it takes 10 resources to produce 1 ton of cocoa and 13½ resources to produce 1 ton of rice. Thus, given its 200 units of resources, Ghana can produce 20 tons of cocoa and no rice, 15 tons of rice and no cocoa, or any combination in between on its PPF (the line GG' in Figure 6.2). In South Korea it takes 40 resources to produce 1 ton of cocoa and 20 resources to produce 1 ton of rice. Thus, South Korea can produce 5 tons of cocoa and no rice, 10 tons of rice and no cocoa, or any combination on its PPF (the line KK' in Figure 6.2). Again assume that without trade, each country uses half its resources to produce rice and half to produce cocoa. Thus, without trade, Ghana will produce 10 tons of cocoa and 7.5 tons of rice (point A in Figure 6.2), while South Korea will produce 2.5 tons of cocoa and 5 tons of rice (point B in Figure 6.2).

In light of Ghana's absolute advantage in the production of both goods, why should it trade with South Korea? Although Ghana has an absolute advantage in the production of both cocoa and rice, it has a comparative advantage only in the production of cocoa: Ghana can

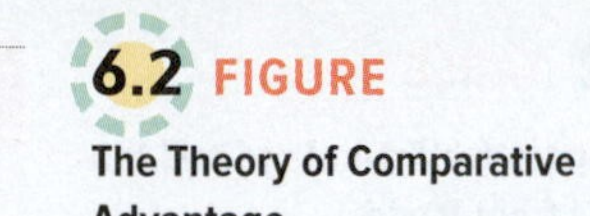

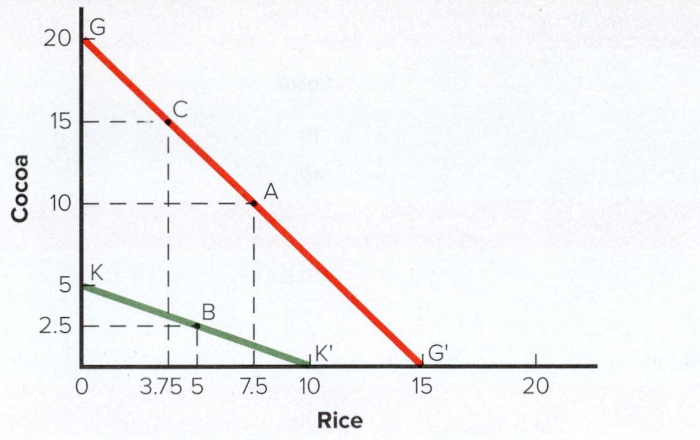

The Theory of Comparative Advantage.

produce 4 times as much cocoa as South Korea, but only 1.5 times as much rice. Ghana is *comparatively* more efficient at producing cocoa than it is at producing rice.

Without trade the combined production of cocoa will be 12.5 tons (10 tons in Ghana and 2.5 in South Korea), and the combined production of rice will also be 12.5 tons (7.5 tons in Ghana and 5 tons in South Korea). Without trade each country must consume what it produces. By engaging in trade, the two countries can increase their combined production of rice and cocoa, and consumers in both nations can consume more of both goods.

THE GAINS FROM TRADE Imagine that Ghana exploits its comparative advantage in the production of cocoa to increase its output from 10 tons to 15 tons. This uses up 150 units of resources, leaving the remaining 50 units of resources to use in producing 3.75 tons of rice (point C in Figure 6.2). Meanwhile, South Korea specializes in the production of rice, producing 10 tons. The combined output of both cocoa and rice has now increased. Before specialization, the combined output was 12.5 tons of cocoa and 12.5 tons of rice. Now it is 15 tons of cocoa and 13.75 tons of rice (3.75 tons in Ghana and 10 tons in South Korea). The source of the increase in production is summarized in Table 6.2.

Not only is output higher, but both countries also can now benefit from trade. If Ghana and South Korea swap cocoa and rice on a one-to-one basis, with both countries choosing to exchange 4 tons of their export for 4 tons of the import, both countries are able to consume more cocoa and rice than they could before specialization and trade (see Table 6.2). Thus, if Ghana exchanges 4 tons of cocoa with South Korea for 4 tons of rice, it is still left with 11 tons of cocoa, which is 1 ton more than it had before trade. The 4 tons of rice it gets from South Korea in exchange for its 4 tons of cocoa, when added to the 3.75 tons it now produces domestically, leave it with a total of 7.75 tons of rice, which is 0.25 ton more than it had before specialization. Similarly, after swapping 4 tons of rice with Ghana, South Korea still ends up with 6 tons of rice, which is more than it had before specialization. In addition, the tons of cocoa it receives in exchange is 1.5 tons more than it produced before trade. Thus, consumption of cocoa and rice can increase in both countries as a result of specialization and trade.

The basic message of the theory of comparative advantage is that *potential world production is greater with unrestricted free trade than it is with restricted trade.* Ricardo's theory suggests that consumers in all nations can consume more if there are no restrictions on trade. This occurs even in countries that lack an absolute advantage in the production of any good. In other words, to an even greater degree than the theory of absolute advantage, *the theory of comparative advantage suggests that trade is a positive-sum game in which all countries that participate realize economic gains.* As such, this theory provides a strong rationale for encouraging free trade. So powerful is Ricardo's theory that it remains a major intellectual weapon for those who argue for free trade.

6.2 TABLE

Comparative Advantage and the Gains from Trade

	Cocoa	Rice
Resources Required to Produce 1 Ton of Cocoa and Rice		
Ghana	10	13.33
South Korea	40	20
Production and Consumption Without Trade		
Ghana	10.0	7.5
South Korea	2.5	5.0
Total production	12.5	12.5
Production with Specialization		
Ghana	15.0	3.75
South Korea	0.0	10.0
Total production	15.0	13.75
Consumption after Ghana Trades 4 Tons of Cocoa for 4 Tons of South Korean Rice		
Ghana	11.0	7.75
South Korea	4.0	6.0
Increase in Consumption as a Result of Specialization and Trade		
Ghana	1.0	0.25
South Korea	1.5	1.0

LO 6-3

Recognize why many economists believe that unrestricted free trade between nations will raise the economic welfare of countries that participate in a free trade system.

QUALIFICATIONS AND ASSUMPTIONS

The conclusion that free trade is universally beneficial is a rather bold one to draw from such a simple model. Our simple model includes many unrealistic assumptions:

1. We have assumed a simple world in which there are only two countries and two goods. In the real world, there are many countries and many goods.
2. We have assumed away transportation costs between countries.
3. We have assumed away differences in the prices of resources in different countries. We have said nothing about exchange rates, simply assuming that cocoa and rice could be swapped on a one-to-one basis.
4. We have assumed that resources can move freely from the production of one good to another within a country. In reality, this is not always the case.
5. We have assumed constant returns to scale; that is, that specialization by Ghana or South Korea has no effect on the amount of resources required to produce one ton of cocoa or rice. In reality, both diminishing and increasing returns to specialization exist. The amount of resources required to produce a good might decrease or increase as a nation specializes in production of that good.
6. We have assumed that each country has a fixed stock of resources and that free trade does not change the efficiency with which a country uses its resources. This static assumption makes no allowances for the dynamic changes in a country's stock of resources and in the efficiency with which the country uses its resources that might result from free trade.
7. We have assumed away the effects of trade on income distribution within a country.

Given these assumptions, can the conclusion that free trade is mutually beneficial be extended to the real world of many countries, many goods, positive transportation costs, volatile exchange rates, immobile domestic resources, nonconstant returns to specialization, and dynamic changes? Although a detailed extension of the theory of comparative advantage is beyond the scope of this book, economists have shown that the basic result derived from our simple model can be generalized to a world composed of many countries producing many different goods.[5] Despite the shortcomings of the Ricardian model, research suggests that the basic proposition that countries will export the goods that they are most efficient at producing is borne out by the data.[6]

However, once all the assumptions are dropped, the case for unrestricted free trade, while still positive, has been argued by some economists associated with the "new trade theory" to lose some of its strength.[7] We return to this issue later in this chapter and in the next when we discuss the new trade theory. In a recent and widely discussed analysis, the Nobel Prize–winning economist Paul Samuelson argued that contrary to the standard interpretation, in certain circumstances the theory of comparative advantage predicts that a rich country might actually be *worse* off by switching to a free trade regime with a poor nation.[8] We consider Samuelson's critique in the next section.

EXTENSIONS OF THE RICARDIAN MODEL

Let us explore the effect of relaxing three of the assumptions identified earlier in the simple comparative advantage model. Next, we relax the assumptions that resources move freely from the production of one good to another within a country, that there are constant returns to scale, and that trade does not change a country's stock of resources or the efficiency with which those resources are utilized.

Immobile Resources

In our simple comparative model of Ghana and South Korea, we assumed that producers (farmers) could easily convert land from the production of cocoa to rice and vice versa. While this assumption may hold for some agricultural products, resources do not always shift quite so easily from producing one good to another. A certain amount of friction is involved. For example, embracing a free trade regime for an advanced economy such as the United States often implies that the country will produce less of some labor-intensive goods, such as textiles, and more of some knowledge-intensive goods, such as computer software or biotechnology products. Although the country as a whole will gain from such a shift, textile producers will lose. A textile worker in South Carolina is probably not qualified to write software for Microsoft. Thus, the shift to free trade may mean that she becomes unemployed or has to accept another less attractive job, such as working at a fast-food restaurant.

Resources do not always move easily from one economic activity to another. The process creates friction and human suffering too. While the theory predicts that the benefits of free trade outweigh the costs by a significant margin, this is of cold comfort to those who bear the costs. Accordingly, political opposition to the adoption of a free trade regime typically comes from those whose jobs are most at risk. In the United States, for example, textile workers and their unions have long opposed the move toward free trade precisely because this group has much to lose from free trade. Governments often ease the transition toward free trade by helping retrain those who lose their jobs as a result. The pain caused by the movement toward a free trade regime is a short-term phenomenon, while the gains from trade once the transition has been made are both significant and enduring.

Diminishing Returns

The simple comparative advantage model developed above assumes constant returns to specialization. By **constant returns to specialization** we mean the units of resources required to produce a good (cocoa or rice) are assumed to remain constant no matter where one is on a country's production possibility frontier (PPF). Thus, we assumed that it always took Ghana 10 units of resources to produce 1 ton of cocoa. However, it is more realistic to assume diminishing returns to specialization. Diminishing returns to specialization occur when more units of resources are required to produce each additional unit. While 10 units of resources may be sufficient to increase Ghana's output of cocoa from 12 tons to 13 tons, 11 units of resources may be needed to increase output from 13 to 14 tons, 12 units of resources to increase output from 14 tons to 15 tons, and so on. Diminishing

Constant Returns to Specialization
The units of resources required to produce a good are assumed to remain constant no matter where one is on a country's production possibility frontier.

FIGURE 6.3

Ghana's PPF Under Diminishing Returns.

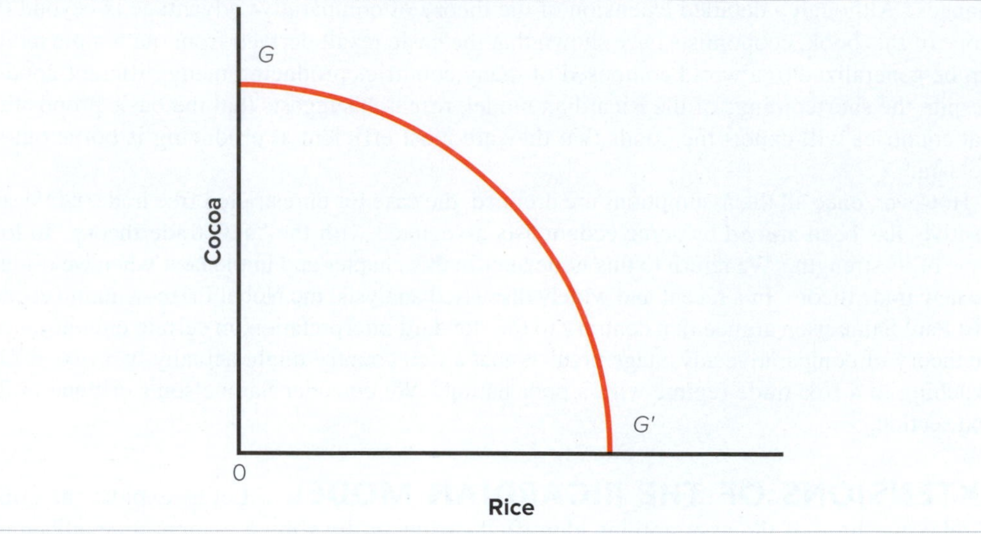

returns imply a convex PPF for Ghana (see Figure 6.3), rather than the straight line depicted in Figure 6.2.

It is more realistic to assume diminishing returns for two reasons. First, not all resources are of the same quality. As a country tries to increase its output of a certain good, it is increasingly likely to draw on more marginal resources whose productivity is not as great as those initially employed. The result is that it requires ever more resources to produce an equal increase in output. For example, some land is more productive than other land. As Ghana tries to expand its output of cocoa, it might have to utilize increasingly marginal land that is less fertile than the land it originally used. As yields per acre decline, Ghana must use more land to produce 1 ton of cocoa.

A second reason for diminishing returns is that different goods use resources in different proportions. For example, imagine that growing cocoa uses more land and less labor than growing rice and that Ghana tries to transfer resources from rice production to cocoa production. The rice industry will release proportionately too much labor and too little land for efficient cocoa production. To absorb the additional resources of labor and land, the cocoa industry will have to shift toward more labor-intensive methods of production. The effect is that the efficiency with which the cocoa industry uses labor will decline, and returns will diminish.

Diminishing returns show that it is not feasible for a country to specialize to the degree suggested by the simple Ricardian model outlined earlier. Diminishing returns to specialization suggest that the gains from specialization are likely to be exhausted before specialization is complete. In reality, most countries do not specialize, but instead produce a range of goods. However, the theory predicts that it is worthwhile to specialize until that point where the resulting gains from trade are outweighed by diminishing returns. Thus, the basic conclusion that unrestricted free trade is beneficial still holds, although because of diminishing returns, the gains may not be as great as suggested in the constant returns case.

LO 6-3

Recognize why many economists believe that unrestricted free trade between nations will raise the economic welfare of countries that participate in a free trade system.

Dynamic Effects and Economic Growth

The simple comparative advantage model assumed that trade does not change a country's stock of resources or the efficiency with which it utilizes those resources. This static assumption makes no allowances for the dynamic changes that might result from trade. If we relax this assumption, it becomes apparent that opening an economy to trade is likely to generate dynamic gains of two sorts.[9] First, free trade might increase a country's stock of resources as increased supplies of labor and capital from abroad become available for use within the country. For example, this has been occurring in eastern Europe since the early 1990s, with many Western businesses investing significant capital in the former communist countries.

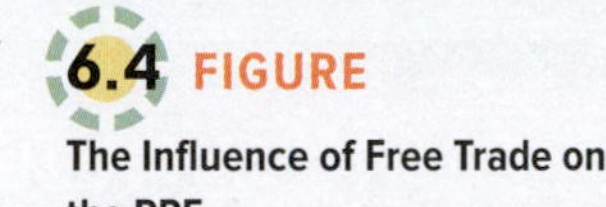
FIGURE 6.4

The Influence of Free Trade on the PPF.

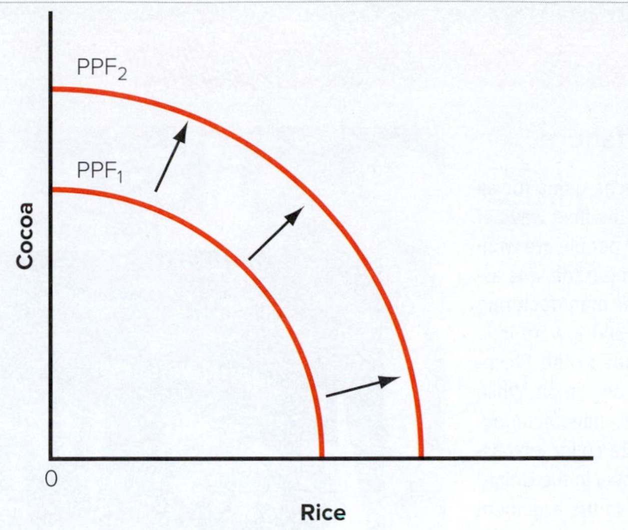

Second, free trade might also increase the efficiency with which a country uses its resources. Gains in the efficiency of resource utilization could arise from a number of factors. For example, economies of large-scale production might become available as trade expands the size of the total market available to domestic firms. Trade might make better technology from abroad available to domestic firms; better technology can increase labor productivity or the productivity of land. (The so-called green revolution had this effect on agricultural outputs in developing countries.) Also, opening an economy to foreign competition might stimulate domestic producers to look for ways to increase their efficiency. Again, this phenomenon has arguably been occurring in the once-protected markets of eastern Europe, where many former state monopolies have had to increase the efficiency of their operations to survive in the competitive world market.

Dynamic gains in both the stock of a country's resources and the efficiency with which resources are utilized will cause a country's PPF to shift outward. This is illustrated in Figure 6.4, where the shift from PPF1 to PPF2 results from the dynamic gains that arise from free trade. As a consequence of this outward shift, the country in Figure 6.4 can produce more of both goods than it did before introduction of free trade. The theory suggests that opening an economy to free trade not only results in static gains of the type discussed earlier but also results in dynamic gains that stimulate economic growth. If this is so, then one might think that the case for free trade becomes stronger still, and in general it does. However, as noted, one of the leading economic theorists of the twentieth century, Paul Samuelson, argued that in some circumstances, dynamic gains can lead to an outcome that is not so beneficial.

The Samuelson Critique

Paul Samuelson's critique looks at what happens when a rich country—the United States—enters into a free trade agreement with a poor country—China—that rapidly improves its productivity after the introduction of a free trade regime (i.e., there is a dynamic gain in the efficiency with which resources are used in the poor country). Samuelson's model suggests that in such cases, the lower prices that U.S. consumers pay for goods imported from China following the introduction of a free trade regime *may* not be enough to produce a net gain for the U.S. economy if the dynamic effect of free trade is to lower real wage rates in the United States. As he stated in a *New York Times* interview, "Being able to purchase groceries 20 percent cheaper at Wal-Mart (due to international trade) does not necessarily make up for the wage losses (in America)."[10]

Samuelson goes on to note that he is particularly concerned about the ability to offshore service jobs that traditionally were not internationally mobile, such as software debugging, call-center jobs, accounting jobs, and even medical diagnosis of MRI scans (see the accompanying Country Focus for details). Recent advances in communications technology have

country FOCUS

Moving U.S. White-Collar Jobs Offshore

Economists have long argued that free trade produces gains for all countries that participate in a free trading system. As the next wave of globalization sweeps through the U.S. economy, many people are wondering if this is true. During the 1980s and 1990s, free trade was associated with the movement of low-skill, blue-collar manufacturing jobs out of rich countries such as the United States and toward low-wage countries—textiles to Costa Rica, athletic shoes to the Philippines, steel to Brazil, electronic products to Thailand, and so on. While many observers bemoaned the "hollowing out" of U.S. manufacturing, economists stated that high-skill and high-wage white-collar jobs associated with the knowledge-based economy would stay in the United States. Computers might be assembled in Thailand, so the argument went, but they would continue to be designed in Silicon Valley by highly skilled U.S. engineers, and software applications would be written in the United States by programmers at Apple, Microsoft, Adobe, Oracle, and the like.

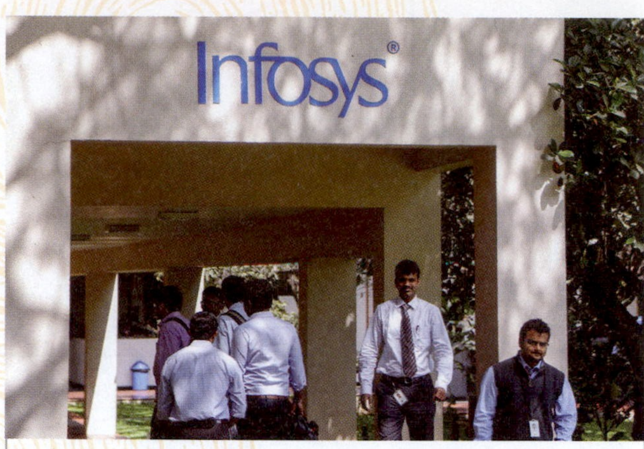

Companies like Infosys in India provide many jobs through servicing U.S.-based companies.

Source: © Vivek Prakash/Bloomberg/Getty Images

Developments over the past several decades have people questioning this assumption. Many American companies have been moving white-collar, knowledge-based jobs to developing nations where they can be performed for a fraction of the cost. During the long economic boom of the 1990s, Bank of America had to compete with other organizations for the scarce talents of information technology specialists, driving annual salaries to more than $100,000. However, with business under pressure during the 2000s, the bank cut nearly 5,000 jobs from its 25,000-strong, U.S.-based information technology workforce. Some of these jobs were transferred to India, where work that costs $100 an hour in the United States could be done for $20 an hour.

One beneficiary of Bank of America's downsizing is Infosys Technologies Ltd., a Bangalore, India, information technology firm where 250 engineers now develop information technology applications for the bank. Other Infosys employees are busy processing home loan applications for U.S. mortgage companies. Nearby in the offices of another Indian firm, Wipro Ltd., radiologists interpret 30 CT scans a day for Massachusetts General Hospital that are sent over the Internet. At yet another Bangalore business, engineers earn $10,000 a year designing leading-edge semiconductor chips for Texas Instruments. Nor is India the only beneficiary of these changes.

Some architectural work also is being outsourced to lower-cost locations. Flour Corp., a California-based construction company, employs some 1,200 engineers and drafters in the Philippines, Poland, and India to turn layouts of industrial facilities into detailed specifications. For a Saudi Arabian chemical plant Flour is designing, 200 young engineers based in the Philippines earning less than $3,000 a year collaborate in real time over the Internet with elite U.S. and British engineers who make up to $90,000 a year. Why does Flour do this? According to the company, the answer is simple. Doing so reduces the prices of a project by 15 percent, giving the company a cost-based competitive advantage in the global market for construction design. Most disturbing of all for future job growth in the United States, some high-tech start-ups are outsourcing significant work right from inception. For example, Zoho Corporation, a California-based start-up offering online web applications for small businesses, has about 20 employees in the United States and more than 1,000 in India!

Sources: P. Engardio, A. Bernstein, and M. Kripalani, "Is Your Job Next?," *BusinessWeek,* February 3, 2003, pp. 50–60; "America's Pain, India's Gain," *The Economist,* January 11, 2003, p. 57; M. Schroeder and T. Aeppel, "Skilled Workers Mount Opposition to Free Trade, Swaying Politicians," *The Wall Street Journal,* October 10, 2003, pp. A1, A11; D. Clark, "New U.S. Fees on Visas Irk Outsources," *The Wall Street Journal,* August 16, 2010, p. 6; J. R. Hagerty, "U.S. Loses High Tech Jobs as R&D Shifts to Asia," *The Wall Street Journal,* January 18, 2012, p. B1.

made this possible, effectively expanding the labor market for these jobs to include educated people in places such as India, the Philippines, and China. When coupled with rapid advances in the productivity of foreign labor due to better education, the effect on middle-class wages in the United States, according to Samuelson, may be similar to mass inward migration into the country: It will lower the market clearing wage rate, *perhaps* by enough to outweigh the positive benefits of international trade.

Having said this, it should be noted that Samuelson concedes that free trade has historically benefited rich counties (as data discussed later seem to confirm). Moreover, he notes that introducing protectionist measures (e.g., trade barriers) to guard against the theoretical possibility that free trade may harm the United States in the future may produce a situation that is worse than the disease they are trying to prevent. To quote Samuelson: "Free trade may turn out pragmatically to be still best for each region in comparison to lobbyist-induced tariffs and quotas which involve both a perversion of democracy and non-subtle deadweight distortion losses."[11]

One recent study found evidence in support of Samuelson's thesis. The study looked at every county in the United States for its manufacturers' exposure to competition from China.[12] The researchers found that regions most exposed to China tended not only to lose more manufacturing jobs but also to see overall employment decline. Areas with higher exposure to China also had larger increases in workers receiving unemployment insurance, food stamps, and disability payments. The costs to the economy from the increased government payments amounted to two-thirds of the gains from trade with China. In other words, many of the ways trade with China has helped the United States—such as providing inexpensive goods to U.S. consumers—have been wiped out. Even so, the authors of this study argued that in the long run, free trade is a good thing. They note, however, that the rapid rise of China has resulted in some large adjustment costs that, in the short run, significantly reduce the gains from trade.

Other economists have dismissed Samuelson's fears.[13] While not questioning his analysis, they note that as a practical matter, developing nations are unlikely to be able to upgrade the skill level of their workforce rapidly enough to give rise to the situation in Samuelson's model. In other words, they will quickly run into diminishing returns. However, such rebuttals are at odds with recent data suggesting that Asian countries are rapidly upgrading their educational systems. For example, about 56 percent of the world's engineering degrees awarded in 2008 were in Asia, compared with 4 percent in the United States![14]

Evidence for the Link Between Trade and Growth

Many economic studies have looked at the relationship between trade and economic growth.[15] In general, these studies suggest that as predicted by the standard theory of comparative advantage, countries that adopt a more open stance toward international trade enjoy higher growth rates than those that close their economies to trade. Jeffrey Sachs and Andrew Warner created a measure of how "open" to international trade an economy was and then looked at the relationship between "openness" and economic growth for a sample of more than 100 countries from 1970 to 1990.[16] Among other findings, they reported:

> We find a strong association between openness and growth, both within the group of developing and the group of developed countries. Within the group of developing countries, the open economies grew at 4.49 percent per year, and the closed economies grew at 0.69 percent per year. Within the group of developed economies, the open economies grew at 2.29 percent per year, and the closed economies grew at 0.74 percent per year.[17]

A study by Wacziarg and Welch updated the Sachs and Warner data through the late 1990s. They found that over the period 1950–1998, countries that liberalized their trade regimes experienced, on average, increases in their annual growth rates of 1.5 percent compared to preliberalization times.[18] An exhaustive survey of 61 studies published between 1967 and 2009 concluded: "The macroeconomic evidence provides dominant support for the positive and significant effects of trade on output and growth."[19]

The message seems clear: Adopt an open economy and embrace free trade, and your nation will be rewarded with higher economic growth rates. Higher growth will raise income levels and living standards. This last point has been confirmed by a study that looked at the relationship between trade and growth in incomes. The study, undertaken by Jeffrey Frankel and David Romer, found that on average, a 1 percentage point increase in the ratio of a country's trade to its gross domestic product increases income per person by at least 0.5 percent.[20] For every 10 percent increase in the importance of international trade in an economy, average income levels will rise by at least 5 percent. Despite the short-term adjustment costs associated with adopting a free trade regime, trade would seem to produce greater economic growth and higher living standards in the long run, just as the theory of Ricardo would lead us to expect.[21]

test PREP

Use SmartBook to help retain what you have learned. Access your Instructor's Connect course to check out SmartBook or go to learnsmartadvantage.com for help.

LO 6-2

Summarize the different theories explaining trade flows between nations.

Heckscher-Ohlin Theory

Ricardo's theory stresses that comparative advantage arises from differences in productivity. Thus, whether Ghana is more efficient than South Korea in the production of cocoa depends on how productively it uses its resources. Ricardo stressed labor productivity and argued that differences in labor productivity between nations underlie the notion of comparative advantage. Swedish economists Eli Heckscher (in 1919) and Bertil Ohlin (in 1933) put forward a different explanation of comparative advantage. They argued that comparative advantage arises from differences in national factor endowments.[22] By **factor endowments** they meant the extent to which a country is endowed with such resources as land, labor, and capital. Nations have varying factor endowments, and different factor endowments explain differences in factor costs; specifically, the more abundant a factor, the lower its cost. The Heckscher-Ohlin theory predicts that countries will export those goods that make intensive use of factors that are locally abundant, while importing goods that make intensive use of factors that are locally scarce. Thus, the Heckscher-Ohlin theory attempts to explain the pattern of international trade that we observe in the world economy. Like Ricardo's theory, the Heckscher-Ohlin theory argues that free trade is beneficial. Unlike Ricardo's theory, however, the Heckscher-Ohlin theory argues that the pattern of international trade is determined by differences in factor endowments, rather than differences in productivity.

Factor Endowments
A country's endowment with resources such as land, labor, and capital.

The Heckscher-Ohlin theory has commonsense appeal. For example, the United States has long been a substantial exporter of agricultural goods, reflecting in part its unusual abundance of arable land. In contrast, China has excelled in the export of goods produced in labor-intensive manufacturing industries. This reflects China's relative abundance of low-cost labor. The United States, which lacks abundant low-cost labor, has been a primary importer of these goods. Note that it is relative, not absolute, endowments that are important; a country may have larger absolute amounts of land and labor than another country but be relatively abundant in one of them.

THE LEONTIEF PARADOX

The Heckscher-Ohlin theory has been one of the most influential theoretical ideas in international economics. Most economists prefer the Heckscher-Ohlin theory to Ricardo's theory because it makes fewer simplifying assumptions. Because of its influence, the theory has been subjected to many empirical tests. Beginning with a famous study published in 1953 by Wassily Leontief (winner of the Nobel Prize in economics in 1973), many of these tests have raised questions about the validity of the Heckscher-Ohlin theory.[23] Using the Heckscher-Ohlin theory, Leontief postulated that because the United States was relatively abundant in capital compared to other nations, the United States would be an exporter of capital-intensive goods and an importer of labor-intensive goods. To his surprise, however, he found that U.S. exports were less capital intensive than U.S. imports. Because this result was at variance with the predictions of the theory, it has become known as the *Leontief paradox.*

No one is quite sure why we observe the Leontief paradox. One possible explanation is that the United States has a special advantage in producing new products or goods made with innovative technologies. Such products may be less capital intensive than products whose technology has had time to mature and become suitable for mass production. Thus, the United States may be exporting goods that heavily use skilled labor and innovative entrepreneurship, such as computer software, while importing heavy manufacturing products that use large

Should Factor Endowments or Productivity Drive Trade?

Ricardo's theory of trade suggests that it makes sense for a country to specialize in production of those products that it produces most efficiently and to buy the products that it produces less efficiently from other countries, even if this means that the country is buying products that in reality it could produce more efficiently itself. This means that Ricardo showed that a country can derive advantages by trade even though it has an absolute advantage in producing all products. The Heckscher-Ohlin theory of trade suggests that comparative advantage for a country arises from differences in national factor endowments (i.e., the extent to which a country is endowed with such resources as land, labor, and capital). Ricardo's argument focused on relative productivity, while Heckscher-Ohlin's argument focused on having important resources. If you can only have one of the two—better relative productivity or lots of resources such as land, labor, and capital—which would you prefer, any why?

amounts of capital. Some empirical studies tend to confirm this.[24] Still, tests of the Heckscher-Ohlin theory using data for a large number of countries tend to confirm the existence of the Leontief paradox.[25]

This leaves economists with a difficult dilemma. They prefer the Heckscher-Ohlin theory on theoretical grounds, but it is a relatively poor predictor of real-world international trade patterns. On the other hand, the theory they regard as being too limited, Ricardo's theory of comparative advantage, actually predicts trade patterns with greater accuracy. The best solution to this dilemma may be to return to the Ricardian idea that trade patterns are largely driven by international differences in productivity. Thus, one might argue that the United States exports commercial aircraft and imports textiles not because its factor endowments are especially suited to aircraft manufacture and not suited to textile manufacture, but because the United States is relatively more efficient at producing aircraft than textiles. A key assumption in the Heckscher-Ohlin theory is that technologies are the same across countries. This may not be the case. Differences in technology may lead to differences in productivity, which in turn, drives international trade patterns.[26] Thus, Japan's success in exporting automobiles from the 1970s onward has been based not only on the relative abundance of capital but also on its development of innovative manufacturing technology that enabled it to achieve higher productivity levels in automobile production than other countries that also had abundant capital. More recent empirical work suggests that this theoretical explanation may be correct.[27] The new research shows that once differences in technology across countries are controlled for, countries do indeed export those goods that make intensive use of factors that are locally abundant, while importing goods that make intensive use of factors that are locally scarce. In other words, once the impact of differences of technology on productivity is controlled for, the Heckscher-Ohlin theory seems to gain predictive power.

Use SmartBook to help retain what you have learned. Access your Instructor's Connect course to check out SmartBook or go to learnsmartadvantage.com for help.

The Product Life-Cycle Theory

Summarize the different theories explaining trade flows between nations.

Raymond Vernon initially proposed the product life-cycle theory in the mid-1960s.[28] Vernon's theory was based on the observation that for most of the twentieth century, a very large proportion of the world's new products had been developed by U.S. firms and sold first in the U.S. market (e.g., mass-produced automobiles, televisions, instant cameras, photocopiers, personal computers, and semiconductor chips). To explain this, Vernon argued that the wealth and size of the U.S. market gave U.S. firms a strong incentive to develop new consumer products. In addition, the high cost of U.S. labor gave U.S. firms an incentive to develop cost-saving process innovations.

Just because a new product is developed by a U.S. firm and first sold in the U.S. market, it does not follow that the product must be produced in the United States. It could be produced abroad at some low-cost location and then exported back into the United States. However, Vernon argued that most new products were initially produced in America. Apparently, the pioneering firms believed it was better to keep production facilities close to the market and to the firm's center of decision making, given the uncertainty and risks inherent in introducing new products. Also, the demand for most new products tends to be based on nonprice factors. Consequently, firms can charge relatively high prices for new products, which obviates the need to look for low-cost production sites in other countries.

Vernon went on to argue that early in the life cycle of a typical new product, while demand is starting to grow rapidly in the United States, demand in other advanced countries is limited to high-income groups. The limited initial demand in other advanced countries does not make it worthwhile for firms in those countries to start producing the new product, but it does necessitate some exports from the United States to those countries.

Over time, demand for the new product starts to grow in other advanced countries (e.g., Great Britain, France, Germany, and Japan). As it does, it becomes worthwhile for foreign producers to begin producing for their home markets. In addition, U.S. firms might set up production facilities in those advanced countries where demand is growing. Consequently, production within other advanced countries begins to limit the potential for exports from the United States.

As the market in the United States and other advanced nations matures, the product becomes more standardized, and price becomes the main competitive weapon. As this occurs, cost considerations start to play a greater role in the competitive process. Producers based in advanced countries where labor costs are lower than in the United States (e.g., Italy and Spain) might now be able to export to the United States. If cost pressures become intense, the process might not stop there. The cycle by which the United States lost its advantage to other advanced countries might be repeated once more, as developing countries (e.g., Thailand) begin to acquire a production advantage over advanced countries. Thus, the locus of global production initially switches from the United States to other advanced nations and then from those nations to developing countries.

The consequence of these trends for the pattern of world trade is that over time, the United States switches from being an exporter of the product to an importer of the product as production becomes concentrated in lower-cost foreign locations.

PRODUCT LIFE-CYCLE THEORY IN THE TWENTY-FIRST CENTURY Historically, the product life-cycle theory seems to be an accurate explanation of international trade patterns. Consider photocopiers; the product was first developed in the early 1960s by Xerox in the United States and sold initially to U.S. users. Originally, Xerox exported photocopiers from the United States, primarily to Japan and the advanced countries of western Europe. As demand began to grow in those countries, Xerox entered into joint ventures to set up production in Japan (Fuji-Xerox) and Great Britain (Rank-Xerox). In addition, once Xerox's patents on the photocopier process expired, other foreign competitors began to enter the market (e.g., Canon in Japan and Olivetti in Italy). As a consequence, exports from the United States declined, and U.S. users began to buy some photocopiers from lower-cost foreign sources, particularly Japan. More recently, Japanese companies found that manufacturing costs are too high in their own country, so they have begun to switch production to developing countries such as Thailand. Thus, initially the United States and now other advanced countries (e.g., Japan and Great Britain) have switched from being exporters of photocopiers to importers. This evolution in the pattern of international trade in photocopiers is consistent with the predictions of the product life-cycle theory that mature industries tend to go out of the United States and into low-cost assembly locations.

However, the product life-cycle theory is not without weaknesses. Viewed from an Asian or European perspective, Vernon's argument that most new products are developed and introduced in the United States seems ethnocentric and increasingly dated. Although it may be true that during U.S. dominance of the global economy (from 1945 to 1975), most new products were introduced in the United States, there have always been important exceptions. These exceptions appear to have become more common in recent years. Many new products are now first introduced in Japan (e.g., video-game consoles) or South Korea (e.g., Samsung smartphones). Moreover, with the increased globalization and integration of the world economy discussed in Chapter 1, an increasing number of new products (e.g., tablet computers, smartphones, and digital cameras) are now introduced simultaneously in the United States and many European and Asian nations. This may be accompanied by globally dispersed production, with particular components of a new product being produced in those locations around the globe where the mix of factor costs and skills is most favorable (as predicted by the theory of comparative advantage). In sum, although Vernon's theory may be useful for explaining the pattern of international trade during the period of American global dominance, its relevance in the modern world seems more limited.

Use SmartBook to help retain what you have learned. Access your Instructor's Connect course to check out SmartBook or go to learnsmartadvantage.com for help.

New Trade Theory

Summarize the different theories explaining trade flows between nations.

Economies of Scale

Cost advantages associated with large-scale production.

The new trade theory began to emerge in the 1970s when a number of economists pointed out that the ability of firms to attain economies of scale might have important implications for international trade.[29] **Economies of scale** are unit cost reductions associated with a large scale of output. Economies of scale have a number of sources, including the ability to spread fixed costs over a large volume and the ability of large-volume producers to utilize specialized employees and equipment that are more productive than less specialized employees and equipment. Economies of scale are a major source of cost reductions in many industries, from computer software to automobiles and from pharmaceuticals to aerospace. For example, Microsoft realizes economies of scale by spreading the fixed costs of developing new versions of its Windows operating system, which runs to about $10 billion, over the 2 billion or so personal computers on which each new system is ultimately installed. Similarly, automobile companies realize economies of scale by producing a high volume of automobiles from an assembly line where each employee has a specialized task.

New trade theory makes two important points: First, through its impact on economies of scale, trade can increase the variety of goods available to consumers and decrease the average cost of those goods. Second, in those industries in which the output required to attain economies of scale represents a significant proportion of total world demand, the global market may be able to support only a small number of enterprises. Thus, world trade in certain products may be dominated by countries whose firms were first movers in their production.

INCREASING PRODUCT VARIETY AND REDUCING COSTS

Recognize why many economists believe that unrestricted free trade between nations will raise the economic welfare of countries that participate in a free trade system.

Imagine first a world without trade. In industries where economies of scale are important, both the variety of goods that a country can produce and the scale of production are limited by the size of the market. If a national market is small, there may not be enough demand to enable producers to realize economies of scale for certain products. Accordingly, those products may not be produced, thereby limiting the variety of products available to consumers. Alternatively, they may be produced but at such low volumes that unit costs and prices are considerably higher than they might be if economies of scale could be realized.

Now consider what happens when nations trade with each other. Individual national markets are combined into a larger world market. As the size of the market expands due to trade, individual firms may be able to better attain economies of scale. The implication, according to new trade theory, is that each nation may be able to specialize in producing a narrower range of products than it would in the absence of trade, yet by buying goods that it does not make from other countries, each nation can simultaneously increase the *variety* of goods available to its consumers and *lower the costs* of those goods; thus, trade offers an opportunity for mutual gain even when countries do not differ in their resource endowments or technology.

Suppose there are two countries, each with an annual market for 1 million automobiles. By trading with each other, these countries can create a combined market for 2 million cars. In this combined market, due to the ability to better realize economies of scale, more varieties (models) of cars can be produced, and cars can be produced at a lower average cost, than in either market alone. For example, demand for a sports car may be limited to 55,000 units in each national market, while a total output of at least 100,000 per year may be required to realize significant scale economies. Similarly, demand for a minivan may be 80,000 units in each national market, and again a total output of at least 100,000 per year may be required to realize significant scale economies. Faced with limited domestic market demand, firms in each nation may decide not to produce a sports car, because the costs of doing so at such low volume are too great. Although they may produce minivans, the cost of doing so will be higher, as will prices, than if significant economies of scale had been attained. Once the two countries decide to trade, however, a firm in one nation may specialize in producing sports cars, while a firm in the other nation may produce minivans. The combined demand for 110,000 sports cars and 160,000 minivans allows each firm to realize scale economies. Consumers in this case benefit from having access to a product (sports cars) that was not available before international trade and from the lower price for a product (minivans) that could not be

Can We Continue to Rely on Economies of Scale?

Economies of scale are unit cost reductions associated with a large scale of output. As we discuss in the text, economies of scale have a number of sources, including the ability to spread fixed costs over a large volume and the ability of large-volume producers to utilize specialized employees and equipment that are more productive than less specialized employees and equipment. Economies of scale have been a major source of cost reductions in many industries—from computer software to automobiles and from pharmaceuticals to aerospace. But some of these economies of scale advantages were realized when production platforms for computers, automobiles, and so on were used for years and spread across large numbers of customers. With more and more innovations coming on the market faster and faster every year and more and more customers wanting customized products (even if the customization is small), how can companies continue to rely on economies of scale as a strategic advantage? Will large, mass market–type companies that are selling large quantities of specific products always have economies of scale advantages vis-à-vis small and medium-sized companies?

produced at the most efficient scale before international trade. Trade is thus mutually beneficial because it allows the specialization of production, the realization of scale economies, the production of a greater variety of products, and lower prices.

ECONOMIES OF SCALE, FIRST-MOVER ADVANTAGES, AND THE PATTERN OF TRADE

A second theme in new trade theory is that the pattern of trade we observe in the world economy may be the result of economies of scale and first-mover advantages. **First-mover advantages** are the economic and strategic advantages that accrue to early entrants into an industry.[30] The ability to capture scale economies ahead of later entrants, and thus benefit from a lower cost structure, is an important first-mover advantage. New trade theory argues that for those products where economies of scale are significant and represent a substantial proportion of world demand, the first movers in an industry can gain a scale-based cost advantage that later entrants find almost impossible to match. Thus, the pattern of trade that we observe for such products may reflect first-mover advantages. Countries may dominate in the export of certain goods because economies of scale are important in their production and because firms located in those countries were the first to capture scale economies, giving them a first-mover advantage.

First-Mover Advantages

Advantages accruing to the first to enter a market.

For example, consider the commercial aerospace industry. In aerospace, there are substantial scale economies that come from the ability to spread the fixed costs of developing a new jet aircraft over a large number of sales. It has cost Airbus some $15 billion to develop its new superjumbo jet, the 550-seat A380. To recoup those costs and break even, Airbus will have to sell at least 250 A380 planes. If Airbus can sell more than 350 A380 planes, it will apparently be a profitable venture. Total demand over the next 20 years for this class of aircraft is estimated to be between 400 and 600 units. Thus, the global market can probably profitably support only one producer of jet aircraft in the superjumbo category. It follows that the European Union might come to dominate in the export of very large jet aircraft, primarily because a European-based firm, Airbus, was the first to produce a superjumbo jet aircraft and realize scale economies. Other potential producers, such as Boeing, might be shut out of the market because they will lack the scale economies that Airbus will enjoy. By pioneering this market category, Airbus may have captured a *first-mover advantage* based on *scale economies* that will be difficult for rivals to match, and that will result in the European Union becoming the *leading exporter* of very large jet aircraft.

IMPLICATIONS OF NEW TRADE THEORY

New trade theory has important implications. The theory suggests that nations may benefit from trade even when they do not differ in resource endowments or technology. Trade allows a nation to specialize in the production of certain products, attaining scale economies and lowering the costs of producing those products, while buying products that it does not produce from other nations that specialize in the production of other products. By this mechanism, the variety of products available to consumers in each nation is increased, while the average costs of those products should fall, as should their price, freeing resources to produce other goods and services.

The theory also suggests that a country may predominate in the export of a good simply because it was lucky enough to have one or more firms among the first to produce that good. Because they are able to gain economies of scale, the first movers in an industry may get a lock on the world market that discourages subsequent entry. First-movers' ability to benefit from increasing returns creates a barrier to entry. In the commercial aircraft industry, the fact that Boeing and Airbus are already in the industry and have the benefits of economies of scale discourages new entry and reinforces the dominance of America and Europe in the trade of midsize and large jet aircraft. This dominance is further reinforced because global demand may not be sufficient to profitably support another producer of midsize and large jet aircraft in the industry. So although Japanese firms might be able to compete in the market, they have decided not to enter the industry but to ally themselves as major subcontractors with primary producers (e.g., Mitsubishi Heavy Industries is a major subcontractor for Boeing on the 777 and 787 programs).

New trade theory is at variance with the Heckscher-Ohlin theory, which suggests a country will predominate in the export of a product when it is particularly well endowed with those factors used intensively in its manufacture. New trade theorists argue that the United States is a major exporter of commercial jet aircraft not because it is better endowed with the factors of production required to manufacture aircraft but because one of the first movers in the industry, Boeing, was a U.S. firm. The new trade theory is not at variance with the theory of comparative advantage. Economies of scale increase productivity. Thus, the new trade theory identifies an important source of comparative advantage.

This theory is quite useful in explaining trade patterns. Empirical studies seem to support the predictions of the theory that trade increases the specialization of production within an industry, increases the variety of products available to consumers, and results in lower average prices.[31] With regard to first-mover advantages and international trade, a study by Harvard business historian Alfred Chandler suggests the existence of first-mover advantages is an important factor in explaining the dominance of firms from certain nations in specific industries.[32] The number of firms is very limited in many global industries, including the chemical industry, the heavy construction-equipment industry, the heavy truck industry, the tire industry, the consumer electronics industry, the jet engine industry, and the computer software industry.

Perhaps the most contentious implication of the new trade theory is the argument that it generates for government intervention and strategic trade policy.[33] New trade theorists stress the role of luck, entrepreneurship, and innovation in giving a firm first-mover advantages. According to this argument, the reason Boeing was the first mover in commercial jet aircraft manufacture—rather than firms such as Great Britain's De Havilland and Hawker Siddeley or Holland's Fokker, all of which could have been—was that Boeing was both lucky and innovative. One way Boeing was lucky is that De Havilland shot itself in the foot when its Comet jet airliner, introduced two years earlier than Boeing's first jet airliner, the 707, was found to be full of serious technological flaws. Had De Havilland not made some serious technological mistakes, Great Britain might have become the world's leading exporter of commercial jet aircraft. Boeing's innovativeness was demonstrated by its independent development of the technological know-how required to build a commercial jet airliner. Several new trade theorists have pointed out, however, that Boeing's R&D was largely paid for by the U.S. government; the 707 was a spin-off from a government-funded military program (the entry of Airbus into the industry was also supported by significant government subsidies). Herein is a rationale for government intervention; by the sophisticated and judicious use of subsidies, could a government increase the chances of its domestic firms becoming first movers in newly emerging industries, as the U.S. government apparently did with Boeing (and the European Union did with Airbus)? If this is possible, and the new trade theory suggests it might be, we have an economic rationale for a proactive trade policy that is at variance with the free trade prescriptions of the trade theories we have reviewed so far. We consider the policy implications of this issue in Chapter 7.

Use SmartBook to help retain what you have learned. Access your Instructor's Connect course to check out SmartBook or go to learnsmartadvantage.com for help.

National Competitive Advantage: Porter's Diamond

Summarize the different theories explaining trade flows between nations.

Michael Porter, the famous Harvard strategy professor, has also written extensively on international trade.[34] Porter and his team looked at 100 industries in 10 nations. Like the work of the new trade theorists, Porter's work was driven by a belief that existing theories of international trade told only part of the story. For Porter, the essential task was to explain why a nation achieves international success in a particular industry. Why does Japan do so well in the automobile industry? Why does Switzerland excel in the production and export of precision instruments and pharmaceuticals? Why do Germany and the United States do so well in the chemical industry? These questions cannot be answered easily by the Heckscher-Ohlin theory, and the theory of comparative advantage offers only a partial explanation. The theory of comparative advantage would say that Switzerland excels in the production and export of precision instruments because it uses its resources very productively in these industries. Although this may be correct, this does not explain why Switzerland is more productive in this industry than Great Britain, Germany, or Spain. Porter tries to solve this puzzle.

Porter theorizes that four broad attributes of a nation shape the environment in which local firms compete, and these attributes promote or impede the creation of competitive advantage (see Figure 6.5). These attributes are:

- *Factor endowments*—a nation's position in factors of production, such as skilled labor or the infrastructure necessary to compete in a given industry.

FIGURE

The Determinants Of National Competitive Advantage: Porter's Diamond.

Source: Michael E. Porter, *The Competitive Advantage of Nations* (New York: Free Press, 1990; republished with a new introduction, 1998), p. 72.

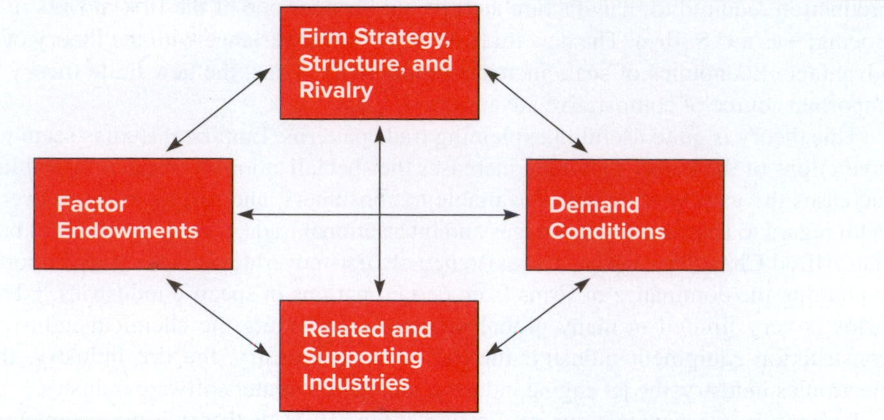

- *Demand conditions*—the nature of home demand for the industry's product or service.
- *Related and supporting industries*—the presence or absence of supplier industries and related industries that are internationally competitive.
- *Firm strategy, structure, and rivalry*—the conditions governing how companies are created, organized, and managed and the nature of domestic rivalry.

Porter speaks of these four attributes as constituting the *diamond.* He argues that firms are most likely to succeed in industries or industry segments where the diamond is most favorable. He also argues that the diamond is a mutually reinforcing system. The effect of one attribute is contingent on the state of others. For example, Porter argues favorable demand conditions will not result in competitive advantage unless the state of rivalry is sufficient to cause firms to respond to them.

Porter maintains that two additional variables can influence the national diamond in important ways: chance and government. Chance events, such as major innovations, can reshape industry structure and provide the opportunity for one nation's firms to supplant another's. Government, by its choice of policies, can detract from or improve national advantage. For example, regulation can alter home demand conditions, antitrust policies can influence the intensity of rivalry within an industry, and government investments in education can change factor endowments.

FACTOR ENDOWMENTS Factor endowments lie at the center of the Heckscher-Ohlin theory. While Porter does not propose anything radically new, he does analyze the characteristics of factors of production. He recognizes hierarchies among factors, distinguishing between *basic factors* (e.g., natural resources, climate, location, and demographics) and *advanced factors* (e.g., communication infrastructure, sophisticated and skilled labor, research facilities, and technological know-how). He argues that advanced factors are the most significant for competitive advantage. Unlike the naturally endowed basic factors, advanced factors are a product of investment by individuals, companies, and governments. Thus, government investments in basic and higher education, by improving the general skill and knowledge level of the population and by stimulating advanced research at higher education institutions, can upgrade a nation's advanced factors.

The relationship between advanced and basic factors is complex. Basic factors can provide an initial advantage that is subsequently reinforced and extended by investment in advanced factors. Conversely, disadvantages in basic factors can create pressures to invest in advanced factors. An obvious example of this phenomenon is Japan, a country that lacks arable land and mineral deposits and yet through investment has built a substantial endowment of advanced factors. Porter notes that Japan's large pool of engineers (reflecting a much higher number of engineering graduates per capita than almost any other nation) has been vital to Japan's success in many manufacturing industries.

DEMAND CONDITIONS Porter emphasizes the role home demand plays in upgrading competitive advantage. Firms are typically most sensitive to the needs of their closest customers. Thus, the characteristics of home demand are particularly important in shaping the attributes of domestically made products and in creating pressures for innovation and quality. Porter argues that a nation's firms gain competitive advantage if their domestic consumers are sophisticated and demanding. Such consumers pressure local firms to meet high standards of product quality and to produce innovative products. For example, Porter notes that Japan's sophisticated and knowledgeable buyers of cameras helped stimulate the Japanese camera industry to improve product quality and to introduce innovative models.

RELATED AND SUPPORTING INDUSTRIES The third broad attribute of national advantage in an industry is the presence of suppliers or related industries that are internationally competitive. The benefits of investments in advanced factors of production by related and supporting industries can spill over into an industry, thereby helping it achieve a strong competitive position internationally. Swedish strength in fabricated steel products (e.g., ball bearings and cutting tools) has drawn on strengths in Sweden's specialty steel industry. Technological leadership in the U.S. semiconductor industry provided the basis for U.S. success in personal computers and several other technically advanced electronic products. Similarly, Switzerland's success in pharmaceuticals is closely related to its previous international success in the technologically related dye industry.

One consequence of this process is that successful industries within a country tend to be grouped into clusters of related industries. This was one of the most pervasive findings of Porter's study. One such cluster Porter identified was in the German textile and apparel sector, which included high-quality cotton, wool, synthetic fibers, sewing machine needles, and a wide range of textile machinery. Such clusters are important because valuable knowledge can flow between the firms within a geographic cluster, benefiting all within that cluster. Knowledge flows occur when employees move between firms within a region and when national industry associations bring employees from different companies together for regular conferences or workshops.[35]

FIRM STRATEGY, STRUCTURE, AND RIVALRY The fourth broad attribute of national competitive advantage in Porter's model is the strategy, structure, and rivalry of firms within a nation. Porter makes two important points here. First, different nations are characterized by different management ideologies, which either help them or do not help them build national competitive advantage. For example, Porter noted the predominance of engineers in top management at German and Japanese firms. He attributed this to these firms' emphasis on improving manufacturing processes and product design. In contrast, Porter noted a predominance of people with finance backgrounds leading many U.S. firms. He linked this to U.S. firms' lack of attention to improving manufacturing processes and product design. He argued that the dominance of finance led to an overemphasis on maximizing short-term financial returns. According to Porter, one consequence of these different management ideologies was a relative loss of U.S. competitiveness in those engineering-based industries where manufacturing processes and product design issues are all-important (e.g., the automobile industry).

Porter's second point is that there is a strong association between vigorous domestic rivalry and the creation and persistence of competitive advantage in an industry. Vigorous domestic rivalry induces firms to look for ways to improve efficiency, which makes them better international competitors. Domestic rivalry creates pressures to innovate, to improve

How Important Is Education?

Both the Heckscher-Ohlin and Michael Porter theories of trade focus to a large degree on "factor endowments." The Heckscher-Ohlin theory specifies endowments such as resources as land, labor, and capital as being critical, while the Porter theory recognizes hierarchies among these factor endowments. Education- related endowments such as skilled labor, research facilities, and technological know-how are what Porter calls "advanced factors." A long-standing argument across multiple governmental organizations, research studies, and prominent individuals is that education drives economic, social, and environmental well-being of countries (i.e., countries adopt sustainability principles the more educated the people in the country are relative to people in the global marketplace—see Chapter 5). The extension of this argument is that education helps people become better citizens of a country. But, what do you think education does to a customer's product needs and wants? Do they want more foreign products if they have more years of education (e.g., graduate degree) compared with fewer years of education (e.g., high school)? Or does education not influence the type of products bought by customers (i.e., foreign-made or home-country made)?

Sources: T. Healy and S. Cote, "The Well-Being of Nations: The Role of Human and Social Capital," Organisation for Economic Cooperation and Development (OECD) (2001); S. Samuel, "Importance of Education in a Country's Progress," HowToLearn.com, March 13, 2013; K. Matsui, "The Economic Benefits of Educating Women," *Bloomberg Businessweek*, March 7, 2013.

quality, to reduce costs, and to invest in upgrading advanced factors. All this helps create world-class competitors. Porter cites the case of Japan:

> Nowhere is the role of domestic rivalry more evident than in Japan, where it is all-out warfare in which many companies fail to achieve profitability. With goals that stress market share, Japanese companies engage in a continuing struggle to outdo each other. Shares fluctuate markedly. The process is prominently covered in the business press. Elaborate rankings measure which companies are most popular with university graduates. The rate of new product and process development is breathtaking.[36]

LO 6-4
Explain the arguments of those who maintain that government can play a proactive role in promoting national competitive advantage in certain industries.

EVALUATING PORTER'S THEORY

Porter contends that the degree to which a nation is likely to achieve international success in a certain industry is a function of the combined impact of factor endowments, domestic demand conditions, related and supporting industries, and domestic rivalry. He argues that the presence of all four components is usually required for this diamond to boost competitive performance (although there are exceptions). Porter also contends that government can influence each of the four components of the diamond—either positively or negatively. Factor endowments can be affected by subsidies, policies toward capital markets, policies toward education, and so on. Government can shape domestic demand through local product standards or with regulations that mandate or influence buyer needs. Government policy can influence supporting and related industries through regulation and influence firm rivalry through such devices as capital market regulation, tax policy, and antitrust laws.

If Porter is correct, we would expect his model to predict the pattern of international trade that we observe in the real world. Countries should be exporting products from those industries where all four components of the diamond are favorable, while importing in those areas where the components are not favorable. Is he correct? We simply do not know. Porter's theory has not been subjected to detailed empirical testing. Much about the theory rings true, but the same can be said for the new trade theory, the theory of comparative advantage, and the Heckscher-Ohlin theory. It may be that each of these theories, which complement each other, explains something about the pattern of international trade.

test PREP
Use SmartBook to help retain what you have learned. Access your Instructor's Connect course to check out SmartBook or go to learnsmartadvantage.com for help.

FOCUS ON MANAGERIAL IMPLICATIONS

LOCATION, FIRST-MOVER ADVANTAGES, AND GOVERNMENT POLICY

LO 6-5
Understand the important implications that international trade theory holds for business practice.

Why does all this matter for business? There are at least three main implications for international businesses of the material discussed in this chapter: location implications, first-mover implications, and government policy implications.

Location

Underlying most of the theories we have discussed is the notion that different countries have particular advantages in different productive activities. Thus, from a profit perspective, it makes sense for a firm to disperse its productive activities to those countries where, according to the theory of international trade, they can be performed most efficiently. If design can be performed most efficiently in France, that is where design facilities should be located; if the manufacture of basic components can be performed most efficiently in Singapore, that is where they should be manufactured; and if final assembly can be performed most efficiently in China, that is where final assembly should be performed. The result is a global web of productive activities, with different activities being performed in different locations around the globe depending on considerations of comparative advantage, factor endowments, and the like. If the firm does not do this, it may find itself at a competitive disadvantage relative to firms that do.

First-Mover Advantages

According to the new trade theory, firms that establish a first-mover advantage with regard to the production of a particular new product may subsequently dominate global trade in that product. This is particularly true in industries where the global market can profitably support only a limited number of firms, such as the aerospace market, but early commitments may also seem to be important in less concentrated industries. For the individual firm, the clear message is that it pays to invest substantial financial resources in trying to build a first-mover, or early-mover, advantage, even if that means several years of losses before a new venture becomes profitable. The idea is to preempt the available demand, gain cost advantages related to volume, build an enduring brand ahead of later competitors, and, consequently, establish a long-term sustainable competitive advantage. Although the details of how to achieve this are beyond the scope of this book, many publications offer strategies for exploiting first-mover advantages and for avoiding the traps associated with pioneering a market (first-mover disadvantages).[37]

Government Policy

The theories of international trade also matter to international businesses because firms are major players on the international trade scene. Business firms produce exports, and business firms import the products of other countries. Because of their pivotal role in international trade, businesses can exert a strong influence on government trade policy, lobbying to promote free trade or trade restrictions. The theories of international trade claim that promoting free trade is generally in the best interests of a country, although it may not always be in the best interest of an individual firm. Many firms recognize this and lobby for open markets.

For example, when the U.S. government announced its intention to place a tariff on Japanese imports of liquid crystal display (LCD) screens in the 1990s, IBM and Apple Computer protested strongly. Both IBM and Apple pointed out that (1) Japan was the lowest-cost source of LCD screens; (2) they used these screens in their own laptop computers; and (3) the proposed tariff, by increasing the cost of LCD screens, would increase the cost of laptop computers produced by IBM and Apple, thus making them less competitive in the world market. In other words, the tariff, designed to protect U.S. firms, would be self-defeating. In response to these pressures, the U.S. government reversed its posture.

Unlike IBM and Apple, however, businesses do not always lobby for free trade. In the United States, for example, restrictions on imports of steel have periodically been put into place in response to direct pressure by U.S. firms on the government. In some cases, the government has responded to pressure by getting foreign companies to agree to "voluntary" restrictions on their imports, using the implicit threat of more comprehensive formal trade barriers to get them to adhere to these agreements (historically, this has occurred in the automobile industry). In other cases, the government used what are called "antidumping" actions to justify tariffs on imports from other nations (these mechanisms will be discussed in detail in Chapter 7).

As predicted by international trade theory, many of these agreements have been self-defeating, such as the voluntary restriction on machine tool imports agreed to in 1985. Shielded from international competition by import barriers, the U.S. machine tool industry had no incentive to increase its efficiency. Consequently, it lost many of its export markets to more efficient foreign competitors. Because of this misguided action, the U.S. machine tool industry shrunk during the period when the agreement was in force. For anyone schooled in international trade theory, this was not surprising.[38]

Finally, Porter's theory of national competitive advantage also contains policy implications. Porter's theory suggests that it is in the best interest of business for a firm to invest in upgrading advanced factors of production (for example, to invest in better training for its employees) and to increase its commitment to research and development. It is also in the best interests of business to lobby the government to adopt policies that have a favorable impact on each component of the national diamond. Thus, according to Porter, businesses should urge government to increase investment in education, infrastructure, and basic research (since all these enhance advanced factors) and to adopt policies that promote strong competition within domestic markets (since this makes firms stronger international competitors, according to Porter's findings).

Key Terms

free trade, p. 155
new trade theory, p. 156
mercantilism, p. 157
zero-sum game, p. 157
absolute advantage, p. 158
constant returns to specialization, p. 163
factor endowments, p. 168
economies of scale, p. 170
first-mover advantages, p. 172
balance-of-payments accounts, p. 181
current account, p. 182
current account deficit, p. 182
current account surplus, p. 182
capital account, p. 182
financial account, p. 182

Summary

This chapter reviewed a number of theories that explain why it is beneficial for a country to engage in international trade and explained the pattern of international trade observed in the world economy. The theories of Smith, Ricardo, and Heckscher-Ohlin all make strong cases for unrestricted free trade. In contrast, the mercantilist doctrine and, to a lesser extent, the new trade theory can be interpreted to support government intervention to promote exports through subsidies and to limit imports through tariffs and quotas.

In explaining the pattern of international trade, this chapter shows that, with the exception of mercantilism, which is silent on this issue, the different theories offer largely complementary explanations. Although no one theory may explain the apparent pattern of international trade, taken together, the theory of comparative advantage, the Heckscher-Ohlin theory, the product life-cycle theory, the new trade theory, and Porter's theory of national competitive advantage do suggest which factors are important. Comparative advantage tells us that productivity differences are important; Heckscher-Ohlin tells us that factor endowments matter; the product life-cycle theory tells us that where a new product is introduced is important; the new trade theory tells us that increasing returns to specialization and first-mover advantages matter; and Porter tells us that all these factors may be important insofar as they affect the four components of the national diamond. The chapter made the following points:

1. Mercantilists argued that it was in a country's best interests to run a balance-of-trade surplus. They viewed trade as a zero-sum game, in which one country's gains cause losses for other countries.
2. The theory of absolute advantage suggests that countries differ in their ability to produce goods efficiently. The theory suggests that a country should specialize in producing goods in areas where it has an absolute advantage and import goods in areas where other countries have absolute advantages.
3. The theory of comparative advantage suggests that it makes sense for a country to specialize in producing those goods that it can produce most efficiently, while buying goods that it can produce relatively less efficiently from other countries—even if that means buying goods from other countries that it could produce more efficiently itself.
4. The theory of comparative advantage suggests that unrestricted free trade brings about increased world production, that is, that trade is a positive-sum game.
5. The theory of comparative advantage also suggests that opening a country to free trade stimulates economic growth, which creates dynamic gains from trade. The empirical evidence seems to be consistent with this claim.
6. The Heckscher-Ohlin theory argues that the pattern of international trade is determined by differences in factor endowments. It predicts that countries will export those goods that make intensive use of locally abundant factors and will import goods that make intensive use of factors that are locally scarce.
7. The product life-cycle theory suggests that trade patterns are influenced by where a new product is introduced. In an increasingly integrated global economy, the product life-cycle theory seems to be less predictive than it once was.
8. New trade theory states that trade allows a nation to specialize in the production of certain goods, attaining scale economies and lowering the costs of producing those goods, while buying goods that it does not produce from other nations that are similarly specialized. By this mechanism, the variety of goods available to consumers in each nation is increased, while the average costs of those goods should fall.
9. New trade theory also states that in those industries where substantial economies of scale imply that the world market will profitably support only a few firms, countries may predominate in the export of certain products simply because they had a firm that was a first mover in that industry.
10. Some new trade theorists have promoted the idea of strategic trade policy. The argument is that government, by the sophisticated and judicious use of subsidies, might be able to increase the chances of domestic firms becoming first movers in newly emerging industries.

11. Porter's theory of national competitive advantage suggests that the pattern of trade is influenced by four attributes of a nation: *(a)* factor endowments, *(b)* domestic demand conditions, *(c)* related and supporting industries, and *(d)* firm strategy, structure, and rivalry.
12. Theories of international trade are important to an individual business firm primarily because they can help the firm decide where to locate its various production activities.
13. Firms involved in international trade can and do exert a strong influence on government policy toward trade. By lobbying government, business firms can promote free trade or trade restrictions.

Critical Thinking and Discussion Questions

1. Mercantilism is a bankrupt theory that has no place in the modern world. Discuss.
2. Is free trade fair? Discuss!
3. Unions in developed nations often oppose imports from low-wage countries and advocate trade barriers to protect jobs from what they often characterize as "unfair" import competition. Is such competition "unfair"? Do you think that this argument is in the best interests of (*a*) the unions, (*b*) the people they represent, and/or (*c*) the country as a whole?
4. What are the potential costs of adopting a free trade regime? Do you think governments should do anything to reduce these costs? What?
5. Reread the Country Focus "Is China a Neo-mercantilist Nation?"
   a. Do you think China is pursuing an economic policy that can be characterized as neo-mercantilist?
   b. What should the United States, and other countries, do about this?
6. Reread the Country Focus on moving U.S. white-collar jobs offshore.
   a. Who benefits from the outsourcing of skilled white-collar jobs to developing nations? Who are the losers?
   b. Will developed nations like the United States suffer from the loss of high-skilled and high-paying jobs?
   c. Is there a difference between the transference of high-paying white-collar jobs, such as computer programming and accounting, to developing nations, and low-paying blue-collar jobs? If so, what is the difference, and should government do anything to stop the flow of white-collar jobs out of the country to countries such as India?
7. Drawing upon the new trade theory and Porter's theory of national competitive advantage, outline the case for government policies that would build national competitive advantage in biotechnology. What kinds of policies would you recommend that the government adopt? Are these policies at variance with the basic free trade philosophy?
8. The world's poorest countries are at a competitive disadvantage in every sector of their economies. They have little to export. They have no capital; their land is of poor quality; they often have too many people given available work opportunities; and they are poorly educated. Free trade cannot possibly be in the interests of such nations. Discuss.

globalEDGE Research Task

globalEDGE.msu.edu

Use the globalEDGE™ website (**globaledge.msu.edu**) to complete the following exercises:

1. The *World Trade Organization International Trade Statistics* is an annual report that provides comprehensive, comparable, and updated statistics on trade in merchandise and commercial services. The report allows an assessment of world trade flows by country, region, and main product or service categories. Using the most recent statistics available, identify the top 10 countries that lead in the export and import of merchandise trade, respectively. Which countries appear in the top 10 in both exports and imports? Can you explain why these countries appear at the top of both lists?
2. Food in an integral part of understanding different countries, cultures, and lifestyles. You run a chain of high-end premium restaurants in the United States, and you are looking for unique Australian wines you can import. However, you must first identify which *Australian suppliers* can provide you with premium wines. After searching through the Australian supplier directory, identify three to four companies that can be potential suppliers. Then develop a list of criteria you would need to ask these companies to select which one to work with.

Creating the World's Biggest Free Trade Zone closing case

In his February 12, 2013, State of the Union address, President Barack Obama committed the United States to negotiating a free trade deal with the European Union (EU). The proposed agreement is known as the Transatlantic Trade and Investment Partnership (TTIP). The United States and the 28 countries that are members of the EU already make up the world's largest and richest trading partnership, accounting for about 60 percent of global GDP, 33 percent of world trade in goods, and 42 percent of world trade in services. Moreover, both the United States and EU are members of the World Trade Organization, and many trade tariffs between the two economic blocks are already low. Nevertheless, the announcement was greeted with approval on both sides of the Atlantic and, unusually for President Obama, from both sides of the political divide in the United States.

The reason for the enthusiasm for the proposed TTIP can be traced to acceptance of the key axiom of international trade theory—trade is a good thing for all countries involved in a free trade agreement. Free trade is a positive-sum game; it is equivalent to the rising tide that lifts all boats. Both the United States and the EU have struggled with low economic growth, persistently high unemployment, and large government deficits. A new free trade deal could help economies on both sides of the Atlantic grow faster, thereby reducing unemployment, without costing another dime in government spending. A trade deal is in effect a cost-free stimulus package.

How big the economic impact will be remains to be seen. For both the United States and the EU, average tariffs (taxes) on imported goods are currently close to 3 percent by most measures. Further reduction could nonetheless stimulate additional trade, and there are some areas where tariffs are much higher, notably on agricultural goods. Beyond tariff reductions, there are many nontariff barriers to international trade that could be reduced or eliminated as the result of a deal. One example is found in the automobile industry, where the EU and United States both employ equally strict but different safety standards. This means that to sell in both the EU and United States, automobile manufacturers must adhere to two different sets of regulations. Similarly, pharmaceutical firms currently have to submit new drugs to two sets of safety tests, one in the United States and one in the EU. Such regulatory requirements are functionally equivalent to an import tariff insofar as they raise the costs of business and international trade. By some calculations, nontariff barriers such as these are equivalent to a traditional import tariff of 10 to 20 percent. Initial estimates suggest that a comprehensive and ambitious agreement that covers both tariff and nontariff barriers to trade will boost annual GDP growth by about 0.5 percent per annum on both sides of the Atlantic, producing an additional $200 billion a year in economic activity. Talks on the TTIP began in July 2013 and currently are expected to be completed sometime in 2019 or 2020.

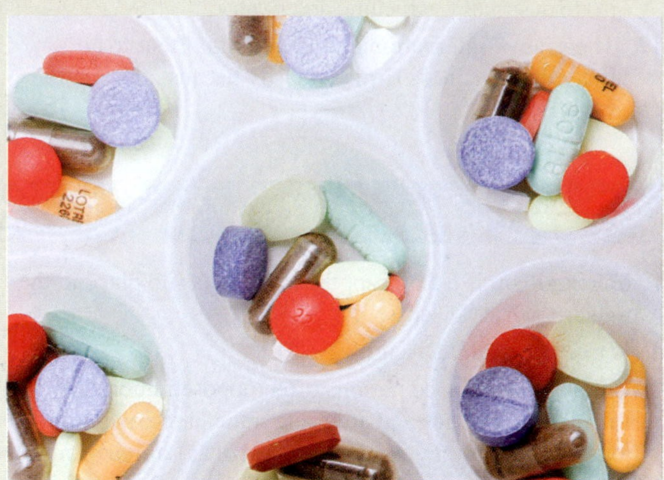

Generic drugs manufactured by Indian firms help the country emerge as a major exporter of pharmaceuticals.

Source: © Image Source/Getty Images RF

Sources: "Transatlantic Trading," *The Economist*, February 2013; Andrew Walker, "EU and US Free Trade Talks Launched," *BBC News*, February 13, 2013; Paul Ames, "Parmesan Cheese: Thorn in US-EU Free Trade Deal?," *GlobalPost.com*, February 25, 2013; Henry Chu, "U.S., EU Resume Negotiations on Free Trade Agreement," *Los Angeles Times*, November 11, 2013.

CASE DISCUSSION QUESTIONS

1. What are the benefits of the proposed TTIP?
2. Can you think of any drawbacks associated with the TTIP?
3. Two decades ago when the United States entered into the North American Free Trade Agreement with Canada and Mexico, there was significant opposition from organized labor and some politicians. There does not seem to be the same level of opposition to the TTIP. Why do you think this is so?
4. The Trans Pacific Partnership (TTP) has met with significant political resistance in the United States (see the opening case), while the TTIP has not (at least as yet). Why do you think this is the case?

appendix

International Trade and the Balance of Payments

International trade involves the sale of goods and services to residents in other countries (exports) and the purchase of goods and services from residents in other countries (imports). A country's **balance-of-payments accounts** keep track of the payments to and receipts from other countries for a particular time period. These include payments to foreigners for imports of goods and services, and receipts from foreigners for goods and services exported to them. A summary copy of the U.S. balance-of-payments accounts for 2014 is given in Table A.1. In this appendix, we briefly describe the form of the balance-of-payments accounts, and we discuss whether a current account deficit, often a cause of much concern in the popular press, is something to worry about.

Balance-of-Payments Accounts
National accounts that track both payments to and receipts from foreigners.

A.1 TABLE
U.S. Balance-of-Payments Accounts, 2014

Current Account	$ Millions
Exports of goods, services, and income receipts (credits)	$3,306,574
Goods	1,632,639
Services	710,565
Primary income receipts	823,535
Secondary income receipts	410,016
Imports of goods, services, and income (debits)	**3,696,100**
Goods	2,374,101
Services	477,428
Primary income payments	585,369
Secondary income payments	259,202
Capital Account	
Capital transfer receipts	0
Capital transfer debits	45
Financial Account	
Net U.S. acquisition of financial assets	792,145
Net U.S. incurrence of liabilities	977,421
Net financial derivatives	−54,372
Statistical discrepancy	149,923
Balances	
Balance on current account	−389,526
Balance on capital account	−45
Balance on financial account	−239,648

Bureau of Economic Analysis.

BALANCE-OF-PAYMENTS ACCOUNTS Balance-of-payments accounts are divided into three main sections: the current account, the capital account, and the financial account (to confuse matters, what is now called the capital account until recently was part of the current account, and the financial account used to be called the capital account). The **current account** records transactions that pertain to four categories, all of which can be seen in Table A.1. The first category, goods, refers to the export or import of physical goods (e.g., agricultural foodstuffs, autos, computers, chemicals). The second category is the export or import of services (e.g., intangible products such as banking and insurance services). The third category, primary income receipts or payments, refers to income from foreign investments or payments to foreign investors (e.g., interest and dividend receipts or payments). The third category also includes payments that foreigners have made to U.S. residents for work performed outside the United States and payments that U.S. entities make to foreign residents. The fourth category, secondary income receipts or payments, refers to the transfer of a good, service, or asset to the U.S. government or U.S. private entities, or the transfer to a foreign government or entity in the case of payments (this includes tax payments, foreign pension payments, cash transfers, etc.).

Current Account

In the balance of payments, records transactions involving the export or import of goods and services.

A **current account deficit** occurs when a country imports more goods, services, and income than it exports. A **current account surplus** occurs when a country exports more goods, services, and income than it imports. Table A.1 shows that in 2014 the United States ran a current account deficit of $389.5 billion. This is often a headline-grabbing figure and is widely reported in the news media. In recent years, the U.S. current account deficit has been fairly significant, primarily because America imports far more physical goods than it exports. (The United States typically runs a surplus on trade in services and on income payments.)

Current Account Deficit

The current account of the balance of payments is in deficit when a country imports more goods and services than it exports.

Current Account Surplus

The current account of the balance of payments is in surplus when a country exports more goods and services than it imports.

The 2006 current account deficit of $803 billion was the largest on record and was equivalent to about 6.5 percent of the country's GDP. The deficit has shrunk since then, and the 2014 current account deficit represented just 2.2 percent of GDP. Many people find the fact that the United States runs a persistent deficit on its current account to be disturbing, the common assumption being that high import of goods displaces domestic production, causes unemployment, and reduces the growth of the U.S. economy. However, the issue is more complex than this. Fully understanding the implications of a large and persistent deficit requires that we look at the rest of the balance-of-payments accounts.

The **capital account** records one-time changes in the stock of assets. As noted earlier, until recently this item was included in the current account. The capital account includes capital transfers, such as debt forgiveness and migrants' transfers (the goods and financial assets that accompany migrants as they enter or leave the country). In the big scheme of things, this is a relatively small figure amounting to $45 million in 2014.

Capital Account

Records one-time changes in the stock of assets.

The **financial account** (formerly the capital account) records transactions that involve the purchase or sale of assets. Thus, when a German firm purchases stock in a U.S. company or buys a U.S. bond, the transaction enters the U.S. balance of payments as a credit on the financial account. This is because capital is flowing into the country. When capital flows out of the United States, it enters the financial account as a debit.

Financial Account

In balance of payments, transactions that involve the purchase or sale of assets.

The financial account is comprised of a number of elements. The net U.S. acquisition of financial assets includes the change in foreign assets owned by the U.S. government (e.g., U.S. official reserve assets) and the change in foreign assets owned by private individuals and corporations (including changes in assets owned through foreign direct investment). As can be seen from Table A.1, in 2014 there was a $792 billion increase in U.S. ownership of foreign assets, which tells us that the U.S. government and U.S. private entities were purchasing more foreign assets than they were selling. The net U.S. incurrence of liabilities refers to the change in U.S. assets owned by foreigners. In 2014 foreigners increased their holdings of U.S. assets by $977 billion, signifying that foreigners were net acquirers of U.S. stocks, bonds (including Treasury bills), and physical assets such as real estate.

A basic principle of balance-of-payments accounting is double-entry bookkeeping. Every international transaction automatically enters the balance of payments twice—once as a credit and once as a debit. Imagine that you purchase a car produced in Japan by Toyota for $20,000.

Because your purchase represents a payment to another country for goods, it will enter the balance of payments as a debit on the current account. Toyota now has the $20,000 and must do something with it. If Toyota deposits the money at a U.S. bank, Toyota has purchased a

U.S. asset—a bank deposit worth $20,000—and the transaction will show up as a $20,000 credit on the financial account. Or Toyota might deposit the cash in a Japanese bank in return for Japanese yen. Now the Japanese bank must decide what to do with the $20,000. Any action that it takes will ultimately result in a credit for the U.S. balance of payments. For example, if the bank lends the $20,000 to a Japanese firm that uses it to import personal computers from the United States, then the $20,000 must be credited to the U.S. balance-of-payments current account. Or the Japanese bank might use the $20,000 to purchase U.S. government bonds, in which case it will show up as a credit on the U.S. balance-of-payments financial account.

Thus, any international transaction automatically gives rise to two offsetting entries in the balance of payments. Because of this, the sum of the current account balance, the capital account, and the financial account balance should always add up to zero. In practice, this does not always occur due to the existence of "statistical discrepancies," the source of which need not concern us here (note that in 2014, the statistical discrepancy amounted to $149.9 billion).

DOES THE CURRENT ACCOUNT DEFICIT MATTER? As discussed earlier, there is some concern when a country is running a deficit on the current account of its balance of payments.[39] In recent years, a number of rich countries, including most notably the United States, have run persistent current account deficits. When a country runs a current account deficit, the money that flows to other countries can then be used by those countries to purchase assets in the deficit country. Thus, when the United States runs a trade deficit with China, the Chinese use the money that they receive from U.S. consumers to purchase U.S. assets such as stocks, bonds, and the like. Put another way, a deficit on the current account is financed by selling assets to other countries; that is, by increasing liabilities on the financial account. Thus, the persistent U.S. current account deficit is being financed by a steady sale of U.S. assets (stocks, bonds, real estate, and whole corporations) to other countries. In short, countries that run current account deficits become net debtors.

For example, as a result of financing its current account deficit through asset sales, the United States must deliver a stream of interest payments to foreign bondholders, rents to foreign landowners, and dividends to foreign stockholders. One might argue that such payments to foreigners drain resources from a country and limit the funds available for investment within the country. Since investment within a country is necessary to stimulate economic growth, a persistent current account deficit can choke off a country's future economic growth. This is the basis of the argument that persistent deficits are bad for an economy. However, things are not this simple. For one thing, in an era of global capital markets, money is efficiently directed toward its highest value uses, and over the past quarter of a century, many of the highest value uses of capital have been in the United States. So even though capital is flowing out of the United States in the form of payments to foreigners, much of that capital finds its way right back into the country to fund productive investments in the United States. In short, it is not clear that the current account deficit chokes off U.S. economic growth. In fact, notwithstanding the 2008–2009 recession, the U.S. economy has grown substantially over the past 30 years, despite running a persistent current account deficit and despite financing that deficit by selling U.S. assets to foreigners. This is precisely because foreigners reinvest much of the income earned from U.S. assets and from exports to the United States right back into the United States. This revisionist view, which has gained in popularity in recent years, suggests that a persistent current account deficit might not be the drag on economic growth it was once thought to be.[40]

Having said this, there is still a nagging fear that at some point, the appetite that foreigners have for U.S. assets might decline. If foreigners suddenly reduced their investments in the United States, what would happen? In short, instead of reinvesting the dollars that they earn from exports and investment in the United States back into the country, they would sell those dollars for another currency, European euros, Japanese yen, or Chinese yuan, for example, and invest in euro-, yen-, and yuan-denominated assets instead. This would lead to a fall in the value of the dollar on foreign exchange markets, and that in turn would increase the price of imports and lower the price of U.S. exports, making them more competitive, which should reduce the overall level of the current account deficit. Thus, in the long run, the persistent U.S. current account deficit could be corrected via a reduction in the value of the U.S. dollar. The concern is that such adjustments may not be smooth. Rather than a controlled decline in the value of the dollar, the dollar might suddenly lose a significant amount of its value in a very short time, precipitating a "dollar crisis."[41] Because the U.S. dollar is the world's major reserve currency and is held by many foreign governments and banks, any dollar crisis could deliver a body blow to the world economy and at the very least trigger a global economic slowdown. That would not be a good thing.

Endnotes

1. H. W. Spiegel, *The Growth of Economic Thought* (Durham, NC: Duke University Press, 1991).
2. M. Solis, "The Politics of Self-Restraint: FDI Subsidies and Japanese Mercantilism," *The World Economy* 26 (February 2003), pp. 153–70.
3. S. Hollander, *The Economics of David Ricardo* (Buffalo: University of Toronto Press, 1979).
4. D. Ricardo, *The Principles of Political Economy and Taxation* (Homewood, IL: Irwin, 1967, first published in 1817).
5. For example, R. Dornbusch, S. Fischer, and P. Samuelson, "Comparative Advantage: Trade and Payments in a Ricardian Model with a Continuum of Goods," *American Economic Review* 67 (December 1977), pp. 823–39.
6. B. Balassa, "An Empirical Demonstration of Classic Comparative Cost Theory," *Review of Economics and Statistics,* 1963, pp. 231–38.
7. See P. R. Krugman, "Is Free Trade Passé?" *Journal of Economic Perspectives* 1 (Fall 1987), pp. 131–44.
8. P. Samuelson, "Where Ricardo and Mill Rebut and Confirm Arguments of Mainstream Economists Supporting Globalization," *Journal of Economic Perspectives* 18, no. 3 (Summer 2004), pp. 135–46.
9. P. Samuelson, "The Gains from International Trade Once Again," *Economic Journal* 72 (1962), pp. 820–29.
10. S. Lohr, "An Elder Challenges Outsourcing's Orthodoxy," *The New York Times*, September 9, 2004, p. C1.
11. Samuelson, "Where Ricardo and Mill Rebut and Confirm Arguments of Mainstream Economists Supporting Globalization," p. 143.
12. D. H. Autor, D. Dorn, and Gordon H. Hanson, "The China Syndrome: Local Labor Market Effects of Import Competition in the United States," *MIT Working Paper,* August 2011.
13. See A. Dixit and G. Grossman, "Samuelson Says Nothing about Trade Policy," Princeton University, 2004, accessed from http://depts.washington.edu/teclass/ThinkEcon/readings/Kalles/Dixit%20and%20Grossman%20on%20Samuelson.pdf.
14. J. R. Hagerty, "U.S. Loses High Tech Jobs as R&D Shifts to Asia," *The Wall Street Journal,* January 18, 2012, p. B1.
15. For example, J. D. Sachs and A. Warner, "Economic Reform and the Process of Global Integration," *Brookings Papers on Economic Activity,* 1995, pp. 1–96; J. A. Frankel and D. Romer, "Does Trade Cause Growth?," *American Economic Review* 89, no. 3 (June 1999), pp. 379–99; D. Dollar and A. Kraay, "Trade, Growth and Poverty," working paper, Development Research Group, World Bank, June 2001. Also, for an accessible discussion of the relationship between free trade and economic growth, see T. Taylor, "The Truth about Globalization," *Public Interest,* Spring 2002, pp. 24–44; D. Acemoglu, S. Johnson, and J. Robinson, "The Rise of Europe: Atlantic Trade, Institutional Change and Economic Growth," *American Economic Review* 95, no. 3 (2005), pp. 547–79; T. Singh, "Does International Trade Cause Economic Growth?," *The World Economy* 33, no. 11 (2010), pp. 1517–64.
16. Sachs and Warner, "Economic Reform and the Process of Global Integration."
17. Ibid., pp. 35–36.
18. R. Wacziarg and K. H. Welch, "Trade Liberalization and Growth: New Evidence," *National Bureau of Economic Research Working Paper Series,* working paper no. 10152, December 2003.
19. Singh, "Does International Trade Cause Economic Growth?", pp. 1517–64.
20. Frankel and Romer, "Does Trade Cause Growth?"
21. A recent skeptical review of the empirical work on the relationship between trade and growth questions these results. See Francisco Rodriguez and Dani Rodrik, "Trade Policy and Economic Growth: A Skeptic's Guide to the Cross-National Evidence," *National Bureau of Economic Research Working Paper Series,* working paper no. 7081 (April 1999). Even these authors, however, cannot find any evidence that trade hurts economic growth or income levels.
22. B. Ohlin, *Interregional and International Trade* (Cambridge, MA: Harvard University Press, 1933). For a summary, see R. W. Jones and J. P. Neary, "The Positive Theory of International Trade," in *Handbook of International Economics,* R. W. Jones and P. B. Kenen, eds. (Amsterdam: North Holland, 1984).
23. W. Leontief, "Domestic Production and Foreign Trade: The American Capital Position Re-examined," *Proceedings of the American Philosophical Society* 97 (1953), pp. 331–49.
24. R. M. Stern and K. Maskus, "Determinants of the Structure of U.S. Foreign Trade," *Journal of International Economics* 11 (1981), pp. 207–44.
25. See H. P. Bowen, E. E. Leamer, and L. Sveikayskas, "Multicountry, Multifactor Tests of the Factor Abundance Theory," *American Economic Review* 77 (1987), pp. 791–809.
26. D. Trefler, "The Case of the Missing Trade and Other Mysteries," *American Economic Review* 85, (December 1995), pp. 1029–46.
27. D. R. Davis and D. E. Weinstein, "An Account of Global Factor Trade," *American Economic Review* 91, no. 5 (December 2001), pp. 1423–52.
28. R. Vernon, "International Investments and International Trade in the Product Life Cycle," *Quarterly Journal of Economics,* May 1966, pp. 190–207; R. Vernon and L. T. Wells, *The Economic Environment of International Business,* 4th ed. (Englewood Cliffs, NJ: Prentice Hall, 1986).
29. For a good summary of this literature, see E. Helpman and P. Krugman, *Market Structure and Foreign Trade: Increasing Returns, Imperfect Competition, and the International Economy*

(Boston: MIT Press, 1985). Also see P. Krugman, "Does the New Trade Theory Require a New Trade Policy?" *World Economy* 15, no. 4 (1992), pp. 423–41.

30. M. B. Lieberman and D. B. Montgomery, "First-Mover Advantages," *Strategic Management Journal* 9 (Summer 1988), pp. 41–58; W. T. Robinson and Sungwook Min, "Is the First to Market the First to Fail?" *Journal of Marketing Research* 29 (2002), pp. 120–28.
31. J. R. Tybout, "Plant and Firm Level Evidence on New Trade Theories," *National Bureau of Economic Research Working Paper Series,* working paper no. 8418 (August 2001), www.nber.org; S. Deraniyagala and B. Fine, "New Trade Theory versus Old Trade Policy: A Continuing Enigma," *Cambridge Journal of Economics* 25 (November 2001), pp. 809–25.
32. A. D. Chandler, *Scale and Scope* (New York: Free Press, 1990).
33. Krugman, "Does the New Trade Theory Require a New Trade Policy?"
34. M. E. Porter, *The Competitive Advantage of Nations* (New York: Free Press, 1990). For a good review of this book, see R. M. Grant, "Porter's Competitive Advantage of Nations: An Assessment," *Strategic Management Journal* 12 (1991), pp. 535–48.
35. B. Kogut, ed., *Country Competitiveness: Technology and the Organizing of Work* (New York: Oxford University Press, 1993).
36. Porter, *The Competitive Advantage of Nations*, p. 121.
37. Lieberman and Montgomery, "First-Mover Advantages." See also Robinson and Min, "Is the First to Market the First to Fail?"; W. Boulding and M. Christen, "First Mover Disadvantage," *Harvard Business Review,* October 2001, pp. 20–21; R. Agarwal and M. Gort, "First Mover Advantage and the Speed of Competitive Entry," *Journal of Law and Economics* 44 (2001), pp. 131–59.
38. C. A. Hamilton, "Building Better Machine Tools," *Journal of Commerce,* October 30, 1991, p. 8; and "Manufacturing Trouble," *The Economist,* October 12, 1991, p. 71.
39. P. Krugman, *The Age of Diminished Expectations* (Cambridge, MA: MIT Press, 1990).
40. D. Griswold, "Are Trade Deficits a Drag on U.S. Economic Growth?," *Free Trade Bulletin,* March 12, 2007; O. Blanchard, "Current Account Deficits in Rich Countries," *National Bureau of Economic Research Working Paper Series,* working paper no. 12925, February 2007.
41. S. Edwards, "The U.S. Current Account Deficit: Gradual Correction or Abrupt Adjustment?," *National Bureau of Economic Research Working Paper Series,* working paper no. 12154, April 2006.

Government Policy and International Trade

learning objectives

After reading this chapter, you will be able to:

LO7-1 Identify the policy instruments used by governments to influence international trade flows.

LO7-2 Understand why governments sometimes intervene in international trade.

LO7-3 Summarize and explain the arguments against strategic trade policy.

LO7-4 Describe the development of the world trading system and the current trade issue.

LO7-5 Explain the implications for managers of developments in the world trading system.

Source: © Si wei/AP Images

Is China Dumping Its Excess Steel Production?

opening case

In the 15 years up to 2015, China increased its steel production fivefold as it forged the steel products demanded by its huge boom in construction and infrastructure spending. By 2015, the country produced 800 million tons of steel a year, half of the world's annual output. However, in 2015 the bottom fell out of the Chinese domestic market for steel. The economy slowed down, and the government shifted its priorities away from massive infrastructure investments and toward boosting consumer spending. By the end of 2015, Chinese steelmakers were estimated to be producing 300 million more tons of steel a year than required for domestic consumption.

With prices for steel slumping, China's largest 101 steel firms lost over $12 billion in 2015, roughly twice what they made in profits during 2014. Not surprisingly, the Chinese are seeking to export this unwanted product, even if it is at a loss. China exported more than 100 million tons of steel for the first time in 2015, making its steel exports alone larger than the production of any other country in the world except for Japan. The prices for Chinese steel products appear to be at least 10 percent lower outside of China than within the country.

Those low-priced exports are having a devastating impact on steelmakers around the globe. American producers have responded by clamoring for action from the U.S. Commerce Department to stop what they perceive to be the illegal dumping of steel products below the costs of production. Moreover, they have argued that cheap steel from China has also persuaded producers in India, Italy, South Korea, and Taiwan to dump their excess production on the world market, further harming U.S. producers. In November 2015, the Commerce Department ruled that all of these countries except Taiwan were dumping steel and placed duties as high as 236 percent on some imports of foreign steel. In late December, the Commerce Department ruled that China was also selling corrosion-resistant steel at unfairly low prices and placed an *additional* 256 percent tariff on such imports. This erected a huge barrier to certain Chinese steel imports into the United States.

The European Union has been contemplating similar steps. The United Kingdom has been particularly hard hit by Chinese imports. Chinese imports now take 45 percent of the UK market for steel rebar, up from nothing in 2010. Overall, steel imports from China doubled between 2014 and 2015. The UK lost some 4,000 steelmaking jobs in the second half of 2015 as the Chinese grabbed market share. Elsewhere in Europe, the Luxembourg-based steel giant ArcelorMittal blamed dumping by Chinese firms for a $8 billion loss in 2015. In response, in January 2016, the EU placed a 13 percent tariff on imports of Chinese steel. EU steelmakers called this totally inadequate, particularly given the much large tariffs levied in the United States. For its

–continued

part, the Chinese government remained unmoved. In fact, it may have added fuel to the fire in December 2015, when it cut export taxes on several types of steel, signaling perhaps that it was doubling down on a strategy to encourage domestic producers to export their surplus production rather than close mills. ●

Sources: Sonja Elmquist, "U.S. Calls for 256% Tariff on Imports of Steel from China," *Bloomberg News*, December 22, 2015; "China's Soaring Steel Exports May Presage a Trade War," *The Economist*, December 9, 2015; "Steel Imports from China Investigated by the European Commission," *BBC News*, February 12, 2016; Ivana Kottasova, "Europe Tries to Protect Steel Jobs with Tariffs on Chinese Imports," *CNN Money*, January 29, 2016.

Introduction

Free Trade
The absence of barriers to the free flow of goods and services between countries.

The review of the classical trade theories of Smith, Ricardo, and Heckscher-Ohlin in Chapter 6 showed that in a world without trade barriers, trade patterns are determined by the relative productivity of different factors of production in different countries. Countries will specialize in products that they can make most efficiently, while importing products that they can produce less efficiently. Chapter 6 also laid out the intellectual case for free trade. Remember, **free trade** refers to a situation in which a government does not attempt to restrict what its citizens can buy from or sell to another country. As we saw in Chapter 6, the theories of Smith, Ricardo, and Heckscher-Ohlin predict that the consequences of free trade include both static economic gains (because free trade supports a higher level of domestic consumption and more efficient utilization of resources) and dynamic economic gains (because free trade stimulates economic growth and the creation of wealth).

This chapter looks at the political reality of international trade. Although many nations are nominally committed to free trade, they tend to intervene in international trade to protect the interests of politically important groups or promote the interests of key domestic producers. For example, the opening case suggest that Chinese steelmakers, who are struggling with slumping domestic demand, have been dumping excess steel production on the world market. They may even have been encouraged to do this by the Chinese government, which recently cut taxes on the export of certain steel products. This has caused significant hardship to steel producers around the world, particularly in the European Union and the United States. In both regions, steelmakers have lobbied government agencies for protection from what they see as unfair competition. Those agencies have responded by placing tariffs on the imports of certain Chinese steel products. Thus in the steel industry, political realities have resulted in a departure for the time being from the theoretical ideal of unimpeded free trade.

This chapter explores the political and economic reasons that governments have for intervening in international trade. When governments intervene, they often do so by restricting imports of goods and services into their nation, while adopting policies that promote domestic production and exports. Normally, their motives are to protect domestic producers. In recent years, social issues have intruded into the decision-making calculus. In the United States, for example, a movement is growing to ban imports of goods from countries that do not abide by the same labor, health, and environmental regulations as the United States.

General Agreement on Tariffs and Trade (GATT)
International treaty that committed signatories to lowering barriers to the free flow of goods across national borders and led to the WTO.

This chapter starts by describing the range of policy instruments that governments use to intervene in international trade. A detailed review of governments' various political and economic motives for intervention follows. In the third section of this chapter, we consider how the case for free trade stands up in view of the various justifications given for government intervention in international trade. Then we look at the emergence of the modern international trading system, which is based on the **General Agreement on Tariffs and Trade (GATT)** and its successor, the World Trade Organization. The GATT and WTO are the creations of a series of multinational treaties. The final section of this chapter discusses the implications of this material for management practice.

LO 7-1
Identify the policy instruments used by governments to influence international trade flows.

Instruments of Trade Policy

Trade policy uses seven main instruments: tariffs, subsidies, import quotas, voluntary export restraints, local content requirements, administrative policies, and antidumping duties. Tariffs are the oldest and simplest instrument of trade policy. As we shall see later in this chapter, they are also the instrument that the GATT and WTO have been most successful in limiting. A fall in tariff barriers in recent decades has been accompanied by a rise in nontariff barriers, such as subsidies, quotas, voluntary export restraints, and antidumping duties.

Tariff
A tax levied on imports.

Specific Tariff
Tariff levied as a fixed charge for each unit of good imported.

Ad Valorem Tariff
A tariff levied as a proportion of the value of an imported good.

TARIFFS

A **tariff** is a tax levied on imports (or exports). Tariffs fall into two categories. **Specific tariffs** are levied as a fixed charge for each unit of a good imported (e.g., $3 per barrel of oil). **Ad valorem tariffs** are levied as a proportion of the value of the imported good. In most cases, tariffs are placed on imports to protect domestic producers from foreign competition by raising the price of imported goods. However, tariffs also produce revenue for the government. Until the income tax was introduced, for example, the U.S. government received most of its revenues from tariffs.

Did You Know?
Did you know that the high price of SUVs in the US is the result of the "chicken tariff"?

Visit your Connect SmartBook® to view a short video explanation from the authors.

The important thing to understand about an import tariff is who suffers and who gains. The government gains, because the tariff increases government revenues. Domestic producers gain, because the tariff affords them some protection against foreign competitors by increasing the cost of imported foreign goods. Consumers lose because they must pay more for certain imports. For example, in 2002 the U.S. government placed an ad valorem tariff of 8 to 30 percent on imports of foreign steel. The idea was to protect domestic steel producers from cheap imports of foreign steel. In this case, however, the effect was to raise the price of steel products in the United States between 30 and 50 percent. A number of U.S. steel consumers, ranging from appliance makers to automobile companies, objected that the steel tariffs would raise their costs of production and make it more difficult for them to compete in the global marketplace. Whether the gains to the government and domestic producers exceed the loss to consumers depends on various factors, such as the amount of the tariff, the importance of the imported good to domestic consumers, the number of jobs saved in the protected industry, and so on. In the steel case, many argued that the losses to steel consumers apparently outweighed the gains to steel producers. In November 2003, the World Trade Organization declared that the tariffs represented a violation of the WTO treaty, and the United States removed them in December of that year. Whether the tariffs imposed by the United States and the European Union on Chinese steel imports in 2015 and 2016 will similarly be declared illegal by the WTO remains to be seen (see the opening case).

In general, two conclusions can be derived from economic analysis of the effect of import tariffs.[1] First, tariffs are generally pro-producer and anticonsumer. While they protect producers from foreign competitors, this restriction of supply also raises domestic prices. For example, a study by Japanese economists calculated that tariffs on imports of foodstuffs, cosmetics, and chemicals into Japan cost the average Japanese consumer about $890 per year in the form of higher prices. Almost all studies find that import tariffs impose significant costs on domestic consumers in the form of higher prices. Second, import tariffs reduce the overall efficiency of the world economy. They reduce efficiency because a protective tariff encourages domestic firms to produce products at home that, in theory, could be produced more efficiently abroad. The consequence is an inefficient utilization of resources.

Sometimes tariffs are levied on exports of a product from a country. Export tariffs are less common than import tariffs. In general, export tariffs have two objectives: first, to raise revenue for the government, and second, to reduce exports from a sector, often for political reasons. For example, in 2004 China imposed a tariff on textile exports. The primary objective was to moderate the growth in exports of textiles from China, thereby alleviating tensions with other trading partners. China also had tariffs on steel exports but removed many of those in late 2015.

Which Country Is Really the Most Globally Competitive?

The World Economic Forum is an independent international organization committed to improving the state of the world by engaging business, political, academic, and other leaders of society to shape global, regional, and industry agendas. The World Economic Forum also conducts global economic research and annually publishes country competitive rankings. Over the years, northern and western European countries have dominated the top 10 most globally competitive nations. The United States and Japan typically also hold strong positions. But is it really fair that the "global competitiveness" ranking indicates that relatively small Nordic countries such as Finland and Sweden are viewed as being as competitive as the United States and Japan? Should larger countries, with more people and a larger economy be given preferential treatment in ranking such as when the topic is on "global competitiveness"?

Source: www.weforum.org.

Subsidy

Government financial assistance to a domestic producer.

SUBSIDIES A **subsidy** is a government payment to a domestic producer. Subsidies take many forms, including cash grants, low-interest loans, tax breaks, and government equity participation in domestic firms. By lowering production costs, subsidies help domestic producers in two ways: (1) competing against foreign imports and (2) gaining export markets. Agriculture tends to be one of the largest beneficiaries of subsidies in most countries. The European Union has been paying out about €44 billion annually ($55 billion) in farm subsidies. The farm bill that passed the U.S. Congress in 2007 contained subsidies of $289 billion for the next 10 years. The Japanese also have a long history of supporting inefficient domestic producers with farm subsidies. According to the World Trade Organization, in mid-2000 countries spent some $300 billion on subsidies, $250 billion of which was spent by 21 developed nations.[2] In response to a severe sales slump following the global financial crisis, between mid-2008 and mid-2009, some developed nations gave $45 billion in subsidies to their automobile makers. While the purpose of the subsidies was to help them survive a very difficult economic climate, one of the consequences was to give subsidized companies an unfair competitive advantage in the global auto industry. Somewhat ironically given the government bailouts of U.S. auto companies during the global financial crisis, in 2012 the Obama administration filed a complaint with the WTO arguing that the Chinese were illegally subsidizing exports of autos and auto parts. Details are given in the Country Focus feature.

The main gains from subsidies accrue to domestic producers, whose international competitiveness is increased as a result. Advocates of strategic trade policy (which, as you will recall from Chapter 6, is an outgrowth of the new trade theory) favor subsidies to help domestic firms achieve a dominant position in those industries in which economies of scale are important and the world market is not large enough to profitably support more than a few firms (aerospace and semiconductors are two such industries). According to this argument, subsidies can help a firm achieve a first-mover advantage in an emerging industry (just as U.S. government subsidies, in the form of substantial R&D grants, allegedly helped Boeing). If this is achieved, further gains to the domestic economy arise from the employment and tax revenues that a major global company

country FOCUS

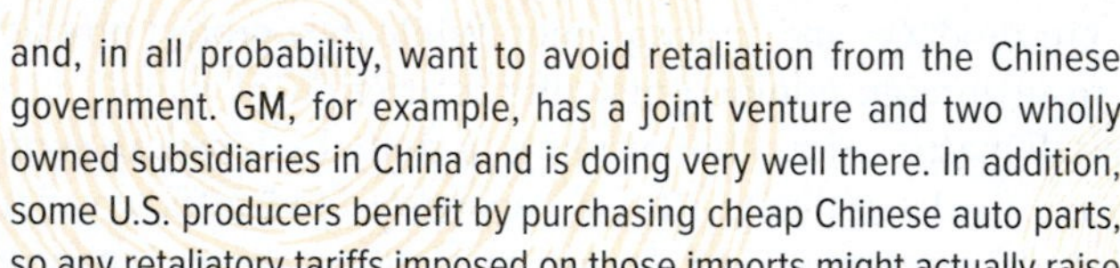

Are the Chinese Illegally Subsidizing Auto Exports?

In late 2012, during the presidential election campaign, the Obama administration filed a complaint against China with the World Trade Organization. The complaint claims that China is providing export subsidies to its auto and auto parts industries. The subsidies include cash grants for exporting, grants for R&D, subsidies to pay interest on loans, and preferential tax treatment.

The United States estimates the value of the subsidies to be at least $1 billion between 2009 and 2011. The complaint also points out that in the years 2002 through 2011, the value of China's exports of autos and auto parts increased more than ninefold from $7.4 billion to $69.1 billion. The United States was China's largest market for exports of auto parts during this period. The United States is asserting that, to some degree, this growth may have been helped by subsidies. The complaint goes on to claim that these subsidies have hurt producers of automobiles and auto parts in the United States. This is a large industry in the United States, employing over 800,000 people and generating some $350 billion in sales.

While some in the labor movement applauded the move, the response from U.S. auto companies and auto parts producers was muted. One reason for this is that many U.S. producers do business in China and, in all probability, want to avoid retaliation from the Chinese government. GM, for example, has a joint venture and two wholly owned subsidiaries in China and is doing very well there. In addition, some U.S. producers benefit by purchasing cheap Chinese auto parts, so any retaliatory tariffs imposed on those imports might actually raise their costs.

More cynical observers saw the move as nothing more than political theater. The week before the complaint was filed, the Republican presidential candidate, Mitt Romney, had accused the Obama administration of "failing American workers" by not labeling China a currency manipulator. So perhaps the complaint was in part simply another move on the presidential campaign chessboard. In any event, the WTO does not move rapidly, and the case was still under consideration in early 2016. Indeed, in February 2014, the United States expanded its complaint with the WTO against China, arguing that the country had an illegal export subsidy program that includes not only autos and auto parts but also textile, apparel, and footwear, advanced materials and metals, specialty chemicals, medical products, and agriculture.

Source: James Healey, "U.S. Alleges Unfair China Auto Subsidies in WTO Action," *USA Today*, September 17, 2012; M. A. Memoli, "Obama to Tell WTO That China Illegally Subsidizes Auto Imports," *Los Angeles Times*, September 17, 2012; Vicki Needham, "US Launches Trade Case against China's Export Subsidy Program," *The Hill*, February 11, 2014.

can generate. However, government subsidies must be paid for, typically by taxing individuals and corporations.

Whether subsidies generate national benefits that exceed their national costs is debatable. In practice, many subsidies are not that successful at increasing the international competitiveness of domestic producers. Rather, they tend to protect the inefficient and promote excess production. One study estimated that if advanced countries abandoned subsidies to farmers, global trade in agricultural products would be 50 percent higher and the world as a whole would be better off by $160 billion.[3] Another study estimated that removing all barriers to trade in agriculture (both subsidies and tariffs) would raise world income by $182 billion.[4] This increase in wealth arises from the more efficient use of agricultural land.

IMPORT QUOTAS AND VOLUNTARY EXPORT RESTRAINTS An **import quota** is a direct restriction on the quantity of some good that may be imported into a country. The restriction is usually enforced by issuing import licenses to a group of individuals or firms. For example, the United States has a quota on cheese imports. The only firms allowed to import cheese are certain trading companies, each of which is allocated the right to import a maximum number of pounds of cheese each year. In some cases, the right to sell is given directly to the governments of exporting countries.

Import Quota
A direct restriction on the quantity of a good that can be imported into a country.

A common hybrid of a quota and a tariff is known as a tariff rate quota. Under a **tariff rate quota**, a lower tariff rate is applied to imports within the quota than those over the quota. For example, as illustrated in Figure 7.1, an ad valorem tariff rate of 10 percent might be levied on 1 million tons of rice imports into South Korea, after which an out-of-quota rate of 80 percent might be applied. Thus, South Korea might import 2 million tons of rice, 1 million at a 10 percent tariff rate and another 1 million at an 80 percent tariff. Tariff rate quotas are common in agriculture, where their goal is to limit imports over quota.

Tariff Rate Quota
Lower tariff rates applied to imports within the quota than those over the quota.

A variant on the import quota is the voluntary export restraint. A **voluntary export restraint (VER)** is a quota on trade imposed by the exporting country, typically at the request of the importing country's government. For example, in 2012 Brazil imposed what amounts to voluntary export restraints on shipments of vehicles from Mexico to Brazil. The two countries have a decade-old free trade agreement, but a surge in vehicles heading to Brazil from Mexico prompted Brazil to raise its protectionist walls. Mexico has agreed to quotas on Brazil-bound vehicle exports for the next three years.[5] Foreign producers agree to VERs because they fear more damaging punitive tariffs or import quotas might follow if they do not. Agreeing to a VER is seen as a way to make the best of a bad situation by appeasing protectionist pressures in a country.

Voluntary Export Restraint (VER)
A quota on trade imposed from the exporting country's side, instead of the importer's; usually imposed at the request of the importing country's government.

As with tariffs and subsidies, both import quotas and VERs benefit domestic producers by limiting import competition. As with all restrictions on trade, quotas do not benefit consumers.

FIGURE
Hypothetical Tariff Rate Quota.

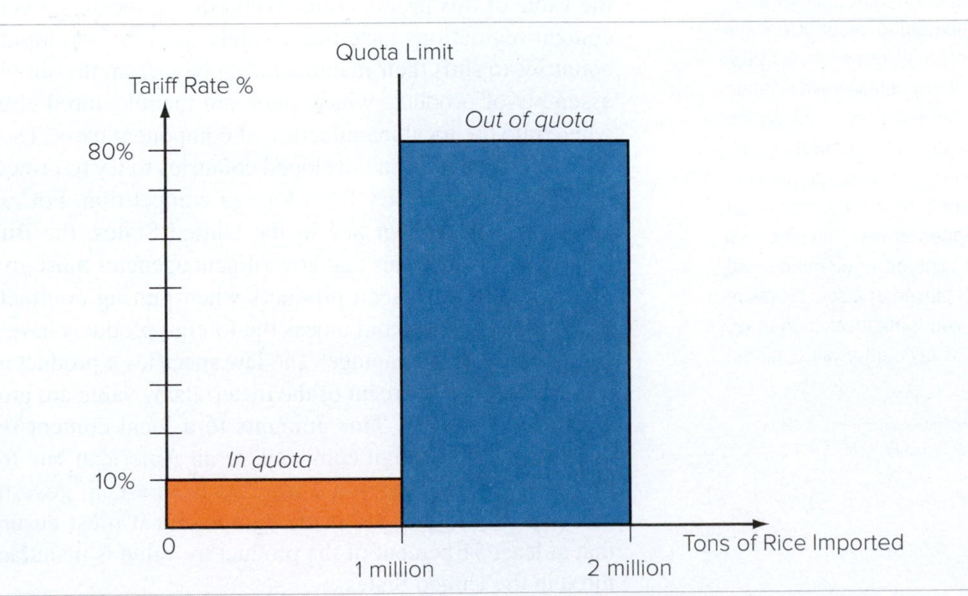

An import quota or VER always raises the domestic price of an imported good. When imports are limited to a low percentage of the market by a quota or VER, the price is bid up for that limited foreign supply. The extra profit that producers make when supply is artificially limited by an import quota is referred to as a **quota rent**.

Quota Rent

Extra profit producers make when supply is artificially limited by an import quota.

If a domestic industry lacks the capacity to meet demand, an import quota can raise prices for *both* the domestically produced and the imported good. This happened in the U.S. sugar industry, in which a tariff rate quota system has long limited the amount foreign producers can sell in the U.S. market. According to one study, import quotas have caused the price of sugar in the United States to be as much as 40 percent greater than the world price.[6] These higher prices have translated into greater profits for U.S. sugar producers, which have lobbied politicians to keep the lucrative agreement. They argue U.S. jobs in the sugar industry will be lost to foreign producers if the quota system is scrapped.

Export Tariff

A tax placed on the export of a good.

EXPORT TARIFFS AND BANS

An **export tariff** is a tax placed on the export of a good. The goal behind an export tariff is to discriminate *against* exporting in order to ensure that there is sufficient supply of a good within a country. For example, in the past China has placed an export tariff on the export of grain to ensure that there is sufficient supply in China. Similarly, during its infrastructure building boom, China had an export tariff in place on certain kinds of steel products to ensure that there was sufficient supply of steel within the country. The steel tariffs were removed in late 2015 (see the opening case). Since most countries try to encourage exports, export tariffs are relatively rare.

Export Ban

A policy that partially or entirely restricts the export of a good.

Local Content Requirement (LCR)

A requirement that some specific fraction of a good be produced domestically.

An **export ban** is a policy that partially or entirely restricts the export of a good. One well-known example was the ban on exports of U.S. crude oil production that was enacted by Congress in 1975. At the time, OPEC was restricting the supply of oil in order to drive up prices and punish Western nations for their support of Israel during conflicts between Arab nations and Israel. The export ban in the United States was seen as a way of ensuring a sufficient supply of domestic oil at home, thereby helping to keep the domestic price down and boosting national security. The ban was lifted in 2015 after lobbying from American oil producers, who believed that they could get a higher prices for some of their output if they were allowed to sell on world markets.

LOCAL CONTENT REQUIREMENTS

A **local content requirement (LCR)** is a requirement that some specific fraction of a good be produced domestically. The requirement can be expressed either in physical terms (e.g., 75 percent of component parts for this product must be produced locally) or in value terms (e.g., 75 percent of the value of this product must be produced locally). Local content regulations have been widely used by developing countries to shift their manufacturing base from the simple assembly of products whose parts are manufactured elsewhere into the local manufacture of component parts. They have also been used in developed countries to try to protect local jobs and industry from foreign competition. For example, a little-known law in the United States, the Buy America Act, specifies that government agencies must give preference to American products when putting contracts for equipment out to bid unless the foreign products have a significant price advantage. The law specifies a product as "American" if 51 percent of the materials by value are produced domestically. This amounts to a local content requirement. If a foreign company, or an American one for that matter, wishes to win a contract from a U.S. government agency to provide some equipment, it must ensure that at least 51 percent of the product by value is manufactured in the United States.

Is Having a Local Content Requirement a Good Idea?

Local content requirements refer to a specific fraction of a product that needs to be manufactured domestically. Basically, LCRs establish a minimum level of local content required under trade law when giving foreign companies the right to manufacture in a particular place. In the wake of the economic downturn in 2008, many economists feared that some governments would institute protectionist policies similar to the tariff escalations during the Great Depression of the 1930s. However, most public policy officials avoided traditional forms of protection (e.g., tariffs, quotas). This led some observers to underestimate the degree of protectionism. Instead, what had happened was that so-called nontariff barriers in the form of local content requirements had become increasingly popular. As a (1) citizen of a specific country and (2) as a global customer, do you think local content requirements help you as a citizen of a country, as a global customer, as both, or as neither?

Source: G. C. Hufbauer and J. J. Scott, "Local Content Requirements: A Global Problem Washington, D.C.," *Peterson Institute for Global Economics,* 2013.

Local content regulations provide protection for a domestic producer of parts in the same way an import quota does: by limiting foreign competition. The aggregate economic effects are also the same; domestic producers benefit, but the restrictions on imports raise the prices of imported components. In turn, higher prices for imported components are passed on to consumers of the final product in the form of higher final prices. So as with all trade policies, local content regulations tend to benefit producers and not consumers.

ADMINISTRATIVE POLICIES In addition to the formal instruments of trade policy, governments of all types sometimes use informal or administrative policies to restrict imports and boost exports. **Administrative trade policies** are bureaucratic rules designed to make it difficult for imports to enter a country. It has been argued that the Japanese are the masters of this trade barrier. In recent decades, Japan's formal tariff and nontariff barriers have been among the lowest in the world. However, critics charge that the country's informal administrative barriers to imports more than compensate for this. For example, at one point, the Netherlands exported tulip bulbs to almost every country in the world except Japan. In Japan, customs inspectors insisted on checking every tulip bulb by cutting it vertically down the middle, and even Japanese ingenuity could not put any back together. Federal Express also initially had a tough time expanding its global express shipping services into Japan because Japanese customs inspectors insist on opening a large proportion of express packages to check for pornography, a process that delayed an "express" package for days. As with all instruments of trade policy, administrative instruments benefit producers and hurt consumers, who are denied access to possibly superior foreign products.

Administrative Trade Policies
Administrative policies, typically adopted by government bureaucracies, that can be used to restrict imports or boost exports.

ANTIDUMPING POLICIES In the context of international trade, **dumping** is variously defined as selling goods in a foreign market at below their costs of production or as selling goods in a foreign market at below their "fair" market value. There is a difference between these two definitions; the fair market value of a good is normally judged to be greater than the costs of producing that good because the former includes a "fair" profit margin. Dumping is viewed as a method by which firms unload excess production in foreign markets. Some dumping may be the result of predatory behavior, with producers using substantial profits from their home markets to subsidize prices in a foreign market with a view to driving indigenous competitors out of that market. Once this has been achieved, so the argument goes, the predatory firm can raise prices and earn substantial profits. An example of dumping is given in the opening case.

Dumping
Selling goods in a foreign market for less than their cost of production or below their "fair" market value.

Antidumping policies are designed to punish foreign firms that engage in dumping. The ultimate objective is to protect domestic producers from unfair foreign competition. Although antidumping policies vary from country to country, the majority are similar to those used in the United States. If a domestic producer believes that a foreign firm is dumping production in the U.S. market, it can file a petition with two government agencies, the Commerce Department and the International Trade Commission (ITC). If a complaint has merit, the Commerce Department may impose an antidumping duty on the offending foreign imports (antidumping duties are often called **countervailing duties**). These duties, which represent a special tariff, can be fairly substantial and stay in place for up to five years. The accompanying Management Focus discusses how a firm, U.S. Magnesium, used antidumping legislation to gain protection from unfair foreign competitors.

Antidumping Policies
Designed to punish foreign firms that engage in dumping and thus protect domestic producers from unfair foreign competition.

Countervailing Duties
Antidumping duties.

Use SmartBook to help retain what you have learned. Access your Instructor's Connect course to check out SmartBook or go to learnsmartadvantage.com for help.

The Case for Government Intervention

LO 7-2
Understand why governments sometimes intervene in international trade.

Now that we have reviewed the various instruments of trade policy that governments can use, it is time to look at the case for government intervention in international trade. Arguments for government intervention take two paths: political and economic. Political arguments for intervention are concerned with protecting the interests of certain groups within a nation (normally producers), often at the expense of other groups (normally consumers), or with achieving some political objective that lies outside the sphere of economic relationships, such as protecting the environment or human rights. Economic arguments for intervention are typically concerned with boosting the overall wealth of a nation (to the benefit of all, both producers and consumers).

management FOCUS

Protecting U.S. Magnesium

In February 2004, U.S. Magnesium, the sole surviving U.S. producer of magnesium, a metal that is primarily used in the manufacture of certain automobile parts and aluminum cans, filed a petition with the U.S. International Trade Commission contending that a surge in imports had caused material damage to the U.S. industry's employment, sales, market share, and profitability. According to U.S. Magnesium, Russian and Chinese producers had been selling the metal at prices significantly below market value. During 2002 and 2003, imports of magnesium into the United States rose 70 percent, while prices fell by 40 percent, and the market share accounted for by imports jumped to 50 percent from 25 percent.

"The United States used to be the largest producer of magnesium in the world," a U.S. Magnesium spokesperson said at the time of the filing. "What's really sad is that you can be state of the art and have modern technology, and if the Chinese, who pay people less than 90 cents an hour, want to run you out of business, they can do it. And that's why we are seeking relief."*

During a yearlong investigation, the ITC solicited input from various sides in the dispute. Foreign producers and consumers of magnesium in the United States argued that falling prices for magnesium during 2002 and 2003 simply reflected an imbalance between supply and demand due to additional capacity coming on stream not from Russia or China but from a new Canadian plant that opened in 2001 and from a planned Australian plant. The Canadian plant shut down in 2003, the Australian plant never came on stream, and prices for magnesium rose again in 2004.

Magnesium consumers in the United States also argued to the ITC that imposing antidumping duties on foreign imports of magnesium would raise prices in the United States significantly above world levels. A spokesperson for Alcoa, which mixes magnesium with aluminum to make alloys for cans, predicted that if antidumping duties were imposed, high magnesium prices in the United States would force Alcoa to move some production out of the United States. Alcoa also noted that in 2003, U.S. Magnesium was unable to supply all of Alcoa's needs, forcing the company to turn to imports. Consumers of magnesium in the automobile industry asserted that high prices in the United States would drive engineers to design magnesium out of automobiles or force manufacturing elsewhere, which would ultimately hurt everyone.

The six members of the ITC were not convinced by these arguments. In March 2005, the ITC ruled that both China and Russia had been dumping magnesium in the United States. The government decided to impose duties ranging from 50 percent to more than 140 percent on imports of magnesium from China. Russian producers faced duties ranging from 19 percent to 22 percent. The duties were to be levied for five years, after which the ITC would revisit the situation. The ITC revoked the antidumping order on Russia in February 2011 but decided to continue placing them on Chinese producers.

According to U.S. Magnesium, the favorable ruling would allow the company to reap the benefits of nearly $50 million in investments made in its manufacturing plant and enable the company to boost its capacity by 28 percent by the end of 2005. Commenting on the favorable ruling, a U.S. Magnesium spokesperson noted, "Once unfair trade is removed from the marketplace we'll be able to compete with anyone."** U.S. Magnesium's customers and competitors, however, did not view the situation as one of unfair trade. While the imposition of antidumping duties no doubt will help to protect U.S. Magnesium and the 400 people it employs from foreign competition, magnesium consumers in the United States are left wondering if they will be the ultimate losers.

*D. Anderton, "U.S. Magnesium Lands Ruling on Unfair Imports," *Deseret News*, October 1, 2004, p. D10.

**S. Oberbeck, "U.S. Magnesium Plans Big Utah Production Expansion," *Salt Lake Tribune*, March 30, 2005.

Sources: D. Anderton, "U.S. Magnesium Lands Ruling on Unfair Imports," *Deseret News*, October 1, 2004, p. D10; "U.S. Magnesium and Its Largest Consumers Debate before U.S. ITC," *Platt's Metals Week*, February 28, 2005, p. 2; S. Oberbeck, "U.S. Magnesium Plans Big Utah Production Expansion," *Salt Lake Tribune*, March 30, 2005; "US to Keep Anti-dumping Duty on China Pure Magnesium," *Chinadaily.com*, September 13, 2012.

POLITICAL ARGUMENTS FOR INTERVENTION Political arguments for government intervention cover a range of issues, including preserving jobs, protecting industries deemed important for national security, retaliating against unfair foreign competition, protecting consumers from "dangerous" products, furthering the goals of foreign policy, and advancing the human rights of individuals in exporting countries.

Protecting Jobs and Industries Perhaps the most common political argument for government intervention is that it is necessary for protecting jobs and industries from unfair foreign competition. The tariffs placed on imports of foreign steel by President George W. Bush in 2002 were designed to do this (many steel producers were located in states that Bush needed to win reelection in 2004). A political motive also underlay establishment of the Common Agricultural Policy (CAP) by the European Union. The CAP was designed to protect the jobs of Europe's politically powerful farmers by restricting imports and guaranteeing prices. However, the higher prices that resulted from the CAP have cost Europe's consumers dearly. This is true of many attempts to protect jobs and industries through government intervention. For example, the imposition of steel tariffs in 2002 raised steel prices for American consumers, such as automobile companies, making them less competitive in the global marketplace.

Protecting National Security Countries sometimes argue that it is necessary to protect certain industries because they are important for national security. Defense-related industries often get this kind of attention (e.g., aerospace, advanced electronics, and semiconductors). Although not as common as it used to be, this argument is still made. Those in favor of protecting the U.S. semiconductor industry from foreign competition, for example, argue that semiconductors are now such important components of defense products that it would be dangerous to rely primarily on foreign producers for them. In 1986, this argument helped persuade the federal government to support Sematech, a consortium of 14 U.S. semiconductor companies that accounted for 90 percent of the U.S. industry's revenues. Sematech's mission was to conduct joint research into manufacturing techniques that could be parceled out to members. The government saw the venture as so critical that Sematech was specially protected from antitrust laws. Initially, the U.S. government provided Sematech with $100 million per year in subsidies. By the mid-1990s, however, the U.S. semiconductor industry had regained its leading market position, largely through the personal computer boom and demand for microprocessor chips made by Intel. In 1994, the consortium's board voted to seek an end to federal funding, and since 1996, the consortium has been funded entirely by private money.[7]

Retaliating Some argue that governments should use the threat to intervene in trade policy as a bargaining tool to help open foreign markets and force trading partners to "play by the rules of the game." The U.S. government has used the threat of punitive trade sanctions to try to get the Chinese government to enforce its intellectual property laws. Lax enforcement of these laws had given rise to massive copyright infringements in China that had been costing U.S. companies such as Microsoft hundreds of millions of dollars per year in lost sales revenues. After the United States threatened to impose 100 percent tariffs on a range of Chinese imports and after harsh words between officials from the two countries, the Chinese agreed to tighter enforcement of intellectual property regulations.[8]

If it works, such a politically motivated rationale for government intervention may liberalize trade and bring with it resulting economic gains. It is a risky strategy, however. A country that is being pressured may not back down and instead may respond to the imposition of punitive tariffs by raising trade barriers of its own. This is exactly what the Chinese government threatened to do when pressured by the United States, although it ultimately did back down. If a government does not back down, the results could be higher trade barriers all around and an economic loss to all involved.

Protecting Consumers Many governments have long had regulations to protect consumers from unsafe products. The indirect effect of such regulations often is to limit or ban the importation of such products. For example, in 2003 several countries, including Japan and South Korea, decided to ban imports of American beef after a single case of mad cow disease was found in Washington state. The ban was designed to protect consumers from what was seen to be

Trade Law

Government policy and international trade is the core focus of Chapter 7. This topic area has far-ranging implications, such as trade policy, free trade, and the world's international trading system. Basically, we are talking about a lot of legalistic aspects starting at the government level and moving all the way to what organizations and even individuals can and cannot do globally when trading. The globalEDGE™ section "Trade Law" (globaledge.msu.edu/global-resources/trade-law) is a unique compilation of globalEDGE™ partner-designed "compendiums of trade laws," country- and region-specific trade law, free online learning modules created for globalEDGE™ on various aspects of trade law, and much more. One fascinating resource related to trade law is the Anti-Counterfeiting and Product Protection Program (A-CAPPP). A-CAPPP includes counterfeiting-related webinars, presentations, and research-related materials and working papers. Do you know what counterfeiting is? Take a look at the "Trade Law" section of globalEDGE™ and especially the A-CAPPP site to become more familiar with the topic. (Is China really as bad as many in the international community think?)

country FOCUS

Trade in Hormone-Treated Beef

In the 1970s, scientists discovered how to synthesize certain hormones and use them to accelerate the growth rate of livestock animals, reduce the fat content of meat, and increase milk production. Bovine somatotropin (BST), a growth hormone produced by cattle, was first synthesized by the biotechnology firm Genentech. Injections of BST could be used to supplement an animal's own hormone production and increase its growth rate. These hormones became popular among farmers, who found they could cut costs and help satisfy consumer demands for leaner meat. Although these hormones occurred naturally in animals, consumer groups in several countries soon raised concerns about the practice. They argued that the use of hormone supplements was unnatural and that the health consequences of consuming hormone-treated meat were unknown but might include hormonal irregularities and cancer.

The European Union responded to these concerns in 1989 by banning the importation of hormone-treated meat and the use of growth-promoting hormones in the production of livestock. The ban was controversial because a reasonable consensus existed among scientists that the hormones posed no health risk. Although the EU banned hormone-treated meat, many other countries did not, including big meat-producing countries such as Australia, Canada, New Zealand, and the United States. The use of hormones soon became widespread in these countries. According to trade officials outside the EU, the European ban constituted an unfair restraint on trade. As a result of this ban, exports of meat to the EU fell. For example, U.S. red meat exports to the EU declined from $231 million in 1988 to $98 million in 1994. The complaints of meat exporters were bolstered in 1995, when Codex Alimentarius, the international food standards body of the UN's Food and Agriculture Organization and the World Health Organization, approved the use of growth hormones. In making this decision, Codex reviewed the scientific literature and found no evidence of a link between the consumption of hormone-treated meat and human health problems, such as cancer.

Fortified by such decisions, in 1995 the United States pressed the EU to drop the import ban on hormone-treated beef. The EU refused, citing "consumer concerns about food safety." In response, Canada and the United States filed formal complaints with the World Trade Organization. They were soon joined by a number of other countries, including Australia and New Zealand. The WTO created a trade panel of three independent experts. After reviewing evidence and hearing from a range of experts and representatives of both parties, the panel in May 1997 ruled that the EU ban on hormone-treated beef was illegal because it had no scientific justification.

This ruling left the EU in a difficult position. Legally, the EU had to lift the ban or face punitive sanctions, but the ban had wide public support in Europe. The EU feared that lifting the ban could produce a consumer backlash. Instead, the EU did nothing. In February 1999, the United States asked the WTO for permission to impose punitive sanctions on the EU. The WTO responded by allowing the United States to impose punitive tariffs valued at $125 million on EU exports to the United States. The EU decided to accept these tariffs rather than lift the ban on hormone-treated beef. In 2012, the EU struck a deal with the United States that allowed it to keep the ban in place, in return for increasing its import quota of high-quality non-hormone-treated beef from the United States. In response, the United States lifted its punitive tariffs on EU food exports, thereby ending one of the longest-running trade disputes in history.

Sources: C. Southey, "Hormones Fuel a Meaty EU Row," *Financial Times*, September 7, 1995, p. 2; E. L. Andrews, "In Victory for U.S., European Ban on Treated Beef Is Ruled Illegal," *The New York Times*, May 9, 1997, p. A1; R. Baily, "Food and Trade: EU Fear Mongers' Lethal Harvest," *Los Angeles Times*, August 18, 2002, p. M3; Scott Miller, "EU Trade Sanctions Have Dual Edge," *The Wall Street Journal*, February 26, 2004, p. A3; G. Reilhac, "Lawmakers Approve Rise in Imports of Hormone Free Beef," *Reuters*, March 14, 2012.

an unsafe product. Together, Japan and South Korea accounted for about $2 billion of U.S. beef sales, so the ban had a significant impact on U.S. beef producers. After two years, both countries lifted the ban, although they placed stringent requirements on U.S. beef imports to reduce the risk of importing beef that might be tainted by mad cow disease (e.g., Japan required that all beef must come from cattle under 21 months of age). The accompanying Country Focus describes how the European Union banned the sale and importation of hormone-treated beef. The ban was motivated by a desire to protect European consumers from the possible health consequences of eating meat from animals treated with growth hormones.

Furthering Foreign Policy Objectives Governments sometimes use trade policy to support their foreign policy objectives.[9] A government may grant preferential trade terms to a country with which it wants to build strong relations. Trade policy has also been used several times to pressure or punish "rogue states" that do not abide by international law or norms. Iraq labored under extensive trade sanctions after the UN coalition defeated the country in the 1991 Gulf War until the 2003 invasion of Iraq by U.S.-led forces. The theory is that such pressure might persuade the rogue state to mend its ways, or it might hasten a change of government. In the case of Iraq, the sanctions were seen as a way of forcing that country to comply with several UN resolutions. The United States has maintained long-running trade sanctions against Cuba (despite the move by the Obama administration to "normalize" relations with Cuba, these sanctions are still in place). Their principal function is to impoverish Cuba in the hope that the resulting economic hardship will lead to the downfall of Cuba's communist government and its replacement with a more democratically inclined (and pro-U.S.) regime. The United States has also had trade sanctions in place against Libya and Iran, both of which were accused of supporting terrorist action against U.S. interests and building weapons of mass destruction. In late 2003, the sanctions against Libya seemed to yield some returns when that country announced it would terminate a program to build nuclear weapons. The U.S. government responded by relaxing those sanctions. Similarly, the U.S. government used trade sanctions to pressure the Iranian government to halt its alleged nuclear weapons program. Following a 2015 agreement to limit Iran's nuclear program, it relaxed some of those sanctions.

Other countries can undermine unilateral trade sanctions. The U.S. sanctions against Cuba, for example, have not stopped other Western countries from trading with Cuba. The U.S. sanctions have done little more than help create a vacuum into which other trading nations, such as Canada and Germany, have stepped.

Protecting Human Rights

Protecting and promoting human rights in other countries is an important element of foreign policy for many democracies. Governments sometimes use trade policy to try to improve the human rights policies of trading partners. For example, as discussed in Chapter 5, the U.S. government long had trade sanctions in place against the nation of Myanmar, in no small part due to the poor human rights practices in that nation. In late 2012, the United States said that it would ease trade sanctions against Myanmar in response to democratic reforms in that country. Similarly, in the 1980s and 1990s, Western governments used trade sanctions against South Africa as a way of pressuring that nation to drop its apartheid policies, which were seen as a violation of basic human rights.

ECONOMIC ARGUMENTS FOR INTERVENTION

With the development of the new trade theory and strategic trade policy (see Chapter 6), the economic arguments for government intervention have undergone a renaissance in recent years. Until the early 1980s, most economists saw little benefit in government intervention and strongly advocated a free trade policy. This position has changed at the margins with the development of strategic trade policy, although as we will see in the next section, there are still strong economic arguments for sticking to a free trade stance.

The Infant Industry Argument

The **infant industry argument** is by far the oldest economic argument for government intervention. Alexander Hamilton proposed it in 1792. According to this argument, many developing countries have a potential comparative advantage in manufacturing, but new manufacturing industries cannot initially compete with established industries in developed countries. To allow manufacturing to get a toehold, the argument is that governments should temporarily support new industries (with tariffs, import quotas, and subsidies) until they have grown strong enough to meet international competition.

Infant Industry Argument
New industries in developing countries must be temporarily protected from international competition to help them reach a position where they can compete on world markets with the firms of developed nations.

This argument has had substantial appeal for the governments of developing nations during the past 50 years, and the GATT has recognized the infant industry argument as a legitimate reason for protectionism. Nevertheless, many economists remain critical of this argument for two main reasons. First, protection of manufacturing from foreign competition does no good unless the protection helps make the industry efficient. In case after case, however, protection seems to have done little more than foster the development of inefficient industries that have little hope of ever competing in the world market. Brazil, for example, built the world's 10-largest auto industry behind tariff barriers and quotas. Once those barriers were removed in the late 1980s, however, foreign imports soared, and the industry was forced to face up to the fact that after 30 years of protection, the Brazilian auto industry was one of the world's most inefficient.[10]

Second, the infant industry argument relies on an assumption that firms are unable to make efficient long-term investments by borrowing money from the domestic or international capital market. Consequently, governments have been required to subsidize long-term investments. Given the development of global capital markets over the past 20 years, this assumption no longer looks as valid as it once did. Today, if a developing country has a potential comparative advantage in a manufacturing industry, firms in that country should be able to borrow

Even though the United States holds trade sanctions with Cuba, other Western countries continue to trade with the island nation.

Source: © Adalberto Roque/AFP/Getty Images

money from the capital markets to finance the required investments. Given financial support, firms based in countries with a potential comparative advantage have an incentive to endure the necessary initial losses in order to make long-run gains without requiring government protection. Many Taiwanese and South Korean firms did this in industries such as textiles, semiconductors, machine tools, steel, and shipping. Thus, given efficient global capital markets, the only industries that would require government protection would be those that are not worthwhile.

Strategic Trade Policy

Some new trade theorists have proposed the strategic trade policy argument.[11] We reviewed the basic argument in Chapter 6 when we considered the new trade theory. The new trade theory argues that in industries in which the existence of substantial economies of scale implies that the world market will profitably support only a few firms, countries may predominate in the export of certain products simply because they have firms that were able to capture first-mover advantages. The long-term dominance of Boeing in the commercial aircraft industry has been attributed to such factors.

Strategic Trade Policy

Government policy aimed at improving the competitive position of a domestic industry and/or domestic firm in the world market.

The **strategic trade policy** argument has two components. First, it is argued that by appropriate actions, a government can help raise national income if it can somehow ensure that the firm or firms that gain first-mover advantages in an industry are domestic rather than foreign enterprises. Thus, according to the strategic trade policy argument, a government should use subsidies to support promising firms that are active in newly emerging industries. Advocates of this argument point out that the substantial R&D grants that the U.S. government gave Boeing in the 1950s and 1960s probably helped tilt the field of competition in the newly emerging market for passenger jets in Boeing's favor. (Boeing's first commercial jet airliner, the 707, was derived from a military plane.) Similar arguments have been made with regard to Japan rise to dominance in the production of liquid crystal display screens (used in computers). Although these screens were invented in the United States, the Japanese government, in cooperation with major electronics companies, targeted this industry for research support in the late 1970s and early 1980s. The result was that Japanese firms, not U.S. firms, subsequently captured first-mover advantages in this market.

The second component of the strategic trade policy argument is that it might pay a government to intervene in an industry by helping domestic firms overcome the barriers to entry created by foreign firms that have already reaped first-mover advantages. This argument underlies government support of Airbus, Boeing's major competitor. Formed in 1966 as a consortium of four companies from Great Britain, France, Germany, and Spain, Airbus had less than 5 percent of the world commercial aircraft market when it began production in the mid-1970s. By 2015, it was splitting the market with Boeing. How did Airbus achieve this? According to the U.S. government, the answer is a $15 billion subsidy from the governments of Great Britain, France, Germany, and Spain.[12] Without this subsidy, Airbus would never have been able to break into the world market.

If these arguments are correct, they support a rationale for government intervention in international trade. Governments should target technologies that may be important in the future and use subsidies to support development work aimed at commercializing those technologies. Furthermore, government should provide export subsidies until the domestic firms have established first-mover advantages in the world market. Government support may also be justified if it can help domestic firms overcome the first-mover advantages enjoyed by foreign competitors and emerge as viable competitors in the world market (as in the Airbus and semiconductor examples). In this case, a combination of home-market protection and export-promoting subsidies may be needed.

Use SmartBook to help retain what you have learned. Access your Instructor's Connect course to check out SmartBook or go to learnsmartadvantage.com for help.

The Revised Case for Free Trade

LO 7-3

Summarize and explain the arguments against strategic trade policy.

The strategic trade policy arguments of the new trade theorists suggest an economic justification for government intervention in international trade. This justification challenges the rationale for unrestricted free trade found in the work of classic trade theorists such as Adam Smith and David Ricardo. In response to this challenge to economic orthodoxy, a number of economists—including some of those responsible for the development of the new trade theory, such as Paul Krugman—point out that although strategic trade policy looks appealing in theory, in practice it may be unworkable. This response to the strategic trade policy argument constitutes the revised case for free trade.[13]

RETALIATION AND TRADE WAR Krugman argues that a strategic trade policy aimed at establishing domestic firms in a dominant position in a global industry is a beggar-thy-neighbor policy that boosts national income at the expense of other countries. A country that attempts to use such policies will probably provoke retaliation. In many cases, the resulting trade war between two or more interventionist governments will leave all countries involved worse off than if a hands-off approach had been adopted in the first place. If the U.S. government were to respond to the Airbus subsidy by increasing its own subsidies to Boeing, for example, the result might be that the subsidies would cancel each other out. In the process, both European and U.S. taxpayers would end up supporting an expensive and pointless trade war, and both Europe and the United States would be worse off.

Krugman may be right about the danger of a strategic trade policy leading to a trade war. The problem, however, is how to respond when one's competitors are already being supported by government subsidies; that is, how should Boeing and the United States respond to the subsidization of Airbus? According to Krugman, the answer is probably not to engage in retaliatory action but to help establish rules of the game that minimize the use of trade-distorting subsidies. This is what the World Trade Organization seeks to do.

DOMESTIC POLICIES Governments do not always act in the national interest when they intervene in the economy; politically important interest groups often influence them. The European Union's support for the Common Agricultural Policy (CAP), which arose because of the political power of French and German farmers, is an example. The CAP benefits inefficient farmers and the politicians who rely on the farm vote but not consumers in the EU, who end up paying more for their foodstuffs. Thus, a further reason for not embracing strategic trade policy, according to Krugman, is that such a policy is almost certain to be captured by special-interest

test PREP

Use SmartBook to help retain what you have learned. Access your Instructor's Connect course to check out SmartBook or go to learnsmartadvantage.com for help.

LO 7-4

Describe the development of the world trading system and the current trade issue.

groups within the economy, which will distort it to their own ends. Krugman concludes that in the United States,

> To ask the Commerce Department to ignore special-interest politics while formulating detailed policy for many industries is not realistic; to establish a blanket policy of free trade, with exceptions granted only under extreme pressure, may not be the optimal policy according to the theory but may be the best policy that the country is likely to get.[14]

Development of the World Trading System

Strong economic arguments support unrestricted free trade. While many governments have recognized the value of these arguments, they have been unwilling to unilaterally lower their trade barriers for fear that other nations might not follow suit. Consider the problem that two neighboring countries, say, Brazil and Argentina, face when deciding whether to lower trade barriers between them. In principle, the government of Brazil might favor lowering trade barriers, but it might be unwilling to do so for fear that Argentina will not do the same. Instead, the government might fear that the Argentineans will take advantage of Brazil's low barriers to enter the Brazilian market while continuing to shut Brazilian products out of their market through high trade barriers. The Argentinean government might believe that it faces the same dilemma. The essence of the problem is a lack of trust. Both governments recognize that their respective nations will benefit from lower trade barriers between them, but neither government is willing to lower barriers for fear that the other might not follow.[15]

Such a deadlock can be resolved if both countries negotiate a set of rules to govern cross-border trade and lower trade barriers. But who is to monitor the governments to make sure they are playing by the trade rules? And who is to impose sanctions on a government that cheats? Both governments could set up an independent body to act as a referee. This referee could monitor trade between the countries, make sure that no side cheats, and impose sanctions on a country if it does cheat in the trade game.

While it might sound unlikely that any government would compromise its national sovereignty by submitting to such an arrangement, since World War II an international trading framework has evolved that has exactly these features. For its first 50 years, this framework was known as the General Agreement on Tariffs and Trade (GATT). Since 1995, it has been known as the World Trade Organization (WTO). Here, we look at the evolution and workings of the GATT and WTO.

FROM SMITH TO THE GREAT DEPRESSION As noted in Chapter 5, the theoretical case for free trade dates to the late eighteenth century and the work of Adam Smith and David Ricardo. Free trade as a government policy was first officially embraced by Great Britain in 1846, when the British Parliament repealed the Corn Laws. The Corn Laws placed a high tariff on imports of foreign corn. The objectives of the Corn Laws tariff were to raise government revenues and to protect British corn producers. There had been annual motions in Parliament in favor of free trade since the 1820s, when David Ricardo was a member. However, agricultural protection was withdrawn only as a result of a protracted debate when the effects of a harvest failure in Great Britain were compounded by the imminent threat of famine in Ireland. Faced with considerable hardship and suffering among the populace, Parliament narrowly reversed its long-held position.

During the next 80 years or so, Great Britain, as one of the world's dominant trading powers, pushed the case for trade liberalization, but the British government was a voice in the wilderness. Its major trading partners did not reciprocate the British policy of unilateral free trade. The only reason Britain kept this policy for so long was that

Do You Believe in Free Trade Agreements?

The benefits of free trade agreements are often hard to see. At the same time, the benefits of protecting certain industries and/or companies from foreign competition are often very visible. Given these scenarios, many people often argue that free trade agreements are bad for their country. Perhaps as a result, many governments impose many tariffs, quotas, and other nontariff barriers to trade. For example, the common perception is that by establishing trade barriers, a country keeps the jobs at home instead of jobs being shipped overseas. But is this really true?

Source: D. J. Boudreaux, *The Benefits of Free Trade: Addressing the Myths* (Washington, DC: Mercatus Center, George Mason University, 2013).

as the world's largest exporting nation, it had far more to lose from a trade war than did any other country.

By the 1930s, the British attempt to stimulate free trade was buried under the economic rubble of the Great Depression. Economic problems were compounded in 1930, when the U.S. Congress passed the Smoot-Hawley tariff. Aimed at avoiding rising unemployment by protecting domestic industries and diverting consumer demand away from foreign products, the **Smoot-Hawley Act** erected an enormous wall of tariff barriers. Almost every industry was rewarded with its "made-to-order" tariff. The Smoot-Hawley Act had a damaging effect on employment abroad. Other countries reacted by raising their own tariff barriers. U.S. exports tumbled in response, and the world slid further into the Great Depression.[16]

Smoot-Hawley Act

Enacted in 1930 by the U.S. Congress, this act erected a wall of tariff barriers against imports into the United States.

1947–1979: GATT, TRADE LIBERALIZATION, AND ECONOMIC GROWTH

Economic damage caused by the beggar-thy-neighbor trade policies that the Smoot-Hawley Act ushered in exerted a profound influence on the economic institutions and ideology of the post–World War II world. The United States emerged from the war both victorious and economically dominant. After the debacle of the Great Depression, opinion in the U.S. Congress had swung strongly in favor of free trade. Under U.S. leadership, the GATT was established in 1947.

The GATT was a multilateral agreement whose objective was to liberalize trade by eliminating tariffs, subsidies, import quotas, and the like. From its foundation in 1947 until it was superseded by the WTO, the GATT's membership grew from 19 to more than 120 nations. The GATT did not attempt to liberalize trade restrictions in one fell swoop; that would have been impossible. Rather, tariff reduction was spread over eight rounds.

In its early years, the GATT was by most measures very successful. For example, the average tariff declined by nearly 92 percent in the United States between the Geneva Round of 1947 and the Tokyo Round of 1973–1979. Consistent with the theoretical arguments first advanced by Ricardo and reviewed in Chapter 5, the move toward free trade under the GATT appeared to stimulate economic growth.

1980–1993: PROTECTIONIST TRENDS

During the 1980s and early 1990s, the trading system erected by the GATT came under strain as pressures for greater protectionism increased around the world. There were three reasons for the rise in such pressures during the 1980s. First, the economic success of Japan during that time strained the world trading system (much as the success of China has created strains today). Japan was in ruins when the GATT was created. By the early 1980s, however, it had become the world's second-largest economy and its largest exporter. Japan's success in such industries as automobiles and semiconductors might have been enough to strain the world trading system. Things were made worse by the widespread perception in the West that despite low tariff rates and subsidies, Japanese markets were closed to imports and foreign investment by administrative trade barriers.

Second, the world trading system was strained by the persistent trade deficit in the world's largest economy, the United States. The consequences of the U.S. deficit included painful adjustments in industries such as automobiles, machine tools, semiconductors, steel, and textiles, where domestic producers steadily lost market share to foreign competitors. The resulting unemployment gave rise to renewed demands in the U.S. Congress for protection against imports.

A third reason for the trend toward greater protectionism was that many countries found ways to get around GATT regulations. Bilateral voluntary export restraints (VERs) circumvent GATT agreements, because neither the importing country nor the exporting country complains to the GATT bureaucracy in Geneva—and without a complaint, the GATT bureaucracy can do nothing. Exporting countries agreed to VERs to avoid more damaging punitive tariffs. One of the best-known examples is the automobile VER between Japan and the United States, under which Japanese producers promised to limit their auto imports into the United States as a way of defusing growing trade tensions. According to a World Bank study, 16 percent of the imports of industrialized countries in 1986 were subjected to nontariff trade barriers such as VERs.[17]

THE URUGUAY ROUND AND THE WORLD TRADE ORGANIZATION

Against the background of rising pressures for protectionism, in 1986 GATT members embarked on their eighth round of negotiations to reduce tariffs, the Uruguay Round (so named because it occurred in Uruguay). This was the most ambitious round of negotiations yet. Until then, GATT rules had applied only to trade in manufactured goods and commodities. In the Uruguay Round, member countries sought to extend GATT rules to cover trade in services. They also sought to write rules governing the protection of intellectual property, to reduce agricultural subsidies, and to strengthen the GATT's monitoring and enforcement mechanisms.

The Uruguay Round dragged on for seven years before an agreement was reached on December 15, 1993. It went into effect July 1, 1995. The Uruguay Round contained the following provisions:

1. Tariffs on industrial goods were to be reduced by more than one-third, and tariffs were to be scrapped on more than 40 percent of manufactured goods.
2. Average tariff rates imposed by developed nations on manufactured goods were to be reduced to less than 4 percent of value, the lowest level in modern history.
3. Agricultural subsidies were to be substantially reduced.
4. GATT fair trade and market access rules were to be extended to cover a wide range of services.
5. GATT rules also were to be extended to provide enhanced protection for patents, copyrights, and trademarks (intellectual property).
6. Barriers on trade in textiles were to be significantly reduced over 10 years.
7. The World Trade Organization was to be created to implement the GATT agreement.

The World Trade Organization

The WTO acts as an umbrella organization that encompasses the GATT along with two new sister bodies, one on services and the other on intellectual property. The WTO's General Agreement on Trade in Services (GATS) has taken the lead to extending free trade agreements to services. The WTO's Agreement on Trade-Related Aspects of Intellectual Property Rights (TRIPS) is an attempt to narrow the gaps in the way intellectual property rights are protected around the world and to bring them under common international rules. WTO has taken over responsibility for arbitrating trade disputes and monitoring the trade policies of member countries. While the WTO operates on the basis of consensus as the GATT did, in the area of dispute settlement, member countries are no longer able to block adoption of arbitration reports. Arbitration panel reports on trade disputes between member countries are automatically adopted by the WTO unless there is a consensus to reject them. Countries that have been found by the arbitration panel to violate GATT rules may appeal to a permanent appellate body, but its verdict is binding. If offenders fail to comply with the recommendations of the arbitration panel, trading partners have the right to compensation or, in the last resort, to impose (commensurate) trade sanctions. Every stage of the procedure is subject to strict time limits. Thus, the WTO has something that the GATT never had—teeth.[18]

WTO: EXPERIENCE TO DATE

By 2016, the WTO had 162 members, including China, which joined at the end of 2001, and Russia, which joined in 2012. WTO members collectively account for 98 percent of world trade. Since its formation, the WTO has remained at the forefront of efforts to promote global free trade. Its creators expressed the belief that the enforcement mechanisms granted to the WTO would make it more effective at policing global trade rules than the GATT had been. The great hope was that the WTO might emerge as an effective advocate and facilitator of future trade deals, particularly in areas such as services. The experience so far has been mixed. After a strong early start, since the late 1990s the WTO has been unable to get agreements to further reduce barriers to international trade and trade and investment. There has been very slow progress with the current round of trade talks (the Doha Round). There was also a shift back toward some limited protectionism following the global financial crisis of 2008–2009. These developments have raised a number of questions about the future direction of the WTO.

WTO as Global Police

The first two decades in the life of the WTO suggest that its policing and enforcement mechanisms are having a positive effect.[19] Between 1995 and 2015, more than 415 trade disputes between member countries were brought to the WTO.[20] This record compares with a total of 196 cases handled by the GATT over almost half a century. Of the cases brought to the WTO, three-fourths have been resolved by informal consultations between the disputing countries. Resolving the remainder has involved more formal procedures, but these have been largely successful. In general, countries involved have adopted the WTO's recommendations. The fact that countries are using the WTO represents an important vote of confidence in the organization's dispute resolution procedures.

Should a Standard Process Be in Place for Import Licenses?

Import licenses are permits granted before a product is imported. The administrative procedures for obtaining the licenses should be simple, neutral, equitable, and transparent. Where possible, they should be given automatically and quickly, and even if they are nonautomatic, they should not obstruct trade unnecessarily. Australia, Turkey, the European Union, Norway, Thailand, the United States, New Zealand, Costa Rica, Colombia, Peru, Chinese Taipei, Japan, the Republic of Korea, Switzerland, and Canada said their producers and traders reported that exports to Argentina have declined or been delayed by Argentina's licensing processes and requirements, which some described as "protectionist." Should there be a standardized process and timeline for processing import licenses in member countries of the World Trade Organization?

Source: World Trade Organization, "Members Continue to Criticize Argentina's Import Licensing," 2012; www.wto.org/english/news_e/news12_e/impl_27apr12_e.htm.

Expanded Trade Agreements As explained earlier, the Uruguay Round of GATT negotiations extended global trading rules to cover trade in services. The WTO was given the role of brokering future agreements to open up global trade in services. The WTO was also encouraged to extend its reach to encompass regulations governing foreign direct investment, something the GATT had never done. Two of the first industries targeted for reform were the global telecommunication and financial services industries.

In February 1997, the WTO brokered a deal to get countries to agree to open their telecommunication markets to competition, allowing foreign operators to purchase ownership stakes in domestic telecommunication providers and establishing a set of common rules for fair competition. Most of the world's biggest markets—including the United States, European Union, and Japan—were fully liberalized by January 1, 1998, when the pact went into effect. All forms of basic telecommunication service are covered, including voice telephone, data, and satellite and radio communications. Many telecommunication companies responded positively to the deal, pointing out that it would give them a much greater ability to offer their business customers one-stop shopping—a global, seamless service for all their corporate needs and a single bill.

This was followed in December 1997 with an agreement to liberalize cross-border trade in financial services. The deal covered more than 95 percent of the world's financial services market. Under the agreement, which took effect at the beginning of March 1999, 102 countries pledged to open (to varying degrees) their banking, securities, and insurance sectors to foreign competition. In common with the telecommunication deal, the accord covers not just cross-border trade but also foreign direct investment. Seventy countries agreed to dramatically lower or eradicate barriers to foreign direct investment in their financial services sector. The United States and the European Union (with minor exceptions) are fully open to inward investment by foreign banks, insurance, and securities companies. As part of the deal, many Asian countries made important concessions that allow significant foreign participation in their financial services sectors for the first time.

THE FUTURE OF THE WTO: UNRESOLVED ISSUES AND THE DOHA ROUND

Since the successes of the 1990s, the World Trade Organization has struggled to make progress on the international trade front. Confronted by a slower growing world economy after 2001, many national governments have been reluctant to agree to a fresh round of policies designed to reduce trade barriers. Political opposition to the WTO has been growing in many nations. As the public face of globalization, some politicians and nongovernmental organizations blame the WTO for a variety of ills, including high unemployment, environmental degradation, poor working conditions in developing nations, falling real wage rates among the lower paid in developed nations, and rising income inequality. The rapid rise of China as a dominant trading nation has also played a role here. Reflecting sentiments like those toward Japan 25 years ago, many perceive China as failing to play by the international trading rules, even as it embraces the WTO.

Against this difficult political backdrop, much remains to be done on the international trade front. Four issues at the forefront of the current agenda of the WTO are antidumping policies, the high level of protectionism in agriculture, the lack of strong protection for intellectual property rights in many nations, and continued high tariff rates on nonagricultural goods and services in many nations. We shall look at each in turn before discussing the latest round of talks between WTO members aimed at reducing trade barriers, the Doha Round, which began in 2001 and is ongoing.

Antidumping Actions Antidumping actions proliferated during the 1990s and 2000s. WTO rules allow countries to impose antidumping duties on foreign goods that are being sold cheaper than at home or below their cost of production when domestic producers can show that they are being harmed. Unfortunately, the rather vague definition of what constitutes "dumping" has proved to be a loophole that many countries are exploiting to pursue protectionism.

Between 1995 and mid-2015, WTO members had reported implementation of some 4,757 antidumping actions to the WTO. India initiated the largest number of antidumping actions, some 740; the EU initiated 468 over the same period, and the United States, 527. China accounted for 1,052 complaints, South Korea for 349, the United States for 266, Taiwan for 265, and Japan for 187. Antidumping actions seem to be concentrated in certain sectors of the economy, such as basic metal industries (e.g., aluminum and steel), chemicals, plastics, and machinery and electrical equipment.[21] These sectors account for approximately 70 percent of all antidumping actions reported to the WTO. Since 1995, these four sectors have been characterized by periods of intense competition and excess productive capacity, which have led to low prices and profits (or losses) for firms in those industries. It is not unreasonable, therefore, to hypothesize that the high level of antidumping actions in these industries represents an attempt by beleaguered manufacturers to use the political process in their nations to seek protection from foreign competitors, which they claim are engaging in unfair competition. While some of these claims may have merit, the process can become very politicized as representatives of businesses and their employees lobby government officials to "protect domestic jobs from unfair foreign competition," and government officials, mindful of the need to

Removing barriers to trade and subsidies in agricultural products should benefit consumers.
Source: © Mark Elias/Bloomberg/Getty Images

get votes in future elections, oblige by pushing for antidumping actions. The WTO is clearly worried by the use of antidumping policies, suggesting that it reflects persistent protectionist tendencies and pushing members to strengthen the regulations governing the imposition of antidumping duties.

Protectionism in Agriculture

Another focus of the WTO has been the high level of tariffs and subsidies in the agricultural sector of many economies. Tariff rates on agricultural products are generally much higher than tariff rates on manufactured products or services. For example, the average tariff rates on nonagricultural products among developed nations are around 4 percent. On agricultural products, however, the average tariff rates are 21.2 percent for Canada, 15.9 percent for the European Union, 18.6 percent for Japan, and 10.3 percent for the United States.[22] The implication is that consumers in these countries are paying significantly higher prices than necessary for agricultural products imported from abroad, which leaves them with less money to spend on other goods and services.

The historically high tariff rates on agricultural products reflect a desire to protect domestic agriculture and traditional farming communities from foreign competition. In addition to high tariffs, agricultural producers also benefit from substantial subsidies. According to estimates from the Organisation for Economic Co-operation and Development (OECD), government subsidies on average account for about 17 percent of the cost of agricultural production in Canada, 21 percent in the United States, 35 percent in the European Union, and 59 percent in Japan.[23] OECD countries spend more than $300 billion a year in agricultural subsidies.

Not surprisingly, the combination of high tariff barriers and subsidies introduces significant distortions into the production of agricultural products and international trade of those products. The net effect is to raise prices to consumers, reduce the volume of agricultural trade, and encourage the overproduction of products that are heavily subsidized (with the government typically buying the surplus). Because global trade in agriculture currently amounts to around 10 percent of total merchandized trade, the WTO argues that removing tariff barriers and subsidies could significantly boost the overall level of trade, lower prices to consumers, and raise global economic growth by freeing consumption and investment resources for more productive uses. According to estimates from the International Monetary Fund, removal of tariffs and subsidies on agricultural products would raise global economic welfare by $128 billion annually.[24] Others suggest gains as high as $182 billion.[25]

The biggest defenders of the existing system have been the advanced nations of the world, which want to protect their agricultural sectors from competition by low-cost producers in developing nations. In contrast, developing nations have been pushing hard for reforms that would allow their producers greater access to the protected markets of the developed nations. Estimates suggest that removing all subsidies on agricultural production alone in OECD countries could return to the developing nations of the world three times more than all the foreign aid they currently receive from the OECD nations.[26] In other words, free trade in agriculture could help jump-start economic growth among the world's poorer nations and alleviate global poverty.

Protection of Intellectual Property

Another issue that has become increasingly important to the WTO has been protecting intellectual property. The 1995 Uruguay agreement that established the WTO also contained an agreement to protect intellectual property (the Trade-Related Aspects of Intellectual Property Rights, or TRIPS, agreement). The TRIPS regulations oblige WTO members to grant and enforce patents lasting at least 20 years and copyrights lasting 50 years. Rich countries had to comply with the rules within a year. Poor countries, in which such protection was generally much weaker, had five years' grace, and the very poorest had 10 years. The basis for this agreement was a strong belief among signatory nations that the protection of intellectual property through patents, trademarks, and copyrights must be an essential element of the international trading system. Inadequate protections for intellectual property reduce the incentive for innovation. Because innovation is a central engine of economic growth and rising living standards, the argument has been that a multilateral agreement is needed to protect intellectual property.

Without such an agreement, it is feared that producers in a country—let's say, India—might market imitations of patented innovations pioneered in a different country—say, the United States. This can affect international trade in two ways. First, it reduces the export opportunities in India for the original innovator in the United States. Second, to the extent that the Indian producer is able to export its pirated imitation to additional countries, it also reduces the export opportunities in those countries for the U.S. inventor. Also, one can argue that because the size of the total world market for the innovator is reduced, its incentive to pursue risky and expensive innovations is also reduced. The net effect would be less innovation in the world economy and less economic growth.

Market Access for Nonagricultural Goods and Services

Although the WTO and the GATT have made big strides in reducing the tariff rates on nonagricultural products, much work remains. Although most developed nations have brought their tariff rates on industrial products down to an average of 3.8 percent of value, exceptions still remain. In particular, while average tariffs are low, high tariff rates persist on certain imports into developed nations, which limit market access and economic growth. For example, Australia and South Korea, both OECD countries, still have bound tariff rates of 15.1 percent and 24.6 percent, respectively, on imports of transportation equipment (*bound tariff rates* are the highest rate that can be charged, which is often, but not always, the rate that is charged). In contrast, the bound tariff rates on imports of transportation equipment into the United States, European Union, and Japan are 2.7 percent, 4.8 percent, and 0 percent, respectively. A particular area for concern is high tariff rates on imports of selected goods from developing nations into developed nations.

In addition, tariffs on services remain higher than on industrial goods. The average tariff on business and financial services imported into the United States, for example, is 8.2 percent, into the EU it is 8.5 percent, and into Japan it is 19.7 percent.[27] Given the rising value of cross-border trade in services, reducing these figures can be expected to yield substantial gains.

The WTO would like to bring down tariff rates still further and reduce the scope for the selective use of high tariff rates. The ultimate aim is to reduce tariff rates to zero. Although this might sound ambitious, 40 nations have already moved to zero tariffs on information technology goods, so a precedent exists. Empirical work suggests that further reductions in average tariff rates toward zero would yield substantial gains. One estimate by economists at the World Bank suggests that a broad global trade agreement coming out of the Doha negotiations could increase world income by $263 billion annually, of which $109 billion would go to poor countries.[28] Another estimate from the OECD suggests a figure closer to $300 billion annually.[29] See the accompanying Country Focus for estimates of the benefits to the American economy from free trade.

Looking farther out, the WTO would like to bring down tariff rates on imports of nonagricultural goods into developing nations. Many of these nations use the infant industry argument to justify the continued imposition of high tariff rates; however, ultimately these rates need to come down for these nations to reap the full benefits of international trade. For example, the bound tariff rates of 53.9 percent on imports of transportation equipment into India and 33.6 percent on imports into Brazil, by raising domestic prices, help protect inefficient domestic producers and limit economic growth by reducing the real income of consumers who must pay more for transportation equipment and related services.

A New Round of Talks: Doha

In 2001, the WTO launched a new round of talks between member states aimed at further liberalizing the global trade and investment framework. For this meeting, it picked the remote location of Doha in the Persian Gulf state of Qatar. The talks were originally scheduled to last three years, although they have already gone on for 14 years and are currently stalled.

The Doha agenda includes cutting tariffs on industrial goods and services, phasing out subsidies to agricultural producers, reducing barriers to cross-border investment, and limiting the use of antidumping laws. The talks are currently ongoing. They have been characterized by halting progress punctuated by significant setbacks and missed deadlines. A September 2003 meeting in

country FOCUS

Estimating the Gains from Trade for America

A study published by the Institute for International Economics tried to estimate the gains to the American economy from free trade. According to the study, due to reductions in tariff barriers under the GATT and WTO since 1947, by 2003 the gross domestic product (GDP) of the United States was 7.3 percent higher than would otherwise be the case. The benefits of that amounted to roughly $1 trillion a year, or $9,000 extra income for each American household per year.

The same study tried to estimate what would happen if America concluded free trade deals with all its trading partners, reducing tariff barriers on all goods and services to zero. Using several methods to estimate the impact, the study concluded that additional annual gains of between $450 billion and $1.3 trillion could be realized. This final march to free trade, according to the authors of the study, could safely be expected to raise incomes of the average American household by an additional $4,500 per year.

The authors also tried to estimate the scale and cost of employment disruption that would be caused by a move to universal free trade. Jobs would be lost in certain sectors and gained in others if the country abolished all tariff barriers. Using historical data as a guide, they estimated that 226,000 jobs would be lost every year due to expanded trade, although some two-thirds of those losing jobs would find reemployment after a year. Reemployment, however, would be at a wage that was 13 to 14 percent lower. The study concluded that the disruption costs would total some $54 billion annually, primarily in the form of lower lifetime wages to those whose jobs were disrupted as a result of free trade. Offset against this, however, must be the higher economic growth resulting from free trade, which creates many new jobs and raises household incomes, creating another $450 billion to $1.3 trillion annually in *net* gains to the economy. In other words, the estimated annual gains from trade are far greater than the estimated annual costs associated with job disruption, and more people benefit than lose as a result of a shift to a universal free trade regime.

Sources: S. C. Bradford, P. L. E. Grieco, and G. C. Hufbauer, "The Payoff to America from Global Integration," in *The United States and the World Economy: Foreign Policy for the Next Decade*, C. F. Bergsten, ed. (Washington, DC: Institute for International Economics, 2005).

Cancún, Mexico, broke down, primarily because there was no agreement on how to proceed with reducing agricultural subsidies and tariffs; the EU, United States, and India, among others, proved less than willing to reduce tariffs and subsidies to their politically important farmers, while countries such as Brazil and certain West African nations wanted free trade as quickly as possible. In 2004, both the United States and the EU made a determined push to start the talks again. Since then, however, little progress has been made, and the talks are in deadlock, primarily because of disagreements over how deep the cuts in subsidies to agricultural producers should be. As of early 2015, the goal was to reduce tariffs for manufactured and agricultural goods by 60 to 70 percent and to cut subsidies to half of their current level—but getting nations to agree to these goals was proving exceedingly difficult.

MULTILATERAL AND BILATERAL TRADE AGREEMENTS In response to the apparent failure of the Doha Round to progress, many nations have pushed forward with **multilateral or bilateral trade agreements**, which are reciprocal trade agreements between two or more partners. For example, in 2014 Australia and China entered into a bilateral free trade agreement. Similarly, in March 2012 the United States entered into a bilateral free trade agreement with South Korea. Under this agreement, 80 percent of U.S. exports of consumer and industrial products became duty free, and 95 percent of bilateral trade in industrial and consumer products will be duty free by 2017. The agreement is estimated to boost U.S. GDP by some $10 to $12 billion. The United States is currently pursuing two major multilateral trade agreements, one with 11 other Pacific Rim countries including Australia, New Zealand, Japan, Malaysia, and Chile, and another with the European Union.

Multilateral or Bilateral Trade Agreements
Reciprocal trade agreements between two or more partners.

Multilateral and bilateral trade agreements are designed to capture gain from trade beyond those agreements currently attainable under WTO treaties. Multilateral and bilateral trade agreements are allowed under WTO rules, and countries entering into these agreements are required to notify the WTO. As of 2015, some 406 regional or bilateral trade agreements were in force. Reflecting the lack of progress on the Doha Round, the number of such agreements has increased significantly since the early 2000s, when fewer than 100 were in force.

test PREP

Use SmartBook to help retain what you have learned. Access your Instructor's Connect course to check out SmartBook or go to learnsmartadvantage.com for help.

FOCUS ON MANAGERIAL IMPLICATIONS

TRADE BARRIERS, FIRM STRATEGY, AND POLICY IMPLICATIONS

LO 7-5

Explain the implications for managers of developments in the world trading system.

What are the implications for business practice? Why should the international manager care about the political economy of free trade or about the relative merits of arguments for free trade and protectionism? There are two answers to this question. The first concerns the impact of trade barriers on a firm's strategy. The second concerns the role that business firms can play in promoting free trade or trade barriers.

Trade Barriers and Firm Strategy

To understand how trade barriers affect a firm's strategy, consider first the material in Chapter 6. Drawing on the theories of international trade, we discussed how it makes sense for the firm to disperse its various production activities to those countries around the globe where they can be performed most efficiently. Thus, it may make sense for a firm to design and engineer its product in one country, to manufacture components in another, to perform final assembly operations in yet another country, and then export the finished product to the rest of the world.

Clearly, trade barriers constrain a firm's ability to disperse its productive activities in such a manner. First and most obvious, tariff barriers raise the costs of exporting products to a country (or of exporting partly finished products between countries). This may put the firm at a competitive disadvantage to indigenous competitors in that country. In response, the firm may then find it economical to locate production facilities in that country so that it can compete on even footing. Second, quotas may limit a firm's ability to serve a country from locations outside that country. Again, the response by the firm might be to set up production facilities in that country—even though it may result in higher production costs. Such reasoning was one of the factors behind the rapid expansion of Japanese automaking capacity in the United States during the 1980s and 1990s. This followed the establishment of a VER agreement between the United States and Japan that limited U.S. imports of Japanese automobiles.

Third, to conform to local content regulations, a firm may have to locate more production activities in a given market than it would otherwise. Again, from the firm's perspective, the consequence might be to raise costs above the level that could be achieved if each production activity were dispersed to the optimal location for that activity. And finally, even when trade barriers do not exist, the firm may still want to locate some production activities in a given country to reduce the threat of trade barriers being imposed in the future.

All these effects are likely to raise the firm's costs above the level that could be achieved in a world without trade barriers. The higher costs that result need not translate into a significant competitive disadvantage relative to other foreign firms, however, if the countries imposing trade barriers do so to the imported products of all foreign firms, irrespective of their national origin. But when trade barriers are targeted at exports from a particular nation, firms based in that nation are at a competitive disadvantage to firms of other nations. The firm may deal with such targeted trade barriers by moving production into the country imposing barriers. Another strategy may be to move production to countries whose exports are not targeted by the specific trade barrier.

Finally, the threat of antidumping action limits the ability of a firm to use aggressive pricing to gain market share in a country. Firms in a country also can make strategic use of antidumping measures to limit aggressive competition from low-cost foreign producers. For example, the U.S. steel industry has been very aggressive in bringing antidumping actions against foreign steelmakers, particularly in times of weak global demand for steel and excess capacity. In 1998 and 1999, the United States faced a surge in low-cost steel imports as a severe recession in Asia left producers there with excess capacity. The U.S. producers filed several complaints with the International Trade Commission. One argued that Japanese producers of hot rolled steel were selling it at below cost in the United States. The ITC agreed and levied tariffs ranging from 18 to 67 percent on imports of certain steel products from Japan (these tariffs are separate from the steel tariffs discussed earlier).[30]

Policy Implications

As noted in Chapter 6, business firms are major players on the international trade scene. Because of their pivotal role in international trade, firms can and do exert a strong influence on government policy toward trade. This influence can encourage protectionism, or it can encourage the government to support the WTO and push for open markets and freer trade among all nations. Government policies with regard to international trade can have a direct impact on business.

Consistent with strategic trade policy, examples can be found of government intervention in the form of tariffs, quotas, antidumping actions, and subsidies helping firms and industries establish a competitive advantage in the world economy. In general, however, the arguments contained in this chapter and in Chapter 6 suggest that government intervention has three drawbacks. Intervention can be self-defeating because it tends to protect the inefficient rather than help firms become efficient global competitors. Intervention is dangerous; it may invite retaliation and trigger a trade war. Finally, intervention is unlikely to be well executed, given the opportunity for such a policy to be captured by special-interest groups. Does this mean that business should simply encourage government to adopt a laissez-faire free trade policy?

Most economists would probably argue that the best interests of international business are served by a free trade stance but not a laissez-faire stance. It is probably in the best long-run interests of the business community to encourage the government to aggressively promote greater free trade by, for example, strengthening the WTO. Business probably has much more to gain from government efforts to open protected markets to imports and foreign direct investment than from government efforts to support certain domestic industries in a manner consistent with the recommendations of strategic trade policy.

This conclusion is reinforced by a phenomenon we touched on in Chapter 1—the increasing integration of the world economy and internationalization of production that has occurred over the past two decades. We live in a world where many firms of all national origins increasingly depend on globally dispersed production systems for their competitive advantage. Such systems are the result of freer trade. Freer trade has brought great advantages to firms that have exploited it and to consumers who benefit from the resulting lower prices. Given the danger of retaliatory action, business firms that lobby their governments to engage in protectionism must realize that by doing so they may be denying themselves the opportunity to build a competitive advantage by constructing a globally dispersed production system. By encouraging their governments to engage in protectionism, their own activities and sales overseas may be jeopardized if other governments retaliate. This does not mean a firm should never seek protection in the form of antidumping actions and the like, but it should review its options carefully and think through the larger consequences.

Key Terms

free trade, p. 188
General Agreement on Tariffs and Trade (GATT), p. 188
tariff, p. 189
specific tariff, p. 189
ad valorem tariff, p. 189
subsidy, p. 190
import quota, p. 191
tariff rate quota, p. 191
voluntary export restraint (VER), p. 191
quota rent, p. 192
export credit, p. 192
export ban, p. 192
local content requirement (LCR), p. 192
administrative trade policies, p. 193
dumping, p. 193
antidumping policies, p. 193
countervailing duties, p. 193
infant industry argument, p. 197
strategic trade policy, p. 198
Smoot-Hawley Act, p. 201
multilateral or bilateral trade agreements, p. 207

Summary

This chapter described how the reality of international trade deviates from the theoretical ideal of unrestricted free trade reviewed in Chapter 6. In this chapter, we reported the various instruments of trade policy, reviewed the political and economic arguments for government intervention in international trade, reexamined the economic case for free trade in light of the strategic trade policy argument, and looked at the evolution of the world trading framework. While a policy of free trade may not always be the theoretically optimal policy (given the arguments of the new trade theorists), in practice it is probably the best policy for a government to pursue. In particular, the long-run interests of business and consumers may be best served by strengthening international institutions such as the WTO. Given the danger that isolated protectionism might escalate into a trade war, business probably has far more to gain from government efforts to open protected markets to imports and foreign direct investment (through the WTO) than from government efforts to protect domestic industries from foreign competition. The chapter made the following points:

1. Trade policies such as tariffs, subsidies, antidumping regulations, and local content requirements tend to be pro-producer and anticonsumer. Gains accrue to producers (who are protected from foreign competitors), but consumers lose because they must pay more for imports.
2. There are two types of arguments for government intervention in international trade: political and economic. Political arguments for intervention are concerned with protecting the interests of certain groups, often at the expense of other groups, or with promoting goals with regard to foreign policy, human rights, consumer protection, and the like. Economic arguments for intervention are about boosting the overall wealth of a nation.
3. A common political argument for intervention is that it is necessary to protect jobs. However, political intervention often hurts consumers, and it can be self-defeating. Countries sometimes argue that it is important to protect certain industries for reasons of national security. Some argue that government should use the threat to intervene in trade policy as a bargaining tool to open foreign markets. This can be a risky policy; if it fails, the result can be higher trade barriers.
4. The infant industry argument for government intervention contends that to let manufacturing get a toehold, governments should temporarily support new industries. In practice, however, governments often end up protecting the inefficient.
5. Strategic trade policy suggests that with subsidies, government can help domestic firms gain first-mover advantages in global industries where economies of scale are important. Government subsidies may also help domestic firms overcome barriers to entry into such industries.
6. The problems with strategic trade policy are twofold: (*a*) Such a policy may invite retaliation, in which case all will lose, and (*b*) strategic trade policy may be captured by special-interest groups, which will distort it to their own ends.
7. The GATT was a product of the postwar free trade movement. The GATT was successful in lowering trade barriers on manufactured goods and commodities. The move toward greater free trade under the GATT appeared to stimulate economic growth.
8. The completion of the Uruguay Round of GATT talks and the establishment of the World Trade Organization have strengthened the world trading system by extending GATT rules to services, increasing protection for intellectual property, reducing agricultural subsidies, and enhancing monitoring and enforcement mechanisms.
9. Trade barriers act as a constraint on a firm's ability to disperse its various production activities to optimal locations around the globe. One response to trade barriers is to establish more production activities in the protected country.
10. Business may have more to gain from government efforts to open protected markets to imports and foreign direct investment than from government efforts to protect domestic industries from foreign competition.

Critical Thinking and Discussion Questions

1. Do you think governments should consider human rights when granting preferential trading rights to countries? What are the arguments for and against taking such a position?
2. Whose interests should be the paramount concern of government trade policy: the interests of producers (businesses and their employees) or those of consumers?

3. Given the arguments relating to the new trade theory and strategic trade policy, what kind of trade policy should business be pressuring government to adopt?

4. You are an employee of a U.S. firm that produces personal computers in Thailand and then exports them to the United States and other countries for sale. The personal computers were originally produced in Thailand to take advantage of relatively low labor costs and a skilled workforce. Other possible locations considered at the time were Malaysia and Hong Kong. The U.S. government decides to impose punitive 100 percent ad valorem tariffs on imports of computers from Thailand to punish the country for administrative trade barriers that restrict U.S. exports to Thailand. How should your firm respond? What does this tell you about the use of targeted trade barriers?

5. Reread the Management Focus "Protecting U.S. Magnesium." Who gains most from the antidumping duties levied by the United States on imports of magnesium from China and Russia? Who are the losers? Are these duties in the best national interests of the United States?

globalEDGE Research Task

globalEDGE.msu.edu

Use the globalEDGE™ website (globaledge.msu.edu) to complete the following exercises:

1. You work for a pharmaceutical company that hopes to provide products and services in New Zealand. Yet management's current knowledge of this country's trade policies and barriers is limited. After searching a resource that summarizes the *import and export regulations,* outline the most important foreign trade barriers your firm's managers must keep in mind while developing a strategy for entry into New Zealand's pharmaceutical market.

2. The number of member nations of the World Trade Organization has increased considerably in recent years. In addition, some nonmember countries have observer status in the WTO. Such status requires accession negotiations to begin within five years of attaining this preliminary position. Visit the WTO's website to identify a list of current members and observers. Identify the last five countries that joined the WTO as members. Also, examine the list of current observer countries. Do you notice anything in particular about the countries that have recently joined or have observer status?

Sugar Subsidies Drive Candy Makers Abroad

closing case

Back in the 1930s at the height of the Great Depression, the U.S. government stepped in to support the U.S. sugar industry with a combination of subsidies, price supports, import quotas, and tariffs. These actions were meant to be temporary, but as of 2015 they are still in place. Under policies approved in the 2008 farm bill, the government guarantees 85 percent of the market for U.S. producers, primarily farmers growing sugar beets and cane. The remaining 15 percent is allocated for imports from certain countries at a preferential tariff rate. The government also sets a floor price for sugar. If the price falls below the floor, the government steps in to purchase excess supply, driving the price back up again. The surplus is then sold at a loss to producers of ethanol. A significant U.S. sugar harvest in 2013 required the government to spend some $300 million to prop up U.S. sugar prices. As a result of these policies, between 2010 and 2013, the U.S. sugar price has averaged between 64 and 92 percent higher than the world price of sugar.

American sugar producers say that the federal programs are necessary to keep big sugar-producing countries such as Brazil, India, and Thailand from flooding the U.S. market and driving them out of business. Opponents of the practice include numerous small candy producers. Many of them complain about the high U.S. price for sugar. Increasingly, they have responded by moving production offshore. For example, the Spangler Candy Company, the maker of Dum Dums, has moved 200 jobs from Ohio to Juarez, Mexico, where it makes candy canes that are then imported back into the United States. Similarly, Adams & Brooks, a California-based candy company, has shifted two-thirds of its production across the border to Mexico in response to higher U.S. sugar prices.

A recent academic study suggest that the U.S. sugar policies primarily benefit 4,700 sugar producers, while imposing costs of $2.9 to $3.5 billion per annum on U.S. consumers due to higher sugar prices. The same research predicts that removing the support programs would lead to the net creation of 17,000 to 20,000 new jobs in the United States, while dramatically reducing imports of products containing sugar.

Given the benefits of removing sugar support programs and all the talk about deregulation and reducing the budget deficit in Congress, many observers thought that 2013 would be the year that the sugar programs were finally abandoned. The farm bill was up for renewal, and the sugar support programs were held up as an example of how wasteful government subsidies are. However, sugar producers spent some $20 million on political lobbying between 2011 and 2013. Partly due to their influence, the U.S. Senate voted 54 to 45 against any reform in the sugar programs. The majority included 20 out of 45 Republican senators, most of whom publicly rail against this kind of government intervention. Apparently, however, political expediency required that they support intervention in this case.

Sources: George F. Will, "Congress Needs to Stop Subsidies to Sugar Farmers," *The Washington Post,* June 7, 2013; Ron Nixon, "American Candy Makers, Pinched by Inflated Sugar Prices, Look Abroad," *The New York Times,* October 30, 2013; J. Beghinand and A. Elobeid, "The Impact of the U.S. Sugar Program Redux," Iowa State Working Paper 13-WP 538, May 2013, www.card.iastate.edu/publications/dbs/pdffiles/13wp538.pdf.

CASE DISCUSSION QUESTIONS

1. Who benefits from subsidies to U.S. sugar producers? Who loses?
2. Do the benefits of U.S. government support to the U.S. sugar industry outweigh the losses?
3. What do you think would happen if the U.S. government removed all support for U.S. sugar producers?
4. Government support programs for sugar producers were introduced in the 1930s, yet they are still in place today, long after the original rationale disappeared. What does this tell you about political decisions relating to international trade?
5. If you had the power to make changes here, what would you do and why?

Endnotes

1. For a detailed welfare analysis of the effect of a tariff, see P. R. Krugman and M. Obstfeld, *International Economics: Theory and Policy* (New York: HarperCollins, 2000), ch. 8.
2. World Trade Organization, *World Trade Report 2006* (Geneva: WTO, 2006).
3. The study was undertaken by Kym Anderson of the University of Adelaide. See "A Not So Perfect Market," *The Economist: Survey of Agriculture and Technology,* March 25, 2000, pp. 8–10.
4. K. Anderson, W. Martin, and D. van der Mensbrugghe, "Distortions to World Trade: Impact on Agricultural Markets and Farm Incomes," *Review of Agricultural Economics* 28 (Summer 2006), pp. 168–94.
5. J. B. Teece, "Voluntary Export Restraints Are Back; They Didn't Work the Last Time," *Automotive News,* April 23, 2012.
6. G. Hufbauer and Z. A. Elliott, *Measuring the Costs of Protectionism in the United States* (Washington, DC: Institute for International Economics, 1993).
7. Alan Goldstein, "Sematech Members Facing Dues Increase; 30% Jump to Make Up for Loss of Federal Funding," *Dallas Morning News,* July 27, 1996, p. 2F.
8. N. Dunne and R. Waters, "U.S. Waves a Big Stick at Chinese Pirates," *Financial Times,* January 6, 1995, p. 4.
9. Peter S. Jordan, "Country Sanctions and the International Business Community," *American Society of International Law Proceedings of the Annual Meeting* 20, no. 9 (1997), pp. 333–42.
10. "Brazil's Auto Industry Struggles to Boost Global Competitiveness," *Journal of Commerce,* October 10, 1991, p. 6A.
11. For reviews, see J. A. Brander, "Rationales for Strategic Trade and Industrial Policy," in *Strategic Trade Policy and the New International Economics,* P. R. Krugman, ed. (Cambridge, MA: MIT Press, 1986); P. R. Krugman, "Is Free Trade Passé?," *Journal of Economic Perspectives* 1 (1987), pp. 131–44; P. R. Krugman, "Does the New Trade Theory Require a New Trade Policy?," *World Economy* 15, no. 4 (1992), pp. 423–41.
12. "Airbus and Boeing: The Jumbo War," *The Economist,* June 15, 1991, pp. 65–66.
13. For details, see Krugman, "Is Free Trade Passé?" and Brander, "Rationales for Strategic Trade and Industrial Policy."
14. Krugman, "Is Free Trade Passé?"
15. This dilemma is a variant of the famous prisoner's dilemma, which has become a classic metaphor for the difficulty of achieving cooperation between self-interested and mutually suspicious entities. For a good general introduction, see A. Dixit and B. Nalebuff, *Thinking Strategically: The Competitive Edge in Business, Politics, and Everyday Life* (New York: Norton, 1991).
16. Note that the Smoot-Hawley Act did not cause the Great Depression. However, the beggar-thy-neighbor trade policies that it ushered in certainly made things worse. See J. Bhagwati, *Protectionism* (Cambridge, MA: MIT Press, 1988).
17. World Bank, *World Development Report* (New York: Oxford University Press, 1987).
18. Frances Williams, "WTO—New Name Heralds New Powers," *Financial Times,* December 16, 1993, p. 5; Frances Williams, "GATT's Successor to Be Given Real Clout," *Financial Times,* April 4, 1994, p. 6.
19. W. J. Davey, "The WTO Dispute Settlement System: The First Ten Years," *Journal of International Economic Law,* March 2005, pp. 17–28.
20. Information provided on WTO website, www.wto.org/english/tratop_e/dispu_e/dispu_status_e.htm.

21. Data at www.wto.org/english/tratop_e/adp_e/adp_e.htm.
22. World Trade Organization, *Annual Report by the Director General* 2003 (Geneva: WTO, 2003).
23. Ibid.
24. Ibid.
25. Anderson et al., "Distortions to World Trade."
26. World Trade Organization, *Annual Report 2002* (Geneva: WTO, 2002).
27. S. C. Bradford, P. L. E. Grieco, and G. C. Hufbauer, "The Payoff to America from Global Integration," in *The United States and the World Economy: Foreign Policy for the Next Decade,* C. F. Bergsten, ed. (Washington, DC: Institute for International Economics, 2005).
28. World Bank, *Global Economic Prospects* 2005 (Washington, DC: World Bank, 2005).
29. "Doha Development Agenda," *OECD Observer,* September 2006, pp. 64–67.
30. "Punitive Tariffs Are Approved on Imports of Japanese Steel," *The New York Times,* June 12, 1999, p. A3.

Foreign Direct Investment

learning objectives

After reading this chapter, you will be able to:

LO8-1 Recognize current trends regarding foreign direct investment (FDI) in the world economy.

LO8-2 Explain the different theories of FDI.

LO8-3 Understand how political ideology shapes a government's attitudes toward FDI.

LO8-4 Describe the benefits and costs of FDI to home and host countries.

LO8-5 Explain the range of policy instruments that governments use to influence FDI.

LO8-6 Identify the implications for managers of the theory and government policies associated with FDI.

Source: © Silviu Doroftei/ZUMA Press/London/Newscom

Burberry Shifts Its Strategy in Japan

opening case

Burberry, the icon British luxury apparel company best known for its high fashion outwear, has been operating in Japan for nearly half a century. Until recently, its branded products were sold under a licensing agreement with Sanyo Shokai. The Japanese company had considerable discretion as to how it utilized the Burberry brand. It sold everything from golf bags to miniskirts and Burberry-clad Barbie dolls in its 400 stores around the country, typically at prices significantly below those Burberry charged for its high-end products in the United Kingdom.

For a long time, it looked like a good deal for Burberry. Sanyo Shokai did all of the market development in Japan, generating revenues of around $800 million a year and paying Burberry $80 million in annual royalty payments. However, by 2007 Burberry's CEO, Angela Ahrendts, was becoming increasingly dissatisfied with the Japanese licensing deal and 22 others like it in countries around the world. In Ahrendts's view, the licensing deals were diluting Burberry's core brand image. Licensees such as Sanyo Shokai were selling a wide range of products at a much lower price point than Burberry charged for products in its own stores. "In luxury,"Ahrendts once remarked, "ubiquity will kill you—it means that you're not really luxury anymore."* Moreover, with an increasing number of customers buying Burberry products online and on trips to Britain, where the brand was considered very upmarket, Ahrendts felt that it was crucial for Burberry to tightly control its global brand image.

Ahrendts was determined to rein in licensees and regain control of Burberry's sales in foreign markets, even if it mean taking a short-term hit to sales. She started off the process of terminating licensees before leaving Burberry to run Apple's retail division in 2014. Her hand-picked successor as CEO, Christopher Bailey, who rose through the design function at Burberry, has continued to pursue this strategy.

In Japan, the license was terminated in 2015. Sanyo Shokai was required to close nearly 400 licensed Burberry stores. Burberry is not giving up on Japan, however. After all, Japan is the world's second-largest market for luxury goods. Instead, the company will now sell products through a limited number of wholly owned stores. The goal is to have 35 to 50 stores in the most exclusive locations in Japan by 2018. They will offer only high-end products, such as Burberry's classic $1,800 trench coat. In general, the price point will be 10 times higher than was common for most Burberry products in Japan. The company realizes the move is risky and fully expects sales to initially fall before rising again as it rebuilds its brand, but CEO Bailey argues that the move is absolutely necessary if Burberry is to have a coherent global brand image for its luxury products. •

*Angela Ahrendts, "Burberry's CEO on Turning an Aging British Icon into a Global Luxury Brand," *Harvard Business Review*, January-February 2013.

Sources: Kathy Chu and Megumi Fujikawa, "Burberry Gets a Grip on Brand in Japan," *The Wall Street Journal*, August 15-16, 2015; Angela hrendts, "Burberry's CEO on Turning an Aging British Icon into a Global Luxury Brand," *Harvard Business Review*, January-February 2013; Tim Blanks, "The Designer Who Would be CEO," *The Wall Street Journal Magazine*, June 18, 2015.

Introduction

Foreign direct investment (FDI) occurs when a firm invests directly in facilities to produce or market a good or service in a foreign country. According to the U.S. Department of Commerce, FDI occurs whenever a U.S. citizen, organization, or affiliated group takes an interest of 10 percent or more in a foreign business entity. Once a firm undertakes FDI, it becomes a multinational enterprise.

The opening case suggests some of the reasons why firms undertake FDI. Burberry, the high-end British fashion retailer, had long operated in Japan under a licensing agreement with local retailer, Sanyo Shokai. However, Burberry came to the realization that its lack of control over how its Japanese licensee utilized the icon Burberry name has damaged the company's global brand image. Specifically, Sanyo Shokai sold a wide range of products under the Burberry brand at much lower price points than Burberry would charge for its high-end luxury goods in its British stores. In order to regain control of its brand, Burberry ended the licensing agreement, requiring Sanyo Shokai to close some 400 licensed stores in Japan. Burberry will now operate 35 to 50 wholly owned stores in upscale locations in Japan. They will sell a limited line of luxury fashion products at a much higher price point. In other words, Burberry is investing directly in the Japanese market in order to control how its brand is used in that market, to regain control over its global brand image, and to generate sales for its high-end apparel, both in Japan and elsewhere.

This chapter begins by looking at the importance of FDI in the world economy. Next, we shall review the theories that have been used to explain why firms like Burberry undertake foreign direct investment. The chapter then moves on to look at government policy toward foreign direct investment. The chapter closes with a section on implications for management practice.

LO 8-1

Recognize current trends regarding foreign direct investment (FDI) in the world economy.

Foreign Direct Investment in the World Economy

When discussing foreign direct investment, it is important to distinguish between the flow of FDI and the stock of FDI. The **flow of FDI** refers to the amount of FDI undertaken over a given time period (normally a year). The **stock of FDI** refers to the total accumulated value of foreign-owned assets at a given time. We also talk of **outflows of FDI**, meaning the flow of FDI out of a country, and **inflows of FDI**, the flow of FDI into a country.

Flow of FDI

The amount of foreign direct investment undertaken over a given time period (normally one year).

Stock of FDI

The total accumulated value of foreign-owned assets at a given time.

Outflows of FDI

Flow of foreign direct investment out of a country.

Inflows of FDI

Flow of foreign direct investment into a country.

TRENDS IN FDI The past 35 years have seen a marked increase in both the flow and stock of FDI in the world economy. The average yearly outflow of FDI increased from \$25 billion in 1975 to \$1.34 trillion in 2014 (see Figure 8.1).[1] Over the past 30 years, the flow of FDI has accelerated faster than the growth in world trade and world output. For example, between 1992 and 2014, the total flow of FDI from all countries increased around ninefold, while world trade by value grew fourfold and world output by around 60 percent.[2] As a result of the strong FDI flows, by 2014 the global stock of FDI was about \$25 trillion. The foreign

8.1 FIGURE

FDI Outflows, 1980–2014 (\$ billions).

Source: UNCTAD statistical data set. http://unctadstat.unctad.org.

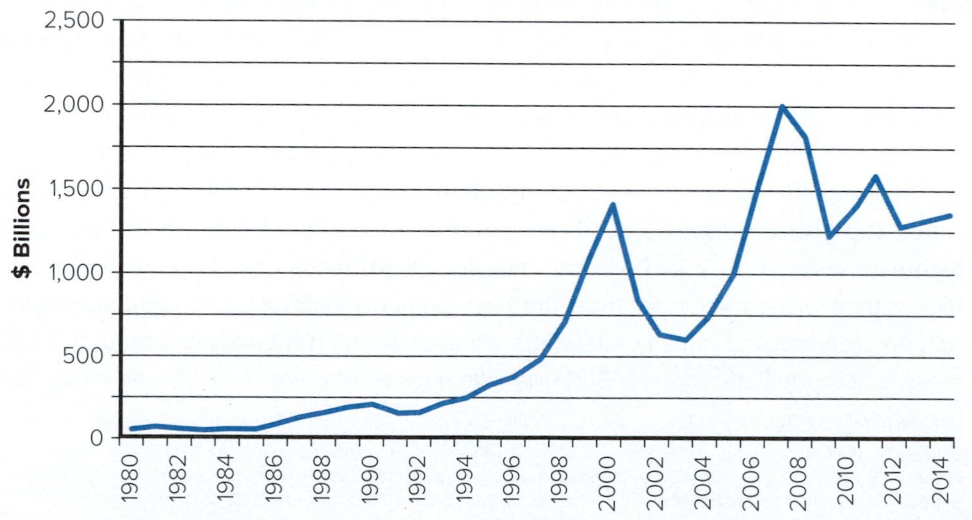

affiliates of multinationals had more than $28 trillion in global sales and accounted for one-third of all cross-border trade in goods and services.[3] Clearly by any measure, FDI is a very important phenomenon.

FDI has grown more rapidly than world trade and world output for several reasons. First, despite the general decline in trade barriers over the past 30 years, firms still fear protectionist pressures. Executives see FDI as a way of circumventing future trade barriers. Second, much of the increase in FDI has been driven by the political and economic changes that have been occurring in many of the world's developing nations. The general shift toward democratic political institutions and free market economies that we discussed in Chapter 3 has encouraged FDI. Across much of Asia, eastern Europe, and Latin America, economic growth, economic deregulation, privatization programs that are open to foreign investors, and removal of many restrictions on FDI have made these countries more attractive to foreign multinationals. According to the United Nations, some 90 percent of the 2,700 changes made worldwide between 1992 and 2009 in the laws governing foreign direct investment created a more favorable environment for FDI.[4]

The globalization of the world economy is also having a positive effect on the volume of FDI. Many firms see the whole world as their market, and they are undertaking FDI in an attempt to make sure they have a significant presence in many regions of the world. For example, a third of the revenues and as much as 40 percent of the profits of firms in the S&P 500 index are generated abroad. For reasons that we explore later in this book, many firms now believe it is important to have production facilities close to their major customers. This too creates pressure for greater FDI.

THE DIRECTION OF FDI

Historically, most FDI has been directed at the developed nations of the world as firms based in advanced countries invested in the others' markets (see Figure 8.2). During the 1980s and 1990s, the United States was often the favorite target for FDI inflows. The United States has been an attractive target for FDI because of its large and wealthy domestic markets, its dynamic and stable economy, a favorable political environment, and the openness of the country to FDI. Investors include firms based in Great Britain, Japan, Germany, Holland, and France. Inward investment into the United States remained high during the 2000s and stood at $92 billion in 2014. The developed nations of the European Union have also been recipients of significant FDI inflows, principally from the United States and other member states of the EU. In 2014, inward investment into the EU was $258 billion. The United Kingdom and France have historically been the largest recipients of inward FDI.[5]

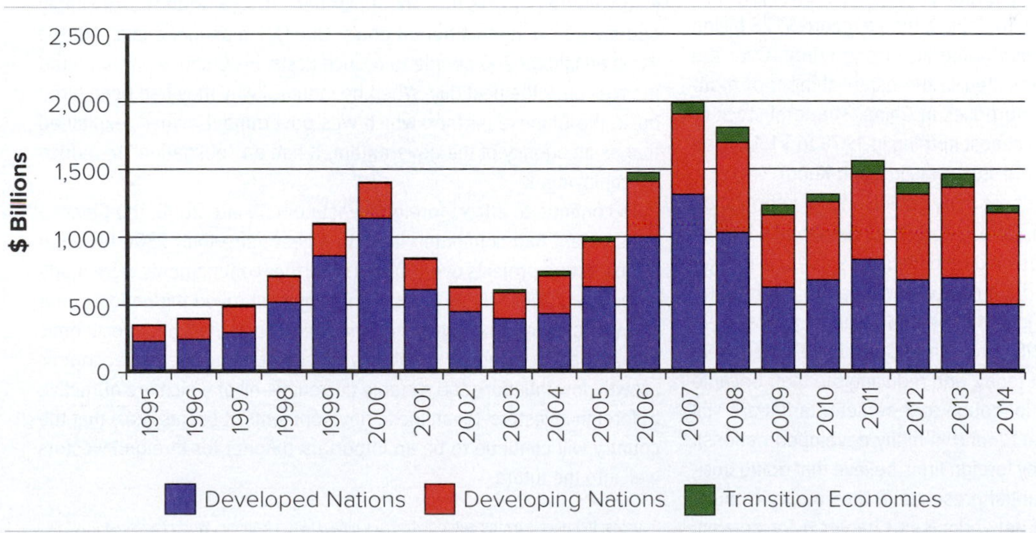

8.2 FIGURE

FDI Inflows by Region, 1995–2014 ($ billions).

Source: United Nations World Investment Report, various editions.

Even though developed nations still account for the largest share of FDI inflows, FDI into developing nations and the transition economies of eastern Europe and the old Soviet Union has increased markedly (see Figure 8.2). Most recent inflows into developing nations have been targeted at the emerging economies of Southeast Asia. Driving much of the increase has been the growing importance of China as a recipient of FDI, which attracted about $60 billion of FDI in 2004 and rose steadily to hit a record $128 billion in 2014.[6] The reasons for the strong flow of investment into China are discussed in the accompanying Country Focus. Latin America is the next most important region in the developing world for FDI inflows. In 2014, total inward investments into this region reached $160 billion. Brazil has historically been the top recipient of inward FDI in Latin America. At the other end of the scale, Africa has long received the smallest amount of inward investment, $54 billion in 2014. In recent years, Chinese enterprises have emerged as major investors in Africa, particularly in extraction industries, where they seem to be trying to ensure future supplies of valuable raw materials. The inability of Africa to attract greater investment is in part a reflection of the political unrest, armed conflict, and frequent changes in economic policy in the region.[7]

Did You Know?
Did you know that America is the world's largest foreign investor?

Visit your Connect SmartBook® to view a short video explanation from the authors.

THE SOURCE OF FDI Since World War II, the United States has consistently been the largest source country for FDI. Other important source countries include the United Kingdom, France, Germany, the Netherlands, and Japan. Collectively, these six countries accounted for 60 percent of all FDI outflows for 1998–2014 (see Figure 8.3). As might be expected, these countries also predominate in rankings of the world's largest multinationals.[8] These nations dominate primarily because they were the most developed nations with the largest economies during

country FOCUS

Foreign Direct Investment in China

Beginning in late 1978, China's leadership decided to move the economy away from a centrally planned socialist system to one that was more market driven. The result has been 35 years of sustained high economic growth rates of around 8–10 percent, compounded annually. This growth attracted substantial foreign investment. Starting from a tiny base, foreign investment increased to an annual average rate of $2.7 billion between 1985 and 1990 and then surged to $40 billion annually in the late 1990s, making China the second-biggest recipient of FDI inflows in the world after the United States. The growth has continued, with inward investments into China hitting a record $128 billion in 2014 (with another $103 billion going into Hong Kong). Over the past 20 years, this inflow has resulted in the establishment of more than 300,000 foreign-funded enterprises in China. The total stock of FDI in mainland China grew from almost nothing in 1978 to $1.1 trillion in 2014 (another $1.5 trillion of FDI stock was in Hong Kong).

The reasons for this investment are fairly obvious. With a population of more than 1.3 billion people, China represents the world's largest market. Historically, import tariffs made it difficult to serve this market via exports, so FDI was required if a company wanted to tap into the country's huge potential. China joined the World Trade Organization in 2001. As a result, average tariff rates on imports have fallen from 15.4 percent to about 8 percent today, and reducing the tariff became a motive for investing in China (although at 8 percent, tariffs are still above the average of 3.5 percent found in many developed nations). Notwithstanding tariff rates, many foreign firms believe that doing business in China requires a substantial presence in the country to build *guanxi,* the crucial relationship networks (see Chapter 4 for details). Furthermore, a combination of relatively inexpensive labor and tax incentives, particularly for enterprises that establish themselves in special economic zones, makes China an attractive base from which to serve Asian or world markets with exports (although rising labor costs in China are now making this less important).

Less obvious, at least to begin with, was how difficult it would be for foreign firms to do business in China. China may have a huge population, but despite decades of rapid growth, it is still relatively poor. The lack of purchasing power translates into a relatively immature market for many Western consumer goods outside affluent urban areas such as Shanghai. Other problems include a highly regulated environment, which can make it problematic to conduct business transactions, and shifting tax and regulatory regimes. Then there are problems with local joint-venture partners that are inexperienced, opportunistic, or simply operate according to different goals. One U.S. manager explained that when he laid off 200 people to reduce costs, his Chinese partner hired them all back the next day. When he inquired why they had been hired back, the Chinese partner, which was government-owned, explained that as an agency of the government, it had an "obligation" to reduce unemployment.

To continue to attract foreign investment, in late 2000, the Chinese government had committed itself to invest more than $800 billion in infrastructure projects over 10 years. Further commitments were made in the late 2000s. These investments have improved the nation's poor highway system. The government has been pursuing a macroeconomic policy that includes an emphasis on maintaining steady economic growth, low inflation, and a stable currency—all of which are attractive to foreign investors. Given these developments, it seems likely that the country will continue to be an important magnet for foreign investors well into the future.

Sources: Interviews by the author while in China; United Nations, *World Investment Report, 2015;* Linda Ng and C. Tuan, "Building a Favorable Investment Environment: Evidence for the Facilitation of FDI in China," *The World Economy,* 2002, pp. 1095–114; S. Chan and G. Qingyang, "Investment in China Migrates Inland," *Far Eastern Economic Review,* May 2006, pp. 52–57.

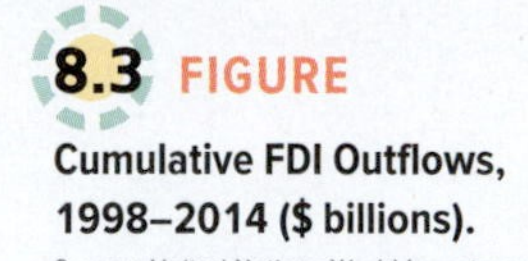

8.3 FIGURE

Cumulative FDI Outflows, 1998–2014 ($ billions).

Source: United Nations World Investment Report, various editions.

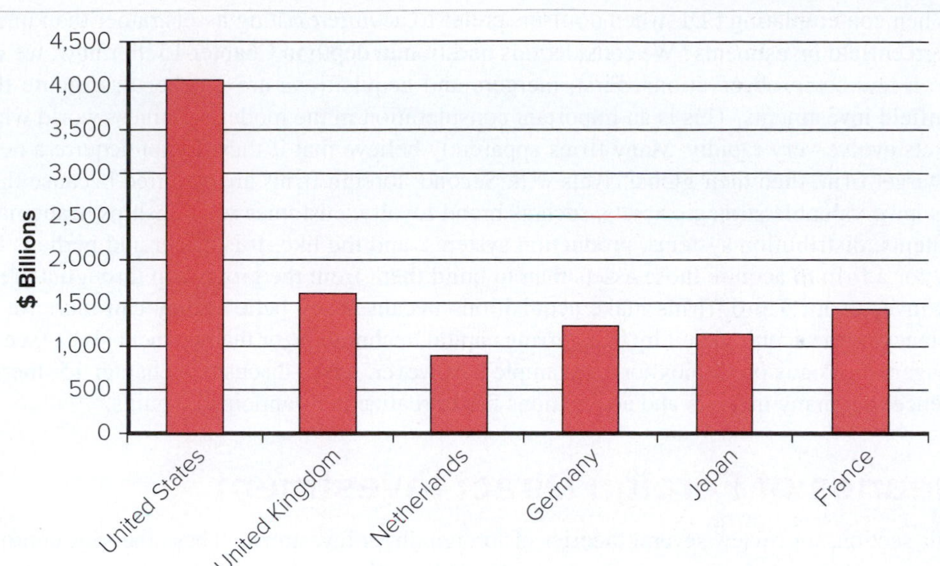

much of the postwar period and therefore home to many of the largest and best-capitalized enterprises. Many of these countries also had a long history as trading nations and naturally looked to foreign markets to fuel their economic expansion. Thus, it is no surprise that enterprises based there have been at the forefront of foreign investment trends.

That being said, it is noteworthy that Chinese firms have started to emerge as major foreign investors. In 2005, Chinese firms invested some $12 billion internationally. Since then, the figure has risen steadily, reaching $116 billion in 2014. Firms based in Hong Kong accounted for another $142 billion of outward FDI in 2014. Much of the outward investment by Chinese firms has been directed at extractive industries in less developed nations (e.g., China has been a major investor in African countries). A major motive for these investments has been to gain access to raw materials, of which China is one of the world's largest consumers. There are signs, however, that Chinese firms are starting to turn their attention to more advanced nations. In 2014, Chinese firms invested $13 billion in the United States, up from $146 million in 2003. Perhaps even more striking, in the first six weeks of 2016, Chinese firms announced takeover bids of Western firms valued at $81.5 billion, with half of this value involving takeovers of U.S. enterprises.[9]

Greenfield Investment

Establishing a new operation in a foreign country.

THE FORM OF FDI: ACQUISITIONS VERSUS GREENFIELD INVESTMENTS

FDI takes on two main forms. The first is a **greenfield investment**, which involves the establishment of a new operation in a foreign country. The second involves acquiring or merging with an existing firm in the foreign country. UN estimates indicate that some 40 to 80 percent of all FDI inflows were in the form of mergers and acquisitions between 1998 and 2014.[10] However, FDI flows into developed nations differ markedly from those into developing nations. In the case of developing nations, only about one-third or less of FDI is in the form of cross-border mergers and acquisitions. The lower percentage of mergers and acquisitions may simply reflect the fact that there are fewer target firms to acquire in developing nations.

Which Is Better, an Acquisition or a Greenfield Investment?

A greenfield investment is an establishment of a new operation in a foreign country (i.e., a parent company starts a new venture in a foreign country by building new production facilities from the ground up). The acquisition approach refers to buying or merging operations with an existing firm in a foreign country. In the text of Chapters 8 and 13, we discuss reasons for greenfield and acquisition-based investments in a foreign country. While mergers and acquisitions (M&A) are typically quicker to execute than building something from literally the ground up, M&A often fail to gain the advantages expected. The failure rate of M&A is somewhere between 50 and 83 percent. At the same time, the trend shows that both the number of M&A and the sums of money spent on M&A are increasingly consistently every year. If you were making the decision, would you prefer to make a greenfield investment or to engage in either a merger or acquisition in a foreign country?

Source: Y. Weber, C. Oberg, and S. Tarba, "The M&A Paradox: Factors of Success and Failure in Mergers and Acquisitions," *Comprehensive Guide to Mergers & Acquisitions, A: Managing the Critical Success Factors Across Every Stage of the M&A Process* (Upper Saddle River, NJ: FT Press, 2013).

When contemplating FDI, when do firms prefer to acquire existing assets rather than undertake greenfield investments? We consider this question in depth in Chapter 15. For now, we will make a few basic observations. First, mergers and acquisitions are quicker to execute than greenfield investments. This is an important consideration in the modern business world where markets evolve very rapidly. Many firms apparently believe that if they do not acquire a desirable target firm, then their global rivals will. Second, foreign firms are acquired because those firms have valuable strategic assets, such as brand loyalty, customer relationships, trademarks or patents, distribution systems, production systems, and the like. It is easier and perhaps less risky for a firm to acquire those assets than to build them from the ground up through a greenfield investment. Third, firms make acquisitions because they believe they can increase the efficiency of the acquired unit by transferring capital, technology, or management skills (see the Management Focus on Cemex for an example). However, as we discuss in Chapter 15, there is evidence that many mergers and acquisitions fail to realize their anticipated gains.[11]

test PREP

Use SmartBook to help retain what you have learned. Access your Instructor's Connect course to check out SmartBook or go to learnsmartadvantage.com for help.

LO 8-2

Explain the different theories of FDI.

Theories of Foreign Direct Investment

In this section, we review several theories of foreign direct investment. These theories approach the various phenomena of foreign direct investment from three complementary perspectives. One set of theories seeks to explain why a firm will favor direct investment as a means of entering a foreign market when two other alternatives, exporting and licensing, are open to it. Another set of theories seeks to explain why firms in the same industry often undertake foreign direct investment at the same time and why they favor certain locations over others as targets for foreign direct investment. Put differently, these theories attempt to explain the observed *pattern* of foreign direct investment flows. A third theoretical perspective, known as the **eclectic paradigm**, attempts to combine the two other perspectives into a single holistic explanation of foreign direct investment (this theoretical perspective is *eclectic* because the best aspects of other theories are taken and combined into a single explanation).

Eclectic Paradigm

Argument that combining location-specific assets or resource endowments and the firm's own unique assets often requires FDI; it requires the firm to establish production facilities where those foreign assets or resource endowments are located.

WHY FOREIGN DIRECT INVESTMENT?

Why do firms go to the trouble of establishing operations abroad through foreign direct investment when two alternatives, exporting and licensing, are available to them for exploiting the profit opportunities in a foreign market? **Exporting** involves producing goods at home and then shipping them to the receiving country for sale. **Licensing** involves granting a foreign entity (the licensee) the right to produce and sell the firm's product in return for a royalty fee on every unit sold. The question is important, given that a cursory examination of the topic suggests that foreign direct investment may be both expensive and risky compared with exporting and licensing. FDI is expensive because a firm must bear the costs of establishing production facilities in a foreign country or of acquiring a foreign enterprise. FDI is risky because of the problems associated with doing business in a different culture where the rules of the game may be very different. Relative to indigenous firms, there is a greater probability that a foreign firm undertaking FDI in a country for the first time will make costly mistakes due to its ignorance. When a firm exports, it need not bear the costs associated with FDI, and it can reduce the risks associated with selling abroad by using a native sales agent. Similarly, when a firm allows another enterprise to produce its products under license, the licensee bears the costs or risks (this is why fashion retailer Burberry originally entered Japan via a licensing contract with a Japanese retailer: see the opening case). So why do so many firms apparently prefer FDI over either exporting or licensing? The answer can be found by examining the limitations of exporting and licensing as means for capitalizing on foreign market opportunities.

Exporting

Sale of products produced in one country to residents of another country.

Licensing

Occurs when a firm (the licensor) licenses the right to produce its product, use its production processes, or use its brand name or trademark to another firm (the licensee). In return for giving the licensee these rights, the licensor collects a royalty fee on every unit the licensee sells.

Limitations of Exporting

The viability of an exporting strategy is often constrained by transportation costs and trade barriers. When transportation costs are added to production costs, it becomes unprofitable to ship some products over a large distance. This is particularly true of products that have a low value-to-weight ratio and that can be produced in almost any location. For such products, the attractiveness of exporting decreases, relative to either FDI or licensing. This is the case, for example, with cement. Thus, Cemex, the large Mexican cement maker, has expanded internationally by pursuing FDI, rather than exporting (see the accompanying

RANKINGS

Cross-border investments have been ramped up to a relatively large degree in the last decade. Even with the economic downturn that started in 2008, the world continued to see a great deal of foreign direct investment by companies in the last decade. Now, when the economic prosperity is likely to be better, given that we are removed from those downturn days, the expectation is that more foreign direct investment will be considered by companies. On globalEDGE™, there are myriad opportunities to gain more knowledge about foreign direct investment (FDI). The "Rankings" section is a great starting point (globaledge.msu.edu/global-resources/rankings). In this section, globalEDGE™ features several reports by A.T. Kearney—with one of them squarely centered on foreign direct investment and a "confidence index" for FDI. The companies that participate in the regular study account for more than $2 trillion in annual global revenue! Which countries are in the top three in the investment confidence index, and do you agree that the three countries are the best ones to invest in if you were running a company?

Management Focus). For products with a high value-to-weight ratio, however, transportation costs are normally a minor component of total landed cost (e.g., electronic components, personal computers, medical equipment, computer software, etc.) and have little impact on the relative attractiveness of exporting, licensing, and FDI.

management FOCUS

Foreign Direct Investment by Cemex

Over the last two decades, Mexico's largest cement manufacturer, Cemex, has transformed itself from a primarily Mexican operation into the second-largest cement company in the world behind Lafarge Group of France. Cemex has long been a powerhouse in Mexico and currently controls more than 60 percent of the market for cement in that country. Cemex's domestic success has been based in large part on an obsession with efficient manufacturing and a focus on customer service that is tops in the industry.

Cemex is a leader in using information technology to match production with consumer demand. The company sells ready-mixed cement that can survive for only about 90 minutes before solidifying, so precise delivery is important. But Cemex can never predict with total certainty what demand will be on any given day, week, or month. To better manage unpredictable demand patterns, Cemex developed a system of seamless information technology—including truck-mounted global positioning systems, radio transmitters, satellites, and computer hardware—that allows it to control the production and distribution of cement like no other company can, responding quickly to unanticipated changes in demand and reducing waste. The results are lower costs and superior customer service, both differentiating factors for Cemex.

Cemex's international expansion strategy was driven by a number of factors. First, the company wished to reduce its reliance on the Mexican construction market, which was characterized by very volatile demand. Second, the company realized there was tremendous demand for cement in many developing countries, where significant construction was being undertaken or needed. Third, the company believed that it understood the needs of construction businesses in developing nations better than the established multinational cement companies, all of which were from developed nations. Fourth, Cemex believed that it could create significant value by acquiring inefficient cement companies in other markets and transferring its skills in customer service, marketing, information technology, and production management to those units.

The company embarked in earnest on its international expansion strategy in the early 1990s. Initially, Cemex targeted other developing nations, acquiring established cement makers in Venezuela, Colombia, Indonesia, the Philippines, Egypt, and several other countries. It also purchased two stagnant companies in Spain and turned them around. Bolstered by the success of its Spanish ventures, Cemex began to look for expansion opportunities in developed nations. In 2000, Cemex purchased Houston-based Southland, one of the largest cement companies in the United States, for $2.5 billion. Following the Southland acquisition, Cemex had 56 cement plants in 30 countries, most of which were gained through acquisitions. In all cases, Cemex devoted great attention to transferring its technological, management and marketing know-how to acquired units, thereby improving their performance.

In 2004, Cemex made another major foreign investment move, purchasing RMC of Great Britain for $5.8 billion. RMC was a huge multinational cement firm with sales of $8 billion, only 22 percent of which were in the United Kingdom, and operations in more than 20 other nations, including many European nations where Cemex had no presence. Finalized in March 2005, the RMC acquisition transformed Cemex into a global powerhouse in the cement industry. Today it generates more than $15 billion in annual sales and operations in 50 countries. Only about a third of the company's sales are now generated in Mexico.

Sources: C. Piggott, "Cemex's Stratospheric Rise," *Latin Finance*, March 2001, p. 76; J. F. Smith, "Making Cement a Household Word," *Los Angeles Times*, January 16, 2000, p. C1; D. Helft, "Cemex Attempts to Cement Its Future," *The Industry Standard*, November 6, 2000; Diane Lindquist, "From Cement to Services," *Chief Executive*, November 2002, pp. 48–50; "Cementing Global Success," *Strategic Direct Investor*, March 2003, p. 1; M. T. Derham, "The Cemex Surprise," *Latin Finance*, November 2004, pp. 1–2; "Holcim Seeks to Acquire Aggregate," *The Wall Street Journal*, January 13, 2005, p. 1; J. Lyons, "Cemex Prowls for Deals in Both China and India," *The Wall Street Journal*, January 27, 2006, p. C4; S. Donnan, "Cemex Sells 25 Percent Stake in Semen Gresik," *FT.com*, May 4, 2006, p. 1.

Transportation costs aside, some firms undertake foreign direct investment as a response to actual or threatened trade barriers such as import tariffs or quotas. By placing tariffs on imported goods, governments can increase the cost of exporting relative to foreign direct investment and licensing. Similarly, by limiting imports through quotas, governments increase the attractiveness of FDI and licensing. For example, the wave of FDI by Japanese auto companies in the United States that started in the mid 1980s and continues to this day has been partly driven by protectionist threats from Congress and by tariffs on the importation of Japanese vehicles, particularly light trucks (SUVs), which still face a 25 percent import tariff into the United States. For Japanese auto companies, these factors decreased the profitability of exporting and increased that of foreign direct investment. In this context, it is important to understand that trade barriers do not have to be physically in place for FDI to be favored over exporting. Often, the desire to reduce the threat that trade barriers might be imposed is enough to justify foreign direct investment as an alternative to exporting.

Internalization Theory
Marketing imperfection approach to foreign direct investment.

Market Imperfections
Imperfections in the operation of the market mechanism.

Limitations of Licensing

A branch of economic theory known as **internalization theory** seeks to explain why firms often prefer foreign direct investment over licensing as a strategy for entering foreign markets (this approach is also known as the **market imperfections** approach).[12] According to internalization theory, licensing has three major drawbacks as a strategy for exploiting foreign market opportunities. First, *licensing may result in a firm's giving away valuable technological know-how to a potential foreign competitor*. For example, in the 1960s, RCA licensed its leading-edge color television technology to a number of Japanese companies, including Matsushita and Sony. At the time, RCA saw licensing as a way to earn a good return from its technological know-how in the Japanese market without the costs and risks associated with foreign direct investment. However, Matsushita and Sony quickly assimilated RCA's technology and used it to enter the U.S. market to compete directly against RCA. As a result, RCA is now a minor player in its home market, while Matsushita and Sony have a much bigger market share.

A second problem is that *licensing does not give a firm the tight control over manufacturing, marketing, and strategy in a foreign country that may be required to maximize its profitability.* With licensing, control over manufacturing, marketing, and strategy are granted to a licensee in return for a royalty fee. However, for both strategic and operational reasons, a firm may want to retain control over these functions. One reason for wanting control over the *strategy* of a foreign entity is that a firm might want its foreign subsidiary to price and market very aggressively as a way of keeping a foreign competitor in check. Unlike a wholly owned subsidiary, a licensee would probably not accept such an imposition, because it would likely reduce the licensee's profit, or it might even cause the licensee to take a loss. Another reason for wanting control over the *strategy* of a foreign entity is to make sure that the entity does not damage the firm's brand. This was the primary reason fashion retailer Burberry terminated its licensing agreement in Japan and switched to a strategy of direct ownership of its own retail stores in the Japanese market (see the opening case for details).

One reason for wanting control over the *operations* of a foreign entity is that the firm might wish to take advantage of differences in factor costs across countries, producing only part of its final product in a given country, while importing other parts from where they can be produced at lower cost. Again, a licensee would be unlikely to accept such an arrangement, since it would limit the licensee's autonomy. For reasons such as these, when tight control over a foreign entity is desirable, foreign direct investment is preferable to licensing.

A third problem with licensing arises when the firm's competitive advantage is based not as much on its products as on the management, marketing, and manufacturing capabilities that produce those products. The problem here is that *such capabilities are often not amenable to licensing*. While a foreign licensee may be able to physically reproduce the firm's product under license, it often may not be able to do so as efficiently as the firm could itself. As a result, the licensee may not be able to fully exploit the profit potential inherent in a foreign market.

For example, consider Toyota, a company whose competitive advantage in the global auto industry is acknowledged to come from its superior ability to manage the overall process of designing, engineering, manufacturing, and selling automobiles—that is, from its management and organizational capabilities. Indeed, Toyota is credited with pioneering the development of a new production process, known as *lean production,* that enables it to produce higher-quality automobiles at a lower cost than its global rivals.[13] Although Toyota could license certain products, its real competitive advantage comes from its management and process capabilities. These kinds of skills are difficult to articulate or codify; they certainly cannot be written down in a simple licensing contract. They are organization-wide and have been developed over the years. They are not embodied in any one individual but instead are widely dispersed throughout the company. Put another way, Toyota's skills are embedded in its organizational culture, and culture is something that cannot be licensed. Thus, if Toyota were to allow a foreign entity to produce its cars under license, the chances are that the entity could not do so as efficiently as could Toyota. In turn, this would limit the ability of the foreign entity to fully develop the market potential of that product. Such reasoning underlies Toyota's preference for direct investment in foreign markets, as opposed to allowing foreign automobile companies to produce its cars under license.

All of this suggests that when one or more of the following conditions holds, markets fail as a mechanism for selling know-how and FDI is more profitable than licensing: (1) when the firm has valuable know-how that cannot be adequately protected by a licensing contract, (2) when the firm needs tight control over a foreign entity to maximize its market share and earnings in that country, and (3) when a firm's skills and know-how are not amenable to licensing.

Advantages of Foreign Direct Investment

It follows that a firm will favor foreign direct investment over exporting as an entry strategy when transportation costs or trade barriers make exporting unattractive. Furthermore, the firm will favor foreign direct investment over licensing (or franchising) when it wishes to maintain control over its technological know-how, or over its operations and business strategy, or when the firm's capabilities are simply not amenable to licensing, as may often be the case.

THE PATTERN OF FOREIGN DIRECT INVESTMENT

Observation suggests that firms in the same industry often undertake foreign direct investment at about the same time. Also, firms tend to direct their investment activities toward the same target markets. The two theories we consider in this section attempt to explain the patterns that we observe in FDI flows.

Strategic Behavior

One theory is based on the idea that FDI flows are a reflection of strategic rivalry between firms in the global marketplace. An early variant of this argument was expounded by F. T. Knickerbocker, who looked at the relationship between FDI and rivalry in oligopolistic industries.[14] An **oligopoly** is an industry composed of a limited number of large firms (e.g., an industry in which four firms control 80 percent of a domestic market would be defined as an oligopoly). A critical competitive feature of such industries is interdependence of the major players: What one firm does can have an immediate impact on the major competitors, forcing a response in kind. By cutting prices, one firm in an oligopoly can take market share away from its competitors, forcing them to respond with similar price cuts to retain their market share. Thus, the interdependence between firms in an oligopoly leads to imitative behavior; rivals often quickly imitate what a firm does in an oligopoly.

Oligopoly
An industry composed of a limited number of large firms.

Imitative behavior can take many forms in an oligopoly. One firm raises prices, and the others follow; one expands capacity, and the rivals imitate lest they be left at a disadvantage in the future. Knickerbocker argued that the same kind of imitative behavior characterizes FDI. Consider an oligopoly in the United States in which three firms—A, B, and C—dominate the market. Firm A establishes a subsidiary in France. Firms B and C decide that if successful, this new subsidiary may knock out their export business to France and give a first-mover advantage to firm A. Furthermore, firm A might discover some competitive asset in France that it could repatriate to the United States to torment firms B and C on their native soil. Given these possibilities, firms B and C decide to follow firm A and establish operations in France.

Studies that have looked at FDI by U.S. firms show that firms based in oligopolistic industries tended to imitate each other's FDI.[15] The same phenomenon has been observed with regard to FDI undertaken by Japanese firms.[16] For example, Toyota and Nissan responded to investments by Honda in the United States and Europe by undertaking their own FDI in the United States and Europe. Research has also shown that models of strategic behavior in a global oligopoly can explain the pattern of FDI in the global tire industry.[17]

Multipoint Competition

Arises when two or more enterprises encounter each other in different regional markets, national markets, or industries.

Knickerbocker's theory can be extended to embrace the concept of multipoint competition. **Multipoint competition** arises when two or more enterprises encounter each other in different regional markets, national markets, or industries.[18] Economic theory suggests that rather like chess players jockeying for advantage, firms will try to match each other's moves in different markets to try to hold each other in check. The idea is to ensure that a rival does not gain a commanding position in one market and then use the profits generated there to subsidize competitive attacks in other markets.

Although Knickerbocker's theory and its extensions can help explain imitative FDI behavior by firms in oligopolistic industries, it does not explain why the first firm in an oligopoly decides to undertake FDI rather than to export or license. Internalization theory addresses this phenomenon. The imitative theory also does not address the issue of whether FDI is more efficient than exporting or licensing for expanding abroad. Again, internalization theory addresses the efficiency issue. For these reasons, many economists favor internalization theory as an explanation for FDI, although most would agree that the imitative explanation tells an important part of the story.

THE ECLECTIC PARADIGM

The eclectic paradigm has been championed by the British economist John Dunning.[19] Dunning argues that in addition to the various factors discussed earlier, location-specific advantages are also of considerable importance in explaining both the rationale for and the direction of foreign direct investment. By **location-specific advantages**, Dunning means the advantages that arise from utilizing resource endowments or assets that are tied to a particular foreign location and that a firm finds valuable to combine with its own unique assets (such as the firm's technological, marketing, or management capabilities). Dunning accepts the argument of internalization theory that it is difficult for a firm to license its own unique capabilities and know-how. Therefore, he argues that combining location-specific assets or resource endowments with the firm's own unique capabilities often requires foreign direct investment. That is, it requires the firm to establish production facilities where those foreign assets or resource endowments are located.

Location-Specific Advantages

Advantages that arise from using resource endowments or assets that are tied to a particular foreign location and that a firm finds valuable to combine with its own unique assets (such as the firm's technological, marketing, or management know-how).

An obvious example of Dunning's arguments are natural resources, such as oil and other minerals, which are by their character specific to certain locations. Dunning suggests that to exploit such foreign resources, a firm must undertake FDI. Clearly, this explains the FDI undertaken by many of the world's oil companies, which have to invest where oil is located in order to combine their technological and managerial capabilities with this valuable location-specific resource. Another obvious example is valuable human resources, such as low-cost, highly skilled labor. The cost and skill of labor varies from country to country. Because labor is not internationally mobile, according to Dunning it makes sense for a firm to locate production facilities in those countries where the cost and skills of local labor are most suited to its particular production processes.

However, Dunning's theory has implications that go beyond basic resources such as minerals and labor. Consider Silicon Valley, which is the world center for the computer and semiconductor industry. Many of the world's major computer and semiconductor companies—such as Apple Computer, Hewlett-Packard, Oracle, Google, and Intel—are located close to each other in the Silicon Valley region of California. As a result, much of the cutting-edge research and product development in computers and semiconductors occurs there. According to Dunning's arguments, knowledge being generated in Silicon Valley with regard to the design and manufacture of computers and semiconductors is available nowhere else in the world. To be sure, that knowledge is commercialized as it diffuses throughout the world, but the leading edge of knowledge generation in the computer and semiconductor industries is to be found in Silicon Valley. In Dunning's language, this means that Silicon Valley has a *location-specific advantage* in the generation of knowledge related to the computer and semiconductor industries. In part, this advantage comes from the sheer concentration of intellectual talent in this area, and in part, it arises from a network of informal contacts that allows firms to benefit from each other's knowledge generation. Economists refer to such knowledge "spillovers" as **externalities**, and there is a well-established theory suggesting that firms can benefit from such externalities by locating close to their source.[20]

Externalities

Knowledge spillovers.

test PREP

Use SmartBook to help retain what you have learned. Access your Instructor's Connect course to check out SmartBook or go to learnsmartadvantage.com for help.

Insofar as this is the case, it makes sense for foreign computer and semiconductor firms to invest in research and, perhaps, production facilities so they too can learn about and utilize valuable new knowledge before those based elsewhere, thereby giving them a competitive advantage in the global marketplace.[21] Evidence suggests that European, Japanese, South Korean, and

Taiwanese computer and semiconductor firms are investing in the Silicon Valley region precisely because they wish to benefit from the externalities that arise there.[22] Others have argued that direct investment by foreign firms in the U.S. biotechnology industry has been motivated by desires to gain access to the unique location-specific technological knowledge of U.S. biotechnology firms.[23] Dunning's theory, therefore, seems to be a useful addition to those outlined previously, because it helps explain how location factors affect the direction of FDI.[24]

Silicon Valley, where Google is based, has long been known as the epicenter of the computer and semiconductor industry.

Source: © Phillip Bond/Alamy Stock Photo

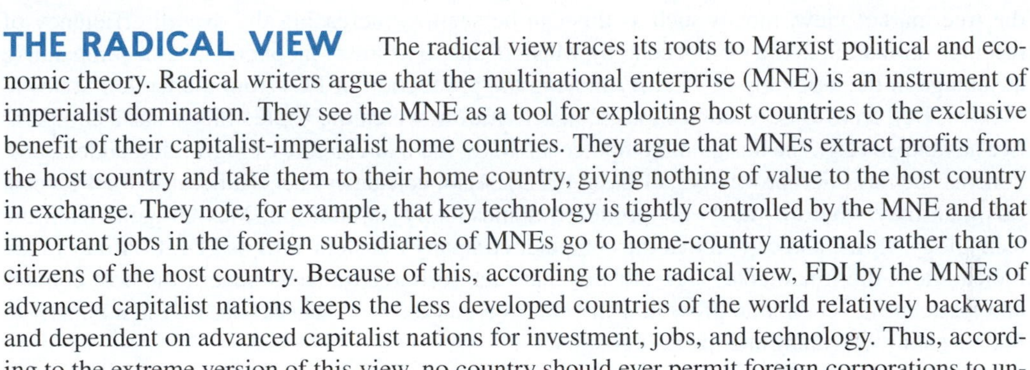

Political Ideology and Foreign Direct Investment

Historically, political ideology toward FDI within a nation has ranged from a dogmatic radical stance that is hostile to all inward FDI at one extreme to an adherence to the noninterventionist principle of free market economics at the other. Between these two extremes is an approach that might be called *pragmatic nationalism*.

LO 8-3

Understand how political ideology shapes a government's attitudes toward FDI.

THE RADICAL VIEW

The radical view traces its roots to Marxist political and economic theory. Radical writers argue that the multinational enterprise (MNE) is an instrument of imperialist domination. They see the MNE as a tool for exploiting host countries to the exclusive benefit of their capitalist-imperialist home countries. They argue that MNEs extract profits from the host country and take them to their home country, giving nothing of value to the host country in exchange. They note, for example, that key technology is tightly controlled by the MNE and that important jobs in the foreign subsidiaries of MNEs go to home-country nationals rather than to citizens of the host country. Because of this, according to the radical view, FDI by the MNEs of advanced capitalist nations keeps the less developed countries of the world relatively backward and dependent on advanced capitalist nations for investment, jobs, and technology. Thus, according to the extreme version of this view, no country should ever permit foreign corporations to undertake FDI, because they can never be instruments of economic development, only of economic domination. Where MNEs already exist in a country, they should be immediately nationalized.[25]

From 1945 until the 1980s, the radical view was very influential in the world economy. Until the collapse of communism between 1989 and 1991, the countries of eastern Europe were opposed to FDI. Similarly, communist countries elsewhere—such as China, Cambodia, and Cuba—were all opposed in principle to FDI (although, in practice, the Chinese started to allow FDI in mainland China in the 1970s). Many socialist countries—particularly in Africa, where one of the first actions of many newly independent states was to nationalize foreign-owned enterprises—also embraced the radical position. Countries whose political ideology was more nationalistic than socialistic further embraced the radical position. This was true in Iran and India, for example, both of which adopted tough policies restricting FDI and nationalized many foreign-owned enterprises. Iran is a particularly interesting case because its Islamic government, while rejecting Marxist theory, has essentially embraced the radical view that FDI by MNEs is an instrument of imperialism.

By the early 1990s, the radical position was in widespread retreat. There seem to be three reasons for this: (1) the collapse of communism in eastern Europe; (2) the generally abysmal economic performance of those countries that embraced the

Are They Friends or Not—India and Pakistan?

For many years, since the partition of British India in 1947 and the creation of India and Pakistan, these two South Asian countries have been involved in numerous wars, border skirmishes, and military stand-offs. The dispute for Kashmir has been the main reason in most interactions, with a notable exception being the Indo-Pakistani War of 1971, when the conflict started because of turmoil in East Pakistan (now called Bangladesh). However, in trying to improve the economic ties between the two nations, India recently announced that it will allow FDI from Pakistan, paving the way for industries from the neighboring country to set up businesses in the growing Indian market. While this is a prime example of how free markets are promoting trade between countries that have not traditionally enjoyed stable political relationships with each other, the question is also on what grounds cross-border interaction is founded. What do you think? Can countries that have been long-standing enemies normalize their relationship simply based on foreign direct investment opportunities?

Source: www.hindustantimes.com.

radical position, and a growing belief by many of these countries that FDI can be an important source of technology and jobs and can stimulate economic growth; and (3) the strong economic performance of those developing countries that embraced capitalism rather than radical ideology (e.g., Singapore, Hong Kong, and Taiwan). Despite this, the radical view lingers on in some countries, such as Venezuela, where the government of Hugo Chávez and his successor, Nicolás Maduro, both viewed foreign multinationals as an instrument of domination.

THE FREE MARKET VIEW The free market view traces its roots to classical economics and the international trade theories of Adam Smith and David Ricardo (see Chapter 6). The intellectual case for this view has been strengthened by the internalization explanation of FDI. The free market view argues that international production should be distributed among countries according to the theory of comparative advantage. Countries should specialize in the production of those goods and services that they can produce most efficiently. Within this framework, the MNE is an instrument for dispersing the production of goods and services to the most efficient locations around the globe. Viewed this way, FDI by the MNE increases the overall efficiency of the world economy.

Imagine that Dell decided to move assembly operations for many of its personal computers from the United States to Mexico to take advantage of lower labor costs in Mexico. According to the free market view, moves such as this can be seen as increasing the overall efficiency of resource utilization in the world economy. Mexico, due to its lower labor costs, has a comparative advantage in the assembly of PCs. By moving the production of PCs from the United States to Mexico, Dell frees U.S. resources for use in activities in which the United States has a comparative advantage (e.g., the design of computer software, the manufacture of high value-added components such as microprocessors, or basic R&D). Also, consumers benefit because the PCs cost less than they would if they were produced domestically. In addition, Mexico gains from the technology, skills, and capital that the computer company transfers with its FDI. Contrary to the radical view, the free market view stresses that such resource transfers benefit the host country and stimulate its economic growth. Thus, the free market view argues that FDI is a benefit to both the source country and the host country.

PRAGMATIC NATIONALISM In practice, many countries have adopted neither a radical policy nor a free market policy toward FDI but instead a policy that can best be described as pragmatic nationalism.[26] The pragmatic nationalist view is that FDI has both benefits and costs. FDI can benefit a host country by bringing capital, skills, technology, and jobs, but those benefits come at a cost. When a foreign company rather than a domestic company produces products, the profits from that investment go abroad. Many countries are also concerned that a foreign-owned manufacturing plant may import many components from its home country, which has negative implications for the host country's balance-of-payments position.

Recognizing this, countries adopting a pragmatic stance pursue policies designed to maximize the national benefits and minimize the national costs. According to this view, FDI should be allowed so long as the benefits outweigh the costs. Japan offers an example of pragmatic nationalism. Until the 1980s, Japan's policy was probably one of the most restrictive among countries adopting a pragmatic nationalist stance. This was due to Japan's perception that direct entry of foreign (especially U.S.) firms with ample managerial resources into the Japanese markets could hamper the development and growth of its own industry and technology.[27] This belief led Japan to block the majority of applications to invest in Japan. However, there were always exceptions to this policy. Firms that had important technology were often permitted to undertake FDI if they insisted that they would neither license their technology to a Japanese firm nor enter into a joint venture with a Japanese enterprise. IBM and Texas Instruments were able to set up wholly owned subsidiaries in Japan by adopting this negotiating position. From the perspective of the Japanese government, the benefits of FDI in such cases—the stimulus that these firms might impart to the Japanese economy—outweighed the perceived costs.

Another aspect of pragmatic nationalism is the tendency to aggressively court FDI believed to be in the national interest by, for example, offering subsidies to foreign MNEs in the form of tax breaks or grants. The countries of the European Union often seem to be competing with each other to attract U.S. and Japanese FDI by offering large tax breaks and subsidies. Britain has been the most successful at attracting Japanese investment in the automobile industry. Nissan, Toyota, and Honda now have major assembly plants in Britain and use the country as their base for serving the rest of Europe—with obvious employment and balance-of-payments benefits for Britain. Similarly, within the United States, individual states often compete with each other to attract FDI, offering generous financial incentives in the form of tax breaks to foreign companies looking to set up operations in the country.

SHIFTING IDEOLOGY

Recent years have seen a marked decline in the number of countries that adhere to a radical ideology. Although few countries have adopted a pure free market policy stance, an increasing number of countries are gravitating toward the free market end of the spectrum and have liberalized their foreign investment regime. This includes many countries that 30 years ago were firmly in the radical camp (e.g., the former communist countries of eastern Europe, many of the socialist countries of Africa, and India) and several countries that until recently could best be described as pragmatic nationalists with regard to FDI (e.g., Japan, South Korea, Italy, Spain, and most Latin American countries). One result has been the surge in the volume of FDI worldwide, which, as we noted earlier, has been growing twice as fast as the growth in world trade. Another result has been an increase in the volume of FDI directed at countries that have recently liberalized their FDI regimes, such as China, India, and Vietnam.

As a counterpoint, there is some evidence of a shift to a more hostile approach to foreign direct investment in some nations. Venezuela and Bolivia have become increasingly hostile to foreign direct investment. In 2005 and 2006, the governments of both nations unilaterally rewrote contracts for oil and gas exploration, raising the royalty rate that foreign enterprises had to pay the government for oil and gas extracted in their territories. Following his election victory in 2006, Bolivian president Evo Morales nationalized the nation's gas fields and stated that he would evict foreign firms unless they agreed to pay about 80 percent of their revenues to the state and relinquish production oversight. In some developed nations, there is increasing evidence of hostile reactions to inward FDI as well. In Europe in 2006, there was a hostile political reaction to the attempted takeover of Europe's largest steel company, Arcelor, by Mittal Steel, a global company controlled by the Indian entrepreneur Lakshmi Mittal. In mid-2005, China National Offshore Oil Company withdrew a takeover bid for Unocal of the United States after highly negative reaction in Congress about the proposed takeover of a "strategic asset" by a Chinese company.

test PREP

Use SmartBook to help retain what you have learned. Access your Instructor's Connect course to check out SmartBook or go to learnsmartadvantage.com for help.

Benefits and Costs of FDI

Describe the benefits and costs of FDI to home and host countries.

To a greater or lesser degree, many governments can be considered pragmatic nationalists when it comes to FDI. Accordingly, their policy is shaped by a consideration of the costs and benefits of FDI. Here, we explore the benefits and costs of FDI, first from the perspective of a host (receiving) country and then from the perspective of the home (source) country. In the next section, we look at the policy instruments governments use to manage FDI.

HOST-COUNTRY BENEFITS

The main benefits of inward FDI for a host country arise from resource-transfer effects, employment effects, balance-of-payments effects, and effects on competition and economic growth.

Resource-Transfer Effects

Foreign direct investment can make a positive contribution to a host economy by supplying capital, technology, and management resources that would otherwise not be available and thus boost that country's economic growth rate.

With regard to capital, many MNEs, by virtue of their large size and financial strength, have access to financial resources not available to host-country firms. These funds may be available from internal company sources, or, because of their reputation, large MNEs may find it easier to borrow money from capital markets than host-country firms would.

Does Foreign Direct Investment Promote Growth?

There are multiple reasons for companies to make foreign direct investments. Lowering the cost of production, increasing capacity (volume) of production, and strategically locating production facilities to serve world regions are some of the many reasons for FDI by a company. For the host countries that receive the investment by multinational corporations, the logic is that the influx of capital and increase in tax revenues will benefit the host country in the form of new infrastructure, increased knowledge, and general economic development. However, the evidence so far is very mixed on the value of FDI to the host, ranging from beneficial to detrimental. What do you think? Does FDI promote growth in the host country?

Source: L. Alfaro, A. Chanda, S. Kalemli-Ozcan, and S. Sayek, *Does Foreign Direct Investment Promote Growth? Exploring the Role of Financial Markets on Linkages* (Cambridge, MA: Harvard Business School, 2009), www.people.hbs.edu/lalfaro/fdiandlinkages.pdf.

As for technology, you will recall from Chapter 3 that technology can stimulate economic development and industrialization. Technology can take two forms, both of which are valuable. Technology can be incorporated in a production process (e.g., the technology for discovering, extracting, and refining oil), or it can be incorporated in a product (e.g., personal computers). However, many countries lack the research and development resources and skills required to develop their own indigenous product and process technology. This is particularly true in less developed nations. Such countries must rely on advanced industrialized nations for much of the technology required to stimulate economic growth, and FDI can provide it.

Research supports the view that multinational firms often transfer significant technology when they invest in a foreign country.[28] For example, a study of FDI in Sweden found that foreign firms increased both the labor and total factor productivity of Swedish firms that they acquired, suggesting that significant technology transfers had occurred (technology typically boosts productivity).[29] Also, a study of FDI by the Organisation for Economic Co-operation and Development (OECD) found that foreign investors invested significant amounts of capital in R&D in the countries in which they had invested, suggesting that not only were they transferring technology to those countries but they may also have been upgrading existing technology or creating new technology in those countries.[30]

Foreign management skills acquired through FDI may also produce important benefits for the host country. Foreign managers trained in the latest management techniques can often help improve the efficiency of operations in the host country, whether those operations are acquired or greenfield developments. Beneficial spin-off effects may also arise when local personnel who are trained to occupy managerial, financial, and technical posts in the subsidiary of a foreign MNE leave the firm and help establish indigenous firms. Similar benefits may arise if the superior management skills of a foreign MNE stimulate local suppliers, distributors, and competitors to improve their own management skills.

Employment Effects

Another beneficial employment effect claimed for FDI is that it brings jobs to a host country that would otherwise not be created there. The effects of FDI on employment are both direct and indirect. Direct effects arise when a foreign MNE employs a number of host-country citizens. Indirect effects arise when jobs are created in local suppliers as a result of the investment and when jobs are created because of increased local spending by employees of the MNE. The indirect employment effects are often as large as, if not larger than, the direct effects. For example, when Toyota decided to open a new auto plant in France, estimates suggested the plant would create 2,000 direct jobs and perhaps another 2,000 jobs in support industries.[31]

Job creation is a result of FDI. These French workers assemble cars at Toyota's Valenciennes manufacturing plant.

Source: © Philippe Huguen/AFP/Getty Images

Cynics argue that not all the "new jobs" created by FDI represent net additions in employment. In the case of FDI by Japanese auto companies in the United States, some argue that the jobs created by this investment have been more than offset by the jobs lost in U.S.-owned auto companies, which have lost market share to their Japanese competitors. As a consequence of such substitution effects, the net number of new jobs created by FDI may not be as great as initially claimed by an MNE. The issue of the likely net gain in employment may be a major negotiating point between an MNE wishing to undertake FDI and the host government.

When FDI takes the form of an acquisition of an established enterprise in the host economy as opposed to a greenfield investment, the immediate effect may be to reduce employment as the multinational tries to restructure the operations of the acquired unit to improve its operating efficiency. However, even in such cases, research suggests that once the initial period of restructuring is over, enterprises acquired by foreign firms tend to increase their employment base at a faster rate than domestic rivals. An OECD study found that foreign firms created new jobs at a faster rate than their domestic counterparts.[32]

Balance-of-Payments Effects FDI's effect on a country's balance-of-payments accounts is an important policy issue for most host governments. A country's **balance-of-payments accounts** track both its payments to and its receipts from other countries. Governments normally are concerned when their country is running a deficit on the current account of their balance of payments. The **current account** tracks the export and import of goods and services. A current account deficit, or *trade deficit* as it is often called, arises when a country is importing more goods and services than it is exporting. Governments typically prefer to see a current account surplus than a deficit. The only way in which a current account deficit can be supported in the long run is by selling off assets to foreigners (for a detailed explanation of why this is the case, see the appendix to Chapter 6). For example, the persistent U.S. current account deficit since the 1980s has been financed by a steady sale of U.S. assets (stocks, bonds, real estate, and whole corporations) to foreigners. Because national governments invariably dislike seeing the assets of their country fall into foreign hands, they prefer their nation to run a current account surplus. There are two ways in which FDI can help a country achieve this goal.

Balance-of-Payments Accounts
National accounts that track both payments to and receipts from foreigners.

Current Account
In the balance of payments, records transactions involving the export or import of goods and services.

First, if the FDI is a substitute for imports of goods or services, the effect can be to improve the current account of the host country's balance of payments. Much of the FDI by Japanese automobile companies in the United States and Europe, for example, can be seen as substituting for imports from Japan. Thus, the current account of the U.S. balance of payments has improved somewhat because many Japanese companies are now supplying the U.S. market from production facilities in the United States, as opposed to facilities in Japan. Insofar as this has reduced the need to finance a current account deficit by asset sales to foreigners, the United States has clearly benefited.

A second potential benefit arises when the MNE uses a foreign subsidiary to export goods and services to other countries. According to a UN report, inward FDI by foreign multinationals has been a major driver of export-led economic growth in a number of developing and developed nations.[33] For example, in China exports increased from $26 billion in 1985 to $2.3 trillion in 2014. Much of this dramatic export growth was due to the presence of foreign multinationals that invested heavily in China.

Effect on Competition and Economic Growth Economic theory tells us that the efficient functioning of markets depends on an adequate level of competition between producers. When FDI takes the form of a greenfield investment, the result is to establish a new enterprise, increasing the number of players in a market and thus consumer choice. In turn, this can increase the level of competition in a national market, thereby driving down prices and increasing the economic welfare of consumers. Increased competition tends to stimulate capital investments by firms in plant, equipment, and R&D as they struggle to gain an edge over their rivals. The long-term results may include increased productivity growth, product and process innovations, and greater economic growth.[34] Such beneficial effects seem to have occurred in the South Korean retail sector following the liberalization of FDI regulations in 1996. FDI by large Western discount stores—including Walmart, Costco, Carrefour, and Tesco—seems to have encouraged indigenous discounters such as E-Mart to improve the efficiency of their own operations. The results have included more competition and lower prices, which benefit South Korean consumers.

FDI's impact on competition in domestic markets may be particularly important in the case of services, such as telecommunications, retailing, and many financial services, where exporting is often not an option because the service has to be produced where it is delivered.[35] For example, under a 1997 agreement sponsored by the World Trade Organization, 68 countries accounting for more than 90 percent of world telecommunications revenues pledged to start opening their markets to foreign investment and competition and to abide by common rules for fair competition in telecommunications. Before this agreement, most of the world's telecommunications markets were closed to foreign competitors, and in most countries, the market was monopolized by a single carrier, which was often a state-owned enterprise. The agreement has dramatically increased the level of competition in many national telecommunications markets, producing two major benefits. First, inward investment has increased competition and stimulated investment in the modernization of telephone networks around the world, leading to better service. Second, the increased competition has resulted in lower prices.

HOST-COUNTRY COSTS

Three costs of FDI concern host countries. They arise from possible adverse effects on competition within the host nation, adverse effects on the balance of payments, and the perceived loss of national sovereignty and autonomy.

Adverse Effects on Competition

Host governments sometimes worry that the subsidiaries of foreign MNEs may have greater economic power than indigenous competitors. If it is part of a larger international organization, the foreign MNE may be able to draw on funds generated elsewhere to subsidize its costs in the host market, which could drive indigenous companies out of business and allow the firm to monopolize the market. Once the market is monopolized, the foreign MNE could raise prices above those that would prevail in competitive markets, with harmful effects on the economic welfare of the host nation. This concern tends to be greater in countries that have few large firms of their own (generally, less developed countries). It tends to be a relatively minor concern in most advanced industrialized nations.

In general, while FDI in the form of greenfield investments should increase competition, it is less clear that this is the case when the FDI takes the form of acquisition of an established enterprise in the host nation, as was the case when Cemex acquired RMC in Britain (see the Management Focus). Because an acquisition does not result in a net increase in the number of players in a market, the effect on competition may be neutral. When a foreign investor acquires two or more firms in a host country and subsequently merges them, the effect may be to reduce the level of competition in that market, create monopoly power for the foreign firm, reduce consumer choice, and raise prices. For example, in India, Hindustan Lever Ltd., the Indian subsidiary of Unilever, acquired its main local rival, Tata Oil Mills, to assume a dominant position in the bath soap (75 percent) and detergents (30 percent) markets. Hindustan Lever also acquired several local companies in other markets, such as the ice cream makers Dollops, Kwality, and Milkfood. By combining these companies, Hindustan Lever's share of the Indian ice cream market went from zero to 74 percent.[36] However, although such cases are of obvious concern, there is little evidence that such developments are widespread. In many nations, domestic competition authorities have the right to review and block any mergers or acquisitions that they view as having a detrimental impact on competition. If such institutions are operating effectively, this should be sufficient to make sure that foreign entities do not monopolize a country's markets.

Adverse Effects on the Balance of Payments

The possible adverse effects of FDI on a host country's balance-of-payments position are twofold. First, set against the initial capital inflow that comes with FDI must be the subsequent outflow of earnings from the foreign subsidiary to its parent company. Such outflows show up as capital outflow on balance-of-payments accounts. Some governments have responded to such outflows by restricting the amount of earnings that can be repatriated to a foreign subsidiary's home country. A second concern arises when a foreign subsidiary imports a substantial number of its inputs from abroad, which results in a debit on the current account of the host country's balance of payments. One criticism leveled against Japanese-owned auto assembly operations in the United States, for example, is that they tend to import many component parts from Japan. Because of this, the favorable impact of this FDI on the current account of the U.S. balance-of-payments position may not be as great as initially supposed. The Japanese auto companies responded to these criticisms by pledging to purchase 75 percent of their component parts from U.S.-based manufacturers (but not necessarily U.S.-owned manufacturers). When the Japanese auto company Nissan invested in the United Kingdom, Nissan responded to concerns about local content by pledging to increase the proportion of local content to 60 percent and subsequently raising it to more than 80 percent.

Possible Effects on National Sovereignty and Autonomy Some host governments worry that FDI is accompanied by some loss of economic independence. The concern is that key decisions that can affect the host country's economy will be made by a foreign parent that has no real commitment to the host country and over which the host country's government has no real control. Most economists dismiss such concerns as groundless and irrational. Political scientist Robert Reich has noted that such concerns are the product of outmoded thinking because they fail to account for the growing interdependence of the world economy.[37] In a world in which firms from all advanced nations are increasingly investing in each other's markets, it is not possible for one country to hold another to "economic ransom" without hurting itself.

HOME-COUNTRY BENEFITS

The benefits of FDI to the home (source) country arise from three sources. First, the home country's balance of payments benefits from the inward flow of foreign earnings. FDI can also benefit the home country's balance of payments if the foreign subsidiary creates demands for home-country exports of capital equipment, intermediate goods, complementary products, and the like.

Second, benefits to the home country from outward FDI arise from employment effects. As with the balance of payments, positive employment effects arise when the foreign subsidiary creates demand for home-country exports. Thus, Toyota's investment in auto assembly operations in Europe has benefited both the Japanese balance-of-payments position and employment in Japan, because Toyota imports some component parts for its European-based auto assembly operations directly from Japan.

Third, benefits arise when the home-country MNE learns valuable skills from its exposure to foreign markets that can subsequently be transferred back to the home country. This amounts to a reverse resource-transfer effect. Through its exposure to a foreign market, an MNE can learn about superior management techniques and superior product and process technologies. These resources can then be transferred back to the home country, contributing to the home country's economic growth rate.[38]

HOME-COUNTRY COSTS

Against these benefits must be set the apparent costs of FDI for the home (source) country. The most important concerns center on the balance-of-payments and employment effects of outward FDI. The home country's balance of payments may suffer in three ways. First, the balance of payments suffers from the initial capital outflow required to finance the FDI. This effect, however, is usually more than offset by the subsequent inflow of foreign earnings. Second, the current account of the balance of payments suffers if the purpose of the foreign investment is to serve the home market from a low-cost production location. Third, the current account of the balance of payments suffers if the FDI is a substitute for direct exports. Thus, insofar as Toyota's assembly operations in the United States are intended to substitute for direct exports from Japan, the current account position of Japan will deteriorate.

With regard to employment effects, the most serious concerns arise when FDI is seen as a substitute for domestic production. This was the case with Toyota's investments in the United States and Europe. One obvious result of such FDI is reduced home-country employment. If the labor market in the home country is already tight, with little unemployment, this concern may not be that great. However, if the home country is suffering from unemployment, concern about the export of jobs may arise. For example, one objection frequently raised by U.S. labor leaders to the free trade pact among the United States, Mexico, and Canada (see Chapter 9) is that the United States would lose hundreds of thousands of jobs as U.S. firms invest in Mexico to take advantage of cheaper labor and then export back to the United States.[39]

Is FDI a Form of Colonialism or Ethical Investing?

Some critics of globalization suggest that FDI is an advanced form of colonialism that destroys local cultures in developing countries. What these critics say may have some limited validity, but it isn't the whole picture. Take Freeport McMoRan, a U.S.-based mining company with operations in West Papua (the former Irian Jaya), Indonesia, where the world's largest gold, mineral, and copper reserves have been found. Freeport formed a joint venture with the Indonesian government to mine a concession, an isolated tract of land the size of Massachusetts on a remote island, half of which is the country of Papua New Guinea. Freeport has brought education, Internet connections, world-class health care, and the modern world to the isolated local tribes in West Papua, nomadic peoples who wear loincloths and hunt in the forest. Their traditional, subsistence way of life is threatened, while at the same time, they gain from their share of the operation's profits, from their increased health care and education, and from local employment opportunities with FCX. Is this colonialism or a kind of ethical investing?

Source: www.corpwatch.org.

INTERNATIONAL TRADE THEORY AND FDI When assessing the costs and benefits of FDI to the home country, keep in mind the lessons of international trade theory (see Chapter 6). International trade theory tells us that home-country concerns about the negative economic effects of offshore production may be misplaced. The term **offshore production** refers to FDI undertaken to serve the home market. Far from reducing home-country employment, such FDI may actually stimulate economic growth (and hence employment) in the home country by freeing home-country resources to concentrate on activities where the home country has a comparative advantage. In addition, home-country consumers benefit if the price of the particular product falls as a result of the FDI. Also, if a company were prohibited from making such investments on the grounds of negative employment effects while its international competitors reaped the benefits of low-cost production locations, it would undoubtedly lose market share to its international competitors. Under such a scenario, the adverse long-run economic effects for a country would probably outweigh the relatively minor balance-of-payments and employment effects associated with offshore production.

Offshore Production
FDI undertaken to serve the home market.

test PREP
Use SmartBook to help retain what you have learned. Access your Instructor's Connect course to check out SmartBook or go to learnsmartadvantage.com for help.

LO 8-5
Explain the range of policy instruments that governments use to influence FDI.

Government Policy Instruments and FDI

We have reviewed the costs and benefits of FDI from the perspective of both home country and host country. We now turn our attention to the policy instruments that home (source) countries and host countries can use to regulate FDI.

HOME-COUNTRY POLICIES Through their choice of policies, home countries can both encourage and restrict FDI by local firms. We look at policies designed to encourage outward FDI first. These include foreign risk insurance, capital assistance, tax incentives, and political pressure. Then we will look at policies designed to restrict outward FDI.

Encouraging Outward FDI Many investor nations now have government-backed insurance programs to cover major types of foreign investment risk. The types of risks insurable through these programs include the risks of expropriation (nationalization), war losses, and the inability to transfer profits back home. Such programs are particularly useful in encouraging firms to undertake investments in politically unstable countries.[40] In addition, several advanced countries also have special funds or banks that make government loans to firms wishing to invest in developing countries. As a further incentive to encourage domestic firms to undertake FDI, many countries have eliminated double taxation of foreign income (i.e., taxation of income in both the host country and the home country). Last, and perhaps most significant, a number of investor countries (including the United States) have used their political influence to persuade host countries to relax their restrictions on inbound FDI. For example, in response to direct U.S. pressure, Japan relaxed many of its formal restrictions on inward FDI. In response to further U.S. pressure, Japan relaxed its informal barriers to inward FDI. One beneficiary of this trend was Toys "R" Us, which, after five years of intensive lobbying by company and U.S. government officials, opened its first retail stores in Japan in December 1991. By 2012, Toys "R" Us had more than 170 stores in Japan, and its Japanese operation, in which Toys "R" Us retained a controlling stake, had a listing on the Japanese stock market.

Restricting Outward FDI Virtually all investor countries, including the United States, have exercised some control over outward FDI from time to time. One policy has been to limit capital outflows out of concern for the country's balance of payments. From the early 1960s until 1979, for example, Britain had exchange-control regulations that limited the amount of capital a firm could take out of the country. Although the main intent of such policies was to improve the British balance of payments, an important secondary intent was to make it more difficult for British firms to undertake FDI.

In addition, countries have occasionally manipulated tax rules to try to encourage their firms to invest at home. The objective behind such policies is to create jobs at home rather than in other nations. At one time, Britain adopted such policies. The British advanced corporation tax system taxed British companies' foreign earnings at a higher rate than their domestic earnings. This tax code created an incentive for British companies to invest at home.

Finally, countries sometimes prohibit national firms from investing in certain countries for political reasons. Such restrictions can be formal or informal. For example, formal U.S. rules prohibited U.S. firms from investing in countries such as Cuba and Iran, whose political ideology and actions are judged to be contrary to U.S. interests. Similarly, during the 1980s, informal pressure was applied to dissuade U.S. firms from investing in South Africa. In this case, the objective was to pressure South Africa to change its apartheid laws, which happened during the early 1990s.

HOST-COUNTRY POLICIES

Host countries adopt policies designed both to restrict and to encourage inward FDI. As noted earlier in this chapter, political ideology has determined the type and scope of these policies in the past. In the last decade of the twentieth century, many countries moved quickly away from adhering to some version of the radical stance and prohibiting much FDI toward a situation where a combination of free market objectives and pragmatic nationalism took hold.

Encouraging Inward FDI

It is common for governments to offer incentives to foreign firms to invest in their countries. Such incentives take many forms, but the most common are tax concessions, low-interest loans, and grants or subsidies. Incentives are motivated by a desire to gain from the resource-transfer and employment effects of FDI. They are also motivated by a desire to capture FDI away from other potential host countries. For example, in the mid-1990s, the governments of Britain and France competed with each other on the incentives they offered Toyota to invest in their respective countries. In the United States, state governments often compete with each other to attract FDI. For example, Kentucky offered Toyota an incentive package worth $147 million to persuade it to build its U.S. automobile assembly plants there. The package included tax breaks, new state spending on infrastructure, and low-interest loans.[41]

Restricting Inward FDI

Host governments use a wide range of controls to restrict FDI in one way or another. The two most common are ownership restraints and performance requirements. Ownership restraints can take several forms. In some countries, foreign companies are excluded from specific fields. They are excluded from tobacco and mining in Sweden and from the development of certain natural resources in Brazil, Finland, and Morocco. In other industries, foreign ownership may be permitted although a significant proportion of the equity of the subsidiary must be owned by local investors. Foreign ownership is restricted to 25 percent or less of an airline in the United States. In India, foreign firms were prohibited from owning media businesses until 2001, when the rules were relaxed, allowing foreign firms to purchase up to 26 percent of an Indian newspaper.

The rationale underlying ownership restraints seems to be twofold. First, foreign firms are often excluded from certain sectors on the grounds of national security or competition. Particularly in less developed countries, the feeling seems to be that local firms might not be able to develop unless foreign competition is restricted by a combination of import tariffs and controls on FDI. This is a variant of the infant industry argument discussed in Chapter 7.

Second, ownership restraints seem to be based on a belief that local owners can help maximize the resource-transfer and employment benefits of FDI for the host country. Until the 1980s, the Japanese government prohibited most FDI but allowed joint ventures between Japanese firms and foreign MNEs if the MNE had a valuable technology. The Japanese government clearly believed such an arrangement would speed up the subsequent diffusion of the MNE's valuable technology throughout the Japanese economy.

Performance requirements can also take several forms. Performance requirements are controls over the behavior of the MNE's local subsidiary. The most common performance requirements are related to local content, exports, technology transfer, and local participation in top management. As with certain ownership restrictions, the logic underlying performance requirements is that such rules help maximize the benefits and minimize the costs of FDI for the host country. Many countries employ some form of performance requirements when it suits their objectives. However, performance requirements tend to be more common in less developed countries than in advanced industrialized nations.[42]

INTERNATIONAL INSTITUTIONS AND THE LIBERALIZATION OF FDI

Until the 1990s, there was no consistent involvement by multinational institutions in the governing of FDI. This changed with the formation of the World Trade Organization in 1995. The WTO embraces the promotion of international trade in services. Because many services have to be produced where they are sold, exporting is not an option (e.g., one cannot export McDonald's hamburgers or consumer banking services). Given this, the WTO has become involved in regulations governing FDI. As might be expected for an institution created to promote free trade, the thrust of the WTO's efforts has been to push for the liberalization of regulations governing FDI, particularly in services. Under the auspices of the WTO, two extensive multinational agreements were reached in 1997 to liberalize trade in telecommunications and financial services. Both these agreements contained detailed clauses that require signatories to liberalize their regulations governing inward FDI, essentially opening their markets to foreign telecommunications and financial services companies. The WTO has had less success trying to initiate talks aimed at establishing a universal set of rules designed to promote the liberalization of FDI. Led by Malaysia and India, developing nations have so far rejected efforts by the WTO to start such discussions.

Use SmartBook to help retain what you have learned. Access your Instructor's Connect course to check out SmartBook or go to learnsmartadvantage.com for help.

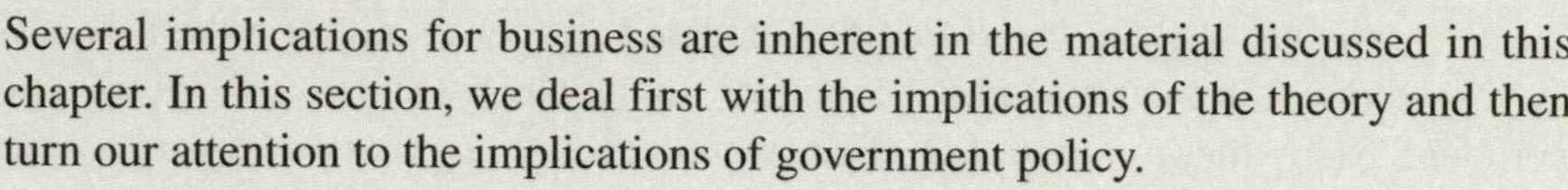

FDI AND GOVERNMENT POLICY

LO 8-6
Identify the implications for managers of the theory and government policies associated with FDI.

Several implications for business are inherent in the material discussed in this chapter. In this section, we deal first with the implications of the theory and then turn our attention to the implications of government policy.

The Theory of FDI

The implications of the theories of FDI for business practice are straightforward. First, the location-specific advantages argument associated with John Dunning does help explain the *direction* of FDI. However, the location-specific advantages argument does not explain *why* firms prefer FDI to licensing or to exporting. In this regard, from both an explanatory and a business perspective, perhaps the most useful theories are those that focus on the limitations of exporting and licensing—that is, internalization theories. These theories are useful because they identify with some precision how the relative profitability of foreign direct investment, exporting, and licensing varies with circumstances. The theories suggest that exporting is preferable to licensing and FDI so long as transportation costs are minor and trade barriers are trivial. As transportation costs or trade barriers increase, exporting becomes unprofitable, and the choice is between FDI and licensing. Because FDI is more costly and more risky than licensing, other things being equal, the theories argue that licensing is preferable to FDI. Other things are seldom equal, however. Although licensing may work, it is not an attractive option when one or more of the following conditions exist: (1) the firm has valuable know-how that cannot be adequately protected by a licensing contract, (2) the firm needs tight control over a foreign entity to maximize its market share and earnings in that country, and (3) a firm's skills and capabilities are not amenable to licensing. Figure 8.4 presents these considerations as a decision tree.

Firms for which licensing is not a good option tend to be clustered in three types of industries:

1. High-technology industries in which protecting firm-specific expertise is of paramount importance and licensing is hazardous.
2. Global oligopolies, in which competitive interdependence requires that multinational firms maintain tight control over foreign operations so that they have the ability to launch coordinated attacks against their global competitors.
3. Industries in which intense cost pressures require that multinational firms maintain tight control over foreign operations (so that they can disperse manufacturing to locations around the globe where factor costs are most favorable in order to minimize costs).

Although empirical evidence is limited, the majority of studies seem to support these conjectures.[43] In addition, licensing is not a good option if the competitive advantage of a firm is based upon managerial or marketing knowledge that is embedded in the routines of the firm or the skills of its managers and that is difficult to codify in a "book of blueprints." This would seem to be the case for firms based in a fairly wide range of industries.

Firms for which licensing is a good option tend to be in industries whose conditions are opposite to those just specified. That is, licensing tends to be more common, and more profitable, in fragmented, low-technology industries in which globally dispersed manufacturing is not an option. A good example is the fast-food industry. McDonald's has expanded globally by using a franchising

A Decision Framework.

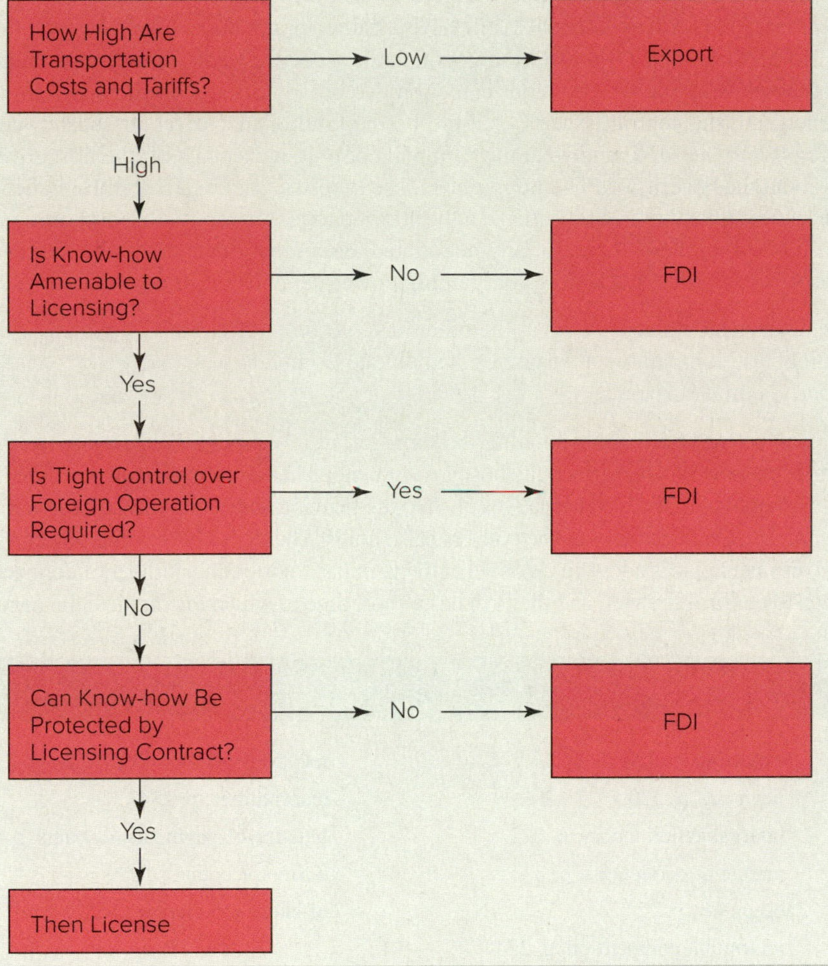

strategy. Franchising is essentially the service-industry version of licensing, although it normally involves much longer-term commitments than licensing. With franchising, the firm licenses its brand name to a foreign firm in return for a percentage of the franchisee's profits. The franchising contract specifies the conditions that the franchisee must fulfill if it is to use the franchisor's brand name. Thus, McDonald's allows foreign firms to use its brand name so long as they agree to run their restaurants on exactly the same lines as McDonald's restaurants elsewhere in the world. This strategy makes sense for McDonald's because (1) like many services, fast food cannot be exported; (2) franchising economizes the costs and risks associated with opening up foreign markets; (3) unlike technological know-how, brand names are relatively easy to protect using a contract; (4) there is no compelling reason for McDonald's to have tight control over franchisees; and (5) McDonald's know-how, in terms of how to run a fast-food restaurant, is amenable to being specified in a written contract (e.g., the contract specifies the details of how to run a McDonald's restaurant).

Finally, it should be noted that the product life-cycle theory and Knickerbocker's theory of FDI tend to be less useful from a business perspective. The problem with these two theories is that they are descriptive rather than analytical. They do a good job of describing the historical evolution of FDI, but they do a relatively poor job of identifying the factors that influence the relative profitability of FDI, licensing, and exporting. Indeed, the issue of licensing as an alternative to FDI is ignored by both these theories.

Government Policy

A host government's attitude toward FDI should be an important variable in decisions about where to locate foreign production facilities and where to make a foreign direct investment. Other things being equal, investing in countries that have permissive policies toward FDI is clearly preferable to investing in countries that restrict FDI.

However, often the issue is not this straightforward. Despite the move toward a free market stance in recent years, many countries still have a rather pragmatic stance toward FDI. In such cases, a firm considering FDI must often negotiate the specific terms of the investment with the country's government. Such negotiations center on two broad issues. If the host government is trying to attract FDI, the central issue is likely to be the kind of incentives the host government is prepared to offer to the MNE and what the firm will commit in exchange. If the host government is uncertain about the benefits of FDI and might choose to restrict access, the central issue is likely to be the concessions that the firm must make to be allowed to go forward with a proposed investment.

To a large degree, the outcome of any negotiated agreement depends on the relative bargaining power of both parties. Each side's bargaining power depends on three factors:

- The value each side places on what the other has to offer.
- The number of comparable alternatives available to each side.
- Each party's time horizon.

From the perspective of a firm negotiating the terms of an investment with a host government, the firm's bargaining power is high when the host government places a high value on what the firm has to offer, the number of comparable alternatives open to the firm is greater, and the firm has a long time in which to complete the negotiations. The converse also holds. The firm's bargaining power is low when the host government places a low value on what the firm has to offer, the number of comparable alternatives open to the firm is fewer, and the firm has a short time in which to complete the negotiations.[44]

Key Terms

flow of FDI, p. 216
stock of FDI, p. 216
outflows of FDI, p. 216
inflows of FDI, p. 216
greenfield investment, p. 219
eclectic paradigm, p. 220
exporting, p. 220
licensing, p. 220
internalization theory, p. 222
market imperfections, p. 222
oligopoly, p. 223
multipoint competition, p. 224
location-specific advantages, p. 224
externalities, p. 224
balance-of-payments accounts, p. 229
current account, p. 229
offshore production, p. 232

Summary

This chapter reviewed theories that attempt to explain the pattern of FDI between countries and to examine the influence of governments on firms' decisions to invest in foreign countries. The chapter made the following points:

1. Any theory seeking to explain FDI must explain why firms go to the trouble of acquiring or establishing operations abroad when the alternatives of exporting and licensing are available to them.
2. High transportation costs or tariffs imposed on imports help explain why many firms prefer FDI or licensing over exporting.
3. Firms often prefer FDI to licensing when (*a*) a firm has valuable know-how that cannot be adequately protected by a licensing contract, (*b*) a firm needs tight control over a foreign entity in order to maximize its market share and earnings in that country, and (*c*) a firm's skills and capabilities are not amenable to licensing.
4. Knickerbocker's theory suggests that much FDI is explained by imitative behavior by rival firms in an oligopolistic industry.
5. Dunning has argued that location-specific advantages are of considerable importance in explaining the nature and direction of FDI. According to Dunning, firms undertake FDI to exploit resource endowments or assets that are location-specific.
6. Political ideology is an important determinant of government policy toward FDI. Ideology ranges from a radical stance that is hostile to FDI to a noninterventionist, free market stance. Between the two extremes is an approach best described as pragmatic nationalism.
7. Benefits of FDI to a host country arise from resource-transfer effects, employment effects, and balance-of-payments effects.
8. The costs of FDI to a host country include adverse effects on competition and balance of payments and a perceived loss of national sovereignty.
9. The benefits of FDI to the home (source) country include improvement in the balance of payments as a result of the inward flow of foreign earnings, positive employment effects when the foreign subsidiary creates

demand for home-country exports, and benefits from a reverse resource-transfer effect. A reverse resource-transfer effect arises when the foreign subsidiary learns valuable skills abroad that can be transferred back to the home country.

10. The costs of FDI to the home country include adverse balance-of-payments effects that arise from the initial capital outflow and from the export substitution effects of FDI. Costs also arise when FDI exports jobs abroad.
11. Home countries can adopt policies designed to both encourage and restrict FDI. Host countries try to attract FDI by offering incentives, and try to restrict FDI by dictating ownership restraints and requiring that foreign MNEs meet specific performance requirements.

Critical Thinking and Discussion Questions

1. In 2008, inward FDI accounted for some 63.7 percent of gross fixed capital formation in Ireland but only 4.1 percent in Japan (*gross fixed capital formation* refers to investments in fixed assets such as factories, warehouses, and retail stores). What do you think explains this difference in FDI inflows into the two countries?
2. Compare and contrast these explanations of FDI: internalization theory and Knickerbocker's theory of FDI. Which theory do you think offers the best explanation of the historical pattern of FDI? Why?
3. What are the strengths of the eclectic theory of FDI? Can you see any shortcomings? How does the eclectic theory influence management practice?
4. Read the Management Focus on Cemex, and then answer the following questions:
   a. Which theoretical explanation, or explanations, of FDI best explains Cemex's FDI?
   b. What is the value that Cemex brings to a host economy? Can you see any potential drawbacks of inward investment by Cemex in an economy?
   c. Cemex has a strong preference for acquisitions over greenfield ventures as an entry mode. Why?
5. You are the international manager of a U.S. business that has just developed a revolutionary new personal computer that can perform the same functions as existing PCs but costs only half as much to manufacture. Several patents protect the unique design of this computer. Your CEO has asked you to formulate a recommendation for how to expand into western Europe. Your options are (*a*) to export from the United States, (*b*) to license a European firm to manufacture and market the computer in Europe, or (*c*) to set up a wholly owned subsidiary in Europe. Evaluate the pros and cons of each alternative, and suggest a course of action to your CEO.

globalEDGE Research Task

globalEDGE.msu.edu

Use the globalEDGE™ website (globaledge.msu.edu) to complete the following exercises:

1. The *World Investment Report* published annually by UNCTAD provides a summary of recent trends in FDI as well as quick access to comprehensive investment statistics. Identify the table of *largest transnational corporations* from developing and transition countries. The ranking is based on the foreign assets each corporation owns. Based only on the top 20 companies, provide a summary of the countries and industries represented. Do you notice any common traits from your analysis? Did any industries or countries in the top 20 surprise you? Why?
2. An integral part of successful foreign direct investment is to understand the target market opportunities as well as the nature of the risk inherent in possible investment projects, particularly in developing countries. You work for a company that builds wastewater and sanitation infrastructure in such countries. *The Multilateral Investment Guarantee Agency (MIGA)* provides insurance for risky projects in these markets. Identify the sector brief for the water and wastewater sector, and prepare a report to identify the major risks projects in this sector tend to face and how MIGA can assist in such projects.

Volkswagen in Russia

closing case

In the mid-2000s, Volkswagen announced that it would invest directly in automobile production in Russia. The decision to invest was driven by a number of factors. Russia's economy was growing rapidly at the time and living standards were rising, while the level of car ownership per capita was still low by European standards. This suggested that demand for cars would grow rapidly going forward. Indeed, forecasts predicted that by 2020, Russia would surpass Germany to become the largest car market in Europe. Moreover, Volkswagen's global rivals, including most notably Toyota, General Motors, and Ford, were also investing in production facilities in Russia, so Volkswagen felt that it had to make direct investments in order to avoid being preempted by its rivals.

The Russian government also created incentives for carmakers to invest directly in Russian production facilities, allowing them to avoid import tariffs and a punitive tax on imports of parts if they produced at least 25,000 cars in the country. In 2011, the government announced that it would keep tariffs on imported components at 0.3 percent if a foreign automaker built at least 300,000 in the country by 2020 and produced 60 percent of the value of the car locally.

Spurred on by such incentives, in 2007 Volkswagen opened a plant in Kaluga, 160 miles southwest of Moscow, to build some of its VW and Skoda car brands. The plant was projected to have a peak capacity of 150,000 units a year and employ 3,000 people. Initially all vehicles at the plant were assembled from semi-knocked-down kits imported from Germany. In October 2009, however, the plant launched full-scale production, including welding and painting of vehicles. In October 2011, Volkswagen announced that, together with a local partner, GAZ Group, it would open a second plant near St. Petersburg, as it strove to reach the 300,000 units of local production by 2020. In 2013, Volkswagen made an additional investment in Kaluga when it pledged 300 million euros to build an engine plant near to its assembly operation. The engine plant opened in September 2015.

All told, by this point Volkswagen had invested over $1 billion in production in Russia. General Motors and Toyota had also announced investments of over $1 billion to boost Russian production up to 300,000 units by 2020, and Fiat had indicated that it would make investments to bring its Russian production up to 300,000 as well. In total, foreign carmakers had invested over $5 billion in Russian assembly operations by 2014. Meanwhile, analysts continued to predict that the Russian car market would grow at a healthy pace and exceed that of Germany by 2020.

In 2014, however, the market took a sharp turn for the worse. Russia is a major oil producer. Since the mid-2000s, much of the country's economic growth had been powered by high oil prices. In the second half of 2014, however, global oil prices started to fall rapidly as increased production in America and weak demand in China conspired to create a global glut of oil. By early 2016, oil prices had fallen 80 percent from their peak. To make matters worse, following hard on the heals of its hostile takeover of the Crimea region from Ukraine, Russia had become embroiled in a smoldering civil war in eastern Ukraine. Western nations responded to what they perceived as Russian aggression by imposing sanctions on Russia. Hit by these twin blows, the Russian economy weakened significantly in 2014 and 2015, and the ruble declined precipitously, losing 50 percent of its value against the U.S. dollar. Suddenly the bright hopes that foreign automakers had for the Russian market seemed to be tarnished.

Faced with falling demand, Volkswagen cut production at its Kaluga plant to 120,000 vehicles from a planned 150,000. With the new engine plant scheduled to come on line and no resolution to Russia's economic crisis insight, Volkswagen's excess capacity problem may get worse. Looking forward, Volkswagen has to decide whether to keep investing in Russia in order to hit the magic 300,000 local output figure by 2020 or to pull back from a market whose future suddenly looks highly uncertain. At this point, it looks as if Volkswagen is staying the course. In late 2015, a Volkswagen board member noted that "We need to continue to strengthen our partnership (in Russia) despite the current situation".*

*"Volkswagen Bets on Long-Term Russian Growth with New Engine Plant," *Reuters*, September 4, 2015, http://www.reuters.com.

Sources: Sarah Sloat, "Volkswagen to Halt Production at Russian Plant for 10 Days," *The Wall Street Journal*, September 7, 2014; Clare Nuttall, "Foreign Car Firms Invest Heavily in Russia," *The Telegraph*, April 28, 2011; Staff reporter, "Volkswagen Russia Shows the Way," *Automotive Supply Chain*, July 2, 2013; Staff reporter, "Volkswagen Slashes Car Production at Russian Plat," *Reuters*, September 7, 2014.

CASE DISCUSSION QUESTIONS

1. What factors underlay the decision by Volkswagen to invest directly in automobile production in Russia? Why was FDI preferable to exporting from existing factories in Germany?
2. Which theory (or theories) of FDI best explain Volkswagen's FDI in Russia?
3. How do you think FDI by foreign automobile companies might benefit the Russian economy? Is there any potential downside to Russia from this inflow of FDI?
4. Russia is largely dependent on oil exports to drive its economy forward. Given the sharp fall in global oil prices that occurred in 2014 and 2015, what impact do you think this will have on FDI into Russia?
5. Volkswagen has signaled that it is going to stay the course in Russia, despite current political and economic headwinds. Why do you think it made this decision? What are the pros and cons of this decision? In your opinion, is it the correct decision?

Endnotes

1. United Nations, *World Investment Report, 2013*; United Nations Conference on Trade and Investment, "Global Flows of Foreign Direct Investment Exceeding Pre-Crisis Levels in 2011," *Global Investment Trends Monitor*, January 24, 2012.
2. World Trade Organization, *International Trade Statistics, 2012* (Geneva: WTO, 2012); United Nations, *World Investment Report, 2012*.
3. United Nations, *World Investment Report, 2013.*
4. United Nations, *World Investment Report, 2010* (New York and Geneva: United Nations, 2010).
5. United Nations, *World Investment Report, 2015*; UN Conference on Trade and Investment, "Global Flows of Foreign Direct Investment."
6. Ibid.
7. United Nations, *World Investment Report, 2015.*
8. Ibid.
9. M. Caruso-Cabrera, "Chinese Investment in US May Break Record in 2015," *CNBC*, January 4, 2015; Shayndi Raice and William Mauldin, "Chinese Deals Draw Scrutiny in Washington," *Wall Street Journal*, February 19, 2016.
10. United Nations, *World Investment Report, 2015.*
11. See D. J. Ravenscraft and F. M. Scherer, *Mergers, Selloffs and Economic Efficiency* (Washington, DC: Brookings Institution, 1987); A. Seth, K. P. Song, and R. R. Pettit, "Value Creation and Destruction in Cross-Border Acquisitions," *Strategic Management Journal* 23 (2002), pp. 921–40.
12. For example, see S. H. Hymer, *The International Operations of National Firms: A Study of Direct Foreign Investment*

(Cambridge, MA: MIT Press, 1976); A. M. Rugman, *Inside the Multinationals: The Economics of Internal Markets* (New York: Columbia University Press, 1981); D. J. Teece, "Multinational Enterprise, Internal Governance, and Industrial Organization," *American Economic Review* 75 (May 1983), pp. 233–38; C. W. L. Hill and W. C. Kim, "Searching for a Dynamic Theory of the Multinational Enterprise: A Transaction Cost Model," *Strategic Management Journal* 9 (special issue, 1988), pp. 93–104; A. Verbeke, "The Evolutionary View of the MNE and the Future of Internalization Theory," *Journal of International Business Studies* 34 (2003), pp. 498–501; J. H. Dunning, "Some Antecedents of Internalization Theory," *Journal of International Business Studies* 34 (2003), pp. 108–28.

13. J. P. Womack, D. T. Jones, and D. Roos, *The Machine That Changed the World* (New York: Rawson Associates, 1990).
14. The argument is most often associated with F. T. Knickerbocker, *Oligopolistic Reaction and Multinational Enterprise* (Boston: Harvard Business School Press, 1973).
15. The studies are summarized in R. E. Caves, *Multinational Enterprise and Economic Analysis*, 2d ed. (Cambridge, UK: Cambridge University Press, 1996).
16. See R. E. Caves, "Japanese Investment in the US: Lessons for the Economic Analysis of Foreign Investment," *The World Economy* 16 (1993), pp. 279–300; B. Kogut and S. J. Chang, "Technological Capabilities and Japanese Direct Investment in the United States," *Review of Economics and Statistics* 73 (1991), pp. 401–43; J. Anand and B. Kogut, "Technological Capabilities of Countries, Firm Rivalry, and Foreign Direct Investment," *Journal of International Business Studies*, 1997, pp. 445–65.
17. K. Ito and E. L. Rose, "Foreign Direct Investment Location Strategies in the Tire Industry," *Journal of International Business Studies* 33 (2002), pp. 593–602.
18. H. Haveman and L. Nonnemaker, "Competition in Multiple Geographical Markets," *Administrative Science Quarterly* 45 (2000), pp. 232–67; L. Fuentelsaz and J. Gomez, "Multipoint Competition, Strategic Similarity and Entry into Geographic Markets," *Strategic Management Journal* 27 (2006), pp. 447–57.
19. J. H. Dunning, *Explaining International Production* (London: Unwin Hyman, 1988).
20. P. Krugman. "Increasing Returns and Economic Geography," *Journal of Political Economy* 99, no. 3 (1991), pp. 483–99.
21. J. M. Shaver and F. Flyer, "Agglomeration Economies, Firm Heterogeneity, and Foreign Direct Investment in the United States," *Strategic Management Journal* 21 (2000), pp. 1175–93.
22. J. H. Dunning and R. Narula, "Transpacific Foreign Direct Investment and the Investment Development Path," *South Carolina Essays in International Business*, May 1995.
23. W. Shan and J. Song, "Foreign Direct Investment and the Sourcing of Technological Advantage: Evidence from the Biotechnology Industry," *Journal of International Business Studies*, 1997, pp. 267–84.
24. For some additional evidence, see L. E. Brouthers, K. D. Brouthers, and S. Warner, "Is Dunning's Eclectic Framework Descriptive or Normative?," *Journal of International Business Studies* 30 (1999), pp. 831–44.
25. For elaboration, see S. Hood and S. Young, *The Economics of the Multinational Enterprise* (London: Longman, 1979); P. M. Sweezy and H. Magdoff, "The Dynamics of U.S. Capitalism," *Monthly Review Press*, 1972.
26. For an example of this policy as practiced in China, see L. G. Branstetter and R. C. Freenstra, "Trade and Foreign Direct Investment in China: A Political Economy Approach," *Journal of International Economics* 58 (December 2002), pp. 335–58.
27. M. Itoh and K. Kiyono, "Foreign Trade and Direct Investment," in *Industrial Policy of Japan*, ed. R. Komiya, M. Okuno, and K. Suzumura (Tokyo: Academic Press, 1988).
28. X. J. Zhan and T. Ozawa, *Business Restructuring in Asia: Cross Border M&As in Crisis Affected Countries* (Copenhagen: Copenhagen Business School, 2000); I. Costa, S. Robles, and R. de Queiroz, "Foreign Direct Investment and Technological Capabilities," *Research Policy* 31 (2002), pp. 1431–43; B. Potterie and F. Lichtenberg, "Does Foreign Direct Investment Transfer Technology across Borders?," *Review of Economics and Statistics* 83 (2001), pp. 490–97; K. Saggi, "Trade, Foreign Direct Investment and International Technology Transfer," *World Bank Research Observer* 17 (2002), pp. 191–235.
29. K. M. Moden, "Foreign Acquisitions of Swedish Companies: Effects on R&D and Productivity," Research Institute of International Economics, 1998, mimeo.
30. "Foreign Friends," *The Economist*, January 8, 2000, pp. 71–72.
31. A. Jack, "French Go into Overdrive to Win Investors," *Financial Times*, December 10, 1997, p. 6.
32. "Foreign Friends."
33. United Nations, *World Investment Report, 2014* (New York and Geneva: United Nations, 2014).
34. R. Ram and K. H. Zang, "Foreign Direct Investment and Economic Growth," *Economic Development and Cultural Change* 51 (2002), pp. 205–25.
35. United Nations, *World Investment Report, 2014* (New York and Geneva: United Nations, 2014).
36. United Nations, *World Investment Report, 2000* (New York and Geneva: United Nations, 2000).
37. R. B. Reich, *The Work of Nations: Preparing Ourselves for the 21st Century* (New York: Knopf, 1991).
38. This idea has been articulated, although not quite in this form, by C. A. Bartlett and S. Ghoshal, *Managing across Borders: The Transnational Solution* (Boston: Harvard Business School Press, 1989).
39. P. Magnusson, "The Mexico Pact: Worth the Price?," *BusinessWeek*, May 27, 1991, pp. 32–35.
40. C. Johnston, "Political Risk Insurance," in *Assessing Corporate Political Risk*, ed. D. M. Raddock (Totowa, NJ: Rowman & Littlefield, 1986).
41. M. Tolchin and S. Tolchin, *Buying into America: How Foreign Money Is Changing the Face of Our Nation* (New York: Times Books, 1988).
42. L. D. Qiu and Z. Tao, "Export, Foreign Direct Investment and Local Content Requirements," *Journal of Development Economics* 66 (October 2001), pp. 101–25.
43. See R. E. Caves, *Multinational Enterprise and Economic Analysis* (Cambridge, UK: Cambridge University Press, 1982).
44. For a good general introduction to negotiation strategy, see M. H. Bazerman and M. A. Neale, *Negotiating Rationally* (New York: Free Press, 1992); A. Dixit and B. Nalebuff, *Thinking Strategically: The Competitive Edge in Business, Politics, and Everyday Life* (New York: Norton, 1991); H. Raiffa, *The Art and Science of Negotiation* (Cambridge, MA: Harvard University Press, 1982).

Regional Economic Integration

learning objectives

After reading this chapter, you will be able to:

- **LO9-1** Describe the different levels of regional economic integration.
- **LO9-2** Understand the economic and political arguments for regional economic integration.
- **LO9-3** Understand the economic and political arguments against regional economic integration.
- **LO9-4** Explain the history, current scope, and future prospects of the world's most important regional economic agreements.
- **LO9-5** Understand the implications for management practice that are inherent in regional economic integration agreements.

Source: © APA Images/SIPA/SIPA France/Sharm El Sheikh/Egypt/Newscom

The Push Toward Free Trade in Africa

opening case

On June 10, 2015, representatives from 26 African nations signed an agreement pledging to work together to establish a free trade area that would remove or reduce many tariffs and eliminate time-consuming customs procedures between them. Know as the Tripartite Free Trade Area (TFTA), this common market would encompass more than 630 million people and link together three existing regional trading blocks in Southern and Eastern Africa with a combined gross domestic product of $1.2 trillion and over $102 billion in trade between member states.

The existing regional trading blocks are the East African Community, created in 2000; the Southern African Development Community, created in 1980; and an overlapping Common Market for Eastern and Southern Africa, which also took shape in the 1980s. The East Africa Community has made some progress fostering trade between its member countries, which include Kenya, Tanzania, and Uganda. Countries in the Southern African Development Community have a common set of external tariffs, and several member states use the South African rand, the most liquid and widely traded currency on the continent.

However, the existing patchwork of African trading blocks—there are some 17 in all, with many countries being members of more than one—has made it difficult to realize the gains from trade that could flow from an expanded single market. An African firm selling goods on the continent still faces an average tariff of 8.7 percent, compared with a 2.5 percent tariff on goods sold overseas. Other costs of intra-African trade include often-lengthy stops at borders for customs inspection, excessive customs-related bureaucracy and red tape, and a lack of adequate physical infrastructure, including roads and railways. There are also some vexing local content requirements. The South African Development Community, for example, requires that clothes traded within the region are both manufactured and sourced there to qualify for lower tariffs. However, since few textiles are produced in the region, the rules have stifled trade in garments.

For all these reasons, African countries are more likely to trade with Europe and America than they are with each other. Only 12 percent of Africa trade is with other countries on the continent. By comparison, some 60 percent of Europe's trade is within its own continent, as is 40 percent of North American trade.

The thinking behind the TFTA is that harmonizing rules, reducing tariffs, and streamlining or removing customs procedures will allow African firms to sell more goods and services to their neighbors, enabling them to achieve greater economies of scale and lower costs, which would benefit all parties to the agreement. On the other hand, such agreements may prove difficult to reach and, if the past is any guide, even more difficult to implement, given political realities on the ground. Some observers think that the TFTA is too ambitious an undertaking and that focusing effort on improving the three existing regional groups

–continued

would yield more gains. It's easier, they argue, to reach an agreement between five adjacent member states, as in the case of the East African Community, than 26 very different countries scattered over the entire continent. •

Sources: "Intra-African Trade: The Road Less Travelled," *The Economist*, April 17, 2013; Martin Stevis and Patrick McGroarty, "African Leaders Pledge to Create a Free Trade Zone," *The Wall Street Journal*, June 10, 2015; "Trade Within Africa: Tear Down These Walls," *The Economist*, February 27, 2016.

Introduction

Regional Economic Integration
Agreements among countries in a geographic region to reduce and ultimately remove tariff and nontariff barriers to the free flow of goods, services, and factors or production between each other.

The past two decades have witnessed a proliferation of regional trade blocs that promote **regional economic integration**. World Trade Organization (WTO) members are required to notify the WTO of any regional trade agreements in which they participate. By 2016, nearly all members had notified the WTO of participation in one or more regional trade agreements. The total number currently in force is close to 2016.[1]

Consistent with the predictions of international trade theory and particularly the theory of comparative advantage (see Chapter 6), agreements designed to promote freer trade within regions are believed to produce gains from trade for all member countries. The General Agreement on Tariffs and Trade (GATT) and its successor, the World Trade Organization, also seek to reduce trade barriers. However, the WTO has a global perspective and 162 members, which can make reaching an agreement extremely difficult. By entering into regional agreements, groups of countries aim to reduce trade barriers more rapidly than can be achieved under the auspices of the WTO. This has become an increasingly important policy approach in recent years, given the failure of the WTO to make any progress with its latest round of trade talks, the Doha Round, initiated in 2001 but currently in limbo (see Chapter 7). Given the failure of the Doha Round, national governments have felt that they can better advance their trade agenda through multilateral agreements than through the WTO.

Nowhere has the movement toward regional economic integration been more ambitious than in Europe. On January 1, 1993, the European Union formally removed many barriers to doing business across borders within the EU in an attempt to create a single market with 340 million consumers. Today, the EU has a population of more than 500 million and a gross domestic product of more than $18.5 trillion, making it slightly larger than the United States in economic terms. That being said, the recent vote by the British to negotiate an exit from the EU has cast a dark cloud over the future of the European project.

Similar moves toward regional integration are being pursued elsewhere in the world. Canada, Mexico, and the United States have implemented NAFTA. Ultimately, this aims to remove all barriers to the free flow of goods and services among the three countries. While the implementation of NAFTA has resulted in job losses in some sectors of the U.S. economy, in aggregate and consistent with the predictions of international trade theory, most economists argue that the benefits of greater regional trade outweigh any costs. South America too has moved toward regional integration. For example, in 1991, Argentina, Brazil, Paraguay, and Uruguay implemented an agreement known as Mercosur to start reducing barriers to trade between each other, and although progress within Mercosur has been halting, the institution is still in place. As described in the opening case, there are also ongoing attempts at regional economic integration in Africa, where 26 countries recently signed an agreement to try and reduce tariffs and costly customs processes in order to stimulate economic growth in the region.

While the move toward regional economic integration is generally seen as a good thing, some worry that it will lead to a world in which regional trade blocs compete against each other. In this future scenario, free trade will exist within each bloc, but each bloc will protect its market from outside competition with high tariffs. The specter of the EU and NAFTA turning into economic fortresses that shut out foreign producers through high tariff barriers is worrisome to those who believe in unrestricted free trade. If such a situation were to materialize, the resulting decline in trade between blocs could more than offset the gains from free trade within blocs.

Regional Trade Agreements

Regional economic integration is the focus of Chapter 9, and the value-added portion of globalEDGE™ that captures the ongoing development of major trade agreements worldwide is called "Regional Trade Agreements" (globaledge.msu.edu/global-resources/regional-trade-agreements). In this section of globalEDGE™, the most critical agreements of the some 300 that exist today are included, with direct access to the home pages for each agreement. The landing page for "Regional Trade Agreements" also includes globalEDGE™'s own "Trade Bloc Insights," which takes the user to a wealth of information and data (e.g., overview of each agreement, its history, countries included in the membership, related agreements, online resources, statistics, and an executive summary of what the agreement entails). In Chapter 9, we cover several of the trade agreements to provide an overview of the global marketplace. But which agreements are not covered in detail in the book and which ones are covered on globalEDGE? (*Hint: African trade agreements.*) What do you know about, for example, ECOWAS and SADC? How many members are in ECOWAS and SADC, respectively, and are any of these agreements overlapping? When were the treaties (trade agreements) of ECOWAS and SADC started?

With these issues in mind, this chapter explores the economic and political debate surrounding regional economic integration, paying particular attention to the economic and political benefits and costs of integration; reviews progress toward regional economic integration around the world; and maps the important implications of regional economic integration for the practice of international business. Before tackling these objectives, we first need to examine the levels of integration that are theoretically possible.

Levels of Economic Integration

LO 9-1

Describe the different levels of regional economic integration.

Several levels of economic integration are possible in theory (see Figure 9.1). From least integrated to most integrated, they are a free trade area, a customs union, a common market, an economic union, and, finally, a full political union.

Free Trade Area

A group of countries committed to removing all barriers to the free flow of goods and services between each other but pursuing independent external trade policies.

In a **free trade area**, all barriers to the trade of goods and services among member countries are removed. In the theoretically ideal free trade area, no discriminatory tariffs, quotas, subsidies, or administrative impediments are allowed to distort trade between members. Each country, however, is allowed to determine its own trade policies with regard to nonmembers. Thus, for

9.1 FIGURE

Levels of Economic Integration.

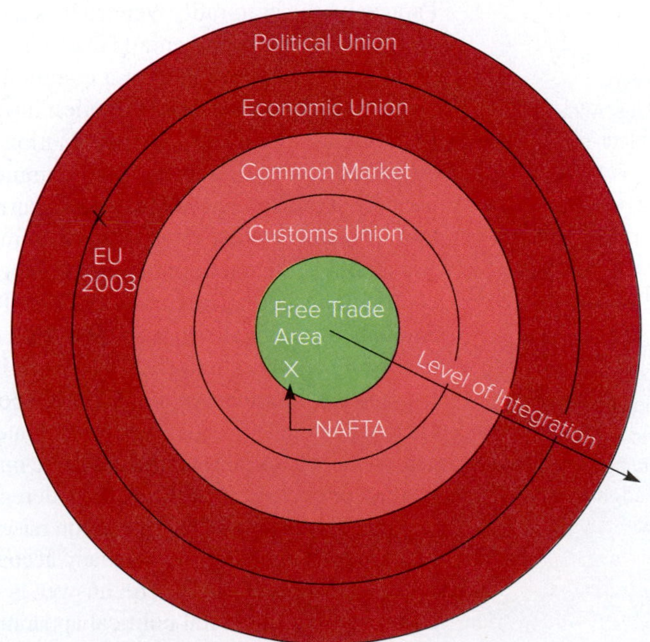

example, the tariffs placed on the products of nonmember countries may vary from member to member. Free trade agreements are the most popular form of regional economic integration, accounting for almost 90 percent of regional agreements.[2]

European Free Trade Association (EFTA)

A free trade association including Norway, Iceland, Liechtenstein, and Switzerland.

Customs Union

A group of countries committed to (1) removing all barriers to the free flow of goods and services between each other and (2) the pursuit of a common external trade policy.

Common Market

A group of countries committed to (1) removing all barriers to the free flow of goods, services, and factors of production between each other; and (2) the pursuit of a common external trade policy.

Economic Union

A group of countries committed to (1) removing all barriers to the free flow of goods, services, and factors of production between each other; (2) the adoption of a common currency; (3) the harmonization of tax rates; and (4) the pursuit of a common external trade policy.

Political Union

A central political apparatus coordinates economic, social, and foreign policy.

The most enduring free trade area in the world is the **European Free Trade Association (EFTA)**. Established in January 1960, the EFTA currently joins four countries—Norway, Iceland, Liechtenstein, and Switzerland—down from seven in 1995 (three EFTA members—Austria, Finland, and Sweden—joined the EU on January 1, 1996). The EFTA was founded by those western European countries that initially decided not to be part of the European Community (the forerunner of the EU). Its original members included Austria, Great Britain, Denmark, Finland, and Sweden, all of which are now members of the EU. The emphasis of the EFTA has been on free trade in industrial goods. Agriculture was left out of the arrangement, each member being allowed to determine its own level of support. Members are also free to determine the level of protection applied to goods coming from outside the EFTA. Other free trade areas include the North American Free Trade Agreement, which we discuss in depth later in the chapter.

The customs union is one step farther along the road to full economic and political integration. A **customs union** eliminates trade barriers between member countries and adopts a common external trade policy. Establishment of a common external trade policy necessitates significant administrative machinery to oversee trade relations with nonmembers. Most countries that enter into a customs union desire even greater economic integration down the road. The EU began as a customs union, but it has now moved beyond this stage. Other customs unions include the current version of the Andean Community (formerly known as the Andean Pact) among Bolivia, Colombia, Ecuador, and Peru. The Andean Community established free trade between member countries and imposes a common tariff, of 5 to 20 percent, on products imported from outside.[3]

The next level of economic integration, a **common market**, has no barriers to trade among member countries, includes a common external trade policy, and allows factors of production to move freely among members. Labor and capital are free to move because there are no restrictions on immigration, emigration, or cross-border flows of capital among member countries. Establishing a common market demands a significant degree of harmony and cooperation on fiscal, monetary, and employment policies. Achieving this degree of cooperation has proved very difficult. For years, the European Union functioned as a common market, although it has now moved beyond this stage. Mercosur—the South American grouping of Argentina, Brazil, Paraguay, and Uruguay—hopes to eventually establish itself as a common market. Venezuela was accepted as a full member of Mercosur subject to ratification by the governments of the four existing members. As of early 2016, Paraguay has yet to ratify Venezuela's membership.

An economic union entails even closer economic integration and cooperation than a common market. Like the common market, an **economic union** involves the free flow of products and factors of production among member countries and the adoption of a common external trade policy, but it also requires a common currency, harmonization of members' tax rates, and a common monetary and fiscal policy. Such a high degree of integration demands a coordinating bureaucracy and the sacrifice of significant amounts of national sovereignty to that bureaucracy. The EU is an economic union, although an imperfect one because not all members of the EU have adopted the euro, the currency of the EU; differences in tax rates and regulations across countries still remain; and some markets, such as the market for energy, are still not fully deregulated.

The move toward economic union raises the issue of how to make a coordinating bureaucracy accountable to the citizens of member nations. The answer is through **political union** in which a central political apparatus coordinates the economic, social, and foreign policy of the member states.

Should Regional Economic Integration Be Based on Culture?

A free trade area is a group of countries committed to removing all barriers to the free flow of goods and services while at the same time pursuing independent external trade policies. A free trade area can be of the form of a customs union, common market, economic union, or political union. The European Union is an economic union—although some would say that the EU is striving for the approach of a political union as well. The EU, in reality, is an imperfect economic union because not all members of the EU have adopted the common currency, the euro, and countries differ in a variety of economic measures (e.g., taxes, regulations). But the most obvious reason the EU is an imperfect market is that the cultures of the independent countries in many cases are very different, from the Nordic countries to the southern European countries to the former eastern bloc European countries, and so on. Do you think regional economic integration should be more based on similarity in culture of the nations involved, or are market-based economic indicators the most appropriate?

The EU is on the road toward at least partial political union. The European Parliament, which plays an important role in the EU, has been directly elected by citizens of the EU countries since the late 1970s. In addition, the Council of Ministers (the controlling, decision-making body of the EU) is composed of government ministers from each EU member. The United States provides an example of even closer political union; in the United States, independent states are effectively combined into a single nation.

test PREP

Use SmartBook to help retain what you have learned. Access your Instructor's Connect course to check out SmartBook or go to learnsmartadvantage.com for help.

The Case for Regional Integration

LO 9-2

Understand the economic and political arguments for regional economic integration.

The case for regional integration is both economic and political, and it is typically not accepted by many groups within a country, which explains why most attempts to achieve regional economic integration have been contentious and halting. In this section, we examine the economic and political cases for integration and two impediments to integration. In the next section, we look at the case against integration.

THE ECONOMIC CASE FOR INTEGRATION The economic case for regional integration is straightforward. We saw in Chapter 6 how economic theories of international trade predict that unrestricted free trade will allow countries to specialize in the production of goods and services that they can produce most efficiently. The result is greater world production than would be possible with trade restrictions. That chapter also revealed how opening a country to free trade stimulates economic growth, which creates dynamic gains from trade. Chapter 8 detailed how foreign direct investment (FDI) can transfer technological, marketing, and managerial know-how to host nations. Given the central role of knowledge in boosting economic growth, opening a country to FDI also is likely to stimulate economic growth. In sum, economic theories suggest that free trade and investment is a positive-sum game, in which all participating countries stand to gain.

Given this, the theoretical ideal is an absence of barriers to the free flow of goods, services, and factors of production among nations. However, as we saw in Chapters 7 and 8, a case can be made for government intervention in international trade and FDI. Because many governments have accepted part or all of the case for intervention, unrestricted free trade and FDI have proved to be only an ideal. Although international institutions such as the WTO have been moving the world toward a free trade regime, success has been less than total. In a world of many nations and many political ideologies, it is very difficult to get all countries to agree to a common set of rules.

Against this background, regional economic integration can be seen as an attempt to achieve additional gains from the free flow of trade and investment between countries beyond those attainable under global agreements such as the WTO. It is easier to establish a free trade and investment regime among a limited number of adjacent countries than among the world community. Coordination and policy harmonization problems are largely a function of the number of countries that seek agreement. The greater the number of countries involved, the more perspectives that must be reconciled, and the harder it will be to reach agreement. Thus, attempts at regional economic integration are motivated by a desire to exploit the gains from free trade and investment.

THE POLITICAL CASE FOR INTEGRATION The political case for regional economic integration also has loomed large in several attempts to establish free trade areas, customs unions, and the like. Linking neighboring economies and making them increasingly dependent on each other creates incentives for political cooperation between the neighboring states and reduces the potential for violent conflict. In addition, by grouping their economies, the countries can enhance their political weight in the world.

These considerations underlay the 1957 establishment of the European Community (EC), the forerunner of the EU. Europe had suffered two devastating wars in the first half of the twentieth century, both arising out of the unbridled ambitions of nation-states. Those who have sought a united Europe have always had a desire to make another war in Europe unthinkable. Many Europeans also believed that after World War II, the European nation-states were no longer large enough to hold their own in world markets and politics. The need for a united Europe to deal with the United States and the politically alien Soviet Union loomed large in the minds of many of the

EC's founders.[4] A long-standing joke in Europe is that the European Commission should erect a statue to Joseph Stalin, for without the aggressive policies of the former dictator of the old Soviet Union, the countries of western Europe may have lacked the incentive to cooperate and form the EC.

IMPEDIMENTS TO INTEGRATION Despite the strong economic and political arguments in support, integration has never been easy to achieve or sustain for two main reasons. First, although economic integration aids the majority, it has its costs. While a nation as a whole may benefit significantly from a regional free trade agreement, certain groups may lose. Moving to a free trade regime can involve painful adjustments. Due to the establishment of NAFTA, some Canadian and U.S. workers in such industries as textiles, which employ low-cost, low-skilled labor, lost their jobs as Canadian and U.S. firms moved production to Mexico. The promise of significant net benefits to the Canadian and U.S. economies as a whole is little comfort to those who lose as a result of NAFTA. Such groups have been at the forefront of opposition to NAFTA and will continue to oppose any widening of the agreement.

A second impediment to integration arises from concerns over national sovereignty. For example, Mexico's concerns about maintaining control of its oil interests resulted in an agreement with Canada and the United States to exempt the Mexican oil industry from any liberalization of foreign investment regulations achieved under NAFTA. Concerns about national sovereignty arise because close economic integration demands that countries give up some degree of control over such key issues as monetary policy, fiscal policy (e.g., tax policy), and trade policy. This has been a major stumbling block in the EU. To achieve full economic union, the EU introduced a common currency, the euro, controlled by a central EU bank. Although most member states have signed on, Great Britain remains an important holdout. A politically important segment of public opinion in that country opposes a common currency on the grounds that it would require relinquishing control of the country's monetary policy to the EU, which many British perceive as a bureaucracy run by foreigners. In 1992, the British won the right to opt out of any single currency agreement, and as of 2016, the British government has yet to reverse its decision—and it does not seem likely to do so, given the sovereign debt crisis in Europe and the strains it has placed on the euro (more on this later). Indeed, in 2016, the British held a referendum on their continuing membership of the EU (discussed later in the chapter). Concerns over national sovereignty, particularly with regard to immigration policy, were the major factor persuading the British government that a referendum was necessary.

Use SmartBook to help retain what you have learned. Access your Instructor's Connect course to check out SmartBook or go to learnsmartadvantage.com for help.

The Case Against Regional Integration

Understand the economic and political arguments against regional economic integration.

Although the tide has been running in favor of regional free trade agreements in recent years, some economists have expressed concern that the benefits of regional integration have been oversold, while the costs have often been ignored.[5] They point out that the benefits of regional integration are determined by the extent of trade creation, as opposed to trade diversion. **Trade creation** occurs when high-cost domestic producers are replaced by low-cost producers within the free trade area. It may also occur when higher-cost external producers are replaced by lower-cost external producers within the free trade area. **Trade diversion** occurs when lower-cost external suppliers are replaced by higher-cost suppliers within the free trade area. A regional free trade agreement will benefit the world only if the amount of trade it creates exceeds the amount it diverts.

Trade Creation
Trade created due to regional economic integration; occurs when high-cost domestic producers are replaced by low-cost foreign producers within a free trade area.

Trade Diversion
Trade diverted due to regional economic integration; occurs when low-cost foreign suppliers outside a free trade area are replaced by higher-cost suppliers within a free trade area.

Suppose the United States and Mexico imposed tariffs on imports from all countries, and then they set up a free trade area, scrapping all trade barriers between themselves but maintaining tariffs on imports from the rest of the world. If the United States began to import textiles from Mexico, would this change be for the better? If the United States previously produced all its own textiles at a higher cost than Mexico, then the free trade agreement has shifted production to the cheaper source. According to the theory of comparative advantage, trade has been created within the regional grouping, and there would be no decrease in trade with the rest of the world. Clearly, the change would be for the better. If, however, the United States previously imported textiles from Costa Rica, which produced them more cheaply than either Mexico or the United States, then trade has been diverted from a low-cost source—a change for the worse.

In theory, WTO rules should ensure that a free trade agreement does not result in trade diversion. These rules allow free trade areas to be formed only if the members set tariffs that are not higher or more restrictive to outsiders than the ones previously in effect. However, as we saw in Chapter 7, GATT and the WTO do not cover some nontariff barriers. As a result, regional trade blocs could emerge whose markets are protected from outside competition by high nontariff barriers. In such cases, the trade diversion effects might outweigh the trade creation effects. The only way to guard against this possibility, according to those concerned about this potential, is to increase the scope of the WTO so it covers nontariff barriers to trade. There is no sign that this is going to occur anytime soon, however, so the risk remains that regional economic integration will result in trade diversion.

Use SmartBook to help retain what you have learned. Access your Instructor's Connect course to check out SmartBook or go to learnsmartadvantage.com for help.

Regional Economic Integration in Europe

LO 9-4
Explain the history, current scope, and future prospects of the world's most important regional economic agreements.

Europe has two trade blocs—the European Union and the European Free Trade Association. Of the two, the EU is by far the more significant, not just in terms of membership (the EU currently has 28 members, although the British have voted to exit the union; the EFTA has four) but also in terms of economic and political influence in the world economy. Many have argued that the EU as an emerging economic and political superpower of the same order as the United States. Accordingly, we will concentrate our attention on the EU.[6]

EVOLUTION OF THE EUROPEAN UNION The **European Union (EU)** is the product of two political factors: (1) the devastation of western Europe during two world wars and the desire for a lasting peace, and (2) the European nations' desire to hold their own on the world's political and economic stage. In addition, many Europeans were aware of the potential economic benefits of closer economic integration of the countries.

European Union (EU)
An economic and political union of 28 countries (2015) that are located in Europe.

The forerunner of the EU, the European Coal and Steel Community, was formed in 1951 by Belgium, France, West Germany, Italy, Luxembourg, and the Netherlands. Its objective was to remove barriers to intragroup shipments of coal, iron, steel, and scrap metal. With the signing of the **Treaty of Rome** in 1957, the European Community (EC) was established. The name changed again in 1993 when the European Community became the European Union following the ratification of the Maastricht Treaty (discussed later).

Treaty of Rome
The 1957 treaty that established the European Community.

The Treaty of Rome provided for the creation of a common market. Article 3 of the treaty laid down the key objectives of the new community, calling for the elimination of internal trade barriers and the creation of a common external tariff and requiring member states to abolish obstacles to the free movement of factors of production among the members. To facilitate the free movement of goods, services, and factors of production, the treaty provided for any necessary harmonization of the member states' laws. Furthermore, the treaty committed the EC to establish common policies in agriculture and transportation.

The community grew in 1973, when Great Britain, Ireland, and Denmark joined. These three were followed in 1981 by Greece; in 1986 by Spain and Portugal; and in 1995 by Austria, Finland, and Sweden—bringing the total membership to 15 (East Germany became part of the EC after the reunification of Germany in 1990). Another 10 countries joined the EU on May 1, 2004—eight of them from eastern Europe plus the small Mediterranean nations of Malta and Cyprus. Bulgaria and Romania joined in 2007 and Croatia in 2013, bringing the total number of member states to 28 (see Map 9.1). Through these enlargements, the EU has become a global economic superpower.

POLITICAL STRUCTURE OF THE EUROPEAN UNION The economic policies of the EU are formulated and implemented by a complex and still-evolving political structure. The four main institutions in this structure are the European Commission, the Council of the European Union, the European Parliament, and the Court of Justice.[7]

The **European Commission** is responsible for proposing EU legislation, implementing it, and monitoring compliance with EU laws by member states. Headquartered in Brussels, Belgium, it is run by a group of commissioners appointed by each member country for five-year renewable terms. Currently, there are 28 commissioners, one from each member state. A president of the

European Commission
Responsible for proposing EU legislation, implementing it, and monitoring compliance.

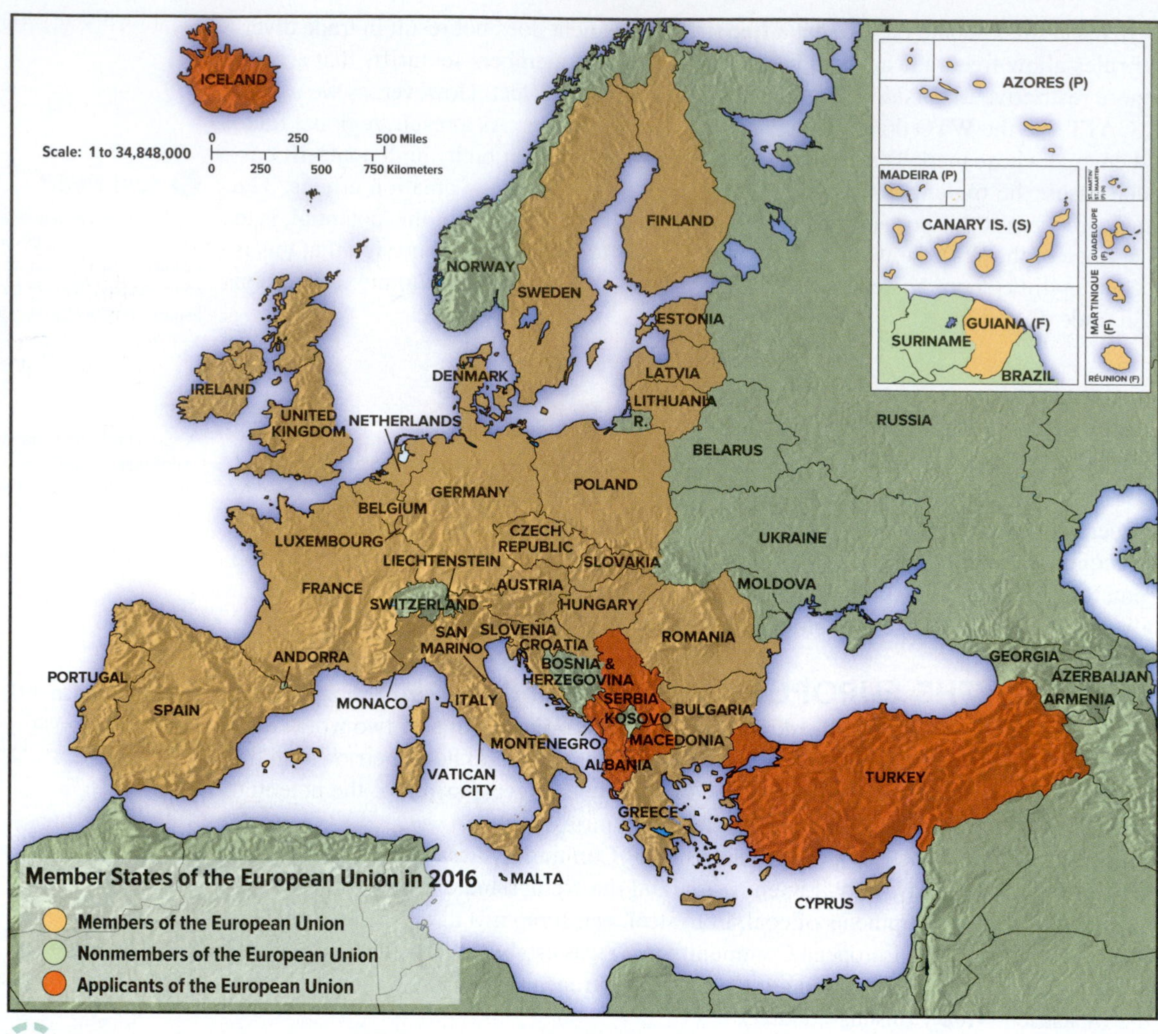

9.1 MAP

Member States of the European Union in 2016.

Source: European Union, 1995–2013.

commission is chosen by member states, and the president then chooses other members in consultation with the states. The entire commission has to be approved by the European Parliament before it can begin work. The commission has a monopoly in proposing European Union legislation. The commission makes a proposal, which goes to the Council of the European Union and then to the European Parliament. The council cannot legislate without a commission proposal in front of it. The commission is also responsible for implementing aspects of EU law, although in practice much of this must be delegated to member states. Another responsibility of the commission is to monitor member states to make sure they are complying with EU laws. In this policing role, the commission will normally ask a state to comply with any EU laws that are being broken. If this persuasion is not sufficient, the commission can refer a case to the Court of Justice.

The European Commission's role in competition policy has become increasingly important to business in recent years. Since 1990, when the office was formally assigned a role in competition policy, the EU's competition commissioner has been steadily gaining influence as the chief regulator of competition policy in the member nations of the EU. As with antitrust authorities in the United States, which include the Federal Trade Commission and the Department of Justice, the role of the competition commissioner is to ensure that no one enterprise uses its market power to drive out competitors and monopolize markets. In 2009, for example, the commission fined Intel a record €1.06 billion for abusing its market power in the computer chip market. (See the Management Focus for details.) The previous record for a similar abuse was €497 billion imposed on Microsoft in 2004 for blocking competition in markets for server computers and media

management FOCUS

The European Commission and Intel

In May 2009, the European Commission announced that it had imposed a record €1.06 billion ($1.45 billion) fine on Intel for anticompetitive behavior. This fine was the result of an investigation into Intel's competitive conduct during the period from October 2002 to December 2007. During this period, Intel's market share of microprocessor sales to personal computer manufacturers consistently exceeded 70 percent. According to the commission, Intel illegally used its market power to ensure that its major rival, AMD, was at a competitive disadvantage, thereby harming "millions of European consumers."

The commission charged that Intel granted major rebates to PC manufacturers—including Acer, Dell, Hewlett-Packard, Lenovo, and NEC—on the condition that they purchased all or almost all their supplies from Intel. Intel also made payments to some manufacturers in exchange for them postponing, canceling, or putting restrictions on the introduction or distribution of AMD-based products. Intel also apparently made payments to Media Saturn Holdings, the owner of Media Markt chain of superstores, for selling only Intel-based computers in Germany, Belgium, and other countries.

Under the order, Intel had to change its practices immediately, pending any appeal. The company was also required to write a bank guarantee for the fine, although that guarantee is held in a bank until the appeal process is exhausted.

For its part, Intel immediately appealed the ruling. The company insisted that it had never coerced computer makers and retailers with inducements and maintained that it had never paid to stop AMD products from reaching the market in Europe. Although Intel acknowledges that it did offer rebates, it claimed that they were never conditional on specific actions by manufacturers and retailers aimed to limit AMD. In June 2014, an EU court rejected Intel's appeal and upheld the judgment against the company.

Sources: M. Hachman, "EU Hits Intel with $1.45 Billion Fine for Antitrust Violations," *PCMAG.com*, May 13, 2009; J. Kanter, "Europe Fines Intel $1.45 billion in Antitrust Case," *The New York Times*, May 14, 2009; T. Fairless, "EU Court Upholds Record Fine Against Intel," *The Wall Street Journal*, June 12, 2014.

software. The commissioner also reviews proposed mergers and acquisitions to make sure they do not create a dominant enterprise with substantial market power.[8] For example, in 2000 a proposed merger between Time Warner of the United States and EMI of the United Kingdom, both music recording companies, was withdrawn after the commission expressed concerns that the merger would reduce the number of major record companies from five to four and create a dominant player in the $40 billion global music industry. Similarly, the commission blocked a proposed merger between two U.S. telecommunication companies, WorldCom and Sprint, because their combined holdings of Internet infrastructure in Europe would give the merged companies so much market power that the commission argued the combined company would dominate that market.

European Council
The heads of state of EU members and the president of the European Commission.

The **European Council** represents the interests of member states. It is clearly the ultimate controlling authority within the EU because draft legislation from the commission can become EU law only if the council agrees. The council is composed of one representative from the government of each member state. The membership, however, varies depending on the topic being discussed. When agricultural issues are being discussed, the agriculture ministers from each state attend council meetings; when transportation is being discussed, transportation ministers attend; and so on. Before 1987, all council issues had to be decided by unanimous agreement among member states. This often led to marathon council sessions and a failure to make progress or reach agreement on commission proposals. In an attempt to clear the resulting logjams, the Single European Act formalized the use of majority voting rules on issues "which have as their object the establishment and functioning of a single market." Most other issues, however, such as tax regulations and immigration policy, still require unanimity among council members if they are to become law. The votes that a country gets in the council are related to the size of the country. For example, Britain, a large country, has 29 votes, whereas Denmark, a much smaller state, has seven votes.

European Parliament
Elected EU body that provides consultation on issues proposed by the European Commission.

As of 2016, the **European Parliament** has 751 members and is directly elected by the populations of the member states. The parliament, which meets in Strasbourg, France, is primarily a consultative rather than legislative body. It debates legislation proposed by the commission and forwarded to it by the council. It can propose amendments to that legislation, which the commission and ultimately the council are not obliged to take up but often will. The power of the parliament recently has been increasing, although not by as much as parliamentarians would like. The European Parliament now has the right to vote on the appointment of commissioners as well as veto some laws (such as the EU budget and single-market legislation).

One major debate waged in Europe during the past few years is whether the council or the parliament should ultimately be the most powerful body in the EU. Some in Europe expressed concern over the democratic accountability of the EU bureaucracy. One side argued that the answer to this apparent democratic deficit lay in increasing the power of the parliament, while others think that true democratic legitimacy lies with elected governments, acting through the Council of the European Union.[9] After significant debate, in December 2007, the member states signed a new treaty, the **Treaty of Lisbon**, under which the power of the European Parliament was increased. When it took effect in December 2009, for the first time in history the European Parliament was the co-equal legislator for almost all European laws.[10] The Treaty of Lisbon also created a new position, a president of the European Council, who serves a 30-month term and represents the nation-states that make up the EU.

Treaty of Lisbon
A European Union–sanctioned treaty that will allow the European Parliament to become the co-equal legislator for almost all European laws.

Court of Justice
Supreme appeals court for EU law.

The **Court of Justice**, which is comprised of one judge from each country, is the supreme appeals court for EU law. Like commissioners, the judges are required to act as independent officials, rather than as representatives of national interests. The commission or a member country can bring other members to the court for failing to meet treaty obligations. Similarly, member countries, member companies, or member institutions can bring the commission or council to the court for failure to act according to an EU treaty.

THE SINGLE EUROPEAN ACT

The Single European Act was born of a frustration among members that the community was not living up to its promise. By the early 1980s, it was clear that the EC had fallen short of its objectives to remove barriers to the free flow of trade and investment among member countries and to harmonize the wide range of technical and legal standards for doing business. Against this background, many of the EC's prominent businesspeople mounted an energetic campaign in the early 1980s to end the EC's economic divisions. The EC responded by creating the Delors Commission. Under the chairperson Jacques Delors, the commission proposed that all impediments to the formation of a single market be eliminated by December 31, 1992. The result was the Single European Act, which became EC law in 1987.

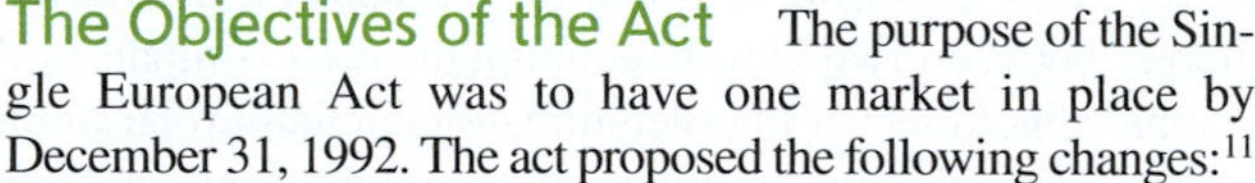

The Objectives of the Act

The purpose of the Single European Act was to have one market in place by December 31, 1992. The act proposed the following changes:[11]

- Remove all frontier controls among EC countries, thereby abolishing delays and reducing the resources required for complying with trade bureaucracy.
- Apply the principle of "mutual recognition" to product standards. A standard developed in one EC country should be accepted in another, provided it met basic requirements in such matters as health and safety.
- Institute open public procurement to nonnational suppliers, reducing costs directly by allowing lower-cost suppliers into national economies and indirectly by forcing national suppliers to compete.
- Lift barriers to competition in the retail banking and insurance businesses, which should drive down the costs of financial services, including borrowing, throughout the EC.
- Remove all restrictions on foreign exchange transactions between member countries by the end of 1992.
- Abolish restrictions on cabotage—the right of foreign truckers to pick up and deliver goods within another member state's borders—by the end of 1992. Estimates suggested this would reduce the cost of haulage within the EC by 10 to 15 percent.

Is Greece a Good Member of the European Union?

In April 2014, Greece held its first bond sale since 2010, raising about $4.2 billion as investors flocked to secure bonds from the hard-hit country. Greece stopped issuing bonds in 2010 amid the country's economic crisis. The 2014 bonds sale was hailed as a sign that Greece is recovering and heading in the right direction. As most observers agree, Greece has struggled to deal with its financial crisis, and has, among many measures, taken on more than $330 billion worth of bailouts and implemented various austerity measures to fix the country's finances. The government's bond sale is a return to international markets for Greece and a step toward the country reducing its dependence on foreign aid—a crucial step to regain confidence from investors and other countries. The bond sale's success is a reason for optimism in Greece and throughout Europe, especially the European Union countries, as it not only shows investors renewed confidence in the Greek economy, but perhaps also in the euro zone's recovery in general. Do you think that the European Union is only as strong as its weakest link or as strong as its strongest country?

Source: T. Ford, "globalEDGE Blog: High Demand for Greece's Return to Bond Market," April 11, 2014, http://globalEDGE.msu.edu.

All those changes were expected to lower the costs of doing business in the EC, but the single-market program was also expected to have more complicated supply-side effects. For example, the expanded market was predicted to give EC firms greater opportunities to exploit economies of scale. In addition, it was thought that the increase in competitive intensity brought about by removing internal barriers to trade and investment would force EC firms to become more efficient. To signify the importance of the Single European Act, the European Community also decided to change its name to the European Union once the act took effect.

Impact The Single European Act has had a significant impact on the EU economy.[12] The act provided the impetus for the restructuring of substantial sections of European industry. Many firms have shifted from national to pan-European production and distribution systems in an attempt to realize scale economies and better compete in a single market. The results have included faster economic growth than would otherwise have been the case.

However, 25 years after the formation of a single market, the reality still falls short of the ideal. An example is given in the accompanying Country Focus, which describes the slow progress toward establishing a fully functioning single market for financial services in the EU. Thus, although the EU is undoubtedly moving toward a single marketplace, established legal, cultural, and language differences among nations mean that implementation has been uneven.

country FOCUS

Creating a Single Market in Financial Services

The European Union in 1999 embarked upon an ambitious action plan to create a single market in financial services by January 1, 2005. Launched a few months after the euro, the EU's single currency, the goal was to dismantle barriers to cross-border activity in financial services, creating a continentwide market for banking services, insurance services, and investment products. In this vision of a single Europe, a citizen of France might use a German firm for basic banking services, borrow a home mortgage from an Italian institution, buy auto insurance from a Dutch enterprise, and keep her savings in mutual funds managed by a British company. Similarly, an Italian firm might raise capital from investors across Europe and use a German firm as its lead underwriter to issue stock for sale through stock exchanges in London and Frankfurt.

One main benefit of a single market, according to its advocates, would be greater competition for financial services, which would give consumers more choices and lower prices, and require financial service firms in the EU to become more efficient, thereby increasing their global competitiveness. Another major benefit would be the creation of a single European capital market. The increased liquidity of a larger capital market would make it easier for firms to borrow funds, lowering their cost of capital (the price of money) and stimulating business investment in Europe, which would create more jobs. A European Commission study suggested that the creation of a single market in financial services would increase the EU's gross domestic product by 1.1 percent a year, creating an additional €130 billion in wealth over a decade. Total business investment would increase by 6 percent annually in the long run, private consumption by 0.8 percent, and total employment by 0.5 percent a year.

Creating a single market has been anything but easy. The financial markets of different EU member states historically have been segmented from each other, and each has its own regulatory framework. In the past, EU financial services firms rarely did business across national borders because of a host of different national regulations with regard to taxation, oversight, accounting information, cross-border takeovers, and the like—all of which had to be harmonized. To complicate matters, long-standing cultural and linguistic barriers complicated the move toward a single market. While in theory an Italian might benefit by being able to purchase homeowner's insurance from a British company, in practice he might be predisposed to purchase it from a local enterprise, even if the price were higher.

By 2014, the EU had made significant progress. More than 40 measures designed to create a single market in financial services had become EU law, and others were in the pipeline. The new rules embraced issues as diverse as the conduct of business by investment firms, stock exchanges, and banks; disclosure standards for listing companies on public exchanges; and the harmonization of accounting standards across nations. However, there had also been some significant setbacks. Most notably, legislation designed to make it easier for firms to make hostile cross-border acquisitions was defeated, primarily due to opposition from German members of the European Parliament, making it more difficult for financial service firms to build pan-European operations. In addition, national governments have still reserved the right to block even friendly cross-border mergers between financial service firms.

The critical issue now is enforcement of the rules that have been put in place. Some believe that it will be years before the full benefits of the new regulations become apparent. In the meantime, the changes may impose significant costs on financial institutions as they attempt to deal with the new raft of regulations.

Sources: C. Randzio-Plath, "Europe Prepares for a Single Financial Market," *Intereconomic,* May–June 2004, pp. 142–46; T. Buck, D. Hargreaves, and P. Norman, "Europe's Single Financial Market," *Financial Times,* January 18, 2005, p. 17; "The Gate-Keeper," *The Economist,* February 19, 2005, p. 79; P. Hofheinz, "A Capital Idea: The European Union Has a Grand Plan to Make Its Financial Markets More Efficient," *The Wall Street Journal,* October 14, 2002, p. R4; "Banking on McCreevy: Europe's Single Market," *The Economist,* November 26, 2005, p. 91; "A New Financial System for Europe; Financial Reform at the Service of Growth; State of Play," The European Commission, http://ec.europa.eu.

Maastricht Treaty

Treaty agreed to in 1992, but not ratified until January 1, 1994, that committed the 12 member states of the European Community to a closer economic and political union.

THE ESTABLISHMENT OF THE EURO

In February 1992, EC members signed the **Maastricht Treaty**, which committed them to adopting a common currency by January 1, 1999.[13] The euro is now used by 19 of the 28 member states of the European Union; these 19 states are members of what is often referred to as the *euro zone*. It encompasses 330 million EU citizens and includes the powerful economies of Germany and France. Many of the countries that joined the EU on May 1, 2004, and the two that joined in 2007 originally planned to adopt the euro when they fulfilled certain economic criteria—a high degree of price stability, a sound fiscal situation, stable exchange rates, and converged long-term interest rates (the current members had to meet the same criteria). However, the events surrounding the EU sovereign debt crisis of 2010–2012 persuaded many of these countries to put their plans on hold, at least for the time being (further details provided later).

Establishment of the euro was an amazing political feat with few historical precedents. It required participating national governments to give up their own currencies and national control over monetary policy. Governments do not routinely sacrifice national sovereignty for the greater good, indicating the importance that the Europeans attach to the euro. By adopting the euro, the EU has created the second most widely traded currency in the world after that of the U.S. dollar. Some believe that the euro could come to rival the dollar as the most important currency in the world.

Three long-term EU members—Great Britain, Denmark, and Sweden—are still sitting on the sidelines. The countries agreeing to the euro locked their exchange rates against each other January 1, 1999. Euro notes and coins were not actually issued until January 1, 2002. In the interim, national currencies circulated in each participating state. However, in each country, the national currency stood for a defined amount of euros. After January 1, 2002, euro notes and coins were issued and the national currencies were taken out of circulation. By mid-2002, all prices and routine economic transactions within the euro zone were in euros.

Benefits of the Euro

Europeans decided to establish a single currency in the EU for a number of reasons. First, they believe that businesses and individuals realize significant savings from having to handle one currency, rather than many. These savings come from lower foreign exchange and hedging costs. For example, people going from Germany to France no longer have to pay a commission to a bank to change German deutsche marks into French francs. Instead, they are able to use euros. According to the European Commission, such savings amount to 0.5 percent of the European Union's GDP.

Second, and perhaps more important, the adoption of a common currency makes it easier to compare prices across Europe. This has been increasing competition because it has become easier for consumers to shop around. For example, if a German finds that cars sell for less in France than Germany, he may be tempted to purchase from a French car dealer rather than his local car dealer. Alternatively, traders may engage in arbitrage to exploit such price differentials, buying cars in France and reselling them in Germany. The only way that German car dealers will be able to hold onto business in the face of such competitive pressures will be to reduce the prices they charge for cars. As a consequence of such pressures, the introduction of a common currency has led to lower prices, which translates into substantial gains for European consumers.

Third, faced with lower prices, European producers have been forced to look for ways to reduce their production costs to maintain their profit margins. The introduction of a common currency, by increasing competition, has produced long-run gains in the economic efficiency of European companies.

Fourth, the introduction of a common currency has given a boost to the development of a highly liquid pan-European capital market. Over time, the development of such a capital market should lower the cost of capital and lead to an increase in both the level of investment and the efficiency with which investment funds are allocated. This could be especially helpful to smaller companies that have historically had difficulty borrowing money from domestic banks. For example, the capital market of Portugal is very small and illiquid, which makes it extremely difficult for bright Portuguese entrepreneurs with a good idea to borrow money at a reasonable price. However, in theory, such companies can now tap a much more liquid pan-European capital market.

Finally, the development of a pan-European, euro-denominated capital market will increase the range of investment options open to both individuals and institutions. For example, it will now be much easier for individuals and institutions based in, let's say, Holland to invest in Italian or French companies. This will enable European investors to better diversify their risk, which again lowers the cost of capital, and should also increase the efficiency with which capital resources are allocated.[14]

Can the Euro Survive?

It seems like experts and interested observers are always debating the merits of the euro and its likelihood of survival. The answers lie in examining several interesting facts of the European Union. First, the lack of a European treasury is a missing piece of the puzzle. Without it, the ECB is limited in the assistance it can provide to euro zone member-states. In theory, the European Central Bank (ECB) could bail out those member-states burdened with excessive debt by printing more money. However, that would require the approval of all of the EU member countries (not just the countries that that use the euro as their national currency). Germany is typically opposed to any measure that may light the fires of inflation. Some of the EU members also think it is unfair to bail out those states that have lived beyond their means for many years. It is difficult to compare the difficulties within the EU to those of other nations that have faced similar problems and survived. But the basic question remains, will the euro survive?

Source: http://seekingalpha.com.

Costs of the Euro The drawback, for some, of a single currency is that national authorities have lost control over monetary policy. Thus, it is crucial to ensure that the EU's monetary policy is well managed. The Maastricht Treaty called for establishment of the independent European Central Bank (ECB), similar in some respects to the U.S. Federal Reserve, with a clear mandate to manage monetary policy so as to ensure price stability. The ECB, based in Frankfurt, is meant to be independent from political pressure—although critics question this. Among other things, the ECB sets interest rates and determines monetary policy across the euro zone.

The implied loss of national sovereignty to the ECB underlies the decision by Great Britain, Denmark, and Sweden to stay out of the euro zone. Many in these countries are suspicious of the ECB's ability to remain free from political pressure and to keep inflation under tight control.

In theory, the design of the ECB should ensure that it remains free of political pressure. The ECB is modeled on the German Bundesbank, which historically has been the most independent and successful central bank in Europe. The Maastricht Treaty prohibits the ECB from taking orders from politicians. The executive board of the bank, which consists of a president, vice president, and four other members, carries out policy by issuing instructions to national central banks. The policy itself is determined by the governing council, which consists of the executive board plus the central bank governors from the euro zone countries. The governing council votes on interest rate changes. Members of the executive board are appointed for eight-year nonrenewable terms, insulating them from political pressures to get reappointed. So far, the ECB has established a solid reputation for political independence.

According to critics, another drawback of the euro is that the EU is not what economists would call an optimal currency area. In an **optimal currency area**, similarities in the underlying structure of economic activity make it feasible to adopt a single currency and use a single exchange rate as an instrument of macroeconomic policy. Many of the European economies in the euro zone, however, are very dissimilar. For example, Finland and Portugal have different wage rates, tax regimes, and business cycles, and they may react very differently to external economic shocks. A change in the euro exchange rate that helps Finland may hurt Portugal. Obviously, such differences complicate macroeconomic policy. For example, when euro economies are not growing in unison, a common monetary policy may mean that interest rates are too high for depressed regions and too low for booming regions.

Optimal Currency Area
Region in which similarities in economic activity make a single currency and exchange rate feasible instruments of macroeconomic policy.

One way of dealing with such divergent effects within the euro zone is for the EU to engage in fiscal transfers, taking money from prosperous regions and pumping it into depressed regions. Such a move, however, opens a political can of worms. Would the citizens of Germany forgo their "fair share" of EU funds to create jobs for underemployed Greece workers? Not surprisingly, there is strong political opposition to such practices.

The Euro Experience Since its establishment January 1, 1999, the euro has had a volatile trading history against the world's major currency, the U.S. dollar. After starting life in 1999 at €1 = $1.17, the euro steadily fell until it reached a low of €1 = $0.83 in October 2000, leading critics to claim the euro was a failure. A major reason for the fall in the euro's value was that international investors were investing money in booming U.S. stocks and bonds and taking money out of Europe to finance this investment. In other words, they were selling euros to buy dollars so that they could invest in dollar-denominated assets. This increased the demand for dollars and decreased the demand for the euro, driving the value of the euro down.

The fortunes of the euro began improving in late 2001, when the dollar weakened; the currency stood at a robust all-time high of €1 = $1.54 in early March 2008. One reason for the rise in the value of the euro was that the flow of capital into the United States stalled as the U.S. financial markets fell during 2007 and 2008. Many investors were now taking money out of the United States by selling dollar-denominated assets such as U.S. stocks and bonds and purchasing euro-denominated assets. Falling demand for U.S. dollars and rising demand for euros translated into a fall in the value of the dollar against the euro. Furthermore, in a vote of confidence in both the euro and the ability of the ECB to manage monetary policy within the euro zone, many foreign central banks added more euros to their supply of foreign currencies. In the first three years of its life, the euro never reached the 13 percent of global reserves made up by the deutsche mark and other former euro zone currencies. The euro didn't jump that hurdle until early 2002, but by 2011, it stood at 26.3 percent.[15]

Since 2008 however, the euro has weakened, reflecting persistent concerns over slow economic growth and large budget deficits among several EU member states, particularly Greece, Portugal, Ireland, Italy, and Spain. During the 2000s, all these governments had sharply increased their government debt to finance public spending. Government debt as a percentage of GDP hit record levels in many of these nations. By 2010, private investors became increasingly concerned that these nations would not be able to service their sovereign debt, particularly given the economic slowdown following the 2008–2009 global financial crisis. They sold off government bonds of troubled nations, driving down bond prices and driving up the cost of government borrowing (bond prices and interest rates are inversely related). This led to fears that several national governments, particularly Greece, might default on their sovereign debt, plunging the euro zone into an economic crisis. To try and stave off such a sovereign debt crisis, in May 2010, the euro zone nations and the International Monetary Fund (IMF) agreed to a €110 billion bailout package to help rescue Greece. In November 2010, the EU and IMF agreed to a bailout package for Ireland of €85 billion; in May 2011, euro zone countries and the IMF instituted a €78 billion bailout plan for Portugal. In return for these loans, all three countries had to agree to sharp reductions in government spending, which meant slower economic growth and high unemployment until government debt was reduced to more sustainable levels. While Italy and Spain did not request bailout packages, both countries were forced by falling bond prices to institute austerity programs that required big reductions in government spending. The euro zone nations also set up a permanent bailout fund—the European Stability Mechanism—worth about €500 billion,

The weakened value of the euro against the U.S. dollar has been a cause for concern among many nations.

Source: © Martin Leissl/Bloomberg/Getty Images

country FOCUS

The Greek Sovereign Debt Crisis

When the euro was established, some critics worried that free-spending countries in the euro zone (such as Italy and Greece) might borrow excessively, running up large public-sector deficits that they could not finance. This would then rock the value of the euro, requiring their more sober brethren, such as Germany or France, to step in and bail out the profligate nation. In 2010, this worry became a reality as a financial crisis in Greece hit the value of the euro.

The financial crisis had its roots in a decade of free spending by the Greek government, which ran up a high level of debt to finance extensive spending in the public sector. Much of the spending increase could be characterized as an attempt by the government to buy off powerful interest groups in Greek society, from teachers and farmers to public-sector employees, rewarding them with high pay and extensive benefits. To make matters worse, the government misled the international community about the level of its indebtedness. In October 2009, a new government took power and quickly announced that the 2009 public-sector deficit, which had been projected to be around 5 percent, would actually be 12.7 percent. The previous government had apparently been cooking the books.

This shattered any faith that international investors might have had in the Greek economy. Interest rates on Greek government debt quickly surged to 7.1 percent, about 4 percentage points higher than the rate on German bonds. Two of the three international rating agencies also cut their ratings on Greek bonds and warned that further downgrades were likely. The main concern now was that the Greek government might not be able to refinance some €20 billion of debt that would mature in April or May 2010. A further concern was that the Greek government might lack the political willpower to make the large cuts in public spending necessary to bring down the deficit and restore investor confidence.

Nor was Greece alone in having large public-sector deficits. Three other euro zone countries—Spain, Portugal, and Ireland—also had large debt loads, and interest rates on their bonds surged as investors sold out. This raised the specter of financial contagion, with large-scale defaults among the weaker members of the euro zone. If this did occur, the EU and IMF would most certainly have to step in and rescue the troubled nations. With this possibility, once considered very remote, investors started to move money out of euros, and the value of the euro started to fall on the foreign exchange market.

Recognizing that the unthinkable might happen—and that without external help, Greece might default on its government debt, pushing the EU and the euro into a major crisis—in May 2010, the euro zone countries, led by Germany, along with the IMF agreed to lend Greece up to €110 billion. These loans were judged sufficient to cover Greece's financing needs for three years. In exchange, the Greek government agreed to implement a series of strict austerity measures. These included tax increases, major cuts in public-sector pay, reductions in benefits enjoyed by public-sector employees (e.g., the retirement age was increased to 65 from 61, and limits were placed on pensions), and reductions in the number of public-sector enterprises from 6,000 to 2,000. However, the Greek economy contracted so fast in 2010 and 2011 that tax revenues plunged. By the end of 2011, the Greek economy was almost 29 percent smaller than it had been in 2005, while unemployment approached 20 percent. The contracting tax base limited the ability of the government to pay down debt. By early 2012, yields on 10-year Greek government debt reached 34 percent, indicating that many investors now expected Greece to default on its sovereign debt. This forced the Greek government to seek further aid from the euro zone countries and the IMF. As a condition for a fresh €130 billion bailout plan, the Greek government had to get holders of Greek government bonds to agree to the biggest sovereign debt restructuring in history, In effect, bondholders agreed to write off 53.5 percent of the debt they held.

While the Greek government did not technically default on its sovereign debt, to many it seemed as if the EU and IMF had orchestrated an orderly partial default. By early 2014, it looked as if the Greek economy had finally turned a corner and was on the way to recovery. Yields on 10-year bonds had fallen blow 8 percent, and the government was running a budget surplus before interest payments.

Unfortunately, things took a turn for the worse in 2014, when it became clear that despite economic progress, Greece did not have the funds to replay its creditors on time and would have to issue new bonds in order to do so. Following a decision to call a snap election, in January 2015, a radical left-wing "anti-bailout" party was swept into power. The financial minister of the new government suggested that Greece should default on its scheduled debt repayments to its largest creditor, Germany. This initiated a crisis in the euro zone and helped precipitate a sharp decline in the value of the euro against the U.S. dollar. Following further negotiations, Greece's creditors agreed to a third bailout in late 2015 but only after Greece agreed to implement further austerity measures and economic reforms. Whether this will prove to be any more successful than the prior two bailouts remains to be seen.

Sources: "A Very European Crisis," *The Economist,* February 6, 2010, pp. 75–77; L. Thomas, "Is Debt Trashing the Euro?" *The New York Times,* February 7, 2010, pp. 1, 7; "Bite the Bullet," *The Economist,* January 15, 2011, pp. 77–79; "The Wait Is Over," *The Economist,* March 17, 2012, pp. 83–84; "Aegean Stables," *The Economist,* January 11, 2014; Liz Alderman, "Greece's Debt Crisis Explained," The New York Times, November 8, 2015.

which was designed to restore confidence in the euro. As detailed in the accompanying Country Focus, by 2012 Greece had been granted two more bailout packages in an attempt to forestall a full-blown default on payment of its sovereign debt.

As might be expected, the economic turmoil led to a decline in the value of the euro. By early 2016, the dollar-euro exchange rate stood at €1 = $1.11, significantly below its 2008 level but still somewhat better than the exchange rate in early 2000. The euro also declined by 20 to 30 percent against most of the world's other major currencies between late 2008 and early 2016.

More troubling perhaps for the long-run success of the euro, many of the newer EU nations that had committed to adopting the euro put their plans on hold. Countries like Poland and the

Czech Republic had no desire to join the euro zone and then have their taxpayers help bail out the profligate governments of countries like Italy and Greece. To compound matters, the sovereign debt crisis had exposed a deep flaw in the euro zone: it was difficult for fiscally more conservative nations like Germany to limit profligate spending by the governments of other nations that might subsequently create strains and impose costs on the entire euro zone. The Germans in particular found themselves in the unhappy position of having to underwrite loans to bail out the governments of Greece, Portugal, and Ireland. This started to erode support for the euro in the stronger EU states. To try to correct this flaw, 25 of the then 27 countries in the EU signed a fiscal pact in January 2012 that made it more difficult for member states to break tight new rules on government deficits (the United Kingdom and Czech Republic abstained; Croatia joined in 2013). Whether such actions will be sufficient to get the euro back on track remains to be seen.

ENLARGMENT OF THE EUROPEAN UNION Enlargement of the EU into eastern Europe has been discussed since the collapse of communism at the end of the 1980s, and by the end of the 1990s, 13 countries had applied to become EU members. To qualify for EU membership, the applicants had to privatize state assets, deregulate markets, restructure industries, and tame inflation. They also had to enshrine complex EU laws into their own systems, establish stable democratic governments, and respect human rights.[16] In December 2002, the EU formally agreed to accept the applications of 10 countries, and they joined May 1, 2004. The new members included the Baltic countries, the Czech Republic, and the larger nations of Hungary and Poland. The only new members not in eastern Europe were the Mediterranean island nations of Malta and Cyprus. Their inclusion in the EU expanded the union to 25 states, stretching from the Atlantic to the borders of Russia; added 23 percent to the landmass of the EU; brought 75 million new citizens into the EU, building an EU with a population of 450 million people; and created a single continental economy with a GDP of close to €11 trillion. In 2007, Bulgaria and Romania joined, and in 2013, Croatia joined, bringing total membership to 28 nations.

The new members were not able to adopt the euro for several years, and free movement of labor among the new and existing members was prohibited until then. Consistent with theories of free trade, the enlargement should create added benefits for all members. However, given the small size of the eastern European economies (together they amount to only 5 percent of the GDP of current EU members), the initial impact will probably be small. The biggest notable change might be in the EU bureaucracy and decision-making processes, where budget negotiations among 28 nations are bound to prove more problematic than negotiations among 15 nations.

Left standing at the door is Turkey. Turkey, which has long lobbied to join the union, presents the EU with some difficult issues. The country has had a customs union with the EU since 1995, and about half its international trade is already with the EU. However, full membership has been denied because of concerns over human rights issues (particularly Turkish policies toward its Kurdish minority). In addition, some on the Turkish side suspect the EU is not eager to let a primarily Muslim nation of 74 million people, which has one foot in Asia, join the EU. The EU formally indicated in December 2002 that it would allow the Turkish application to proceed with no further delay in December 2004 if the country improved its human rights record to the satisfaction of the EU. In December 2004, the EU agreed to allow Turkey to start accession talks in October 2005, but those talks are stalled, and at this point, it is unclear when the nation will join.

Croatia is the 28th nation to join the EU.

Source: © Frederik Florin/AFP/Getty Images

BRITISH EXIT FROM THE EUROPEAN UNION

On June 23, 2016, the British electorate voted in a national referendum to leave the EU. Under the Treaty of Lisbon, the British now have two years to negotiate the terms of exit with the EU. While the British have enjoyed the benefits of free trade within Europe, a segment of the population has never been comfortable with the loss of national sovereignty implied by membership within the EU. The British have often railed against regulations imposed by the EU bureaucracy in Brussels, and more recently, immigration has become a key issue. Immigration from within the EU hit record levels in 2015. Much of that immigration has been from eastern Europe. Many of the immigrants have been low skilled and work in restaurants, hotels and retail stores. The campaign for leaving the EU claimed that exit would allow the British to "take back control" of immigration. In the referendum, London, Scotland, and Northern Island voted to stay in the EU, whereas most of the rest of the country voted for exit. The vote was also split by age and education. The younger and more educated voted to stay in the EU, while the older and less educated voted to leave.

The impending exit of Britain creates an existential problem for the EU. Britain is the EU's second largest national economy. It is seen by many smaller member countries as an important counterweight to the economic power of Germany. In the aftermath of the British vote, right-wing politicians in Holland, Denmark, and France also called for referendums on continuing EU membership, raising fears that the British vote might trigger a "rush for the exits." While this seems unlikely to occur, there is little doubt that an EU without Britain will lose some of its economic and political clout on the world stage, and the EU itself will be diminished. Given the importance of immigration in the British vote, further expansion of the EU now seems unlikely, particularly with regard to Turkey. As for Britain, most experts predict that the country will bear significant short- to medium-term costs as a result of this decision. Britain is now less likely to attract inward investment from foreign multinationals, some multinationals may move operations to other EU countries to maintain access to the single market, and exports to the EU may fall, London risks losing its position as the financial capital of Europe, and economic growth will probably be lower than it otherwise might have been. Furthermore, given that the Scots voted by a large margin to stay in the EU, this once again raises the possibility of Scottish independence from the United Kingdom. In the long run, whether Britain benefits from exit depends on its ability to negotiate trade deals with the EU and other major economic powers, including the United States, Japan, and China, to replace the benefits it will lose by exiting from the EU. In a world that is becoming increasingly resistant to free trade deals, there is no guarantee that the British will be able to do this.

Use SmartBook to help retain what you have learned. Access your Instructor's Connect course to check out SmartBook or go to learnsmartadvantage.com for help.

Regional Economic Integration in the Americas

LO 9-4

Explain the history, current scope, and future prospects of the world's most important regional economic agreements.

No other attempt at regional economic integration comes close to the EU in its boldness or its potential implications for the world economy, but regional economic integration is on the rise in the Americas. The most significant attempt is the North American Free Trade Agreement. In addition to NAFTA, several other trade blocs are in the offing in the Americas (see Map 9.2), the most significant of which appear to be the Andean Community and Mercosur.

THE NORTH AMERICAN FREE TRADE AGREEMENT

The governments of the United States and Canada in 1988 agreed to enter into a free trade agreement, which took effect January 1, 1989. The goal of the agreement was to eliminate all tariffs on bilateral trade between Canada and the United States by 1998. This was followed in 1991 by talks among the United States, Canada, and Mexico aimed at establishing a **North American Free Trade Agreement (NAFTA)** for the three countries. The talks concluded in August 1992 with an agreement in principle, and the following year, the agreement was ratified by the governments of all three countries. The agreement became law January 1, 1994.[17]

North American Free Trade Agreement (NAFTA)

Free trade area among Canada, Mexico, and the United States.

NAFTA'S Contents

The contents of NAFTA include the following:

- Abolition by 2004 of tariffs on 99 percent of the goods traded among Mexico, Canada, and the United States.
- Removal of most barriers on the cross-border flow of services, allowing financial institutions, for example, unrestricted access to the Mexican market by 2000.
- Protection of intellectual property rights.
- Removal of most restrictions on foreign direct investment among the three member countries, although special treatment (protection) will be given to Mexican energy and railway industries, American airline and radio communications industries, and Canadian culture.
- Application of national environmental standards, provided such standards have a scientific basis. Lowering of standards to lure investment is described as being inappropriate.
- Establishment of two commissions with the power to impose fines and remove trade privileges when environmental standards or legislation involving health and safety, minimum wages, or child labor are ignored.

9.2 MAP

Economic Integration in the Americas.

The Case for NAFTA Proponents of NAFTA have argued that the free trade area should be viewed as an opportunity to create an enlarged and more efficient productive base for the entire region. Advocates acknowledge that one effect of NAFTA would be that some U.S. and Canadian firms would move production to Mexico to take advantage of lower labor costs. (In 2004, the average hourly labor cost in Mexico was still one-tenth of that in the United States and Canada.) Movement of production to Mexico, they argued, was most likely to occur in low-skilled, labor-intensive manufacturing industries in which Mexico might have a comparative advantage. Advocates of NAFTA argued that many would benefit from such a trend. Mexico would benefit from much-needed inward investment and employment. The United States and Canada would benefit because the increased incomes of the Mexicans would allow them to import more U.S. and Canadian goods, thereby increasing demand and making up for the jobs lost in industries that moved production to Mexico. U.S. and Canadian consumers would benefit from the lower prices of products made in Mexico. In addition, the international competitiveness of U.S. and Canadian firms that moved production to Mexico to take advantage of lower labor costs would be enhanced, enabling them to better compete with Asian and European rivals.

The Case against NAFTA

Those who opposed NAFTA claimed that ratification would be followed by a mass exodus of jobs from the United States and Canada into Mexico as employers sought to profit from Mexico's lower wages and less strict environmental and labor laws. According to one extreme opponent, Ross Perot, up to 5.9 million U.S. jobs would be lost to Mexico after NAFTA in what he famously characterized as a "giant sucking sound." Most economists, however, dismissed these numbers as being absurd and alarmist. They argued that Mexico would have to run a bilateral trade surplus with the United States of close to $300 billion for job loss on such a scale to occur—and $300 billion was the size of Mexico's GDP. In other words, such a scenario seemed implausible.

More sober estimates of the impact of NAFTA ranged from a net creation of 170,000 jobs in the United States (due to increased Mexican demand for U.S. goods and services) and an increase of $15 billion per year to the joint U.S. and Mexican GDP to a net loss of 490,000 U.S. jobs. To put these numbers in perspective, employment in the U.S. economy was predicted to grow by 18 million from 1993 to 2003. As most economists repeatedly stressed, NAFTA would have a small impact on both Canada and the United States. It could hardly be any other way, because the Mexican economy was only 5 percent of the size of the U.S. economy. Signing NAFTA required the largest leap of economic faith from Mexico rather than Canada or the United States. Falling trade barriers would expose Mexican firms to highly efficient U.S. and Canadian competitors that, when compared to the average Mexican firm, had far greater capital resources, access to highly educated and skilled workforces, and much greater technological sophistication. The short-run outcome was likely to be painful economic restructuring and unemployment in Mexico. But advocates of NAFTA claimed there would be long-run dynamic gains in the efficiency of Mexican firms as they adjusted to the rigors of a more competitive marketplace. To the extent that this occurred, they argued, Mexico's economic growth rate would accelerate, and Mexico might become a major market for Canadian and U.S. firms.[18]

Did You Know?

Did you know that NAFTA was thought to produce a "giant sucking sound?"

Visit your Connect SmartBook® to view a short video explanation from the authors.

Environmentalists also voiced concerns about NAFTA. They pointed to the sludge in the Rio Grande and the smog in the air over Mexico City and warned that Mexico could degrade clean air and toxic waste standards across the continent. They pointed out that the lower Rio Grande was the most polluted river in the United States and that, with NAFTA, chemical waste and sewage would increase along its course from El Paso, Texas, to the Gulf of Mexico.

There was also opposition in Mexico to NAFTA from those who feared a loss of national sovereignty. Mexican critics argued that their country would be dominated by U.S. firms that would not really contribute to Mexico's economic growth but instead would use Mexico as a low-cost assembly site while keeping their high-paying, high-skilled jobs north of the border.

NAFTA: The Results

Studies of NAFTA's impact suggest its initial effects muted, and both advocates and detractors may have been guilty of exaggeration.[19] On average, studies indicate that NAFTA's overall impact has been small but positive.[20] NAFTA was meant to increase trade between the three member states, and that it appears to have done. From 1993 to 2005, trade among NAFTA's partners grew by 250 percent.[21] Canada and Mexico are now among the top three trading partners of the United States (the other is China), suggesting the economies of the three NAFTA nations have become more closely integrated. In 1990, U.S. trade with Canada and Mexico accounted for about a quarter of total U.S. trade. By 2005, the figure was close to one-third. Canada's trade with its NAFTA partners increased from about 70 percent to more than 80 percent of all Canadian foreign trade between 1993 and 2005, while Mexico's trade with NAFTA increased from 66 percent to 80 percent over the same period.

As NAFTA Nurtures Mexican Economy, Illegal Immigration Dwindles?

The large wave of immigration from Mexico to the United States that began four decades ago, most of it unauthorized, has to a large degree ended. As a report from the Pew Hispanic Center confirms, net migration from Mexico to the United States sank to about zero in the past five years. Did the North American Free Trade Agreement (NAFTA) play a role? Yes and no. Actually, the number of Mexicans living illegally in the United States shot up from 2.5 million in 1995, the year after NAFTA took effect, to 11 million in 2013. The main reason was the booming U.S. economy, which generated huge demands for labor just as the share of Mexico's population aged 15 to 39, prime migration years, was peaking at about 75 percent. Migration plummeted after 2005 because of reduced U.S. demand for labor and the slowing of Mexican population growth but also because NAFTA started to pay off in the form of dynamic new export industries in Mexico, such as automobile manufacturing. Do you think there will be continued decline in immigration of people from Mexico to the United States in future years because of the NAFTA agreement, or will the immigration decline (or potential increase) be due to factors that are not tied to NAFTA?

Source: www.lehighvalleylive.com.

America's trade with Mexico increased 506 percent between 1993 and 2012, compared with 279 percent for non-NAFTA countries. All three countries also experienced strong productivity growth in the first 10 years NAFTA was in place. In Mexico, labor productivity has increased by 50 percent. The passage of NAFTA may well have contributed to this.

Estimates suggest that employment effects of NAFTA have been moderate to small. By far the most pessimistic estimate of job losses comes from a study published by the left-leaning Economic Policy Institute. This study suggests that the United States lost about 850,000 jobs between 1993 and 2013 due to NAFTA, or 42,500 jobs a year on average. To put this loss in context, between 1992 and 2000, the U.S. economy created 2.86 million jobs *every year* on average. Other studies suggest that NAFTA had a far more moderate job impact in the United States. A review of the evidence by the OECD, for example, concluded that "the net employment effects were relatively small, although there were adjustments across sectors displacing workers."[22]

A study of the welfare effects of NAFTA, which take into account its impact on national income, suggest that Mexico and the United States saw small welfare gains of 1.31 percent and 0.08 percent, respectively, while Canada suffered a welfare loss of 0.06 percent%. The same study noted that real wages increased for all NAFTA members, with Mexico registering the largest gain. This study supports the general conclusion that contrary to political rhetoric, the impact of NAFTA has been quite small.[23]

Andean Community

A 1969 agreement among Bolivia, Chile, Ecuador, Colombia, and Peru to establish a customs union.

THE ANDEAN COMMUNITY

Bolivia, Chile, Ecuador, Colombia, and Peru signed an agreement in 1969 to create the Andean Pact. The **Andean Community** was largely based on the EU model but was far less successful at achieving its stated goals. The integration steps begun in 1969 included an internal tariff reduction program, a common external tariff, a transportation policy, a common industrial policy, and special concessions for the smallest members, Bolivia and Ecuador.

By the mid-1980s, the Andean Pact had all but collapsed and had failed to achieve any of its stated objectives. There was no tariff-free trade among member countries, no common external tariff, and no harmonization of economic policies. Political and economic problems seem to have hindered cooperation among member countries. The countries of the Andean Pact have had to deal with low economic growth, hyperinflation, high unemployment, political unrest, and crushing debt burdens. In addition, the dominant political ideology in many of the Andean countries during this period tended toward the radical-socialist end of the political spectrum. Because such an ideology is hostile to the free market economic principles on which the Andean Pact was based, progress toward closer integration could not be expected.

The tide began to turn in the late 1980s when, after years of economic decline, the governments of Latin America began to adopt free market economic policies. In 1990, the heads of the five current members of the Andean Community—Bolivia, Ecuador, Peru, Colombia, and Venezuela—met in the Galápagos Islands. The resulting Galápagos Declaration effectively relaunched the Andean Pact, which was renamed the Andean Community in 1997. The declaration's objectives included the establishment of a free trade area by 1992, a customs union by 1994, and a common market by 1995. This last milestone has not been reached. A customs union was implemented in 1995—although Peru opted out and Bolivia received preferential treatment until 2003. The Andean Community now operates as a customs union. In December 2005, it signed an agreement with Mercosur to restart stalled negotiations on the creation of a free trade area between the two trading blocs. Those negotiations are proceeding at a slow pace. In late 2006, Venezuela withdrew from the Andean Community as part of that country's attempts to join Mercosur.

Mercosur

Pact among Argentina, Brazil, Paraguay, and Uruguay to establish a free trade area.

MERCOSUR

Mercosur originated in 1988 as a free trade pact between Brazil and Argentina. The modest reductions in tariffs and quotas accompanying this pact reportedly helped bring about an 80 percent increase in trade between the two countries in the late 1980s.[24] This success encouraged the expansion of the pact in March 1990 to include Paraguay and Uruguay. In 2006, the pact was further expanded when Venezuela joined Mercosur, although it may take years for Venezuela to become fully integrated into the pact. As of early 2014, Paraguay had yet to ratify the agreement allowing Venezuela to become a full member of Mercosur.

The initial aim of Mercosur was to establish a full free trade area by the end of 1994 and a common market sometime thereafter. In December 1995, Mercosur's members agreed to a five-year program under which they hoped to perfect their free trade area and move toward a full customs union—something that has yet to be achieved.[25] For its first eight years or so, Mercosur seemed to be making a positive contribution to the economic growth rates of its member states. Trade among the four core members quadrupled between 1990 and 1998. The combined GDP of the four member states grew at an annual average rate of 3.5 percent between 1990 and 1996, a performance that is significantly better than the four attained during the 1980s.[26]

However, Mercosur had its critics, including Alexander Yeats, a senior economist at the World Bank, who wrote a stinging critique.[27] According to Yeats, the trade diversion effects of Mercosur outweigh its trade creation effects. Yeats pointed out that the fastest-growing items in intra-Mercosur trade were cars, buses, agricultural equipment, and other capital-intensive goods that are produced relatively inefficiently in the four member countries. In other words, Mercosur countries, insulated from outside competition by tariffs that run as high as 70 percent of value on motor vehicles, are investing in factories that build products that are too expensive to sell to anyone but themselves. The result, according to Yeats, is that Mercosur countries might not be able to compete globally once the group's external trade barriers come down. In the meantime, capital is being drawn away from more efficient enterprises. In the near term, countries with more efficient manufacturing enterprises lose because Mercosur's external trade barriers keep them out of the market.

Mercosur hit a significant roadblock in 1998, when its member states slipped into recession and intrabloc trade slumped. Trade fell further in 1999, following a financial crisis in Brazil that led to the devaluation of the Brazilian real, which immediately made the goods of other Mercosur members 40 percent more expensive in Brazil, their largest export market. At this point, progress toward establishing a full customs union all but stopped. Things deteriorated further in 2001, when Argentina, beset by economic stresses, suggested the customs union be temporarily suspended. Argentina wanted to suspend Mercosur's tariff so that it could abolish duties on imports of capital equipment, while raising those on consumer goods to 35 percent (Mercosur had established a 14 percent import tariff on both sets of goods). Brazil agreed to this request, effectively halting Mercosur's quest to become a fully functioning customs union.[28] Hope for a revival arose in 2003, when new Brazilian President Lula da Silva announced his support for a revitalized and expanded Mercosur modeled after the EU with a larger membership, a common currency, and a democratically elected Mercosur parliament.[29] In 2010, the members of Mercosur did agree on a common customs code to avoid outside goods having to pay tariffs more than once, an important step toward achieving a full customs union. Since 2010, however, Mercosur has made little forward progress, and the jury is still out on whether it will become a fully functioning customs union.

CENTRAL AMERICAN COMMON MARKET, CAFTA, AND CARICOM Two other trade pacts in the Americas have not made much progress. In the early 1960s, Costa Rica, El Salvador, Guatemala, Honduras, and Nicaragua attempted to set up a **Central American Common Market**. It collapsed in 1969, when war broke out between Honduras and El Salvador after a riot at a soccer match between teams from the two countries. Since then, the member countries have made some progress toward reviving their agreement (the five founding members were joined by the Dominican Republic). The proposed common market was given a boost in 2003, when the United States signaled its intention to enter into bilateral free trade negotiations with the group. These culminated in a 2004 agreement to establish a free trade agreement between the six countries and the United States. Known as the **Central America Free Trade Agreement (CAFTA)**, the aim is to lower trade barriers between the United States and the six countries for most goods and services.

A customs union was to have been created in 1991 between the English-speaking Caribbean countries under the auspices of the Caribbean Community. Referred to as **CARICOM,** it was established in 1973. However, it repeatedly failed to progress toward economic integration. A formal commitment to economic and monetary union was adopted by CARICOM's member states in 1984, but since then, little progress has been made. In October 1991, the CARICOM governments failed, for the third consecutive time, to meet a deadline for establishing a common external tariff. Despite this, CARICOM expanded to 15 members by 2005. In early 2006, six CARICOM members established the **Caribbean Single Market and Economy (CSME)**. Modeled on the EU's single market, CSME's goal is to lower trade barriers and harmonize macroeconomic and monetary policy between member states.[30]

Central American Common Market
A trade pact among Costa Rica, El Salvador, Guatemala, Honduras, and Nicaragua, which began in the early 1960s but collapsed in 1969 due to war.

Central America Free Trade Agreement (CAFTA)
The agreement of the member states of the Central American Common Market joined by the Dominican Republic to trade freely with the United States.

CARICOM
An association of English-speaking Caribbean states that are attempting to establish a customs union.

Caribbean Single Market and Economy (CSME)
The six CARICOM members that agreed to lower trade barriers and harmonize macroeconomic and monetary policies.

 **test PREP**

Use SmartBook to help retain what you have learned. Access your Instructor's Connect course to check out SmartBook or go to learnsmartadvantage.com for help.

LO 9-4

Explain the history, current scope, and future prospects of the world's most important regional economic agreements.

Regional Economic Integration Elsewhere

Numerous attempts at regional economic integration have been tried throughout Asia, Africa, and elsewhere. One of the most significant is the Association of Southeast Asian Nations (ASEAN), although there have been numerous attempts to establish free trade agreements in Africa (see the opening case), and there are ongoing efforts to establish free trade agreements between the United States and 11 other nations bordering the Pacific (the Trans Pacific Partnership or TPP), and the United States and the European Union (the Transatlantic Trade and Investment Partnership or TTIP).

Association of Southeast Asian Nations (ASEAN)

Formed in 1967, an attempt to establish a free trade area among Brunei, Cambodia, Indonesia, Laos, Malaysia, Myanmar, the Philippines, Singapore, Vietnam, and Thailand.

ASSOCIATION OF SOUTHEAST ASIAN NATIONS

Formed in 1967, the **Association of Southeast Asian Nations (ASEAN)** includes Brunei, Cambodia, Indonesia, Laos, Malaysia, Myanmar, Philippines, Singapore, Thailand, and Vietnam. Laos, Myanmar, Vietnam, and Cambodia have all joined recently, creating a regional grouping of 600 million people with a combined GDP of some $2 trillion (see Map 9.3). The basic objective of ASEAN is to foster freer trade among member countries and to achieve cooperation in their industrial policies. Progress so far has been limited, however.

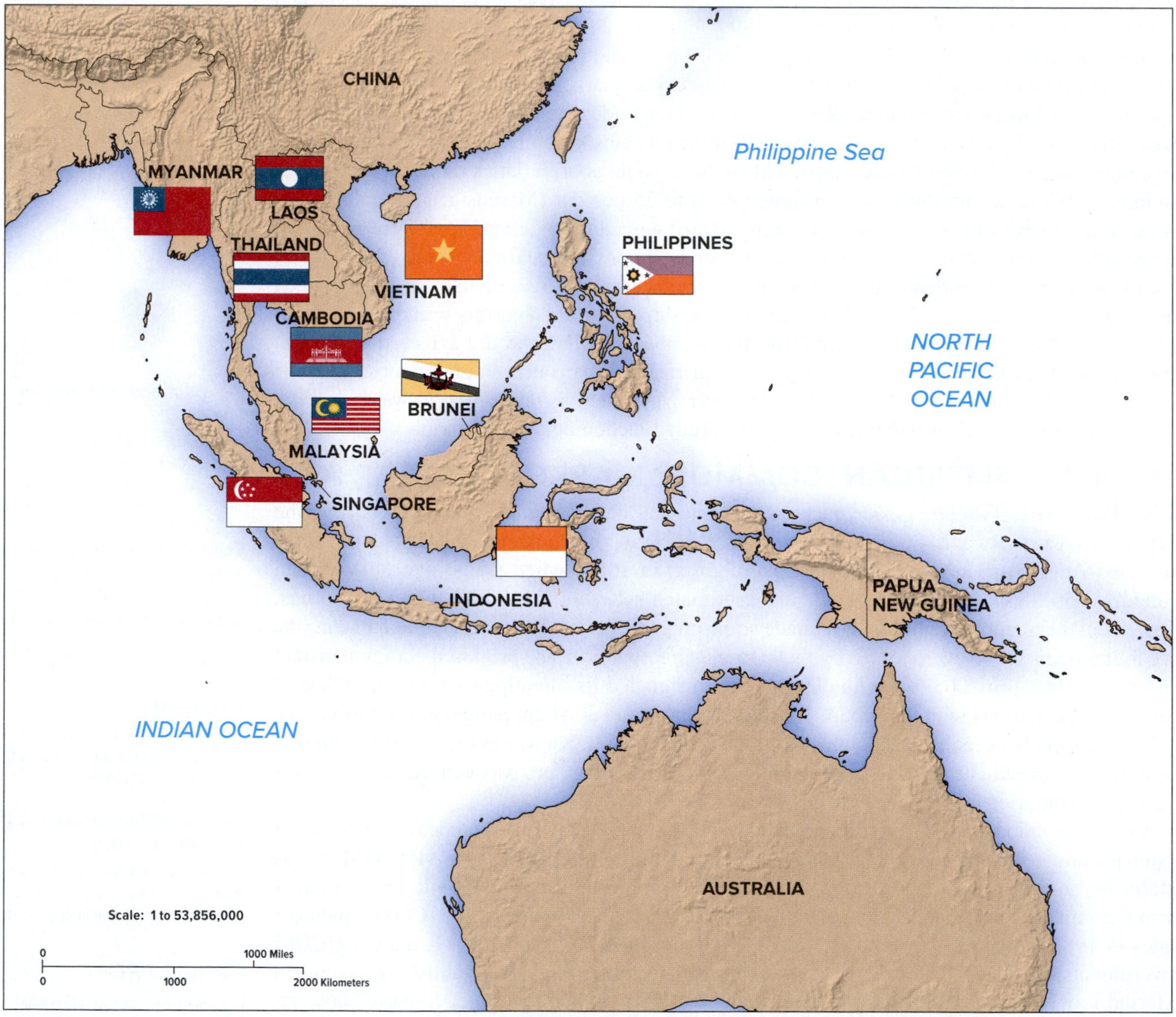

CHINA
Philippine Sea
MYANMAR
LAOS
THAILAND
VIETNAM
PHILIPPINES
CAMBODIA
NORTH PACIFIC OCEAN
BRUNEI
MALAYSIA
SINGAPORE
INDONESIA
PAPUA NEW GUINEA
INDIAN OCEAN
AUSTRALIA
Scale: 1 to 53,856,000
0 1000 Miles
0 1000 2000 Kilometers

9.3 MAP

ASEAN Countries.

Until recently, only 5 percent of intra-ASEAN trade consisted of goods whose tariffs had been reduced through an ASEAN preferential trade arrangement. This may be changing. In 2003, an ASEAN Free Trade Area (AFTA) among the six original members of ASEAN came into full effect. The AFTA has cut tariffs on manufacturing and agricultural products to less than 5 percent. However, there are some significant exceptions to this tariff reduction. Malaysia, for example, refused to bring down tariffs on imported cars until 2005 and then agreed to lower the tariff only to 20 percent, not the 5 percent called for under the AFTA. Malaysia wanted to protect Proton, an inefficient local carmaker, from foreign competition. Similarly, the Philippines has refused to lower tariff rates on petrochemicals, and rice, the largest agricultural product in the region, will remain subject to higher tariff rates until at least 2020.[33]

Notwithstanding such issues, ASEAN and AFTA are at least progressing toward establishing a free trade zone. Vietnam joined the AFTA in 2006, Laos and Myanmar in 2008, and Cambodia in 2010. The goal was to reduce import tariffs among the six original members to zero by 2010 and to do so by 2015 for the newer members (although important exceptions to that goal, such as tariffs on rice, will persist).

ASEAN signed a free trade agreement with China that removes tariffs on 90 percent of traded goods. This went into effect January 1, 2010. Trade between China and ASEAN members more than tripled during the first decade of the twenty-first century, and this agreement should spur further growth.[34]

REGIONAL TRADE BLOCS IN AFRICA African countries have been experimenting with regional trade blocs for half a century. Nominally there are now 17 trade blocs on the African continent. Many countries are members of more than one group. Although the number of trade groups is impressive, progress toward the establishment of meaningful trade blocs has been slow.

Many of these groups have been dormant for years. Significant political turmoil in several African nations has persistently impeded any meaningful progress. Also, deep suspicion of free trade exists in several African countries. The argument most frequently heard is that because these countries have less developed and less diversified economies, they need to be "protected" by tariff barriers from unfair foreign competition. Given the prevalence of this argument, it has been hard to establish free trade areas or customs unions.

A meaningful attempt to reenergize the free trade movement in Africa occurred in early 2001, when Kenya, Uganda, and Tanzania, member states of the East African Community (EAC), committed themselves to relaunching their bloc, 24 years after it collapsed. The three countries, with 80 million inhabitants, intend to establish a customs union, regional court, legislative assembly, and, eventually, a political federation.

Their program includes cooperation on immigration, road and telecommunication networks, investment, and capital markets. However, while local business leaders welcomed the relaunch as a positive step, they were critical of the EAC's failure in practice to make progress on free trade. At the EAC treaty's signing in November 1999, members gave themselves four years to negotiate a customs union, with a draft slated for the end of 2001. But that fell far short of earlier plans for an immediate free trade zone, shelved after Tanzania and Uganda, fearful of Kenyan competition, expressed concerns that the zone could create imbalances similar to those that contributed to the breakup of the first community.[36] Nevertheless, in 2005 the EAC did start to implement a customs union. In 2007, Burundi and Rwanda joined the EAC. The EAC established a common market in 2010 and is now striving toward an eventual goal of monetary union.

In 2015, in what is a promising sign, representatives from 26 African nations signed an agreement pledging to work together to establish a free trade area that would remove or reduce many tariffs and eliminate time-consuming customs procedures between them. Know as the Tripartite Free Trade Area (TFTA), this common market would encompass more than 630 million people and link together three existing regional trading blocks in Southern and Eastern Africa with a combined gross domestic product of $1.2 trillion and over $102 billion in trade between member states (see the opening case for further details).

OTHER TRADE AGREEMENTS As noted in Chapter 7, following the failure of the Doha Round of talks to extend the WTO, the United States and many other nations have placed renewed emphasis on bilateral and multilateral trade agreements. The United States is currently pursuing two major multilateral trade agreements, the Trans Pacific Partnership (TPP) with 11other Pacific Rim countries, including Australia, New Zealand, Japan, South Korea, Malaysia, and Chile, and the Transatlantic Trade and Investment Partnership (TTIP) with the European Union. While the TTIP is still in negotiation, the 12 nations negotiating the TPP have signed an agreement. The TPP agreement must now be ratified by legislators in the 12 nations before it can be implemented. If it is ratified and put into effect, the TPP will reduce tariff rates on some 18,000 items traded between the signatory states. Since U.S. tariff rates are already low, most of the tariff reductions will occur in other nations, which arguably could disproportionately favor the United States. Despite this, there is strong political opposition to the TPP in the United States, and ratification is uncertain at this point in time.

test PREP

Use SmartBook to help retain what you have learned. Access your Instructor's Connect course to check out SmartBook or go to learnsmartadvantage.com for help.

FOCUS ON MANAGERIAL IMPLICATIONS

REGIONAL ECONOMIC INTEGRATION THREATS

LO 9-5

Understand the implications for business that are inherent in regional economic integration agreements.

Currently, the most significant developments in regional economic integration are occurring in the EU and NAFTA. Although some of the Latin American trade blocs, ASEAN, and the proposed TPP may have economic significance in the future, developments in the EU and NAFTA currently have more profound implications for business practice. Accordingly, in this section, we concentrate on the business implications of those two groups. Similar conclusions, however, could be drawn with regard to the creation of a single market anywhere in the world.

Opportunities

The creation of a single market through regional economic integration offers significant opportunities because markets that were formerly protected from foreign competition are increasingly open. Additional opportunities arise from the inherent lower costs of doing business in a single market—as opposed to 28 national markets in the case of the EU or three national markets in the case of NAFTA. Free movement of goods across borders, harmonized product standards, and simplified tax regimes make it possible for firms based in the EU and the NAFTA countries to realize potentially significant cost economies by centralizing production in those EU and NAFTA locations where the mix of factor costs and skills is optimal. Rather than producing a product in each of the 28 EU countries or the three NAFTA countries, a firm may be able to serve the whole EU or North American market from a single location. This location must be chosen carefully, of course, with an eye on local factor costs and skills.

Even after the removal of barriers to trade and investment, enduring differences in culture and competitive practices often limit the ability of companies to realize cost economies by centralizing production in key locations and producing a standardized product for a single multiple-country market. Consider the case of Atag Holdings NV, a Dutch maker of kitchen appliances.[37] Atag thought it was well placed to benefit from the single market but found it tough going. Atag's plant is just 1 mile from the German border and near the center of the EU's population. The company thought it could cater to both the "potato" and "spaghetti" belts—marketers' terms for consumers in northern and southern Europe—by producing two main product lines and selling these standardized "euro-products" to "euro-consumers." The main benefit of doing so is the economy of scale derived from mass production of a standardized range of products. Atag quickly discovered that the "euro-consumer" was a myth. Consumer preferences vary much more across nations than Atag had thought. Consider ceramic cooktops: Atag planned to market just two varieties throughout the EU but found it needed 11. Belgians, who cook in huge pots, require extra-large burners. Germans like oval pots and burners to fit. The French need small burners and very low temperatures for simmering sauces and broths. Germans like oven knobs on the top; the French want them on the front. Most Germans and French prefer black and white ranges; the British demand a range of colors, including peach, pigeon blue, and mint green.

Threats

Just as the emergence of single markets creates opportunities for business, it also presents a number of threats. For one thing, the business environment within each grouping has become more competitive. The lowering of barriers to trade and investment among countries has led to increased price competition throughout the EU and NAFTA. The next Management Focus feature looked at how this process played out in the North American market for tomatoes following the introduction of NAFTA.

Over time, price differentials across nations will decline in a single market. This is a direct threat to any firm doing business in EU or NAFTA countries. To survive in the tougher single-market environment, firms must take advantage of the opportunities offered by the creation of a single market to rationalize their production and reduce their costs. Otherwise, they will be at a severe disadvantage.

A further threat to firms outside these trading blocs arises from the likely long-term improvement in the competitive position of many firms within the areas. This is particularly relevant in the EU, where many firms have historically been limited by a high-cost structure in their ability to compete globally with North American and Asian firms. The creation of a single market and the resulting increased competition in the EU produced serious attempts by many EU firms to reduce their cost structure by rationalizing production. This transformed many EU companies into more efficient global competitors. The message for non-EU businesses is that they need to respond to the emergence of more capable European competitors by reducing their own cost structures.

management FOCUS

NAFTA's Tomato Wars

When the North America Free Trade Agreement (NAFTA) went into effect in December 1992 and tariffs on imported tomatoes were dropped, U.S. tomato producers in Florida feared that they would lose business to lower-cost producers in Mexico. So they lobbied the government to set a minimum floor price for tomatoes imported from Mexico. The idea was to stop Mexican producers from cutting prices below the floor to gain share in the U.S. market. In 1996, the United States and Mexico agreed on basic floor price of 21.69 cents a pound.

At the time, both sides declared themselves to be happy with the deal. As it turns out, the deal didn't offer much protection for U.S. tomato growers. In 1992, the year before NAFTA was passed, Mexican producers exported 800 million pounds of tomatoes to the United States. By 2011, they were exporting 2.8 billion pounds of tomatoes, an increase of 3.5 times. The value of Mexican tomato exports almost tripled over the same period to $2 billion. In contrast, tomato production in Florida has fallen by 41 percent since NAFTA went into effect. Florida growers complained that they could not compete against low wages and lax environmental oversight in Mexico. They also alleged that Mexican growers were dumping tomatoes in the U.S. market at below the cost of production, with the goal of driving U.S. producers out of business.

In 2012, Florida growers petitioned the U.S. Department of Commerce to scrap the 1996 minimum price agreement, which would then free them up to file an antidumping case against Mexican producers. In September 2012, the Commerce Department announced a preliminary decision to scrap the agreement. At first glance, it looked as if the Florida growers were going to get their way. It soon became apparent, however, that the situation was more complex than appeared at first glance. More than 370 business and trade groups in the United States—from small family-run importers to meat and vegetable producers and Walmart stores—wrote or signed letters to the Commerce Department in favor of continuing the 1996 agreement.

Among the letter writers was Kevin Ahern, the CEO of Ahern Agribusiness in San Diego. His company sells about $20 million a year in tomato seeds and transplants to Mexican farmers. In a letter sent to the *New York Times,* Ahern noted that "yes, Mexico produces their tomatoes on average at a lower cost than Florida; that's what we call competitive advantage."* Without the agreement, Ahern claimed, his business would suffer. Another U.S. company, NatureSweet Ltd., grows cherry and grape tomatoes under 1,200 acres of greenhouses in Mexico for the American market. It employs 5,000 people, although all but 100 work in Mexico. The CEO, Bryant Ambelang, said that his company couldn't survive without NAFTA. In his view, Mexican-grown tomatoes were more competitive because of lower labor costs, good weather, and more than a decade of investment in greenhouse technology. In a similar vein, Scott DeFife, a representative of the U.S. National Restaurant Association, stated, "people want tomato-based dishes all the time. . . . You plan over the course of the year where you are going to get your supply in the winter, spring, fall." Without tomatoes from Mexico, a winter freeze in Florida, for example, would send prices shooting up, he said.

Faced with a potential backlash from U.S. importers, and U.S. producers with interests in Mexico, the Commerce Department pulled back from its initial conclusion that the agreement should be scrapped. Instead, in early 2013, it reached an agreement with Mexican growers to raise the minimum floor price from 21.69 cents a pound to 31 cents a pound. The new agreement also established even higher prices for specialty tomatoes and tomatoes grown in controlled environments. This was clearly aimed at Mexican growers, who have invested billions to grow tomatoes in greenhouses. Florida tomatoes are largely picked green and treated with gas to change their color.

*Source: E. Malkin, "Mexico Finds Unlikely Allies in Trade Fight," *The New York Times,* December 25, 2012, p. B1.

Sources: E. Malkin, "Mexico Finds Unlikely Allies in Trade Fight," *The New York Times,* December 25, 2012, p. B1; S. Strom, "United States and Mexico Reach Tomato Deal, Averting a Trade War," *The New York Times,* February 3, 2013; J. Margolis, "NAFTA 20 Years After: Florida's Tomato Growers Struggling," *The World,* December 1, 2012.

Another threat to firms outside of trading areas is the threat of being shut out of the single market by the creation of a "trade fortress." The charge that regional economic integration might lead to a fortress mentality is most often leveled at the EU. Although the free trade philosophy underpinning the EU theoretically argues against the creation of any fortress in Europe, occasional signs indicate the EU may raise barriers to imports and investment in certain "politically sensitive" areas, such as autos. Non-EU firms might be well advised, therefore, to set up their own EU operations. This could also occur in the NAFTA countries, but it seems less likely.

Finally, the emerging role of the European Commission in competition policy suggests the EU is increasingly willing and able to intervene and impose conditions on companies proposing mergers and acquisitions. This is a threat insofar as it limits the ability of firms to pursue the corporate strategy of their choice. The commission may require significant concessions from businesses as a precondition for allowing proposed mergers and acquisitions to proceed. While this constrains the strategic options for firms, it should be remembered that in taking such action, the commission is trying to maintain the level of competition in Europe's single market, which should benefit consumers.

Key Terms

regional economic integration, p. 242
free trade area, p. 243
European Free Trade Association (EFTA), p. 244
customs union, p. 244
common market, p. 244
economic union, p. 244
political union, p. 244
trade creation, p. 246
trade diversion, p. 246
European Union, p. 247
Treaty of Rome, p. 247
European Commission, p. 247
European Council, p. 249
European Parliament, p. 249
Treaty of Lisbon, p. 250
Court of Justice, p. 250
Maastricht Treaty, p. 252
optimal currency area, p. 253
North American Free Trade Agreement (NAFTA), p. 257
Andean Community, p. 260
Mercosur, p. 260
Central American Common Market, p. 261
Central America Free Trade Agreement (CAFTA), p. 261
CARICOM, p. 261
Caribbean Single Market and Economy (CSME), p. 261
Association of Southeast Asian Nations (ASEAN), p. 262

Summary

This chapter pursued three main objectives: to examine the economic and political debate surrounding regional economic integration; to review the progress toward regional economic integration in Europe, the Americas, and elsewhere; and to distinguish the important implications of regional economic integration for the practice of international business. The chapter made the following points:

1. A number of levels of economic integration are possible in theory. In order of increasing integration, they include a free trade area, a customs union, a common market, an economic union, and full political union.
2. In a free trade area, barriers to trade among member countries are removed, but each country determines its own external trade policy. In a customs union, internal barriers to trade are removed, and a common external trade policy is adopted. A common market is similar to a customs union, except that a common market also allows factors of production to move freely among countries. An economic union involves even closer integration, including the establishment of a common currency and the harmonization of tax rates. A political union is the logical culmination of attempts to achieve ever-closer economic integration.
3. Regional economic integration is an attempt to achieve economic gains from the free flow of trade and investment between neighboring countries.
4. Integration is not easily achieved or sustained. Although integration brings benefits to the majority, it is never without costs for the minority. Concerns over national sovereignty often slow or stop integration attempts. In 2016, these concerns resulted in Britain voting for exit from the EU.
5. Regional integration will not increase economic welfare if the trade creation effects in the free trade area are outweighed by the trade diversion effects.
6. The Single European Act sought to create a true single market by abolishing administrative barriers to the free flow of trade and investment among EU countries.
7. Seventeen EU members now use a common currency, the euro. The economic gains from a common currency come from reduced exchange costs, reduced risk associated with currency fluctuations, and increased price competition within the EU.

8. Increasingly, the European Commission is taking an activist stance with regard to competition policy, intervening to restrict mergers and acquisitions that it believes will reduce competition in the EU.
9. Although no other attempt at regional economic integration comes close to the EU in terms of potential economic and political significance, various other attempts are being made in the world. The most notable include NAFTA in North America, the Andean Community and Mercosur in Latin America, and ASEAN in Southeast Asia.
10. The creation of single markets in the EU and North America means that many markets that were formerly protected from foreign competition are now more open. This creates major investment and export opportunities for firms within and outside these regions.
11. The free movement of goods across borders, the harmonization of product standards, and the simplification of tax regimes make it possible for firms based in a free trade area to realize potentially enormous cost economies by centralizing production in those locations within the area where the mix of factor costs and skills is optimal.
12. The lowering of barriers to trade and investment among countries within a trade group will probably be followed by increased price competition.

Critical Thinking and Discussion Questions

1. NAFTA has produced significant net benefits for the Canadian, Mexican, and U.S. economies. Discuss.
2. What are the economic and political arguments for regional economic integration? Given these arguments, why don't we see more substantial examples of integration in the world economy?
3. What in general was the effect of the creation of a single market and a single currency within the EU on competition within the EU? Why?
4. Do you think it is correct for the European Commission to restrict mergers between American companies that do business in Europe? (For example, the European Commission vetoed the proposed merger between WorldCom and Sprint, both U.S. companies, and it carefully reviewed the merger between AOL and Time Warner, again both U.S. companies.)
5. What were the causes of the 2010–2012 sovereign debt crisis in the EU? What does this crisis tell us about the weaknesses of the euro? Do you think the euro will survive the sovereign debt crisis?
6. How should a U.S. firm that currently exports only to ASEAN countries respond to the creation of a single market in this regional grouping?
7. How should a firm with self-sufficient production facilities in several ASEAN countries respond to the creation of a single market? What are the constraints on its ability to respond in a manner that minimizes production costs?
8. After a promising start, Mercosur, the major Latin American trade agreement, has faltered and made little progress since 2000. What problems are hurting Mercosur? What can be done to solve these problems?
9. Read the Management Focus feature in this chapter, "NAFTA's Tomato Wars," then answer the following questions:
    - Was the establishment of a minimum floor price for tomatoes consistent with the free trade principles enshrined in the NAFTA agreement?
    - Why, despite the establishment of a minimum floor price, have imports from Mexico grown over the years?
    - Who benefits from the importation of tomatoes grown in Mexico? Who suffers?
    - Do you think that Mexican producers were dumping tomatoes in the United States?
    - Was the Commerce Department right to establish a new minimum floor price, rather than scrap the agreement and file an antidumping suit? Who would have benefited from an antidumping suit against Mexican tomato producers? Who would have suffered?
    - What do you think will be the impact of the new higher floor price? Who benefits from the higher floor price? Who suffers?
    - What do you think is the optimal government policy response here? Explain your answer.

globalEDGE Research Task

globalEDGE.msu.edu

Use the globalEDGE™ website (globaledge.msu.edu) to complete the following exercises:

1. The World Trade Organization maintains a database of *regional trade agreements.* You can search this database to identify all agreements that a specific country participates in. Search the database to identify the trade agreements that Japan currently participates in. What patterns do you see? Which region (or regions) of the world does Japan seem to be focusing on in its trade endeavors?

2. Your company has assigned you with the task of investigating the various trade blocs in Africa to see if your company can benefit from these trade agreements while expanding into African markets. The first trade bloc you come across is *COMESA*. Prepare a short executive summary for your company, explaining the level of integration the bloc has currently achieved, the level it aspires to accomplish, and the relationships it has with other African trade blocs.

Regional Trade Deals and the Mexican Auto Industry — closing case

Mexico's automobile industry is booming. Bolstered by $19 billion in new investment from foreign carmakers, including Nissan, Honda, Volkswagen, and Mazda, vehicle production doubled between 2009 and 2014 to an estimated 3.2 million vehicles. This investment surge has transformed Mexico into the eighth-largest automaker in the world, and it's not over yet. In 2014 and 2015, Toyota, Mercedes-Benz, Hyundai-Kia, BMW, and Volkswagen all outlined plans to build new state-of-the-art factories in Mexico. Audi is also constructing a $1.3 billion factory that is slated for producing luxury sport-utility vehicles. The Audi factory is scheduled to open in 2016. Taken together, these new factories represent another $20 billion in investment that will push Mexico past Brazil and South Korea to become the sixth-largest car producer in the world by 2020 with an annual output of 4.7 million vehicles (for comparison, the U.S. industry makes some 11.5 million autos a year).

The initial stimulus for the dramatic growth of the Mexican auto industry was the establishment of the North American Free Trade Agreement (NAFTA) in 1994. Prior to NAFTA, Mexico's auto industry was small and protected from foreign competition by high tariff barriers. Car prices in Mexico were two to three times higher than in the United States. Not only were cars in Mexico more expensive, exporting or importing cars and parts was also very tough. Shipments got delayed at the border and were difficult to move around because of poor infrastructure, which is a major problem in an industry in which tight logistics is critical. NAFTA removed most tariff and nontariff barriers to trade between Mexico, the United States, and Canada. This initially led to a flood of low-priced auto imports into Mexico from the United States, but it also gave auto manufacturers based in Mexico duty-free access to the large U.S. market next door. With labor costs in Mexico just a fraction of those in the United States, auto manufacturers now had to consider Mexico when planning new plants to serve the North American market.

Mexico's shift to free trade didn't stop with NAFTA. Mexico spent much of the 2000s hammering out free trade deals with over 40 other countries, including the 28 states of the European Union, Japan, and Brazil. These deals give auto factories based in Mexico duty-free access to markets that contain 60 percent of the world's economic output, and they have helped transform Mexico into the fourth-largest auto exporter in the world. Eighty percent of the cars now produced in Mexico are exported to other countries, two-thirds of them to the United States. This unprecedented network of regional trade agreements has given Mexico an important edge when it comes to attracting new investment. For example, when BMW ships cars to Europe from its 20-year-old plant in South Carolina, it is hit with a 10 percent import duty. For a $50,000 car, that amounts to $5,000, which is a much bigger factor than differences in labor costs. A factory in Mexico can supply both the U.S. and the EU markets with duty-free automobiles. This was a major factor behind BMW's 2014 decision to build a new factory in central Mexico rather than the United States, far outweighing the $500 a car labor cost advantage that Mexico currently enjoys over the United States. The new BMW factory will supply the U.S. and EU markets, as well as Latin America. Indeed, because of differences in trade barriers, a car exported from the United States to Brazil costs 55 percent more than one exported from Mexico.

As Mexico's auto industry has grown, auto-part suppliers have also followed manufacturers to Mexico. The large auto parts supplier Delphi, for example, has 30 factories in Mexico and generates revenues of $3 billion in the country. Employment at Delphi's facilities doubled to 24,000 between 2007 and 2014. Infrastructure has also improved dramatically, and customs clearance at the border is now quick and efficient.

All of this bodes well for the future of the Mexican auto industry. However, not everyone is happy with what has happened. Some argue that growth in Mexico has come at the expense of factories in the United States, which has had negative impact on employment growth in the U.S. auto industry. When BMW decided to build a factory in central Mexico, for example, it meant that it would not be expanding its South Carolina plant. The South Carolina plant will continue to operate, and no plants have been closed as a result of the growth of production in Mexico, but it is true that new plants are increasingly being located south of the border.

Sources: Joann Muller, "America's Car Capital Will Soon Be . . . Mexico," *Forbes*, July 20, 2014; Dudley Althaus and William Boston, "Trade Pacts Give Mexico an Edge," *The Wall Street Journal*, March 18, 2015; Sonari Glinton, "How NAFTA Drove the Auto Industry South," *National Public Radio*, December 8, 2013; Serena Maria Daniels, "Twenty Years after NAFTA, a Mini Detroit Rises in Mexico," *Bridge*, September 25, 2014.

CASE DISCUSSION QUESTIONS

1. What was the *initial* impact of NAFTA on the U.S. and Mexican automobile markets? Who benefited most from this?
2. How did the impact of NAFTA start to change location decisions by automobile manufacturers over the years? How did this start to impact automobile production in Mexico and the United States?
3. Mexico has been very proactive in signing regional free trade deals in addition to NAFTA. How has this strategy impacted automobile consumers and producers in Mexico? How has it impacted automobile consumers and producers in the United States?
4. What lessons can United States policy makers draw from the growing success of the Mexican automobile industry that can be applied to future free trade deals, such as the deal currently being negotiated between the United States and the European Union?

Endnotes

1. Information taken from World Trade Organization website and current as of April 2016, www.wto.org.
2. Ibid.
3. The Andean Community has been through a number of changes since its inception. The latest version was established in 1991. See "Free-Trade Free for All," *The Economist,* January 4, 1991, p. 63.
4. D. Swann, *The Economics of the Common Market,* 6th ed. (London: Penguin Books, 1990).
5. See J. Bhagwati, "Regionalism and Multilateralism: An Overview," Columbia University Discussion Paper 603, Department of Economics, Columbia University, New York; A. de la Torre and M. Kelly, "Regional Trade Arrangements," International Monetary Fund Occasional Paper 93, March 1992; J. Bhagwati, "Fast Track to Nowhere," *The Economist,* October 18, 1997, pp. 21–24; Jagdish Bhagwati, *Free Trade Today* (Princeton and Oxford: Princeton University Press, 2002); B. K. Gordon, "A High Risk Trade Policy," *Foreign Affairs* 82 no. 4 (July–August 2003), pp. 105–15.
6. N. Colchester and D. Buchan, *Europower: The Essential Guide to Europe's Economic Transformation in 1992* (London: The Economist Books, 1990); and Swann, *Economics of the Common Market.*
7. Swann, *Economics of the Common Market;* Colchester and Buchan, *Europower*; "The European Union: A Survey," *The Economist*, October 22, 1994; "The European Community: A Survey," *The Economist,* July 3, 1993; and the European Union website at http://europa.eu.int.
8. E. J. Morgan, "A Decade of EC Merger Control," *International Journal of Economics and Business,* November 2001, pp. 451–73.
9. "The European Community: A Survey," 1993.
10. Tony Barber, "The Lisbon Reform Treaty," *FT.com*, December 13, 2007.
11. "One Europe, One Economy," *The Economist,* November 30, 1991, pp. 53–54; and "Market Failure: A Survey of Business in Europe," *The Economist,* June 8, 1991, pp. 6–10.
12. Alan Riley, "The Single Market Ten Years On," *European Policy Analyst,* December 2002, pp. 65–72.
13. See C. Wyploze, "EMU: Why and How It Might Happen," *Journal of Economic Perspectives* 11 (1997), pp. 3–22; M. Feldstein, "The Political Economy of the European Economic and Monetary Union," *Journal of Economic Perspectives* 11 (1997), pp. 23–42.
14. "One Europe, One Economy;" Feldstein, "The Political Economy of the European Economic and Monetary Union."
15. "Euro Still the World's Second Reserve Currency," *The Economic Times,* July 22, 2011.
16. Details regarding conditions of membership and the progression of enlargement negotiations can be found at http://europa.eu/pol/enlarg/index_en.htm.
17. "What Is NAFTA?," *Financial Times,* November 17, 1993, p. 6; S. Garland, "Sweet Victory," *BusinessWeek,* November 29, 1993, pp. 30–31.
18. "NAFTA: The Showdown," *The Economist*, November 13, 1993, pp. 23–36.
19. N. C. Lustog, "NAFTA: Setting the Record Straight," *The World Economy,* 1997, pp. 605–14; G. C. Hufbauer and J. J. Schott, *NAFTA Revisited: Achievements and Challenges* (Washington, DC: Institute for International Economics, 2005).
20. W. Thorbecke and C. Eigen-Zucchi, "Did NAFTA Cause a Giant Sucking Sound?," *Journal of Labor Research,* Fall 2002, pp. 647–58; G. Gagne, "North American Free Trade, Canada, and U.S. Trade Remedies: An Assessment after Ten Years," The World Economy, 2000, pp. 77–91; Hufbauer and Schott, *NAFTA Revisited; J. Romalis,* "NAFTA's and Custfa's Impact on International Trade," *Review of Economics and Statistics* 98, no. 3 (2007), pp. 416–35; "NAFTA at 20: Ready to Take Off Again?," *The Economist,* January 4, 2014.
21. All trade figures from U.S. Department of Commerce Trade Stat Express website at http://tse.export.gov/.
22. C. J. O'Leary, R. W. Eberts, and B. M. Pittelko, "Effects of NAFTA on US Employment and Policy Responses: A Product of the International Collaborative Initiative on Trade and Employment (ICITE)," *OECD Trade Policy Papers,* no. 131 (Paris: OECD Publishing, 2012).
23. L. Caliendo and F. Parro, "Estimates of the trade and welfare effects of NAFTA", *Review of Economic Studies,* July 2014.
24. "The Business of the American Hemisphere," *The Economist,* August 24, 1991, pp. 37–38.
25. "NAFTA Is Not Alone," *The Economist,* June 18, 1994, pp. 47–48.
26. "Murky Mercosur," *The Economist,* July 26, 1997, pp. 66–67.
27. See M. Philips, "South American Trade Pact under Fire," *The Wall Street Journal,* October 23, 1996, p. A2; A. J. Yeats, *Does Mercosur's Trade Performance Justify Concerns about the Global Welfare-Reducing Effects of Free Trade Arrangements? Yes!* (Washington, DC: World Bank, 1996); D. M. Leipziger et al., "Mercosur: Integration and Industrial Policy," *The World Economy,* 1997, pp. 585–604.
28. "Another Blow to Mercosur," *The Economist,* March 31, 2001, pp. 33–34.
29. "Lula Lays Out Mercosur Rescue Mission," *Latin America Newsletters,* February 4, 2003, p. 7.
30. "CARICOM Single Market Begins," *EIU Views,* February 3, 2006.
31. "Every Man for Himself: Trade in Asia," *The Economist,* November 2, 2002, pp. 43–44.
32. L. Gooch, "Asian Free-Trade Zone Raises Hopes," *The New York Times,* January 1, 2010, p. B3.
33. M. Turner, "Trio Revives East African Union," *Financial Times,* January 16, 2001, p. 4.
34. T. Horwitz, "Europe's Borders Fade," *The Wall Street Journal,* May 18, 1993, pp. A1, A12; "A Singular Market," *The Economist,* October 22, 1994, pp. 10–16; "Something Dodgy in Europe's Single Market," *The Economist,* May 21, 1994, pp. 69–70.

The Foreign Exchange Market

learning objectives

After reading this chapter, you will be able to:

- **LO10-1** Describe the functions of the foreign exchange market.
- **LO10-2** Understand what is meant by spot exchange rates.
- **LO10-3** Recognize the role that forward exchange rates play in insuring against foreign exchange risk.
- **LO10-4** Understand the different theories explaining how currency exchange rates are determined and their relative merits.
- **LO10-5** Identify the merits of different approaches toward exchange rate forecasting.
- **LO10-6** Compare and contrast the differences among translation, transaction, and economic exposure, and explain the implications for management practice.

Source: © ICP-Tech/incamerastock/Alamy Stock Photo

Apple's Earnings Hit by Strong Dollar

opening case

When Apple reported its fourth quarter earnings in January 2016, they contained a nasty surprise. According to CEO Tim Cook, the strong U.S. dollar had cost Apple nearly $5 billion in revenue. If currency moves were excluded, Apple would have generated $80.8 billion in revenue in the quarter ending December 31, 2015. Instead, it reported $75.9 billion in revenue, knocking down what would have been an 8 percent increase to just 2 percent.

Although the U.S. dollar has been trending higher against most currencies since 2012, the appreciation has accelerated since September 2014. For a company like Apple, which gets 66 percent of its revenues from outside of the United States, this can have a major impact. Since September 2014, according to Cook, the appreciation in the value of the dollar against most of the world's currencies has meant that $100 of Apple's revenues outside of the United States translated into just $85 by January 2016.

With regard to specific currencies, between September 1, 2014, and March 21, 2016, the U.S. dollar appreciated by 17 percent against the euro, 15 percent against the British pound, 5 percent against the Chinese yuan, 21 percent against the Canadian dollar, 33 percent against the Mexican peso, 62 percent against the Brazilian real, and 82 percent against the Russian ruble. Cook referred to these moves, and others like them, as constituting "extreme conditions unlike anything we have seen before just about everywhere we look."*

Apple has tried to protect the dollar value of its overseas sales by buying currency forward to hedge against future increases, but the appreciation of the dollar has been faster than forecasted, and Apple's hedging activity has been insufficient to protect the value of its overseas earnings. To shore up its revenues and protect profit margins, in some markets the company has turned to price increases. But there is only so far that Apple can push this strategy before people stop buying its phones.

Nor is Apple alone is feeling the pain from a sustained increase in the value of the dollar on foreign exchange markets. Numerous other major technology enterprises, including Microsoft, Google, IBM, and Oracle, have also reported lower revenues and earnings due to the translation effects of the strong dollar. Large technology companies are particularly hard hit by the appreciating dollar because they generate 59 percent of their revenue outside of the United States on average, compared to 48 percent for companies within the broader S&P 500 index.

So why is the dollar so strong? There are several reasons. First, the U.S. economy has performed better than most since the great recession of 2008–2009, making it a more attractive destination for foreign

*Mark DeCambre, "Apple Chief Tim Cook: We're Seeing Extreme Conditions Everywhere We Look", *Market Watch*, January 27, 2016.

–continued

capital. The U.S. economy, for example, has consistently outperformed the economies of all major European nations, Japan, Australia, and Canada. Foreigners have responding by investing more in the United States, and the inflow of capital has driven up the value of the dollar. Second, governments in Europe and Japan have responded to slow growth by lowering interest rates and expanding their domestic money supply. The purpose of such "quantitative easing" is to try to encourage consumption and investment. At the same time, interest rates in the United States have started to inch up as the economy continues to expand. Investors have responded by moving money to the United States to take advantage of favorable interest rate differentials.

Third, several developing nations have seen their economies hammered by adverse developments, which has put downward pressure on their currencies. The rapid fall in the price of oil since mid-2015, for example, has hit major oil exporting nations such as Russia hard. In Brazil, a serious corruption scandal coupled with economic mismanagement has translated into a lack of consumer confidence, slow economic growth, and a weak currency. In China, a slowdown in the rate of economic growth from 10 percent per annum to around 6 percent per annum is exposing structural flaws in the economy, including excessive debt and too many poorly managed state-owned enterprises, resulting in an outflow of capital. The Chinese reportedly spent $500 billion trying to prop up the value of the yuan against the U.S. dollar in 2015 and another $80 billion in January 2016. Despite this aggressive action, the yuan has depreciated against the dollar, although by less than most other major currencies.

The conditions that have led to an increase in the value of the dollar are unlikely to change in the near future. For companies like Apple, this means that they must adopt strategies to hedge against further increases. At the same time, too much hedging can expose the company to significant financial risks if the dollar does not move in the predicted direction. It is crucial, therefore, for Apple to get its hedging strategy right. •

Sources: B. White, "Here Is Why the Dollar Is So Strong and What It Means for Investors," *Business Insider*, January 30, 2015; D. Clark, "Strong Dollar Batters Earnings for U.S. Tech Firms," *The Wall Street Journal*, January 31, 2016; Mark DeCambre, "Apple Chief Tim Cook: We're Seeing Extreme Conditions Everywhere We Look," *Market Watch*, January 27, 2016.

Introduction

Like many enterprises in the global economy, Apple is affected by changes in the value of currencies on the foreign exchange market. As described in the opening case, Apple's revenues and profits were reduced in 2015 by increases in the value of the dollar against most of the world's other currencies. The case illustrates that what happens in the foreign exchange market can have a fundamental impact on the sales, profits, and strategy of an enterprise. Accordingly, it is very important for managers to understand how the foreign exchange works and what the impact of changes in currency exchange rates might be for their enterprise.

This chapter has three main objectives. The first is to explain how the foreign exchange market works. The second is to examine the forces that determine exchange rates and to discuss the degree to which it is possible to predict future exchange rate movements. The third objective is to map the implications for international business of exchange rate movements. This chapter is the first of three that deal with the international monetary system and its relationship to international business. Chapter 11 explores the institutional structure of the international monetary system. The institutional structure is the context within which the foreign exchange market functions. As we shall see, changes in the institutional structure of the international monetary system can exert a profound influence on the development of foreign exchange markets.

Foreign Exchange Market
A market for converting the currency of one country into that of another country.

Exchange Rate
The rate at which one currency is converted into another.

The **foreign exchange market** is a market for converting the currency of one country into that of another country. An **exchange rate** is simply the rate at which one currency is converted into another. For example, Toyota uses the foreign exchange market to convert the dollars it earns from selling cars in the United States into Japanese yen. Without the foreign exchange market, international trade and international investment on the scale that we see today would be impossible;

globalEDGE Database of International Business Statistics

The "global money system" can have a significant effect on how companies operate globally. Often companies have to deal with exchange rates, monetary systems, and the capital market on both country and regional levels. But the influences of countries on the regional and global money system are significant (i.e., countries set the tone for the parameters of the foreign exchange market and the international monetary system). The globalEDGE™ Database of International Business Statistics (DIBS) includes time-series data beginning in the 1990s until today and covers more than 200 countries and more than 5,000 data variables. Countries, regions, and the world use these types of data points to drive the global money system, and everyone who is interested in better understanding the global capital market needs to know about them! Register free on globalEDGE™ to gain access to the DIBS database right now; students have free access to DIBS, and DIBS can be found at http://globaledge.msu.edu/tools-and-data/dibs

companies would have to resort to barter. The foreign exchange market is the lubricant that enables companies based in countries that use different currencies to trade with each other.

We know from earlier chapters that international trade and investment have their risks. Some of these risks exist because future exchange rates cannot be perfectly predicted. The rate at which one currency is converted into another can change over time. For example, at the start of 2001, one U.S. dollar bought 1.065 euros, but by early 2014, one U.S. dollar bought only 0.74 euro. The dollar had fallen sharply in value against the euro. This made American goods cheaper in Europe, boosting export sales. At the same time, it made European goods more expensive in the United States, which hurt the sales and profits of European companies that sold goods and services to the United States. The pricing advantage enjoyed by U.S. companies, however, disappeared during the second half of 2014 and 2015 as economic weakness in Europe and a stronger U.S. economy resulted in a sharp fall in the value of the euro. By March 2016, one U.S. dollar bought 0.89 euro. Rapid changes in currency values such as these often take managers by surprise, and if they have not hedged against the possible risk, sales and profits can be significantly impacted.

One function of the foreign exchange market is to provide some insurance against the risks that arise from such volatile changes in exchange rates, commonly referred to as *foreign exchange risk*. Although the foreign exchange market offers some insurance against foreign exchange risk, it cannot provide complete insurance. It is not unusual for international businesses to suffer losses (or gains) because of unpredicted changes in exchange rates. Currency fluctuations can make seemingly profitable trade and investment deals unprofitable, and vice versa.

We begin this chapter by looking at the functions and the form of the foreign exchange market. This includes distinguishing among spot exchanges, forward exchanges, and currency swaps. Then we consider the factors that determine exchange rates. We also look at how foreign trade is conducted when a country's currency cannot be exchanged for other currencies, that is, when its currency is not convertible. The chapter closes with a discussion of these things in terms of their implications for business.

The Functions of the Foreign Exchange Market

LO 10-1
Describe the functions of the foreign exchange market.

The foreign exchange market serves two main functions. The first is to convert the currency of one country into the currency of another. The second is to provide some insurance against **foreign exchange risk**, or the adverse consequences of unpredictable changes in exchange rates.[1]

Foreign Exchange Risk
The risk that changes in exchange rates will hurt the profitability of a business deal.

CURRENCY CONVERSION Each country has a currency in which the prices of goods and services are quoted. In the United States, it is the dollar ($); in Great Britain, the pound (£); in France, Germany, and the other 17 members of the euro zone it is the euro (€); in Japan, the yen (¥); and so on. In general, within the borders of a particular country, one must use the national currency. A U.S. tourist cannot walk into a store in Edinburgh, Scotland, and use U.S. dollars to buy a bottle of Scotch whisky. Dollars are not recognized as legal tender in Scotland; the tourist must use British pounds. Fortunately, the tourist can go to a bank and exchange her dollars for pounds. Then she can buy the whisky.

Should Countries Be Free to Set Currency Policy?

Exchange rates are critically important in the global economy. They affect the price of every country's imports and exports, companies' foreign direct investment, and—directly or indirectly—people's spending behaviors. In recent years, disagreements among countries over exchange rates have become much more widespread. Some government officials and analysts even suggest that there is a "currency war" among certain countries. The main issue is whether or not some countries are using exchange rate policies to undermine free currency markets and whether they intentionally, in essence, devalue their currency to gain a trade advantage at the expense of other countries. A weaker currency makes exports inexpensive (or at least cheaper) to foreigners, which can lead to higher exports and job creation in the export sector.

Source: Nelson, R. M., "Current Debates over Exchange Rates: Overview and Issues for Congress," *Congressional Research Service*, November 12, 2013.

When a tourist changes one currency into another, she is participating in the foreign exchange market. The exchange rate is the rate at which the market converts one currency into another. For example, an exchange rate of €1 = $1.12 specifies that 1 euro buys 1.12 U.S. dollars. The exchange rate allows us to compare the relative prices of goods and services in different countries. A U.S. tourist wishing to buy a bottle of Scotch whisky in Edinburgh may find that she must pay £30 for the bottle, knowing that the same bottle costs $45 in the United States. Is this a good deal? Imagine the current pound/dollar exchange rate is £1.00 = $2.00 (i.e., one British pound buys $2.00). Our intrepid tourist takes out her calculator and converts £30 into dollars. (The calculation is 30 × 2.) She finds that the bottle of Scotch costs the equivalent of $60. She is surprised that a bottle of Scotch whisky could cost less in the United States than in Scotland (alcohol is taxed heavily in Great Britain).

Tourists are minor participants in the foreign exchange market; companies engaged in international trade and investment are major ones. International businesses have four main uses of foreign exchange markets. First, the payments a company receives for its exports, the income it receives from foreign investments, or the income it receives from licensing agreements with foreign firms may be in foreign currencies. To use those funds in its home country, the company must convert them to its home country's currency. Consider the Scotch distillery that exports its whisky to the United States. The distillery is paid in dollars, but because those dollars cannot be spent in Great Britain, they must be converted into British pounds. Similarly, Toyota sells its cars in the United States for dollars; it must convert the U.S. dollars it receives into Japanese yen to use them in Japan.

Currency Speculation
Involves short-term movement of funds from one currency to another in hopes of profiting from shifts in exchange rates.

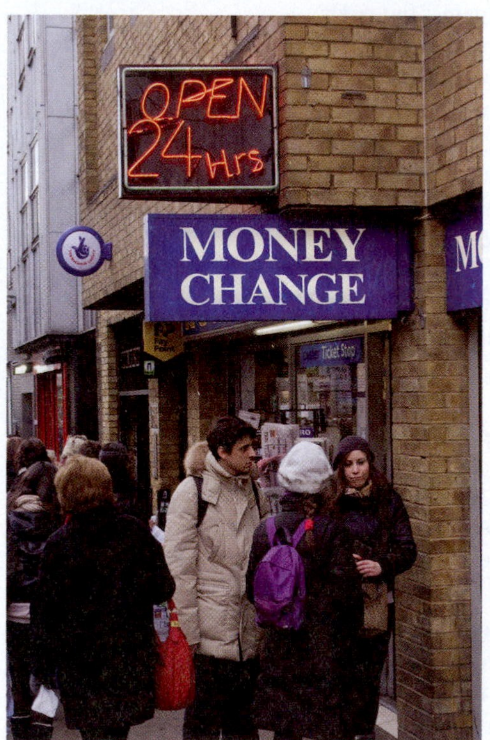

Every time tourists change money in a foreign country they are participating in the foreign exchange market.

Source: © Ed Brown/Alamy Stock Photo

Second, international businesses use foreign exchange markets when they must pay a foreign company for its products or services in its country's currency. For example, Dell buys many of the components for its computers from Malaysian firms. The Malaysian companies must be paid in Malaysia's currency, the ringgit, so Dell must convert money from dollars into ringgit to pay them.

Third, international businesses also use foreign exchange markets when they have spare cash that they wish to invest for short terms in money markets. For example, consider a U.S. company that has $10 million it wants to invest for three months. The best interest rate it can earn on these funds in the United States may be 2 percent. Investing in a South Korean money market account, however, may earn 6 percent. Thus, the company may change its $10 million into Korean won and invest it in South Korea. Note, however, that the rate of return it earns on this investment depends not only on the Korean interest rate but also on the changes in the value of the Korean won against the dollar in the intervening period.

Currency speculation is another use of foreign exchange markets. **Currency speculation** typically involves the short-term movement of funds from one currency to another in the hopes of profiting from shifts in exchange rates. Consider again a U.S. company with $10 million to invest for three months. Suppose the company suspects that the U.S. dollar is overvalued against the Japanese yen. That is, the company expects the value of the dollar to depreciate (fall) against that of the yen. Imagine the current dollar/yen exchange rate is $1 = ¥120. The company exchanges its $10 million into yen, receiving ¥1.2 billion ($10 million × 120 = ¥1.2 billion). Over the next three months, the value of the dollar depreciates against the yen until $1 = ¥100. Now the company exchanges its

¥1.2 billion back into dollars and finds that it has $12 million. The company has made a $2 million profit on currency speculation in three months on an initial investment of $10 million! In general, however, companies should beware, for speculation by definition is a very risky business. The company cannot know for sure what will happen to exchange rates. While a speculator may profit handsomely if his speculation about future currency movements turns out to be correct, he can also lose vast amounts of money if it turns out to be wrong.

A kind of speculation that has become more common in recent years is known as the **carry trade**. The carry trade involves borrowing in one currency where interest rates are low and then using the proceeds to invest in another currency where interest rates are high. For example, if the interest rate on borrowings in Japan is 1 percent, but the interest rate on deposits in American banks is 6 percent, it can make sense to borrow in Japanese yen, convert the money into U.S. dollars, and deposit it in an American bank. The trader can make a 5 percent margin by doing so, minus the transaction costs associated with changing one currency into another. The speculative element of this trade is that its success is based on a belief that there will be no adverse movement in exchange rates (or interest rates for that matter) that will make the trade unprofitable. However, if the yen were to rapidly increase in value against the dollar, then it would take more U.S. dollars to repay the original loan, and the trade could fast become unprofitable. The dollar/yen carry trade was actually very significant during the mid-2000s, peaking at more than $1 trillion in 2007, when some 30 percent of trade on the Tokyo foreign exchange market was related to the carry trade.[2] This carry trade declined in importance during 2008–2009 because interest rate differentials were falling as U.S. rates came down, making the trade less profitable.

Carry Trade
A kind of speculation that involves borrowing in one currency where interest rates are low and then using the proceeds to invest in another currency where interest rates are high.

INSURING AGAINST FOREIN EXCHANGE RISK

A second function of the foreign exchange market is to provide insurance against foreign exchange risk, which is the possibility that unpredicted changes in future exchange rates will have adverse consequences for the firm. When a firm insures itself against foreign exchange risk, it is engaging in *hedging*. To explain how the market performs this function, we must first distinguish among spot exchange rates, forward exchange rates, and currency swaps.

LO 10-2
Understand what is meant by spot exchange rates.

Spot Exchange Rates

When two parties agree to exchange currency and execute the deal immediately, the transaction is referred to as a spot exchange. Exchange rates governing such "on the spot" trades are referred to as spot exchange rates. The **spot exchange rate** is the rate at which a foreign exchange dealer converts one currency into another currency on a particular day. Thus, when our U.S. tourist in Edinburgh goes to a bank to convert her dollars into pounds, the exchange rate is the spot rate for that day.

Spot Exchange Rate
The exchange rate at which a foreign exchange dealer will convert one currency into another that particular day.

Spot exchange rates are reported on a real-time basis on many financial websites. An exchange rate can be quoted in two ways: as the amount of foreign currency one U.S. dollar will buy or as the value of a dollar for one unit of foreign currency. Thus, on March 21, 2016, at 12:30 p.m., Eastern Standard Time, one U.S. dollar bought €0.89, and one euro bought $1.12.

Spot rates change continually, often on a minute-by-minute basis (although the magnitude of changes over such short periods is usually small). The value of a currency is determined by the interaction between the demand and supply of that currency relative to the demand and supply of other currencies. For example, if lots of people want U.S. dollars and dollars are in short supply, and few people want British pounds and pounds are in plentiful supply, the spot exchange rate for converting dollars into pounds will change. The dollar is likely to appreciate against the pound (or the pound will depreciate against the dollar). Imagine the spot exchange rate is £1 = $2.00 when the market opens. As the day progresses, dealers demand more dollars and fewer pounds. By the end of the day, the spot exchange rate might be £1 = $1.98. Each pound now buys fewer dollars than at the start of the day. The dollar has appreciated, and the pound has depreciated.

Forward Exchange Rates

Changes in spot exchange rates can be problematic for an international business. For example, a U.S. company that imports high-end cameras from Japan knows that in 30 days it must pay yen to a Japanese supplier when a shipment arrives. The company will pay the Japanese supplier ¥200,000 for each camera, and the current dollar/yen spot exchange rate is $1 = ¥120. At this rate, each camera costs the importer $1,667 (i.e., 1,667 = 200,000/120). The importer knows she can sell the camera the day they arrive for $2,000 each,

LO 10-3
Recognize the role that forward exchange rates play in insuring against foreign exchange risk.

which yields a gross profit of $333 on each ($2,000 − $1,667). However, the importer will not have the funds to pay the Japanese supplier until the cameras are sold. If, over the next 30 days, the dollar unexpectedly depreciates against the yen, say, to $1 = ¥95, the importer will still have to pay the Japanese company ¥200,000 per camera but in dollar terms that would be equivalent to $2,105 per camera, which is more than she can sell the cameras for. A depreciation in the value of the dollar against the yen from $1 = ¥120 to $1 = ¥95 would transform a profitable deal into an unprofitable one.

Forward Exchange
When two parties agree to exchange currency and execute a deal at some specific date in the future.

Forward Exchange Rate
The exchange rate governing a forward exchange transaction.

To *insure* or *hedge* against this risk, the U.S. importer might want to engage in a forward exchange. A **forward exchange** occurs when two parties agree to exchange currency and execute the deal at some specific date in the future. Exchange rates governing such future transactions are referred to as **forward exchange rates**. For most major currencies, forward exchange rates are quoted for 30 days, 90 days, and 180 days into the future. In some cases, it is possible to get forward exchange rates for several years into the future. Returning to our camera importer example, let us assume the 30-day forward exchange rate for converting dollars into yen is $1 = ¥110. The importer enters into a 30-day forward exchange transaction with a foreign exchange dealer at this rate and is guaranteed that she will have to pay no more than $1,818 for each camera (1,818 = 200,000/110). This guarantees her a profit of $182 per camera ($2,000 − $1,818). She also insures herself against the possibility that an unanticipated change in the dollar/yen exchange rate will turn a profitable deal into an unprofitable one.

Currency Swap
Simultaneous purchase and sale of a given amount of foreign exchange for two different value dates.

In this example, the spot exchange rate ($1 = ¥120) and the 30-day forward rate ($1 = ¥110) differ. Such differences are normal; they reflect the expectations of the foreign exchange market about future currency movements. In our example, the fact that $1 bought more yen with a spot exchange than with a 30-day forward exchange indicates foreign exchange dealers expected the dollar to depreciate against the yen in the next 30 days. When this occurs, we say the dollar is selling at a discount on the 30-day forward market (i.e., it is worth less than on the spot market). Of course, the opposite can also occur. If the 30-day forward exchange rate were $1 = ¥130, for example, $1 would buy more yen with a forward exchange than with a spot exchange. In such a case, we say the dollar is selling at a premium on the 30-day forward market. This reflects the foreign exchange dealers' expectations that the dollar will appreciate against the yen over the next 30 days.

In sum, when a firm enters into a forward exchange contract, it is taking out insurance against the possibility that future exchange rate movements will make a transaction unprofitable by the time that transaction has been executed. Although many firms routinely enter into forward exchange contracts to hedge their foreign exchange risk, sometimes this can work against the company. An example is given in the accompanying Management Focus, which explains how the hedging strategy adopted by the Brazilian regional jet manufacturer, Embraer, backfired.

Should Currency Speculation Be Allowed?

Currency speculation involves the short-term movement of funds from one currency to another in the hopes of profiting from shifts in exchange rates. Sometimes this speculation is done as what is called a carry trade. As we describe in Chapter 10, this involves borrowing in one currency where interest rates are low and then using the proceeds to invest in another currency where interest rates are high. In effect, it can be argued that currency speculation tactics may have a strong negative effect on some countries' economic foundation (e.g., Iceland, Thailand). For years, Iceland was a respected country for its unmatchable standards of living. The 2008 economic turmoil threw the island nation's currency off the cliff. The hedge funds closed in, and the government had to try to fight off the predators. Several years later, Iceland is still feeling the effect of these currency woes, albeit the country is now in recovery mode and progressing in a positive direction. But the issue remains that large-scale currency speculation has the potential to adversely affect global markets. So, should currency speculation be allowed?

Source: A. Jung and C. Pauly, "Currency Woes: Crashing the Party of Icelandic Prosperity," *Spiegel Online International*, April 10, 2008.

Currency Swaps

The preceding discussion of spot and forward exchange rates might lead you to conclude that the option to buy forward is very important to companies engaged in international trade—and you would be right. According to the most recent data, forward instruments account for almost two-thirds of all foreign exchange transactions, while spot exchanges account for about one-third.[3] However, the vast majority of these forward exchanges are not forward exchanges of the type we have been discussing but rather a more sophisticated instrument known as currency swaps.

A **currency swap** is the simultaneous purchase and sale of a given amount of foreign exchange for two different value dates. Swaps are transacted between international businesses and their banks, between banks, and between governments

management FOCUS

Embraer and the Gyrations of the Brazilian Real

For many years, Brazil was a country battered by persistently high inflation. As a result, the value of its currency, the real, depreciated steadily against the U.S. dollar. This changed in the early 2000s, when the Brazilian government was successful in bringing down annual inflation rates into the single digits. Lower inflation, coupled with policies that paved the way for the expansion of the Brazilian economy, resulted in a steady appreciation of the real against the U.S. dollar. In May 2004, 1 real bought \$0.3121; by August 2008, 1 real bought \$0.65, an appreciation of more than 100 percent.

The appreciation of the real against the dollar was a mixed bag for Embraer, the world's largest manufacturer of regional jets of up to 110 seats and one of Brazil's most prominent industrial companies. Embraer purchases many of the parts that go into its jets, including the engines and electronics, from U.S. manufacturers. As the real appreciated against the dollar, these parts cost less when translated into reals, which benefited Embraer's profit margins. However, the company also prices its aircraft in U.S. dollars, as do all manufacturers in the global market for commercial jet aircraft. So, as the real appreciated against the dollar, Embraer's dollar revenues were compressed when exchanged back into reals.

To try to deal with the impact of currency appreciation on its revenues, in the mid-2000s, Embraer started to hedge against future appreciation of the real by buying forward contracts (forward contracts give the holder the right to exchange one currency—in this case, dollars—for another—in this case, reals—at some point in the future at a predetermined exchange rate). If the real had continued to appreciate, this would have been a great strategy for Embraer because the company could have locked in the rate at which sales made in dollars were exchanged back into reals. Unfortunately for Embraer, as the global financial crisis unfolded in 2008, investors fled to the dollar, which they viewed as a safe haven, and the real *depreciated* against the dollar. Between August 2008 and November 2008, the value of the real fell by almost 40 percent against the dollar. But for the hedging, this depreciation would have actually increased Embraer's revenues in reals. Embraer, however, had locked itself into a much higher real/dollar exchange rate, and the company was forced to take a \$121 million loss on what was essentially a bad currency bet.

Since the shock of 2008, Embraer has cut back on currency hedging, and most of its dollar sales and purchases are not hedged. This makes Embraer's sales revenues very sensitive to the real/dollar exchange rate. By 2010, the Brazilian real was once more appreciating against the U.S. dollar, which pressured Embraer's revenues. By 2012, however, the Brazilian economy was stagnating, while inflation was starting to increase again. This led to a sustained fall in the value of the real, which fell from 1 real = \$0.644 in July 2011 to 1 real = \$0.40 by January 2014, a depreciation of 38 percent. What was bad for the Brazilian currency, however, was good for Embraer, whose stock price surged to the highest price since February 2008 on speculation that the decline on the real would lead to a boost in Embraer's revenues when expressed in reals.

Sources: D. Godoy, "Embraer Rallies as Brazilian Currency Weakens," *Bloomberg,* May 31, 2013; K. Kroll, "Embraer Fourth Quarter Profits Plunge 44% on Currency Woes," *Cleveland.com,* March 27, 2009; "A Fall from Grace: Brazil's Mediocre Economy," *The Economist,* June 8, 2013; "Brazil's Economy: The Deterioration," *The Economist,* December 7, 2013.

when it is desirable to move out of one currency into another for a limited period without incurring foreign exchange risk. A common kind of swap is spot against forward. Consider a company such as Apple. Imagine Apple assembles laptop computers in the United States, but the screens are made in Japan. Apple also sells some of the finished laptops in Japan. So, like many companies, Apple both buys from and sells to Japan. Imagine Apple needs to change \$1 million into yen to pay its supplier of laptop screens today. Apple knows that in 90 days it will be paid ¥120 million by the Japanese importer that buys its finished laptops. It will want to convert these yen into dollars for use in the United States. Let us say today's spot exchange rate is \$1 = ¥120 and the 90-day forward exchange rate is \$1 = ¥110. Apple sells \$1 million to its bank in return for ¥120 million. Now Apple can pay its Japanese supplier. At the same time, Apple enters into a 90-day forward exchange deal with its bank for converting ¥120 million into dollars. Thus, in 90 days Apple will receive \$1.09 million (¥120 million/110 = \$1.09 million). Because the yen is trading at a premium on the 90-day forward market, Apple ends up with more dollars than it started with (although the opposite could also occur). The swap deal is just like a conventional forward deal in one important respect: It enables Apple to insure itself against foreign exchange risk. By engaging in a swap, Apple knows today that the ¥120 million payment it will receive in 90 days will yield \$1.09 million.

 **test PREP**

Use SmartBook to help retain what you have learned. Access your Instructor's Connect course to check out SmartBook or go to learnsmartadvantage.com for help.

The Nature of the Foreign Exchange Market

The foreign exchange market is not located in any one place. It is a global network of banks, brokers, and foreign exchange dealers connected by electronic communications systems. When companies wish to convert currencies, they typically go through their own banks rather than entering the market directly. The foreign exchange market has been growing at a rapid pace, reflecting a general growth in the volume of cross-border trade and investment (see Chapter 1). In March 1986, the average total value of global foreign exchange trading was about $200 billion per day. By April 2013, the last date for which we have solid data, it had hit $5.3 trillion a day.[4] The most important trading centers are London (37 percent of activity), New York (18 percent of activity), and Zurich, Tokyo, and Singapore (all with around 5 to 6 percent of activity).[5] Major secondary trading centers include Frankfurt, Paris, Hong Kong, and Sydney.

London's dominance in the foreign exchange market is due to both history and geography. As the capital of the world's first major industrial trading nation, London had become the world's largest center for international banking by the end of the nineteenth century, a position it has retained. Today, London's central position between Tokyo and Singapore to the east and New York to the west has made it the critical link between the East Asian and New York markets. Due to the particular differences in time zones, London opens soon after Tokyo closes for the night and is still open for the first few hours of trading in New York.[6]

Arbitrage
The purchase of securities in one market for immediate resale in another to profit from a price discrepancy.

Two features of the foreign exchange market are of particular note. The first is that the market never sleeps. Tokyo, London, and New York are all shut for only three hours out of every 24. During these three hours, trading continues in a number of minor centers, particularly San Francisco and Sydney, Australia. The second feature of the market is the integration of the various trading centers. High-speed computer linkages among trading centers around the globe have effectively created a single market. The integration of financial centers implies there can be no significant difference in exchange rates quoted in the trading centers. For example, if the yen/dollar exchange rate quoted in London at 3 p.m. is ¥120 = $1, the yen/dollar exchange rate quoted in New York at the same time (10 a.m. New York time) will be identical. If the New York yen/dollar exchange rate were ¥125 = $1, a dealer could make a profit through **arbitrage**, buying a currency low and selling it high. For example, if the prices differed in London and New York as given, a dealer in New York could take $1 million and use that to purchase ¥125 million. She could then immediately sell the ¥125 million for dollars in London, where the transaction would yield $1.041666 million, allowing the trader to book a profit of $41,666 on the transaction. If all dealers tried to cash in on the opportunity, however, the demand for yen in New York would rise, resulting in an appreciation of the yen against the dollar such that the price differential between New York and London would quickly disappear. Because foreign exchange dealers are always watching their computer screens for arbitrage opportunities, the few that arise tend to be small, and they disappear in minutes.

Use SmartBook to help retain what you have learned. Access your Instructor's Connect course to check out SmartBook or go to learnsmartadvantage.com for help.

Another feature of the foreign exchange market is the important role played by the U.S. dollar. Although a foreign exchange transaction can involve any two currencies, most transactions involve dollars on one side. This is true even when a dealer wants to sell a nondollar currency and buy another. A dealer wishing to sell Korean won for Brazilian real, for example, will usually sell the won for dollars and then use the dollars to buy real. Although this may seem a roundabout way of doing things, it is actually cheaper than trying to find a holder of real who wants to buy won. Because the volume of international transactions involving dollars is so great, it is not hard to find dealers who wish to trade dollars for won or real.

Due to its central role in so many foreign exchange deals, the dollar is a vehicle currency. In 2013, 87 percent of all foreign exchange transactions involved dollars on one side of the transaction. After the dollar, the most important vehicle currencies were the euro (33 percent), the Japanese yen (23 percent), and the British pound (12 percent)—reflecting the historical importance of these trading entities in the world economy.

Understand the different theories explaining how currency exchange rates are determined and their relative merits.

Economic Theories of Exchange Rate Determination

At the most basic level, exchange rates are determined by the demand and supply of one currency relative to the demand and supply of another. For example, if the demand for dollars outstrips the supply of them and if the supply of Japanese yen is greater than the demand for them, the dollar/yen exchange rate will change. The dollar will appreciate against the yen (the yen will depreciate against the dollar). However, while differences in relative demand and supply explain the determination of exchange rates, they do so only in a superficial sense. This simple explanation does not reveal what factors underlie the demand for and supply of a currency. Nor does it tell us when the demand for dollars will exceed the supply (and vice versa) or when the supply of Japanese yen will exceed demand for them (and vice versa). Neither does it show under what conditions a currency is in demand or under what conditions it is not demanded. In this section, we will review economic theory's answers to these questions. This will give us a deeper understanding of how exchange rates are determined.

If we understand how exchange rates are determined, we may be able to forecast exchange rate movements. Because future exchange rate movements influence export opportunities, the profitability of international trade and investment deals, and the price competitiveness of foreign imports, this is valuable information for an international business. Unfortunately, there is no simple explanation. The forces that determine exchange rates are complex, and no theoretical consensus exists, even among academic economists who study the phenomenon every day. Nonetheless, most economic theories of exchange rate movements seem to agree that three factors have an important impact on future exchange rate movements in a country's currency: the country's price inflation, its interest rate, and market psychology.[7]

PRICES AND EXCHANGE RATES

To understand how prices are related to exchange rate movements, we first need to discuss an economic proposition known as the law of one price. Then we will discuss the theory of purchasing power parity (PPP), which links changes in the exchange rate between two countries' currencies to changes in the countries' price levels.

The Law of One Price

The **law of one price** states that in competitive markets free of transportation costs and barriers to trade (such as tariffs), identical products sold in different countries must sell for the same price when their price is expressed in terms of the same currency.[8] For example, if the exchange rate between the British pound and the dollar is £1 = $2, a jacket that retails for $80 in New York should sell for £40 in London (because $80/$2 = £40). Consider what would happen if the jacket cost £30 in London ($60 in U.S. currency). At this price, it would pay a trader to buy jackets in London and sell them in New York (an example of *arbitrage*). The company initially could make a profit of $20 on each jacket by purchasing it for £30 ($60) in London and selling it for $80 in New York (we are assuming away transportation costs and trade barriers). However, the increased demand for jackets in London would raise their price in London, and the increased supply of jackets in New York would lower their price there. This would continue until prices were equalized. Thus, prices might equalize when the jacket cost £35 ($70) in London and $70 in New York (assuming no change in the exchange rate of £1 = $2).

Law of One Price
In competitive markets free of transportation costs and barriers to trade, identical products sold in different countries must sell for the same price when their price is expressed in the same currency.

Purchasing Power Parity

If the law of one price were true for all goods and services, the *purchasing power parity (PPP)* exchange rate could be found from any individual set of prices. By comparing the prices of identical products in different currencies, it would be possible to determine the "real" or PPP exchange rate that would exist if markets were efficient. (An **efficient market** has no impediments to the free flow of goods and services, such as trade barriers.)

Efficient Market
A market where prices reflect all available information.

A less extreme version of the PPP theory states that given relatively efficient markets—that is, markets in which few impediments to international trade exist—the price of a "basket of goods" should be roughly equivalent in each country. To express the PPP theory in symbols, let P$ be the U.S. dollar price of a basket of particular goods and P¥ be the price of the same basket of goods in Japanese yen. The PPP theory predicts that the dollar/yen exchange rate, E$/¥, should be equivalent to

$$E_{\$/¥} = P_{\$}/P_{¥}$$

Thus, if a basket of goods costs $200 in the United States and ¥20,000 in Japan, PPP theory predicts that the dollar/yen exchange rate should be $200/¥20,000 or $0.01 per Japanese yen (i.e., $1 = ¥100).

Every year, the news magazine *The Economist* publishes its own version of the PPP theorem, which it refers to as the "Big Mac Index." *The Economist* has selected McDonald's Big Mac as a proxy for a "basket of goods" because it is produced according to more or less the same recipe in about 120 countries. The Big Mac PPP is the exchange rate that would have hamburgers costing the same in each country. According to *The Economist,* comparing a country's actual exchange

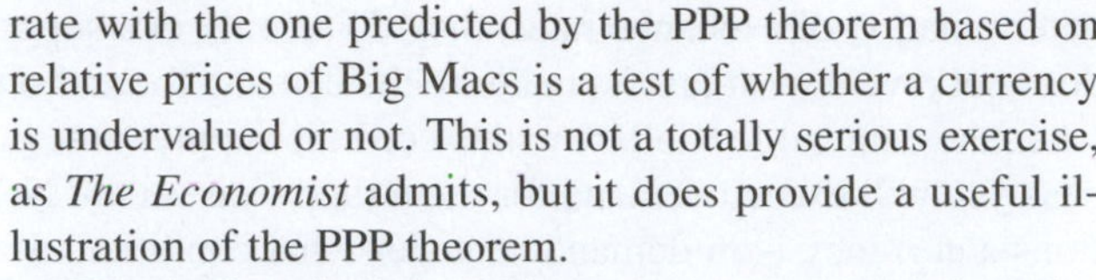

China Renminbi as Reserve Currency: Yuan a Bet?

Given China's importance in international trade, it is very likely that the role of the yuan will continue to expand in the foreign exchange market. A study from the Brookings Institution suggests that in the long run, the ascendance of the yuan to reserve-currency standing is likely. A so-called reserve currency is a currency that is held in significant quantities by governments and institutions as a part of their foreign exchange reserves and that is commonly used in international financial transactions. China is the only country whose currency does not have reserve status. Getting there will require overcoming two main challenges. First, it will take exchange rate flexibility and financial market development to improve the cost–benefit tradeoff of the yuan. Second, it will take strengthening the Chinese banking system. The potential costs of having a reserve currency include reduced control of the currency's external value and possibly a more volatile exchange rate. Given these challenges and constraints, do you think the yuan will become a reserve currency that can compete with, for example, the U.S. dollar and the euro (which make up about 90 percent of allocated currency reserves globally)?

Source: http://blogs.reuters.com.

rate with the one predicted by the PPP theorem based on relative prices of Big Macs is a test of whether a currency is undervalued or not. This is not a totally serious exercise, as *The Economist* admits, but it does provide a useful illustration of the PPP theorem.

To calculate the index, *The Economist* converts the price of a Big Mac in a country into dollars at current exchange rates and divides that by the average price of a Big Mac in America. According to the PPP theorem, the prices should be the same. If they are not, it implies that the currency is either overvalued against the dollar or undervalued. For example, in January 2016, the average price of a Big Mac in the United States was \$4.93, while it was \$3.35 in Brazil, \$2.68 in China, and \$5.21 in Norway. This suggests that the Brazilian *real* is undervalued by 23 percent and the Chinese *yuan* in undervalued by 46 percent, while the Norwegian krona is overvalued by 5.7 percent!

The next step in the PPP theory is to argue that the exchange rate will change if relative prices change. For example, imagine there is no price inflation in the United States, while prices in Japan are increasing by 10 percent a year. At the beginning of the year, a basket of goods costs \$200 in the United States and ¥20,000 in Japan, so the dollar/yen exchange rate, according to PPP theory, should be \$1 = ¥100. At the end of the year, the basket of goods still costs \$200 in the United States, but it costs ¥22,000 in Japan. PPP theory predicts that the exchange rate should change as a result. More precisely, by the end of the year:

$$E_{\$/¥} = \$200/¥22{,}000$$

Thus, ¥1 = \$0.0091 (or \$1 = ¥110). Because of 10 percent price inflation, the Japanese yen has depreciated by 10 percent against the dollar. One dollar will buy 10 percent more yen at the end of the year than at the beginning.

Money Supply and Price Inflation

In essence, PPP theory predicts that changes in relative prices will result in a change in exchange rates. Theoretically, a country in which price inflation is running wild should expect to see its currency depreciate against that of countries in which inflation rates are lower. If we can predict what a country's future inflation rate is likely to be, we can also predict how the value of its currency relative to other currencies—its exchange rate—is likely to change. The growth rate of a country's money supply determines its likely future inflation rate.[9] Thus, in theory at least, we can use information about the growth in money supply to forecast exchange rate movements.

Inflation is a monetary phenomenon. It occurs when the quantity of money in circulation rises faster than the stock of goods and services—that is, when the money supply increases faster than output increases. Imagine what would happen if everyone in the country was suddenly given \$10,000 by the government. Many people would rush out to spend their extra money on those things they had always wanted—new cars, new furniture, better clothes, and so on. There would be a surge in demand for goods and services. Car dealers, department stores, and other providers of goods and services would respond to this upsurge in demand by raising prices. The result would be price inflation.

A government increasing the money supply is analogous to giving people more money. An increase in the money supply makes it easier for banks to borrow from the government and for individuals and companies to borrow from banks. The resulting increase in credit causes increases in demand for goods and services. Unless the output of goods and services is growing at a rate similar to that of the money supply, the result will be inflation. This relationship has been observed time after time in country after country.

So now we have a connection between the growth in a country's money supply, price inflation, and exchange rate movements. Put simply, *when the growth in a country's money supply is faster than the growth in its output, price inflation is fueled.* The PPP theory tells us that a country with a high inflation rate will see depreciation in its currency exchange rate. In one of the clearest historical examples, in the mid-1980s, Bolivia experienced *hyperinflation*—an explosive and seemingly uncontrollable price inflation in which money loses value very rapidly. Table 10.1 presents data on Bolivia's money supply, inflation rate, and its peso's exchange rate with the U.S. dollar during the period of hyperinflation. The exchange rate is actually the "black market" exchange rate, because the Bolivian government prohibited converting the peso to other currencies during the period. The data show that the growth in money supply, the rate of price inflation, and the depreciation of the peso against the dollar all moved in step with each other. This is just what PPP theory and monetary economics predict. Between April 1984 and July 1985, Bolivia's money supply increased by 17,433 percent, prices increased by 22,908 percent, and the value of the peso against the dollar fell by 24,662 percent! In October 1985, the Bolivian government instituted a dramatic stabilization plan—which included the introduction of a new currency and tight control of the money supply—and by 1987, the country's annual inflation rate was down to 16 percent.[10]

Another way of looking at the same phenomenon is that an increase in a country's money supply, which increases the amount of currency available, changes the relative demand-and-supply

10.1 TABLE

Macroeconomic Data for Bolivia, April 1984 to October 1985

Source: Juan-Antonio Morales, "Inflation Stabilization in Bolivia," *Inflation Stabilization: The Experience of Israel, Argentina, Brazil, Bolivia, and Mexico*, ed. Michael Bruno et al. (Cambridge, MA: MIT Press, 1988).

Month	Money Supply (billions of pesos)	Price Level Relative to 1982 (average = 1)	Exchange Rate (pesos per dollar)
1984			
April	270	21.1	3,576
May	330	31.1	3,512
June	440	32.3	3,342
July	599	34.0	3,570
August	718	39.1	7,038
September	889	53.7	13,685
October	1,194	85.5	15,205
November	1,495	112.4	18,469
December	3,296	180.9	24,515
1985			
January	4,630	305.3	73,016
February	6,455	863.3	141,101
March	9,089	1,078.6	128,137
April	12,885	1,205.7	167,428
May	21,309	1,635.7	272,375
June	27,778	2,919.1	481,756
July	47,341	4,854.6	885,476
August	74,306	8,081.0	1,182,300
September	103,272	12,647.6	1,087,440
October	132,550	12,411.8	1,120,210

Women shop at an outdoor market in La Paz, Boliva. Bolivia's inflation rate is much lower today than it was in 1985 but must be carefully monitored.

Source: © Noah Friedman-Rudovsky/Bloomberg/Getty Images

conditions in the foreign exchange market. If the U.S. money supply is growing more rapidly than U.S. output, dollars will be relatively more plentiful than the currencies of countries where monetary growth is closer to output growth. As a result of this relative increase in the supply of dollars, the dollar will depreciate on the foreign exchange market against the currencies of countries with slower monetary growth.

Government policy determines whether the rate of growth in a country's money supply is greater than the rate of growth in output. A government can increase the money supply simply by telling the country's central bank to issue more money. Governments tend to do this to finance public expenditure (building roads, paying government workers, paying for defense, etc.). A government could finance public expenditure by raising taxes, but because nobody likes paying more taxes and because politicians do not like to be unpopular, they have a natural preference for expanding the money supply. Unfortunately, there is no magic money tree. The result of *excessive* growth in money supply is typically price inflation. However, this has not stopped governments around the world from expanding the money supply, with predictable results. If an international business is attempting to predict future movements in the value of a country's currency on the foreign exchange market, it should examine that country's policy toward monetary growth. If the government seems committed to controlling the rate of growth in money supply, the country's future inflation rate may be low (even if the current rate is high) and its currency should not depreciate too much on the foreign exchange market. If the government seems to lack the political will to control the rate of growth in money supply, the future inflation rate may be high, which is likely to cause its currency to depreciate. Historically, many Latin American governments have fallen into this latter category, including Argentina, Bolivia, and Brazil. More recently, many of the newly democratic states of eastern Europe made the same mistake. In late 2010, when the U.S. Federal Reserve decided to promote growth by expanding the U.S. money supply using a technique known as quantitative easing, critics charged that this too would lead to inflation and a decline in the value of the U.S. dollar on foreign exchange markets, but are they right? For a discussion of this, see the accompanying Country Focus.

Empirical Tests of PPP Theory

PPP theory predicts that exchange rates are determined by relative prices and that changes in relative prices will result in a change in exchange rates. A country in which price inflation is running wild should expect to see its currency depreciate against that of countries with lower inflation rates. This is intuitively appealing, but is it true in practice? There are several good examples of the connection between a country's price inflation and exchange rate position (such as Bolivia). However, extensive empirical testing of PPP theory has yielded mixed results.[11] While PPP theory seems to yield relatively accurate predictions in the long run, it does not appear to be a strong predictor of short-run movements in exchange rates covering time spans of five years or less.[12] In addition, the theory seems to best predict exchange rate changes for countries with high rates of inflation and underdeveloped capital markets. The theory is less useful for predicting short-term exchange rate movements between the currencies of advanced industrialized nations that have relatively small differentials in inflation rates.

The failure to find a strong link between relative inflation rates and exchange rate movements has been referred to as the purchasing power parity puzzle. Several factors may explain the failure of PPP theory to predict exchange rates more accurately.[13] PPP theory assumes away transportation costs and barriers to trade. In practice, these factors are significant, and they tend to create significant price differentials between countries. Transportation costs are certainly not trivial for many goods. Moreover, as we saw in Chapter 7, governments routinely intervene in international trade, creating tariff and nontariff barriers to cross-border trade. Barriers to trade limit the ability of traders to use arbitrage to equalize prices for the country FOCUS

Quantitative Easing, Inflation, and the Value of the U.S. Dollar

In fall 2010, the U.S. Federal Reserve (the Fed) decided to expand the U.S. money supply by entering the open market and purchasing $600 billion in U.S. government bonds from bondholders, a technique known as *quantitative easing*. Where did the $600 billion come from? The Fed simply created new bank reserves and used this cash to pay for the bonds. It had, in effect, printed money. The Fed took this action in an attempt to stimulate the U.S. economy, which, in the aftermath of the 2008–2009 global financial crisis, was struggling with low economic growth and high unemployment rates. The Fed had already tried to stimulate the economy by lowering short-term interest rates, but these were already close to zero, so it decided to lower medium- to longer-term rates; its tool for doing this was to pump $600 billion into the economy, increasing the supply of money and lowering its price, the interest rate. The Fed pursued further rounds of quantitative easing in 2011 through to 2013. In 2014 with the U.S. economy getting stronger and unemployment falling below 6 percent, the Fed progressively reduced its bond buying program. It ended the program in October 2014. By that time, the Fed had effectively pumped more than $3.5 trillion into the U.S. economy.

Critics were quick to attack the Fed's moves. Many claimed that the policy of expanding the money supply would fuel inflation and lead to a decline in the value of the U.S. dollar on the foreign exchange market. Some even called the policy a deliberate attempt by the Fed to debase the value of the U.S. currency, thereby driving down its value and promoting U.S. exports, which, if true, would be a form of mercantilism.

However, these charges may be unfounded for two reasons. First, at the time, the core U.S. inflation rate was the lowest in 50 years. In fact, the Fed actually feared the risk of deflation (a persistent fall in prices), which is a very damaging phenomenon. When prices are falling, people hold off their purchases because they know that goods will be cheaper tomorrow than they are today. This can result in a collapse in aggregate demand and high unemployment. The Fed felt that a little inflation—say, 2 percent per year—might be a good thing. Second, U.S. economic growth had been weak, unemployment was high, and there was excess productive capacity in the economy. Consequently, if the injection of money into the economy did stimulate demand, this would not translate into price inflation because the first response of businesses would be to expand output to utilize their excess capacity. Defenders of the Fed argued that the important point, which the critics seemed to be missing, was that expanding the money supply leads to only higher price inflation when unemployment is relatively low and there is not much excess capacity in the economy, a situation that did not exist in fall 2010. As for the currency market, its reaction was muted. At the beginning of November 2010, just before the Fed announced its policy, a trade-weighted index of the value of the dollar against a basket of other major currencies stood at 72. At the end of January 2014, it stood at 78—a slight appreciation. In short, currency traders did not seem to be selling off the dollar or reflecting worries about high inflation rates.

By March 2016, with the program over, there was no sign of a surge in price inflation in the U.S. economy. Indeed, inflation rates remained near historic lows. Moreover, far from weakening, the U.S. dollar had increased in value against most currencies, and the index value stood at 92. The Fed, it would seem, had been right and the critics were wrong.

Sources: P. Wallsten and S. Reddy, "Fed's Bond Buying Plan Ignites Growing Criticism," *The Wall Street Journal*, November 15, 2010; S. Chan, "Under Attack, the Fed Defends Policy of Buying Bonds," *International Herald Tribune*, November 17, 2010; "What QE Means for the World; Positive Sum Currency Wars," *The Economist*, February 14, 2013.

same product in different countries, which is required for the law of one price to hold. Government intervention in cross-border trade, by violating the assumption of efficient markets, weakens the link between relative price changes and changes in exchange rates predicted by PPP theory.

PPP theory may not hold if many national markets are dominated by a handful of multinational enterprises that have sufficient market power to be able to exercise some influence over prices, control distribution channels, and differentiate their product offerings between nations.[14] In fact, this situation seems to prevail in a number of industries. In such cases, dominant enterprises may be able to exercise a degree of pricing power, setting different prices in different markets to reflect varying demand conditions. This is referred to as price discrimination. For price discrimination to work, arbitrage must be limited. According to this argument, enterprises with some market power may be able to control distribution channels and therefore limit the unauthorized resale (arbitrage) of products purchased in another national market. They may also be able to limit resale (arbitrage) by differentiating otherwise identical products among nations along some line, such as design or packaging.

For example, even though the version of Microsoft Office sold in China may be less expensive than the version sold in the United States, the use of arbitrage to equalize prices may be limited because few Americans would want a version that was based on Chinese characters. The design differentiation between Microsoft Office for China and for the United States means

What About the Starbucks Index, a Good Idea?

To test the Big Mac index, which applies the purchasing power parity (PPP) theory using the price of a Big Mac in various markets to determine the equilibrium value of the foreign currency, *The Economist* established a Starbucks index in 2004. Like the Big Mac, a cup of Starbucks coffee can be found in many foreign markets and can be seen as a proxy for a basket of goods. The results of the Starbucks index followed the Big Mac index in most markets, except in Asia, where the former indicated that the dollar was at parity with the Chinese yuan. The Big Mac index suggested that the yuan was heavily undervalued. Neither of these consumer items is a good proxy for a basket of goods, but comparing their relative prices with exchange rates is an interesting and playful approach to quickly grasping how under- or overvalued the foreign currency is against the dollar. This obviously does not take into account whether you think a McDonald's Big Mac or a Starbucks cup of coffee is overpriced or relatively cheap where you live! What would be a good product, sold worldwide, that can replace the Big Mac and Starbucks indices?

that the law of one price would not work for Microsoft Office, even if transportation costs were trivial and tariff barriers between the United States and China did not exist. If the inability to practice arbitrage were widespread enough, it would break the connection between changes in relative prices and exchange rates predicted by the PPP theorem and help explain the limited empirical support for this theory.

Another factor of some importance is that governments also intervene in the foreign exchange market in attempting to influence the value of their currencies. We look at why and how they do this in Chapter 11. For now, the important thing to note is that governments regularly intervene in the foreign exchange market, and this further weakens the link between price changes and changes in exchange rates. One more factor explaining the failure of PPP theory to predict short-term movements in foreign exchange rates is the impact of investor psychology and other factors on currency purchasing decisions and exchange rate movements. We discuss this issue in more detail later in this chapter.

INTEREST RATES AND EXCHANGE RATES

Economic theory tells us that interest rates reflect expectations about likely future inflation rates. In countries where inflation is expected to be high, interest rates also will be high, because investors want compensation for the decline in the value of their money. This relationship was first formalized by economist Irvin Fisher and is referred to as the Fisher effect. The **Fisher effect** states that a country's "nominal" interest rate (i) is the sum of the required "real" rate of interest (r) and the expected rate of inflation over the period for which the funds are to be lent (I). More formally,

Fisher Effect

Nominal interest rates (i) in each country equal the required real rate of interest (r) and the expected rate of inflation over the period of time for which the funds are to be lent (I). That is, $i = r + I$.

$$i = r + I$$

For example, if the real rate of interest in a country is 5 percent and annual inflation is expected to be 10 percent, the nominal interest rate will be 15 percent. As predicted by the Fisher effect, a strong relationship seems to exist between inflation rates and interest rates.[15]

We can take this one step further and consider how it applies in a world of many countries and unrestricted capital flows. When investors are free to transfer capital between countries, real interest rates will be the same in every country. If differences in real interest rates did emerge between countries, arbitrage would soon equalize them. For example, if the real interest rate in Japan was 10 percent and only 6 percent in the United States, it would pay investors to borrow money in the United States and invest it in Japan. The resulting increase in the demand for money in the United States would raise the real interest rate there, while the increase in the supply of foreign money in Japan would lower the real interest rate there. This would continue until the two sets of real interest rates were equalized.

It follows from the Fisher effect that if the real interest rate is the same worldwide, any difference in interest rates between countries reflects differing expectations about inflation rates. Thus, if the expected rate of inflation in the United States is greater than that in Japan, U.S. nominal interest rates will be greater than Japanese nominal interest rates.

International Fisher Effect (IFE)

For any two countries, the spot exchange rate should change in an equal amount but in the opposite direction to the difference in nominal interest rates between countries.

Because we know from PPP theory that there is a link (in theory, at least) between inflation and exchange rates and because interest rates reflect expectations about inflation, it follows that there must also be a link between interest rates and exchange rates. This link is known as the international Fisher effect. The **international Fisher effect (IFE)** states that for any two countries, the spot exchange rate should change in an equal amount but in the opposite direction to the difference in nominal interest rates between the two countries. Stated more formally, the change in the spot exchange rate between the United States and Japan, for example, can be modeled as follows:

$$\frac{S_1 - S_2}{S_2} \times 100 = i_{\$} - i_{¥}$$

where $i_{\$}$ and $i_{¥}$ are the respective nominal interest rates in the United States and Japan, S_1 is the spot exchange rate at the beginning of the period, and S_2 is the spot exchange rate at the end of the period. If the U.S. nominal interest rate is higher than Japan's, reflecting greater expected inflation rates, the value of the dollar against the yen should fall by that interest rate differential in the future. So if the interest rate in the United States is 10 percent and in Japan it is 6 percent, we would expect the value of the dollar to depreciate by 4 percent against the Japanese yen.

Do interest rate differentials help predict future currency movements? The evidence is mixed; as in the case of PPP theory, in the long run, there seems to be a relationship between interest rate differentials and subsequent changes in spot exchange rates. However, considerable short-run deviations occur. Like PPP, the international Fisher effect is not a good predictor of short-run changes in spot exchange rates.[16]

INVESTOR PSYCHOLOGY AND BANDWAGON EFFECTS

Empirical evidence suggests that neither PPP theory nor the international Fisher effect is particularly good at explaining short-term movements in exchange rates. One reason may be the impact of investor psychology on short-run exchange rate movements. Evidence reveals that various psychological factors play an important role in determining the expectations of market traders as to likely future exchange rates.[17] In turn, expectations have a tendency to become self-fulfilling prophecies.

A particularly famous example of this mechanism occurred in September 1992, when the international financier George Soros made a huge bet against the British pound. Soros borrowed billions of pounds, using the assets of his investment funds as collateral, and immediately sold those pounds for German deutsche marks (this was before the advent of the euro). This technique, known as short selling, can earn the speculator enormous profits if he can subsequently buy back the pounds he sold at a much better exchange rate and then use those pounds, purchased cheaply, to repay his loan. By selling pounds and buying deutsche marks, Soros helped start pushing down the value of the pound on the foreign exchange markets. More importantly, when Soros started shorting the British pound, many foreign exchange traders, knowing Soros's reputation, jumped on the bandwagon and did likewise. This triggered a classic **bandwagon effect** with traders moving as a herd in the same direction at the same time. As the bandwagon effect gained momentum, with more traders selling British pounds and purchasing deutsche marks in expectation of a decline in the pound, their expectations became a self-fulfilling prophecy. Massive selling forced down the value of the pound against the deutsche mark. In other words, the pound declined in value not so much because of any major shift in macroeconomic fundamentals but because investors followed a bet placed by a major speculator, George Soros.

Bandwagon Effect
Movement of traders like a herd, all in the same direction and at the same time, in response to each other's perceived actions.

According to a number of studies, investor psychology and bandwagon effects play an important role in determining short-run exchange rate movements.[18] However, these effects can be hard to predict. Investor psychology can be influenced by political factors and by microeconomic events, such as the investment decisions of individual firms, many of which are only loosely linked to macroeconomic fundamentals, such as relative inflation rates. Also, bandwagon effects can be both triggered and exacerbated by the idiosyncratic behavior of politicians. Something like this seems to have occurred in Southeast Asia during 1997 when, one after another, the currencies of Thailand, Malaysia, South Korea, and Indonesia lost between 50 and 70 percent of their value against the U.S. dollar in a few months.

SUMMARY OF EXCHANGE RATE THEORIES

Relative monetary growth, relative inflation rates, and nominal interest rate differentials are all moderately good predictors of long-run changes in exchange rates. They are poor predictors of short-run changes in exchange rates, however, perhaps because of the impact of psychological factors, investor expectations, and bandwagon effects on short-term currency movements. This information is useful for an international business. Insofar as the long-term profitability of foreign investments, export opportunities, and the price competitiveness of foreign imports are all influenced by long-term movements in exchange rates, international businesses would be advised to pay attention to countries' differing monetary growth, inflation, and interest rates. International businesses that engage in foreign exchange transactions on a day-to-day basis could benefit by knowing some predictors of short-term foreign exchange rate movements. Unfortunately, short-term exchange rate movements are difficult to predict.

Use SmartBook to help retain what you have learned. Access your Instructor's Connect course to check out SmartBook or go to learnsmartadvantage.com for help.

Identify the merits of different approaches toward exchange rate forecasting.

Exchange Rate Forecasting

A company's need to predict future exchange rate variations raises the issue of whether it is worthwhile for the company to invest in exchange rate forecasting services to aid decision making. Two schools of thought address this issue. The efficient market school argues that forward exchange rates do the best possible job of forecasting future spot exchange rates and, therefore, investing in forecasting services would be a waste of money. The other school of thought, the inefficient market school, argues that companies can improve the foreign exchange market's estimate of future exchange rates (as contained in the forward rate) by investing in forecasting services. In other words, this school of thought does not believe the forward exchange rates are the best possible predictors of future spot exchange rates.

THE EFFICIENT MARKET SCHOOL

Forward exchange rates represent market participants' collective predictions of likely spot exchange rates at specified future dates. If forward exchange rates are the best possible predictor of future spot rates, it would make no sense for companies to spend additional money trying to forecast short-run exchange rate movements. Many economists believe the foreign exchange market is efficient at setting forward rates.[19] An efficient market is one in which prices reflect all available public information. (If forward rates reflect all available information about likely future changes in exchange rates, a company cannot beat the market by investing in forecasting services.)

If the foreign exchange market is efficient, forward exchange rates should be unbiased predictors of future spot rates. This does not mean the predictions will be accurate in any specific situation. It means inaccuracies will not be consistently above or below future spot rates; they will be random. Many empirical tests have addressed the efficient market hypothesis. Although most of the early work seems to confirm the hypothesis (suggesting that companies should not waste their money on forecasting services), some studies have challenged it.[20] There is some evidence that forward rates are not unbiased predictors of future spot rates and that more accurate predictions of future spot rates can be calculated from publicly available information.[21]

Did You Know?

Did you know that the U.S. dollar has been one of the strongest currencies in the world since the great recession of 2008–2009?

Visit your Connect SmartBook® to view a short video explanation from the authors.

THE INEFFICIENT MARKET SCHOOL

Citing evidence against the efficient market hypothesis, some economists believe the foreign exchange market is inefficient. An **inefficient market** is one in which prices do not reflect all available information. In an inefficient market, forward exchange rates will not be the best possible predictors of future spot exchange rates.

Inefficient Market

One in which prices do not reflect all available information.

If this is true, it may be worthwhile for international businesses to invest in forecasting services (as many do). The belief is that professional exchange rate forecasts might provide better predictions of future spot rates than forward exchange rates do. However, the track record of professional forecasting services is not that good.[22] For example, forecasting services did not predict the 1997 currency crisis that swept through Southeast Asia, nor did they predict the rise in the value of the dollar that occurred during late 2008, a period when the United States fell into a deep financial crisis that some thought would lead to a decline in the value of the dollar (it appears that the dollar rose because it was seen as a relatively safe currency in a time when many nations were experiencing economic trouble).

APPROACHES TO FORECASTING

Assuming the inefficient market school is correct that the foreign exchange market's estimate of future spot rates can be improved, on what basis should forecasts be prepared? Here again, there are two schools of thought. One adheres to fundamental analysis, while the other uses technical analysis.

Fundamental Analysis Fundamental analysis draws on economic theory to construct sophisticated econometric models for predicting exchange rate movements. The variables contained in these models typically include those we have discussed, such as relative money supply growth rates, inflation rates, and interest rates. In addition, they may include variables related to balance-of-payments positions.

Running a deficit on a balance-of-payments current account (a country is importing more goods and services than it is exporting) creates pressures that may result in the depreciation of the country's currency on the foreign exchange market.[23] Consider what might happen if the United States were running a persistent current account balance-of-payments deficit (as it has been). Because the United States would be importing more than it was exporting, people in other countries would be increasing their holdings of U.S. dollars. If these people were willing to hold their dollars, the dollar's exchange rate would not be influenced. However, if these people converted their dollars into other currencies, the supply of dollars in the foreign exchange market would increase (as would demand for the other currencies). This shift in demand and supply would create pressures that could lead to the depreciation of the dollar against other currencies.

This argument hinges on whether people in other countries are willing to hold dollars. This depends on such factors as U.S. interest rates, the return on holding other dollar-denominated assets such as stocks in U.S. companies, and, most important, inflation rates. So, in a sense, the balance-of-payments situation is not a fundamental predictor of future exchange rate movements. But what makes financial assets such as stocks and bonds attractive? The answer is prevailing interest rates and inflation rates, both of which affect underlying economic growth and the real return to holding U.S. financial assets. Given this, we are back to the argument that the fundamental determinants of exchange rates are monetary growth, inflation rates, and interest rates.

Technical Analysis Technical analysis uses price and volume data to determine past trends, which are expected to continue into the future. This approach does not rely on a consideration of economic fundamentals. Technical analysis is based on the premise that there are analyzable market trends and waves and that previous trends and waves can be used to predict future trends and waves. Since there is no theoretical rationale for this assumption of predictability, many economists compare technical analysis to fortune-telling. Despite this skepticism, technical analysis has gained favor in recent years.[24]

test PREP

Use SmartBook to help retain what you have learned. Access your Instructor's Connect course to check out SmartBook or go to learnsmartadvantage.com for help.

Currency Convertibility

Until this point, we have assumed that the currencies of various countries are freely convertible into other currencies. Due to government restrictions, a significant number of currencies are not freely convertible into other currencies. A country's currency is said to be **freely convertible** when the country's government allows both residents and nonresidents to purchase unlimited amounts of a foreign currency with it. A currency is said to be **externally convertible** when only nonresidents may convert it into a foreign currency without any limitations. A currency is **nonconvertible** when neither residents nor nonresidents are allowed to convert it into a foreign currency.

Freely Convertible Currency
A country's currency is freely convertible when the government of that country allows both residents and nonresidents to purchase unlimited amounts of foreign currency with the domestic currency.

Externally Convertible Currency
Limitations on the ability of residents to convert domestic currency, though nonresidents can convert their holdings of domestic currency into foreign currency.

Nonconvertible Currency
A currency is not convertible when both residents and nonresidents are prohibited from converting their holdings of that currency into another currency.

Free convertibility is not universal. Many countries place some restrictions on their residents' ability to convert the domestic currency into a foreign currency (a policy of external convertibility). Restrictions range from the relatively minor (such as restricting the amount of foreign currency they may take with them out of the country on trips) to the major (such as restricting domestic businesses' ability to take foreign currency out of the country). External convertibility restrictions can limit domestic companies' ability to invest abroad, but they present few problems for foreign companies wishing to do business in that country. For example, even if the Japanese government tightly controlled the ability of its residents to convert the yen into U.S. dollars, all U.S. businesses with deposits in Japanese banks may at any time convert all their yen into dollars and take them out of the country. Thus, a U.S. company with a subsidiary in Japan is assured that it will be able to convert the profits from its Japanese operation into dollars and take them out of the country.

Serious problems arise, however, under a policy of nonconvertibility. This was the practice of the former Soviet Union, and it continued to be the practice in Russia for several years after the collapse of the Soviet Union. When strictly applied, nonconvertibility means that although a U.S. company doing business in a country such as Russia may be able to generate significant ruble profits, it may not convert those rubles into dollars and take them out of the country. Obviously, this is not desirable for international business.

Governments limit convertibility to preserve their foreign exchange reserves. A country needs an adequate supply of these reserves to service its international debt commitments and to purchase imports. Governments typically impose convertibility restrictions on their currency when they fear that free convertibility will lead to a run on their foreign exchange reserves. This occurs when residents and nonresidents rush to convert their holdings of domestic currency into a foreign currency—a phenomenon generally referred to as **capital flight**. Capital flight is most likely to occur when the value of the domestic currency is depreciating rapidly because of hyperinflation or when a country's economic prospects are shaky in other respects. Under such circumstances, both residents and nonresidents tend to believe that their money is more likely to hold its value if it is converted into a foreign currency and invested abroad. Not only will a run on foreign exchange reserves limit the country's ability to service its international debt and pay for imports, but it will also lead to a precipitous depreciation in the exchange rate as residents and nonresidents unload their holdings of domestic currency on the foreign exchange markets (thereby increasing the market supply of the country's currency). Governments fear that the rise in import prices resulting from currency depreciation will lead to further increases in inflation. This fear provides another rationale for limiting convertibility.

Capital Flight
Converting domestic currency into a foreign currency.

Companies can deal with the nonconvertibility problem by engaging in countertrade. **Countertrade** refers to a range of barter-like agreements by which goods and services can be traded for other goods and services. Countertrade can make sense when a country's currency is nonconvertible. For example, consider the deal that General Electric struck with the Romanian government when that country's currency was nonconvertible. When General Electric won a contract for a $150 million generator project in Romania, it agreed to take payment in the form of Romanian goods that could be sold for $150 million on international markets. In a similar case, the Venezuelan government negotiated a contract with Caterpillar under which Venezuela would trade 350,000 tons of iron ore for Caterpillar heavy construction equipment. Caterpillar subsequently traded the iron ore to Romania in exchange for Romanian farm products, which it then sold on international markets for dollars.[25]

Countertrade
The trade of goods and services for other goods and services.

How important is countertrade? Twenty years ago, a large number of nonconvertible currencies existed in the world, and countertrade was quite significant. However, in recent years, many governments have made their currencies freely convertible, and the percentage of world trade that involves countertrade is probably significantly below 5 percent.[26]

Use SmartBook to help retain what you have learned. Access your Instructor's Connect course to check out SmartBook or go to learnsmartadvantage.com for help.

FOCUS ON MANAGERIAL IMPLICATIONS

LO 10-6
Compare and contrast the differences among translation, transaction, and economic exposure, and what managers can do to manage each type of exposure.

FOREIGN EXCHANGE RATE RISK

This chapter contains a number of clear implications for business. First, it is critical that international businesses understand the influence of exchange rates on the profitability of trade and investment deals. Adverse changes in exchange rates can make apparently profitable deals unprofitable. As noted, the risk introduced into international business transactions by changes in exchange rates is referred to as foreign exchange risk. Foreign exchange risk is usually divided into three main categories: transaction exposure, translation exposure, and economic exposure.

Transaction Exposure

Transaction exposure is the extent to which the income from individual transactions is affected by fluctuations in foreign exchange values. Such exposure includes obligations for the purchase or sale of goods and services at previously agreed prices and the borrowing or lending of funds in foreign currencies. For example, suppose in 2004, an American airline agreed to purchase 10 Airbus 330 aircraft for €120 million each for a total price of €1.20 billion, with delivery scheduled for 2008 and payment due then. When the contract was signed in 2004, the dollar/euro exchange rate stood at $1 = €1.10, so the American airline anticipated paying $1.09 billion for the 10 aircraft when they were delivered (€1.2 billion/1.1 = $1.09 billion). However, imagine that the value of the dollar depreciates against the euro over the intervening period, so that a dollar buys only €0.80 in 2008 when payment is due ($1 = €0.80). Now the total cost in U.S. dollars is $1.5 billion (€1.2 billion/0.80 = $1.5 billion), an increase of $0.41 billion! The transaction exposure here is $0.41 billion, which is the money lost due to an adverse movement in exchange rates between the time when the deal was signed and when the aircraft were paid for.

Transaction Exposure
The extent to which income from individual transactions is affected by fluctuations in foreign exchange values.

Translation Exposure

Translation exposure is the impact of currency exchange rate changes on the reported financial statements of a company. Translation exposure is concerned with the present measurement of past events. The resulting accounting gains or losses are said to be unrealized—they are "paper" gains and losses—but they are still important. Consider a U.S. firm with a subsidiary in Mexico. If the value of the Mexican peso depreciates significantly against the dollar, this would substantially reduce the dollar value of the Mexican subsidiary's equity. In turn, this would reduce the total dollar value of the firm's equity reported in its consolidated balance sheet. This would raise the apparent leverage of the firm (its debt ratio), which could increase the firm's cost of borrowing and potentially limit its access to the capital market. Similarly, if an American firm has a subsidiary in the European Union and the value of the euro depreciates rapidly against that of the dollar over a year, this will reduce the dollar value of the euro profit made by the European subsidiary, resulting in negative translation exposure. In fact, many U.S. firms suffered from significant negative translation exposure in Europe during 2000, precisely because the euro did depreciate rapidly against the dollar. In 2002–2007, the euro rose in value against the dollar. This positive translation exposure boosted the dollar profits of American multinationals with significant operations in Europe. Between mid-2014 and early 2015, the euro slumped in value against the dollar, compressing the dollar profits of American multinationals with significant European exposure.

Translation Exposure
The extent to which the reported consolidated results and balance sheets of a corporation are affected by fluctuations in foreign exchange values.

Economic Exposure

Economic exposure is the extent to which a firm's future international earning power is affected by changes in exchange rates. Economic exposure is concerned with the long-run effect of changes in exchange rates on future prices, sales, and costs. This is distinct from transaction exposure, which is concerned with the effect of exchange rate changes on individual transactions, most of which are short-term affairs that will be executed within a few weeks or months. Consider the effect of wide swings in the value of the dollar on many U.S. firms' international competitiveness. The rapid rise in the value of the dollar on the foreign exchange market in the 1990s hurt the price competitiveness of many U.S. producers in world markets. U.S. manufacturers that relied heavily on exports saw their export volume and world market share decline. The reverse phenomenon occurred in 2000–2009, when the dollar declined against most major currencies. The fall in the value of the dollar helped increase the price competitiveness of U.S. manufacturers in world markets. Between mid-2014 and early 2015, the dollar increased significantly in value against most major currencies, decreasing the price competitiveness of U.S. exporters.

Economic Exposure
The extent to which a firm's future international earning power is affected by changes in exchange rates.

Reducing Translation and Transaction Exposure

A number of tactics can help firms minimize their transaction and translation exposure. These tactics primarily protect short-term cash flows from adverse changes in exchange rates. We have already discussed two of these tactics at length in the chapter, entering into forward exchange rate contracts and buying swaps. In addition to buying forward and using swaps, firms can minimize their foreign exchange exposure through leading and lagging payables and receivables—that is, paying suppliers and collecting payment from customers early or late depending on expected exchange rate movements. A **lead strategy** involves attempting to collect foreign currency receivables (payments from customers) early when a foreign currency is expected to depreciate and paying foreign currency payables (to suppliers) before they are due when a currency is expected to appreciate. A **lag strategy** involves delaying collection of foreign currency receivables if that currency is expected to appreciate and delaying payables if the currency is expected to depreciate. Leading and lagging involve accelerating payments from weak-currency to strong-currency countries and delaying inflows from strong-currency to weak-currency countries.

Lead Strategy

Collecting foreign currency receivables early when a foreign currency is expected to depreciate and paying foreign currency payables before they are due when a currency is expected to appreciate.

Lag Strategy

Delaying the collection of foreign currency receivables if that currency is expected to appreciate and delaying payables if that currency is expected to depreciate.

Lead and lag strategies can be difficult to implement, however. The firm must be in a position to exercise some control over payment terms. Firms do not always have this kind of bargaining power, particularly when they are dealing with important customers who are in a position to dictate payment terms. Also, because lead and lag strategies can put pressure on a weak currency, many governments limit leads and lags. For example, some countries set 180 days as a limit for receiving payments for exports or making payments for imports.

Reducing Economic Exposure

Reducing economic exposure requires strategic choices that go beyond the realm of financial management. The key to reducing economic exposure is to distribute the firm's productive assets to various locations so the firm's long-term financial well-being is not severely affected by adverse changes in exchange rates. This is a strategy that firms both large and small sometimes pursue. For example, during the 2000s, fearing that the euro would continue to strengthen against the U.S. dollar, some European firms that did significant business in the United States set up local production facilities in that market to ensure that a rising euro does not put them at a competitive disadvantage relative to their local rivals. Similarly, Toyota has production plants distributed around the world in part to make sure that a rising yen does not price Toyota cars out of local markets. Caterpillar has also pursued this strategy, setting up factories around the world that can act as a hedge against the possibility that a strong dollar will price Caterpillar's exports out of foreign markets. In 2008, 2009, and 2014–2015, all periods of dollar strength, this real hedge proved to be very useful.

Other Steps for Managing Foreign Exchange Risk

A firm needs to develop a mechanism for ensuring it maintains an appropriate mix of tactics and strategies for minimizing its foreign exchange exposure. Although there is no universal agreement as to the components of this mechanism, a number of common themes stand out.[27] First, central control of exposure is needed to protect resources efficiently and ensure that each subunit adopts the correct mix of tactics and strategies. Many companies have set up inhouse foreign exchange centers. Although such centers may not be able to execute all foreign exchange deals—particularly in large, complex multinationals where myriad transactions may be pursued simultaneously—they should at least set guidelines for the firm's subsidiaries to follow.

Second, firms should distinguish between, on one hand, transaction and translation exposure and, on the other, economic exposure. Many companies seem to focus on reducing their transaction and translation exposure and pay scant attention to economic exposure, which may have more profound long-term implications.[28] Firms need to develop strategies for dealing with economic exposure. For example, Stanley Black & Decker, the maker of power tools, has a strategy for actively managing its economic risk. The key to Stanley Black & Decker's strategy is flexible sourcing. In response to foreign exchange movements, Stanley Black & Decker can move production from one location to another to offer the most competitive pricing. Stanley Black & Decker manufactures in more than a dozen locations around the world—in Europe, Australia, Brazil, Mexico, and Japan. More than 50 percent of the company's productive assets are based outside North America. Although each of Stanley Black & Decker's factories focuses on one or two products to achieve economies of scale, there is considerable overlap. On average, the company runs its factories at no more than 80 percent capacity, so most are able to switch rapidly from producing one product to producing another or to add a product. This allows a factory's production to be changed in response to foreign exchange movements. For example, if the dollar depreciates against other currencies, the amount of imports into the United States from overseas subsidiaries can be reduced and the amount of exports from U.S. subsidiaries to other locations can be increased.[29]

Third, the need to forecast future exchange rate movements cannot be overstated, though, as we saw earlier in the chapter, this is a tricky business. No model comes close to perfectly predicting future movements in foreign exchange rates. The best that can be said is that in the short run, forward exchange rates provide the best predictors of exchange rate movements, and in the long run, fundamental economic factors—particularly relative inflation rates—should be watched because they influence exchange rate movements. Some firms attempt to forecast exchange rate movements in-house; others rely on outside forecasters. However, all such forecasts are imperfect attempts to predict the future.

Fourth, firms need to establish good reporting systems so the central finance function (or in-house foreign exchange center) can regularly monitor the firm's exposure positions. Such reporting systems should enable the firm to identify any exposed accounts, the exposed position by currency of each account, and the time periods covered.

Finally, on the basis of the information it receives from exchange rate forecasts and its own regular reporting systems, the firm should produce monthly foreign exchange exposure reports. These reports should identify how cash flows and balance sheet elements might be affected by forecasted changes in exchange rates. The reports can then be used by management as a basis for adopting tactics and strategies to hedge against undue foreign exchange risks.

Surprisingly, some of the largest and most sophisticated firms don't take such precautionary steps, exposing themselves to very large foreign exchange risks.

Key Terms

foreign exchange market, p. 272
exchange rate, p. 272
foreign exchange risk, p. 273
currency speculation, p. 274
carry trade, p. 275
spot exchange rate, p. 275
forward exchange, p. 276
forward exchange rate, p. 276
currency swap, p. 276
arbitrage, p. 278
law of one price, p. 279
efficient market, p. 279
Fisher effect, p. 284
international Fisher effect, p. 284
bandwagon effect, p. 285
inefficient market, p. 286
freely convertible currency, p. 287
externally convertible currency, p. 287
nonconvertible currency, p. 287
capital flight, p. 288
countertrade, p. 288
transaction exposure, p. 289
translation exposure, p. 289
economic exposure, p. 289
lead strategy, p. 290
lag strategy, p. 290

Summary

This chapter explained how the foreign exchange market works, examined the forces that determine exchange rates, and then discussed the implications of these factors for international business. Given that changes in exchange rates can dramatically alter the profitability of foreign trade and investment deals, this is an area of major interest to international business. The chapter made the following points:

1. One function of the foreign exchange market is to convert the currency of one country into the currency of another. A second function of the foreign exchange market is to provide insurance against foreign exchange risk.
2. The spot exchange rate is the exchange rate at which a dealer converts one currency into another currency on a particular day.
3. Foreign exchange risk can be reduced by using forward exchange rates. A forward exchange rate is an exchange rate governing future transactions. Foreign exchange risk can also be reduced by engaging in currency

swaps. A swap is the simultaneous purchase and sale of a given amount of foreign exchange for two different value dates.

4. The law of one price holds that in competitive markets that are free of transportation costs and barriers to trade, identical products sold in different countries must sell for the same price when their price is expressed in the same currency.
5. Purchasing power parity (PPP) theory states the price of a basket of particular goods should be roughly equivalent in each country. PPP theory predicts that the exchange rate will change if relative prices change.
6. The rate of change in countries' relative prices depends on their relative inflation rates. A country's inflation rate seems to be a function of the growth in its money supply.
7. The PPP theory of exchange rate changes yields relatively accurate predictions of long-term trends in exchange rates but not of short-term movements. The failure of PPP theory to predict exchange rate changes more accurately may be due to transportation costs, barriers to trade and investment, and the impact of psychological factors such as bandwagon effects on market movements and short-run exchange rates.
8. Interest rates reflect expectations about inflation. In countries where inflation is expected to be high, interest rates also will be high.
9. The international Fisher effect states that for any two countries, the spot exchange rate should change in an equal amount but in the opposite direction to the difference in nominal interest rates.
10. The most common approach to exchange rate forecasting is fundamental analysis. This relies on variables such as money supply growth, inflation rates, nominal interest rates, and balance-of-payments positions to predict future changes in exchange rates.
11. In many countries, the ability of residents and nonresidents to convert local currency into a foreign currency is restricted by government policy. A government restricts the convertibility of its currency to protect the country's foreign exchange reserves and to halt any capital flight.
12. Nonconvertibility of a currency makes it very difficult to engage in international trade and investment in the country. One way of coping with the nonconvertibility problem is to engage in countertrade—to trade goods and services for other goods and services.
13. The three types of exposure to foreign exchange risk are transaction exposure, translation exposure, and economic exposure.
14. Tactics that insure against transaction and translation exposure include buying forward, using currency swaps, and leading and lagging payables and receivables.
15. Reducing a firm's economic exposure requires strategic choices about how the firm's productive assets are distributed around the globe.

Critical Thinking and Discussion Questions

1. The interest rate on South Korean government securities with one-year maturity is 4 percent, and the expected inflation rate for the coming year is 2 percent. The interest rate on U.S. government securities with one-year maturity is 7 percent, and the expected rate of inflation is 5 percent. The current spot exchange rate for Korean won is \$1 = W1,200. Forecast the spot exchange rate one year from today. Explain the logic of your answer.
2. Two countries, Great Britain and the United States, produce just one good: beef. Suppose the price of beef in the United States is \$2.80 per pound and in Britain it is £3.70 per pound.
   a. According to PPP theory, what should the dollar/pound spot exchange rate be?
   b. Suppose the price of beef is expected to rise to \$3.10 in the United States and to £4.65 in Britain. What should the one-year forward dollar/pound exchange rate be?
   c. Given your answers to parts *a* and *b*, and given that the current interest rate in the United States is 10 percent, what would you expect the current interest rate to be in Britain?
3. Reread the Management Focus on Embraer, then answer the following questions:
   a. What does the recent economic history of Brazil tell you about the relationship between price inflation and exchange rates? What other factors might determine exchange rates for the Brazilian real?
   b. Is a decline in value of the real against the U.S. dollar good for Embraer, bad for Embraer, or a mixed bag? Explain your answer.
   c. What kind of foreign exchange rate risks is Embraer exposed to? Can Embraer reduce these risks? How?
   d. Do you think Embraer's decision to try and hedge against further appreciation of the real in the early 2000s was a good decision? What was the alternative?
   e. Since 2008, Embraer has significantly reduced its dollar hedging operations. Is this wise?
   f. Between mid-2014 and early 2015, the real depreciated significantly against the U.S. dollar. What do you think the impact was on Embraer?

4. You manufacture wine goblets. In mid-June, you receive an order for 10,000 goblets from Japan. Payment of ¥400,000 is due in mid-December. You expect the yen to rise from its present rate of $1 = ¥130 to $1 = ¥100 by December. You can borrow yen at 6 percent a year. What should you do?
5. You are the CFO of a U.S. firm whose wholly owned subsidiary in Mexico manufactures component parts for your U.S. assembly operations. The subsidiary has been financed by bank borrowings in the United States. One of your analysts told you that the Mexican peso is expected to depreciate by 30 percent against the dollar on the foreign exchange markets over the next year. What actions, if any, should you take?

globalEDGE Research Task

globaledge.msu.edu

Use the globalEDGE™ website (globaledge.msu.edu) to complete the following exercises:

1. One of your company's essential suppliers is located in Japan. Your company needs to make a 1 million Japanese yen payment in six months. Considering that your company primarily operates in U.S. dollars, you are assigned the task of deciding on a strategy to minimize your transaction exposure. Identify the spot and *forward exchange rates* between the two currencies. What factors influence your decision to use each? Which one would you choose? How many dollars must you spend to acquire the amount of yen required?
2. Sometimes analysts use the price of specific products in different locations to compare currency valuation and purchasing power. For example, *The Economist*'s Big Mac Index compares the purchasing power parity of many countries based on the price of a Big Mac. Using Google, locate the latest edition of this index that is accessible. Identify the five countries (and their currencies) with the lowest purchasing power parity according to this classification. Which currencies, if any, are overvalued?

Subaru's Sales Boom Thanks to the Weaker Yen

closing case

For the Japanese carmaker Subaru, a sharp fall in the value of yen against the U.S. dollar has turned a problem—the lack of U.S. production—into an unexpected sales boom. Subaru, which is a niche player in the global auto industry, has long bucked the trend among its Japanese rivals of establishing significant manufacturing facilities in the North American market. Instead, the company has chosen to concentrate most of its manufacturing in Japan in order to achieve economies of scale at its home plants, exporting its production to the United States. Subaru still makes 80 percent of its vehicles at home, compared with 21 percent for Honda.

Back in 2012, this strategy was viewed as something of a liability. In those days, one U.S. dollar bought only 80 Japanese yen. The strong yen meant that Subaru cars were being priced out of the U.S. market. Japanese companies like Honda and Toyota, which had substantial production in the United States, gained business at Subaru's expense. But from 2012 onward, with Japan mired in recession and consumer prices falling, the country's central bank repeatedly cut interest rates in an attempt to stimulate the economy. As interest rates fell in Japan, investors moved money out of the country, selling yen and buying the U.S. dollar. They used those dollars to invest in U.S. stocks and bonds where they anticipated a greater return. As a consequence, the price of yen in terms of dollars fell. By December 2015, one dollar bought 120 yen, representing a 50 percent fall in the value of the yen against the U.S. dollar since 2012.

For Subaru, the depreciation in the value of the yen has given it a pricing advantage and driven a sales boom. Demand for Subaru cars in the United States has been so strong that the automaker has been struggling to keep up. The profits of Subaru's parent company, Fuji Heavy Industries, have surged. In February 2015, Fuji announced that it would earn record operating profits of around ¥410 billion ($3.5 billion) for the financial year ending March 2015. Subaru's profit margin has increased to 14.4 percent, compared with 5.6 percent for Honda, a company that is heavily dependent on U.S. production. The good times continued in 2015, with Subaru posting record profits in the quarter ending December 31, 2015.

Despite its current pricing advantage, Subaru is moving to increase its U.S. production. It plans to expand its sole plant in the United States, in Indiana, by March 2017, with a goal of making 310,000 a year, up from 200,000 currently. When asked why it is doing this, Subaru's management notes that the yen will not stay weak against the dollar forever, and it is wise to expand local production as a hedge against future increases in the value of the yen. Indeed, when the Bank of Japan decided to set a key interest rate below zero in early February 2016, the yen started to appreciate against the U.S. dollar, presumably on expectations that negative interest rates would finally help stimulate Japan's sluggish economy. By late March 2016, the yen had appreciated against the dollar and was trading at $1=112 yen.

Sources: Chang-Ran Kim, "Subaru-Maker, Fuji Heavy Lifts Profit View on Rosy US Sales, Weak Yen," *Reuters*, February 3, 2015; Yoko Kubota, "Why Subaru's Profit Is Surging," *The Wall Street Journal*, November 14, 2014; Doron Levin, "Subaru Profit Soaring on Weaker Yen," *Market Watch*, November 15, 2014; Y. Kubato, "Weaker Yen Drives Subaru Maker's Profit Higher," *The Wall Street Journal*, February 4, 2016.

CASE DISCUSSION QUESTIONS

1. Why do you think that historically, Subaru chose to export production from Japan, rather than set up manufacturing facilities in the United States like its Japanese rivals?
2. What are the currency risks associated with Subaru's export strategy? What are the potential benefits?
3. Why did Subaru's sales and profits surge in 2014 and 2015?
4. Is Subaru wise to expand its U.S. production capacity? What other strategies could the company use to hedge against adverse changes in exchange rates? What are the pros and cons of the different hedging strategies Subaru might adopt?

Endnotes

1. For a good general introduction to the foreign exchange market, see R. Weisweiller, *How the Foreign Exchange Market Works* (New York: New York Institute of Finance, 1990). A detailed description of the economics of foreign exchange markets can be found in P. R. Krugman and M. Obstfeld, *International Economics: Theory and Policy* (New York: HarperCollins, 1994).
2. "The Domino Effect," *The Economist,* July 5, 2008, p. 85.
3. Bank for International Settlements, *Tri-annual Central Bank Survey of Foreign Exchange and Derivatives Market Activity, April 2013* (Basle, Switzerland: BIS, September 2013).
4. Ibid.
5. Ibid.
6. M. Dickson, "Capital Gain: How London Is Thriving as It Takes on the Global Competition," *Financial Times,* March 27, 2006, p. 11.
7. For a comprehensive review, see M. Taylor, "The Economics of Exchange Rates," *Journal of Economic Literature* 33 (1995), pp. 13–47.
8. Krugman and Obstfeld, *International Economics*.
9. M. Friedman, *Studies in the Quantity Theory of Money* (Chicago: University of Chicago Press, 1956). For an accessible explanation, see M. Friedman and R. Friedman, *Free to Choose* (London: Penguin Books, 1979), chap. 9.
10. Juan-Antonio Morales, "Inflation Stabilization in Bolivia," in *Inflation Stabilization: The Experience of Israel, Argentina, Brazil, Bolivia, and Mexico,* ed. Michael Bruno et al. (Cambridge, MA: MIT Press, 1988); *The Economist, World Book of Vital Statistics* (New York: Random House, 1990).
11. For reviews and various articles, see H. J. Edison, J. E. Gagnon, and W. R. Melick, "Understanding the Empirical Literature on Purchasing Power Parity," *Journal of International Money and Finance* 16 (February 1997), pp. 1–18; J. R. Edison, "Multi-country Evidence on the Behavior of Purchasing Power Parity under the Current Float," *Journal of International Money and Finance* 16 (February 1997), pp. 19–36; K. Rogoff, "The Purchasing Power Parity Puzzle," *Journal of Economic Literature* 34 (1996), pp. 647–68; D. R. Rapach and M. E. Wohar, "Testing the Monetary Model of Exchange Rate Determination: New Evidence from a Century of Data," *Journal of International Economics,* December 2002, pp. 359–85; M. P. Taylor, "Purchasing Power Parity," *Review of International Economics,* August 2003, pp. 436–56.
12. M. Obstfeld and K. Rogoff, "The Six Major Puzzles in International Economics," *National Bureau of Economic Research Working Paper Series,* paper no. 7777, July 2000.
13. Ibid.
14. See M. Devereux and C. Engel, "Monetary Policy in the Open Economy Revisited: Price Setting and Exchange Rate Flexibility," *National Bureau of Economic Research Working Paper Series,* paper no. 7665, April 2000. See also P. Krugman, "Pricing to Market When the Exchange Rate Changes," in *Real Financial Economics,* ed. S. Arndt and J. Richardson (Cambridge, MA: MIT Press, 1987).
15. For a summary of the evidence, see the survey by Taylor, "The Economics of Exchange Rates."
16. R. E. Cumby and M. Obstfeld, "A Note on Exchange Rate Expectations and Nominal Interest Differentials: A Test of the Fisher Hypothesis," *Journal of Finance,* June 1981, pp. 697–703; L. Coppock and M. Poitras, "Evaluating the Fisher Effect in Long Term Cross Country Averages," *International Review of Economics and Finance* 9 (2000), pp. 181–203.
17. Taylor, "The Economics of Exchange Rates." See also R. K. Lyons, *The Microstructure Approach to Exchange Rates* (Cambridge, MA: MIT Press, 2002).
18. See H. L. Allen and M. P. Taylor, "Charts, Noise, and Fundamentals in the Foreign Exchange Market," *Economic Journal* 100 (1990), pp. 49–59; T. Ito, "Foreign Exchange Rate Expectations: Micro Survey Data," *American Economic Review* 80 (1990), pp. 434–49; T. F. Rotheli, "Bandwagon Effects and Run Patterns in Exchange Rates," *Journal of International Financial Markets, Money and Institutions* 12, no. 2 (2002), pp. 157–66.
19. For example, see E. Fama, "Forward Rates as Predictors of Future Spot Rates," *Journal of Financial Economics,* October 1976, pp. 361–77.
20. L. Kilian and M. P. Taylor, "Why Is It So Difficult to Beat the Random Walk Forecast of Exchange Rates?" *Journal of International Economics* 20 (May 2003), pp. 85–103; R. M. Levich, "The Efficiency of Markets for Foreign Exchange," in *International Finance,* ed. G. D. Gay and R. W. Kold (Richmond, VA: Robert F. Dane, Inc., 1983).
21. J. Williamson, The *Exchange Rate System* (Washington, DC: Institute for International Economics, 1983); R. H. Clarida, L. Sarno, M. P. Taylor, and G. Valente, "The Out of Sample Success of Term Structure Models as Exchange Rate

Predictors," *Journal of International Economics* 60 (May 2003), pp. 61–84.

22. Kilian and Taylor, "Why Is It So Difficult to Beat the Random Walk Forecast of Exchange Rates?"
23. Rogoff, "The Purchasing Power Parity Puzzle."
24. C. Engel and J. D. Hamilton, "Long Swings in the Dollar: Are They in the Data and Do Markets Know It?" *American Economic Review,* September 1990, pp. 689–713.
25. J. R. Carter and J. Gagne, "The Do's and Don'ts of International Countertrade," *Sloan Management Review,* Spring 1988, pp. 31–37.
26. D. S. Levine, "Got a Spare Destroyer Lying Around?" *World Trade* 10 (June 1997), pp. 34–35; Dan West, "Countertrade," *Business Credit,* April 2001, pp. 64–67.
27. For details on how various firms manage their foreign exchange exposure, see the articles contained in the special foreign exchange issue of *Business International Money Report,* December 18, 1989, pp. 401–12.
28. Ibid.
29. S. Arterian, "How Black & Decker Defines Exposure," *Business International Money Report,* December 18, 1989, pp. 404, 405, 409.

Part 4 The Global Monetary System

The International Monetary System

learning objectives

After reading this chapter, you will be able to:

- **LO11-1** Describe the historical development of the modern global monetary system.
- **LO11-2** Explain the role played by the World Bank and the IMF in the international monetary system.
- **LO11-3** Compare and contrast the differences between a fixed and a floating exchange rate system.
- **LO11-4** Identify exchange rate regimes used in the world today and why countries adopt different exchange rate regimes.
- **LO11-5** Understand the debate surrounding the role of the IMF in the management of financial crises.
- **LO11-6** Explain the implications of the global monetary system for management practice.

China's Exchange Rate Regime

opening case

For years, there have been claims from politicians in the United States that the Chinese actively manipulate their currency, the yuan, keeping its value low against the dollar and other major currencies in order to boost Chinese exports. In November 2015, for example, presidential hopeful Donald Trump claimed that "the wanton manipulation of China's currency" is "robbing Americans of billions of dollars in capital and millions of jobs.".* But is this claim true? Would it even be possible for China to manipulate the foreign exchange markets to artificially depress the value of their currency? To answer these questions, one needs to look at the history of exchange rate determination for China and understand something about how the international monetary system actually works.

For most of its history, the Chinese yuan was pegged to the U.S. dollar at a fixed exchange rate. When China started to open up its economy to foreign trade and investment in the 1980s, the yuan was devalued by the Chinese government in order to improve the competitiveness of Chinese exports. Thus, the official yuan/USD pegged exchange rate was increased from 1.50 yuan per U.S. dollar in 1980 to 8.62 *yuan* per U.S. dollar in 1994. With China's exports growing and the country running a growing current account trade surplus, pressure began to increase for China to let its currency appreciate. In response, between 1997 and 2005, the exchange rate was fixed at 8.27 yuan per U.S. dollar, which represented a small appreciation. One could argue that during this period, China's currency was indeed undervalued and that this was the result of government policy.

By the 2000s, China's growing importance in the global economy and the rise of its export-led economy led to calls for the country to reevaluate its fixed exchange rate policy. In response, in July 2005, the country adopted a managed floating exchange rate system. Under this system, the exchange rate for the yuan was set with reference to a basket of foreign currencies that included the U.S. dollar, the euro, the Japanese yen, and the British pound. The daily exchange rate was allowed to float within a narrow band of 0.3 percent around the central parity. The daily band was extended to 0.5 percent in 2007, 1 percent in 2012, and 2 percent in 2014.

Over time, this managed float system allowed for the appreciation of the Chinese yuan. For example, against the U.S. dollar, the exchange rate changed from 8.27 yuan per dollar in mid-2005 to 6.0875 yuan per U.S. dollar on July 20, 2015, representing an appreciation of 26 percent. More generally, the effective exchange rate index of the yuan against a basket of more than 60 other currencies increased from 86.3 in July 2005 to 123.8 by early 2016, representing as appreciation of 43 percent. The yuan has appreciated by

*Matthew Slaughter, "The Myths of China's Currency Manipulation," *The Wall Street Journal*, January 8, 2016.

–continued

less than this against the U.S. dollar primarily because the U.S. dollar has also been relatively strong and appreciated against many other currencies over the same time period.

This data suggests that far from artificially trying to keep their currency undervalued, since July 2005, the Chinese have allowed the yuan to increase in value against other currencies, albeit within the constraints imposed by the managed float. In late 2015, this commitment was put to the test when a slowdown in the rate of growth of the Chinese economy led to an outflow of capital from China, which put downward pressure on the yuan. The Chinese responded by trying to maintain the value of the yuan, using their foreign exchange reserves, which are primarily held in U.S. dollars, to buy yuan on the open market and shore up its value. Reports suggest that China spent $500 billion in 2015 to shore up the value of the yuan and another $100 billion in January 2016 alone. These actions reduced China's foreign exchange reserves to $3.23 trillion, the lowest level since 2012. One reason for China to protect the value of the yuan against the dollar: a large number of Chinese companies have dollar-denominated debt. If the yuan falls against the dollar, the price of serving that debt goes up when translated into yuan. This could stress the financials of those companies (possibly pushing some into bankruptcy) and make it more difficult for China to hit the government's economic growth targets. ●

Sources: T. Hult, "The U.S. Shouldn't Fret over Cheaper Yuan," *Time*, August 14, 2015; "The Yuan and the Markets," *The Economist*, January 16, 2016; Madison Gesiotto, "The Negative Effects of China's Currency Manipulation Explained," *Washington Times*, November 13, 2015; Matthew Slaughter, "The Myths of China's Currency Manipulation," *The Wall Street Journal*, January 8, 2016; "The Curious Case of China's Currency," *The Economist*, August 11, 2015.

Introduction

International Monetary System
Institutional arrangements countries adopt to govern exchange rates.

Floating Exchange Rate
A system under which the exchange rate for converting one currency into another is continuously adjusted depending on the laws of supply and demand.

Pegged Exchange Rate
Currency value is fixed relative to a reference currency.

Dirty-Float System
A system under which a country's currency is nominally allowed to float freely against other currencies but in which the government will intervene, buying and selling currency, if it believes that the currency has deviated too far from its fair value.

Fixed Exchange Rate
A system under which the exchange rate for converting one currency into another is fixed.

In this chapter, we look at the international monetary system and its role in determining exchange rates. The **international monetary system** refers to the institutional arrangements that govern exchange rates. In Chapter 10, we assumed the foreign exchange market was the primary institution for determining exchange rates and the impersonal market forces of demand and supply determined the relative value of any two currencies (i.e., their exchange rate). Furthermore, we explained that the demand and supply of currencies is influenced by their respective countries' relative inflation rates and interest rates. When the foreign exchange market determines the relative value of a currency, we say that the country is adhering to a **floating exchange rate** regime. Four of the world's major trading currencies—the U.S. dollar, the European Union's euro, the Japanese yen, and the British pound—are all free to float against each other. Thus, their exchange rates are determined by market forces and fluctuate against each other day to day, if not minute to minute. However, the exchange rates of many currencies are not determined by the free play of market forces; other institutional arrangements are adopted.

Many of the world's developing nations peg their currencies, primarily to the dollar or the euro. A **pegged exchange rate** means the value of the currency is fixed relative to a reference currency, such as the U.S. dollar, and then the exchange rate between that currency and other currencies is determined by the reference currency exchange rate. As noted in the opening case, China operated with a pegged exchange rate system until July 2005.

Other countries, while not adopting a formal pegged rate, try to hold the value of their currency within some range against an important reference currency such as the U.S. dollar or a "basket" of currencies. This is often referred to as a **managed float system** or a **dirty-float system**. It is a float because, in theory, the value of the currency is determined by market forces, but it is a managed (or dirty) float (as opposed to a clean float) because the central bank of a country will intervene in the foreign exchange market to try to maintain the value of its currency if it depreciates too rapidly against an important reference currency. As described in the opening case, this has been the policy adopted by the Chinese since July 2005. The value of the Chinese currency, the yuan, has been linked to a basket of other currencies—including the dollar, yen, and euro—and it is allowed to vary in value against individual currencies, but only within limits.

Still other countries have operated with a **fixed exchange rate,** in which the values of a set of currencies are fixed against each other at some mutually agreed-on exchange rate. Before the

globalEDGE Blog

The international monetary system captures our attention because here we are talking about the institutional arrangements that govern exchange rates, and this is a tricky business in which countries have leverage to influence their country's currency value but do not necessarily always use it. The options for how the value, or "rate," is set for a currency are many: floating exchange rate, pegged exchange rate, dirty float, and fixed exchange rate are the ones covered in Chapter 11. We start the chapter by some history related to the "gold standard," a practice that takes us back to ancient times. Technically, no country uses the gold standard any longer but many, including the United States, hold substantial gold reserves. The international monetary system depends on a lot of variables (see the globalEDGE™ Database of International Business Statistics, which we covered in Chapter 10); today, these variables also include "behavioral" (perception) issues in addition to hard, concrete data. The globalEDGE™ Blog has been a favored "international business" vehicle to stay current on important topics, often related to monetary issues. Check out the globalEDGE™ Blog (globaledge.msu.edu/blog), see what is covered on monetary issues, and engage with people from around the world on issues that are of interest to you.

introduction of the euro in 1999, several member states of the European Union operated with fixed exchange rates within the context of the **European Monetary System (EMS).** For a quarter of a century after World War II, the world's major industrial nations participated in a fixed exchange rate system. Although this system collapsed in 1973, some still argue that the world should attempt to reestablish it.

European Monetary System (EMS)
EU system designed to create a zone of monetary stability in Europe, control inflation, and coordinate exchange rate policies of EU countries.

This chapter explains how the international monetary system works and points out its implications for international business. To understand how the system works, we must review its evolution. We begin with a discussion of the gold standard and its breakup during the 1930s. Then we discuss the 1944 Bretton Woods conference. The Bretton Woods conference also created two major international institutions that play a role in the international monetary system—the International Monetary Fund (IMF) and the World Bank. The IMF was given the task of maintaining order in the international monetary system; the World Bank's role was to promote development. Today, both these institutions continue to play major roles in the world economy and in the international monetary system. As we will see in the closing case, the IMF has stepped in to help Ukraine navigate its way through an economic crisis caused by political turmoil and a civil war in eastern Ukraine. The Bretton Woods system of fixed exchange rates collapsed in 1973. Since then, the world has operated with a mixed system in which some currencies are allowed to float freely, but many are either managed by government intervention or pegged to another currency.

Finally, we discuss the implications of all this material for international business. We will see how the exchange rate policy adopted by a government can have an important impact on the outlook for business operations in a given country. We also look at how the policies adopted by the IMF can have an impact on the economic outlook for a country and, accordingly, on the costs and benefits of doing business in that country.

The Gold Standard

LO 11-1
Describe the historical development of the modern global monetary system.

The gold standard had its origin in the use of gold coins as a medium of exchange, unit of account, and store of value—a practice that dates to ancient times. When international trade was limited in volume, payment for goods purchased from another country was typically made in gold or silver. However, as the volume of international trade expanded in the wake of the Industrial Revolution, a more convenient means of financing international trade was needed. Shipping large quantities of gold and silver around the world to finance international trade seemed impractical. The solution adopted was to arrange for payment in paper currency and for governments to agree to convert the paper currency into gold on demand at a fixed rate.

MECHANICS OF THE GOLD STANDARD

Pegging currencies to gold and guaranteeing convertibility is known as the **gold standard.** By 1880, most of the world's major trading nations, including Great Britain, Germany, Japan, and the United States, had adopted the

Gold Standard
The practice of pegging currencies to gold and guaranteeing convertibility.

gold standard. Given a common gold standard, the value of any currency in units of any other currency (the exchange rate) was easy to determine.

For example, under the gold standard, one U.S. dollar was defined as equivalent to 23.22 grains of "fine" (pure) gold. Thus, one could, in theory, demand that the U.S. government convert that one dollar into 23.22 grains of gold. Because there are 480 grains in an ounce, one ounce of gold cost $20.67 (480/23.22). The amount of a currency needed to purchase one ounce of gold was referred to as the **gold par value.** The British pound was valued at 113 grains of fine gold. In other words, one ounce of gold cost £4.25 (480/113). From the gold par values of pounds and dollars, we can calculate what the exchange rate was for converting pounds into dollars; it was £1 = $4.87 (i.e., $20.67/£4.25).

Gold Par Value

The amount of currency needed to purchase one ounce of gold.

STRENGTH OF THE GOLD STANDARD

The great strength claimed for the gold standard was that it contained a powerful mechanism for achieving balance-of-trade equilibrium by all countries.[1] A country is said to be in **balance-of-trade equilibrium** when the income its residents earn from exports is equal to the money its residents pay to other countries for imports (the current account of its balance of payments is in balance). Suppose there are only two countries in the world, Japan and the United States. Imagine Japan's trade balance is in surplus because it exports more to the United States than it imports from the United States. Japanese exporters are paid in U.S. dollars, which they exchange for Japanese yen at a Japanese bank. The Japanese bank submits the dollars to the U.S. government and demands payment of gold in return. (This is a simplification of what would occur, but it will make our point.)

Balance-of-Trade Equilibrium

Reached when the income a nation's residents earn from exports equals money paid for imports.

Under the gold standard, when Japan has a trade surplus, there is a net flow of gold from the United States to Japan. These gold flows automatically reduce the U.S. money supply and swell Japan's money supply. As we saw in Chapter 10, there is a close connection between money supply growth and price inflation. An increase in money supply will raise prices in Japan, while a decrease in the U.S. money supply will push U.S. prices downward. The rise in the price of Japanese goods will decrease demand for these goods, while the fall in the price of U.S. goods will increase demand for these goods. Thus, Japan will start to buy more from the United States, and the United States will buy less from Japan, until a balance-of-trade equilibrium is achieved.

This adjustment mechanism seems so simple and attractive that even today, nearly 80 years after the final collapse of the gold standard, some people believe the world should return to a gold standard.

THE PERIOD BETWEEN THE WARS: 1918–1939

The gold standard worked reasonably well from the 1870s until the start of World War I in 1914, when it was abandoned. During the war, several governments financed part of their massive military expenditures by printing money. This resulted in inflation, and by the war's end in 1918, price levels were higher everywhere. The United States returned to the gold standard in 1919, Great Britain in 1925, and France in 1928.

Great Britain returned to the gold standard by pegging the pound to gold at the prewar gold parity level of £4.25 per ounce, despite substantial inflation between 1914 and 1925. This priced British goods out of foreign markets, which pushed the country into a deep depression. When foreign holders of pounds lost confidence in Great Britain's commitment to maintaining its currency's value, they began converting their holdings of pounds into gold. The British government saw that it could not satisfy the demand for gold without seriously depleting its gold reserves, so it suspended convertibility in 1931.

Use SmartBook to help retain what you have learned. Access your Instructor's Connect course to check out SmartBook or go to learnsmartadvantage.com for help.

The United States followed suit and left the gold standard in 1933 but returned to it in 1934, raising the dollar price of gold from $20.67 per ounce to $35.00 per ounce. Because more dollars were needed to buy an ounce of gold than before, the implication was that the dollar was worth less. This effectively amounted to a devaluation of the dollar relative to other currencies. Thus, before the devaluation, the pound/dollar exchange rate was £1 = $4.87, but after the devaluation it was £1 = $8.24. By reducing the price of U.S. exports and increasing the price of imports, the government was trying to create employment in the United States by boosting output (the U.S. government was basically using the exchange rate as an instrument of trade policy—something it now accuses China of doing). However, a number of other countries adopted a similar tactic, and in the cycle of competitive devaluations that soon emerged, no country could win.

The net result was the shattering of any remaining confidence in the system. With countries devaluing their currencies at will, one could no longer be certain how much gold a currency could buy. Instead of holding onto another country's currency, people often tried to change it into gold immediately, lest the country devalue its currency in the intervening period. This put pressure on the gold reserves of various countries, forcing them to suspend gold convertibility. By the start of World War II in 1939, the gold standard was dead.

The Bretton Woods System

LO 11-2
Explain the role played by the World Bank and the IMF in the international monetary system.

In 1944, at the height of World War II, representatives from 44 countries met at Bretton Woods, New Hampshire, to design a new international monetary system. With the collapse of the gold standard and the Great Depression of the 1930s fresh in their minds, these statesmen were determined to build an enduring economic order that would facilitate postwar economic growth. There was consensus that fixed exchange rates were desirable. In addition, the conference participants wanted to avoid the senseless competitive devaluations of the 1930s, and they recognized that the gold standard would not ensure this. The major problem with the gold standard as previously constituted was that no multinational institution could stop countries from engaging in competitive devaluations.

The agreement reached at Bretton Woods established two multinational institutions—the International Monetary Fund (IMF) and the World Bank. The task of the IMF would be to maintain order in the international monetary system and that of the World Bank would be to promote general economic development. The Bretton Woods agreement also called for a system of fixed exchange rates that would be policed by the IMF. Under the agreement, all countries were to fix the value of their currency in terms of gold but were not required to exchange their currencies for gold. Only the dollar remained convertible into gold—at a price of $35 per ounce. Each country decided what it wanted its exchange rate to be vis-à-vis the dollar and then calculated the gold par value of the currency based on that selected dollar exchange rate. All participating countries agreed to try to maintain the value of their currencies within 1 percent of the par value by buying or selling currencies (or gold) as needed. For example, if foreign exchange dealers were selling more of a country's currency than demanded, that country's government would intervene in the foreign exchange markets, buying its currency in an attempt to increase demand and maintain its gold par value.

Another aspect of the Bretton Woods agreement was a commitment not to use devaluation as a weapon of competitive trade policy. However, if a currency became too weak to defend, a devaluation of up to 10 percent would be allowed without any formal approval by the IMF. Larger devaluations required IMF approval.

Does the World Bank Make Global Markets Less Competitive?

The World Bank was created in 1944 as an international financial institution of the United Nations that would provide loans to developing countries for capital investments in the country. Broadly, the World Bank's official goal is the reduction of poverty in the global marketplace. According to its Articles of Agreement, all of the World Bank's decisions must be guided by a commitment to the promotion of foreign investment and international trade and to the facilitation of capital investment. These goals are admirable to most people and countries, but what effect does lending to developing countries have on the rest of the world? Would it be better or worse if lending was only based on risk assessments and financial opportunities of countries in a free market system?

THE ROLE OF THE IMF

The IMF Articles of Agreement were heavily influenced by the worldwide financial collapse, competitive devaluations, trade wars, high unemployment, hyperinflation in Germany and elsewhere, and general economic disintegration that occurred between the two world wars. The aim of the Bretton Woods agreement, of which the IMF was the main custodian, was to try to avoid a repetition of that chaos through a combination of discipline and flexibility.

Discipline

A fixed exchange rate regime imposes discipline in two ways. First, the need to maintain a fixed exchange rate puts a brake on competitive devaluations and brings stability to the world trade environment. Second, a fixed exchange rate regime imposes monetary discipline on countries, thereby curtailing price inflation. For example, consider what would happen under a fixed exchange rate regime if Great Britain rapidly increased its money supply by printing pounds. As explained in Chapter 10, the increase in money supply would lead to price inflation. Given fixed exchange rates, inflation would make British goods uncompetitive in world markets, while the prices of imports would become more attractive in Great Britain. The result would be a widening trade deficit in Great Britain, with the country importing more than it exports. To correct this trade imbalance under a fixed exchange rate regime, Great Britain would be required to restrict the rate of growth in its money supply to bring price inflation back under control. Thus, fixed exchange rates are seen as a mechanism for controlling inflation and imposing economic discipline on countries.

Flexibility Although monetary discipline was a central objective of the Bretton Woods agreement, it was recognized that a rigid policy of fixed exchange rates would be too inflexible. It would probably break down just as the gold standard had. In some cases, a country's attempts to reduce its money supply growth and correct a persistent balance-of-payments deficit could force the country into recession and create high unemployment. The architects of the Bretton Woods agreement wanted to avoid high unemployment, so they built limited flexibility into the system. Two major features of the IMF Articles of Agreement fostered this flexibility: IMF lending facilities and adjustable parities.

The IMF stood ready to lend foreign currencies to members to tide them over during short periods of balance-of-payments deficits, when a rapid tightening of monetary or fiscal policy would hurt domestic employment. A pool of gold and currencies contributed by IMF members provided the resources for these lending operations. A persistent balance-of-payments deficit can lead to a depletion of a country's reserves of foreign currency, forcing it to devalue its currency. By providing deficit-laden countries with short-term foreign currency loans, IMF funds would buy time for countries to bring down their inflation rates and reduce their balance-of-payments deficits. The belief was that such loans would reduce pressures for devaluation and allow for a more orderly and less painful adjustment.

Countries were to be allowed to borrow a limited amount from the IMF without adhering to any specific agreements. However, extensive drawings from IMF funds would require a country to agree to increasingly stringent IMF supervision of its macroeconomic policies. Heavy borrowers from the IMF must agree to monetary and fiscal conditions set down by the IMF, which typically included IMF-mandated targets on domestic money supply growth, exchange rate policy, tax policy, government spending, and so on.

The system of adjustable parities allowed for the devaluation of a country's currency by more than 10 percent if the IMF agreed that a country's balance of payments was in "fundamental disequilibrium." The term *fundamental disequilibrium* was not defined in the IMF's Articles of Agreement, but it was intended to apply to countries that had suffered permanent adverse shifts in the demand for their products. Without devaluation, such a country would experience high unemployment and a persistent trade deficit until the domestic price level had fallen far enough to restore a balance-of-payments equilibrium. The belief was that devaluation could help sidestep a painful adjustment process in such circumstances.

THE ROLE OF THE WORLD BANK

The official name for the World Bank is the International Bank for Reconstruction and Development (IBRD). When the Bretton Woods participants established the World Bank, the need to reconstruct the war-torn economies of Europe was foremost in their minds. The bank's initial mission was to help finance the building of Europe's economy by providing low-interest loans. As it turned out, the World Bank was overshadowed in this role by the Marshall Plan, under which the United States lent money directly to European nations to help them rebuild. So the bank turned its attention to development and began lending money to third-world nations. In the 1950s, the bank concentrated on public-sector projects. Power stations, road building, and other transportation investments were much in favor. During the 1960s, the bank also began to lend heavily in support of agriculture, education, population control, and urban development.

Use SmartBook to help retain what you have learned. Access your Instructor's Connect course to check out SmartBook or go to learnsmartadvantage.com for help.

The bank lends money under two schemes. Under the IBRD scheme, money is raised through bond sales in the international capital market. Borrowers pay what the bank calls a market rate of interest—the bank's cost of funds plus a margin for expenses. This "market" rate is lower than commercial banks' market rate. Under the IBRD scheme, the bank offers low-interest loans to risky customers whose credit rating is often poor, such as the governments of underdeveloped nations.

A second scheme is overseen by the International Development Association (IDA), an arm of the bank created in 1960. Resources to fund IDA loans are raised through subscriptions from wealthy members such as the United States, Japan, and Germany. IDA loans go only to the poorest countries. Borrowers have up to 50 years to repay at an interest rate of less than 1 percent a year. The world's poorest nations receive grants and interest-free loans.

The Collapse of the Fixed Exchange Rate System

LO 11-1

Describe the historical development of the modern global monetary system.

The system of fixed exchange rates established at Bretton Woods worked well until the late 1960s, when it began to show signs of strain. The system finally collapsed in 1973, and since then, we have had a managed-float system. To understand why the system collapsed, one must appreciate the special role of the U.S. dollar in the system. As the only currency that could be converted into gold and as the currency that served as the reference point for all others, the dollar occupied a central place in the system. Any pressure on the dollar to devalue could wreak havoc with the system, and that is what occurred.

Most economists trace the breakup of the fixed exchange rate system to the U.S. macroeconomic policy package of 1965–1968.[2] To finance both the Vietnam conflict and his welfare programs, President Lyndon Johnson backed an increase in U.S. government spending that was not financed by an increase in taxes. Instead, it was financed by an increase in the money supply, which led to a rise in price inflation from less than 4 percent in 1966 to close to 9 percent by 1968. At the same time, the rise in government spending had stimulated the economy. With more money in their pockets, people spent more—particularly on imports—and the U.S. trade balance began to deteriorate.

The increase in inflation and the worsening of the U.S. foreign trade position gave rise to speculation in the foreign exchange market that the dollar would be devalued. Things came to a head in spring 1971, when U.S. trade figures showed that for the first time since 1945, the United States was importing more than it was exporting. This set off massive purchases of German deutsche marks in the foreign exchange market by speculators who guessed that the mark would be revalued against the dollar. On a single day, May 4, 1971, the Bundesbank (Germany's central bank) had to buy $1 billion to hold the dollar/deutsche mark exchange rate at its fixed exchange rate, given the great demand for deutsche marks. On the morning of May 5, the Bundesbank purchased another $1 billion during the first hour of foreign exchange trading! At that point, the Bundesbank faced the inevitable and allowed its currency to float.

In the weeks following the decision to float the deutsche mark, the foreign exchange market became increasingly convinced that the dollar would have to be devalued. However, devaluation of the dollar was no easy matter. Under the Bretton Woods provisions, any other country could change its exchange rates against all currencies simply by fixing its dollar rate at a new level. But as the key currency in the system, the dollar could be devalued only if all countries agreed to simultaneously revalue against the dollar. Many countries did not want this, because it would make their products more expensive relative to U.S. products.

To force the issue, President Richard Nixon announced in August 1971 that the dollar was no longer convertible into gold. He also announced that a new 10 percent tax on imports would remain in effect until U.S. trading partners agreed to revalue their currencies against the dollar. This brought the trading partners to the bargaining table, and in December 1971, an agreement was reached to devalue the dollar by about 8 percent against foreign currencies. The import tax was then removed. The problem was not solved, however. The U.S. balance-of-payments position continued to deteriorate throughout 1973, while the nation's money supply continued to expand at an

Should We Go Back to the Gold Standard?

Nixon's decision to not link the dollar to gold is the "primary cause of the troubles we have [today]," says Porter Stansberry, founder of Stansberry & Associates Investment Research. "The purpose of gold is to make sure credit growth is restrained and limited to real growth and productivity." Since 1971, the amount of debt in the United States has skyrocketed, while the value of the dollar has tumbled. Moving away from gold "allows people who have borrowed money to pay it back in currency that's worth less," Stansberry says. Unfortunately, "it's hugely disruptive to our economy." His idea is that the United States and other countries should go back to a gold (or silver) standard. On the other hand, "Why should we limit the amount of currency floating in circulation by a rock we have to dig out of the ground and store?" asks James Altucher of Formula Capital. "Gold is ultimately a limited resource." Why should we arbitrarily pick this yellow rock and limit the world's economy by it? Innovation happens because we've been able to extend credit . . . beyond what gold would allow us. And it's through debt and lending that companies grow." Who do you agree with: Stansberry, who argues for the gold standard, or Altucher, who argues for today's currency system?

Source: Aaron Task, "40 Years Later: Should America Go Back to the Gold Standard?" *Yahoo! Finance*, August 19, 2011. http://finance.yahoo.com.

inflationary rate. Speculation continued to grow that the dollar was still overvalued and that a second devaluation would be necessary. In anticipation, foreign exchange dealers began converting dollars to deutsche marks and other currencies. After a massive wave of speculation in February 1973, which culminated with European central banks spending $3.6 billion on March 1 to try to prevent their currencies from appreciating against the dollar, the foreign exchange market was closed. When the foreign exchange market reopened March 19, the currencies of Japan and most European countries were floating against the dollar, although many developing countries continued to peg their currency to the dollar, and many do to this day. At that time, the switch to a floating system was viewed as a temporary response to unmanageable speculation in the foreign exchange market. But it is now more than 40 years since the Bretton Woods system of fixed exchange rates collapsed, and the temporary solution looks permanent.

The Bretton Woods system had an Achilles' heel: The system could not work if its key currency, the U.S. dollar, was under speculative attack. The Bretton Woods system could work only as long as the U.S. inflation rate remained low and the United States did not run a balance-of-payments deficit. Once these things occurred, the system soon became strained to the breaking point.

LO 11-1
Describe the historical development of the modern global monetary system.

The Floating Exchange Rate Regime

The floating exchange rate regime that followed the collapse of the fixed exchange rate system was formalized in January 1976, when IMF members met in Jamaica and agreed to the rules for the international monetary system that are in place today.

THE JAMAICA AGREEMENT The Jamaica meeting revised the IMF's Articles of Agreement to reflect the new reality of floating exchange rates. The main elements of the Jamaica agreement include the following:

- Floating rates were declared acceptable. IMF members were permitted to enter the foreign exchange market to even out "unwarranted" speculative fluctuations.
- Gold was abandoned as a reserve asset. The IMF returned its gold reserves to members at the current market price, placing the proceeds in a trust fund to help poor nations. IMF members were permitted to sell their own gold reserves at the market price.
- Total annual IMF quotas—the amount member countries contribute to the IMF—were increased to $41 billion. (Since then, they have been increased to $767 billion, while the membership of the IMF has been expanded to include 188 countries. Non-oil-exporting, less developed countries were given greater access to IMF funds.)

EXCHANGE RATES SINCE 1973 Since March 1973, exchange rates have become much more volatile and less predictable than they were between 1945 and 1973.[3] This volatility has been partly due to a number of unexpected shocks to the world monetary system, including:

- The oil crisis in 1971, when the Organization of the Petroleum Exporting Countries (OPEC) quadrupled the price of oil. The harmful effect of this on the U.S. inflation rate and trade position resulted in a further decline in the value of the dollar.
- The loss of confidence in the dollar that followed a sharp rise in the U.S. inflation rate in 1977–1978.
- The oil crisis of 1979, when OPEC once again increased the price of oil dramatically: this time, it was doubled.
- The unexpected rise in the dollar between 1980 and 1985, despite a deteriorating balance-of-payments picture.
- The rapid fall of the U.S. dollar against the Japanese yen and German deutsche mark between 1985 and 1987, and against the yen between 1993 and 1995.
- The partial collapse of the European Monetary System in 1992.
- The 1997 Asian currency crisis, when the Asian currencies of several countries—including South Korea, Indonesia, Malaysia, and Thailand—lost between 50 and 80 percent of their value against the U.S. dollar in a few months.
- The global financial crisis of 2008–2010 and the sovereign debt crisis in the European Union during 2010–2011.

Figure 11.1 summarizes how the value of the U.S. dollar has fluctuated against an index of trading currencies between January 1973 and February 2016. (The index, which was set equal to 100 in March 1973, is a weighted average of the foreign exchange values of the U.S. dollar against a basket of other currencies.) An interesting phenomenon in Figure 11.1 is the rapid rise in the value of the dollar between 1980 and 1985 and its subsequent fall between 1985 and 1988. A similar, though less pronounced, rise and fall in the value of the dollar occurred between 1995 and 2012. You will also notice a sharp uptick in the value of the dollar between mid-2014 and early 2016. We briefly discuss the rise and fall of the dollar during these periods, because this tells us something about how the international monetary system has operated in recent years.[4]

The rise in the value of the dollar between 1980 and 1985 occurred when the United States was running a large and growing trade deficit, importing substantially more than it exported. Conventional wisdom would suggest that the increased supply of dollars in the foreign exchange market as a result of the trade deficit should lead to a reduction in the value of the dollar, but as shown in Figure 11.1, it increased in value. Why?

A number of favorable factors overcame the unfavorable effect of a trade deficit. Strong economic growth in the United States attracted heavy inflows of capital from foreign investors seeking high returns on capital assets. High real interest rates attracted foreign investors seeking high returns on financial assets. At the same time, political turmoil in other parts of the world, along with relatively slow economic growth in the developed countries of Europe, helped create the view that the United States was a good place to invest. These inflows of capital increased the demand for dollars in the foreign exchange market, which pushed the value of the dollar upward against other currencies.

The fall in the value of the dollar between 1985 and 1988 was caused by a combination of government intervention and market forces. The rise in the dollar, which priced U.S. goods out of foreign markets and made imports relatively cheap, had contributed to a dismal trade picture. In 1985, the United States posted a then-record-high trade deficit of more than $160 billion. This led to growth in demands for protectionism in the United States. In September 1985, the finance ministers and central bank governors of the so-called Group of Five major industrial countries (Great Britain, France, Japan, Germany, and the United States) met at the Plaza Hotel in New York City and reached what was later referred to as the Plaza Accord. They announced that it would be desirable for most major currencies to appreciate vis-à-vis the U.S. dollar and pledged to intervene in the foreign exchange markets, selling dollars, to encourage this objective. The dollar had already begun to weaken during summer 1985, and this announcement further accelerated the decline.

11.1 FIGURE

Major Currencies Dollar Index, 1973–2016.

Source: Data from www.federalreserve.gov.

The dollar continued to decline until 1987. The governments of the Group of Five began to worry that the dollar might decline too far, so the finance ministers of the Group of Five met in Paris in February 1987 and reached a new agreement known as the Louvre Accord. They agreed that exchange rates had been realigned sufficiently and pledged to support the stability of exchange rates around their current levels by intervening in the foreign exchange markets when necessary to buy and sell currency. Although the dollar continued to decline for a few months after the Louvre Accord, the rate of decline slowed, and by early 1988, the decline had ended.

Except for a brief speculative flurry around the time of the Persian Gulf War in 1991, the dollar was relatively stable for the first half of the 1990s. However, in the late 1990s, the dollar again began to appreciate against most major currencies, including the euro after its introduction, even though the United States was still running a significant balance-of-payments deficit. Once again, the driving force for the appreciation in the value of the dollar was that foreigners continued to invest in U.S. financial assets, primarily stocks and bonds, and the inflow of money drove up the value of the dollar on foreign exchange markets. The inward investment was due to a belief that U.S. financial assets offered a favorable rate of return.

By 2002, however, foreigners had started to lose their appetite for U.S. stocks and bonds, and the inflow of money into the United States slowed. Instead of reinvesting dollars earned from exports to the United States in U.S. financial assets, they exchanged those dollars for other currencies, particularly euros, to invest them in non-dollar-denominated assets. One reason for this was the continued growth in the U.S. trade deficit, which hit a record $791 billion in 2005 (by 2011, it had fallen to $540 billion). Although the U.S. trade deficits had been setting records for decades, this deficit was the largest ever when measured as a percentage of the country's GDP (6.3 percent of GDP in 2005).

The record deficit meant that even more dollars were flowing out of the United States into foreign hands, and those foreigners were less inclined to reinvest those dollars in the United States at a rate required to keep the dollar stable. This growing reluctance of foreigners to invest in the United States was in turn due to several factors. First, there was a slowdown in U.S. economic activity during 2001–2002. Second, the U.S. government's budget deficit expanded rapidly after 2001. This led to fears that ultimately the budget deficit would be financed by an expansionary monetary policy that could lead to higher price inflation. Third, from 2003 onward, U.S. government officials began to "talk down" the value of the dollar, in part because the administration believed that a cheaper dollar would increase exports and reduce imports, thereby improving the U.S. balance of trade position.[5] Foreigners saw this as a signal that the U.S. government would not intervene in the foreign exchange markets to prop up the value of the dollar, which increased their reluctance to reinvest dollars earned from export sales in U.S. financial assets. As a result of these factors, demand for dollars weakened, and the value of the dollar slid on the foreign exchange markets—hitting an index value of 80.5 in June 2011, the lowest value since the index began in 1973. Some believed that the dollar would have fallen even further had not oil-producing states recycled the dollars they were earning from sales of crude oil back into the U.S. economy. At the time, these states were benefiting from high oil prices (oil is priced in US dollars), and they chose to invest the dollars they earned back into the United States, rather than selling them for another currency (see the Country Focus for details).

Interestingly, from mid-2008 through early 2009, the dollar staged a moderate rally against major currencies, despite the fact that the American economy was suffering from a serious financial crisis. The reason seems to be that despite America's problems, things were even worse in many other countries, and foreign investors saw the dollar as a safe haven and put their money in low-risk U.S. assets, particularly low-yielding U.S. government bonds. This rally faltered in mid-2009 as investors became worried about the level of U.S. indebtedness. However, between 2014 and early 2016, the dollar yet again increased significantly in value, primarily because of the strength of the U.S. economy, which had emerged from the great financial crisis of 2008–2009 in better shape than any other major developed nation, with higher economic growth rates and lower levels of unemployment.

Did You Know?
Did you know that China has recently been trying to stop its currency from falling in value on foreign exchange markets?

Visit your Connect SmartBook® to view a short video explanation from the authors.

This review tells us that in recent history, both market forces and government intervention have determined the value of the dollar. Under a floating exchange rate regime, market forces

country FOCUS

The U.S. Dollar, Oil Prices, and Recycling Petrodollars

Between 2004 and 2008, global oil prices surged. They peaked at $147 a barrel in July 2008, up from about $20 in 2001, before falling sharply back to a $34 to $48 range by early 2009. From 2010 onward, they increased again, rising to over $100 a barrel in early 2014, before falling back to around $30 a barrel by early 2016. The rise was due to a combination of greater-than-expected demand for oil, particularly from rapidly developing giants such as China and India; tight supplies; and perceived geopolitical risks in the Middle East, the world's largest oil-producing region. The fall since mid-2014 was due to the combination of a weak global economy and rapidly increasing production from shale oil fields in the United States.

The surge in oil prices between 2004 and 2009 was a windfall for oil-producing countries. Collectively, they earned around $700 billion in oil revenues in 2005 and well over $1 trillion in 2007 and 2008—some 64 percent of which went to members of OPEC. Saudi Arabia, the world's largest oil producer, reaped a major share. Because oil is priced in U.S. dollars, the rise in oil prices translated into a substantial increase in the dollar holdings of oil producers (the dollars earned from the sale of oil are often referred to as *petrodollars*). In essence, rising oil prices represent a net transfer of dollars from oil consumers in countries such as the United States to oil producers in Russia, Saudi Arabia, and Venezuela. What did they do with these dollars?

One option for producing countries was to spend their petrodollars on public-sector infrastructure, such as health services, education, roads, and telecommunications systems. Among other things, this could boost economic growth in those countries and pull in foreign imports, which would help counterbalance the trade surpluses enjoyed by oil producers and support global economic growth. Spending did indeed pick up in many oil-producing countries. However, according to the IMF, OPEC members spent only about 40 percent of their windfall profits from higher oil prices in 2002–2007 (an exception was Venezuela, whose leader, Hugo Chávez, was on a spending spree until his death in early 2013). The last time oil prices increased sharply in 1979, oil producers significantly ramped up spending on infrastructure, only to find themselves saddled with excessive debt when oil prices collapsed a few years later. This time they were more cautious—an approach that seems wise given the rapid fall in oil prices during late 2008 and again in late 2014.

Another option was for oil producers to invest a good chunk of the dollars they earned from oil sales in dollar-denominated assets, such as U.S. bonds, stocks, and real estate. This did happen. OPEC members in particular funneled dollars back into U.S. assets, mostly low-risk government bonds. The implication is that by recycling their petrodollars, oil producers helped finance the large and growing current account deficit of the United States, enabling it to pay its large oil import bill.

A third possibility for oil producers was to invest in non-dollar-denominated assets, including European and Japanese bonds and stocks. This, too, happened. Also, some OPEC investors had purchased not just small equity positions but entire companies. In 2005, for example, Dubai International Capital purchased the Tussauds Group, a British theme-park firm, and DP World of Dubai purchased P&O, Britain's biggest port and ferries group. Despite examples such as these, the bulk of petrodollars appear to have been recycled into dollar-denominated assets. In part, this was because U.S. interest rates increased throughout 2004–2007 and in part because the United States was viewed as a safe haven in economically troubled times. However, if the flow of petrodollars should dry up, which could occur if oil prices continue to stay around their 2015 lows, the value of the dollar could be negatively impacted going forward.

Sources: "Recycling the Petrodollars; Oil Producers' Surpluses," *The Economist*, November 12, 2005, pp. 101–02; S. Johnson, "Dollar's Rise Aided by OPEC Holdings," *Financial Times*, December 5, 2005, p. 17; "The Petrodollar Puzzle," *The Economist*, June 9, 2007, p. 86.

have produced a volatile dollar exchange rate. Governments have sometimes responded by intervening in the market—buying and selling dollars—in an attempt to limit the market's volatility and to correct what they see as overvaluation (in 1985) or potential undervaluation (in 1987) of the dollar. In addition to direct intervention, statements from government officials have frequently influenced the value of the dollar. The dollar may not have declined by as much as it did in 2004, for example, had not U.S. government officials publicly ruled out any action to stop the decline. Paradoxically, a signal not to intervene can affect the market. The frequency of government intervention in the foreign exchange market explains why the current system is sometimes thought of as a **managed-float system** or a dirty-float system.

Managed-Float System
System under which some currencies are allowed to float freely, but the majority are either managed by government intervention or pegged to another currency.

Use SmartBook to help retain what you have learned. Access your Instructor's Connect course to check out SmartBook or go to learnsmartadvantage.com for help.

Fixed Versus Floating Exchange Rates

Compare and contrast the differences between a fixed and a floating exchange rate system.

The breakdown of the Bretton Woods system has not stopped the debate about the relative merits of fixed versus floating exchange rate regimes. Disappointment with the system of floating rates in recent years has led to renewed debate about the merits of fixed exchange rates. This section reviews the arguments for fixed and floating exchange rate regimes.[6] We discuss the case for floating rates before studying why many critics are disappointed with the experience under floating exchange rates and yearn for a system of fixed rates.

THE CASE FOR FLOATING EXCHANGE RATES

The case in support of floating exchange rates has three main elements: monetary policy autonomy, automatic trade balance adjustments, and economic recovery following a severe economic crisis.

Monetary Policy Autonomy

It is argued that under a fixed system, a country's ability to expand or contract its money supply as it sees fit is limited by the need to maintain exchange rate parity. Monetary expansion can lead to inflation, which puts downward pressure on a fixed exchange rate (as predicted by the PPP theory; see Chapter 10). Similarly, monetary contraction requires high interest rates (to reduce the demand for money). Higher interest rates lead to an inflow of money from abroad, which puts upward pressure on a fixed exchange rate. Thus, to maintain exchange rate parity under a fixed system, countries were limited in their ability to use monetary policy to expand or contract their economies.

Advocates of a floating exchange rate regime argue that removal of the obligation to maintain exchange rate parity would restore monetary control to a government. If a government faced with unemployment wanted to increase its money supply to stimulate domestic demand and reduce unemployment, it could do so unencumbered by the need to maintain its exchange rate. While monetary expansion might lead to inflation, this would lead to a depreciation in the country's currency. If PPP theory is correct, the resulting currency depreciation on the foreign exchange markets should offset the effects of inflation. Although under a floating exchange rate regime, domestic inflation would have an impact on the exchange rate, it should have no impact on businesses' international cost competitiveness due to exchange rate depreciation. The rise in domestic costs should be exactly offset by the fall in the value of the country's currency on the foreign exchange markets. Similarly, a government could use monetary policy to contract the economy without worrying about the need to maintain parity.

Trade Balance Adjustments

Under the Bretton Woods system, if a country developed a permanent deficit in its balance of trade (importing more than it exported) that could not be corrected by domestic policy, this would require the IMF to agree to currency devaluation. Critics of this system argue that the adjustment mechanism works much more smoothly under a floating exchange rate regime. They argue that if a country is running a trade deficit, the imbalance between the supply and demand of that country's currency in the foreign exchange markets (supply exceeding demand) will lead to depreciation in its exchange rate. In turn, by making its exports cheaper and its imports more expensive, exchange rate depreciation should correct the trade deficit.

Crisis Recovery

Advocates of floating exchange rates also argue that exchange rate adjustments can help a country to deal with economic crises. When a country is hit by a severe economic crisis, its currency typically declines on foreign exchange markets. The reason for this is that investors respond to the crisis by taking their money out of the country, selling the local currency, and driving down its value. At some point, however, the currency becomes so cheap that it starts to stimulate exports. This is what occurred in Iceland after the krona lost 50 percent of its value against the U.S. dollar and euro following a banking crisis in 2008. By 2009, exports of fish and aluminum from Iceland were booming, which helped pull the Icelandic economy out of a recession. A similar process occurred in South Korean after the 1997 Asian banking crisis. The value of the South Korean won plunged to 1,700 per dollar from around 800. In turn, the cheap won helped South Korea increase its exports and resulted in an export-led economic recovery. On the other hand, in both countries, the declining value of the currency did raise import prices and led to an increase in inflation, so there is a price that has to be paid for an export-led recovery due to falling currency values.

A contrast can be drawn with the recent situation in Greece, where the economy imploded following the 2008–2009 global financial crisis and has struggled to recover. Part of the problem in Greece is that it gave up its own currency to adopt the euro in 2001, and the euro has remained quite strong; thus, Greece cannot rely on a falling local currency to boost exports and stimulate economic recovery.

THE CASE FOR FIXED EXCHANGE RATES

The case for fixed exchange rates rests on arguments about monetary discipline, speculation, uncertainty, and the lack of connection between the trade balance and exchange rates.

Monetary Discipline

We have already discussed the nature of monetary discipline inherent in a fixed exchange rate system when we discussed the Bretton Woods system. The need to maintain fixed exchange rate parity ensures that governments do not expand their money supplies at inflationary rates. While advocates of floating rates argue that each country should be allowed to choose its own inflation rate (the monetary autonomy argument), advocates of fixed rates argue that governments all too often give in to political pressures and expand the monetary supply far too rapidly, causing unacceptably high price inflation. A fixed exchange rate regime would ensure that this does not occur.

Speculation

Critics of a floating exchange rate regime also argue that speculation can cause fluctuations in exchange rates. They point to the dollar's rapid rise and fall during the 1980s, which they claim had nothing to do with comparative inflation rates and the U.S. trade deficit but everything to do with speculation. They argue that when foreign exchange dealers see a currency depreciating, they tend to sell the currency in the expectation of future depreciation, regardless of the currency's longer-term prospects. As more traders jump on the bandwagon, the expectations of depreciation are realized. Such destabilizing speculation tends to accentuate the fluctuations around the exchange rate's long-run value. It can damage a country's economy by distorting export and import prices. Thus, advocates of a fixed exchange rate regime argue that such a system will limit the destabilizing effects of speculation.

Uncertainty

Speculation also adds to the uncertainty surrounding future currency movements that characterizes floating exchange rate regimes. The unpredictability of exchange rate movements in the post–Bretton Woods era has made business planning difficult, and it adds risk to exporting, importing, and foreign investment activities. Given a volatile exchange rate, international businesses do not know how to react to the changes—and often they do not react. Why change plans for exporting, importing, or foreign investment after a 6 percent fall in the dollar this month, when the dollar may rise 6 percent next month? This uncertainty, according to the critics, dampens the growth of international trade and investment. They argue that a fixed exchange rate, by eliminating such uncertainty, promotes the growth of international trade and investment. Advocates of a floating system reply that the forward exchange market ensures against the risks associated with exchange rate fluctuations (see Chapter 10), so the adverse impact of uncertainty on the growth of international trade and investment has been overstated.

Trade Balance Adjustments and Economic Recovery

Those in favor of floating exchange rates argue that floating rates help adjust trade imbalances and can assist with economic recovery after a crisis. Critics question the closeness of the link between the exchange rate, the trade balance and economic growth. They claim trade deficits are determined by the balance between savings and investment in a country, not by the external value of its currency.[7] They argue that depreciation in a currency will lead to inflation (due to the resulting increase in import prices). This inflation, they state, will wipe out any apparent gains in cost competitiveness that arise from currency depreciation. In other words, a depreciating exchange rate will not boost exports and reduce imports, as advocates of floating rates claim; it will simply boost price inflation. In support of this argument, those who favor fixed rates point out that the 40 percent drop in the value of the dollar between 1985 and 1988 did not correct the U.S. trade deficit. In reply, advocates of a floating exchange rate regime argue that between 1985 and 1992, the U.S. trade deficit fell from more than $160 billion to about $70 billion, and they attribute this in part to the decline in the value of the dollar. Moreover, the experience of countries like South Korea and Iceland seems to suggest that floating rates can help a country recover from a severe economic crisis.

Floating or Fixed Exchange Rates?

In Chapter 11, we have included a lot of material on the positives and negatives of floating and fixed exchange rates. The case for a floating exchange rate includes monetary policy autonomy, trade balance adjustments, and crisis recovery issues. The case for a fixed exchange rate includes monetary discipline, speculation issues, uncertainty, trade balance adjustments and economic recovery. We conclude these topics with a short section on "who is right" without actually addressing this very complex issue. But, what do you think? Who is right? Should we have a floating or fixed exchange rate system?

Use SmartBook to help retain what you have learned. Access your Instructor's Connect course to check out SmartBook or go to learnsmartadvantage.com for help.

WHO IS RIGHT? Which side is right in the vigorous debate between those who favor a fixed exchange rate and those who favor a floating exchange rate? Economists cannot agree. Business, as a major player on the international trade and investment scene, has a large stake in the resolution of the debate. Would international business be better off under a fixed regime, or are flexible rates better? The evidence is not clear.

However, a fixed exchange rate regime modeled along the lines of the Bretton Woods system probably will not work. Speculation ultimately broke the system, a phenomenon that advocates of fixed rate regimes claim is associated with floating exchange rates! Nevertheless, a different kind of fixed exchange rate system might be more enduring and might foster the stability that would facilitate more rapid growth in international trade and investment. In the next section, we look at potential models for such a system and the problems with such systems.

LO 11-4

Identify exchange rate regimes used in the world today and why countries adopt different exchange rate regimes.

Exchange Rate Regimes in Practice

Governments around the world pursue a number of different exchange rate policies. These range from a pure "free float" in which the exchange rate is determined by market forces to a pegged system that has some aspects of the pre-1973 Bretton Woods system of fixed exchange rates. Some 21 percent of the IMF's members allow their currency to float freely. Another 23 percent intervene in only a limited way (the so-called managed float as practiced by China, among other nations—see the opening case). A further 5 percent of IMF members now have no separate legal tender of their own (this figure excludes the European Union countries that have adopted the euro). These are typically smaller states, mostly in Africa or the Caribbean, that have no domestic currency and have adopted a foreign currency as legal tender within their borders, typically the U.S. dollar or the euro. The remaining countries use more inflexible systems, including a fixed peg arrangement (43 percent) under which they peg their currencies to other currencies, such as the U.S. dollar or the euro, or to a basket of currencies. Other countries have adopted a system under which their exchange rate is allowed to fluctuate against other currencies within a target zone (an adjustable peg system). In this section, we look more closely at the mechanics and implications of exchange rate regimes that rely on a currency peg or target zone.

PEGGED EXCHANGE RATES Under a pegged exchange rate regime, a country will peg the value of its currency to that of a major currency so that, for example, as the U.S. dollar rises in value, its own currency rises too. Pegged exchange rates are popular among many of the world's smaller nations. As with a full fixed exchange rate regime, the great virtue claimed for a pegged exchange rate is that it imposes monetary discipline on a country and leads to low inflation. For example, if Belize pegs the value of the Belizean dollar to that of the U.S. dollar so that US$1 = B$1.97, then the Belizean government must make sure the inflation rate in Belize is similar to that in the United States. If the Belizean inflation rate is greater than the U.S. inflation rate, this will lead to pressure to devalue the Belizean dollar (i.e., to alter the peg). To maintain the peg, the Belizean government would be required to rein in inflation. Of course, for a pegged exchange rate to impose monetary discipline on a country, the country whose currency is chosen for the peg must also pursue sound monetary policy.

Evidence shows that adopting a pegged exchange rate regime moderates inflationary pressures in a country. An IMF study concluded that countries with pegged exchange rates had an average annual inflation rate of 8 percent, compared with 14 percent for intermediate regimes and 16 percent for floating regimes.[8] However, many countries operate with only a nominal peg and in practice are willing to devalue their currency rather than pursue a tight monetary policy. It can be very difficult for a smaller country to maintain a peg against another currency if capital is flowing out of the country and foreign exchange traders are speculating against the currency. Something like this occurred in 1997, when a combination of adverse capital flows and currency speculation forced several Asian countries, including Thailand and Malaysia, to abandon pegs against the U.S. dollar and let their currencies float freely. Malaysia and Thailand would not have been in this position had they dealt with a number of problems that began to arise in their economies during the 1990s, including excessive private-sector debt and expanding current account trade deficits.

CURRENCY BOARDS Hong Kong's experience during the 1997 Asian currency crisis added a new dimension to the debate over how to manage a pegged exchange rate. During late 1997, when other Asian currencies were collapsing, Hong Kong maintained the value of its currency against the U.S. dollar at about $1 = HK$7.80 despite several concerted speculative attacks. Hong Kong's currency board has been given credit for this success. A country that introduces a **currency board** commits itself to converting its domestic currency on demand into another currency at a fixed exchange rate. To make this commitment credible, the currency board holds reserves of foreign currency equal at the fixed exchange rate to at least 100 percent of the domestic currency issued. The system used in Hong Kong means its currency must be fully backed by the U.S. dollar at the specified exchange rate. This is still not a true fixed exchange rate regime, because the U.S. dollar, and by extension the Hong Kong dollar, floats against other currencies, but it has some features of a fixed exchange rate regime.

Currency Board
Means of controlling a country's currency.

Under this arrangement, the currency board can issue additional domestic notes and coins only when there are foreign exchange reserves to back it. This limits the ability of the government to print money and, thereby, create inflationary pressures. Under a strict currency board system, interest rates adjust automatically. If investors want to switch out of domestic currency into, for example, U.S. dollars, the supply of domestic currency will shrink. This will cause interest rates to rise until it eventually becomes attractive for investors to hold the local currency again. In the case of Hong Kong, the interest rate on three-month deposits climbed as high as 20 percent in late 1997, as investors switched out of Hong Kong dollars and into U.S. dollars. The dollar peg held, however, and interest rates declined again.

test PREP
Use SmartBook to help retain what you have learned. Access your Instructor's Connect course to check out SmartBook or go to learnsmartadvantage.com for help.

Since its establishment in 1983, the Hong Kong currency board has weathered several storms, including the latest. This success persuaded several other countries in the developing world to consider a similar system. Argentina introduced a currency board in 1991 (but abandoned it in 2002), and Bulgaria, Estonia, and Lithuania have all gone down this road in recent years. Despite interest in the arrangement, however, critics are quick to point out that currency boards have their drawbacks.[9] If local inflation rates remain higher than the inflation rate in the country to which the currency is pegged, the currencies of countries with currency boards can become noncompetitive and overvalued (this is what happened in the case of Argentina, which had a currency board). Also, under a currency board system, government lacks the ability to set interest rates. Interest rates in Hong Kong, for example, are effectively set by the U.S. Federal Reserve. In addition, economic collapse in Argentina in 2001 and the subsequent decision to abandon its currency board dampened much of the enthusiasm for this mechanism of managing exchange rates.

Crisis Management by the IMF

LO 11-5
Understand the debate surrounding the role of the IMF in the management of financial crises.

Many observers initially believed that the collapse of the Bretton Woods system in 1973 would diminish the role of the IMF within the international monetary system. The IMF's original function was to provide a pool of money from which members could borrow, short term, to adjust their balance-of-payments position and maintain their exchange rate. Some believed the demand for short-term loans would be considerably diminished under a floating exchange rate regime. A trade deficit would presumably lead to a decline in a country's exchange rate, which would help reduce imports and boost exports. No temporary IMF adjustment loan would be needed. Consistent with this, after 1973, most industrialized countries tended to let the foreign exchange market determine exchange rates in response to demand and supply. Since the early 1970s, the rapid development of global capital markets has generally allowed developed countries such as Great Britain and the United States to finance their deficits by borrowing private money, as opposed to drawing on IMF funds.

Despite these developments, the activities of the IMF have expanded over the past 30 years. By 2016, the IMF had 188 members, 33 of which had some kind of IMF program in place. In 1997, the institution implemented its largest rescue packages until that date, committing more than $110 billion in short-term loans to three troubled Asian countries—South Korea, Indonesia, and Thailand. This was followed by additional IMF rescue packages in Turkey, Russia, Argentina, and Brazil. IMF loans increased again in late 2008 as the global financial crisis took hold. Between 2008 and 2010, the IMF made more than $100 billion in loans to troubled economies such as Latvia, Greece, and Ireland. In April 2009, in response to the growing financial crisis, major IMF members agreed to triple the institution's resources from $250 billion to $750 billion, thereby giving the IMF the financial leverage to act aggressively in times of global financial crisis.

The IMF's activities have expanded because periodic financial crises have continued to hit many economies in the post–Bretton Woods era. The IMF has repeatedly lent money to nations experiencing financial crises, requesting in return that the governments enact certain macroeconomic policies. Critics of the IMF claim these policies have not always been as beneficial as the IMF might have hoped and, in some cases, may have made things worse. Following the IMF loans to several Asian economies, these criticisms reached new levels, and a vigorous debate was waged as to the appropriate role of the IMF. In this section, we discuss some of the main challenges the IMF has had to deal with over the past three decades and review the ongoing debate over the role of the IMF.

Currency Crisis
Occurs when a speculative attack on the exchange value of a currency results in a sharp depreciation in the value of the currency or forces authorities to expend large volumes of international currency reserves and sharply increase interest rates to defend the prevailing exchange rate.

Banking Crisis
A loss of confidence in the banking system that leads to a run on banks, as individuals and companies withdraw their deposits.

Foreign Debt Crisis
Situation in which a country cannot service its foreign debt obligations, whether private-sector or government debt.

FINANCIAL CRISES IN THE POST–BRETTON WOODS ERA A number of broad types of financial crises have occurred over the past 30 years, many of which have required IMF involvement. A **currency crisis** occurs when a speculative attack on the exchange value of a currency results in a sharp depreciation in the value of the currency or forces authorities to expend large volumes of international currency reserves and sharply increase interest rates to defend the prevailing exchange rate. This happened in Brazil in 2002, and the IMF stepped in to help stabilize the value of the Brazilian currency on foreign exchange markets by lending it foreign currency. A **banking crisis** refers to a loss of confidence in the banking system that leads to a run on banks, as individuals and companies withdraw their deposits. This is what happened in Iceland in 2008. The experience of Iceland with the IMF is discussed in depth in the next Country Focus feature. A **foreign debt crisis** is a situation in which a country cannot service its foreign debt obligations, whether private-sector or government debt. This happened to Greece, Ireland, and Portugal in 2010.

country FOCUS

The IMF and Iceland's Economic Recovery

When the global financial crisis hit in 2008, tiny Iceland suffered more than most. The country's three biggest banks had been expanding at a breakneck pace since 2000, when the government privatized the banking sector. With a population of around 320,000, Iceland was too small for the banking sector's ambitions, so the banks started to expand into other Scandinavian countries and the United Kingdom. They entered local mortgage markets, purchased foreign financial institutions, and opened foreign branches, attracting depositors by offering high interest rates. The expansion was financed by debt, much of it structured as short-term loans that had to be regularly refinanced. By early 2008, the three banks held debts that amounted to almost six times the value of the entire economy of Iceland! So long as they could periodically refinance this debt, it was not a problem. However, in 2008, global financial markets imploded following the bankruptcy of Lehman Brothers and the collapse of the U.S. housing market. In the aftermath, financial markets froze. The Icelandic banks found that they could not refinance their debt, and they faced bankruptcy.

The Icelandic government lacked the funds to bail out the banks, so it decided to let the big three fail. In quick succession, the local stock market plunged 90 percent and unemployment increased ninefold. The krona, Iceland's currency, plunged on foreign exchange markets, pushing up the price of imports, and inflation soared to 18 percent. Iceland appeared to be in free fall. The economy shrank by almost 7 percent in 2009 and another 4 percent in 2010.

To stem the decline, the government secured $10 billion in loans from the International Monetary Fund (IMF) and other countries. The Icelandic government stepped in to help local depositors, seizing the domestic assets of the Icelandic banks and using IMF and other loans to backstop deposit guarantees. Far from implementing austerity measures to solve the crisis, the Icelandic government looked for ways to shore up consumer spending. For example, the government provided means-tested subsidies to reduce the mortgage interest expenses of borrowers. The idea was to stop domestic consumer spending from imploding and further depressing the economy.

With the financial system stabilized, thanks to the IMF and other foreign loans, what happened next is an object lesson in the value of having a floating currency. The fall in the value of the krona helped boost Iceland's exports, such as fish and aluminum, while depressing demand for costly imports, such as automobiles. By 2009, the krona was worth half as much against the U.S. dollar and euro as it was in 2007 before the crisis. Iceland's exports surged and imports slumped. While the high cost of imports did stoke inflation, booming exports started to pump money back into the Icelandic economy. In 2011, the economy grew again at a 3.1 percent annual rate. This was followed by 2.7 percent growth in 2012 and 4 percent growth in 2013, while unemployment fell from a high of nearly 10 percent to 4.4 percent at the end of 2013.

Sources: Charles Forelle, "In European Crisis, Iceland Emerges as an Island of Recovery," *The Wall Street Journal*, May 19, 2012, pp. A1, A10; "Coming in from the Cold," *The Economist*, December 16, 2010; Charles Duxbury, "Europe Gets Cold Shoulder in Iceland," *The Wall Street Journal*, April 26, 2012; "Iceland," *The World Factbook 2013* (Washington, DC: Central Intelligence Agency, 2013).

These crises tend to have common underlying macroeconomic causes: high relative price inflation rates, a widening current account deficit, excessive expansion of domestic borrowing, high government deficits, and asset price inflation (such as sharp increases in stock and property prices).[10] At times, elements of currency, banking, and debt crises may be present simultaneously, as in the 1997 Asian crisis, the 2000–2002 Argentinean crisis, and the 2010 crisis in Ireland.

To assess the frequency of financial crises, the IMF looked at the macroeconomic performance of a group of 53 countries from 1975 to 1997 (22 of these countries were developed nations, and 31 were developing countries).[11] The IMF found there had been 158 currency crises, including 55 episodes in which a country's currency declined by more than 25 percent. There were also 54 banking crises. The IMF's data suggest that developing nations were more than twice as likely to experience currency and banking crises as developed nations. It is not surprising, therefore, that most of the IMF's loan activities since the mid-1970s have been targeted toward developing nations.

In 1997, several Asian currencies started to fall sharply as international investors came to the realization that there was a speculative investment bubble in the region. They took their money out of local currencies, changing it into U.S. dollars, and those currencies started to fall precipitously. The currency declines started in Thailand and then, in a process of contagion, quickly spread to other countries in the region. Stabilizing those currencies required massive help from the IMF. In the case of South Korea, local enterprises had built up huge debt loads as they invested heavily in new industrial capacity. By 1997, they found they had too much industrial capacity and could not generate the income required to service their debt. South Korean banks and companies had also made the mistake of borrowing in dollars, much of it in the form of short-term loans that would come due within a year. Thus, when the Korean won started to decline in fall 1997 in sympathy with the problems elsewhere in Asia, South Korean companies saw their debt obligations balloon. Several large companies were forced to file for bankruptcy. This triggered a decline in the South Korean currency and stock market that was difficult to halt.

With its economy on the verge of collapse, the South Korean government requested $20 billion in standby loans from the IMF on November 21. As the negotiations progressed, it became apparent that South Korea was going to need far more than $20 billion. On December 3, 1997, the IMF and South Korean government reached a deal to lend $55 billion to the country.

Christine Lagarde heads the IMF.

Source: © Stephen Jaffe/IMF/Handout/Getty Images News/Getty Images

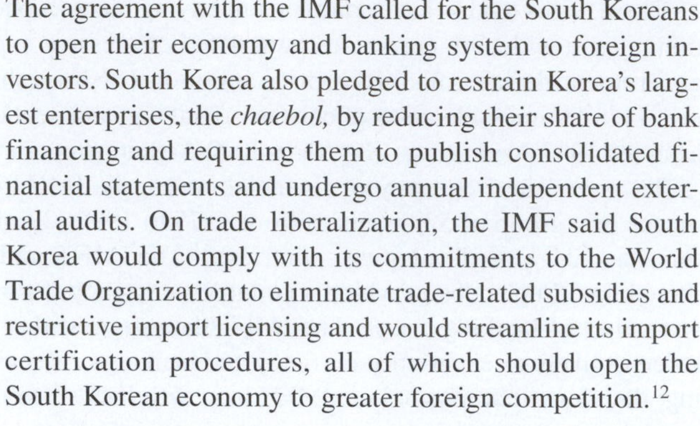

Is the International Monetary Fund (IMF) Needed?

The International Monetary Fund (IMF) is an organization of 188 countries working to foster global monetary cooperation, secure financial stability, facilitate international trade, promote high employment and sustainable economic growth, and reduce poverty around the world. It is a specialized agency of the United Nations but has its own charter, governing structure, and finances. Its members are represented through a quota system broadly based on their relative size in the global economy. The Board of Governors, the highest decision-making body of the IMF, consists of one governor and one alternate governor for each member country. The governor is appointed by the member country and is usually the minister of finance or the governor of the central bank. Chapter 11 includes a lot of material on the IMF, the debate about its positive and negative effects on world markets, and its policy prescriptions. Based on this material, should the IMF's one-size fits-all approach (see the section on "Inappropriate Policies" in this chapter) be evaluated? If yes, how would you change it? If no, why not?

Source: http://www.imf.org.

The agreement with the IMF called for the South Koreans to open their economy and banking system to foreign investors. South Korea also pledged to restrain Korea's largest enterprises, the *chaebol,* by reducing their share of bank financing and requiring them to publish consolidated financial statements and undergo annual independent external audits. On trade liberalization, the IMF said South Korea would comply with its commitments to the World Trade Organization to eliminate trade-related subsidies and restrictive import licensing and would streamline its import certification procedures, all of which should open the South Korean economy to greater foreign competition.[12]

EVALUATING THE IMF'S POLICY PRESCRIPTIONS

By 2016, the IMF had programs in more than 30 countries that were struggling with economic and/or currency crises. All IMF loan packages come with conditions attached. Until very recently, the IMF has insisted on a combination of tight macroeconomic policies, including cuts in public spending, higher interest rates, and tight monetary policy. It has also often pushed for the deregulation of sectors formerly protected from domestic and foreign competition, privatization of state-owned assets, and better financial reporting from the banking sector. These policies are designed to cool overheated economies by reining in inflation and reducing government spending and debt. This set of policy prescriptions has come in for tough criticisms from many observers, and the IMF itself has started to change its approach.[13]

Inappropriate Policies

One criticism is that the IMF's traditional policy prescriptions represent a "one-size-fits-all" approach to macroeconomic policy that is inappropriate for many countries. In the case of the 1997 Asian crisis, critics argue that the tight macroeconomic policies imposed by the IMF were not well suited to countries that are suffering not from excessive government spending and inflation but from a private-sector debt crisis with deflationary undertones.[14]

In South Korea, for example, the government had been running a budget surplus for years (it was 4 percent of South Korea's GDP in 1994–1996), and inflation was low at about 5 percent. South Korea had the second-strongest financial position of any country in the Organisation for Economic Co-operation and Development. Despite this, critics say, the IMF insisted on applying the same policies that it applies to countries suffering from high inflation. The IMF required South Korea to maintain an inflation rate of 5 percent. However, given the collapse in the value of its currency and the subsequent rise in price for imports such as oil, critics claimed inflationary pressures would inevitably increase in South Korea. So to hit a 5 percent inflation rate, the South Koreans would be forced to apply an unnecessarily tight monetary policy. Short-term interest rates in South Korea did jump from 12.5 to 21 percent immediately after the country signed its initial deal with the IMF. Increasing interest rates made it even more difficult for companies to service their already excessive short-term debt obligations, and critics used this as evidence to argue that the cure prescribed by the IMF may actually increase the probability of widespread corporate defaults, not reduce them.

At the time, the IMF rejected this criticism. According to the IMF, the central task was to rebuild confidence in the won. Once this was achieved, the won would recover from its oversold levels, reducing the size of South Korea's dollar-denominated debt burden when expressed in won and making it easier for companies to service their debt. The IMF also argued that by requiring South Korea to remove restrictions on foreign direct investment, foreign capital would flow into the country to take advantage of cheap assets. This, too, would increase demand for the Korean currency and help improve the dollar/won exchange rate.

South Korea did recover fairly quickly from the crisis, supporting the position of the IMF. While the economy contracted by 7 percent in 1998, by 2000, it had rebounded and grew at a 9 percent rate (measured by growth in GDP). Inflation, which peaked at 8 percent in 1998, fell to 2 percent by 2000, and unemployment fell from 7 to 4 percent over the same period. The won hit a low of $1 = W1,812 in early 1998 but by 2000 was back to an exchange rate of around $1 = W1,200, at which it seems to have stabilized.

Moral Hazard A second criticism of the IMF is that its rescue efforts are exacerbating a problem known to economists as moral hazard. **Moral hazard** arises when people behave recklessly because they know they will be saved if things go wrong. Critics point out that many Japanese and Western banks were far too willing to lend large amounts of capital to overleveraged Asian companies during the boom years of the 1990s. These critics argue that the banks should now be forced to pay the price for their rash lending policies, even if that means some banks must close.[15] Only by taking such drastic action, the argument goes, will banks learn the error of their ways and not engage in rash lending in the future. By providing support to these countries, the IMF is reducing the probability of debt default and in effect bailing out the banks whose loans gave rise to this situation.

Moral Hazard
Arises when people behave recklessly because they know they will be saved if things go wrong.

This argument ignores two critical points. First, if some Japanese or Western banks with heavy exposure to the troubled Asian economies were forced to write off their loans due to widespread debt default, the impact would have been difficult to contain. The failure of large Japanese banks, for example, could have triggered a meltdown in the Japanese financial markets. That would almost inevitably lead to a serious decline in stock markets around the world, which was the very risk the IMF was trying to avoid by stepping in with financial support. Second, it is incorrect to imply that some banks have not had to pay the price for rash lending policies. The IMF insisted on the closure of banks in South Korea, Thailand, and Indonesia after the 1997 Asian financial crisis. Foreign banks with short-term loans outstanding to South Korean enterprises have been forced by circumstances to reschedule those loans at interest rates that do not compensate for the extension of the loan maturity.

Lack of Accountability The final criticism of the IMF is that it has become too powerful for an institution that lacks any real mechanism for accountability.[16] The IMF has determined macroeconomic policies in those countries, yet according to critics such as noted economist Jeffrey Sachs, the IMF, with a staff of less than 1,000, lacks the expertise required to do a good job. Evidence of this, according to Sachs, can be found in the fact that the IMF was singing the praises of the Thai and South Korean governments only months before both countries lurched into crisis. Then the IMF put together a draconian program for South Korea without having deep knowledge of the country. Sachs's solution to this problem is to reform the IMF so it makes greater use of outside experts and its operations are open to greater outside scrutiny.

Observations As with many debates about international economics, it is not clear which side is correct about the appropriateness of IMF policies. There are cases where one can argue that IMF policies had been counterproductive or only had limited success. For example, one might question the success of the IMF's involvement in Turkey given that the country has had to implement some 18 IMF programs since 1958! But the IMF can also point to some notable accomplishments, including its success in containing the Asian crisis, which could have rocked the global international monetary system to its core, and its actions in 2008–2010 to contain the global financial crisis, quickly stepping in to rescue Iceland, Ireland, Greece, and Latvia. Similarly, many observers give the IMF credit for its deft handling of politically difficult situations, such as the Mexican peso crisis, and for successfully promoting a free market philosophy.

Several years after the IMF's intervention, the economy of Asia recovered. Certainly, the kind of catastrophic implosion that might have occurred had the IMF not stepped in had been averted, and although some countries still faced considerable problems, it is not clear that the IMF should take much blame for this. The IMF cannot force countries to adopt the policies required to correct economic mismanagement. While a government may commit to taking corrective action in return for an IMF loan, internal political problems may make it difficult for a government to act on that commitment. In such cases, the IMF is caught between a rock and a hard place, because if it decided to withhold money, it might trigger financial collapse and the kind of contagion that it seeks to avoid.

Finally, it is notable that in recent years the IMF has started to change its policies. In response to the global financial crisis of 2008–2009, the IMF began to urge countries to adopt policies that included fiscal stimulus and monetary easing—the direct opposite of what the fund traditionally advocated. Some economists in the fund are also now arguing that higher inflation rates might be a good thing, if the consequence is greater growth in aggregate demand, which would help pull nations out of recessionary conditions. The IMF, in other words, is starting to display the very flexibility in policy responses that its critics claim it lacks. While the traditional policy of tight controls on fiscal policy and tight monetary policy targets might be appropriate for countries suffering from high inflation rates, the Asian economic crisis and the 2008–2009 global financial crisis were caused not by high inflation rates but by excessive debt, and the IMF's "new approach" seems tailored to deal with this.[17]

test PREP

Use SmartBook to help retain what you have learned. Access your Instructor's Connect course to check out SmartBook or go to learnsmartadvantage.com for help.

FOCUS ON MANAGERIAL IMPLICATIONS

LO 11-6

Explain the implications of the global monetary system for currency management and business strategy.

CURRENCY MANAGEMENT, BUSINESS STRATEGY, AND GOVERNMENT RELATIONS

The implications for international businesses of the material discussed in this chapter fall into three main areas: currency management, business strategy, and corporate–government relations.

Currency Management

An obvious implication with regard to currency management is that companies must recognize that the foreign exchange market does not work quite as depicted in Chapter 10. The current system is a mixed system in which a combination of government intervention and speculative activity can drive the foreign exchange market. Companies engaged in significant foreign exchange activities need to be aware of this and to adjust their foreign exchange transactions accordingly. For example, the currency management unit of Caterpillar claims it made millions of dollars in the hours following the announcement of the Plaza Accord by selling dollars and buying currencies that it expected to appreciate on the foreign exchange market following government intervention.

Under the present system, speculative buying and selling of currencies can create very volatile movements in exchange rates (as exhibited by the rise and fall of the dollar during the 1980s and the Asian currency crisis of the late 1990s). Contrary to the predictions of the purchasing power parity theory (see Chapter 10), exchange rate movements during the 1980s and 1990s often did not seem to be strongly influenced by relative inflation rates. Insofar as volatile exchange rates increase foreign exchange risk, this is not good news for business. On the other hand, as we saw in Chapter 10, the foreign exchange market has developed a number of instruments, such as the forward market and swaps, that can help ensure against foreign exchange risk. Not surprisingly, use of these instruments has increased markedly since the breakdown of the Bretton Woods system in 1973.

Business Strategy

The volatility of the current global exchange rate regime presents a conundrum for international businesses. Exchange rate movements are difficult to predict, and yet their movement can have a major impact on a business's competitive position. For a detailed example, see the accompanying Management Focus on Airbus. Faced with uncertainty about the future value of currencies, firms can utilize the forward exchange market, which Airbus has done. However, the forward exchange market is far from perfect as a predictor of future exchange rates (see Chapter 10). It is also difficult, if not impossible, to get adequate insurance coverage for exchange rate changes that might occur several years in the future. The forward market tends to offer coverage for exchange rate changes a few months—not years—ahead. Given this, it makes sense to pursue strategies that will increase the company's strategic flexibility in the face of unpredictable exchange rate

management FOCUS

Airbus and the Euro

Airbus had reason to celebrate in 2003; for the first time in the company's history, it delivered more commercial jet aircraft than long-time rival Boeing. Airbus delivered 305 planes in 2003, compared to Boeing's 281. The celebration, however, was muted because the strength of the euro against the U.S. dollar was casting a cloud over the company's future. Airbus, which is based in Toulouse, France, prices planes in dollars, just as Boeing has always done. But more than half of Airbus' costs are in euros. So as the dollar drops in value against the euro—and it dropped by more than 50 percent between 2002 and the end of 2009—Airbus' costs rise in proportion to its revenue, squeezing profits in the process.

In the short run, the fall in the value of the dollar against the euro did not hurt Airbus. The company fully hedged its dollar exposure in 2005 and was mostly hedged for 2006. However, anticipating that the dollar would stay weak against the euro, Airbus started to take other steps to reduce its economic exposure to a strong European currency. Recognizing that raising prices is not an option given the strong competition from Boeing, Airbus decided to focus on reducing its costs. As a step toward doing this, Airbus gave U.S. suppliers a greater share of work on new aircraft models, such as the A380 superjumbo and the A350. It also shifted supply work on some of its older models from European to American-based suppliers. This increased the proportion of its costs that were in dollars, making profits less vulnerable to a rise in the value of the euro and reducing the costs of building an aircraft when they were converted back into euros.

In addition, Airbus pushed its European-based suppliers to start pricing in U.S. dollars. Because the costs of many suppliers were in euros, the suppliers found that to comply with Airbus' wishes, they too had to move more work to the United States or to countries whose currency is pegged to the U.S. dollar. Thus, one large French-based supplier, Zodiac, announced that it was considering acquisitions in the United States. Not only was Airbus pushing suppliers to price components for commercial jet aircraft in dollars, but the company was also requiring suppliers to its A400M program, a military aircraft that will be sold to European governments and priced in euros, to price components in U.S. dollars. Beyond these steps, the CEO of EADS, Airbus' parent company, publicly stated it might be prepared to assemble aircraft in the United States if that would help win important U.S. contracts. While this strategy made good sense for years, it worked against Airbus between mid-2014 and 2015 as the dollar rose rapidly against the euro.

Wings are assembled at the Airbus SAS factory in Broughton, United Kingdom. Completed wings are transported to Toulouse, France, or Hamburg, Germany, for final assembly.

Source: © Christopher Furlong/Getty Images News/Getty Images

Sources: D. Michaels, "Airbus Deliveries Top Boeing's; But Several Obstacles Remain," *The Wall Street Journal*, January 16, 2004, p. A9; J. L. Gerondeau, "Airbus Eyes U.S. Suppliers as Euro Gains," *Seattle Times*, February 21, 2004, p. C4; "Euro's Gains Create Worries in Europe," *HoustonChronicle.com*, January 13, 2004, p. 3; K. Done, "Soft Dollar and A380 Hitches Lead to EADS Losses," *Financial Times*, November 9, 2006, p. 32.

movements—that is, to pursue strategies that reduce the economic exposure of the firm (which we first discussed in Chapter 10).

Maintaining strategic flexibility can take the form of dispersing production to different locations around the globe as a real hedge against currency fluctuations (this seems to be what Airbus has considered). Consider the case of Daimler-Benz, Germany's export-oriented automobile and aerospace company. In June 1995, the company stunned the German business community when it announced it expected to post a severe loss in 1995 of about $720 million. The cause was Germany's strong currency, which had appreciated by 4 percent against a basket of major currencies since the beginning of 1995 and had risen by more than 30 percent against the U.S. dollar since late 1994. By mid-1995, the exchange rate against the dollar stood at $1 = DM1.38. Daimler's management believed it could not make money with an exchange rate under $1 = DM1.60. Daimler's senior managers concluded the appreciation of the mark against the dollar was probably permanent, so they decided to move substantial production outside of Germany and increase purchasing of foreign components. The idea was to reduce the vulnerability of the company to future exchange rate movements. Even before the company's acquisition of Chrysler Corporation in 1998, the Mercedes-Benz division planned to produce 10 percent of its cars outside Germany by 2000, mostly in the United States. Similarly, the move by Japanese automobile companies to expand their productive capacity in the United States and Europe can be seen in the context of the increase in the value of the yen between 1985 and 1995, which raised the price of Japanese exports. For the Japanese companies, building production capacity overseas was a hedge against continued appreciation of the yen (as well as against trade barriers).

Another way of building strategic flexibility and reducing economic exposure involves contracting out manufacturing. This allows a company to shift suppliers from country to country in response to changes in relative costs brought about by exchange rate movements. However, this kind of strategy may work only for low-value-added manufacturing (e.g., textiles), in which the individual manufacturers have few if any firm-specific skills that contribute to the value of the product. It may be less appropriate for high-value-added manufacturing, in which firm-specific technology and skills add significant value to the product (e.g., the heavy equipment industry) and in which switching costs are correspondingly high. For high-value-added manufacturing, switching suppliers will lead to a reduction in the value that is added, which may offset any cost gains arising from exchange rate fluctuations.

The roles of the IMF and the World Bank in the current international monetary system also have implications for business strategy. Increasingly, the IMF has been acting as the macroeconomic police of the world economy, insisting that countries seeking significant borrowings adopt IMF-mandated macroeconomic policies. These policies typically include anti-inflationary monetary policies and reductions in government spending. In the short run, such policies usually result in a sharp contraction of demand. International businesses selling or producing in such countries need to be aware of this and plan accordingly. In the long run, the kind of policies imposed by the IMF can promote economic growth and an expansion of demand, which create opportunities for international business.

Corporate-Government Relations

As major players in the international trade and investment environment, businesses can influence government policy toward the international monetary system. For example, intense government lobbying by U.S. exporters helped convince the U.S. government that intervention in the foreign exchange market was necessary. With this in mind, business can and should use its influence to promote an international monetary system that facilitates the growth of international trade and investment. Whether a fixed or floating regime is optimal is a subject for debate. However, exchange rate volatility such as the world experienced during the 1980s and 1990s creates an environment less conducive to international trade and investment than one with more stable exchange rates. Therefore, it would seem to be in the interests of international business to promote an international monetary system that minimizes volatile exchange rate movements, particularly when those movements are unrelated to long-run economic fundamentals.

Key Terms

international monetary system, p. 298
floating exchange rate, p. 298
pegged exchange rate, p. 298
dirty-float system, p. 298
fixed exchange rate, p. 298
European Monetary System (EMS), p. 299
gold standard, p. 299
gold par value, p. 300
balance-of-trade equilibrium, p. 300
managed-float system, p. 307
currency board, p. 311
currency crisis, p. 312
banking crisis, p. 312
foreign debt crisis, p. 312
moral hazard, p. 315

Summary

This chapter explained the workings of the international monetary system and pointed out its implications for international business. The chapter made the following points:

1. The gold standard is a monetary standard that pegs currencies to gold and guarantees convertibility to gold. It was thought that the gold standard contained an automatic mechanism that contributed to the simultaneous achievement of a balance-of-payments equilibrium by all countries. The gold standard broke down during the 1930s as countries engaged in competitive devaluations.
2. The Bretton Woods system of fixed exchange rates was established in 1944. The U.S. dollar was the central

currency of this system; the value of every other currency was pegged to its value. Significant exchange rate devaluations were allowed only with the permission of the International Monetary Fund (IMF). The role of the IMF was to maintain order in the international monetary system (*a*) to avoid a repetition of the competitive devaluations of the 1930s and (*b*) to control price inflation by imposing monetary discipline on countries.

3. The fixed exchange rate system collapsed in 1973, primarily due to speculative pressure on the dollar following a rise in U.S. inflation and a growing U.S. balance-of-trade deficit.
4. Since 1973, the world has operated with a floating exchange rate regime, and exchange rates have become more volatile and far less predictable. Volatile exchange rate movements have helped reopen the debate over the merits of fixed and floating systems.
5. The case for a floating exchange rate regime claims (*a*) such a system gives countries autonomy regarding their monetary policy and (*b*) floating exchange rates facilitate smooth adjustment of trade imbalances.
6. The case for a fixed exchange rate regime claims (*a*) the need to maintain a fixed exchange rate imposes monetary discipline on a country; (*b*) floating exchange rate regimes are vulnerable to speculative pressure; (*c*) the uncertainty that accompanies floating exchange rates dampens the growth of international trade and investment; and (*d*) far from correcting trade imbalances, depreciating a currency on the foreign exchange market tends to cause price inflation.
7. In today's international monetary system, some countries have adopted floating exchange rates; some have pegged their currency to another currency, such as the U.S. dollar; and some have pegged their currency to a basket of other currencies, allowing their currency to fluctuate within a zone around the basket.
8. In the post–Bretton Woods era, the IMF has continued to play an important role in helping countries navigate their way through financial crises by lending significant capital to embattled governments and by requiring them to adopt certain macroeconomic policies.
9. An important debate is occurring over the appropriateness of IMF-mandated macroeconomic policies. Critics charge that the IMF often imposes inappropriate conditions on developing nations that are the recipients of its loans.
10. The current managed-float system of exchange rate determination has increased the importance of currency management in international businesses.
11. The volatility of exchange rates under the current managed-float system creates both opportunities and threats. One way of responding to this volatility is for companies to build strategic flexibility and limit their economic exposure by dispersing production to different locations around the globe by contracting out manufacturing (in the case of low-value-added manufacturing) and other means.

Critical Thinking and Discussion Questions

1. Why did the gold standard collapse? Is there a case for returning to some type of gold standard? What is it?
2. What opportunities might current IMF lending policies to developing nations create for international businesses? What threats might they create?
3. Do you think the standard IMF policy prescriptions of tight monetary policy and reduced government spending are always appropriate for developing nations experiencing a currency crisis? How might the IMF change its approach? What would the implications be for international businesses?
4. Debate the relative merits of fixed and floating exchange rate regimes. From the perspective of an international business, what are the most important criteria in a choice between the systems? Which system is the more desirable for an international business?
5. Imagine that Canada, the United States, and Mexico decide to adopt a fixed exchange rate system. What would be the likely consequences of such a system for (*a*) international businesses and (*b*) the flow of trade and investment among the three countries?
6. Reread the Country Focus on the U.S. dollar, oil prices, and recycling petrodollars, then answer the following questions:
   a. What will happen to the value of the U.S. dollar if oil producers decide to invest most of their earnings from oil sales in domestic infrastructure projects?
   b. What factors determine the relative attractiveness of dollar-, euro-, and yen- denominated assets to oil producers flush with petrodollars? What might lead them to direct more funds toward non-dollar-denominated assets?
   c. What will happen to the value of the U.S. dollar if OPEC members decide to invest more of their petrodollars toward non-dollar-denominated assets, such as euro-denominated stocks and bonds?
   d. In addition to oil producers, China is also accumulating a large stock of dollars, currently estimated to total $3.3 trillion. What would happen to the value of the dollar if China and oil-producing nations all shifted out of dollar-denominated assets at the same time? What would be the consequence for the U.S. economy?

globalEDGE Research Task

globalEDGE.msu.edu

Use the globalEDGE™ website (globaledge.msu.edu) to complete the following exercises:

1. The *Global Financial Stability Report* is a semiannual report published by the International Capital Markets division of the International Monetary Fund. The report includes an assessment of the risks facing the global financial markets. Locate and download the latest report to get an overview of the most important issues currently under discussion. Also, download a report from five years ago. How do issues from five years ago compare with financial issues identified in the current report?
2. An important element to understanding the international monetary system is keeping updated on current growth trends worldwide. A German colleague told you yesterday that *Deutsche Bank Research* provides an effective way to stay informed on important topics in international finance from a European perspective. One area of focus for the site is emerging markets and economic and financial challenges faced by these markets. Find an emerging market research report for analysis. On which emerging market region did you choose to focus? What are the key takeaways from your chosen report?

The IMF and Ukraine's Economic Crisis

closing case

Back in late 2013, the then-president of Ukraine, Viktor Yanukovych, suspended preparations for the implementation of a trade agreement with the European Union, opting instead for closer ties with Russia. Yanukovych's decision resulted in mass protests in the capital city Kiev and elsewhere in western Ukraine, where closer ties with the West were seen as a necessary counterbalance to the growing influence of its powerful neighbor to the east, the increasingly autocratic Russia of Vladimir Putin. These protests ultimately led to Yanukovych's ouster from office in February 2014. Following his removal, unrest enveloped the largely Russian-speaking provinces of eastern and southern Ukraine from which he had drawn his support. In March 2014, the autonomous region of Crimea was annexed by Russia, while a civil war between the new Ukrainian government and pro-Russian separatists developed in eastern Ukraine.

The result was an economic disaster for Ukraine. In 2014, the country's GDP shrank by nearly 10 percent. The currency, the hryvina, fell by more than 50 percent against other currencies as capital fled the country. As the costs of imports rose, inflation jumped from 1 to 25 percent. In a desperate attempt to support the value of its currency, Ukraine's central bank bought hryvina on the foreign exchange market, selling its foreign currency reserves to do so. Ukraine's foreign exchange reserves declined from more than $16 billion in mid-2014 to under $6 billion by early 2015. Moreover, the country was facing debt repayments of at least $10 billion and gas import bills from Russia, while its own banking system was shattered.

In an attempt to pull Ukraine out of an economic tailspin, in April 2014, the International Monetary Fund (IMF) pledged to contribute $17 billion in loans to the country over two years, of which about $5 billion was disbursed in 2014. It wasn't enough. The currency continued to lose value, inflation increased, unemployment rose, and the economy shrank. In early March 2015, the IMF deepened its involvement in the country, putting together a package of additional financial support. The IMF agreed to a four-year deal to loan $17.5 billion to Ukraine. The deal was expected to unlock another $20 billion in loans from the United States and the European Union.

In return for these funds, which were to be used to support the value of the hryvina in foreign exchange markets, Ukraine had to agree to a raft of policies imposed at the bequest of the IMF. The country agreed to maintain a free floating exchange rate and to pursue a tight monetary policy aimed at restoring price stability. The state-owned natural gas company, Naftogaz, was also required to increase its prices by as much as 200 percent. Naftogaz had been buying natural gas at market prices from Russia and selling it at deeply subsidized prices to Ukrainians. This money-losing transaction had been financed by issuing debt, which the government could no longer service. Indeed, a growing debt burden and excessive government spending were major problems facing the country. These problems only got worse as the economy contracted and the tax base contracted. At the insistence of the IMF, the Ukrainian government also agreed to cut spending on unemployment and disability insurance, to reduce the salaries of state workers, and to cut state pensions.

The IMF believed that while these austerity policies would result in the economy shrinking by a further 5 percent in 2015, the economy would start growing again in 2016. Unfortunately, conditions in Ukraine deteriorated further in 2015. After some initial success, the Ukrainian government pulled back from implementing the full raft of austerity policies proposed by the IMF. To make matters worse, there was evidence that some of the IMF loans were being syphoned off or squandered by corrupt government officials. In October 2015, the IMF responded by halting its dispersal of funds under the loan program and pressuring Ukraine to institute economic reforms and tackle government corruption. With funds from the IMF on hold, the Ukrainian economy continued to decline, shrinking by an estimated 11 percent in 2015. Unemployment continued to rise, and the inflation rate jumped to around 50 percent.

In February 2016, Christine Lagarde, the managing director of the IMF, stated, "Without a substantial new effort to invigorate governance reforms and fight corruption, it is hard to see how the IMF supported program can continue to be successful."* Lagarde's comments followed the resignation

*Larry Elliott, "IMF Warns Ukraine It Will Halt $40 Billion Bailout Unless Corruption Stops," *The Guardian,* February 10, 2016.

of Ukraine's economic minister after he accused a senior aide to the president of blocking anticorruption reforms. For its part, the Ukrainian government pledged to step up its efforts to fight political corruption and introduce economic reforms but cautioned that changes could not be made overnight.

Sources: Andrew Mayeda, "IMF Approves Ukraine Aid Package of about $17.5 Billion," *Bloomberg Business*, March 11, 2015; Staff reporter, "IMF Signs Off on $17.5 Billion Loan for Ukraine in Second Attempt to Stave Off Bankruptcy," *Reuters*, March 11, 2015; Staff reporter, "The New Greece in the East," *The Economist*, March 12, 2015; Larry Elliott, "IMF Warns Ukraine It Will Halt $40 Billion Bailout Unless Corruption Stops," *The Guardian*, February 10, 2016.

CASE DISCUSSION QUESTIONS

1. Why do you think Viktor Yanukovych walked away from a trade agreement with the EU in favor of closer ties with Russia? What did he gain by doing this? What did he lose?
2. What were the root causes of Ukraine's currency crisis? Without help from the IMF, what might have happened?
3. Were the policy recommendations made by the IMF reasonable?
4. Why do you think the Ukrainian government balked at fully implementing the IMF policies?
5. Was the IMF right to suspend disbursement of monies under its loan program in October 2015? Under what conditions should the IMF resume making loans?
6. What might happen if the IMF discontinues its loan program to Ukraine, as it has threatened to do?
7. Could the IMF have done anything differently to avoid the situation it now finds itself in?

Endnotes

1. The argument goes back to eighteenth-century philosopher David Hume. See D. Hume, "On the Balance of Trade," reprinted in *The Gold Standard in Theory and in History*, ed. B. Eichengreen (London: Methuen, 1985).
2. R. Solomon, *The International Monetary System, 1945–1981* (New York: Harper & Row, 1982).
3. International Monetary Fund, *World Economic Outlook, 2005* (Washington, DC: IMF, May 2005).
4. For an extended discussion of the dollar exchange rate in the 1980s, see B. D. Pauls, "US Exchange Rate Policy: Bretton Woods to the Present," *Federal Reserve Bulletin*, November 1990, pp. 891–908.
5. R. Miller, "Why the Dollar Is Giving Way," *BusinessWeek*, December 6, 2004, pp. 36–37.
6. For a feel for the issues contained in this debate, see P. Krugman, *Has the Adjustment Process Worked?* (Washington, DC: Institute for International Economics, 1991); "Time to Tether Currencies," *The Economist*, January 6, 1990, pp. 15–16; P. R. Krugman and M. Obstfeld, *International Economics: Theory and Policy* (New York: HarperCollins, 1994); J. Shelton, *Money Meltdown* (New York: Free Press, 1994); S. Edwards, "Exchange Rates and the Political Economy of Macroeconomic Discipline," *American Economic Review* 86, no. 2 (May 1996), pp. 159–63.
7. The argument is made by several prominent economists, particularly Stanford University's Robert McKinnon. See R. McKinnon, "An International Standard for Monetary Stabilization," *Policy Analyses in International Economics* 8 (1984). The details of this argument are beyond the scope of this book. For a relatively accessible exposition, see P. Krugman, *The Age of Diminished Expectations* (Cambridge, MA: MIT Press, 1990).
8. A. R. Ghosh and A. M. Gulde, "Does the Exchange Rate Regime Matter for Inflation and Growth?" *Economic Issues*, no. 2 (1997).
9. "The ABC of Currency Boards," *The Economist*, November 1, 1997, p. 80.
10. International Monetary Fund, *World Economic Outlook, 1998* (Washington, DC: IMF, 1998).
11 Ibid.
12. T. S. Shorrock, "Korea Starts Overhaul; IMF Aid Hits $55 Billion," *Journal of Commerce*, December 8, 1997, p. 3A.
13. See J. Sachs, "Economic Transition and Exchange Rate Regime," *American Economic Review* 86, no. 92 (May 1996), pp. 147–52; J. Sachs, "Power unto Itself," *Financial Times*, December 11, 1997, p. 11.
14. Sachs, "Power unto Itself."
15. Martin Wolf, "Same Old IMF Medicine," *Financial Times*, December 9, 1997, p. 12.
16. Sachs, "Power unto Itself."
17. "New Fund, Old Fundamentals," *The Economist*, May 2, 2009, p. 78.

The Strategy of International Business

learning objectives

- **LO12-1** Explain the concept of strategy.
- **LO12-2** Recognize how firms can profit by expanding globally.
- **LO12-3** Understand how pressures for cost reductions and pressures for local responsiveness influence strategic choice.
- **LO12-4** Identify the different strategies for competing globally and their pros and cons.
- **LO12-5** Explain the pros and cons of using strategic alliances to support global strategies.

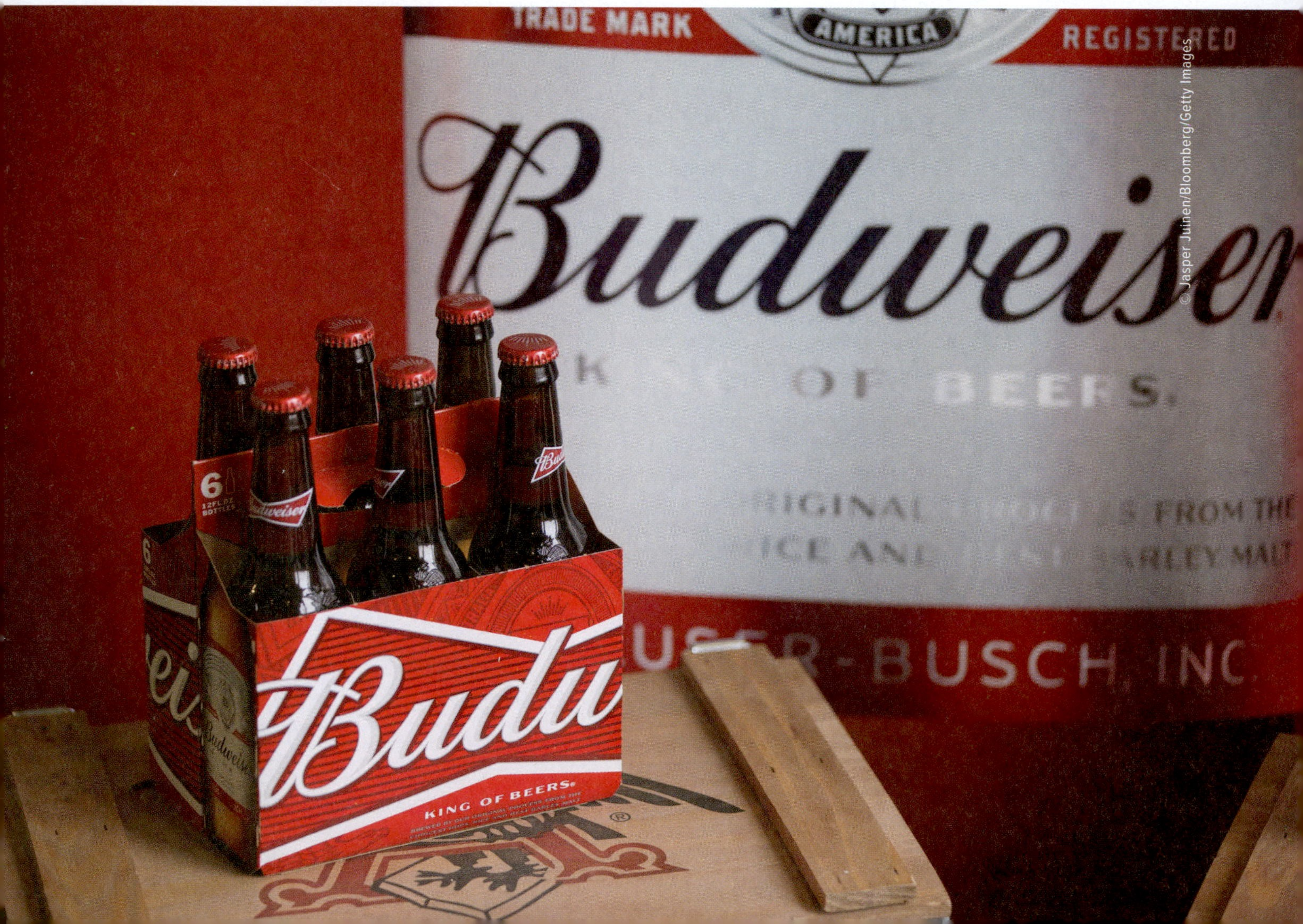

AB InBev and Beer Globally

opening case

The company AB InBev may not sound familiar to everyone, but spelled out, its name likely becomes clearer to most people, especially the beer-loving population of the world. Anheuser-Busch InBev originates from the Den Hoorn brewery in Leuven, Belgium, which dates back to 1366, and the pioneering spirit of the Anheuser & Co brewery, with origins in St. Louis, Missouri, since 1852. Today, AB InBev is the leading global brewer and one of the world's top consumer products companies.

AB InBev has operations in 25 countries, sales in more than 100 countries, revenue of $44 billion, 155,000 employees, and seven of the top 10 most valuable beer brands. These seven brands are: Budweiser, Bud Light, Stella Artois, Skol, Corona, Brahma, and Modelo Especial. Budweiser, Corona, and Stella Artois are marketed as "global brands," while Beck's, Leffe, and Hoegaarden are considered "international brands" in AB InBev's brand portfolio. The company also has 15 "local champions," which represent leadership in their respective local markets. These local brands include Jupiler (most popular beer in Belgium), Quilmes (original Argentinean lager since 1890), and Harbin (from the oldest brewery in North China), among the portfolio. In total, AB InBev's portfolio consists of more than 200 brands.

With more than 200 brands and strong coverage internationally of the different brands, strategically AB InBev is a unique and highly organized global company. Carlos Brito (CEO) and Olivier Goudet (chairman of the board) have stated that the company's ambition is to build a great, enduring company for the next 100 years. The core management team consists of the CEO, nine Executive Board members, and six zone presidents. The six zone presidents have responsibility for Latin America South, Latin America North, Asia Pacific, North America, Mexico, and Europe.

Using this management structure, AB InBev has built leading positions in the important beer profit markets in the world through a combination of organic growth and selected, value-enhancing acquisitions. The company follows a focus brands strategy in which the majority of the resources are devoted to those brands that have the greatest long-term growth potential. Investment behind the brands is fueled by a disciplined approach to cost management and efficiency. AB InBev has a strong track record of industry-leading margins and cash flow generation. In 2015, this led to growth of 12.6 percent of the company's three global brands (Budweiser, Corona, and Stella Artois), for example, and strong earnings in North America and most of Latin America.

The foundation for AB InBev's global strategy is the company's "Dream-People-Culture" approach. The goal is that despite having operations in many countries around the world, with different national cultures, AB InBev operates as one company, with one dream and one culture uniting them. There is also a focus on

–continued

having the right people in the right place at the right time. This culture is built on ownership, informality, candor, transparency, and meritocracy.

Strategically, AB InBev has 10 principles driving everything they do. At the core, AB InBev is focused on a shared dream that energizes everyone to work in the same direction to be the best beer company in the world, bring people together, and aspire for the betterment of the world. Additional principles cover people strengths, quality of teams, striving for increased satisfaction, consumer focus, ownership, common sense and simplicity, cost management, leadership, and hard work and responsibility. ●

Sources: D. Leonard, "Can Craft Beer Survive AB InBev?" *Bloomberg Business*, June 25, 2015; V. Wong, "Why AB InBev and Big Brewers Are Betting on Hard Cider," *Bloomberg Business*, May 13, 2013; J. Colley, "The Big Beer Merger Won't Bring Down the Price of a Pint," *Newsweek*, October 18, 2015; C. Purdy, "There's a Less Obvious Reason Why AB InBev Is Buying Up Craft Breweries," *Quartz*, December 23, 2015; *AB InBev Annual Report* 2015. annualreport.ab-inbev.com.

Introduction

The primary concern so far in the chapters that we have covered has been on aspects of the larger environment in which companies compete in the global marketplace. Sometimes we call this the global macro environment, and the initial set of chapters covers these macro topics in detail. The macro environment discussion has included an overview of globalization, national differences, the global trade and investment environment, and the global monetary system. We also placed a strong emphasis on managerial implications associated with each of the macro topics, with separate sections in each of the macro chapters on what the macro topics mean for managerial strategy and action globally. This managerial focus was complemented with management focus and country focus illustrations throughout to capture the relevant learning in relation to running a global company.

With this chapter and the remainder of the book, our focus shifts from the macro environment to the company itself and, in particular, to the actions managers can take to compete more effectively as an international business. This chapter looks at how firms can increase their profitability by expanding their operations in foreign markets; this is international business strategy. We discuss the different strategies that firms pursue when competing internationally, consider the pros and cons of these strategies, and study the various factors that affect a firm's choice of strategy. We also look at why firms often enter into strategic alliances with their global competitors, and we discuss the benefits, costs, and risks of strategic alliances.

The strategy of global beer manufacturer AB InBev, which was discussed in the opening case, gives us a preview of some of the key issues addressed in the strategy chapter. AB InBev's basic strategy is to first categorize their brand portfolio into global brands, international brands, and local brands. Budweiser, Corona, and Stella Artois are marketed as "global brands" while Beck's, Leffe, and Hoegaarden are considered "international brands" in AB InBev's brand portfolio. This brand categorization of their portfolio of more than 200 brands has resulted in seven of the top 10 most valuable beer brands being owned by AB InBev. These seven brands are Budweiser, Bud Light, Stella Artois, Skol, Corona, Brahma, and Modelo Especial.

The categorization of the various AB InBev products helps the company compete globally by strategically leveraging unique aspects of each beer in the market in which it sells. As you noticed, very few of their beer brands are sold globally. Had AB InBev strategically tried to make all brands global and expanded into a large number of countries by using exactly the same segmentation strategy and retailing formula, and selling the same set of products (see the closing case on IKEA's global strategy as a contrast to AB InBev's), the likelihood of success (profitability) would have been much lower.

Global strategy has for a long time been focused on value creation, strategic positioning, value chain operations, global expansion opportunities, cost pressures, and choosing a strategy that fits with the core business model of a company in its industry. AB InBev (opening case) and IKEA (closing case) have both been very successful in their global strategy development and implementation but for vastly different strategic reasons. For each company, value creation and strategic positioning were the initial drivers of success, and these topics are covered in the next section of this chapter.

The final topic in the chapter is strategic alliances. **Strategic alliances** are cooperative agreements between potential or actual competitors. The term is often used to embrace a variety of agreements between actual or potential competitors, including cross-shareholding deals, licensing arrangements, formal joint ventures, and informal cooperative arrangements. The motives for entering strategic alliances are varied, but they often include market access, hence the overlap with the topic of entering foreign markets, which we cover in detail in Chapter 13.

Strategic Alliances
Cooperative agreements between potential or actual competitors.

Strategy and the Firm

LO 12-2
Explain the concept of strategy.

Before we discuss the strategies that managers in the multinational enterprise can pursue, we need to review some basic principles of strategy. A firm's **strategy** can be defined as the actions that managers take to attain the goals of the firm. For most firms, the preeminent goal is to maximize the value of the firm for its owners, its shareholders (subject to the constraint that this is done in a legal, ethical, and socially responsible manner; see Chapter 5 for details). To maximize the value of a firm, managers must pursue strategies that increase the *profitability* of the enterprise and its rate of *profit growth* over time (see Figure 12.1). **Profitability** can be measured in a number of ways, but for consistency, we shall define it as the rate of return that the firm makes on its invested capital (ROIC), which is calculated by dividing the net profits of the firm by total invested capital.[1] **Profit growth** is measured by the percentage increase in net profits over time. In general, higher profitability and a higher rate of profit growth will increase the value of an enterprise and thus the returns garnered by its owners, the shareholders.[2]

Strategy
Actions managers take to attain the firm's goals.

Profitability
A ratio or rate of return concept.

Profit Growth
The percentage increase in net profits over time.

Managers can increase the profitability of the firm by pursuing strategies that lower costs or by pursuing strategies that add value to the firm's products, which enables the firm to raise prices. Managers can increase the rate at which the firm's profits grow over time by pursuing strategies to sell more products in existing markets or by pursuing strategies to enter new markets. As we shall see, expanding internationally can help managers boost the firm's profitability *and* increase the rate of profit growth over time.

VALUE CREATION

The way to increase the profitability of a firm is to create more value. The amount of value a firm creates is measured by the difference between its costs of production and the value that consumers perceive in its products. In general, the more value customers place on a firm's products, the higher the price the firm can charge for those products. However, the price a firm charges for a good or service is typically less than the value placed on that good or service by the customer. This is because the customer captures some of that value in the form of what economists call a consumer surplus.[3] The customer is able to do this because the firm is competing with other firms for the customer's business, so the firm must charge a

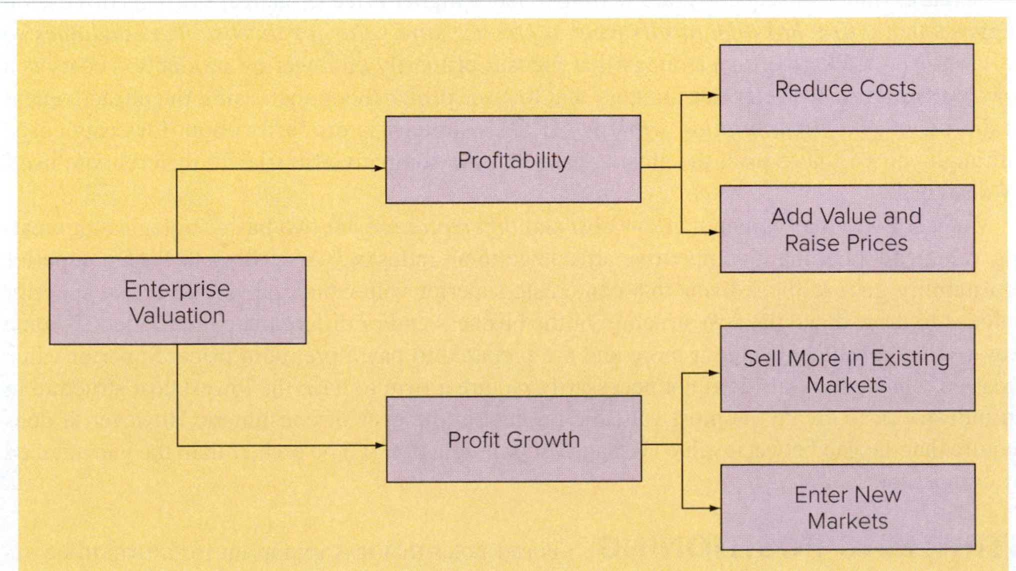

12.1 FIGURE

Determinants of Enterprise Value

Source: C. W. L. Hill and G. T. M. Hult, G. T. M., *International Business: Competing in the Global Marketplace* (New York: McGraw-Hill Education, 2017).

12.2 FIGURE

Value Creation

Source: C. W. L. Hill and G. T. M. Hult, *International Business: Competing in the Global Marketplace* (New York: McGraw-Hill Education, 2017).

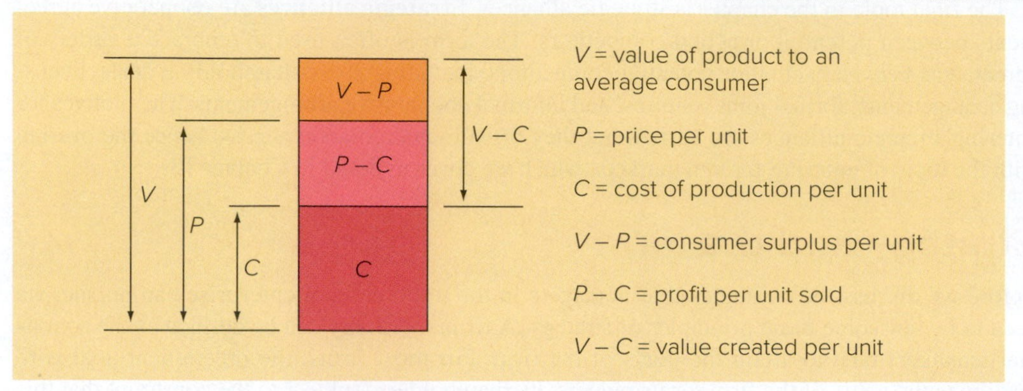

lower price than it could were it a monopoly supplier. Also, it is normally impossible to segment the market to such a degree that the firm can charge each customer a price that reflects that individual's assessment of the value of a product, which economists refer to as a customer's reservation price. For these reasons, the price that gets charged tends to be less than the value placed on the product by many customers.

Did You Know?

Did you know FedEx's global strategy focuses on more than transportation?

Visit your Connect SmartBook® to view a short video explanation from the authors.

Figure 12.2 illustrates these concepts. The value of a product to an *average* consumer is *V*, the average price that the firm can charge a consumer for that product given competitive pressures and its ability to segment the market is *P*, and the average unit cost of producing that product is *C* (*C* comprises all relevant costs, including the firm's cost of capital). The firm's profit per unit sold (π) is equal to $P - C$, while the consumer surplus per unit is equal to $V - P$ (another way of thinking of the consumer surplus is as "value for the money"; the greater the consumer surplus, the greater the value for the money the consumer gets). The firm makes a profit so long as *P* is greater than *C*, and its profit will be greater the lower *C* is *relative* to *P*. The difference between *V* and *P* is in part determined by the intensity of competitive pressure in the marketplace: the lower the intensity of competitive pressure, the higher the price charged relative to *V*.[4] In general, the higher the firm's profit per unit sold is, the greater its profitability will be, all else being equal.

Value Creation
Performing activities that increase the value of goods or services to consumers.

The firm's **value creation** is measured by the difference between *V* and *C* ($V - C$); a company creates value by converting inputs that cost *C* into a product on which consumers place a value of *V*. A company can create more value ($V - C$) either by lowering production costs, *C*, or by making the product more attractive through superior design, styling, functionality, features, reliability, after-sales service, and the like, so that consumers place a greater value on it (*V* increases) and, consequently, are willing to pay a higher price (*P* increases). This discussion suggests that *a firm has high profits when it creates more value for its customers and does so at a lower cost.* We refer to a strategy that focuses primarily on lowering production costs as a *low-cost strategy*. We refer to a strategy that focuses primarily on increasing the attractiveness of a product as a *differentiation strategy*.[5] IKEA's strategy is primarily about lowering costs, although you will note from the closing case that the company also tries to differentiate itself by design.

Michael Porter has argued that *low cost* and *differentiation* are two basic strategies for creating value and attaining a competitive advantage in an industry.[6] According to Porter, superior profitability goes to those firms that can create superior value, and the way to create superior value is to drive down the cost structure of the business and/or differentiate the product in some way so that consumers value it more and are prepared to pay a premium price. Superior value creation relative to rivals does not necessarily require a firm to have the lowest cost structure in an industry or to create the most valuable product in the eyes of consumers. However, it does require that the gap between value (*V*) and cost of production (*C*) be greater than the gap attained by competitors.

STRATEGIC POSITIONING Porter notes that it is important for a firm to be explicit about its choice of strategic emphasis with regard to value creation (differentiation) and

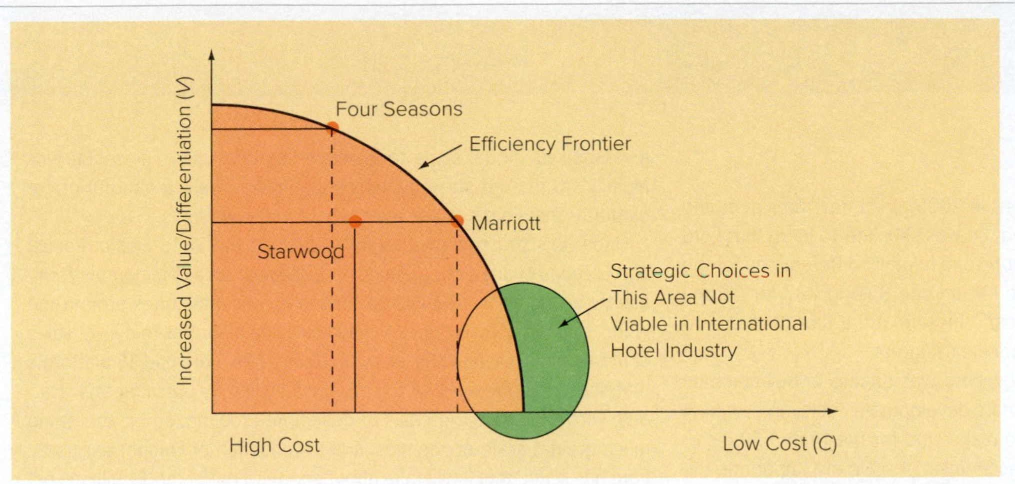

12.3 FIGURE

Strategic Choice in the International Hotel Industry

Source: C. W. L. Hill and G. T. M. Hult, *International Business: Competing in the Global Marketplace* (New York: McGraw-Hill Education, 2017).

low cost, and to configure its internal operations to support that strategic emphasis.[7] Figure 12.3 illustrates his point. The convex curve in Figure 12.3 is what economists refer to as an efficiency frontier. The efficiency frontier shows all of the different positions that a firm can adopt with regard to adding value to the product (*V*) and low cost (*C*), assuming that its internal operations are configured efficiently to support a particular position (note that the horizontal axis in Figure 12.3 is reverse scaled; moving along the axis to the right implies lower costs). The efficiency frontier has a convex shape because of diminishing returns. Diminishing returns imply that when a firm already has significant value built into its product offering, increasing value by a relatively small amount requires significant additional costs. The converse also holds: when a firm already has a low-cost structure, it has to give up a lot of value in its product offering to get additional cost reductions.

Figure 12.3 plots three hotel firms with a global presence that cater to international travelers: Four Seasons, Marriott International, and Starwood (Starwood owns the Sheraton and Westin chains). Four Seasons positions itself as a luxury chain and emphasizes the value of its product offering, which drives up its costs of operations. Marriott and Starwood are positioned more in the middle of the market. Both emphasize sufficient value to attract international business travelers but are not luxury chains like Four Seasons. In Figure 12.3, Four Seasons and Marriott are shown to be on the efficiency frontier, indicating that their internal operations are well configured to their strategy and run efficiently. Starwood is inside the frontier, indicating that its operations are not running as efficiently as they might be and that its costs are too high. This implies that Starwood is less profitable than Four Seasons and Marriott and that its managers must take steps to improve the company's performance.

Porter emphasizes that it is very important for management to decide where the company wants to be positioned with regard to value (*V*) and cost (*C*), to configure operations accordingly, and to manage them efficiently to make sure the firm is operating on the efficiency frontier. However, not all positions on the efficiency frontier are viable. In the international hotel industry, for example, there might not be enough demand to support a chain that emphasizes very low cost and strips all the value out of its product offering (see Figure 12.3). International travelers are relatively affluent and expect a degree of comfort (value) when they travel away from home.

A central tenet of the basic strategy paradigm is that to maximize its profitability, a firm must do three things: (1) pick a position on the efficiency frontier that is viable in the sense that there is enough demand to support that choice; (2) configure its internal operations, such as manufacturing, marketing, logistics, information systems, human resources, and so on, so that they support that position; and (3) make sure that the firm has the right organization structure in place to execute its strategy. *The strategy, operations, and organization of the firm must all be consistent with each other if it is to attain a competitive advantage and garner superior profitability.* By operations, we mean the different value creation activities a firm undertakes, which we shall review next.

management FOCUS

Ford Creating Value

When Alan Mulally arrived at Ford in 2006 as its new president and CEO after a long career at Boeing, he was shocked to learn that Ford produced one Ford Focus for Europe and a totally different one for the United States. "Can you imagine having one Boeing 737 for Europe and one 737 for the United States?"* he said at the time. And 2014–appointed President and CEO Mark Fields agrees.

Due to the old product strategy, Ford was unable to buy common parts for the vehicles, could not share development costs, and couldn't use its European Focus plants to make cars for the United States or vice versa. In a business where economies of scale are important, the result was high costs. Nor were these problems limited to the Ford Focus. The strategy of designing and building different cars for different regions was the standard approach at Ford.

Ford's long-standing strategy of regional models was based upon the assumption that consumers in different regions had different tastes and preferences, which required considerable local customization. Americans, it was argued, loved their trucks and SUVs, while Europeans preferred smaller, fuel-efficient cars. Notwithstanding such differences, Mulally still could not understand why small car models like the Focus or the Escape SUV, which were sold in different regions, were not built on the same platform and did not share common parts. In truth, the strategy probably had more to do with the autonomy of different regions within Ford's organization—a fact that was deeply embedded in Ford's history as one of the oldest multinational corporations.

When the global financial crisis rocked the world's automobile industry in 2008–2009 and precipitated the steepest drop in sales since the Great Depression, Mulally decided that Ford had to change its long-standing practices in order to get its costs under control. Moreover, he felt that there was no way that Ford would be able to compete effectively in the large developing markets of China and India unless Ford leveraged its global scale to produce low-cost cars. The result was Mulally's One Ford strategy, which aimed to create a handful of car platforms that Ford can use everywhere in the world.

Under this strategy, new models—such as the 2013 Fiesta, Focus, and Escape—share a common design, are built on a common platform, use the same parts, and will be built in identical factories around the world. Ultimately, Ford hopes to have only five platforms to deliver sales of more than 9 million vehicles by 2020. In 2006, Ford had 15 platforms that accounted for sales of 6.6 million vehicles. By pursuing this strategy, Ford can share the costs of design and tooling, and it can attain much greater scale economies in the production of component parts. Ford has stated that it will take about one-third out of the $1 billion cost of developing a new car model and should significantly reduce its $50 billion annual budget for component parts. Moreover, because the factories producing these cars are identical in all respects, useful knowledge acquired through experience in one factory can quickly be transferred to other factories, resulting in systemwide cost savings.

What Ford hopes is that this strategy will bring down costs sufficiently to enable Ford to make greater profit margins in developed markets and be able to achieve good profit margins at lower price points in hypercompetitive developing nations, such as China (now the world's largest car market), where Ford currently trails its global rivals such as General Motors and Volkswagen. Indeed, the strategy is central to current President and CEO Mark Field's goal for growing Ford's sales to 9.4 million vehicles by 2020.

*M. Ramsey, "Ford SUV Marks New World Car Strategy," *The Wall Street Journal*, November 16, 2011.

Sources: N. Bunkley, "Ford Sets Goal of 9.4M Global Sales by 2020," *Automotive News*, September 29, 2014; M. Ramsey, "Ford SUV Marks New World Car Strategy," *The Wall Street Journal*, November 16, 2011; B. Vlasic, "Ford Strategy Will Call for Stepping Up Expansion, Especially in Asia," *The New York Times*, June 7, 2011; "Global Manufacturing Strategy Gives Ford Competitive Advantage," *Ford Motor Company website*. http://media.ford.com.

Operations
The various value creation activities a firm undertakes.

OPERATIONS: THE FIRM AS A VALUE CHAIN The **operations** of a firm can be thought of as a value chain composed of a series of distinct value creation activities, including production, marketing and sales, materials management, research and development, human resources, information systems, and the firm infrastructure. We can categorize these value creation activities, or operations, as primary activities and support activities (see Figure 12.4).[8] As noted earlier, if a firm is to implement its strategy efficiently and position itself on the efficiency frontier shown in Figure 12.3, it must manage these activities effectively and in a manner that is consistent with its strategy.

Primary Activities Primary activities have to do with the design, creation, and delivery of the product; its marketing; and its support and after-sale service. Following normal practice, in the value chain illustrated in Figure 12.4, the primary activities are divided into four functions: research and development, production, marketing and sales, and customer service.

Research and development (R&D) is concerned with the design of products and production processes. Although we think of R&D as being associated with the design of physical products and production processes in manufacturing enterprises, many service companies also undertake R&D. For example, banks compete with each other by developing new financial products and new ways of delivering those products to customers. Online banking and smart debit cards are two examples of product development in the banking industry. Earlier examples of innovation in

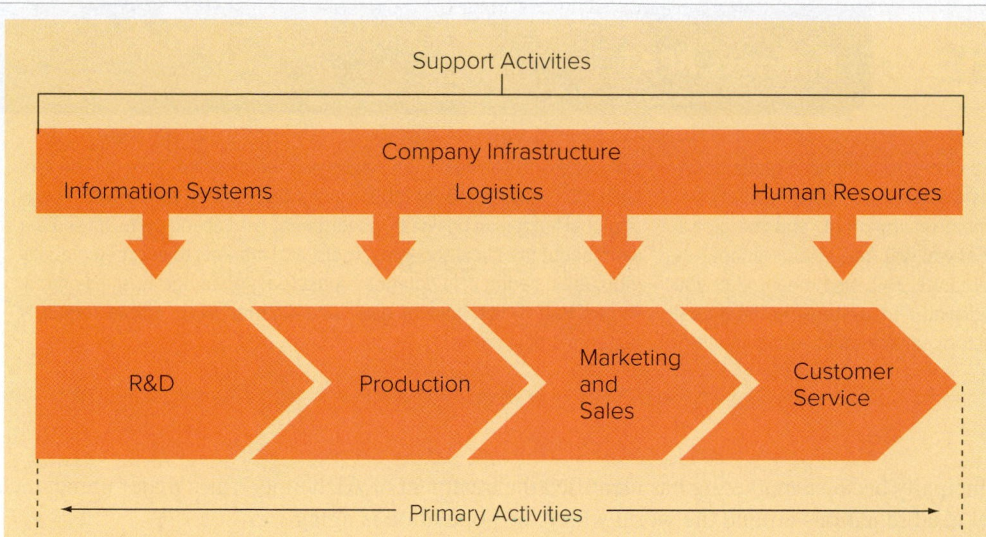

12.4 FIGURE

The Value Chain

Source: C. W. L. Hill and G. T. M. Hult, *International Business: Competing in the Global Marketplace* (New York: McGraw-Hill Education, 2017).

the banking industry included automated teller machines, credit cards, and debit cards. Through superior product design, R&D can increase the functionality of products, which makes them more attractive to consumers (raising *V*). Alternatively, R&D may result in more efficient production processes, thereby cutting production costs (lowering *C*). Either way, the R&D function can create value.

A Caterpillar motor factory in Germany helps to ensure product after-sales and service outside the United States.

© Bernd Wustneck/picture-alliance/dpa/AP Images

Production is concerned with the creation of a good or service. For physical products, when we talk about production, we generally mean manufacturing. Thus, we can talk about the production of an automobile. For services such as banking or health care, "production" typically occurs when the service is delivered to the customer (e.g., when a bank originates a loan for a customer, it is engaged in "production" of the loan). For a retailer such as Walmart, "production" is concerned with selecting the merchandise, stocking the store, and ringing up the sale at the cash register. For MTV, production is concerned with the creation, programming, and broadcasting of content, such as music videos and thematic shows. The production activity of a firm creates value by performing its activities efficiently so lower costs result (lower *C*) and/or by performing them in such a way that a higher-quality product is produced (which results in higher *V*).

The marketing and sales functions of a firm can help to create value in several ways. Through brand positioning and advertising, the marketing function can increase the value (*V*) that consumers perceive to be contained in a firm's product. If these create a favorable impression of the firm's product in the minds of consumers, they increase the price that can be charged for the firm's product. For example, Ford produced a high-value version of its Ford Expedition SUV. Sold as the Lincoln Navigator and priced around $10,000 higher, the Navigator has the same body, engine, chassis, and design as the Expedition, but through skilled advertising and marketing, supported by some fairly minor features changes (e.g., more accessories and the addition of a Lincoln-style engine grille and nameplate), Ford has fostered the perception that the Navigator is a "luxury SUV." This marketing strategy has increased the perceived value (*V*) of the Navigator relative to the Expedition and enables Ford to charge a higher price for the car (*P*).

Marketing and sales can also create value by discovering consumer needs and communicating them back to the R&D function of the company, which can then design products that better match those needs. For example, the allocation of research budgets at Pfizer, the world's largest pharmaceutical company, is determined by the marketing function's assessment of the potential market size associated with solving unmet medical needs. Thus, Pfizer is currently directing significant monies to R&D efforts aimed at finding treatments for Alzheimer's disease,

globalEDGE Business BEAT

In Chapter 12, we are bringing you closer to running a globally oriented company based on the issues we have covered on country differences, global trade and investment environment, and the global money system. This is where many of you will "make your money" as strategic decision makers in corporations. This also means that you need to know what is current, important, and strategic in the global marketplace; your company's products or services; and your company's uniqueness in satisfying the needs and wants of customers. The globalEDGE™ Business Beat (gBB) covers discussions with a wide range of global leaders in business, government, and academe to spread the word about the latest thoughts, tools, and markets to succeed globally (http://globaledge.msu.edu/get-connected/globaledge-business-beat). Tomas Hult is the host of gBB, and Charles W. L. Hill is regularly featured on the show.

principally because marketing has identified the treatment of Alzheimer's as a major unmet medical need in nations around the world where the population is aging.

The role of the enterprise's service activity is to provide after-sale service and support. This function can create a perception of superior value (*V*) in the minds of consumers by solving customer problems and supporting customers after they have purchased the product. Caterpillar, the U.S.-based manufacturer of heavy earthmoving equipment, can get spare parts to any point in the world within 24 hours, thereby minimizing the amount of downtime its customers have to suffer if their Caterpillar equipment malfunctions. This is an extremely valuable capability in an industry where downtime is very expensive. It has helped to increase the value that customers associate with Caterpillar products and thus the price that Caterpillar can charge.

Support Activities

The support activities of the value chain provide inputs that allow the primary activities to occur (see Figure 12.4). In terms of attaining a competitive advantage, support activities can be as important as, if not more important than, the primary activities of the firm. Consider information systems: these systems refer to the electronic systems for managing inventory, tracking sales, pricing products, selling products, dealing with customer service inquiries, and so on. Information systems, when coupled with the communications features of the Internet, can alter the efficiency and effectiveness with which a firm manages its other value creation activities. Dell, for example, has used its information systems to attain a competitive advantage over rivals. When customers place an order for a Dell product over the firm's website, that information is immediately transmitted, via the Internet, to suppliers, who then configure their production schedules to produce and ship that product so that it arrives at the right assembly plant at the right time. These systems have reduced the amount of inventory that Dell holds at assembly plants to under two days, which is a major source of cost savings.

The logistics function controls the transmission of physical materials through the value chain, from procurement through production and into distribution. The efficiency with which this is carried out can significantly reduce cost (lower *C*), thereby creating more value. The combination of logistics systems and information systems is a particularly potent source of cost savings in many enterprises, such as Dell, where information systems tell Dell on a real-time basis where in its global logistics network parts are, when they will arrive at an assembly plant, and thus how production should be scheduled.

The human resource function can help create more value in a number of ways. It ensures that the company has the right mix of skilled people to perform its value creation activities effectively. The human resource function also ensures that people are adequately trained, motivated, and compensated to perform their value creation tasks. In a multinational enterprise, one of the things human resources can do to boost the competitive position of the firm is to take advantage of its transnational reach to identify, recruit, and develop a cadre of skilled managers, regardless of their nationality, who can be groomed to take on senior management positions. They can find the very best, wherever they are in the world. Indeed, the senior management ranks of many multinationals are becoming increasingly diverse, as managers from a variety of national backgrounds have ascended to senior leadership positions.

The final support activity is the company infrastructure, or the context within which all the other value creation activities occur. The infrastructure includes the organizational structure, control systems, and culture of the firm. Because top management can exert considerable influence in shaping these aspects of a firm, top management should also be viewed as part of the firm's infrastructure. Through strong leadership, top management can consciously shape the infrastructure of a firm and through that the performance of all its value creation activities.

Is Education Creating Value for You?

The concept of a value chain can be used to examine the role your education plays in your life plans, if you look closely at your personal development plans (education, internship, work, physical and emotional fitness, and extracurricular activities) and think about them in terms of primary and support activities. If we use the logic that the amount of value you receive from your education is the difference between the costs (e.g., tuition, time, lost income) and what you receive in the form of education (e.g., knowledge, tools, networks), how does your choice of major area of focus in your education fit into your personal development strategy? How do your choices of how you spend your time fit into your value chain? Do you ever spend time doing things that do not support the strategic goals of your personal value chain? But, most importantly, what is the one thing you should do more of to drive the value higher for yourself today and in the future?

Organization: The Implementation of Strategy

The strategy of a firm is implemented through its organization. For a firm to have superior ROIC, its organization must support its strategy and operations. The term **organization architecture** can be used to refer to the totality of a firm's organization, including formal organizational structure, control systems and incentives, organizational culture, processes, and people.[9] Figure 12.5 illustrates these different elements. By **organizational structure**, we mean three things: first, the formal division of the organization into subunits such as product divisions, national operations, and functions (most organizational charts display this aspect of structure); second, the location of decision-making responsibilities within that structure (e.g., centralized or decentralized); and third, the establishment of integrating mechanisms to coordinate the activities of subunits including cross functional teams and or pan-regional committees.

Controls are the metrics used to measure the performance of subunits and make judgments about how well managers are running those subunits. **Incentives** are the devices used to reward appropriate managerial behavior. Incentives are very closely tied to performance metrics. For example, the incentives of a manager in charge of a national operating subsidiary might be linked to the performance of that company. Specifically, she might receive a bonus if her subsidiary exceeds its performance targets.

Processes are the manner in which decisions are made and work is performed within the organization. Examples are the processes for formulating strategy, for deciding how to allocate resources within a firm, or for evaluating the performance of managers and giving feedback. Processes are conceptually distinct from the location of decision-making responsibilities within an organization, although both involve decisions. While the CEO might have ultimate responsibility for deciding what the strategy of the firm should be (i.e., the decision-making responsibility is centralized), the process he or she uses to make that decision might include the solicitation of ideas and criticism from lower-level managers.

Organizational culture is the norms and value systems that are shared among the employees of an organization. Just as societies have cultures (see Chapter 4 for details), so do organizations. Organizations are societies of individuals who come together to perform collective tasks. They have their own distinctive patterns of culture and subculture.[10] As we shall see, organizational culture can have a profound impact on how a firm performs. Finally, by **people** we mean not just the employees of the organization but also the strategy used to recruit, compensate, and retain those individuals and the type of people that they are in terms of their skills, values, and orientation (discussed in depth in Chapter 17).

As illustrated by the arrows in Figure 12.5, the various components of an organization's architecture are not independent of each other: Each component shapes, and is shaped by, other components of architecture. An obvious example is the strategy regarding people. This can be used proactively to hire individuals whose internal values are consistent with those that the firm wishes to emphasize in its organization culture. Thus, the people component of architecture can be used to reinforce (or not) the prevailing culture of the organization. If a firm is going to maximize its profitability, it must pay close attention to achieving internal consistency among the various components of its architecture, and the architecture must support the strategy and operations of the firm.

Organization Architecture
The totality of a firm's organization, including formal organizational structure, control systems and incentives, organizational culture, processes, and people.

Organizational Structure
The three-part structure of an organization, including its formal division into subunits such as product divisions, its location of decision-making responsibilities within that structure, and the establishment of integrating mechanisms to coordinate the activities of all subunits.

Controls
The metrics used to measure the performance of subunits and make judgments about how well managers are running those subunits.

Incentives
The devices used to reward appropriate managerial behavior.

Processes
The manner in which decisions are made and work is performed within any organization.

Organizational Culture
The values and norms shared among an organization's employees.

People
The employees of the organization, the strategy used to recruit, compensate, and retain those individuals, and the type of people that they are in terms of their skills, values, and orientation.

12.5 FIGURE
Organization Architecture

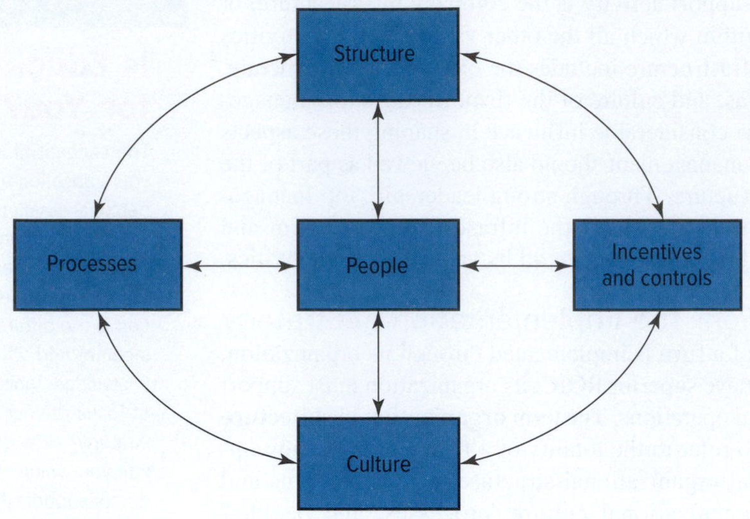

In Sum: Strategic Fit

In sum, as we have repeatedly stressed, for a firm to attain superior performance and earn a high return on capital, its strategy (as captured by its desired strategic position on the efficiency frontier) must make sense given market conditions (there must be sufficient demand to support that strategic choice). The operations of the firm must be configured in a way that supports the strategy of the firm, and the organization architecture of the firm must match the operations and strategy of the firm. In other words, as illustrated in Figure 12.6, market conditions, strategy, operations, and organization must all be consistent with each other, or fit each other, for superior performance to be attained.

Of course, the issue is more complex than illustrated in Figure 12.6. For example, the firm can influence market conditions through its choice of strategy—it can create demand by leveraging core skills to create new market opportunities. In addition, shifts in market conditions caused by new technologies, government action such as deregulation, demographics, or social trends can mean that the strategy of the firm no longer fits the market. In such circumstances, the firm must change its strategy, operations, and organization to fit the new reality—which can be an extraordinarily difficult challenge. And last but by no means least, international expansion adds another layer of complexity to the strategic challenges facing the firm. We shall now consider this.

test PREP

Use LearnSmart to help retain what you have learned. Access your instructor's Connect course to check out LearnSmart or go to learnsmartadvantage.com for help.

12.6 FIGURE
Strategic Fit

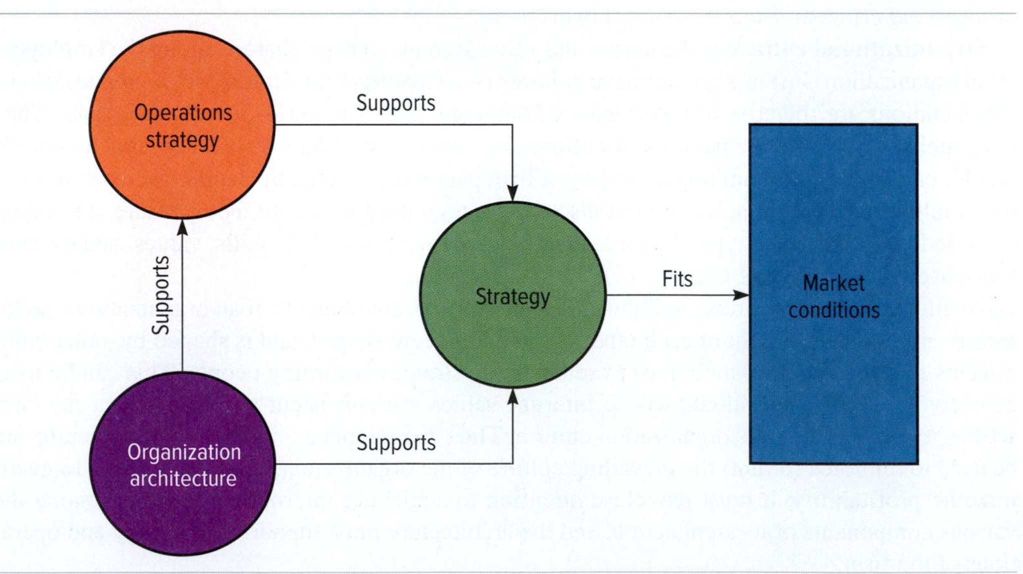

Global Expansion, Profitability, and Profit Growth

LO 12-2

Recognize how firms can profit by expanding globally.

Expanding globally allows firms to increase their profitability and rate of profit growth in ways not available to purely domestic enterprises.[11] Firms that operate internationally are able to:

1. Expand the market for their domestic product offerings by selling those products in international markets.
2. Realize location economies by dispersing individual value creation activities to those locations around the globe where they can be performed most efficiently and effectively.
3. Realize greater cost economies from experience effects by serving an expanded global market from a central location, thereby reducing the costs of value creation.
4. Earn a greater return by leveraging any valuable skills developed in foreign operations and transferring them to other entities within the firm's global network of operations.

As we will see, however, a firm's ability to increase its profitability and profit growth by pursuing these strategies is constrained by the need to customize its product offering, marketing strategy, and business strategy to differing national or regional conditions—that is, by the imperative of localization.

EXPANDING THE MARKET: LEVERAGING PRODUCTS AND COMPETENCIES

A company can increase its growth rate by taking goods or services developed at home and selling them internationally. Almost all multinationals started out doing just this. For example, Procter & Gamble developed most of its best-selling products (such as Pampers disposable diapers and Ivory soap) in the United States and subsequently sold them around the world. Likewise, although Microsoft developed its software in the United States, from its earliest days the company has always focused on selling that software in international markets. Automobile companies such as Volkswagen and Toyota also grew by developing products at home and then selling them in international markets. The returns from such a strategy are likely to be greater if indigenous competitors in the nations that a company enters lack comparable products. Thus, Toyota increased its profits by entering the large automobile markets of North America and Europe, offering products that differed from those offered by local rivals (Ford and GM) in their superior quality and reliability.

The success of many multinational companies that expand in this manner is based not just upon the goods or services that they sell in foreign nations but also upon the core competencies that underlie the development, production, and marketing of those goods or services. The term **core competence** refers to skills within the firm that competitors cannot easily match or imitate.[12] These skills may exist in any of the firm's value creation activities: production, marketing, R&D, human resources, logistics, general management, and so on. Such skills are typically expressed in product offerings that other firms find difficult to match or imitate. Core competencies are the bedrock of a firm's competitive advantage. They enable a firm to reduce the costs of value creation and/or to create perceived value in such a way that premium pricing is possible. For example, Toyota has a core competence in the production of cars. It is able to produce high-quality, well-designed cars at a lower delivered cost than any other firm in the world. The competencies that enable Toyota to do this seem to reside primarily in the firm's production and logistics functions.[13] Similarly, IKEA has a core competence in the design of stylish and affordable furniture that can be manufactured at a low cost and flat-packed, McDonald's has a core competence in managing fast-food operations (it seems to be one of the most skilled firms in the world in this industry), and Procter & Gamble (P&G) has a core competence in developing and marketing name-brand consumer products (it is one of the most skilled firms in the world in this business.

Core Competence

Firm skills that competitors cannot easily match or imitate.

Because core competencies are, by definition, the source of a firm's competitive advantage, the successful global expansion by manufacturing companies such as Toyota and P&G was based not just on leveraging products and selling them in foreign markets but also on the transfer of core competencies to foreign markets in which indigenous competitors lacked them. The same can be said of companies engaged in the service sectors of an economy, such as financial institutions, retailers like , restaurant chains, and hotels. Expanding the market for their services often means replicating their business model in foreign nations (albeit with some changes to account for local differences, which we will discuss in more detail shortly). Firms such as Starbucks and IKEA, for example, expanded rapidly outside of their home markets in the United States by taking the basic business model that they developed at home and using that as a blueprint for establishing international operations.

P&G's core competency in marketing is evidenced in this photo of Olay men's skin care products for sale in a Shanghai, China, supermarket.

Source: © Imaginechina/AP Images

LOCATION ECONOMIES Earlier chapters revealed that countries differ along a range of dimensions—including the economic, political, legal, and cultural—and that these differences can either raise or lower the costs of doing business in a country. The theory of international trade also teaches that due to differences in factor costs, certain countries have a comparative advantage in the production of certain products. Japan might excel in the production of automobiles and consumer electronics; the United States in the production of computer software, pharmaceuticals, biotechnology products, and financial services; Switzerland in the production of precision instruments and pharmaceuticals; South Korea in the production of semiconductors; and Vietnam in the production of apparel.[14]

For a firm that is trying to survive in a competitive global market, this implies that *trade barriers and transportation costs* permitting, the firm will benefit by basing each value creation activity it performs at that location where economic, political, and cultural conditions—including relative factor costs—are most conducive to the performance of that activity. Thus, if the best designers for a product live in France, a firm should base its design operations in France. If the most productive labor force for assembly operations is in Mexico, assembly operations should be based in Mexico. If the best marketers are in the United States, the marketing strategy should be formulated in the United States. And so on.

Location Economies

Cost advantages from performing a value creation activity at the optimal location for that activity.

Firms that pursue such a strategy can realize what we refer to as **location economies,** which are the economies that arise from performing a value creation activity in the optimal location for that activity, wherever in the world that might be (transportation costs and trade barriers permitting). Locating a value creation activity in the optimal location for that activity can have one of two effects. *It can lower the costs of value creation and help the firm to achieve a low-cost position, and/or it can enable a firm to differentiate its product offering from those of competitors.* In terms of Figure 12.2, it can lower C and/or increase V (which, in general, supports higher pricing), both of which boost the profitability of the enterprise.

For an example of how this works in an international business, consider Clear Vision, a manufacturer and distributor of eyewear. Started by David Glassman, the firm now generates annual gross revenues of more than $100 million. Not exactly small, but no corporate giant either, Clear Vision is a multinational firm with production facilities on three continents and customers around the world. Clear Vision began its move toward becoming a multinational when its sales were still less than $20 million. At the time, the U.S. dollar was very strong, and this made U.S.-based manufacturing expensive. Low-priced imports were taking an ever-larger share of the U.S. eyewear market, and Clear Vision realized it could not survive unless it also began to import. Initially, the firm bought from independent overseas manufacturers, primarily in Hong Kong. However, the firm became dissatisfied with these suppliers' product quality and delivery. As Clear Vision's volume of imports increased, Glassman decided the best way to guarantee quality and delivery was to set up Clear Vision's own manufacturing operation overseas. Accordingly, Clear Vision found a Chinese partner, and together they opened a manufacturing facility in Hong Kong, with Clear Vision being the majority shareholder.

The choice of the Hong Kong location was influenced by its combination of low labor costs, a skilled workforce, and tax breaks given by the Hong Kong government. The firm's objective at this point was to lower production costs by locating value creation activities at an appropriate location. After a few years, however, the increasing industrialization of Hong Kong and a growing labor shortage had pushed up wage rates to the extent that it was no longer a low-cost location. In response, Glassman and his Chinese partner moved part of their manufacturing to a plant in mainland China to take advantage of the lower wage rates there. Again, the goal was to lower production costs. The parts for eyewear frames manufactured at this plant are shipped to the

Hong Kong factory for final assembly and then distributed to markets in North and South America. The Hong Kong factory employs 80 people and the China plant between 300 and 400.

At the same time, Clear Vision was looking for opportunities to invest in foreign eyewear firms with reputations for fashionable design and high quality. Its objective was not to reduce production costs but to launch a line of high-quality, differentiated, "designer" eyewear. Clear Vision did not have the design capability in-house to support such a line, but Glassman knew that certain foreign manufacturers did. As a result, Clear Vision invested in factories in Japan, France, and Italy, holding a minority shareholding in each case. These factories now supply eyewear for Clear Vision's Status Eye division, which markets high-priced designer eyewear.[15]

Thus, to deal with a threat from foreign competition, Clear Vision adopted a strategy intended to lower its cost structure (lower *C*): shifting its production from a high-cost location, the United States, to a low-cost location, first Hong Kong and later China. Then Clear Vision adopted a strategy intended to increase the perceived value of its product (increase *V*) so it could charge a premium price (*P*). Reasoning that premium pricing in eyewear depended on superior design, its strategy involved investing capital in French, Italian, and Japanese factories that had reputations for superior design. In sum, Clear Vision's strategies included some actions intended to reduce its costs of creating value and other actions intended to add perceived value to its product through differentiation. The overall goal was to increase the value created by Clear Vision and thus the profitability of the enterprise. To the extent that these strategies were successful, the firm should have attained a higher profit margin and greater profitability than if it had remained a U.S.-based manufacturer of eyewear.

Global Web

When different stages of value chain are dispersed to those locations around the globe where value added is maximized or where costs of value creation are minimized.

Creating a Global Web

Generalizing from the Clear Vision example, one result of this kind of thinking is the creation of a **global web** of value creation activities, with different stages of the value chain being dispersed to those locations around the globe where perceived value is maximized or where the costs of value creation are minimized.[16] Consider Lenovo's ThinkPad laptop computers (Lenovo is the Chinese computer company that purchased IBM's personal computer operations in 2005).[17] This product is designed in the United States by engineers because Lenovo believes that the United States is the best location in the world to do the basic design work. The case, keyboard, and hard drive are made in Thailand; the display screen and memory in South Korea; the built-in wireless card in Malaysia; and the microprocessor in the United States. In each case, these components are manufactured and sourced from the optimal location given current factor costs. These components are then shipped to an assembly operation in China, where the product is assembled before being shipped to the United States for final sale. Lenovo assembles the ThinkPad in Mexico because managers have calculated that due to low labor costs, the costs of assembly can be minimized there. The marketing and sales strategy for North America is developed by Lenovo personnel in the United States, primarily because managers believe that due to their knowledge of the local marketplace, U.S. personnel add more value to the product through their marketing efforts than personnel based elsewhere.

In theory, a firm that realizes location economies by dispersing each of its value creation activities to its optimal location should have a competitive advantage vis-à-vis a firm that bases all of its value creation activities at a single location. It should be able to better differentiate its product offering (thereby raising perceived value, *V*) and lower its cost structure (*C*) than its single-location competitor. In a world where competitive pressures are increasing, such a strategy may become an imperative for survival.

Some Caveats

Introducing transportation costs and trade barriers complicates this picture. Due to favorable factor endowments, New Zealand may have a comparative advantage for automobile assembly operations, but high transportation costs would make it an uneconomical location from which to serve global markets. Another caveat concerns the importance of assessing political and economic risks when making location decisions. Even if a country looks very attractive as a production location when measured against all the standard criteria, if its government is unstable or totalitarian, the firm might be advised not to base production there. (Political risk is discussed in Chapter 3.) Similarly, if the government appears to be pursuing inappropriate economic policies that could lead to foreign exchange risk, that might be another reason for not basing production in that location, even if other factors look favorable.

12.7 FIGURE

The Experience Curve

Source: C. W. L. Hill and G. T. M. Hult, *International Business: Competing in the Global Marketplace* (New York: McGraw-Hill Education, 2017).

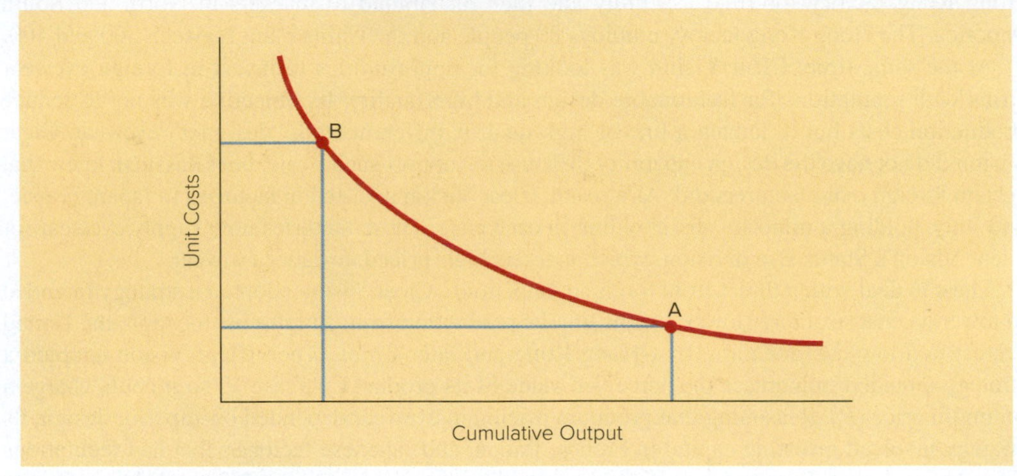

Experience Curve

Systematic production cost reductions that occur over the life of a product.

EXPERIENCE EFFECTS

The **experience curve** refers to systematic reductions in production costs that have been observed to occur over the life of a product.[18] A number of studies have observed that a product's production costs decline by some quantity about each time *cumulative* output doubles. The relationship was first observed in the aircraft industry, where each time cumulative output of airframes was doubled, unit costs typically declined to 80 percent of their previous level.[19] Thus, production cost for the fourth airframe would be 80 percent of production cost for the second airframe, the eighth airframe's production costs 80 percent of the fourth's, the sixteenth's 80 percent of the eighth's, and so on. Figure 12.7 illustrates this experience curve relationship between unit production costs and *cumulative* output (the relationship is for *cumulative* output over time and *not* output in any one period, such as a year). Two things explain this: learning effects and economies of scale.

Learning Effects

Cost savings from learning by doing.

Learning Effects

Learning effects refer to cost savings that come from learning by doing. Labor, for example, learns by repetition how to carry out a task, such as assembling airframes, most efficiently. Labor productivity increases over time as individuals learn the most efficient ways to perform particular tasks. Equally important in new production facilities, management typically learns how to manage the new operation more efficiently over time. Hence, production costs decline due to increasing labor productivity and management efficiency, which increases the firm's profitability.

Learning effects tend to be more significant when a technologically complex task is repeated because there is more that can be learned about the task. Thus, learning effects will be more significant in an assembly process involving 1,000 complex steps than in one of only 100 simple steps. No matter how complex the task, however, learning effects typically disappear after a while. It has been suggested that they are important only during the start-up period of a new process and that they cease after two or three years.[20] Any decline in the experience curve after such a point is due to economies of scale.

Economies of Scale

Cost advantages associated with large-scale production.

Economies of Scale

Economies of scale refer to the reductions in unit cost achieved by producing a large volume of a product. Attaining economies of scale lowers a firm's unit costs and increases its profitability. Economies of scale have a number of sources. One is the ability to spread fixed costs over a large volume.[21] Fixed costs are the costs required to set up a production facility, develop a new product, and the like. They can be substantial. For example, the fixed cost of establishing a new production line to manufacture semiconductor chips now exceeds $5 billion. Similarly, according to one estimate, developing a new drug and bringing it to market costs about $800 million and takes about 12 years.[22] The only way to recoup such high fixed costs may be to sell the product worldwide, which reduces average unit costs by spreading fixed costs over a larger volume. The more rapidly that cumulative sales volume is built up, the more rapidly fixed costs can be amortized over a large production volume and the more rapidly unit costs will fall.

Second, a firm may not be able to attain an efficient scale of production unless it serves global markets. In the automobile industry, for example, an efficiently scaled factory is one designed to produce about 200,000 units a year. Automobile firms would prefer to produce a single model from each factory because this eliminates the costs associated with switching production from one model to another. If domestic demand for a particular model is only 100,000 units a year, the inability to attain a 200,000-unit output will drive up average unit costs. By serving international markets as well, however, the firm may be able to push production volume up to 200,000 units a year, thereby reaping greater scale economies, lowering unit costs, and boosting profitability. By serving domestic and international markets from its production facilities, a firm may be able to utilize those facilities more intensively. For example, if Intel sold microprocessors only in the United States, it might be able to keep its factories open for only one shift five days a week. By serving international markets from the same factories, Intel can utilize its productive assets more intensively, which translates into higher capital productivity and greater profitability.

Finally, as global sales increase the size of the enterprise, its bargaining power with suppliers increases as well, which may allow it to attain economies of scale in purchasing, bargaining down the cost of key inputs and boosting profitability that way. For example, Walmart has used its enormous sales volume as a lever to bargain down the price it pays suppliers for merchandise sold through its stores.

Strategic Significance

The strategic significance of the experience curve is clear. Moving down the experience curve allows a firm to reduce its cost of creating value (to lower *C* in Figure 12.2) and increase its profitability. The firm that moves down the experience curve most rapidly will have a cost advantage vis-á-vis its competitors. Firm A in Figure 12.7, because it is farther down the experience curve, has a clear cost advantage over firm B.

Many of the underlying sources of experience-based cost economies are plant-based. This is true for most learning effects as well as for the economies of scale derived by spreading the fixed costs of building productive capacity over a large output, attaining an efficient scale of output, and utilizing a plant more intensively. Thus, one key to progressing downward on the experience curve as rapidly as possible is to increase the volume produced by a single plant as rapidly as possible. Because global markets are larger than domestic markets, a firm that serves a global market from a single location is likely to build accumulated volume more quickly than a firm that serves only its home market or that serves multiple markets from multiple production locations. Thus, serving a global market from a single location is consistent with moving down the experience curve and establishing a low-cost position. In addition, to get down the experience curve rapidly, a firm may need to price and market aggressively so demand will expand rapidly. It will also need to build sufficient production capacity for serving a global market. Also, the cost advantages of serving the world market from a single location will be even more significant if that location is the optimal one for performing the particular value creation activity.

Once a firm has established a low-cost position, it can act as a barrier to new competition. Specifically, an established firm that is well down the experience curve, such as firm A in Figure 12.7, can price so that it is still making a profit while new entrants, which are farther up the curve, are suffering losses. Intel is one of the masters of this kind of strategy. The costs of building a state-of-the-art facility to manufacture microprocessors are so large (now around $5 billion) that to make this investment pay Intel *must* pursue experience curve effects, serving world markets from a limited number of plants to maximize the cost economies that derive from scale and learning effects.

LEVERAGING SUBSIDIARY SKILLS

Implicit in our earlier discussion of core competencies is the idea that valuable skills are developed first at home and then transferred to foreign operations. However, for more mature multinationals that have already established a network of subsidiary operations in foreign markets, the development of valuable skills can just as well occur in foreign subsidiaries.[23] Skills can be created anywhere within a multinational's global network of operations, wherever people have the opportunity and incentive to try new ways of doing things. The creation of skills that help to lower the costs of production or to enhance perceived value and support higher product pricing is not the monopoly of the corporate center.

Leveraging the skills created within subsidiaries and applying them to other operations within the firm's global network may create value. McDonald's is increasingly finding that its foreign franchisees are a source of valuable new ideas. Faced with slow growth in France, its local franchisees began to experiment not only with the menu but also with the layout and theme of restaurants. Gone are the ubiquitous golden arches; gone too are many of the utilitarian chairs and tables and other plastic features of the fast-food giant. Many McDonald's restaurants in France now have hardwood floors, exposed brick walls, and even armchairs. The menu, too, has been changed to include premier sandwiches, such as chicken on focaccia bread, priced some 30 percent higher than the average hamburger. In France at least, the strategy seems to be working. Following the change, increases in same-store sales rose from 1 percent annually to 3.4 percent, and France is now the second-largest national market for McDonald's. Impressed with the impact, McDonald's executives are considering similar changes at other McDonald's restaurants in markets where same-store sales growth is sluggish, including the United States.[24]

For the managers of the multinational enterprise, this phenomenon creates important new challenges. First, they must have the humility to recognize that valuable skills that lead to competencies can arise anywhere within the firm's global network, not just at the corporate center. Second, they must establish an incentive system that encourages local employees to acquire new skills. This is not as easy as it sounds. Creating new skills involves a degree of risk. Not all new skills add value. For every valuable idea created by a McDonald's subsidiary in a foreign country, there may be several failures. The management of the multinational must install incentives that encourage employees to take the necessary risks. The company must reward people for successes and not sanction them unnecessarily for taking risks that did not pan out. Third, managers must have a process for identifying when valuable new skills have been created in a subsidiary. And finally, they need to act as facilitators, helping to transfer valuable skills within the firm.

PROFITABILITY AND PROFIT GROWTH SUMMARY We have seen how firms that expand globally can increase their profitability and profit growth by entering new markets where indigenous competitors lack similar competencies, by lowering costs and adding value to their product offering through the attainment of location economies, by exploiting experience curve effects, and by transferring valuable skills among their global network of subsidiaries. For completeness, it should be noted that strategies that increase profitability may also expand a firm's business and thus enable it to attain a higher rate of profit growth. For example, by simultaneously realizing location economies and experience effects, a firm may be able to produce a more highly valued product at a lower unit cost, thereby boosting profitability. The increase in the perceived value of the product may also attract more customers, thereby growing revenues and profits as well. Furthermore, rather than raising prices to reflect the higher perceived value of the product, the firm's managers may elect to hold prices low in order to increase global market share and attain greater scale economies (in other words, they may elect to offer consumers better "value for money"). Such a strategy could increase the firm's rate of profit growth even further, because consumers will be attracted by prices that are low relative to value. The strategy might also increase profitability if the scale economies that result from market share gains are substantial. In sum, managers need to keep in mind the complex relationship between profitability and profit growth when making strategic decisions about pricing.

Use LearnSmart to help retain what you have learned. Access your instructor's Connect course to check out LearnSmart or go to learnsmartadvantage.com for help.

LO 12-3

Understand how pressures for cost reductions and pressures for local responsiveness influence strategic choice.

Cost Pressures and Pressures for Local Responsiveness

Firms that compete in the global marketplace typically face two types of competitive pressure that affect their ability to realize location economies and experience effects and to leverage products and transfer competencies and skills within the enterprise. They face *pressures for cost reductions* and *pressures to be locally responsive* (see Figure 12.8).[25] These competitive pressures place conflicting demands on a firm. Responding to pressures for cost reductions requires that a firm try to minimize its unit costs. But responding to pressures to be locally responsive requires that a firm differentiate its product offering and marketing strategy from country to country (or in some cases, region to region) in an effort to accommodate the diverse demands

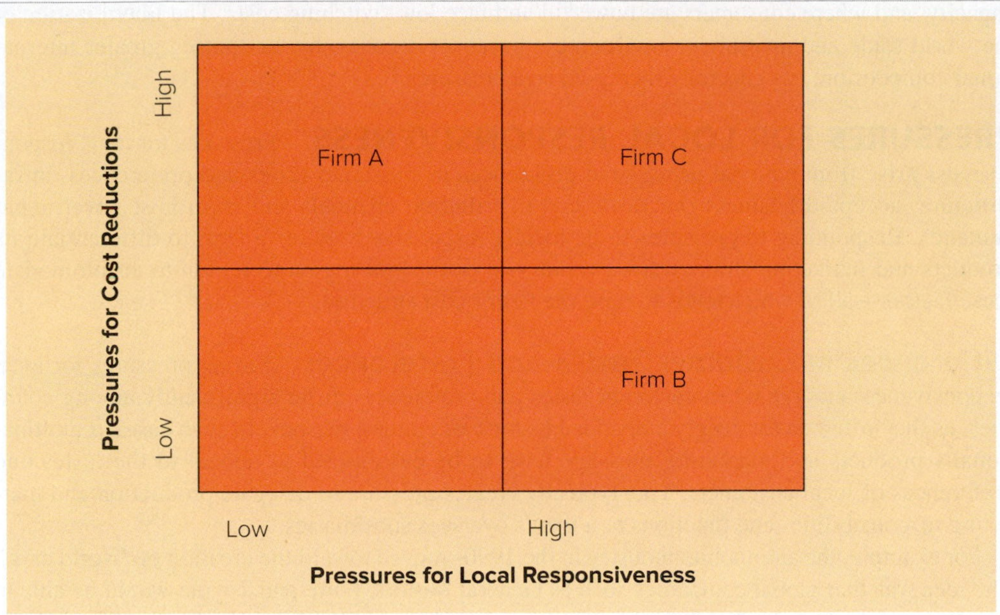

12.8 FIGURE

Pressures for Cost Reductions and Local Responsiveness

Source: C. W. L. Hill and G. T. M. Hult, *International Business: Competing in the Global Marketplace* (New York: McGraw-Hill Education, 2017).

arising from national (or regional) differences in consumer tastes and preferences, business practices, distribution channels, competitive conditions, and government policies. Because differentiation across countries can involve significant duplication and a lack of product standardization, it may raise costs.

While some enterprises, such as firm A in Figure 12.8, face high pressures for cost reductions and low pressures for local responsiveness, and others, such as firm B, face low pressures for cost reductions and high pressures for local responsiveness, many companies are in the position of firm C. They face high pressures for *both* cost reductions and local responsiveness. Dealing with these conflicting and contradictory pressures is a difficult strategic challenge, primarily because being locally responsive tends to raise costs.

 **test PREP**

Use LearnSmart to help retain what you have learned. Access your instructor's Connect course to check out LearnSmart or go to learnsmartadvantage.com for help.

PRESSURES FOR COST REDUCTIONS

In competitive global markets, international businesses often face pressures for cost reductions. Responding to pressures for cost reduction requires a firm to try to lower the costs of value creation. A manufacturer, for example, might mass-produce a standardized product at the optimal locations in the world, wherever that might be, to realize economies of scale, learning effects, and location economies. Alternatively, a firm might outsource certain functions to low-cost foreign suppliers in an attempt to reduce costs. Thus, many computer companies have outsourced their telephone-based customer service functions to India, where qualified technicians who speak English can be hired for a lower wage rate than in the United States. In the same manner, a retailer such as Walmart might push its suppliers (manufacturers) to do the same. (The pressure that Walmart has placed on its suppliers to reduce prices has been cited as a major cause of the trend among North American manufacturers to shift production to China.[26]) A service business such as a bank might respond to cost pressures by moving some back-office functions, such as information processing, to developing nations where wage rates are lower.

Pressures for cost reduction can be particularly intense in industries producing commodity-type products where meaningful differentiation on nonprice factors is difficult and price is the main competitive weapon. This tends to be the case for products that serve universal needs. **Universal needs** exist when the tastes and preferences of consumers in different nations or regions are similar, if not identical. This is the case for conventional commodity products such as bulk chemicals, petroleum, steel, sugar, and the like. It also tends to be the case for many industrial and consumer products—for example, smartphones, semiconductor chips, personal computers, and liquid crystal display screens. Pressures for cost reductions are also intense in industries where major competitors are based in low-cost locations, where there is persistent excess

Universal Needs

Needs that are the same all over the world, such as steel, bulk chemicals, and industrial electronics.

capacity, and where consumers are powerful and face low switching costs. The liberalization of the world trade and investment environment in recent decades, by facilitating greater international competition, has generally increased cost pressures.[27]

PRESSURES FOR LOCAL RESPONSIVENESS

Pressures for local responsiveness arise from national or regional differences in consumer tastes and preferences, infrastructure, accepted business practices, and distribution channels and from host-government demands. Responding to pressures to be locally responsive requires a firm to differentiate its products and marketing strategy from country to country or region to region to accommodate these factors—all of which tends to raise the firm's cost structure.

Differences in Customer Tastes and Preferences

Strong pressures for local responsiveness emerge when customer tastes and preferences differ significantly among countries, as they often do for deeply embedded historic or cultural reasons. In such cases, a multinational's products and marketing message have to be customized to appeal to the tastes and preferences of local customers. This typically creates pressure to delegate production and marketing responsibilities and functions to a firm's overseas subsidiaries.

For example, the automobile industry in the 1990s moved toward the creation of "world cars." The idea was that global companies such as General Motors, Ford, and Toyota would be able to sell the same basic vehicle the world over, sourcing it from centralized production locations. If successful, the strategy would have enabled automobile companies to reap significant gains from global scale economies. However, this strategy frequently ran aground upon the hard rocks of consumer reality. Consumers in different automobile markets seem to have different tastes and preferences, and they demand different types of vehicles. North American consumers show a strong demand for pickup trucks. This is particularly true in the South and West of the United States, where many families have a pickup truck as a second or third car. But in European countries, pickup trucks are seen purely as utility vehicles and are purchased primarily by firms rather than individuals. As a consequence, the product mix and marketing message needs to be tailored to consider the different nature of demand in North America and Europe.

Some have argued that customer demands for local customization are on the decline worldwide.[28] According to this argument, modern communications and transport technologies have created the conditions for a convergence of the tastes and preferences of consumers from different nations. The result is the emergence of enormous global markets for standardized consumer products. The worldwide acceptance of McDonald's hamburgers, Coca-Cola, Gap clothes, Apple iPhones, and Microsoft's Xbox—all of which are sold globally as standardized products—are often cited as evidence of the increasing homogeneity of the global marketplace.

However, this argument may not hold in many consumer goods markets. Significant differences in consumer tastes and preferences still exist across nations, regions, and cultures. Managers in international businesses do not yet have the luxury of being able to ignore these differences, and they may not for a long time to come. For an example of a company that has discovered how important pressures for local responsiveness can still be, read the accompanying Management Focus on MTV Networks.

Differences in Infrastructure and Traditional Practices

Pressures for local responsiveness arise from differences in infrastructure or traditional practices among countries, creating a need to customize products accordingly. Fulfilling this need may require the delegation of manufacturing and production functions to foreign subsidiaries. For example, in North America, consumer electrical systems are based on 110 volts, whereas in some European countries, 240-volt systems are standard. Thus, domestic electrical appliances have to be customized for this difference in infrastructure. Traditional practices also often vary across nations. For example, in Britain, people drive on the left-hand side of the road, creating a demand for right-hand-drive cars, whereas in France (and the rest of Europe), people drive on the right-hand side of the road and therefore want left-hand-drive cars. Obviously, automobiles have to be customized to accommodate this difference in traditional practice.

Although many national and regional differences in infrastructure are rooted in history, some are quite recent. For example, in the wireless telecommunications industry, different technical

management FOCUS

Local Responsiveness at MTV Networks

MTV Networks has become a symbol of globalization. Established in 1981, the U.S.-based TV network has been expanding outside of its North American base since 1987, when it opened MTV Europe. Today, MTV Networks figures that every second of every day, more than 2 million people are watching MTV around the world, the majority outside the United States. Despite its international success, MTV's global expansion got off to a weak start. In the 1980s, when the main programming fare was still music videos, it piped a single feed across Europe almost entirely composed of American programming with English-speaking veejays. Naively, the network's U.S. managers thought Europeans would flock to the American programming. But while viewers in Europe shared a common interest in a handful of global superstars, their tastes turned out to be surprisingly local. After losing share to local competitors, who focused more on local tastes, MTV changed its strategy in the 1990s. It broke its service into "feeds" aimed at national or regional markets. While MTV Networks exercises creative control over these different feeds and while all the channels have the same familiar frenetic look and feel of MTV in the United States, a significant share of the programming and content is now local.

Today, an increasing share of programming is local in conception. Although a lot of programming ideas still originate in the United States, with staples such as *The Real World* having equivalents in different countries, an increasing share of programming is local in conception. In Italy, *MTV Kitchen* combines cooking with a music countdown. *Erotica* airs in Brazil and features a panel of youths discussing sex. The Indian channel produces 21 homegrown shows hosted by local veejays who speak "Hinglish," a city-bred version of Hindi and English. Many feeds still feature music videos by locally popular performers. This localization push reaped big benefits for MTV, allowing the network to capture viewers back from local imitators.

Sources: M. Gunther, "MTV's Passage to India," *Fortune,* August 9, 2004, pp. 117–22; B. Pulley and A. Tanzer, "Sumner's Gemstone," *Forbes,* February 21, 2000, pp. 107–11; K. Hoffman, "Youth TV's Old Hand Prepares for the Digital Challenge," *Financial Times,* February 18, 2000, p. 8; Summer M. Redstone, Presentation delivered to Salomon Smith Barney, 11th Annual Global Entertainment Media, Telecommunications Conference, Scottsdale, AZ, January 8, 2001. *www.viacom.com; Viacom 10K Statement,* 2005.

standards exist in different parts of the world. A technical standard known as GSM is common in Europe, and an alternative standard, CDMA, is more common in the United States and parts of Asia. Equipment designed for GSM will not work on a CDMA network and vice versa. Thus, companies in this industry—such as Apple, Nokia, Motorola, Samsung, and Ericsson—that manufacture smartphones or infrastructure such as switches need to customize their product offering according to the technical standard prevailing in a given country or region.

Differences in Distribution Channels A firm's marketing strategies may have to be responsive to differences in distribution channels among countries, which may necessitate the delegation of marketing functions to national subsidiaries. In the pharmaceutical industry, for example, the British and Japanese distribution systems are radically different from the U.S. system. British and Japanese doctors will not accept or respond favorably to a U.S.-style high-pressure sales force. Thus, pharmaceutical companies have to adopt different marketing practices in Britain and Japan compared with the United States—soft sell versus hard sell. Similarly, Poland, Brazil, and Russia all have similar per capita income on a purchasing power parity basis, but there are big differences in distribution systems across the three countries. In Brazil, supermarkets account for 36 percent of food retailing, in Poland for 18 percent, and in Russia for less than 1 percent.[29] These differences in channels require that companies adapt their own distribution and sales strategies.

Host-Government Demands Economic and political demands imposed by host-country governments may require local responsiveness. For example, pharmaceutical companies are subject to local clinical testing, registration procedures, and pricing restrictions—all of which make it necessary that the manufacturing and marketing of a drug should meet local requirements. Because governments and government agencies control a significant proportion of the health care budget in most countries, they are in a powerful position to demand a high level of local responsiveness.

More generally, threats of protectionism, economic nationalism, and local content rules (which require that a certain percentage of a product should be manufactured locally) dictate that international businesses manufacture locally. For example, consider Bombardier, the Canadian-based manufacturer of railcars, aircraft, jet boats, and snowmobiles. Bombardier has 12 railcar factories across Europe. Critics of the company argue that the resulting duplication of manufacturing facilities leads to high costs and helps explain why Bombardier makes lower profit margins on its railcar operations than on its other business lines. In reply, managers at Bombardier argue that in Europe, informal rules with regard to local content favor people who use local workers. To sell railcars in Germany, they claim, you must manufacture in Germany. The same goes for Belgium, Austria, and France. To try to address its cost structure in Europe, Bombardier has centralized its engineering and purchasing functions, but it has no plans to centralize manufacturing.[30]

The Rise of Regionalism

Traditionally, we have tended to think of pressures for local responsiveness as being derived from *national* differences in tastes and preferences, infrastructure, and the like. While this is still often the case, there is also a tendency toward the convergence of tastes, preferences, infrastructure, distribution channels, and host-government demands within a broader *region* that is composed of two or more nations.[31] We tend to see this when there are strong pressures for convergence due to, for example, a shared history and culture or the establishment of a trading block where there are deliberate attempts to harmonize trade policies, infrastructure, regulations, and the like.

The most obvious example of a region is the European Union and particularly the euro zone countries within that trade block, where there are institutional forces that are pushing toward convergence (see Chapter 9 for details). The creation of a single EU market—with a single currency, common business regulations, standard infrastructure, and so on—cannot help but result in the reduction of certain national differences among countries within the EU and the creation of one regional rather than several national markets. Indeed, at the economic level at least, that is the explicit intent of the EU.

Another example of regional convergence is North America, which includes the United States, Canada, and, to some extent in some product markets, Mexico. Canada and the United States share history, language, and much of their culture, and both are members of NAFTA. Mexico is clearly different in many regards, but its proximity to the United States, along with its membership in NAFTA, implies that for some product markets (e.g., automobiles), it might be reasonable to consider Mexico as part of a relatively homogenous regional market. We might also talk about the Latin America region, where shared Spanish history, cultural heritage, and language (with the exception of Brazil, which was colonized by the Portuguese) mean that national differences are somewhat moderated. It can also be argued that greater China, which includes the city-states of Honk Kong and Singapore along with Taiwan, is a coherent region, as is much of the Middle East, where a strong Arab culture and shared history may limit national differences. Similarly, Russia and some of the former states of the Soviet Union, such as Belarus and Ukraine, might be considered part of a larger regional market, at least for some products.

Taking a regional perspective is important because it may suggest that localization at the regional rather than the national level is the appropriate strategic response. For example, rather than produce cars for each national market within the Europe or North America, it makes far more sense for car manufacturers to build cars for the European or North American regions. The ability to standardize product offering within a region allows for the attainment of greater scale economies, and hence lower costs, than if each nation had to have its own offering. At the same time, this perspective should not be pushed too far. There are still deep and profound cultural differences among the France, Germany, and Italy—all members of the EU—that may in turn require some degree of local customization at the *national* level. Managers must thus make a judgment call about the appropriate level of aggregation, given (1) the product market they are looking at and (2) the nature of national differences and trends for regional convergence. What might make sense for automobiles, for example, might not be appropriate for packaged food products.

Use LearnSmart to help retain what you have learned. Access your instructor's Connect course to check out LearnSmart or go to learnsmartadvantage.com for help.

Identify the different strategies for competing globally and their pros and cons.

Choosing a Strategy

Pressures for local responsiveness imply that it may not be possible for a firm to realize the full benefits from economies of scale, learning effects, and location economies. It may not be possible to serve the global marketplace from a single low-cost location, producing a globally standardized product and marketing it worldwide to attain the cost reductions associated with experience effects. The need to customize the product offering to local conditions, whether national or

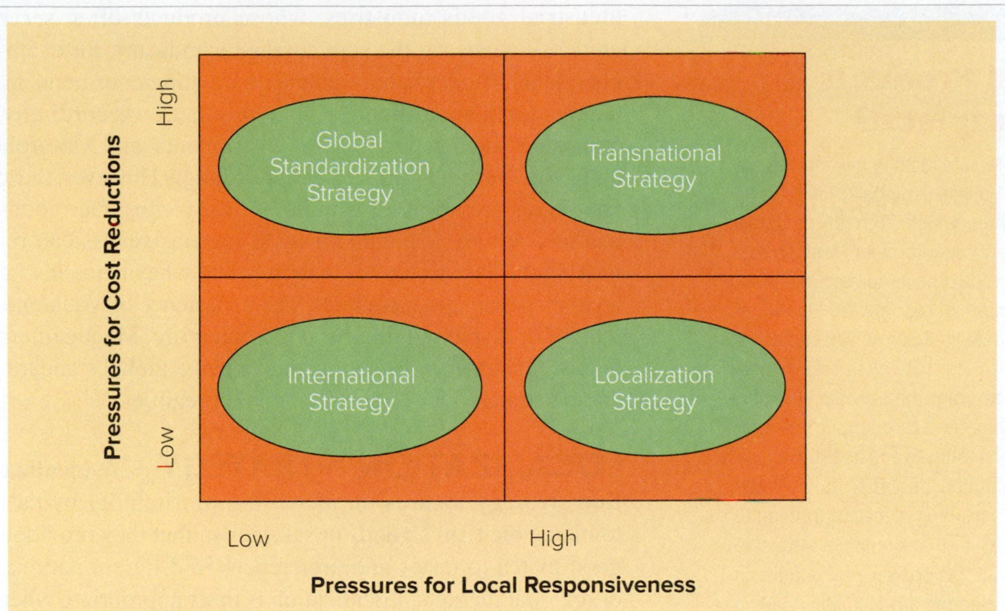

12.9 FIGURE

Four Basic Strategies

Source: C. W. L. Hill and G. T. M. Hult, *International Business: Competing in the Global Marketplace* (New York: McGraw-Hill Education, 2017).

regional, may work against the implementation of such a strategy. For example, as noted, automobile firms have found that Japanese, American, and European consumers demand different kinds of cars, and this necessitates producing products that are customized for regional markets. In response, firms such as Honda, Ford, and Toyota are pursuing a strategy of establishing top-to-bottom design and production facilities in each of these regions so that they can better serve local demands. Although such customization brings benefits, it also limits the ability of a firm to realize significant scale economies and location economies.

In addition, pressures for local responsiveness imply that it may not be possible to leverage skills and products associated with a firm's core competencies wholesale from one nation or region to another. Concessions often have to be made to local conditions. Despite being depicted as "poster child" for the proliferation of standardized global products, even McDonald's has found that it has to customize its product offerings (i.e., its menu) to account for national differences in tastes and preferences.

How do differences in the strength of pressures for cost reductions versus those for local responsiveness affect a firm's choice of strategy? Firms typically choose among four main strategic postures when competing internationally. These can be characterized as a global standardization strategy, a localization strategy, a transnational strategy, and an international strategy.[32] The appropriateness of each strategy varies, given the extent of pressures for cost reductions and local responsiveness. Figure 12.9 illustrates the conditions under which each of these strategies is most appropriate.

GLOBAL STANDARDIZATION STRATEGY

Firms that pursue a **global standardization strategy** focus on increasing profitability and profit growth by reaping the cost reductions that come from economies of scale, learning effects, and location economies; that is, their strategic goal is to pursue a low-cost strategy on a global scale. The production, marketing, and R&D activities of firms pursuing a global standardization strategy are concentrated in a few favorable locations. Firms pursuing a global standardization strategy try not to customize their product offering and marketing strategy to local conditions because customization involves shorter production runs and the duplication of functions, which tends to raise costs. Instead, they prefer to market a standardized product worldwide so that they can reap the maximum benefits from economies of scale and learning effects. They also tend to use their cost advantage to support aggressive pricing in world markets.

Global Standardization Strategy
A firm focuses on increasing profitability and profit growth by reaping the cost reductions that come from economies of scale, learning effects, and location economies.

This strategy makes most sense when there are strong pressures for cost reductions and demands for local responsiveness are minimal. Increasingly, these conditions prevail in many

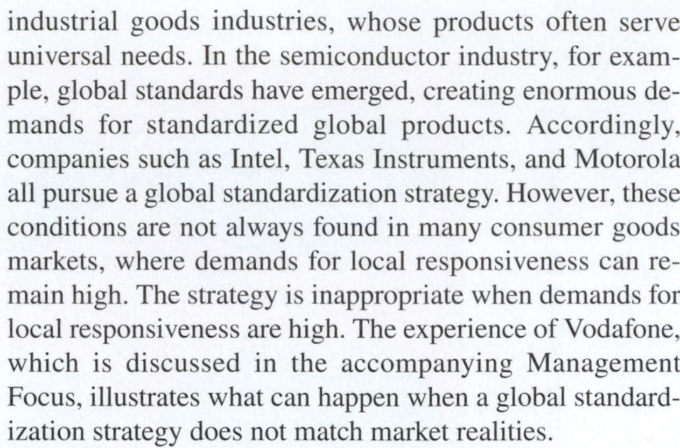

industrial goods industries, whose products often serve universal needs. In the semiconductor industry, for example, global standards have emerged, creating enormous demands for standardized global products. Accordingly, companies such as Intel, Texas Instruments, and Motorola all pursue a global standardization strategy. However, these conditions are not always found in many consumer goods markets, where demands for local responsiveness can remain high. The strategy is inappropriate when demands for local responsiveness are high. The experience of Vodafone, which is discussed in the accompanying Management Focus, illustrates what can happen when a global standardization strategy does not match market realities.

LOCALIZATION STRATEGY A **localization strategy** focuses on increasing profitability by customizing the firm's goods or services so that they provide a good match to tastes and preferences in different national or regional markets. Localization is most appropriate when there are substantial differences across nations or regions with regard to consumer tastes and preferences and where cost pressures are not too intense. By customizing the product offering to local demands, the firm increases the value of that product in the local market. On the downside, because it involves some duplication of functions and smaller production runs, customization limits the ability of the firm to capture the cost reductions associated with mass-producing a standardized product for global consumption. The strategy may make sense, however, if the added value associated with local customization supports higher pricing, which enables the firm to recoup its higher

More Customized Products in the Global Marketplace?

The Coca-Cola Company's (TCCC) Minute Maid Pulpy became the cola giant's 14th brand to reach $1 billion in global retail sales (in 2011). As opposed to cola carbonates, which often rely on global brand recognition and cross-generational formulas for success, Minute Maid Pulpy has relied on product development and innovations inspired by local flavors and textures. Toward the end of 2004, Minute Maid released Minute Maid Pulpy, which contained less than 24 percent actual fruit juice, but TCCC was able to retail the product at a much lower price point than products with a higher content of fruit juice. In China and throughout the Asia-Pacific region, consumer notions of freshness and health are connected much more to the consumption of actual fruit. Minute Maid Pulpy acknowledged this by including pieces of fruit in the drink, thereby creating a thicker texture that would not appeal to most North American consumers but has proven very popular in this region of the world. In customizing the product, Minute Maid Pulpy went from the 10th most popular fruit/vegetable juice brand in China in 2004 to first by the time it had achieved $1 billion in total sales in 2011. But isn't the world becoming more globalized? Do we still need large multinational corporations customizing their products to local markets?

Source: http://blog.euromonitor.com.

Localization Strategy
Increasing profitability by customizing the firm's goods and services so that they provide a good match to tastes and preferences in different national markets.

management FOCUS

Vodafone in Japan

In 2002, Vodafone Group of the United Kingdom, the world's largest provider of wireless telephone service, made a big splash by paying $14 billion to acquire J-Phone, the number-three player in Japan's fast-growing market for wireless communications services. J-Phone was considered a hot property, having just launched Japan's first cell phones that were embedded with digital cameras, winning over large numbers of young people who wanted to e-mail photos to their friends. Four years later, after losing market share to local competitors, Vodafone sold J-Phone and took an $8.6 billion charge against earnings related to the sale. What went wrong?

According to analysts, Vodafone's mistake was to focus too much on building a global brand and not enough on local market conditions in Japan. In the early 2000s, Vodafone's vision was to offer consumers in different countries the same technology so that they could take their phones with them when they traveled across international borders. The problem, however, was that Japan's most active cell phone users—many of them young people who don't regularly travel abroad—care far less about this capability than about game playing and other features that are embedded in their cell phones.

Vodafone's emphasis on global services meant that it delayed its launch in Japan of phones that use 3G technology, which allowed users to do things such as watch video clips and teleconference on their cell phones. The company, in line with its global branding ambitions, had decided to launch 3G cell phones that worked both inside and outside Japan. The delay was costly. Its Japanese competitors launched 3G phones a year ahead of Vodafone. Although these phones only worked in Japan, they rapidly gained share as consumers adopted these leading-edge devices. When Vodafone did finally introduce a 3G phone, design problems associated with making a phone that worked globally meant that the supply of phones was limited, and the launch fizzled despite strong product reviews, simply because consumers could not get the phones.

Sources: C. Bryan-Low, "Vodafone's Global Ambitions Got Hung Up in Japan," *The Wall Street Journal,* March 18, 2006, p. A1; G. Parket, "Going Global Can Hit Snags Vodafone Finds," *The Wall Street Journal,* June 16, 2004, p. B1.

costs, or if it leads to substantially greater local demand, enabling the firm to reduce costs through the attainment of some scale economies in the local market.

At the same time, firms still have to keep an eye on costs. Firms pursuing a localization strategy still need to be efficient and, whenever possible, to capture some scale economies from their global reach. As noted earlier, many automobile companies have found that they have to customize some of their product offerings to local market demands—for example, producing large pickup trucks for North American consumers and small fuel-efficient cars for Europeans and Japanese. At the same time, these multinationals try to get some scale economies from their global volume by using common vehicle platforms and components across many different models and manufacturing those platforms and components at efficiently scaled factories that are optimally located. By designing their products in this way, these companies have been able to localize their product offering, yet simultaneously capture some scale economies, learning effects, and location economies.

TRANSNATIONAL STRATEGY We have argued that a global standardization strategy makes most sense when cost pressures are intense and demands for local responsiveness are limited. Conversely, a localization strategy makes most sense when demands for local responsiveness are high, but cost pressures are moderate or low. What happens, however, when the firm simultaneously faces both strong cost pressures and strong pressures for local responsiveness? How can managers balance the competing and inconsistent demands such divergent pressures place on the firm? According to some researchers, the answer is to pursue what has been called a transnational strategy.

Two of these researchers, Christopher Bartlett and Sumantra Ghoshal, argue that in the modern global environment, competitive conditions are so intense that to survive, firms must do all they can to respond to pressures for cost reductions and local responsiveness.[33] They must try to realize location economies and experience effects, leverage products internationally, transfer core competencies and skills within the company, and simultaneously pay attention to pressures for local responsiveness.[34] Bartlett and Ghoshal note that in the modern multinational enterprise, core competencies and skills do not reside just in the home country but can develop in any of the firm's worldwide operations. Thus, they maintain that the flow of skills and product offerings should not be all one way, from home country to foreign subsidiary. Rather, the flow should also be from foreign subsidiary to home country and from foreign subsidiary to foreign subsidiary. Transnational enterprises, in other words, must also focus on leveraging subsidiary skills.

In essence, firms that pursue a **transnational strategy** are trying to simultaneously achieve low costs through location economies, economies of scale, and learning effects; differentiate their product offering across geographic markets to account for local differences; and foster a multidirectional flow of skills between different subsidiaries in the firm's global network of operations. As attractive as this may sound in theory, the strategy is not an easy one to pursue because it places conflicting demands on the company. Differentiating the product to respond to local demands in different geographic markets raises costs, which runs counter to the goal of reducing costs. Companies such as 3M and ABB (one of the world's largest engineering conglomerates) have tried to embrace a transnational strategy and found it difficult to implement.

Transnational Strategy
Attempt to simultaneously achieve low costs through location economies, economies of scale, and learning effects while also differentiating product offerings across geographic markets to account for local differences and fostering multidirectional flows of skills between different subsidiaries in the firm's global network of operations.

How best to implement a transnational strategy is one of the most complex questions that large multinationals are grappling with today. Few, if any, enterprises have perfected this strategic posture. But some clues as to the right approach can be derived from a number of companies. For an example, consider the case of Caterpillar. The need to compete with low-cost competitors such as Komatsu of Japan forced Caterpillar to look for greater cost economies. However, variations in construction practices and government regulations across countries and regions mean that Caterpillar also has to be responsive to local demands. Therefore, Caterpillar confronted significant pressures for cost reductions *and* for local responsiveness.

To deal with cost pressures, Caterpillar redesigned its products to use many identical components and invested in a few large-scale component manufacturing facilities, sited at favorable locations, to fill global demand and realize scale economies. At the same time, the company augments the centralized manufacturing of components with assembly plants in each of its major

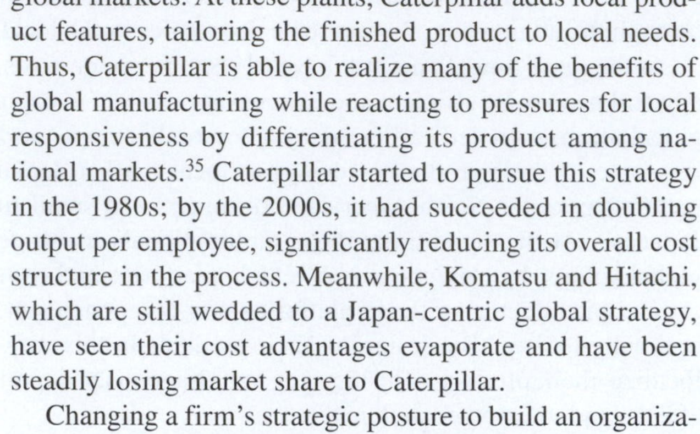

global markets. At these plants, Caterpillar adds local product features, tailoring the finished product to local needs. Thus, Caterpillar is able to realize many of the benefits of global manufacturing while reacting to pressures for local responsiveness by differentiating its product among national markets.[35] Caterpillar started to pursue this strategy in the 1980s; by the 2000s, it had succeeded in doubling output per employee, significantly reducing its overall cost structure in the process. Meanwhile, Komatsu and Hitachi, which are still wedded to a Japan-centric global strategy, have seen their cost advantages evaporate and have been steadily losing market share to Caterpillar.

Changing a firm's strategic posture to build an organization capable of supporting a transnational strategy is a complex and challenging task. Some would say it is too complex because the strategy implementation problems of creating a viable organizational structure and control systems to manage this strategy are immense.

Is Citigroup Now the Best in Financials?

Recent earnings reports of the financials showed a separation between the more internationally focused business models of Bank of America and Citigroup from the more domestically focused growth strategies of JP Morgan and Wells Fargo. The banking sector in the United States is heavily saturated, and the financials that rely primarily on the domestic economy for growth continue to struggle. Today, when you look at Citigroup's business model, the company looks like an international bank headquartered in the United States because the company gets nearly 70 percent of its revenue overseas. The company is strongly positioned in almost every major emerging market economy, with bold plans for continued future growth. In Latin America, for instance, Eduardo Cruz, one of the most respected executives in the banking industry, continues to successfully build out Citigroup's retail and investment banking presence. Also, in Asia, where Citigroup has its largest international footprint, the company continues to be similarly successful in building out its core banking business across the region, with a particularly strong retail franchise in India. Based on the material in Chapter 12, do you think Citigroup is using a global standardization strategy, localization strategy, transnational strategy, or international strategy? And, perhaps more interestingly, is Citigroup now the best in financials?

Source: http://seekingalpha.com.

International Strategy
Trying to create value by transferring core competencies to foreign markets where indigenous competitors lack those competencies.

INTERNATIONAL STRATEGY

Sometimes it is possible to identify multinational firms that find themselves in the fortunate position of being confronted with low cost pressures and low pressures for local responsiveness. Many of these enterprises have pursued an **international strategy,** taking products first produced for their domestic market and selling them internationally with only minimal local customization. The distinguishing feature of many such firms is that they are selling a product that serves universal needs, but they do not face significant competitors; thus, unlike firms pursuing a global standardization strategy, they are not confronted with pressures to reduce their cost structure. Xerox found itself in this position in the 1960s, after its invention and commercialization of the photocopier. The technology underlying the photocopier was protected by strong patents, so for several years, Xerox did not face competitors—it had a monopoly. The product serves universal needs, and it was highly valued in most developed nations. Thus, Xerox was able to sell the same basic product the world over, charging a relatively high price for that product. Because Xerox did not face direct competitors, it did not have to deal with strong pressures to minimize its cost structure.

Enterprises pursuing an international strategy have followed a similar developmental pattern as they expanded into foreign markets. They tend to centralize product development functions such as R&D at home. However, they also tend to establish manufacturing and marketing functions in each major country or geographic region in which they do business. The resulting duplication can raise costs, but this is less of an issue if the firm does not face strong pressures for cost reductions. Although they may undertake some local customization of product offering and marketing strategy, this tends to be rather limited in scope. Ultimately, in most firms that pursue an international strategy, the head office retains fairly tight control over marketing and product strategy.

Firms that have pursued this strategy include Procter & Gamble and Microsoft. Historically, Procter & Gamble developed innovative new products in Cincinnati and then transferred them wholesale to local markets (see the accompanying Management Focus). Similarly, the bulk of Microsoft's product development work occurs in Redmond, Washington, where the company is headquartered. Although some localization work is undertaken elsewhere, this is limited to producing foreign-language versions of popular Microsoft programs.

THE EVOLUTION OF STRATEGY

The Achilles' heel of the international strategy is that over time, competitors inevitably emerge, and if managers do not take proactive steps

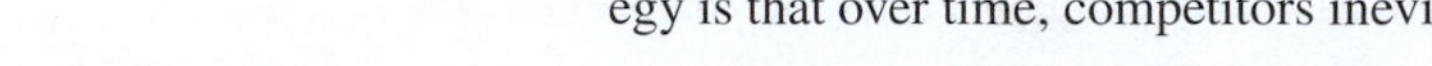

management FOCUS

Evolution of Strategy at Procter & Gamble

Founded in 1837, Cincinnati-based Procter & Gamble (P&G) has long been one of the world's most international companies. Today, P&G is a global colossus in the consumer products business with annual sales in excess of $80 billion, some 54 percent of which are generated outside of the United States. P&G sells more than 300 brands—including Ivory soap, Tide, Pampers, IAMS pet food, Crisco, and Folgers—to consumers in 180 countries. Historically, the strategy at P&G was well established. The company developed new products in Cincinnati and then relied on semiautonomous foreign subsidiaries to manufacture, market, and distribute those products in different nations. In many cases, foreign subsidiaries had their own production facilities and tailored the packaging, brand name, and marketing message to local tastes and preferences. For years, this strategy delivered a steady stream of new products and reliable growth in sales and profits. By the 1990s, however, profit growth at P&G was slowing.

The essence of the problem was simple; P&G's costs were too high because of extensive duplication of manufacturing, marketing, and administrative facilities in different national subsidiaries. The duplication of assets made sense in the world of the 1960s, when national markets were segmented from each other by barriers to cross-border trade. Products produced in Great Britain, for example, could not be sold economically in Germany due to high tariff duties levied on imports into Germany. By the 1980s, however, barriers to cross-border trade were falling rapidly worldwide and fragmented national markets were merging into larger regional or global markets. Also, the retailers through which P&G distributed its products were growing larger and more global, such as Walmart, Tesco from the United Kingdom, and Carrefour from France. These emerging global retailers were demanding price discounts from P&G.

In the 1990s, P&G embarked on a major reorganization in an attempt to control its cost structure and recognize the new reality of emerging global markets. The company shut down some 30 manufacturing plants around the globe, laid off 13,000 employees, and concentrated production in fewer plants that could better realize economies of scale and serve regional markets. It wasn't enough! Profit growth remained sluggish, so in 1999, P&G launched its second reorganization of the decade. Named "Organization 2005," the goal was to transform P&G into a truly global company. The company tore up its old organization, which was based on countries and regions, and replaced it with one based on seven self-contained global business units, ranging from baby care to food products. Each business unit was given complete responsibility for generating profits from its products and for manufacturing, marketing, and product development. Each business unit was told to rationalize production, concentrating it in fewer larger facilities; to try to build global brands wherever possible, thereby eliminating marketing differences among countries; and to accelerate the development and launch of new products. P&G announced that as a result of this initiative, it would close another 10 factories and lay off 15,000 employees, mostly in Europe where there was still extensive duplication of assets. The annual cost savings were estimated to be about $800 million. P&G planned to use the savings to cut prices and increase marketing spending in an effort to gain market share and thus further lower costs through the attainment of scale economies. This time, the strategy seemed to be working. For most of the 2000s, P&G reported strong growth in both sales and profits. Significantly, P&G's global competitors, such as Unilever, Kimberly-Clark, and Colgate-Palmolive, were struggling during the same time period.

Sources: J. Neff, "P&G Outpacing Unilever in Five-Year Battle," *Advertising Age*, November 3, 2003, pp. 1–3; G. Strauss, "Firm Restructuring into Truly Global Company," *USA Today*, September 10, 1999, p. B2; *Procter & Gamble 10K Report*, 2005; M. Kolbasuk McGee, "P&G Jump-Starts Corporate Change," *Information Week*, November 1, 1999, pp. 30–34.

to reduce their firm's cost structure, it will be rapidly outflanked by efficient global competitors. This is what happened to Xerox. Japanese companies such as Canon ultimately invented their way around Xerox's patents, produced their own photocopiers in very efficient manufacturing plants, priced them below Xerox's products, and rapidly took global market share from Xerox. In the final analysis, Xerox's demise was not due to the emergence of competitors—because, ultimately, that was bound to occur—but due to its failure to proactively reduce its cost structure in advance of the emergence of efficient global competitors. The message in this story is that an international strategy may not be viable in the long term and to survive, firms need to shift toward a global standardization strategy or a transnational strategy in advance of competitors (see Figure 12.10).

The same can be said about a localization strategy. Localization may give a firm a competitive edge, but if it is simultaneously facing aggressive competitors, the company will also have to reduce its cost structure, and the only way to do that may be to shift toward a transnational strategy. This is what Procter & Gamble has been doing (see the accompanying Management Focus). Thus, as competition intensifies, international and localization strategies tend to become less viable, and managers need to orient their companies toward either a global standardization strategy or a transnational strategy.

test PREP

Use LearnSmart to help retain what you have learned. Access your instructor's Connect course to check out LearnSmart or go to learnsmartadvantage.com for help.

12.10 FIGURE

Changes in Strategy Over Time

Source: C. W. L. Hill and G. T. M. Hult, *International Business: Competing in the Global Marketplace* (New York: McGraw-Hill Education, 2017).

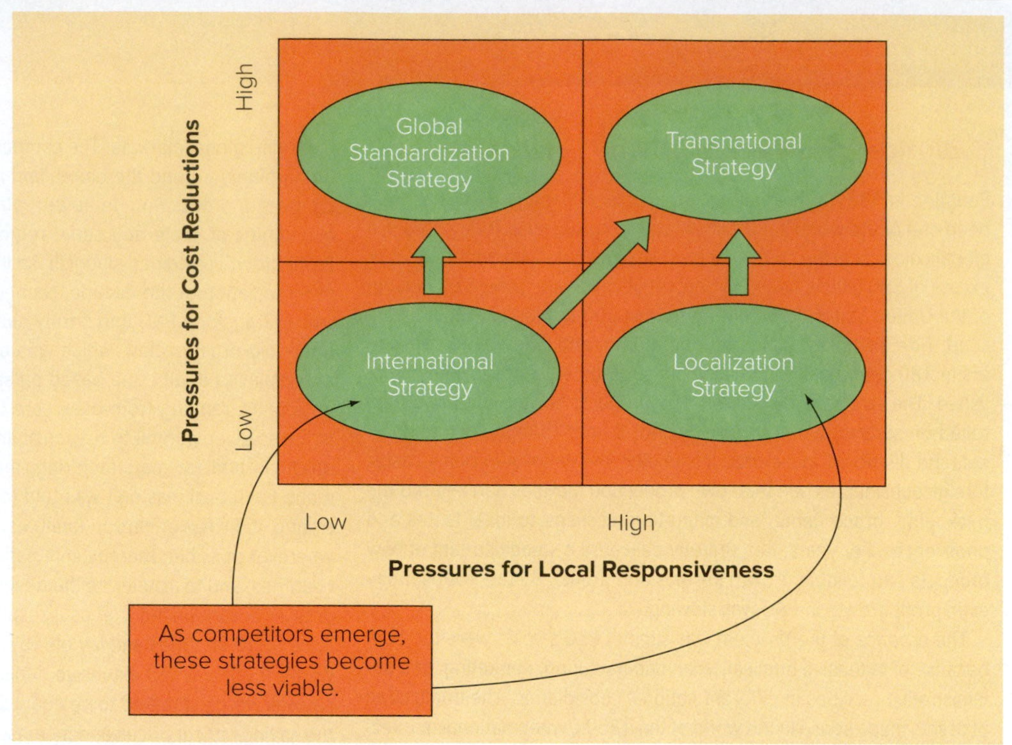

LO 12-5

Explain the pros and cons of using strategic alliances to support global strategies.

Strategic Alliances

Strategic alliances refer to cooperative agreements between potential or actual competitors. In this section, we are concerned specifically with strategic alliances between firms from different countries. Strategic alliances run the range from formal joint ventures, in which two or more firms have equity stakes (e.g., Fuji Xerox), to short-term contractual agreements, in which two companies agree to cooperate on a particular task (such as developing a new product). Collaboration between competitors is fashionable; recent decades have seen an explosion in the number of strategic alliances.

THE ADVANTAGES OF STRATEGIC ALLIANCES Firms ally themselves with actual or potential competitors for various strategic purposes.[36] First, strategic alliances may facilitate entry into a foreign market. For example, many firms believe that if they are to successfully enter the Chinese market, they need a local partner who understands business conditions and who has good connections (or *guanxi*—see Chapter 4). Thus, Warner Brothers entered into a joint venture with two Chinese partners to produce and distribute films in China. As a foreign film company, Warner found that if it wanted to produce films on its own for the Chinese market, it had to go through a complex approval process for every film, and it had to farm out distribution to a local company, which made doing business in China very difficult. Due to the participation of Chinese firms, however, the joint-venture films will go through a streamlined approval process, and the venture will be able to distribute any films it produces. Also, the joint venture will be able to produce films for Chinese TV, something that foreign firms are not allowed to do.[37]

A moviegoer walks past a poster of the Warner Bros movie *Gravity* in Shanghai, China. The strategic alliance between Warner Brothers and their Chinese partners has helped streamline the process for film distribution.

Source: © Imaginechina/Corbis

Strategic alliances also allow firms to share the fixed costs (and associated risks) of developing new products or processes. An alliance between Boeing and a number of Japanese companies to build Boeing's latest commercial jetliner, the 787, was motivated by Boeing's desire to share the estimated $8 billion investment required to develop the aircraft.

Third, an alliance is a way to bring together complementary skills and assets that neither company could easily develop on its own.[38] In 2003, for example, Microsoft and Toshiba established an alliance aimed at developing embedded microprocessors (essentially tiny computers) that can perform a variety of entertainment functions in an automobile (e.g., run a backseat DVD player or a wireless Internet connection). The processors run a version of Microsoft's Windows operating system. Microsoft brings its software engineering skills to the alliance and Toshiba its skills in developing microprocessors.[39]

Fourth, it can make sense to form an alliance that will help the firm establish technological standards for the industry that will benefit the firm. For example, in 2011, Nokia, one of the leading makers of smartphones, entered into an alliance with Microsoft under which Nokia agreed to license and use Microsoft's Windows Mobile operating system in Nokia's phones. The motivation for the alliance was in part to help establish Windows Mobile as the industry standard for smartphones as opposed to the rival operating systems such as Apple's iPhone and Google's Android. Unfortunately for Microsoft, the Nokia's Windows phones failed to gain sufficient market share. In 2013, Microsoft decided to acquire Nokia's mobile phone business and bring it in house so that it could ensure a continued aggressive push into the smartphone hardware business.

Was Nokia a Risky Purchase for Microsoft?

Microsoft Corporation's acquisition of Nokia Corporation's devices and services business was seen as a bold but risky gamble in the software giant's bid for a larger footprint in the fast-growing mobile market. Initially, it relied heavily on a strategic alliance with Nokia, which in 2011 announced that it was embracing Microsoft's Windows Phone as its main operating system. This partnership produced Lumia, a Windows-based Nokia phone. It has won upbeat reviews but remains an insignificant player in a market dominated by Apple's iPhone and other devices based on Google's Android operating system. Nokia got caught in a tough transition from its phones based on its Symbian operating system to Windows-based devices, and this transition has been more painful than Nokia anticipated. Despite the somewhat rocky start to their alliance, in September 2013, Microsoft and Nokia announced that the two companies "have decided to enter into a transaction whereby Microsoft will purchase substantially all of Nokia's Devices and Services business, license Nokia's patents, and license and use Nokia's mapping services."* Experts, the markets, and customers are skeptical. Was Nokia a risky purchase for Microsoft?

*"Microsoft to Acquire Nokia's Devices and Services Business, License Nokia's Patents and Mapping Services," *Microsoft News Center*, September 3, 2013.

Source: "Microsoft to Acquire Nokia's Devices and Services Business, License Nokia's Patents and Mapping Services," *Microsoft News Center*, September 3, 2013.

THE DISADVANTAGES OF STRATEGIC ALLIANCES

The advantages we have discussed can be very significant. Despite this, some have criticized strategic alliances on the grounds that they give competitors a low-cost route to new technology and markets.[40] For example, two decades ago, critics argued that many strategic alliances between U.S. and Japanese firms were part of an implicit Japanese strategy to keep high-paying, high-value-added jobs in Japan while gaining the project engineering and production process skills that underlie the competitive success of many U.S. companies.[41] They argued that Japanese success in the machine tool and semiconductor industries was built on U.S. technology acquired through strategic alliances. And they argued that U.S. managers were aiding the Japanese by entering alliances that channel new inventions to Japan and provide a U.S. sales and distribution network for the resulting products. Although such deals may generate short-term profits, so the argument goes, in the long run, the result is to "hollow out" U.S. firms, leaving them with no competitive advantage in the global marketplace. The same arguments are now made regarding alliances with Chinese firms.

These critics have a point; alliances have risks. Unless a firm is careful, it can give away more than it receives. But there are so many examples of apparently successful alliances between firms—including alliances between U.S. and Japanese firms—that the critics' position seems extreme. It is difficult to see how the Microsoft–Toshiba alliance, the Boeing–Mitsubishi alliance for the 787, and the Fuji–Xerox alliance fit the critics' thesis. In these cases, both partners seem to have gained from the alliance. Why do some alliances benefit both firms while others benefit one firm and hurt the other? The next section provides an answer to this question.

MAKING ALLIANCES WORK

The failure rate for international strategic alliances seems to be high. One study of 49 international strategic alliances found that two-thirds run into serious managerial and financial troubles within two years of their formation and that although many of these problems are solved, 33 percent are ultimately rated as failures by the parties involved.[42] The success of an alliance seems to be a function of three main factors: partner selection, alliance structure, and the manner in which the alliance is managed.

Partner Selection One key to making a strategic alliance work is to select the right ally. A good ally, or partner, has three characteristics. First, a good partner helps the firm achieve its strategic goals, whether they are market access, sharing the costs and risks of product development, or gaining access to critical core competencies. The partner must have capabilities that the firm lacks and that it values. Second, a good partner shares the firm's vision for the purpose of the alliance. If two firms approach an alliance with radically different agendas, the chances are great that the relationship will not be harmonious, will not flourish, and will end in divorce. Third, a good partner is unlikely to try to opportunistically exploit the alliance for its own ends, that is, to expropriate the firm's technological know-how while giving away little in return. In this respect, firms with reputations for "fair play" to maintain probably make the best allies. For example, companies such as General Electric are involved in so many strategic alliances that it would not pay the company to trample over individual alliance partners.[43] This would tarnish GE's reputation of being a good ally and would make it more difficult for GE to attract alliance partners. Because IBM attaches great importance to its alliances, it is unlikely to engage in the kind of opportunistic behavior that critics highlight. Similarly, their reputations make it less likely (but by no means impossible) that such Japanese firms as Sony, Toshiba, and Fuji, which have histories of alliances with non-Japanese firms, would opportunistically exploit an alliance partner.

To select a partner with these three characteristics, a firm needs to conduct comprehensive research on potential alliance candidates. To increase the probability of selecting a good partner, the firm should:

1. Collect as much pertinent, publicly available information on potential allies as possible.
2. Gather data from informed third parties. These include firms that have had alliances with the potential partners, investment bankers that have had dealings with them, and former employees.
3. Get to know the potential partner as well as possible before committing to an alliance. This should include face-to-face meetings between senior managers (and perhaps middle-level managers) to ensure that the chemistry is right.

Alliance Structure A partner having been selected, the alliance should be structured so that the firm's risks of giving too much away to the partner are reduced to an acceptable level. First, alliances can be designed to make it difficult (if not impossible) to transfer technology not meant to be transferred. The design, development, manufacture, and service of a product manufactured by an alliance can be structured so as to wall off sensitive technologies to prevent their leakage to the other participant. In a long-standing alliance between General Electric and Snecma to build commercial aircraft engines for single-aisle commercial jet aircraft, for example, GE reduced the risk of excess transfer by walling off certain sections of the production process. The modularization effectively cut off the transfer of what GE regarded as key competitive technology, while permitting Snecma access to final assembly. Formed in 1974, the alliance has been remarkably successful, and today it dominates the market for jet engines used on the Boeing 737 and Airbus 320.[44] Similarly, in the alliance between Boeing and the Japanese to build the 767, Boeing walled off research, design, and marketing functions considered central to its competitive position, while allowing the Japanese to share in production technology. Boeing also walled off new technologies not required for 767 production.[45]

Second, contractual safeguards can be written into an alliance agreement to guard against the risk of opportunism by a partner. (Opportunism includes the theft of technology and/or markets.) For example, TRW Inc. entered into three strategic alliances with large Japanese auto component suppliers to produce seat belts, engine valves, and steering gears for sale to Japanese-owned auto assembly plants in the United States. TRW put clauses in each of its alliance contracts that barred the Japanese firms from competing with TRW to supply U.S.-owned auto companies with component parts. By doing this, TRW protected itself against the possibility that the Japanese companies were entering into the alliances merely to gain access to the North American market to compete with TRW in its home market.

Third, both parties to an alliance can agree in advance to swap skills and technologies that the other covets, thereby ensuring a chance for equitable gain. Cross-licensing agreements are one way to achieve this goal. Fourth, the risk of opportunism by an alliance partner can be reduced if the firm extracts a significant credible commitment from its partner in advance. The long-term alliance between Xerox and Fuji to build photocopiers for the Asian market perhaps best illustrates this. Rather than enter into an informal agreement or a licensing arrangement (which Fuji Photo initially wanted), Xerox insisted that Fuji invest in a 50/50 joint venture to serve Japan and East Asia. This venture constituted such a significant investment in people, equipment, and facilities that Fuji Photo was committed from the outset to making the alliance work in order to earn a return on its investment. By agreeing to the joint venture, Fuji essentially made a credible commitment to the alliance. Given this, Xerox felt secure in transferring its photocopier technology to Fuji.[46]

Managing the Alliance Once a partner has been selected and an appropriate alliance structure has been agreed on, the task facing the firm is to maximize its benefits from the alliance. As in all international business deals, an important factor is sensitivity to cultural differences (see Chapter 4). Many differences in management style are attributable to cultural differences, and managers need to make allowances for these in dealing with their partner. Beyond this, maximizing the benefits from an alliance seems to involve building trust between partners and learning from partners.[47]

Managing an alliance successfully requires building interpersonal relationships between the firms' managers, or what is sometimes referred to as *relational capital*.[48] This is one lesson that can be drawn from a successful strategic alliance between Ford and Mazda. Ford and Mazda set up a framework of meetings within which their managers not only discuss matters pertaining to the alliance but also have time to get to know each other better. The belief is that the resulting friendships help build trust and facilitate harmonious relations between the two firms. Personal relationships also foster an informal management network between the firms. This network can then be used to help solve problems arising in more formal contexts (such as in joint committee meetings between personnel from the two firms).

Academics have argued that a major determinant of how much acquiring knowledge a company gains from an alliance is its ability to learn from its alliance partner.[49] For example, in a five-year study of 15 strategic alliances between major multinationals, Gary Hamel, Yves Doz, and C. K. Prahalad focused on a number of alliances between Japanese companies and Western (European or American) partners.[50] In every case in which a Japanese company emerged from an alliance stronger than its Western partner, the Japanese company had made a greater effort to learn. Few Western companies studied seemed to want to learn from their Japanese partners. They tended to regard the alliance purely as a cost-sharing or risk-sharing device, rather than as an opportunity to learn how a potential competitor does business.

Consider the alliance between General Motors and Toyota constituted in 1985 to build the Chevrolet Nova. This alliance was structured as a formal joint venture, called New United Motor Manufacturing Inc., and each party had a 50 percent equity stake. The venture owned an auto plant in Fremont, California. According to one Japanese manager, Toyota quickly achieved most of its objectives from the alliance: "We learned about U.S. supply and transportation. And we got the confidence to manage U.S. workers."[51] All that knowledge was then transferred to Georgetown, Kentucky, where Toyota opened its own plant in 1988. Possibly all GM got was a new product, the Chevrolet Nova. Some GM managers complained that the knowledge they gained through the alliance with Toyota has never been put to good use inside GM. They believe they should have been kept together as a team to educate GM's engineers and workers about the Japanese system. Instead, they were dispersed to various GM subsidiaries.

To maximize the learning benefits of an alliance, a firm must try to learn from its partner and then apply the knowledge within its own organization. It has been suggested that all operating employees should be well briefed on the partner's strengths and weaknesses and should understand how acquiring particular skills will bolster their firm's competitive position. Hamel and Prahalad note that this is already standard practice among Japanese companies. They made this observation:

> We accompanied a Japanese development engineer on a tour through a partner's factory. This engineer dutifully took notes on plant layout, the number of production stages, the rate at which the line was running, and the number of employees. He recorded all this despite the fact that he had no manufacturing responsibility in his own company, and that the alliance did not encompass joint manufacturing. Such dedication greatly enhances learning.[52]

Use LearnSmart to help retain what you have learned. Access your instructor's Connect course to check out LearnSmart or go to learnsmartadvantage.com for help.

Key Terms

strategic alliances, p. 325
strategy, p. 325
profitability, p. 325
profit growth, p. 325
value creation, p. 326
operations, p. 328
organization architecture, p. 331
organizational structure, p. 331
controls, p. 331
incentives, p. 331
processes, p. 331
organizational culture, p. 331
people, p. 331
core competence, p. 333
location economies, p. 334
global web, p. 335
experience curve, p. 336
learning effects, p. 336
economies of scale, p. 336
universal needs, p. 339
global standardization strategy, p. 343
localization strategy, p. 344
transnational strategy, p. 345
international strategy, p. 346

Summary

This chapter reviewed basic principles of strategy and the various ways in which firms can profit from global expansion, and it looked at the strategies that firms that compete globally can adopt. The chapter made the following points:

1. A strategy can be defined as the actions that managers take to attain the goals of the firm. For most firms, the preeminent goal is to maximize shareholder value. Maximizing shareholder value requires firms to focus on increasing their profitability and the growth rate of profits over time.
2. International expansion may enable a firm to earn greater returns by transferring the product offerings derived from its core competencies to markets where indigenous competitors lack those product offerings and competencies.
3. It may pay a firm to base each value creation activity it performs at that location where factor conditions are most conducive to the performance of that activity. We refer to this strategy as focusing on the attainment of location economies.
4. By rapidly building sales volume for a standardized product, international expansion can assist a firm in moving down the experience curve by realizing learning effects and economies of scale.
5. A multinational firm can create additional value by identifying valuable skills created within its foreign subsidiaries and leveraging those skills within its global network of operations.
6. The best strategy for a firm to pursue often depends on a consideration of the pressures for cost reductions and for local responsiveness.
7. Firms pursuing an international strategy transfer the products derived from core competencies to foreign markets, while undertaking some limited local customization.
8. Firms pursuing a localization strategy customize their product offering, marketing strategy, and business strategy to national conditions.
9. Firms pursuing a global standardization strategy focus on reaping the cost reductions that come from experience curve effects and location economies.
10. Many industries are now so competitive that firms must adopt a transnational strategy. This involves a simultaneous focus on reducing costs, transferring skills and products, and boosting local responsiveness. Implementing such a strategy may not be easy.
11. Strategic alliances are cooperative agreements between actual or potential competitors.
12. The advantages of alliances are that they facilitate entry into foreign markets, enable partners to share the fixed costs and risks associated with new products and processes, facilitate the transfer of complementary skills between companies, and help firms establish technical standards.
13. A disadvantage of a strategic alliance is that the firm risks giving away technological know-how and market access to its alliance partner in return for very little.
14. The disadvantages associated with alliances can be reduced if the firm selects partners carefully, paying close attention to the firm's reputation and the structure of the alliance so as to avoid unintended transfers of know-how.
15. Keys to making alliances work seem to be building trust and informal communications networks between partners and taking proactive steps to learn from alliance partners.

Critical Thinking and Discussion Questions

1. In a world of zero transportation costs, no trade barriers, and nontrivial differences between nations with regard to factor conditions, firms must expand internationally if they are to survive. Discuss.
2. Plot the position of the following firms on Figure 12.8: Procter & Gamble, IBM, Apple, Coca-Cola, Dow Chemical, U.S. Steel, McDonald's. In each case, justify your answer.
3. In what kind of industries does a localization strategy make sense? When does a global standardization strategy make most sense?
4. Reread the Management Focus on Procter & Gamble and then answer the following questions:
   a. What strategy was Procter & Gamble pursuing when it first entered foreign markets in the period up until the 1980s?
   b. Why do you think this strategy became less viable in the 1990s?
   c. What strategy does P&G appear to be moving toward? What are the benefits of this strategy? What are the potential risks associated with it?
5. What do you see as the main organizational problems that are likely to be associated with implementation of a transnational strategy?

globalEDGE Research Task

globalEDGE.msu.edu

Use the globalEDGE™ website (globaledge.msu.edu) to complete the following exercises:

1. Several classifications and rankings of the world's largest companies are prepared by a variety of sources. Find one such *composite ranking* system, and identify the criteria that are used to rank the top global companies. Extract the list of the top 20 ranked companies, paying particular attention to their home countries.
2. The top management of your company, a manufacturer and marketer of smartphones, has decided to pursue international expansion opportunities in eastern Europe. To ensure success, management's goal is to enter into countries with a high level of *global connectedness*. Identify the top three eastern European countries in which your company can market its current product line. Prepare an executive summary to support your recommendations.

IKEA and Its Strategy of International Business — closing case

Walk into an IKEA store anywhere in the world, and you would recognize it instantly. The warehouse-type stores all sell the same broad range of affordable home furnishings, kitchens, and accessories. Most of the products are instantly recognizable as IKEA merchandise, with their clean yet tasteful lines and functional design.

The outside of the store will be wrapped in the blue and yellow colors of the Swedish flag. The store itself will be laid out as a maze that requires customers to walk through every department before they reach the checkout stations. Immediately before the checkout, there is an in-store warehouse where customers can pick up the items they purchased. The furniture is all flat, packed for ease of transportation, and requires assembly by the customer. If you look at the customers in the store, you will see that many of them are in their 20s and 30s. IKEA sells to the same basic customers all across the world: young, upwardly mobile people who are looking for tasteful yet inexpensive "disposable" furniture.

A global network of about 978 suppliers based in 50 countries manufactures most of the 12,000 products that IKEA sells. IKEA itself focuses on the design of products and works closely with suppliers to bring down manufacturing costs. Developing a new product line can be a painstaking process that takes years. IKEA's designers will develop a prototype design—a small couch, for example—look at the price that rivals charge for a similar piece, and then work with suppliers to figure out a way to cut prices by 40 percent without compromising on quality. IKEA also manufactures about 10 percent of what it sells in-house and uses the knowledge gained to help its suppliers improve their productivity, thereby lowering costs across the entire supply chain.

It's a formula that has worked remarkably well. From its roots in Scandinavia, in 2015 IKEA had grown to become the largest furniture retailer in the world with 328 stores in 28 countries and revenues of $36 billion (32 billion euro). IKEA had 771 million store visits and 1.9 billion online visits (IKEA.com). With its Swedish heritage, IKEA is particularly strong in Europe, where it has more than 200 stores, but it also has around 50 stores in North America. Its strongest growth recently has been in China, where it had 17 stores, and Russia, where it had 14 stores.

Look a little closer, however, and you will see subtle differences between the IKEA offerings in North America, Europe, and China. In North

America, sizes are different to reflect the American demand for bigger beds, furnishings, and kitchenware. This adaptation to local tastes and preferences was the result of a painful learning experience for IKEA. When the company first entered the United States in the late 1980s, it thought that consumers would flock to their stores the same way that they had in Europe. At first they did, but they didn't buy as much, and sales fell short of expectations. IKEA discovered that its European-style sofas were not big enough, wardrobe drawers were not deep enough, glasses were too small, and kitchens didn't fit U.S. appliances. So the company set about redesigning its offerings to better match American tastes and was rewarded with accelerating sales growth.

Lesson learned, when IKEA entered China in the 2000s, it made adaptations to the local market. The store layout reflects the layout of many Chinese apartments, where most people live, and because many Chinese apartments have balconies, IKEA's Chinese stores include a balcony section. IKEA has also had to shift its locations in China, where car ownership lags behind that in Europe and North America. In the West, IKEA stores are located in suburban areas and have lots of parking space. In China, stores are located near public transportation, and IKEA offers a delivery service so that Chinese customers can get their purchases home.

Sources: J. Leland, "How the Disposable Sofa Conquered America," *The New York Times Magazine,* October 5, 2005, p. 45; "The Secret of IKEA's Success," *The Economist,* February 24, 2011; B. Torekull, *Leading by Design: The IKEA Story* (New York: HarperCollins, 1998); P. M. Miller, "IKEA with Chinese Characteristics," *Chinese Business Review,* July–August 2004, pp. 36–69.

CASE DISCUSSION QUESTIONS

1. Why do you think IKEA uses a floorplan that "forces" the customers to move along a certain path in the store?
2. Is it appropriate for IKEA to customize their furniture to each geographic location, for example, differences between U.S. and European furniture? Some companies do not make these changes, but IKEA does; why?
3. IKEA entered the United States in 1985 and China in 1998. But the company started in 1958; why did it take so long to move into the United States and China? Why do you think IKEA is not in more than 28 countries today (there are almost 200 countries in the world)?

Endnotes

1. More formally, ROIC = Net profit after tax/Capital, where capital includes the sum of the firm's equity and debt. This way of calculating profitability is highly correlated with return on assets.
2. T. Copeland, T. Koller, and J. Murrin, *Valuation: Measuring and Managing the Value of Companies* (New York: John Wiley & Sons, 2000).
3. The concept of consumer surplus is an important one in economics. For a more detailed exposition, see D. Besanko, D. Dranove, and M. Shanley, *Economics of Strategy* (New York: John Wiley & Sons, 1996).
4. However, $P = V$ only in the special case in which the company has a perfect monopoly and in which it can charge each customer a unique price that reflects the value of the product to that customer (i.e., where perfect price discrimination is possible). More generally, except in the limiting case of perfect price discrimination, even a monopolist will see most consumers capture some of the value of a product in the form of a consumer surplus.
5. This point is central to the work of Michael Porter, *Competitive Advantage* (New York: Free Press, 1985). See also chap. 4 in P. Ghemawat, *Commitment: The Dynamic of Strategy* (New York: Free Press, 1991).
6. M. E. Porter, *Competitive Strategy* (New York: Free Press, 1980).
7. M. E. Porter, "What Is Strategy?" *Harvard Business Review,* On-point Enhanced Edition article, February 1, 2000.
8. Porter, *Competitive Advantage.*
9. D. Naidler, M. Gerstein, and R. Shaw, *Organization Architecture* (San Francisco: Jossey-Bass, 1992).
10. G. Morgan, *Images of Organization* (Beverly Hills, CA: Sage Publications, 1986).
11. Empirical evidence does seem to indicate that, on average, international expansion is linked to greater firm profitability. For some recent examples, see M. A. Hitt, R. E. Hoskisson, and H. Kim, "International Diversification, Effects on Innovation and Firm Performance," *Academy of Management Journal* 40, no. 4 (1997), pp. 767–98; and S. Tallman and J. Li, "Effects of International Diversity and Product Diversity on the Performance of Multinational Firms," *Academy of Management Journal* 39, no. 1 (1996), pp. 179–96.
12. This concept has been popularized by G. Hamel and C. K. Prahalad, *Competing for the Future* (Boston: Harvard Business School Press, 1994). The concept is grounded in the resource-based view of the firm; for a summary, see J. B. Barney, "Firm Resources and Sustained Competitive Advantage," *Journal of Management* 17 (1991), pp. 99–120; and K. R. Conner, "A Historical Comparison of Resource-Based Theory and Five Schools of Thought within Industrial Organization Economics: Do We Have a New Theory of the Firm?" *Journal of Management* 17 (1991), pp. 121–54.
13. J. P. Womack, D. T. Jones, and D. Roos, *The Machine That Changed the World* (New York: Rawson Associates, 1990).
14. M. E. Porter, *The Competitive Advantage of Nations* (New York: Free Press, 1990).
15. Example is based on C. S. Trager, "Enter the Mini-Multinational," *Northeast International Business,* March 1989, pp. 13–14.
16. See R. B. Reich, *The Work of Nations* (New York: Alfred A. Knopf, 1991); and P. J. Buckley and N. Hashai, "A Global System View of Firm Boundaries," *Journal of International Business Studies,* January 2004, pp. 33–50.
17. D. Barboza, "An Unknown Giant Flexes Its Muscles," *The New York Times,* December 4, 2004, pp. B1, B3.
18. G. Hall and S. Howell, "The Experience Curve from an Economist's Perspective," *Strategic Management Journal* 6 (1985), pp. 197–212.
19. A. A. Alchain, "Reliability of Progress Curves in Airframe Production," *Econometrica* 31 (1963), pp. 697–98.

20. Hall and Howell, "The Experience Curve from an Economist's Perspective."

21. For a full discussion of the source of scale economies, see D. Besanko, D. Dranove, and M. Shanley, *Economics of Strategy* (New York: John Wiley & Sons, 1996).

22. This estimate was provided by the Pharmaceutical Manufacturers Association.

23. See J. Birkinshaw and N. Hood, "Multinational Subsidiary Evolution: Capability and Charter Change in Foreign Owned Subsidiary Companies," *Academy of Management Review* 23 (October 1998), pp. 773–95; A. K. Gupta and V. J. Govindarajan, "Knowledge Flows within Multinational Corporations," *Strategic Management Journal* 21 (2000), pp. 473–96; V. J. Govindarajan and A. K. Gupta, *The Quest for Global Dominance* (San Francisco: Jossey Bass, 2001); T. S. Frost, J. M. Birkinshaw, and P. C. Ensign, "Centers of Excellence in Multinational Corporations," *Strategic Management Journal* 23 (2002), pp. 997–1018; and U. Andersson, M. Forsgren, and U. Holm, "The Strategic Impact of External Networks," *Strategic Management Journal* 23 (2002), pp. 979–96.

24. S. Leung, "Armchairs, TVs and Espresso: Is It McDonald's?" *The Wall Street Journal,* August 30, 2002, pp. A1, A6; and E. Beardsley, "Why McDonald's in France Doesn't Feel Like Fast Food," *NPR,* January 24, 2012.

25. C. K. Prahalad and Yves L. Doz, *The Multinational Mission: Balancing Local Demands and Global Vision* (New York: Free Press, 1987). Also see J. Birkinshaw, A. Morrison, and J. Hulland, "Structural and Competitive Determinants of a Global Integration Strategy," *Strategic Management Journal* 16 (1995), pp. 637–55; and P. Ghemawat, *Redefining Global Strategy* (Boston: Harvard Business School Press, 2007).

26. J. E. Garten, "Wal-Mart Gives Globalization a Bad Name," *BusinessWeek,* March 8, 2004, p. 24.

27. Prahalad and Doz, *The Multinational Mission.* Prahalad and Doz actually talk about local responsiveness rather than local customization.

28. T. Levitt, "The Globalization of Markets," *Harvard Business Review,* May–June 1983, pp. 92–102.

29. W. W. Lewis, *The Power of Productivity* (Chicago: University of Chicago Press, 2004).

30. C. J. Chipello, "Local Presence Is Key to European Deals," *The Wall Street Journal,* June 30, 1998, p. A15.

31. For an extended discussion see: G. S. Yip and G. Tomas M. Hult, *Total Global Strategy* (Boston: Pearson, 2012), and A. M. Rugman and A. Verbeke, "A Perspective on Regional and Global Strategies of Multinational Enterprises," *Journal of International Business Studies* 35, no. 1 (2004), pp. 3–18.

32. C. A. Bartlett and S. Ghoshal, *Managing Across Borders: The Transnational Solution* (Boston: Harvard Business School Press, 1998).

33. Ibid.

34. Pankaj Ghemawat makes a similar argument, although he does not use the term *transnational*. See Ghemawat, *Redefining Global Strategy*.

35. T. Hout, M. E. Porter, and E. Rudden, "How Global Companies Win Out," *Harvard Business Review,* September–October 1982, pp. 98–108.

36. See K. Ohmae, "The Global Logic of Strategic Alliances," *Harvard Business Review,* March–April 1989, pp. 143–54; G. Hamel, Y. L. Doz, and C. K. Prahalad, "Collaborate with Your Competitors and Win!" *Harvard Business Review,* January–February 1989, pp. 133–39; W. Burgers, C. W. L. Hill, and W. C. Kim, "Alliances in the Global Auto Industry," *Strategic Management Journal* 14 (1993), pp. 419–32; and P. Kale, H. Singh, and H. Perlmutter, "Learning and Protection of Proprietary Assets in Strategic Alliances: Building Relational Capital," *Strategic Management Journal* 21 (2000), pp. 217–37.

37. L. T. Chang, "China Eases Foreign Film Rules," *The Wall Street Journal,* October 15, 2004, p. B2.

38. B. L. Simonin, "Transfer of Marketing Know-How in International Strategic Alliances," *Journal of International Business Studies,* 1999, pp. 463–91; and J. W. Spencer, "Firms' Knowledge Sharing Strategies in the Global Innovation System," *Strategic Management Journal* 24 (2003), pp. 217–33.

39. C. Souza, "Microsoft Teams with MIPS, Toshiba," *EBN,* February 10, 2003, p. 4.

40. Kale, Singh, and Perlmutter, "Learning and Protection of Proprietary Assets."

41. R. B. Reich and E. D. Mankin, "Joint Ventures with Japan Give Away Our Future," *Harvard Business Review,* March–April 1986, pp. 78–90.

42. J. Bleeke and D. Ernst, "The Way to Win in Cross-Border Alliances," *Harvard Business Review,* November–December 1991, pp. 127–35.

43. C. H. Deutsch, "The Venturesome Giant," *The New York Times,* October 5, 2007, pp. C1, C8.

44. "Odd Couple: Jet Engines," *The Economist,* May 5, 2007, pp. 79–80.

45. W. Roehl and J. F. Truitt, "Stormy Open Marriages Are Better," *Columbia Journal of World Business,* Summer 1987, pp. 87–95.

46. B. Gomes-Casseres and K. McQuade, "Xerox and Fuji Xerox," Cambridge, MA: Harvard Business School Case, February 15, 1991.

47. See T. Khanna, R. Gulati, and N. Nohria, "The Dynamics of Learning Alliances: Competition, Cooperation, and Relative Scope," *Strategic Management Journal* 19 (1998), pp. 193–210; and Kale, Singh, and Perlmutter, "Learning and Protection of Proprietary Assets in Strategic Alliances."

48. Kale, Singh, and Perlmutter, "Learning and Protection of Proprietary Assets in Strategic Alliances."

49. Hamel, Doz, and Prahalad, "Collaborate with Your Competitors and Win!"; Khanna, Gulati, and Nohria, "The Dynamics of Learning Alliances"; and E. W. K. Tang, "Acquiring Knowledge by Foreign Partners from International Joint Ventures in a Transition Economy: Learning by Doing and Learning Myopia," *Strategic Management Journal* 23 (2002), pp. 835–54.

50. Hamel, Doz, and Prahalad, "Collaborate with Your Competitors and Win!"

51. B. Wysocki, "Cross-Border Alliances Become Favorite Way to Crack New Markets," *The Wall Street Journal,* March 4, 1990, p. A1.

52. G. Hamel and C. K. Prahalad, *Competing for the Future* (Boston, MA: Harvard Business School Press, 1994).

Entering Foreign Markets

learning objectives

After reading this chapter, you will be able to:

LO13-1 Explain the three basic decisions that firms contemplating foreign expansion must make: which markets to enter, when to enter those markets, and on what scale.

LO13-2 Compare and contrast the different modes that firms use to enter foreign markets.

LO13-3 Identify the factors that influence a firm's choice of entry mode.

LO13-4 Recognize the pros and cons of acquisitions versus greenfield ventures as an entry strategy.

Credit: © Don Heupel/AP Images

Cutco Corporation—Sharpening Your Market Entry

opening case

The name Cutco comes from "Cooking UTensils COmpany," a name once owned by Alcoa. Alcoa is a U.S. company now concentrating on work with lightweight metals and advanced manufacturing techniques. Together with W.R. Case & Sons Cutlery Company, Alcoa created the joint venture Alcas Corporation in 1949, which subsequently became Cutco Corporation in 2009.

Cutco Corporation includes the wholly owned subsidiaries of Vector Marketing Corporation, which it acquired in 1985, and Cutco Cutlery Corporation. Vector Marketing is the U.S.-based sales arm of Cutco Corporation, which is headquartered in Olean, New York. More than 700 manufacturing and administrative employees work at the Olean location.

Cutco is now the largest manufacturer of high-quality kitchen cutlery in the United States and Canada. The product line includes kitchen knives and utensils, shears, flatware, cookware, and sporting knives. Look around your house and your friends' houses, and you are likely to see one of their well-known blocks of knives in the kitchen! The price for one of the blocks with a dozen or so knives ranges from about $100 to upwards of a couple of thousand dollars. Some 16 million people have bought Cutco knives.

Originally, Cutco was created as product for Wear-Ever Aluminum (a company focused on cookware), which at the time was a division of Alcoa. Cutco evolved from there, eventually adding its signature Wedge-Lock handle and Double-D recessed edge on some of its knives. Two things that have never changed are Cutco's commitment to fine craftsmanship and the Forever Guarantee. The guarantee means what it implies—that Cutco stands behind its knives' performance and sharpness forever. They also have a forever guarantee of replacing their knives for any misuse or abuse at half the cost.

Cutco, as it operates today, was formed in 1982 following a management buyout that took the company private. As with any employee or manager buyout, it was a leap of faith for the team that bought the company. But, based on the company's story, it was also the moment that secured Cutco's future for generations to come. In this process, in 1985, Vector Marketing Corporation became the exclusive marketer of Cutco products directly to consumers via sales representatives located throughout the United States and Canada. Cutco International Inc. is responsible for international marketing.

Annual sales for Cutco now stand at about $200 million worldwide, but mainly in the United States and Canada. The product line includes more than 100 choices under the Cutco name alone. The extended line includes kitchen utensils, gadgets and flatware, sporting and pocket knives, and garden tools. For the Cutco line, the products are marketed via what is called "direct selling" (marketing of products directly to the consumer away from a fixed retail location). Internationally, outside North America, Cutco has

–continued

independent office arrangements in Australia, Costa Rica, Germany, South Korea, and the United Kingdom. Puerto Rico also has independently run sales locations.

In the United States and Canada, Vector Marketing Corporation typically employ college students in the 18-to-24 age range part-time during the school year and full-time during the summers to be part of their direct sales force. The sales pitch to students is good pay, flexible schedules, personal growth, no experience needed, great training, and engagement with quality products. In fact, 85 percent of the sales force at Cutco is college-aged individuals.

This sales force is a drastic change from the early days of the company. Early on, Cutco had hundreds of small independent sellers of the company's knives and other products. Vector Marketing became one of these sellers in 1981 and stayed in this role until 1984. In 1985, Cutco bought out Vector Marketing, and Vector became the sole channel for sales across the United States. As a core member of the Direct Selling Association, Vector Marketing Corporation drives Cutco sales using college-aged students who they pay $12 to $20 per hour in a direct-to-customer business model. But internationally, Cutco products are still sold via a myriad of independent sellers in Australia, Costa Rica, Germany, South Korea, and the United Kingdom. •

Sources: Cutco website. http://www.cutco.com; Vector Marketing Corporation. http://vectormarketing.com; "Company Overview of Cutco Corporation," *Bloomberg Business*, March 24, 2016; J. Berghoff, *Cutting Edge Sales: Confessions of Success, Influence & Self-Fulfillment from the World's Finest Knife Dealers* (Morgan James Publishing, New York, 2009); "Bringing Help to Haiti: Vector Marketing Sales Record Holder Michael Arrieta," *PRweb*, September 15, 2015.

Introduction

This chapter is concerned with two closely related topics: (1) the decision of which foreign markets to enter, when to enter them, and on what scale; and (2) the choice of entry mode. In addition, we covered strategic alliances in Chapter 12 when we discussed the strategy of international business, which also has implications for entering foreign markets. Specifically, a company can engage in a strategic alliance to enter a foreign market, and this becomes the company's internationalization strategy. However, most companies are not strategic and instead chose a market entry mode that requires lower levels of commitment and involvement. This includes choices between entering foreign markets by exporting, licensing, or franchising. Strategic alliances, like joint ventures, which we cover as a market entry form in this chapter, require greater involvement and commitment.

Did You Know?
Did you know increasingly more companies are born global?

Visit your Connect SmartBook® to view a short video explanation from the authors.

At the basic level, any firm thinking about foreign expansion must first struggle with the issue of which foreign market or markets to enter and the timing and scale of entry. The choice of which markets to enter should be driven by an assessment of the potential for relative long-run growth and profit. For example, in the opening case, the choice of mode for entering a foreign market is a major issue with which Cutco seemingly wrestles even today. The case illustrates a variety of options facing Cutco Corporation. Should they stay with the direct selling model, as in the United States and Canada, or go with independent sellers, as they do in Australia, Costa Rica, Germany, South Korea, and the United Kingdom? The ultimate decision—if the company were to expand more internationally than the few markets they are in now—is a matter of both business model and modes of foreign market entry. The choice is not an easy one. Right now, Cutco has different approaches domestically in the United States and Canada vis-à-vis their international operations.

In a different situation than Cutco is facing, Starbucks was enticed by its long-term growth potential and decided to enter China in 1999. In number of Starbucks stores, China is the second-most important market after the United States, ahead of Canada, Japan, and the United Kingdom. And China continues to be a strategic market focus for Starbucks, with the company planning several hundred more store openings in the near future. The Starbucks experience is highlighted in the closing case of this chapter.

The various modes for serving foreign markets are exporting, licensing, or franchising to host-country firms, establishing joint ventures with a host-country firm, setting up a new wholly owned subsidiary in a host country to serve its market, and acquiring an established enterprise in

Interactive Rankings

Entering foreign markets is the focus of Chapter 13. The selection of country markets to choose from is getting larger for many product categories as more countries see their populations' purchasing power growing. With almost 200 countries in the world, the data are overwhelming, and even the starting point for analysis is not always an easy decision. The Interactive Rankings on globalEDGE™ can serve as a great pictorial view of the world on some 50 important variables in categories covering the economy, energy, government, health, infrastructure, labor, people, and trade and investment (globaledge.msu.edu/tools-and-data/interactive-rankings). Active data maps such as the Interactive Rankings maps are a good starting point for analysis to evaluate data for a specific country as well as the countries around it in a region. This allows for a focus on entry into one market now and a strategy for expansion later on to nearby countries with similar characteristics. Which are the top three countries for Internet users?

the host nation to serve that market. Each of these options has advantages and disadvantages. The magnitude of the advantages and disadvantages associated with each entry mode is determined by a number of factors, including transportation costs, trade barriers, political risks, economic risks, business risks, costs, and firm strategy. The optimal entry mode varies by situation, depending on these factors. Thus, whereas some firms may best serve a given market by exporting, other firms may better serve the market by setting up a new wholly owned subsidiary or by acquiring an established enterprise.

Starbucks, for example, seems to have had a preference for entering into joint ventures with local partners and then licensing its format to the joint venture. Cutco, on the other hand, adopted different models for domestic and international sales. From Starbuck's perspective, the company opted for the joint venture in order to benefit from its joint-venture partners' local expertise, which has helped the company better configure its store format and menu to the tastes and preferences of local customers. In China, for example, its partners urged Starbucks to capitalize on the tea-drinking culture of the country by using popular local ingredients such as green tea. This helped get consumers through the door, and once they frequented the stores, they quickly developed a taste for Starbucks coffee. Local expertise was also a driving force behind Cutco's independent sellers in Australia, Costa Rica, Germany, South Korea, and the United Kingdom. But, since 1985, Cutco has strongly preferred the "direct-selling" model described in the opening case.

Basic Entry Decisions

LO 13-1
Explain the three basic decisions that firms contemplating foreign expansion must make: which markets to enter, when to enter those markets, and on what scale.

A firm contemplating foreign expansion must make three basic decisions: which markets to enter, when to enter those markets, and on what scale.[1]

WHICH FOREIGN MARKETS? There are now almost 200 countries in the world, and they do not all hold the same profit potential for a firm contemplating foreign expansion. Ultimately, the choice must be based on an assessment of a nation's long-run revenue potential. This potential is a function of several factors, many of which we have studied in earlier chapters. Chapters 2 and 3 looked in detail at the economic and political factors that influence the potential attractiveness of a foreign market. The attractiveness of a country as a potential market for an international business depends on balancing the benefits, costs, and risks associated with doing business in that country.

Chapters 2 and 3 also noted that the long-run economic benefits of doing business in a country are a function of factors such as the size of the market (in terms of demographics), the present wealth (purchasing power) of consumers in that market, and the likely future wealth of consumers, which depends on economic growth rates. While some markets are very large when measured by number of consumers (e.g., China, India, Brazil, Russia, and Indonesia), one must also look at living standards and economic growth. On this basis, China and India, while relatively poor, are growing so rapidly that they are attractive targets for inward investment. Alternatively, weak growth in Indonesia implies that this populous nation is a far less attractive target for inward investment. As we saw in Chapters 2 and 3, likely future economic growth rates appear to be a function of a free market system and a country's capacity for growth (which may be greater in less developed nations). Also, the costs and risks associated with doing business in a foreign country are typically lower in economically advanced and politically stable democratic nations, and they are greater in less developed and politically unstable nations.

The discussion in Chapters 2 and 3 suggests that, other things being equal, the benefit–cost–risk trade-off is likely to be most favorable in politically stable developed and developing nations that have free market systems and where there is not a dramatic upsurge in either inflation rates or private-sector debt. The trade-off is likely to be least favorable in politically unstable developing nations that operate with a mixed or command economy or in developing nations where speculative financial bubbles have led to excess borrowing.

Another important factor is the value an international business can create in a foreign market. This depends on the suitability of its product offering to that market and the nature of indigenous competition.[2] If the international business can offer a product that has not been widely available in that market and that satisfies an unmet need, the value of that product to consumers is likely to be much greater than if the international business simply offers the same type of product that indigenous competitors and other foreign entrants are already offering. Greater value translates into an ability to charge higher prices and/or to build sales volume more rapidly. By considering such factors, a firm can rank countries in terms of their attractiveness and long-run profit potential. Preference is then given to entering markets that rank highly. For example, Tesco, the large British grocery chain, has been aggressively expanding its foreign operations, primarily by focusing on emerging markets that lack strong indigenous competitors (see the accompanying Management Focus).

TIMING OF ENTRY

Once attractive markets have been identified, it is important to consider the **timing of entry**. Entry is early when an international business enters a foreign market before other foreign firms and late when it enters after other international businesses have already established themselves. The advantages frequently associated with entering a market early are commonly known as **first-mover advantages**.[3] One first-mover advantage is the ability to preempt rivals and capture demand by establishing a strong brand name. This desire has driven the rapid expansion by Tesco into developing nations (see the Management Focus). A second advantage is the ability to build sales volume in that country and ride down the experience curve ahead of rivals, giving the early entrant a cost advantage over later entrants. This cost advantage may enable the early entrant to cut prices below that of later entrants, thereby driving them out of the market. A third advantage is the ability of early entrants to create switching costs that tie customers into their products or services. Such switching costs make it difficult for later entrants to win business.

Timing of Entry
Entry is early when a firm enters a foreign market before other foreign firms and late when a firm enters after other international businesses have established themselves.

First-Mover Advantages
Advantages accruing to the first to enter a market.

There can also be disadvantages associated with entering a foreign market before other international businesses. These are often referred to as **first-mover disadvantages**.[4] These disadvantages may give rise to **pioneering costs**, costs that an early entrant has to bear that a later entrant can avoid. Pioneering costs arise when the business system in a foreign country is so different from that in a firm's home market that the enterprise has to devote considerable effort, time, and expense to learning the rules of the game. Pioneering costs include the costs of business failure if the firm, due to its ignorance of the foreign environment, makes major mistakes. A certain liability is associated with being a foreigner, and this liability is greater for foreign firms that enter a national market early.[5] Research seems to confirm that the probability of survival increases if an international business enters a national market after several other foreign firms have already done so.[6] The late entrant may benefit by observing and learning from the mistakes made by early entrants.

First-Mover Disadvantages
Disadvantages associated with entering a foreign market before other international businesses.

Pioneering Costs
Costs an early entrant bears that later entrants avoid, such as the time and effort in learning the rules, failure due to ignorance, and the liability of being a foreigner.

Pioneering costs also include the costs of promoting and establishing a product offering, including the costs of educating customers. These can be significant when the product being promoted is unfamiliar to local consumers. In contrast, later entrants may be able to ride on an early entrant's investments in learning and customer education by watching how the early entrant proceeded in the market, by avoiding costly mistakes made by the early entrant, and by exploiting the market potential created by the early entrant's investments in customer education. For example, KFC introduced the Chinese to American-style fast food, but a later entrant, McDonald's, has capitalized on the market in China by correcting mistakes that KFC made and implementing a better approach.

management FOCUS

Tesco's International Growth Strategy

Tesco, founded in 1919 by Jack Cohen, is a British multinational grocery and merchandise retailer. It is the largest grocery retailer in the United Kingdom, with a 28 percent share of the local market, and the second-largest retailer in the world after Walmart measured by revenue. In 2015, Tesco had sales of more than $71 billion, more than 500,000 employees, and 6,814 stores.

In its home market of the United Kingdom (with a headquarters in Chestnut, Hertfordshire, England), the company's strengths are reputed to come from strong competencies in marketing and store site selection, logistics and inventory management, and its own label product offerings. By the early 1990s, these competencies had already given the company a leading position in the United Kingdom. The company was generating strong free cash flows, and senior managers had to decide how to use that cash. One strategy they settled on was overseas expansion.

As they looked at international markets, they soon concluded the best opportunities were not in established markets, such as those in North America and western Europe, where strong local competitors already existed, but in the emerging markets of eastern Europe and Asia, where there were few capable competitors but strong underlying growth trends. Tesco's first international foray was into Hungary in 1994, when it acquired an initial 51 percent stake in Global, a 43-store, state-owned grocery chain. By 2015, Tesco was the market leader in Hungary, with more than 200 stores and additional openings planned. In 1995, Tesco acquired 31 stores in Poland from Stavia; a year later, it added 13 stores purchased from Kmart in the Czech Republic and Slovakia; and the following year, it entered the Republic of Ireland. Tesco now has more than 450 stores in Poland, some 80 stores in the Czech Republic, more than 120 stores in Slovakia, and more than 100 stores in Ireland.

Tesco's Asian expansion began in 1998 in Thailand when it purchased 75 percent of Lotus, a local food retailer with 13 stores. Building on that base, Tesco had more than 380 stores in Thailand by 2015. In 1999, the company entered South Korea when it partnered with Samsung to develop a chain of hypermarkets. This was followed by entry into Taiwan in 2000, Malaysia in 2002, Japan in 2003, and China in 2004. The move into China came after three years of careful research and discussions with potential partners. Like many other Western companies, Tesco was attracted to the Chinese market by its large size and rapid growth. In the end, Tesco settled on a 50–50 joint venture with Hymall, a hypermarket chain that is controlled by Ting Hsin, a Taiwanese group, which had been operating in China for six years. In 2014, Tesco combined its 131 stores in China in a joint venture with the state-run China Resources Enterprise (CRE) and its nearly 3,000 stores. Tesco owns 20 percent of the joint venture.

As a result of these moves, by 2015 Tesco generated sales of $25 billion outside the United Kingdom (its UK annual revenues were $46 billion). The addition of international stores has helped make Tesco the second-largest company in the global grocery market behind only Walmart (Tesco is also behind Carrefour of France if profits are used). Of the three, however, Tesco may be the most successful internationally. By 2015, all its foreign ventures were making money.

Tesco is the largest grocery retailer in the United Kingdom and the second-largest retailer worldwide after Walmart.

Source: © Guang Niu/Getty Images

In explaining the company's success, Tesco's managers have detailed a number of important factors. First, the company devotes considerable attention to transferring its core capabilities in retailing to its new ventures. At the same time, it does not send in an army of expatriate managers to run local operations, preferring to hire local managers and support them with a few operational experts from the United Kingdom. Second, the company believes that its partnering strategy in Asia has been a great asset. Tesco has teamed up with good companies that have a deep understanding of the markets in which they are participating but that lack Tesco's financial strength and retailing capabilities. Consequently, both Tesco and its partners have brought useful assets to the venture, increasing the probability of success. As the venture becomes established, Tesco has typically increased its ownership stake in its partner. For example, by 2015 Tesco owned 100 percent of Homeplus, its South Korean hypermarket chain, but when the venture was established, Tesco owned 51 percent. Third, the company has focused on markets with good growth potential but that lack strong indigenous competitors, which provides Tesco with ripe ground for expansion.

Sources: P. N. Child, "Taking Tesco Global," *The McKenzie Quarterly*, no. 3, 2002; H. Keers, "Global Tesco Sets Out Its Stall in China," *Daily Telegraph*, July 15, 2004, p. 31; K. Burgess, "Tesco Spends Pounds 140m on Chinese Partnership," *Financial Times*, July 15, 2004, p. 22; J. McTaggart, "Industry Awaits Tesco Invasion," *Progressive Grocer*, March 1, 2006, pp. 8–10; Tesco's annual reports, www.tesco.com; P. Sonne, "Five Years and $1.6 Billion Later, Tesco Decides to Quit US," *The Wall Street Journal*, December 6, 2012; "Tesco Set to Push Ahead in the United States," *The Wall Street Journal*, October 6, 2010, p. 19.

Is First-Mover Advantage Always a Good Thing?

Timing of entry into a foreign market is one of the most critical aspects of going international. Popularized by Marvin Lieberman and David Montgomery in 1988, first-mover advantage was an idea that resonated with every company. But, 10 years later, in 1998, Lieberman and Montgomery actually backed off their own idea that taking advantage of being the first mover was always a good strategy. At this time, it was too late: Venture capitalists, companies, people, and many scholars had already latched on to the positive things about being first in a new foreign market and stressed this approach over any other timing of entry. Now we are some 15 years into the twenty-first century, and the realization is that first-mover advantages also come with pioneering costs. If you had a choice of being the first-mover into a new emerging foreign market (e.g., Turkey) and being the fifth company entering that market with your product, what would you choose and why?

Sources: M. B. Lieberman and D. B. Montgomery, "First-Mover Advantages," *Strategic Management Journal*, 9 (1988), pp. 41–58; M. B. Lieberman and D. B. Montgomery, "First-Mover (Dis)Advantages: Retrospective and Link with the Resource-Based View," *Strategic Management Journal*, 19 (1998), pp. 1111–25.

An early entrant may be put at a severe disadvantage, relative to a later entrant, if regulations change in a way that diminishes the value of an early entrant's investments. This is a serious risk in many developing nations where the rules that govern business practices are still evolving. Early entrants can find themselves at a disadvantage if a subsequent change in regulations invalidates prior assumptions about the best business model for operating in that country.

SCALE OF ENTRY AND STRATEGIC COMMITMENTS Another issue that an international business needs to consider when contemplating market entry is the scale of entry. Entering a market on a large scale involves the commitment of significant resources and implies rapid entry. Consider the entry of the Dutch insurance company ING into the U.S. insurance market in 1999. ING had to spend several billion dollars to acquire its U.S. operations. Not all firms have the resources necessary to enter on a large scale, and even some large firms prefer to enter foreign markets on a small scale and then build slowly as they become more familiar with the market.

The consequences of entering on a significant scale—entering rapidly—are associated with the value of the resulting strategic commitments.[7] A strategic commitment has a long-term impact and is difficult to reverse. Deciding to enter a foreign market on a significant scale is a major strategic commitment. Strategic commitments, such as rapid large-scale market entry, can have an important influence on the nature of competition in a market. For example, by entering the U.S. financial services market on a significant scale, ING signaled its commitment to the market. This will have several effects. On the positive side, it will make it easier for the company to attract customers and distributors (such as insurance agents). The scale of entry gives both customers and distributors reasons for believing that ING will remain in the market for the long run. The scale of entry may also give other foreign institutions considering entry into the United States pause; now they will have to compete not only against indigenous institutions in the United States but also against an aggressive and successful European institution. On the negative side, by committing itself heavily to one country, the United States, ING may have fewer resources available to support expansion in other desirable markets, such as Japan. The commitment to the United States limits the company's strategic flexibility.

As suggested by the ING example, significant strategic commitments are neither unambiguously good nor bad. Rather, they tend to change the competitive playing field and unleash a number of changes, some of which may be desirable and some of which will not be. It is important for a firm to think through the implications of large-scale entry into a market and act accordingly. Of particular relevance is trying to identify how actual and potential competitors might react to large-scale entry into a market. Also, the large-scale entrant is more likely than the small-scale entrant to be able to capture first-mover advantages associated with demand preemption, scale economies, and switching costs.

The value of the commitments that flow from rapid large-scale entry into a foreign market must be balanced against the resulting risks and lack of flexibility associated with significant commitments. But strategic inflexibility can also have value. A famous example from military history illustrates the value of inflexibility. When Hernán Cortés landed in Mexico, he ordered his men to burn all but one of his ships. Cortés reasoned that by eliminating their only method of retreat, his men had no choice but to fight hard to win against the Aztecs—and ultimately they did.[8]

Balanced against the value and risks of the commitments associated with large-scale entry are the benefits of a small-scale entry. Small-scale entry allows a firm to learn about a foreign market while limiting the firm's exposure to that market. Small-scale entry is a way to gather information about a foreign market before deciding whether to enter on a significant scale and how best to enter. By giving the firm time to collect information, small-scale entry reduces the risks associated with a subsequent large-scale entry. But the lack of commitment associated with small-scale entry may make it more difficult for the small-scale entrant to build market share and to capture first-mover or early-mover advantages. The risk-averse firm that enters a foreign market on a small scale may limit its potential losses, but it may also miss the chance to capture first-mover advantages.

MARKET ENTRY SUMMARY

There are no "right" decisions here, just decisions that are associated with different levels of risk and reward. Entering a large developing nation such as China or India before most other international businesses in the firm's industry and entering on a large scale will be associated with high levels of risk. In such cases, the liability of being foreign is increased by the absence of prior foreign entrants whose experience can be a useful guide. At the same time, the potential long-term rewards associated with such a strategy are great. The early large-scale entrant into a major developing nation may be able to capture significant first-mover advantages that will bolster its long-run position in that market.[9] In contrast, entering developed nations such as Australia or Canada after other international businesses in the firm's industry and entering on a small scale to first learn more about those markets will be associated with much lower levels of risk. However, the potential long-term rewards are also likely to be lower because the firm is essentially forgoing the opportunity to capture first-mover advantages and because the lack of commitment signaled by small-scale entry may limit its future growth potential.

This section has been written largely from the perspective of a business based in a developed country considering entry into foreign markets. Christopher Bartlett and Sumantra Ghoshal have pointed out the ability that businesses based in emerging countries have to enter foreign markets and become global players.[10] Although such firms tend to be late entrants into foreign markets and although their resources may be limited, Bartlett and Ghoshal argue that such late movers can still succeed against well-established global competitors by pursuing appropriate strategies. In particular, companies based in emerging countries should use the entry of foreign multinationals as an opportunity to learn from these competitors by benchmarking their operations and performance against them. Furthermore, a local company may be able to find ways to differentiate itself from a foreign multinational, for example, by focusing on market niches that the multinational ignores or is unable to serve effectively if it has a standardized global product offering. Having improved its performance through learning and differentiated its product offering, the firm from an emerging country may then be able to pursue its own international expansion strategy. Even though the firm may be a late entrant into many countries, by benchmarking and then differentiating itself from early movers in global markets, the firm from the emerging country may still be able to build a strong international business presence. A good example of how this can work is given in the accompanying Management Focus, which looks at how Jollibee, a Philippines-based fast-food chain, has started to build a global presence in a market dominated by U.S. multinationals such as McDonald's and KFC.

test PREP

Use SmartBook to help retain what you have learned. Access your Instructor's Connect course to check out SmartBook or go to learnsmartadvantage.com for help.

Entry Modes

Compare and contrast the different modes that firms use to enter foreign markets.

Once a firm decides to enter a foreign market, the question arises as to the best mode of entry. Firms can use six different modes to enter foreign markets: exporting, turnkey projects, licensing, franchising, establishing joint ventures with a host-country firm, or setting up a new wholly owned subsidiary in the host country. Each entry mode has advantages and disadvantages. Managers need to consider these carefully when deciding which to use.[11]

EXPORTING

Many manufacturing firms begin their global expansion as exporters and only later switch to another mode for serving a foreign market. We take a close look at the mechanics of exporting in Chapter 14. Here we focus on the advantages and disadvantages of exporting as an entry mode.

management FOCUS

The Jollibee Phenomenon

Jollibee Foods Corporation, abbreviated JFC and more popularly known as Jollobee, is one of the Philippines' phenomenal business success stories. Jollibee, which stands for "Jolly Bee," began operations in 1975 as a two-branch ice cream parlor. It later expanded its menu to include hot sandwiches and other meals. Encouraged by early success, Jollibee Foods Corporation was incorporated in 1978, with a network that had grown to seven outlets. In 1981, when Jollibee had 11 stores, McDonald's began to open stores in Manila. Many observers thought Jollibee would have difficulty competing against McDonald's. However, Jollibee saw this as an opportunity to learn from a very successful global competitor. Jollibee benchmarked its performance against that of McDonald's and started to adopt operational systems similar to those used at McDonald's to control its quality, cost, and service at the store level. This helped Jollibee improve its performance.

As it came to better understand McDonald's business model, Jollibee began to look for a weakness in McDonald's global strategy. Jollibee executives concluded that McDonald's fare was too standardized for many locals and that the local firm could gain share by tailoring its menu to local tastes. Jollibee's hamburgers were set apart by a secret mix of spices blended into the ground beef to make the burgers sweeter than those produced by McDonald's, appealing more to Philippine tastes. It also offered local fare, including various rice dishes, pineapple burgers, and banana *langka* and peach mango pies for desserts. By pursuing this strategy, Jollibee maintained a leadership position over the global giant. By 2015, Jollibee had over 801 stores in the Philippines for its Jollibee brand and some 2,040 total stores across all of its brands (e.g., Jollibee, Chowking, Greenwich, Red Ribbon, Mang INasal, and Burger King), a market share of more than 60 percent, and revenues in excess of $600 million. McDonald's, in contrast, had about 400 stores.

The international expansion started in the mid-1980s. Jollibee's initial ventures were into neighboring Asian countries such as Indonesia, where it pursued the strategy of localizing the menu to better match local tastes, thereby differentiating itself from McDonald's. In 1987, Jollibee entered the Middle East, where a large contingent of expatriate Filipino workers provided a ready-made market for the company. The strategy of focusing on expatriates worked so well that in the late 1990s, Jollibee decided to enter another foreign market where there was a large Filipino population—the United States.

Between 1999 and 2016, Jollibee opened 32 stores in the United States, 20 of which are in California. Even though many believe the U.S. fast-food market is saturated, the stores have performed well. While the initial clientele was strongly biased toward the expatriate Filipino community, where Jollibee's brand awareness is high, non-Filipinos increasingly are coming to the restaurant. In the San Francisco store, which has been open the longest, more than half the customers are now non-Filipino. Today, Jollibee has some 500 international stores and a potentially bright future as a niche player in a market that has historically been dominated by U.S. multinationals.

Sources: "Jollibee Battles Burger Giants in US Market," *Philippine Daily Inquirer*, July 13, 2000; M. Ballon, "Jollibee Struggling to Expand in U.S.," *Los Angeles Times*, September 16, 2002, p. C1; J. Hookway, "Burgers and Beer," *Far Eastern Economic Review*, December 2003, pp. 72–74; S. E. Lockyer, "Coming to America," *Nation's Restaurant News*, February 14, 2005, pp. 33–35; Erik de la Cruz, "Jollibee to Open 120 New Stores This Year, Plans India," *Inquirer Money*, July 5, 2006, business.inquirer.net; www.jollibee.com.ph.

Exporting
Sale of products produced in one country to residents of another country.

Advantages

Exporting has two distinct advantages. First, it avoids the often substantial costs of establishing manufacturing operations in the host country. Second, exporting may help a firm achieve experience curve and location economies (see Chapter 12). By manufacturing the product in a centralized location and exporting it to other national markets, the firm may realize substantial scale economies from its global sales volume. This is how many Japanese automakers made inroads into the U.S. market.

Disadvantages

Exporting has a number of drawbacks. First, exporting from the firm's home base may not be appropriate if lower-cost locations for manufacturing the product can be found abroad (i.e., if the firm can realize location economies by moving production elsewhere). Thus, particularly for firms pursuing global or transnational strategies, it may be preferable to manufacture where the mix of factor conditions is most favorable from a value creation perspective and to export to the rest of the world from that location. This is not so much an argument against exporting as an argument against exporting from the firm's home country. Many U.S. electronics firms have moved some of their manufacturing to the Far East because of the availability of low-cost, highly skilled labor. They then export from that location to the rest of the world, including the United States.

A second drawback to exporting is that high transportation costs can make exporting uneconomical, particularly for bulk products. One way of getting around this is to manufacture bulk products regionally. This strategy enables the firm to realize some economies from large-scale production and at the same time to limit its transportation costs. For example, many multinational chemical firms manufacture their products regionally, serving several countries from one facility.

Another drawback is that tariff barriers can make exporting uneconomical. Similarly, the threat of tariff barriers by the host-country government can make it very risky. A fourth drawback to exporting arises when a firm delegates its marketing, sales, and service in each country where it does business to another company. This is a common approach for manufacturing firms that are just beginning to expand internationally. The other company may be a local agent, or it may be another multinational with extensive international distribution operations. Local agents often carry the products of competing firms and so have divided loyalties. In such cases, the local agent may not do as good a job as the firm would if it managed its marketing itself. Similar problems can occur when another multinational takes on distribution.

The way around such problems is to set up wholly owned subsidiaries in foreign nations to handle local marketing, sales, and service. By doing this, the firm can exercise tight control over marketing and sales in the country while reaping the cost advantages of manufacturing the product in a single location or a few choice locations.

TURNKEY PROJECTS

Firms that specialize in the design, construction, and start-up of turnkey plants are common in some industries. In a **turnkey project**, the contractor agrees to handle every detail of the project for a foreign client, including the training of operating personnel. At completion of the contract, the foreign client is handed the "key" to a plant that is ready for full operation—hence, the term *turnkey*. This is a means of exporting process technology to other countries. Turnkey projects are most common in the chemical, pharmaceutical, petroleum-refining, and metal-refining industries, all of which use complex, expensive production technologies.

Turnkey Project
A project in which a firm agrees to set up an operating plant for a foreign client and hand over the "key" when the plant is fully operational.

Advantages

The know-how required to assemble and run a technologically complex process, such as refining petroleum or steel, is a valuable asset. Turnkey projects are a way of earning great economic returns from that asset. The strategy is particularly useful where foreign direct investment (FDI) is limited by host-government regulations. For example, the governments of many oil-rich countries have set out to build their own petroleum-refining industries, so they restrict FDI in their oil-refining sectors. But because many of these countries lack petroleum-refining technology, they gain it by entering into turnkey projects with foreign firms that have the technology. Such deals are often attractive to the selling firm because without them, they would have no way to earn a return on their valuable know-how in that country. A turnkey strategy can also be less risky than conventional FDI. In a country with unstable political and economic environments, a longer-term investment might expose the firm to unacceptable political and/or economic risks (e.g., the risk of nationalization or of economic collapse).

Disadvantages

Three main drawbacks are associated with a turnkey strategy. First, the firm that enters into a turnkey deal will have no long-term interest in the foreign country. This can be a disadvantage if that country subsequently proves to be a major market for the output of the process that has been exported. One way around this is to take a minority equity interest in the operation. Second, the firm that enters into a turnkey project with a foreign enterprise may inadvertently create a competitor. For example, many of the Western firms that sold oil-refining technology to firms in Saudi Arabia, Kuwait, and other Gulf states now find themselves competing with these firms in the world oil market. Third, if the firm's process technology is a source of competitive advantage, then selling this technology through a turnkey project is also selling competitive advantage to potential and/or actual competitors.

LICENSING

A **licensing agreement** is an arrangement whereby a licensor grants the rights to intangible property to another entity (the licensee) for a specified period, and in return, the licensor receives a royalty fee from the licensee.[12] Intangible property includes patents, inventions, formulas, processes, designs, copyrights, and trademarks. For example, to enter the Japanese market, Xerox, inventor of the photocopier, established a joint venture with Fuji Photo that is known as Fuji Xerox. Xerox then licensed its xerographic know-how to Fuji Xerox. In return, Fuji Xerox paid Xerox a royalty fee equal to 5 percent of the net sales revenue that Fuji Xerox earned from the sales of photocopiers based on Xerox's patented know-how. In the Fuji Xerox case, the license was originally granted for 10 years, and it has been renegotiated and

Licensing Agreement
Arrangement in which a licensor grants the rights to intangible property to a licensee for a specified period and receives a royalty fee in return.

Exporting or Licensing?

In Chapter 13, we discuss as series of advantages and disadvantages of exporting and licensing (as well as turnkey projects, franchising, joint ventures, and wholly owned subsidiaries as other entry mode choices). Exporting refers to the sale of products produced in one country to residents of another country. Licensing refers to an arrangement in which a licensor grants the rights to intangible property to the licensee for a specified period and receives a royalty fee in return. Both of these modes of entry into a foreign market have unique advantages and disadvantages. Oftentimes, selecting exporting or licensing depends on myriad factors—one being the global mindset of the business owner. Assume you have a choice to enter three emerging markets—Bolivia, Chile, and Peru, neighboring countries in South America. You have a great product, with lots of technological innovation and a lightweight packaging. Would you opt for exporting or licensing, and why?

extended several times since. The licensing agreement between Xerox and Fuji Xerox also limited Fuji Xerox's direct sales to the Asian Pacific region (although Fuji Xerox does supply Xerox with photocopiers that are sold in North America under the Xerox label).[13]

Advantages In the typical international licensing deal, the licensee puts up most of the capital necessary to get the overseas operation going. Thus, a primary advantage of licensing is that the firm does not have to bear the development costs and risks associated with opening a foreign market. Licensing is very attractive for firms lacking the capital to develop operations overseas. In addition, licensing can be attractive when a firm is unwilling to commit substantial financial resources to an unfamiliar or politically volatile foreign market. Licensing is also often used when a firm wishes to participate in a foreign market but is prohibited from doing so by barriers to investment. This was one of the original reasons for the formation of the Fuji Xerox joint venture. Xerox wanted to participate in the Japanese market but was prohibited from setting up a wholly owned subsidiary by the Japanese government. So Xerox set up the joint venture with Fuji and then licensed its know-how to the joint venture.

Finally, licensing is frequently used when a firm possesses some intangible property that might have business applications, but it does not want to develop those applications itself. For example, Bell Laboratories at AT&T originally invented the transistor circuit in the 1950s, but AT&T decided it did not want to produce transistors, so it licensed the technology to a number of other companies, such as TI (Texas Instruments). Similarly, Coca-Cola has licensed its famous trademark to clothing manufacturers, which have incorporated the design into clothing. Harley-Davidson licenses its brand to Wolverine World Wide to make footwear that embodies the spirit of the open road, which Harley-Davidson emphasizes in its advertisements and product positioning.

Disadvantages Licensing has three serious drawbacks. First, it does not give a firm the tight control over manufacturing, marketing, and strategy that is required for realizing experience curve and location economies. Licensing typically involves each licensee setting up its own production operations. This severely limits the firm's ability to realize experience curve and location economies by producing its product in a centralized location. When these economies are important, licensing may not be the best way to expand overseas.

Second, competing in a global market may require a firm to coordinate strategic moves across countries by using profits earned in one country to support competitive attacks in another. By its very nature, licensing limits a firm's ability to do this. A licensee is unlikely to allow a multinational firm to use its profits (beyond those due in the form of royalty payments) to support a different licensee operating in another country.

A third problem with licensing is one that we encountered in Chapter 8 when we reviewed the economic theory of foreign direct investment (FDI). This is the risk associated with licensing technological know-how to foreign companies. Technological know-how constitutes the basis of many multinational firms' competitive advantage. Most firms wish to maintain control over how their know-how is used, and a firm can quickly lose control over its technology by licensing it. Many firms have made the mistake of thinking they could maintain control over their know-how within the framework of a licensing agreement. RCA Corporation, for example, once licensed its color TV technology to Japanese firms including Matsushita and Sony. The Japanese firms quickly assimilated the technology, improved on it, and used it to enter the U.S. market, taking substantial market share away from RCA.

There are ways of reducing this risk. One way is by entering into a cross-licensing agreement with a foreign firm. Under a cross-licensing agreement, a firm might license some valuable intangible property to a foreign partner, but in addition to a royalty payment, the firm might also request that the foreign partner license some of its valuable know-how to the firm. Such agreements are believed to reduce the risks associated with licensing technological know-how, since the licensee realizes that if it violates the licensing contract (by using the knowledge obtained to compete directly with the licensor), the licensor can do the same to it. Cross-licensing agreements enable firms to hold each other hostage, which reduces the probability that they will behave opportunistically toward each other.[14] Such cross-licensing agreements are increasingly common in high-technology industries.

Another way of reducing the risk associated with licensing is to follow the Fuji Xerox model and link an agreement to license know-how with the formation of a joint venture in which the licensor and licensee take important equity stakes. Such an approach aligns the interests of licensor and licensee, because both have a stake in ensuring that the venture is successful. Thus, the risk that Fuji Photo might appropriate Xerox's technological know-how and then compete directly against Xerox in the global photocopier market was reduced by the establishment of a joint venture in which both Xerox and Fuji Photo had an important stake.

FRANCHISING

Franchising is similar to licensing, although franchising tends to involve longer-term commitments than licensing. **Franchising** is basically a specialized form of licensing in which the franchiser not only sells intangible property (normally a trademark) to the franchisee but also insists that the franchisee agree to abide by strict rules as to how it does business. The franchiser will also often assist the franchisee to run the business on an ongoing basis. As with licensing, the franchiser typically receives a royalty payment, which amounts to some percentage of the franchisee's revenues. Whereas licensing is pursued primarily by manufacturing firms, franchising is employed primarily by service firms.[15]

Franchising
A specialized form of licensing in which the franchiser sells intangible property to the franchisee and insists on rules to conduct the business.

Advantages

McDonald's is a good example of a firm that has grown and taken advantage of a franchising strategy. McDonald's strict rules as to how franchisees should operate a restaurant extend to control over the menu, cooking methods, staffing policies, and design and location. McDonald's also organizes the supply chain for its franchisees and provides management training and financial assistance.[16] Overall, the advantages of franchising as an entry mode are very similar to those of licensing. The firm is relieved of many of the costs and risks of opening a foreign market on its own. Instead, the franchisee typically assumes those costs and risks. This creates a good incentive for the franchisee to build a profitable operation as quickly as possible.

Thus, using a franchising strategy, a service firm can build a global presence quickly and at a relatively low cost and risk, as McDonald's has. Two Men and a Truck—a Lansing, Michigan–headquartered moving company—effectively used the franchising concept to scale up from a local company to a U.S. nationwide company almost immediately in 1989 after its inception in 1985. Now, the company has 320 locations worldwide.

Disadvantages

The disadvantages of franchising are less pronounced than with licensing. Since franchising is often used by service companies, there is no reason to consider the need for coordination of manufacturing to achieve experience curve and location economies. But franchising may inhibit the firm's ability to take profits out of one country to support competitive attacks in another. A more significant disadvantage of franchising is quality control. The foundation of franchising arrangements is that the firm's brand name conveys a message to consumers about the quality of the firm's product. Thus, a business traveler checking in at a Four Seasons hotel in Hong Kong can reasonably expect the same quality of room, food, and service that she would receive in New York. The Four Seasons name is supposed to guarantee consistent product quality. This presents a problem in that foreign franchisees may not be as

So, You Think You Want to Own a Franchise?

Franchising is a specialized form of licensing in which the franchiser not only sells intangible property to the franchisee but also insists that the franchisee agree to abide by strict rules as to how it does business. Some of the advantages of franchising include branding, advertising, reputation, and headquarters/company support for development of the infrastructure needed to operate the franchise business. Some of the disadvantages of franchising include restrictions on territory and pricing, not being completely independent, franchise fee and ongoing royalty payments, and dependence on other franchise owners for nurturing the brand. Well-known worldwide franchise systems include Subway, 7-Eleven, Pizza Hut, and McDonald's. Assume you are interested in being an international entrepreneur. Would franchising be your choice of starting a business?

Source: T. Hult, D. Closs, and D. Frayer, *Global Supply Chain Management: Leveraging Processes, Measurements, and Tools for Strategic Corporate Advantage* (New York: McGraw-Hill Education, 2014).

concerned about quality as they are supposed to be, and the result of poor quality can extend beyond lost sales in a particular foreign market to a decline in the firm's worldwide reputation. For example, if the business traveler has a bad experience at the Four Seasons in Hong Kong, she may never go to another Four Seasons hotel and may urge her colleagues to do likewise. The geographic distance of the firm from its foreign franchisees can make poor quality difficult to detect. In addition, the sheer numbers of franchisees—in the case of McDonald's, tens of thousands—can make quality control difficult. Due to these factors, quality problems may persist.

One way around this disadvantage is to set up a subsidiary in each country in which the firm expands. The subsidiary might be wholly owned by the company or a joint venture with a foreign company. The subsidiary assumes the rights and obligations to establish franchises throughout the particular country or region. McDonald's, for example, establishes a master franchisee in many countries. Typically, this master franchisee is a joint venture between McDonald's and a local firm. The proximity and the smaller number of franchises to oversee reduce the quality control challenge. In addition, because the subsidiary (or master franchisee) is at least partly owned by the firm, the firm can place its own managers in the subsidiary to help ensure that it is doing a good job of monitoring the franchises. This organizational arrangement has proven very satisfactory for McDonald's, KFC, and others.

Joint Venture

A cooperative undertaking between two or more firms.

JOINT VENTURES

A **joint venture** entails establishing a firm that is jointly owned by two or more otherwise independent firms. Fuji Xerox, for example, was set up as a joint venture between Xerox and Fuji Photo. Establishing a joint venture with a foreign firm has long been a popular mode for entering a new market. The most typical joint venture is a 50–50 venture, in which there are two parties, each of which holding a 50 percent ownership stake and contributing a team of managers to share operating control. This was the case with the Fuji–Xerox joint venture until 2001; it is now a 25–75 venture with Xerox holding 25 percent. The GM SAIC venture in China was a 50–50 venture until 2010, which it became a 51–49 venture, with SAIC holding the 51 percent stake. Some firms, however, have sought joint ventures in which they have a majority share and thus tighter control.[17]

Advantages

Joint ventures have a number of advantages. First, a firm benefits from a local partner's knowledge of the host country's competitive conditions, culture, language, political systems, and business. Thus, for many U.S. firms, joint ventures have involved the U.S. company providing technological know-how and products and the local partner providing the marketing expertise and the local knowledge necessary for competing in that country. Second, when the development costs and/or risks of opening a foreign market are high, a firm might gain by sharing these costs and or risks with a local partner. Third, in many countries, political considerations make joint ventures the only feasible entry mode. Research suggests joint ventures with local partners face a low risk of being subject to nationalization or other forms of adverse government interference.[18] This appears to be because local equity partners, who may have some influence on host-government policy, have a vested interest in speaking out against nationalization or government interference.

Disadvantages

Despite these advantages, there are major disadvantages with joint ventures. First, as with licensing, a firm that enters into a joint venture risks giving control of its technology to its partner. Thus, a proposed joint venture in 2002 between Boeing and Mitsubishi Heavy Industries to build a new wide-body jet (the 787) raised fears that Boeing might unwittingly give away its commercial airline technology to the Japanese. However, joint-venture agreements can be constructed to minimize this risk. One option is to hold majority ownership in the venture. This allows the dominant partner to exercise greater control over its technology. But it can be difficult to find a foreign partner who is willing to settle for minority ownership. Another option is to "wall off" from a partner technology that is central to the core competence of the firm, while sharing other technology.

A second disadvantage is that a joint venture does not give a firm the tight control over subsidiaries that it might need to realize experience curve or location economies. Nor does it give a firm the tight control over a foreign subsidiary that it might need for engaging in coordinated global attacks against its rivals. Consider the entry of Texas Instruments (TI) into the Japanese semiconductor market. When TI established semiconductor facilities in Japan, it did so for the dual purpose of checking Japanese manufacturers' market share and limiting their cash available for invading TI's global market. In other words, TI was engaging in global strategic coordination. To implement this strategy, TI's subsidiary in Japan had to be prepared to take instructions from corporate headquarters regarding competitive strategy. The strategy also required the Japanese subsidiary to run at a loss if necessary. Few, if any, potential joint-venture partners would have been willing to accept such conditions, since it would have necessitated a willingness to accept a negative return on investment. Indeed, many joint ventures establish a degree of autonomy that would make such direct control over strategic decisions all but impossible to establish.[19] Thus, to implement this strategy, TI set up a wholly owned subsidiary in Japan.

A third disadvantage with joint ventures is that the shared ownership arrangement can lead to conflicts and battles for control between the investing firms if their goals and objectives change or if they take different views as to what the strategy should be. This was apparently not a problem with the Fuji Xerox joint venture. According to Yotaro Kobayashi, the former chair of Fuji Xerox, a primary reason is that both Xerox and Fuji Photo adopted an arm's-length relationship with Fuji Xerox, giving the venture's management considerable freedom to determine its own strategy.[20] However, much research indicates that conflicts of interest over strategy and goals often arise in joint ventures. These conflicts tend to be greater when the venture is between firms of different nationalities, and they often end in the dissolution of the venture.[21] Such conflicts tend to be triggered by shifts in the relative bargaining power of venture partners. For example, in the case of ventures between a foreign firm and a local firm, as a foreign partner's knowledge about local market conditions increases, it depends less on the expertise of a local partner. This increases the bargaining power of the foreign partner and ultimately leads to conflicts over control of the venture's strategy and goals.[22] Some firms have sought to limit such problems by entering into joint ventures in which one partner has a controlling interest.

WHOLLY OWNED SUBSIDIARIES

In a **wholly owned subsidiary**, the firm owns 100 percent of the stock. Establishing a wholly owned subsidiary in a foreign market can be done two ways. The firm either can set up a new operation in that country, often referred to as a greenfield venture, or it can acquire an established firm in that host nation and use that firm to promote its products.[23] For example, ING's strategy for entering the U.S. insurance market was to acquire established U.S. enterprises, rather than try to build an operation from the ground floor.

Wholly Owned Subsidiary
A subsidiary in which the firm owns 100 percent of the stock.

Advantages

There are several clear advantages of wholly owned subsidiaries. First, when a firm's competitive advantage is based on technological competence, a wholly owned subsidiary will often be the preferred entry mode because it reduces the risk of losing control over that competence. (See Chapter 8 for more details.) Many high-tech firms prefer this entry mode for overseas expansion (e.g., firms in the semiconductor, electronics, and pharmaceutical industries). Second, a wholly owned subsidiary gives a firm tight control over operations in different countries. This is necessary for engaging in global strategic coordination (i.e., using profits from one country to support competitive attacks in another).

Third, a wholly owned subsidiary may be required if a firm is trying to realize location and experience curve economies (as firms pursuing global and transnational strategies try to do). As we saw in Chapter 11, when cost pressures are intense, it may pay a firm to configure its value chain in such a way that the value added at each stage is maximized. Thus, a national subsidiary may specialize in manufacturing only part of the product line or certain components of the end product, exchanging parts and products with other subsidiaries in the firm's global system. Establishing such a global production system requires a high degree of control over the operations of each affiliate. The various operations must be prepared to accept centrally determined decisions as to how they will produce, how much they will produce, and how their output will be priced for transfer to the next operation. Because licensees or joint-venture partners are unlikely to accept such a subservient role, establishing wholly owned subsidiaries may be necessary. Finally, establishing a wholly owned subsidiary gives the firm a 100 percent share in the profits generated in a foreign market.

Disadvantage

Establishing a wholly owned subsidiary is generally the most costly method of serving a foreign market from a capital investment standpoint. Firms doing this must bear the full capital costs and risks of setting up overseas operations. The risks associated with

Use SmartBook to help retain what you have learned. Access your Instructor's Connect course to check out SmartBook or go to learnsmartadvantage.com for help.

Identify the factors that influence a firm's choice of entry mode.

learning to do business in a new culture are less if the firm acquires an established host-country enterprise. However, acquisitions raise additional problems, including those associated with trying to marry divergent corporate cultures. These problems may more than offset any benefits derived by acquiring an established operation. Because the choice between greenfield ventures and acquisitions is such an important one, we discuss it in more detail later in the chapter.

Selecting an Entry Mode

As the preceding discussion demonstrated, all the entry modes have advantages and disadvantages, as summarized in Table 13.1. Thus, trade-offs are inevitable when selecting an entry mode. For example, when considering entry into an unfamiliar country with a track record for discriminating against foreign-owned enterprises when awarding government contracts, a firm might favor a joint venture with a local enterprise. Its rationale might be that the local partner will help it establish operations in an unfamiliar environment and will help the company win government contracts. However, if the firm's core competence is based on proprietary technology, entering a joint venture might risk losing control of that technology to the joint-venture partner, in which case the strategy may seem unattractive. Despite the existence of such trade-offs, it is possible to make some generalizations about the optimal choice of entry mode.[24]

CORE COMPETENCIES AND ENTRY MODE

We saw in Chapter 12 that firms often expand internationally to earn greater returns from their core competencies, transferring the skills and products derived from their core competencies to foreign markets where indigenous

13.1 TABLE

Advantages and Disadvantages of Entry Modes

Entry Mode	Advantages	Disadvantages
Exporting	Ability to realize location and experience curve economies Increased speed and flexibility of engaging target markets	High transport costs Trade barriers Problems with local marketing agents
Turnkey contracts	Ability to earn returns from process technology skills in countries where FDI is restricted	Creation of efficient competitors Lack of long-term market presence
Licensing	Low development costs and risks Moderate involvement and commitment	Lack of control over technology Inability to realize location and experience curve economies Inability to engage in global strategic coordination
Franchising	Low development costs and risks Possible circumvention of import barriers, and strong sales potential	Lack of control over quality Inability to engage in global strategic coordination
Joint ventures	Access to local partner's knowledge Shared development costs and risks Politically acceptable Typically no ownership restrictions	Lack of control over technology Inability to engage in global strategic coordination Inability to realize location and experience economies
Wholly owned subsidiaries	Protection of technology Ability to engage in global strategic coordination Ability to realize location and experience economies	High costs and risks Need for more human and nonhuman resources, and interaction and integration with local employees

competitors lack those skills. The optimal entry mode for these firms depends to some degree on the nature of their core competencies. A distinction can be drawn between firms whose core competency is in technological know-how and those whose core competency is in management know-how.

Technological Know-How As was observed in Chapter 8, if a firm's competitive advantage (its core competence) is based on control over proprietary technological know-how, licensing and joint-venture arrangements should be avoided if possible to minimize the risk of losing control over that technology. Thus, if a high-tech firm sets up operations in a foreign country to profit from a core competency in technological know-how, it will probably do so through a wholly owned subsidiary. This rule should not be viewed as hard and fast, however. Sometimes a licensing or joint-venture arrangement can be structured to reduce the risk of licensees or joint-venture partners expropriating technological know-how. Another exception exists when a firm perceives its technological advantage to be only transitory, when it expects rapid imitation of its core technology by competitors. In such cases, the firm might want to license its technology as rapidly as possible to foreign firms to gain global acceptance for its technology before the imitation occurs.[25] Such a strategy has some advantages. By licensing its technology to competitors, the firm may deter them from developing their own, possibly superior, technology. Further, by licensing its technology, the firm may establish its technology as the dominant design in the industry. This may ensure a steady stream of royalty payments. However, the attractions of licensing are frequently outweighed by the risks of losing control over technology, and if this is a risk, licensing should be avoided.

Management Know-How The competitive advantage of many service firms is based on management know-how (e.g., McDonald's, Starbucks). For such firms, the risk of losing control over the management skills to franchisees or joint-venture partners is not that great. These firms' valuable asset is their brand name, and brand names are generally well protected by international laws pertaining to trademarks. Given this, many of the issues arising in the case of technological know-how are of less concern here. As a result, many service firms favor a combination of franchising and master subsidiaries to control the franchises within particular countries or regions. The master subsidiaries may be wholly owned or joint ventures, but most service firms have found that joint ventures with local partners work best for the master controlling subsidiaries. A joint venture is often politically more acceptable and brings a degree of local knowledge to the subsidiary.

PRESSURES FOR COST REDUCTIONS AND ENTRY MODE

The greater the pressures for cost reductions, the more likely a firm will want to pursue some combination of exporting and wholly owned subsidiaries. By manufacturing in those locations where factor conditions are optimal and then exporting to the rest of the world, a firm may be able to realize substantial location and experience curve economies. The firm might then want to export the finished product to marketing subsidiaries based in various countries. These subsidiaries will typically be wholly owned and have the responsibility for overseeing distribution in their particular countries. Setting up wholly owned marketing subsidiaries is preferable to joint-venture arrangements and to using foreign marketing agents because it gives the firm tight control that might be required for coordinating a globally dispersed value chain. It also gives the firm the ability to use the profits generated in one market to improve its competitive position in another market. In other words, firms pursuing global standardization or transnational strategies tend to prefer establishing wholly owned subsidiaries.

test PREP

Use SmartBook to help retain what you have learned. Access your Instructor's Connect course to check out SmartBook or go to learnsmartadvantage.com for help.

Greenfield Venture or Acquisition?

LO 13-4

Recognize the pros and cons of acquisitions versus greenfield ventures as an entry strategy.

A firm can establish a wholly owned subsidiary in a country by building a subsidiary from the ground up, the so-called greenfield strategy, or by acquiring an enterprise in the target market.[26] The volume of cross-border acquisitions has been growing at a rapid rate for two decades. Over most of the past decades, between 40 and 80 percent of all foreign direct investment (FDI) inflows have been in the form of mergers and acquisitions.[27]

PROS AND CONS OF ACQUISITIONS

Acquisitions have three major points in their favor. First, they are quick to execute. By acquiring an established enterprise, a firm can

management FOCUS

General Motors on the Upswing

The late 2000s were not kind to General Motors Corporation (GM), but the company is on a much-needed upswing. The Chinese market, in particular, is becoming one of the most important foreign markets for GM. General Motors, of course, is a U.S.-based multinational corporation headquartered in Detroit, Michigan. GM was founded in 1908 in Flint, Michigan, and Mary Barra is the company's CEO. In 2015, GM had revenues of $156 billion and more than 216,000 employees, produced almost 10 million vehicles, and consisted of four core divisions (Buick, Chevrolet, Cadillac, and GMC).

Hurt by a deep recession in the United States and plunging vehicle sales, GM capped off the 2000s decade, where it had progressively lost market share to foreign rivals such as Toyota, by entering Chapter 11 bankruptcy. Between 1980, when it dominated the U.S. market, and 2009, when it entered bankruptcy protection, GM saw its U.S. market share slip from 44 to just 19 percent. The troubled company emerged from bankruptcy a few months later a smaller enterprise with fewer brands, and yet going forward, some believe that the new GM could be a much more profitable enterprise. One major reason for this optimism was the success of its joint ventures in China.

GM entered China in 1997 with a $1.6 billion investment to establish a joint venture with the state-owned Shanghai Automotive Industry Corporation (SAIC) to build Buick sedans. At the time, the Chinese market was tiny (fewer than 400,000 cars were sold in 1996), but GM was attracted by the enormous potential in a country of more than 1.4 billion people that was experiencing rapid economic growth. While the company initially recognized that it had much to learn about the Chinese market and would probably lose money for a few years in the early years, GM executives believed it was crucial to establish operations and to team up with SAIC (one of the early leaders in China's emerging automobile industry) before its global rivals did. The decision to enter a joint venture was not a hard one. Not only did GM lack knowledge and connections in China, but Chinese government regulations made it all but impossible for a foreign automaker to go it alone in the country.

While GM was not alone in investing in China—many of the world's major automobile companies entered into some kind of Chinese joint venture during this time period—it was among the largest investors. Only Volkswagen, whose management shared GM's view, made a similar-sized investment. Other companies adopted a more cautious approach, investing smaller amounts and setting more limited goals.

By 2007, GM had expanded the range of its partnership with SAIC to include vehicles sold under the names of Chevrolet, Cadillac, and Wuling. The two companies had also established the Pan-Asian Technical Automotive Center to design cars and components not just for China but also for other Asian markets. At this point, it was already clear that both the Chinese market and the joint venture were exceeding GM's initial expectations. Not only was the venture profitable, but it was also selling more than 900,000 cars and light trucks in 2007, an 18 percent increase over 2006, placing it second only to Volkswagen in the market among foreign nameplates. Equally impressive, some 8 million cars and light trucks were sold in China in 2007, making China the second-largest car market in the world, ahead of Japan and behind the United States. In 2015, GM sold about 3.16 million vehicles in China, up from some 2.4 million vehicles sold in 2010.

Much of the venture's success could be attributed to its strategy of designing vehicles explicitly for the Chinese market. For example, together with SAIC, GM produced a tiny minivan, the Wuling Sunshine. The van costs $3,700, has a 0.8-liter engine, hits a top speed of 60 mph, and weighs less than 1,000 kilograms—a far cry from the heavy SUVs GM was known for in the United States. For China, the vehicle was perfect, making it the best seller in the light truck sector.

It is the future, however, that has people excited. From a market of about 9 million passenger and commercial vehicles sold in China in 2008 to 23.5 million in 2014, the Chinese vehicle market is booming compared with those in the United States and Europe. China has now become GM's largest market in vehicles sold. GM also plans to expand its Chinese dealer network to more than 5,000, and it plans to have 17 assembly plants in China by the end of 2015, more than the 12 it has in the United States. Driving this expansion are forecasts from GM that demand in China will reach 35 million vehicles a year by 2022, a huge increase from the 23.5 million vehicles sold in 2014. Underlying these forecasts are the still relatively low vehicle penetration rates in China. China has about 85 vehicles per 1,000 people compared to around 800 vehicles for every 1,000 people in the United States.

Sources: S. Schifferes, "Cracking China's Car Market," BBC News, May 17, 2007; N. Madden, "Led by Buick, Carmaker Learning Fine Points of Regional China Tastes," *Automotive News*, September 15, 2008, pp. 186–90; "GM Posts Record Sales in China," *Toronto Star*, January 5, 2010, p. B4; "GM's Sales in China Top US," *Investor's Business Daily*, January 25, 2011, p. A1; K. Naughton, "GM's China Bet Mimics Toyota's Bet on U.S. Last Century," Bloomberg.com, April 29, 2013.

rapidly build its presence in the target foreign market. When the German automobile company Daimler-Benz decided it needed a bigger presence in the U.S. automobile market, it did not increase that presence by building new factories to serve the United States, a process that would have taken years. Instead, it acquired the third-largest U.S. automobile company, Chrysler, and merged the two operations to form DaimlerChrysler (Daimler spun off Chrysler into a private equity firm in 2007). When the Spanish telecommunications service provider Telefónica wanted to build a service presence in Latin America, it did so through a series of acquisitions, purchasing telecommunications companies in Brazil and Argentina. In these cases, the firms made acquisitions because they knew that was the quickest way to establish a sizable presence in the target market.

Second, in many cases, firms make acquisitions to preempt their competitors. The need for preemption is particularly great in markets that are rapidly globalizing, such as telecommunications, where a combination of deregulation within nations and liberalization of regulations governing cross-border foreign direct investment has made it much easier for enterprises to enter foreign markets through acquisitions. Such markets may see concentrated waves of acquisitions as firms race each other to attain global scale. In the telecommunications industry, for example, regulatory changes triggered what can be called a feeding frenzy, with firms entering each other's markets via acquisitions to establish a global presence. These included the $56 billion acquisition of AirTouch Communications in the United States by the British company Vodafone, which was the largest acquisition ever; the $13 billion acquisition of One 2 One in Britain by the German company Deutsche Telekom; and the $6.4 billion acquisition of Excel Communications in the United States by Teleglobe of Canada.[28] A similar wave of cross-border acquisitions occurred in the global automobile industry, with Daimler acquiring Chrysler, Ford acquiring Volvo (and then selling Volvo as well), and Renault acquiring Nissan.

Third, managers may believe acquisitions to be less risky than greenfield ventures. When a firm makes an acquisition, it buys a set of assets that are producing a known revenue and profit stream. In contrast, the revenue and profit stream that a greenfield venture might generate is uncertain because it does not yet exist. When a firm makes an acquisition in a foreign market, it not only acquires a set of tangible assets, such as factories, logistics systems, and customer service systems, but it also acquires valuable intangible assets, including a local brand name and managers' knowledge of the business environment in that nation. Such knowledge can reduce the risk of mistakes caused by ignorance of the national culture.

Despite the arguments for engaging in acquisitions, many acquisitions often produce disappointing results.[29] For example, a study by Mercer Management Consulting looked at 150 acquisitions worth more than $500 million each.[30] The Mercer study concluded that 50 percent of these acquisitions eroded shareholder value, while another 33 percent created only marginal returns. Only 17 percent were judged to be successful. Similarly, a study by KPMG, an accounting and management consulting company, looked at 700 large acquisitions. The study found that while some 30 percent of these actually created value for the acquiring company, 31 percent destroyed value, and the remainder had little impact.[31] A similar study by McKinsey & Company estimated that some 70 percent of mergers and acquisitions failed to achieve expected revenue synergies.[32] In a seminal study of the postacquisition performance of acquired companies, David Ravenscraft and Mike Scherer concluded that on average, the profits and market shares of acquired companies declined following acquisition.[33] They also noted that a smaller but substantial subset of those companies experienced traumatic difficulties, which ultimately led to their being sold by the acquiring company. Ravenscraft and Scherer's evidence suggests that many acquisitions destroy rather than create value. While most research has looked at domestic acquisitions, the findings probably also apply to cross-border acquisitions.[34]

Why Do Acquisitions Fail? Acquisitions fail for several reasons. First, the acquiring firms often overpay for the assets of the acquired firm. The price of the target firm can get bid up if more than one firm is interested in its purchase, as is often the case. In addition, the management of the acquiring firm is often too optimistic about the value that can be created via an acquisition and is thus willing to pay a significant premium over a target firm's market capitalization. This is called the "hubris hypothesis" of why acquisitions fail. The hubris hypothesis postulates that top managers typically overestimate their ability to create value from an acquisition, primarily because rising to the top of a corporation has given them an exaggerated sense of their own capabilities.[35] For example, Daimler acquired Chrysler in 1998 for $40 billion, a premium of 40 percent over the market value of Chrysler before the takeover bid. Daimler paid this much because it thought it could use Chrysler to help it grow market share in the United States. At the time, Daimler's management issued bold announcements about the "synergies" that would be created from combining the operations of the two companies. However, within a year of the acquisition, Daimler's German management was faced with a crisis at Chrysler, which was suddenly losing money due to weak sales in the United States. In retrospect, Daimler's management had been far too optimistic about the potential for future demand in the U.S. auto market and about the opportunities for creating value from "synergies." Daimler acquired Chrysler at the end of a multiyear boom in U.S. auto sales and paid a large premium over Chrysler's market value just before demand slumped (and in 2007, in an admission of failure, Daimler sold its Chrysler unit to a private equity firm, now owned by Fiat Chrysler Automobiles).[36]

Second, many acquisitions fail because there is a clash between the cultures of the acquiring and acquired firms. After an acquisition, many acquired companies experience high management turnover, possibly because their employees do not like the acquiring company's way of doing things.[37] This happened at DaimlerChrysler; many senior managers left Chrysler in the first year after the merger. Apparently, Chrysler executives disliked the dominance in decision making by Daimler's German managers, while the Germans resented that Chrysler's American managers were paid two to three times as much as their German counterparts. These cultural differences created tensions, which ultimately exhibited themselves in high management turnover at Chrysler.[38] The loss of management talent and expertise can materially harm the performance of the acquired unit.[39] This may be particularly problematic in an international business, where management of the acquired unit may have valuable local knowledge that can be difficult to replace.

Third, many acquisitions fail because attempts to realize gains by integrating the operations of the acquired and acquiring entities often run into roadblocks and take much longer than forecast. Differences in management philosophy and company culture can slow the integration of operations. Differences in national culture may exacerbate these problems. Bureaucratic haggling between managers also complicates the process. Again, this reportedly occurred at DaimlerChrysler, where grand plans to integrate the operations of the two companies were bogged down by endless committee meetings and by simple logistical considerations such as the six-hour time difference between Detroit and Germany. By the time an integration plan had been worked out, Chrysler was losing money, and Daimler's German managers suddenly had a crisis on their hands.

Finally, many acquisitions fail due to inadequate preacquisition screening.[40] Many firms decide to acquire other firms without thoroughly analyzing the potential benefits and costs. They often move with undue haste to execute the acquisition, perhaps because they fear another competitor may preempt them. After the acquisition, however, many acquiring firms discover that instead of buying a well-run business, they have purchased a troubled organization. This may be a particular problem in cross-border acquisitions because the acquiring firm may not fully understand the target firm's national culture and business system.

Reducing the Risks of Failure These problems can all be overcome if the firm is careful about its acquisition strategy.[41] Screening of the foreign enterprise to be acquired, including a detailed auditing of operations, financial position, and management culture, can help to make sure the firm (1) does not pay too much for the acquired unit, (2) does not uncover any nasty surprises after the acquisition, and (3) acquires a firm whose organization culture is not antagonistic to that of the acquiring enterprise. It is also important for the acquirer to allay any concerns that management in the acquired enterprise might have. The objective should be to reduce unwanted management attrition after the acquisition. Finally, managers must move rapidly after an acquisition to put an integration plan in place and to act on that plan. Some people in both the acquiring and acquired units will try to slow or stop any integration efforts, particularly when losses of employment or management power are involved, and managers should have a plan for dealing with such impediments before they arise.

PROS AND CONS OF GREENFIELD VENTURES The big advantage of establishing a greenfield venture in a foreign country is that it gives the firm a much greater ability to build the kind of subsidiary company that it wants. For example, it is much easier to build an organization culture from scratch than it is to change the culture of an acquired unit. Similarly, it is much easier to establish a set of operating routines in a new subsidiary than it is to convert the operating routines of an acquired unit. This is a very important advantage for many international businesses, where transferring products, competencies, skills, and know-how from the established operations of the firm to the new subsidiary are principal ways of creating value. For example, when Lincoln Electric, the U.S. manufacturer of arc welding equipment, first ventured overseas in the mid-1980s, it did so by acquisitions, purchasing arc welding equipment companies in Europe. However, Lincoln's competitive advantage in the United States was based on a strong organizational culture and a unique set of incentives that encouraged its employees to do everything possible to increase productivity. Lincoln found through bitter experience that it was almost impossible to transfer its organizational culture and incentives to acquired firms, which had their own distinct organizational cultures and incentives. As a result, the firm switched its entry strategy in the mid-1990s and began to enter foreign countries by establishing greenfield ventures, building operations from the ground up. While this strategy takes more time to execute, Lincoln has found that it yields greater long-run returns than the acquisition strategy.

Set against this significant advantage are the disadvantages of establishing a greenfield venture. Greenfield ventures are slower to establish. They are also risky. As with any new venture, a degree of uncertainty is associated with future revenue and profit prospects. However, if the firm has already been successful in other foreign markets and understands what it takes to do business in other countries, these risks may not be that great. For example, having already gained great knowledge about operating internationally, the risk to McDonald's of entering yet another country is probably not that great. Also, greenfield ventures are less risky than acquisitions in the sense that there is less potential for unpleasant surprises. A final disadvantage is the possibility of being preempted by more aggressive global competitors who enter via acquisitions and build a big market presence that limits the market potential for the greenfield venture.

How Risky Would Indonesia Be for a New Greenfield Investment?

Business is all about risk, the right risks. Choosing which risks to accept and which to avoid is at the heart of international business. These risks increase and become more interesting with entry into foreign markets. David Conklin discusses the idea of managing risk through planned uncertainty. By "planned uncertainty," he means an awareness of contingencies, with possible what-if scenarios developed in advance. The key idea here is that through an ongoing monitoring of the various risk areas, decision makers can have much of the data they may need to address a number of possible outcomes. Of course, we have to know what uncertainty to plan for, and we don't know what we don't know. Planning for everything is impossible, but what Conklin suggests is that planned uncertainty is a way of thinking. Given that we don't know the future, this way of thinking may be helpful in career development and other parts of our lives. Who ever said business wasn't like surfing? So, as just one country example, how big do you think the risk is by entering Indonesia with a new greenfield investment?

Sources: D. Conklin, "Analyzing and Managing Country Risks," *Ivey Business Journal: Improving the Practice of Management*, January/February 1992. Also, see "Indices" for countries on globalEDGE.msu.edu.

WHICH CHOICE? The choice between acquisitions and greenfield ventures is not an easy one. Both modes have their advantages and disadvantages. In general, the choice will depend on the circumstances confronting the firm. If the firm is seeking to enter a market where there are already well-established incumbent enterprises and where global competitors are also interested in establishing a presence, it may pay the firm to enter via an acquisition. In such circumstances, a greenfield venture may be too slow to establish a sizable presence. However, if the firm is going to make an acquisition, its management should be cognizant of the risks associated with acquisitions that were discussed earlier and consider these when determining which firms to purchase. It may be better to enter by the slower route of a greenfield venture than to make a bad acquisition.

If the firm is considering entering a country where there are no incumbent competitors to be acquired, then a greenfield venture may be the only mode. Even when incumbents exist, if the competitive advantage of the firm is based on the transfer of organizationally embedded competencies, skills, routines, and culture, it may still be preferable to enter via a greenfield venture. Things such as skills and organizational culture, which are based on significant knowledge that is difficult to articulate and codify, are much easier to embed in a new venture than they are in an acquired entity, where the firm may have to overcome the established routines and culture of the acquired firm. Thus, as our earlier examples suggest, firms such as McDonald's and Lincoln Electric prefer to enter foreign markets by establishing greenfield ventures.

test PREP

Use SmartBook to help retain what you have learned. Access your Instructor's Connect course to check out SmartBook or go to learnsmartadvantage.com for help.

Key Terms

timing of entry, p. 360
first-mover advantages, p. 360
first-mover disadvantages, p. 360
pioneering costs, p. 360
exporting, p. 364
turnkey project, p. 365
licensing agreement, p. 365
franchising, p. 367
joint venture, p. 368
wholly owned subsidiary, p. 369

Summary

The chapter made the following points:

1. Basic entry decisions include identifying which markets to enter, when to enter those markets, and on what scale.
2. The most attractive foreign markets tend to be found in politically stable developed and developing nations that have free market systems and where there is no dramatic upsurge in either inflation rates or private-sector debt.

3. There are several advantages associated with entering a national market early, before other international businesses have established themselves. These advantages must be balanced against the pioneering costs that early entrants often have to bear, including the greater risk of business failure.
4. Large-scale entry into a national market constitutes a major strategic commitment that is likely to change the nature of competition in that market and limit the entrant's future strategic flexibility. Although making major strategic commitments can yield many benefits, there are also risks associated with such a strategy.
5. There are six modes of entering a foreign market: exporting, creating turnkey projects, licensing, franchising, establishing joint ventures, and setting up a wholly owned subsidiary.
6. Exporting has the advantages of facilitating the realization of experience curve economies and of avoiding the costs of setting up manufacturing operations in another country. Disadvantages include high transport costs, trade barriers, and problems with local marketing agents.
7. Turnkey projects allow firms to export their process know-how to countries where foreign direct investment (FDI) might be prohibited, thereby enabling the firm to earn a greater return from this asset. The disadvantage is that the firm may inadvertently create efficient global competitors in the process.
8. The main advantage of licensing is that the licensee bears the costs and risks of opening a foreign market. Disadvantages include the risk of losing technological know-how to the licensee and a lack of tight control over licensees.
9. The main advantage of franchising is that the franchisee bears the costs and risks of opening a foreign market. Disadvantages center on problems of quality control of distant franchisees.
10. Joint ventures have the advantages of sharing the costs and risks of opening a foreign market and of gaining local knowledge and political influence. Disadvantages include the risk of losing control over technology and a lack of tight control.
11. The advantages of wholly owned subsidiaries include tight control over technological know-how. The main disadvantage is that the firm must bear all the costs and risks of opening a foreign market.
12. The optimal choice of entry mode depends on the firm's strategy. When technological know-how constitutes a firm's core competence, wholly owned subsidiaries are preferred, since they best control technology. When management know-how constitutes a firm's core competence, foreign franchises controlled by joint ventures seem to be optimal. When the firm is pursuing a global standardization or transnational strategy, the need for tight control over operations to realize location and experience curve economies suggests wholly owned subsidiaries are the best entry mode.
13. When establishing a wholly owned subsidiary in a country, a firm must decide whether to do so by a greenfield venture strategy or by acquiring an established enterprise in the target market.
14. Acquisitions are quick to execute, may enable a firm to preempt its global competitors, and involve buying a known revenue and profit stream. Acquisitions may fail when the acquiring firm overpays for the target, when the cultures of the acquiring and acquired firms clash, when there is a high level of management attrition after the acquisition, and when there is a failure to integrate the operations of the acquiring and acquired firm.
15. The advantage of a greenfield venture in a foreign country is that it gives the firm a much greater ability to build the kind of subsidiary company that it wants. For example, it is much easier to build an organization culture from scratch than it is to change the culture of an acquired unit.

Critical Thinking and Discussion Questions

1. Review the Management Focus on Tesco. Then answer the following questions:
   a. Why did Tesco's initial international expansion strategy focus on developing nations?
   b. How does Tesco create value in its international operations?
   c. In Asia, Tesco has a history of entering into joint-venture agreements with local partners. What are the benefits of doing this for Tesco? What are the risks? How are those risks mitigated?
   d. When Tesco decided to enter the United States, this represented a departure from its historic strategy of focusing on developing nations. Why do you think Tesco made this decision? How is the U.S. market different from other markets that Tesco has entered?
2. Licensing proprietary technology to foreign competitors is the best way to give up a firm's competitive advantage. Discuss.
3. Discuss how the need for control over foreign operations varies with firms' strategies and core competencies. What are the implications for the choice of entry mode?
4. A small Canadian firm that has developed valuable new medical products using its unique biotechnology know-how is trying to decide how best to serve the European Union market. Its choices are given below. The cost of

investment in manufacturing facilities will be a major one for the Canadian firm, but it is not outside its reach. If these are the firm's only options, which one would you advise it to choose? Why?

a. Manufacture the products at home, and let foreign sales agents handle marketing.
b. Manufacture the products at home, and set up a wholly owned subsidiary in Europe to handle marketing.
c. Enter into an alliance with a large European pharmaceutical firm. The products would be manufactured in Europe by the 50–50 joint venture and marketed by the European firm.

globalEDGE Research Task

globalEDGE.msu.edu

Use the globalEDGE™ website (globaledge.msu.edu) to complete the following exercises:

1. *Entrepreneur* magazine annually publishes a ranking of the *top global franchises.* Provide a list of the top 25 companies that pursue franchising as their preferred mode of international expansion. Study one of these companies in detail, and describe its business model, its international expansion pattern, desirable qualifications in possible franchisees, and the support and training the company typically provides.
2. The U.S. Commercial Service prepares reports known as the *Country Commercial Guide* for countries of interest to U.S. investors. Utilize the *Country Commercial Guide* for Russia to gather information on this country's energy and mining industry. Considering that your company has plans to enter Russia in the foreseeable future, select the most appropriate entry method. Be sure to support your decision with the information collected.

Starbucks Entering Foreign Markets

closing case

Forty years ago, Starbucks was a single store in Seattle's Pike Place Market selling premium roasted coffee. Today, it is a global roaster and retailer of coffee with some 21,536 stores, 43 percent of which are in 63 countries outside the United States. China (1,716 stores), Canada (1,330 stores), Japan (1,079 stores), and the United Kingdom (808 stores) are large markets internationally for Starbucks.

Starbucks set out on its current course in the 1980s when the company's director of marketing, Howard Schultz, came back from a trip to Italy enchanted with the Italian coffeehouse experience. Schultz, who later became CEO, persuaded the company's owners to experiment with the coffeehouse format—and the Starbucks experience was born. The strategy was to sell the company's own premium roasted coffee and freshly brewed espresso-style coffee beverages, along with a variety of pastries, coffee accessories, teas, and other products, in a tastefully designed coffeehouse setting. From the outset, the company focused on selling "a third place experience," rather than just the coffee. The formula led to spectacular success in the United States, where Starbucks went from obscurity to one of the best-known brands in the country in a decade. Thanks to Starbucks, coffee stores became places for relaxation, chatting with friends, reading the newspaper, holding business meetings, or (more recently) browsing the web.

In 1995, with 700 stores across the United States, Starbucks began exploring foreign market opportunities. The first target market was Japan. The company established a joint venture with a local retailer, Sazaby Inc. Each company held a 50 percent stake in the venture, Starbucks Coffee of Japan. Starbucks initially invested $10 million in this venture, its first foreign direct investment. The Starbucks format was then licensed to the venture, which was charged with taking over responsibility for growing Starbucks' presence in Japan.

© Imagebroker/Alamy Stock Photo

To make sure the Japanese operations replicated the "Starbucks experience" in North America, Starbucks transferred some employees to the Japanese operation. The licensing agreement required all Japanese store managers and employees to attend training classes similar to those given to U.S. employees. The agreement also required that stores adhere to the design parameters established in the United States. In 2001, the company introduced a stock option plan for all Japanese employees, making it the first company in Japan to do so. Skeptics doubted that Starbucks would be able to replicate its North American success overseas, but by June 2015, Starbucks had some 1,079 stores and a profitable business in Japan.

After Japan, the company embarked on an aggressive foreign investment program. In 1998, it purchased Seattle Coffee, a British coffee chain with 60 retail stores, for $84 million. An American couple originally from Seattle had started Seattle Coffee with the intention of establishing a Starbucks-like chain in Britain. In the late 1990s, Starbucks opened stores in Taiwan, Singapore, Thailand, New Zealand, South Korea, Malaysia, and—most significantly—China. In Asia, Starbucks' most common strategy was to license its format to a local operator in return for initial licensing fees and royalties on store revenues. As in Japan, Starbucks insisted on an intensive employee-training program and strict specifications regarding the format and layout of the store.

By 2002, Starbucks was pursuing an aggressive expansion in mainland Europe. As its first entry point, Starbucks chose Switzerland. Drawing on its experience in Asia, the company entered into a joint venture with a Swiss company, Bon Appetit Group, Switzerland's largest food service company. Bon Appetit was to hold a majority stake in the venture, and Starbucks would license its format to the Swiss company using a similar agreement to those it had used successfully in Asia. This was followed by a joint venture in other countries. The United Kingdom leads the charge in Europe with 808 Starbucks stores.

By 2014, Starbucks emphasized the rapid growth of its operations in China, where it had 1,716 stores and planned to roll out another 500 in three years. The success of Starbucks in China has been attributed to a smart partnering strategy. China is not one homogeneous market; the culture of northern China is very different from that of the east, and consumer spending power inland is not on par with that of the big coastal cities. To deal with this complexity, Starbucks entered into three different joint ventures: in the north with Beijong Mei Da coffee, in the east with Taiwan-based UniPresident, and in the south with Hong Kong-based Maxim's Caterers. Each partner brought different strengths and local expertise that helped the company gain insights into the tastes and preferences of local Chinese customers, and to adapt accordingly. Starbucks now believes that China will become its second-largest market after the United States by 2020.

Sources: Starbucks 10K, various years; C. McLean, "Starbucks Set to Invade Coffee-Loving Continent," *Seattle Times,* October 4, 2000, p. E1; J. Ordonez, "Starbucks to Start Major Expansion in Overseas Market," *The Wall Street Journal,* October 27, 2000, p. B10; S. Homes and D. Bennett, "Planet Starbucks," BusinessWeek, September 9, 2002, pp. 99–110; "Starbucks Outlines International Growth Strategy," *Business Wire,* October 14, 2004; A. Yeh, "Starbucks Aims for New Tier in China," *Financial Times,* February 14, 2006, p. 17; C. Matlack, "Will Global Growth Help Starbucks?" *BusinessWeek,* July 2, 2008; H. H. Wang, "Five Things Starbucks Did to Get China Right," *Forbes,* July 10, 2012.

CASE DISCUSSION QUESTIONS

1. Starbucks prefers a combination approach to foreign market entry: the use of joint ventures and licensing. Do you agree with this approach? Why or why not?
2. Many would argue that Starbucks coffee is expensive, and yet customers get "value" for their money. How do you think Starbucks has been able to transfer this business model and value proposition to international markets?
3. Why did Starbucks not just go with a licensing approach internationally? Is the the preference for joint ventures in strategic target markets coupled with licensing unique?
4. To stay competitive worldwide, what do you think Starbucks has to focus on in the next decade from a market entry standpoint and from a value proposition to customers?

Endnotes

1. For interesting empirical studies that deal with the issues of timing and resource commitments, see T. Isobe, S. Makino, and D. B. Montgomery, "Resource Commitment, Entry Timing, and Market Performance of Foreign Direct Investments in Emerging Economies," *Academy of Management Journal* 43, no. 3 (2000), pp. 468–84; and Y. Pan and P. S. K. Chi, "Financial Performance and Survival of Multinational Corporations in China," *Strategic Management Journal* 20, no. 4 (1999), pp. 359–74. A complementary theoretical perspective on this issue can be found in V. Govindarjan and A. K. Gupta, *The Quest for Global Dominance* (San Francisco: Jossey-Bass, 2001). Also see F. Vermeulen and H. Barkeme, "Pace, Rhythm and Scope: Process Dependence in Building a Profitable Multinational Corporation," *Strategic Management Journal* 23 (2002), pp. 637–54.
2. This can be reconceptualized as the resource base of the entrant, relative to indigenous competitors. For work that focuses on this issue, see W. C. Bogner, H. Thomas, and J. McGee, "A Longitudinal Study of the Competitive Positions and Entry Paths of European Firms in the U.S. Pharmaceutical Market," *Strategic Management Journal* 17 (1996), pp. 85–107; D. Collis, "A Resource-Based Analysis of Global Competition," *Strategic Management Journal* 12 (1991), pp. 49–68; and S. Tallman, "Strategic Management Models and Resource-Based Strategies among MNEs in a Host Market," *Strategic Management Journal* 12 (1991), pp. 69–82.
3. For a discussion of first-mover advantages, see M. Lieberman and D. Montgomery, "First-Mover Advantages," *Strategic Management Journal* 9 (Summer Special Issue, 1988), pp. 41–58.
4. J. M. Shaver, W. Mitchell, and B. Yeung, "The Effect of Own Firm and Other Firm Experience on Foreign Direct Investment Survival in the United States, 1987–92," *Strategic Management Journal* 18 (1997), pp. 811–24.
5. S. Zaheer and E. Mosakowski, "The Dynamics of the Liability of Foreignness: A Global Study of Survival in the Financial Services Industry," *Strategic Management Journal* 18 (1997), pp. 439–64.
6. Shaver et al., "The Effect of Own Firm and Other Firm Experience."
7. P. Ghemawat, *Commitment: The Dynamics of Strategy* (New York: Free Press, 1991).
8. R. Luecke, *Scuttle Your Ships before Advancing* (Oxford: Oxford University Press, 1994).
9. Isobe et al., "Resource Commitment, Entry Timing, and Market Performance"; Pan and Chi, "Financial Performance and Survival of Multinational Corporations in China"; Govindarjan and Gupta, *The Quest for Global Dominance*.
10. Christopher Bartlett and Sumantra Ghoshal, "Going Global: Lessons from Late Movers," *Harvard Business Review,* March–April 2000, pp. 132–45.
11. This section draws on numerous studies, including C. W. L. Hill, P. Hwang, and W. C. Kim, "An Eclectic Theory of the Choice of International Entry Mode," *Strategic Management Journal* 11 (1990), pp. 117–28; C. W. L. Hill and W. C. Kim, "Searching for a Dynamic Theory of the Multinational Enterprise: A Transaction Cost Model," *Strategic Management Journal* 9 (Special Issue on Strategy Content, 1988), pp. 93–104; E. Anderson and

H. Gatignon, "Modes of Foreign Entry: A Transaction Cost Analysis and Propositions," *Journal of International Business Studies* 17 (1986), pp. 1–26; F. R. Root, *Entry Strategies for International Markets* (Lexington, MA: D. C. Heath, 1980); A. Madhok, "Cost, Value and Foreign Market Entry: The Transaction and the Firm," *Strategic Management Journal* 18 (1997), pp. 39–61; K. D. Brouthers and L. B. Brouthers, "Acquisition or Greenfield Start-Up?" *Strategic Management Journal* 21, no. 1 (2000), pp. 89–97; X. Martin and R. Salmon, "Knowledge Transfer Capacity and Its Implications for the Theory of the Multinational Enterprise," *Journal of International Business Studies,* July 2003, p. 356; and A. Verbeke, "The Evolutionary View of the MNE and the Future of Internalization Theory," *Journal of International Business Studies,* November 2003, pp. 498–515.

12. For a general discussion of licensing, see F. J. Contractor, "The Role of Licensing in International Strategy," *Columbia Journal of World Business,* Winter 1982, pp. 73–83.
13. See E. Terazono and C. Lorenz, "An Angry Young Warrior," *Financial Times,* September 19, 1994, p. 11; and K. McQuade and B. Gomes-Casseres, "Xerox and Fuji-Xerox," Harvard Business School Case No. 9-391-156.
14. O. E. Williamson, *The Economic Institutions of Capitalism* (New York: Free Press, 1985).
15. J. H. Dunning and M. McQueen, "The Eclectic Theory of International Production: A Case Study of the International Hotel Industry," *Managerial and Decision Economics* 2 (1981), pp. 197–210.
16. Andrew E. Serwer, "McDonald's Conquers the World," *Fortune,* October 17, 1994, pp. 103–16.
17. For an excellent review of the basic theoretical literature of joint ventures, see B. Kogut, "Joint Ventures: Theoretical and Empirical Perspectives," *Strategic Management Journal* 9 (1988), pp. 319–32. More recent studies include T. Chi, "Option to Acquire or Divest a Joint Venture," Strategic Management Journal 21, no. 6 (2000), pp. 665–88; H. Merchant and D. Schendel, "How Do International Joint Ventures Create Shareholder Value?" *Strategic Management Journal* 21, no. 7 (2000), pp. 723–37; H. K. Steensma and M. A. Lyles, "Explaining IJV Survival in a Transitional Economy though Social Exchange and Knowledge Based Perspectives," *Strategic Management Journal* 21, no. 8 (2000), pp. 831–51; and J. F. Hennart and M. Zeng, "Cross Cultural Differences and Joint Venture Longevity," *Journal of International Business Studies,* December 2002, pp. 699–717.
18. D. G. Bradley, "Managing against Expropriation," *Harvard Business Review,* July–August 1977, pp. 78–90.
19. J. A. Robins, S. Tallman, and K. Fladmoe-Lindquist, "Autonomy and Dependence of International Cooperative Ventures," *Strategic Management Journal,* October 2002, pp. 881–902.
20. Speech given by Tony Kobayashi at the University of Washington Business School, October 1992.
21. A. C. Inkpen and P. W. Beamish, "Knowledge, Bargaining Power, and the Instability of International Joint Ventures," *Academy of Management Review* 22 (1997), pp. 177–202; and S. H. Park and G. R. Ungson, "The Effect of National Culture, Organizational Complementarity, and Economic Motivation on Joint Venture Dissolution," *Academy of Management Journal* 40 (1997), pp. 279–307.
22. Inkpen and Beamish, "Knowledge, Bargaining Power, and the Instability of International Joint Ventures."
23. See Brouthers and Brouthers, "Acquisition or Greenfield Start-Up?"; and J. F. Hennart and Y. R. Park, "Greenfield versus Acquisition: The Strategy of Japanese Investors in the United States," *Management Science,* 1993, pp. 1054–70.
24. This section draws on Hill et al., "An Eclectic Theory of the Choice of International Entry Mode."
25. C. W. L. Hill, "Strategies for Exploiting Technological Innovations: When and When Not to License," *Organization Science* 3 (1992), pp. 428–41.
26. See Brouthers and Brouthers, "Acquisition or Greenfield Start-Up?"; and J. Anand and A. Delios, "Absolute and Relative Resources as Determinants of International Acquisitions," *Strategic Management Journal,* February 2002, pp. 119–34.
27. United Nations, *World Investment Report,* 2010 (New York and Geneva: United Nations, 2010).
28. Ibid.
29. For evidence on acquisitions and performance, see R. E. Caves, "Mergers, Takeovers, and Economic Efficiency," *International Journal of Industrial Organization* 7 (1989), pp. 151–74; M. C. Jensen and R. S. Ruback, "The Market for Corporate Control: The Scientific Evidence," *Journal of Financial Economics* 11 (1983), pp. 5–50; R. Roll, "Empirical Evidence on Takeover Activity and Shareholder Wealth," in *Knights, Raiders and Targets,* ed. J. C. Coffee, L. Lowenstein, and S. Rose (Oxford: Oxford University Press, 1989); A. Schleifer and R. W. Vishny, "Takeovers in the 60s and 80s: Evidence and Implications," *Strategic Management Journal* 12 (Winter 1991 Special Issue), pp. 51–60; T. H. Brush, "Predicted Changes in Operational Synergy and Post-acquisition Performance of Acquired Businesses," *Strategic Management Journal* 17 (1996), pp. 1–24; and A. Seth, K. P. Song, and R. R. Pettit, "Value Creation and Destruction in Cross-Border Acquisitions," *Strategic Management Journal* 23 (October 2002), pp. 921–40.
30. J. Warner, J. Templeman, and R. Horn, "The Case against Mergers," *BusinessWeek,* October 30, 1995, pp. 122–34.
31. "Few Takeovers Pay Off for Big Buyers," *Investor's Business Daily,* May 25, 2001, p. 1.
32. S. A. Christofferson, R. S. McNish, and D. L. Sias, "Where Mergers Go Wrong," *The McKinsey Quarterly* 2 (2004), pp. 92–110.
33. D. J. Ravenscraft and F. M. Scherer, *Mergers, Selloffs, and Economic Efficiency* (Washington, DC: Brookings Institution, 1987).
34. See P. Ghemawat and F. Ghadar, "The Dubious Logic of Global Mega-Mergers," *Harvard Business Review,* July–August 2000, pp. 65–72.
35. R. Roll, "The Hubris Hypothesis of Corporate Takeovers," *Journal of Business* 59 (1986), pp. 197–216.
36. "Marital Problems," *The Economist,* October 14, 2000.
37. See J. P. Walsh, "Top Management Turnover Following Mergers and Acquisitions," *Strategic Management Journal* 9 (1988), pp. 173–83.
38. B. Vlasic and B. A. Stertz, *Taken for a Ride: How Daimler-Benz Drove Off with Chrysler* (New York: HarperCollins, 2000).
39. See A. A. Cannella and D. C. Hambrick, "Executive Departure and Acquisition Performance," *Strategic Management Journal* 14 (1993), pp. 137–52.
40. P. Haspeslagh and D. Jemison, *Managing Acquisitions* (New York: Free Press, 1991).
41. Ibid.

Exporting, Importing, and Countertrade

learning objectives

After reading this chapter, you will be able to:

- **LO14-1** Explain the promises and risks associated with exporting.
- **LO14-2** Identify the steps managers can take to improve their firm's export performance.
- **LO14-3** Identify information sources and government programs that exist to help exporters.
- **LO14-4** Recognize the basic steps involved in export financing.
- **LO14-5** Describe how countertrade can be used to facilitate exporting.

Dwight Burdette/Wikimedia Commons

Two Men and a Truck

opening case

By some accounts, moving is ranked as the third-most stressful event a person can experience, after death of a relative and divorce. Two Men and a Truck started as an after-school business for two high school boys in Lansing, Michigan. As a small business focused on local moving services, the company began in 1985 with $350, a hand-drawn logo, and an advertisement in a local community newspaper.

In 1989, Melanie Bergeron, the daughter of founder Mary Ellen Sheets, opened the first franchised office of Two Men and a Truck in her hometown of Atlanta, Georgia. Melanie is now board chair, with Brig Sorber as the chief executive officer and Jon Sorber as executive vice president. Randy Shacka, who joined the company as an intern in 2001, was promoted in 2012 to president. This is the first president of the company who did not come from the family.

Two Men and a Truck is no longer "two men and a truck." The company has grown both domestically and internationally to most of the United States and some 320 locations worldwide. Two Men and a Truck is the fastest-growing franchised moving company in the United States, with more than $300 million in sales, 2,100 moving trucks, and some 6,000 workers. The average franchise grosses about $1.5 million annually. Bergeron said that "we never imagined being in the moving business—that is, until my mom and my brothers Brig and Jon scraped together some money to buy a truck to help raise extra cash for college."

Two Men and a Truck has remained branded as "Two Men and a Truck" in all parts of the world in which it operates franchises (e.g., Canada, Ireland, the United Kingdom). Names such as "Two Blokes and a Lorry" do not appeal to them! The company has decided to stick to the core American brand name because "that's what master franchisers and their investors want," said Bergeron. "The customers are less interested in whether it's a U.S. brand . . . the appeal is the opposite . . . it's a local [franchise] company that will be available when I need them. . . . They want the U.S. brand power and mystique."*

In going international to new markets, Two Men and a Truck's primary factors to evaluate are the size of the middle class in a country and the population's mobility. They use software tools to help pinpoint income levels by neighborhood and whether the housing market is primarily based on single- or multifamily units. The market for Two Men and a Truck is best where there is a good mix of both. In addition, Bergeron said that two other key areas in determining locations in which to operate include obtaining accurate market research and identifying potential master franchisees.

* D. Barry, "Melanie Bergeron, Chair of the Board of Two Men and a Truck," *Exporters: The Wit and Wisdom of Small Businesspeople Who Sell Globally* (Washington, DC: U.S. Commerce Department. 2013).

–continued

In the case of Two Men and a Truck going international, the industry itself also represented a challenge. There are plenty of moving businesses worldwide; why should franchisees represent Two Men and a Truck? The company's answer to this market differentiation problem is its exceptional focus on customer service and a sophisticated web-based tracking system. Quality control, labor costs, and cycle time to complete a move are core performance metrics in the system. In fact, the company has become known in its industry for faster and better analytics to run the business. It has installed a private cloud system to make its business operations more efficient, using business analytics to capture and identify growth opportunities worldwide. •

Sources: D. Barry, "Melanie Bergeron, Chair of the Board of Two Men and a Truck," *Exporters: The Wit and Wisdom of Small Businesspeople Who Sell Globally* (Washington, DC: U.S. Commerce Department, 2013); C. Boulton, "Moving Company Gets a Lift from Faster Analytics," *The Wall Street Journal*, August 20, 2013; A. Wittrock, "Two Men and a Truck Wins State Grant, Plans $4 Million Expansion of Lansing-Area Headquarters," *MLive.com*, February 27, 2013.

Introduction

Chapter 13 reviewed exporting from a strategic perspective as a part of the chapter topic on entering foreign markets. We considered exporting as just one of a range of strategic options for profiting from international expansion. This chapter is more concerned with the nuts and bolts of exporting, along with tackling importing and countertrade. But exporting, in particular, is a tremendously important mode of foreign market entry, preferred by more than 90 percent of all companies engaging in the global marketplace. As such, we specifically look at how to export. As the opening case about Two Men and a Truck makes clear, exporting is not just for large enterprises; many small firms such as Two Men and a Truck and Lulu's Desserts (the closing case in this chapter) have benefited significantly from the market opportunities stemming from exporting to a variety of worldwide locations.

Did You Know?
Did you know you can call Sweden and chat with a random Swede?

Visit your Connect SmartBook® to view a short video explanation from the authors.

The volume of export activity in the world economy has increased as exporting has become easier from a large number of countries. Even countries now export themselves, such as Sweden with its award-winning "Calling Sweden" number. In a positive move for international trade, the gradual decline in trade barriers under the umbrella of GATT and now the World Trade Organization or WTO (see Chapter 7), along with regional economic agreements such as the European Union (EU) and the North American Free Trade Agreement (NAFTA) (see Chapter 9), has significantly increased export opportunities. At the same time, modern communication and transportation technologies have alleviated the logistical problems associated with exporting. Over the last two decades, firms have increasingly used the Internet and international air express services to reduce the costs, distance, and cycle time associated with exporting. Consequently, it is not unusual to find thriving exporters among small companies. In fact, of U.S. companies that trade internationally, some 85 percent of them are small and medium-sized enterprises (SMEs), and they generally do so via exporting.

Nevertheless, exporting remains a challenge for many firms. Take the United States as an example. Fewer than 1 percent of all U.S. firms trade across their country borders to other countries, and those companies that do engage in trade do so with typically one other country (about 60 percent of all U.S. companies that export trade only with one other country). This means knowledge, data, and experience oftentimes are lacking, and smaller enterprises, in particular, can find the exporting process intimidating.

The firm wishing to export must identify foreign market opportunities, avoid a host of unanticipated problems that are often associated with doing business in a foreign market, familiarize itself with the mechanics of export and import financing, learn where it can get financing and export credit insurance, and learn how it should deal with foreign exchange risk. The process can be made more problematic by currencies that are not freely convertible. Arranging payment for exports to countries with weak currencies can be a problem. Countertrade allows payment for exports to be made through goods and services rather than money. This chapter discusses all these issues, with the exception of foreign exchange risk, which was covered in Chapter 10.

In Chapter 13, we dealt with the scale of market entry and strategic commitments in going international. Essentially, our focus was on involvement and commitment when engaging in the international marketplace. What we find is that the first international level for both involvement and

commitment was the exporting (outbound international activity) and importing (inbound international activity) options. The remaining options for involvement and commitment, although they overlapped in some areas, were a bit different (Chapter 13 discusses turnkey projects, licensing, franchising, joint ventures, and wholly owned subsidiaries—the latter also a production facility focus in Chapter 15). That places a lot of emphasis on exporting and importing as modes of operations for many companies, and we think that this area deserves a bit more coverage; this chapter is devoted to digging deeper into the knowledge of operations ("nuts and bolts") of exporting and importing as well as the unique case of countertrade. This is, after all, the lowest level of involvement and the lowest level of commitment a company can make when going international: selling to foreign markets (exporting) or purchasing raw materials, component parts, or finished goods for operations (importing).

The bottom line is that as the global marketplace becomes more viable for many companies over time, companies must also adapt to this opportunity by strategically engaging in exporting (see Chapter 13) and operationally go about seeking opportunities globally. This could mean using suppliers from developing nations, importing products from new sources, or exporting products to new markets. Companies that have traditionally operated within national or regional trading groups may feel ill equipped to extend their market horizon. This may be as simple as feeling unable to select and manage a foreign supplier or not knowing how to sell products in a new country. But keep in mind that, by some accounts, 90 percent of the products and services that are needed locally are not produced locally; they are shipped in from somewhere else. As such, market opportunities are globally available everywhere and exporting and importing fill these voids.[1]

The chapter opens in the next section by considering the promise and pitfalls of exporting. The logic for both exporting and importing is very similar. Readiness to export and/or import is a large part of the story, as illustrated in Figure 14.1.[2]

For Which Product Is Autarky a Good Choice for Countries?

The word *autarky* refers to the quality and belief that a country should be self-sufficient and avoid trade and/or external assistance with other nations. Many economists regard autarky as an idealistic, but impractical, goal of countries. Basically, it sounds like a nice idea to be self-sufficient and practice autarky. In reality, throughout history countries have tried to achieve autarky but soon discovered they could not produce the wide range of products and services customers in their population want and need. These countries also found out that manufacturing products at competitive prices over the long term became a daunting task. In fact, those countries found themselves worse off economically than nations that engaged in international trade. So, a word to the wise; unless your country can efficiently produce everything it needs, the country needs to engage in international trade. A more logical and achievable possibility is to focus on being self-sufficient in certain areas, for certain products or services. Which product or service do you think a country should strive to be self-sufficient in?

Source: J. Heathcote, "Financial Autarky and International Business Cycles," *Journal of Monetary Economics 9* (2002), pp. 601–627.

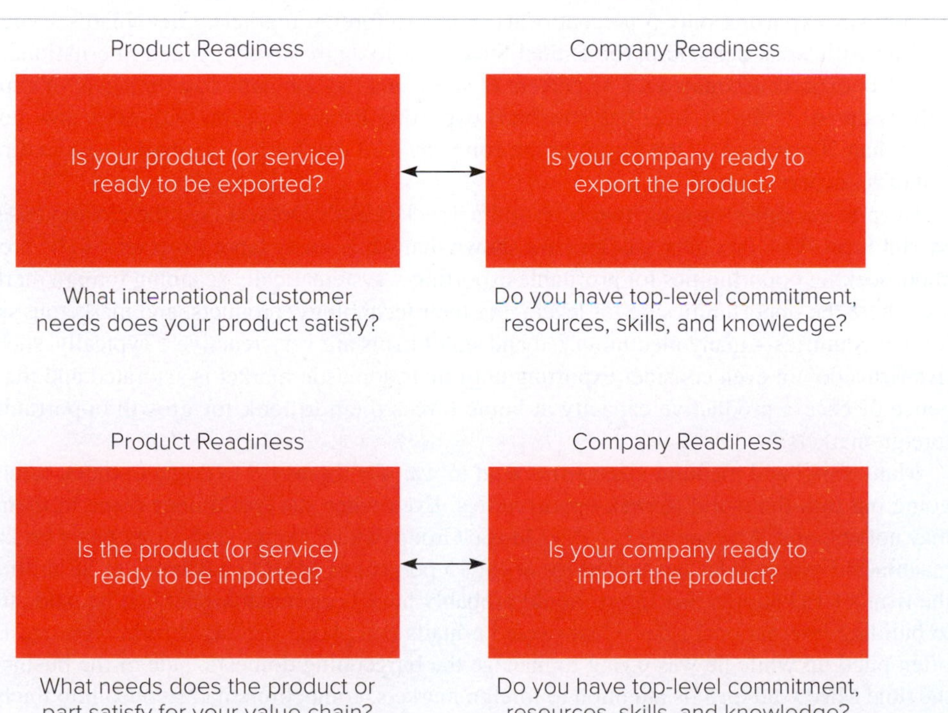

14.1 FIGURE

Product Readiness and Company Readiness to Export or Import.

Source: Adapted from T. Hult, D. Closs, and D. Frayer, *Global Supply Chain Management: Leveraging Processes, Measurements, and Tools for Strategic Corporate Advantage* (New York: McGraw-Hill, 2014).

Export Tutorials

Exporting, importing, and countertrade are the focus areas of Chapter 14. The exporting entry mode choice, also discussed in Chapter 13, is the most often used way to conduct cross-border trade for companies. The vast majority of small and medium-sized enterprises, for example, use exporting as their way to expand to international markets. But that begs the question of whether the company is ready to export and whether the product the company plans to export is ready to be exported. The "Export Tutorials" section of globalEDGE™ (globaledge.msu.edu/reference-desk/export-tutorials) includes CORE as a diagnostic tool to assess "company readiness to export." The "Export Tutorials" section also has a lengthy set of questions and answers to the most common exporting-related questions in the categories of government regulations, financial considerations, sales and marketing, and logistics. For example, one question deals with whether a company needs a license to export. Assume you are based in the United States. How can you identify the relevant commodity jurisdiction for a product?

LO 14-1
Explain the promises and risks associated with exporting.

The Promise and Pitfalls of Exporting

The great promise of exporting is that large revenue and profit opportunities are to be found in foreign markets for most firms in most industries. This was true for Two Men and a Truck in the opening case The international market is normally so much larger than the firm's domestic market that exporting is nearly always a way to increase the revenue and profit base of a company. By expanding the size of the market, exporting can enable a firm to achieve economies of scale, thereby lowering its unit costs. Firms that do not export often lose out on significant opportunities for growth and cost reduction.[3]

Consider the case of Marlin Steel Wire Products, a Baltimore manufacturer of wire baskets and fabricated metal items with revenues of about $5 million. Among its products are baskets to hold dedicated parts for aircraft engines and automobiles. Its engineers design custom wire baskets for the assembly lines of companies such as Boeing and Toyota. It has a reputation for producing high-quality products for these niche markets. Like many small businesses, Marlin did not have a history of exporting. However, Marlin decided to engage globally in the export market, shipping small numbers of products to Mexico and Canada.

Marlin President and CEO Drew Greenblatt soon realized that export sales could be the key to growth. In 2008, when the global financial crisis hit and America slid into a serious recession, Marlin was exporting only 5 percent of its orders to foreign markets. Greenblatt's strategy for dealing with weak demand in the United States was to aggressively expand international sales. By 2010, exports accounted for 17 percent of sales, and the company had set a goal of exporting half its output.[4] Marlin Steel has now been exporting for eight years, with sales now going to more than 20 countries. One-fourth of the company's 33 employees are employed as a direct result of its export success.

Despite examples such as Two Men and a Truck, Lulu's Dessert (see the closing case), and Marlin Steel Wire Products, studies have shown that while many large firms tend to be proactive about seeking opportunities for profitable exporting—systematically scanning foreign markets to see where the opportunities lie for leveraging their technology, products, and marketing skills in foreign countries—many medium-sized and small firms are very reactive.[5] Typically, such reactive firms do not even consider exporting until their domestic market is saturated and the emergence of excess productive capacity at home forces them to look for growth opportunities in foreign markets.

Many small and medium-sized firms tend to wait for the world to come to them, rather than going out into the world to seek opportunities. Even when the world does come to them, they may not respond. An example is MMO Music Group, which makes sing-along tapes for karaoke machines. Foreign sales accounted for about 15 percent of MMO's revenues of $8 million, but the firm's CEO admits this figure would probably have been much higher had he paid attention to building international sales. Unanswered e-mails and phone messages from Asia and Europe often piled up while he was trying to manage the burgeoning domestic side of the business. By the time MMO did turn its attention to foreign markets, competitors had stepped into the breach, and MMO found it tough going to build export volume.[6]

MMO's experience is common, and it suggests a need for firms to become more proactive about seeking export opportunities. One reason more firms are not proactive is that they are unfamiliar with foreign market opportunities; they simply do not know how big the opportunities actually are or where they might lie. Simple ignorance of the potential opportunities is a huge barrier to exporting.[7] Also, many would-be exporters, particularly smaller firms, are often intimidated by the complexities and mechanics of exporting to countries where business practices, language, culture, legal systems, and currency are very different from those in the home market.[8] This combination of unfamiliarity and intimidation probably explains why exporters still account for only a tiny percentage of U.S. firms, less than 5 percent of firms with fewer than 500 employees, according to the Small Business Administration.[9]

To make matters worse, many neophyte exporters run into significant problems when first trying to do business abroad, and this sours them on future exporting ventures. Common pitfalls include poor market analysis, a poor understanding of competitive conditions in the foreign market, a failure to customize the product offering to the needs of foreign customers, a lack of an effective distribution program, a poorly executed promotional campaign, and problems securing financing.[10] Novice exporters tend to underestimate the time and expertise needed to cultivate business in foreign countries.[11] Few realize the amount of management resources that have to be dedicated to this activity. Many foreign customers require face-to-face negotiations on their home turf. An exporter may have to spend months learning about a country's trade regulations, business practices, and more before a deal can be closed. The accompanying Management Focus, which documents the experience of Ambient Technologies and the Panama Canal, illustrates cultural and language barriers for exporters but also the advantages of small exporters in many cases.

 **test PREP**

Use SmartBook to help retain what you have learned. Access your Instructor's Connect course to check out SmartBook or go to learnsmartadvantage.com for help.

Exporters often face voluminous paperwork, complex formalities, and many potential delays and errors. According to a United Nations report on trade and development, a typical international trade

management FOCUS

Ambient Technologies and the Panama Canal

Ambient Technologies, Inc. (ATI) has a core business in the areas of geology, geophysics, and drilling services. Carlos Lemos, CEO, started the business in 1993 after having previously worked for a very large consulting company for 22 years. Instead of continuing with the larger company, Lemos decided to use his Brazilian heritage and "live the American dream" by starting his own entrepreneurial venture. He says, "We support other companies that are looking to find information that's below the ground, whether it's groundwater related, whether it's construction related, whether it's engineering related, whether it is anything related with infrastructure issues, mining."

The highest-profile project that Ambient Technologies is working on right now is the Panama Canal expansion. This expansion project involves the construction of two new sets of locks: one on the Pacific side and one on the Atlantic side of the existing Panama Canal, which opened in 1914. Each lock will have three water chambers, and each chamber will have three water reutilization basins. The Panama Canal project also includes the widening and deepening of existing navigational channels in Gatun Lake and the deepening of the Culebra Cut. Additionally, in order to open a new 3.8-mile- (6.1-kilometer-) long access channel to connect the Pacific locks and the Culebra Cut, four dry excavation projects are executed.

Ambient Technologies is performing all of the drilling underneath where the new set of locks is going to be, as the third set of locks is being built next to the existing locks. These locks will accommodate the much larger ships in service today as well as the increased traffic flow through the Panama Canal. Lemos says that "it's a huge, huge, huge operation because it also involves a lot of retention basins because they're circulating the water instead of just simply discharging it to the ocean."* Ambient Technologies is drilling as part of the Panama Canal project because the project team found some geological faults. Basically, Ambient Technologies is needed to make sure the Panama Canal design is appropriate and takes into account any fault concerns; Ambient Technologies even suggests relocation of parts of the project such as Gatun Lake.

Lemos and Ambient Technologies were honored recently at the White House for their activities in exporting from the United States to other countries. Interestingly, Lemos says that even though he is a native of Brazil and speaks the language fluently (Portuguese), he still faced lots of problems and issues when exporting initially to Brazil. He found an easier time exporting to smaller countries, which were more comfortable working with smaller companies like Ambient Technologies. Lemos found these types of smaller countries in Central America. Panama became a target market but also Colombia. This like-mindedness is a common success factor for many small and medium-sized companies that export to new markets: Success is often most easily found where customers and market characteristics are similar to the home environment.

*D. Barry, "Melanie Bergeron, Chair of the Board of Two Men and a Truck," *Exporters: The Wit and Wisdom of Small Businesspeople Who Sell Globally* (Washington, DC: U.S. Commerce Department, 2013).

Source: D. Barry, "Melanie Bergeron, Chair of the Board of Two Men and a Truck," *Exporters: The Wit and Wisdom of Small Businesspeople Who Sell Globally* (Washington, DC: U.S. Commerce Department, 2013).

transaction may involve 30 parties, 60 original documents, and 360 document copies, all of which have to be checked, transmitted, reentered into various information systems, processed, and filed. The UN has calculated that the time involved in preparing documentation, along with the costs of common errors in paperwork, often amounts to 10 percent of the final value of goods exported.[12]

LO 14-2

Identify the steps managers can take to improve their firm's export performance.

Improving Export Performance

Inexperienced exporters have a number of ways to gain information about foreign market opportunities and avoid common pitfalls that tend to discourage and frustrate novice exporters.[13] In this section, we look at information sources for exporters to increase their knowledge of foreign market opportunities, we consider a number of service providers, we review various exporting strategies that can increase the probability of successful exporting, and we illustrate four globalEDGE™ Diagnostic Tools that can help exporters. We begin, however, with a look at how several nations try to help domestic firms export.

INTERNATIONAL COMPARISONS One big impediment to exporting is the simple lack of knowledge of the opportunities available. Often, there are many markets for a firm's product, but because they are in countries separated from the firm's home base by culture, language, distance, and time, the firm does not know of them. Identifying export opportunities is made even more complex because almost 200 countries with widely differing cultures compose the world of potential opportunities. Faced with such complexity and diversity, firms sometimes hesitate to seek export opportunities.

The way to overcome ignorance is to collect information. In Germany—one of the world's most successful exporting nations—trade associations, government agencies, and commercial banks gather information, helping small firms identify export opportunities. A similar function is provided by the Japanese Ministry of International Trade and Industry (**MITI**), which is always on the lookout for export opportunities. In addition, many Japanese firms are affiliated in some way with the ***sogo shosha,*** Japan's great trading houses. The *sogo shosha* have offices all over the world, and they proactively, continuously seek export opportunities for their affiliated companies large and small.[14]

MITI
Japan's Ministry of International Trade and Industry.

Sogo Shosha
Japanese trading companies; a key part of the *keiretsu,* the large Japanese industrial groups.

German and Japanese firms can draw on the large reservoirs of experience, skills, information, and other resources of their respective export-oriented institutions. Unlike their German and Japanese competitors, many U.S. firms are relatively blind when they seek export opportunities; they are information-disadvantaged. In part, this reflects historical differences. Both Germany and Japan have long made their living as trading nations, whereas until recently, the United States has been a relatively self-contained continental economy in which international trade played a minor role. This is changing; both imports and exports now play a greater role in the U.S. economy than they did 20 years ago. However, the United States has not yet evolved an institutional structure for promoting exports similar to that of either Germany or Japan.

INFORMATION SOURCES Despite institutional disadvantages, U.S. firms can increase their awareness of export opportunities. The most comprehensive source of information is the U.S. Department of Commerce and its district offices all over the country (U.S. Export Assistance Centers, USEAC). Within that department are two organizations dedicated to providing businesses with intelligence and assistance for attacking foreign markets: U.S. and Foreign Commercial Service and International Trade Administration (ITA). ITA regularly publishes *A Guide to Exporting* (most recently edited by Doug Barry, 2015). This is the "Official Government Resource to Small and Medium-Sized Companies" in their exporting quest.

The U.S. and Foreign Commercial Service and International Trade Administration are governmental agencies that provide the potential exporter with a "best prospects" list, which gives the names and addresses of potential distributors in foreign markets along with businesses they are in, the products they handle, and their contact person. In addition, the Department of Commerce has assembled a "comparison shopping service" for countries that are major markets for U.S. exports. For a small fee, a firm can receive a customized market research survey on a product of its choice. This survey provides information on marketability, the competition, comparative prices, distribution channels, and names of potential sales representatives. Each study is conducted on-site by an officer of the Department of Commerce.

The Department of Commerce also organizes trade events that help potential exporters make foreign contacts and explore export opportunities. The department organizes exhibitions at international trade fairs, which are held regularly in major cities worldwide. The department also has a matchmaker program, in which department representatives accompany groups of U.S. businesspeople abroad to meet with qualified agents, distributors, and customers. Affiliated with the U.S. Department of Commerce and its USEAC offices is a set of District Export Councils (DEC; connected also via the National District Export Council). DECs are composed of some 1,500 volunteers appointed by the U.S. Secretary of Commerce to help U.S. business be more competitive internationally.

Another governmental organization, the Small Business Administration (SBA), can help potential exporters (see the accompanying Management Focus for examples of the SBA's work). The SBA employs 76 district international trade officers and 10 regional international trade officers throughout the United States, as well as a 10-person international trade staff in Washington, DC. Among the SBA's no-fee services are Small Business Development Centers (SBDC), Service Corps of Retired Executives (SCORE), and Export Legal Assistance Network (ELAN). The SBDCs around the country provide a full range of export assistance to business, particularly small companies new to exporting. Through SCORE, the SBA oversees some 11,500 volunteers with international trade experience to provide one-on-one counseling to active and new-to-export businesses. The SBA also coordinates ELAN, nationwide group of international trade attorneys who provide free initial consultations to small businesses on export-related matters.

The United States has also established a set of 17 Centers for International Business Education and Research (CIBERs), which assist with exporting needs. The CIBERs were created by the U.S. Congress under the Omnibus Trade and Competitiveness Act of 1988 to increase and promote the nation's capacity for international understanding and competitiveness. Administered by the U.S. Department of Education, the CIBER network links the human resource and technological needs of the U.S. business community with the international education, language training, and research capacities of universities across the country. The 17 CIBERs, including the University of Washington and Michigan State University (www2.ed.gov/programs/iegpscibe), serve as regional and national resources to businesspeople, students, and teachers at all levels. Many countries around the world are trying to replicate the U.S. CIBER initiative (e.g., the European Union).

Additionally, nearly every U.S. state, country regions, and many large cities maintain active trade commissions whose purpose is to promote exports. Most of these provide business counseling, information gathering, technical assistance, and financing. Unfortunately, many have fallen victim to budget cuts or to turf battles for political and financial support with other export agencies.

A number of private organizations are also beginning to provide more assistance to would-be exporters. Commercial banks and major accounting firms are more willing to assist small firms in starting export operations than they were a decade ago. In addition, large multinationals that have been successful in the global arena are typically willing to discuss opportunities overseas with the owners or managers of small firms.[15]

Is Chinese Exporting the Next Edge for the Country?

With hundreds of television sets stacked high, Changhong Electronics' warehouse in Shunde resembles many other storage depots in southern China, but their destinations reveal an important shift in global trade patterns. While Changhong's smaller sets are headed for Europe, its 50-inch plasma screens, which dominate the warehouse, will be shipped to South Africa. Fast growth in developing countries and sluggish Western economies are prompting these companies to abandon their obsession with the United States and Europe and to try to capitalize on rapidly growing markets in Asia, Africa, and Latin America. The so-called China price—a vastly lower price because of low labor costs and the low cost of capital for large government-owned companies—now applies to industrial goods, not just consumer goods. Experts believe that cheap Chinese exports could provide a boost to investment in the developing world, just as they once did to consumption in the developed world. Can China boost investment in the developing world and also boost its own economy?

Source: R. Jacob, "Chinese Exporters Seek New Markets," *Financial Times*, June 12, 2012 (http://www.ft.com/cms/s/0/4dc14e6c-b381-11e1-a3db-00144feabdc0.html#axzz4GBucgVYu).

SERVICE PROVIDERS

Most companies that engage in international trade enlist the help of export–import service providers, but there are many choices. Let's look at the main ones: freight forwarders, export management companies, export trading companies, export packaging companies, customs brokers, confirming houses, export agents and merchants, piggyback marketing, and economic processing zones.

Exporting with Government Assistance

Exporting can seem like a daunting prospect, but the reality is that in the United States, as in many other countries, many small enterprises have built profitable export businesses. For example, Landmark Systems of Virginia had virtually no domestic sales before it entered the European market. Landmark had developed a software program for IBM mainframe computers and located an independent distributor in Europe to represent its product. In the first year, 80 percent of sales were attributed to exporting. In the second year, sales jumped from $100,000 to $1.4 million—with 70 percent attributable to exports. Landmark is not alone; governmental data suggest that in the United States, more than 97 percent of the 240,000 firms that export are small or medium-sized businesses that employ fewer than 500 people. Their share of total U.S. exports has grown steadily and is around 30 percent today.

To help jump-start the exporting process, many small companies have drawn on the expertise of governmental agencies, financial institutions, and export management companies. Consider the case of Novi Inc., a California-based business. Company president Michael Stoff tells how he utilized the services of the U.S. Small Business Administration (SBA) Office of International Trade to start exporting:

"When I began my business venture, Novi Inc., I knew that my Tune-Tote (a stereo system for bicycles) had the potential to be successful in international markets. Although I had no prior experience in this area, I began researching and collecting information on international markets. I was willing to learn, and by targeting key sources for information and guidance, I was able to penetrate international markets in a short period of time. One vital source I used from the beginning was the SBA. Through SBA, I was directed to a program that dealt specifically with business development—the Service Corps of Retired Executives (SCORE). I was assigned an adviser who had run his own import/export business for 30 years. The services of SCORE are provided on a continual basis and are free.

"As I began to pursue exporting, my first step was a thorough marketing evaluation. I targeted trade shows with a good presence of international buyers. I also went to DOC [Department of Commerce] for counseling and information about the rules and regulations of exporting. I advertised my product in *Commercial News USA,* distributed through United States embassies to buyers worldwide. I utilized DOC's World Traders Data Reports to get background information on potential foreign buyers. As a result, I received 60 to 70 inquiries about Tune-Tote from around the world. Once I completed my research and evaluation of potential buyers, I decided which ones would be most suitable to market my product internationally. Then I decided to grant exclusive distributorship. In order to effectively communicate with my international customers, I invested in a fax. I chose a U.S. bank to handle international transactions. The bank also provided guidance on methods of payment and how best to receive and transmit money. This is essential know-how for anyone wanting to be successful in foreign markets."*

In just one year of exporting, export sales at Novi topped $1 million and increased 40 percent in the second year of operations. Today, Novi Inc. is a large distributor of wireless intercom systems that exports to more than 10 countries.

*Michael Stoff, President of Novi, Inc.

Source: U.S. Department of Commerce, "A Profile of U.S. Exporting Companies, 2000–2001," February 2003, www.census.gov/foreign-trade/aip/index.html#profile; *The 2007 National Exporting Strategy* (Washington, DC: U.S. International Trade Commission, 2007).

Freight forwarders are mainly in business to orchestrate transportation for companies that are shipping internationally. Their primary task is to combine smaller shipments into a single large shipment to minimize the shipping cost. Freight forwarders also provide other services that are beneficial to the exporting firm, such as documentation, payment, and carrier selection.

Export Management Company (EMC)

Export specialist that acts as an export marketing department for client firms.

An **export management company (EMC)**offers services to companies that have not previously exported products. EMCs offer a full menu of services to handle all aspects of exporting, similar to having an internal exporting department within your own firm. For example, EMCs deal with export documents and operate as the firm's agent and distributor; this may include selling the products directly or operating a sales unit to process sales orders.

Export trading companies export products for companies that contract with them. They identify and work with companies in foreign countries that will market and sell the products. They provide comprehensive exporting services, including export documentation, logistics, and transportation.

Export packaging companies, or export packers for short, provide services to companies that are unfamiliar with exporting. For example, some countries require packages to meet certain specifications, and the export packaging firm's knowledge of these requirements is invaluable to new exporters in particular. The export packer can also advise companies on appropriate design and materials for the packaging of their items. Export packers can assist companies in minimizing packaging to maximize the number of items to be shipped.

Customs brokers can help companies avoid the pitfalls involved in customs regulations. The customs requirements of many countries can be difficult for new or infrequent exporters to understand, and the knowledge and experience of the customs broker can be very important.

For example, many countries have certain laws and documentation regulations concerning imported items that are not always obvious to the exporter. Customs brokers can offer a firm a complete package of services that are essential when a firm is exporting to a large number of countries.

Confirming houses, sometimes called buying agents, represent foreign companies that want to buy your products. Typically, they try to get the products they want at the lowest prices and are paid a commission by their foreign clients. A good place to find these potential exporting linkages is via government embassies.

Export agents, merchants, and remarketers buy products directly from the manufacturer and package and label the products in accordance with their own wishes and specifications. They then sell the products internationally through their own contacts under their own names and assume all risks. The effort it takes for you to market the product internationally is very small, but you also lose any control over the marketing, promotion, and positioning of your product.

Piggyback marketing is an arrangement whereby one firm distributes another firm's products. For example, a firm may have a contract to provide an assortment of products to an overseas client, but it does not have all the products requested. In such cases, another firm can piggyback its products to fill the contract's requirements. Successful piggybacking usually requires complementary products and the same target market of customers.

There are now more than 600 export processing zones (EPZs) in the world, and they exist in more than 100 countries. The EPZs include foreign trade zones (FTZs), special economic zones, bonded warehouses, free ports, and customs zones. Many companies use EPZs to receive shipments of products that are then reshipped in smaller lots to customers throughout the surrounding areas. Founded in 1978 by the United Nations, the World Economic Processing Zones Association (wepza.org) is a private nonprofit organization dedicated to the improvement of the efficiency of all EPZs.

EXPORT STRATEGY

In addition to using export service providers, a firm can reduce the risks associated with exporting if it is careful about its choice of export strategy.[16] A few guidelines can help firms improve their odds of success. For example, one of the most successful exporting firms in the world, 3M (originally, Minnesota Mining & Manufacturing Company), has built its export success on three main principles: enter on a small scale to reduce risks, add additional product lines once the exporting operations start to become successful, and hire locals to promote the firm's products (3M's export strategy is profiled in the accompanying Management Focus). Another successful exporter, Red Spot Paint & Varnish Company, emphasizes the importance of cultivating personal relationships when trying to build an export business.

The probability of exporting successfully can be increased dramatically by taking a handful of simple strategic steps. First, particularly for the novice exporter, it helps to hire an EMC or at least an experienced export consultant to identify opportunities and navigate the paperwork and regulations so often involved in exporting. Second, it often makes sense to initially focus on one market or a handful of markets. Learn what is required to succeed in those markets before moving to other markets. The firm that enters many markets at once runs the risk of spreading its limited management resources too thin. The result of such a shotgun approach to exporting may be a failure to become established in any one market.

Third, as with 3M, it often makes sense to enter a foreign market on a small scale to reduce the costs of any subsequent failure. Most important, entering on a small scale provides the time and opportunity to learn about the foreign country before making significant capital commitments to that market. Fourth, the exporter needs to recognize the time and managerial commitment involved in building export sales and should hire additional personnel to oversee this activity. Fifth, in many countries, it is important to devote a lot of attention to building strong and enduring relationships with local distributors and/or customers. Sixth, as 3M often does, it is important to hire local personnel to help the firm establish itself in a foreign market. Local people are likely to have a much greater sense of how to do business in a given country than a manager from an exporting firm who has previously never set foot in that country. Seventh, several studies have suggested the firm needs to be proactive about seeking export opportunities.[17] Armchair exporting does not work! The world will not normally beat a pathway to your door.

Finally, it is important for the exporter to retain the option of local production. Once exports reach a sufficient volume to justify cost-efficient local production, the exporting firm should

management FOCUS

3M's Export Strategy

3M, which makes more than 55,000 products including tape, sandpaper, medical products, and the ever-present Post-it notes, is one of the world's great multinational operations. Today, more than 60 percent of the firm's revenues are generated outside the United States. Although the bulk of these revenues came from foreign-based operations, 3M remains a major exporter with more than $30 billion in sales, operations in 65 countries, and sales in more than 200 countries. The company often uses its exports to establish an initial presence in a foreign market, only building foreign production facilities once sales volume rises to a level that justifies local production.

The export strategy is built around simple principles. One is known as "FIDO," which stands for *f*irst *i*n (to a new market) *d*efeats *o*thers. The essence of FIDO is to gain an advantage over other exporters by getting into a market first and learning about that country and how to sell there before others do. A second principle is "make a little, sell a little," which is the idea of entering on a small scale with a very modest investment and pushing one basic product, such as reflective sheeting for traffic signs in Russia or scouring pads in Hungary. Once 3M believes it has learned enough about the market to reduce the risk of failure to reasonable levels, it adds additional products.

A third principle at 3M is to hire local employees to sell the firm's products. The company normally sets up a local sales subsidiary to handle its export activities in a country. It then staffs this subsidiary with local hires because it believes they are likely to have a much better idea than American expatriates of how to sell in their own country. Because of the implementation of this principle, fewer than 200 of 3M's 40,000-plus foreign employees are U.S. expatriates.

Another common practice at 3M is to formulate global strategic plans for the export and eventual overseas production of its products. Within the context of these plans, 3M gives local managers considerable autonomy to find the best way to sell the product within their country. Thus, when 3M first exported its Post-it notes, it planned to "sample the daylights" out of the product, but it also told local managers to find the best way of doing this. Local managers hired office cleaning crews to pass out samples in Great Britain and Germany; in Italy, office products distributors were used to pass out free samples; in Malaysia, local managers employed young women to go from office to office handing out samples of the product. In typical 3M fashion, when the volume of Post-it notes was sufficient to justify it, exports from the United States were replaced by local production. Thus, after several years, 3M found it worthwhile to set up production facilities in France to produce Post-it notes for the European market.

Sourcese: "3M Science of Applied Life." www.3m.com; R. L. Rose, "Success Abroad," *The Wall Street Journal*, March 29, 1991, p. A1; T. Eiben, "US Exporters Keep on Rolling," *Fortune*, June 14, 1994, pp. 128–31; "3M Company, A Century on Innovation," 3M, 2002, 2005, 2015; 10K form. www.3m.com.

consider establishing production facilities in the foreign market. Such localization helps foster good relations with the foreign country and can lead to greater market acceptance. Exporting is often not an end in itself but merely a step on the road toward establishment of foreign production (again, 3M provides an example of this philosophy).

globalEDGE™ DIAGNOSTIC TOOLS In Chapter 1, we introduced the globalEDGE™ website (globaledge.msu.edu), a product of the International Business Center in the Eli Broad College of Business at Michigan State University. globalEDGE™ has been the top-ranked website in the world for international business resources on Google since 2004. Businesspeople, public policy makers, academics, and college students have been using globalEDGE™ in some form since 1994, when it first started as "International Business Resources on the World Wide Web." Some 10 million people now use globalEDGE™, with about 1.5 million active users. The site is free, including the "Diagnostic Tools" section. In that section of the site, there are four diagnostic tools that focus on helping companies export. Each tool has been developed through sophisticated research and Delphi studies with business executives. The tools are CORE, PARTNER, DISTRIBUTOR, and FREIGHT.

CORE (Company Readiness to Export) assists firms in self-assessment of their exporting proficiency, evaluates both the firm's and the intended product's readiness to be taken internationally, and systematically identifies the firm's strengths and weaknesses within the context of exporting (see Figure 14.2). The CORE tool also serves as a tutorial in exporting, and it has been the most successful and most widely used of the tools created by the International Business Center.

PARTNER (International Partner Selection) assists in the analysis and evaluation of potential international partners. It covers a wide variety of types of partnerships: joint ventures, licensees, franchisees, contract manufacturers, and R&D partnerships. It is based on a multidimensional set of criteria that includes trust and relationship factors as well as operational criteria and contains

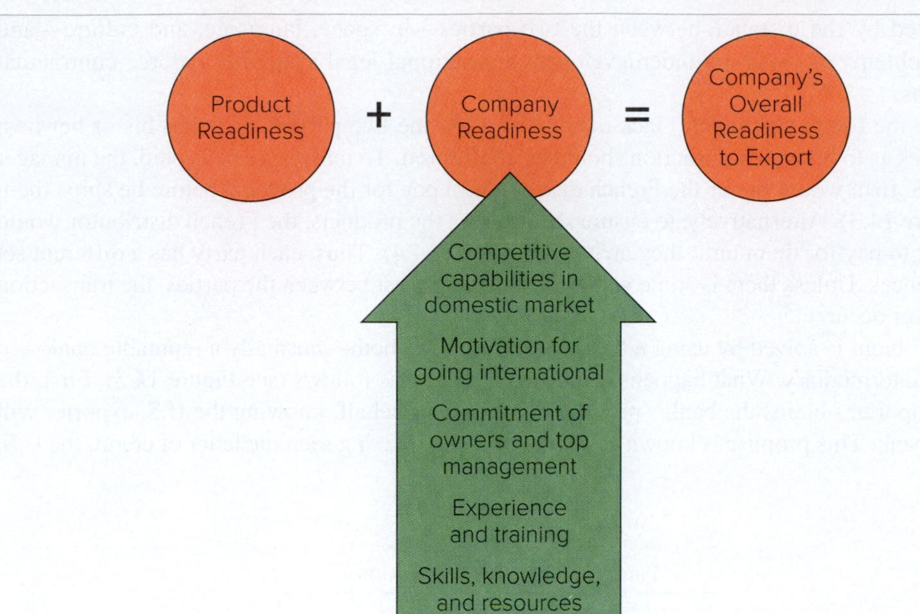

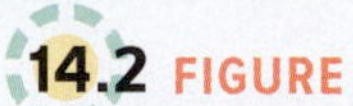

14.2 FIGURE

Company Readiness to Export.

Source: C. W. L. Hill and G. T. M. Hult, *International Business: Competing in the Global Marketplace* (New York: McGraw-Hill Education, 2017).

individually identified strengths and weaknesses of each partner. DISTRIBUTOR (Foreign Distributor Selection) helps exporting firms evaluate and compare foreign distributor or agent candidates, given the type of product being sold and the market characteristics, and indicates areas that may require ongoing training and management throughout the life of the relationship. FREIGHT (Freight Forwarder Selection) assists companies in selecting the most appropriate international freight forwarder for their type and volume of business based on six sets of criteria; it evaluates each candidate, highlights the candidates' strengths and weaknesses, and compares the various candidates.

test PREP

Use SmartBook to help retain what you have learned. Access your Instructor's Connect course to check out SmartBook or go to learnsmartadvantage.com for help.

Export and Import Financing

LO 14-4

Recognize the basic steps involved in export financing.

Mechanisms for financing exports and imports have evolved over the centuries in response to a problem that can be particularly acute in international trade: the lack of trust that exists when one must put faith in a stranger. In this section, we examine the financial devices that have evolved to cope with this problem in the context of international trade: the letter of credit, the draft (or bill of exchange), and the bill of lading. Then we trace the 14 steps of a typical export–import transaction.[18]

LACK OF TRUST Firms engaged in international trade have to trust someone they may have never seen, who lives in a different country, who speaks a different language, who abides by (or does not abide by) a different legal system, and who could be very difficult to track down if he or she defaults on an obligation. Consider a U.S. firm exporting to a distributor in France. The U.S. businessperson might be concerned that if he ships the products to France before he receives payment from the French businessperson, she might take delivery of the products and not pay him. Conversely, the French importer might worry that if she pays for the products before they are shipped, the U.S. firm might keep the money and never ship the products or might ship defective products. Neither party to the exchange completely trusts the other. This lack of trust is

How Trusting Can You Be?

In Chapter 14, we discuss the fact that firms that are engaged in international trade have to trust someone they may have never seen, who lives in a different country, who speaks a different language, who abides by (or does not abide by) a different legal system, and who could be very difficult to track down if he or she defaults on an obligation. Basically, there is a lot of potential for unknown issues to arise and for complications to happen, given the lack of established trust between trading partners. With almost 200 countries in the world, lots of cultural values and beliefs, and many potential avenues to run into complications, how much trust would you place on a relationship that involved (1) an organization from a country like yours (e.g., Swedish people doing business with Danish people) or (2) an organization from a country very different from yours (e.g., a Canadian doing business with someone from Turkey)?

exacerbated by the distance between the two parties—in space, language, and culture—and by the problems of using an underdeveloped international legal system to enforce contractual obligations.

Due to the (quite reasonable) lack of trust between the two parties, each has his or her own preferences as to how the transaction should be configured. To make sure he is paid, the manager of the U.S. firm would prefer the French distributor to pay for the products before he ships them (see Figure 14.3). Alternatively, to ensure she receives the products, the French distributor would prefer not to pay for them until they arrive (see Figure 14.4). Thus, each party has a different set of preferences. Unless there is some way of establishing trust between the parties, the transaction might never occur.

The problem is solved by using a third party trusted by both—normally a reputable bank—to act as an intermediary. What happens can be summarized as follows (see Figure 14.5). First, the French importer obtains the bank's promise to pay on her behalf, knowing the U.S. exporter will trust the bank. This promise is known as a letter of credit. Having seen the letter of credit, the U.S.

14.3 FIGURE

Preference of the U.S. Exporter.

Source: C. W. L. Hill and G. T. M. Hult, *International Business: Competing in the Global Marketplace* (New York: McGraw-Hill Education, 2017).

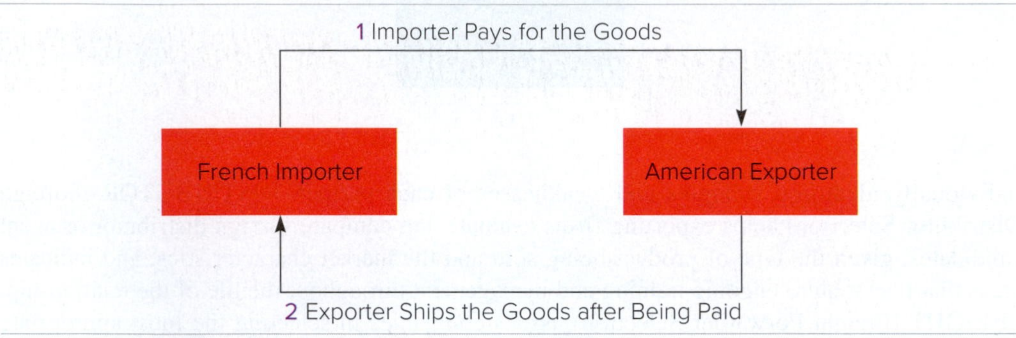

14.3 FIGURE

Preference of the French Importer.

Source: C. W. L. Hill and G. T. M. Hult, *International Business: Competing in the Global Marketplace* (New York: McGraw-Hill Education, 2017).

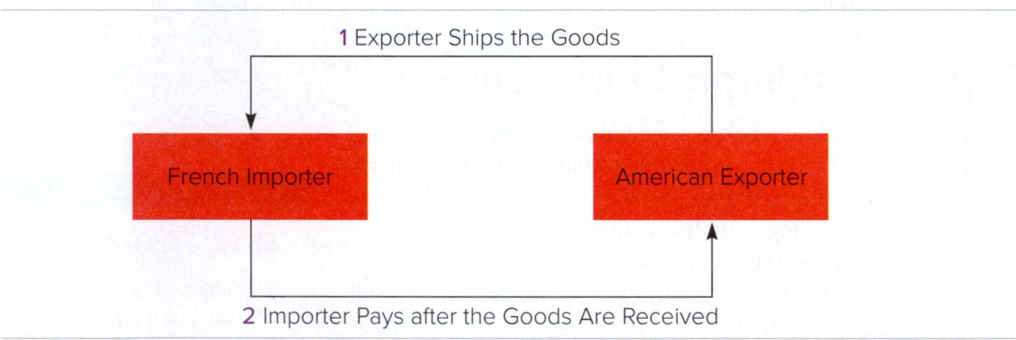

14.5 FIGURE

The Use of a Third Party.

Source: C. W. L. Hill and G. T. M. Hult, *International Business: Competing in the Global Marketplace* (New York: McGraw-Hill Education, 2017).

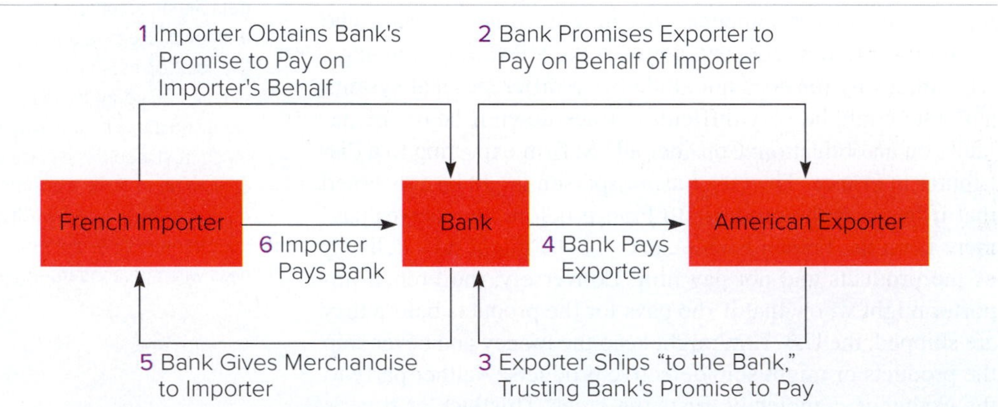

exporter now ships the products to France. Title to the products is given to the bank in the form of a document called a bill of lading. In return, the U.S. exporter tells the bank to pay for the products, which the bank does. The document for requesting this payment is referred to as a draft. The bank, having paid for the products, now passes the title on to the French importer, whom the bank trusts. At that time or later, depending on their agreement, the importer reimburses the bank. In the remainder of this section, we examine how this system works in more detail.

LETTER OF CREDIT A letter of credit, abbreviated as L/C, stands at the center of international commercial transactions. Issued by a bank at the request of an importer, the **letter of credit** states that the bank will pay a specified sum of money to a beneficiary, normally the exporter, on presentation of particular, specified documents.

Letter of Credit
Issued by a bank, indicating that the bank will make payments under specific circumstances.

Consider again the example of the U.S. exporter and the French importer. The French importer applies to her local bank, say, the Bank of Paris, for the issuance of a letter of credit. The Bank of Paris then undertakes a credit check of the importer. If the Bank of Paris is satisfied with her creditworthiness, it will issue a letter of credit. However, the Bank of Paris might require a cash deposit or some other form of collateral from her first. In addition, the Bank of Paris will charge the importer a fee for this service. Typically, this amounts to between 0.5 and 2 percent of the value of the letter of credit, depending on the importer's creditworthiness and the size of the transaction. (As a rule, the larger the transaction, the lower the percentage.)

Assume the Bank of Paris is satisfied with the French importer's creditworthiness and agrees to issue a letter of credit. The letter states that the Bank of Paris will pay the U.S. exporter for the merchandise as long as it is shipped in accordance with specified instructions and conditions. At this point, the letter of credit becomes a financial contract between the Bank of Paris and the U.S. exporter. The Bank of Paris then sends the letter of credit to the U.S. exporter's bank, say, the Bank of New York. The Bank of New York tells the exporter that it has received a letter of credit and that he can ship the merchandise. After the exporter has shipped the merchandise, he draws a draft against the Bank of Paris in accordance with the terms of the letter of credit, attaches the required documents, and presents the draft to his own bank, the Bank of New York, for payment. The Bank of New York then forwards the letter of credit and associated documents to the Bank of Paris. If all the terms and conditions contained in the letter of credit have been complied with, the Bank of Paris will honor the draft and will send payment to the Bank of New York. When the Bank of New York receives the funds, it will pay the U.S. exporter.

As for the Bank of Paris, once it has transferred the funds to the Bank of New York, it will collect payment from the French importer. Alternatively, the Bank of Paris may allow the importer some time to resell the merchandise before requiring payment. This is not unusual, particularly when the importer is a distributor and not the final consumer of the merchandise, since it helps the importer's cash flow. The Bank of Paris will treat such an extension of the payment period as a loan to the importer and will charge an appropriate rate of interest.

The great advantage of this system is that both the French importer and the U.S. exporter are likely to trust reputable banks, even if they do not trust each other. Once the U.S. exporter has seen a letter of credit, he knows that he is guaranteed payment and will ship the merchandise. Also, an exporter may find that having a letter of credit will facilitate obtaining pre-export financing. For example, having seen the letter of credit, the Bank of New York might be willing to lend the exporter funds to process and prepare the merchandise for shipping to France. This loan may not have to be repaid until the exporter has received his payment for the merchandise. As for the French importer, she does not have to pay for the merchandise until the documents have arrived and unless all conditions stated in the letter of credit have been satisfied. The drawback for the importer is the fee she must pay the Bank of Paris for the letter of credit. In addition, because the letter of credit is a financial liability against her, it may reduce her ability to borrow funds for other purposes.

DRAFT A draft, sometimes referred to as a **bill of exchange**, is the instrument normally used in international commerce to effect payment. A **draft** is simply an order written by an exporter instructing an importer, or an importer's agent, to pay a specified amount of money at a specified time. In the example of the U.S. exporter and the French importer, the exporter writes a draft that instructs the Bank of Paris, the French importer's agent, to pay for the merchandise shipped to France. The person or business initiating the draft is known as the maker (in this case,

Bill of Exchange
An order written by an exporter instructing an importer, or an importer's agent, to pay a specified amount of money at a specified time.

Draft
An order written by an exporter telling an importer what and when to pay.

the U.S. exporter). The party to whom the draft is presented is known as the drawee (in this case, the Bank of Paris).

International practice is to use drafts to settle trade transactions. This differs from domestic practice in which a seller usually ships merchandise on an open account, followed by a commercial invoice that specifies the amount due and the terms of payment. In domestic transactions, the buyer can often obtain possession of the merchandise without signing a formal document acknowledging his or her obligation to pay. In contrast, due to the lack of trust in international transactions, payment or a formal promise to pay is required before the buyer can obtain the merchandise.

Sight Draft
A draft payable on presentation to the drawee.

Time Draft
A promise to pay by the accepting party at some future date.

Drafts fall into two categories, sight drafts and time drafts. A **sight draft** is payable on presentation to the drawee. A **time draft** allows for a delay in payment—normally 30, 60, 90, or 120 days. It is presented to the drawee, who signifies acceptance of it by writing or stamping a notice of acceptance on its face. Once accepted, the time draft becomes a promise to pay by the accepting party. When a time draft is drawn on and accepted by a bank, it is called a *banker's acceptance*. When it is drawn on and accepted by a business firm, it is called a *trade acceptance*.

Time drafts are negotiable instruments; that is, once the draft is stamped with an acceptance, the maker can sell the draft to an investor at a discount from its face value. Imagine that the agreement between the U.S. exporter and the French importer calls for the exporter to present the Bank of Paris (through the Bank of New York) with a time draft requiring payment 120 days after presentation. The Bank of Paris stamps the time draft with an acceptance. Imagine further that the draft is for $100,000.

The exporter can either hold onto the accepted time draft and receive $100,000 in 120 days or sell it to an investor, say, the Bank of New York, for a discount from the face value. If the prevailing discount rate is 7 percent, the exporter could receive $97,700 by selling it immediately (7 percent per year discount rate for 120 days for $100,000 equals $2,300, and $100,000 – $2,300 = $97,700). The Bank of New York would then collect the full $100,000 from the Bank of Paris in 120 days. The exporter might sell the accepted time draft immediately if he needed the funds to finance merchandise in transit and/or to cover cash flow shortfalls.

Bill of Lading
A document issued to an exporter by a common carrier transporting merchandise. It serves as a receipt, a contract, and a document of title.

BILL OF LADING

The third key document for financing international trade is the bill of lading. The **bill of lading** is issued to the exporter by the common carrier transporting the merchandise. It serves three purposes: it is a receipt, a contract, and a document of title. As a receipt, the bill of lading indicates that the carrier has received the merchandise described on the face of the document. As a contract, it specifies that the carrier is obligated to provide a transportation service in return for a certain charge. As a document of title, it can be used to obtain payment or a written promise of payment before the merchandise is released to the importer. The bill of lading can also function as collateral against which funds may be advanced to the exporter by its local bank before or during shipment and before final payment by the importer.

A TYPICAL INTERNATIONAL TRADE TRANSACTION

Now that we have reviewed the elements of an international trade transaction, let us see how the process works in a typical case, sticking with the example of the U.S. exporter and the French importer. The typical transaction involves 14 steps (see Figure 14.6).

1. The French importer places an order with the U.S. exporter and asks the American if he would be willing to ship under a letter of credit.
2. The U.S. exporter agrees to ship under a letter of credit and specifies relevant information such as prices and delivery terms.
3. The French importer applies to the Bank of Paris for a letter of credit to be issued in favor of the U.S. exporter for the merchandise the importer wishes to buy.
4. The Bank of Paris issues a letter of credit in the French importer's favor and sends it to the U.S. exporter's bank, the Bank of New York.
5. The Bank of New York advises the exporter of the opening of a letter of credit in his favor.
6. The U.S. exporter ships the goods to the French importer on a common carrier. An official of the carrier gives the exporter a bill of lading.

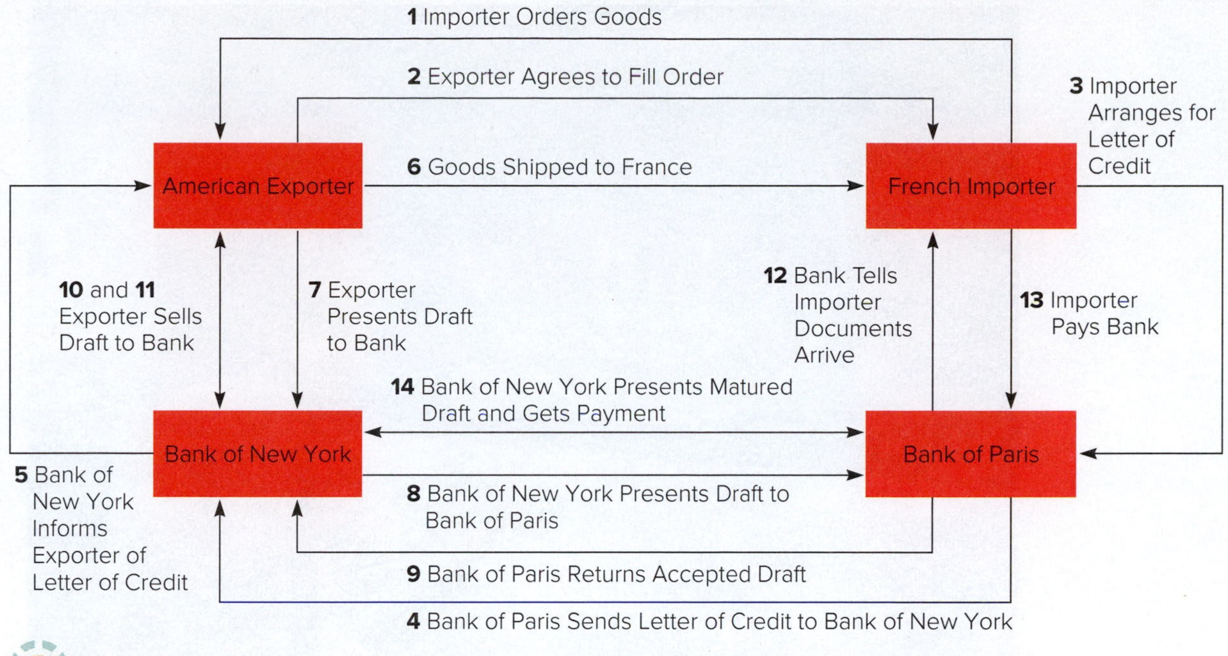

14.6 FIGURE

A Typical International Trade Transaction.

Source: C. W. L. Hill and G. T. M. Hult, *International Business: Competing in the Global Marketplace* (New York: McGraw-Hill Education, 2017).

7. The U.S. exporter presents a 90-day time draft drawn on the Bank of Paris in accordance with its letter of credit and the bill of lading to the Bank of New York. The exporter endorses the bill of lading so title to the goods is transferred to the Bank of New York.
8. The Bank of New York sends the draft and bill of lading to the Bank of Paris. The Bank of Paris accepts the draft, taking possession of the documents and promising to pay the now-accepted draft in 90 days.
9. The Bank of Paris returns the accepted draft to the Bank of New York.
10. The Bank of New York tells the U.S. exporter that it has received the accepted bank draft, which is payable in 90 days.
11. The exporter sells the draft to the Bank of New York at a discount from its face value and receives the discounted cash value of the draft in return.
12. The Bank of Paris notifies the French importer of the arrival of the documents. She agrees to pay the Bank of Paris in 90 days. The Bank of Paris releases the documents so the importer can take possession of the shipment.
13. In 90 days, the Bank of Paris receives the importer's payment, so it has funds to pay the maturing draft.
14. In 90 days, the holder of the matured acceptance (in this case, the Bank of New York) presents it to the Bank of Paris for payment. The Bank of Paris pays.

test PREP

Use SmartBook to help retain what you have learned. Access your Instructor's Connect course to check out SmartBook or go to learnsmartadvantage.com for help.

Export Assistance

LO 14-3

Identify information sources and government programs that exist to help exporters.

Prospective U.S. exporters can draw on two forms of government-backed assistance to help finance their export programs. They can get financing aid from the Export-Import Bank and export credit insurance from the Foreign Credit Insurance Association (similar programs are available in most countries).

EXPORT-IMPORT BANK **Export-Import Bank (Ex-Im Bank)** is a wholly owned U.S. government corporation that was established in 1934. Its mission is to assist in the financing of U.S. exports of products and services to support U.S. employment and market competitiveness. Based on its charter and mandate from the U.S. Congress, the Ex-Im Bank's financing must have a "reasonable assurance of repayment" and should supplement, and not

Export-Import Bank (Ex-Im Bank)
Agency of the U.S. government whose mission is to provide aid in financing and facilitate exports and imports.

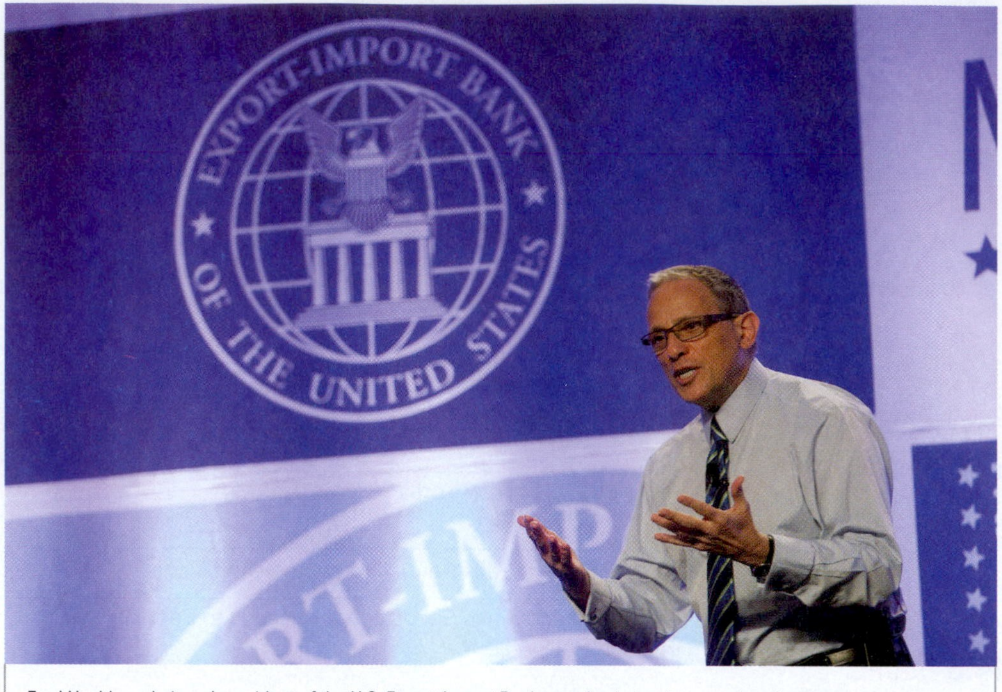

Fred Hochber, chair and president of the U.S. Export-Import Bank, speaks during its annual conference.
© Bloomberg/Getty Images

test PREP

Use SmartBook to help retain what you have learned. Access your Instructor's Connect course to check out SmartBook or go to learnsmartadvantage.com for help.

compete with, private capital lending. The Ex-Im Bank also follows the international rules for government-backed export credit activity under the Organisation for Economic Co-operation and Development (OECD).

In fiscal year 2014, the Ex-Im Bank reported authorizing about $20.5 billion for 3,746 transactions of finance and insurance to support some $27.5 billion in U.S. exports and 164,000 U.S. jobs. Ex-Im Bank's overall exposure was $112 billion in that year, below the $140 billion statutory cap for fiscal year 2014. Overall, Ex-Im Bank pursues its mission with various loan and loan-guarantee programs. The agency guarantees repayment of medium- and long-term loans that U.S. commercial banks make to foreign borrowers for purchasing U.S. exports. The Ex-Im Bank guarantee makes the commercial banks more willing to lend cash to foreign enterprises. This facilitates cross-border trade by U.S. companies. About 85 percent of the banks' transactions support small businesses (under 500 employees).

Ex-Im Bank also has a direct lending operation under which it lends dollars to foreign borrowers for use in purchasing U.S. exports. In some cases, it grants loans that commercial banks would not if it sees a potential benefit to the United States in doing so. The foreign borrowers use the loans to pay U.S. suppliers and repay the loan to the Ex-Im Bank with interest. Using the structure of the U.S. Ex-Im Bank, many countries now have their own export-import banks to facilitate cross-border trade (e.g., China, India).

EXPORT CREDIT INSURANCE For reasons outlined earlier, exporters clearly prefer to get letters of credit from importers. However, sometimes an exporter who insists on a letter of credit will lose an order to one who does not require a letter of credit. Thus, when the importer is in a strong bargaining position and able to play competing suppliers against each other, an exporter may have to forgo a letter of credit.[19] The lack of a letter of credit exposes the exporter to the risk that the foreign importer will default on payment. The exporter can insure against this possibility by buying export credit insurance. If the customer defaults, the insurance firm will cover a major portion of the loss.

In the United States, export credit insurance is provided by the Foreign Credit Insurance Association (FCIA), an association of private commercial institutions operating under the guidance of the Export-Import Bank. The FCIA provides coverage against commercial risks and political risks. Losses due to commercial risk result from the buyer's insolvency or payment default. Political losses arise from actions of governments that are beyond the control of either buyer or seller. Marlin, the small Baltimore manufacturer of wire baskets discussed earlier, credits export credit insurance with giving the company the confidence to push ahead with export sales. For a premium of roughly half a percentage of the price of a sale, Marlin has been able to insure itself against the possibility of nonpayment by a foreign buyer.[20]

Countertrade

LO 14-5
Describe how countertrade can be used to facilitate exporting.

Countertrade is an alternative means of structuring an international sale when conventional means of payment are difficult, costly, or nonexistent. We first encountered countertrade in Chapter 10's discussion of currency convertibility. A government may restrict the convertibility of its currency to preserve its foreign exchange reserves so they can be used to service international debt commitments and purchase crucial imports.[21] This is problematic for exporters. Nonconvertibility implies that the exporter may not be paid in his or her home currency, and few exporters would desire payment in a currency that is not convertible. Countertrade is a common solution.[22] **Countertrade** denotes a range of barterlike agreements; its principle is to trade goods and services for other goods and services when they cannot be traded for money. Some examples of countertrade are:

Countertrade
The trade of goods and services for other goods and services.

- An Italian company that manufactures power-generating equipment, ABB SAE Sadelmi SpA, was awarded a 720 million baht ($17.7 million) contract by the Electricity Generating Authority of Thailand. The contract specified that the company had to accept 218 million baht ($5.4 million) of Thai farm products as part of the payment.
- Saudi Arabia agreed to buy ten 747 jets from Boeing with payment in crude oil, discounted at 10 percent below posted world oil prices.
- General Electric won a contract for a $150 million electric generator project in Romania by agreeing to market $150 million of Romanian products in markets to which Romania did not have access.
- The Venezuelan government negotiated a contract with Caterpillar under which Venezuela would trade 350,000 tons of iron ore for Caterpillar earthmoving equipment.
- Albania offered such items as spring water, tomato juice, and chrome ore in exchange for a $60 million fertilizer and methanol complex.
- Philip Morris shipped cigarettes to Russia, for which it received chemicals that can be used to make fertilizer. Philip Morris shipped the chemicals to China, and in return, China shipped glassware to North America for retail sale by Philip Morris.[23]

THE POPULARITY OF COUNTERTRADE

Countertrade emerged in the 1960s as a way for the old Soviet Union and the then-communist states of eastern Europe, whose currencies were generally nonconvertible, to purchase imports. During the 1980s, the technique grew in popularity among many developing nations that lacked the foreign exchange reserves required to purchase necessary imports. Today, reflecting their own shortages of foreign exchange reserves, some successor states to the former Soviet Union and the eastern European communist nations periodically engage in countertrade to purchase their imports. Estimates of the percentage of world trade covered by some sort of countertrade agreement range from highs of 8 and 10 percent by value to lows of around 2 percent.[24] The precise figure is

Is Countertrade an Appropriate Way of Trading Today?

Countertrades can take many forms, and there are several examples of how it works internationally. For instance, the Malaysian government recently bought 20 diesel electric locomotives from General Electric. Officials of the government said that GE will be paid with palm oil supplied by a plantation company. The company will supply about 200,000 metric tons of palm oil over a period of 30 months. No money changed hands, and no third parties were involved. As another example, in order to save foreign exchange reserves, the Philippine government offered some creditors tinned tuna to repay part of a state $4 billion debt. In other examples, General Motors Corporation sold $12 million worth of locomotive and diesel engines to Yugoslavia and took cash and $4 million in Yugoslavian cutting tools as payment. Plus, McDonnell Douglas agreed to a compensation deal with Thailand for eight top-of-the-line F/A–18 strike aircraft. Thailand agreed to pay $578 million of the total cost in cash, and McDonnell Douglas agreed to accept $93 million in a mixed bag of goods, including Thai rubber, ceramics, furniture, frozen chicken, and canned fruit. To some, these types of trading contracts are strange, and to some they are normal, especially if we go back in time. But what about today? Should the global marketplace engage in these types of nonmonetary trades?

Source: S. Rama, "Types of Counter Trade," 2011, http://www.citeman.com.

unknown, but it is probably at the very low end of these estimates, given the increasing liquidity of international financial markets and wider currency convertibility. However, a short-term spike in the volume of countertrade can follow periodic financial crises. For example, countertrade activity increased notably after the Asian financial crisis of 1997. That crisis left many Asian nations with little hard currency to finance international trade. In the tight monetary regime that followed the crisis in 1997, many Asian firms found it very difficult to get access to export credit to finance their own international trade. Thus, they turned to the only option available to them—countertrade.

Given that countertrade is a means of financing international trade, albeit a minor one, prospective exporters may have to engage in this technique from time to time to gain access to certain international markets. The governments of developing nations sometimes insist on a certain amount of countertrade.[25]

TYPES OF COUNTERTRADE

With its roots in the simple trading of goods and services for other goods and services, countertrade has evolved into a diverse set of activities that can be categorized as five distinct types of trading arrangements: barter, counterpurchase, offset, switch trading, and compensation or buyback.[26] Many countertrade deals involve not just one arrangement but elements of two or more.

Barter
The direct exchange of goods or services between two parties without a cash transaction.

Barter

Barter is the direct exchange of goods and/or services between two parties without a cash transaction. Although barter is the simplest arrangement, it is not common. Its problems are twofold. First, if goods are not exchanged simultaneously, one party ends up financing the other for a period. Second, firms engaged in barter run the risk of having to accept goods they do not want, cannot use, or have difficulty reselling at a reasonable price. For these reasons, barter is viewed as the most restrictive countertrade arrangement. It is primarily used for one-time-only deals in transactions with trading partners who are not creditworthy or trustworthy.

Counterpurchase
A reciprocal buying agreement.

Counterpurchase

Counterpurchase is a reciprocal buying agreement. It occurs when a firm agrees to purchase a certain amount of materials back from a country to which a sale is made. Suppose a U.S. firm sells some products to China. China pays the U.S. firm in dollars, but in exchange, the U.S. firm agrees to spend some of its proceeds from the sale on textiles produced by China. Thus, although China must draw on its foreign exchange reserves to pay the U.S. firm, it knows it will receive some of those dollars back because of the counterpurchase agreement. In one counterpurchase agreement, Rolls-Royce sold jet parts to Finland. As part of the deal, Rolls-Royce agreed to use some of the proceeds from the sale to purchase Finnish-manufactured TV sets that it would then sell in Great Britain.

Offset
Agreement to purchase goods and services with a specified percentage of proceeds from an original sale in that country from any firm in the country.

Offset

An **offset** is similar to a counterpurchase insofar as one party agrees to purchase goods and services with a specified percentage of the proceeds from the original sale. The difference is that this party can fulfill the obligation with any firm in the country to which the sale is being made. From an exporter's perspective, this is more attractive than a straight counterpurchase agreement because it gives the exporter greater flexibility to choose the goods that it wishes to purchase.

Switch Trading
Use of a specialized third-party trading house in a countertrade arrangement.

Switch Trading

The term **switch trading** refers to the use of a specialized third-party trading house in a countertrade arrangement. When a firm enters a counterpurchase or offset agreement with a country, it often ends up with what are called counterpurchase credits, which can be used to purchase goods from that country. Switch trading occurs when a third-party trading house buys the firm's counterpurchase credits and sells them to another firm that can better use them. For example, a U.S. firm concludes a counterpurchase agreement with Poland for which it receives some number of counterpurchase credits for purchasing Polish goods. The U.S. firm cannot use and does not want any Polish goods, however, so it sells the credits to a third-party trading house at a discount. The trading house finds a firm that can use the credits and sells them at a profit.

In one example of switch trading, Poland and Greece had a counterpurchase agreement that called for Poland to buy the same U.S.-dollar value of goods from Greece that it sold to Greece.

However, Poland could not find enough Greek goods that it required, so it ended up with a dollar-denominated counterpurchase balance in Greece that it was unwilling to use. A switch trader bought the right to 250,000 counterpurchase dollars from Poland for $225,000 and sold them to a European sultana (grape) merchant for $235,000, who used them to purchase sultanas from Greece.

A subsea oil and gas tree is lowered into a testing pool at a GE plant in Montrose, United Kingdom. Large, diverse, global companies like GE can benefit from countertrade agreements.

Source: © Simon Dawson/Bloomberg/Getty Images

Compensation or Buybacks

A **buyback** occurs when a firm builds a plant in a country—or supplies technology, equipment, training, or other services to the country—and agrees to take a certain percentage of the plant's output as partial payment for the contract. For example, Occidental Petroleum negotiated a deal with Russia under which Occidental would build several ammonia plants in Russia and as partial payment receive ammonia over a 20-year period.

Buyback

Agreement to accept a percentage of a plant's output as payment for contract to build a plant.

PROS AND CONS OF COUNTERTRADE

Countertrade's main attraction is that it can give a firm a way to finance an export deal when other means are not available. Given the problems that many developing nations have in raising the foreign exchange necessary to pay for imports, countertrade may be the only option available when doing business in these countries. Even when countertrade is not the only option for structuring an export transaction, many countries prefer countertrade to cash deals. Thus, if a firm is unwilling to enter a countertrade agreement, it may lose an export opportunity to a competitor that is willing to make a countertrade agreement.

In addition, a countertrade agreement may be required by the government of a country to which a firm is exporting goods or services. Boeing often has to accept to counterpurchase agreements to capture orders for its commercial jet aircraft. For example, in exchange for gaining an order from Air India, Boeing may be required to purchase certain component parts, such as aircraft doors, from an Indian company. Taking this one step further, Boeing can use its willingness to enter into a counterpurchase agreement as a way of winning orders in the face of intense competition from its global rival, Airbus. Thus, countertrade can become a strategic marketing weapon.

However, the drawbacks of countertrade agreements are substantial. Other things being equal, firms would normally prefer to be paid in hard currency. Countertrade contracts may involve the exchange of unusable or poor-quality goods that the firm cannot dispose of profitably. For example, a few years ago, one U.S. firm got burned when 50 percent of the television sets it received in a countertrade agreement with Hungary were defective and could not be sold. In addition, even if the goods it receives are of high quality, the firm still needs to dispose of them profitably. To do this, countertrade requires the firm to invest in an in-house trading department dedicated to arranging and managing countertrade deals. This can be expensive and time-consuming.

Given these drawbacks, countertrade is most attractive to large, diverse multinational enterprises that can use their worldwide network of contacts to dispose of goods acquired in countertrading. The masters of countertrade are Japan's giant trading firms, the *sogo shosha,* which use their vast networks of affiliated companies to profitably dispose of goods acquired through countertrade agreements. The trading firm of Mitsui & Company, for example, has about 120 affiliated companies in almost every sector of the manufacturing and service industries. If one of Mitsui's affiliates receives goods in a countertrade agreement that it cannot consume, Mitsui & Company will normally be able to find another affiliate that can profitably use them. Firms affiliated with one of Japan's *sogo shosha* often have a competitive advantage in countries where countertrade agreements are preferred.

 **test PREP**

Use SmartBook to help retain what you have learned. Access your Instructor's Connect course to check out SmartBook or go to learnsmartadvantage.com for help.

Western firms that are large, diverse, and have a global reach (e.g., General Electric, Philip Morris, and 3M) have similar profit advantages from countertrade agreements. Indeed, 3M has established its own trading company—3M Global Trading Inc.—to develop and manage the company's international countertrade programs. Unless there is no alternative, small and medium-sized exporters should probably try to avoid countertrade deals because they lack the worldwide network of operations that may be required to profitably utilize or dispose of goods acquired through them.[27]

Key Terms

MITI, p. 386

sogo shosha, p. 386

export management company (EMC), p. 388

letter of credit, p. 393

bill of exchange, p. 393

draft, p. 393

sight draft, p. 394

time draft, p. 394

bill of lading, p. 394

Export-Import Bank (Ex-Im Bank), p. 395

countertrade, p. 397

barter, p. 398

counterpurchase, p. 398

offset, p. 398

switch trading, p. 398

buyback, p. 399

Summary

This chapter examined the steps that firms must take to establish themselves as exporters. The chapter made the following points:

1. One big impediment to exporting is ignorance of foreign market opportunities.
2. Neophyte exporters often become discouraged or frustrated with the exporting process because they encounter many problems, delays, and pitfalls.
3. The way to overcome ignorance is to gather information. In the United States, a number of institutions, the most important of which is the U.S. Department of Commerce, can help firms gather information in the matchmaking process. Export management companies can also help identify export opportunities.
4. Many of the pitfalls associated with exporting can be avoided if a company hires an experienced export service provider (e.g., export management company) and if it adopts the appropriate export strategy.
5. Firms engaged in international trade must do business with people they cannot trust and people who may be difficult to track down if they default on an obligation. Due to the lack of trust, each party to an international transaction has a different set of preferences regarding the configuration of the transaction.
6. The problems arising from lack of trust between exporters and importers can be solved by using a third party that is trusted by both, normally a reputable bank.
7. A letter of credit is issued by a bank at the request of an importer. It states that the bank promises to pay a beneficiary, normally the exporter, on presentation of documents specified in the letter.
8. A draft is the instrument normally used in international commerce to effect payment. It is an order written by an exporter instructing an importer or an importer's agent to pay a specified amount of money at a specified time.
9. Drafts are either sight drafts or time drafts. Time drafts are negotiable instruments.
10. A bill of lading is issued to the exporter by the common carrier transporting the merchandise. It serves as a receipt, a contract, and a document of title.
11. U.S. exporters can draw on two types of government-backed assistance to help finance their exports: loans from the Export-Import Bank and export credit insurance from the Foreign Credit Insurance Association.
12. Countertrade includes a range of barterlike agreements. It is primarily used when a firm exports to a country whose currency is not freely convertible and may lack the foreign exchange reserves required to purchase the imports.
13. The main attraction of countertrade is that it gives a firm a way to finance an export deal when other means are not available. A firm that insists on being paid in hard currency may be at a competitive disadvantage vis-à-vis one that is willing to engage in countertrade.
14. The main disadvantage of countertrade is that the firm may receive unusable or poor-quality goods that cannot be disposed of profitably.

Critical Thinking and Discussion Questions

1. A firm based in California wants to export a shipload of finished lumber to the Philippines. The would-be importer cannot get sufficient credit from domestic sources to pay for the shipment but insists that the finished lumber can quickly be resold in the Philippines for a profit. Outline the steps the exporter should take to effect this export to the Philippines.
2. You are the assistant to the CEO of a small technology firm that manufactures quality, premium-priced, stylish clothing. The CEO has decided to see what the

advice as to the steps the company should take. What advice would you give the CEO?

opportunities are for exporting and has asked you for advice as to the steps the company should take. What advice would you give the CEO?

3. An alternative to using a letter of credit is export credit insurance. What are the advantages and disadvantages of using export credit insurance rather than a letter of credit for exporting *(a)* a luxury yacht from California to Canada and *(b)* machine tools from New York to Ukraine?
4. How do you explain the use of countertrade? Under what scenarios might its use increase further by 2020? Under what scenarios might its use decline?
5. How might a company make strategic use of countertrade schemes as a marketing weapon to generate export revenues? What are the risks associated with pursuing such a strategy?

globalEDGE Research Task

globalEDGE.msu.edu

Use the globalEDGE™ website (globaledge.msu.edu) to complete the following exercises:

1. One way that exporters analyze conditions in emerging markets is through the use of macroeconomic indicators. The Market Potential Index (MPI) is a yearly study conducted by Michigan State University's International Business Center to compare the market potential of country markets for U.S. exporters. Provide a description of the dimensions used in the index. Which of the dimensions would have greater importance for a company that markets wireless devices? What about a company that sells clothing?
2. You work in the sales department of a company that manufactures and sells medical implants. A Brazilian company contacted your department and expressed interest in purchasing a large quantity of your products. The Brazilian company requested an FOB price quote. One of your colleagues mentioned to you that FOB is part of a collection of international shipping terms called "Incoterms," but that was all he knew. Find the *Export Tutorials* on the globalEDGE™ site, and find a more detailed explanation of Incoterms. For an FOB quote, what line items will you need to include in your price quote, in addition to the price your company will charge for the products?

Exporting Desserts

closing case

The opening line of the "About" section of Lulu's Dessert's website—www.lulusdessert.com—is "pull up a chair and join in the festival of flavors with Lulu's Gelatin Desserts,"* Taking basic ingredients and creating a myriad of flavors has led to worldwide exporting success for Lulu's Dessert Corporation. Started in 1982 in a 700-square-foot storefront in Torrance, California, followed by exporting to Mexico in 1992, the company is a gelatin dessert business with core customer target markets in the United States and Mexico but with exporting to several countries worldwide. Lulu is the nickname of the founder, Maria de Lourdes Sobrino.

"Lulu" thought of the idea of ready-to-eat flavored gelatin desserts when she was looking for the popular dessert in local stores. At the time, she was living in the United States, but originally she came from Mexico. The ready-to-eat flavored gelatin desserts were a staple in her native Mexico, but the concept was a novelty when she introduced it to American grocers. Today, Lulu's Desserts can be found in a variety of well-known stores (e.g., Albertsons, Safeway, Walmart).

Back in the early 1980s, Lulu identified and recognized a need for gelatin desserts, filled it with what has now become 45 ready-to-eat products of different sizes and flavors, and transformed the food industry by creating the first ready-to-eat gelatin category based largely on her mother's recipes. The business concept has become quite a "spoon spectacular" since Lulu first began, with a catch line for the company of "more fun for your spoon."

The party started out very small with just Lulu making her mother's gelatin recipe desserts, with an initial production of 300 cups of gelatin per day. Ultimately, the party grew so big that Lulu could not handle it by herself and had to negotiate help from established markets and wholesale distributors. Lulu wanted everyone within reach to enjoy her festival of flavors. In going international, Lulu spent some 10 years trying to gain international sales but continued to run into all kinds of problems and issues. After the trial-and-error decade, she found assistance from the U.S. Export-Import Bank services and now has deeper confidence in her abilities to export products worldwide.

Over the years, Lulu has kept making more and more varieties of her gelatin desserts. A carnival of colors of three-layer gelatins, fruit parfaits, and festive containers of wild new colors and flavors have become identifying marks. This exporting innovation led Bill Hopkins of *USA Today* to call Maria de Lourdes Sobrino "the queen of ready-to-eat gelatins and a force

*"Welcome to Lulu's Dessert," www.lulusdessert.com.

in the surging number of Hispanic Entrepreneurs."** Hal Lancaster of the *Wall Street Journal* also recognized her as an innovator and very successful entrepreneur in "getting out and selling customers your dream."***

Today, with its exporting worldwide but especially to Mexico and sales across the United States, Lulu's Dessert's core focus is on five product categories, including the original Mexican gelatin cup, rice pudding Mexican-style cup, the original creamy gelatin cup, parfait treats gelatin cups, and caramel flan cups. The flavors include such exotic descriptors as Fruit Fantasia, Orange Blast, Creamy Vanilla with Cinnamon, and Sugar Free-De-Light.

**"Welcome to Lulu's Dessert," www.lulusdessert.com.

***Hal Lancaster, "Your Business, Yourself Successful Marketing Means Getting Out and Selling Customers Your Dream," *The Wall Street Journal*, June 18, 2001.

Source: D. Barry, "Maria de Lourdes Sobrino, Founder, LuLu's Dessert," *Exporters: The Wit and Wisdom of Small Businesspeople Who Sell Globally* (Washington, DC: U.S. Commerce Department, 2013); J. Hopkins, "Bad Times Spawn Great Start-Ups," *USA Today*, December 18, 2001; "Welcome to Lulu's Dessert," www.lulusdessert.com.

CASE DISCUSSION QUESTIONS

1. Desserts are often very localized in taste. Beyond the United States and Mexico, where do you think Lulu's Dessert products would be favorable received by customers?
2. Lulu's Dessert used the U.S. Export-Import Bank services to help with knowledge and market segmentation for her desserts as a part of exporting the company products. The Ex-Im Bank receives lots of positive and negative reviews in the United States; do you think it is helpful that the United States has an export-import bank to assist U.S. companies?
3. Do you think franchising is a foreign market entry option for Lulu's Dessert? Why or why not?
4. How would you use business analytics to identify exporting opportunities for Lulu's Dessert?

Endnotes

1. T. Hult, D. Closs, and D. Frayer, *Global Supply Chain Management: Leveraging Processes, Measurements, and Tools for Strategic Corporate Advantage* (New York: McGraw-Hill, 2014).
2. Ibid.
3. R. A. Pope, "Why Small Firms Export: Another Look," *Journal of Small Business Management* 40 (2002), pp. 17–26.
4. M. C. White, "Marlin Steel Wire Products," *Slate Magazine,* November 10, 2010.
5. S. T. Cavusgil, "Global Dimensions of Marketing," in *Marketing,* ed. P. E. Murphy and B. M. Enis (Glenview, IL: Scott, Foresman, 1985), pp. 577–99.
6. S. M. Mehta, "Enterprise: Small Companies Look to Cultivate Foreign Business," *The Wall Street Journal,* July 7, 1994, p. B2.
7. P. A. Julien and C. Ramagelahy, "Competitive Strategy and Performance of Exporting SMEs," *Entrepreneurship Theory and Practice* (2003), pp. 227–94.
8. W. J. Burpitt and D. A. Rondinelli, "Small Firms' Motivations for Exporting: To Earn and Learn?" *Journal of Small Business Management* 38 (2000), pp. 1–14; J. D. Mittelstaedt, G. N. Harben, and W. A. Ward, "How Small Is Too Small?," *Journal of Small Business Management* 41 (2003), pp. 68–85.
9. Small Business Administration, "The State of Small Business 1999–2000: Report to the President," 2001; D. Ransom, "Obama's Math: More Exports Equals More Jobs," *The Wall Street Journal,* February 6, 2010.
10. A. O. Ogbuehi and T. A. Longfellow, "Perceptions of U.S. Manufacturing Companies Concerning Exporting," *Journal of Small Business Management* 32 (1994), pp. 37–59; and U.S. Small Business Administration, "Guide to Exporting," www.sba.gov/oit/info/Guide-to-Exporting/index.html.
11. R. W. Haigh, "Thinking of Exporting?" *Columbia Journal of World Business* 29 (December 1994), pp. 66–86.
12. F. Williams, "The Quest for More Efficient Commerce," *Financial Times,* October 13, 1994, p. 7.
13. See Burpitt and Rondinelli, "Small Firms' Motivations for Exporting"; C. S. Katsikeas, L. C. Leonidou, and N. A. Morgan, "Firm Level Export Performance Assessment," *Academy of Marketing Science* 28 (2000), pp. 493–511.
14. M. Y. Yoshino and T. B. Lifson, *The Invisible Link* (Cambridge, MA: MIT Press, 1986).
15. L. W. Tuller, *Going Global* (Homewood, IL: Business One–Irwin, 1991).
16. M. A. Raymond, J. Kim, and A. T. Shao. "Export Strategy and Performance," *Journal of Global Marketing* 15 (2001), pp. 5–29; P. S. Aulakh, M. Kotabe, and H. Teegen, "Export Strategies and Performance of Firms from Emerging Economies," *Academy of Management Journal* 43 (2000), pp. 342–61.
17. J. Francis and C. Collins-Dodd, "The Impact of Firms' Export Orientation on the Export Performance of High-Tech Small and Medium Sized Enterprises," *Journal of International Marketing* 8 (2000), pp. 84–103.
18. J. Koch, "Integration of U.S. Small Businesses into the Export Trade Sector Using Available Financial Tools and Resources," *Business Credit* 109, no. 10 (2007), pp. 64–68.
19. For a review of the conditions under which a buyer has power over a supplier, see M. E. Porter, *Competitive Strategy* (New York: Free Press, 1980).
20. White, "Marlin Steel Wire Products."
21. *Exchange Agreements and Exchange Restrictions* (Washington, DC: International Monetary Fund, 1989).
22. It's also sometimes argued that countertrade is a way of reducing the risks inherent in a traditional money-for-goods transaction, particularly with entities from emerging economies. See C. J. Choi, S. H. Lee, and J. B. Kim, "A Note of Countertrade: Contractual Uncertainty and Transactional Governance in

Emerging Economies," *Journal of International Business Studies* 30, no. 1 (1999), pp. 189–202.

23. J. R. Carter and J. Gagne, "The Do's and Don'ts of International Countertrade," *Sloan Management Review,* Spring 1988, pp. 31–37; W. Maneerungsee, "Countertrade: Farm Goods Swapped for Italian Electricity," *Bangkok Post,* July 23, 1998.
24. Estimate from the American Countertrade Association at www.countertrade.org/index.htm. See also D. West, "Countertrade," *Business Credit* 104, no. 4 (2001), pp. 64–67; B. Meyer, "The Original Meaning of Trade Meets the Future of Barter," *World Trade* 13 (January 2000), pp. 46–50.
25. Carter and Gagne, "Do's and Don'ts of International Countertrade."
26. For details, see Carter and Gagne, "Do's and Don'ts of International Countertrade"; J. F. Hennart, "Some Empirical Dimensions of Countertrade," *Journal of International Business Studies,* 21, no. 2 (1990), pp. 240–60; West, "Countertrade."
27. D. J. Lecraw, "The Management of Counter-Trade: Factors Influencing Success," *Journal of International Business Studies,* Spring 1989, pp. 41–59.

Part 6 International Business Functions

Global Production and Supply Chain Management

learning objectives

After reading this chapter, you will be able to:

LO15-1 Explain why global production and supply chain management decisions are of central importance to many global companies.

LO15-2 Explain how country differences, production technology, and production factors all affect the choice of where to locate production activities.

LO15-3 Recognize how the role of foreign subsidiaries in production can be enhanced over time as they accumulate knowledge.

LO15-4 Identify the factors that influence a firm's decision of whether to source supplies from within the company or from foreign suppliers.

LO15-5 Understand the functions of logistics and purchasing (sourcing) within global supply chains.

LO15-6 Describe what is required to efficiently manage a global supply chain.

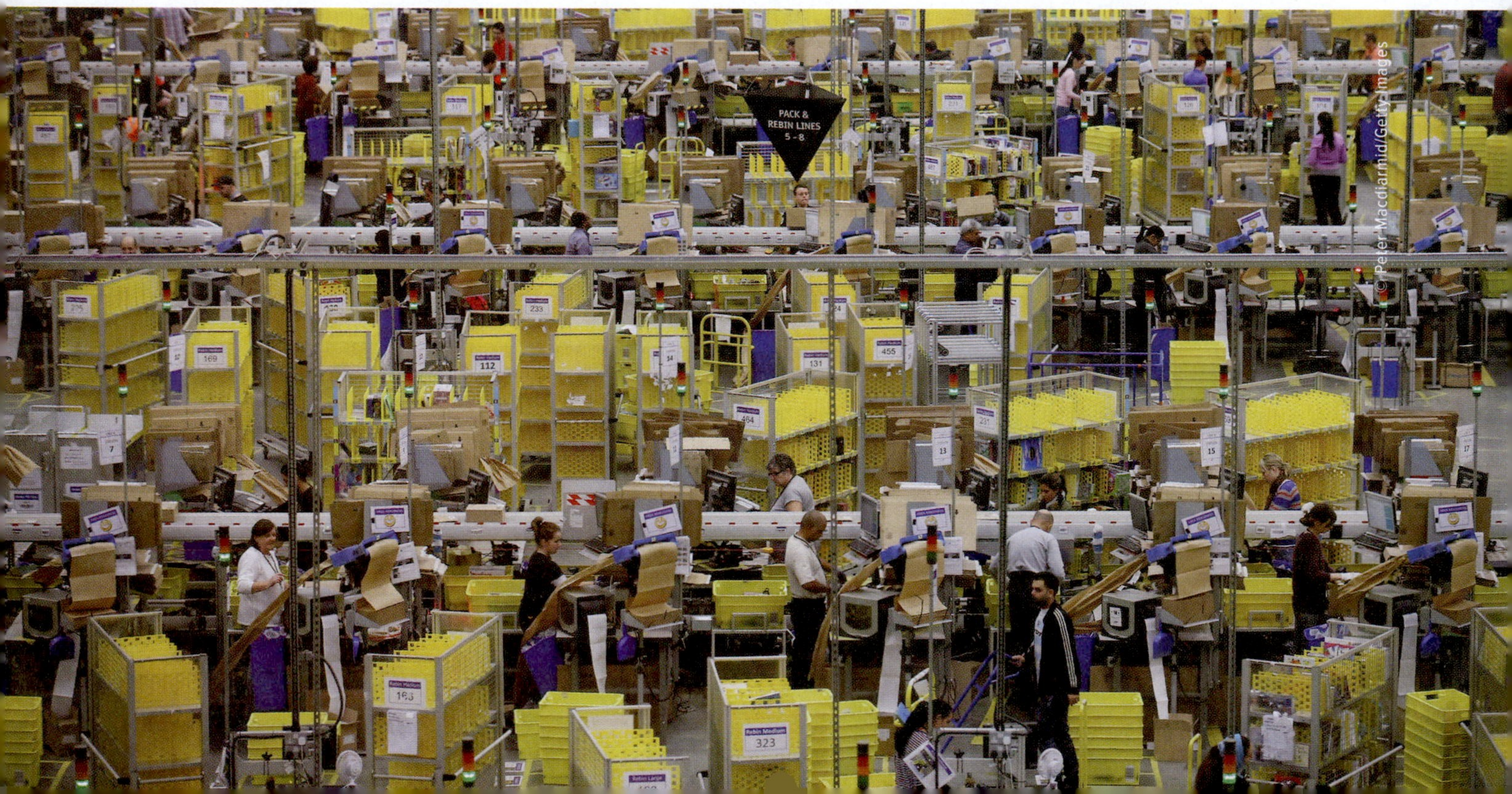

Amazon—A Leader in Global Supply Chain Management

opening case

Amazon.com, Inc.—typically referred to as just Amazon—was the number one company in the latest "Gartner Global Supply Chain Top 25" ranking (Apple and P&G earned Master status and were listed separately above the top 25 companies). This is the first time in the last five years Amazon has been elevated to the top position, although they have been a mainstay in the top 5. Other regular entries in the top five companies with the best global supply chains include Apple, P&G, McDonald's, and Unilever.

Amazon is based in Seattle, Washington, in the northwest corner of the United States. It has now become the largest online retailer in the United States, and it surpassed Walmart as the most valuable retailer in 2015 by market capitalization. The company started in 1994 as an online bookstore but has diversified to a variety of products, including music downloads, furniture, food, and basically almost all consumer electronics. These days, customers can seemingly buy almost anything they need via the Amazon platform. In the United States alone in 2016, more than 130 million customers per month visited Amazon.com. But this massive availability of products also puts a strain on Amazon's global supply chains.

As customers, we have come to expect that Amazon will deliver whatever we buy in the shortest cycle time possible, often no more than two days, especially if a customer is signed up for Amazon Prime. The Amazon Prime service includes free two-day shipping (on many products), video streaming, music, photos, and the Kindle lending library for an annual fee (currently $99). All these services are welcomed by customers, but the free two-day shipping is really what drives the Amazon Prime service.

The free two-day shipping (and a myriad of other shipping alternatives for a fee) requires Amazon to leverage its inventory management practices, global supply chains, and technology to cost effectively reach customers. Delivery speed and efficiency require Amazon to have strategically located fulfillment centers worldwide that can be used by select vendors on the Amazon platform. This includes strict requirements for packaging, labeling, and shipment. Amazon stores these vendors' products in bulk or in individual "pickable" locations.

So far, in addition to the United States, Amazon has retail websites for Australia, Brazil, Canada, China, France, Germany, India, Italy, Japan, Mexico, Netherlands, Spain, the United Kingdom, and Ireland. And the Amazon Prime service places great strain on Amazon's supply chains where it is available in its worldwide locations (e.g., Canada, France, Germany, Italy, Japan, and the United Kingdom).

–continued

In addition, Amazon's customer service centers span some 15 countries worldwide. Plus, the company operates retail websites for international brands such as Sears Canada, Bebe Stores, Marks & Spencer, Mothercare, and Lacoste. This means that Amazon is benefiting from both its global supply chains for delivery of vendors' products and its service as a technology supply chain vendor to businesses. •

Sources: V. Walt, "How Jeff Bezos Aims to Conquer the Next Trillion-dollar Market," *Fortune*, January 1, 2016; B. Stone, "The Secrets of Bezos: How Amazon Became the Everything Store," *Bloomberg Business*, October 10, 2013; *Amazon.com*; A. Cuthbertson, "Amazon Buries Zombie Apocalypse Clause in Terms of Service," *Newsweek*, February 11, 2016.

Introduction

As trade barriers fall and global markets develop, many firms increasingly confront a set of interrelated issues. First, where in the world should production activities be located? Should they be concentrated in a single country, or should they be dispersed around the globe, matching the type of activity with country differences in factor costs, tariff barriers, political risks, and the like to minimize costs and maximize value added? Single country strategies may be efficient operationally but oftentimes become ineffective strategically. For example, what if the company focused all of its attention on one country for production and that country became politically or economically unstable? Some redundancy is usually the best approach in both global production and supply chain management practices, and such redundancy often demands that a company spreads its production and supply chains across countries.

Second, what should be the long-term strategic role of foreign production sites? Should the firm abandon a foreign site if factor costs change, moving production to another more favorable location, or is there value to maintaining an operation at a given location even if underlying economic conditions change? Value can come from cost inefficiencies. Moving factory locations from one country to another solely due to cost considerations is usually not a strategic move. Successful companies typically evaluate cost considerations along with quality, flexibility, and time issues At the same time, cost is one of the most important considerations and serves as the starting point for discussion of making a strategic move from one country to a more advantageous production home.

Third, should the firm own foreign production activities, or is it better to outsource those activities to independent vendors? Outsourcing means less control, but it can be cost-efficient. Fourth, how should a globally dispersed supply chain be managed, and what is the role of information technology in the management of global logistics, purchasing (sourcing), and operations? Fifth, similar to issues of production, should the company manage global supply chains itself, or should it outsource the management to enterprises that specialize in this activity? There are myriad options for supply chain management by third parties. Few companies want to manage the full supply chain from raw material to delivering the product to the end-customer. The question, though, is what portion of the supply chain should be managed by third parties and what portion should be managed by the company itself.

The example of Amazon's inventory management practices, global supply chains, and technology to cost effectively reach customers, which were discussed in the opening case, touch on some of these issues. Likewise, the closing case on Apple covers aspects of global supply chains. Like many modern products, different components for Apple's consumer electronics are manufactured in

Which Career Would You Choose in Global Supply Chain Management?

With increased outsourcing and overseas production sites and customers, supply chain management is a growing field. The Council of Supply Chain Management Professionals (CSCMP), a professional association with more than 8,500 members worldwide, says the industry offers a promising outlook. What's more, potential employers are everywhere: manufacturers and distributors; government agencies; consulting firms; the transport industry; universities and colleges; service firms such as banks, hospitals, and hotels; and third-party logistics providers. The basic career options in global supply chains include its main functions of logistics, purchasing (sourcing), production and operations management, and marketing channels. Which functional area would you choose if you decided to get a job in supply chain management and why? For more information about the organization and careers in this field, visit the CSCMP website at www.cscmp.org and its careers site, www.careersinsupplychain.org.

different locations to produce a low-cost product at a great value for the price paid by the customers. In choosing which company should make which components, Apple was guided by the need to keep the cost of the component parts low so that it could price aggressively and gain market share from its global rivals, such as Samsung.

As the Amazon and Apple examples illustrate, companies also need to be very careful when deciding on supply chain partners globally, and they need to think about the *total costs* of their supply chains. A total cost focus of a global supply chain ensures that the goal is not to strive for the lowest cost possible at each stage of the supply chain (each node in the chain) but instead strive for the lowest total cost to the customer, and by extension greatest value, at the end of the product supply chain. This means that all aspects of cost—including integration and coordination of companies in the supply chain—have been incorporated in addition to the cost of raw material, component parts, and assembly worldwide. And these cost issues, as they relate to global logistics and global purchasing—both considered supply chains functions in a company—have been strategically and tactically addressed.

Strategy, Production, and Supply Chain Management

LO 15-1

Explain why global production and supply chain management decisions are of central importance to many global companies.

Chapter 12 introduced the concept of the value chain and discussed a number of value creation activities, including production, marketing, logistics, R&D, human resources, and information systems. This chapter focuses on two of these value creation activities—**production** and **supply chain management**—and attempts to clarify how they might be performed internationally to (1) lower the costs of value creation and (2) add value by better serving customer needs. Production is sometimes also referred to as manufacturing or operations when discussed in relation to global supply chains. We also discuss the contributions of information technology to these activities, which has become particularly important in a globally integrated world. The remaining chapters in this text look at other value creation activities in the international context (marketing, R&D, and human resource management).

Production
Activities involved in creating a product.

Supply Chain Management
The integration and coordination of logistics, purchasing, operations, and market channel activities from raw material to the end-customer.

Did You Know?
Did you know global supply chains are not just about transportation?

Visit your Connect SmartBook® to view a short video explanation from the authors.

In Chapter 12, we stated that production is concerned with the creation of a good or service. We used the term *production* to denote both service and manufacturing activities, because either a service or a physical product can be produced. Although in this chapter we focus more on the production of physical goods, we should not forget that the term can also be applied to services. This has become more evident in recent years, with the continued pattern among U.S. firms to outsource the "production" of certain service activities to developing nations where labor costs are lower (e.g., the trend among many U.S. companies to outsource customer care services to places such as India, where English is widely spoken and labor costs are much lower). Supply chain management is the integration and coordination of logistics, purchasing, operations, and market channel activities from raw material to the end-customer. Production and supply chain management are closely linked because a firm's ability to perform its production activities efficiently depends on a timely supply of high-quality material and information inputs, for which

Outsourcing

This chapter tackles a number of issues related to production, make-or-buy decisions, sourcing, and logistics. Outsourcing is one of the most commonly discussed topics in news media and on the Internet related to production and supply chains. In effect, the word *outsourcing* sometimes even creates an "us against them" mentality (i.e., should the company outsource production or other activities to entities outside its country borders, or should it use only domestic operations?). Often, the answer is more of a political issue than a strategic resource issue. To stay competitive, companies typically opt for the best value to infuse in their supply chains. The "Outsourcing" section on globalEDGE™ ensures that you have an updated set of data and knowledge on outsourcing (globaledge.msu.edu/global-resources/outsourcing). For example, did you know that there is an International Association of Outsourcing Professionals? Do you know what it does, its goals, and how many members it has worldwide?

Purchasing

The part of the supply chain that includes the worldwide buying of raw material, component parts, and products used in manufacturing of the company's products and services.

Logistics

The part of the supply chain that plans, implements, and controls the effective flows and inventory of raw material, component parts, and products used in manufacturing.

purchasing and **logistics** are critical functions. Purchasing represents the part of the supply chain that involves worldwide buying of raw material, component parts, and products used in manufacturing of the company's products and services. Logistics is the part of the supply chain that plans, implements, and controls the effective flows and inventory of raw material, component parts, and products used in manufacturing.

The production and supply chain management functions (purchasing, logistics) of an international firm have a number of important strategic objectives.[1] One is to ensure that the total cost of moving from raw materials to finished goods is as low as possible for the value provided to the end-customer. Dispersing production activities to various locations around the globe where each activity can be performed most efficiently can lower the total costs. Costs can also be cut by managing the global supply chain efficiently to better match supply and demand. This involves both coordination and integration of the supply chain functions *inside* a global company (e.g., purchasing, logistics, production and operations management) and across the independent organizations (e.g., suppliers) involved in the chain. For example, efficient logistics practices reduce the amount of inventory in the system, increase inventory turnover, and facilitate the appropriate transportation modes being used. Maximizing purchasing operations enhances the order fulfillment and delivery, outsourcing initiatives, and supplier selections. Efficient operations ensure that the right location of production is made, establishes which production priorities should be stressed, and facilitates a high-quality outcome of the supply chain.

Upstream Supply Chain

The portion of the supply chain from raw materials to the production facility.

Downstream Supply Chain

The portion of the supply chain from the production facility to the end-customer.

Another strategic objective shared by production and supply chain management is to increase product (or service) quality by establishing process-based quality standards and eliminating defective raw material, component parts, and products from the manufacturing process and the supply chain.[2] In this context, *quality* means *reliability,* implying that ultimately the finished product has no defects and performs well. These quality assurances should be embedded in both the **upstream** and **downstream** portions of the global supply chain. The upstream supply chain includes all of the organizations (e.g., suppliers) and resources that are involved in the portion of the supply chain from raw materials to the production facility (this is sometimes also called the inbound supply chain). The downstream supply chain includes all of the organizations (e.g., wholesaler, retailer) that are involved in the portion of the supply chain from the production facility to the end-customer (this is also sometimes called the outbound supply chain). Through the upstream and downstream chains, the objectives of reducing costs and increasing quality are not independent of each other. As illustrated in Figure 15.1, the firm that improves its quality control will also reduce its costs of value creation. Improved quality control reduces costs by:

- Increasing productivity because time is not wasted producing poor-quality products that cannot be sold, leading to a direct reduction in unit costs.
- Lowering rework and scrap costs associated with defective products.
- Reducing the warranty costs and time associated with fixing defective products.

15.1 FIGURE

The Relationship Between Quality and Costs.

Source: David A. Gandin, "What Does Product Quality Really Mean?," *MIT Sloan Management Review*, Fall 1984, pp. 25–43.

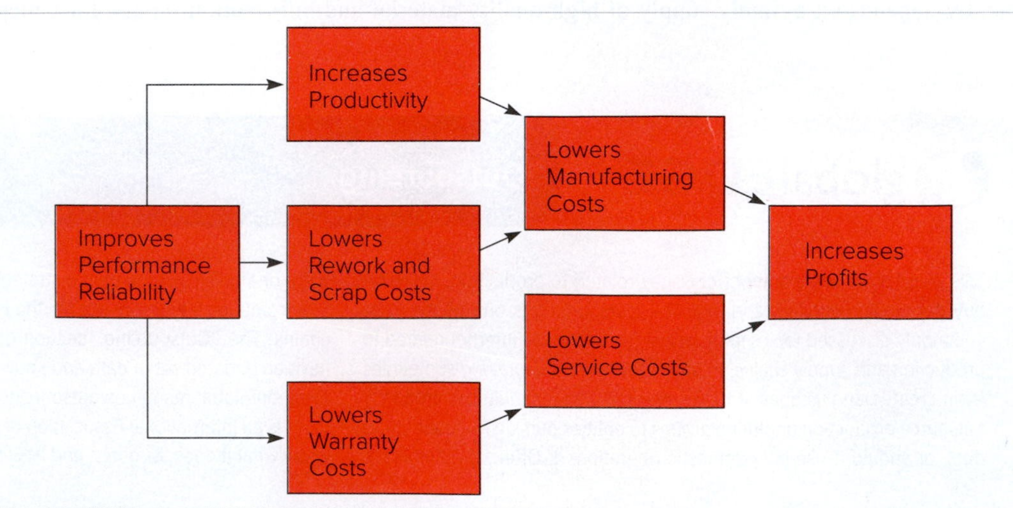

The effect is to lower the total costs of value creation by reducing both production and after-sales service costs. This creates an increased overall reliability in global production and supply chain management.

The principal tool that most managers now use to increase the reliability of their product offering is the Six Sigma quality improvement methodology. Six Sigma is a direct descendant of the **total quality management (TQM)** philosophy that was widely adopted, first by Japanese companies and then American companies, during the 1980s and early 1990s.[3] The TQM philosophy was developed by a number of American consultants such as W. Edward Deming, Joseph Juran, and A. V. Feigenbaum.[4] Deming identified a number of steps that should be part of any TQM program. He argued that management should embrace the philosophy that mistakes, defects, and poor-quality materials are not acceptable and should be eliminated. He suggested that the quality of supervision should be improved by allowing more time for supervisors to work with employees and by providing them with the tools they need to do the job. Deming recommended that management should create an environment in which employees will not fear reporting problems or recommending improvements. He believed that work standards should not only be defined as numbers or quotas but also include some notion of quality to promote the production of defect-free output. He argued that management has the responsibility to train employees in new skills to keep pace with changes in the workplace. In addition, he believed that achieving better quality requires the commitment of everyone in the company.

Total Quality Management (TQM)

Management philosophy that takes as its central focus the need to improve the quality of a company's products and services.

Six Sigma, the modern successor to TQM, is a statistically based philosophy that aims to reduce defects, boost productivity, eliminate waste, and cut costs throughout a company. Six Sigma programs have been adopted by several major corporations, such as Motorola, General Electric, and Honeywell. Sigma comes from the Greek letter that statisticians use to represent a standard deviation from a mean; the higher the number of "sigmas," the smaller the number of errors. At six sigmas, a production process would be 99.99966 percent accurate, creating just 3.4 defects per million units. While it is almost impossible for a company to achieve such perfection, Six Sigma quality is a goal to strive toward. The Six Sigma program is particularly informative in structuring global processes that multinational corporations can follow in quality and productivity initiatives. As such, increasingly companies are adopting Six Sigma programs to try to boost their product quality and productivity.[5]

Six Sigma

Statistically based methodology for improving product quality.

The growth of international standards has also focused greater attention on the importance of product quality. In Europe, for example, the European Union requires that the quality of a firm's manufacturing processes and products be certified under a quality standard known as **ISO 9000** before the firm is allowed access to the EU marketplace. Although the ISO 9000 certification process has proved to be somewhat bureaucratic and costly for many firms, it does focus management attention on the need to improve the quality of products and processes.[6]

ISO 9000

Certification process that requires certain quality standards that must be met.

In addition to lowering costs and improving quality, two other objectives have particular importance in international businesses. First, production and supply chain functions must be able to accommodate demands for local responsiveness. As we saw in Chapter 12, demands for local responsiveness arise from national differences in consumer tastes and preferences, infrastructure, distribution channels, and host-government demands. Demands for local responsiveness create pressures to decentralize production activities to the major national or regional markets in which the firm does business or to implement flexible manufacturing processes that enable the firm to customize the product coming out of a factory according to the market in which it is to be sold.

Use SmartBook to help retain what you have learned. Access your Instructor's Connect course to check out SmartBook or go to learnsmartadvantage.com for help.

Second, production and supply chain management must be able to respond quickly to shifts in customer demand. In recent years, time-based competition has grown more important.[7] When consumer demand is prone to large and unpredictable shifts, the firm that can adapt most quickly to these shifts will gain an advantage.[8] As we shall see, both production and supply chain management play critical roles here.

Where to Produce

Explain how country differences, production technology, and production factors all affect the choice of where to locate production activities.

An essential decision facing an international firm is where to locate its production activities to best minimize costs and improve product quality. For the firm contemplating international production, a number of factors must be considered. These factors can be grouped under three broad headings: country factors, technological factors, and production factors.[9]

COUNTRY FACTORS We reviewed country-specific factors in some detail earlier in the book. Political and economic systems, culture, and relative factor costs differ from country to country. In Chapter 6, we saw that due to differences in factor costs, some countries have a comparative advantage for producing certain products. In Chapters 2, 3, and 4, we saw how differences in political and economic systems—and national culture—influence the benefits, costs, and risks of doing business in a country. Other things being equal, a firm should locate its various manufacturing activities where the economic, political, and cultural conditions—including relative factor costs—are conducive to the performance of those activities (for an example, see the accompanying Management Focus, which looks at the Philips investment in

management FOCUS

Philips Investments in China

The Dutch consumer electronics, lighting, semiconductor, and medical equipment conglomerate Koninklijke Philips NV has been operating factories in China since 1985, when the country first opened its markets to foreign investors. When Philips initially entered China, it had dreams of Chinese consumers snapping up its products by the millions. However, the company soon found out that the reason it liked China—low wage rates—also meant that few Chinese workers could afford to buy its products. So Philips hit on a new strategy: Keep the factories in China, but export most of the goods to developed nations.

The initial attractions of China to Philips included low wage rates, an educated workforce, a robust Chinese economy, a stable exchange rate that is linked to the U.S. dollar through a managed float, a rapidly expanding industrial base that includes many other Western and Chinese companies that Philips uses as suppliers, and easier access to world markets given China's entry into the World Trade Organization in 2001. By the early 2000s, Philips employed some 30,000 people in China either directly or indirectly at joint ventures. Philips exported nearly two-thirds of the $7 billion in products that its Chinese factories were producing. At this point, 25 percent of everything that Philips made worldwide came from China.

As time passed, Philips started to give its Chinese factories a greater role in product development. In the TV business, for example, basic development used to occur in the Netherlands but was moved to Singapore in the early 1990s. In the early 2000s, Philips transferred TV development work to a new R&D center in Suzhou near Shanghai. Similarly, basic product development work on LCD screens for cell phones was shifted to Shanghai. In 2011, in a testament to just how important China had become to Philips, the company moved the global headquarters of its domestic appliances business from Amsterdam to Shanghai. By this point, China was far more than just an export base. Demand in China had accelerated rapidly, and the country was now the second-largest market for Philips.

Employees work at a Philips booth during a trade show in Shanghai, China.

Source: © Weng lei- Imaginechina/AP Images

Some worry that Philips and companies pursuing a similar strategy might be overdoing it. Too much dependence on China could be dangerous if political, economic, or other problems disrupt production and the company's ability to supply global markets. Some observers believe that it might be better if the manufacturing facilities of companies were more geographically diverse as a hedge against problems in China. These fears have taken on added importance recently as labor costs have accelerated in China due to labor shortages. According to estimates, labor costs have been growing by 20 percent per year since the 2000s. On the other hand, there is a silver lining to this cloud: Chinese consumption of many of the products that Philips makes there is now rising rapidly.

Sources: B. Einhorn, "Philips' Expanding Asia Connections," *BusinessWeek Online*, November 27, 2003; K. Leggett and P. Wonacott, "The World's Factory: A Surge in Exports from China Jolts the Global Industry," *The Wall Street Journal*, October 10, 2002, p. A1; J. Blau, "Philips Tears Down Eindhoven R&D Fence," *Research Technology Management*, 50, no. 6, 2007, pp. 9–11; L. Baijia, "Philips Elevates China's Market Status," *China Daily*, May 26, 2011; Philips NV website. www.philips.com.

China). In Chapter 12, we referred to the benefits derived from such a strategy as location economies. We argued that one result of the strategy is the creation of a global web of value creation activities.

Also important in some industries is the presence of global concentrations of activities at certain locations. In Chapter 8, we discussed the role of location externalities in influencing foreign direct investment decisions. Externalities include the presence of an appropriately skilled labor pool and supporting industries.[10] Such externalities can play an important role in deciding where to locate production activities. For example, because of a cluster of semiconductor manufacturing plants in Taiwan, a pool of labor with experience in the semiconductor business has developed. In addition, the plants have attracted a number of supporting industries, such as the manufacturers of semiconductor capital equipment and silicon, which have established facilities in Taiwan to be near their customers. This implies that there are real benefits to locating in Taiwan, as opposed to another location that lacks such externalities. Other things being equal, the externalities make Taiwan an attractive location for semiconductor manufacturing facilities. The same process is now under way in two Indian cities, Hyderabad and Bangalore, where both Western and Indian information technology companies have established operations. For example, locals refer to a section of Hyderabad as "Cyberabad," where Microsoft, IBM, Infosys, and Qualcomm (among others) have major facilities.

Of course, other things are not equal. Differences in relative factor costs, political economy, culture, and location externalities are important, but other factors also loom large. Formal and informal trade barriers obviously influence location decisions (see Chapter 7), as do transportation costs and rules and regulations regarding foreign direct investment (see Chapter 8). For example, although relative factor costs may make a country look attractive as a location for performing a manufacturing activity, regulations prohibiting foreign direct investment may eliminate this option. Similarly, a consideration of factor costs might suggest that a firm should source production of a certain component from a particular country, but trade barriers could make this uneconomical.

Another important country factor is expected future movements in its exchange rate (see Chapters 10 and 11). Adverse changes in exchange rates can quickly alter a country's attractiveness as a manufacturing base. Currency appreciation can transform a low-cost location into a high-cost location. Many Japanese corporations had to grapple with this problem during the 1990s and early 2000s. The relatively low value of the yen on foreign exchange markets between 1950 and 1980 helped strengthen Japan's position as a low-cost location for manufacturing. More recently, however, the yen's steady appreciation against the dollar increased the dollar cost of products exported from Japan, making Japan less attractive as a manufacturing location. In response, many Japanese firms moved their manufacturing offshore to lower-cost locations in East Asia.

TECHNOLOGICAL FACTORS The type of technology a firm uses to perform specific manufacturing activities can be pivotal in location decisions. For example, because of technological constraints, in some cases it is necessary to perform certain manufacturing activities in only one location and serve the world market from there. In other cases, the technology may make it feasible to perform an activity in multiple locations. Three characteristics of a manufacturing technology are of interest here: the level of fixed costs, the minimum efficient scale, and the flexibility of the technology.

Fixed Costs As noted in Chapter 12, in some cases the fixed costs of setting up a production plant are so high that a firm must serve the world market from a single location or from very few locations. For example, it now costs up to $5 billion to set up a state-of-the-art plant to manufacture semiconductor chips. Given this, other things being equal, serving the world market from a single plant sited at a single (optimal) location can make sense.

Conversely, a relatively low level of fixed costs can make it economical to perform a particular activity in several locations at once. This allows the firm to better accommodate demands for local responsiveness. Manufacturing in multiple locations may also help the firm avoid becoming too dependent on one location. Being too dependent on one location is particularly risky in a world of floating exchange rates. Many firms disperse their manufacturing plants to different locations as a "real hedge" against potentially adverse moves in currencies.

Minimum Efficient Scale The concept of economies of scale tells us that as plant output expands, unit costs decrease. The reasons include the greater utilization of capital equipment and the productivity gains that come with specialization of employees within the plant.[11] However, beyond a certain level of output, few additional scale economies are available. Thus, the "unit cost curve" declines with output until a certain output level is reached, at which point further increases in output realize little reduction in unit costs. The level of output at which most plant-level scale economies are exhausted is referred to as the **minimum efficient scale** of output. This is the scale of output a plant must operate to realize all major plant-level scale economies (see Figure 15.2).

Minimum Efficient Scale
The level of output at which most plant-level scale economies are exhausted.

The implications of this concept are as follows: The larger the minimum efficient scale of a plant relative to total global demand, the greater the argument for centralizing production in a single location or a limited number of locations. Alternatively, when the minimum efficient scale of production is low relative to global demand, it may be economical to manufacture a product at several locations. For example, the minimum efficient scale for a plant to manufacture personal computers is about 250,000 units a year, while the total global demand exceeds 35 million units a year. The low level of minimum efficient scale in relation to total global demand makes it economically feasible for companies such as Dell and Lenovo to assemble PCs in multiple locations.

As in the case of low fixed costs, the advantages of a low minimum efficient scale include allowing the firm to accommodate demands for local responsiveness or to hedge against currency risk by manufacturing the same product in several locations.

Flexible Manufacturing and Mass Customization Central to the concept of economies of scale is the idea that the best way to achieve high efficiency, and hence low unit costs, is through the mass production of a standardized output. The trade-off implicit in this idea is between unit costs and product variety. Producing greater product variety from a factory implies shorter production runs, which in turn implies an inability to realize economies of scale. That is, wide product variety makes it difficult for a company to increase its production efficiency and thus reduce its unit costs. According to this logic, the way to increase efficiency and drive down unit costs is to limit product variety and produce a standardized product in large volumes.

Flexible Manufacturing Technology
Manufacturing technology designed to improve job scheduling, reduce setup time, and improve quality control.

Lean Production
See flexible manufacturing technology.

This view of production efficiency has been challenged by the rise of flexible manufacturing technologies. The term **flexible manufacturing technology**—or **lean production**, as it is often called—covers a range of manufacturing technologies designed to (1) reduce setup

15.2 FIGURE

Typical Unit Cost Curve.

Source: C. W. L. Hill and G. T. M. Hult, *International Business: Competing in the Global Marketplace* (New York: McGraw-Hill Education, 2017).

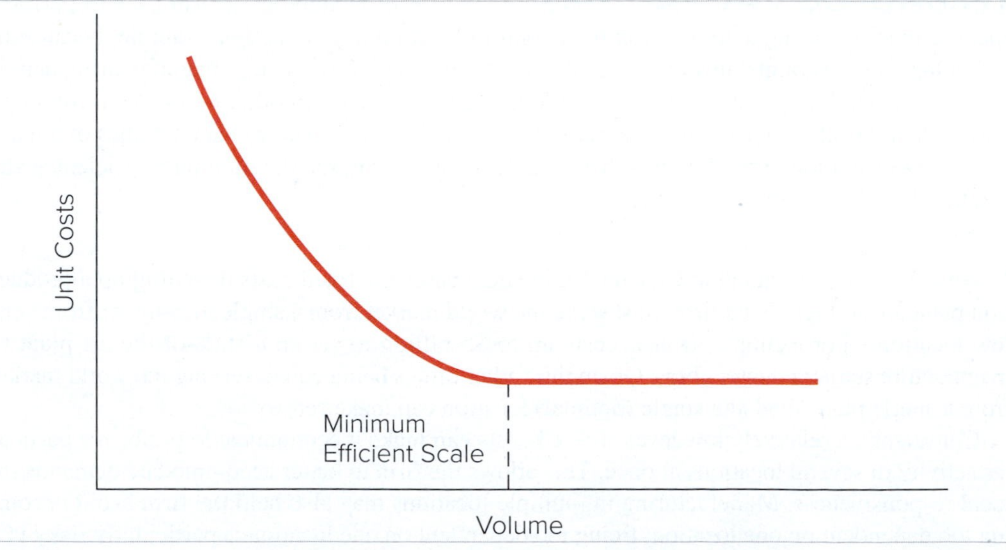

times for complex equipment, (2) increase the utilization of individual machines through better scheduling, and (3) improve quality control at all stages of the manufacturing process.[12] Flexible manufacturing technologies allow the company to produce a wider variety of end products at a unit cost that at one time could be achieved only through the mass production of a standardized output. Research suggests the adoption of flexible manufacturing technologies may actually increase efficiency and lower unit costs relative to what can be achieved by the mass production of a standardized output while enabling the company to customize its product offering to a much greater extent than was once thought possible. The term **mass customization** has been coined to describe the ability of companies to use flexible manufacturing technology to reconcile two goals that were once thought to be incompatible: low cost and product customization.[13] Flexible manufacturing technologies vary in their sophistication and complexity.

Mass Customization
The production of a variety of end products at a unit cost that could once be achieved only through mass production of a standardized output.

One of the most famous examples of a flexible manufacturing technology, Toyota's production system, has been credited with making Toyota the most efficient auto company in the world. (Despite Toyota's recent problems with sudden uncontrolled acceleration, the company continues to be an efficient producer of high-quality automobiles, according to J.D. Power, which produces an annual quality survey. Toyota's Lexus models continue to top J.D. Power's quality rankings.[14]) Toyota's flexible manufacturing system was developed by one of the company's engineers, Taiichi Ohno. After working at Toyota for five years and visiting Ford's U.S. plants, Ohno became convinced that the mass production philosophy for making cars was flawed. He saw numerous problems with mass production.

First, long production runs created massive inventories that had to be stored in large warehouses. This was expensive, both because of the cost of warehousing and because inventories tied up capital in unproductive uses. Second, if the initial machine settings were wrong, long production runs resulted in the production of a large number of defects (i.e., waste). Third, the mass production system was unable to accommodate consumer preferences for product diversity.

In response, Ohno looked for ways to make shorter production runs economical. He developed a number of techniques designed to reduce setup times for production equipment (a major source of fixed costs). By using a system of levers and pulleys, he reduced the time required to change dies on stamping equipment from a full day in 1950 to three minutes by 1971. This made small production runs economical, which allowed Toyota to respond better to consumer demands for product diversity. Small production runs also eliminated the need to hold large inventories, thereby reducing warehousing costs. Plus, small product runs and the lack of inventory meant that defective parts were produced only in small numbers and entered the assembly process immediately. This reduced waste and helped trace defects back to their source to fix the problem. In sum, these innovations enabled Toyota to produce a more diverse product range at a lower unit cost than was possible with conventional mass production.[15]

Flexible machine cells are another common flexible manufacturing technology. A flexible machine cell is a grouping of various types of machinery, a common materials handler, and a centralized cell controller (computer). Each cell normally contains four to six machines capable of performing a variety of operations. The typical cell is dedicated to the production of a family of parts or products. The settings on machines are computer controlled, which allows each cell to switch quickly between the production of different parts or products.

Flexible Machine Cells
Flexible manufacturing technology in which a grouping of various machine types, a common materials handler, and a centralized cell controller produce a family of products.

Improved capacity utilization and reductions in work in progress (i.e., stockpiles of partly finished products) and in waste are major efficiency benefits of flexible machine cells. Improved capacity utilization arises from the reduction in setup times and from the computer-controlled coordination of production flow between machines, which eliminates bottlenecks. The tight coordination between machines also reduces work-in-progress inventory. Reductions in waste are due to the ability of computer-controlled machinery to identify ways to transform inputs into outputs while producing a minimum of unusable waste material. While freestanding machines might be in use 50 percent of the time, the same machines when grouped into a cell can be used more than 80 percent of the time and produce the same end product with half the waste. This increases efficiency and results in lower costs.

The effects of installing flexible manufacturing technology on a company's cost structure can be dramatic. The Ford Motor Company has been introducing flexible manufacturing technologies into its automotive plants around the world. These new technologies should allow Ford to

Should Nestlé Continue to Invest Heavily in Turkey?

According to Nestlé Turkey's CEO Hans Ulrich Mayer, Turkey has been a great place to invest. "Turkey has been the recipient of several Nestlé investments many times greater than we invest in other markets,"* reported Mayer. Nestlé has invested about $500 million in Turkey over the last four years, and following its successful breakfast cereal investment in 2011, the company intends to go on investing because of the strong Turkish economy compared to other European economies. Nestlé products sold in Turkey, ranging from pet food to chocolates, are manufactured in Turkey and also exported to North Africa and the Middle East. Given the political situation in Turkey, should Nestlé continue to establish increased production (i.e., expand its production facility) in delivering to North Africa and the Middle East, or should it establish production elsewhere?

Invest in Turkey. www.spotblue.co.uk.

Source: *Invest in Turkey.* www.spotblue.co.uk.

produce multiple models from the same line and to switch production from one model to another much more quickly than in the past, allowing Ford to take $2 billion out of its cost structure.[16]

Besides improving efficiency and lowering costs, flexible manufacturing technologies enable companies to customize products to the demands of small consumer groups—at a cost that at one time could be achieved only by mass-producing a standardized output. Thus, the technologies help a company achieve mass customization, which increases its customer responsiveness. Most important for international business, flexible manufacturing technologies can help a firm customize products for different national markets. The importance of this advantage cannot be overstated. When flexible manufacturing technologies are available, a firm can manufacture products customized to various national markets at a single factory sited at the optimal location. And it can do this without absorbing a significant cost penalty. Thus, firms no longer need to establish manufacturing facilities in each major national market to provide products that satisfy specific consumer tastes and preferences, part of the rationale for a localization strategy (Chapter 12).

PRODUCTION FACTORS

Several production factors feature prominently into the reasons why production facilities are located and used in a certain way worldwide. They include (1) product features, (2) locating production facilities, and (3) strategic roles for production facilities.

Product Features

Two product features affect location decisions. The first is the product's *value-to-weight* ratio because of its influence on transportation costs. Many electronic components and pharmaceuticals have high value-to-weight ratios; they are expensive, and they do not weigh very much. Thus, even if they are shipped halfway around the world, their transportation costs account for a very small percentage of total costs. Given this, other things being equal, there is great pressure to produce these products in the optimal location and to serve the world market from there. The opposite holds for products with low value-to-weight ratios. Refined sugar, certain bulk chemicals, paint, and petroleum products all have low value-to-weight ratios; they are relatively inexpensive products that weigh a lot. Accordingly, when they are shipped long distances, transportation costs account for a large percentage of total costs. Thus, other things being equal, there is great pressure to make these products in multiple locations close to major markets to reduce transportation costs.

The other product feature that can influence location decisions is whether the product serves universal needs, needs that are the same all over the world. Examples include many industrial products (e.g., industrial electronics, steel, bulk chemicals) and modern consumer products (e.g., Apple's iPhone or iPad, Amazon's Kindle, Lenovo's ThinkPad, Sony's Cyber-shot camera, Microsoft's Xbox). Because there are few national differences in consumer taste and preference for such products, the need for local responsiveness is reduced. This increases the attractiveness of concentrating production at an optimal location.

LO 15-3
Recognize how the role of foreign subsidiaries in production can be enhanced over time as they accumulate knowledge.

Locating Production Facilities

There are two basic strategies for locating production facilities: (1) concentrating them in a centralized location and serving the world market from there or (2) decentralizing them in various regional or national locations that are close to major markets. The appropriate strategic choice is determined by the various country-specific, technological, and product factors discussed in this section and summarized in Table 15.1.

15.1 TABLE

Location Strategy and Production

	Concentrated Production Favored	Decentralized Production Favored
Country Factors		
Differences in political economy	Substantial	Few
Differences in culture	Substantial	Few
Differences in factor costs	Substantial	Few
Trade barriers	Few	Substantial
Location externalities	Important in industry	Not important in industry
Exchange rates	Stable	Volatile
Technological Factors		
Fixed costs	High	Low
Minimum efficient scale	High	Low
Flexible manufacturing technology	Available	Not available
Product Factors		
Value-to-weight ratio	High	Low
Serves universal needs	Yes	No

As can be seen, concentration of production makes most sense when:

- Differences among countries in factor costs, political economy, and culture have a substantial impact on the costs of manufacturing in various countries.
- Trade barriers are low.
- Externalities arising from the concentration of like enterprises favor certain locations.
- Important exchange rates are expected to remain relatively stable.
- The production technology has high fixed costs and high minimum efficient scale relative to global demand or flexible manufacturing technology exists.
- The product's value-to-weight ratio is high.
- The product serves universal needs.

Alternatively, decentralization of production is appropriate when:

- Differences among countries in factor costs, political economy, and culture do not have a substantial impact on the costs of manufacturing in various countries.
- Trade barriers are high.
- Location externalities are not important.
- Volatility in important exchange rates is expected.
- The production technology has low fixed costs and low minimum efficient scale, and flexible manufacturing technology is not available.
- The product's value-to-weight ratio is low.
- The product does not serve universal needs (i.e., significant differences in consumer tastes and preferences exist among nations).

In practice, location decisions are seldom clear-cut. For example, it is not unusual for differences in factor costs, technological factors, and product factors to point toward concentrated production, while a combination of trade barriers and volatile exchange rates points toward decentralized production. This seems to be the case in the world automobile industry. Although the availability of flexible manufacturing and cars' relatively high value-to-weight ratios suggest concentrated manufacturing, the combination of formal and informal trade barriers and the uncertainties of the world's current floating exchange rate regime (see Chapter 10) have inhibited firms' ability to pursue this strategy. For these reasons, several automobile companies have established "top-to-bottom" manufacturing operations in three major regional markets: Asia, North America, and western Europe.

Strategic Roles for Production Facilities

The growth of global production among multinational companies has been tremendous over the past two decades, outdoing the growth of home country production by more than 10-fold.[17] In essence, since the early 1990s, multinationals have opted to set up production facilities outside their home country 10 times for every 1 time they have opted to create such facilities at home. There is a clear strategic rational for this; multinationals are trying to capture the gains associated with a dispersed global production system. This trend is expected to continue going forward. Thus, managers need to be ready to make the decision to open up a new production facility outside of their home base and decide where to locate the facility.

Global Learning
The flow of skills and product offerings from foreign subsidiary to home country and from foreign subsidiary to foreign subsidiary.

When making these decisions, managers need to think about the strategic role assigned to a foreign factory. A major consideration here is the importance of **global learning**—the idea that valuable knowledge does not reside just in a firm's domestic operations; it may also be found in its foreign subsidiaries. Foreign factories that upgrade their capabilities over time are creating valuable knowledge that might benefit the whole corporation. Foreign factories can have one of a number of strategic roles or designations, including (1) offshore factory, (2) source factory, (3) server factory, (4) contributor factory, (5) outpost factory, and (6) lead factory.[18]

Offshore Factory
A factory that is developed and set up mainly for producing component parts or finished goods at a lower cost than producing them at home or in any other market.

An **offshore factory** is one that is developed and set up mainly for producing component parts or finished goods at a lower cost than producing them at home or in any other market. At an offshore factory, investments in technology and managerial resources should ideally be kept to a minimum to achieve greater cost-efficiencies. Basically, the best offshore factory should involve minimal everything—from engineering to development to engaging with suppliers to negotiating prices to any form of strategic decisions being made at that facility. In reality, we expect at least some strategic decisions to include input from the offshore factory personnel.

Source Factory
A factory whose primary purpose is also to drive down costs in the global supply chain.

The primary purpose of a **source factory** is also to drive down costs in the global supply chain. The main difference between a source factory and an offshore factory is the strategic role of the factory, which is more significant for a source factory than for an offshore factory. Managers of a source factory have more of a say in certain decisions, such as purchasing raw materials and component parts used in the production at the source factory. They also have strategic input into production planning, process changes, logistics issues, product customization, and implementation of newer designs when needed. Centrally, a source factory is at the top of the standards in the global supply chain, and these factories are used and treated just like any factory in the global firm's home country. This also means that source factories should be located where production costs are low, where infrastructure is well developed, and where it is relatively easy to find a knowledgeable and skilled workforce to make the products.

Server Factory
A factory linked into the global supply chain for a global firm to supply specific country or regional markets around the globe.

A **server factory** is linked into the global supply chain for a global firm to supply specific country or regional markets around the globe. This type of factory—often with the same standards as the top factories in the global firm's system—is set up to overcome intangible and tangible barriers in the global marketplace. For example, a server factory may be intended to overcome tariff barriers, reduce taxes, and reinvest money made in the region. Another obvious reason for a server factory is to reduce or eliminate costly global supply chain operations that would be needed if the factory were located much farther away from the end customers. Managers at a server factory typically have more authority to make minor customizations to please their customers, but they still do not have much more input than managers in an offshore factory relative to the home country factories of the same global firm.

Contributor Factory
A factory that serves a specific country or world region.

A **contributor factory** also serves a specific country or world region. The main difference between a contributor factory and a server factory is that a contributor factory has responsibilities for product and process engineering and development. This type of factory also has much more of a choice in terms of which suppliers to use for raw materials and component parts. In fact, a contributor factory often competes with the global firm's home factories for testing new ideas and products. A contributor factory has its own infrastructure when it comes to development, engineering, and production. This means that a contributor factory is very much stand-alone in terms of what it can do and how it contributes to the global firm's supply chain efforts.

An **outpost factory** can be viewed as an intelligence-gathering unit. This means that an outpost factory is often placed near a competitor's headquarters or main operations, near the most demanding customers, or near key suppliers of unique and critically important parts. An outpost factory also has a function to fill in production; it often operates as a server and/or offshore factory as well. The outpost factory can be very much connected to the idea of selecting countries for operations based on the countries' strategic importance rather than on the production logic of a location. Maintaining and potentially even enhancing the position of the global firm in strategic countries is sometimes viewed as a practical factor. For example, the fact that Nokia has its headquarters in Finland may result in another mobile phone manufacturer locating some operations in Finland, even though the country market is rather small (about 5.5 million people).

Outpost Factory
A factory that can be viewed as an intelligence-gathering unit.

A **lead factory** is intended to create new processes, products, and technologies that can be used throughout the global firm in all parts of the world. This is where cutting-edge production should take place or at least be tested for implementation in other parts of the firm's production network. Given the lead factory's prominent role in setting a high bar for how the global firm wants to provide products to customers, we also expect that it will be located in an area where highly skilled employees can be found (or where they want to locate). A lead factory scenario also implies that managers and employees at the site have a direct connection to and say in which suppliers to use, what designs to implement, and other issues that are of critical importance to the core competencies of the global firm.

Lead Factory
A factory that is intended to create new processes, products, and technologies that can be used throughout the global firm in all parts of the world.

THE HIDDEN COSTS OF FOREIGN LOCATIONS

There may be some "hidden costs" to basing production in a foreign location. Numerous anecdotes suggest that high employee turnover, shoddy workmanship, poor product quality, and low productivity are significant issues in some outsourcing locations.[19]

Microsoft, for example, established a major facility in Hyderabad, India, for four very good reasons: (1) The wage rate of software programmers in India is one-third of that in the United States; (2) India has an excellent higher education system that graduates many computer science majors every year; (3) there was already a high concentration of information technology companies and workers in Hyderabad; and (4) many of Microsoft's highly skilled Indian employees, after spending years in the United States, wanted to return home, and Microsoft saw the Hyderabad facility as a way of holding on to this valuable human capital.

However, the company found that the turnover rate among its Indian employees is higher than in the United States. Demand for software programmers in India is high, and many employees are prone to switch jobs to get better pay. Although Microsoft has tried to limit turnover by offering good benefits and long-term incentive pay, such as stock grants to high performers who stay with the company, many of the Indians who were hired locally apparently place little value on long-term incentives and prefer higher current pay. High employee turnover, of course, has a negative impact on productivity. One Microsoft manager in India noted that 40 percent of his core team had left within the past 12 months, making it very difficult to stay on track with development projects.[20]

Microsoft is not alone in experiencing this problem. The manager of an electronics company that outsourced the manufacture of wireless headsets to China noted that after four years of frustrations with late deliveries and poor quality, his company decided to move production *back* to the United States. In his words: "On the face of it, labor costs seemed so much lower in China that the decision to move production there was a very easy one. In retrospect, I wish we had looked much closer at productivity and workmanship. We have actually lost market share because of this decision."[21] Another example of this phenomenon is given in the accompanying Management Focus, which looks at H&M, the Swedish retail-clothing giant. The lesson here is that within the global supply chain infrastructure, one key aspect of H&M is the ordering timing of each product. Specifically, ordering each product at the optimal moment is an important part of H&M achieving the right balance among price, cycle time, and quality.

Use SmartBook to help retain what you have learned. Access your Instructor's Connect course to check out SmartBook or go to learnsmartadvantage.com for help.

management FOCUS

H&M and Their Order Timing

David Beckham, Freja Beha, Beyoncé, Gisele Bündchen, Georgia May Jagger, Miranda Kerr, Madonna, Vanessa Paradis, Katy Perry, Lana Del Rey, Rihanna, and Anja Rubik represent just a partial list of well-known people around the world who have worked with H&M (do you recognize all of them?). But let's move on from the name-dropping to Hennes & Mauritz, or H&M as it is more commonly known. H&M is a Swedish multinational retail-clothing giant known for its fashion clothing for women, men, teenagers, and children. H&M has effectively used superstar celebrities such as Beckham, Beyoncé, and Bündchen for years to carry their advertising message worldwide. Behind the scenes, H&M's global supply chains are equally well orchestrated and are as high powered as its advertising campaigns.

H&M Hennes & Mauritz AB is now the full name of the company (it started simply as "Hennes" in 1947 in a small Swedish town called Västerås). The idea for the company emerged when, in 1946, Erling Persson, the company's founder, came up with the idea of offering fashionable clothing at relatively low prices while he was on a business trip to the United States. At that time, Persson decided to focus on women's clothing only, and Hennes, which means "her" or "hers" in Swedish, was started. A couple of decades later, in 1968, Hennes acquired the building and inventory of hunting equipment retailer Mauritz Widforss. A supply of men's clothing was also part of the inventory. This resulted in menswear being included in the company's collection—and gave birth to Hennes & Maurits (H&M). H&M now has some 3,200 stores in 54 countries and approximately 116,000 employees. It is the second-largest clothing retailer in the world after Spain-based Inditex (parent company of ZARA) and ahead of U.S.-based Gap Inc.

H&M comprises six different brands, although the H&M brand is the most recognizable worldwide. The other brands are COS, Monki, Weekday, Cheap Monday, and & Other Stories. H&M designs sustainable fashion for all people at relatively modest prices and sells its products in 54 countries and online in an additional 10 markets. COS explores the concept of style over fashion and sells its products in stores and online in 38 countries. Monki is promoted as a fashion experience and is offered in 30 markets in stores and online. Weekday is a jeans-focused fashion destination with sales in 25 markets. Cheap Monday combines "influences from street fashion and subculture with a catwalk vibe"* and is offered in some 20 markets. The last brand, called "& Other Stories," was launched in 2013 and focuses on personal expression and styling, with availability in 17 markets. The collection of these brands, driven by the H&M collection and its footprint in 64 countries, presents a unique global supply chain challenge for the company.

The collections of clothing are created by a team of 160 in-house designers and 100 pattern makers. The design and pattern team is large and diverse, representing different age groups and nationalities. H&M's design process is about "striking the right balance between fashion, quality and the best price . . . and it always involves sustainability awareness."** H&M does not own its own factories but instead works with around 900 independent suppliers to implement the team's designs into reality. These independent suppliers are mostly located in Europe and Asia. They manufacture all of H&M's products, and they also generally source fabrics and other components needed to create the fashion statements we have come to know from the H&M brands. Some 80 people in the H&M organization are dedicated to constantly auditing the working conditions at the factories of suppliers, including safety and quality testing, and ensuring that chemicals requirements are met.

Within the global supply chain infrastructure, one key aspect of H&M is the ordering of each product. Specifically, ordering each product at the optimal moment is an important part of H&M achieving the right balance among price, cycle time, and quality. To realize the effectiveness needed to ultimately sell fashion-oriented clothing at affordable prices, H&M works closely with long-term partners and invests significant resources into the sustainability of the work needed in its supply chains. In these areas, the company strives to promote lasting improvements in working conditions and environmental impact throughout the footprint that it makes worldwide. Through its 900 suppliers, H&M is connected to some 1,900 factories and about 1.6 million workers.

*H&M website. http://hm.com.

**H&M website. http://hm.com.

Sources: H&M website. http://hm.com; L. Siegle, "Is H&M the New Home of Ethical Fashion?," *The Observer*, April 7, 2012; G. Petro, "The Future of Fashion Retailing—The H&M Approach," Forbes, November 5, 2012; K. Stock, "H&M's New Store Blitz Moves Faster Than Its Digital Expansion," *Bloomberg Businessweek*, March 17, 2014; M. Kerppola, R. Moody, L. Zheng, and A. Liu, "H&M's Global Supply Chain Management Sustainability: Factories and Fast Fashion," *GlobaLens*, a division of the William Davidson Institute at the University of Michigan, February 8, 2014.

Identify the factors that influence a firm's decision of whether to source supplies from within the company or from foreign suppliers.

Make-or-Buy Decisions

The **make-or-buy decision** for a global firm is the strategic decision concerning whether to produce an item in-house ("make") or purchase it from an outside supplier ("buy"). Make-or-buy decisions are made at both the strategic and operational levels, with the strategic level being focused on the long term and the operational level being more focused on the short term. In some ways, the make-or-buy decision is also the starting point for operations' influence on global supply chains. That is, someone in the chain—within one firm—has to take the lead in deciding whether the global firm should make the product in-house or buy it from an external supplier. If the decision is to make it in-house, there are certain implications for that firm's global supply chains (e.g., where to purchase raw materials and component parts). If the decision is to buy the product, that decision also has certain implications (e.g., quality control and competitive priorities management).

Make-or-Buy Decision

The strategic decision concerning whether to produce an item in-house ("make") or purchase it from an outside supplier ("buy").

A number of things are involved in determining which decision is the correct one for a particular global firm in a particular situation. At a broad level, issues of product success, specialized knowledge, and strategic fit can lead to the make (produce) decision. For example, if the item or part is critical to the success of the product, including perceptions among primary stakeholders, such a scenario skews the decision in favor of make. Another reason for a make decision is that the item or part requires specialized design or production skills and/or equipment and reliable alternatives are very scarce. Strategic fit is also important. If the item or part strategically fits within the firm's current and/or planned core competencies, then it should be a make decision for the global firm.

However, these are strategic decisions at a general level. In reality, the make-or-buy decision is often based largely on two critical factors: cost and production capacity. Cost issues include such things as acquiring raw materials, component parts, and any other inputs into the process, along with the costs of finishing the product. The production capacity is really presented as an opportunity cost. That is, does the firm have the capacity to produce the product at a cost that is at least no higher than the cost of buying it from an external supplier? And if the product is made in-house, what opportunity cost would be incurred as a result (e.g., what product or item was the firm unable to produce because of limited production capacity)? Unfortunately, many, and perhaps most, global companies think that cost and production capacity are the only factors playing into the make-or-buy decision. This is simply not true!

Do You Expect a Trend in Bringing Jobs Back from Overseas?

The United States may be on the verge of bringing back manufacturing jobs from China. Outsourcing manufacturing to China is not as cheap as it used to be. Many companies, especially in the auto and furniture industries, moved plants overseas once China opened its doors to free trade and foreign investment in the last few decades. Labor was cheaper for American companies—less than $1 per hour by some estimates at the time. Today, labor costs in China have risen dramatically, and shipping and fuel costs have skyrocketed. As China's economy has expanded and as China has built new factories all across the country, the demand for workers has risen. As a result, wages are up as new companies compete to hire the best workers. Experts note that the fears that U.S. manufacturing is in decline are overstated and that the United States is still a manufacturing giant. However, both China and the United States each account for about 20 percent global manufacturing value added. The U.S. share of about 20 percent of global manufacturing value added "has declined only slightly over the past three decades," according to the Boston Consulting Group. With these estimates in mind, do you expect more and more outsourced jobs to be "insourced" in the future?

"Made in America Again," Boston Consulting Group, 2012. http://www.bcg.com/documents/file84471.pdf

Cost and production capacity are just the two main drivers behind make-or-buy choices made by global companies when they engage in global supply chains. The decision of whether to buy or make a product is a much more complex and research-intensive process than the typical global firm may expect, though. For example, how many times have we heard, "Let's move our production to China because we can get the same quality for a dime-on-the-dollar cost, and that will free up production capacity that we can use to focus on other products"? Of course, dime-on-the-dollar cost is not relevant because we have to take into account the costs of quality control measures that have to be instituted, raw materials that have to be purchased far away from home, foreign entry requirements, multiple-party contracts, management responsibilities for the outsourced production operations, and so on. Ultimately, we are unlikely to end up with a dime-on-the-dollar cost, but where do we end up and how do we get there? In other words, what are the core elements that we should be evaluating when we are determining whether the correct decision is to make or to buy?

To facilitate the make-or-buy decision, we have captured the dynamics of this choice in two figures that center on either operationally favoring a make decision or operationally favoring a buy decision (Figures 15.3 and 15.4). As shown, the core elements in both cases are cost and production capacity. However, the other elements differ for each of the decisions and influence the choice differently. This means that we need to evaluate each decision separately, not jointly. In fact, through this process, we may end up thinking that both a make decision and a buy decision would be acceptable and strategically logical for our firm. Keep in mind that this simply means that we have a choice; if both choices seem positive for your firm, choose the one that is the best strategic fit with the least opportunity cost structure.

The elements that favor a make decision—beyond the core elements of cost and production capacity—include quality control, proprietary technology, having control, excess capacity, limited suppliers, assurance of continual supply, and industry drivers (see Figure 15.3). So, the starting point is lower (or at least no greater) cost than what we can expect when we outsource the production to an external party in another country (or another external party in general).

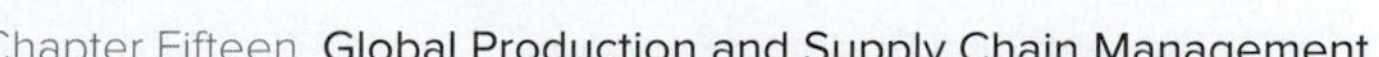

15.3 FIGURE

Operationally Favoring a Make Decision.

Source: C. W. L. Hill and G. T. M. Hult, *International Business: Competing in the Global Marketplace* (New York: McGraw-Hill Education, 2017).

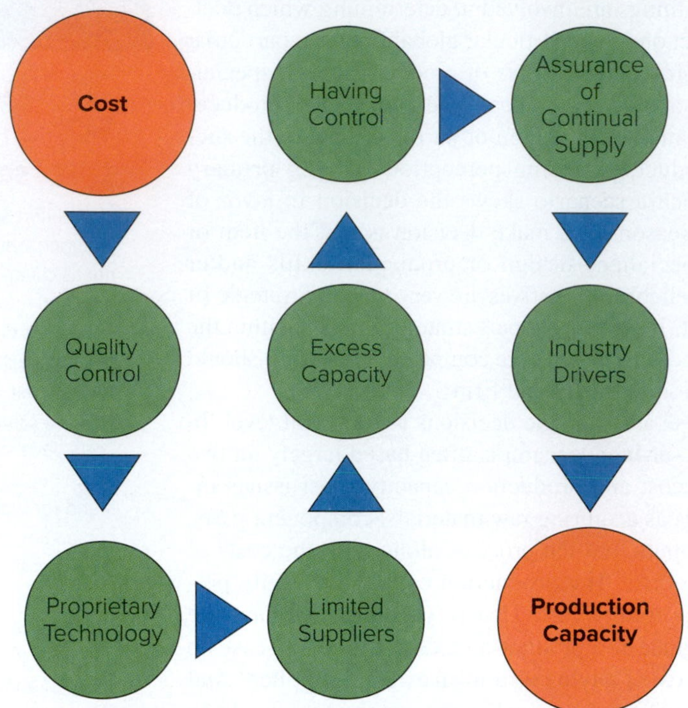

15.4 FIGURE

Operationally Favoring a Buy Decision.

Source: C. W. L. Hill and G. T. M. Hult, *International Business: Competing in the Global Marketplace* (New York: McGraw-Hill Education, 2017).

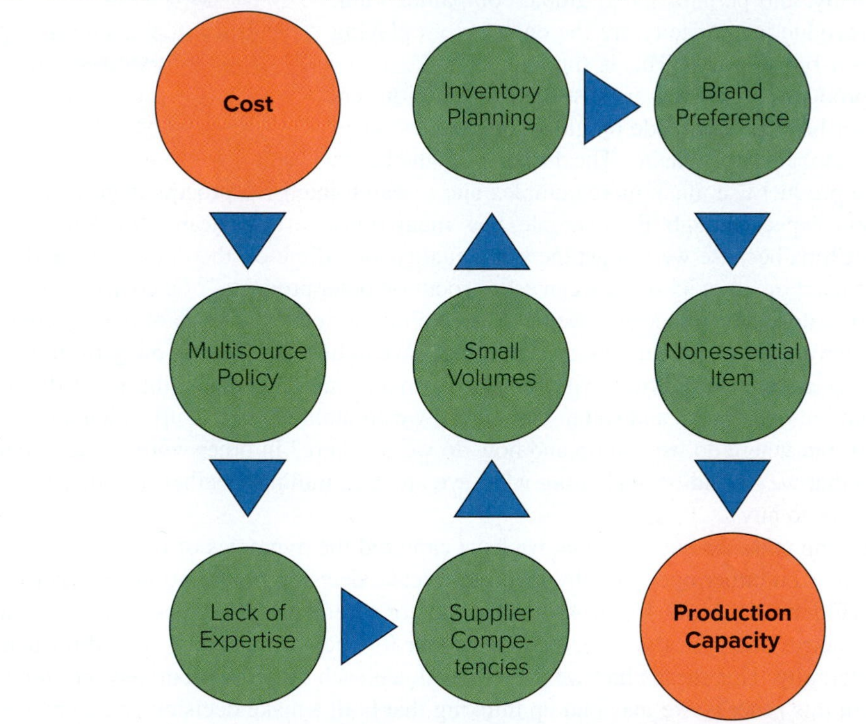

The limitation is that we must have excess production capacity or capacity that is best used by our firm for making the product in-house.

After the cost and production capacity decisions have been explored and made (really, after the cost and production hurdles have been overcome), the next set of decisions follows logically from the path in Figure 15.3. For example, if quality control is important to the global firm, cannot be relied on fully if the part is outsourced, and is at the center of the strategic core that customers expect from the firm, then the quality control issue favors a make decision. If there is proprietary technology involved in making the product that cannot or should not be shared with outsourcing parties, then the decision has to be make.

The idea that limited suppliers may influence the make-or-buy choice in the direction of the make selection is important as well. Specifically, it could be that some suppliers do not want to work with certain companies in certain parts of the world. It could also be that a supplier cannot, because of various restrictions on production or location or because of international barriers, follow the production of your firm's products to wherever you see fit to locate your production lines.

Naturally, if the firm has excess capacity that otherwise would not be productively used, the decision should favor a make choice to allow that excess capacity to be used for the benefit of the firm in the global marketplace. Some companies also simply want to have control over certain elements of their production processes. This affects the make-or-buy decision in favor of the make choice.

A make decision is also favored if there is any chance that supply cannot be guaranteed if the firm moves its production overseas. And, finally, the industry globalization drivers may dictate that a make decision should be the choice for various trust and commitment reasons involving your industry and the marketplace that you engage with in order to find success.

Now, some of these elements that favor make can probably influence a buy decision as well. Naturally, if one of the make elements is not in favor of the make decision (e.g., if there is no excess capacity), this would suggest that the global firm should think more seriously about a buy decision. However, again, the buy decision also involves a number of other elements that are not necessarily factors in the make decision (see Figure 15.4). As with the make decision, after the cost and production capacity decisions have been considered and made, the next set of decisions for the buy choice follow logically from the path in Figure 15.4. For example, if the global firm has minimal restrictions on which firms or companies it can source raw materials and component parts from, then a buy decision is more likely because outsourcing production also increases the likelihood that other and/or more suppliers in those parts of the world will be used.

Another good reason to choose a buy scenario is if the firm lacks the needed expertise to make a product or component part and the supplier or outsourced production choice has that expertise. Supplier competencies can affect the decision in favor of a buy choice as well, especially if those competencies reside closer to the production facility that you buy from than the ones that will be available if you make the product. Small volumes would also be a reason favoring a buy decision; cost-efficiencies can seldom be achieved when only small volumes are produced.

Inventory planning is also of critical importance. Even if your firm can make the product equally well in terms of quality and expectations set, perhaps a better choice is to buy simply in order to strategically manage inventory (which is a cost center in the global supply chain). In certain cases, even brand preference is a reason to go with a buy decision; for example, many computer users favor Intel microchips in their computers, so many of the large computer manufacturers opt to buy chips from Intel instead of making them in-house for that reason (this was truer in the 1990s and 2000s than it is now, but it is still a factor). And, of course, if the item to be made is a so-called nonessential item that has little effect on the firm's core competencies and what the customers expect in terms of uniqueness, this is a factor in favor of a buy decision.

 **test PREP**

Use SmartBook to help retain what you have learned. Access your Instructor's Connect course to check out SmartBook or go to learnsmartadvantage.com for help.

Global Supply Chain Functions

 **LO 15-5**

Understand the functions of logistics and purchasing (sourcing) within global supply chains.

To this point in the chapter, we have emphasized global production, a component of the operations management of a supply chain. Issues such as where to produce, the strategic role of a foreign production site, and the make-or-buy decisions are the core aspects of global production. In addition to global production, three additional supply chain functions need to be developed in concert with global production. They are logistics, purchasing (sourcing), and the company's distribution strategy (i.e., marketing channels). The latter—distribution strategy—is addressed in Chapter 18, where we discuss marketing and R&D. Here we address logistics and purchasing. From earlier in this chapter, we know that production and supply chain management are closely linked because a firm's ability to perform its production activities depends on information inputs and a timely supply of high-quality material (raw material, component parts, and even finished products that are used in the manufacturing of new products). Logistics and purchasing are critical functions in ensuring that materials are ordered and delivered and that an appropriate level of inventory is managed.

How Much Relationship Building Do You Really Want to Do?

Like manufacturers, professional service firms have also been learning how to better manage their delivery on a global basis. For example, some global services firms are dealing with other global firms in a new way, using one supplier for all their service-related needs around the world. The traditional approach involved the development of market-specific relationships, so the same multinational client would have a number of individual service relationships, one in each major market for each company division. Under a global account management approach, one relationship has a global span—and one contract. Such supply chain practices allow for more effective relationship management, a better sense of what the client needs, more product extension opportunities, and better pricing and economies. But global account management also takes time, energy, and resources. How many "global accounts" do you think would be ideal for a global company? What is the minimum and maximum number of global account relationships a large multinational corporation should have (e.g., Microsoft)?

GLOBAL LOGISTICS From earlier in this chapter, we know that logistics is the part of the supply chain that plans, implements, and controls the effective flows and inventory of raw material, component parts, and products used in manufacturing. The core activities performed in logistics are (1) global distribution center management, (2) inventory management, (3) packaging and materials handling, (4) transportation, and (5) reverse logistics. Each of these core logistics is described in the next paragraphs.

A **global distribution center** (or warehouse) is a facility that positions and allows customization of products for delivery to worldwide wholesalers or retailers or directly to consumers anywhere in the world. Distribution centers (DCs) are used by manufacturers, importers, exporters, wholesalers, retailers, transportation companies, and customs agencies to store products and provide a location where customization can be facilitated. When warehousing shifted from passive storage of products to strategic assortments and processing, the term *distribution center* became more widely used to capture this strategic and dynamic aspect of not only storing but also of adding value to products that are being warehoused or staged. A DC is at the center of the global supply chain; specifically, the order-processing part of the order-fulfillment process. DCs are the foundation of a global supply network because they allow either a single location or satellite warehouses to store quantities and assortments of products and allow for value-added customization. They should be located strategically in the global marketplace, considering the aggregate total labor and transportation cost of moving products from plants or suppliers through the distribution center and then delivering them to customers.

Global Distribution Center
A facility that positions and allows customization of products for delivery to worldwide wholesalers or retailers or directly to consumers anywhere in the world; also called a global distribution warehouse.

Global Inventory Management
The decision-making process regarding the raw materials, work-in-process (component parts), and finished goods inventory for a multinational corporation.

Global inventory management can be viewed as the decision-making process regarding the raw materials, work-in-process (component parts), and finished goods inventory for a multinational corporation. The decisions include how much inventory to hold, in what form to hold it, and where to locate it in the supply chain. Examining the largest 20,910 global companies with headquarters in 105 countries, we find that these companies, on average across all industries, carry 14.41 percent of their total assets in some form of inventory.[22] These companies have 32.30 percent of their inventory in raw materials, 17.94 percent of their inventory in work-in-process, and 49.76 percent of their inventory in finished goods.[23] At the company level, Toyota (www.toyota.com) from Japan, one of the largest automobile firms in the world, has 8.71 percent of its total assets in inventory, with a mix of 25.87, 13.62, and 60.50 percent in raw materials, work-in-process, and finished vehicles, respectively. Another example is Sinopec (www.sinopec.com), a petroleum firm and the largest firm in China. Sinopec has 21.46 percent of its total assets in inventory, with a mix of 36.58, 42.50, and 20.92 percent in raw materials and component parts, work-in-process, and finished goods, respectively. Note that Sinopec maintains a much higher percentage of its inventories in work-in-process and a much lower percentage in finished goods than Toyota does. This suggests that petroleum firms want more flexibility in deciding exactly how to formulate the finished product. The company's global inventory strategy must effectively trade off the service and economic benefits of making products in large quantities and positioning them near customers against the risk of having too much stock or the wrong items.

Packaging
The container that holds the product itself. It can be divided into primary, secondary, and transit packaging.

Packaging comes in all shapes, sizes, forms, and uses. It can be divided into three different types: primary, secondary, and transit. *Primary packaging* holds the product itself. These are the packages brought home from the store, usually a retailer, by the end-consumer. *Secondary packaging* (sometimes called case-lot packaging) is designed to contain several primary packages. Bulk buying or warehouse store customers may take secondary packages home (e.g., from Sam's Club), but this is not the typical mode for retailers. Retailers can also use secondary packaging as an aid when stocking shelves in the store. *Transit packaging* comes into use when a number of primary and secondary packages are assembled on a pallet or unit load for transportation. Unit-load packaging—through palletizing, shrink-wrapping, or containerization—is the outer packaging envelope that allows for easier handling or product transfer among international suppliers, manufacturers, distribution centers, retailers, and any other intermediaries in the global supply chain.

Regardless of where the product is in the global supply chain, packaging is intended to achieve a set of multilayered functions. These can be grouped into (1) perform, (2) protect, and (3) inform.[24] *Perform* refers to (1) the ability of the product in the package to handle being transported between nodes in the global supply chain, (2) the ability of the product to be stored for typical lengths of time for a particular product category, and (3) the package providing the convenience expected by both the supply chain partners and the end-customers. *Protect* refers to the package's ability to (1) contain the products properly, (2) preserve the products to maintain their freshness or newness, and (3) provide the necessary security and safety to ensure that the products reach their end destination in their intended shape. *Inform* refers to the package's inclusion of (1) logical and sufficient instructions for the use of the products inside the package, including specific requirements to satisfy local regulations, (2) a statement of a compelling product guarantee, and (3) information about service for the product if and when it is needed.

Transportation refers to the movement of raw material, component parts, and finished goods throughout the global supply chain. It typically represents the largest percentage of any logistics budget and an even greater percentage for global companies because of the distances involved. Global supply chains are directly or indirectly responsible for transporting raw materials from their suppliers to the production facilities, work-in-process and finished goods inventories between plants and distribution centers, and finished goods from distribution centers to customers. The primary drivers of transportation rates and the resulting aggregate cost are distance, transport mode (ocean, air, or land), size of load, load characteristics, and oil prices. As would be expected, longer distances require more fuel and more time from vehicle operators, so transport rates increase with distance. Transport mode influences rates because of the different technologies involved. Ocean is the least expensive because of the size of the vehicles used and the low friction of water. Land is the next least expensive, with rail being less expensive than motor carriers. Air is the most expensive because there is a substantial charge for defying gravity. Transportation rates are heavily influenced by economies of scale, so larger shipments are typically relatively less expensive than smaller shipments. The characteristics of the shipment also influence transportation rates through such factors as product density, value, perishability, potential for damage, and other such factors. Finally, oil prices have a major impact on transportation rates because anywhere from 10 to 40 percent of most carrier costs, depending on the mode, are related to fuel.

Transportation
The movement of inventory through the supply chain.

Reverse logistics is the process of planning, implementing, and controlling the efficient, cost-effective flow of raw materials, in-process inventory, finished goods, and related information from the point of consumption to the point of origin for the purpose of recapturing value or proper disposal. The ultimate goal is to optimize the after-market activity or make it more efficient, thus saving money and environmental resources. Reverse logistics is critically important in global supply chains. For example, product returns cost manufacturers and retailers more than \$100 billion per year in the United States, or an average of 3.8 percent in lost profits.[25] Overall, manufacturers spend about 9 to 14 percent of their sales revenue on returns. Even more staggering, each year, consumers in America return more than the GDP of two-thirds of the nations in the world. Just these sample numbers suggest that reverse logistics is an incredibly important part of the global supply chain.

Reverse Logistics
The process of moving inventory from the point of consumption to the point of origin in supply chains for the purpose of recapturing value or proper disposal.

GLOBAL PURCHASING

As defined in the introduction to this chapter, purchasing represents the part of the supply chain that involves worldwide buying of raw material, component parts, and products used in manufacturing of the company's products and services. The core activities performed in purchasing include development of an appropriate strategy for global purchasing and selecting the type of purchasing strategy best suited for the company.

There are five strategic levels—from domestic to international to global—that can be undertaken by a global company.[26] Level I is simply companies engaging in domestic purchasing activities only. Often, these companies stay close to their home base in their domestic market when purchasing raw materials, component parts, and the like for their operations (e.g., a Michigan firm purchasing raw materials, such as cherries, from another Michigan firm). Levels II and III are both considered "international purchasing," but of various degrees and forms. Companies that are at level II engage in international purchasing activities only as needed. This means that their approach to international purchasing is often reactive and uncoordinated among the buying locations within the firm and/or across the various units that make up the firm, such as strategic business units and functional units. Companies at level III engage in international purchasing activities as part of the firm's overall supply chain management strategy. As such, at the level III stage, companies begin to recognize that a well-formulated and well-executed worldwide international purchasing strategy can be very effective in elevating the firm's competitive edge in the marketplace. Levels IV and V both involve "global purchasing" to various degrees. Level IV refers to global purchasing activities that are integrated across worldwide locations. This involves integration and coordination of purchasing strategies across the firm's buying locations worldwide. With level IV, we are now dealing with a sophisticated form of worldwide purchasing. Level V involves engaging in global purchasing activities that are integrated across worldwide locations and functional groups. Broadly, this means that the firm integrates and coordinates the purchasing of common items, purchasing processes, and supplier selection efforts globally, for example.

Beyond the domestic, international, and global purchasing strategies in levels I through V, purchasing includes a number of basic choices that companies make in deciding how to engage with markets.[27] The starting point is a choice of internal purchasing versus external purchasing—in other words, "how to purchase." We find that roughly 35 percent of the purchasing in global companies today is internal (i.e., from sources within their own company), with 65 percent being classified as external (i.e., from sources outside their company). The next decision, in both internal and external purchasing, is to figure out "where to purchase" (domestically or globally). This takes us ultimately to the "types of purchasing" (where and how) and the four choices for purchasing strategy: domestic internal purchasing, global internal purchasing, domestic external purchasing, and global external purchasing.

Use SmartBook to help retain what you have learned. Access your Instructor's Connect course to check out SmartBook or go to learnsmartadvantage.com for help.

Outsourcing Terms and Options

Outsourcing	A multinational corporation buys products or services from one of its suppliers that produces them somewhere else, whether domestically or globally. In that sense, it also refers to external purchasing in relation to purchasing strategy.
Insourcing	A multinational corporation decides to stop outsourcing products or services and instead starts to produce them internally; insourcing is the opposite of outsourcing. Thus it refers to internal purchasing in the context of purchasing strategy.
Offshoring	A multinational corporation buys products or services from one of its suppliers that produces them somewhere globally (outside the MNCs home country). Offshoring is thus a form of global external purchasing in terms of purchasing strategy.
Offshore outsourcing	A multinational corporation buys products or services from one of its suppliers in a country other than the one in which the product is manufactured or the service is developed. This again is a form of global external purchasing in terms of purchasing strategy.
Nearshoring	A multinational corporation transfers business or information technology processes to suppliers in a nearby country, often one that shares a border with the firm's own country. While nearshoring is not a purchasing activity per se, it involves facilitating global external purchasing.
Co-sourcing	A multinational corporation uses both its own employees from inside the firm and an external supplier to perform certain tasks, often in concert with each other. This applies to all four forms of purchasing strategy. It implies that the relationship between the firm and its supplier is rather strategic in nature—often, this involves the top suppliers in a particular product or component category.

The types of purchasing activities and strategies just discussed come with a set of generic options for the "international arena." But we all know that outsourcing and offshoring, along with many by-products and other similar yet quite different options, exist in the purchasing world today. At this stage of the text, we feel it is important to go over the outsourcing-related terms and options that companies have, especially the following terms that are often confusing to understand, develop strategy around, and implement: outsourcing, insourcing, offshoring, offshore outsourcing, nearshoring, and co-sourcing (see Table 15.2).

Managing a Global Supply Chain

LO 15-6

Describe what is required to efficiently manage a global supply chain.

The potential for reducing costs through more efficient supply chain management is enormous. For the typical manufacturing enterprise, material costs account for between 50 and 70 percent of revenues, depending on the industry. Even a small reduction in these costs can have a substantial impact on profitability. According to one estimate, for a firm with revenues of $1 million, a return on investment rate of 5 percent, and materials costs that are 50 percent of sales revenues, a $15,000 increase in total profits could be achieved either by increasing sales revenues 30 percent or by reducing materials costs by 3 percent.[28] In a saturated market, it would be much easier to reduce materials costs by 3 percent than to increase sales revenues by 30 percent. As such, managing global supply chains is one of the strategically most important areas for a global company. Four main areas are of concern in managing a global supply chain, including the role of just-in-time inventory, the role of information technology, coordination in global supply chains, and interorganizational relationships in global supply chains.

ROLE OF JUST-IN-TIME INVENTORY

Pioneered by Japanese firms during that country's remarkable economic transformation during the 1960s and 1970s, just-in-time inventory systems now play a major role in most manufacturing firms. The basic philosophy behind **just-in-time (JIT)** inventory systems is to economize on inventory holding costs by having materials arrive at a manufacturing plant just in time to enter the production process and not before. The major cost savings comes from speeding up inventory turnover. This reduces inventory holding costs, such as warehousing and storage costs. It means the company can reduce the amount of working capital it needs to finance inventory, freeing capital for other uses and/or lowering the total capital requirements of the enterprise. Other things being equal, this will boost the company's profitability as measured by return on capital invested. It also means the company is less likely to have excess unsold inventory that it has to write off against earnings or price low to sell.

Just In Time (JIT)

Inventory logistics system designed to deliver parts to a production process as they are needed, not before.

In addition to the cost benefits, JIT systems can also help firms improve product quality. Under a JIT system, parts enter the manufacturing process immediately; they are not warehoused. This allows defective inputs to be spotted right away. The problem can then be traced to the supply source and fixed before more defective parts are produced. Under a more traditional system, warehousing parts for weeks before they are used allows many defective parts to be produced before a problem is recognized.

The drawback of a JIT system is that it leaves a firm without a buffer stock of inventory. Although buffer stocks are expensive to store, they can help a firm respond quickly to increases in demand and tide a firm over shortages brought about by disruption among suppliers. Such a disruption occurred after the September 11, 2001, attacks on the World Trade Center and Pentagon, when the subsequent shutdown of international air travel and shipping left many firms that relied on globally dispersed suppliers and tightly managed "just-in-time" supply chains without a buffer stock of inventory. A less pronounced but similar situation occurred again in April 2003, when the outbreak of the pneumonia-like severe acute respiratory syndrom (SARS) virus in China resulted in the temporary shutdown of several plants operated by foreign companies and disrupted their global supply chains. Similarly, in late 2004, record imports into the United States left several major West Coast shipping ports clogged with too many ships from Asia that could not be unloaded fast enough, which disrupted the finely tuned supply chains of several major U.S. enterprises.[29]

There are ways of reducing the risks associated with a global supply chain that operates on just-in-time principles. To reduce the risks associated with depending on one supplier for an important input, some firms source these inputs from several suppliers located in different countries. While this does not help in the case of an event with global ramifications, such as September 11, 2001, it does help manage country-specific supply disruptions, which are more common. Strategically, all global companies need to build in some degree of redundancy in supply chains by having multiple options for suppliers.

ROLE OF INFORMATION TECHNOLOGY Web- and cloud-based information systems play a crucial role in modern materials management. By tracking component parts as they make their way across the globe toward an assembly plant, information systems enable a firm to optimize its production scheduling according to when components are expected to arrive. By locating component parts in the supply chain precisely, good information systems allow the firm to accelerate production when needed by pulling key components out of the regular supply chain and having them flown to the manufacturing plant.

Firms now typically use some form of supply chain information system to coordinate the flow of materials into manufacturing, through manufacturing, and out to customers. There are a variety of options for global supply chains. Electronic data interchange (EDI) refers to the electronic interchange of data between two or more companies. Enterprise resource planning (ERP) is a wide-ranging business planning and control system that includes supply chain-related subsystems (e.g., materials requirements planning, or MRP). Collaborative planning, forecasting, and replenishment (CPFR) was developed to fill the interorganizational connections that ERP cannot fill. Vendor management of inventory (VMI) allows for a holistic overview of the supply chain with a single point of control for all inventory management. A warehouse management system (WMS) often operates in concert with ERP systems; for example, an ERP system defines material requirements, and these are transmitted to a distribution center for a WMS.

Before the emergence of the Internet as a major communication medium, firms and their suppliers normally had to purchase expensive proprietary software solutions to implement EDI systems. The ubiquity of the Internet and the availability of web- and cloud-based applications have made most of these proprietary solutions obsolete. Less expensive systems that are much easier to install and manage now dominate the market for global supply chain management software. These systems have transformed the management of globally dispersed supply chains, allowing even small firms to achieve a much better balance between supply and demand, thereby reducing the inventory in their systems and reaping the associated economic benefits. Importantly, with most firms now using these systems, those that do not will find themselves at a competitive disadvantage. This has implications for small and medium-sized companies that may not always have the resources to implement the most sophisticated supply chain information systems.

COORDINATION IN GLOBAL SUPPLY CHAINS Consider how to turn an aircraft, and think in terms of coordination and leverage points. That is, aircraft are typically steered using an integrated system of ailerons on the wings and the rudder at the tail of the aircraft. In comparison to the aircraft, the ailerons and the rudder seem very small. However, leverage allows the coordinated effort of the ailerons and the rudder to turn the aircraft. In other words, putting the right combination of a little leverage on the right places together with a coordinated effort leads to incredible maneuvering ability for the plane. Global supply chains are the same. Integration and coordination are critically important. **Global supply chain coordination** refers to shared decision-making opportunities and operational collaboration of key global supply chain activities.

Global Supply Chain Coordination
The shared decision-making opportunities and operational collaboration of key global supply chain activities.

Shared decision making—such as joint consideration of replenishment, inventory holding costs, collaborative planning, costs of different processes, frequency of orders, batch size, and product development—creates a more integrated, coherent, efficient, and effective global supply chain. This includes shared decision making by supply chain members both inside an organization (e.g., logistics, purchasing, operations, and marketing channels employees) and across organizations (e.g., raw materials producers, transportation companies, manufacturers, wholesalers, retailers). *Shared* decision making is not *joint* decision making; it is decision making involving joint considerations. Shared decision making helps in resolving potential conflicts among global supply chain members and fosters a culture of coordination and integration. In most supply chains, certain parties are more influential, and shared decision making, at a minimum, should include the critically important chain members.

To achieve operational integration and collaboration within a global supply chain, six operational objectives should be addressed: responsiveness, variance reduction, inventory reduction, shipment consolidation, quality, and life-cycle support.[30] *Responsiveness* refers to a global firm's ability to satisfy customers' requirements across global supply chain functions in a timely manner. *Variance reduction* refers to integrating a control system across global supply chain functions to eliminate global supply chain disruptions. *Inventory reduction* refers to integrating an inventory system, controlling asset commitment, and turning velocity across global supply chain functions. *Shipment consolidation* refers to using various programs to combine small shipments and provide timely, consolidated movement. This includes multiunit coordination across global supply chain functions. *Quality* refers to integrating a system so that it achieves zero defects throughout global supply chains. Finally, *life-cycle support* refers to integrating the activities of reverse logistics, recycling, after-market service, product recall, and product disposal across global supply chain functions.

INTERORGANIZATIONAL RELATIONSHIPS

Interorganizational relationships have been studied and talked about in various contexts for decades. The two keys are trust and commitment. If we always had 100 percent trust within relationships and 100 percent commitment to them, most global supply chains would ultimately be efficient and effective. But we don't! However, by looking at the building blocks for global supply chains, we would also assume that not all relationships are equally valuable and that they should not be treated as if they were. Two examples centered on upstream/inbound and downstream/outbound supply chain activities can effectively be used to illustrate this point. Figure 15.5 focuses on the upstream (or inbound) supply chain relationships, and Figure 15.6 focuses on the downstream (or outbound) supply chain relationships.

For the upstream/inbound portion of the global supply chain, the three logical scenarios of interacting organizations are labeled as vendors, suppliers, and partners. Each scenario is based on the degree of coordination, integration, and transactional versus relationship emphasis that the firm should adopt in partnering with other entities in the global supply chain. For instance, a firm

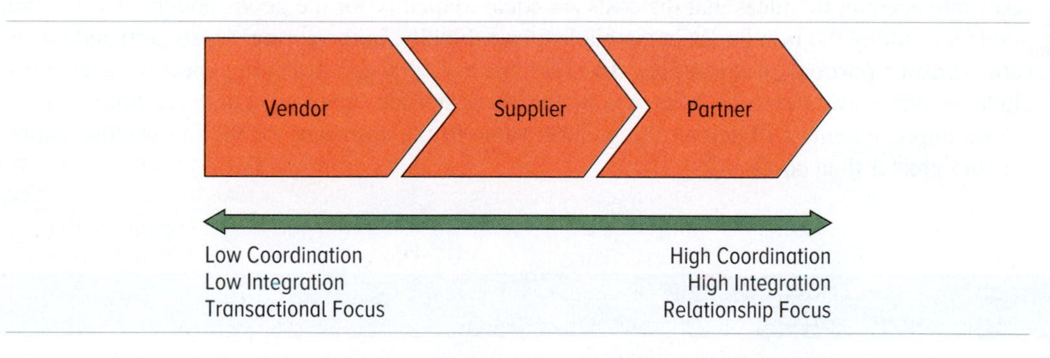

FIGURE

Upstream/Inbound Relationships.

Source: C. W. L. Hill and G. T. M. Hult, *International Business: Competing in the Global Marketplace* (New York: McGraw-Hill Education, 2017).

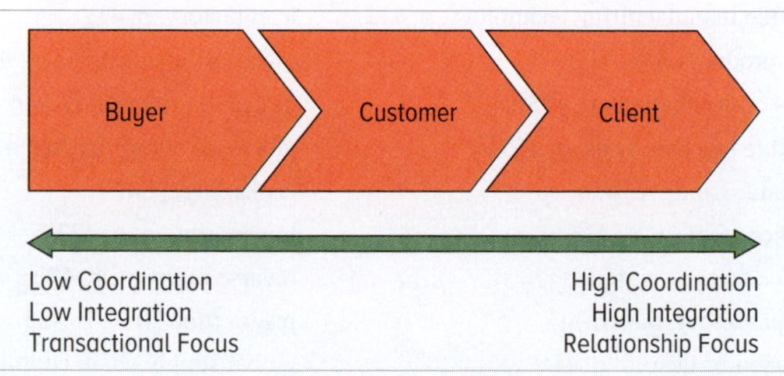

15.6 FIGURE

Downstream/Outbound Relationships.

Source: C. W. L. Hill and G. T. M. Hult, *International Business: Competing in the Global Marketplace* (New York: McGraw-Hill Education, 2017).

uses vendors to obtain raw materials and component parts through a transactional relationship that can change easily. A given firm may use suppliers to obtain raw materials and parts and maintain a relationship with those suppliers based on experience and performance. Another firm may engage with partners to obtain raw materials and parts, maintaining a relationship based on trust and commitment.

For the downstream/outbound portion of the global supply chain, the three logical scenarios of interacting organizations are labeled as buyers, customers, and clients. As with the upstream/inbound examples, each downstream/outbound scenario is based on the degree of coordination, integration, and transactional versus relationship focus that the firm should adopt in partnering with other entities in the global supply chain. One firm may sell products and parts to buyers through a transactional relationship that can change easily. Another firm may sell products and parts to customers and maintain a relationship that is based on experience and performance. Yet another firm may sell products and parts to clients and maintain a relationship that is based on trust and commitment.

Having reviewed the three scenarios for the upstream/inbound and downstream/outbound portions of the global supply chain, let's look at the emphasis a global company should place on the relationships with each entity: the benefits to be expected, favorable points of distinction, and resonating focus in the relationship.[31] First, however, some basics on value are appropriate. Value between nodes and actors in global supply chains is a function of the cost (money and nonmoney resources) given up in return for the quality (products, services, information, trust, and commitment) received. Basically, greater value is achieved if the quality is greater while the cost remains the same or is reduced or when the cost is reduced and the quality remains constant.

A global company should allocate 20 percent of its efforts to the vendor category, 30 percent to the supplier category, and 50 percent to the partner category in the upstream/inbound portion of the global supply chain. Likewise, a global company should allocate 20 percent of its efforts to the buyer category, 30 percent to the customer category, and 50 percent to the client category in the downstream/outbound portion of the chain. In the vendor (upstream) and buyer (downstream) portions of the supply chain, the benefits that can be expected include those typical of a transactional exchange (costs equal to quality for the goods bought but not necessarily the best goods in the marketplace). In the supplier (upstream) and customer (downstream) stages, the expectation is that the firm will receive all the favorable points that the raw materials, component parts, and/or products have relative to the next best alternative in the global marketplace. This takes into account the ideas that the costs are equal to quality for the goods bought and that the goods are among the best goods in the marketplace. Finally, in the partner (upstream) and client (downstream) portions of the supply chain, the benefits that the firm can expect to receive include the one or two points of difference for the raw materials, component parts, and/or products whose improvements will deliver the greatest value to the customer for the foreseeable future (quality greater than cost).

test PREP

Use SmartBook to help retain what you have learned. Access your Instructor's Connect course to check out SmartBook or go to learnsmartadvantage.com for help.

Key Terms

production, p. 407
supply chain management, p. 407
purchasing, p. 408
logistics, p. 408
upstream supply chain, p. 408
downstream supply chain, p. 408
total quality management (TQM), p. 409
Six Sigma, p. 409
ISO 9000, p. 409
minimum efficient scale, p. 412
flexible manufacturing technology, p. 412
lean production, p. 412
mass customization, p. 413
flexible machine cells, p. 413
global learning, p. 416
offshore factory, p. 416
source factory, p. 416
server factory, p. 416
contributor factory, p. 416
outpost factory, p. 417
lead factory, p. 417
make-or-buy decision, p. 418
global distribution center, p. 422
global inventory management, p. 422
packaging, p. 422
transportation, p. 423
reverse logistics, p. 423
just in time (JIT), p. 425
global supply chain coordination, p. 426

Summary

This chapter explained how global production and supply chain management can improve the competitive position of an international business by lowering the total costs of value creation and by performing value creation activities in such ways that customer service is enhanced and value added is maximized. We looked closely at five issues central to global production and supply chain management: where to produce, the strategic role of foreign production sites, what to make and what to buy, global supply chain functions, and managing a global supply chain. The chapter made the following points:

1. The choice of an optimal production location must consider country factors, technological factors, and production factors.
2. Country factors include the influence of factor costs, political economy, and national culture on production costs, along with the presence of location externalities.
3. Technological factors include the fixed costs of setting up production facilities, the minimum efficient scale of production, and the availability of flexible manufacturing technologies that allow for mass customization.
4. Production factors include product features, locating production facilities, and strategic roles for production facilities.
5. Location strategies either concentrate or decentralize manufacturing. The choice should be made in light of country, technological, and production factors. All location decisions involve trade-offs.
6. Foreign factories can improve their capabilities over time, and this can be of immense strategic benefit to the firm. Managers need to view foreign factories as potential centers of excellence and encourage and foster attempts by local managers to upgrade factory capabilities.
7. An essential issue in many international businesses is determining which component parts should be manufactured in-house and which should be outsourced to independent suppliers. Both making and buying component parts are primarily based on cost considerations and production capacity constraints, but each decision (make or buy) is also influenced by several different factors.
8. The core global supply chain functions are logistics, purchasing (sourcing), production (and operations management), and marketing channels.
9. Logistics is the part of the supply chain that plans, implements, and controls the effective flows and inventory of raw material, component parts, and products used in manufacturing. The core activities performed in logistics are to manage global distribution centers, inventory management, packaging and materials handling, transportation, and reverse logistics.
10. Purchasing represents the part of the supply chain that involves worldwide buying of raw material, component parts, and products used in manufacturing of the company's products and services. The core activities performed in purchasing include development of an appropriate strategy for global purchasing and selecting the type of purchasing strategy best suited for the company.
11. Managing a supply chain involves orchestrating effective just-in-time inventory systems, using information technology, coordination among functions and entities in the chain, and developing interorganizational relationships.
12. Just-in-time systems generate major cost savings by reducing warehousing and inventory holding costs and by reducing the need to write off excess inventory. In addition, JIT systems help the firm spot defective parts and remove them from the manufacturing process quickly, thereby improving product quality.
13. Information technology, particularly Internet-based electronic data interchange, plays a major role in materials management. EDI facilitates the tracking of inputs, allows the firm to optimize its production schedule, lets the firm and its suppliers communicate in real time, and eliminates the flow of paperwork between a firm and its suppliers.
14. Global supply chain coordination refers to shared decision-making opportunities and operational collaboration of key global supply chain activities.
15. The depth and involvement in interorganizational relationships in global supply chains should be based on the degree of coordination, integration, and transactional versus relationship emphasis that the firm should adopt in partnering with other entities in the global supply chain.

Critical Thinking and Discussion Questions

1. An electronics firm is considering how best to supply the world market for microprocessors used in consumer and industrial electronic products. A manufacturing plant costs about $500 million to construct and requires a highly skilled workforce. The total value of the world market for this product over the next 10 years is estimated to be between $10 billion and $15 billion. The tariffs prevailing in this industry are currently low. What kind of location(s) should the firm favor for its plant(s)?

2. A chemical firm is considering how best to supply the world market for sulfuric acid. A manufacturing plant costs about $20 million to construct and requires a moderately skilled workforce. The total value of the world market for this product over the next 10 years is estimated to be between $20 billion and $30 billion. The tariffs prevailing in this industry are moderate. What kind of location(s) should the firm seek for its plant(s)?
3. A firm must decide whether to make a component part in-house or to contract it out to an independent supplier. Manufacturing the part requires a nonrecoverable investment in specialized assets. The most efficient suppliers are located in countries with currencies that many foreign exchange analysts expect to appreciate substantially over the next decade. What are the pros and cons of *(a)* manufacturing the component in-house and *(b)* outsourcing manufacturing to an independent supplier? Which option would you recommend? Why?
4. Reread the Management Focus on Philips in China and then answer the following questions:
   a. What are the benefits to Philips of shifting so much of its global production to China?
   b. What are the risks associated with a heavy concentration of manufacturing assets in China?
   c. What strategies might Philips adopt to maximize the benefits and mitigate the risks associated with moving so much product?
5. Explain how the global supply chain functions of *(a)* logistics and *(b)* purchasing can be used to strategically leverage the global supply chains for a manufacturing company producing mobile phones.
6. What type of interorganizational relationship should a global company consider in the *(a)* inbound portion of its supply chains if the goal is to buy commodity-oriented component parts for its own production and *(b)* outbound portion of its supply chains if the goal is to establish a strong partnership in reaching end-customers?

globalEDGE Research Task

globalEDGE.msu.edu

Use the globalEDGE™ website (globaledge.msu.edu) to complete the following exercises:

1. The globalization of production makes many people aware of the differences in manufacturing costs worldwide. The U.S. Department of Labor's Bureau of International Labor Affairs publishes the *Chartbook of International Labor Comparisons.* Locate the latest edition of this report, and identify the hourly compensation costs for manufacturing workers in China, Brazil, Mexico, Turkey, Germany, and the United States.
2. The World Bank's Logistics Performance Index (LPI) assesses the trade logistics environment and performance of countries. Locate the most recent LPI ranking. What components for each country are examined to construct the index? Identify the top 10 logistics performers. Prepare an executive summary highlighting the key findings from the LPI. How are these findings helpful for companies trying to build a competitive supply chain network?

Apple: The Best Supply Chains in the World?

closing case

For eight straight years, Apple has been recognized as having the best worldwide supply chains in the "Gartner Global Supply Chain Top 25" ranking. In the most recent ranking, Apple was actually classified above the ranking as a "Master" (Amazon.com was the listed the number one company). The Master status recognizes the accomplishments and capabilities of long-term global supply chain leaders in the Gartner Global Supply Chain Top 25. Companies qualify for the Masters category if their score places them in the top five rankings for at least seven out of the past 10 years.

Numerous accolades have also been made about Apple's supply chain strategy, operations, and results. For example, Apple's supply chains "best demonstrate leadership in applying demand-driven principles to drive business results."* "Apple dominates because it consistently brings both operational and innovation excellence to bear in some of the most competitive markets in the world."* Basically, Apple gets a lot of credit in the supply chain profession for being able to ramp up volumes both in hardware and software while also uniquely helping redefine the consumer electronics market (e.g., iPhone, iPad, MacBook).

*D. Hofman, "The Gartner Supply Chain Top 25," 2013, www.gartner.com/technology.

Apple is the world's second-largest information technology company by revenue after Samsung and the second-largest mobile phone producer also after Samsung. In Interbrand's *Best Global Brands* report, Apple is now also the most valuable brand in the world. It overtook Coca-Cola in 2013 for the number one position after Coca-Cola's 13-year run at the top and has stayed at the top every year since that time. Apple has an estimated brand value of more than $170 billion. "Few brands have enabled so many people to do so much so easily, which is why Apple has legions of adoring fans."* These "fans" or customers have downloaded apps for Apple's electronic gadgets more than 60 billion times.

The company's general supply chain model follows the path of most large multinational corporations' supply chains. They do research and development to cultivate new technologies and/or to acquire intellectual property needed for future products. They test the product concepts via marketing research, product testing, and total cost analysis. After that, Apple typically does a prelaunch of new products, where global production, sourcing commitments, inventory management, and so on are evaluated. The product launch involves doing demand forecasts, resolving potential backlogs, and ensuring that the products are in the hands of its customers in as fast a cycle time as possible. After the launch, monitoring starts with periodic reviews of inventory, demand, life cycle status, and component cost forecasts.

A number of factors make Apple's global supply chains world leading. First, early on, Apple took steps to manage the total value created in its global supply chains by managing its suppliers and all other providers within the chains. Predetermined expectations of suppliers, exclusivity in supplier arrangements, and volume guarantees ensured a supply chain infrastructure that could support Apple's aggressive market leadership. Apple's relationship building with its network partners is also a strength that has helped with increased scaling of production and resulted in improved quality in the manufacturing processes. Plus, and not to be underestimated, Apple has amassed lots of cash! The available cash funds have partially been used to place high-volume orders, which strengthen supplier relationships, and in other ways maintain global supply chain leadership.

Using its supply chain infrastructure, Apple has managed to solve most of the challenges it has faced. For example, while the global economic downturn in 2008 presented problems for virtually all companies, Apple came through it in great shape. At the time, CEO Steve Jobs said, "We're armed with the strongest product line in our history, the most talented employees and the best customers in our industry. . . . Apple just reported one of the best quarters in its history."* Other challenges that Apple is facing include obtaining enough quality components for its consumer electronics, potential for supply chain disruptions (natural and people created), dependence on third-party logistics providers, and inventory management issues. In each case, so far, Apple has strategically solved major issues to the satisfaction of the marketplace (the company consistently ranks at the top in "customer satisfaction" in the American Customer Satisfaction Index).

However, everything is not all rosy or positive about Apple. The company's reputation has taken a few hits recently. For example, Apple was found guilty by a U.S. court of conspiring with publishers to set the price of e-books that were bought using iTunes. The ongoing feud with Samsung regarding various patents keeps lingering year-by-year, and worldwide customers are almost fanatically taking sides for or against Apple. There have also been allegations about the treatment of employees at Foxconn in China (one of the Apple suppliers). Plus, there was a U.S. Senate hearing that investigated Apple's "highly questionable" tax minimization strategies. Now, on the more positive side, Apple has a portfolio of potential blockbuster products, welcomed upgrades, and innovative services in the making that are sure to remind its fans why they favor Apple products.

The challenges attached to these new offerings are sure to test Apple's leadership in both brand value and best global supply chains. To some degree, the future challenges are clear. To stay at the top of its industry, Apple has to succeed in slowing Samsung's momentum and capturing the booming Chinese mobile phone market. As always with Apple, as set in our expectations over the years by Steve Jobs's "one more thing" announcements, CEO Tim Cook and the new Apple leadership team must keep communicating to the market that their vision, innovations, and leadership can drive the idea that Apple's best days are ahead. As one way to do this, Apple is on a hiring binge in Asia, adding hundreds of engineers and supply chain managers to its staff in Shangai and Taipei as it seeks to increase the speed at which it introduces new products. Plus, with Cook as the CEO, Apple has a global production and supply chain management expert at the helm who constantly scrutinizes Apple's supply chains, production operations, and fair labor practices.

*Angela Moscaritolo, "Apple Unseats Coca-Cola as World's No. 1 Brand of 2013," PC Magazine, September 30, 2013, http://in.pcmag.com.

*"Apple Reports Fourth Quarter Results," https://www.apple.com.

Sources: D. Hofman, "The Gartner Supply Chain Top 25," 2013, www.gartner.com/technology; "Interbrand's Best Global Brands 2013," www.interbrand.com; "Apple Is the World's Most Valuable Brand at $98 Billion," *The Huffington Post,* September 30, 2013; "Apple Reports Fourth Quarter Results," *Apple Press Info,* October 21, 2008; E. Doe, "Apple Goes on Hiring Binge in Asia to Speed Product Releases," *The Wall Street Journal,* March 3, 2014 (http://www.wsj.com/articles/SB10001424052702304360704579416660215507816); *American Customer Satisfaction Index,* http://theacsi.org; "Fixing Apple's Supply Chains," *The New York Times,* April 2, 2012 (http://query.nytimes.com/gst/fullpage.html?res=9C03EED91F3FF931A35757C0A9649D8B63).

CASE DISCUSSION QUESTIONS

1. According to Interbrand's analysis, Apple's brand is valued at more than $170 billion, while Google in second place is valued at $120 billion and Coca-Cola in third is at $78 billion (2015). Do you agree that Apple should be so far ahead of its nearest brand competition? What about Samsung, which is larger in size (Samsung is valued at $45 billion)?
2. With Steve Jobs, Apple's legendary founder and CEO, passing away in 2011, what can we expect from Apple in the future? Will they be as innovative? Will they maintain brand value leadership? Will they run the top global supply chains in the world?
3. Apple products have usually been priced above their competition and sold for their value, intrigue, and market leadership. Some would say Samsung is catching up on many of these fronts and even passing Apple perhaps. Do you think Apple can charge a price premium for their products much longer?
4. Apple's global supply chains make their business thrive. There is secrecy among suppliers, superior quality standards by every party involved in Apple's supply chains, and a total value focus that ultimately makes the customers happy. Is this a sustainable business model for their global supply chains?

Endnotes

1. T. Hult, D. Closs, and D. Frayer, Global Supply Chain Management: Leveraging Processes, *Measurements, and Tools for Strategic Corporate Advantage* (New York: McGraw-Hill Professional, 2014).
2. D. A. Garvin, "What Does Product Quality Really Mean," *Sloan Management Review* 26 (Fall 1984), pp. 25–44.
3. See the articles published in the special issue of the *Academy of Management Review on Total Quality Management* 19, no. 3 (1994). The following article provides a good overview of many of the issues involved from an academic perspective: J. W. Dean and D. E. Bowen, "Management Theory and Total Quality," *Academy of Management Review* 19 (1994), pp. 392–418. Also see T. C. Powell, "Total Quality Management as Competitive Advantage," *Strategic Management Journal* 16 (1995), pp. 15–37; S. B. Han et al., "The Impact of ISO 9000 on TQM and Business Performance," *Journal of Business and Economic Studies* 13, no. 2 (2007), pp. 1–25.
4. For general background information, see "How to Build Quality," The Economist, September 23, 1989, pp. 91–92; A. Gabor, *The Man Who Discovered Quality* (New York: Penguin, 1990); P. B. Crosby, *Quality Is Free* (New York: Mentor, 1980); M. Elliot et al., "A Quality World, a Quality Life," *Industrial Engineer, January* 2003, pp. 26–33.
5. G. T. Lucier and S. Seshadri, "GE Takes Six Sigma Beyond the Bottom Line," *Strategic Finance,* May 2001, pp. 40–46; and U. D. Kumar et al., "On the Optimal Selection of Process Alternatives in a Six Sigma Implementation," *International Journal of Production Economics* 111, no. 2 (2008), pp. 456–70.
6. M. Saunders, "U.S. Firms Doing Business in Europe Have Options in Registering for ISO 9000 Quality Standards," *Business America,* June 14, 1993, p. 7; and Han et al., "The Impact of ISO 9000."
7. G. Stalk and T. M. Hout, *Competing against Time* (New York: Free Press, 1990).
8. N. Tokatli, "Global Sourcing: Insights from the Global Clothing Industry—The Case of Zara, a Fast Fashion Retailer," *Journal of Economic Geography* 8, no. 1 (2008), pp. 21–39.
9. Diana Farrell, "Beyond Offshoring," *Harvard Business Review,* December 2004, pp. 1–8; and M. A. Cohen and H. L. Lee, "Resource Deployment Analysis of Global Manufacturing and Distribution Networks," *Journal of Manufacturing and Operations Management* 2 (1989), pp. 81–104.
10. P. Krugman, "Increasing Returns and Economic Geography," *Journal of Political Economy* 99, no. 3 (1991), pp. 483–99; J. M. Shaver and F. Flyer, "Agglomeration Economies, Firm Heterogeneity, and Foreign Direct Investment in the United States," *Strategic Management Journal* 21 (2000), pp. 1175–93; and R. E. Baldwin and T. Okubo, "Heterogeneous Firms, Agglomeration Economies, and Economic Geography," *Journal of Economic Geography* 6, no. 3 (2006), pp. 323–50.
11. For a review of the technical arguments, see D. A. Hay and D. J. Morris, *Industrial Economics: Theory and Evidence* (Oxford, UK: Oxford University Press, 1979). See also C. W. L. Hill and G. R. Jones, *Strategic Management: An Integrated Approach* (Boston: Houghton Mifflin, 2004).
12. See P. Nemetz and L. Fry, "Flexible Manufacturing Organizations: Implications for Strategy Formulation," *Academy of Management Review* 13 (1988), pp. 627–38; N. Greenwood, *Implementing Flexible Manufacturing Systems* (New York: Halstead Press, 1986); J. P. Womack, D. T. Jones, and D. Roos, *The Machine That Changed the World* (New York: Rawson Associates, 1990); and R. Parthasarthy and S. P. Seith, "The Impact of Flexible Automation on Business Strategy and Organizational Structure," *Academy of Management Review* 17 (1992), pp. 86–111.
13. B. J. Pine, *Mass Customization: The New Frontier in Business Competition* (Boston: Harvard Business School Press, 1993); S. Kotha, "Mass Customization: Implementing the Emerging Paradigm for Competitive Advantage," *Strategic Management Journal* 16 (1995), pp. 21–42; J. H. Gilmore and B. J. Pine II, "The Four Faces of Mass Customization," *Harvard Business Review,* January–February 1997, pp. 91–101; M. Zerenler and D. Ozilhan, "Mass Customization Manufacturing: The Drivers and Concepts," *Journal of American Academy of Business* 12, no. 1 (2007), pp. 230–62.
14. "Toyota Motor Corporation Captures Ten Segment Awards," J. D. Power press release, March 19, 2009, http://businesscenter.jdpower.com/news/pressrelease.aspx?ID52009043.
15. M. A. Cusumano, *The Japanese Automobile Industry* (Cambridge, MA: Harvard University Press, 1989); T. Ohno, *Toyota Production System* (Cambridge, MA: Productivity Press, 1990); Womack et al., *The Machine That Changed the World.*
16. P. Waurzyniak, "Ford's Flexible Push," *Manufacturing Engineering,* September 2003, pp. 47–50.
17. Hult et al., *Global Supply Chain Management.*
18. F. Kasra, "Making the Most of Foreign Factories," in *World View,* ed. J. E. Garten (Boston: Harvard Business School Press, 2000).
19. "The Boomerang Effect," *The Economist,* April 21, 2012; Charles Fishman, "The Insourcing Boom," *The Atlantic,* December 2012.
20. This anecdote was told to one of the authors by a Microsoft manager while the author was visiting Microsoft facilities in Hyderabad, India.
21. Interview by one of the authors. The manager was a former executive MBA student of the author.
22. Hult et al., *Global Supply Chain Management.*
23. Ibid.
24. D. A. Beeton, *Technology Roadmapping in the Packaging Sector* (Cambridge, UK: Institute for Manufacturing, University of Cambridge, 2004).
25. J. A. Peterson and V. Kumar, "Can Product Returns Make You Money?," *MIT Sloan Management Review* 51, no. 3 (2013), pp. 85–89.

26. Hult et al., *Global Supply Chain Management;* R. J. Trent and R. M. Monczka, "Achieving Excellence in Global Sourcing," *MIT Sloan Management Review* 47, no. 1 (2005), pp. 24–32.
27. M. Kotabe and K. Helsen, *Global Marketing Management* (Hoboken, NJ: Wiley, 2010).
28. H. F. Busch, "Integrated Materials Management," *IJPD & MM* 18 (1990), pp. 28–39.
29. T. Aeppel, "Manufacturers Cope with the Costs of Strained Global Supply Lines," *The Wall Street Journal, December* 8, 2004, p. A1.
30. D. J. Bowersox, D. J. Closs, M. B. Cooper, and J. C. Bowersox, *Supply Chain Logistics Management* (New York: McGraw-Hill Companies, 2012).
31. J. C. Anderson, J. A. Narus, and W. van Rossum, "Customer Value Propositions in Business Markets," *Harvard Business Review,* March 2006, pp. 1–10.

Part 6 International Business Functions

Global Marketing and R&D

learning objectives

After reading this chapter, you will be able to:

- **LO16-1** Explain why it might make sense to vary the attributes of a product from country to country.
- **LO16-2** Recognize why and how a firm's distribution strategy might vary among countries.
- **LO16-3** Identify why and how advertising and promotional strategies might vary among countries.
- **LO16-4** Explain why and how a firm's pricing strategy might vary among countries.
- **LO16-5** Understand how to configure the marketing mix globally.
- **LO16-6** Understand the importance of international market research.
- **LO16-7** Describe how globalization is affecting product development.

© Newscast/AP Images

Domino's Global Marketing

opening case

Domino's made its name by pioneering home delivery service of pizza in the United States. The company was founded in 1960 in Ypsilanti, Michigan, by Tom Monaghan and his brother, Jim. Domino's Pizza was sold to Bain Capital in 1998 and went public in 2004. Before that, on May 12, 1983, Domino's opened its first store internationally—in Winnipeg, Canada. And, in 2012, Domino's Pizza removed the word "Pizza" from the logo to emphasize its non-pizza products. Its current menu features a variety of Italian-American entrées, side dishes, and desserts.

You can now order Domino's with your Apple iPhone, with Amazon's Echo, and of course in any way you want online. "Ordering via Amazon Echo marks Domino's eighth platform in the suite of AnyWare technology," said Dennis Maloney, Domino's vice president and chief digital officer. "We want to continue making ordering pizza as convenient as possible, and this is no exception."* Domino's has been constantly adding new ways to order items in recent years, including options to order via emoji, Twitter, text, and smart TV.

Strategically, beyond digitalization of ordering, the growth for Domino's has been overseas. With the U.S. fast-food market saturated and consumer demand weak, Domino's has been looking to international markets for growth opportunities. Today, almost all new store openings are outside the United States. On August 3, 2015, Domino's opened its 12,000th store, and they now have about 5,000 stores the United States, 750 in the United Kingdom, 650 in India, 400 in Canada, and the remaining spread out in 80 countries. On October 5, 2015, Dominos even opened its first store in Milan, Italy—the birthplace of pizza. "I am beyond excited to celebrate this huge milestone for Domino's," said Patrick Doyle, Domino's president and CEO. "We've been opening new stores around the world at a steady clip—building beautiful and customer-friendly pizza theaters with our new image."†

Its plans call for 4 to 6 percent growth in stores per year for the next few years (some 500 new stores annually, with the majority in foreign markets). Given this expansion and clear international growth strategy, perhaps even more amazing is the 76 straight quarters of same-store sales growth in Domino's international stores. The company reported global retail sales of more than $8.9 billion in the last year, comprised of more than $4.1 billion in the United States and nearly $4.8 billion internationally. Perhaps more impressive, Domino's has opened more than 3,000 new stores around the globe since March 2010.

As Domino's expands its international businesses, there are some things that the company has kept the same as in the United States, and there are some things that are very different. What is the same is the

*L. Lorenzetti, "There's a New Way to Order Dominos This Super Bowl Sunday," *Fortune*, February 3, 2016.

†Patrick Doyle

–continued

basic business model of home delivery. This sets it apart from many of its rivals, which changed their basic offering when they entered foreign markets. For example, when Yum! Brands Inc. introduced Pizza Hut into China, it radically altered the format, establishing Pizza Hut Casual Dining, a chain that offers a vast selection of American fare—including ribs, spaghetti, and steak—in a full-service setting. Pizza Hut adopted this format because table service was what the locals were used to, but Domino's isn't interested. "We go in there with a tried-and-true business model of delivery and carry-out pizza that we deploy around the world," stated Richard Allison, Domino's executive vice president-international. "In emerging markets, we've got more tables than you would find in the U.S., but we have no plans to lean toward a casual dining model where the server comes out and takes an order."*

This general strategy is backed up by CEO Doyle, who said, "The joy of pizza is that bread, sauce, and cheese works fundamentally everywhere, except maybe China, where dairy wasn't a big part of their diet until lately." He continued, "It's easy to just change toppings market to market . . . in Asia, it's seafood and fish . . . it's curry in India . . . but half the toppings are standard offerings around the world." Only eight restaurant chains worldwide have more than 10,000 outlets, and Domino's is one of them. "Local knowledge and ownership are critical to our success overseas,"† Doyle said.

Bottom line, Domino's is the overall pizza-sales leader in the global marketplace and has established operations with some 7,000 store units worldwide. At this time, Domino's is also making a run for the top pizza spot in the United States, which now is held by Pizza Hut (with Papa John's at number three). This entrepreneurial leadership is best captured by Ronnie Asmar, director of new store development for STA Management in Southfield, Michigan, which owns 33 Domino's outlets. He said, "We come from an entrepreneurial family in the hospitality industry, and Domino's has been an awesome partner."†

And Domino's appear to lead the market in other ways as well. Domino's appear to have captured, integrated, and found an edge in the social media world we live in now better than its competition. For example, Mitch Speiser, a securities analyst for Buckingham Research in New York said, "Domino's mobile app for ordering pizza is better than its rivals'."† Information technology also helps drive sales for Domino's vis-à-vis local pizza entrepreneurs. At this time, about 58 percent of Domino's orders are digital in the United Kingdom and about 40 percent in the United States.

On the other hand, some things vary from country to country. In the United States, pizza is viewed as casual food, frequently mentioned in the same breath as beer and football. In Japan, it's viewed as more upscale fare. This is reflected in the offering. Japanese pizzas come with toppings that the average American couldn't fathom. Domino's has sold a $50 pizza in Japan featuring foie gras. Other premium toppings include snow crab, Mangalitsa pork with Bordeaux sauce, and beef stew with fresh mozzarella. Japanese consumers value aesthetics and really care about the look of food, so presentation is key. Patrons expect every slice to have precisely the same amount of toppings, which must be uniformly spaced. Shrimp, for example, are angled with the tails pointing the same way. Domino's developed their business in South Korea in much the same manner as in Japan.

Now, even with these unique toppings in Japan, pizza consumption is relatively low in Japan: the average Japanese pizza customer only consumes the product four times a year. To boost this, Domino's has been working to create more occasions to enjoy it. For example, on Valentine's Day, its Japanese stores deliver heart-shaped pizzas in pink boxes. Heart-shaped pizzas also appear on Mother's Day. This culture of superb pizzas with high-quality toppings was actually an initiative that was initially demanded by their U.S customer base; over an 18-month period during 2009 to 2011, Domino's remade itself and its pizzas—at the same time, it stayed short of adding more than 10 percent in cost to the pizza ingredients.

But back to Japan! To promote the offering in Japan, rather than spending money on commercials, Domino's tried to create news, such as topics that people talk about. If the topic is fun and hot, Domino's believes that people will talk about it, which ultimately translates into better sales. One promotion in

*A. Gasparro, "Domino's Sticks to Its Ways Abroad," *The Wall Street Journal*, April 17, 2012, p. B10.

†D. Buss, "Domino's Global Growth Feeds Pizza Chain's Rising Success," *Forbes*, March 9, 2013.

particular received heavy coverage. The chain offered 2.5 million yen (about $31,000) for one hour's work at a Domino's store. In all, about 12,000 people applied for the "job." The lucky winner was a rural housewife who had never eaten pizza. She flew to a small island to deliver pizza to schoolchildren, who were also new to pizza. The event received heavy news coverage—free advertising, in other words! As its international focus is now larger and advertisement funds are being allocated accordingly, Domino's is moving much more toward TV commercials in its promotional efforts to complement other promotional efforts. This includes efforts in Japan, India, and a variety of countries.

Domino's today has focused on branding itself with high-quality ingredients, efficiency but at a speed that fosters quality, and a devotion to maintaining a cultural fabric that allows for a strong entrepreneurial mindset among employees and franchisees. The company captures the global marketplace effectively, either as a first-mover or as a strong follower. "For Domino's the development and eventual channelization of industries is important strategically," said Michael Lawton, then CFO of Domino's. He continued: "It led the company to decide in some foreign markets that the best alternative was to let someone else introduce the pizza category with a sit-down concept and then Domino's moved in and captured their part of the industry as delivery and carry-out developed."* In other cases, Domino's led the market entry into foreign countries. These decision choices make for great global strategy. Domino's has certainly captured the "taste" of the global marketplace! •

*Michael Lawton

Source: L. Lorenzetti, "There's a New Way to Order Domino's This Super Bowl Sunday," *Fortune*, February 3, 2016 (http://fortune.com/2016/02/03/dominos-amazon-echo-ordering/); "Domino's Opens 12,000th Store," *PR Newswire*, August 3, 2015; "Domino's Opens Its 12,000th Store Worldwide," *QSR*, August 3, 2015; A. Gasparro, "Domino's Sticks to Its Ways Abroad," *The Wall Street Journal*, April 17, 2012, p. B10; A. C. Beattie, "In Japan, Pizza Is Recast as a Meal for Special Occasions," *Advertising Age*, April 2, 2012, p. 16; A. Gasparro, "Domino's Sees Bigger Slice Overseas," *The Wall Street Journal*, February 29, 2012, p. B7; R. Shah, "How Domino's Pizza Is Taking a Bite Out of India," *Getting More Awesome*, www.gettingmoreawesome.com; D. Buss, "Domino's Global Growth Feeds Pizza Chain's Rising Success," *Forbes*, March 9, 2013 (http://www.forbes.com/sites/dalebuss/2013/03/09/dominos-global-growth-feeds-pizza-chains-growing-success/#4a633c0b842c).

Introduction

Chapter 15 looked at the roles of global production and supply chain management in an international business. This chapter continues our focus on specific business functions by examining the roles of global marketing and research and development (R&D). We focus on how marketing and R&D can be performed so they will reduce the costs of value creation and add value by better serving customer needs in the global marketplace. This includes distribution strategy (sometimes also called marketing channels), which is part of global supply chains that we discussed in Chapter 15.

Get Insights by Industry

When conducting research and development (R&D) and creating international marketing campaigns, the vast majority of global companies focus on the customers' needs in a particular industry. Industries worldwide are classified according to the Harmonized Commodity Description and Coding System, or simply HS Codes, which are maintained by the World Customs Organization. The HS Codes are divided into about 20 sections for its roughly 5,000 commodity groups. The "Get Insights by Industry" section on globalEDGE™ (http://globaledge.msu.edu/global-insights/by/industry) is a great source for international business–related resources, statistics, risk assessments, regulatory agencies, corporations, and events for these 20 industry sectors. An interesting aspect of each industry section on globalEDGE™ is the rating provided of the industry's level of fragmentation. Highly concentrated industries are dominated by many large firms that are capable of shaping the industry's direction and price levels. Highly fragmented industries have many companies involved, with none of them really large enough to be able to influence the industry's direction or price levels. Which do you think is more fragmented: consumer products or technology? Check out the industry section on globalEDGE™ for an answer.

In Chapter 12, we spoke of the tension existing in most international businesses between the need to reduce costs and, at the same time, respond to local conditions, which tends to raise costs. This tension continues to be a persistent theme in this chapter. Basically, the world is becoming more globalized in some respects but remains different in others. A global marketing strategy that views the world's consumers as similar in their tastes and preferences is consistent with the mass production of a standardized output. By mass-producing a standardized output—whether it be soap, semiconductor chips, or high-end apparel—the firm can realize substantial unit cost reductions from experience curve effects and other economies of scale.

At the same time, ignoring country differences in consumer tastes and preferences can lead to failure. Some industries are more ripe for globalization than others; check out the globalEDGE™ "Get Insights by Industry" section for comparisons. Strategically, the global marketing function of a company needs to determine when product standardization is appropriate, how standardized it can be, and when it is not in the business's best interest to standardize a product too much. And, even if product standardization is appropriate, the way in which a product is positioned in a market and the promotions and messages used to sell that product may still have to be customized so that they resonate with local consumers.

In some way, the pizza-making portion of the food industry is becoming more and more standardized around the world, but ingredients remain very different in many markets. Pepperoni is a clear favorite in the United States. But bananas (Sweden), pickled ginger (India), mackerel (Russia), green peas (Brazil), eel (Japan), flambée (France), curry (Pakistan), shrimp (Australia), and coconut (Costa Rica) may not strike a chord with all customers worldwide. At the same time, the making of the pizza is largely standardized.

So, we are now in a time when homogenization of customers' needs and wants, especially of younger populations across developed and emerging nations, help marketing professionals sell products and services globally. To some degree, the globalization of product and service needs is age-dependent. Younger people want more similar products worldwide and actually expect to be able to buy any products anywhere and get them immediately. Globalization is also industry-dependent in that some industries are more likely to be able to standardize their products and value proposition (e.g., electronics) than other industries (e.g., furniture), at least not to the same degree, based on customers' desired. This chapter is exciting as a learning experience since globalization has increased the pressure on marketing to deliver on product quality and availability in a far-spanning way worldwide, with effective distribution strategies, appropriate communication strategies, and competitive pricing strategies.

We consider marketing and R&D within the same chapter because of their close relationship. A critical aspect of the marketing function is identifying gaps in the market so that the firm can develop new products to fill those gaps. Developing new products requires R&D—thus the linkage between marketing and R&D. A firm should develop new products with market needs in mind, and marketing is best suited to define those needs for R&D personnel, given, among many things, its closeness to the market via front-line customer service personnel. Also, marketing personnel are well suited to communicate to R&D personnel whether to produce globally standardized or locally customized products. The reason marketing is so well positioned to communicate with R&D about (1) customer needs and wants, and (2) degree of product standardization or customization needed is that the marketing function is responsible for the international marketing research that is conducted by the global company. Overall, our thinking here is in line with long-standing research that maintains that a major contributor to the success of new-product introductions is a close relationship between marketing and R&D.[1]

In this chapter, we begin by reviewing the debate on the globalization of markets. Then we discuss the issue of market segmentation. Next, we look at four elements that constitute a firm's marketing mix: product attributes, distribution strategy, communication strategy, and pricing strategy (these are sometimes called the 4 Ps for product, place, promotion, and price in many basic marketing textbooks). The **marketing mix** is the set of choices the firm offers to its targeted markets. Many firms vary their marketing mix from country to country, depending on differences in national culture, economic development, product standards, distribution channels, and so on. The best way to think about the marketing mix is that it represents the tactical activities and behaviors that are implemented by a global company based on its international marketing strategy

Marketing Mix

Choices about product attributes, distribution strategy, communication strategy, and pricing strategy that a firm offers its targeted markets.

to offer the best possible "mix" of product, distribution, communication, and price to a specific target market in a country or region.

Given the importance of the marketing mix and having the right products, we include three sections on those topics in this chapter after we provide a detailed discussion of the marketing mix elements. First, we have a section on configuring an appropriate marketing mix for each unique international market segment. This includes a set of sample questions to ask for each of the marketing mix elements (product, distribution, communication, and price) to gauge how standardized or customized a marketing mix should be for a certain international market segment. Next, we discuss international market research as a way to better understand how to configure the marketing mix for international market segments. Third, we focus a discussion on product development issues, with a particular emphasis on new-product development. Here we integrate R&D, marketing, and production issues along with management issues such as cross-functional teams.

Globalization of Markets and Brands

In a now-classic *Harvard Business Review* article, the late Theodore Levitt wrote lyrically about the globalization of world markets. Levitt's arguments have become something of a lightning rod in the debate about the extent of globalization. According to Levitt,

> A powerful force drives the world toward a converging commonality, and that force is technology. It has proletarianized communication, transport, and travel. The result is a new commercial reality—the emergence of global markets for standardized consumer products on a previously unimagined scale of magnitude.
>
> Gone are accustomed differences in national or regional preferences. The globalization of markets is at hand. With that, the multinational commercial world nears its end, and so does the multinational corporation. The multinational corporation operates in a number of countries and adjusts its products and practices to each—at high relative costs. The global corporation operates with resolute consistency—at low relative cost—as if the entire world were a single entity; it sells the same thing in the same way everywhere.
>
> Commercially, nothing confirms this as much as the success of McDonald's from the Champs Élysées to the Ginza, of Coca-Cola in Bahrain and Pepsi-Cola in Moscow, and of rock music, Greek salad, Hollywood movies, Revlon cosmetics, Sony television, and Levi's jeans everywhere.
>
> Ancient differences in national tastes or modes of doing business disappear. The commonalty of preference leads inescapably to the standardization of products, manufacturing, and the institutions of trade and commerce.[2]

This is eloquent and evocative writing, but is Levitt correct? The rise of the global media phenomenon from CNN to MTV and the ability of such media to help shape a global culture would seem to lend weight to Levitt's argument. If Levitt is correct, his argument has major implications for the marketing strategies pursued by international businesses. However, many academics feel that Levitt overstates his case.[3] Although Levitt may have a point when it comes to many basic industrial products, such as steel, bulk chemicals, and semiconductor chips, globalization in the sense used by Levitt seems to be the exception rather than the rule in many consumer goods markets and industrial markets. Even a firm such as McDonald's, which Levitt holds up as the archetypal example of a consumer products firm that sells a standardized product worldwide, modifies its menu from country to country in light of local consumer preferences. In select Arab countries and Pakistan, for example, McDonald's sells the McArabia, a chicken sandwich on Arabian-style bread, and in France, the Croque McDo, a hot ham and cheese sandwich.[4]

On the other hand, Levitt is probably correct to assert that modern transportation and communications technologies are facilitating a convergence of certain tastes and preferences among consumers in the more advanced countries of the world, and this has become even more prevalent since he wrote his article. Our movie example in the opening case of this chapter highlights such a convergence in tastes. By extension, in the long run, technological and other forces may lead to the evolution of a global culture. At present, however, the continuing persistence of some unique cultural and economic differences between nations acts as a brake on many trends toward the standardization of consumer tastes and preferences across nations. While we see more

Will Toyota Stay Number 1?

Yundong, or Cloud Action, is Toyota China's first-ever strategic plan for its business in China. China is the "most important" market in the world, but the Japanese carmaker has less than 10 percent of the auto market, far behind global rivals such as General Motors and Volkswagen. The auto giant aims to become a company "that is beyond consumers' expectations and creates happiness and fortune for consumers and the regions where it operates," emphasizing local responsiveness to Chinese customers but still maintaining a global strategy. The Yundong plan combines the company's global strategy and local marketing operation, which will bring advanced technologies to the local market, improve the local management and marketing system, and build "exciting" products "that touch the hearts of Chinese consumers and are beyond their expectations"* according to company officials. China is clearly an important market if Toyota is to maintain the overall worldwide leadership in auto sales. Do you think Toyota will capture a significant share of the Chinese auto market? And do you think Toyota can maintain its number one position in the worldwide auto market?

*www.chinadaily.com.cn.

Sources: J. Korceniewski, "Toyota Is World's Top-Selling Automaker for Second Year in a Row," *Autoblog*, January 26, 2014 (http://www.autoblog.com/2014/01/26/toyota-worlds-largest-automaker-2014/).

homogenization and standardization of needs and wants among younger people, typically 40 years and younger, there are still wide gaps in tastes among older people. What will be interesting to find out is if this increased homogenization among younger people will remain when they become older. Some indications exist that standardization of needs and wants stays with people when they become older, but, at least anecdotally, we also see people adopt more culturally specific needs as they grow older.

So, we may never see a world where globalization is fully spread across the almost 200 countries that exist (see globaledge.msu.edu for a comparison of information and data on the countries in the world). Some writers have argued that the rise of global culture does not mean that consumers share the same tastes and preferences.[5] Rather, people in different nations, often with conflicting viewpoints, are increasingly participating in a shared "global" conversation, drawing on shared symbols that include global brands from Nike and Dove to Coca-Cola and Sony but also Toyota, the world's largest automobile maker. But the way in which these brands are perceived, promoted, and used still varies from country to country, depending on local differences in tastes and preferences.

Another reason it appears that globalization is spreading is that certain products simply exist everywhere—but that does not mean consumers everywhere prefer those products over more local options if such product alternatives existed. Better technology, production processes, and innovation may lead to better local product alternatives in the future that can compete with global products. If so, international marketing is going to be even more critical than it already is for global and local companies. Furthermore, trade barriers and differences in product and technical standards also constrain a firm's ability to sell a standardized product to a global market using a standardized marketing strategy. We discuss the sources of these differences in subsequent sections when we look at how products must be altered from country to country. In short, Levitt's fully standardized international marketplace is some way off in many industries.

test PREP

Use SmartBook to help retain what you have learned. Access your Instructor's Connect course to check out SmartBook or go to learnsmartadvantage.com for help.

Market Segmentation

Market Segmentation
Identifying groups of consumers whose purchasing behavior differs from others in important ways.

Market segmentation refers to identifying distinct groups of consumers whose needs, wants, and purchasing behavior differ from others in important ways. Markets can be segmented in numerous ways: by geography, demography (e.g., gender, age, income, race, education level), sociocultural factors (e.g., social class, values, religion, lifestyle choices), and psychological factors (e.g., personality). Because different segments exhibit different needs, wants, and patterns of purchasing behavior, firms often adjust their marketing mix from segment to segment. Thus, the precise design of a product, the pricing strategy, the distribution channels used, and the choice of communication strategy may all be varied from segment to segment. The goal is to optimize the fit between the purchasing behavior of consumers in a given segment and the marketing mix, thereby maximizing sales to that segment. Automobile companies, for example, use a different marketing mix to sell cars to different socioeconomic segments. Thus, Toyota uses its Lexus division to sell high-priced luxury cars to high-income consumers while selling its entry-level models, such as the Toyota Corolla, to lower-income consumers. Similarly, computer manufacturers will offer different computer models, embodying different combinations of product attributes and price points, to appeal to consumers from different market segments (e.g., business users and home users).

When managers in an international business consider market segmentation in foreign countries, they need to be cognizant of two main issues: the differences between countries in the structure of market segments and the existence of segments that transcend national borders. For example, some companies opt to target a country with a number of different product options based on the multiple unique market segments in a country. Other companies opt to target one unique market segment in a country that also has parallels in other countries. A segment that spans multiple countries, transcending national boarders, is often called an **intermarket segment**. Strategically, marketing managers have marketing mix options with these two choices. Targeting one country and its multiple potential market segments with multiple marketing mixes allows a company to focus on the cultural characteristics of one country (or the characteristics of a manageable set of countries). Targeting many countries and the intermarket segment that has characteristics that are largely the same across countries allows a company to focus on the cultural characteristics that are universal for certain customers across countries.

Intermarket Segment
A segment of customers that spans multiple countries, transcending national borders.

These are important choices because the structure of the many potential market segments may differ significantly from country to country as well as within countries. In fact, an important market segment in a foreign country may have no parallel in the firm's home country, and vice versa. In such a case, the focus cannot be on an intermarket segment, at least not one involving the home-country market. The firm may have to develop a unique marketing mix to appeal to the needs, wants, and purchasing behavior of a certain segment in a given country. An example of such a market segment is given in the accompanying Management Focus, which looks at the African Brazilian market segment in Brazil that, as you will see, is very different from the African American segment in the United States. In another example, a research project identified a segment of consumers in China in the 45-to-55 age range that has few parallels in other countries.[6] This group came of age during China's Cultural Revolution in the late 1960s and early 1970s. The group's values have been shaped by their members' experiences during the Cultural Revolution. They tend to be highly sensitive to price and respond negatively to new products and

management FOCUS

Marketing to Black Brazil

Brazil is home to the largest black population outside Nigeria. Nearly half of the 206 million people in Brazil are of African (15 million) or mixed race (79 million) origins. Despite this, until recently have businesses made any effort to target this numerically large segment of the population. Part of the reason is rooted in economics.

Black Brazilians have historically been poorer than Brazilians of European origin (91 million people) and thus have not received the same attention as whites. But after a decade of relatively strong economic performance in Brazil, with the exception of 2013–2015, an emerging black middle class is beginning to command the attention of consumer product companies. To take advantage of this, companies such as Unilever have introduced a range of skin care products and cosmetics aimed at black Brazilians, and Brazil's largest toy company introduced a black Barbie-like doll, Susi Olodum, sales of which quickly caught up with sales of a similar white doll.

But there is more to the issue than simple economics. Unlike the United States, where a protracted history of racial discrimination gave birth to the civil rights movement, fostered black awareness, and produced an identifiable subculture in U.S. society, the history of blacks in Brazil has been very different. Although Brazil did not abolish slavery until 1888, racism in Brazil historically has been much subtler than in the United States. Brazil has never excluded blacks from voting nor has it had a tradition of segregating the races. Historically, too, the government encouraged intermarriage between whites and blacks. Partly due to this more benign history, Brazil has not had a black rights movement similar to that in the United States, and racial self-identification is much weaker. Surveys routinely find that African Brazilian consumers decline to categorize themselves as either black or white; instead, they choose one of dozens of skin tones and see themselves as being part of a culture that transcends race. Indeed, only 15 million of Brazil's population classify themselves as "Afro-Brazilian," while 79 million classify themselves as *pardo,* or brown Brazilians of mixed race ancestry including white, African, and Amerindian descent.

This subtler racial dynamic has important implications for market segmentation and tailoring the marketing mix in Brazil. Unilever had to face this issue when launching a Vaseline Intensive Care lotion for black consumers in Brazil. The company learned in focus groups that for the product to resonate with nonwhite women, its promotions had to feature women of different skin tones, excluding neither whites nor blacks. The campaign Unilever devised features three women with different skin shades at a fitness center. The bottle says the lotion is for "tan and black skin," a description that could include many white women considering that much of the population lives near the beach. Unilever learned that the segment exists, but it is more difficult to define and requires subtler marketing messages than the African American segment in the United States or middle-class segments in Africa.

Sources: A. Tarde, "African-Oriented Market Is Growing Despite the Economic Crisis," *Black Women of Brazil*, January 7, 2016 (https://blackwomenofbrazil.co/2016/01/07/african-oriented-market-is-growing-despite-the-economic-crisis/); "Brazil Population 2016," *World Population Review*, http://worldpopulationreview.com; M. Jordan, "Marketers Discover Black Brazil," *The Wall Street Journal*, November 24, 2000, pp. A11, A14.

most forms of marketing. Thus, firms doing business in China may need to customize their marketing mix to address the unique values and purchasing behavior of the group. The existence of such a segment constrains the ability of firms to standardize their global marketing strategy.

In contrast, the existence of market segments that transcend national borders clearly enhances the ability of an international business to view the global marketplace as a single entity and pursue a global strategy—selling a standardized product worldwide and using the same basic marketing mix to help position and sell that product in a variety of national markets. For a segment to transcend national borders, consumers in that segment must have some compelling similarities along important dimensions—such as age, values, lifestyle choices—and those similarities must translate into similar needs, wants, and purchasing behavior. If this is true, the company can globalize its marketing mix efforts by adopting the so-called intermarket segment to target customers' needs, wants, and purchasing behavior. Although such segments clearly exist in certain industrial markets, they have historically been rarer in consumer markets.

The forecast, however, is that these intermarket segments will become more and more common with the increased globalization among younger consumers (40 years and younger) in the developed- and emerging-country markets. For example, one emerging global segment that is attracting the attention of international marketers of consumer goods is the global teenage segment. Global media are paving the way for a global youth segment. Evidence that such a segment exists comes from a study of the cultural attitudes and purchasing behavior of more than 6,500 teenagers in 26 countries.[7] The findings suggest that teens and young adults around the world are increasingly living parallel lives that share many common values. It follows that they are likely to purchase the same kind of consumer goods and for the same reasons.

Use SmartBook to help retain what you have learned. Access your Instructor's Connect course to check out SmartBook or go to learnsmartadvantage.com for help.

LO 16-1
Explain why it might make sense to vary the attributes of a product from country to country.

Product Attributes

A product can be viewed as a bundle of attributes.[8] For example, the attributes that make up a car include power, design, quality, performance, fuel consumption, and comfort; the attributes of a hamburger include taste, texture, and size; a hotel's attributes include atmosphere, quality, comfort, and service. Products sell well when their attributes match consumer needs (and when their prices are appropriate). BMW cars sell well to people who have high needs for luxury, quality, and performance precisely because BMW builds those attributes into its cars. If consumer needs were the same the world over, a firm could simply sell the same product worldwide. However, consumer needs vary from country to country, depending on culture and the level of economic development. A firm's ability to sell the same product worldwide is further constrained by countries' differing product standards. This section reviews each of these issues and discusses how they influence product attributes.

CULTURAL DIFFERENCES

We discussed countries' cultural differences in Chapter 4. Countries differ along a whole range of dimensions, including social structure, language, religion, and education. These differences have important implications for marketing strategy. For example, "hamburgers" do not sell well in Islamic countries, where the consumption of ham is forbidden by Islamic law (thus, the sandwich's name is changed). The most important aspect of cultural differences is probably the impact of tradition. Tradition is particularly important in foodstuffs and beverages. For example, reflecting differences in traditional eating habits, the Findus frozen food division of Nestlé, the Swiss food giant, markets fish cakes and fish fingers in Great Britain, but beef bourguignon and coq au vin in France and vitéllo con funghi and braviola in Italy. In addition to its normal range of products, Coca-Cola in Japan markets Georgia, a cold coffee in a can, and Aquarius, a tonic drink, both of which appeal to traditional Japanese tastes.

Coca-Cola responded to Japan's traditional tastes with the beverage Georgia, a cold coffee in a can.

Source: © Phillip Augustavo/Alamy Stock Photo

For historical and idiosyncratic reasons, a range of other cultural differences exist among countries. For example, scent preferences differ from one country to another. SC Johnson, a manufacturer of waxes and polishes, encountered resistance to its lemon-scented Pledge furniture polish among older consumers in Japan. Careful market research revealed the polish smelled similar to a latrine disinfectant used widely in Japan. Sales rose sharply after the scent was adjusted.[9]

There is some evidence of the trends Levitt talked about. Tastes and preferences are becoming more cosmopolitan. Coffee is gaining ground against tea in Japan and Great Britain, while American-style frozen dinners have become popular in Europe (with some fine-tuning to local tastes). Taking advantage of these trends, Nestlé has found that it can market its instant coffee, spaghetti bolognese, and Lean Cuisine frozen dinners in essentially the same manner in both North America and western Europe. However, there is no market for Lean Cuisine dinners in most of the rest of the world, and there may not be for years or decades. Although some cultural convergence has occurred, particularly among the advanced industrial nations of North America and western Europe, Levitt's global culture characterized by standardized tastes and preferences is still a long way off.

ECONOMIC DEVELOPMENT

Just as important as differences in culture are differences in the level of economic development. We discussed the extent of country differences in economic development in Chapter 3. Consumer behavior is influenced by the level of economic development of a country. Firms based in highly developed countries such as the United States tend to build a lot of extra performance attributes into their products. These extra attributes are not usually demanded by consumers in less developed nations, where the preference is for more basic products. Thus, cars sold in less developed nations typically lack many of the features found in developed nations, such as air-conditioning, power steering, power windows, radios, and CD players. For most consumer durables, product reliability may be a more important attribute in less developed nations, where such a purchase may account for a major proportion of a consumer's income, than it is in advanced nations.

Contrary to Levitt's suggestions, consumers in the most developed countries are often not willing to sacrifice their preferred attributes for lower prices. Consumers in the most advanced countries often shun globally standardized products that have been developed with the lowest common denominator in mind. They are willing to pay more for products that have additional features and attributes customized to their tastes and preferences. For example, demand for top-of-the-line four-wheel-drive sport-utility vehicles—such as Chrysler's Jeep, Ford's Explorer, and Toyota's Land Cruiser—has been largely restricted to the United States. This is due to a combination of factors, including the high income level of U.S. consumers, the country's vast distances, the relatively low cost of gasoline, and the culturally grounded "outdoor" theme of American life.

PRODUCT AND TECHNICAL STANDARDS

Even with the forces that are creating some convergence of consumer tastes and preferences among advanced, industrialized nations, Levitt's vision of global markets may still be a long way off because of national differences in product and technological standards. However, if anything, the increased development and implementation of regional trade agreements, often taking into account technical standards setting, may influence certain regional markets to become more globalized, as Levitt suggested.

For now, differing government-mandated product standards can often result in companies ruling out mass production and marketing of a fully global and standardized product. Differences in technical standards also constrain the globalization of markets. Some of these differences result from idiosyncratic decisions made long ago, rather than from government actions, but their long-term effects are profound. For example, DVD equipment manufactured for sale in the United States will not

Can Spotify and Coca-Cola Leverage Their Partnership for Sales?

Swedish music-streaming service Spotify has gained access to Coca-Cola's global marketing engine, and Coca-Cola can use Spotify tunes in its online marketing. Spotify is hoping that Coke will teach the world to click its play button. The Swedish digital music service has a broad-ranging marketing deal with Coca-Cola Co. that could help turbocharge the number of people who are exposed to, and ultimately sign up for, Spotify. For Spotify, getting access to Coca-Cola's formidable global marketing engine will come in handy as it expands its international footprint. In return, Coca-Cola can now use Spotify's service to instantly add music to its online marketing repertoire. For instance, the drink giant can add songs to its Facebook page via Spotify without having to negotiate licenses for each tune (Spotify already has financial agreements with major record labels to pay royalties for every song that is played on its digital service). These co-branding deals sometimes motivate customers to buy more from each company—if you are a fan of Spotify, you may buy more from Coca-Cola, and vice versa. If your favorite company co-branded with a company you have never bought from, would you try that company's products?

Sources: A. Pham, "Spotify and Coca-Cola Form Marketing Partnership," *Los Angeles Times*, April 18, 2012 (http://articles.latimes.com/2012/apr/18/business/la-fi-ct-spotify-coca-cola-20120419); "Spotify and Coca-Cola Partner to Share Music with the World," *Spotify Press Release.* http://press.spotify.com.

play DVDs recorded on equipment manufactured for sale in Great Britain, Germany, and France (and vice versa). Different technical standards for television signal frequency emerged in the 1950s that require television and video equipment to be customized to prevailing standards. RCA stumbled in the 1970s when it failed to account for this in its marketing of TVs in Asia. Although several Asian countries adopted the U.S. standard, Singapore, Hong Kong, and Malaysia adopted the British standard. People who bought RCA TVs in those countries could receive a picture but no sound![10]

LO 16-2

Recognize why and how a firm's distribution strategy might vary among countries.

Distribution Strategy

A critical element of a firm's marketing mix is its distribution strategy: the means it chooses for delivering the product to the consumer. The way the product is delivered is determined by the firm's entry strategy, discussed in Chapter 15. This section examines a typical distribution system, discusses how its structure varies between countries, and looks at how appropriate distribution strategies vary from country to country.

Figure 16.1 illustrates a typical distribution system consisting of a channel that includes a wholesale distributor and a retailer. If the firm manufactures its product in the particular country, it can sell directly to the consumer, to the retailer, or to the wholesaler. The same options are available to a firm that manufactures outside the country. Plus, this firm may decide to sell to an import agent, which then deals with the wholesale distributor, the retailer, or the consumer. Later in the chapter, we consider the factors that determine the firm's choice of channel.

DIFFERENCES BETWEEN COUNTRIES

The four main differences between distribution systems worldwide are retail concentration, channel length, channel exclusivity, and channel quality.

Retail Concentration

In some countries, the retail system is very concentrated, but it is fragmented in others. In a **concentrated retail system**, a few retailers supply most of the market. A **fragmented retail system** is one in which there are many retailers, none of which has a major share of the market. Many of the differences in concentration are rooted in history and tradition. In the United States, the importance of the automobile and the relative youth of many urban areas have resulted in a retail system centered on large stores or shopping malls to which people can drive. This has facilitated system concentration. Japan, with a much greater population density and a large number of urban centers that grew up before the automobile, has a more fragmented retail system, with many small stores serving local neighborhoods and to which people frequently

Concentrated Retail System

A retail system in which a few retailers supply most of the market.

Fragmented Retail System

A retail system in which there are many retailers, none of which has a major share of the market.

16.1 FIGURE

A Typical Distribution System.

Source: C. W. L. Hill and G. T. M. Hult, *International Business: Competing in the Global Marketplace* (New York: McGraw-Hill Education, 2017).

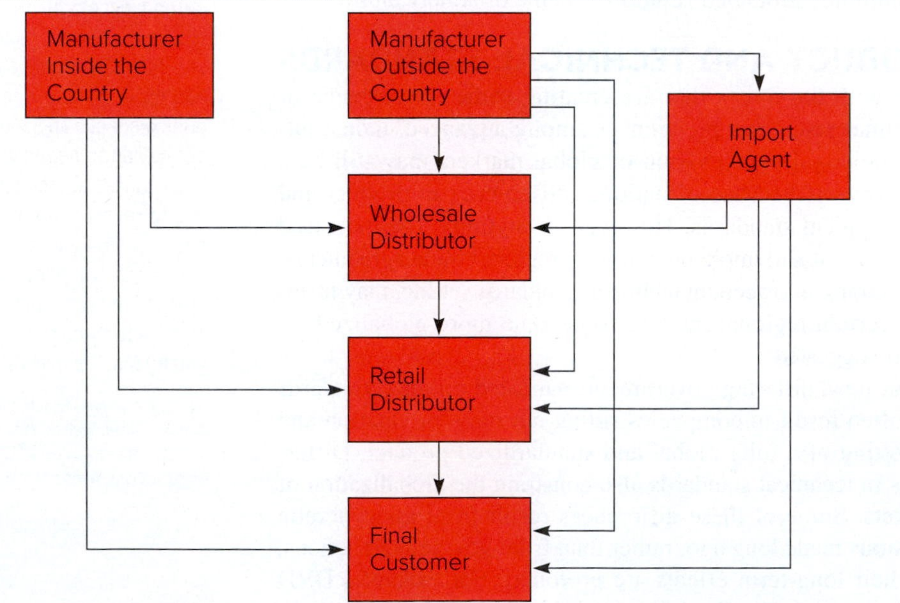

walk. In addition, the Japanese legal system protects small retailers. Small retailers can try to block the establishment of a large retail outlet by petitioning their local government.

There is a tendency for greater retail concentration in developed countries. Three factors that contribute to this are the increases in car ownership, the number of households with refrigerators and freezers, and the number of two-income households. All these factors have changed shopping habits and facilitated the growth of large retail establishments sited away from traditional shopping areas. The last decade has seen consolidation in the global retail industry, with companies such as Walmart and Carrefour attempting to become global retailers by acquiring retailers in different countries. This has increased retail concentration.

In contrast, retail systems are very fragmented in many developing countries, which can make for interesting distribution challenges. In rural China, large areas of the country can be reached only by traveling rutted dirt roads. In India, Unilever has to sell to retailers in 600,000 rural villages, many of which cannot be accessed via paved roads, which means products can reach their destination only by bullock, bicycle, or cart. In neighboring Nepal, the terrain is so rugged that even bicycles and carts are not practical, and businesses rely on yak trains and the human back to deliver products to thousands of small retailers.

Channel Length

Channel length refers to the number of intermediaries between the producer (or manufacturer) and the consumer. If the producer sells directly to the consumer, the channel is very short. If the producer sells through an import agent, a wholesaler, and a retailer, a long channel exists. The choice of a short or long channel is, in part, a strategic decision for the producing firm. However, some countries have longer distribution channels than others. The most important determinant of channel length is the degree to which the retail system is fragmented. Fragmented retail systems tend to promote the growth of wholesalers to serve retailers, which lengthens channels.

Channel Length
The number of intermediaries that a product has to go through before it reaches the final consumer.

The more fragmented the retail system, the more expensive it is for a firm to make contact with each individual retailer. Imagine a firm that sells toothpaste in a country where there are more than a million small retailers, as in rural India. To sell directly to the retailers, the firm would have to build a huge sales force. This would be very expensive, particularly because each sales call would yield a very small order. But suppose a few hundred wholesalers in the country supply retailers not only with toothpaste but also with all other personal care and household products. Because these wholesalers carry a wide range of products, they get bigger orders with each sales call, making it worthwhile for them to deal directly with the retailers. Accordingly, it makes economic sense for the firm to sell to the wholesalers and the wholesalers to deal with the retailers.

Because of such factors, countries with fragmented retail systems also tend to have long channels of distribution, sometimes with multiple layers. The classic example is Japan, where there are often two or three layers of wholesalers between the firm and retail outlets. In countries such as Great Britain, Germany, and the United States, where the retail systems are far more concentrated, channels are much shorter. When the retail sector is very concentrated, it makes sense for the firm to deal directly with retailers, cutting out wholesalers. A relatively small sales force is required to deal with a concentrated retail sector, and the orders generated from each sales call can be large. Such circumstances tend to prevail in the United States, where large food companies may sell directly to supermarkets rather than going through wholesale distributors.

Another factor that is shortening channel length in some countries is the entry of large discount superstores, such as Carrefour, Walmart, and Tesco. The business model of these retailers is, in part, based on the idea that in an attempt to lower prices, they cut out wholesalers and instead deal directly with manufacturers. Thus, when Walmart entered Mexico, its policy of dealing directly with manufacturers, instead of buying merchandise through wholesalers, helped shorten distribution channels in that nation. Similarly, Japan's historically long distribution channels are now being shortened by the rise of large retailers, some of them foreign-owned, such as Toys "R" Us and Walmart, and some of them indigenous enterprises that are imitating the American model, all of which are progressively cutting out wholesalers and dealing directly with manufacturers.

Channel Exclusivity

An **exclusive distribution channel** is one that is difficult for outsiders to access. For example, it is often difficult for a new firm to get access to shelf space

Exclusive Distribution Channel
A distribution channel that outsiders find difficult to access.

in supermarkets. This occurs because retailers tend to prefer to carry the products of established manufacturers of foodstuffs with national reputations rather than gamble on the products of unknown firms. The exclusivity of a distribution system varies among countries. Japan's system is often held up as an example of a very exclusive system. In Japan, relationships among manufacturers, wholesalers, and retailers often go back decades. Many of these relationships are based on the understanding that distributors will not carry the products of competing firms. In return, the distributors are guaranteed an attractive markup by the manufacturer. As many U.S. and European manufacturers have learned, the close ties that result from this arrangement can make access to the Japanese market difficult. However, it is possible to break into the Japanese market with a new consumer product. Procter & Gamble did during the 1990s with its Joy brand of dish soap. P&G was able to overcome a tradition of exclusivity for two reasons. First, after two decades of lackluster economic performance, Japan is changing. In their search for profits, retailers are far more willing than they have been historically to violate the old norms of exclusivity. Second, P&G has been in Japan long enough and has a broad enough portfolio of consumer products to give it considerable leverage with distributors, enabling it to push new products out through the distribution channel.

Channel Quality

The expertise, competencies, and skills of established retailers in a nation and their ability to sell and support the products of international businesses.

Channel Quality

Channel quality refers to the expertise, competencies, and skills of established retailers in a nation and their ability to sell and support the products of international businesses. Although the quality of retailers is good in most developed nations, in emerging markets and less developed nations from Russia to Indonesia, channel quality is variable at best. The lack of a high-quality channel may impede market entry, particularly in the case of new or sophisticated products that require significant point-of-sale assistance and after-sales services and support. When channel quality is poor, an international business may have to devote considerable attention to upgrading the channel, for example, by providing extensive education and support to existing retailers and, in extreme cases, by establishing its own channel. Thus, after pioneering its Apple retail store concept in the United States, Apple opened retail stores in several nations—including the United Kingdom, France, Germany, Japan, and China—to provide point-of-sales education, service, and support for its popular iPhone, iPad, and MacBook products. Apple believes that this strategy will help it gain market share in these nations.

CHOOSING A DISTRIBUTION STRATEGY

A choice of distribution strategy determines which channel the firm will use to reach potential consumers. Should the firm try to sell directly to the consumer? Or should it go through retailers, go through a wholesaler, use an import agent, or invest in establishing its own channel? The optimal strategy is determined by the relative costs and benefits of each alternative, which vary from country to country, depending on the four factors we have just discussed: retail concentration, channel length, channel exclusivity, and channel quality.

Because each intermediary in a channel adds its own markup to the products, there is generally a critical link among channel length, the final selling price, and the firm's profit margin. The longer a channel, the greater the aggregate markup, and the higher the price that consumers are charged for the final product. To ensure that prices do not get too high as a result of markups by multiple intermediaries, a firm might be forced to operate with lower profit margins. Thus, if price is an important competitive weapon, and if the firm does not want to see its profit margins squeezed, other things being equal, the firm would prefer to use a shorter channel.

However, the benefits of using a longer channel may outweigh these drawbacks. As we have seen, one benefit of a longer channel is that it cuts selling costs when the retail sector is very fragmented. Thus, it makes sense for an international business to use longer channels in countries where the retail sector is fragmented and shorter channels in countries where the retail sector is concentrated. Another benefit of using a longer channel is market access—the ability to enter an exclusive channel. Import agents may have long-term relationships with wholesalers, retailers, or important consumers and thus be better able to win orders and get access to a distribution system. Similarly, wholesalers may have long-standing relationships with retailers and be better able to persuade them to carry the firm's product than the firm itself would.

Import agents are not limited to independent trading houses; any firm with a strong local reputation could serve as well. For example, to break down channel exclusivity and gain greater access to the Japanese market, when Apple Computer originally entered Japan, it signed distribution agreements with five large Japanese firms, including business equipment giant Brother Industries, stationery leader Kokuyo, Mitsubishi, Sharp, and Minolta. These firms use their own long-established distribution relationships with consumers, retailers, and wholesalers to push Apple computers through the Japanese distribution system. Today, Apple has supplemented this strategy with its own stores in the country.

If such an arrangement is not possible, the firm might want to consider other, less traditional alternatives to gaining market access. Frustrated by channel exclusivity in Japan, some foreign manufacturers of consumer goods have attempted to sell directly to Japanese consumers using direct mail and catalogs. Finally, if channel quality is poor, a firm should consider what steps it could take to upgrade the quality of the channel, including establishing its own distribution channel.

test PREP

Use SmartBook to help retain what you have learned. Access your Instructor's Connect course to check out SmartBook or go to learnsmartadvantage.com for help.

Communication Strategy

LO 16-3

Identify why and how advertising and promotional strategies might vary among countries.

Another critical element in the marketing mix is communicating the attributes of the product to prospective customers. A number of communication channels are available to a firm, including direct selling, sales promotion, direct marketing, and advertising. A firm's communication strategy is partly defined by its choice of channel. Some firms rely primarily on direct selling, others on point-of-sale promotions or direct marketing, and others on mass advertising; still others use several channels simultaneously to communicate their message to prospective customers. This section looks first at the barriers to international communication. Then, we survey the various factors that determine which communication strategy is most appropriate in a particular country. After that, we discuss global advertising.

BARRIERS TO INTERNATIONAL COMMUNICATION

International communication occurs whenever a firm uses a marketing message to sell its products in another country. The effectiveness of a firm's international communication can be jeopardized by three potentially critical variables: cultural barriers, source effects, and noise levels.

Cultural Barriers

Cultural barriers can make it difficult to communicate messages across cultures. We discussed some sources and consequences of cultural differences between nations in Chapter 4 and in the previous section of this chapter. Because of cultural differences, a message that means one thing in one country may mean something quite different in another. Benetton, the Italian clothing manufacturer and retailer, ran into cultural problems with its advertising. The company launched a worldwide advertising campaign with the theme "United Colors of Benetton" that had won awards in France. One of its ads featured a black woman breast-feeding a white baby, and another one showed a black man and a white man handcuffed together. Benetton was surprised when the ads were attacked by U.S. civil rights groups for promoting white racial domination. Benetton withdrew its ads and fired its advertising agency, Eldorado of France.

The best way for a firm to overcome cultural barriers is to develop cross-cultural literacy (see Chapter 4). In addition, it should use local input, such as a local advertising agency, in developing its marketing message. If the firm uses direct selling rather than advertising to communicate its message, it should develop a local sales force whenever possible. Cultural differences limit a firm's ability to use the same marketing

Is the Google Advertising Model Viable in the Long Term?

Google's share of the Internet ads is at about 33 percent of the $117 billion market, making it the undisputed Goliath of online advertising. Google also continues to grow, thanks to acquisitions such as DoubleClick, YouTube, and even drone company Titan Aerospace. Facebook is solidly in the number two spot in Internet ads but is gaining market share (it has about 5 percent of the online ad market). Google is also a heavyweight in mobile ads with about 56 percent of the $16 billion market (Facebook has about 13 percent of this market). Research experts predict that new ad dollars will come from emerging markets such as China, Russia, and Indonesia. Over the next three years, about half of all global ad growth will come from 10 developing markets—with Brazil, Russia, India, and China combined accounting for 33 percent. Currently, there are four markets in which Internet ads account for more than 30 percent of total spending: Canada, Norway, Sweden, and the United Kingdom. Basically, the world is shifting its ad spending to the Internet and similar options. With that in mind, where can global companies reach you via advertisements if they wanted to target you? And do you think the Google advertisement business model is viable as a way to reach customers for the long term?

Source: A. Efrati, "In Online Ads, There's Google—and Then Everybody Else," *The Wall Street Journal*, June 13, 2013 (http://blogs.wsj.com/digits/2013/06/13/in-online-ads-theres-google-and-then-everybody-else/).

message and selling approach worldwide. What works well in one country may be offensive in another.

Source Effects
Effects that occur when the receiver of the message (i.e., a potential consumer) evaluates the message on the basis of status or image of the sender.

Source and Country of Origin Effects

Source effects occur when the receiver of the message (the potential consumer in this case) evaluates the message on the basis of status or image of the sender. Source effects can be damaging for an international business when potential consumers in a target country have a bias against foreign firms. For example, a wave of "Japan bashing" swept the United States in the early 1990s. Worried that U.S. consumers might view its products negatively, Honda responded by creating ads that emphasized the U.S. content of its cars to show how "American" the company had become.

Many international businesses try to counter negative source effects by deemphasizing their foreign origins. When the French antiglobalization protester José Bové was hailed as a hero by some in France for razing a partly built McDonald's in 1999, the French franchisees of McDonald's responded with an ad depicting a fat, ignorant American who could not understand why McDonald's France used locally produced food that wasn't genetically modified. The edgy ad worked, and McDonald's French operations are now among the most robust in the company's global network.[11]

Country of Origin Effects
A subset of source effects, the extent to which the place of manufacturing influences product evaluations.

A subset of source effects is referred to as **country of origin effects**, or the extent to which the place of manufacturing influences product evaluations. Research suggests that the consumer may use country of origin as a cue when evaluating a product, particularly if he or she lacks more detailed knowledge of the product. For example, one study found that Japanese consumers tended to rate Japanese products more favorably than U.S. products across multiple dimensions, even when independent analysis showed that they were actually inferior.[12] When a negative country of origin effect exists, an international business may have to work hard to counteract this effect by, for example, using promotional messages that stress the positive performance attributes of its product.

Source effects and country of origin effects are not always negative. French wine, Italian clothes, and German luxury cars benefit from nearly universal positive source effects. In such cases, it may pay a firm to emphasize its foreign origins.

Noise
The number of other messages competing for a potential consumer's attention.

Noise Levels

Noise tends to reduce the probability of effective communication. **Noise** refers to the number of other messages competing for a potential consumer's attention, and this too varies across countries. In highly developed countries such as the United States, noise is extremely high. Fewer firms vie for the attention of prospective customers in developing countries; thus, the noise level is lower.

PUSH VERSUS PULL STRATEGIES

Push Strategy
A marketing strategy emphasizing personal selling rather than mass media advertising.

Pull Strategy
A marketing strategy emphasizing mass media advertising as opposed to personal selling.

The main decision with regard to communications strategy is the choice between a push strategy and a pull strategy. A **push strategy** emphasizes personal selling rather than mass media advertising in the promotional mix. Although effective as a promotional tool, personal selling requires intensive use of a sales force and is relatively costly. A **pull strategy** depends more on mass media advertising to communicate the marketing message to potential consumers.

Although some firms employ only a pull strategy and others only a push strategy, still other firms combine direct selling with mass advertising to maximize communication effectiveness. Factors that determine the relative attractiveness of push and pull strategies include product type relative to consumer sophistication, channel length, and media availability.

Product Type and Consumer Sophistication

Firms in consumer goods industries that are trying to sell to a large segment of the market generally favor a pull strategy. Mass communication has cost advantages for such firms; thus, they rarely use direct selling. Exceptions can be found in poorer nations with low literacy levels, where direct selling may be the only way to reach consumers (see the Management Focus on Unilever). Firms that sell industrial products or other complex products favor a push strategy. Direct selling allows the firm to educate potential consumers about the features of the product. This may not be necessary in advanced nations where a complex product has been in use for some time, where the product's

management FOCUS

Unilever Among India's Poor

Unilever, one of the world's largest and oldest consumer products companies, has long had a substantial presence in many of the world's poorer nations, such as India. Outside major urban areas, low-income, unsophisticated consumers, illiteracy, fragmented retail distribution systems, and the lack of paved roads have made for difficult marketing challenges. Despite this, Unilever has built a significant presence among impoverished rural populations by adopting innovative selling strategies.

India's large rural population is dispersed among some 600,000 villages, more than 500,000 of which cannot be reached by a motor vehicle. Some 91 percent of the rural population lives in villages of fewer than 2,000 people, and of necessity, rural retail stores are very small and carry limited stock. The population is desperately poor, making perhaps a dollar a day, and two-thirds of that income is spent on food, leaving about 30 cents a day for other items. Literacy levels are low, and TVs are rare, making traditional media ineffective. Despite these drawbacks, Hindustan Lever, Unilever's Indian subsidiary, has made a concerted effort to reach the rural poor. Although the revenues generated from rural sales are small, Unilever hopes that as the country develops and income levels rise, the population will continue to purchase the Unilever brands that they are familiar with, giving the company a long-term competitive advantage.

To contact rural consumers, Hindustan Lever tries to establish a physical presence wherever people frequently gather in numbers. This means ensuring that advertisements are seen in places where people congregate and make purchases, such as at village wells and weekly rural markets, and where they consume products, such as at riverbanks where people gather to wash their clothes using (the company hopes) Unilever soap. It is not uncommon to see the village well plastered with advertisements for Unilever products. The company also takes part in weekly rural events, such as market day, at which farm produce is sold and family provisions purchased. Hindustan Lever salespeople will visit these gatherings, display their products, explain how they work, give away some free samples, make a few sales, and seed the market for future demand.

An ad for Lux soap sits in front of a vegetable seller in Mumbai, India.

Source: © Prashanth Vishwanathan/Bloomberg/Getty Images

The backbone of Hindustan Lever's selling effort, however, is a rural distribution network that encompasses 100 factories, 7,500 distributors, and an estimated 3 million retail stores, many of which are little more than a hole in a wall or a stall at a market. The total stock of Unilever products in these stores may be no more than a few sachets of shampoo and half a dozen bars of soap. A depot in each of India's states feeds products to major wholesalers, which then sell directly to retailers in thousands of small towns and villages that can be reached by motor vehicles. If access via motor vehicles is not possible, the major wholesalers sell to smaller second-tier wholesalers, which then handle distribution to India's 500,000 inaccessible rural villages, reaching them by bicycle, bullock cart, or baskets carried on a human back.

Sources: I. Kottasova, "Unilever Settles India Mercury Poisoning Claims," *CNN Money*, March 9, 2016; K. Merchant, "Striving for Success—One Sachet at a Time," *Financial Times*, December 11, 2000, p. 14; M. Turner, "Bicycle Brigade Takes Unilever to the People," *Financial Times*, August 17, 2000, p. 8; "Brands Thinking Positively," *Brand Strategy*, December 2003, pp. 28–29; "The Legacy That Got Left on the Shelf," *The Economist*, February 2, 2008, pp. 77–79.

attributes are well understood, where consumers are sophisticated, and where high-quality channels exist that can provide point-of-sale assistance. However, customer education may be important when consumers have less sophistication toward the product, which can be the case in developing nations or in advanced nations when a new complex product is being introduced, or where high-quality channels are absent or scarce.

Channel Length The longer the distribution channel, the more intermediaries there are that must be persuaded to carry the product for it to reach the consumer. This can lead to inertia in the channel, which can make entry difficult. Using direct selling to push a product through many layers of a distribution channel can be expensive. In such circumstances, a firm may try to pull its product through the channels by using mass advertising to create consumer demand; once demand is created, intermediaries will feel obliged to carry the product.

In Japan, products often pass through two, three, or even four wholesalers before they reach the final retail outlet. This can make it difficult for foreign firms to break into the

Japanese market. Not only must the foreign firm persuade a Japanese retailer to carry its product, but it may also have to persuade every intermediary in the chain to carry the product. Mass advertising may be one way to break down channel resistance in such circumstances. However, in countries such as India, which has a very long distribution channel to serve its massive rural population, mass advertising may not work because of low literacy levels, in which case the firm may need to fall back on direct selling or rely on the goodwill of distributors (see the Management Focus on Unilever).

Media Availability

A pull strategy relies on access to advertising media. In the United States, a large number of media are available, including print media (newspapers and magazines), broadcasting media (television and radio), and the Internet. The rise of cable television in the United States has facilitated extremely focused advertising (e.g., MTV for teens and young adults, Lifetime for women, ESPN for sports enthusiasts). The same is true of the Internet, with different websites attracting different kinds of users, and companies such as Google transforming the ability of companies to do targeted advertising. While this level of media sophistication is now found in many other developed countries, it is still not universal. Even many advanced nations have far fewer electronic media available for advertising than the United States. In Scandinavia, for example, no commercial television or radio stations existed until recently; all electronic media were state owned and carried no commercials, although this has now changed with the advent of satellite television deregulation. In many developing nations, the situation is even more restrictive because mass media of all types are typically more limited. A firm's ability to use a pull strategy is limited in some countries by media availability. In such circumstances, a push strategy is more attractive. For example, Unilever uses a push strategy to sell consumer products in rural India, where few mass media are available (see the Management Focus).

Media availability is limited by law in some cases. Few countries allow advertisements for tobacco and alcohol products on television and radio, though they are usually permitted in print media. When the leading Japanese whiskey distiller, Suntory, entered the U.S. market, it had to do so without television, its preferred medium. The firm spends about $50 million annually on television advertising in Japan. Similarly, while advertising pharmaceutical products directly to consumers is allowed in the United States, it is prohibited in many other advanced nations. In such cases, pharmaceutical firms must rely heavily on advertising and direct-sales efforts focused explicitly at doctors to get their products prescribed.

The Push-Pull Mix

The optimal mix between push and pull strategies depends on product type and consumer sophistication, channel length, and media sophistication. Push strategies tend to be emphasized:

- For industrial products or complex new products.
- When distribution channels are short.
- When few print or electronic media are available.

Pull strategies tend to be emphasized:

- For consumer goods.
- When distribution channels are long.
- When sufficient print and electronic media are available to carry the marketing message.

GLOBAL ADVERTISING

In recent years, largely inspired by the work of visionaries such as Theodore Levitt, there has been much discussion about the pros and cons of standardizing advertising worldwide.[13] One of the most successful standardized campaigns in history was Philip Morris' promotion of Marlboro cigarettes. The campaign was instituted in the 1950s, when the brand was repositioned, to assure smokers that the flavor would be unchanged by the addition of a filter. The campaign theme of "Come to where the flavor is: Come to Marlboro country" was a worldwide success. Marlboro built on this when it introduced "the Marlboro man," a rugged cowboy smoking his Marlboro while riding his horse through the great outdoors.

This ad proved successful in almost every major market around the world, and it helped propel Marlboro to the top of the world market.

For Standardized Advertising

The support for global advertising is threefold. First, it has significant economic advantages. Standardized advertising lowers the costs of value creation by spreading the fixed costs of developing the advertisements over many countries. For example, Coca-Cola's advertising agency, McCann Erickson, claims to have saved Coca-Cola more than $100 million over 20 years by using certain elements of its campaigns globally.

Second, there is the concern that creative talent is scarce, so one large effort to develop a campaign will produce better results than 40 or 50 smaller efforts. A third justification for a standardized approach is that many brand names are global. With the substantial amount of international travel today and the considerable overlap in media across national borders, many international firms want to project a single brand image to avoid confusion caused by local campaigns. This is particularly important in regions such as western Europe, where travel across borders is almost as common as travel across state lines in the United States.

Against Standardized Advertising

There are two main arguments against globally standardized advertising. First, as we have seen repeatedly in this chapter and in Chapter 4, cultural differences among nations are such that a message that works in one nation can fail miserably in another. Cultural diversity makes it extremely difficult to develop a single advertising theme that is effective worldwide. Messages directed at the culture of a given country may be more effective than global messages.

Second, advertising regulations may block implementation of standardized advertising. For example, Kellogg could not use a television commercial it produced in Great Britain to promote its cornflakes in many other European countries. A reference to the iron and vitamin content of its cornflakes was not permissible in the Netherlands, where claims relating to health and medical benefits are outlawed. A child wearing a Kellogg T-shirt had to be edited out of the commercial before it could be used in France because French law forbids the use of children in product endorsements. The key line "Kellogg's makes their cornflakes the best they have ever been" was disallowed in Germany because of a prohibition against competitive claims.[14]

Dealing with Country Differences

Some firms are experimenting with capturing some benefits of global standardization while recognizing differences in countries' cultural and legal environments. A firm may select some features to include in all its advertising campaigns and localize other features. By doing so, it may be able to save on some costs and build international brand recognition and yet customize its advertisements to different cultures.

Nokia, the Finnish cell phone manufacturer, has tried to do this. Historically, Nokia had used a different advertising campaign in different markets. In 2004, however, the company launched a global advertising campaign that used the slogan "1001 reasons to have a Nokia imaging phone." Nokia did this to reduce advertising costs, capture some economies of scale, and establish a consistent global brand image. At the same time, Nokia tweaked the advertisements for different cultures. The campaign used actors from the region where the ad ran to reflect the local population, though they said the same lines. Local settings were also modified when showcasing the phones by, for example, using a marketplace when advertising in Italy or a bazaar when advertising in the Middle East.[15] Another example of this process is given in the accompanying Management Focus, which looks at how Unilever built a global brand for its Dove products while still tweaking the message to consider local sensibilities.

Use SmartBook to help retain what you have learned. Access your Instructor's Connect course to check out SmartBook or go to learnsmartadvantage.com for help.

Pricing Strategy

Explain why and how a firm's pricing strategy might vary among countries.

International pricing strategy is an important component of the overall international marketing mix.[16] This section looks at three aspects of international pricing strategy. First, we examine the case for pursuing price discrimination, charging different prices for the same product in different countries. Second, we look at what might be called strategic pricing. Third, we review regulatory factors, such as government-mandated price controls and antidumping regulations that limit a firm's ability to charge the prices it would prefer in a country.

management FOCUS

Dove's Global "Real Beauty" Campaign

About a decade ago, Dove was not a beauty brand; it was a bar of soap that was positioned and sold differently in different markets. Unilever, the company that marketed Dove, was a storied consumer product multinational with global reach, had a strong position in fast-growing developing nations, and had a reputation for customizing products to conditions prevailing in local markets. In India, for example, women often oil their hair before washing it, so Western shampoos that do not remove the oil have not sold well. Unilever reformulated its shampoo for India and was rewarded with market leadership.

But sometimes Unilever went too far. It used different formulations for shampoo in Hong Kong and mainland China, for example, even though hair and washing habits were very similar in both markets. Unilever would also often vary the packaging and marketing message in similar products, even for its most commoditized products. The company tended to exaggerate complexity, and its financial performance was suffering.

A decade later, Unilever's financial performance has improved, in no small part because it has shifted toward a more global emphasis, and the Dove brand has led the way. The Dove story dates to 2003, when the global brand director, Silvia Lagnado, who was based in New York, decided to move the positioning of Dove from one based on the product to one of an entire beauty brand. The basic message: The brand should stand for the real beauty of all women. Dove's mission was to make women feel more beautiful every day by widening the stereotypical definition of beauty and inspiring them to take care of themselves.

But how was this mission to be executed? Following a series of workshops held around the globe that asked brand managers and advertising agency partners to find ways to communicate an inclusive definition of beauty, the Canadian brand manager asked 67 female photographers to submit work that best reflects real beauty. The photographs are stunning portraits not of models but of women from all walks of life who come in all shapes, sizes, and ages. It led to a coffee table book and traveling exhibition, called the Dove Photo Tour, which garnered a lot of positive press in Canada. Silvia Lagnado realized that the Canadians were on to something.

Around the same time, the German office of Unilever's advertising agency, Ogilvy and Mather Worldwide, came up with a concept for communicating "real beauty" based on photographs showing, instead of skinny models, ordinary women in their underwear. The original German advertisements quickly made their way to the United Kingdom, where a London newspaper article stated the campaign was not advertising; it was politics. Lagnado was not surprised by this. She had commissioned research that revealed only 2 percent of women worldwide considered themselves beautiful and that half thought their weight was too high.

In 2004, the "Dove Campaign for Real Beauty" was launched globally. This was a radical shift for Unilever and the Dove brand, which until then had left marketing in the hands of local brand managers. The Real Beauty campaign was tweaked to take local sensibilities into account. For example, it was deemed better not to show women touching each other in America, while in Latin America, tactile women do not shock anybody, so touching was seen as acceptable. Recently, the "Dove Campaign for Real Beauty" celebrated its 10th anniversary as an enormously successful global marketing campaign despite some even calling for "Dove to put its real beauty campaign to rest."

Instead, the "Dove Campaign for Real Beauty" has also been complemented by the launch of the Dove "self-esteem fund," a worldwide campaign to persuade girls and young women to embrace a more positive image of themselves. Unilever made an online video, uploaded to YouTube, called *Onslaught,* which was critical of the beauty industry and ended with the slogan, "Talk to your daughter before the beauty industry does." Another video, *Evolution,* showed how the face of a girl can be changed, partly through computer graphics, to create an image of beauty. The video ended with the tag line, "No wonder our perception of beauty is distorted." Made for very little money, the YouTube videos created a viral buzz around the campaign that helped transform Dove into one of Unilever's leading brands. By its use of such techniques, the campaign has become a model for how to revitalize and build a new global brand.

Sources: T. Garcia, "It's Time for Dove to Put Its Real Beauty Campaign to Rest," PR Newservice, April 15, 2015; "The Legacy That Got Left on the Shelf," *The Economist*, February 2, 2008, pp. 77–79; R, Rothenberg, "Dove Effort Gives Package-Goods Marketers Lessons for the Future," *Advertising Age*, March 5, 2007, p. 18; J. Neff, "A Real Beauty: Dove's Viral Makes Big Splash for No Cash," *Advertising Age*, 2006, volume 77, number 4, pp. 1–2; K. Mazurkewich, "Dove Story: You Know the Name, and Some of the Story," *Strategy*, January 2007, pp. 37–39.

PRICE DISCRIMINATION Price discrimination exists whenever consumers in different countries are charged different prices for the same product or for slightly different variations of the product.[17] Price discrimination involves charging whatever the market will bear; in a competitive market, prices may have to be lower than in a market where the firm has a monopoly. Price discrimination can help a company maximize its profits. It makes economic sense to charge different prices in different countries.

Two conditions are necessary for profitable price discrimination. First, the firm must be able to keep its national markets separate. If it cannot do this, individuals or businesses may undercut its attempt at price discrimination by engaging in arbitrage. Arbitrage occurs when an individual or business capitalizes on a price differential for a firm's product between two countries by purchasing the product in the country where prices are lower and reselling it in the country where prices are higher. For example, many automobile firms have long practiced price discrimination in Europe. A Ford Escort once cost $2,000 more in Germany than it did in Belgium. This policy broke down when car dealers bought Escorts in Belgium and drove them to Germany, where they sold them at a profit for slightly less than Ford was selling Escorts in Germany. To protect the market share of its German auto dealers, Ford had to bring its German prices into line with those being charged in Belgium. Ford could not keep these markets separate, unlike in Britain where the need for right-hand-drive cars keep the market separate from the rest of Europe.

The second necessary condition for profitable price discrimination is different price elasticities of demand in different countries. The **price elasticity of demand** is a measure of the responsiveness of demand for a product to change in price. Demand is said to be **elastic** when a small change in price produces a large change in demand; it is said to be **inelastic** when a large change in price produces only a small change in demand. Figure 16.2 illustrates elastic and inelastic demand curves. Generally, a firm can charge a higher price in a country where demand is inelastic.

The elasticity of demand for a product in a given country is determined by a number of factors, of which income level and competitive conditions are the two most important. Price elasticity tends to be greater in countries with low income levels. Consumers with limited incomes tend to be very price conscious; they have less to spend, so they look much more closely at price. Thus, price elasticity for products such as personal computers is greater in countries such as India, where a PC is still a luxury item, than in the United States, where it is now considered a necessity. The same is true of the software that resides on those PCs; thus, to sell more software in India, Microsoft has had to introduce low-priced versions of its products into that market, such as Windows Starter Edition.

In general, the more competitors there are, the greater consumers' bargaining power will be and the more likely consumers will be to buy from the firm that charges the lowest price. Thus, many competitors cause high elasticity of demand. In such circumstances, if a firm raises its prices above those of its competitors, consumers will switch to the competitors' products. The opposite is true when a firm faces few competitors. When competitors are limited, consumers'

Is iPhone the Next BlackBerry?

BlackBerry accounted for less than half a percentage point of sales in the United States in the last quarter of 2013, down from its dominating position as the market leader just a few years ago. The rise of Apple and Samsung in the mobile phone market has made BlackBerry nearly irrelevant. At the same time, Apple is in a fierce battle against Android and Windows-based phones. Apple's smartphone market share has steadily declined in the global marketplace. Apple has also traditionally maintained higher prices for the iPhone by leveraging its brand value and gaining maximum profits during the process. Analysts believe that Apple could gain by showing some price flexibility on the iPhone, especially for weaker economies. Another initiative that Apple could take is to come up with a cheaper iPhone with lower specifications than the current iPhones. Where will Apple's iPhone be by the year 2020? Will it still be a strong force in the mobile phone market, or will it be the next BlackBerry?

Sources: S. Rodriguez, "BlackBerry Accounts for Less Than 0.5% of Smartphone Sales," *Los Angeles Times*, January 31, 2014 (http://articles.latimes.com/2014/jan/31/business/la-fi-tn-blackberry-smartphone-sales-fourth-quarter-20140131); J. Pepitone, "New BlackBerry CEO Optimistic Despite Loss," *CNNMoney*, December 30, 2013; L. Whitney, "iPhone Market Share Shrinks as Android, Windows Phone Grow," *CNET*, January 6, 2014.

Price Elasticity of Demand
A measure of how responsive demand for a product is to changes in price.

Elastic
A small change in price produces a large change in demand.

Inelastic
When a large change in price produces only a small change in demand.

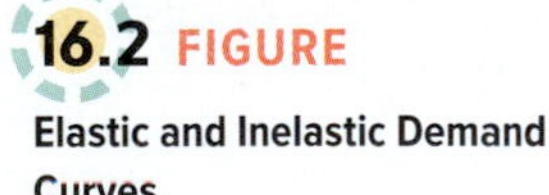

Elastic and Inelastic Demand Curves.

Source: C. W. L. Hill and G. T. M. Hult, *International Business: Competing in the Global Marketplace* (New York: McGraw-Hill Education, 2017).

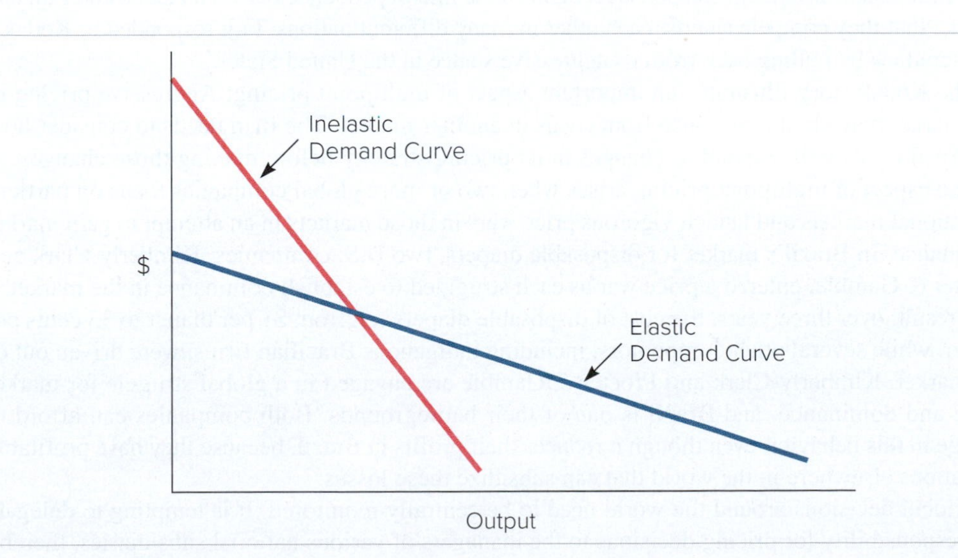

bargaining power is weaker, and price is less important as a competitive weapon. Thus, a firm may charge a higher price for its product in a country where competition is limited than in one where competition is intense.

Strategic Pricing

The concept containing the three aspects: predatory pricing, multipoint pricing, and experience curve pricing.

STRATEGIC PRICING

The concept of **strategic pricing** has three aspects, which we refer to as predatory pricing, multipoint pricing, and experience curve pricing. Both predatory pricing and experience curve pricing may violate antidumping regulations. After we review predatory and experience curve pricing, we will look at antidumping rules and other regulatory policies.

Predatory Pricing

Reducing prices below fair market value as a competitive weapon to drive weaker competitors out of the market ("fair" being cost plus some reasonable profit margin).

Predatory Pricing

Predatory pricing is the use of price as a competitive weapon to drive weaker competitors out of a national market. Once the competitors have left the market, the firm can raise prices and enjoy high profits. For such a pricing strategy to work, the firm must normally have a profitable position in another national market, which it can use to subsidize aggressive pricing in the market it is trying to monopolize. Historically, many Japanese firms were accused of pursuing such a policy. The argument ran like this: Because the Japanese market was protected from foreign competition by high informal trade barriers, Japanese firms could charge high prices and earn high profits at home. They then used these profits to subsidize aggressive pricing overseas, with the goal of driving competitors out of those markets. Once this had occurred, so it is claimed, the Japanese firms then raised prices. Matsushita was accused of using this strategy to enter the U.S. TV market. As one of the major TV producers in Japan, Matsushita earned high profits at home. It then used these profits to subsidize the losses it made in the United States during its early years there, when it priced low to increase its market penetration. Ultimately, Matsushita became the world's largest manufacturer of TVs.[18]

Multipoint Pricing Strategy

Multipoint pricing becomes an issue when two or more international businesses compete against each other in two or more national markets. Multipoint pricing was an issue for Kodak and Fujifilm because the companies long competed against each other around the world in the market for silver halide film.[19] **Multipoint pricing** refers to the fact that a firm's pricing strategy in one market may have an impact on its rivals' pricing strategy in another market. Aggressive pricing in one market may elicit a competitive response from a rival in another market. For example, Fuji launched an aggressive competitive attack against Kodak in the U.S. company's home market in January 1997, cutting prices on multiple-roll packs of 35-mm film by as much as 50 percent.[20] This price cutting resulted in a 28 percent increase in shipments of Fuji color film during the first six months of 1997, while Kodak's shipments dropped by 11 percent. This attack created a dilemma for Kodak: the company did not want to start price discounting in its largest and most profitable market. Kodak's response was to aggressively cut prices in Fuji's largest market, Japan. This strategic response recognized the interdependence between Kodak and Fuji and the fact that they compete against each other in many different nations. Fuji responded to Kodak's counterattack by pulling back from its aggressive stance in the United States.

Multipoint Pricing

Occurs when a pricing strategy in one market may have an impact on a rival's pricing strategy in another market.

The Kodak story illustrates an important aspect of multipoint pricing: Aggressive pricing in one market may elicit a response from rivals in another market. The firm needs to consider how its global rivals will respond to changes in its pricing strategy before making those changes. A second aspect of multipoint pricing arises when two or more global companies focus on particular national markets and launch vigorous price wars in those markets in an attempt to gain market dominance. In Brazil's market for disposable diapers, two U.S. companies, Kimberly-Clark and Procter & Gamble, entered a price war as each struggled to establish dominance in the market.[21] As a result, over three years, the cost of disposable diapers fell from $1 per diaper to 33 cents per diaper, while several other competitors, including indigenous Brazilian firms, were driven out of the market. Kimberly-Clark and Procter & Gamble are engaged in a global struggle for market share and dominance, and Brazil is one of their battlegrounds. Both companies can afford to engage in this behavior, even though it reduces their profits in Brazil, because they have profitable operations elsewhere in the world that can subsidize these losses.

Pricing decisions around the world need to be centrally monitored. It is tempting to delegate full responsibility for pricing decisions to the managers of various national subsidiaries, thereby reaping the benefits of decentralization. However, because pricing strategy in one part of the world can elicit a competitive response in another, central management needs to at least monitor and approve pricing decisions in a given national market, and local managers need to recognize that their actions can affect competitive conditions in other countries.

Experience Curve Pricing

We first encountered the experience curve in Chapter 12. As a firm builds its accumulated production volume over time, unit costs fall due to experience effects. Learning effects and economies of scale underlie the experience curve. Price comes into the picture because aggressive pricing (along with aggressive promotion and advertising) can build accumulated sales volume rapidly and thus move production down the experience curve. Firms farther down the experience curve have a cost advantage vis-à-vis those farther up the curve.

Many firms pursuing an **experience curve pricing** strategy on an international scale will price low worldwide in attempting to build global sales volume as rapidly as possible, even if this means taking large losses initially. Such a firm believes that in several years, when it has moved down the experience curve, it will be making substantial profits and have a cost advantage over its less aggressive competitors.

Experience Curve Pricing
Aggressive pricing designed to increase volume and help the firm realize experience curve economies.

REGULATORY INFLUENCES ON PRICES

The ability to engage in either price discrimination or strategic pricing may be limited by national or international regulations. Most important, a firm's freedom to set its own prices is constrained by antidumping regulations and competition policy.

Antidumping Regulations

Both predatory pricing and experience curve pricing can run afoul of antidumping regulations. Dumping occurs whenever a firm sells a product for a price that is less than the cost of producing it. Most regulations, however, define dumping more vaguely. For example, a country is allowed to bring antidumping actions against an importer under Article 6 of GATT as long as two criteria are met: sales at "less than fair value" and "material injury to a domestic industry." The problem with this terminology is that it does not indicate what a fair value is. The ambiguity has led some to argue that selling abroad at prices below those in the country of origin, as opposed to below cost, is dumping.

Such logic led the Bush administration to place a 20 percent duty on imports of foreign steel in 2001. Foreign manufacturers protested that they were not selling below cost. Admitting that their prices were lower in the United States than some other countries, they argued that this simply reflected the intensely competitive nature of the U.S. market (i.e., different price elasticities).

Antidumping rules set a floor under export prices and limit firms' ability to pursue strategic pricing. The rather vague terminology used in most antidumping actions suggests that a firm's ability to engage in price discrimination also may be challenged under antidumping legislation.

Competition Policy

Most developed nations have regulations designed to promote competition and to restrict monopoly practices. These regulations can be used to limit the prices a firm can charge in a given country. For example, at one time the Swiss pharmaceutical manufacturer Hoffmann–La Roche had a monopoly on the supply of Valium and Librium tranquilizers. The company was investigated by the British Monopolies and Mergers Commission, which is responsible for promoting fair competition in Great Britain. The commission found that Hoffmann–La Roche was overcharging for its tranquilizers and ordered the company to reduce its prices 50 to 60 percent and repay excess profit of $30 million. Hoffmann–La Roche maintained unsuccessfully that it was merely engaging in price discrimination. Similar actions were later brought against Hoffmann–La Roche by the German cartel office and by the Dutch and Danish governments.[22]

Use SmartBook to help retain what you have learned. Access your Instructor's Connect course to check out SmartBook or go to learnsmartadvantage.com for help.

Configuring the Marketing Mix

Understand how to configure the marketing mix globally.

A firm might vary aspects of its marketing mix from country to country to take into account local differences in culture, economic conditions, competitive conditions, product and technical standards, distribution systems, government regulations, and the like. Such differences may require variation in product attributes, distribution strategy, communication strategy, and pricing strategy.

Did You Know?

Did you know "Pure Michigan" is a global brand?

Visit your Connect SmartBook® to view a short video explanation from the authors.

The cumulative effect of these factors made it rare that a firm would adopt the same marketing mix worldwide just a few years ago, and it holds true in many cases still. But we are also seeing a new generation of customers—younger customers—worldwide who appear more and more willing to engage in a "global" way in what they want, need, and use in their daily lives. The global branding of Marvel's movies (see the accompanying Management Focus) is one illustration where a global approach to marketing has worked beneficially vis-à-vis competition from Warner Bros. films (e.g., *Batman, Man of Steel*).

Beyond the movie industry, the financial services industry is often thought of as one in which global standardization of the marketing mix is the norm. A financial services company such as American Express sells the same basic charge card service worldwide, utilizes the same basic fee structure for that product, and adopts the same basic global advertising message ("Don't leave home without it"). That said, Amex also runs into differences in national regulations, which means that it still has to vary aspects of its communication strategy from country to country.

management FOCUS

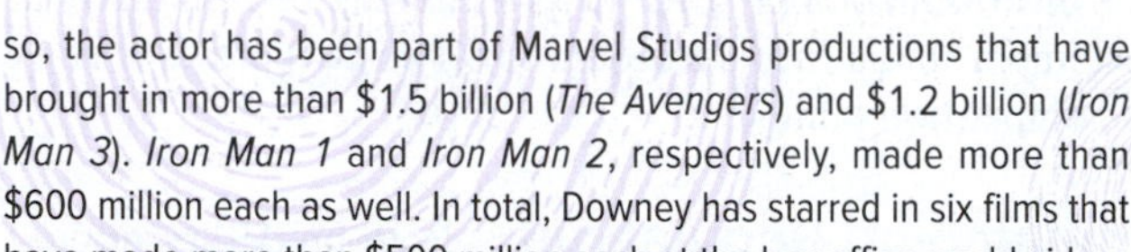

Global Branding of Marvel' s Movies

In a global brand move, the post-credits to the original *Iron Man* movie had SHIELD director Nick Fury visit Tony Stark's home. Fury told Stark that Iron Man is not "the only superhero in the world" and that he wanted to discuss the "Avenger's Initiative."

The Avengers and *Iron Man* movie franchises have made billions of dollars for Marvel Studios, a television and motion picture studio that is a wholly owned subsidiary of the Walt Disney Company. They have also contributed heavily to making Robert Downey, Jr., one of the highest paid actors in Hollywood. Downey was born in 1965 in the United States. He made his movie debut at the age of five when he appeared in his father's movie titled *Pound*. The "up-and-down-and-up" career of Downey is also a fascinating global brand story. He is riding high with three incredible multisequel franchises—*Iron Man*, *The Avengers*, and *Sherlock Holmes*. But the focus here is on *The Avengers* and *Iron Man*.

Iron Man premiered April 30, 2008, in international markets and a few days later in the United States. Amazingly, the movie had been in development since 1990 at Universal Pictures, 20th Century Fox, and New Line Cinema. Marvel Studios reacquired the rights to the movie in 2006. The basic plot has playboy, philanthropist, and genius Tony Stark (played by Downey) as the "superhero." Iron Man is a fictional character that first appeared in the Marvel Comics *Tales of Suspense* in 1963. The character itself was created by Stan Lee. *Iron Man 2* was released in 2010, and *Iron Man 3* was released in 2013, with plans for additional sequels after more *Avengers* movies.

The Avengers premiered on April 11, 2012, at the El Capitan Theatre in Hollywood. The film was developed beginning in 2005, is based on the Marvel Comics superhero team with the same name, and was written and directed by Joss Whedon. *The Avengers* is a superhero team with familiar heroes such as Iron Man, Captain America, Hulk, Thor, Black Widow, Hawkeye, and so on. No one really plays *the* superhero, although Scarlett Johansson's role as Black Widow was important to the movie franchise; it set the release date back from 2011 to 2012 to accommodate her inclusion. The second installment of the *Avengers* franchise came out on May 1, 2015, in the United States (*The Avengers: Age of Ultron*).

While the movie character Iron Man is heavily connected to Downey, he also plays an integral part of Tony Stark in *The Avengers*. In doing so, the actor has been part of Marvel Studios productions that have brought in more than $1.5 billion (*The Avengers*) and $1.2 billion (*Iron Man 3*). *Iron Man 1* and *Iron Man 2*, respectively, made more than $600 million each as well. In total, Downey has starred in six films that have made more than $500 million each at the box office worldwide.

Clearly, the connection between Tony Stark as Iron Man in the *Iron Man* franchise and in the *Avengers* franchise is perhaps not needed for the movie plot in *The Avengers* or its sequel. Marvel Comics has drawn from more than 100 characters for its Avengers superheroes since 1963, but Iron Man was one of the original ones (along with Ant-Man, the Wasp, Thor, and the Hulk). The global branding success of Tony Stark as played by Downey across these two brands is also very advantageous for Marvel Studios' global branding.

Marvel Studios was originally known as Marvel Films from 1963 to 1996. Given that Marvel Studios is part of the Walt Disney empire, it operates jointly with Walt Disney Studios on distribution and marketing of Iron Man and Avengers movies. Other high-profile projects of Marvel Studios have included the X-Men, Spider-Man, and Captain America franchises, with more to come. Anything embedded in the global branding of the Walt Disney Company has tremendous potential, reach, and longevity.

Walter Elias "Walt" Disney was an American business mogul as well as animator, cartoonist, director, philanthropist, producer, screenwriter, and voice actor who lived from 1901 to 1966. An international icon, he started Disney Brothers Cartoon Studio with his brother, Roy O. Disney, in 1923. The current name of the Walt Disney Company has been around since 1986. Disney has one of the largest and most well-known studios in the world. It also operates numerous related businesses, such as the ABC broadcast TV network, cable TV networks (e.g., Disney Channel, ESPN), publishing, merchandising, theater divisions, theme parks (e.g., Disney World, Disneyland), and much more. Mickey Mouse is the primary symbol of the Walt Disney Company and one of the most globally recognized brands ever!

Sources: K. Buchanan and J. Wolk, "How Vulture Ranked Its 2013 Most Valuable Stars List," *Vulture.com*, October 22, 2013; T. Culpan, "HTC Said to Hire Robert Downey Jr. for $12 Million Ad Campaign," *Bloomberg Businessweek*, June 20, 2013; C. Isidore, "Avengers Set to Rescue Disney and Hollywood," *CNNMoney*, May 7, 2012; "Iron Man 3: Clank Clank Bang Bang," *The Wall Street Journal*, May 2, 2013 (http://www.wsj.com/articles/SB10001424127887324266904578458760734514122); http://marvel.com/universe/Iron_Man; http://marvel.com/universe/Avengers.

Similarly, while McDonald's is often thought of as the quintessential example of a firm that sells the same basic standardized product worldwide, in reality it varies one important aspect of its marketing mix—its menu—from country to country. McDonald's also varies its distribution strategy. In Canada and the United States, most McDonald's are located in areas that are easily accessible by car, whereas in more densely populated and less automobile-reliant societies of the world, such as Japan and Great Britain, location decisions are driven by the accessibility of a restaurant to pedestrian traffic. Because countries typically still differ along one or more of the dimensions discussed earlier, some customization of the marketing mix is normal.

Basically, there are significant opportunities for standardization along one or more elements of the marketing mix.[23] Firms may find that it is possible and desirable to standardize their global advertising message or core product attributes to realize substantial cost economies. They may find it desirable to customize their distribution and pricing strategy to take advantage of local differences. In reality, the "customization versus standardization" debate is not an all-or-nothing issue; it frequently makes sense to standardize some aspects of the marketing mix and customize others, depending on conditions in various national marketplaces.

Table 16.1 illustrates issues that should be evaluated to assess how standardized or customized the marketing mix needs to be for various international market segments. Keep in mind that a truly "globalized" product—a product that is 100 percent standardized across worldwide markets—is generally an illusion, but companies can come close by leveraging certain marketing mix attributes and customizing others.

Use SmartBook to help retain what you have learned. Access your Instructor's Connect course to check out SmartBook or go to learnsmartadvantage.com for help.

International Market Research

Understand the importance of international market research.

International Market Research

The systematic collection, recording, analysis, and interpretation of data to provide knowledge that is useful for decision making in a global company.

To effectively configure the marketing mix and answer questions such as those in Table 16.1, global companies conduct international marketing research. **International market research** is defined as the systematic collection, recording, analysis, and interpretation of data to provide knowledge that is useful for decision making in a global company. Compared with market research that is domestic only, international market research involves additional issues such as (1) translation of questionnaires and reports into appropriate foreign languages and (2) accounting for cultural and environmental differences in data collection. In this section, some of the more prominent international market research companies are highlighted; the basic steps and issues in conducting international market research are then discussed.

International market research is one of the most critical aspects of understanding the global marketplace. Given this importance, global companies often have their own in-house marketing research department to continually assess customers' needs, wants, and purchasing behavior. In addition, global companies also typically undertake ongoing data collection to assess customers' satisfaction with products and services offered. J.D. Power (www.jdpower.com) and the CFI Group (www.cfigroup.com) are two of the most prominent customer-satisfaction measurement companies. In addition, for large-scale projects such as better understanding a new country market, global companies often work with outside marketing research firms for input. A sample of prominent international market research firms includes Nielsen, Kantar, Ipsos, and the NPD Group.

- Nielsen (www.nielsen.com) is an international market research company with headquarters in New York in the United States and Diemen in the Netherlands. The company was founded in 1923, is active in more than 100 countries, employs about 40,000 people, and has revenue of about $6 billion annually. Nielsen says on its website that "Whether you're eyeing markets in the next town or across continents, we understand the importance of knowing what consumers watch and buy."*
- Kantar (www.kantar.com) is an international market research company based in London. The company was founded in 1993 as the market research, insight, and consultancy division of WPP (an advertising and public relations firm). It operates in more than 100 countries, employs some 28,000 people, and has revenues of about $4 billion annually. As a conglomerate of research companies, Kantar works with more than half of the Fortune 500 companies (a *kantar* is a measure for cotton that is still used in the ports of Egypt today).

*The Nielsen Company. http://www.nielsen.com.

16.1 TABLE

Questions to Address to Configure the Marketing Mix

Mix Element	Sample Questionsto Address
Product Strategy	
Product core	Do the customers have similar product needs across international market segments?
Product adoption	How is the product bought by customers in the international market segments targeted?
Product management	How are established products versus new products managed for customers in the international market segments?
Product branding	What is the perception of the product brand by customers in the international market segments?
Distribution Strategy	
Distribution channels	Where is the product typically bought by customers in the international market segments?
Wholesale distribution	What is the role of wholesalers for the international market segments targeted?
Retail distribution	What is the availability of different types of retail stores in the international markets for the customer segments targeted?
Communication Strategy	
Advertising	How is product awareness created for a product to reach customers in the international market segments targeted?
Publicity	What role does publicity (e.g., public relations) play among customers in the international market segments targeted?
Mass media	What role do various media (e.g., TV, radio, newspapers, magazines, billboards) have in reaching customers in the international market segments targeted?
Social media	What role do various social media (e.g., Facebook, Twitter, blogs, virtual communities), mainly focused on user-generated content, have in communicating with customers in the international market segments targeted?
Sales promotion	Are rebates, coupons, and other sale offers a widespread activity to motivate customers in the international market segments targeted to buy a company's products?
Pricing Strategy	
Value	Is the price of a product critical to the customer's understanding (or perception) of the value of the product itself among customers in the international market segments?
Demand	Is the demand for the product among customers in the international market segments targeted similar to domestic demands?
Costs	Are the fixed and variable costs of the product the same when targeting customers in the international market segments (e.g., are there variable costs that change significantly when going international)?
Retail price	Are there trade tariffs, nontariff barriers, and/or other regulatory influences on price that will influence the pricing equation used to determine the retail price to customers in the international market segments?

- Ipsos (www.ipsos.com) is an international market research company based in Paris, France. The company was founded in 1975, has offices in some 90 countries, employs about 15,000 people, and has revenue of about $2 billion annually. Ipsos is now the only major international market research firm that is controlled and operated by market researchers; it focuses on a mantra of BQC ("better, quicker, cheaper") as a way to be competitive in the global marketplace.
- NPD Group (www.npd.com), formerly known as National Purchase Diary, is an international market research firm based in Port Washington, New York. The company was founded in 1967, has 25 worldwide offices, employs about 5,000 people, and is a privately held company (estimated to have revenues of about $500 million annually). NPD Group is known for its retail tracking services and market size and trends analysis. Today, it tracks businesses that represent more than $1 trillion in sales worldwide.

Nielsen, Kantar, Ipsos, and the NPD Group, along with many other market research firms, follow a similar process when conducting international market research. The basic data that companies want collected in international market research include (1) data on the country and potential market segments (geography, demography, sociocultural factors, and psychological factors); (2) data to forecast customer demands within specific country or world region (social, economic, consumer, and industry trends); and (3) data to make marketing mix decisions (product, distribution, communication, and price). The data collection needed to address these three areas always entails give-and-take in terms of time, cost, and available data collection techniques. The process, however, is somewhat universal across both domestic and international settings and includes (1) defining the research objectives, (2) determining the data sources, (3) assessing the costs and benefits of the research, (4) collecting the data, (5) analyzing and interpreting the research, and (6) reporting the research findings.[24] Each step is discussed in more detail in the following paragraphs (see Figure 16.3).

Defining the research objectives includes both (1) defining the research problem and (2) setting objectives for the international market research. At the outset of any international market research project, one of the problem areas is to have a baseline understanding of a country market or target segment that is sufficient enough to properly capture what should be done and what can be accomplished with the research. Oftentimes, the research starts with a relatively vague idea of the research problem and the objectives, subsequently refined when a better understanding of country markets and potential customer segments has been reached and more data have been collected.[25] One of the most critical aspects of the early stages of international market research is a willingness to refine the research problem and objectives throughout the process; not doing so may lead to unwanted conclusions. For example, not understanding the scope of the research problem (i.e., children turning to more electronic devices and video games) and accompanying objectives led Mattel Inc., the world's largest toy maker by sales, to suffer dismal holiday season sales in 2013. While the NPD Group reported that U.S. toy sales dropped just 1 percent in the last quarter of 2013, Mattel's CEO, Bryan G. Stockton, concluded that "our product innovations and our marketing programs were not strong enough."[26]

Determining the data sources that will address specific research problems and ultimately achieve the objectives is often not an easy task, especially if the international market research spans more than one country market. In market research, we talk about two forms of data that can be used: primary and secondary data.[27] Primary data refers to data collected by the global company and/or its recruited international market research agency for the purpose of addressing the research problem and objectives defined by the company. Given the costs of collecting international data, most companies try to avoid duplicating similar data that have been collected previously. However, for more than half of the world's countries, so-called secondary data that can be helpful can be tough to come by, are often unreliable, and typically do not address what global companies require to better understand the needs, wants, and purchasing

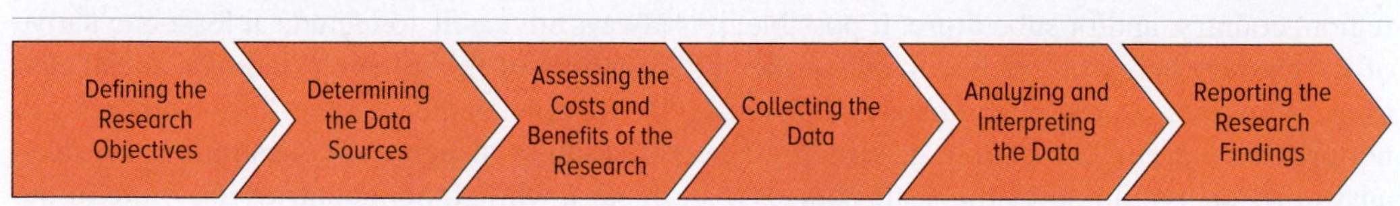

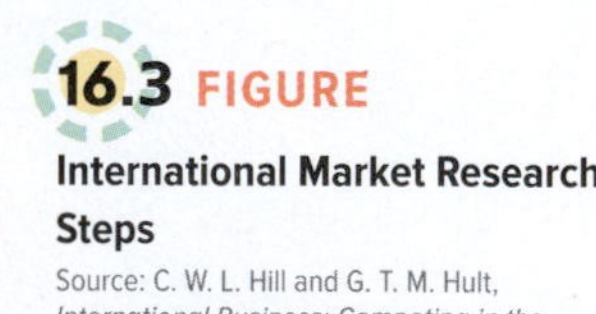

16.3 FIGURE

International Market Research Steps

Source: C. W. L. Hill and G. T. M. Hult, *International Business: Competing in the Global Marketplace* (New York: McGraw-Hill Education, 2017).

behaviors of targeted customers. Secondary data refers to data that have been collected previously by organizations, people, or agencies for purposes other than specifically addressing the research problem and objectives at hand. Overall, the data used in international market research should be evaluated based on (1) availability, (2) comparability across countries and potential market segments, (3) reliability (whether the research produces consistent results), and (4) validity (whether the research measures what it set out to measure). globalEDGE.msu.edu is a great starting point for secondary data on countries and industries, among many data categories, and the research firms mentioned earlier (i.e., Nielsen, Kantar, Ipsos, and the NPD Group) are great organizations used by many global companies for primary data collection worldwide.

Assessing the costs and benefits of the research often relates to the cost of collecting primary data that can address the research problem and objectives directly versus using available secondary data. If secondary data are available, such data are typically available as a less costly alternative to collecting primary data. The costs that drive up the spending in primary data collections broadly include survey development and sampling frame issues. For the survey, the questions have to be developed so that they clearly communicate the attitudes, attributes, or characteristics about a product or customer issue in such a way that the respondent recognizes the value. This also means overcoming any barriers or differences in language, answer choices, and cultural values and beliefs. For example, the most common way of converting a survey question into another language is to have the question translated into the foreign language (e.g., from English to Spanish) and then back-translated into English again by another person. The two English versions are then compared to ensure similarity in the back-translated version with the original. For the sampling frame, one of the core issues internationally is to make sure that comparable samples can be drawn in the countries in which international market research is conducted. This includes identifying reliable lists or groups of potential people to survey and cultivating potential people to respond to the survey.[28]

Collecting the data simply refers to gathering data via primary or secondary methods that address the research problem and objectives that the global company has established. The two mechanisms to collect data are quantitative and qualitative data collection. Quantitative methods include experiments, clinical trials, observing and recording events, and administering surveys with closed-end questions. The goal of quantitative methods is to systematically gain an understanding of customers' needs, wants, and purchase behavior via numerical data and computational techniques. A popular way of collecting quantitative data today is to use online surveys and consumer mail panels. Most large international market research firms have access to global customer mail panels and potential sampling frames that target both business-to-business customers and end-customers. Qualitative methods include in-depth interviews, observation methods, and document reviews. Here, the focus is broad-based questions aimed at gaining a depth understanding of customers' needs, wants, and purchase behaviors.

Analyzing and interpreting the research begins when the data have been collected. Assuming the survey is reliable and valid, whether the data come from primary or secondary data collection methods, analyzing and interpreting the data is an important step in the international market research process. It takes a fairly high degree of knowledge—both statistically and culturally—to analyze and interpret international market research. First, statistically the goal should be to use the technique that best addresses the research problem—often stated in the form of research questions or hypothesis (a specified relationship between study variables). There is a plethora of quantitative and qualitative methods of analyzing data, often taught in sophisticated marketing research programs around the world.[29] In these programs, software such as SAS, SPSS, LISREL, and Smart-PLS are used for quantitative analysis, and ATLAS.ti and MAXQDA are used for qualitative methods. Second, the researcher interpreting the findings must be in tune culturally with the values, beliefs, norms, and artifacts that affect a respondent's answers in a certain world region, country, and/or subculture. If possible, it is always advisable to include at least one native of the country being researched to add to the understanding of the research findings, social customs, semantics, attitudes, and business customs. For example, some societies have a tendency to not provide extreme answers (e.g., strongly agree or strongly disagree) to questions but instead answer by using middle-of-the-scale choices (e.g., Japan), while other countries use more of the extreme answer choices (e.g., the United States).

Reporting the research findings is a way to communicate the overall results of the international market research project. Such reports often include information about customers, competitors, countries, the industry, and the environment that affect how the global company develops an appropriate marketing mix for the targeted international market segment. Ultimately, the focus will be on how best to reach customers by addressing their needs, wants, and purchasing behavior in a way that is competitive vis-à-vis existing competitors and potential new entrants into the market. Ideally, top executives who receive the report should have been part of the formulation of the research problem and objectives earlier on in the international market research process. Preferably, they should also take part in some of the fieldwork to collect the data to better understand the voices of customers. If critical employee levels of the global company—from front-line service employees to market researchers to top executives—are insiders of the culture in which the customers are targeted, a lot of misunderstanding and faulty market research can be prevented. The worst-case scenario would be if customers misunderstand the questions and managers misunderstand the answers! One such example was the case of the Toyota accelerator debacle in 2010; Toyota had issues with accelerator pedals that could get stuck, causing vehicles to speed unintentionally.[30] Toyota was slow to correct the problems with the accelerator due to a disconnect between identifying the problem (i.e., it did not know why the accelerator pedals got stuck), analyzing the damage, and reporting it to senior management for rectification. Culturally, Japan prides itself on quality products, which means that disclosing poor quality, assuming responsibility, communicating with senior management, and fixing the problem are very difficult tasks within a Japanese firm.

Use SmartBook to help retain what you have learned. Access your Instructor's Connect course to check out SmartBook or go to learnsmartadvantage.com for help.

Product Development

Describe how globalization is affecting product development.

So far in this chapter, we have discussed several issues related to globalization of markets and brands, characteristics of the marketing mix (product attributes, distribution strategy, communication strategy, and pricing strategy), configuring the marketing mix, and international market research. These issues represent the core of this chapter's discussion of international marketing and R&D. However, firms that successfully develop and market new products can earn enormous returns, and this final section of the chapter addresses the interplay among international marketing, R&D, and manufacturing. Examples of firms that have been very successful at mastering the interplay among international marketing, R&D, and manufacturing include DuPont, which has produced a steady stream of successful innovations such as cellophane, nylon, Freon, and Teflon (nonstick coating); Sony, whose successes include the Walkman, the compact disc, the PlayStation, and the Blu-ray high-definition DVD player; Pfizer, the drug company that during the 1990s produced several major new drugs, including Viagra; 3M, which has applied its core competency in tapes and adhesives to developing a wide range of new products; Intel, which has consistently managed to lead in the development of innovative microprocessors to run personal computers; and Apple, with its string of hits, including the iPod, iPhone, and iPad. These and other success stories warrant a specific focus. As such, we draw on the material up to this point in the chapter and combine it with the global production material in Chapter 15 to illustrate this interplay of marketing, R&D, and manufacturing.

In today's world, competition is as much about technological innovation as anything else. The pace of technological change has accelerated since the Industrial Revolution in the eighteenth century, and it continues to do so today. The result has been a dramatic shortening of product life cycles. Technological innovation is both creative and destructive.[31] An innovation can make established products obsolete overnight. But an innovation can also make a host of new products possible. Witness changes in the electronics industry. For 40 years before the early 1950s, vacuum tubes were a major component in radios and then in record players and early computers. The advent of transistors destroyed the market for vacuum tubes, but at the same time, it created new opportunities connected with transistors. Transistors took up far less space than vacuum tubes, creating a trend toward miniaturization that continues today. The transistor held its position as the major component in the electronics industry for just a decade. Microprocessors were developed in the 1970s, and the market for transistors declined rapidly. The microprocessor created yet another set of new-product opportunities: handheld calculators (which destroyed the market for slide rules), compact disc players (which destroyed the market for analog record players), personal computers (which destroyed the market for typewriters), and mobile phones (which are making landline phones obsolete).

This "creative destruction" unleashed by technological change makes it critical that a firm stay on the leading edge of technology, lest it lose out to a competitor's innovations. As explained next, this not only creates a need for the firm to invest in R&D but also requires the firm to establish R&D activities at those locations where expertise is concentrated. As we shall see, leading-edge technology on its own is not enough to guarantee a firm's survival. The firm must also apply that technology to developing products that satisfy consumer needs, and it must design the product so that it can be manufactured in a cost-effective manner. To do that, the firm needs to build close links among R&D, marketing, and manufacturing. This is difficult enough for the domestic firm, but it is even more problematic for the international business competing in an industry where consumer tastes and preferences differ from country to country.[32] With all of this in mind, we move on to examine locating R&D activities and building links among R&D, marketing, and manufacturing.

THE LOCATION OF R&D

Ideas for new products are stimulated by the interactions of scientific research, demand conditions, and competitive conditions. Other things being equal, the rate of new-product development seems to be greater in countries where:

- More money is spent on basic and applied research and development.
- Underlying demand is strong.
- Consumers are affluent.
- Competition is intense.[33]

Basic and applied research and development discovers new technologies and then commercializes them. Strong demand and affluent consumers create a potential market for new products. Intense competition among firms stimulates innovation as the firms try to beat their competitors and reap potentially enormous first-mover advantages that result from successful innovation.

For most of the post–World War II period, the country that ranked highest on these criteria was the United States. The United States devoted a greater proportion of its gross domestic product to R&D than any other country did. Its scientific establishment was the largest and most active in the world. U.S. consumers were the most affluent, the market was large, and competition among U.S. firms was brisk. Due to these factors, the United States was the market where most new products were developed and introduced. Accordingly, it was the best location for R&D activities; it was where the action was.

Over the past 25 years, things have been changing quickly. The U.S. monopoly on new-product development has weakened considerably. Although U.S. firms are still at the leading edge of many new technologies, Asian and European firms are also strong players. Companies such as Sony, Sharp, Samsung, Ericsson, Nokia, and Philips have often driven product innovation in their respective industries. In addition, Japan, the European Union, and increasingly parts of China and other developing nations are large, affluent markets, and the wealth gap between them and the United States is closing.

As a result, it is often no longer appropriate to consider the United States as the lead market. In video games, for example, Japan is often the lead market, with companies such as Sony and Nintendo introducing their latest video-game players in Japan some six months before they introduce them in the United States. However, it often is questionable whether any developed nation can be considered the lead market. To succeed in today's high-technology industries, it is often necessary to simultaneously introduce new products in all major industrialized markets. When Intel introduces a new microprocessor, for example, it does not first introduce it in the United States and then roll it out in Europe a year later. It introduces it simultaneously around the world. The same is true of Microsoft with new versions of its Windows operating systems or Samsung with a new smartphone.

Because leading-edge research is now carried out in many locations around the world, the argument for centralizing R&D activity in the United States is not as strong as it was three decades ago. (It used to be argued that centralized R&D eliminated duplication.) Much leading-edge research is now occurring in Asia and Europe. Dispersing R&D activities to those locations allows a firm to stay close to the center of leading-edge activity to gather scientific and competitive information and to draw on local scientific resources.[34] This may result in some duplication of R&D activities, but the cost disadvantages of duplication are outweighed by the advantages of dispersion.

For example, to expose themselves to the research and new-product development work being done in Japan, many U.S. firms have set up satellite R&D centers in Japan. U.S. firms that have established R&D facilities in Japan include Corning, Texas Instruments, IBM, Procter & Gamble, Pfizer, DuPont, Monsanto, and Microsoft.[35] The National Science Foundation (NSF) has documented a sharp increase in the proportion of total R&D spending by U.S. firms that is now done abroad.[36] For example, Bristol-Myers Squibb has 12 facilities in five countries. At the same time, to internationalize their own research and gain access to U.S. talent, many European and Asian firms are investing in U.S.-based research facilities, according to the NSF.

INTEGRATING R&D, MARKETING, AND PRODUCTION Although a firm that is successful at developing new products may earn enormous returns, new-product development has a high failure rate. One study of product development in 16 companies in the chemical, drug, petroleum, and electronics industries suggested that only about 20 percent of R&D projects result in commercially successful products or processes.[37] Another in-depth case study of product development in three companies (one in chemicals and two in drugs) reported that about 60 percent of R&D projects reached technical completion, 30 percent were commercialized, and only 12 percent earned an economic profit that exceeded the company's cost of capital.[38] Along the same lines, another study concluded that one in nine major R&D projects, or about 11 percent, produced commercially successful products.[39] In sum, the evidence suggests that only 10 to 20 percent of major R&D projects give rise to commercially successful products. Well-publicized product failures include Apple Computer's Newton personal digital assistant, Sony's Betamax format in the video player and recorder market, and Sega's Dreamcast videogame console.

The reasons for such high failure rates are various and include development of a technology for which demand is limited, failure to adequately commercialize promising technology, and inability to manufacture a new product cost effectively. Firms can reduce the probability of making such mistakes by insisting on tight cross-functional coordination and integration among three core functions involved in the development of new products: R&D, marketing, and production.[40] Tight cross-functional integration among R&D, production, and marketing can help a company ensure that:

1. Product development projects are driven by customer needs.
2. New products are designed for ease of manufacture.
3. Development costs are kept in check.
4. Time to market is minimized.

Close integration between R&D and marketing is required to ensure that product development projects are driven by the needs of customers. A company's customers can be a primary source of new-product ideas. Identification of customer needs, particularly unmet needs, can set the context within which successful product innovation occurs. As the point of contact with customers, the marketing function of a company can provide valuable information in this regard. Integration of R&D and marketing is crucial if a new product is to be properly commercialized. Without integration of R&D and marketing, a company runs the risk of developing products for which there is little or no demand.

Integration between R&D and production can help a company design products with manufacturing requirements in mind. Designing for manufacturing can lower costs and increase product quality. Integrating R&D and production can also help lower development costs and speed products to market. If a new product is not designed with manufacturing capabilities in mind, it may prove too difficult to build. Then the product will have to be redesigned, and both overall development costs and the time it takes to bring the product to market may increase significantly. Making design changes during product planning could increase overall development costs by 50 percent and add 25 percent to the time it takes to bring the product to market.[41] Many quantum product innovations require new processes to manufacture them, which makes it all the more important to achieve close integration between R&D and production. Minimizing time to market and development costs may require the simultaneous development of new products and new processes.[42]

CROSS-FUNCTIONAL TEAMS One way to achieve cross-functional integration is to establish cross-functional product development teams composed of representatives from R&D, marketing, and production. Because these functions may be located in different countries, the team will sometimes have a multinational membership. The objective of a team should be to take a product development project from the initial concept development to market introduction. A number of attributes seem to be important for a product development team to function effectively and meet all its development milestones.[43]

First, the team should be led by a "heavyweight" project manager who has high status within the organization and who has the power and authority required to get the financial and human resources the team needs to succeed. The leader should be dedicated primarily, if not entirely, to the project. He or she should be someone who believes in the project (a champion) and who is skilled at integrating the perspectives of different functions and at helping personnel from different functions and countries work together for a common goal. The leader should also be able to act as an advocate of the team to senior management.

Second, the team should be composed of at least one member from each key function. The team members should have a number of attributes, including an ability to contribute functional expertise, high standing within their function, a willingness to share responsibility for team results, and an ability to put functional and national advocacy aside. It is generally preferable if core team members are 100 percent dedicated to the project for its duration. This ensures their focus on the project, not on the ongoing work of their function.

Third, the team members should physically be in one location if possible to create a sense of camaraderie and to facilitate communication. This presents problems if the team members are drawn from facilities in different nations. One solution is to transfer key individuals to one location for the duration of a product development project. Fourth, the team should have a clear plan and clear goals, particularly with regard to critical development milestones and development budgets. The team should have incentives to attain those goals, such as receiving pay bonuses when major development milestones are hit. Fifth, each team needs to develop its own processes for communication and conflict resolution. For example, one product development team at Quantum Corporation, a California-based manufacturer of hard drives for personal computers, instituted a rule that all major decisions would be made and conflicts resolved at meetings that were held every Monday afternoon. This simple rule helped the team meet its development goals. In this case, it was also common for team members to fly in from Japan, where the product was to be manufactured, to the U.S. development center for the Monday morning meetings.[44]

BUILDING GLOBAL R&D CAPABILITIES The need to integrate R&D and marketing to adequately commercialize new technologies poses special problems in the international business because commercialization may require different versions of a new product to be produced for various countries.[45] To do this, the firm must build close links between its R&D centers and its various country operations. A similar argument applies to the need to integrate R&D and production, particularly in those international businesses that have dispersed production activities to different locations around the globe in consideration of relative factor costs and the like.

Integrating R&D, marketing, and production in an international business may require R&D centers in North America, Asia, and Europe that are linked by formal and informal integrating mechanisms with marketing operations in each country in their regions and with the various manufacturing facilities. In addition, the international business may have to establish cross-functional teams whose members are dispersed around the globe. This complex endeavor requires the company to utilize formal and informal integrating mechanisms to knit its far-flung operations together so they can produce new products in an effective and timely manner.

While there is no one best model for allocating product development responsibilities to various centers, one solution adopted by many international businesses involves establishing a global network of R&D centers. Within this model, fundamental research is undertaken at basic research centers around the globe. These centers are normally located in regions or cities where valuable scientific knowledge is being created and where there is a pool of skilled research talent (e.g., Silicon Valley in the United States, Cambridge in England, Kobe in Japan, Singapore). These centers are the innovation engines of the firm. Their job is to develop the basic technologies that become new products.

These technologies are picked up by R&D units attached to global product divisions and are used to generate new products to serve the global marketplace. At this level, commercialization of the technology and design for manufacturing are emphasized. If further customization is needed so the product appeals to the tastes and preferences of consumers in individual markets, such redesign work will be done by an R&D group based in a subsidiary in that country or at a regional center that customizes products for several countries in the region.

Hewlett-Packard has seven basic research centers located in Palo Alto, California; Bristol, England; Haifa, Israel; Beijing, China; Singapore; Bangalore, India; and St. Petersburg, Russia.[46] These labs are the seedbed for technologies that ultimately become new products and businesses. They are the company's innovation engines. The Palo Alto center, for example, pioneered HP's thermal ink-jet technology. The products are developed by R&D centers associated with HP's global product divisions. Thus, HP's Consumer Products Group, which has its worldwide headquarters in San Diego, California, designs, develops, and manufactures a range of imaging products using HP-pioneered thermal ink-jet technology. Subsidiaries might then customize the product so that it best matches the needs of important national markets. HP's subsidiary in Singapore, for example, is responsible for the design and production of thermal ink-jet printers for Japan and other Asian markets. This subsidiary takes products originally developed in San Diego and redesigns them for the Asian market. In addition, the Singapore subsidiary has taken the lead from San Diego in the design and development of certain portable thermal ink-jet printers. HP delegated this responsibility to Singapore because this subsidiary has acquired important competencies in the design and production of thermal ink-jet products, so it has become the best place in the world to undertake this activity.

 **test PREP**

Use SmartBook to help retain what you have learned. Access your Instructor's Connect course to check out SmartBook or go to learnsmartadvantage.com for help.

John Maltabes, research engineer at Hewlett-Packard, takes out a thin, flexible electronic display that has etched resistors and uses self-aligned imprint lithography technology for testing at Hewlett-Packard Laboratories.

Source: © Tony Avelar/The Christian Science Monitor/Getty Images

Key Terms

marketing mix, p. 438
market segmentation, p. 440
intermarket segment, p. 441
concentrated retail system, p. 444
fragmented retail system, p. 444
channel length, p. 445
exclusive distribution channel, p. 445
channel quality, p. 446
source effects, p. 448
country of origin effects, p. 448
noise, p. 448
push strategy, p. 448
pull strategy, p. 448
price elasticity of demand, p. 453
elastic, p. 453
inelastic, p. 453
strategic pricing, p. 454
predatory pricing, p. 454
multipoint pricing, p. 454
experience curve pricing, p. 455
international market research, p. 457

Summary

This chapter discussed the marketing and R&D functions in international business. A persistent theme of the chapter is the tension that exists between the need to reduce costs and the need to be responsive to local conditions, which raises costs. The chapter made the following points:

1. Theodore Levitt argued that due to the advent of modern communications and transport technologies, consumer tastes and preferences are becoming global, which is creating global markets for standardized consumer products. However, this position is regarded as extreme by many experts, who argue that substantial differences still exist between customers from different countries and cultures.
2. Market segmentation refers to the process of identifying distinct groups of consumers whose needs, wants, and purchasing behavior differs from each other in important ways. Managers in an international business need to be aware of two main issues relating to segmentation: the extent to which there are differences between countries in the structure of market segments and the existence of segments that transcend national borders (i.e., intermarket segments).
3. A product can be viewed as a bundle of attributes. Product attributes often need to be varied from country to country to satisfy different consumer tastes and preferences.
4. Country differences in consumer tastes and preferences are due to differences in culture and economic development. In addition, differences in product and technical standards may require the firm to customize product attributes from country to country.
5. A distribution strategy decision is an attempt to define the optimal channel for delivering a product to the consumer. In the global supply chain, the marketing channel is a part of the downstream (also called outbound) portion of the supply chain (refer to Chapter 17).
6. Significant country differences exist in distribution systems. In some countries, the retail system is concentrated; in others, it is fragmented. In some countries, channel length is short; in others, it is long. Access to distribution channels is difficult to achieve in some countries, and the quality of the channel may be poor, especially in less developed nations.
7. A critical element in the marketing mix is communication strategy, which defines the process the firm will use in communicating the attributes of its product to prospective customers.
8. Barriers to international communication include cultural differences, source effects, and noise levels.
9. A communication strategy is either a push strategy or a pull strategy. A push strategy emphasizes personal selling, and a pull strategy emphasizes mass media advertising. Whether a push strategy or a pull strategy is optimal depends on the type of product, consumer sophistication, channel length, and media availability.
10. A globally standardized advertising campaign, which uses the same marketing message all over the world, has economic advantages, but it fails to account for differences in culture and advertising regulations.
11. Price discrimination exists when consumers in different countries are charged different prices for the same product. Price discrimination can help a firm maximize its profits. For price discrimination to be effective, the national markets must be separate and their price elasticities of demand must differ.
12. Predatory pricing is the use of profit gained in one market to support aggressive pricing in another market to drive competitors out of that market.
13. Multipoint pricing refers to the fact that a firm's pricing strategy in one market may affect rivals' pricing strategies in another market. Aggressive pricing in one market may elicit a competitive response from a rival in another market that is important to the firm.
14. Experience curve pricing is the use of aggressive pricing to build accumulated volume as rapidly as possible to quickly move the firm down the experience curve.
15. International market research involves (*a*) defining the research objectives, (*b*) determining the data sources, (*c*) assessing the costs and benefits of the research, (*d*) collecting the data, (e) analyzing and interpreting the research, and (*f*) reporting the research findings.
16. New-product development is a high-risk, potentially high-return activity. To build a competency in

new-product development, an international business must do two things: disperse R&D activities to those countries where new products are being pioneered and integrate R&D with marketing and manufacturing.

17. Achieving tight integration among R&D, marketing, and manufacturing requires the use of cross-functional teams.

Critical Thinking and Discussion Questions

1. Imagine that you are the marketing manager for a U.S. manufacturer of disposable diapers. Your firm is considering entering the Brazilian market. Your CEO believes the advertising message that has been effective in the United States will suffice in Brazil. Outline some possible objections to this. Your CEO also believes that the pricing decisions in Brazil can be delegated to local managers. Why might she be wrong?
2. Within 20 years, we will have seen the emergence of enormous global markets for standardized consumer products. Do you agree with this statement? Justify your answer.
3. You are the marketing manager of a food products company that is considering entering the Indian market. The retail system in India tends to be very fragmented. Also, retailers and wholesalers tend to have long-term ties with Indian food companies; these ties make access to distribution channels difficult. What distribution strategy would you advise the company to pursue? Why?
4. Price discrimination is indistinguishable from dumping. Discuss the accuracy of this statement.
5. You work for a company that designs and manufactures personal computers. Your company's R&D center is in Michigan. The computers are manufactured under contract in Taiwan. Marketing strategy is delegated to the heads of three regional groups: a North American group (based in Chicago), a European group (based in Paris), and an Asian group (based in Singapore). Each regional group develops the marketing approach within its region. In order of importance, the largest markets for your products are North America, Germany, Great Britain, China, and Australia. Your company is experiencing problems in its product development and commercialization process. Products are late to market, the manufacturing quality is poor, costs are higher than projected, and market acceptance of new products is less than hoped for. What might be the source of these problems? How would you fix them?

globalEDGE Research Task

http://globalEDGE.msu.edu

Use the globalEDGE™ website (globaledge.msu.edu) to complete the following exercises:

1. The consumer purchase of specific brands is an indication of the relationship that develops over time between a company and its customers. Locate and retrieve the most current ranking of *best global brands*. Identify the criteria used. Which countries appear to dominate the top 100 global brands list? Why do you think this is the case? Now look at which sectors appear to dominate the list, and try to identify the reasons. Prepare a short report identifying the countries that possess global brands and the potential reasons for success.
2. Part of developing a long-term R&D strategy is to locate facilities in countries that are widely known to be competitive. Your company seeks to develop R&D facilities in Asia to counter recent competitor responses. A publication that evaluates economies based on their competitiveness is the Global Competitiveness Report. Locate this report, and develop a presentation for the top management team that presents the benefits and drawbacks for the top five Asian economies listed.

Burberry's Reinventing Its Global Marketing

closing case

Burberry, the icon British luxury apparel retailer founded in 1856 by Thomas Burberry and famed for its trench coats and plaid-patterned accessories, has been on a roll in recent years. In the late 1990s, one critic described Burberry as "an outdated business with a fashion cache of almost zero." But by 2016, Burberry was widely recognized as one of the world's premier luxury brands with a strong presence in many of the world's richest cities, some 500 retail stores, about 10,800 employees, and revenues in excess of $3.6 billion.

Two successive American CEOs were behind Burberry's transformation. The first, Rose Marie Bravo, joined the company in 1997 from Saks Fifth Avenue. Bravo saw immense hidden value in the Burberry brand. One of her first moves was to hire world-class designers to reenergize the brand. The company also shifted its orientation toward a younger, hipper demographic, perhaps best exemplified by the ads featuring supermodel Kate Moss that helped to reposition the brand. By the time Bravo retired in 2006, she had transformed Burberry into what one commentator called an "achingly hip," high-end fashion brand whose raincoats, clothes, handbags, and other accessories were must-have items for younger, well-heeled, fashion-conscious consumers worldwide.

Bravo was succeeded by Angela Ahrendts, whose career had taken her from a small town in Indiana and a degree at Ball State University, through Warnaco and LizClaiborne, to become the CEO of Burberry at age 46. Ahrendts realized that for all of Bravo's success, Burberry still faced significant problems. The company had long pursued a licensing strategy, allowing partners in other countries to design and sell their own offerings under the Burberry label. This lack of control over the offering was hurting its brand equity. The Spanish partner, for example, was selling casual wear that bore no relationship to what was being designed in London. So long as this state of affairs continued, Burberry would struggle to build a unified global brand.

Ahrendts's solution was to start acquiring partners and/or buying back licensing rights in order to regain control over the brand. Hand in hand with this, she pushed for an aggressive expansion of the company's retail store strategy. The company's core demographics under Ahrendts remained the well-heeled, younger, fashion-conscious set. To reach this demographic, Burberry has focused on 25 of the world's wealthier cities. Key markets include New York, London, and Beijing, which according to Burberry, account for more than half the global luxury fashion trade. As a result of this strategy, the number of retail stores increased from 211 in 2007 to 497 in 2015.

Another aspect of Burberry's strategy has been to embrace digital marketing tools to reach its tech-savvy customer base. Indeed, there are few luxury brand companies that have utilized digital technology as aggressively as Burberry. Burberry has simulcast its runway shows in 3-D in New York, Los Angeles, Dubai, Paris, and Tokyo. Viewers at home can stream the shows over the Internet and post comments in real time. Outerwear and bags are made available through "click and buy" technology, with delivery several months before they reach the stores. Burberry had more than 17 million Facebook fans as of 2016. At "The Art of the Trench," a company-run social media site, people can submit photos of themselves in the company's icon rainwear.

The global marketing strategy seems to be working. Between 2007 and 2016, revenues at Burberry increased from some $1.3 billion to $3.6 billion, and this increase also happened against the background of a global economic slowdown in the 2008-to-2010 period.

In April 2014, Angela Ahrendts was replaced as CEO by Christopher Bailey (Ahrendts took a position as senior vice president of retail and online at Apple, Inc.). Bailey, with a heritage from Halifax, United Kingdom, first started with Burberry's in May 2001 as a creative director. One of the branding decisions that happened on his creative director watch was to remove the Burberry brand's iconic check pattern from virtually all Burberry products, leaving only 10 percent of the products with the famous check pattern. He also masterminded the design of Burberry's largest store, 121 Regent Street in London, United Kingdom, which opened in 2012 as a bricks-and-mortar incarnation of the brand's website.

Sources: S. Davis, "Burberry's Blurred Lines: The Integrated Customer Experience," *Forbes*, March 27, 2014; A. Ahrendts, "Burberry's CEO on Turning an Aging British Icon into a Global Luxury Brand," *Harvard Business Review*, January-February 2013; Nancy Hass, "Earning Her Stripes," *The Wall Street Journal*, September 9, 2010; "Burberry Shines as Aquascutum Fades," *The Wall Street Journal*, April 17, 2010; Peter Evans, "Burberry Sales Ease from Blistering Pace," *The Wall Street Journal*, April 17, 2010; "Burberry Case Study," *Market Line*, www.marketline.com.

CASE DISCUSSION QUESTIONS

1. The centralized brand management that happened under the watch of Angela Ahrendts was a strategic move that resulted in a better brand equity. Is this a move that should remain a staple of the company's brand strategy, or what decisions/strategies should Burberry be making moving forward?
2. With the leadership of Angela Ahrendts and Christopher Bailey, Burberry brand's iconic check pattern became less of a marketing focus than even before. What role in design and marketing should the Burberry check pattern play in the future? Does the target market matter in this decision?
3. Is it time for Burberry to focus more intensely on markets outside its core 25 wealthy cities? What about its demographic focus on well-heeled, younger, fashion-conscious set?
4. Should Burberry's be focused on new brick-and-mortar stores, as new CEO Christopher Bailey did with the opening of Burberry's largest store, 121 Regent Street in London, or should they focus on more online sales worldwide? Are high-end products (clothing such as Burberry's) better sold in stores or online, or both?

Endnotes

1. See R. W. Ruekert and O. C. Walker, "Interactions between Marketing and R&D Departments in Implementing Different Business-Level Strategies," *Strategic Management Journal* 8 (1987), pp. 233–48; and K. B. Clark and S. C. Wheelwright, *Managing New Product and Process Development* (New York: Free Press, 1993).
2. T. Levitt, "The Globalization of Markets," *Harvard Business Review*, May–June 1983, pp. 92–102.
3. For example, see S. P. Douglas and Y. Wind, "The Myth of Globalization," *Columbia Journal of World Business*, Winter 1987, pp. 19–29; C. A. Bartlett and S. Ghoshal, *Managing across Borders: The Transnational Solution* (Boston: Harvard Business School Press, 1989); V. J. Govindarajan and A. K. Gupta, *The Quest for Global Dominance* (San Francisco: Jossey-Bass, 2001); J. Quelch, "The Return of the Global Brand," *Harvard Business Review*, August 2003, pp. 1–3; P. J. Ghemawat, *Redefining Global Strategy* (Boston: Harvard Business School Press, 2007).
4. J. Tagliabue, "U.S. Brands Are Feeling Global Tension," *The New York Times*, March 15, 2003, p. C3.
5. D. B. Holt, J. A. Quelch, and E. L. Taylor, "How Global Brands Compete," *Harvard Business Review*, September 2004.
6. J. T. Landry, "Emerging Markets: Are Chinese Consumers Coming of Age?" *Harvard Business Review*, May–June 1998, pp. 17–20.
7. C. Miller, "Teens Seen as the First Truly Global Consumers," *Marketing News*, March 27, 1995, p. 9.
8. This approach was originally developed in K. Lancaster, "A New Approach to Demand Theory," *Journal of Political Economy* 74 (1965), pp. 132–57.
9. V. R. Alden, "Who Says You Can't Crack Japanese Markets?" *Harvard Business Review*, January–February 1987, pp. 52–56.
10. "RCA's New Vista: The Bottom Line," *BusinessWeek*, July 4, 1987, p. 44.

11. C. Matlack and P. Gogoi, "What's This? The French Love McDonald's?" *BusinessWeek*, January 13, 2003, pp. 50–51.
12. Z. Gurhan-Cvanli and D. Maheswaran, "Cultural Variation in Country of Origin Effects," *Journal of Marketing Research,* August 2000, pp. 309–17.
13. See M. Laroche, V. H. Kirpalani, F. Pons, and L. Zhou, "A Model of Advertising Standardization in Multinational Corporations," *Journal of International Business Studies* 32 (2001), pp. 249–66; and D. A. Aaker and E. Joachimsthaler, "The Lure of Global Branding," *Harvard Business Review*, November–December 1999, pp. 137–44.
14. "Advertising in a Single Market," *The Economist,* March 24, 1990, p. 64.
15. R. G. Matthews and D. Pringle, "Nokia Bets One Global Message Will Ring True in Many Markets," *The Wall Street Journal,* September 27, 2004, p. B6.
16. R. J. Dolan and H. Simon, *Power Pricing* (New York: Free Press, 1999).
17. B. Stottinger, "Strategic Export Pricing: A Long Winding Road," *Journal of International Marketing* 9 (2001), pp. 40–63; S. Gil-Pareja, "Export Process Discrimination in Europe and Exchange Rates," *Review of International Economics,* May 2002, pp. 299–312; and G. Corsetti and L. Dedola, "A Macro Economic Model of International Price Discrimination," *Journal of International Economics,* September 2005, pp. 129–40.
18. These allegations were made on a PBS *Frontline* documentary telecast in the United States in May 1992.
19. Y. Tsurumi and H. Tsurumi, "Fujifilm-Kodak Duopolistic Competition in Japan and the United States," *Journal of International Business Studies* 30 (1999), pp. 813–30.
20. G. Smith and B. Wolverton, "A Dark Moment for Kodak," *BusinessWeek,* August 4, 1997, pp. 30–31.
21. R. Narisette and J. Friedland, "Disposable Income: Diaper Wars of P&G and Kimberly-Clark Now Heat Up in Brazil," *The Wall Street Journal,* June 4, 1997, p. A1.
22. J. F. Pickering, *Industrial Structure and Market Conduct* (London: Martin Robertson, 1974).
23. S. P. Douglas, C. Samuel Craig, and E. J. Nijissen, "Integrating Branding Strategy across Markets," *Journal of International Marketing* 9, no. 2 (2001), pp. 97–114.
24. We summarized the basic steps in the international market research process. Detailed discussions of similar processes can be found in P. Cateora, M. Gilly, and J. Graham, *International Marketing* (New York: McGraw-Hill, 2013); V. Kumar, *International Marketing Research* (Upper Saddle River, NJ: Pearson Prentice Hall, 2000); and C. S. Craig and S. P. Douglas, *International Marketing Research* (West Sussex, UK: Wiley, 2005).
25. B. Pedersen, T. Pedersen, and M. Lyles, "Closing the Knowledge Gaps in Foreign Markets," *Journal of International Business Studies* 39 (2008), pp. 1097–13.
26. P, Ziobro, "Mattel Takes a Hit as Barbie Sales Slump," *The Wall Street Journal,* January 31, 2014.
27. Kumar, *International Marketing Research*; Craig and Douglas, *International Marketing Research.*
28. A-W. Harzing, "Response Rates in International Mail Surveys: Results of a 22-Country Study," *International Business Review* 6 (1997), pp. 641–65.
29. Kumar, *International Marketing Research*; Craig and Douglas, *International Marketing Research*; J. Hair, W. Black, B. Babin, and R. Anderson, *Multivariate Data Analysis* (Upper Saddle River, NJ: Pearson Prentice Hall, 2010); and J. Hair, T. Hult, C. Ringle, and M. Sarstedt, *A Primer on Partial Least Squares Structural Equation Modeling (PLS-SEM)* (Los Angeles, CA: Sage, 2014).
30. N. Bunkley, "Toyota Issues a 2nd Recall," *The New York Times*, January 21, 2010.
31. The phrase was first used by economist Joseph Schumpeter in *Capitalism, Socialism, and Democracy* (New York: Harper Brothers, 1942).
32. S. Kotabe, S. Srinivasan, and P. S. Aulakh. "Multinationality and Firm Performance: The Moderating Role of R&D and Marketing," *Journal of International Business Studies* 33 (2002), pp. 79–97.
33. D. C. Mowery and N. Rosenberg, *Technology and the Pursuit of Economic Growth* (Cambridge, UK: Cambridge University Press, 1989); M. E. Porter, *The Competitive Advantage of Nations* (New York: Free Press, 1990).
34. W. Kuemmerle, "Building Effective R&D Capabilities Abroad," Harvard Business Review, March–April 1997, pp. 61–70; and C. Le Bas and C. Sierra, "Location versus Home Country Advantages in R&D Activities," *Research Policy* 31 (2002), pp. 589–609.
35. "When the Corporate Lab Goes to Japan," *The New York Times*, April 28, 1991, sec. 3, p. 1.
36. D. Shapley, "Globalization Prompts Exodus," *Financial Times*, March 17, 1994, p. 10.
37. E. Mansfield, "How Economists See R&D," *Harvard Business Review,* November–December 1981, pp. 98–106.
38. Ibid.
39. G. A. Stevens and J. Burley, "Piloting the Rocket of Radical Innovation," *Research Technology Management* 46 (2003), pp. 16–26.
40. K. B. Clark and S. C. Wheelwright, *Managing New Product and Process Development* (New York: Free Press, 1993); and M. A. Shilling and C. W. L. Hill, "Managing the New Product Development Process," *Academy of Management Executive* 12, no. 3 (1998), pp. 67–81.
41. O. Port, "Moving Past the Assembly Line," *BusinessWeek Special Issue: Reinventing America*, 1992, pp. 177–80.
42. K. B. Clark and T. Fujimoto, "The Power of Product Integrity," *Harvard Business Review,* November–December 1990, pp. 107–18; Clark and Wheelwright, *Managing New Product and Process Development;* S. L. Brown and K. M. Eisenhardt, "Product Development: Past Research, Present Findings, and Future Directions," *Academy of Management Review* 20 (1995), pp. 348–78; G. Stalk and T. M. Hout, *Competing against Time* (New York: Free Press, 1990).
43. Shilling and Hill, "Managing the New Product Development Process."
44. C. Christensen, "Quantum Corporation—Business and Product Teams," Harvard Business School case no. 9-692-023.
45. R. Nobel and J. Birkinshaw, "Innovation in Multinational Corporations: Control and Communication Patterns in International R&D Operations," *Strategic Management Journal* 19 (1998), pp. 479–96.
46. Information comes from the company's website; also see K. Ferdows, "Making the Most of Foreign Factories," *Harvard Business Review*, March–April 1997, pp. 73–88.

Global Human Resource Management

learning objectives

After reading this chapter, you will be able to:

LO17-1 Summarize the strategic role of human resource management in the international business.

LO17-2 Identify the pros and cons of different approaches to staffing policy in the international business.

LO17-3 Explain why managers may fail to thrive in foreign postings.

LO17-4 Recognize how management development and training programs can increase the value of human capital in the international business firm.

LO17-5 Explain how and why performance appraisal systems might vary across nations.

LO17-6 Understand how and why compensation systems might vary across nations.

LO17-7 Understand how organized labor can influence strategic choices in international business firms.

© Michael Bezjian/Getty Images

A Global Team at Mary Kay Inc.

opening case

Founded in 1963 by Mary Kay Ash, the company bearing her name, Mary Kay Inc., is an American privately owned multilevel marketing company that sells cosmetic products in more than 35 countries. Mary Kay Ash's son, Richard Rogers, is board chair, and David Holl is president and CEO. The multilevel marketing model adopted by Mary Kay Inc. involves "beauty consultants" (distributors) selling directly to customers in their local community. The direct selling approach and local focus create a unique global workforce model for Mary Kay Inc.

The company's global independent sales force exceeds 3.5 million distributors, with some $4 billion in wholesale sales worldwide. Since opening its first international operations in Australia in 1971, Mary Kay has expanded to more than 35 countries on five continents. Mary Kay also consistently ranks as one of the top brands in the United States. The pink color has become associated with Mary Kay—from its beginning as a "Mary Kay pink" color on the 1968 Cadillac Mary Kay bought herself as a reward after five successful years of the company.

As part of the Mary Kay rewards program, in 1969 five pink Cadillacs were also rewarded to top salespeople. From this start, recognition of people has been an integral part of the Mary Kay culture and experience. The idea is that recognizing achievements heightens ambition among the workforce, and success globally becomes a cultural value system. Pink Cadillacs to diamond bumblebees to Mary Kay porcelain dolls to trips to exotic locations such as Australia, England, Greece, and China motivate the Mary Kay beauty distributors.

This people focus is a staple of the Mary Kay global philosophy. "A company is only as good as its people. . . . [I]n order to grow and progress in the sales force, you don't move upward, you expand outward. This gives the independent sales force a deep sense of personal worth."* With these people principles, today somewhere in the world, a Mary Kay sales party (independent beauty consultants direct selling in their local communities) is held every hour. It is not sales per se, it is a "party."

The similarities among Mary Kay operations globally outweigh any country-to-country differences. And, importantly, just as the original reasoning was for founding the company in the United States, Mary Kay is an important factor in the employment of women in the workforce in many countries, particularly in developing nations. While the products may vary to meet the needs and preferences of local consumers in the global marketplace, they are held to the same rigid quality-control standards whether they are purchased in the United States, Brazil, China, or Russia. This quality backing gives the independent beauty consultants assurances that they are part of a trustworthy Mary Kay Inc. team. •

*Mary Kay Ash, *The Mary Kay Way: Timeless Principles from America's Greatest Woman Entrepreneur* (Hoboken, NJ: Wiley, 2008).

Sources: G. Ostega, *It's Not Where You Start, It's Where You Finish: The Success Secrets of a Top Member of the Mary Kay Independent Sales Force* (Hoboken, NJ: Wiley, 2005); *Mary Kay Global.* www.marykay.com; "The Story of Mary Kay Inc." www.marykaymuseum.com; Mary Kay Ash, *The Mary Kay Way: Timeless Principles from America's Greatest Woman Entrepreneur* (Hoboken, NJ: Wiley, 2008).

Introduction

Human Resource Management (HRM)
Activities an organization conducts to use its human resources effectively.

Did You Know?
Did you know the world population is now 7 billion?

Visit your Connect SmartBook® to view a short video explanation from the authors.

This chapter continues our focus on business functions within a company engaged in a global marketplace of some 7 billion people by looking at global human resource management. **Human resource management (HRM)** refers to the activities an organization carries out to use its human resources effectively.[1] These activities include determining the firm's human resource strategy, staffing, performance evaluation, management development, compensation, and labor relations.

None of these global HRM activities is performed in a vacuum, however; all are related to the global strategy of the firm. As we will see in this chapter, HRM has an important strategic component.[2] Through its influence on the character, development, quality, and productivity of the firm's human resources, the HRM function can help the firm achieve its primary strategic goals of reducing the costs of value creation and adding value by better serving customers. A good example of this is given in the opening case, which looks at how Mary Kay Inc. uses human resources in a highly unique and strategic way to build and sustain a competitive advantage over rivals.

Irrespective of the desire of managers in multinational companies such as Mary Kay Inc. to build a truly global enterprise with a global workforce, the reality is that HRM practices still have to be modified to national contexts. The strategic role of HRM is complex enough in a purely domestic firm, but it is more complex in an international business, where staffing, management development, performance evaluation, and compensation activities are complicated by profound differences between countries in labor markets, culture, legal systems, economic systems, and the like (see Chapters 2, 3, and 4). For example,

- Compensation practices may vary from country to country, depending on prevailing management customs.
- Labor laws may prohibit union organization in one country and mandate it in another.
- Equal employment legislation may be strongly pursued in one country and not in another.

Expatriate Manager
A national of one country appointed to a management position in another country.

If it is to build a cadre of managers capable of managing a multinational enterprise, the HRM function must deal with a host of issues. It must decide how to staff key management posts in the company, how to develop managers so that they are familiar with the nuances of doing business in different countries, how to compensate people in different nations, and how to evaluate the performance of managers based in different countries. HRM must also deal with a myriad of issues related to expatriate managers. (An **expatriate manager** is a citizen of one country who is working abroad in one of the firm's subsidiaries.) It must decide when to use expatriates, determine whom to send on expatriate postings, be clear about the reasons why, compensate expatriates appropriately, and make sure that they are adequately debriefed and reoriented once they return home.

This chapter looks closely at the role of HRM in an international business. It begins by briefly discussing the strategic role of HRM. Then we turn our attention to four major tasks of the HRM function: staffing policy, management training and development, performance appraisal, and compensation policy. We point out the strategic implications of each task. The chapter closes with a look at international labor relations and the relationship between the firm's management of labor relations and its overall strategy.

LO 17-1
Summarize the strategic role of human resource management in the international business.

Strategic Role of Global HRM

A large and expanding body of academic research suggests that a strong fit between human resource practices and strategy is required for high profitability.[3] You will recall from Chapter 12 that superior performance requires not only the right strategy, but the strategy must also be supported by the right organizational architecture. Strategy is implemented through organization. As shown in Figure 17.1, people are the linchpin of a firm's organizational architecture. For a firm to outperform its rivals in the global marketplace, it must have the right people in the right postings (see the opening case on Mary Kay Inc. and the closing case on Siemens for examples). Those people must be trained appropriately so that they have the skill sets required to perform their jobs effectively and so that they behave in a manner that is congruent with the desired culture of the firm. Their compensation packages must create incentives for them to take actions that are consistent with the strategy of the firm, and the performance appraisal system the firm uses must measure the behavior that the firm wants to encourage.

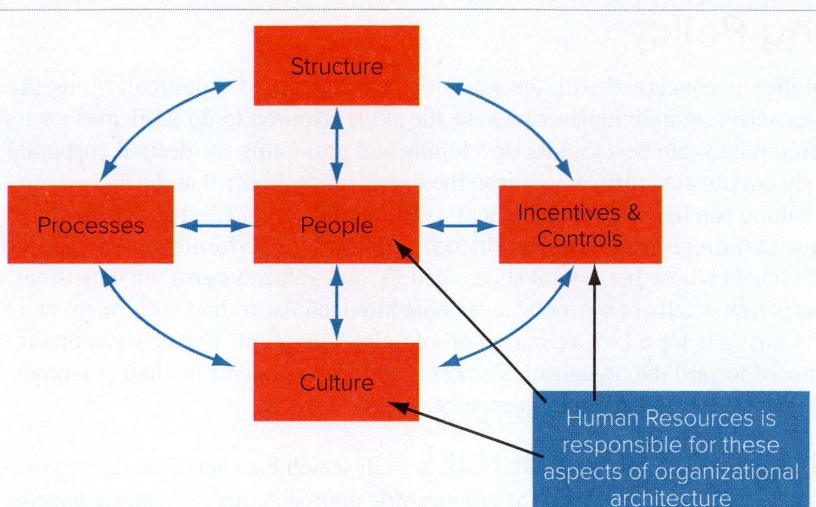

17.1 FIGURE

The Role of Human Resources in Shaping Organizational Architecture.

Source: C. W. L. Hill and G. T. M. Hult, *International Business: Competing in the Global Marketplace* (New York: McGraw-Hill Education, 2017).

As indicated in Figure 17.1, the HRM function, through its staffing, training, compensation, and performance appraisal activities, has a critical impact on the people, culture, incentive, and control system elements of the firm's organizational architecture (performance appraisal systems are part of the control systems in an enterprise). Thus, HRM professionals have a critically important strategic role. It is incumbent on them to shape these elements of a firm's organizational architecture in a manner that is consistent with the strategy of the enterprise so that the firm can effectively implement its strategy.

In short, superior human resource management can be a sustained source of high productivity and competitive advantage in the global economy. At the same time, research suggests that many international businesses have room for improving the effectiveness of their HRM function. In one study of competitiveness among 326 large multinationals, the authors found that human resource management was one of the weakest capabilities in most firms, suggesting that improving the effectiveness of international HRM practices might have substantial performance benefits.[4]

In Chapter 12, we examined four strategies pursued by international businesses: localization strategy, global standardization strategy, transnational strategy, and international strategy. In this chapter, we will see that success also requires HRM policies to be congruent with the firm's strategy. For example, a transnational strategy imposes different requirements for staffing, management development, and compensation practices from a localization strategy. Firms pursuing a transnational strategy need to build a strong corporate culture and an informal management network for transmitting information and knowledge within the organization. Through its employee selection, management development, performance appraisal, and compensation policies, the HRM function can help develop these things. Thus, as we have noted, HRM has a critical role to play in implementing strategy. In each section that follows, we review the strategic role of HRM in some detail.

 **test PREP**

Use SmartBook to help retain what you have learned. Access your Instructor's Connect course to check out SmartBook or go to learnsmartadvantage.com for help.

International Internship Directory

People are what make value chains "valuable," and global human resource management, which is the focus of Chapter 17, is a critical part of operating worldwide. The obvious HR issue to us as authors is YOU—the student and reader of this text! Our goal is to provide information and data and infuse our knowledge to each student using the text. globalEDGE™ can help take this knowledge to another level with its International Internship Directory (globaledge.msu.edu/international-internships). The directory is a reference guide for students and others (e.g., faculty, staff, and administrators) to help match students with international internship opportunities offered by universities, governmental agencies, nonprofit groups, private organizations, and corporations. To search for an internship, you can select a type of organization, country, or subject of study (e.g., international business). Check it out. What opportunities can you find based on your interests?

LO 17-2

Identify the pros and cons of different approaches to staffing policy in the international business.

Staffing Policy

Strategy concerned with selecting employees for particular jobs.

Corporate Culture

The organization's norms and value systems.

Staffing Policy

Staffing policy is concerned with the selection of employees for particular jobs. At one level, this involves selecting individuals who have the skills required to do particular jobs. At another level, staffing policy can be a tool for developing and promoting the desired corporate culture of the firm.[5] By **corporate culture**, we mean the organization's norms and value systems. A strong corporate culture can help a firm implement its strategy. General Electric, for example, is not just concerned with hiring people who have the skills required for performing particular jobs; it wants to hire individuals whose behavioral styles, beliefs, and value systems are consistent with those of GE. This is true whether an American is being hired, an Australian, a German, or a Swede and whether the hiring is for a U.S. operation or a foreign operation. The belief is that if employees are predisposed toward the organization's norms and value systems by their personality type, the firm will be able to attain higher performance.

TYPES OF STAFFING POLICIES

Research has identified three types of staffing policies in international businesses: the ethnocentric approach, the polycentric approach, and the geocentric approach.[6] We review each policy and link it to the strategy pursued by the firm. The most attractive staffing policy is probably the geocentric approach, although there are several impediments to adopting it.

Ethnocentric Staffing Policy

A staffing approach within the MNE in which all key management positions are filled by parent-country nationals.

The Ethnocentric Approach

An **ethnocentric staffing policy** is one in which all key management positions are filled by parent-country nationals. This practice was widespread at one time. Firms such as Procter & Gamble, Philips, and Matsushita (now called Panasonic) originally followed it. In the Dutch firm Philips, for example, all important positions in most foreign subsidiaries were at one time held by Dutch nationals, who were referred to by their non-Dutch colleagues as the Dutch Mafia. Historically in many Japanese and South Korean firms, such as Toyota, Matsushita, and Samsung, key positions in international operations have often been held by home-country nationals. For example, according to the Japanese Overseas Enterprise Association, only 29 percent of foreign subsidiaries of Japanese companies had presidents who were not Japanese. In contrast, 66 percent of the Japanese subsidiaries of foreign companies had Japanese presidents.[7] Today, there is evidence that as Chinese enterprises are expanding internationally, they too are using an ethnocentric staffing policy in their foreign operations.[8]

Firms pursue an ethnocentric staffing policy for three reasons. First, the firm may believe the host country lacks qualified individuals to fill senior management positions. This argument is heard most often when the firm has operations in less developed countries. Second, the firm may see an ethnocentric staffing policy as the best way to maintain a unified corporate culture. Many Japanese firms, for example, have traditionally preferred their foreign operations to be headed by expatriate Japanese managers because these managers will have been socialized into the firm's culture while employed in Japan.[9] Procter & Gamble until fairly recently preferred to staff important management positions in its foreign subsidiaries with U.S. nationals who had been socialized into P&G's corporate culture by years of employment in its U.S. operations. Such reasoning tends to predominate when a firm places a high value on its corporate culture.

Third, if the firm is trying to create value by transferring core competencies to a foreign operation, as firms pursuing

Will We See an Influx of Chinese Workers Worldwide?

Asia is among the fastest-growing areas of the world for international students. For example, foreign enrollment of students at universities in Indonesia and South Korea has more than doubled since 2005. In particular, China has become the most popular destination in Asia, and the country ranks third among all countries in hosting international students. Education in China is still a state-run system of public education, where the Ministry of Education is in charge. By some estimates, China has been growing investment in education by some 20 percent annually for more than a decade, and the quality of education has been improved along with this increased spending. This has resulted in Chinese people becoming more knowledgeable about today's global marketplace; adding to the pool of talent are the Chinese who are educated abroad and decide to return home after their education. Collectively, these highly educated Chinese are more likely to want to work for a foreign company than a Chinese company. Companies already recruit Chinese in China for their foreign operations, but how significant do you think the potential influx of Chinese-educated people around the world will become in the next five years?

Source: K. Sheehy, "Explore the World's Top Universities," *U.S. News & World Report*, October 8, 2013 (http://www.usnews.com/education/best-global-universities/articles/2013/10/08/explore-the-worlds-top-universities).

an international strategy are, it may believe that the best way to do this is to transfer parent-country nationals who have knowledge of that competency to the foreign operation. Imagine what might occur if a firm tried to transfer a core competency in marketing to a foreign subsidiary without a corresponding transfer of home-country marketing management personnel. The transfer would probably fail to produce the anticipated benefits because the knowledge underlying a core competency cannot easily be articulated and written down. Such knowledge often has a significant tacit dimension; it is acquired through experience. Just like the great tennis player who cannot instruct others how to become great tennis players simply by writing a handbook, the firm that has a core competency in marketing, or anything else, cannot just write a handbook that tells a foreign subsidiary how to build the firm's core competency anew in a foreign setting. It must also transfer management personnel to the foreign operation to show foreign managers how to become good marketers, for example. The need to transfer managers overseas arises because the knowledge that underlies the firm's core competency resides in the heads of its domestic managers and was acquired through years of experience, not by reading a handbook. Thus, if a firm is to transfer a core competency to a foreign subsidiary, it must also transfer the appropriate managers.

Despite this rationale for pursuing an ethnocentric staffing policy, the policy is now on the wane in most international businesses for two reasons. First, an ethnocentric staffing policy limits advancement opportunities for host-country nationals. This can lead to resentment, lower productivity, and increased turnover among that group. Resentment can be greater still if, as often occurs, expatriate managers are paid significantly more than home-country nationals.

Second, an ethnocentric policy can lead to *cultural myopia,* the firm's failure to understand host-country cultural differences that require different approaches to marketing and management. The adaptation of expatriate managers can take a long time, during which they may make major mistakes. For example, expatriate managers may fail to appreciate how product attributes, distribution strategy, communications strategy, and pricing strategy should be adapted to host-country conditions. The result may be costly blunders. They may also make decisions that are ethically suspect simply because they do not understand the culture in which they are managing.[10] In one highly publicized case in the United States, Mitsubishi Motors was sued by the federal Equal Employment Opportunity Commission for tolerating extensive and systematic sexual harassment in a plant in Illinois. The plant's top management, all Japanese expatriates, denied the charges. The Japanese managers may have failed to realize that behavior that would be viewed as acceptable in Japan was not acceptable in the United States.[11]

The Polycentric Approach

A **polycentric staffing policy** requires host-country nationals to be recruited to manage subsidiaries, while parent-country nationals occupy key positions at corporate headquarters. In many respects, a polycentric approach is a response to the shortcomings of an ethnocentric approach. One advantage of adopting a polycentric approach is that the firm is less likely to suffer from cultural myopia. Host-country managers are unlikely to make the mistakes arising from cultural misunderstandings to which expatriate managers are vulnerable. A second advantage is that a polycentric approach may be less expensive to implement, reducing the costs of value creation. Expatriate managers can be expensive to maintain.

Polycentric Staffing Policy
A staffing policy in an MNE in which host-country nationals are recruited to manage subsidiaries in their own country, while parent-country nationals occupy key positions at corporate headquarters.

A polycentric approach has its drawbacks. Host-country nationals have limited opportunities to gain experience outside their own country and thus cannot progress beyond senior positions in their own subsidiary. As in the case of an ethnocentric policy, this may cause resentment. Perhaps the major drawback with a polycentric approach, however, is the gap that can form between host-country managers and parent-country managers. Language barriers, national loyalties, and a range of cultural differences may isolate the corporate headquarters staff from the various foreign subsidiaries. The lack of management transfers from home to host countries and vice versa can exacerbate this isolation and lead to a lack of integration between corporate headquarters and foreign subsidiaries. The result can be a "federation" of largely independent national units with only nominal links to the corporate headquarters. Within such a federation, the coordination required to transfer core competencies or to pursue experience curve and location economies may be difficult to achieve. Thus, although a polycentric approach may be effective for firms pursuing a localization strategy, it is inappropriate for other strategies.

The federation that may result from a polycentric approach can also be a force for inertia within the firm. After decades of pursuing a polycentric staffing policy, food and detergents giant

Unilever found that shifting from a strategic posture that emphasized localization to a transnational posture was very difficult. Unilever's foreign subsidiaries had evolved into quasi-autonomous operations, each with its own strong national identity. These "little kingdoms" objected strenuously to corporate headquarters' attempts to limit their autonomy and to rationalize global manufacturing.[12]

Geocentric Staffing Policy

A staffing policy where the best people are sought for key jobs throughout an MNE, regardless of nationality.

The Geocentric Approach

A **geocentric staffing policy** seeks the best people for key jobs throughout the organization, regardless of nationality. This policy has a number of advantages. First, it enables the firm to make the best use of its human resources. Second, and perhaps more important, a geocentric policy enables the firm to build a cadre of international executives who feel at home working in a number of cultures. Creation of such a cadre may be a critical first step toward building a strong unifying corporate culture and an informal management network, both of which are required for global standardization and transnational strategies.[13] Firms pursuing a geocentric staffing policy may be better able to create value from the pursuit of experience curve and location economies and from the multidirectional transfer of core competencies than firms pursuing other staffing policies. In addition, the multinational composition of the management team that results from geocentric staffing tends to reduce cultural myopia and to enhance local responsiveness.

In sum, other things being equal, a geocentric staffing policy seems the most attractive. Indeed, in recent years there has been a sharp shift toward adoption of a geocentric staffing policy by many multinationals. For example, India's Tata Group, now more than a $100 billion global conglomerate, runs several of its companies with American and British executives. Japan's Sony Corporation broke 60 years of tradition in 2005 when it installed its first non-Japanese chair and CEO, Howard Stringer, a former CBS president and a U.S. citizen who was born and raised in Wales. American companies increasingly draw their managerial talent from overseas. In 2014, for example, Microsoft appointed Satya Nadella, a native of India, to its CEO position. One study found that by the mid-2000s, 24 percent of the managers among the top 100 to 250 people in U.S. companies were from outside the United States. For European companies, the average was 40 percent.[14]

However, a number of problems limit the firm's ability to pursue a geocentric policy. Many countries want foreign subsidiaries to employ their citizens. To achieve this goal, they use immigration laws to require the employment of host-country nationals if they are available in adequate numbers and have the necessary skills. Most countries, including the United States, require firms to provide extensive documentation if they wish to hire a foreign national instead of a local national. This documentation can be time-consuming, expensive, and at times futile. A geocentric staffing policy also can be expensive to implement. Training and relocation costs increase when transferring managers from country to country. The company may also need a compensation structure with a standardized international base pay level higher than national levels in many countries. In addition, the higher pay enjoyed by managers placed on an international fast track may be a source of resentment within a firm.

Types of Staffing Policies Summary

The advantages and disadvantages of the three approaches to staffing policy are summarized in Table 17.1. Broadly speaking, an ethnocentric approach is compatible with an international strategy, a polycentric approach is compatible with a localization strategy, and a geocentric approach is compatible with both global standardization and transnational strategies. (See Chapter 12 for details of the strategies.)

While the staffing policies described here are well known and widely used among both practitioners and scholars of international businesses, some critics have claimed that the typology is too simplistic and that it obscures the internal differentiation of management practices within international businesses. The critics claim that within some international businesses, staffing policies vary significantly from national subsidiary to national subsidiary; while some are managed on an ethnocentric basis, others are managed in a polycentric or geocentric manner.[15] Other critics note that the staffing policy adopted by a firm is primarily driven by its geographic scope, as opposed to its strategic orientation. Firms that have a broad geographic scope are the most likely to have a geocentric mindset.[16]

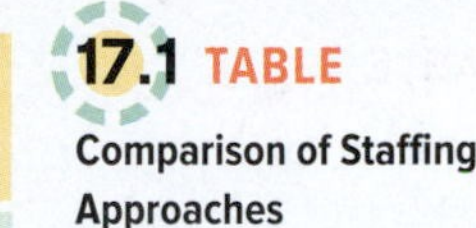

17.1 TABLE

Comparison of Staffing Approaches

Staffing Approach	Strategic Appropriateness	Advantages	Disadvantages
Ethnocentric	International	Overcomes lack of qualified managers in host nation Unifies culture Helps transfer core competencies	Produces resentment in host country Can lead to cultural myopia
Polycentric	Localization	Alleviates cultural myopia Inexpensive to implement	Limits career mobility Isolates headquarters from foreign subsidiaries
Geocentric	Global standardization and transnational	Uses human resources efficiently Helps build strong culture and informal management networks	National immigration policies may limit implementation Expensive

LO 17-3

Explain why managers may fail to thrive in foreign postings.

EXPATRIATE MANAGERS

Two of the three staffing policies we have discussed—the ethnocentric and the geocentric—rely on extensive use of expatriate managers. As defined earlier, expatriates are citizens of one country who are working in another country. Sometimes the term *inpatriates* is used to identify a subset of expatriates who are citizens of a foreign country working in the home country of their multinational employer.[17] Thus, a citizen of Japan who moves to the United States to work at Microsoft would be classified as an inpatriate (Microsoft has large numbers of inpatriates working at its main U.S. location near Seattle). With an ethnocentric policy, the expatriates are all home-country nationals who are transferred abroad. With a geocentric approach, the expatriates need not be home-country nationals; the firm does not base transfer decisions on nationality. A prominent issue in the international staffing literature is **expatriate failure**—the premature return of an expatriate manager to his or her home country.[18] Here, we briefly review the evidence on expatriate failure before discussing a number of ways to minimize the failure rate.

Expatriate Failure

The premature return of an expatriate manager to the home country.

Expatriate Failure Rates

Expatriate failure represents a failure of the firm's selection policies to identify individuals who will not thrive abroad.[19] The consequences include premature return from a foreign posting and high resignation rates, with expatriates leaving their company at about twice the rate of domestic managers.[20] The costs of expatriate failure are high. One estimate is that the average cost per failure to the parent firm can be as high as three times the expatriate's annual domestic salary plus the cost of relocation (which is affected by currency exchange rates and location of assignment). Estimates of the costs of each failure run between $40,000 and $1 million.[21] In addition, approximately 30 to 50 percent of American expatriates, whose average annual compensation package runs to $250,000, stay at their international assignments but are considered ineffective or marginally effective by their firms.[22] In a seminal study undertaken in the 1980s, Rosalie Tung surveyed a number of U.S., European, and Japanese multinationals.[23] Her results, summarized in Table 17.2, show that 76 percent of U.S. multinationals experienced expatriate failure rates of

Would You Send a Woman on an International Assignment?

Would you send a woman expatriate to Saudi Arabia, Japan, Korea, or Kuwait? How are Western women expatriates doing in foreign cultures that have traditionally limited women's public roles? In many cases, women sent to these countries have met with substantial success. Their key challenge is often simply to get the assignments! Once in place, women expatriates are usually successful. This is in part because once in the culture, women expatriates are seen first as expatriates who fall outside the local role for women. In addition, "expat" women also have salience in their new environment—they are noticed—and this can be a distinct business advantage. Locals often take pride in developing business relationships with women expatriates because by doing so, they can suggest that the foreign stereotype of their culture is superficial and incomplete. But cultural barriers still remain, with some cultures having restrictions on what women are allowed to do and not do in business settings and social life. With these lingering potential problems in some countries in the world, would you send a woman on an international assignment?

17.2 TABLE

Expatriate Failure Rates

Source: R. L. Tung, "Selection and Training Procedures of U.S., European, and Japanese Multinationals," *California Management Review,* 25, no. 1 (1982), pp. 51–71.

Recall Rate Percentage	Percentage of Companies
U.S. multinationals	
20–40%	7%
10–20	69
<10	24
European multinationals	
11–15%	3%
6–10	38
<5	59
Japanese multinationals	
11–19%	14%
6–10	10
<5	76

10 percent or more, and 7 percent experienced a failure rate of more than 20 percent. Tung's work also suggests that U.S.-based multinationals experience a much higher expatriate failure rate than either European or Japanese multinationals. However, more recent work suggests that Tung's widely quoted estimates may no longer hold. For example, a study of 136 large multinationals from four different countries undertaken in the late 2000s found that the rate of premature return of expatriate managers had dropped to 6.3 percent and that there was little difference between multinationals from different nations. The authors of this study suggest that multinationals have gotten much better at the selection and training of expatriates since Tung's study.[24]

Tung asked her sample of multinational managers to indicate reasons for expatriate failure. For U.S. multinationals, the reasons, in order of importance, were:

1. Inability of spouse to adjust.
2. Manager's inability to adjust.
3. Other family problems.
4. Manager's personal or emotional maturity.
5. Inability to cope with larger overseas responsibilities.

Managers of European firms gave only one reason consistently to explain expatriate failure: the inability of the manager's spouse to adjust to a new environment. For the Japanese firms, the reasons for failure were:

1. Inability to cope with larger overseas responsibilities.
2. Difficulties with new environment.
3. Personal or emotional problems.
4. Lack of technical competence.
5. Inability of spouse to adjust.

The most striking difference between these lists is that "inability of spouse to adjust" was the top reason for expatriate failure among U.S. and European multinationals but only the fifth reason among Japanese multinationals. Tung comments that this difference was not surprising, given the role and status to which Japanese society traditionally relegates the wife and the fact that most of the Japanese expatriate managers in the study were men.

Since Tung's study, a number of other studies have consistently confirmed that the inability of a spouse to adjust, the inability of the manager to adjust, or other family problems remain major reasons for continuing high levels of expatriate failure.[25] One study by International Orientation Resources, an HRM consulting firm, found that 60 percent of expatriate failures occur due to these three reasons.[26] Another study found that the most common reason for assignment failure is lack of partner (spouse) satisfaction, which was listed by 27 percent of respondents.[27] The inability of expatriate managers to adjust to foreign postings seems to be caused by a lack of cultural skills on the part of the manager being transferred. According to one HRM consulting firm, this is because the expatriate selection process at many firms is fundamentally flawed: "Expatriate assignments rarely fail because the person cannot accommodate to the technical demands of the job. Typically, the expatriate selections are made by line managers based on technical competence. They fail because of family and personal issues and lack of cultural skills that haven't been part of the selection process."[28]

The failure of spouses to adjust to a foreign posting seems to be related to a number of factors. Often, spouses find themselves in a foreign country without the familiar network of family and friends. Language differences make it difficult for them to make new friends. While this may not be a problem for the manager, who can make friends at work, it can be difficult for the spouse, who might feel trapped at home. The problem is often exacerbated by immigration regulations prohibiting the spouse from taking employment. With the recent rise of two-career families in many developed nations, this issue has become much more important. One survey found that 69 percent of expatriates are married, with spouses accompanying them 77 percent of the time. Of those spouses, 49 percent were employed before an assignment and only 11 percent were employed during an assignment.[29] Research suggests that a main reason managers now turn down international assignments is concern over the impact such an assignment might have on their spouse's career.[30] The accompanying Management Focus examines how one large multinational company, Royal Dutch Shell, has tried to come to grips with this issue.

Which Country Do You Want to Go to?

The HSBC Expat Explorer Survey is an interesting way to better understand the friendliness of a country. The Expat Explorer Survey provides an overall ranking based on economics, experience, and raising children in the country (because expatriates are often younger professionals establishing their family lives while abroad). China, Germany, Singapore, Cayman Islands, and Australia are at the top in 2013. Interestingly, of the 24 countries ranked, at the bottom of the ranking are Ireland, Italy, United Kingdom, Kuwait, and Spain. Many rankings are based on how countries see foreign visitors, and visiting instead of staying to work in the country also has implications. According to the World Economic Forum's "friendliest countries" ranking, the attitude of the local population toward foreign visitors is the best in Iceland, New Zealand, Morocco, Macedonia, and Austria. The bottom five countries, from the ranking of 140 countries are Bolivia, Venezuela, Russia, Kuwait, and Latvia. Kuwait is at the bottom both for expats to work and visitors in general for tourism. If you can pick one country in the world to work in and also to visit as a visitor—not at the same time, naturally—which country would it be?

Sources: C. Davis, "The World's Friendliest Countries to Foreigners, According to the World Economic Forum," *The Huffington Post*, April 9, 2013; J. Blanke and T. Chiesa, *The Travel and Tourism Competitiveness Report 2013*, World Economic Forum; *HSBC Expat Explorer Survey*. http://www.expatexplorer.hsbc.com.

Expatriate Selection

One way to reduce expatriate failure rates is by improving selection procedures to screen out inappropriate candidates. In a review of the research on this issue, Mendenhall and Oddou state that a major problem in many firms is that HRM managers tend to equate domestic performance with overseas performance potential.[31] Domestic performance and overseas performance potential are *not* the same thing. An executive who performs well in a domestic setting may not be able to adapt to managing in a different cultural setting. From their review of the research, Mendenhall and Oddou identified four dimensions that seem to predict success in a foreign posting: self-orientation, others-orientation, perceptual ability, and cultural toughness.

1. *Self-orientation.* The attributes of this dimension strengthen the expatriate's self-esteem, self-confidence, and mental well-being. Expatriates with high self-esteem, self-confidence, and mental well-being were more likely to succeed in foreign postings. Mendenhall and Oddou concluded that such individuals were able to adapt their interests in food, sport, and music; had interests outside of work that could be pursued (e.g., hobbies); and were technically competent.
2. *Others-orientation.* The attributes of this dimension enhance the expatriate's ability to interact effectively with host-country nationals. The more effectively the expatriate interacts with host-country nationals, the more likely he or she is to succeed. Two factors seem to be particularly important here: relationship development and willingness to communicate. Relationship development refers to the ability to develop long-lasting friendships with host-country nationals. Willingness to communicate refers to the expatriate's willingness to use the host-country language. Although language fluency helps, an expatriate need not be fluent to show willingness to communicate. Making the effort to use the language is what is

Expatriates at Royal Dutch Shell

Royal Dutch Shell is a global petroleum company with joint headquarters in London and The Hague in the Netherlands. The $400 billion company employs more than 92,000 people, approximately 10,000 of whom are at any one time living and working as expatriates. The expatriates at Shell are a diverse group, made up of more than 70 nationalities and located in some 100 countries. Shell, as a global corporation, has long recognized that the international mobility of its workforce is essential to its success

By the 1990s, however, Shell was finding it harder to recruit key personnel for foreign postings. To discover why, the company interviewed more than 200 expatriate employees and their spouses to determine their biggest concerns. The data were then used to construct a survey that was sent to 17,000 current and former expatriate employees, expatriates' spouses, and employees who had declined international assignments.

The survey registered a phenomenal 70 percent response rate, clearly indicating that many employees thought this was an important issue. According to the survey, five issues had the greatest impact on the willingness of an employee to accept an international assignment. In order of importance, these were (1) separation from children during their secondary education (the children of British and Dutch expatriates were often sent to boarding schools in their home countries while their parents worked abroad), (2) harm done to a spouse's career and employment, (3) failure to recognize and involve a spouse in the relocation decision, (4) failure to provide adequate information and assistance regarding relocation, and (5) health issues. The underlying message was that the family is the basic unit of expatriation, not the individual, and Shell needed to do more to recognize this.

To deal with these issues, Shell implemented a number of programs designed to address some of these problems. To help with the education of children, Shell built elementary schools for Shell employees where there was a heavy concentration of expatriates. As for secondary school education, it worked with local schools, often providing grants, to help them upgrade their educational offerings. It also offered an education supplement to help expatriates send their children to private schools in the host country.

Helping spouses with their careers is a more vexing problem. According to the survey data, half the spouses accompanying Shell staff on assignment were employed until the transfer. When expatriated, only 12 percent were able to secure employment, while a further 33 percent wished to be employed. Shell set up a spouse employment center to address the problem. The center provides career counseling and assistance in locating employment opportunities both during and immediately after an international assignment. The company also agreed to reimburse up to 80 percent of the costs of vocational training, further education, or reaccreditation.

Shell set up a global information and advice network known as "The Outpost" to provide support for families contemplating a foreign posting. The Outpost has its headquarters in The Hague and now runs 45 to 55 local offices around the world (depending on the business). The center recommends schools and medical facilities and provides housing advice and up-to-date information on employment, study, self-employment, and volunteer work.

Sources: L. Doan and B. Powell, "Striking U.S. Oil Workers Reach National Pact with Shell," *Bloomberg Business*, March 12, 2015; E. Smockum, "Don't Forget the Trailing Spouse," *Financial Times*, May 6, 1998, p. 22; V. Frazee, "Tearing Down Roadblocks," *Workforce*, 77, no. 2 (1998), pp. 50–54; C. Sievers, "Expatriate Management," *HR Focus*, 75, no. 3 (1998), pp. 75–76; J. Barbian, "Return to Sender," *Training*, January 2002, pp. 40–43; J. Mainwaring, "Shell Schools: Supporting Expat Families," *Rigzone*, June 21, 2012.

important. Such gestures tend to be rewarded with greater cooperation by host-country nationals.

3. *Perceptual ability.* This is the ability to understand why people of other countries behave the way they do, that is, the ability to empathize. This dimension seems critical for managing host-country nationals. Expatriate managers who lack this ability tend to treat foreign nationals as if they were home-country nationals. As a result, they may experience significant management problems and considerable frustration. As one expatriate executive from Hewlett-Packard observed, as reported by in the Mendenhall and Oddou study: "It took me six months to accept the fact that my staff meetings would start 30 minutes late, and that it would bother no one but me." According to Mendenhall and Oddou, well-adjusted expatriates tend to be nonjudgmental and nonevaluative in interpreting the behavior of host-country nationals and willing to be flexible in their management style, adjusting it as cultural conditions warrant.
4. *Cultural toughness.* This dimension refers to the relationship between the country of assignment and how well an expatriate adjusts to a particular posting. Some countries are much tougher postings than others because their cultures are more unfamiliar and uncomfortable. For example, many Americans regard Great Britain as a relatively easy foreign posting and for good reason—the two cultures have much in common. But many Americans find postings in non-Western cultures, such as India, Southeast Asia, and the

Middle East, to be much tougher.[32] The reasons are many, including poor health care and housing standards, inhospitable climate, lack of Western entertainment, and language difficulties. Also, many cultures are extremely male-dominated and may be particularly difficult postings for female Western managers.

GLOBAL MINDSET Some researchers suggest that a global mindset, one characterized by cognitive complexity and a cosmopolitan outlook, is the fundamental attribute of a global manager. Such managers can deal with high levels of complexity and ambiguity, and are open to the world. In a study of 615 people in the United States in March 2015 (conducted as a research project for the new version of this textbook, *International Business,* 11th edition, by Charles W. L. Hill and G. Tomas M. Hult), people's global mindset was assessed as it is today and what they hope or predict it would be in the next 20 years (margin of error = 3.89 percent). Figure 17.2 illustrates the findings, indicating that people act and behave like global citizens in less than half of what they undertake today but that the expectation is that people's global mindset will improve significantly in the next 20 years.

Given that people are expected to become more globally minded over time, how do you develop these attributes (high levels of complexity, ambiguity, and openness to the world)? Often they are gained in early life, from a family that is bicultural, lives in foreign countries, or learns foreign languages as a regular part of family life. Mendenhall and Oddou note that standard psychological tests can be used to assess the first three of these dimensions, whereas a comparison of cultures can give managers a feeling for the fourth dimension.

Mendenhall and Oddou contend that these four dimensions, in addition to domestic performance, should be considered when selecting a manager for foreign posting. However, practice does not often conform to the authors' recommendations. Tung's research, for example, showed that only 5 percent of the firms in her sample used formal procedures and psychological tests to assess the personality traits and relational abilities of potential expatriates.[33] Research by International Orientation Resources suggests that when selecting employees for foreign assignments, only 10 percent of the 50 Fortune 500 firms surveyed tested for important psychological traits

17.2 FIGURE

Global mindset of Americans

Source: C. W. L. Hill and G. T. M. Hult, *International Business: Competing in the Global Marketplace* (New York: McGraw-Hill Education, 2017).

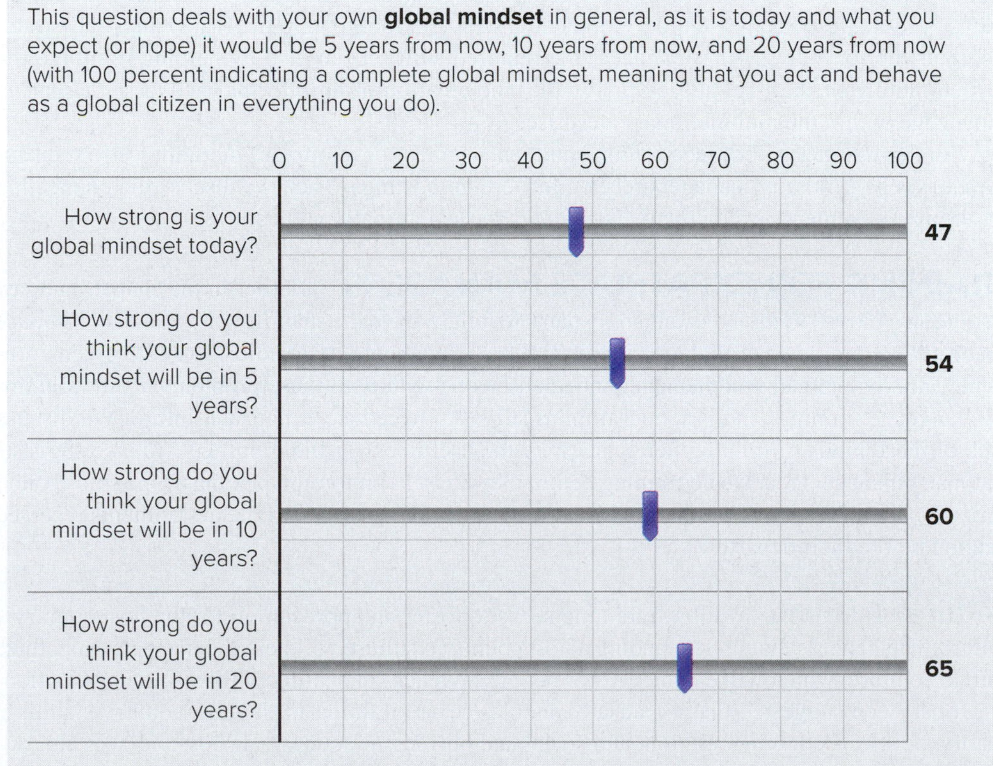

such as cultural sensitivity, interpersonal skills, adaptability, and flexibility. Instead, 90 percent of the time employees were selected on the basis of their technical expertise, not their cross-cultural fluency.[34]

Mendenhall and Oddou do not address the problem of expatriate failure due to a spouse's inability to adjust. According to a number of other researchers, a review of the family situation should be part of the expatriate selection process (see the Management Focus on Royal Dutch Shell for an example).[35] A survey by Windam International, another international HRM consulting firm, found that spouses were included in preselection interviews for foreign postings only 21 percent of the time and that only half of them received any cross-cultural training. The rise of dual-career families has added an additional and difficult dimension to this long-standing problem.[36] Increasingly, spouses wonder why they should have to sacrifice their own career to further that of their partner.[37]

test PREP

Use SmartBook to help retain what you have learned. Access your Instructor's Connect course to check out SmartBook or go to learnsmartadvantage.com for help.

LO 17-4

Recognize how management development and training programs can increase the value of human capital in the international business firm.

Training and Management Development

Selection is just the first step in matching a manager with a job. The next step is training the manager to do the specific job. For example, an intensive training program might be used to give expatriate managers the skills required for success in a foreign posting. However, management development is a much broader concept. It is intended to develop the manager's skills over his or her career with the firm. Thus, as part of a management development program, a manager might be sent on several foreign postings over a number of years to build his or her cross-cultural sensitivity and experience. At the same time, along with other managers in the firm, the person might attend management education programs at regular intervals. The thinking behind job transfers is that broad international experience will enhance the management and leadership skills of executives. Research suggests this may be the case.[38]

Historically, most international businesses have been more concerned with training than with management development. Plus, they tended to focus their training efforts on preparing home-country nationals for foreign postings. Recently, however, the shift toward greater global competition and the rise of transnational firms have changed this. It is increasingly common for firms to provide general management development programs in addition to training for particular posts. In many international businesses, the explicit purpose of these management development programs is strategic. Management development is seen as a tool to help the firm achieve its strategic goals, not only by giving managers the required skill set but also by helping reinforce the desired culture of the firm and by facilitating the creation of an informal network for sharing knowledge within the multinational enterprise.

With this distinction between training and management development in mind, we first examine the types of training managers receive for foreign postings. Then we discuss the connection between management development and strategy in the international business.

TRAINING FOR EXPATRIATE MANAGERS

Earlier in the chapter, we saw that the two most common reasons for expatriate failure were the inability of a manager's spouse to adjust to a foreign environment and the manager's own inability to adjust to a foreign environment. Training can help the manager and spouse cope with both these problems. Cultural training, language training, and practical training all seem to reduce expatriate failure. We discuss each of these kinds of training here.[39] Despite the usefulness of the training, evidence suggests that many managers receive no training before they are sent on foreign postings. One study found that only about 30 percent of managers sent on one- to five-year expatriate assignments received training before their departure.[40]

Cultural Training

Cultural training seeks to foster an appreciation for the host country's culture. The belief is that understanding a host country's culture will help the manager empathize with the culture, which will enhance his or her effectiveness in dealing with host-country nationals. It has been suggested that expatriates should receive training in the host country's culture, history, politics, economy, religion, and social and business practices.[41] If possible, it is also advisable to arrange for a familiarization trip to the host country before the formal transfer, because this seems to ease culture shock. Given the problems related to spouse adaptation, it is important that the spouse, and perhaps the whole family, be included in cultural training programs.

Lenovo decided that English was to be the official language of the company, even though it is a Chinese enterprise.

Source: © Vincent Yu/AP Images

Language Training English is the language of world business; it is quite possible to conduct business all over the world using only English. Notwithstanding the prevalence of English, however, an exclusive reliance on English diminishes an expatriate manager's ability to interact with host-country nationals. As noted earlier, a willingness to communicate in the language of the host country, even if the expatriate is far from fluent, can help build rapport with local employees and improve the manager's effectiveness. Despite this, one study of 74 executives of U.S. multinationals found that only 23 believed knowledge of foreign languages was necessary for conducting business abroad.[42] Those firms that did offer foreign language training for expatriates believed it improved their employees' effectiveness and enabled them to relate more easily to a foreign culture, which fostered a better image of the firm in the host country.

Practical Training Practical training is aimed at helping the expatriate manager and family ease themselves into day-to-day life in the host country. The sooner a routine is established, the better are the prospects that the expatriate and his or her family will adapt successfully. One critical need is for a support network of friends for the expatriate. Where an expatriate community exists, firms often devote considerable effort to ensuring the new expatriate family is quickly integrated into that group. The expatriate community can be a useful source of support and information and can be invaluable in helping the family adapt to a foreign culture.

REPATRIATION OF EXPATRIATES

A largely overlooked but critically important issue in the training and development of expatriate managers is to prepare them for reentry into their home-country organization.[43] Repatriation should be seen as the final link in an integrated, circular process that connects good selection and cross-cultural training of expatriate managers with completion of their term abroad and reintegration into their national organization. However, instead of coming home to share their knowledge and encourage other high-performing managers to take the same international career track, expatriates too often face a different scenario.[44]

Often when they return home after a stint abroad—where they have typically been autonomous, well compensated, and celebrated as a big fish in a little pond—they face an organization that doesn't know what they have done for the past few years, doesn't know how to use their new knowledge, and doesn't particularly care. In the worst cases, reentering employees have to scrounge for jobs, or firms will create standby positions that don't use the expatriate's skills and capabilities and fail to make the most of the business investment the firm has made in that individual.

Research illustrates the extent of this problem. According to one study of repatriated employees, 60 to 70 percent didn't know what their position would be when they returned home. Also, 60 percent said their organizations were vague about repatriation, about their new roles, and about their future career progression within the company; 77 percent of those surveyed took jobs at a lower level in their home organization than in their international assignments.[45] Not surprisingly, 15 percent of returning expatriates leave their firms within a year of arriving home, and 40 percent leave within three years.[46]

The key to solving this problem is good human resource planning. Just as the HRM function needs to develop good selection and training programs for its expatriates, it also needs to develop good programs for reintegrating expatriates back into work life within their home-country organization, for preparing them for changes in their physical and professional landscape, and for utilizing the knowledge they acquired while abroad. For an example of the kind of program that might be used, see the accompanying Management Focus that looks at the repatriation program developed by Monsanto.

Monsanto's Repatriation Program

Monsanto is a global provider of agricultural products with some 22,000 employees and about $15 billion in sales. At any one time, the company will have 100 mid- and higher-level managers on extended postings abroad. Two-thirds of these are Americans posted overseas; the remainder are foreign nationals employed in the United States. At Monsanto, managing expatriates and their repatriation begins with a rigorous selection process and intensive cross-cultural training, both for the managers and for their families. As is the case at many other global companies, the idea is to build an internationally minded cadre of highly capable managers who will lead the organization in the future.

One of the strongest features of this program is that employees and their sending and receiving managers, or sponsors, develop an agreement about how this assignment will fit into the firm's business objectives. The focus is on why employees are going abroad to do the job and what their contribution to Monsanto will be when they return. Sponsoring managers are expected to be explicit about the kind of job opportunities the expatriates will have once they return home.

Once they arrive back in their home country, expatriate managers meet with cross-cultural trainers during debriefing sessions. They are also given the opportunity to showcase their experiences to their peers, subordinates, and superiors in special information exchanges.

However, Monsanto's repatriation program focuses on more than just business; it also attends to the family's reentry. Monsanto has found that difficulties with repatriation often have more to do with personal and family-related issues than with work-related issues. But the personal matters obviously affect an employee's on-the-job performance, so it is important for the company to pay attention to such issues.

This is why Monsanto offers returning employees an opportunity to work through personal difficulties. About three months after they return home, expatriates meet for three hours at work with several colleagues of their choice. The debriefing session is a conversation aided by a trained facilitator who has an outline to help the expatriate cover all the important aspects of the repatriation. The debriefing allows the employee to share important experiences and to enlighten managers, colleagues, and friends about his or her expertise so others within the organization can use some of the global knowledge. According to one participant, "It sounds silly, but it's such a hectic time in the family's life, you don't have time to sit down and take stock of what's happening. You're going through the move, transitioning to a new job, a new house, and the children may be going to a new school. This is a kind of oasis; a time to talk and put your feelings on the table."* Apparently it works; since the program was introduced, the attrition rate among returning expatriates has dropped sharply.

*C. M. Solomon, "Repatriation: Up, Down, or Out?," *Personnel Journal,* January 1995, pp. 28–34.

Sources: A. Walton, "Who Says Monsanto Roundup Ingredient Is 'Probably Carcinogenic': Are They Right?," *Forbes*, March 21, 2015 (http://www.forbes.com/sites/alicegwalton/2015/03/21/monsanto-herbicide-dubbed-probably-carcinogenic-by-world-health-organization-are-they-right/#6f1b4b7726e5); C. M. Solomon, "Repatriation: Up, Down, or Out?," *Personnel Journal,* January 1995, pp. 28–34; J/ Schaefer, E. Hannibal, and J. O'Neill, "How Strategy, Culture and Improved Service Delivery Reshape Monsanto's International Assignment Program," *Journal of Organizational Excellence,* 22, no. 3 (2003), pp. 35–40.

MANAGEMENT DEVELOPMENT AND STRATEGY Management development programs are designed to increase the overall skill levels of managers through a mix of ongoing management education and rotations of managers through a number of jobs within the firm to give them varied experiences. They are attempts to improve the overall productivity and quality of the firm's management resources.

International businesses are increasingly using management development as a strategic tool. This is particularly true in firms pursuing a transnational strategy, as increasing numbers are. Such firms need a strong unifying corporate culture and informal management networks to assist in coordination and control. In addition, transnational firm managers need to be able to detect pressures for local responsiveness—and that requires them to understand the culture of a host country.

Management development programs help build a unifying corporate culture by socializing new managers into the norms and value systems of the firm. In-house company training programs and intense interaction during off-site training can foster esprit de corps—shared experiences, informal networks, perhaps a company language or jargon—as well as develop technical competencies. These training events often include songs, picnics, and sporting events that promote feelings of togetherness. These rites of integration may include "initiation rites" wherein personal culture is stripped, company uniforms are donned (e.g., T-shirts bearing the company logo), and humiliation is inflicted (e.g., a pie in the face). All these activities aim to strengthen a manager's identification with the company.[47]

Bringing managers together in one location for extended periods and rotating them through different jobs in several countries help the firm build an informal management network. Such a network can then be used as a conduit for exchanging valuable performance-enhancing knowledge within the organization.[48] Consider the Swedish telecommunications company

Ericsson. Interunit cooperation is extremely important at Ericsson, particularly for transferring know-how and core competencies from the parent to foreign subsidiaries, from foreign subsidiaries to the parent, and between foreign subsidiaries. To facilitate cooperation, Ericsson transfers large numbers of people back and forth between headquarters and subsidiaries. Ericsson sends a team of 50 to 100 engineers and managers from one unit to another for a year or two. This establishes a network of interpersonal contacts. This policy is effective for both solidifying a common culture in the company and coordinating the company's globally dispersed operations.[49]

Use SmartBook to help retain what you have learned. Access your Instructor's Connect course to check out SmartBook or go to learnsmartadvantage.com for help.

Performance Appraisal

Explain how and why performance appraisal systems might vary across nations.

Performance appraisal systems are used to evaluate the performance of managers against some criteria that the firm judges to be important for the implementation of strategy and the attainment of a competitive advantage. A firm's performance appraisal systems are an important element of its control systems, and control systems are a central component of organizational architecture. A particularly thorny issue in many international businesses is how best to evaluate the performance of expatriate managers.[50] This section looks at this issue and considers guidelines for appraising expatriate performance.

PERFORMANCE APPRAISAL PROBLEMS Unintentional bias makes it difficult to evaluate the performance of expatriate managers objectively. In many cases, two groups evaluate the performance of expatriate managers—host-nation managers and home-office managers—and both are subject to bias. The host-nation managers may be biased by their own cultural frame of reference and expectations. For example, Oddou and Mendenhall report the case of a U.S. manager who introduced participative decision making while working in an Indian subsidiary.[51] The manager subsequently received a negative evaluation from host-country managers because in India, the strong social stratification means managers are seen as experts who should not have to ask subordinates for help. The local employees apparently viewed the U.S. manager's attempt at participatory management as an indication that he was incompetent and did not know his job.

Home-country managers' appraisals may be biased by distance and by their own lack of experience working abroad. Home-office managers are often not aware of what is going on in a foreign operation. Accordingly, they tend to rely on hard data in evaluating an expatriate's performance, such as the subunit's productivity, profitability, or market share. Such criteria may reflect factors outside the expatriate manager's control (e.g., adverse changes in exchange rates, economic downturns). Also, hard data do not take into account many less visible soft variables that are also important, such as an expatriate's ability to develop cross-cultural awareness and to work productively with local managers. Due to such biases, many expatriate managers believe that headquarters management evaluates them unfairly and does not fully appreciate the value of their skills and experience. This could be one reason many expatriates believe a foreign posting does not benefit their careers. In one study of personnel managers in U.S. multinationals, 56 percent of the managers surveyed stated that a foreign assignment is either detrimental or immaterial to one's career.[52]

GUIDELINES FOR PERFORMANCE APPRAISAL Several things can reduce bias in the performance appraisal process.[53] First, most expatriates appear to believe more weight should be given to an on-site manager's appraisal than to an off-site manager's appraisal. Due to proximity, an on-site manager is more likely to evaluate the soft variables that are important aspects of an expatriate's performance. The evaluation may be especially valid when the on-site manager is of the same nationality as the expatriate because cultural bias should be alleviated. In practice, home-office managers often write performance evaluations after receiving input from on-site managers. When this is the case, most experts recommend that a former expatriate who served in the same location should be involved in the appraisal to help reduce bias. Finally, when the policy is for foreign on-site managers to write performance evaluations, home-office managers should be consulted before an on-site manager completes a formal termination evaluation. This gives the home-office manager the opportunity to balance what could be a very hostile evaluation based on a cultural misunderstanding.

 test PREP

Use SmartBook to help retain what you have learned. Access your Instructor's Connect course to check out SmartBook or go to learnsmartadvantage.com for help.

LO 17-6

Understand how and why compensation systems might vary across nations.

Compensation

Two issues are raised in every discussion of compensation practices in an international business. One is how compensation should be adjusted to reflect national differences in economic circumstances and compensation practices. The other issue is how expatriate managers should be paid. From a strategic perspective, the important point is that whatever compensation system is used, it should reward managers for taking actions that are consistent with the strategy of the enterprise (see Mary Kay Inc. in the opening case).

NATIONAL DIFFERENCES IN COMPENSATION Differences exist in the compensation of executives at the same level in various countries. The results of a survey undertaken by Towers Watson, for example, suggest that U.S. CEOs earn, on average, roughly double the pay of non-U.S. CEOs.[54]

National differences in compensation raise a perplexing question for an international business: Should the firm pay executives in different countries according to the prevailing standards in each country, or should it equalize pay on a global basis? The problem does not arise in firms pursuing ethnocentric or polycentric staffing policies. In ethnocentric firms, the issue can be reduced to that of how much home-country expatriates should be paid (which we consider later). As for polycentric firms, the lack of managers' mobility among national operations implies that pay can and should be kept country-specific. There would seem to be no point in paying executives in Great Britain the same as U.S. executives if they never work side by side.

However, this problem is very real in firms with geocentric staffing policies. A geocentric staffing policy is consistent with a transnational strategy. One aspect of this policy is the need for a cadre of international managers that may include many different nationalities. Should all members of such a cadre be paid the same salary and the same incentive pay? For a U.S.-based firm, this would mean raising the compensation of foreign nationals to U.S. levels, which could be expensive. If the firm does not equalize pay, it could cause considerable resentment among foreign nationals who are members of the international cadre and work with U.S. nationals. If a firm is serious about building an international cadre, it may have to pay its international executives the same basic salary irrespective of their country of origin or assignment. Currently, however, this practice is not widespread.

Over the past decade many firms have moved toward a compensation structure that is based on consistent global standards, with employees being evaluated by the same grading system and having access to the same bonus pay and benefits structure irrespective of where they work. Some 85 percent of the companies in a survey by Mercer Management Consulting stated they now have a global compensation strategy in place.[55] McDonald's, which is featured in the accompanying Management Focus, is one such enterprise. Another survey found that two-thirds of multinationals now exercise central control over the benefit plans offered in different nations.[56] However, except for a relative small cadre of internationally mobile executives, base pay in most firms is set with regard to local market conditions.

EXPATRIATE PAY The most common approach to expatriate pay is the balance sheet approach. According to Organizational Resources Counselors, some 80 percent of the 781 companies it surveyed used this approach.[57] This approach equalizes purchasing power across countries so employees can enjoy the same living standard in their foreign posting that they enjoyed at home. In addition, the approach provides financial incentives to offset qualitative differences between assignment locations.[58] Figure 17.3 shows a typical balance sheet. Note that home-country outlays for the employee are designated as income taxes, housing expenses, expenditures for goods and services (food, clothing, entertainment, etc.), and reserves (savings, pension contributions, etc.). The balance sheet approach attempts to provide expatriates with the same standard of living in their host countries as they enjoy at home plus a financial inducement (i.e., premium, incentive) for accepting an overseas assignment.

The components of the typical expatriate compensation package are a base salary, a foreign service premium, allowances of various types, tax differentials, and benefits. We briefly review

management FOCUS

McDonald's Global Compensation Practices

With more than 400,000 managers and senior staff employees in 118 countries around the world, by the early 2000s McDonald's realized it had to develop a consistent global compensation and performance appraisal strategy. As with many companies that have expanded to many corners of the world, McDonald's found itself with a decentralized and inconsistent compensation program. Many reasons existed for this new global HR compensation strategy. Foremost among them was that McDonald's executive of worldwide human resources, Rich Floersch, pointed to a need to have a consistent global HR strategy to attract and retain better people. After months of consultation with global managers to ensure that any new system was formed via a collaborative approach, McDonald's began to roll out its new global compensation program.

One important element of this program calls for the corporate head office to provide local country managers with a menu of business principles to focus on in the coming year. These principles include areas such as customer service, marketing, and restaurant re-imaging. Each country manager then picks three to five areas to focus on for success in the local market. For example, if France is introducing a new menu item, it might create business targets around that for the year. Human resource managers then submit their business cases and targets to senior executives at headquarters for approval. At the end of the year, the country's annual incentive pool is based on how the region met its targets, as well as on the business unit's operating income. A portion of an individual employee's annual bonus is based on that mix.

The other portion of an employee's annual incentive is based on individual performance. McDonald's has always had a performance rating system, but within its new HR management strategy, the company has now introduced global guidelines that suggest 20 percent of employees receive the highest rating, 70 percent the middle, and 10 percent the bottom. By giving guidelines rather than forced ranking, McDonald's hopes to encourage differentiation of performance while allowing for some local flexibility. Also, by providing principles and guidance, and yet allowing local country managers to customize their compensation programs to meet local market demands, McDonald's also claims it has seen a reduction in turnover. The company's own internal surveys suggest more employees now believe that their compensation is fair and reflects local market conditions. Overall, "McDonald's benefits and compensation program is designed to attract, retain and engage talented people who will deliver strong performance and help McDonald's achieve our business goals and objectives."*

McDonald's Total Compensation. www.aboutmcdonalds.com.

Sources: J. Marquez, "McDonald's Rewards Program Leaves Room for Some Local Flavor," *Workforce Management,* April 10, 2006, p. 26; C. Zillman, "McDonald's Loses Big on Labor Ruling," *Forbes*, July 29, 2014; "McDonald's Total Compensation." www.aboutmcdonalds.com; V. Black, "How I Got Here: Rich Floersch of McDonald's," *Bloomberg Business*, August 14, 2012.

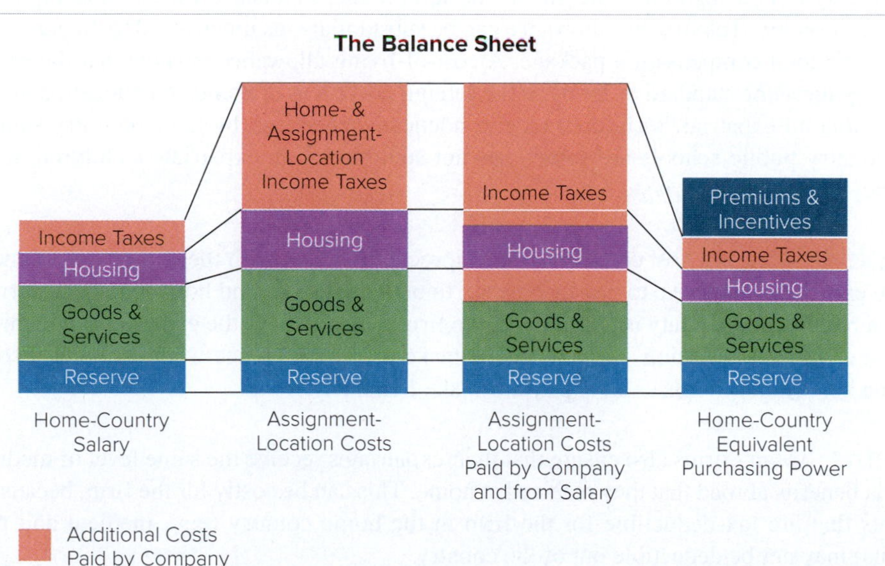

17.3 FIGURE

The Balance Sheet Approach to Expatriate Pay.

Source: C. W. L. Hill and G. T. M. Hult, *International Business: Competing in the Global Marketplace* (New York: McGraw-Hill Education, 2017).

each of these components.[59] An expatriate's total compensation package may amount to three times what he or she would cost the firm in a home-country posting. Because of the high cost of expatriates, many firms have reduced their use of them in recent years. However, a firm's ability to reduce its use of expatriates may be limited, particularly if it is pursuing an ethnocentric or geocentric staffing policy.

Where Would You Go to Find Expat Resources?

Not so many years ago, business professionals whose companies sent them overseas to work had few outside resources to help them become acclimated to their new status as expatriates. Today, however, a wealth of information is available. For example, a simple keyword search online for "expatriate" yields an almost endless supply of links: newspapers and magazines published exclusively for expats; websites catering to expatriates in specific regions or countries; general information sites offering insiders' guides to different countries and their finance, culture, and health care systems; not to mention blogs and chat rooms, forums and groups. The expatriate boom has even fueled an industry offering a broad array of services for expats, from mail forwarding to tax preparation to health and life insurance. One example is globalEDGE™'s section on "Travel/ Living Abroad" (http://globaledge.msu.edu/global-resources/travelliving-abroad). While often good, the examples in this short write-up are all online, removed from the country itself. How much would you trust online information and data as the only source for "getting to know" the new country you have just signed on to spend three years in as an expat?

Base Salary

An expatriate's base salary should normally in the same range as the base salary for a similar position in the home country. At the same time, while an expatriate may have a base salary that he or she would have in their home country, foreign nationals in these expatriate locations do not necessarily get the same salary levels. Oftentimes, developed nations (e.g., Germany, the United States) offer higher base salaries than comparable jobs and positions in the company in other, developing or less developed, countries. The base salary is normally paid in either the home-country currency or in the local currency.

Foreign Service Premium

A foreign service premium is extra pay the expatriate receives for working outside his or her country of origin. It is offered as an inducement to accept foreign postings. It compensates the expatriate for having to live in an unfamiliar country isolated from family and friends, having to deal with a new culture and language, and having to adapt to new work habits and practices. Many firms pay foreign service premiums as a percentage of base salary, ranging from 10 to 30 percent after tax, with 16 percent being the average premium.[60]

Allowances

Four types of allowances are often included in an expatriate's compensation package: hardship, housing, cost of living, and education. A hardship allowance is paid when the expatriate is being sent to a difficult location, usually defined as one where such basic amenities as health care, schools, and retail stores are grossly deficient by the standards of the expatriate's home country. A housing allowance is normally given to ensure that the expatriate can afford the same quality of housing in the foreign country as at home. In locations where housing is expensive (e.g., London, Tokyo), this allowance can be substantial—as much as 10 to 30 percent of the expatriate's total compensation package. A cost-of-living allowance ensures that the expatriate will enjoy the same standard of living in the foreign posting as at home. An education allowance ensures that an expatriate's children receive adequate schooling (by home-country standards). Host-country public schools are sometimes not suitable for an expatriate's children, in which case they must attend a private school.

Taxation

Unless a host country has a reciprocal tax treaty with the expatriate's home country, the expatriate may have to pay income tax to both the home- and host-country governments. When a reciprocal tax treaty is not in force, the firm typically pays the expatriate's income tax in the host country. In addition, firms normally make up the difference when a higher income tax rate in a host country reduces an expatriate's take-home pay.

test PREP

Use SmartBook to help retain what you have learned. Access your Instructor's Connect course to check out SmartBook or go to learnsmartadvantage.com for help.

Benefits

Many firms also ensure that their expatriates receive the same level of medical and pension benefits abroad that they received at home. This can be costly for the firm, because many benefits that are tax-deductible for the firm in the home country (e.g., medical and pension benefits) may not be deductible out of the country.

LO 17-7

Understand how organized labor can influence strategic choices in international business firms.

International Labor Relations

The HRM function of an international business is typically responsible for international labor relations. From a strategic perspective, the key issue in international labor relations is the degree to which organized labor can limit the choices of an international business. A firm's ability to integrate and consolidate its global operations to realize experience curve and location economies can be limited by organized labor, constraining the pursuit of a transnational or global standardization strategy. Prahalad and Doz cite the example of General Motors, which gained peace with labor unions in Germany by agreeing not to integrate and consolidate operations in the most efficient manner.[61] General Motors made substantial investments in Germany—matching its new investments in Austria and Spain—at the demand of the German metalworkers' unions.

One task of the HRM function is to foster harmony and minimize conflict between the firm and organized labor. With this in mind, this section is divided into three parts. First, we review organized labor's concerns about multinational enterprises. Second, we look at how organized labor has tried to deal with these concerns. And third, we look at how international businesses manage their labor relations to minimize labor disputes.

THE CONCERNS OF ORGANIZED LABOR Labor unions generally try to get better pay, greater job security, and better working conditions for their members through collective bargaining with management. Unions' bargaining power is derived largely from their ability to threaten to disrupt production, either by a strike or some other form of work protest (e.g., refusing to work overtime). This threat is credible, however, only insofar as management has no alternative but to employ union labor.

A principal concern of domestic unions about multinational firms is that the company can counter its bargaining power with the power to move production to another country. Ford, for example, clearly threatened British unions with a plan to move manufacturing to continental Europe unless British workers abandoned work rules that limited productivity, showed restraint in negotiating for wage increases, and curtailed strikes and other work disruptions.[62]

Another concern of organized labor is that an international business will keep highly skilled tasks in its home country and farm out only low-skilled tasks to foreign plants. Such a practice makes it relatively easy for an international business to switch production from one location to another as economic conditions warrant. Consequently, the bargaining power of organized labor is once more reduced.

A final union concern arises when an international business attempts to import employment practices and contractual agreements from its home country. When these practices are alien to the host country, organized labor fears the change will reduce its influence and power. This concern has surfaced in response to Japanese multinationals that have been trying to export their style of labor relations to other countries. For example, much to the annoyance of the United Auto Workers, many Japanese auto plants in the United States are not unionized. As a result, union influence in the auto industry is declining.

THE STRATEGY OF ORGANIZED LABOR Organized labor has responded to the increased bargaining power of multinational corporations by taking three actions: (1) trying to establish international labor organizations, (2) lobbying for national legislation to restrict multinationals, and (3) trying to achieve international regulations on multinationals through such organizations as the United Nations. These efforts have not been very successful.

In the 1960s, organized labor began to establish international trade secretariats (ITSs) to provide worldwide links for national unions in particular industries. The long-term goal was to be able to bargain transnationally with multinational firms. Organized labor believed that by coordinating union action across countries through an ITS, it could counter the power of a multinational corporation by threatening to disrupt production on an international scale. For example, Ford's threat to move production from Great Britain to other European locations would not have been credible if the unions in various European countries had united to oppose it.

Employees work on the chassis of an Adam Opel AG car, at a GM factory in Eisenach, Germany.

Source: © Martin Leissl/Bloomberg/Getty Images

However, the ITSs have had virtually no real success. Although national unions may want to cooperate, they also compete with each other to attract investment from international businesses and hence jobs for their members. For example, in attempting to gain new jobs for their members, national unions in the auto industry often court auto firms that are seeking locations for new plants. One reason Nissan chose to build its European production facilities in Great Britain rather than Spain was that the British unions agreed to greater concessions than the Spanish unions did. As a result of such competition between national unions, cooperation is difficult to establish.

A further impediment to cooperation has been the wide variation in union structure. Trade unions developed independently in each country. As a result, the structure and ideology of unions tend to vary significantly from country to country, as does the nature of collective bargaining. For example, in Great Britain, France, and Italy, many unions are controlled by left-wing socialists, who view collective bargaining through the lens of "class conflict." In contrast, most union leaders in Germany, the Netherlands, Scandinavia, and Switzerland are far more moderate politically. The ideological gap between union leaders in different countries has made cooperation difficult. Divergent ideologies are reflected in radically different views about the role of a union in society and the stance unions should take toward multinationals.

Organized labor has also met with only limited success in its efforts to get national and international bodies to regulate multinationals. Such international organizations as the International Labour Organization and the Organisation for Economic Co-operation and Development have adopted codes of conduct for multinational firms to follow in labor relations. However, these guidelines are not as far-reaching as many unions would like. They also do not provide any enforcement mechanisms. Many researchers report that such guidelines are of only limited effectiveness.[63]

APPROACHES TO LABOR RELATIONS

International businesses differ markedly in their approaches to international labor relations. The main difference is the degree to which labor relations activities are centralized or decentralized. Historically, most international businesses have decentralized international labor relations activities to their foreign subsidiaries because labor laws, union power, and the nature of collective bargaining varied so much from country to country. It made sense to decentralize the labor relations function to local managers. The belief was that there was no way central management could effectively handle the complexity of simultaneously managing labor relations in a number of different environments.

Although this logic still holds, the trend is toward greater centralized control. This trend reflects international firms' attempts to rationalize their global operations. The general rise in competitive pressure in industry after industry has made it more important for firms to control their costs. Because labor costs account for such a large percentage of total costs, some firms are now using the threat to move production to another country in their negotiations with unions to change work rules and limit wage increases (as Ford did in Europe). Because such a move would involve major new investments and plant closures, this bargaining tactic requires the input of headquarters management. Thus, the level of centralized input into labor relations is increasing.

In addition, the realization is growing that the way work is organized within a plant can be a major source of competitive advantage. Much of the competitive advantage of Japanese automakers, for example, has been attributed to the use of self-managing teams, job rotation, cross-training, and the like in their Japanese plants.[64] To replicate their domestic performance in foreign plants, the Japanese firms have tried to replicate their work practices there. This often brings them into direct conflict with traditional work practices in those countries, as sanctioned by the local labor unions, so the Japanese firms have often made their foreign investments contingent on the local union accepting a radical change in work practices. To achieve this, the headquarters of many Japanese firms bargains directly with local unions to get union agreement to changes in work rules before committing to an investment. For example, before Nissan decided to invest in northern England, it got a commitment from British unions to agree to a change in traditional work practices. By its very nature, pursuing such a strategy requires centralized control over the labor relations function.

Use SmartBook to help retain what you have learned. Access your Instructor's Connect course to check out SmartBook or go to learnsmartadvantage.com for help.

Key Terms

human resource management (HRM), p. 472
expatriate manager, p. 472
staffing policy, p. 474
corporate culture, p. 474
ethnocentric staffing policy, p. 474
polycentric staffing policy, p. 475
geocentric staffing policy, p. 476
expatriate failure, p. 477

Summary

This chapter focused on human resource management in international businesses. HRM activities include human resource strategy, staffing, performance evaluation, management development, compensation, and labor relations. None of these activities is performed in a vacuum; all must be appropriate to the firm's strategy. The chapter made the following points:

1. Firm success requires HRM policies to be congruent with the firm's strategy and with its formal and informal structure and controls.
2. Staffing policy is concerned with selecting employees who have the skills required to perform particular jobs. Staffing policy can be a tool for developing and promoting a corporate culture.
3. An ethnocentric approach to staffing policy fills all key management positions in an international business with parent-country nationals. The policy is congruent with an international strategy. A drawback is that ethnocentric staffing can result in cultural myopia.
4. A polycentric staffing policy uses host-country nationals to manage foreign subsidiaries and parent-country nationals for the key positions at corporate headquarters. This approach can minimize the dangers of cultural myopia, but it can create a gap between home- and host-country operations. The policy is best suited to a localization strategy.
5. A geocentric staffing policy seeks the best people for key jobs throughout the organization, regardless of their nationality. This approach is consistent with building a strong, unifying culture and informal management network and is well suited to both global standardization and transnational strategies. Immigration policies of national governments may limit a firm's ability to pursue this policy.
6. A prominent issue in the international staffing literature is expatriate failure, defined as the premature return of an expatriate manager to his or her home country. The costs of expatriate failure can be substantial.
7. Expatriate failure can be reduced by selection procedures that screen out inappropriate candidates. The most successful expatriates seem to be those who have high self-esteem and self-confidence, can get along well with others, are willing to attempt to communicate in a foreign language, and can empathize with people of other cultures.
8. Training can lower the probability of expatriate failure. It should include cultural training, language training, and practical training, and it should be provided to both the expatriate manager and the spouse.
9. Management development programs attempt to increase the overall skill levels of managers through a mix of ongoing management education and rotation of managers through different jobs within the firm to give them varied experiences. Management development is often used as a strategic tool to build a strong unifying culture and informal management network, both of which support transnational and global standardization strategies.
10. It can be difficult to evaluate the performance of expatriate managers objectively because of unintentional bias. A firm can take a number of steps to reduce this bias.
11. Country differences in compensation practices raise a difficult question for an international business: Should the firm pay executives in different countries according to the standards in each country or equalize pay on a global basis?
12. The most common approach to expatriate pay is the balance sheet approach. This approach aims to equalize purchasing power so employees can enjoy the same living standard in their foreign posting that they had at home.
13. A key issue in international labor relations is the degree to which organized labor can limit the choices available to an international business. A firm's ability to pursue a transnational or global standardization strategy can be significantly constrained by the actions of labor unions.
14. A principal concern of organized labor is that the multinational can counter union bargaining power with threats to move production to another country.
15. Organized labor has tried to counter the bargaining power of multinationals by forming international labor organizations. In general, these efforts have not been effective.

Critical Thinking and Discussion Questions

1. What are the main advantages and disadvantages of the ethnocentric, polycentric, and geocentric approaches to staffing policy? When is each approach appropriate?
2. Research suggests that many expatriate employees encounter problems that limit both their effectiveness in a foreign posting and their contribution to the company when they return home. What are the main causes and consequences of these problems, and how might a firm reduce the occurrence of such problems?
3. What is the link between an international business's strategy and its human resource management policies, particularly with regard to the use of expatriate employees and their pay scale?
4. In what ways can organized labor constrain the strategic choices of an international business? How can an international business limit these constraints?
5. Reread the Management Focus on McDonald's global compensation practices. How does McDonald's approach help the company take into account local differences when reviewing the performance of different country managers and awarding bonus pay?

globalEDGE Research

TaskglobalEDGE.msu.edu

Use the globalEDGE™ website (globaledge.msu.edu) to complete the following exercises:

1. The impact of strikes and lockouts on business activities can be substantial. Because your manufacturing company is planning to expand its operations in the Asian markets, you have to identify the countries where strikes and lockouts could introduce interruptions to your operations. Using *labor statistics* from the International Labour Organization to develop your report, identify the three Asian countries with the highest number of strikes and lockouts, as well as the total number of lost worker days. What types of precautions can your company take to prevent interruptions from occurring in these markets?
2. You work in the human resource department at the headquarters of a multinational corporation. Your company is about to send a number of managers overseas as expatriates to France and New Zealand. You need to create an executive summary evaluating, comparing, and contrasting the possible issues expats may encounter in these two countries. Your manager tells you that a tool called *Expat Explorer* created by HSBC can assist you in your task.

Siemens and Global Competitiveness

closing case

The German company Siemens is one of the world's great engineering conglomerates, manufacturing everything from hearing aids and medical scanners to giant power generation turbines, wind systems, and locomotives. By the late 2000s, however, Siemens was struggling with subpar performance relative to its global rivals such as General Electric (GE), Honeywell, and United Technologies. In July 2007, Siemens hired Peter Löscher as CEO, replacing Klaus Kleinfeld, and gave him the task of trying to revitalize the organization. Löscher, an Austrian whose career included major leadership positions at GE and Merck, was the first outsider to run Siemens since the company's establishment in 1847.

In 2007, Löscher inherited a global organization of significant complexity. At the time, Siemens had 475,000 employees and revenues of $72 billion, operated in a wide range of industries, and had activities in more than 190 countries. As a comparison, today, Siemens employs about 362,000 people, with revenues of about $79 billion, and covers a similar number of country markets. At the time, Siemens was organized into 12 operating groups, which were further subdivided into 70 business divisions. Although each division had its own product focus, such as wind power or molecular imaging, Siemens worked hard to deliver integrated solutions to customers. This required many of the 70 business divisions to cooperate with each other on large projects.

Siemens also had a strong tradition of local responsiveness. The countries where the company was the most active had their own executive manager, known as "Mr./Ms. Siemens." This individual acted as the country manager for all of Siemens businesses in a specific geography and was also the CEO of the respective local company. The operating group and business division structure was often replicated within the local company. This resulted in a matrix organization, with the head of the power generation business in, for example, Argentina, reporting to the local country CEO and to the global head of the business division.

It was the responsibility of Mr./Ms. Siemens and his or her staff to manage relations with local customers, develop bids for projects, and ensure that business divisions cooperated on the delivery of a project. Local companies were given significant discretion over product specifications for local clients. Thus, the local company in Argentina might bid on a subway project in Buenos Aires, tailor that bid to meet the needs of the local client, and, if the bid was accepted, make sure that there was sufficient cooperation between the different business divisions in order to successfully complete the project.

Löscher could see the virtue in this organization—it tried to meld together global scale at the business level with local responsiveness at the country level—but it was very complex to effectively and efficiently implement. In his view, there were too many direct reports to the corporate headquarters, resulting in significant overload. There was also a serious accountability problem. If the company failed to deliver a project profitably—let's say the subway system in Buenos Aires—who, then, was responsible for that: the local managers or the managers of the business divisions? Löscher believed that country managers had too much power in the structure and the business divisions had too little and were not accountable enough.

In 2008, Löscher changed the organizational structure to deal with these power and accountability issues. He consolidated the operating groups into three main sectors: industry, energy, and health care. The business divisions were placed within their respective sectors. He then organized the 190 country units into 17 regional clusters and gave them primary responsibility for developing a cost-efficient regional infrastructure, focusing on customers and managing sales organizations. Profit and loss responsibility was assigned to the sectors and business divisions. Previously, each operating group and national subsidiary had maintained its own separate profit and loss accounts. This change was a shock to the Mr./Ms. Siemens around the world, who were told that their goal was to contribute toward the global operating income for a sector and business division. While not doing away with local responsiveness, Löscher had effectively reduced the power of country managers within the Siemens structure, making them directly responsible for boosting the profitability of the global businesses.

Löscher went further, instituting a management view process that led to the replacement of half of the company's top 100 managers. Löscher is now directly involved in the appointment of the top 300 management positions at Siemens. He also took out two layers of top management that had no operational accountability in the older company structure. His goal in making these organizational changes has been to replace managers who did not buy into a new way of doing things and to increase the performance accountability of the people who ran the sectors and business divisions.

In August 2013, Joe Kaeser took over as president and CEO of Siemens after a long-term and successful reign by Peter Löscher. Kaeser instituted a "Siemens—Vision 2020" as a follow-up to Löscher's human resource strategy to take the company to the next level. Kaeser joined Siemens in 1980. Today, under Kaeser's leadership, Siemens employs more than 17,500 software engineers. And though much of the conversation about technology revolves around apps and websites, Siemens is focused on using human capital to show how information technology (IT) can add leverage in advanced manufacturing.

Sources: D. Gross, "Siemens CEO Joe Kaeser on the Next Industrial Revolution," *Strategy+Business*, February 9, 2016; T. Ferguson, "Siemens Boss Upbeat on U.S., India—Otherwise Not So Much," *Forbes*, January 12, 2016; J. Kaeser, "Fixing the German Dynamo," *The Economist*, July 26, 2014; B. Kammel and R.Weiss, "How Siemens Got Its Mojo Back," *Bloomberg BusinessWeek*, January 27, 2011; V, J. Racanelli, "The Culture Changer," *Barron's*, March 10, 2012; S. G. Leslie and J. Sorensen, "Siemens: Building a Structure to Drive Performance and Responsibility (A)," *Stanford Business School Case*, October 7, 2010.

CASE DISCUSSION QUESTIONS

1. How would you characterize the strategy for competing internationally that Siemens was pursuing prior to the arrival of Peter Löscher? What were the benefits of this strategy? What were the costs? Why was Siemens pursuing this strategy?
2. What strategy was Peter Löscher trying to get Siemens to pursue with his streamlined "power and accountability" initiative? What are the benefits of this strategy? Can you see any drawbacks?
3. Does the "power and accountability" initiative imply that Siemens will ignore national and regional differences?
4. With the arrival of Joe Kaeser, the focus is much more on apps and websites. How can these individual, customer-based IT features help industrial-based IT companies such as Siemens?

Endnotes

1. P. J. Dowling and R. S. Schuler, *International Dimensions of Human Resource Management* (Boston: PSW-Kent, 1990).
2. J. Millman, M. A. von Glinow, and M. Nathan, "Organizational Life Cycles and Strategic International Human Resource Management in Multinational Companies," *Academy of Management Review* 16 (1991), pp. 318–39; A. Bird and S. Beechler, "Links between Business Strategy and Human Resource Management," *Journal of International Business Studies* 26 (1995), pp. 23–47; B. A. Colbert, "The Complex Resource Based View: Implications for Theory and Practice of Strategic Human Resource Management," *Academy of Management Review* 29 (2004), pp. 341–60; C. J. Collins and K. D. Clark, "Strategic Human Resource Practices, Top Management Team Social Networks, and Firm Performance," *Academy of Management Journal* 46 (2003), pp. 740–60.
3. See Peter Bamberger and Ilan Meshoulam, *Human Resource Strategy: Formulation, Implementation, and Impact* (Thousand Oaks, CA: Sage, 2000); P. M. Wright and S. Snell, "Towards a Unifying Framework for Exploring Fit and Flexibility in Human Resource Management," *Academy of Management Review* 23 (October 1998), pp. 756–72; Colbert, "The Complex Resource-Based View"; R. S. Schuler and S. E. Jackson, "A Quarter Century Review of Human Resource Management in the US: The Growth in Importance of the International Perspective," *Management Review* 16 (2005), pp. 1–25.
4. R. Colman, "HR Management Lags behind at World Class Firms," *CMA Management*, July–August 2002, p. 9.
5. E. H. Schein, *Organizational Culture and Leadership* (San Francisco: Jossey-Bass, 1985).

6. H. V. Perlmutter, "The Tortuous Evolution of the Multinational Corporation," *Columbia Journal of World Business* 4 (1969), pp. 9–18; D. A. Heenan and H. V. Perlmutter, *Multinational Organizational Development* (Reading, MA: Addison-Wesley, 1979); D. A. Ondrack, "International Human Resources Management in European and North American Firms," *International Studies of Management and Organization* 15 (1985), pp. 6–32; T. Jackson, "The Management of People across Cultures: Valuing People Differently," *Human Resource Management* 41 (2002), pp. 455–75.
7. V. Reitman and M. Schuman, "Men's Club: Japanese and Korean Companies Rarely Look Outside for People to Run Their Overseas Operations," *The Wall Street Journal,* September 26, 1996, p. 17.
8. E. Wong, "China's Export of Labor Faces Growing Scorn," The *New York Times,* December 21, 2009, p. A1.
9. S. Beechler and J. Z. Yang, "The Transfer of Japanese Style Management to American Subsidiaries," *Journal of International Business Studies* 25 (1994), pp. 467–91. See also R. Konopaske, S. Warner, and K. E. Neupert, "Entry Mode Strategy and Performance: The Role of FDI Staffing," *Journal of Business Research,* September 2002, pp. 759–70.
10. M. Banai and L. M. Sama, "Ethical Dilemma in MNCs' International Staffing Policies," *Journal of Business Ethics,* June 2000, pp. 221–35.
11. Reitman and Schuman, "Men's Club."
12. C. A. Bartlett and S. Ghoshal, *Managing across Borders: The Transnational Solution* (Boston: Harvard Business School Press, 1989).
13. S. J. Kobrin, "Geocentric Mindset and Multinational Strategy," *Journal of International Business Studies* 25 (1994), pp. 493–511.
14. F. Hansen, "International Business Machine," *Workforce Management,* July 2005, pp. 36–44.
15. P. M. Rosenzweig and N. Nohria, "Influences on Human Resource Management Practices in Multinational Corporations," *Journal of International Business Studies* 25 (1994), pp. 229–51.
16. Kobrin, "Geocentric Mindset and Multinational Strategy."
17. M. Harvey and H. Fung, "Inpatriate Managers: The Need for Realistic Relocation Reviews," *International Journal of Management* 17 (2000), pp. 151–59.
18. S. Black, M. Mendenhall, and G. Oddou, "Toward a Comprehensive Model of International Adjustment," *Academy of Management Review* 16 (1991), pp. 291–317; J. Shay and T. J. Bruce, "Expatriate Managers," *Cornell Hotel & Restaurant Administration Quarterly,* February 1997, pp. 30–40; Y. Baruch and Y. Altman, "Expatriation and Repatriation in MNCs—A Taxonomy," *Human Resource Management* 41 (2002), pp. 239–59.
19. M. G. Harvey, "The Multinational Corporation's Expatriate Problem: An Application of Murphy's Law," *Business Horizons* 26 (1983), pp. 71–78.
20. J. Barbian, "Return to Sender," *Training,* January 2002, pp. 40–43.
21. Barbian, "Return to Sender"; K. Yeaton and N. Hall, "Expatriates: Reducing Failure Rates," *Journal of Corporate Accounting and Finance,* March–April 2008, pp. 75–78.
22. Black et al., "Toward a Comprehensive Model of International Adjustment."
23. R. L. Tung, "Selection and Training Procedures of U.S., European, and Japanese Multinationals," *California Management Review* 25 (1982), pp. 57–71.
24. T. Zsuzzanna and M. Pieperl, "Expatriate Practices in German, Japanese, U.K., and U.S. Multinational Companies: A Comparative Survey of Changes," *Human Resource Management,* January–February 2009, pp. 153–71.
25. H. W. Lee, "Factors That Influence Expatriate Failure," *International Journal of Management* 24 (2007), pp. 403–15.
26. C. M. Solomon, "Success Abroad Depends upon More Than Job Skills," *Personnel Journal,* April 1994, pp. 51–58.
27. C. M. Solomon, "Unhappy Trails," *Workforce,* August 2000, pp. 36–41.
28. Solomon, "Success Abroad Depends upon More Than Job Skills."
29. Solomon, "Unhappy Trails."
30. M. Harvey, "Addressing the Dual-Career Expatriation Dilemma," *Human Resource Planning* 19, no. 4 (1996), pp. 18–32.
31. M. Mendenhall and G. Oddou, "The Dimensions of Expatriate Acculturation: A Review," *Academy of Management Review* 10 (1985), pp. 39–47.
32. I. Torbiorin, *Living Abroad: Personal Adjustment and Personnel Policy in the Overseas Setting* (New York: Wiley, 1982).
33. R. L. Tung, "Selection and Training of Personnel for Overseas Assignments," *Columbia Journal of World Business* 16 (1981), pp. 68–78.
34. Solomon, "Success Abroad."
35. S. Ronen, "Training and International Assignee," in *Training and Career Development,* ed. I. Goldstein (San Francisco: Jossey-Bass, 1985); and Tung, "Selection and Training of Personnel for Overseas Assignments."
36. Solomon, "Success Abroad."
37. Harvey, "Addressing the Dual-Career Expatriation Dilemma"; J. W. Hunt, "The Perils of Foreign Postings for Two," *Financial Times,* May 6, 1998, p. 22.
38. C. M. Daily, S. T. Certo, and D. R. Dalton, "International Experience in the Executive Suite: A Path to Prosperity?" *Strategic Management Journal* 21 (2000), pp. 515–23.
39. Dowling and Schuler, *International Dimensions.*
40. Ibid.
41. G. Baliga and J. C. Baker, "Multinational Corporate Policies for Expatriate Managers: Selection, Training, and Evaluation," *Advanced Management Journal,* Autumn 1985, pp. 31–38.
42. J. C. Baker, "Foreign Language and Departure Training in U.S. Multinational Firms," *Personnel Administrator,* July 1984, pp. 68–70.
43. A 1997 study by the Conference Board looked at this in depth. For a summary, see L. Grant, "That Overseas Job Could Derail Your Career," *Fortune,* April 14, 1997, p. 166. Also see J. S. Black and H. Gregersen, "The Right Way to Manage Expatriates," *Harvard Business Review,* March–April 1999, pp. 52–63.
44. J. S. Black and M. E. Mendenhall, *Global Assignments: Successfully Expatriating and Repatriating International Managers* (San Francisco: Jossey-Bass, 1992); and K. Vermond,

"Expatriates Come Home," *CMA Management,* October 2001, pp. 30–33.

45. Ibid.
46. Figures from the Conference Board study. For a summary, see Grant, "That Overseas Job Could Derail Your Career."
47. S. C. Schneider, "National vs. Corporate Culture: Implications for Human Resource Management," *Human Resource Management* 27 (Summer 1988), pp. 231–46.
48. I. M. Manve and W. B. Stevenson, "Nationality, Cultural Distance and Expatriate Status," *Journal of International Business Studies* 32 (2001), pp. 285–303; and D. Minbaeva et al., "MNC Knowledge Transfer, Subsidiary Absorptive Capacity, and HRM," *Journal of International Business Studies* 34, no. 6 (2003), pp. 586–604.
49. Bartlett and Ghoshal, *Managing across Borders.*
50. See G. Oddou and M. Mendenhall, "Expatriate Performance Appraisal: Problems and Solutions," in *International Human Resource Management,* ed. M. Mendenhall and G. Oddou (Boston: PWS-Kent, 1991); Dowling and Schuler, *International Dimensions;* R. S. Schuler and G.W. Florkowski, "International Human Resource Management," in *Handbook for International Management Research,* ed. B. J. Punnett and O. Shenkar (Oxford: Blackwell, 1996); K. Roth and S. O'Donnell, "Foreign Subsidiary Compensation Strategy: An Agency Theory Perspective," *Academy of Management Journal* 39, no. 3 (1996), pp. 678–703.
51. Oddou and Mendenhall, "Expatriate Performance Appraisal."
52. "Expatriates Often See Little Benefit to Careers in Foreign Stints, Indifference at Home," *The Wall Street Journal,* December 11, 1989, p. B1.
53. Oddou and Mendenhall, "Expatriate Performance Appraisal"; and Schuler and Florkowski, "International Human Resource Management."
54. Towers Perrin, *Towers Perrin Worldwide Total Remuneration Study, 2005–2006,* www.towerswatson.com. Not all researchers agree with this conclusion; see, for example, N. Fernandes et al., "Are US CEOs Paid More? New International Evidence," *The Review of Financial Studies* 26, no. 2 (2013), pp. 323–67.
55. J. Cummings and L. Brannen, "The New World of Compensation," *Business Finance,* June 2005, p. 8.
56. "Multinationals Tighten Control of Benefit Plans," *Workforce Management,* May 2005, p. 5.
57. Organizational Resource Counselors, 2002 *Survey of International Assignment Policies and Practices,* March 2003.
58. C. Reynolds, "Compensation of Overseas Personnel," in *Handbook of Human Resource Administration,* ed. J. J. Famularo (New York: McGraw-Hill, 1986).
59. M. Helms, "International Executive Compensation Practices," in *International Human Resource Management,* ed. M. Mendenhall and G. Oddou (Boston: PWS-Kent, 1991).
60. G. W. Latta, "Expatriate Incentives," *HR Focus* 75, no. 3 (March 1998), p. S3.
61. C. K. Prahalad and Y. L. Doz, *The Multinational Mission* (New York: Free Press, 1987).
62. Ibid.
63. Schuler and Florkowski, "International Human Resource Management."
64. See J. P. Womack, D. T. Jones, and D. Roos, *The Machine That Changed the World* (New York: Rawson Associates, 1990).

glossary

A

absolute advantage A country has an absolute advantage in the production of a product when it is more efficient than any other country at producing it.

ad valorem tariff A tariff levied as a proportion of the value of an imported good.

administrative trade policies Administrative policies, typically adopted by government bureaucracies, that can be used to restrict imports or boost exports.

Andean Community A 1969 agreement among Bolivia, Chile, Ecuador, Colombia, and Peru to establish a customs union.

antidumping policies Designed to punish foreign firms that engage in dumping and thus protect domestic producers from unfair foreign competition.

arbitrage The purchase of securities in one market for immediate resale in another to profit from a price discrepancy.

Association of Southeast Asian Nations (ASEAN) Formed in 1967, an attempt to establish a free trade area among Brunei, Cambodia, Indonesia, Laos, Malaysia, Myanmar, the Philippines, Singapore, Vietnam, and Thailand.

B

balance-of-payments accounts National accounts that track both payments to and receipts from foreigners.

balance-of-trade equilibrium Reached when the income a nation's residents earn from exports equals money paid for imports.

bandwagon effect Movement of traders like a herd, all in the same direction and at the same time, in response to each other's perceived actions.

banking crisis A loss of confidence in the banking system that leads to a run on banks, as individuals and companies withdraw their deposits.

barter The direct exchange of goods or services between two parties without a cash transaction.

bill of exchange An order written by an exporter instructing an importer, or an importer's agent, to pay a specified amount of money at a specified time.

bill of lading A document issued to an exporter by a common carrier transporting merchandise. It serves as a receipt, a contract, and a document of title.

business ethics The accepted principles of right or wrong governing the conduct of businesspeople.

buyback Agreement to accept a percentage of a plant's output as payment for contract to build a plant.

C

capital account In the balance of payments, records transactions involving one-time changes in the stock of assets.

capital account Records one-time changes in the stock of assets.

capital flight Converting domestic currency into a foreign currency.

Caribbean Single Market and Economy (CSME) The six CARICOM members that agreed to lower trade barriers and harmonize macroeconomic and monetary policies.

CARICOM An association of English-speaking Caribbean states that are attempting to establish a customs union.

carry trade A kind of speculation that involves borrowing in one currency where interest rates are low and then using the proceeds to invest in another currency where interest rates are high.

caste system A system of social stratification in which social position is determined by the family into which a person is born, and change in that position is usually not possible during an individual's lifetime.

Central America Free Trade Agreement (CAFTA) The agreement of the member states of the Central American Common Market joined by the Dominican Republic to trade freely with the United States.

Central American Common Market A trade pact among Costa Rica, El Salvador, Guatemala, Honduras, and Nicaragua, which began in the early 1960s but collapsed in 1969 due to war.

channel length The number of intermediaries that a product has to go through before it reaches the final consumer.

channel quality The expertise, competencies, and skills of established retailers in a nation and their ability to sell and support the products of international businesses.

civil law system A system of law based on a very detailed set of written laws and codes.

class consciousness A tendency for individuals to perceive themselves in terms of their class background.

class system A system of social stratification in which social status is determined by the family into which a person is born and by subsequent socioeconomic achievements; mobility between classes is possible.

code of ethics A business's formal statement of ethical priorities.

collectivism A political system that emphasizes collective goals as opposed to individual goals.

command economy An economic system where the allocation of resources, including determination of what goods and services should be produced, and in what quantity, is planned by the government.

common law A system of law based on tradition, precedent, and custom; when law courts interpret common law, they do so with regard to these characteristics.

common market A group of countries committed to (1) removing all barriers to the free flow of goods, services, and factors of production between each other; and (2) the pursuit of a common external trade policy.

communist totalitarianism A version of collectivism advocating that socialism can be achieved only through a totalitarian dictatorship.

Communists Those who believe socialism can be achieved only through revolution and totalitarian dictatorship.

concentrated retail system A retail system in which a few retailers supply most of the market.

constant returns to specialization The units of resources required to produce a good are assumed to remain constant no matter where one is on a country's production possibility frontier.

contract A document that specifies the conditions under which an exchange is to occur and details the rights and obligations of the parties involved.

contract law The body of law that governs contract enforcement.

contributor factory A factory that serves a specific country or world region.

controls The metrics used to measure the performance of subunits and make judgments about how well managers are running those subunits.

Convention on Combating Bribery of Foreign Public Officials in International Business Transactions An OECD convention that establishes legally binding standards to criminalize bribery of foreign public officials in international business transactions and provides for a host of related measures that make this effective.

copyrights The exclusive legal rights of authors, composers, playwrights, artists, and publishers to publish and disperse their work as they see fit.

core competence Firm skills that competitors cannot easily match or imitate.

corporate culture The organization's norms and value systems.

corporate social responsibility (CSR) Refers to the idea that businesspeople should consider the social consequences of economic actions when making business decisions and that there should be a presumption in favor of decisions that have both good economic and social consequences.

counterpurchase A reciprocal buying agreement.

countertrade The trade of goods and services for other goods and services.

countervailing duties Antidumping duties.

country of origin effects A subset of source effects, the extent to which the place of manufacturing influences product evaluations.

Court of Justice Supreme appeals court for EU law.

cross-cultural literacy Understanding how the culture of a country affects the way business is practiced.

cultural relativism The belief that ethics are culturally determined and that firms should adopt the ethics of the cultures in which they operate.

culture A system of values and norms that are shared among a group of people and that when taken together constitute a design for living.

currency board Means of controlling a country's currency.

currency crisis Occurs when a speculative attack on the exchange value of a currency results in a sharp depreciation in the value of the currency or forces authorities to expend large volumes of international currency reserves and sharply increase interest rates to defend the prevailing exchange rate.

currency speculation Involves short-term movement of funds from one currency to another in hopes of profiting from shifts in exchange rates.

currency swap Simultaneous purchase and sale of a given amount of foreign exchange for two different value dates.

current account In the balance of payments, records transactions involving the export or import of goods and services.

current account deficit The current account of the balance of payments is in deficit when a country imports more goods and services than it exports.

current account surplus The current account of the balance of payments is in surplus when a country exports more goods, services, and income than it imports.

customs union A group of countries committed to (1) removing all barriers to the free flow of goods and services between each other and (2) the pursuit of a common external trade policy.

D

democracy Political system in which government is by the people, exercised either directly or through elected representatives.

deregulation Removal of government restrictions concerning the conduct of a business.

dirty-float system A system under which a country's currency is nominally allowed to float freely against other currencies but in which the government will intervene, buying and selling currency, if it believes that the currency has deviated too far from its fair value.

downstream supply chain The portion of the supply chain from the production facility to the end-customer.

draft An order written by an exporter telling an importer what and when to pay.

dumping Selling goods in a foreign market for less than their cost of production or below their "fair" market value.

E

eclectic paradigm Argument that combining location-specific assets or resource endowments and the firm's own unique assets often requires FDI; it requires the firm to establish production facilities where those foreign assets or resource endowments are located.

economic exposure The extent to which a firm's future international earning power is affected by changes in exchange rates.

economic risk The likelihood that events, including economic mismanagement, will cause drastic changes in a country's business environment that adversely affect the profit and other goals of a particular business enterprise.

economic union A group of countries committed to (1) removing all barriers to the free flow of goods, services, and factors of production between each other; (2) the adoption of a common currency; (3) the harmonization of tax rates; and (4) the pursuit of a common external trade policy.

economies of scale Cost advantages associated with large-scale production.

efficient market A market where prices reflect all available information.

elastic A small change in price produces a large change in demand.

entrepreneurs Those who first commercialize innovations.

ethical dilemma A situation in which there is no ethically acceptable solution.

ethical strategy A course of action that does not violate a company's business ethics.

ethical system A set of moral principles, or values, that is used to guide and shape behavior.

ethnocentric staffing policy A staffing approach within the MNE in which all key management positions are filled by parent-country nationals.

ethnocentrism Behavior that is based on the belief in the superiority of one's own ethnic group or culture; often shows disregard or contempt for the culture of other countries.

European Commission Responsible for proposing EU legislation, implementing it, and monitoring compliance.

European Council The heads of state of EU members and the president of the European Commission.

European Free Trade Association (EFTA) A free trade association including Norway, Iceland, Liechtenstein, and Switzerland.

European Monetary System (EMS) EU system designed to create a zone of monetary stability in Europe, control inflation, and coordinate exchange rate policies of EU countries.

European Parliament Elected EU body that provides consultation on issues proposed by the European Commission.

European Union (EU) An economic and political union of 28 countries (2015) that are located in Europe.

exchange rate The rate at which one currency is converted into another.

exclusive distribution channel A distribution channel that outsiders find difficult to access.

expatriate failure The premature return of an expatriate manager to the home country.

expatriate manager A national of one country appointed to a management position in another country.

experience curve Systematic production cost reductions that occur over the life of a product.

experience curve pricing Aggressive pricing designed to increase volume and help the firm realize experience curve economies.

export ban A policy that partially or entirely restricts the export of a good.

export credit A tax placed on the export of a good.

export management company (EMC) Export specialist that acts as an export marketing department for client firms.

Export-Import Bank (Ex-Im Bank) Agency of the U.S. government whose mission is to provide aid in financing and facilitate exports and imports.

exporting Sale of products produced in one country to residents of another country.

external stakeholders Individuals or groups that have some claim on a firm such as customers, suppliers, and unions.

externalities Knowledge spillovers.

externally convertible currency Limitations on the ability of residents to convert domestic currency, though nonresidents can convert their holdings of domestic currency into foreign currency.

F

factor endowments A country's endowment with resources such as land, labor, and capital.

factors of production Inputs into the productive process of a firm, including labor, management, land, capital, and technological know-how.

financial account In balance of payments, transactions that involve the purchase or sale of assets.

financial account In the balance of payments, transactions that involve the purchase or sale of assets.

first-mover advantages Advantages accruing to the first to enter a market.

first-mover disadvantages Disadvantages associated with entering a foreign market before other international businesses.

Fisher effect Nominal interest rates (i) in each country equal the required real rate of interest (r) and the expected rate of inflation over the period of time for which the funds are to be lent (I). That is, $i = r + I$.

fixed exchange rate A system under which the exchange rate for converting one currency into another is fixed.

flexible machine cells Flexible manufacturing technology in which a grouping of various machine types, a common materials handler, and a centralized cell controller produce a family of products.

flexible manufacturing technology Manufacturing technology designed to improve job scheduling, reduce setup time, and improve quality control.

floating exchange rate A system under which the exchange rate for converting one currency into another is continuously adjusted depending on the laws of supply and demand.

flow of FDI The amount of foreign direct investment undertaken over a given time period (normally one year).

folkways Routine conventions of everyday life.

Foreign Corrupt Practices Act (FCPA) U.S. law regulating behavior regarding the conduct of international business in the taking of bribes and other unethical actions.

foreign debt crisis Situation in which a country cannot service its foreign debt obligations, whether private-sector or government debt.

foreign direct investment (FDI) Direct investment in business operations in a foreign country.

foreign exchange market A market for converting the currency of one country into that of another country.

foreign exchange risk The risk that changes in exchange rates will hurt the profitability of a business deal.

forward exchange When two parties agree to exchange currency and execute a deal at some specific date in the future.

forward exchange rate The exchange rate governing a forward exchange transaction.

fragmented retail system A retail system in which there are many retailers, none of which has a major share of the market.

franchising A specialized form of licensing in which the franchiser sells intangible property to the franchisee and insists on rules to conduct the business.

free trade The absence of barriers to the free flow of goods and services between countries.

free trade area A group of countries committed to removing all barriers to the free flow of goods and services between each other but pursuing independent external trade policies.

freely convertible currency A country's currency is freely convertible when the government of that country allows both residents and nonresidents to purchase unlimited amounts of foreign currency with the domestic currency.

G

General Agreement on Tariffs and Trade (GATT) International treaty that committed signatories to lowering barriers to the free flow of goods across national borders and led to the WTO.

geocentric staffing policy A staffing policy where the best people are sought for key jobs throughout an MNE, regardless of nationality.

global distribution center A facility that positions and allows customization of products for delivery to worldwide wholesalers or retailers or directly to consumers anywhere in the world; also called a global distribution warehouse.

global inventory management The decision-making process regarding the raw materials, work-in-process (component parts), and finished goods inventory for a multinational corporation.

global learning The flow of skills and product offerings from foreign subsidiary to home country and from foreign subsidiary to foreign subsidiary.

global standardization strategy A firm focuses on increasing profitability and profit growth by reaping the cost reductions that come from economies of scale, learning effects, and location economies.

global supply chain coordination The shared decision-making opportunities and operational collaboration of key global supply chain activities.

global web When different stages of value chain are dispersed to those locations around the globe where value added is maximized or where costs of value creation are minimized.

globalization Trend away from distinct national economic units and toward one huge global market.

globalization of markets Moving away from an economic system in which national markets are distinct entities, isolated by trade barriers and barriers of distance, time, and culture, and toward a system in which national markets are merging into one global market.

globalization of production Trend by individual firms to disperse parts of their productive processes to different locations around the globe to take advantage of differences in cost and quality of factors of production.

gold par value The amount of currency needed to purchase one ounce of gold.

gold standard The practice of pegging currencies to gold and guaranteeing convertibility.

greenfield investment Establishing a new operation in a foreign country.

greenfield investment The establishment of a new operation in a foreign country.

gross national income (GNI) Measures the total annual income received by residents of a nation.

group An association of two or more individuals who have a shared sense of identity and who interact with each other in structured ways on the basis of a common set of expectations about each other's behavior.

Group of Twenty (G20) Established in 1999, the G20 comprises the finance ministers and central bank governors of the 19 largest economies in the world, plus representatives from the European Union and the European Central Bank.

H

Human Development Index (HDI) An attempt by the United Nations to assess the impact of a number of factors on the quality of human life in a country.

human resource management (HRM) Activities an organization conducts to use its human resources effectively.

I

import quota A direct restriction on the quantity of a good that can be imported into a country.

incentives The devices used to reward appropriate managerial behavior.

individualism An emphasis on the importance of guaranteeing individual freedom and self-expression.

individualism versus collectivism Theory focusing on the relationship between the individual and his or her fellows; in individualistic societies, the ties between individuals are loose and individual achievement is highly valued; in societies where collectivism is emphasized, ties between individuals are tight, people are born into collectives, such as extended families, and everyone is supposed to look after the interests of his or her collective.

inefficient market One in which prices do not reflect all available information.

inelastic When a large change in price produces only a small change in demand.

infant industry argument New industries in developing countries must be temporarily protected from international competition to help them reach a position where they can compete on world markets with the firms of developed nations.

inflows of FDI Flow of foreign direct investment into a country.

innovation Development of new products, processes, organizations, management practices, and strategies.

intellectual property Products of the mind, ideas (e.g., books, music, computer software, designs, technological know-how); intellectual property can be protected by patents, copyrights, and trademarks.

intermarket segment A segment of customers that spans multiple countries, transcending national borders.

internal stakeholders People who work for or own the business such as employees, directors, and stockholders.

internalization theory Marketing imperfection approach to foreign direct investment.

international business Any firm that engages in international trade or investment.

international Fisher effect (IFE) For any two countries, the spot exchange rate should change in an equal amount but in the opposite direction to the difference in nominal interest rates between countries.

international market research The systematic collection, recording, analysis, and interpretation of data to provide knowledge that is useful for decision making in a global company.

International Monetary Fund (IMF) International institution set up to maintain order in the international monetary system.

international monetary system Institutional arrangements countries adopt to govern exchange rates.

international strategy Trying to create value by transferring core competencies to foreign markets where indigenous competitors lack those competencies.

international trade Occurs when a firm exports goods or services to consumers in another country.

ISO 9000 Certification process that requires certain quality standards that must be met.

J

joint venture A cooperative undertaking between two or more firms.

just distribution A distribution of goods and services that is considered fair and equitable.

just in time (JIT) Inventory logistics system designed to deliver parts to a production process as they are needed, not before.

K

Kantian ethics The belief that people should be treated as ends and never as means to the ends of others.

L

lag strategy Delaying the collection of foreign currency receivables if that currency is expected to appreciate and delaying payables if that currency is expected to depreciate.

late-mover disadvantages Handicaps experienced by being a late entrant in a market.

law of one price In competitive markets free of transportation costs and barriers to trade, identical products sold in different countries must sell for the same price when their price is expressed in the same currency.

lead factory A factory that is intended to create new processes, products, and technologies that can be used throughout the global firm in all parts of the world.

lead strategy Collecting foreign currency receivables early when a foreign currency is expected to depreciate and paying foreign currency payables before they are due when a currency is expected to appreciate.

lean production *See* flexible manufacturing technology.

learning effects Cost savings from learning by doing.

legal risk The likelihood that a trading partner will opportunistically break a contract or expropriate intellectual property rights.

legal system System of rules that regulate behavior and the processes by which the laws of a country are enforced and through which redress of grievances is obtained.

letter of credit Issued by a bank, indicating that the bank will make payments under specific circumstances.

licensing Occurs when a firm (the licensor) licenses the right to produce its product, use its production processes, or use its brand name or trademark to another firm (the licensee). In return for giving the licensee these rights, the licensor collects a royalty fee on every unit the licensee sells.

licensing agreement Arrangement in which a licensor grants the rights to intangible property to a licensee for a specified period and receives a royalty fee in return.

local content requirement (LCR) A requirement that some specific fraction of a good be produced domestically.

localization strategy Increasing profitability by customizing the firm's goods and services so that they provide a good match to tastes and preferences in different national markets.

location economies Cost advantages from performing a value creation activity at the optimal location for that activity.

location-specific advantages Advantages that arise from using resource endowments or assets that are tied to a particular foreign location and that a firm finds valuable to combine with its own unique assets (such as the firm's technological, marketing, or management know-how).

logistics The part of the supply chain that plans, implements, and controls the effective flows and inventory of raw material, component parts, and products used in manufacturing.

long-term versus short-term orientation The theory of the extent to which a culture programs its citizens to accept delayed gratification of their material, social, and emotional needs. It captures attitudes toward time, persistence, ordering by status, protection of face, respect for tradition, and reciprocation of gifts and favors.

M

Maastricht Treaty Treaty agreed to in 1992, but not ratified until January 1, 1994, that committed the 12 member states of the European Community to a closer economic and political union.

make-or-buy decision The strategic decision concerning whether to produce an item in-house ("make") or purchase it from an outside supplier ("buy").

managed-float system System under which some currencies are allowed to float freely, but the majority are either managed by government intervention or pegged to another currency.

market economy An economic system in which the interaction of supply and demand determines the quantity in which goods and services are produced.

market imperfections Imperfections in the operation of the market mechanism.

market segmentation Identifying groups of consumers whose purchasing behavior differs from others in important ways.

marketing mix Choices about product attributes, distribution strategy, communication strategy, and pricing strategy that a firm offers its targeted markets.

masculinity versus femininity Theory of the relationship between gender and work roles. In masculine cultures, sex roles are sharply differentiated and traditional "masculine values" such as achievement and the effective exercise of power determine cultural ideals; in feminine cultures, sex roles are less sharply distinguished, and little differentiation is made between men and women in the same job.

mass customization The production of a variety of end products at a unit cost that could once be achieved only through mass production of a standardized output.

mercantilism An economic philosophy advocating that countries should simultaneously encourage exports and discourage imports.

Mercosur Pact among Argentina, Brazil, Paraguay, and Uruguay to establish a free trade area.

minimum efficient scale The level of output at which most plant-level scale economies are exhausted.

MITI Japan's Ministry of International Trade and Industry.

Moore's law The power of microprocessor technology doubles and its costs of production fall in half every 18 months.

moral hazard Arises when people behave recklessly because they know they will be saved if things go wrong.

mores Norms seen as central to the functioning of a society and to its social life.

multilateral or bilateral trade agreements Reciprocal trade agreements between two or more partners.

multinational enterprise (MNE) A firm that owns business operations in more than one country.

multipoint competition Arises when two or more enterprises encounter each other in different regional markets, national markets, or industries.

multipoint pricing Occurs when a pricing strategy in one market may have an impact on a rival's pricing strategy in another market.

N

naive immoralist One who asserts that if a manager of a multinational sees that firms from other nations are not following ethical norms in a host nation, that manager should not either.

new trade theory The observed pattern of trade in the world economy may be due in part to the ability of firms in a given market to capture first-mover advantages.

noise The number of other messages competing for a potential consumer's attention.

nonconvertible currency A currency is not convertible when both residents and nonresidents are prohibited from converting their holdings of that currency into another currency.

norms Social rules and guidelines that prescribe appropriate behavior in particular situations.

North American Free Trade Agreement (NAFTA) Free trade area among Canada, Mexico, and the United States.

O

offset Agreement to purchase goods and services with a specified percentage of proceeds from an original sale in that country from any firm in the country.

offshore factory A factory that is developed and set up mainly for producing component parts or finished goods at a lower cost than producing them at home or in any other market.

offshore production FDI undertaken to serve the home market.

oligopoly An industry composed of a limited number of large firms.

operations The various value creation activities a firm undertakes.

optimal currency area Region in which similarities in economic activity make a single currency and exchange rate feasible instruments of macroeconomic policy.

organization architecture The totality of a firm's organization, including formal organizational structure, control systems and incentives, organizational culture, processes, and people.

organizational culture The values and norms shared among an organization's employees.

organizational structure The three-part structure of an organization, including its formal division into subunits such as product divisions, its location of decision-making responsibilities within that structure, and the establishment of integrating mechanisms to coordinate the activities of all subunits.

outflows of FDI Flow of foreign direct investment out of a country.

outpost factory A factory that can be viewed as an intelligence-gathering unit.

P

packaging The container that holds the product itself. It can be divided into primary, secondary, and transit packaging.

Paris Convention for the Protection of Industrial Property International agreement to protect intellectual property.

patent Grants the inventor of a new product or process exclusive rights to the manufacture, use, or sale of that invention.

pegged exchange rate Currency value is fixed relative to a reference currency.

people The employees of the organization, the strategy used to recruit, compensate, and retain those individuals, and the type of people that they are in terms of their skills, values, and orientation.

pioneering costs Costs an early entrant bears that later entrants avoid, such as the time and effort in learning the rules, failure due to ignorance, and the liability of being a foreigner.

political economy The political, economic, and legal systems of a country.

political risk The likelihood that political forces will cause drastic changes in a country's business environment that will adversely affect the profit and other goals of a particular business enterprise.

political system System of government in a nation.

political union A central political apparatus coordinates economic, social, and foreign policy.

polycentric staffing policy A staffing policy in an MNE in which host-country nationals are recruited to manage subsidiaries in their own country, while parent-country nationals occupy key positions at corporate headquarters.

power distance Theory of how a society deals with the fact that people are unequal in physical and intellectual capabilities. High power distance cultures are found in countries that let inequalities grow over time into inequalities of power and wealth; low power distance cultures are found in societies that try to play down such inequalities as much as possible.

predatory pricing Reducing prices below fair market value as a competitive weapon to drive weaker competitors out of the market ("fair" being cost plus some reasonable profit margin).

price elasticity of demand A measure of how responsive demand for a product is to changes in price.

private action Violation of property rights through theft, piracy, blackmail, and the like by private individuals or groups.

privatization The sale of state-owned enterprises to private investors.

processes The manner in which decisions are made and work is performed within any organization.

product liability Involves holding a firm and its officers responsible when a product causes injury, death, or damage.

product safety laws Set certain safety standards to which a product must adhere.

production Activities involved in creating a product.

profit growth The percentage increase in net profits over time.

profitability A ratio or rate of return concept.

property rights Bundle of legal rights over the use to which a resource is put and over the use made of any income that may be derived from that resource.

public action The extortion of income or resources of property holders by public officials, such as politicians and government bureaucrats.

pull strategy A marketing strategy emphasizing mass media advertising as opposed to personal selling.

purchasing The part of the supply chain that includes the worldwide buying of raw material, component parts, and products used in manufacturing of the company's products and services.

purchasing power parity (PPP) An adjustment in gross domestic product per capita to reflect differences in the cost of living.

push strategy A marketing strategy emphasizing personal selling rather than mass media advertising.

Q

quota rent Extra profit producers make when supply is artificially limited by an import quota.

R

regional economic integration Agreements among countries in a geographic region to reduce and ultimately remove tariff and nontariff barriers to the free flow of goods, services, and factors of production between each other.

religion A system of shared beliefs and rituals concerned with the realm of the sacred.

representative democracy A political system in which citizens periodically elect individuals to represent them in government.

reverse logistics The process of moving inventory from the point of consumption to the point of origin in supply chains for the purpose of recapturing value or proper disposal.

right-wing totalitarianism A political system in which political power is monopolized by a party, group, or individual that generally permits individual economic freedom but restricts individual political freedom, including free speech, often on the grounds that it would lead to the rise of communism.

righteous moralist One who claims that a multinational's home-country standards of ethics are the appropriate ones for companies to follow in foreign countries.

rights theories Twentieth-century theories that recognize that human beings have fundamental rights and privileges that transcend national boundaries and cultures.

S

server factory A factory linked into the global supply chain for a global firm to supply specific country or regional markets around the globe.

sight draft A draft payable on presentation to the drawee.

Six Sigma Statistically based methodology for improving product quality.

Smoot-Hawley Act Enacted in 1930 by the U.S. Congress, this act erected a wall of tariff barriers against imports into the United States.

Social Democrats Those committed to achieving socialism by democratic means.

social mobility The extent to which individuals can move out of the social strata into which they are born.

social strata Hierarchical social categories often based on family background, occupation, and income.

social structure The basic social organization of a society.

Socialists Those who believe in public ownership of the means of production for the common good of society.

society Group of people who share a common set of values and norms.

sogo shosha Japanese trading companies; a key part of the *keiretsu*, the large Japanese industrial groups.

source effects Effects that occur when the receiver of the message (i.e., a potential consumer) evaluates the message on the basis of status or image of the sender.

source factory A factory whose primary purpose is also to drive down costs in the global supply chain.

specific tariff Tariff levied as a fixed charge for each unit of good imported.

spot exchange rate The exchange rate at which a foreign exchange dealer will convert one currency into another that particular day.

staffing policy Strategy concerned with selecting employees for particular jobs.

stakeholders The individuals or groups that have an interest, stake, or claim in the actions and overall performance of a company.

stock of FDI The total accumulated value of foreign-owned assets at a given time.

strategic alliances Cooperative agreements between potential or actual competitors.

strategic pricing The concept containing the three aspects: predatory pricing, multipoint pricing, and experience curve pricing.

strategic trade policy Government policy aimed at improving the competitive position of a domestic industry and/or domestic firm in the world market.

strategy Actions managers take to attain the firm's goals.

subsidy Government financial assistance to a domestic producer.

supply chain management The integration and coordination of logistics, purchasing, operations, and market channel activities from raw material to the end-customer.

sustainable strategies Strategies that not only help the multinational firm make good profits but that do so without harming the environment, while simultaneously ensuring that the corporation acts in a socially responsible manner with regard to its multiple stakeholders.

switch trading Use of a specialized third-party trading house in a countertrade arrangement.

T

tariff A tax levied on imports.

tariff rate quota Lower tariff rates applied to imports within the quota than those over the quota.

theocratic law system A system of law based on religious teachings.

theocratic totalitarianism A political system in which political power is monopolized by a party, group, or individual that governs according to religious principles.

time draft A promise to pay by the accepting party at some future date.

timing of entry Entry is early when a firm enters a foreign market before other foreign firms and late when a firm enters after other international businesses have established themselves.

total quality management (TQM) Management philosophy that takes as its central focus the need to improve the quality of a company's products and services.

totalitarianism Form of government in which one person or political party exercises absolute control over all spheres of human life and opposing political parties are prohibited.

trade creation Trade created due to regional economic integration; occurs when high-cost domestic producers are replaced by low-cost foreign producers within a free trade area.

trade diversion Trade diverted due to regional economic integration; occurs when low-cost foreign suppliers outside a free trade area are replaced by higher-cost suppliers within a free trade area.

trademarks The designs and names, often officially registered, by which merchants or manufacturers designate and differentiate their products.

transaction exposure The extent to which income from individual transactions is affected by fluctuations in foreign exchange values.

translation exposure The extent to which the reported consolidated results and balance sheets of a corporation are affected by fluctuations in foreign exchange values.

transnational strategy Attempt to simultaneously achieve low costs through location economies, economies of scale, and learning effects while also differentiating product offerings across geographic markets to account for local differences and fostering multidirectional flows of skills between different subsidiaries in the firm's global network of operations.

transportation The movement of inventory through the supply chain.

Treaty of Lisbon A European Union–sanctioned treaty that will allow the European Parliament to become the co-equal legislator for almost all European laws.

Treaty of Rome The 1957 treaty that established the European Community.

tribal totalitarianism A political system in which a party, group, or individual that represents the interests of a particular tribe (ethnic group) monopolizes political power.

turnkey project A project in which a firm agrees to set up an operating plant for a foreign client and hand over the "key" when the plant is fully operational.

U

uncertainty avoidance Extent to which cultures socialize members to accept ambiguous situations and to tolerate uncertainty.

United Nations (UN) An international organization made up of 193 countries headquartered in New York City, formed in 1945 to promote peace, security, and cooperation.

United Nations Convention on Contracts for the International Sale of Goods (CISG) A set of rules governing certain aspects of the making and performance of commercial contracts between sellers and buyers who have their places of businesses in different nations.

Universal Declaration of Human Rights A United Nations document that lays down the basic principles of human rights that should be adhered to.

universal needs Needs that are the same all over the world, such as steel, bulk chemicals, and industrial electronics.

upstream supply chain The portion of the supply chain from raw materials to the production facility.

utilitarian approaches to ethics These hold that the moral worth of actions or practices is determined by their consequences.

V

value creation Performing activities that increase the value of goods or services to consumers.

values Abstract ideas about what a society believes to be good, right, and desirable.

voluntary export restraint (VER) A quota on trade imposed from the exporting country's side, instead of the importer's; usually imposed at the request of the importing country's government.

W

wholly owned subsidiary A subsidiary in which the firm owns 100 percent of the stock.

World Bank International institution set up to promote general economic development in the world's poorer nations.

World Intellectual Property Organization An international organization whose members sign treaties to agree to protect intellectual property.

World Trade Organization (WTO) The organization that succeeded the General Agreement on Tariffs and Trade (GATT) as a result of the successful completion of the Uruguay Round of GATT negotiations.

Z

zero-sum game A situation in which an economic gain by one country results in an economic loss by another.

name index

T

subject index

C

D

E

F

G

H

I

J

K

L

M

N

O

P

Q

R

S

U

V

W

Z

ACRONYM	PROPER NAME
ADB	Asian Development Bank
AfDB	African Development Bank
AFIC	Asian Finance and Investment Corporation
AFTA	ASEAN Free Trade Area
ASEAN	Association of Southeast Asian Nations
ATPA	Andean Trade Preference Act
BIS	Bank for International Settlements
BOP	Balance of Payments
CIM	Computer-Integrated Manufacturing
CIS	Commonwealth of Independent States
CISG	UN Convention on Contracts for the International Sale of Goods
CEMA	Council for Mutual Economic Assistance
CRA	Country Risk Assessment
DB	Development Bank
DC	Developed Country
DFIs	Development Finance Institutions
DISC	Domestic International Sales Corporation
EBRD	European Bank for Reconstruction and Development
ECOWAS	Economic Community of West African States
EMU	Economic and Monetary Union
EEA	European Economic Area
EFTA	European Free Trade Association
EMs	Export Management Companies
EMCF	European Monetary Cooperation Fund
EMS	European Monetary System
EPO	European Patent Organization
ETC	Export Trading Company
ETUC	European Trade Union Confederation
EU	European Union
FCPA	Foreign Corrupt Practices Act
FDI	Foreign Direct Investment
FSC	Foreign Sales Corporation
FTAA	Free Trade Area of the Americas
FTZ	Foreign Trade Zone
Fx	Foreign Exchange
G7	Group of Seven
GATT	General Agreement on Tariffs and Trade
GC	Global Company
GDP	Gross Domestic Product
GNP	Gross National Product
GSP	Generalized System of Preferences
IAC	International Anti-counterfeiting Coalition
IC	International Company
IDA	International Development Association
IDB	Inter-American Development Bank

ACRONYM	PROPER NAME
IEC	International Electrotechnical Commission
IFC	International Finance Corporation
IMF	International Monetary Fund
IPLC	International Product Life Cycle
IRC	International Revenue Code
ISA	International Seabed Authority
ISO	International Organization for Standardization
ITA	International Trade Administration
JIT	Just-in-Time
JV	Joint Venture
LAIA	Latin American Integration Association (formerly LAFTA)
LDC	Less Developed Country
LIBOR	London Interbank Offer Rate
LOST	Law of the Sea Treaty
Mercosur	Free Trade Agreement between Argentina, Brazil, Paraguay, and Uruguay
MNC	Multinational Company
MNE	Multinational Enterprise
NAFTA	North American Free Trade Agreement
NATO	North Atlantic Treaty Organization
NIC	Newly Industrializing Country
NTBs	Nontariff Barriers
OECD	Organization for Economic Cooperation & Development
OPEC	Organizational of Petroleum Exporting Countries
PPP	Purchasing Power Parity
PRC	People's Republic of China
PTA	Preferential Trade Area for Eastern and Southern Africa
SACC	Southern African Development Coordination Conference
SBA	Small Business Administration
SBC	Strategic Business Center
SBU	Small Business Unit
SDR	Special Drawing Rights
SEZ	Special Economic Zone
TQM	Total Quality Management
UN	United Nations
UNCTAD	UN Conference on Trade and Development
VAT	Value Added Tax
VER	Voluntary Export Restraint
VRAs	Voluntary Restraints Agreements
WEC	World Energy Council
WIPO	World Intellectual Property Organization
WTO	World Trade Organization

COUNTRY	CAPITAL
Afghanistan	Kabul
Albania	Tirana
Algeria	Algiers
Andorra	Andorra La Vella
Angola	Luanda
Antigua and Barbuda	St. John's
Argentina	Buenos Aires
Armenia	Yerevan
Aruba	Oranjestad
Australia	Canberra
Austria	Vienna
Azerbaijan	Baku
Bahamas	Nassau
Bahrain	Manama
Bangladesh	Dhaka
Barbados	Bridgetown
Belarus	Minsk
Belgium	Brussels
Belize	Belmopan
Benin	Porto-Novo
Bermuda	Hamilton
Bhutan	Thimphu
Bolivia	La Paz
Bosnia and Herzegovina	Sarajevo
Botswana	Gaborone
Brazil	Brasilia
Brunei	Bandar Seri Begawan
Bulgaria	Sofia
Burkina Faso	Ouagadougou
Burma	Rangoon
Burundi	Bujumbura
Cambodia	Phnom Penh
Cameroon	Yaounde
Canada	Ottawa
Cape Verde	Praia
Cayman Islands	George Town
Central African Republic	Bangui
Chad	N'Djamena
Chile	Santiago
China	Beijing
Colombia	Bogota
Comoros	Moroni
Democratic Republic of the Congo	Kinshasa
Republic of Congo	Brazzaville
Costa Rica	San Jose
Cote d'Ivoire	Yamoussoukro
Croatia	Zagreb
Cuba	Havana
Cyprus	Nicosia
Czech Republic	Prague
Denmark	Copenhagen
Djibouti	Djibouti
Dominica	Roseau
Dominican Republic	Santo Domingo
Ecuador	Quito
Egypt	Cairo
El Salvador	San Salvador
Equatorial Guinea	Malabo
Eritrea	Asmara
Estonia	Tallinn
Ethiopia	Addis Ababa
Fiji	Suva
Finland	Helsinki
France	Paris
Gabon	Libreville
The Gambia	Banjul

COUNTRY	CAPITAL
Georgia	T'bilisi
Germany	Berlin
Ghana	Accra
Greece	Athens
Grenada	Saint George's
Guatemala	Guatemala City
Guinea	Conakry
Guinea-Bissau	Bissau
Guyana	Georgetown
Haiti	Port-au-Prince
Holy See	Vatican City
Honduras	Tegucigalpa
Hungary	Budapest
Iceland	Reykjavik
India	New Delhi
Indonesia	Jakarta
Iran	Tehran
Iraq	Baghdad
Ireland	Dublin
Israel	Jerusalem
Italy	Rome
Jamaica	Kingston
Japan	Tokyo
Jordan	Amman
Kazakhstan	Astana
Kenya	Nairobi
Kiribati	Tarawa
North Korea	Pyongyang
South Korea	Seoul
Kosovo	Pristina
Kuwait	Kuwait City
Kyrgyzstan	Bishkek
Laos	Vientiane
Latvia	Riga
Lebanon	Beirut
Lesotho	Maseru
Liberia	Monrovia
Libya	Tripoli
Liechtenstein	Vaduz
Lithuania	Vilnius
Luxembourg	Luxembourg
Macedonia	Skopje
Madagascar	Antananarivo
Malawi	Lilongwe
Malaysia	Kuala Lumpur
Maldives	Male
Mali	Bamako
Malta	Valletta
Marshall Islands	Majuro
Mauritania	Nouakchott
Mauritius	Port Louis
Mexico	Mexico City
Federated States of Micronesia	Palikir
Moldova	Chisinau
Monaco	Monaco
Mongolia	Ulaanbaatar
Montenegro	Podgorica
Morocco	Rabat
Mozambique	Maputo
Namibia	Windhoek
Nauru	No Official Capital
Nepal	Kathmandu
Netherlands	Amsterdam
New Zealand	Wellington
Nicaragua	Managua
Niger	Niamey

COUNTRY	CAPITAL
Nigeria	Abuja
Norway	Oslo
Oman	Muscat
Pakistan	Islamabad
Palau	Melekeok
Panama	Panama City
Papua New Guinea	Port Moresby
Paraguay	Asuncion
Peru	Lima
Philippines	Manila
Poland	Warsaw
Portugal	Lisbon
Qatar	Doha
Romania	Bucharest
Russia	Moscow
Rwanda	Kigali
Saint Kitts and Nevis	Basseterre
Saint Lucia	Castries
Saint Vincent and the Grenadines	Kingstown
Samoa	Apia
San Marino	San Marino
Sao Tome and Principe	Sao Tome
Saudi Arabia	Riyadh
Senegal	Dakar
Serbia	Belgrade
Seychelles	Victoria
Sierra Leone	Freetown
Singapore	Singapore
Slovakia	Bratislava
Slovenia	Ljubljana
Solomon Islands	Honiara
Somalia	Mogadishu
South Africa	Pretoria
South Sudan	Juba
Spain	Madrid
Sri Lanka	Colombo
Sudan	Khartoum
Suriname	Paramaribo
Swaziland	Mbabane
Sweden	Stockholm
Switzerland	Bern
Syria	Damascus
Taiwan	Taipei
Tajikistan	Dushanbe
Tanzania	Dar es Salaam
Thailand	Bangkok
Timor-Leste	Dili
Togo	Lome
Tonga	Nuku'alofa
Trinidad and Tobago	Port of Spain
Tunisia	Tunis
Turkey	Ankara
Turkmenistan	Ashgabat
Tuvalu	Funafuti
Uganda	Kampala
Ukraine	Kyiv
United Arab Emirates	Abu Dhabi
United Kingdom	London
United States	Washington, DC
Uruguay	Montevideo
Uzbekistan	Tashkent
Vanuatu	Port-Vila
Venezuela	Caracas
Vietnam	Hanoi
Yemen	Sanaa
Zambia	Lusaka
Zimbabwe	Harare

Note: The list of the 199 "Countries and Capitals" on this page are from http://globaledge.msu.edu/global-insights/by/country. More information about each country can be found on globalEDGE (including statistics, economy, history, government, culture, risk factors, corporations, trade indices, resources, and country memos).

ARCTIC OCEAN
Alaska (U.S.)
CANADA
UNITED STATES
MEXICO
NORTH PACIFIC OCEAN
Tropic of Cancer
Hawaii (U.S.)
Equator
KIRIBATI
Tokelau (N.Z.)
Cook Islands (N.Z.)
SAMOA
American Samoa
TONGA
Niue (N.Z.)
French Polynesia
Pitcairn (U.K.)
Scale: 1 to 105,113,000
GUYANA
French Guiana
SURINAME
COLOMBIA
ECUADOR
PERU
BRAZIL
BOLIVIA
PARAGUAY
ARGENTINA
URUGUAY
CHILE
Tropic of Capricorn
SOUTH PACIFIC OCEAN
SOUTHERN OCEAN
ANTARCTICA
BAHAMAS
DOMINICAN REP.
CUBA
Puerto Rico (U.S.)
ANTIGUA AND BARBUDA
ST. KITTS AND NEVIS
(Fr.) Guadeloupe
DOMINICA
(Fr.) Martinique
ST. LUCIA
BARBADOS
ST. VINCENT AND THE GRENADINES
GRENADA
JAMAICA
HAITI
Caribbean Sea
BELIZE
GUATEMALA
HONDURAS
NICARAGUA
EL SALVADOR
COSTA RICA
PANAMA
TRINIDAD AND TOBAGO
VENEZUELA
Scale: 1 to 41,472,000